Nietzsche, the Aristocratic Rebel

Historical Materialism Book Series

The Historical Materialism Book Series is a major publishing initiative of the radical left. The capitalist crisis of the twenty-first century has been met by a resurgence of interest in critical Marxist theory. At the same time, the publishing institutions committed to Marxism have contracted markedly since the high point of the 1970s. The Historical Materialism Book Series is dedicated to addressing this situation by making available important works of Marxist theory. The aim of the series is to publish important theoretical contributions as the basis for vigorous intellectual debate and exchange on the left.

The peer-reviewed series publishes original monographs, translated texts, and reprints of classics across the bounds of academic disciplinary agendas and across the divisions of the left. The series is particularly concerned to encourage the internationalization of Marxist debate and aims to translate significant studies from beyond the English-speaking world.

For a full list of titles in the Historical Materialism Book Series
available in paperback from Haymarket Books, visit:
https://www.haymarketbooks.org/series_collections/1-historical-materialism

Nietzsche, the Aristocratic Rebel

*Intellectual Biography and
Critical Balance-Sheet*

Domenico Losurdo

With an Introduction by
Harrison Fluss

Translated by
Gregor Benton

Haymarket Books
Chicago, IL

First published in 2019 by Brill Academic Publishers, The Netherlands
© 2020 Koninklijke Brill NV, Leiden, The Netherlands

Published in paperback in 2021 by
Haymarket Books
P.O. Box 180165
Chicago, IL 60618
773-583-7884
www.haymarketbooks.org

ISBN: 978-1-64259-340-2

Distributed to the trade in the US through Consortium Book Sales and
Distribution (www.cbsd.com) and internationally through Ingram
Publisher Services International (www.ingramcontent.com).

This book was published with the generous support of Lannan
Foundation and Wallace Action Fund.

Special discounts are available for bulk purchases by organizations and
institutions. Please call 773-583-7884 or email info@haymarketbooks.org
for more information.

Cover art and design by David Mabb. Cover art is a detail of *Long
Live the New! no. 45*, Kazimir Malevich drawing painted on "Arbutus"
wallpaper by Kathleen Kersey for Morris & Co. Paint and wallpaper on
canvas (2016).

Printed in the United States.

10 9 8 7 6 5 4 3 2 1

Library of Congress Cataloging-in-Publication data is available.

Dedicated to those young and not so young listeners who, over many years, have discussed and helped inspire my interpretation of Nietzsche at the seminars organised by Urbino University and the Istituto Italiano per gli Studi Filosofici

.˙.

Domenico Losurdo (14 November 1941–28 June 2018)

Who cannot make demands on him? Tell me what you need and I will find you a Nietzsche quotation for it [...]. For Germany and against Germany; for peace and against peace; for literature and against literature.

TUCHOLSKY 1985, p. 14

• • •

Every author has a sense in which all the contradictory passages are harmonized, otherwise that author has no sense [...]. One must therefore find a sense in which all the contradictions are reconciled.

PASCAL 1954, af. 558

• • •

Politics is now the organ of thought in its totality.

B, I, 2, p. 258

• • •

Less than ever may we see in Plato a mere artist. [...] We err when we consider Plato to be a representative of the Greek artistic type: while this ability was among the more common, the specifically Platonic, i.e., dialectic-political, was something unique.

KGA, II, 4, p. 14

• • •

One could do us no greater injustice than to assume that for us it is a matter of art alone, as if it were to function as a medicine and narcotic with which we could cure ourselves of all other miserable conditions.

WB, 4, I, 451 [277–8]

• •
•

Contents

PART 3
Nietzsche in His Time: Theory and Practice of Aristocratic Radicalism

PART 5
Nietzsche and the Aristocratic Reaction in Two Historical Epochs

Introduction to the English-Language Edition

Harrison Fluss

After narrating the long reception of Nietzsche from Emma Goldman to Stanley Cavell, Jennifer Ratner-Rosenhagen concludes her *American Nietzsche* in a manner sympathetic to the pragmatist reading of the philosopher's work: There is not one correct understanding of Nietzsche, any more than there is one true philosophical approach. What defines Nietzsche – if anything can define him – is the fundamental 'indeterminacy, perspectivalism and heterogeneity' at the heart of his philosophy, making him eminently congenial to the American traditions of liberalism and pluralism.[1] Nietzsche, thus, is as American as apple pie.

What Ratner-Rosenhagen ignores, however, are the other dimensions to Nietzsche's thinking, dimensions that are just as relevant to the story of an *American* Nietzsche. Nietzsche's responses to race, slavery, and abolitionism are left out of the account, since the Americanism Ratner-Rosenhagen presents us with is thoroughly de-contextualised. It is an Americanism clipped of its apparent inconsistencies and paradoxes, embodied, for instance, in Nietzsche's American precursor, the liberal Emerson. Ratner-Rosenhagen starts her narrative with Nietzsche's love for Emerson, but one should note that Nietzsche not only read Emerson the individualist, but Emerson the elitist and hero-worshipper as well.[2] Nietzsche considered himself to be 'a liberal' at times, but he was also a theorist who promoted hierarchy and rank-ordering.[3] How can the ostensibly progressive values of liberalism and pluralism then be united with the elitist politics Nietzsche represented? Indeed, how can such authoritarian values be compatible with the picture of an anti-foundationalist Nietzsche that concludes Ratner-Rosenhagen's book?

---

1   See Ratner-Rosenhagen's defence of Nietzsche from Allan Bloom. Ratner-Rosenhagen 2012.
2   See Newfield 2012 for a more nuanced view of Emerson's liberalism as a species of anti-democratic elitism.
3   These contradictions inherent to liberalism are analysed in Losurdo 2014. What makes Losurdo's account of American notions of liberty so interesting is the way he shows how such individualist 'liberty' was promoted by ideologues in the antebellum South as defending their right to own slaves. For Losurdo, these Southern apologists participate in a tradition of American liberalism, and, in many ways, Nietzsche does so as well. It is a liberalism that is not necessarily compatible with democracy, but rather entirely compatible with inequality. Losurdo covers Nietzsche's relationship to liberalism (including the young Nietzsche's embrace of German 'national liberalism') throughout the book we are introducing here.

Of course, such an objection to Nietzsche's elitism has already been dismissed as irrelevant countless times, since, according to this wide-ranging academic consensus, the importance of Nietzsche lies in his more rarefied ideas and not in his politics. The political dimensions of his thinking are typically phased out in both continental and analytical philosophy circles. For instance, the Cambridge translation of Nietzsche's writings from his later notebooks (materials which were originally edited under the title *The Will to Power*) is introduced by the volume's editors without considering his political views or statements, as if these were extraneous to his more properly philosophical concerns. Hence, Nietzsche's ideas on the nature of reality, epistemology, and language are highlighted for discussion, but not his criticisms of politics, modern decadence, economics, and criminality. These more terrestrial and topical dimensions of the notebooks are treated as if they were bereft of philosophical significance.[4]

In this domestication process of Nietzsche, the Dionysian and creative meditations on the nature of perception, art, language, and morals, are kept at safe distance from his 'timely' interests in historical events, the domestic and foreign policy of the Second Reich, or even a science as dismal as political economy. But, while Nietzsche is said to lack an essence, this decontextualised portrait ironically essentialises him into a timeless philosopher abstracted from history. As an atemporal philosopher, Nietzsche can become a kind of conceptual tool-box wherein academics, scholars, and others can cherry-pick what they want, leaving the potentially offensive elements of Nietzsche behind. The success behind Nietzsche as an empty signifier arguably lies in how people can see in him whatever they would like to see.

The analytical and continental decontamination of Nietzsche has not gone unchallenged in recent years. Several studies exist which deny the bifurcation of Nietzsche's philosophical thinking from his politics, demonstrating an indelible link between the two. Others have also challenged the attempted synthesis between Nietzsche's thinking and progressive ideas, a synthesis which in the end makes a mockery of both what Nietzsche argued for and those progressive ideas he scorned. We can offer here a brief – but by no means exhaustive – list of some of the most interesting approaches to Nietzsche as a highly political and anti-democratic thinker. These include Fredrick Appel's *Nietzsche Contra Democracy*; William Altman's *Friedrich Wilhelm Nietzsche: The Philosopher of the Second Reich*; Malcolm Bull's *Anti-Nietzsche*; Don Dombowsky's

---

4 See the translator and editor introductions to Nietzsche 2003. For one of the best presentations of an Anglophone approach to the French Nietzsche, see Allison 2000.

Nietzsche's Machiavellian Politics; Ishay Landa's *The Overman in the Market-place: Nietzschean Heroism in Popular Culture*; the late Stanley Rosen's *Mask of Enlightenment: Nietzsche's Zarathustra*; and Geoff Waite's *Nietzsche's Corps/e: Aesthetics, Politics, and the Spectacular Techno-Culture of Everyday Life*.[5] These studies, together with the book being introduced here, have been truly trans-formational for how we read Nietzsche.

Domenico Losurdo's intellectual biography is part of this new wave of criticism and helped to inspire a fair amount of it when the biography first came out in Italian, and then in its German, French, and Portuguese translations.[6] But what makes Losurdo's study so monumental is that it is not another interpretation of Nietzsche, but a *total* reconstruction of Nietzsche's main project. It deserves the title of a reconstruction from its immense scope, since Losurdo attempts not only to explicate Nietzsche's ideas, but also the overall context in which they arose.

But where does Nietzsche's ultimate coherence lie for Losurdo? What is it that persists through the vicissitudes of his written corpus? What is it that endures from his intellectual life? The locus of meaning in Nietzsche's writing is revealed to be, according to Losurdo, in 'his constant eye on social conflict and the threat of socialism' (p. 289). Politics is the main organon of Nietzsche's thinking.

This does not bode well for the consensus view of Nietzsche: the anti-dogmatic and anti-systematic thinker par excellence, with no one fixed doctrine or point of view. To think Nietzsche is to think many Nietzsches.[7] That is

---

5   Rehmann 2004 is a book which demonstrates the largely oxymoronic nature of Left-Nietzsch-eanism, but unfortunately has yet to be rendered into English (though a translation in the Historical Materialism Book Series is forthcoming). Nicolas Gonzalez Varela's contributions to Nietzsche scholarship also deserve an English-speaking audience, particularly for their strong focus on the politics of the young Nietzsche. See his *Nietzsche Contra La Democracia: El Pensamiento Politico de Friedrich Nietzsche 1862–1872*. Mention should be made of Timothy Brennan's analysis of Nietzsche as a colonial thinker of European imperialism in *Borrowed Light: Vico, Hegel, and the Colonies*. Brennan strongly acknowledges the importance of Los-urdo's work on this question.

6   The existence of this English translation is thanks to the wonderful and prodigious efforts of Gregor Benton, who, when no English translation was available, translated many of the Nietzsche quotations in this volume from the original German.

7   This argument for the 'postmodern' Nietzsche is encapsulated well here by Derrida: 'But who ever has said that a person bears a single name? Certainly not Nietzsche ... Next to Kierkegaard, was not Nietzsche one of the few great thinkers who multiplied his names and played with signatures, identities, and masks? And what if that would be the heart of the matter, the causa, the Streitfall (point of dispute) of his thinking?' Derrida 1986. Thanks to Ishay Landa for the reference.

why the apparent boldness of Losurdo's claim needs to be understood. Losurdo is not saying that Nietzsche's writings on philosophy, science, and art come with secondary political effects or that they are linked to Nietzsche's own peculiar brand of nineteenth-century prejudices. Losurdo argues that these discussions of philosophy, science, and art are, for Nietzsche, already political discussions and are framed by a distinct political perspective. Without considering the meaning of that perspective, Nietzsche's supposedly more rarefied interventions must remain, to a large degree, unintelligible. For Losurdo, it is the fundamentally undemocratic intent of Nietzsche's thinking that gives his reflections on philosophy, art, and science their real rigour, significance and unity.

This is the research programme with which Losurdo presents us. But it is important to state, from the outset, some qualifying remarks before introducing some of the main contours of the biography. Losurdo is not simply writing a polemic against Nietzsche. Even though he is portraying Nietzsche warts and all, his book is not a hateful screed, but a study that sets out to restore Nietzsche as a great thinker, however disturbing and reactionary he may be. Losurdo wants us to learn from Nietzsche while being critical, and we will see what this conceptual surplus of Nietzsche entails for critical readers below. Second, Losurdo avoids the mistake of seeing Nietzsche's thought as a direct foreshadowing of National Socialism and argues that it is wrong to write the history of Nietzsche's ideas with the Third Reich functioning as a future anterior. Instead, one must first situate Nietzsche's ideas in their correct historical context, that is, not in the Third, but in the Second Reich. And, while there are echoes of Nietzscheanism in German fascism,[8] it is not an unmediated process.

Losurdo starts with Nietzsche's so-called early period as a young Wagnerite. He demonstrates the essentially political nature of his lectures on *Socrates and Tragedy*, and what would become *The Birth of Tragedy*. These are works written in the shadow of what Nietzsche saw as a disaster of cataclysmic proportions, a disaster that may have augured the end of civilisation as he had known it. From the descriptions of Jacob Burckhardt and Nietzsche's letters as an orderly in the Franco-Prussian war, we see the sense of excitement, dread, and horror towards the Paris Commune.

This is from an early letter of Nietzsche's, written in the immediate defeat of the French Commune, and in a spirit of German chauvinism:

---

8 See for instance Chapter 27, Section 6 of this book, 'Hitler and Rosenberg as interpreters of Nietzsche and Nietzscheanism'. For Nietzsche's influence on fascism as a political movement, see the work of the German scholar Bernhard H.F. Taureck, in particular Taureck 2000. For Nietzsche's influence on the contemporary neo-fascist Alt-Right, see Beiner 2018.

Hope is possible again! Our German mission isn't over yet! I'm in better spirit than ever, for not yet everything has capitulated to Franco-Jewish levelling and 'elegance', and to the greedy instincts of Jetztzeit ('now-time'). There is still bravery, and it's a German bravery that has something else to it than the élan of our lamentable neighbours. Over and above the war between nations, that international hydra which suddenly raised its fearsome heads has alarmed us by heralding quite different battles to come.[9]

We already see the threat of socialism coloured with national-racial characteristics for Nietzsche. The association of the Jews with modern decadence is clearly apparent in these early writings and attitudes. Losurdo goes into intricate detail concerning Nietzsche's early Judeophobia, and the anti-Semitism of his supporters and admirers. He also details his shared attitude towards the Jews with Richard and Cosima Wagner (p. 113).

Losurdo dwells on a relatively unknown episode in Nietzsche's early career, concerning his early lecture on *Socrates and Tragedy*. This is a lecture which Nietzsche would later integrate into his first major work, *The Birth of Tragedy*, and has all the stamps of his collaboration with Wagner. Unfortunately, this lecture has never been translated into English, and we can hope that Losurdo's account will spark more interest in it. But there might be reasons for the hesitation of some. Nietzsche, towards the very end of *Socrates and Tragedy*, states that what he means by the modern 'Socratism' – namely, that spirit of optimism and progress which inspired slave revolts from ancient Alexandria to the Commune – is to be identified with the 'Jewish press' of today. Nietzsche thus fully equates the spirit of modernity he attacks with the spirit of Judaism.

What is interesting about this episode, besides the virulent hostility towards Jews on display, is the Wagners' reaction towards it. They agreed with what Nietzsche argued; truly, it could be said that Nietzsche was reinforcing the same polemic Wagner had started against the Jews as early as 1850. However, they also told Nietzsche to exercise caution, with Cosima Wagner urging prudence:

Do not name the Jews, especially not *en passant*. Later, if you want to engage in this terrible struggle, in God's name, but not at the start, so that not everything on your path turns into confusion and entanglement.

9   Cited in Lukács, p. 325. See also Losurdo's discussion of this letter (p. 42). For another in-depth discussion of Nietzsche's reactions to the Paris Commune, see the French scholar Marc Sautet 1981.

I hope you do not misunderstand me. You will know how much I agree, from the depths of my soul, with your statements, but not now, and not in that way.

> p. 113

Besides their orientation towards Jews, we should highlight the shared nature of Nietzsche and Wagner's critique of modernity for at least this stage of the former's intellectual development. First, Nietzsche's metaphysical reflections in *Socrates and Tragedy* and *Birth of Tragedy* are thoroughly politicised, though the argument relies upon a Schopenhauerian pessimism that Nietzsche will later find problematic. In these early works, it is the unknowable thing-in-itself, the noumenal realm as discovered by Kant, which helps to stem the tide of an optimism that seeks to remake reality into a better world. The metaphysics of pessimism here is thus geared towards a political purpose, of crushing what is for Nietzsche, in essence, the slave revolt of modern thought. For the Schopenhauerian Nietzsche, the Dionysian perspective reveals the essential oneness and primordial unity of all being, but this is a dimension that does not coincide with the actual experiences of the phenomenal world. Any attempt to bridge the noumenal and the phenomenal rationally would mean the death of culture and art. It would amount to the abolition of the unknown and the mystery at the heart of reality. Only an aesthetic sensibility could intuit the two together in tragedy, and not everyone was capable of such sensibility.

Nietzsche earned his polemical spurs at this time against David Friedrich Strauss, the Young Hegelian famous for authoring *The Life of Jesus*. Losurdo reveals Nietzsche's cryptic Judeophobia against 'David' Strauss in his untimely meditation (p. 167), and also the possible influence Strauss exercised over Nietzsche's later break from Wagner's circle. Strauss's tepid rationalism, for Nietzsche, was linked to the decay of Hegelianism and the emergence of a mentality conducive to socialism. But this seemed to change after Nietzsche left Wagner's Bayreuth for good. Instead of attacking the Enlightenment project as pernicious, decadent, and destructive of culture, Nietzsche refashioned it in what scholars consider his so-called 'middle period'.[10] Losurdo traces the positivistic ideas in the later Strauss to ideas in Nietzsche's books like *Human, All-Too-Human* and *Daybreak*.

In these works, Nietzsche has undergone a theoretical revolution, but one that is oriented essentially to the same basic concerns he shared previously with Wagner. But now, the perspective of Wagner and Schopenhauer is deemed

---

10   For an informative discussion of this so-called 'middle period', see Detwiler 1990.

insufficient. In fact, it is worse than insufficient: it concedes too much to the rabble, to democracy, to Christianity, and to the forces of modernity that are undermining the very civilization that Nietzsche originally thought Wagner could help to save. Nietzsche, in this period, rejects the lingering overtones of compassion found in Schopenhauer's metaphysics, and what he perceives as the rabble-rousing nature of Wagner's plays. Losurdo points out that Nietzsche, in his efforts to distance himself from Wagner, even goes so far as to accuse the musician of sharing certain features of the Jews who Wagner hates so much (p. 168).

Nietzsche dedicated *Human, All-Too-Human* to Voltaire, and remoulded the Enlightenment in an elitist vein, throwing to the wayside its democratic and socialistic sides. As Losurdo demonstrates, this was – ironically – an Enlightenment meant to buttress the values of the *Ancien Regime*, and to hinder the progress of the plebeian rabble towards socialism. The true Enlightenment of the French moralists and Voltaire was pitted against the proto-socialism of Jean-Jacques Rousseau. In a colourful metaphor, Nietzsche uncovered the subterranean spiritual force of Rousseauianism behind all modern revolutions: 'In every socialistic upheaval, it is ever the man Rousseau who is moving like the hidden forces imprisoned under Mt. Etna' (p. 250).

No longer was French culture monolithically decadent, modern, and Jewish, as it was for the young Wagnerite Nietzsche. And no longer was Nietzsche imbibing the spirit of a narrow German chauvinism. His views were now distinctively 'European', and more attuned to the needs of what he saw as a true 'Enlightenment'. Nietzsche sought to rescue the French Enlightenment from the clutches of the modern disease of universalising and levelling progressivism, and of turning a critical (and scientific) eye of suspicion towards every doctrine. Nietzsche introduced a new sceptical positivism and naturalistic attitude against the metaphysical underpinnings of socialism. From this, Nietzsche developed sympathy not only for the kind of thinking he originally castigated Strauss for, but also for the anti-socialist liberalism and positivism of his Jewish friend Paul Rée. In this period, Nietzsche found himself in tune with an aristocratic conception of liberalism, and one that shared many affinities with the likes of Alexis de Tocqueville and Benjamin Constant, which Losurdo details at some length.

While Nietzsche did not retain his previous enmity towards the Jews in this period, Losurdo points to traces of Judeophobia that persisted in later years. Nietzsche would eventually cast the war against modernity as a war between Judea and Rome, but Losurdo also notes distinctions Nietzsche made within Judaism and the history of Jews. In Nietzsche's appreciation of the Jews of the Old Testament, he favoured what can be called the Kings against the Prophets.

Or, in other words, Nietzsche lamented the decline of the Jews after the Babylonian captivity in their transformation from a people of warriors to a people
spreading the disease of slave morality through their prophets. But, as Losurdo
puts it,

> [Nietzsche] has no difficulty in identifying with the Jewish ancestry of the
> rulers that, thanks to their national religion, conquers Canaan. And even
> the merchants' god arouses indignation only when he seeks to subordin-
> ate to himself the god of hosts, thereby destroying the ancient and noble
> ideal of *otium et bellum*.
>
>   p. 573

We will return to Nietzsche's positions on the Jews, but it is important to know
how his next conceptual revolution was occasioned by his break with Paul Rée
and Lou Salomé. In this phase, Nietzsche cast off the positivistic and naturalistic appeals to science and Enlightenment. As Losurdo demonstrates, he was
no longer nominalistic or simply relativistic in his scepticism but underwent
a transition from a positivistic attitude to a perspectivalist one. A nominalism
that treated all positions as equal was still adopting too universalistic and neutral a standpoint. For Nietzsche, the one who judged relativistically falsified and
denied life itself, since one cannot escape the need to judge, make distinctions,
and order values. One could not appeal to a neutral ground but had to fall back
on one's own immanent sphere of values, values which could not harbour universalistic pretences. Nietzsche deflated such pretences, showing them to be
emanations of will, or a particular set of valuations.

This move was more radical than it may first appear, but it was consistent with what Losurdo considers Nietzsche's main project. The world itself no
longer could be considered in a positivistic way, or as a set of contingent laws
operating naturalistically. Instead, the scientific attitude emanated from a particular set of interests for Nietzsche: the scientific attitude itself came under
genealogical suspicion. The need to set regular, uniform laws of motion; the
very idea of positing a principle of sufficient reason, or laws of cause and effect,
was ultimately reducible to a way of valuing and seeing the world. Universal
laws of physics were not actually universal but emanated only from a universalising ecology of value. Thus, the scientific worldview, for Nietzsche, became
a *political* and not strictly speaking a scientific project.

This was the new science Nietzsche inaugurated: a science of genealogical
reduction to particular sets of interests and forces. But one can argue that Nietzsche established his own 'metaphysical' doctrines in this period: the will to
power (what Heidegger called the last metaphysics) and the eternal return of

the same. Does this mean Nietzsche was contradicting himself? Perhaps so, but it is key to understand how Nietzsche deployed these ideas. The eternal return of the same was, for instance, specifically an idea for 'the strong' against the weak that would heighten and strengthen the power of the free spirits against the rabble. While Nietzsche sometimes tried to justify the eternal return metaphysically and scientifically, the idea primarily springs from his aristocratic perspectivalism. Since ideas like progress or bettering conditions are condemned as illusory when events are said to recur again and again ad infinitum, the eternal return becomes the perfect weapon against the rabble. Hopes for a better world are derided as unscientific and theological, and the eternal return could act now as a check against the aspirations of the lower orders of society. As Losurdo puts it: 'The doctrine of the eternal return is then configured as the counter-revenge of the ruling classes, who now deride the hopes and illusions of the subaltern classes' (p. 476).

Of course, from Nietzsche's aristocratic position, one did not have to demonstrate rationally the merits of specific ideas, including an idea like the eternal return of the same. The aristocratic perspective, the party of life for which Nietzsche was the herald, did not need reasons to justify itself, but could assert what it believed simply because it believed it. In one of his more Calvinistic moments, Nietzsche even calls 'the aristocratic circle that he summons to distinction "God's elect"' (p. 680).

We can appreciate how constitutive a role Nietzsche's aristocratic radicalism now played in his seemingly rarefied discussions of language, science, and art. All these discussions came politically charged and moreover charged with a particular form of politics that must be understood before we can investigate Nietzsche further. It is the main task of Losurdo's biography to explicate the nature of that politics, and how it was shaped by the German and international context.

In analysing the meaning of Nietzsche's political ideas, Losurdo situates them as part of an overall constellation of reaction against democracy, abolitionism, feminism, and socialism. He compares Nietzsche's criticisms of mass democracy with those of other prominent liberal figures, such as Benjamin Constant, John Stuart Mill, and Alexis de Tocqueville, and sees more affinities between them than stark differences, especially when it comes to understanding the threat of the masses against hierarchy, class, and privilege. Losurdo establishes Nietzsche as part of this liberal tradition that did not necessarily equate liberty with democracy.

But Nietzsche radicalised the tendencies of liberal hatred of mass democracy, pushing in the direction of a robust defence of slavery. It is thus significant to acknowledge that, when Nietzsche argued for rank-ordering, the reassertion of slavery, and even the elimination of decadent races, he was not being metaphorical, but was reacting to what he perceived as real threats to a hierarchical mode of existence. As Losurdo states, Nietzsche's own friends, including Georges Brandes, took him at his word (p. 724).

Slavery was not simply a mental image of bondage, but an actual reality Nietzsche wanted to defend, reinforce, and extend. Nietzsche may be as American as apple pie, but not quite in a reassuring sense. Losurdo's sections on the American Civil War and his discussion of Nietzsche's comments on blacks, abolitionism, and Harriet Beecher Stowe are especially illuminating here. It is particularly the reaction to Stowe that throws light on how Nietzsche feared women as carriers of the revolutionary contagion. Influenced by Taine's writings on women and the French Revolution, Nietzsche saw such allegedly unmasculine values as compassion and sentimentalism as helping to unleash the worst in the female gender:

> Continuation of Christianity by the French Revolution. Rousseau is the seducer: he again removes the chains of woman, who from then on is represented in an ever more interesting way, as suffering. Then the slaves and Mistress Beecher-Stowe. Then the poor and the workers. Then the vicious and the sick – all that is brought to the fore.
>
> p. 919

Losurdo instructively compares Nietzsche's ideas with explicit apologists for antebellum slavery, such as George Fitzhugh. For Fitzhugh, abolitionism against the property of slaves eventually implied a logic that would lead to the abolition of property *in toto*. Fitzhugh was also sensitive to the connections between the abolitionist movement and German Social Democracy, and his criticisms of the abolitionist movement correspond to Nietzsche's own. Both were quick to connect abolitionism to socialist revolution.

Nietzsche's defence of slavery accounts for his opposition to the then new Kaiser Wilhelm II, and his derogatory reference to the young monarch as the 'brown idiot'. Nietzsche used this racial insult to signify how the young Kaiser was planning to embark on a variety of social reforms, including an international crusade to free black slaves in Africa.[11] It is a measure of the anti-

---

11   Not that one should see the Kaiser as a beacon of progressivism. The historical record clearly shows he was not, and his inspired social Christianity was hollow, undergirded with anti-Semitic undertones from Stöcker. For an in-depth discussion on Nietzsche's relationship to political anti-Semitism in the Second Reich, see Holub 2015.

progressivism of Nietzsche that his criticism of the Kaiser included a call for the extension of the anti-socialist laws originally promoted under Bismarck, and other reactionary policies that would curtail, block, and eliminate any moves towards democracy and emancipation. Bismarck himself shared this animus towards the surface progressivism of Wilhelm II, though this was unknown to Nietzsche at the time.[12]

Besides their hostility to socialism and the young Kaiser, another thing Bismarck and Nietzsche shared was a utopian project of mixing the Jewish and Prussian races. As Bismarck put it in 1871, it would be a good policy to cross 'Jewish mares with Prussian stallions'. Nietzsche took a nearly identical position and fantasised about how the new European elite he envisioned should appropriate the genius of the Jewish race for its own ends. But what Nietzsche considered as Jewish weakness, superficiality, and ill-manners had to be purged:

> Their [the Jews'] eye does not convince, their tongue easily runs too quickly and becomes entangled, their anger does not achieve the deep and honourable leonine roar, their stomach cannot deal with carousals, their head with strong wines – their arms and legs do not permit them proud passions (in their hands there often twitch I know not what memories); and even the way a Jew mounts a horse [...] is not without its difficulties, and shows that Jews have never been a knightly race.
>
> p. 545

Nietzsche argued also against the further immigration of Jews to Germany and made distinctions between potential bourgeois Jews to include in the new international ruling order, and more subversive types such as the unclean 'Polish Jews' he referred to in the *Antichrist*. Losurdo, in a virtually exhaustive treatment, discusses Nietzsche's other racial ideas, particularly when it comes to Chinese workers. For Nietzsche, the labour question was resolvable by letting European workers undertake expeditions to colonise the rest of the world, while the European bourgeoisie would import Chinese workers to serve as the necessary labour force for the old world. In a perverse way, Nietzsche became a globalisation theorist *avant la lettre*, and the Chinese people came 'for [Nietz-

---

12   Losurdo's biography is an excellent source for the thoughts and opinions of the 'Iron Chancellor', including a discussion of Bismarck's opposition to the young emperor Wilhelm II. See Chapter 17, Section Four of this study. For a recent discussion of Nietzsche's relationship to Bismarck's own 'grand politics', see Drochon 2018.

sche] to symbolise the humble and servile worker, eager to please, the new type of slaves the masters needed' (p. 204).

Losurdo demonstrates how Nietzsche's treatment of the labour question, capitalism, and exploitation can be useful for Marxists. Nietzsche does not hide the fact that the current mode of production is anything but exploitative, and even uses quasi-Marxist language to illustrate this process of surplus extraction from the workers.[13] But, although Nietzsche was honest about the nature of political economy (and the nature of history as the 'struggle of estates and classes'), he still argued for its absolute unavoidability (p. 830). Workers, for Nietzsche, could not rule, much less constitute a workers' state. They had to work, and they had also to learn to become numb and love their dehumanising drudgery. The message to the bourgeoisie Nietzsche sent in the *Gay Science* was not to abjure exploitation, but to adopt manners germane to a ruling or master class. The problem with the bourgeoisie was not the fact that it exploited the proletariat; the problem was its lack of a noble mentality. Nietzsche cautioned it against vulgar displays of wealth, or democratic habits that would sink it down to the level of its workers. What was important was to maintain the pathos of distance between rulers and ruled. But, in occluding his concrete politics, the dominant image of Nietzscheanism helped to conceal what he defended so vehemently: namely, the bases of our current liberal (and now perhaps 'neoliberal') capitalist order. Losurdo's book furnishes us with an antidote to this ideological obfuscation, or what he calls the 'hermeneutics of innocence' which conceals the nature of Nietzsche's thought as a weapon for power and privilege.[14]

One cannot go into more detail here in the introduction, and one should not mistake this menu for the meal to come. Outlined above are some of the stakes involved, but what is accomplished in the text that follows is a restoration of Nietzsche as a political philosopher to be reckoned with. He is a thinker to be taken in earnest, and a thinker who should be able to shock and disturb without being absorbed uncritically. Losurdo ends the domestication process

---

13   It may be possible that Nietzsche was familiar with Marx and Engels's ideas, albeit through secondary source materials. This piece of information from Thomas Brobjer should help to complement Losurdo's account: 'Nietzsche never mentions Karl Marx or Friedrich Engels, and it is generally assumed that he had no knowledge of them and their kind of thinking and socialism. However, this is not correct. Marx is referred to in at least eleven books, by nine different authors, which Nietzsche read or possessed, and in six of them he is discussed and quoted extensively. In one of them Nietzsche has underlined Karl Marx's name'. Brobjer 2008, p. 70.

14   For a recent discussion of Nietzsche's kinship with the anti-socialist economics of the Austrian school, see Corey Robin's 'Nietzsche's Marginal Children: On Friedrich Hayek'.

that has mummified Nietzsche for so long; that has turned him into a harmless and banal icon, rather than the genuinely disquieting philosopher he was. This is a portrait of Nietzsche as counterrevolutionary; as a class-conscious ideologue of aristocracy, and as an enemy of socialism. It is not a portrait Nietzsche would have found unfamiliar. But it is as an enemy that critical readers can learn from him, because the challenge his perspectivalism poses to progressive ideas is remarkable and potentially devastating. Instead of borrowing half-digested concepts from Nietzsche, his challenge should force us to come to grips with the history of progressive ideas, and their philosophical foundations. For, without a positive philosophical orientation to oppose Nietzsche's criticism, we will fall prey to his critique. In other words, we will end up believing what we believe, simply because we believe it. Only when we can confront, reformulate, and rationally defend the philosophical ideas at the basis of our politics can we stop the process of becoming Nietzschean.[15]

---

15   Domenico Losurdo passed away on 28 June 2018. This has been an immeasurable loss for scholars, activists, and socialists around the world. His thought will endure and his contributions to philosophy and politics will continue to be translated into multiple languages for years to come.

PART 1

Nietzsche in His Time: In Struggle against Socratism and Judaism

∵

Annihilation of Greek culture by the Jewish world.
VII, 83

• • •

Was Socrates Greek at all? Often enough, ugliness is a sign of crossbreeding, of arrested development due to crossbreeding.
GD, 'The Problem of Socrates', 3 [163]

• • •

When Socrates and Plato took the side of virtue and justice, they were Jews and nothing but.
XIII, 331

• • •

Is music drama really dead, dead for good? [...] This is the most serious question of our art, and who, as a German, does not understand the seriousness of this question has fallen victim to the Socratism of our days. [...] This Socratism is the Jewish press: I say nothing more.
XIV, 101

• • •

Somebody once said to me: You, Sir, are a Jew, and as such you don't have a complete mastery of German.
From the draft of an imaginary letter to DAVID FRIEDRICH STRAUSS, VII, 589

• •
•

CHAPTER 1

The Crisis of Culture from Socrates to the Paris Commune

1   *The Birth of Tragedy* as a Re-interpretation of Hellenism?

Let us undertake a sort of intellectual experiment. We are at the beginning of 1872. While browsing through the recent publications in a German bookshop, we run into a book with an unusual and at the same time engaging title: *The Birth of Tragedy out of the Spirit of Music*. We flip through the pages to understand what it is about. The title page catches our attention: it informs us that the author is professor of classical philology at the University of Basel. In the following pages there are frequent references to Greek myths, to Aeschylus, Sophocles and Euripides. We are in a less fortunate situation (or perhaps actually happier) than that of Willamowitz who has known Nietzsche for some time and has no doubts: he believes that he holds in his hands a text of classical philology, and is immediately indignant about the method, or an absence of method, which is unforgivable for a university professor of that discipline; he 'discusses a series of very important questions in the history of Greek literature', but as a 'dreaming professor' rather than as a 'scholarly researcher'.[1]

More cautiously, we hesitate to make a judgement. While turning over the pages of the book again, we notice the 'Foreword to Richard Wagner'. He is praised for the 'magnificent celebratory essay on Beethoven'; furthermore, especially in the last pages, there are frequent references to German music and musicians. So, we are pushed to go back to the subtitle, or rather, to the second part of the book's title: are we dealing with a text of musicology or musical criticism? This perspective also does not present the author in a more positive light. Indeed, a few months later, the author will be obliged to acknowledge bitterly that philologists and musicologists, respectively, label him a 'clown philologist' or a 'music littérateur' (B, II, 3, 13).

In light of the history of the success of the great philosopher we now understand we have encountered, these two judgements are unacceptable. However, we are not always aware that their refutation presupposes a radical change in the way of reading *The Birth of Tragedy*. If we continue to believe that it is 'above

---

1   Wilamowitz-Möllendorf 1989a, pp. 29 f. & 34fn.

all a homage to Wagner',[2] we cannot avoid considering it to be completely ephemeral: far from being enduring, this homage was subsequently entirely overturned, into its opposite.

Nor would an interpretation of the book as a text exclusively engaged in reflecting on the artistic phenomenon in Greece or in general be persuasive.[3] It is true that, immediately after the 'Foreword', the author declares that he wants to contribute to the development of 'the science of aesthetics' (GT, 1; I, 25 [14]), while the penultimate chapter calls for taking 'a bold run-up and vault into a metaphysics of art' (GT, 24; I, 152 [113]). However, absolutising or privileging these themes would mean precluding an understanding of the numerous references to the great political events of the time, starting from the war of two years before, already evoked in the 'Foreword', and, furthermore, called upon as an example of the 'courageous seriousness' of the Prussian-German soldiers and a stimulus of the 'patriotic excitement' of the book's author and readers.

More important than the presence of political references is the fact that they are not at all occasional and external to the aesthetic considerations. Of course, the celebration of ancient tragedy in comparison to melodrama and opera is constant. It is interesting, however, to observe the reasons provided for the condemnation of this 'truly modern genre'. Its foundation is 'a need of a non-aesthetic kind', or even 'an entirely un-aesthetic need'. It consists 'in the optimistic glorification of mankind as such, in the view that primal man was both good and artistic by nature'. It is an ideology that has finally taken on a 'threatening and terrible' configuration 'in the socialist movements of the present' (GT, 19; I, 122–3 [90–1]). From the sky to which, apparently, the 'metaphysics of art' refers, we are forced to go down onto the ground of history and politics; from the contemplation of beauty and 'the science of aesthetics' we are sucked down into the vortex of a dramatic conflict. The conflict is so dramatic that it leaves no space for half-measures: it is not so much about formulating an aesthetic judgement, but rather about 'annihilating [vernichten] opera', that mode of subversive contagion. In order to achieve this result, it is necessary to take up 'arms against that Alexandrian cheerfulness which expresses its favourite idea so naively in opera' (GT, 19; I, 125 [93, trans. modified]). These are definitely militant tones. They can be understood only if we do not lose sight of the fact that Nietzsche, at the end of his conscious life, continued to group together 'opera' and 'revolution' (EH, 'The Birth of Tragedy', 1 [108]). That is,

2 Fink 1993, p. 18.
3 This is the case of Fink 1993, pp. 9–45.

these tones can be understood only if we constantly recall that, from the beginning, aesthetic considerations are strictly intertwined with political reflection, and political struggle.

The denunciation of 'optimism's' catastrophic political effects is accompanied by an impassioned polemic against the very widespread interpretation of the Greek world that projects onto it the ideal – in reality, a modern ideal – of a vacuous and superficial 'serenity'. Furthermore, the recovery of authentic Hellenism and the liquidation of its 'serene' image are developed by referring not only to Hellenic tragedy and art but also to Hellenic religion, as demonstrated by the regular references to Dionysus and Apollo. Two integral world views are thereby compared and contrasted; along with art, they embrace every other aspect of life, not excluding the political dimension.

The Birth of Tragedy cannot really be recuperated by attributing to it the merit of having contributed to a more adequate historical understanding of Hellenism. The contempt for 'today's cultured historiographers', who try 'to appropriate Greek antiquity, alongside other antiquities, "historically"' (GT, 20; I, 130 [96]), is clearly declared. 'Historical evaluation' – as contemporary texts explain – in reality rules out a correct 'interpretation of the problems that are eternally the same' (BA, 5; I, 742), so 'historical interest' betrays culture (BA, 2; I, 677). The point is made in even more drastic terms in a note from 1872: to take 'the historical' seriously means taking seriously the 'false' (VII, 411). Although formulated in relation to the religious phenomenon, this consideration aims at a wider significance.

It is true that, at the time of the publication of the book in question, Nietzsche was also engaged as a philologist and historian in a polemic against the unilaterally serene and Olympic view of the world he loved: 'Goethe's Hellenism is, first, historically false, and second, too weak [*weich*] and effeminate' (VII, 778 [336 = *Unpublished Writings from the Period of Unfashionable Observations*]); it was this weakness of the moderns that repressed Hellenism's acute consciousness of the tragic dimension of existence. This is a thesis implicitly reasserted in the title given to the book's third edition (1878): *The Birth of Tragedy, or Hellenism and Pessimism*. However, the interpreter cannot identify immediately with Nietzsche's self-consciousness, as if before his interpretation there were only that of Goethe or, more appropriately, of Winckelmann, and as if the motive of Hellenic serenity had been shared by everyone.

Actually, Schelling had already emphasised 'the tragic, the streak of profound melancholy that traverses all of paganism'.[4] When we read in Nietzsche

---

4 Schelling 1856–61, Vol. XII, p. 346.

that 'Greek culture is based on a relation of domination by a minoritarian class of the unfree numbering four or five times more' (VIII, 60), we are led to think of Wilhelm von Humboldt, according to whom slavery in ancient Greece was 'an unjust and barbaric means of securing for a part of humanity the highest power and beauty through the sacrifice of another part'.[5] In turn, Hegel continually noted that the foundation and condition of the 'beautiful freedom' of Greece was slavery. In this case as well, as soon as we remove this beautiful veil, we see the emergence of a tragic dimension, which can even assume a truly revolting face, as happened, for instance, in the case of the periodic wild hunting by the Spartans of the helots, with 'inhuman harshness'.[6]

The theme of slavery, and of the sufferings it entails, was also present in Schelling. Calling upon the authority of Aristotle, he denounced the emptiness of the progressivism that ignored the foundation of pain and poverty upon which any culture rested. After the revolution of 1848, *The Philosophy of Mythology* offered a hymn to Dike: this 'power', which signified 'the universal expiation of the human race', generated consternation with its sudden irruption; Sophocles's 'tragic chorus' called upon Antigone to bow down before it.[7]

Greece was even less a synonym of undisturbed serenity for the philosopher who was Nietzsche's immediate predecessor. *The World as Will and Representation* attributed to Plato and Pythagoras the merit of having 'taken up with admiration [...] from India or Egypt' the 'philosophical truth' that aspired and called for aspiration to Nirvana, namely, to 'a state in which there are not four things: birth, old age, sickness and death'.[8] This is a theme that in *The Birth of Tragedy* echoed in the bitter truth of Silenus, who, as we shall see, summarised the ideal to which to aspire in these terms: 'not to be born, not to be, to be nothing'.

Later, Nietzsche himself emphasised, in a self-critical sense, that 'a few formulas [in *The Birth of Tragedy*] are tainted with the cadaverous fragrance of Schopenhauer'. The subtitle added to the third edition is thus reinterpreted in a radical way.

> *Hellenism and Pessimism*: that would have been an unambiguous title: that is, as the first lesson in how the Greeks put pessimism behind them, –

---

5   Humboldt 1903–36a, pp. 118–19.
6   Hegel 1919–20, pp. 629–30.
7   Schelling 1856–61, Vol. XI, pp. 530–1.
8   Schopenhauer 1976–82a, p. 487 (§ 63).

how they overcame it ... Tragedy in particular proves that the Greeks were not pessimists: Schopenhauer was wrong about this as he was wrong about everything.

EH, The Birth of Tragedy 1 [107–8]

Now Nietzsche attributed to his youthful work the merit of having started to break not with the optimistic but much more with the pessimistic vision of Hellenism. Just like aesthetic categories, psychological categories too are unable to explain the genesis and significance of *The Birth of Tragedy*.

2   Tragic Hellenism as Antidote to 'Weak' Modernity

In any case, it was not certainly a preoccupation with philological and historical rigour that inspired and distinguished the young professor of philology of the University of Basel. Wilamowitz's irony regarding the easy transitions from Greece to India or the Buddhist Orient, already present in Schopenhauer, is well known.[9] It could be added that no less surprising are those transitions in Nietzsche that go from the Greece of the VII–V century BC to the Europe of the second half of the nineteenth century. Just as 'Socrates and Euripides serve to explain neo-Latin theatre', the music and the culture of the 'neo-Latin peoples' (VII, 326), so too the Greeks provide the basis for 'understanding the Wagnerian artwork', for Wagner represents the 'rebirth of tragedy' (VII, 372–3).

Another consideration is even more important. The role played by space and time in defining authentic Hellenism seems not to be particularly important. Alexander is its 'coarsened copy' (CV, 5; I, 792); although some centuries older, John's Gospel is, instead, to be considered a 'totally Greek creation', or even 'a product of the same spirit from which the mysteries were born' (VII, 156). It is not so much about investigating the concrete historical manifestations of 'the Hellenic human being' (CV, 5; I, 792) than of comprehending the 'Hellenic essence [*Wesen*]', or even 'the core [*Kern*]' of such an essence (GT, 20; I, 129 [96]). This is the most profound and remote core, indefinable on the basis of the empirical world and appearances, which constitutes the measure by which individual authors are measured and evaluated. The art of Euripides has an 'almost un-Greek artistic character' (ST; I, 540); Socrates and Plato represent a 'rupture with the Greek element', and Plato – as a fragment adds – 'fights against the Hellenic element' (VII, 398–9).

---

9   Wilamowitz-Möllendorff 1972a, p. 212.

Later, by stressing a line of continuity with the evaluations expressed in *The Birth of Tragedy*, Nietzsche again asserted that the two philosophers had to be excluded from authentic Hellenism 'as symptoms of decay, as agents of Greek disintegration, as pseudo-Greek, as anti-Greek' (GD, 'The Problem of Socrates', 2 [162]). Socratism represented the perversion of the most profound 'instincts of the earlier Greeks' (GD, 'The Problem of Socrates', 4 [163]). It was misleading 'to take Plato's ideomania, his nearly religious lunacy about forms, as a development and testimony of "the Greek soul"' (FW, 357 [217]). In reality, the author of the doctrine of ideas 'said no' to 'Greek life' (JGB, 28 [30]). His philosophy turned out to be already soaked with Christianity, which, dispensing with Hellas and classical antiquity, did nothing more than develop and plebeanise Platonism (*infra*, Chapter 15 § 2). Nietzsche argued in similar terms when referring to Epicurus. He was the antithesis of a 'Dionysian pessimist': he was thus completely external to authentic and tragic Hellenism and was instead linked to Christianity; the Christian, indeed, 'is simply a kind of Epicurean and, like him, essentially a romantic' (FW, 370 [235]). In the following years, whole decisive chapters of Greek culture and history would be considered spurious compared to authentic Hellenism. Yet, even now, we encounter the thesis that, considered accurately, 'the degeneration had already started in Hellas' (VIII, 78). Thus, as *The Gay Science* would later conclude: 'We must overcome even the Greeks!' (FW, 340 [194]).

Even the 'two centuries of the tragic epoch' were, in a strict sense, regarded as not always adequate to its essence, or to its more profound and true instincts. The irruption of an 'anti-Greek moment' (PHG, 9; I, 836) was represented by Parmenides: 'the lack of perfume, of colour, of soul, of form, the complete lack of blood, of religiosity, of ethical warmth', which characterised Parmenides's philosophy, were completely incomprehensible 'in a Greek' (PHG, 11; I, 845). Nietzsche ended by recognising, at least to some extent, that the Hellenism he loved was not a historical reality which could be studied with the methods of historical research: 'Hellenism has for us the value that the saints have for Catholics' (VII, 18).

Returning later to the significance of the conceptual couplet of pessimism/optimism, Nietzsche would observe: the 'romantic pessimism' of Wagner and Schopenhauer had nothing to do with the 'Dionysian pessimism' that, in turn, was the 'pessimism of the future' more than of a splendid and remote past (FW, 370 [236]). *The Birth of Tragedy* intended to promote a 'pessimism of strength, a classical pessimism'; however, the word classical 'not in the sense of a historical determination, but a psychological one, opposed to a "romantic" sense' (XIII, 229). More precisely, Hellenism was a philosophical category that functioned as a principle of legitimation or delegitimation of individual authors, of different cultural and political movements and of different stages of history in general and of Greek history itself. This is made unequivocally clear in *Ecce Homo*:

> I have the right to understand myself as the first tragic philosopher. [...] Nobody had ever turned the Dionysian into a philosophical pathos before me: tragic wisdom was missing – I could not find any sign of it, even among the eminent Greek philosophers, those from the two centuries before Socrates. I had some doubts in the case of Heraclitus ...
>
> EH, 'The Birth of Tragedy', 3 [110]

We have seen Nietzsche polemicising against the modern projection of 'serenity' onto the Hellenic world: this polemic puts us on the tracks of a different and opposed projection. In this regard, the philosopher, having left behind the years of *The Birth of Tragedy*, expressed himself with great frankness: 'In what sort of disguise did I present that which I felt to be "Dionysian"! In what a learned and monotonous way, and at the same time not sufficiently erudite to be able to produce the effect of opening a new field of work for generations of philologists!' (XI, 424). Further: 'My philology was only an attempt to find a way out, which I grasped at eagerly: I can't deceive myself about that'; it was an expedient necessitated also by the painful sense of not having a single 'companion' (XII, 57). Or, to quote a text from 1886, it was 'the belief that I was not thus isolated, not alone in seeing as I did' that stimulated the construction, with 'a certain amount of "art", a certain amount of false-coinage', the tragic image of the 'Greeks' (MA, 'Introduction', 1 [5]). It was the solitude painfully experienced in the modern world that pushed Nietzsche to search for improbable companions in pre-Socratic Hellas. In this juvenile attitude there was also a residue of a lack of courage: 'What unhappiness there is to speak as a learned man about something that I could have been able to recount as one who has lived it' (*Erlebter* XI, 427).

In conclusion, to understand Nietzsche's manner of proceeding we need to invert the previously cited aphorism that takes its distance from Goethe (and Winckelmann). Put back on its feet again, that critical judgement on Hellenism loved by those two authors should read as follows: Hellenism 'is above all too weak and not virile, and therefore it is to be considered historically false'. In Nietzsche, authentic Hellenism was built in opposition to everything in the modern world that is weak, flabby and effeminate: it is from this denunciation that we need to start if we want to understand the plot and meaning of *The Birth of Tragedy*. This is confirmed in another confession contained in an aphorism in which, with his juvenile work in mind, Nietzsche wrote: 'Each year I become more and more up-front, in the sense that my vision penetrates ever deeper into this nineteenth century, into this century of great moral hypocrisy' (XI, 423–4). Nietzsche's intellectual path is here defined with great clarity: from the denunciation of the present to the invocation and transfiguration of a very remote past.

3   The Paris Commune and the Threat of a 'Horrifying Destruction' of Culture

But what was it that prompted this escape, or rather, this search for a way out of modernity? What was so worrying in the present that pushed Nietzsche towards an alternative located in ancient Greece? While trying to find the Ariadne's thread that enables us to orientate ourselves in what, for now, appears as a labyrinth, we encounter some pages and a paragraph that stands out from all the others due to its anguished tone: because of 'optimism', culture is going to face a 'horrifying destruction'; 'the belief in the earthly happiness of all' makes society tremble 'down to the very lowest levels', sowing discontent in 'a class of barbaric slaves', a class that, having been seduced by utopian ideas and without any ground whatsoever, now feels 'its existence as injustice [*Unrecht*]' and explodes in endless revolts (GT, 18; I, 117 [86–7]).

The dramatic tone of this warning drives away any doubt. No, we are not in the presence of a philological and historical clarification; more than the optimistic interpretation of Hellenism, it is optimism itself that constituted the target of the polemic in *The Birth of Tragedy*. Nietzsche's preoccupation, or rather his anguish, about a danger not remote or hypothetical, but real and impending, is plainly evident. The reference to the Paris Commune is transparent, an event that a great part of the culture of that time experienced as the threatening announcement of a possible imminent end of culture. Tocqueville had already raised the alarm after the Parisian days of June 1848, 'not only in France, but all over Europe, the soil of European civilization shakes'.[10] The events of 23 years later seemed to confirm the most catastrophic predictions. As Burckhardt observed during a series of lectures that Nietzsche followed with interest, it was an explosion produced by the 'great social question', by then at the centre of political conflict. Order had been restored in France, but it should not be forgotten that 'elsewhere the illness still crawls inside the organism'.[11]

---

10   Tocqueville 1864–7, Vol. IX, p. 570.
11   Burckhardt 1978b, p. 383.

Nietzsche's reading of the Paris Commune as a sort of servile revolt was not unusual in the culture of the time. On the eve of the 1848 revolution, Tocqueville warned against the danger of 'servile wars',[12] thus indirectly comparing modern proletarians and ancient slaves. On the other hand, when the *Birth of Tragedy* was published, the echo of the American Civil War, of a few years prior, was still very much alive. It is no mere coincidence that Marx condemned the protagonists of the repression in France as 'slaveholders',[13] capable of any sort of cruelty when 'the slaves' needed to be brought back into order, while instead Marx celebrated the workers' revolt as 'the war of the enslaved [*geknechtete*]' against their enslavers, the 'only justifiable war in history'.[14]

The correspondence and the fragments contemporary with *The Birth of Tragedy* clarify unequivocally the intensity with which Nietzsche experienced the Paris Commune and how painful and indelible were the imprints left in him by this event. After the news of the fire at the Louvre by the insurgents – as he writes in a letter to Gersdorff of 21 June 1871 – 'I was for some days completely destroyed and drenched in tears and doubts: all scholarly and philosophical-aesthetic existence seemed to me an absurdity, if a single day could wipe out the most noble works of art, or whole periods of art' (B, II, 1, 204). Together with the Louvre – Bagehot soon declared from across the Channel – the insurgents wanted to destroy everything in Paris worthy of seeing and admiring, any evidence of 'culture' and civilised life.[15] Once again we are brought back to what Marx wrote on the opposing side. He was indignant because the ruling classes, while undertaking a merciless repression worthy of Tamerlane, labelled the desperate revolt of Parisian workers an assault and conspiracy against 'culture' undertaken by 'incendiarist' barbarians given to 'vandalism'.[16] Afterwards, the news of the fire was revealed to be false, but it did not modify Nietzsche's state of mind, lyrically expressed in a fragment a few years later: 'Autumn – pain – stubble – campions – asters. Very similar when the Louvre was supposed to have been burnt – feeling the autumn-time of culture. Never a deeper pain' (VIII, 504).

Let us try then to examine *The Birth of the Tragedy*, to read it rapidly in such a way that, without referring to any other text, we take seriously the distressed warning against the mortal danger represented by the servile revolt and the Paris Commune. Both had been nourished by the modern illusion of being able

---

12   Tocqueville 1951, Vol. III, 2, p. 727.
13   Marx and Engels 1975 ff., Vol. 22, p. 343.
14   Marx and Engels 1975 ff., Vol. 22, pp. 348 & 351.
15   Bagehot 1974c, p. 197.
16   Marx and Engels 1975 ff., Vol. 22, pp. 348–52 & 327.

to know and to transform the essence of reality, by banishing the negative and tragic from it. But when did this devastating progressive superstition start? A long time before the Enlightenment to which one generally refers: it is possible to come across the *hybris* of reason and the enlightenment already in Greece. Socrates was the beginning of the 'theoretical human being' (GT, 15; I, 98 [72]) and the 'theoretical optimist' who, with his 'belief that the nature of things can be discovered' and in knowledge (GT, 15; I, 100 [74]), at the same time had the pretension of being 'obliged to correct existence' (GT, 13; I, 89 [66]).

With the advancing tide endlessly swelled by optimism and the expectation of happiness, even the dyke traditionally represented by Christianity started showing worrisome cracks. Christianity itself was infected by the 'optimistic spirit', now identified as the 'the seed of our society's destruction' (GT, 18; I, 117 [87]). So, it was not possible to go only halfway in the critique of this ruinous development. The remedy could not be found in Hellenism either, if the latter continued to be read as synonym of unmoved and unmovable serenity. Such an interpretation, which went back to the early-Christian polemicists (GT, 11; I, 78 [57]), comprehended in reality only one aspect, the Apolline, testified first by sculpture. Tragedy and music, on the other hand, put us in the presence of a different and more profound dimension. Forced to reveal a truth he would have preferred to keep secret, Silenus, companion of Dionysus, cut through the sparkling Apolline veils and revealed the abyss of existence.

> Wretched, ephemeral race, children of chance and tribulation, why do you force me to tell you the very thing which it would be most profitable for you not to hear? The very best thing is utterly beyond your reach: not to have been born, not to be, to be nothing. However, the second best thing for you is: to die soon.
>
> GT, 3; I, 35 [23]

Such a Dionysian truth assumed a transfigured and dreamy expression in Apolline art, which even had a socially beneficial function, insofar as it helped the human being to withstand 'the terrors and horrors of existence' (GT, 3; I, 35 [23]). Yet, this should not make us lose sight of the deepest dimension, the tragic and Dionysian intensity of the Greek world, which found a powerful expression in Aeschylus's *Prometheus*. By destroying the vision of progress belonging to a 'naive humanity', he highlighted 'the whole flood of suffering and tribulations' that the invention of fire already entails (GT, 9; I, 69 [49–50]).

The pretension of terrestrial happiness for everyone, which more and more characterised the modern world, was thus revealed as madness. However, the vision of Socrates triumphed. Alexandrian Hellenism took over from the tragic and Dionysiac; it was decisively inclined 'in correcting the world through knowledge, in life led by science': the renunciation of a 'metaphysical solace' opened the road to the search for an 'earthly harmony', a happiness entrusted to the 'machines' and 'smelting furnaces', as well as to political institutions (GT, 17; I, 115 [85]).

However, a ruinous and incurable contradiction intervened. Like any culture, Alexandrian culture also 'needs a slave-class in order to exist in the long term; as it views existence optimistically, however, it denies the necessity of such a class' and proclaims instead 'human dignity' and 'the dignity of labour' (GT, 18; I, 117 [86]). It thus lays the foundations for the ceaseless and ruinous revolutionary cycle, for the successive waves of servile revolts. So, we need to see in Socrates 'the vortex and turning-point of so-called world history' (GT, 15; I, 100 [74]). The literary *pendant* of the philosopher was constituted by Euripides, in the theatre of whom there already predominated, 'at least as far as principles and convictions are concerned', 'the fifth estate, that of the slaves' (GT, 11; I, 78 [56]): the 'barbaric class' that now, as the revolt it had caused in the heart of Europe revealed, threatened culture as such with 'horrifying destruction'. We were at a turning point of the event that started more than two millennia before.

The meaning of *The Birth of Tragedy* starts to become clear. It could easily have had as its title or subtitle: *The Crisis of Civilisation from Socrates to the Paris Commune*. The terrible event that took place in 1871 had to be studied and traced back to its most remote sources. It was thus necessary to start from the Greek philosopher and from his literary *pendant*, from the two figures that embodied theoretical and practical optimism and whose influence 'has spread out across all posterity to this very day, and indeed into the whole future, like a shadow growing ever longer in the evening sun' (GT, 15; I, 97 [71]).

It is indeed true that the gestation of the *Birth of Tragedy* started before the Paris Commune. However, in Nietzsche's eyes, as well as in the eyes of his contemporaries, the horrible event that took place in France constituted only the culminating moment of a subversion that had been raging for a long time. It is for this reason that, already in the fragments, and in the texts that preceded and prepared the book, the reconstruction of the history of Hellenic culture was indissolubly intertwined with reflections on the history of the revolutions in Europe. The death of tragedy in Greece found its parallel in the development of the great English theatre: after having reached its highest moment at the beginning of the seventeenth century, 'it dies violently in the middle of this century due to political revolution', due, that is, to the first English revolution (VII, 36). The Euripidian tragedy, constructed as it is according to an 'abstract concept', brings us back to France where rationalism started to incubate the revolutionary devastations (VII, 39).

4   The Suicide of Tragic Hellenism as Metaphor for the Suicide of the ancien régime

The Greece of Socrates and Euripides was read by Nietzsche with his eyes constantly turned to the Europe of his time and, in particular, to France devastated by an incessant revolutionary cycle, culminating in the Paris Commune. Only in this way is it possible to understand the harshness of the condemnation of Socrates as a 'plebeian' and 'extremely revolutionary' author (KGA, II, 4, 354) and of Euripides as the spokesperson of the 'fifth state', that is, of the 'ochlocracy' (VII, 35).

On the other hand, the anachronisms in the *Birth of Tragedy* are evident and often conscious. As it denounces, as we have seen, the superstitious faith that Alexandrian culture had in 'machines' and 'smelting furnaces', we cannot help thinking of the foundries and the industrialisation of Germany in the nineteenth century. An echo of the reading of Schopenhauer is noticeable; according to him, those who expected progress and real changes and improvements from politics and science, from 'constitutions and legislations', or from 'steam machines and telegraphs', were to be considered 'unilateral realists, thus optimists and eudemonists'.[17] By endorsing the denunciation of this vision of the world, Nietzsche committed himself to searching for its origins in Socrates and Alexandrian culture. It is interesting to note that, at the same time, although giving a different and contrasting value judgement, Engels proposed a similar argument: neglected by the 'Greeks of classical times', 'the exact natural sciences' took their first steps thanks to the 'Greeks of the Alexandrian period';[18] in this way, the foundations were laid for the development of the productive forces and thus for the overcoming of slavery, ancient or modern.

The Birth of Tragedy saw in Euripides, entirely pervaded by Alexandrianism, the interpreter of the aspirations of slaves or of the 'fifth estate'. Once again, we are projected into nineteenth century Europe. We are led to think of Lassalle, who called attention to the sufferings and role of the proletariat that he characterised as the 'fourth estate [*vierter Stand*]' or, on the opposite side, of an

---

17   Schopenhauer 1976–82b, p. 569.
18   Marx and Engels 1975 ff., Vol. 24, p. 299.

author like Strauss, impatient with the weak energy of authorities against the foolish subversive ambitions of, precisely, the 'fourth estate'.[19]

The Birth of Tragedy blamed Alexandrian culture for having theorised 'human dignity' and 'the dignity of labour'. Yet a fragment from the same period seems to express itself in a markedly different way: it regarded 'two concepts that the Greeks lacked', who, thanks to their capacity to look reality in the face, did not feel the completely modern need to mystify reality with discourses on the 'dignity of labour' (VII, 140). In fact, we are dealing with two slogans that go back to the proclamation of the rights of the human being ratified by the French Revolution, and to the struggles and polemics on slavery, labour and the right to labour that spread like wildfire during the long revolutionary cycle inaugurated by the crisis of the *ancien régime*. On 27 April 1848, the provisional government that arose from the fall of the July monarchy published a solemn proclamation announcing the abolition of slavery in the colonies, condemned as an 'attack on human dignity'.[20]

Alongside the political significance of *The Birth of Tragedy*, we can now begin to see its originality. It projected onto the Greece of the sixth to fifth century BC an event that primarily took place in Europe between the eighteenth and nineteenth centuries. The crisis of classical Hellenism was marked by 'Socratic culture', with its optimism, its belief in the originary goodness of the human being (virtue can be taught to anybody and everyone can learn it), with its faithful expectation of a happy world (GT, 18; I, 117 [89]). Well, said Burckhardt, these were the constitutive elements of the crisis of the *ancien régime*: it was not possible to understand the revolutionary ideology without the 'presupposition of the goodness of human nature', the 'great optimistic will' and the promise of 'realization of universal happiness', with the advent of a society in which 'there won't be misery anymore'.[21] This diagnosis was shared also by Taine, according to whom it was a philosophy characterised by 'promises of earthly happiness' for 'everyone' that gave rise to the troubles in France.[22]

It was an event that started with the rise of the *philosophes*, but the first of them – according to *The Birth of Tragedy* – was Socrates, whose thought was a synonym, as we will see, for the 'dubious enlightenment'. On the other hand, given that a note written in the autumn of 1869 condemned Socrates as a 'fanatic of the dialectic' (*infra*, Chapter 2 §1), we are led to think of Taine's

---

19   Lassalle 1919, pp. 194–6 *et passim*; Strauss 1872, p. 282.
20   Wallon 1974a, p. CLXV (the proclamation is included at the end of the introduction).
21   Burckhardt 1978b, pp. 385, 388 & 391.
22   Taine 1899, Vol. II, p. 18.

condemnation of the protagonists of revolution as 'fanatics of logic'.[23] Quoting and endorsing the analysis of a contemporary of the revolution, the French historian characterised the Jacobins as 'drunk and barbaric helots that usurped the place of Spartans'.[24] Thus we are led back to Nietzsche's distressed warning against a servile revolt that had begun already in Greece.

In a text from the same period as *The Birth of Tragedy*, we read that the mass social base of the Euripidean subversion of tragic Hellenism was constituted by the multifaceted front of the 'young indebted gentlemen, careless good-natured old men, hetairai like something out of Kotzebue, promethean house slaves' (ST; I, 536). Again, we are struck by the similarities with the analysis of the fall of the *ancien régime* in the culture of the time and in particular in Taine. Also in the case of the French historian, the scene was dominated by 'disgraced men, whether for crimes or debts', by people 'who have debts with the butcher, the baker, the wine merchant, etc.',[25] 'footmen, porters, domestic servants of every type', 'servants delighted now to be the masters of their masters',[26] 'ladies of the street', 'prostitutes', 'whores'.[27]

As for the 'careless good-natured old men' to whom Nietzsche's text referred, the denunciation of the gullibility of the old aristocracy, susceptible to being infected by the slogans of the movement that would lead it to ruin and to the scaffold, was a topos in the literature committed to the critique of revolution. The nobility – Tocqueville observed – confused the theories of the Enlightenment and revolution with witticism and funny games in which 'it engaged happily to pass the time'.[28] Only when it was too late did the aristocracy glimpse reality: 'what had entertained its spirit in free time became a terrible revolt against it'.[29] It could be said that there was a sort of suicide of the *ancien régime*, just as one should speak of 'suicide', according to Nietzsche, in the case of Greek tragedy (GT, 11; I, 75 [53]), which naïvely let itself be overcome by a rationalism, or rather, a philosophy of Enlightenment, the danger of which it did not suspect.

On the eve of its collapse, as Taine observed in turn, the aristocracy was 'imbued with humanitarian and radical maxims'.[30] In this moment – he continued – 'an active sympathy filled their souls, the rich feared nothing more

---

23   Taine 1899, Vol. VII, p. 129.
24   Taine 1899, Vol. VI, p. 179 n. 1.
25   Taine 1899, Vol. VI, pp. 172–3 & n. 1; cf. Burckhardt 1978b, p. 410.
26   Taine 1899, Vol. VI, p. 171.
27   Taine 1899, Vol. VI, pp. 169, 174–5 & n. 3.
28   Tocqueville 1951, Vol. II, 1, p. 196 (AR, Book III, Chapter 1).
29   Tocqueville 1951, Vol. II, 2, p. 109.
30   Taine 1899, Vol. II, p. 149.

than to be thought unfeeling'.[31] As they became 'epicurean and philanthropic', the nobles stuffed their mouths with 'great words of freedom, justice, public welfare, human dignity':[32] again we run into a slogan of the young Nietzsche projected onto the Greece of sixth century BC. If we want to exit from the crisis – highlights *The Birth of Tragedy* – we must oppose the 'enfeebled doctrines [*Schwächlichkeitsdoktrinen*]' inherent to 'optimism' and to the 'Socratic culture' (GT, 18; I, 119 [88]).

As confirmation of the interpretative approach suggested here, we can recall two reviews, particularly significant because their author knew and shared the ideas and preoccupations of the friend he was reviewing and even expressed, or was asked to express, as Nietzsche wrote in a letter addressed to him, 'our position' (B, II, 3, 12). Erwin Rohde summarised the significance of *The Birth of Tragedy* in this way: 'From the historical treatment of remote antiquity the author advances through the historical periods to the present'. It was not a logical leap or a digression: 'the theoretical optimism inherited by Socrates' had been transformed in the modern world into 'practical eudaimonism, that, once it has become a shrill claim, more and more threatens to unleash a hell of destructive powers against this decaying culture';[33] it had already resulted in the 'vandalism of socialist barbarians'.[34] The accusation against the Communards of having burned the Louvre returned, alongside the appeal to be conscious of the dramatic situation. Fortunately, not everything was lost. The task of exorcising the spectre of socialism and its vandalistic energy, and of representing a hope for the salvation of culture – the reviewer added, identifying himself once again with the author reviewed – fell to the 'German people', the 'German nation', whose great music seemed to announce the re-emergence of tragic Hellenism and the end of the ruinous cycles that had begun over two millennia before.[35]

If Rohde emphasised that, far from limiting himself to denouncing 'the evil of the present time', the author of *The Birth of Tragedy* 'invites all who live in the diaspora, sad and mindful of the past times, to renewed hope',[36] on the other side, substantially sharing the analysis but inverting its value judgement, Wilamowitz denounced Nietzsche not only as a 'dreaming professor' but also as an

---

31   Taine 1899, Vol. II, p. 158.
32   Taine 1899, Vol. II, p. 132.
33   Rohde 1989a, p. 12.
34   Rohde 1989b, p. 23.
35   Rohde 1989b, p. 26.
36   Rohde 1989b, p. 24.

'apostle and metaphysician'.[37] In the one and the other case, both stressed the fact that the text, hated or loved, was inspired by a strongly political perspective.

5   From the Anti-Napoleonic Wars to *The Birth of Tragedy*

The denunciation of modernity, which is at the core of *The Birth of Tragedy*, had nothing of nostalgic and indolent abandonment to it. It was not only combative but, at this moment, also looked hopefully to the possibility of radical transformation of the present in Germany and in Europe. Here became evident the influence of the other great political event of the time on a work that matured – the 'Foreword' observed – 'amidst all the terrors and sublimities of the war that had just broken out' (GT, 'Foreword'; I, 23 [13]). *The Birth of Tragedy* – as the philosopher would write later – was contemplated for a long time 'in front of the walls of Metz during the cold September nights, when I was serving as a medical orderly'. The book was 'begun in the thunder of the battle of Wörth' (EH, 'The Birth of Tragedy', 1 [108]). The defeat of France announced the possible liquidation of the simultaneously vulgar and ruinous modernity that had started with Socrates and Euripides. Immediately after Sedan, it was legitimate to hope for a radical turn, because the defeat of France was the defeat of the country of the Enlightenment and the Revolution. The victory of the Prussian army had a significance that went far beyond the military context: 'The only productive political force in Germany that doesn't have to be pointed out to anybody has now emerged victorious in the most extraordinary way'. Maybe the cycle that had started with the 'great French Revolution' was concluded, or was about to conclude. Liberalism, at least vulgar liberalism, marked by democratic massification, would be bled to death, together with its 'rough brothers' – that is, socialism and communism – 'thanks to that inflexible power mentioned above [the Prussian-German army]' (VII, 355).

Nietzsche was certainly not alone with this reading of the war that had just finished. In Basel, Burckhardt highlighted 'the weakening of the revolutionary people *kat' exochen*'.[38] Beyond the Rhine, Renan argued in a similar way: a country 'exhausted by democracy' and, more in general, by the 'democratic bedevilment' that had come out of the Revolution had been subjected to humiliating defeat; if Prussia could escape the democratic infection and the 'socialist

37   Wilamowitz-Möllendorff 1972a, pp. 218 n. & p. 214.
38   Burckhardt 1978a, p. 133 (it is a handwritten addition to the manuscript).

democracy', it could undertake a noble 'mission of saving the European social order'.[39] Thanks to their military virtues, the Germans were the only ones able to defend Europe against the threat of subversion.[40]

In the first place, a completely different series of themes that run through *The Birth of Tragedy* refer to the cultural and political history of Germany, starting from the contraposition between the serious and tragic feeling of life, found among Germans, and optimistic superficiality, synonym of a philistine and vulgar view of the world, prevalent among the neo-Latin peoples. According to Wagner, a very important exponent of the dominant ideology in the Germany of the time, Sedan was the victory of the German soldier who, in his industrious and 'serious silence', knew how to 'stop the arrogance' of his enemies, penetrating deeply into enemy territory and into the 'vain heart of France'.[41] Here we encounter a topos that goes back to the epoch of the anti-Napoleonic wars, when Fichte contrasted the intellectual and moral 'seriousness' of the Germans to the 'pleasant game' to which the French reduced culture, while Ernst Moritz Arndt (tireless animator of resistance against the Napoleonic army of occupation) attributed to the Germans a 'profundity', completely unknown to the 'silly [*albern*]' people, that is, cheerful in a superficial and fatuous way, as the French were supposed to be.[42]

Now let us reopen *The Birth of Tragedy*: reacting to the trend of the eighteenth century (the century of the hegemony, including cultural hegemony, of France), Kant and Schopenhauer had 'ushered in an incomparably deeper and more serious consideration of ethical questions and art' (GT, 19; I, 128 [95]). An analogous merit went to Germany in the musical field: with Bach, Beethoven and Wagner, dispensing with the 'jagged arabesques of operatic melody' and of neo-Latin opera, German music appeared as a 'daemon' that 'emerges from unfathomable depths' (GT, 19; I, 127 [94]). The Nietzsche of these years was never tired of rendering homage to the 'virile, serious, melancholic, tough and brave German spirit, that spirit which has remained sane since the epoch of the reformation, the spirit of the miner's son Luther' (BA, 5; I, 749). Again, the fourth *Unfashionable Observation*, while recalling 'the great war of the Germans' of some years before, celebrated 'genuinely and uniquely German cheerfulness [*Heiterkeit*]', a cheerfulness which was not unaware of the seriousness and the tragedy of existence, on the contrary, that was typical of those who, like Luther,

---

39   Renan 1947, Vol. I, pp. 333, 383 & 405.
40   Renan 1947, Vol. I, p. 350.
41   Wagner 1910h, pp. 1–2.
42   Cf. Losurdo 1997a, Chapter VII, 4 (pp. 311 & 315).

Beethoven and Wagner, had 'profoundly suffered from life but have turned to face it once more with the smile of the convalescent' (WB, 8; I, 480–1 [304]).

The vacuous and superficially optimistic feeling of life gave a fundamental value to the pleasantness of exterior appearances. And, according to the anti-Napoleonic journalism, the 'luxus of clothes' and 'the changeable elegance of commodities and their seductive appeal' were at the centre of French concerns.[43] The French – so argued Bismarck – 'have money and elegance, but no individuality, no individual feeling of their own self – they live only in the mass'.[44] These themes can also be found in Nietzsche. The already quoted letter to Gersdorff of 21 June 1871 condemned 'the French-Jewish levelling "elegance"' as well as the 'élan of our deplorable neighbours', an aestheticising posture, very different from authentic 'German courage [*Tapferkeit*]' (B, II, 1, 203).

Arndt again contrasted to the 'falsehood' and 'vanity' of the French not only the 'honour' but also the 'loyalty' of the Germans. Until the end – in the meantime the revolution of 1848 had exploded and failed – he loved to conclude his letters *in deutscher Treue*, with the assurance of his 'German loyalty'.[45] The young Nietzsche also rendered homage to the 'loyalty of the German soldier, which has been experienced recently'; one was to recognise in him 'that resistant strength, hostile to every appearance, from which we can expect another victory over the fashionable pseudo-culture of the "present epoch"' (BA, 2; I, 691 & BA, 3; I, 694).

During these years, Nietzsche's adherence to the ideological themes developed during the anti-Napoleonic agitation, the so-called 'wars for freedom [*Freiheitskriege*]', was explicit and without reservation. The fifth lecture *On the Future of our Educational Institutions* explicitly referred to the *Freiheitskriege*: here the *Burschenschaft* was celebrated, the student movement that, after fighting for the 'freedom of the homeland', once back at university, aimed to free the university also from the 'non-German barbarism, covered artificially under any form of erudition' (BA, 5; I, 748).

The Teutonic and Gallophobic pathos was severe. It could be said that both Wagner and the Fichte of the *Addresses to the German Nation* together had an influence upon the young Nietzsche. It was the merit of the great musician also to feel

> with deep pride the immediacy and inexhaustibility still present in this [German] language even today, the resonant strength of its roots in which

---

43   Cf. Losurdo, 1997a, Chapter IX, 6 (p. 429).
44   In Herre 1983, p. 167.
45   Cf. Losurdo, 1997a, Chapter VII, 2 (p. 307).

he sensed – in contrast to the highly derivative, artificially rhetorical Romance languages – a wonderful inclination and disposition for music, for true music.

WB, 9; I, 486–7 [310]

It is not difficult to catch here the echoes, immediate or mediated, precisely of the Fichtian *Addresses*, committed to celebrate, in contraposition to the French and to their dead language, the 'fundamental originality [*Ursprünglich-keit*]'[46] of the 'people of the living language', able to go down 'to the root where concepts spring from the spiritual nature'.[47] The *Appeal to the Germans* written by Nietzsche in favour of the great musician, or the *Appeal to the German Nation*, as it was defined by its own author (B, II, 3, 165) almost evoking the Fichtean *Addresses*, resonated with accents that clearly referred to the philosopher of the anti-Napoleonic wars: it was necessary to mobilise 'for the good and the honour of the German spirit and of the German name'; those who had kept a 'sense of honour' were not to fail to support a music and art that could constitute 'the most important factor of a new life with an originally German imprint' (MD; I, 893–4 & 896). Later, in a quite different stage of his evolution, Nietzsche would bring together Fichte and Wagner explicitly, though now in the context of a strongly critical judgement, both guilty of exalted 'Teutomania [*Deutschthümelei*]' (XII, 55).

But, during the years of *The Birth of Tragedy*, the adherence to such an ideology seemed to be without reservations, as is confirmed by a note of the summer-autumn in 1873; here he rendered homage to 'the excellent depiction of the Germans and French' which was contained in a *pamphlet* by Goerres (VII, 700 [263= *Unpublished Writings from the Period of Unfashionable Observations*]), one of the most grandiloquent speakers of the Teutomania and Gallophobia developed in the wake of the revolt against Napoleon I and still alive during the conflict with Napoleon III's France. The celebration of *Burschenschaftler*, the members of the student association that played an important role in the revolt and the war against the French occupation, resonated emphatically in the Basel lectures:

In the middle of the jubilation of victory and with thoughts focused on his liberated Fatherland, he solemnly pledged to himself to remain German. German! Now he learnt to understand Tacitus, he understood Kant's

---

46   Fichte 1971, Vol. VII, pp. 342 & 375.
47   Fichte 1971, Vol. VII, pp. 327 & 338–9.

categorical imperative, he delighted in the combative lyric of Karl Maria von Weber.

BA, 5; I, 749–50

6 The young Nietzsche's Adherence to German National Liberalism

The ideological and political collocation here suggested of the author of *The Birth of Tragedy* (and of the lectures *On the Future of our Educational Institutions*) should not be surprising. Let us take a look at his educational experiences. During his period of study in Bonn, Nietzsche, as he wrote in a letter to his sister and to his mother (B, I, 2, 15), went to the cemetery to pay homage at the grave of Ernst Moritz Arndt, the popular hero of the anti-Napoleonic resistance who we have already encountered. The moment in which this visit occurred was very significant. It was October 1864: with the war fought together with Austria to take the Duchies of Schleswig, Holstein and Lauenburg from Denmark, Prussia started the process of unification and hegemonisation of Germany.

Two years later, at news of the outbreak of Bismarck's war against Austria (the former ally), Nietzsche defined himself and signed a letter as a 'Prussian private', ready to take up arms (B, I, 2, 126). He followed the development of military operations with trepidation, keeping a close eye on the reactions of France, to which Austria turned, asking it to guarantee the European 'equilibrium' threatened by the successes of the Prussian army. Yet this 'equilibrium' – as Nietzsche observed in a letter to Gersdorff of 1 July 1866 – would have its 'centre in Paris', and would consecrate the continuity of French politics of hegemony and therefore endangered the 'gratification of our German hopes', now more than ever within reach. If those hopes were frustrated once again due to the intervention in the conflict of other European powers, the 'honour of being killed on the battle field by a French bullet' would be better than another humiliation. Fortunately, the prospects were encouraging: the 'war of destruction' of Austria's power was to be followed by a 'war against France'. Apart from its military and political results, this rendering of accounts would be able to produce in Germany a 'spiritual unity [*Gesinnungseinheit*]' that would reinforce national unity permanently (B, I, 2, 143–4). As can be seen, although indulging in some melodramatic tones, the young Nietzsche revealed a robust sense of historical and political reality; he was aware that the realisation of the political unity of Germany went by way of the liquidation of the Napoleonic ambitions of France, still hard to die; he foresaw and hoped for the test of force that would take place four years later. Finally, the letter to Gersdorff observed that for Prussia and Germany the most favourable situation 'in 50 years' had arrived, namely, since the anti-Napoleonic insurgency of 1813.

At this moment the identification with the political programme of the Iron Chancellor, who had taken up the leadership of the government in Berlin, seemed total. It should not be forgotten that, at the domestic level, Bismarck was the protagonist of a revolution from above, which introduced the parliamentary régime, and at the international level confronted his main antagonist in Napoleon III and Bonapartist France. So, we can now understand the enthusiasm expressed by the young Nietzsche:

> We must be proud to have such an army, yes, even – *horribile dictu* – such a government, which doesn't just put the national programme down on paper, but actively maintains it with maximum energy, with enormous expense of money and blood, even against the great French pretender *Louis le diable*. Any party that approves of these political goals is fundamentally a liberal party.
>
> B, I, 2, 142–3

One month later, in a subsequent letter, emphasising his enthusiasm, Nietzsche seemed very interested in the journalism and political positions of Treitschke (destined soon to become a sort of more or less official ideologue of the Second Reich) and considered himself a member or sympathiser of the 'national-liberal party', in favour of 'the unconditional annexation' of Saxony to Prussia and, more generally, of Bismarck's politics of national unification entrusted to the power and discipline of the Prussian army (B, I, 2, 159). The successive tests of force with which Prussia prepared the construction of the Second Reich in Germany were read, by broad swathes of public opinion, as the continuation of the revolt that had started a few decades earlier against the humiliation France had imposed on the nation. When the war of 1870 exploded, the brilliant professor of classical philology momentarily abandoned university teaching in the neutral Swiss city of Basel, to enlist as a volunteer in the Prussian army. He brought with him the hopes and myths of his time, which were also at the centre of *The Birth of Tragedy*.

7   'German Pessimism', 'Serious View of the World', 'Tragic View of the World'

They were hopes and myths that now experienced a process of simultaneous radicalisation and philosophical systematisation. So, the German 'seriousness'

and 'profundity', to which the anti-Napoleonic press never tired of rendering homage, became the 'serious view of the world' that expressed the 'true
German spirit' (VII, 259) and had its roots in 'German pessimism' (VII, 305).
Emphasising this had great significance also at the political level: 'The French
Revolution arose from faith in the good of nature'. There was the need to derive
the right lesson: 'An optimistic and misled view of the world ends up giving rise
to all sort of horrors' (VII, 280). Against the optimistic worldview that remained
in vogue beyond the Rhine, the young Nietzsche counterposed the 'serious view
of the world [*ernste Weltbetrachtung*] as the only salvation from socialism' (VII,
259).

The 'serious view of the world' of the preparatory notes was configured in
The Birth of Tragedy as the 'tragic view of the world [*tragische Weltbetrachtung*]' (GT, 17; I, 111 [82]). Now dominant, this theme was present in multiple
variations: it was absolutely necessary to recover 'tragic knowledge [*tragische
Erkenntniss*]' (GT, 15; I, 101 [75]), the 'culture' that now was to be described as
'tragic' (GT, 18; I, 118 [97]), the culture of those who dared to be 'tragic human
beings' (GT, 20; I, 132 [98]), up to the heights of the 'tragic hero', whose return
was glimpsed on the horizon (GT, 19; I, 128 [95]).

Far from being recent, the conflict between the two counterposed visions of
the world had already begun to appear in Greece. Although two millennia had
passed since its disappearance, tragic Hellenism was fortunately not dead. It
could arise again; it was already arising in the context of German culture. This
was demonstrated by the music of that new Aeschylus that was Wagner, who
had put an end to the predominance of the opera that had emerged on Latin
soil and which was characterised, as we know, by a ruinous optimistic and subversive impetus. But it is demonstrated also by the philosopher Schopenhauer,
'the philosopher of a rediscovered classicism, of a German Hellenism [...], of a
regenerated Germany' (FS, IV, 213) and Kant, who, by revealing the limits and
conflicts of reason, also shows himself to be completely foreign to the superficiality inherent to the Enlightenment and rationalist optimism. Luther was
interpreted in the same way (GT, 23; I, 147 [109]), as an implacable critic of an
harmonic reason and worldview; he therefore also displayed Dionysian themes
and echoes.

The mortal threat represented by the 'theoretical human being' and 'the
practical optimist' could be eliminated only by the 'Dionysiac human being'
(GT, 7; I, 56 [40]). He was a figure that seemed to become contemporary once
again. 'Dionysus had already been chased from the tragic stage, and, what
is more, by a daemonic power speaking out of the mouth of Euripides' (GT,
12; I, 83 [60]), just as he was pursued at the philosophical level by Socrates.
But Dionysus irrupted once again not only onto the theatrical and musical

stage, but especially on historical and political terrain, thanks to the 'rebirth of tragedy' in the German world (GT, 16; I, 103 [76]), in the Germany that defeated the country of Socratism, optimism and servile revolt.

The German people were thus called to be the inheritor of Greek civilisation, which Nietzsche celebrated in impassioned tones. Sometimes this has been regarded as neoclassicism. But it is a misleading category, and not only because *The Birth of Tragedy*, dedicated to Wagner, concentrated its attention in particular on *Tristan and Isolde*, a decisively romantic work (GT, 21; I, 135–7 [100–3]). There is a more important reason. We are not witnessing the recovery of classical antiquity as such. Unlike in the following years, Nietzsche cast a very severe judgement on the Roman world, characterised, in sharp contrast to Greece, by the 'debilitating chase after worldly power and honour'. Synonym of utilitarian spirit, 'worldliness' found 'its most grandiose, but also most terrifying, expression in the Roman imperium' (GT, 21; I, 133 [99]).

To understand these judgements, we need to refer again to the ideological and political atmosphere of the time. At Wagner's house, Nietzsche discussed Kleist's *Political Catechism*.[48] Kleist was the author who, a few days after the battle of Jena, wrote: 'We are the peoples subjugated by the Romans'.[49] If, as conquerors animated by an unbridled imperial ambition, the French appeared to the eyes of Kleist, Fichte and many others as the 'new Romans', their expansionism and politics of oppressive homogenisation were contested by a people without unity at the political and statal level, weaker at the military level but infinitely richer and deeper at the level of culture and artistic and philosophic creativity, a people which could thus be justly compared to the people of ancient Greece. This theme took on a new vitality in the wake of the French-Prussian war, when the great philologist Ernst Curtius also compared the French to the Romans, celebrating the 'Germans' as the people able to take care of their own particularity, against aggressive universalism, and to 'thwart' any attempt to assassinate the 'freedom of peoples'.[50]

The extremely severe judgement formulated in *The Birth of Tragedy* on the Roman world did not prevent Nietzsche, as we have seen, from referring, in this same period, to Tacitus, admirer of the Germans and their spirit of independence. In this reading, Tacitus became a sort of critic *ante litteram* of Latin civilisation. It is not by chance that Tacitus was the only Latin author loved by

---

48   C. Wagner 1976–82, Vol. I, p. 424.

49   Kleist 1961, Vol. II, p. 770 (letter to Ulrike from Kleist of 24 October 1806).

50   Cf. Losurdo 1997a, Chapter XIII, 12 (p. 573).

Fichte in the *Addresses to the German Nation* and by the protagonists of the
anti-Napoleonic resistance engaged in polemics against the new Romans.[51]

Wagner's attitude was similar to Nietzsche's. He also celebrated the indissoluble link that unified 'Greek ideal' and 'German spirit' and negatively set the
Romans (the inheritance of whom had been assumed by France) against the
Greeks (whose inheritance was claimed by Germany): 'At theatre the Romans
celebrated their gladiator games and the Greeks their tragedies'.[52] Between the
two there was an abyss, the abyss that separated 'civilisation' from authentic
'culture'.

8   The 'German Spirit' as 'Saviour' and 'Redeemer' of *Zivilisation*

It is now clear: the country that was a symbol of subversion but also of 'civilisation' had suffered an irreparable defeat at Sedan. At this point the contrast
between Germany and France was configured as the antithesis between *Kultur*
and *Zivilisation*. Particularly significant in this regard is the letter to Gersdorff,
often quoted, of 21 June 1871. After having celebrated the 'ancient German
health', proved by the army and the nation, Nietzsche went on: '[O]n such a
basis it is possible to build: we can hope again!'. One was not to fail to notice
the 'head of the international hydra that suddenly emerged so monstrously,
as a tell-tale sign of other future struggles'. Yet the catastrophe of the Paris
Commune was the result of a long-term and more general devastation: 'Roman
"civilization", now dominant everywhere, reveals the incredible evil with which
our world is afflicted' (B, II, 1, 203–4).

We are brought back once again to the ideological climate that accompanied
the clash between France and Prussia. At the moment of the explosion of hos-
tilities, Napoleon III addressed his soldiers as follows: 'All France follows you
with its ardent best wishes and the universe is watching you. The fate of freedom and civilization [*civilisation*] depends on our success'.[53] Bismarck laughed
at this claim when, referring to the Commune, he stressed that, without the
intervention of the Prussian 'barbarians', very little would have remained of
the 'capital of art and civilization'.[54] There thus emerged the two counterposed

---

51   Cf. Losurdo 1997a, Chapter I, 5 (p. 55).
52   Wagner 1910i, pp. 36 & 60. This was still an ideological theme of extraordinary vitality in
      the middle of the twentieth century (one thinks of Heidegger), due also to Nietzsche's
      mediation (cf. Losurdo 1991, pp. 146–55).
53   In Sorel 1973, p. 565.
54   Bismarck, n.d., Vol. III, p. 29.

ideologies of the war. While France proclaimed itself the privileged representative of civilisation as such, Germany responded by distinguishing between
superficial 'civilisation' and authentic 'culture', of which German itself had cus-
tody.

This dichotomy also has a long history. During the years of Germany's political and military impotence and its backwardness at the economic level, its
great intellectuals thought it appropriate to discuss different and more essential values than the development of mere material richness. With a polemical
allusion to France, Schleiermacher called upon Germans to clamp down on 'the
rough barbarism and on the cold mundane sense of the century', on the 'mean
empiricism [jämmerliche Empirie]'; 'the ancient national character' of the Germans – Schelling wrote in 1802 – could be awakened only through 'a dominant
religion or philosophy' positioned strictly in opposition to the utilitarianism
beyond the Rhine; Germany – stressed Arndt – was to decisively reject that
'half-spiritual formation, that flat intellectual game, that strips life of all that is
sacred, and nature of every secret'.[55]

As for the clash between the *ancien régime* and the *philosophes*, Nietzsche
argued in a similar way regarding the theme of the clash between 'culture' and
'civilisation': he took it up and radicalised it to the extent of projecting it onto
classical antiquity. The superstitious faith in 'machines' and 'smelting furnaces'
and 'the satisfied pleasure of existence' had imposed themselves since the sunset of tragic Hellenism; yet this vulgar optimism, theoretical and practical, was
now destroyed thanks to 'German philosophy', in particular due to Kant and
Schopenhauer. There had been thus a decisive turning point at Sedan. *The Birth
of Tragedy* proclaimed that without a tragic view of life and 'Dionysiac wisdom'
there was no authentic culture. 'All those things which we now call culture,
education, civilization must some day appear before the judge Dionysus whom
no man can deceive'. Returning to itself and assuming deeply the inheritance
of tragic Hellenism, Germany was to liberate itself once and forever from the
'child's leash [Gängelband] of a romance civilization [romanische Civilisation]'
(GT, 19; I, 128–9 [94]).

We can thus understand the pathos with which the young Nietzsche expressed himself on the 'German essence', a theme, according to Cosima's accounts,
that was at the centre of conversations at Wagner's house and of the shared
hopes that nourished those conversations.[56] It is a theme that appeared in multiple variants in *The Birth of Tragedy*, dedicated to producing a hymn to the

---

55   Cf. Losurdo 1997a, ch. VII, 4, (p. 313).
56   C. Wagner 1976–82, Vol. I, p. 491.

deutsches Wesen, to 'the noble core [*Kern*] of our national character', 'the pure and vigorous core of the German character', the 'magnificent, inwardly healthy, ancient strength' of the 'German spirit [*Geist*]' and 'German genius'. Contrary to 'civilized [*civilisiert*] France', in Germany civilisation and modernity were only a passing and superficial phenomenon that badly obscured 'the Dionysiac capacity of a people'. It was possible to get rid of that phenomenon once and forever by 'rejecting the [neo-]Latin influence' (GT, 23; I, 146–7 [108–9] & 149 [111]: GT, 24; I, 153–4 [114]).

Already having begun with the wars against Napoleon I, the process of reconquering authentic German identity received further impetus from the new and decisive victory over France. Nonetheless, it seems to have stopped halfway. Instead of the radical 'liberation from the neo-Latin element [*Romanismus*]' that the new situation offered and made possible, 'until now there were only reworkings' of this element. Analogous uncertainties and lack of rigour had been seen already in the past. Although conducted against the hegemony of Rome, the Reformation itself could not obtain better results (VII, 329). But now the perspective was more favourable: 'The German spirit fights to rise up to the Greek spirit. [...] And just as it is sure that our Persian wars have just started, so we feel with the same certainty that we live in the epoch of tragedy' (VII, 229–30).

The second Reich was called upon to sweep away once and for all 'the liberal and optimistic view of the world, which has its roots in the doctrines of the French enlightenment and the revolution, namely, in a philosophy completely extraneous to Germany, plainly neo-Latin, flat and anti-metaphysical' (CV, 3; I, 773). 'The German spirit' was somehow the 'redeemer [*Retter*]' (VII, 431 [15 = *Unpublished Writings from the Period of Unfashionable Observations*]), 'the redeeming force [*erlösende Kraft*]' (VII, 429 [14 = *Unpublished Writings from the Period of Unfashionable Observations*). Insofar as it was strongly marked by the demand of happiness and by a vulgar and flat vision of life, civilisation establishes the preconditions for revolution. The 'enormous increasing of material civilization' – as Burckhardt had already observed – was a feature of the 'revolutionary epoch', which had not yet concluded.[57] It is a statement that appeared in the lecture series that Nietzsche also attended.

Wagner expressed himself in similar terms a few years earlier, when he also celebrated the 'German spirit' as the 'saviour [*Erretter*]' that acted as the 'redemptive [*erlösend*]' element against the 'ruin' threatening Europe.[58] The

---

57   Burckhardt 1978b, pp. 378–9.
58   Wagner 1910f, p. 84.

influence exerted by the great musician over the young philologist-philosopher emerges clearly. Wagner insisted that the French constituted 'the dominant people of contemporary *Zivilisation*';[59] they were a people 'modern to the core'.[60] For Wagner as well, the French-Prussian war represented a decisive turning-point: 'While German weapons advanced victorious toward the centre of French civilization, there suddenly emerged among us a feeling of shame at our dependence on this civilization'.[61] It was necessary to come to terms with a long-term devastation, which, in the last analysis, referred back to the 'universal civilization of the Romans'.[62]

The similarity to Nietzsche's pronouncements is clear. According to him, by committing to the 'struggle' not only against the incurable subversism of France, but also against the 'terrible danger' represented by 'the American kind of political hubbub [*Getreibe*]', the 'German spirit' reaffirmed the inheritance of tragic Greece, recovered thanks also to Schopenhauer and Wagner and their 'marvellous unity', and reasserted its authentic identity (VII, 423–5 [8–10 = *Unpublished Writings from the Period of Unfashionable Observations*]). The struggle against modernity and civilisation was, at the same time, a commitment to recovering authentic Germanness. '"Workshops of struggle against the present time" and for the renewal of the German essence' (VII, 262) were needed, without ever losing sight of the 'distinction between what is German and what is pseudo-German [*Afterdeutsch*]' (VII, 256).

9   'Optimism', 'Happiness' and Revolutionary Drift: Nietzsche's Radicalism

'Optimism' and the idea of 'happiness', which stimulated the vulgarisation of modern civilisation and strengthened the tide of revolution, were completely alien to both tragic Hellenism and authentic Germanness.

In fact, the idea of happiness, condemned by Nietzsche for its intrinsic subversive dimension, accompanied and stimulated the entire revolutionary cycle on both sides of the Atlantic. The central role that the idea of happiness played in the Enlightenment is well known, that is, in the philosophy that ideologically prepared the collapse of the *ancien régime*.[63] The American Revolution pro-

---

59   Wagner 1910f, p. 115.
60   Wagner 1910f, p. 118.
61   Wagner 1910f, p. 113.
62   Wagner 1910f, p. 120.
63   Mauzi 1960.

claimed, among truths 'evident in themselves', 'inalienable rights' that included 'Life, Freedom and Pursuit of Happiness', which signified here the tranquil enjoyment of a comfortable private sphere. The process of plebeian radicalisation of the French Revolution was accompanied by a growing pathos of the idea of happiness. In 1793 a new *Declaration of the Rights of Man and of the Citizen* was published. The first article proclaimed: 'The aim of society is the common welfare [*bonheur*]'. Article 21 clarified: 'Public relief is a sacred debt. Society owes maintenance to unfortunate [literally, unhappy: *malheureux*] citizens, either procuring work for them or providing the means of existence for those unable to labour'. Crossing the Atlantic, the negative right to happiness (which guaranteed the private sphere against any external interference) was transformed into positive right (which required public intervention in order to rectify situations of poverty and unhappiness that could not be addressed by other means).

The demand for this positive right found its most passionate formulation in two celebrated discourses pronounced by Saint-Just in *Ventôse* of Year II, a few months before the fatal Thermidor of 1794 that saw him sent to the guillotine together with Robespierre:

> Happiness is a new idea in Europe. [...] Do not accept that there is even a single poor and unhappy person in the state. [...] Europe must understand that you no longer want either an unhappy person or an oppressor in French territory. [...] The unhappy are the powers of the earth; they have the right to speak as masters to the governments that neglect them.[64]

Another revolutionary, Babeuf, cited Saint-Just in this way, bringing together two different discourses, at the moment in which he turned to the judges of the tribunal that shortly afterwards condemned him too to death.[65] It was Babouvism, in its different transformations and configurations, that played a not marginal role in the Paris Commune. There can be no doubt, Nietzsche was right: the idea of happiness exerted a disturbing effect for at least a century, the century that ran from the triumph of the Enlightenment to the catastrophe of 1871. Even beyond this date it did not cease to play a revolutionary role. A terrible threat continued to plague culture: not only the long revolutionary cycle that developed in the West but 'socialism' itself, the new danger with which it

---

64   Saint-Just 1984, pp. 715 & 707 (speech of 13 & 8 *Ventôse* of Year II).
65   Cf. Babeuf 1988, p. 316.

was necessary to settle accounts, was to be conceived as 'a fruit of that optimism' that had already produced so many ruins (VII, 379).

By arguing in this way, Nietzsche was anything but isolated in the culture of his time. Some years before the revolution of 1848, Stirner observed that 'happiness of "people" is what one has been looking for since the Revolution';[66] the cycle was anything but concluded! On the eve of the Paris Commune, Renan arrived at the conclusion that the curse and ruin of France lay in the idea of 'vulgar happiness' and in the claim to realise a society in which 'the individuals that compose it enjoy the greatest possible amount of welfare'.[67] About ten years later, Gumplowicz, a leading exponent of Social Darwinism, pointed out the relation between the 'French revolution, socialism, communism' on the one hand and 'optimistic vision' and hopes of a better and happier social order on the other hand.[68]

On the whole, between the eighteenth and the nineteenth centuries, the denunciation of revolution developed under the aegis of the critique of the idea of happiness. According to Gentz, it amounted to miscognising 'the nature of things' and 'the nature of the human being', aiming to put an end, by means of political transformations, to 'all misery of life', wanting to provide the human being on this earth with 'redemption' and liberation from 'the scenes of pain' in which he was inevitably immersed.[69] The diffusion of these ideological themes underwent a further development following the revolution of 1848 and the workers' revolt of June in Paris: in Germany, national liberals like Zeller and Treitschke assimilated socialism to 'Epicureanism', to the search for the 'maximum possible enjoyment', to the 'overvaluation of material goods' and to the 'greediest materialism';[70] in France, Tocqueville condemned out of hand the 'sensual and socialist' philosophy;[71] in Italy, Rosmini thundered at the 'mundane and carnal happiness' that constituted the illusory end of the different socialist and communist tendencies.[72] It was a condemnation that in 1878 found its consecration in an encyclical of Leo XIII: what was primarily pushing humanity 'almost to its extreme ruin' was 'the ardent desire for terrestrial happiness'.[73]

---

66   Stirner 1981, p. 257.
67   Renan 1947, Vol. I, p. 482.
68   Gumplowicz 1883, p. 301.
69   Gentz 1836–8, Vol. I, pp. 8–9.
70   Cf. Losurdo 1983a, Chapter V, 3.
71   Tocqueville 1951, Vol. XV, 2, pp. 107–8.
72   Rosmini 1840–57c, p. 100.
73   In Giordani 1956, p. 30 (Encyclical *Quod apostolici muneris*).

On the opposite side, the early socialist movement was engaged in demanding, to use Saint-Simon's words, the 'social happiness of the poor',[74] or as
Weitling, an author repeatedly quoted and criticised by Stirner,[75] said, 'human
happiness' and 'terrestrial happiness'. Owen in turn proclaimed: 'THE HAPPI-
NESS OF ALL will be the goal and the object of any part of this organisation
in all the extension of society'.[76] The young Marx also stressed that the social
revolution went by way of the search for 'real happiness' with the consequent
'criticism of the vale of tears' and of the 'illusory happiness' sought in another
world.[77] In this context it is worth quoting an author well known to Nietzsche,
Heinrich Heine: 'The masses do not tolerate anymore their mundane misery
with Christian patience; they want happiness on this earth. Communism is
thus a natural consequence of this changed conception of the world, and it
is spreading across all of Germany'.[78]

So, in what does Nietzsche's originality consist? First, in his effort to go back
as far as possible in the search for the origins of the cycle of subversion. It was
not enough to go back to the Enlightenment. The optimistic vision of the world
was already present in the Renaissance (VII, 280). But what was the Renaissance, if not the 'epoch of the awakening of Alexandrian-Roman antiquity in
the fifteenth century'? Already we run into the 'destruction of myth' and the
'enormous growth in worldliness' at the basis of the search for terrestrial happiness for all and of the cycle of subversion (GT, 23; I, 148–9 [111]). This cycle now
encompassed over two millennia. And, given the perspective of the long duration, the usual distinction-contraposition of the liberal starting point of the
French Revolution and its plebeian and Jacobin radicalisation made no sense.

Apart from the temporal level, Nietzsche's extreme radicalism was also displayed at the spatial level, so to speak. He not only investigated the remote
origins of the ruinous idea of happiness, but also its various and disparate configurations and expressions. We know that optimism was at the foundation
of opera too. More generally, it manifested itself – as Nietzsche points out in
a letter to Gersdorff of 28 September 1869 – 'in the most bizarre forms', not
only in 'socialism' but also in the 'vegetarian doctrine' and even in the practice
of 'cremation', in every attempt to reform and modify human existence, failing to recognise its character of 'complete corruption' (B, II, 1, 58). A few days
earlier, by supporting vegetarianism, under the influence of Schopenhauer but

---

74   Saint-Simon 2003, p. 91.
75   Stirner 1981, pp. 296 & 364.
76   In Bravo 1973, pp. 255–6 & 225; the capitalisation is in Owen's text.
77   Marx and Engels 1975 ff., Vol. 3, p. 176.
78   Heine 1969–78, Vol. V, pp. 197–8.

with a consequentiality foreign to him, Nietzsche collided with Wagner, who even accused him of 'arrogance' for claiming to put into question, by refusing any 'compromise', the entire natural order.[79] After having attempted to resist at Tribschen, the young philologist clearly ended up accepting the argumentations of the musician and even radicalised them: as we see in the letter to Gersdorff, the vegetarian doctrine was one of the many manifestations of the optimistic and revolutionary *hybris* of those who aimed to change and subvert the world. It was a view substantially shared by the interlocutor and addressee of the letter, who posited 'socialism', 'domination of the masses, tyranny of the plebs, community of goods, oppression of all that is spiritually significant' (B, II, 2, 55) in a line of continuity with 'optimism'.

The temporal and spatial pervasiveness of the evil required a remedy commensurate with its extent. It was impossible to be satisfied with the critique of this or that manifestation of the idea of happiness. Schopenhauer was already aware of the inadequacy of such an attitude. He also, like many others, emphasised the relationship between hedonism and communism, the philosophy of which could be summarised as '*Gaudeamus igitur!*', '*edite, bibite, post mortem nulla voluptas*'.[80] Yet, beyond the agitation of this traditional theme, we now witness the elaboration of a whole conception of the world, called upon to liquidate revolutionary optimism once and for all. It was in Germany that the political and philosophical dimensions of the debate were more strictly intertwined.

Taking up cudgels against the author of *The World as Will and Representation*, Dühring denounced the 'particularly disturbing' role 'pessimism' played in the 'social question': it stimulated not only an attitude of waiting and resignation but legitimated a further worsening of the life conditions of the popular masses.[81] There was, then, the necessity of reasserting, already in the title of a book, the 'value of life' and of reasserting it by trying to meet Schopenhauer's challenge. So, the demand of happiness was integrated into an entire philosophy of history. Thus we can explain the formulation of the thesis according to which the 'value enhancement of life' constituted 'the fundamental law of history'.[82]

Nietzsche, on the other hand, who in the following years committed himself to study Dühring 'deeply', beginning with the transcription of long passages from his work (VIII, 129 et sq). in July 1866, while he was still a university stu-

---

79   C. Wagner 1976–82, Vol. I, p. 152.
80   Schopenhauer 1976–82c, Vol. IV, pp. 182, 180 & 190 & Schopenhauer 1976–82b, p. 592.
81   Dühring 1875, p. 348.
82   Dühring 1875, p. 339.

dent, attributed to Schopenhauer the merit of having 'taken off his eyes the bandages of optimism' (B, I, 2, 140). By intervening in the debate on the idea of happiness, *The Birth of Tragedy* already located itself at the philosophical height to which this eminently political debate had been raised by Schopenhauer.

10   An Anti-Pelagian Reconquest of Christianity?

Could Christianity form a dyke to hold back the optimistic and socialist tide, with its dogma of original sin and of the irreparable human poverty consecrated and explained by that dogma? This was the dominant orientation, at the European level, in the conservative or liberal-conservative culture. In Italy, Manzoni identified in Rousseau the starting point of the catastrophe in France: by repressing the catastrophe of original sin and by thus forgetting that a 'truly perfect happiness' was 'reserved for another life' and could not be sought 'in the present life', the francophone philosopher believed he could attribute evil and suffering to 'vicious social institutions'. So, he ended up producing that 'terrible and deplorable disciple' that was Robespierre and favouring the birth of the socialist movement itself.[83] Professed Catholic and Christian circles were not the only ones to call upon the dominant religion in the West to act as a dyke against the revolutionary tide. Already in the years preceding 1789, Rivarol, an author who Nietzsche knew (VIII, 594; XI, 20), saw in Christianity the indispensable instrument for teaching people how to 'bear their bad luck' and to renounce the idea of being 'happy'.[84] Later, Burckhardt set up 'the conflict between the worldview that comes out of the French Revolution and the Church, in particular, the Catholic Church', as 'a conflict that has its deepest basis in the optimism of the former and the pessimism of the latter'.[85]

The wide diffusion of this ideological theme is confirmed by the strong polemics that revolutionary movements deployed against it. Moses Hess thundered against the 'infamous dogma of the imperfection of everything on earth', defined as the 'dogma of our shame', the 'dogma of our slavery'. For Heine, it constituted an essential constitutive element of conservative and reactionary ideology: 'Those that believe in original sin' would not deny 'hereditary privileges'. We have already seen that Marx found the revolutionary project of the realisation of 'real happiness' in the radical 'criticism of the vale of tears'. On

---

83   Manzoni 1963, pp. 741–4.
84   In Groethuysen 1978, Vol. 2, p. 213; Groethuysen 1956, Vol. 1, p. 293.
85   Burckhardt 1978a, p. 150.

other occasions, he polemicised explicitly against those that justified and perpetuated the existing order, with its burden of social and political oppression, through references to the *natura lapsa* of man, as a consequence of his fatal fall: 'It is sheer tautology to assert that if absence of freedom is men's essence, freedom is contrary to his essence'.[86]

Thus, on the one hand as on the other, the theme of original sin was perceived as a trench of decisive strategic importance. But was this trench still defensible or had it in reality already been conquered by the subversive movement? Immediately after the July revolution, a prestigious statesman like Stein pointed out the connection between the new upheavals and the relentless diffusion of the belief that the human being was 'free from original sin'. Called to Berlin to oppose Hegelian philosophy (itself very critical of the 'representation', that is, of the 'myth' of original sin), Schelling, going back to Kant as the theoretician of the 'radical evil of human nature', felt obliged to recall bitterly that, with this doctrine, the philosopher of Königsberg 'alienated the multitude immediately, the consent of which made his name popular for a certain period of time'.[87] Later, Engels knew he could count on attentive interlocutors even in Christian circles when he celebrated primitive Christianity as a progressive phenomenon precisely because in it there was 'not a trace' of 'original sin'.[88]

Schopenhauer's perplexities and oscillations can be understood in this context. On the one hand, he still hoped for a possible reaction of the Christian community against the modern and optimistic infection; on the other hand, he was already searching for a possible alternative. In polemic against those who would have liked to build 'heaven on the earth', he invoked the profound truth contained, even though 'in mythical form', in the biblical account of original sin. It was from here that the strong polemic against all 'optimistic people, enemies of Christianity', stemmed, that is, the enemies of the doctrine of original sin, against all those that began from the premise that the earth could be a 'sojourn of happiness', as if God had created the world so that 'it is very pleasing to roam upon it'. Unfortunately, the theme of the 'profound guilt of the human species due to the mere fact of its existing' had sunk into oblivion in the official churches, prone to a Pelagianism that, with its faith in reason and the human being, continued to nourish the will of living and paved the way towards ruinous utopias founded on the idea of progress. Fortunately, Chris-

---

86   Cf. Losurdo 1997a, Chapter IX, 7; Marx and Engels 1955 ff., Vol. I, pp. 48–9; Marx and Engels 1975 ff., Vol. 1, p. 153.

87   Cf. Losurdo 1997a, Chapter IX, 7.

88   Marx and Engels 1955 ff., Vol. 21, p. 11; cf. also Vol. 22, pp. 459 & 471; Marx and Engels 1975 ff., Vol. 26, p. 114: cf. also Vol. 27, pp. 456 & 468.

tianity at its origins, and especially the oriental religious tradition, took care to remind those who did not remember the truth of guilt and sin.[89] Thus a possible alternative was identified.

In Schopenhauer' wake, the young Nietzsche was also of the opinion that, if there was something to be saved in Christianity, it was precisely the myth of original sin. Certainly, for the philologist-philosopher, who had already several years before read and assimilated Strauss's critique of Christianity,[90] who was filled with admiration for pre-Socratic Greece and did not hesitate to express himself with uninhibited frankness, there was no space for an orthodox return to the biblical story. The fact remained that it was necessary to contest the politically ruinous theme of the original good of nature and the human being, a theme dear to Rousseau, the author Nietzsche followed attentively during the years at Pforta (B, I, 1, 216). In comparison to the 'Enlightenment' view of nature found in the '[neo-]Latin world' – the reference was particularly to *Émile* (VII, 305 & GT, 3; I, 37 [24]) – the young Nietzsche had no doubt that the Christian myth of original sin was more profound.

We know about the socialist implications of opera: emerging during the struggle against the 'old ecclesiastic representation of the human being as corrupted and lost in himself', it could be considered as 'the dogma of opposition of the good human being'. By pursuing the 'paradisiac prospect' of 'the human being in his original goodness [*Urmensch*]' and of 'his rights' (GT, 19; I, 122–3 [91]), by losing sight of 'the fearful gravity of nature as it truly is' and contenting itself with a supposedly 'idyllic reality', opera revealed itself as simultaneously empty and dangerous: what 'the features of opera express is not at all the elegiac pain caused by eternal loss' (GT, 19; I, 125 [92–3]), the eternal loss that the biblical account described in a mythical but still deep way as the consequence of original sin. To some extent, Nietzsche seemed during these years to share Schopenhauer's programme of recovering a Christianity cleansed of Pelagian residues, which could thus be associated with Hinduism. In this sense, in a letter to his sister on 5 November 1865, he pronounced in favour of 'original Christianity', quite different from the 'contemporary, sugary and fuzzy' Christianity (B, I, 2, 95). A few months later, writing to Gersdorff, he affirmed: 'The true Hindus are Christian' and 'the true Christians are Hindus' (B, I, 2, 122). Echoing a clearly Schopenhaurian theme, a text of February 1871 numbered the 'saints' and 'the saint in the desert', along with the artists, among the 'great "individuals"' that understood 'the supreme goal of the world's will' (VII, 354).

---

89   Schopenhauer 1976–82c, Vol. V, p. 306; Schopenhauer 1976–82b, p. 802.
90   Janz 1981, Vol. I, p. 146.

The political significance of this Christianity rediscovered by going back beyond the degenerations of modernity is immediately evident. Thanks to it, it
might be possible to save culture, by relegitimising serfdom or slavery: 'Slavery
[...] was displeasing neither to primitive Christianity nor the old Germans, and
even less did they considered it to be condemnable' (CV, 3; I, 769).

Pagan Hellenism and the Christian Middle Ages were now set against modernity and its crazy pretention to abolish slavery and serfdom. For a long historical period, Christianity might have expressed 'aversion to marriage and
the state', along with slavery, but this had nothing to do with an abolitionist
attitude: 'Emancipation is something completely different' (VII, 267). In other
words, just as it was able to accept marriage and the state, so, after its rise to
power, Christianity had for a long time no difficulty in recognising and accepting the reality of slavery. Polemicising against the demand, often tinged with
evangelical motives, of 'the return of property to the community', a text of 1879
once again blamed 'our socialists' for being actually deeply hostile to the found-
ational lesson of Christianity. They 'bear a grudge against that Jew of antiquity
for saying: thou shalt not steal. In their view the seventh commandment should
read rather: thou shalt not possess' (WS, 285 [381]).

11   Christianity as Subversive and a 'Religion of the Learned'

It was also the belief that Christianity was now a part of the 'religions of the
learned [*Gelehrtenreligionen*]' that increased Nietzsche's doubts about it (GT,
18; I, 117 [87]). 'Religions of the learned' were those linked to a positive dog-
matically fixed content, incapable of development and renewal, forced into
a defensive posture that became ever more frantic. The category here used
recalls the 'learned religion [*gelehrte Religion*]', 'assigned to the care of those
who are learned [*Gelehrten*]', that Kant criticised. Kant contrasted it with 'natural religion', based upon 'universal human reason', 'purely moral religion'. Nietzsche's attitude was quite different. He was influenced by a dichotomy that
Wagner favoured, between authentic culture, rooted in the people and able
to unify the community around it, and pseudo-culture, reduced to the solitary occupation or entertainment of uprooted intellectuals (*infra*, Chapter 4,
§1).

Yet, even when committed to celebrating the ceaseless creativity of myth, in
Religion Within the Limits of Reason Alone Nietzsche could have read Kant's confirmation of the increasing difficulties encountered by Christianity and Christian churches: 'the profession of faith in sacred history', the obligation, imposed
by a 'learned religion', of believing, as if it were in an unquestionable historical

truth, in accounts that referred to a very remote time, all this – Kant argued – 'sharply oppresses conscientious people', who instead would have felt liberated if they were able to adhere freely to a content, starting from a rational inquiry.[91] Yet, from the point of view of *The Birth of Tragedy*, nothing was gained when there was a return from history to reason. A religion that entrusted its destiny to one or the other exposed itself to the corrosive acid of philological and philosophical inquiry and then needed the frantic defence of its exegetes and apologists, thus becoming a 'learned religion', incapable of inspiring and moving a community as a whole and, thus, destined to exhaustion:

> For this is usually how religions die. It happens when the mythical presuppositions of a religion become systematized as a finished sum of historical events under the severe, intellectual gaze of orthodox dogmatism, and people begin to defend anxiously the credibility of the myths while resisting every natural tendency within them to go on living and to throw out new shoots – in other words, when the feeling for myth dies and is replaced by the claim of religion to have historical foundations.
>
> GT, 10; I, 74 [53–4]

This attitude was no different from that of his friend Rohde, who, in his second review of *The Birth of Tragedy*, and inspired by it, asked himself the following rhetorical question:

> Who [could be] so foolish to want to heal the illness of the present with the palliative means of religious formulas from previous centuries? Truly, the community of those who looks with apprehension at this suffering and its illusory lustre – a community that grows smaller with each passing day – can be compared to those Greeks in far off Pontus, of which the orator Dio Chrysostom tells the following story: isolated among hostile Scythian tribes, and themselves in costume and morals half barbarized, they drew strength from the old images of long lost poetic glory in the eternal verses of Homer; but usually, in painful renunciation, they bore the guilt of being born late.[92]

The barbarian Scythians here were the moderns, who had already largely overwhelmed Christianity. Nietzsche expressed himself similarly:

---

91   Kant 1900, Vol. VI, pp. 163–7.
92   Rohde 1989b, p. 24.

On *religion*. I notice an exhaustion, people have grown weary of its meaningful symbols. All the possibilities of Christian life, the most serious and the most insipid, the most harmless and the best thought through, have been tried out; it is time for imitation or for something else. Even ridicule, cynicism, hostility have been played out – what one sees is an ice field when the weather is warming, everywhere the ice is dirty, broken, without luster, covered with puddles, dangerous. Here the only attitude that to me seems appropriate is deference, but total abstinence: in this way I honor that religion, even though it is a dying one. [...] Christianity has been entirely turned over to critical history.

> VII, 711 [273 = *Unpublished Writings from the Period of Unfashionable Observations*

This is a fragment from the summer–autumn of 1873. A subsequent revision seems to have left any doubts behind: more than moribund, Christianity was already dead and was to be consigned not only to 'critical history' but also to 'dissection' (VII, 751 [310 = *Unpublished Writings from the Period of Unfashionable Observations*).

It made no sense, then, to hope for the anti-Pelagian rebirth of a religion in its death throes or even decomposition. Could the Pelagian contamination really be considered a simple incident in the history of Christianity? Was it really able to contain the revolutionary tide, or could it end up making that tide even bigger? If Marx thought that (Christian) religion, despite everything, expressed 'a protest against real suffering' (*infra*, Chapter 14 §2), a similar awareness started to emerge on the side of the enemies of the revolution, although with a different and counterposed value-judgement. In his private conversations, Schopenhauer expressed himself with more frankness than in his public writings. In them he did not limit himself to condemning the Pelagianised and spurious Christianity of its modern representatives, but took aim directly at the figure of its founder: he was 'only a demagogue' or 'a Jewish demagogue'.[93] Dispensing with the despondent tone he affected in public, in Wagner's home Gobineau expressed himself severely regarding the fundamentally plebeian religion that was Christianity, hostile to 'great personalities' (*infra*, Chapter 23 §3).

Nietzsche's judgements had not yet assumed the severity of later years. However, he had already achieved sufficient clarity. We were dealing with a religion that appeared infected by the Enlightenment and 'optimism', to such an extent that it rooted out everything 'profound, esoteric, accessible only to the

---

93   Schopenhauer 1971, p. 105.

individual of real talent'. With its democratic and levelling tendencies, Christianity ended up as a sort of 'democratic ethics' (VII, 45); one could even ask whether it was not 'hostile to its core to any form of culture, and thus necessarily connected to barbarism' (VII, 244).

12   Eva, Persephone and Prometheus: The Reinterpretation of Original Sin

Now it is clear. Nietzsche's originality consists not in diagnosing the revolutionary disease, a diagnosis that ultimately, by condemning the idea of happiness, grasped an essential ideological aspect of the revolutionary cycle, but in the extent of the diagnosis, an integral part of which contained an anamnesis that went a very long way back. Here the spirits began to divide also regarding the remedy. Did it still make sense to continue to hope that Christianity could defeat the disaster that had been raging for more than two millennia? Even if the Christian churches seemed committed to delegitimising progressive subversion by referring back to the myth of original sin, it remained true that the disease, which had already begun in Greece before the advent of Christianity, had continued to rage despite its triumph.

Perhaps it was necessary to seek a more valid and effective alternative. Even before Nietzsche, Schelling referred to themes and myths from classical antiquity, alongside the biblical account. Condemning the revolutionary attempts to realise the 'true state', Schelling's Stuttgart lectures invoked the authority of Plato, to whom they attributed the merit of having brought to maturity the awareness of the 'original curse' that weighed on the human being and political institutions.[94]

Yet the reference to Persephone in the *Philosophy of Mythology* was especially significant: the innocent virgin violated by Hades and dragged down into the underworld represented 'unhappiness *kat' exochen*, the first unhappiness, the original fall';[95] and this unhappiness now appeared so much more ineluctable insofar as it was not the result of moral guilt, as in the case of Eve and Adam. The meaning of this discourse, which was also political, did not escape Schelling's contemporaries. Against the myth of Persephone and of the insuperable 'original unhappiness', favoured by Schelling, but to which later Nietzsche himself would also refer (M, 130), Rosenkranz set the myth of Prometheus,

---

94   Schelling 1856–61, Vol. VII, pp. 461–2.
95   Schelling 1856–61, Vol. XII, p. 160.

THE CRISIS OF CULTURE FROM SOCRATES TO THE PARIS COMMUNE   57

which became – as for the young Marx, though in a less pugnacious form and with reformist rather than revolutionary tones – a symbol of humanity's progress.[96]

Schelling, however, also referred to this latter myth, although moved by quite different political and ideological concerns: 'The destiny of the world and humanity is by nature something tragic'. Against any superficial progressivism, the punishment decreed by Zeus demonstrated the strength of the 'power and violence [*Kratos und Bia*]' inherent in history: the 'great spirit Aeschylus' never forgot this 'eternal tragic element', and thus 'does not want to banish everything that is terrible'.[97] The dream of a political community internally reconciled and based on equality and reciprocal recognition was thus vain. The terrible pain inflicted on Prometheus corresponded to an action that was nevertheless profoundly ethical: 'It is a contradiction that we don't need to overcome; on the contrary, we have to recognize it, and find the right expression for it.'[98]

Nietzsche's reading of this myth was not dissimilar: he urged people to take note, without evasion, of the 'insoluble contradiction', of the 'contradiction at the heart of the world', of the 'block of rock' that necessarily weighed on every culture. In the frank and muscular recognition of this ineluctability lay the main superiority of this myth over the biblical tale which, by blaming the original fall on the 'mendacious pretence' of the snake – woman's 'curiosity', 'openness to seduction' and 'lasciviousness' – was inclined 'simply to explain away' 'the curse in the nature of things' (GT, 9; I, 69–70 [49–50]). The biblical tale was focused on the theme of the incidental and redeemable fall. The *natura lapsa*, the result of the catastrophe, did not seem an insuperable given. The history of Christianity was marked by the recurrent manifestation of tendencies that were inclined to think salvation could find its beginning on earth: in this way the emergence of messianic or revolutionary movements was explained. It was confirmation that the biblical tale was not properly a true 'pessimistic tragedy' (GT, 9; I, 69 [50]).

Yet there was another reason why Nietzsche preferred the myth of Prometheus. To clarify it, we can begin from the harsh criticism Marx addressed to Malthus. Malthus, according to Marx, 'sees human suffering as the punishment or sin and who, in any case, needs a "vale of tears on earth"'.[99] On the other hand, the 'principle of population' he theorised (the enduring and unavoidable inadequacies of resources in relation to population) was a type of 'disguised

---

96   Rosenkranz 1969, pp. VI–VII.
97   Schelling 1856–61, Vol. XI, pp. 486–7.
98   Schelling 1856–61, Vol. XI, p. 485.
99   Marx and Engels 1975 ff., Vol. 31, p. 347.

economic original sin',[100] although one with the unusual characteristic that it was applied selectively: while legitimising the misery of the working class, it did not limit the wealth and enjoyment of the exploiting classes; for the latter – as the *Theories on Surplus-Value* ironically observed – Malthus thought it appropriate and indispensable to 'sweeten the ruling classes sojourn in the vale of tears'.[101]

Christian original sin seemed to make its curse weigh on the world as such, condemning all people to renunciation, to a life gained through work and sweat. When formulated in such general terms, this condemnation started to be perceived as debilitating, not only because of the process of secularisation and the increase in the total social wealth (with the rapid obsolescence of ascetic ideals), but also due to an industrial development that accentuated the polarisation of wealth and poverty. There was no longer the widespread limitation of resources of a fundamentally agrarian society: it was the intertwining of wealth and poverty that now had to be justified, an intertwining that became more and more visible and was more and more perceived as intolerable by the popular masses the more the productive forces developed.

It was precisely to such a challenge that Nietzsche's reading of the myth of Prometheus aimed to respond. It was the 'justification of the evil in human life', of the terrible price civilisation entailed. The meaning of the myth could be summarised in this 'conceptual formula': 'All that exists is just and unjust and is equally justified in both respects' (GT, 9; I, 69 & 71 [50–1]). In other words, to use the more explicit language of the 'Preface' to an 'Unwritten Book' not made available to the wide public, 'the vulture that eats the liver of the Promethean promoter of culture' revealed a deep and unavoidable 'truth': 'slavery belongs to the essence of a culture'. From this curse it was impossible to escape, and it weighed inexorably, although not in an undifferentiated way: 'the misery of those that live from the sweat of their brow has to be increased even further, to make possible for a small number of Olympian men the production of a world of art' (CV, 3; I, 767).

13   'Greek Serenity', 'Sensualism' and Socialism

At this point, perhaps, the goal of the polemic against 'Greek serenity' becomes clearer. What was aimed at was not so much Winckelmann's reading, already

---

100   Marx and Engels 1975 ff., Vol. 35, p. 612n (trans. modified).
101   Marx and Engels 1975 ff., Vol. 31, p. 347.

remote both because of the passage of time and because it was separated from the moment by the conflicts and passions of a long revolutionary cycle that made it wholly obsolete. The target of the condemnation of the 'concept of "Greek serenity"', favoured by 'sensuous writers' (DW, 2; I, 561), was quite different. The reference was in the first place to Heine, explicitly quoted on another occasion and deemed guilty of having theorised and celebrated a supposed 'Greek serenity', understood as synonym of 'invulnerable satisfaction [*Behagen*]' and 'comfortable sensualism' (VII, 351–2). In fact, in opposition to Christianity, the author that was the object of this criticism celebrated in an explicit and recurrent way *griechische Heiterkeit* or *hellenische Heiterkeit*, whose rediscovery in the Renaissance and modernity marked the liberation or the possibility of liberation from a 'millennial yoke'.[102]

Yet, in certain respects, Heine seemed to begin from presuppositions analogous with Nietzsche's. He also thought Christianity was now dying:

> From the moment in which a religion asks for help from philosophy, its end is unavoidable. It tries to defend itself, but drifts ever deeper into corruption. Religion, like any absolutism, should not justify itself. [...] As soon as religion allows the printing of a reasoned catechism, as soon as political absolutism publishes an official state gazette, both are at an end.[103]

We are immediately led to think of *The Birth of Tragedy*'s diagnosis of the mortal disease looming over Christianity as a 'learned religion'. For Heine, however, it was a different factor, and perhaps even more important one, that called forth illness and even unavoidable death. This is clarified in a letter to Heinrich Laube of 10 July 1833:

> The hitherto existing spiritualist religion was beneficial and necessary, as long as the greater part of humanity lived in misery and needed to console itself with a heavenly religion. But since the progresses of industry and the economy have made it possible to free humans from their material misery and to make them happy on earth, since then [...] you understand me. And people will understand us when we say to them that, due to that, they should eat beef instead of potatoes every day, and work less, and dance more. You can be sure of it, men are not donkeys.[104]

---

102   Heine 1969–78, Vol. III, pp. 370 & 684–5; Vol. VI, 1, p. 367.
103   Heine 1969–78, Vol. III, p. 578.
104   Heine 1969–78, Vol. III, p. 884.

Yet the death of Christianity would come to coincide, according to Nietzsche, with the death of culture, which could not do without slaves, a class
of men destined to be sacrificed. At this point, the contrast between the two
authors becomes clear. Yes, both thought Christianity was destined to cede its
position to a sort of pagan or neopagan renaissance. Yet how different was the
political situation and the philosophy of history in which each located this happening! While Nietzsche looked, in a certain sense, with respect at the biblical
theme of original sin, for Heine this represented the most repulsive component, the 'bashful part' of the religion dominant in the West. By conjuring up the
bogeyman of this remote and irremediable fall, this religion wanted to deny
human beings, and especially the poor masses, the right to terrestrial happiness.[105] Now we were on the verge of a radical and beneficial turning point:

> I speak of that religion whose first principles damn the flesh, and which
> not only attributes to spirit predominance over the flesh, but even wants
> to kill it in order to glorify spirit itself; I speak of that religion whose unnat-
> ural mission has introduced sin and hypocrisy into the world, by distort-
> ing with the damnation of the flesh even the most innocent of sensual joys
> into a sin, and by necessarily generating hypocrisy given the impossibility
> of being pure spirit; I speak of that religion that, by urging the refusal of
> all worldly goods, and the imposition of a canine humility and an angelic
> patience, has become the most sure support of despotism. Today men
> have uncovered the essence of this religion, they are no longer enchanted
> by heavenly promises, they know that matter contains something of good
> and is not entirely evil, and they now demand earthly pleasures, this beau-
> tiful divine garden, our inalienable heritage. Precisely because today we
> understand completely the consequences of that absolute spiritualism,
> we are right to maintain that the Christian-Catholic conception of the
> world is exhausted. For every epoch is a sphinx that disappears into the
> abyss as soon as its enigma has been resolved.[106]

We saw Nietzsche condemning Heine as a 'sensualist'. And we know that, in
the liberal and conservative culture of the time, sensualism was in the last
analysis a synonym for socialism. This was also the case in Heine, but with a
different and opposed value-judgement. The category of 'sensualism' now had
a univocally positive meaning.[107] It was a synonym for the 'rehabilitation of

---

105   Heine 1969–78, Vol. III, p. 577.
106   Heine 1969–78, Vol. III, p. 362.
107   Heine 1969–78, Vol. III, pp. 533–4.

matter',[108] for the 'rehabilitation of the flesh',[109] for the demand for the earthly happiness of everyone and, in the first place, for those who had been excluded from it for so long:

> Yes, I say it firmly, those who come after us will be more beautiful and happier than us. As I believe in progress, I believe that humanity is destined to happiness, and I therefore nourish a greater opinion of the divinity than those pious people who imagine that he created humanity only in order to make it suffer. I want to establish already here on earth, with the blessing of free political and industrial institutions, the beatitude that, according to the opinion of the pious, should only occur in heaven on doomsday.[110]

Following the Saint-Simonists, the history of the Occident was read as a 'struggle of spiritualism and sensualism', in which sensualism, 'after a long oppression, seeks to regain its rights'.[111] Marked as a 'sensualist', Heine did not wait to label his adversaries in turn as 'spiritualists':

> We thus assign the name of spiritualism to that outrageous pretentiousness of the spirit that, striving after exclusive glorification, seeks to squash under foot matter, or at least to abuse it: and we give the name sensualism to the opposition that, against it, aims to rehabilitate matter and claims for the senses their rights, without denying the rights of spirit, without even denying the supremacy of spirit.[112]

Once the idea of a suffering God like the Christian one, a God that died on the cross, was consigned to history, one sought to realise terrestrial happiness: 'Whoever sees God suffering bears their own pains more easily'; the modern human being could find no satisfaction in a religion that 'concedes no joy anymore, but only consolation'.[113] A joyful neopagan feeling of life was now called upon to shape earthly existence and social and political relations. Thus, 'the old Greek serenity, the lust for life, which appeared to the Christian as the work of the devil', once again became contemporary.[114]

---

108 Heine 1969–78, Vol. III, p. 568.
109 Heine 1969–78, Vol. III, p. 402.
110 Heine 1969–78, Vol. III, p. 519.
111 Heine 1969–78, Vol. III, p. 771 (it is a passage from the manuscript).
112 Heine 1969–78, Vol. III, p. 556.
113 Heine 1969–78 Vol. II, p. 493.
114 Heine 1969–78, Vol. III, p. 684.

By depriving the dominant religion and ideology of the theme of original sin, neopaganism became a moment of socialist and revolutionary unrest. This was the target of Nietzsche's polemic: for him, a conception that ignored the 'horrifying profundity' at the heart of Greek beauty and serenity remained not only on the 'pure surface' but also in the 'present' (VII, 352). In other words, it was itself infected by modern subversion, precisely that which instead had to be contained and blocked. One can thus understand the severity of the tone:

> Hellenism is the word that provides a solution for all who have looked around for luminous models for their conscious affirmation of the will; thus at long last sensual writers have coined the concept of 'Greek serenity', so that irreverently a dissolute lazy life dares to excuse itself with the word 'Greek', or even to praise itself. In all these representations that lose their way and err from what is most noble to the most vulgar, Hellenism is thought to be too crude and simple, and in a certain sense it is fashioned according to the image of unambiguous and unilateral nations (e.g., the Romans).
>
> DW, 2; I, 561

Heine's Hellenism, in other words, was neo-Latin or, more appropriately, from the neo-Latin world: we were not to forget that the French were the new Romans, the protagonists of the revolutionary cycle that culminated in the Paris Commune. Now it had to be put to an end once and for all thanks to the German victory and the return to tragic Hellenism.

14   The Apolline, the Dionysiac and the Social Question

Nevertheless, in *The Birth of Tragedy* and in contemporary writings, there emerged a theme that at first sight appears different and opposed. We thus unexpectedly run into the description of a Dionysian 'superior community', with peculiar characteristics: 'Now the slave is a freeman, now all the rigid, hostile barriers, which necessity, caprice, or "impudent fashion" have established between human beings, break asunder. Now, hearing this gospel of universal harmony, each person feels himself to be not simply united, reconciled or merged with his neighbour, but quite literally one with him' (GT, 1; I, 29 [18]). Or, to quote a different version of this text, 'all the caste divisions that have been established by necessity and capriciousness disappear', 'the noble and the low born join together' (DW, 1; I, 555).

On this basis, some commentators have felt authorised to suggest a more or less 'revolutionary' or subversive reading of the young Nietzsche. However, he repeatedly insisted on the foreignness to political life in the strict sense of the sphere here at stake: 'the dithyrambic chorus is a chorus of transformed beings who have completely forgotten their civic past and their social position' (GT, 8; I, 61 [43]). A handwritten note is even more explicit: unlike the 'Apolline genius', who had a 'military' and 'political' dimension, 'the Dionysiac genius has nothing to do with the state' (VII, 322). He had nothing to do with 'the world of daily life', or if he had a relation with it, only in the sense that he aimed to make it forgotten, by immersing it in a 'lethargic element'. Far from aiming to contest and annul 'the usual barriers and limits of existence', the periodic 'gulf of oblivion' of the Dionysiac festival served to make them more tolerable (GT, 7; I, 56 [40]). It thus served to consolidate an order and culture that inevitably entailed terrible sacrifices. Indeed, Nietzsche asked himself if in Germany there was anything similar to the 'orgiastic feasts of Dionysus'. He believed he could identify them, on the one hand, in certain medieval processions, which 'went from one city to the next with a ever greater crowd singing and jumping', and, on the other, in 'Carnival plays [*Fastnachtspiel*]' (GMD, I, 521 & 516). The mixing of the ranks, of social roles, of single individualities, transformed and fused in a unitary celebration, which occurred on such occasions, did not in any way place in question the social and political hierarchies of ordinary life, in which individuality had a determined and stable place that could not be changed or exchanged with another, as in a game.

The Birth of Tragedy distinguished 'Dionysiac' from 'political impulses': only the latter had the conquest of power, of honour, of wealth as an object, while the former had to do with ecstasy, understood in the etymological sense of the term, as a coming out of oneself and the cancellation and oblivion of one's singularity (GT, 21; I, 133–4 [98–9]). What was the sociopolitical objective meaning of this distinction of spheres? In the Apolline sphere, art and beauty hid with their splendour the burden of suffering that civilisation entailed. In the Dionysiac sphere, this burden was terribly present but it was not a determined social class, or a determined individual that was subjected to it; it was 'the primordial unity [*Ur-Eine*]', the 'eternally suffering and contradictory' unity (GT, 4; I, 38 [26]); it was the 'metaphysical unity of all things' (BA, 4; I, 716). It was in this sphere, from which the *principium individuationis* was absent, that the superior Dionysian community developed. Yet it had so little to do with politics that it was not even limited to the human being; rather than 'generally human', it was 'universally natural' (DW, 1; I, 555). Thus, 'not only is the bond between human beings renewed by the magic of the Dionysiac, but nature, alienated, inimical, or subjugated, celebrates once more her festival of reconciliation with her lost son, humankind'. Now the individual was dissolved in a 'mysterious primordial unity' that included not only human beings but also the beings of the animal and natural world, united and fused in the 'gospel of universal harmony' (GT, 1; I, 29–30 [18]).

The reading of Schopenhauer was in the background. Not by chance, in a letter to Gersdorff of 7 November 1870, Nietzsche said he had written an essay 'on the Dionysian conception of the world', which analysed 'Greek antiquity' by seeking to understand it on the basis of 'our philosopher' (B, II, 1, 155). Let us now read *The World as Will and Representation*: beyond the sphere of the phenomena and appearances, beyond the veil of Maya, the *principium individuationis* has lost its strength; the will, unique and undivided essence, is 'free from all diversity, even though its appearances in time and space are innumerable'.[115] Now we understand that 'the agony personally experienced or inflicted on others, the evil and the ill always strike upon one and the same essence, even if the appearances in which one or the other appear exist as very different individuals'.[116] As if by magic, the contrasts and disharmony that belong to a world marked by the *principium individuationis* are appeased in the 'calm of the species [*Ruhe der Gattung*]'.[117] This species embraces nature in its entirety, the totality of the real: in this context, there is no room for protests and recriminations by individuals, now reabsorbed into the world of essences, in a unity without cracks.

The young Nietzsche also drew on this ideological arrangement. In his eyes, Schopenhauer was an educator also because he was able to evoke the figure of the 'saint, whose ego has entirely melted away and whose life of suffering is no longer – or almost no longer – felt individually, but only as the deepest feeling of quality, communion, and oneness [*Gleich-Mit und Eins-Gefühl*] with all living things'. He kindled the 'most ardent fire in whose light we no longer understand the word "I"' (SE, 5; I, 382 [213–14]). Such a transfiguration and sympathetic identification with everything made tolerable the sacrifice of innumerable individuals without which culture could not be conceived. The victims sacrificed on the altar of culture were thus reminded of 'new duties', which 'are not the duties of a solitary individual'; 'on the contrary, through them one is integrated into a powerful community [*Gemeinsamkeit*], one that, to be sure, is not held together by external forms and laws, but by a fundamental idea', the preoccupation of promoting the production of genius in its diverse configurations (SE, 5; I, 381–2 [213]).

---

115   Schopenhauer 1976–82a, pp. 173–4.
116   Schopenhauer 1976–82a, p. 455.
117   Schopenhauer 1976–82b, p. 617.

The Dionysian view of the world dared 'to gaze into the terrors of individual existence' but, at the same time, pushed us to comprehend the 'eternal lust and delight of existence', though finding it 'not in appearances but behind them'. A world dominated by the *principium individuationis* unavoidably entailed division into slaves and lords, and therefore the condemnation of one caste to a life of privation and suffering; even the luckiest ones were forced to recognise that 'everything that comes into being must be prepared for painful destruction'. But if, beyond this sphere of appearances, we drew on the 'primordial being itself', the 'world-Will', in its 'exuberant fertility' and 'uncountable excess', despite the losses it continuously entailed, the picture changed radically: although, under the 'sting of these pains', we could become 'become one with the immeasurable, primordial delight in existence'. In this way, 'we are happily alive, not as individuals, but as the *one* living being, with whose procreative lust we have become one' (GT, 17; I, 109 [81]). The tiger and the panther lay down at the feet of the Dionysiac man (GT, 20; I, 132 [98]): but it was not because they had been transformed into innocent and harmless lambs; rather, their aggressivity was recognised, integrated and therefore accepted in the Dionysian economy of the 'everything is one'.

At this level, the subject of pain, happiness and guilt was not the concretely determined individual but the primordial unity. Beginning from these presuppositions, on the occasion of the Paris Commune, Nietzsche refused to blame 'the crime of a struggle against culture' exclusively on the revolutionaries: 'those sinners' in reality were 'only bearers of a universal guilt [*allgemeine Schuld*]', which involved everyone, as well as both past and present. This declaration has sometimes been read as a sort of indulgence for or understanding of the reasons of the Communards, but the same letter polemicised violently against the 'international hydra's head'. More than a moral and political judgement, the attribution of 'universal guilt' was a consideration of a metaphysical character, at the basis of which, in a Schopenhauerian way, there was an 'identity of being [*Dasein*] and being indebted [*Verschuldetsein*]' (CV, 5; I, 785).

We can thus understand why, in the preparatory notes for *The Birth of Tragedy*, the reflections on the 'tragic human being' were strictly intertwined with those related to the 'resolution of the social question' (VII, 121). It was 'fear of socialism' (VII, 412) that stimulated both reflections. The letters of his friend Gersdorff had directed Nietzsche's attention to this movement on many occasions. In these letters, Gersdorff warmly recommended to Nietzsche the study of 'political economy' and, in particular, reading Lassalle: only in this way could he adequately understand the 'so-called social question', the emergence of 'socialism' and 'communism', the increasing restlessness of the 'proletariat', 'this cancer of all high culture [*Hochcultur*]' (B, I, 3, 224–9).

In such a situation of grave danger, 'the only salvation from socialism' could, as we know, be the 'serious', 'tragic' or 'Dionysiac' worldview. The return to the noumenal sphere of the primordial unity, constituted on the basis of the transcendence of all determination and individuation, served to defuse the social question, the power of violence and suffering experienced by a given class of individuals: 'in Dionysiac music and lyric the human being wants to express himself as a species being [*Gattungswesen*]' [...]; he becomes 'a natural human being among natural human beings' (VII, 66). It is worth comparing this with another text: 'those who look more deeply' would recognise the 'transparent lies' implicit in the 'supposed "equal rights for all", in the "fundamental rights of the human being"', of the human being as a species being [*des Gattungswesens Mensch*], in the dignity of labour' (VII, 338). The category of 'species being', which famously played an important role in the communist project of the young Marx, thus appeared to be sometimes affirmed and sometimes rejected by Nietzsche.

In reality, as emerges from the second text, Nietzsche was already fully aware that a loud echo of the French Revolution, of the claim of *égalité* and the proclamation of the rights of the human being as such, lingered on in the category of species and species being. Already in the years of his youth, Nietzsche adopted a strategy that resulted from two movements that at first sight seemed to diverge, but that in reality merged perfectly in the act of destroying a category so charged with revolutionary echoes. In the name of the unrepeatable uniqueness of any individual reality, the nominalist pathos dissolved and reduced to a *flatus vocis* any general concept, starting from the concept of the human being as such (*infra*, Chapters 8 §4 & 21 §2); on the other hand, the human being as such was absorbed within an infinitely broader reality that embraced the entire animal and natural world. The peculiarity of the youthful period is that this second movement developed by referring to nature, or the 'great God Pan' (GT, 11; I, 75 [54]), but also to a community, to a species [*Gattung*] that, following Schopenhauer, was expanded to the point where it included and engulfed the human being as such.

The Dionysiac, finally, had a double function. Ripping up the veil that covered the spectacle of a cruel and merciless nature, it confuted the idea of happiness that accompanied the ruinous trajectory of modernity; it also submerged the sufferings of the sacrificial victims of culture in a category of species, embracing the whole of nature, whose explosive political dimension was defused. Culture presupposed, on the one hand, the view of the tragic dimension of existence with the consequent renunciation of belief in the possibility of the terrestrial happiness of everyone; on the other hand, it presupposed the acceptance of a dimension that entailed the 'breakdown of the *principium individuationis*', the annulment of 'subjectivity', 'complete self-forgetting' by the individual or the slave destined to be sacrificed. It was for this reason that the Dionysiac could be compared to 'intoxication', the intoxication into which the sacrificial victims above all should be immersed (GT, 1; I, 28–30 [17–18]). Freemen and slaves, everyone and anybody, all ultimately belonged to a community, to a universal unity of the will of living that, by means of atrocious suffering and the forgetting of it, achieved its superior goal: the production of beauty, art and culture itself.

15   Athens and Jerusalem; Apollo and Jesus, Dionysus and Apollo

To understand Nietzsche's attitude, we must return to the debate on classical antiquity and Christianity that strongly marked the German culture of his time. Fascinated by the strong earthly and mundane sense that characterised paganism, Heine called for a choice 'between Jerusalem and Athens, between the Holy Sepulchre and the cradle of art, between life in the spirit and spirit in life', between 'Judaism founded on mortification' and Hellenism, which often used art as a 'tribunal' for 'preaching life from those heights'.[118] Here we confront two ideal-typical categories: the joyful affirmation of the 'Hellenes' of yesterday and today were set against asceticism and the 'Nazarene limitation' (embodied above all in the Judeo–Christian tradition).[119] We already know that Nietzsche could not identify with the Jerusalem/Athens dichotomy, that is, Nazarene/Hellene, because it was built on a concept of 'Greek serenity' that tended towards 'optimism' and 'sensualism', thus leading to the revolt of the slaves and modern subversion and devastation.

Wagner, the author of *Art and Revolution*, confronts us with a similar dichotomy. Wagner compared and contrasted Apollo and Jesus, pagan Hellenism and Christianity. After it 'overcame the rude natural religion of the Asian homeland', the 'Greek spirit' found 'its most adequate expression in Apollo'.[120] The Greek society based on the cult of this divinity assigned labour and material production to the 'oriental barbarians' and the slaves. Thus, the space for realising and deploying the principle of 'strength and beauty' of the individual opened up; this principle received its plastic expression in Apollo. It is against this world that Christianity loomed up, refusing and overcoming the laceration

---

118   Heine 1969–78, Vol. IV, pp. 175–6.
119   Heine 1969–78, Vol. IV, pp. 17–18.
120   Wagner 1910a, pp. 9–10.

of the human species and the exclusivity of the 'special humanity [*Sonder-menschentum*]' on which Greek civilisation rested,[121] and thereby affirming the universal fraternity of human beings; nonetheless, the new religion proclaimed this principle within a vision that denied the world, art and life and trampled on the free development of the individual. By treasuring the invention of the 'machine',[122] which could take the place of the unhappy slaves, the contemporary world hoped for the reconciliation of the teachings of the 'two sublime masters of humanity', Jesus and Apollo,[123] and thus hoped to build a society in which the beautiful blossoming of individuality and art no longer came up against the limitations and exclusions of Greece.

Though adopting quite different positions, the Wagner of 1848 and Heine both believed that the contemporary world, overcoming the exclusivity of classical antiquity and treasuring the Christian or the Jewish-Christian doctrine, would spread everywhere the attention to the body and art that constituted the great merit of Greek civilisation. The young Nietzsche had a different approach: in his eyes, the dichotomy that the Wagner of 1849 elaborated had the merit of drawing attention back to slavery, to the real foundation of Greek splendour and civilisation as such, thus refuting the myth of an undifferentiated happiness and 'Greek serenity', which constituted, as the example of Heine showed, a component of revolutionary unrest. Published at a time when its author was himself contaminated by such unrest, *Art and Revolution* argued that machines could replace slaves. Yet this illusion was dissipated in the Wagner who engaged in dialogue with the young Nietzsche and, even before *The Birth of Tragedy*, praised the 'spirit of music' omnipresent in the diverse manifestations of Greek civilisation, but also the 'authentic ancient Dorian State', with its severe 'military order'.[124]

In *The Birth of Tragedy* and other writings of the period, culture rested in a difficult equilibrium between the Dionysiac and Apolline, which at the same time was the problematic relation between Orient and Occident, Asia and Europe. The 'Dionysian festive procession' proceeded from 'from India to Greece' (GT, 20; I, 132 [98]), and Greece was located 'between India and Rome' (GT, 21; I, 133 [99]). Far from celebrating the Dionysiac as such, *The Birth of Tragedy* was concerned to emphasise 'the vast gulf which separated the Dionysiac Greeks from the Dionysiac Barbarians' of the East. Indeed, there was 'no more dangerous power [...] than this crude, grotesque manifestation of the

---

121   Wagner 1910a, p. 26.
122   Wagner 1910a, p. 33.
123   Wagner 1910a, p. 41.
124   Wagner 1910f, p. 121.

Dionysiac' (GT, 2; I, 31–2 [20]), which 'among the Asians means the most crude unleashing of the inferior instincts', with the explosion, at least periodically, of 'all social ties', or 'every statal and social tie' (DW, 1; I, 556, 558). The taming of the Dionysian Orient was the 'highest act of Hellenism' (VII, 118).

Not only Greek culture but culture as such could only be thought of beginning from the subjugation of this barbarian element. It was this act of force that made possible the 'separation and division of the chaotic mass' into castes. There thus emerged 'military castes' (CV, 3; I, 775) and 'the organization of the intellectual castes' (VII, 380 & 413). While the state, of which Apollo was the symbol, held in check the slaves and the 'great masses' with its 'iron grip', (CV, 3; I, 769, 772) it promoted war; beside the education of the warriors, this also provided for the recruitment of the slaves themselves: 'for the state war is a necessity, in the same way that slavery is a necessity for society' (CV, 3; I, 774). Despite its 'horrible origin', it was good that the state constituted 'perhaps the highest and most venerable object for the blind and egoistic masses' (CV, 3; I, 771).

The history of Hellenism was the history of its struggle against the barbarian Dionysiac: 'never was Hellenism in greater danger than during the tempestuous entrance of the new God' (DW, 1; I, 556). It was Apollo with 'his power to tame the Dionysus who came storming out of Asia'; 'it was the Apolline people who restrained this overweening instinct with beauty' (DW, 1; I, 556 e 558). This victory was not achieved once and for all:

> The only explanation I can find for the Doric state and Doric art is that it was a permanent military encampment of the Apolline: only in a state of unremitting resistance to the Titanic-barbaric nature of the Dionysiac could such a cruel and ruthless polity, such a war-like and austere form of education, such a defiantly aloof art, surrounded by battlements, exist for long.
>
> GT, 4; I, 41 [28]

The recognition given to the 'Dionysian view of the world' was not to cause us to forget the recognition accorded to the 'Doric view of the world', or the 'Doric State' and 'Doric art' (GT, 4; I, 41–2 [28]). The struggle was not only a long term one but, at a certain point, ceased to be victorious: 'the Hellenic world of Apollo is gradually overcome from within by the Dionysian powers. Christianity had already discovered itself' (VII, 137).

So, the Dionysiac not subjugated by Apollo and authentic Hellenism was Asian and Oriental barbarism. Nietzsche shared the common representation of the Orient as a synonym of pantheism at the religious level and organicism at the political level, elements that left no space for the emergence of subjectivity. Following Hegel, 'distinction and determination vanish', while 'immersion into lack of consciousness, unity with Brahman, annihilation' occurred; one thinks of the 'Buddhist Nirvana'.[125] Insofar as it entailed 'the obliteration of the moment of self-consciousness in essence [*Wesen*]' and in which the single individuality and every reality was 'thrown into this abyss of annihilation', Spinoza's pantheism was also an expression of an 'oriental vision',[126] or of an 'oriental representation'.[127]

In Nietzsche's eyes, Christianity itself already referred to the Orient in as much as it affirmed the idea of equality between human beings, albeit by conceiving of it in religious terms, deleting differences and making the Dionysian element absolute: 'with the orientalist-Christian movement the old Dionysiac culture flooded the world, and all the work of Hellenism seemed in vain' (VII, 118). The morbid 'development of the Dionysiac' flowed into 'absolute mysticism' (VII, 154), into the total abandonment to an 'ecstatic brooding [*ekstatische Brüte*]' (GT, 21; I, 133–4 [99]). Once it was absolutised, the 'ecstatic' (and Dionysian) element acted in a ruinous way, by dispersing into an indistinct whole the individuality, the *principium individuationis*, the differences and the hierarchies that alone made the state and authentic culture possible.

Why then did the young Nietzsche insist on the limits of an Apolline not nourished by the Dionysiac? In other words, what were the positive elements introduced into culture in general by a Dionysiac purged of its dissolving barbarian capacity? We have considered one aspect in detail. It concerned refuting once and for all optimism, whose ruinous consequences manifested themselves in the incessant revolutionary cycle: the unilateral Apolline vision of Greek antiquity was nothing but the vacuous and superficial optimism that modern interpreters projected onto the past, thus depriving modernity of alternatives. Detached from Dionysus, and from the tragic foundation of existence, Apollo became the flag of 'the Enlightenment' and of 'its political convictions': it was an 'enlightened [*aufgeklärt*] God', the prototype of the 'serene, judicious but slightly unmoral Apollinean' (BA, 3; I, 701–2), with whom modern man tended to identify himself.

Yet this was not all. In these years Nietzsche passionately hoped for a German revival of authentic Hellenism. He thus aimed at a society capable of unity, especially at such crucial moments as that in which Prussia and Germany con-

---

125 Hegel 1969–79, Vol. V, p. 389.
126 Hegel 1969–79, Vol. XX, pp. 185 & 165–6.
127 Hegel 1969–79, Vol. VI, p. 198.

fronted the militarily hegemonic power of continental Europe, the country of 'civilisation' and modern subversion. The Dionysiac also responded to this need. It was the moment of choral unity, or of 'superior community', as we have already seen. It was thanks to it that Greece could face the formidable attack of Persia; without it, no society would be able either to legitimise the permanent recourse to slavery (more or less camouflaged), or to face the challenges of the recurrent crises.

16   Art, Politics and *Kulturkritik*

There is no doubt: Wilamowitz was right when he banished *The Birth of Tragedy* from the field of classical philology. On this Ritschl agreed, as he lapidarily observed in a diary note upon receiving the book of his disciple, or ex-disciple: 'ingenious extravagance'.[128] Regarding the 'extravagance', on the absolute originality of this book, there are no doubts: yet wherein lies its ingenious character, its unquestionable charm?

It is not sufficient, or it can even be misleading, to refer to the splendid prose: Nietzsche himself would later warn against the 'seduction of words' (JGB, 16 [16]). At first sight, *The Birth of Tragedy* comprised arguments that were very disparate: Greek philosophy and tragedy, the thought of Kant and Schopenhauer and the music of Bach, Beethoven and Wagner; Christianity and Buddhism; Greece engaged in the confrontation with Persia and the hopes placed in a Germany returned victorious from the war against France; the anxious warning against optimism and socialism and the contemptuous denunciation of the 'restlessly barbaric turmoil known as "the present"' (GT, 15; I, 102 [75]); the reflections on classical antiquity and the condemnation of any 'frivolous deification of the present' (GT, 23; I, 148–49 [111]).

To give this apparent hotchpotch unity, it is not sufficient either to say that it is a philosophical text. First, this is a very large category, a genus that can subsume species very different one from the other. Above all, with this affirmation we have not yet identified the fundamental theme capable of giving unity to *The Birth of Tragedy* and of understanding it as a philosophical text. I have already emphasised the inadequacy of the interpretation in merely aesthetic terms, which are unable to explain the references to the reality and political (and military) struggle of the time. Once the coexistence of multiple themes

---

128   In Janz 1981, Vol. I, p. 470.

has been acknowledged, we need to identify the central theme, that is, the theme capable of imposing order, a coherent and unitary wholeness, on the apparent chaos.

Is it the aesthetic interest? Ritschl read in the work of his disciple or ex-disciple the celebration of art as a 'world-transforming, redeeming and liberating force' (B, II, 2, 541); in turn, Rohde highlighted in *The Birth of Tragedy* the 'noble aspirations to a truly artistic culture'. Does this confirm and endorse a reading in predominantly aesthetic terms? In reality, Rohde thought the 'new culture' in opposition to the 'rotten culture' of the present and its 'hell of destructive powers'.[129] The invocation of a new artistic culture was, in the first place, a political project that entailed a fight to the death against certain institutions and certain political and social relations and the constructions of very different ones, the liquidation of one ideology and vision of the world and the elaboration and diffusion of a very different one. Not by chance did Nietzsche's friend Romundt write to him to complain that he, Romundt, lived in a 'modern society of civilization that has dispensed with religion, art and metaphysics' (B, II, 2, 454).

Certainly, it was necessary to assume 'the artist as teacher', but only because he could clarify something fundamental that went beyond art: 'Hellenism is the only form in which one can live: the terrible in the mask of the beautiful' (VII, 80). If modern optimism stimulated the revolt of the slaves and the triumph of barbarism, Christian pessimism represented escape from the world. The Greek art-religion revealed, instead, its singular greatness by promoting the 'happiness of existence [*Daseinsseligkeit*]' despite pessimism (VII, 81), despite clear knowledge of the burden of suffering and of pain (slavery and the exhaustion of the masses) at the foundation of culture. In Greece, only art made possible 'glorification of the will' and thus acceptance of the 'cruel reality' that 'builds its victory arches on slavery and annihilation' (VII, 140). On the other hand, the rebirth of authentic art was a precondition for the regeneration of Germany and the revival of its 'mission' in the struggle against civilisation and modernity.

That the theme of art does not have a merely aesthetic meaning and even less that it can be used to immerse The *Birth of Tragedy* in a bath of aesthetic immaculateness, according to the habits of not a few interpreters, is further confirmed by the fact that Nietzsche's reference to art passed over effortlessly into a reference to the sociology of art, as emerges from the analyses and questions about the social forces that inspire or consecrate the success of Euripides

---

129   Rohde 1989a, p. 12 f.

and, after two millennia, of neo-Latin melodrama. This sociology of art ended up, in its turn, as a sociology of political 'parties' that still continued to clash on ideological, cultural and artistic terrain, just as they clashed more than two millennia before, at the time of Socrates and Euripides.

So, we can understand why the 'Foreword' affirmed that there was no 'opposition' between 'patriotic excitement and aesthetic self-indulgence' (GT, 'Foreword'; I, 24 [13]). A text from the same period, going further, stressed that far from a contrast, there was a 'mysterious connection [...] between state and art, between political greed and artistic creation, battlefield and artwork' (CV, 3; I, 772). Aesthetic and political reflections were so strictly intertwined that they were effectively inseparable. If, on the one hand, the category of the 'tragic' referred to Greek tragedy and therefore to art, on the other hand, it also had a clear historical and political connotation. This is confirmed by the faithful and combative announcement of the 'entry of the tragic period of the present' (VII, 281). The very expression 'metaphysics of art' recalled the expression 'metaphysics of genius', which consecrated the 'natural hierarchy in the kingdom of the intellect' (*infra*, Chapter 2 §5). It thus contained a provocative political meaning, the glorification of the aristocracy in the natural and also the sociopolitical order.

Poetry and art signified a naïve and simple relation with nature and instinct, and music in particular represented the undisputed 'dominion of the instinct' (VII, 49). As we shall see, 'simplicity', 'ingenuity', 'instinct' led to the calm acceptance, without artifice and cerebral and moralistic complications, of the natural fact of slavery. The 'metaphysics of art', celebrated with one's gaze fixed on tragic Greece, was not so ethereal as to disdain the legitimation of an institution conceived as repugnant by the weak and anti-artistic modern human being. Only thanks to the 'metaphysics of art' could we understand the value of 'dissonance in music' and in life; so it was 'precisely the tragic myth that has to convince us that even the ugly and the disharmonic are an artistic game'. Slavery was an integral part of the ugliness and disharmony that were inextricably connected to life; it was the mass sacrifice consumed on the altar of the production of genius and art. In this sense, 'only as an aesthetic phenomenon do existence and the world appear justified' (GT, 24; I, 152 [113]). On the other hand, Socrates, philosophical *pendant* of Euripides (expression, as we know, of the 'fifth estate, that of slavery') expressed with its optimism a worldview 'as unartistic as it is parasitic on life' (GT, 24; I, 153 [114]).

So, the principal aspect of this inseparable intertwining was politics. Only thanks to it could we grasp the fundamental unity between the recurrent references to the Paris Commune, the socialist movement and the French-

Prussian war, and the subtle analyses of melodrama, of Aeschylus's and Wagner's tragedy. Indeed, these genres and these literary and musical expressions were themselves interpreted in political terms. The reading of Aeschylus was no less political than that of Socrates, who bore the chief responsibility for the *political* catastrophe of Hellenism, just as the reading of Wagner was no less political than the reading of Rousseau, a main protagonist of a *political* catastrophe not yet over. Nor should we forget that the Euripides targeted by *The Birth of Tragedy* was the author celebrated by Heine as 'democratic'.[130] A few years later, the fourth *Unfashionable Observation* would reject with contempt any merely aesthetic interpretation of the reference to art and the great musician in particular (*infra*, Chapter 6 §10).

Yet it is not enough to stress the centrality of politics in *The Birth of Tragedy*. We have seen that, far from being limited to the immediate situation, it took its cue from the remote past. It aimed to comprehend more than two millennia of history. It is worth recalling that one of the subtitles Nietzsche considered for some time was 'A Contribution to the Philosophy of History' (VII, 84). It was fundamentally in this perspective that, at the end of his conscious life, the author of *Ecce Homo* would reread his youthful work. In it, 'the opposition between Dionysian and Apollonian' was 'translated into metaphysics' and considered to be an Ariadne's thread of history itself; in its tragedy and its tragic age, Hellas turned out to be able to comprehend and affirm the 'unity' of the two moments, and so not to flinch in the face of the power of negativity that was the very foundation of culture, thus overcoming 'pessimism' (EH, 'The Birth of Tragedy', 1 [108]).

The subsequent rethinking of the subtitle can be easily understood: the category 'Philosophy of History' referred to Hegel and his school, entailing the legitimation of the modern, of the world that came out of the French Revolution, the very world that instead had to be put in question and even condemned. However, although subsequently put aside, that subtitle continued to indicate a path that could not be neglected. We encounter here a philosophy of history characterised by the polemic against the 'spirit of the age [*Zeitgeist*]', by the 'critique of the age [*Zeitkritik*]' (VII, 418 & 696); in the last analysis, by the refusal of modernity.

The refusal was even more radical to the extent that it was motivated by the conviction that modernity harboured the seeds of catastrophe. In a letter to his friend Gersdorff of 7 November 1870, Nietzsche was explicit: 'I am very worried about the impending state of affairs for culture [*Culturzustand*]' (B, II, 1, 155).

---

130   Heine 1969–78, Vol. III, p. 416; cf. Losurdo 1997a, Chapter VI, 3 (p. 271).

On the other hand, we have already seen the Paris Commune read as a symptom of the 'autumn of civilization'. A fragment from the summer–autumn of 1873 is even more dramatic:

> Everywhere there are symptoms of an extinction, of a complete eradication. [...] Everything is in the service of an imminent barbarism, art as well as science – where should we look? The great flood of biblical proportions of barbarism is at the gates. Since we actually have nothing to defend, and since we are all involved – what should we do?
>
> VII, 718–19

In any case, a 'new view of culture' (VII, 331) was imposed; the settling of accounts with the present and with the threats that loomed on the horizon could no longer be postponed.

17   An Appeal for a 'Struggle against Civilisation'

The importance here attributed to politics in the genesis of *The Birth of Tragedy* can appear surprising: later, Nietzsche would affirm that the book 'is politically indifferent – "un-German", people would say nowadays' (EH, 'The Birth of Tragedy', 1 [108]). In reality, we have seen the regular presence of the theme of the 'German essence', called upon to recover itself and authentic Hellenism in order to regenerate culture in Germany and in Europe. Moreover, the affirmation of *Ecce Homo* was contradicted by a contemporary fragment: 'this text signals itself as German, as loyal to the Reich – it even still believes in the German spirit!' (XIII, 227). To dissolve any doubt there is *An Attempt at Self-Criticism*, which preceded the re-edition, in 1888, of *The Birth of Tragedy*. On this occasion, Nietzsche regretted that he had hoped for so much from the 'German essence' and its capacity of stimulating liberation from the mediocrity of the modern world (GT, 'An Attempt at Self-Criticism', 6 [10]).

Nothing would be more mistaken than an interpretation of *The Birth of Tragedy* that assimilated its author to those philologists or erudite academics for whom he already displayed such contempt. Some fifteen years later, while reviewing his previous development and the youthful works, Nietzsche would write:

> I have made various attempts, not without dangers, to attract around me people [the reference is particularly to Wagner; DL] with whom I could speak of very rare things: *all my writings until then were nets I had cast:*

I wished to capture people with deep, rich and serene souls. [...] Later I
thought to 'seduce' German youth.

XI, 507

Still in this period, another fragment clarified: 'As a young person I aimed my
Unfashionable Observations at young people, to whom I spoke of my experiences and vows, in order *to lure them into my labyrinth*' (XI, 579). Therefore, as
the italicised phrase in particular highlights, Nietzsche's desire to proselytise
was constant, just as was his aspiration to win over the most promising political
forces (the youth), or the most significant personalities of the time, and to convince them not only and not so much about philosophical ideas, but especially
about 'vows [*Gelöbnisse*]', for a new future – ultimately, for a political project.

The slogan we run into time and time again when analysing the correspondence, the preparatory works and the fragments contemporary with the work
that signals Nietzsche's philosophical debut is worth considering: 'struggle
against civilization' (VII, 385). It is not an isolated idea: 'For the coming period
of culture' – underlined the letter to Gersdorff of 7 November 1870 – 'fighters are necessary: we must maintain ourselves for these battles' (B, II, 1, 156).
A few months earlier, at the outbreak of the French-Prussian war, a letter had
expressed anxiety for the fate of 'our outworn civilization': it could even be the
'beginning of the end!' (B, II, 1, 130). It was an anxiety linked to the development
of the social conflict. A fragment from the preparation of one of the Basel lectures stressed the need to elaborate 'proposals (against socialism)' (VII, 298);
some time later, a 'draft of the *Unfashionable Observations*' listed among the
planned titles, or themes possibly to take into consideration, the 'social crisis'
(VII, 699).

The preoccupation with this crisis already played an important role in The
Birth of Tragedy. In the Basel lectures from the same period, the appeal to
struggle was repeated and loud; the ambition to convince the youth about the
fight being prepared was explicit and declared. There was even a reconnais-
sance of the terrain with an evaluation of the different political forces occupying the battlefield. The enemies were those that identified unproblematically
with the present, those that considered acceptance of the present and their
existence as satisfied philistines as obvious and peaceful: they were the 'self-
evident'. On the opposite side, we saw the 'solitude' and desperation of those
who, considering useless any attempt at resistance and opposition, no longer
felt the 'need to fight'. Between the former and the latter were 'the fighters [*die
Kämpfenden*]', that is, those 'rich in hope' (BA, 'Introduction'; I, 646).

On the one hand, the latter had as their point of reference that 'sublime
fighter', Wagner (GT, Foreword [14]); on the other, Schopenhauer, later includ-

ed in the third *Unfashionable Observation* (dedicated to him) among the 'good and courageous fighters' committed to contesting the ruinous trajectory of optimism and modernity (SE, 3; I, 359 [192]). The fighters who had already taken up position, among whom Nietzsche clearly put himself, had the task of attracting and unifying in a common front of struggle all those who until then had been overpowered by a sense of impotence:

> Find yours, O isolated ones, in whose being [*Dasein*] I believe! You altruists, who suffer the pains of the corruption of the German spirit in yourselves. [...] I call to you. Don't crawl back into the cave of your isolation and your mistrust.
>
> CV 2; I, 763

The situation that had been created made a decision necessary. Everyone was 'at the crossroads' (BA, 4; I, 728). On the one hand were the 'barbarians of the nineteenth century', who, as we shall see, could rely on a terrible momentum. But those that suffered the most because of 'our current barbarism' (CV, 2; I, 763) were not for this reason to abandon themselves to discouragement and desertion on 'the battle field'. It was necessary to rise up to the challenge:

> We want nothing for ourselves: we need not worry about knowing how many individuals will fall in this struggle, nor should that we might be among the first to fall. It is precisely because we take it seriously that we should not take our poor individual persons so seriously; in the moment in which we fall, another will undoubtedly take up the flag in whose honour we believe.
>
> BA 3; I, 695–6

Not only 'discouragement' and the 'escape into solitude' were reproachable. It was also necessary to avoid the attitude of those who were ready for the extreme sacrifice but as an aesthetic gesture, those who did not pose the problem of concretely acting upon reality. Despite this, the situation was not at all desperate; it was possible to have 'faith'. The dominion of modern culture in school and society was anything but stable; on the contrary, 'its time is over, its days are numbered'; it would be enough to begin the struggle and this would immediately cause an 'echo' in a 'thousand courageous souls' (BA, 2; I, 673). Nietzsche wanted to be the herald of this mobilisation, the herald destined to become substantially superfluous thanks to the success of his action. 'If you present yourselves on the battlefield equipped with your armour, who would then want to look back at the herald who called you?' (BA, 'Introduction'; I, 650).

The appeal to mobilisation addressed to those who aimed to fight and defeat the barbarians of modernity already identified a potentially favourable terrain on which to engage in struggle. *The Birth of Tragedy* lamented that sort of abdication or betrayal that occurred 'precisely in those circles whose dignity could consist in drawing inexhaustibly from the Greek stream to the benefit of German education, precisely the teachers in our institutions of higher education' (GT, 20; I, 130 [96]). It was matter of central importance for the future of Germany and cultures such. To quote the letter to Gersdorff once more: 'Sooner or later I want to strip the school system bare' (B, II, 1, 155–6). According to the testimony of Cosima Wagner, their three-headed conversations focused, apart from on the theme of the authentic 'German essence', on the 'reform of educational institutions', which such an essence was called to rescue and regenerate.[131] By defending *The Birth of Tragedy* against Wilamowitz, Richard Wagner stressed the contribution his author could give to the cause 'of our national education', of 'our institutes of German culture', of the 'German spirit', of 'German culture'.

18   Manifesto of the Party of the Tragic View of the World

We should not forget that *The Birth of Tragedy* was contemporaneous with a series of passionate interventions regarding 'the future of our educational institutions'. Once cleansed of the virus of modernity that had already penetrated or been injected into them and once properly reshaped, they could and had to constitute a powerful tool of struggle against the modern devastation. Indeed, the grammar school was the most favourable terrain for the struggle looming on the horizon. Divided into diverse faculties and therefore consigned to specialisation, the university maintained only a very weak echo of classical antiquity. In the grammar school, things were quite different. Here, despite everything, 'the most healthy forces coming from classical antiquity' still operated. With appropriate reforms, these schools could 'transform themselves perhaps into arsenals and workshops of this struggle' 'against the barbarism of the present' (BA, 3; I, 694). On the other hand, if the struggle in the grammar school 'does not lead to victory, all the other educational institutions must fail' (BA, 2; I, 674–5).

---

131   C. Wagner 1976–82, Vol. I, p. 491.

It should be clear, though, that the grammar school was a privileged but not exclusive terrain of struggle. A letter to Rohde gives an idea of Nietzsche's state of mind and of the plans that he linked to the publication of *The Birth of Tragedy* and the lectures in Basel:

> I tell you, in all secrecy and asking you to keep this in confidence, that among other things I am preparing a promemoria on the University of Strasburg, as interpellation of the Reich Council, to be forwarded to Bismarck: here I want to show how a prodigious moment for founding a truly German cultural institute was ignominiously lost, an institute dedicated to the regeneration of the German spirit and to the annihilation of what has been passed off as 'culture' up until today. War and knife! Or rather: war and cannon!
>
> B, II, 1, 279–80

The achievement of victory in the course of this life-and-death struggle presupposed a settling of accounts with the distorted, unilaterally and superficially Apolline view of classical antiquity, denounced by *The Birth of Tragedy* and now to be liquidated, starting from the grammar schools. So, we can understand why the philologists sometimes constituted the target of a strong polemic while at other times they are courted. Nietzsche was explicit: 'What matters to me most is to win the youngest generation of philologists, and it would be a shameful sign for me if I could not manage this' (B, II, 1, 282). Philological work was essential but on condition that the philologists freed themselves from the 'uneasiness [*Unbehaglichkeit*]' they often felt in relation to 'the mysterious and orgiastic sides of antiquity'. It was a question of neutralising the philologist inclined to separate Apollo from Dionysus and to project onto Hellenism his own banal 'Enlightenment' (BA, 3; I, 701–2).

Winning back the educational institutions for authentic Hellenism meant to recover them at the same time for authentic Germanness. In the past, there had been other attempts to revitalise the study of classical antiquity in the grammar schools, but they had failed because of the erudite abstractness that characterised them; they had not been supported by a national movement:

> The failure of the attempt to bring the grammar school into the grand movement of classical culture lay in the un-German and almost foreign or cosmopolitan character of these educational efforts [*Bildungsbemühungen*], in the belief that it is possible to take the native [*heimisch*] soil out from under one's feet and still remain standing upright, in the illusion

that one could leap directly and without bridges into the alien [*entfrem-det*] Hellenic world by disavowing the German and in general the national spirit.

BA, 2; I, 689

With the triumphant conclusion of the war with France, a radically new situation had opened up. The strong movement of national regeneration could stimulate or guarantee the recovery of authentic Hellenism: 'The link that really connects the most inner German essence to the Greek genius is very mysterious and difficult to comprehend, but it is indissoluble'; the genuine German spirit had to attempt to grasp 'the hand of the Greek genius, like one gets a firm foothold in the tide of barbarism' (BA, 2; I, 691 & BA, 3; I, 695).

It was no easy task. To defeat the forces of modernity, courage and a spirit of sacrifice were insufficient, although necessary. Above all else, an appropriate theoretical platform was required: 'level-headed practices [...] lack ideas, and thus they lack a real praxis' (BA, 2; I, 673). At this point, *The Birth of Tragedy* seems like a theoretical manifesto of the party of the tragic view of life. It must be read in close connection with the lectures *On the Future of our Educational Institutions*, which were supposed to clarify – as Nietzsche himself stressed in a letter to his teacher – 'the practical consequence of my views', of the views contained in the just published book, 'filled with hope for the German essence' (B, II, 1, 282). Or in other words, to put it differently: the lectures were 'decisively exhortative and, in comparison with *The Birth* [*of Tragedy*], should be regarded as popular or exoteric' (B, II, 1, 296).

It might seem odd to use the term 'manifesto' of a work that is also fascinating at the literary level. It is useful to bear in mind that *Thus Spoke Zarathustra* would be defined by its author as a 'symphony' (B, III, 1, 353), and also as 'my "manifesto"' (B, III, 1, 482). Art and politics were not at all in contradiction: in Nietzsche's eyes, the literary and poetic seduction exercised by a text was even a precondition of its pedagogical and political efficacy (*infra*, Chapter 28 §7).

As if the term 'manifesto' were not enough, here we speak of 'manifesto' of the 'party of the tragic view of the world'. The definition is fundamentally suggested by Nietzsche himself, who would later boast of having behind him, in the years of *The Birth of Tragedy*, 'the entire Wagnerian party' (B, III, 5, 370). In fact, we see him now calling on his friends to act together to defend the musician and the 'unbelievable seriousness and profundity in his view of the world and art' against the attacks of the 'opposing party' (*infra*, Chapter 3 §1).

There was no doubt about the identity of this party, or rather, of these 'monstrous parties [*ungeheure Parteien*]', committed in a deeply organised way to promoting a servile conformism in the present. In the ruinous hypothesis that the youth to whom Nietzsche spoke had been seduced by this exhibition of strength and capitulate before it, this was the situation that would come about:

> Both before and behind you there would be equal numbers of men who have your own sentiments. And when the leader pronounces a word, it will resonate among the ranks. The first duty in this case: to fight in rank and file [*in Reih' und Glied*]; the second duty: to annihilate [*vernichten*] those who will not stand in rank and file.
>
> BA, 4; I, 728

Clearly, the polemic here targeted German Social Democracy, feared and criticised by a large swathe of public opinion for its military-style centralisation, as well as for the spirit of sacrifice shown by its militants. It was an organisation – as Treitschke would write a few years later – that 'dominates the souls of a completely dependent mass, no longer open to any other influence'.[132] There was no doubt – as Nietzsche said again in the preparatory notes for the Basel lectures – that the most threatening danger was represented by the 'servants of a mass, especially servants of a party', those prepared to 'embrace a party and subordinate their own lives to it', thus working for the 'end of culture' (VII, 244).

A few years later, the third *Unfashionable Observation* returned to the same theme using a similar language. Again, there was a warning against the capacity to seduce of those now defined as 'powerful parties [*mächtige Parteien*]'. Certainly, the young person who allowed himself to be seduced would end up in circumstances by no means disadvantageous. He would not be deprived of 'laurels and rewards'. Above all, he would gain from it a sense of security and irresistible power:

> Equal numbers of like-minded people will stand behind him and in front of him, and when the man in front sounds the battle-cry, it will echo through all the ranks. Here the first duty is 'fighting in rank and file [*in Reih' und Glied*]; the second duty, to treat all those who refuse to join the rank and file as enemies.
>
> SE, 6; I, 402 [232]

The threat to be confronted was even more serious because it assumed a dimension that went far beyond Germany. We know the scream of alarm about the International sounded by Nietzsche on the occasion of the Paris Commune.

---

132   Treitschke 1878, p. 6.

Two years later, his state of mind had not changed, as a letter to Rhode of 10 October 1873 reveals. Here a 'sinister machination' of the 'International' is denounced, which now was about to get its hands on the printing presses and publishing houses of Germany. The whole situation was assuming 'gigantic' dimensions: faced with the enormity of the danger, 'even by letter it is only allowed to whisper about it, not to speak clearly' (B, II, 3, 167–8).

From the very beginning, Nietzsche positioned himself on the terrain of struggle against the socialist movement, in which the threat looming over civilisation reached its apex: how to oppose this terrible war machine, which did not hold back from intimidating and even 'annihilating' not only its enemies but also those who would have liked to remain neutral or at least vacillate? The young professor of philology was no less combative and tenacious than his antagonists, as he called in his turn for the 'annihilation [*vernichten*]' of the opera soaked in revolutionary ideas and feelings. So, we are witnessing a fight in which no punches were pulled. What sort of theoretical platform was necessary for the enemies of civilisation, of modernity and subversion, to achieve victory?

19   Universal History, Universal Judgement, Divine Justice, Theodicy, Cosmodicy

Let us take a general look at the relationship between philosophy and politics established by the 'manifesto' of the party of the tragic worldview. It is worth returning for a moment to Schopenhauer. He insisted that injustice and disharmony were only an appearance that vanished as soon as we reached the essence, there where 'divine justice' 'luminously' dominated, undisturbed and imperturbable: 'If one could put all the pain in the world on one side of a scale, and all the guilt in the world on the other side, the scales would undoubtedly balance'.[133] Recalling a motto of Schiller's, Hegel saw in universal history the last judgement [*das jüngste Gericht*]: he affirmed this already in the first edition of the *Encyclopaedia*, published in Heidelberg in 1817.[134] As a progressive realisation of freedom and progress in the 'consciousness of liberty', universal history was 'the authentic theodicy', the only one able to make sense of the struggles and conflicts,[135] of the 'pain' and '"seriousness" of the negative' that

---

133   Schopenhauer 1976–82a, pp. 480–4.

134   Hegel 1956a, pp. 298–9 (*Enzyclopädie der philosophischen Wissenschaften im Grundrisse*, 1817, § 448).

135   Hegel 1969–79, Vol. XII, pp. 28 & 540.

were intrinsic to the historical process.[136] Published just one year after Hegel's Heidelberg *Encyclopaedia*, *The World as Will and Representation* emphasised that it was not universal history or the history of the world [*Weltgeschichte*] but the world [*Welt*] as such that was the universal judgement [*Weltgericht*]. The reinterpretation of the motto here is very significant. 'Theodicy' (to use Hegel's language) or 'divine justice' (to use Schopenhauer's language) did not manifest itself in the course of the historical process or of the sociopolitical changes that it realised, but was present in the world as such, on condition that one did not stop at the level of appearance and reached through to the essence.

In the young Nietzsche, universal history was even dissolved into 'so-called world history', regarding which *The Birth of Tragedy* (GT, 7 & 15; I, 56 & 100) and the private correspondence (B, II, 1, 190) ironised. It had become a 'superb metaphor' (CV, 1; I, 759); rather than 'divine justice', there was now the tendency to speak of mundane 'eternal justice', before the 'tribunal' of which the Greek state, despite the 'ingenious barbarism', war, slavery and pain connected to it, found 'justification' (CV, 3; I, 771–2). Finally, theodicy disappeared. It referred back to a type of Christianity that was already lifeless, but 'it was never a Hellenic problem' (DW, 2; I, 560). Despite its terrible negativity, the world did not need an external justification that referred to a mysterious divine will to make sense of an evil that was otherwise inexplicable and unacceptable. Instead of 'theodicy', there was 'cosmodicy'. The category already made its appearance in a letter from Rohde written in February 1872 (B, II, 2, 534), but it was Nietzsche that elaborated it fully. It was precisely the terrible conflicts, precisely this 'competition' that 'reveals divine justice', that is inherent to the real. 'Cosmodicy' justified the world not as tending towards the realisation of vague projects of transformation assigned to a supposed universal history but starting from its intrinsic and permanent laws, starting from the 'war between opposites that characterizes it and will always characterize it' (PHG, 5; I, 825).

If we really wanted to talk of theodicy, we were to bear in mind that for the Greeks 'the only satisfactory theodicy' was a tragic one (a synonym in the last analysis for cosmodicy), which led to the acceptance of existence even when it meant toil and misery: 'It is not unworthy of the greatest hero to long to go on living, even as a day-labourer' (GT, 3; I, 36–7 [24]). The reference was to Homer's Achilles, who explicitly declared to prefer living in the world at the service of a leader instead of dominating over all the shadows of Hades.[137]

---

136   Hegel 1969–79, Vol. III, p. 24.
137   *Odyssey*, Book XI, verses 488–91.

These lines were repeatedly quoted by Heine, but as a confirmation of his view of the world, for which the sweetnesses of life, and even of the most mediocre 'philistine', were preferable not only to death but also to the bitter existence of the hero.[138] In the disciple of Hegel, the crisis of Christianity and the process of secularisation on the one hand and the development of the productive forces on the other – in the last analysis, universal history – could proceed to a full justification of the world after the sacrifice of the masses had been rendered obsolete and the appeal to renunciation, to asceticism or the hero's sacrifice had been made ridiculous. The theme of the valley of tears was replaced by the joyful acceptance of existence: by claiming terrestrial happiness for everyone and by legitimising the socialist movement, the new world-view felt the need to proceed backwards in order to rediscover in paganism a culture not deaf to the reasons of life.

Nietzsche also, taking his distance from Christian spiritualism, referred to the 'Olympian gods'. 'They express a religion of life, not of obligation or asceticism or spirituality'. All these forms provided evidence of a 'triumph of existence [*Dasein*]'; here we encountered a 'religion of life'. However, within it, an important place was occupied by the renunciation and pain of the slaves of culture: 'luxuriant nature celebrates its Saturnalia and at the same time its funeral rites'. The figures of Olympus were eloquent in themselves: 'They make no demands: in them what exists is deified, no matter good or bad' (DW, 1–2; I, 558–60). It was a point of decisive importance, unfortunately ignored or repressed by those who, like Heine, reduced Hellenic religion to a sort of 'fantastic superabundance', all under the aegis of a supposed serenity (GT, 3; I, 34–5 [22]).

Against any unilateral optimism, Roman or neo-Latin, it was necessary to keep in mind a fundamental truth: 'the Hellene is neither optimist nor pessimist. He is essentially a man, who really looks upon the horrendous and doesn't deceive himself about it' (VII, 77). Refusing the Christian escape from the world, it was necessary to develop a 'cosmodicy', but not a cosmodicy à la Heine that ignored or claimed to overcome struggle, war and suffering: 'According to Heraclitus, honey is simultaneously sour and sweet, and the world itself is a mixture that has to be continually stirred' (PHG, 5; I, 825).

Later, Nietzsche would write that 'already in *The Birth of Tragedy* and in its doctrine of the Dionysiac [...] Schopenhaurian pessimism appears to have been overcome' (XII, 233). This is a judgement that can, at least partially, be endorsed.

---

138   Heine 1969–78, Vol. II, pp. 253–4; cf. also Vol. VI, 1, pp. 349–50 (in this case, the poem *Der Scheidende*).

If, on the one hand, pessimism played an essential role as an antidote to optimism and to the idea of terrestrial happiness, which stimulated the revolutionary catastrophe, on the other hand, there can be no doubt that *The Birth of Tragedy* aimed not to deny the will to live but to affirm it joyously, despite the sacrifice of slaves that it required.

Another important difference is worth noticing. In Schopenhauer, the perfect balance between 'pain' and 'guilt', discussed in *The World as Will and Representation*, seemed to be valid not only for the species as a whole but also for any 'being [*Wesen*]': 'Whatever befalls it, whatever can only befall it, always befalls it rightly'.[139] Nietzsche, on the other hand, rather than trivialise the sufferings of the sacrificial victims of culture, was concerned to place them in a much broader context that, due to its characteristics of necessity and inevitability, left no space for regrets and moral declamations. The events of the world could be compared to the 'game of the great cosmic child Zeus and to the eternal joke of a destruction of the world and a birth of the world' (CV, 1; I, 758). Individual destiny might well be atrocious; nonetheless, now we had moved onto a much higher level:

> Man is no longer an artist, he has become a work of art: all nature's artistic power reveals itself here, amidst shivers of intoxication, to the highest, most blissful satisfaction of the primordial unity. Here man, the noblest clay, the most precious marble, is kneaded and carved and, to the accompaniment of the chisel-blows of the Dionysiac world-artist, the call of the Eleusinian Mysteries rings out: 'Fall ye to the ground, ye millions? Feelst thou thy Creator, world?'
>
> GT, 1; I, 30 [18–19]

Together with Christian religious transcendence, cosmodicy also liquidated revolutionary transcendence and any project of transformation of the world: it was not possible 'to change the eternal essence of things'; any dream of social and political palingenesis was 'laughable or shameful', just like the pretension 'to set to rights a world so out of joint' (GT, 7; I, 57 [40]). Absorbed and swallowed up in the 'great Pan', the individuals and classes destined to be sacrificed now appeared as primary material for the fantastic and fascinating creations, regardless of the costs involved, of a sort of cosmic artist.

---

139   Schopenhauer 1976–82a, pp. 480–4.

CHAPTER 2

Tradition, Myth and the Critique of Revolution

1   'Prejudice' and 'Instinct': Burke and Nietzsche

In confirmation of the central role the denunciation of the French revolutionary cycle plays in *The Birth of Tragedy* and in contemporary texts and fragments,
it helps to compare the theoretical categories used here and those used in
European culture to condemn or criticise the French Revolution.

According to Nietzsche, tragic Hellas presented us with people able to look
reality in the eyes: 'The Greeks are naïve like nature when they talk about
slaves'; they recognised in them and in their condition an unavoidable prerequisite of culture (VII, 138). Here, naïveté meant 'harmony', that 'unity of
man with nature, to which Schiller applied the now generally accepted art-
word "naïve"' (GT, 3, I, 37 [24]). It was the absence of artifice and the rejection
of abstract schemata that falsified and violated reality: 'There *are* such people
[slaves, DL]: wherever there is a culture. I find it terrible to sacrifice culture to
a schema. Where are people equal? Where are they free?' (VII, 138). And, once
again, the remedy for this senseless mystification was sought in Hellas: 'The
simplicity of that which is Greek: the voice of nature is uncorrupted in regard
of women and slaves' or of the 'defeated enemy' (VII, 127). To speak of nature
was also to speak of instinct: 'Slavery is something instinctive in Hellenism' (VII,
46). At the root of this discourse lay two fundamental and closely intertwined
dichotomies: artifice was set against nature just as muddled intellectualism
was set against healthy instinct; whereas instinct in its simplicity and naïveté
cleaved to nature, reason that was actually synonymous with cerebral contor-
tions resorted to artifice and abstract schemes. Both dichotomies were widely
diffused across European culture and journalism criticising the French Revolution. In a polemic against the slogan of *égalité* that sprang from it, Haller praised
the natural law of inequality and the domination of the many by the few, based
on 'eternal, immutable order of God [*ewige, unabänderliche Ordnung Gottes*]'.[1]

But here we should let Burke speak. Perhaps Nietzsche was not entirely
unacquainted with this author, who enjoyed an extraordinary success in Germany, particularly in romantic culture.[2] Moreover, one should also not neglect

---

1   Hegel 1969–79, Vol. 7, p. 403 (*Grundlinien der Philosophie des Rechts*, § 258 A, fn.).
2   Cf. Losurdo 1997a, p. 5, § 4, and Losurdo 2001, p. 15, § 2.

other possible readings: the great antagonist of the French Revolution natur- ally played a central role in Stirner's *History of the Revolution*.[3] And, above all, Emerson was very enthusiastic about him.[4] In Burke we read that the ideal of *égalité*, the 'abstract' demand for legal equality, violates 'the natural order of things', the 'natural social order', and is guilty of the 'worst of usurpations', that that tramples on the 'prerogatives of Nature' or the 'method of Nature'.[5] More drastic still was Gentz: in his translation, 'method of Nature' became 'divine methods of nature [*göttliche Methodik der Natur*]'.[6] This immediately recalls a similar expression used by Nietzsche, the 'sacred hierarchy of nature [*heilige Naturordnung*]', according to which human beings in their vast majority were 'born to serve and to obey' (BA, 3, I, 698 [74]).

Let us turn now to the second dichotomy, without losing sight of the first. According to Nietzsche, the healthy 'instinct' bore witness to the vain and illus- ory character of *égalité* and of human rights, to the inevitability of slavery. Unfortunately, 'enlightenment despises instinct' (VII, 104). But the 'instinct' meant here immediately calls to mind the wise 'prejudice' Burke proposed in opposition to abstract revolutionary rationalism: '[We English] are generally men of untaught feelings: that, instead of casting away all our old prejudices, we cherish them to a very considerable degree. [...] The whole has emanated from the simplicity of our national character, and from a sort of native plainness and directness of understanding, which for a long time characterized those men who have successfully obtained authority among us.'[7]

The exemplary characteristics of the Greek world Nietzsche highlighted in opposition to modernity ('simplicity' and the ability to listen to the 'voice of nature') were attributed by Burke to the English, naturally directed against modernity, which had found its most ruinous manifestation in the Enlight- enment and the French Revolution. The English were well aware that pre- judice contained a 'latent wisdom', a profound and extensive wisdom that, accumulated over centuries, became 'instinct'.[8] Similarly, in Nietzsche's eyes, Socrates had made the mistake of disregarding 'unconscious wisdom [*unbe- wusste Weisheit*]', 'instinctive wisdom [*instinktive Weisheit*]', 'the instinctive' (ST, I, 542).

---

3   Stirner 1967, Vol. 1, pp. 135 ff., 169 ff.
4   Cf. Parrington 1954, p. 385.
5   Burke 1826, Vol. 5, pp. 104, 79.
6   Gentz 1967, p. 70.
7   Burke 1826, Vol. 5, pp. 168, 172 f.
8   Burke 1826, Vol. 5, pp. 168, 174–6.

In this attitude of suspicion and hostility towards that which existed or was asserted 'only by instinct' lay the potential for dissolution and subversion:

> With these words Socratism condemns existing art and existing ethics in equal measure; wherever it directs its probing gaze, it sees a lack of insight [*Mangel der Einsicht*] and the power of delusion [*Macht des Wahns*], and it concludes from this lack that what exists is inwardly wrong and objectionable.
>
> GT, 13, I, 89 [66]

This brings us back to Burke's polemic against the presumption of the 'enlightened': 'The fact that a system is old seems to them justification and sufficient reason for its destruction. [...] The suspicion that something is old-fashioned is raised by them to a system.'

That is why, according to the English Whig, one was not to 'allow human beings to live and act solely on the basis of the cultivation of their individual rationality, because we suspect that this is very limited in every individual'.[9]

So, Nietzsche concluded his indictment of the Greek early-enlighteners as follows:

> Socrates believed that he was obliged to correct existence, starting from this single point; he, the individual [*der Einzelne*], the forerunner of a completely different culture, art, and morality, steps with a look of disrespect and superiority into a world where we would count ourselves supremely happy if we could even touch the hem of its cloak in awe.
>
> GT, 13, I, 89–90 [66]

Burke mocked the religious 'spirit of proselytism' that at the international level accompanied the project to overthrow the *ancien régime*,[10] and berated revolutionaries for wanting to sanctify 1789 as the 'emancipation year' or – as Burke's German translator put it – the 'year of redemption [*Erlösungsjahr*]'.[11] Nietzsche denounced the 'missionary activity' of Socrates, who even asserted 'his unproductive eristic' with 'the seriousness and dignity of a divine mission' (ST, I, 541). According to Burke, 'fanaticism', or rather the 'dire fanaticism' of revolutionary consciousness, sought to silence 'the common feeling of nature'.[12] This exalted

---

9   Burke 1826, Vol. 5, p. 168 f.
10   Burke 1826, Vol. 7, p. 13 f.; cf. also Losurdo 1996, p. 3, § 4.
11   Burke 1826, Vol. 5, p. 83 and Gentz 1967, p. 73.
12   Burke 1826, Vol. 5, p. 278 f., fn.

and intolerant fanaticism inspired the pathos and the agitation of the Enlightenment as well as the struggles unleashed by the protagonists of 1789 and, *a fortiori*, the Jacobins.[13] These themes are found in Nietzsche, who saw Socrates as a 'fanatic of knowledge [*Erkenntnis*]' (VII, 41), a 'fanatic of dialectics' (VII, 22), or a 'fanatical dialectician' (VII, 17).

A clear line of continuity, from Burke to Nietzsche, characterised the diagnosis of the sickness, but its incidence was now dramatically backdated. The origins of the crusade against 'prejudice' or 'instinct' were now sought and investigated in Greece, more than two millennia before the spread of the Enlightenment in its actual sense. 'Euripides is the poet of Socratic rationalism' (ST, I, 540), and both philosopher and poet were an expression of a 'reckless intellectualism [*verwegene Verständigkeit*]' (ST, I, 537–8) and a 'dubious Enlightenment' (GT, 13, I, 88 [64–5]). Both posed as 'seducers of the people [*Volksverführer*]', as 'supporters of the "good old days"', defenders, in the last analysis, of the *ancien régime*, knew only too well (GT, 13, I, 88 [64–5]). From this turmoil was created an 'enlightened mass [*aufgeklärte Masse*]', a 'bourgeois middle estate [*bürgerlicher Mittelstand*]' and a 'bourgeois mediocrity [*bürgerliche Mittelmässigkeit*]', on which Euripides could found 'his political hopes' (ST, I, 535; SGT, I, 605).

There could be no doubt. The fanaticism of the Enlightenment was already present in ancient Greece, infecting the 'wicked Euripides' and the 'mocking Lucians of the ancient world' (GT, 10, I, 74 [54]). Significantly, this criticism was aimed at an author defined and celebrated by Engels as 'the Voltaire of classical antiquity'.[14] The fanaticism of logic reached its peak in Socrates. The insane pretention that 'everything must be conscious to be ethical' (VII, 41) led not only to the destruction of tragedy (VII, 22) but to the advent of 'democracy', 'victorious to the extent that it is rationalism and combats instinct' (VII, 46).

Plato followed in Socrates' footsteps. Plato

> led a fight to the death against all existing state relations and was a revolutionary of the most radical kind. The requirement to create correct concepts of all things seems innocuous: but the philosopher who thinks he has found them treats all other men as ignorant and immoral and all their institutions as nonsense and obstacles to true thinking. The human being of the right concepts wants to judge and rule. The belief that one is in

---

13   Cf. Losurdo 1996, p. 3, §4.
14   Marx and Engels 1975 ff., Vol. 27, p. 449.

possession of the truth makes one a fanatic. This philosophy was based
on contempt for reality and human beings: it quickly reveals a tyrannical
streak.

KGA, II, 4, 155

And just as in the liberal and conservative culture of the time, Nietzsche's critique of abstract revolutionary ideologies went hand in hand with denouncing
the intellectuals that embodied them: 'I would drive the so-called "intellectuals
[Gebildeten]" from my ideal state, just as Plato did the poets' (VII, 164). These
were the years in which Treitschke expressed the hope that 'the terrors of this
war will, like a cleansing rain, sweep away the sultry haze of modern intellectualism [Überbildung]', of the pseudo-culture of enlightenment and revolution.[15]
Moreover, even Bismarck, taking the denunciation of the nihilist movement as
his starting point, warned against the ruinous effects, in Russia as in Germany,
of Überbildung, of an abstract and intrinsically subversive intellectualism.[16]

The target of both Nietzsche's and Treitschke's and of Bismarck's polemic
was, in the last analysis, the rootless and engagé intellectual who, precisely in
those years in France, was beginning to acquire a consistent sociological and
political meaning. Admittedly, in Nietzsche's view, the point of departure of
and model for this figure could already be found in Socrates. The intellectual
as 'enlightener and dissipator [Aufklärer und Auflöser] of nature and instinct'
had already made his appearance in ancient Greece and was at the same time
animated by 'political passion' (VII, 85) – the 'theoretical human being' not only
pledged to struggle against 'Dionysian wisdom and art' and to 'dissolve myth'
but also intent on 'correcting the world through knowledge' (GT, 17, I, 115 [85]).

2   Hubris of Reason and 'Neocriticistic' Reaction

The crusade against prejudice led to a disenchanting of existing society, which,
with the disappearance of the veneration and respect accumulated over centuries, became a vile body for the experiments of reason. The consequences
of this attitude were disastrous. Burke expressed his 'horror' at those precip-
itate revolutionaries or reformers who did not hesitate to 'cut up the body of
their old parent to put it in the pot of the magician in the hope that poisonous weeds and strange spells could restore him to health and vigour'.[17] Using

---

15   In Fenske 1977, p. 426; cf. also Losurdo 1997a, p. 3, §12.
16   Bismarck n.d., Vol. 3, p. 50.
17   Burke 1826, Vol. 5, p. 183.

a different image but with a similar meaning, Nietzsche said of Socrates, the supposed early enlightener: 'Who is this individual who may dare to negate the nature [*Wesen*] of the Greeks? [...]'.

> [To dispel] our astonished worship? What daemonic force is this that may dare to spill this magic potion in the dust? What demi-god is this, to whom the chorus of the noblest spirits of mankind must call out:
> Woe! Woe!
> You have destroyed
> This lovely world
> With mighty fist;
> It falls, it shatters.
>   GT, 13, I, 90 [66]

Even more relevant than Burke was Taine, who similarly highlighted the disastrous consequences of the Enlightenment crusade against 'prejudice', in a language that once again reminds us of Nietzsche: 'The spell is broken', and with it vanished the prestige and solidity of a political and social order, of an entire world.[18] It was the start of a laceration no longer healable.

The denunciation of the hubris of reason, which suggested that society could be manipulated at will, was widespread among intellectuals engaged in criticising the revolution. A book by a French counterrevolutionary *émigré* had the explicit title *De l'usage de l'abus et de l'esprit philosophique au dix-huitième siècle*.[19] In Germany, Adam Müller polemicised against the philosophers' mad pretention to transform the state into an object of 'their experiments'.[20] Looking principally at Jacobinism and protosocialism, Tocqueville attributed the ruinous *expérimentations* of the French revolutionary cycle to the mad claim of the Enlightenment and rationalism to be able to identify and impose a political 'remedy for this hereditary and incurable evil of poverty and labour'.[21]

To return to Nietzsche's immediate vicinity, we see Rohde describe the Paris Commune as the final outcome of the delusion that 'all abysses can be measured by the chain of logic', of 'purely ethical logic', of theoretical and practical optimism.[22] So the criticist consciousness of the bounds of reason was configured as the sole possible antidote to revolutionary madness. It was thanks to

---

18 Taine, 1899, Vol. II, pp. 17–18 (= Taine, 1986, pp. 387–8).
19 In Baldensperger, 1968, Vol. II, p. 45.
20 Müller, 1935, p. 213.
21 Tocqueville, 1951, Vol. XVI, p. 240.
22 Rohde 1989a, p. 12 and Rohde 1989b, p. 23.

great German philosophy and culture that it had been made available: 'For in our people the presumed omnipotence of logical knowledge has been successfully driven back by Kantian criticism into its ambit of force, which is limited to the phenomenon.'[23]

Thus opined the reviewer of *The Birth of Tragedy*, who extracted the theme from the reviewed work. This warned repeatedly against 'the catastrophe slumbering in the womb of theoretical culture'; one was once and for all to ward off 'the danger' inherent in the claim of the Enlighteners and rationalists to be able to penetrate reality to the hilt. Fortunately, 'great natures with a bent for general problems have applied the tools of science itself, with incredible deliberation, to prove that all understanding, by its very nature, is limited and conditional, thereby rejecting decisively the claim of science to universal validity and universal goals'. Yes, 'the enormous courage and wisdom of Kant and Schopenhauer [has made possible] a victory over the optimism which lies hidden in the nature of logic and which in turn is the hidden foundation of our culture' (GT, 18; I, 117–18 [87]).

Worth noting is that this recognition can be found in the section denouncing the horrors of the Paris Commune and the imminent danger of revolt on the part of the 'class of barbaric slaves'. So, it was of decisive political importance to acquire, in the wake of Kant and Schopenhauer, an awareness of the absurdity of belief 'in our ability to grasp and solve [...] all the puzzles of the universe' (GT, 18, I, 118 [87]). The hubris of reason was the prerequisite for revolutionary social engineering: 'one-sided reason', typical of Socratic rationalism, fed 'a monstrous will [*Ungeheuer*]' (ST, I, 541).

Here we encounter a central theme of *The Birth of Tragedy* and the texts that foreshadowed it: 'Oedipus had to be plunged into a confusing maelstrom of atrocities because his unmeasured [*übermässig*] wisdom solved the riddle of the Sphinx' (GT, 4; I, 40 [27]). But the recourse to the Prometheus myth had an analogous meaning, as a contemporary text in particular explained: 'In Prometheus the Greeks were shown an example of the pernicious effect which the excessive [*übergross*] promotion of human knowledge has both on what is promoted and on those who promote it' (DW, 2, I, 565 [128]). And, once again, we are brought back to the journalism engaged in criticising the revolution: in the words of Gentz, Burke's translator in Germany, 'the overload of knowledge [*Übermass des Wissens*]' could be 'disastrous for humankind', so it was necessary to rein it in.[24]

---

23   Rohde 1989a, p. 12 f.
24   Gentz 1836–8, Vol. 1, p. 2.

In nineteenth-century Germany, references to Kant and the criticism were widespread, as a way of distancing oneself from the hubris of reason attributed to the project of the Enlightenment and revolution. Trendelenburg, an author known to Nietzsche, never tired of emphasising that human knowledge could capture only a 'fragment [*Bruchstück*]' of reality and therefore took the form of a simple 'sketch [*Stückwerk*]'.[25] Nor was the limitation of man's cognitive powers to be a cause for scandal: just as it was not surprising that the human eye could not contemplate the 'heavenly sun [*Himmelssonne*]' but only the 'light of earth [*Erdenhelle*]', so the assertion that human thought could penetrate only 'the circle of the finite and limited' was not to scandalise us.[26]

For Stahl too, reason was to be content with capturing a mere 'fragment [*Bruchstück*]': 'No room should be given to the arrogant thought that the human being can penetrate the eternal will and reveal the secret of all things'; the suggestion that 'a uniform system embracing the entire universe' could be produced was absurd.[27] And, again, and even more clearly, the emphasis on the bounds of reason and the direct or indirect reference to criticism were aimed at the arrogance of reason of the Enlightenment and revolution. Especially after 1848, people took their distance from the revolution by explicitly referring to Kant. Haym, for example, another author known to Nietzsche, explained his intellectual and political evolution and his repudiation of his youthful radicalism as follows:

> The ingenuous belief that in speculative reason we are given an infallible instrument to illuminate the depths of truth, the essence of God and the world, began to waver, and the insight dawned on me that we, with all our knowledge, stand not on a continent that extends to infinity but – on this point I had not believed Kant – on an island surrounded by the sea.[28]

In this sense, Haym already declared in 1863 that the author of the *Critique of Pure Reason* was 'the greatest philosopher ever'.[29] Quite apart from the reference to Kant, the need to guard against 'the presumptuous rashness of intelligence' became a recurring theme in the European culture engaged in criticism of the revolution and its various stages.[30] Nietzsche accused Strauss, who,

---

25   Trendelenburg 1964, Vol. 2, p. 494f.
26   Trendelenburg 1964, Vol. 2, p. 492.
27   Stahl 1963, pp. xxii–xxiv.
28   Haym 1902, p. 147.
29   Haym 1930, p. 212.
30   Guizot 1849, p. 9.

in accord with the prevailing national-liberal culture, attempted to eliminate religion in the name of reason, of failing to stay abreast of the results of the criticism:

> He has no inkling whatsoever of the fundamental antinomy of idealism and of the ultimate relativity of all science and reason. Or: It is precisely reason that should tell him how little reason is able to discover about the essence of things.
>
> VII, 587 [157]

A showdown with Hegel, the merciless critic of this 'criticism' or 'despair of reason' that denied 'the courage of truth, faith in the power of the spirit' and thereby condemned the worldly and earthly to an irremediable opacity, became inevitable.[31] In the assertion of the unknowability of the absolute Hegel spied 'the last step in the humiliation of the human being'.[32] On the other hand, while 'the human being still has faith in the dignity of his spirit, still has the courage to truth', he rejected Kantianism.[33]

This criticism, which in reality was synonymous with a vain and conservative tendency to problematise, was mercilessly condemned by the *Phenomenology*:

> The fear of truth may lead consciousness to conceal itself both from itself and from others behind the appearance of being ever more clever than every thought that a person has from himself or others – as if the hot zeal for truth of itself makes it so difficult, indeed impossible, to find another truth than the unique truth of one's own conceit. This latter conceit understands itself as relativizing every truth in order to return into itself, and feasts on this its personal understanding, knowledgeable about continually dissolving all thoughts and about finding merely the dry ego as a substitute for all content.[34]

That is to say, by liquidating the objectivity of knowledge, the supposed rejection of the dogmatism of the object ended up as the dogmatism of the subject.

Regarding Hegel's 'prometheanism', both his opponents and his disciples were of one mind.[35] It made no sense, said Trendelenburg, clearly referring to

---

31   Hegel 1956b, p. 7 f.
32   Hegel 1966, Vol. 1, 5.
33   Hegel 1966, Vol. 1, p. 42.
34   Hegel 1969–79, Vol. 3, p. 75.
35   Rosenkranz 1963, p. 200.

Hegel, to talk in this context of 'unbelief [*Unglauben*]' or 'laziness [*Trägheit*]' of thought.[36] On the other side, Rosenkranz polemicised sharply against 'the priestly ignoramuses and pietistic blockheads' who never tired of repeating that human reason was limited and knowledge was mere *Stückwerk*.[37]

The 'dream of a blissful omniscience' that Gentz denounced in the revolutionaries[38] seemed to find its philosophical *pendant* in Hegel's philosophy, with its affirmation of the total transparency of reality to reason and its ideal of absolute knowledge. Expressing a tendency widespread on the Hegelian left, Herzen believed he could interpret the dialectic as an 'algebra of revolution' (see below, 17, §1). And, at the time, Nietzsche's hostility towards and even repugnance for Hegel was a hostility towards and repugnance for the 'algebra of revolution'.

3   The Radicalisation of Neo-criticism: Truth as Metaphor

So wherein lies the originality of the young philologist-philosopher? We have already noted the radicality of the historical balance-sheets he drew, especially in the sense that, far from restricting themselves to the present or the immediate past, they went a very long way back. The hubris of reason dated not only from the Enlightenment and the French Revolution. Even the Greeks had experienced 'the uncontrolled desire for knowledge' that 'barbarizes just as much as hatred for knowledge'. For a while, the Greeks had succeeded in a very difficult enterprise, 'they tamed their drive for knowledge, in itself insatiable, by an ideal regard for life' (PHG, 1, I, 807). But in the end, they themselves were overwhelmed. It was the triumph of Socrates, vainly criticised by Aristophanes for his attachment to 'abstract woolgathering' (ST, I, 544). Thus developed a ruinous cycle that, seemingly, could only now be blocked or neutralised. At last, German philosophy had succeeded in creating trouble for 'scientific Socratism [...] by demonstrating its limits' (GT, 19, I, 128 [95]).

But that was not yet all. The condemnation of 'the theoretical human being', who was under the illusion that he could penetrate the innermost essence of things, acquired an unprecedented radicality that, going well beyond Kant, was no longer content with the distinction between phenomenon and noumenon. It was the objectivity of knowledge itself that was at issue. It could no longer claim for itself even the limited scope of the phenomenon. This tendency could already be observed in Schopenhauer, but Nietzsche raised it to new levels. On

36   Trendelenburg 1964, Vol. 2, p. 492.
37   Rosenkranz 1862, Vol. 1, p. 85.
38   Gentz 1836–8, Vol. 1, p. 3.

closer inspection, 'truth' was merely 'a mobile army of metaphors' (WL, 1, I, 880 [146]), even a 'superb metaphor' (CV, 1, I, 759). We have seen how Haym compared knowledge to a tiny island surrounded by a stormy sea – by now, even the island was submerged. Or, to cite the images of other exponents of neocriticism, objective knowledge was unthinkable not only as totality, as Hegel claimed, but even as 'fragment'. We will return later to this radicalisation of the 'criticism'. Two texts dealt with it, *The Pathos of Truth* and *On Truth and Lies in an Extra-Moral Sense*, written shortly after *The Birth of Tragedy*. For the time being, we will consider what the young Nietzsche offered as an alternative to the hubris of reason, which, as we know, he never tired of denouncing. With each wave of the never-ending upheavals in France and Europe starting in 1789, the denunciation of the arrogance and hypertrophy of reason, at the root of subversion, represented an element of continuity in the critique of revolution. Yet while the process of secularisation continued, religion was gradually joined and later supplanted by other antidotes. In the thirties, a modest philosopher, bound to theism and branded by Nietzsche as 'demented' in a brief reference (VII, 510), suggested as an alternative to the 'empty generality of the concept' the idea of 'spiritual, poetic and religious intuition'.[39] Not much different, in the last analysis, was the attitude of Schopenhauer, who proposed art and the religion of compassion as an alternative to reason as instrument of the will to live.

Residual elements of this duplexity can even be found in the young Nietzsche, who criticised the positivistic banality of Strauss for lacking a 'concept of Christianity' (VII, 592 [162]), of its power and capacity of spiritual seduction. *The Birth of Tragedy* celebrated the 'wisdom [*Weisheit*]' that, 'not deceived by the seductive distractions of the sciences, instead [...] turns its unmoved gaze on the total image of the world', showing 'heroic attraction to what is monstrous [*ungeheuer*]' (GT, 18; I, 118–19 [87–8]). This extra-rational, intuitive and sympathetic identification with the totality still retained something of the religious thrill, which then yielded to the 'the lovely madness of artistic enthusiasm', to which Socrates unfortunately was immune (GT, 14, I, 92 [67]).

Sometimes, against the world of history and reason, art and religion were jointly and explicitly invoked: 'I term "supra-historical" those powers that divert one's gaze from what is in the process of becoming to what lends existence to the character of something eternal and stable in meaning, to *art* and *religion*' (HL, 10, I, 330 [163]). Yet the two themes tended to merge into one: 'My religion, if I can still define my attitude in such a way, lies in working for the production

---

39   Weisse 1832, p. 42 f.

of genius' (VIII, 46). Clearly, we were at a turning point: the fight against the hubris of reason was waged above all in the name of art. To quote Rohde, the 'highest act of scientific self-knowledge' to which Kant and Schopenhauer rose paved the way for the 'most noble aspirations to a truly artistic culture'.[40]

For the young Nietzsche, as for the great critics of the revolution, science that developed unilaterally and without control was synonymous with destruction and death. The antidote was a higher 'wisdom', respectful of instincts and a friend of life, and which now coincided with art. 'Socratism despises instinct and therefore art. It denies wisdom precisely where its most particular sphere is to be found.' Precisely because the Socratic world did not recognise 'instinct-ive wisdom', 'unconscious wisdom', it was 'an absurd and inverted world' (ST, I, 542). However, 'art is more powerful than knowledge, for it wants life, and knowledge reaches as its ultimate goal only destruction [*Vernichtung*]' (CV, 1, I, 760).

4   Human Rights and Anthropocentrism

Along with the claim to 'happiness', Nietzsche undertook to criticise and decon-struct the other fundamental slogan that emerged from the French Revolution, that which referred to the 'human being' as such, as title-holder of the right to happiness. Discourses about 'human dignity', the 'dignity of work', 'equal rights for all' and 'fundamental human rights' that wished to erase any distinction between free human beings and slaves, between masters and servants, were 'conceptual hallucinations' (CV, 3, I, 765–6 [165]). To free oneself from this mod-ern rubbish one had to go a decidedly long way back: 'Humanity [*Humanität*] is absolutely a non-Greek concept' (VII, 127). The universal concept of a human being was the abstraction of a reason that had rendered itself autonomous from instinct and instinctive wisdom. Up to this point, we are dealing with a theme widely encountered in the critique of the revolution. More specific to the young Nietzsche is the radicality of the gesture with which the 'human thing [*Menschending*]' was viewed as something 'disgraceful and pathetic' (CV, 3, I, 765 [165]). Particularly significant was the 'fable' Nietzsche told in definitive refutation of the revolutionary project:

> In some remote corner of the universe, flickering in the light of the count-less solar systems into which it had been poured, there was once a planet

---

40   Rohde 1989a, p. 12 f.

on which clever animals invented knowledge. It was the most arrogant and most mendacious minute in the history of the world [*Weltgeschichte*]; but a minute was all it was. After nature had drawn just a few more breaths the planet froze and the clever animals had to die.

WL, 1, I, 875 [141], cf. CV, 1, I, 759–60

In light of this huge expansion of space and time, the discourse about human rights and a human being as such, now become an 'intelligent animal' that lived alongside countless other animals, located on a tiny planet lost in one of the 'infinite solar systems', appeared quixotic or problematic. A few years later, Nietzsche would write: '*Human*! What is the vanity of the vainest of humans against the vanity that the most modest person possesses with regard to the fact that he feels himself, amid nature and the world, as "human"!' (WS, 304 [280]).

Naturally, behind this theme lies a tradition. In Malthus we read:

When we strive to contemplate the system of the universe, when we think that the stars are suns of other systems scattered throughout infinite space, when we reflect that our view perhaps misses a millionth of those balls of light radiating light and life to worlds innumerable, when our minds, unable to grasp the immeasurable, floods, lost and confused, in admiration of the great and incomprehensible power of the Creator, not wallow in maudlin lament that not all are equally congenial climate, that the eternal spring does not reign throughout the year, not all of God's creatures enjoy the same benefits.[41]

There can be no doubt about the anthropocentric assumptions of the discourse of the rights of the human being, axiologically separated from other natural beings and occupying a privileged position. Taine made fun of Rousseau's anthropocentric approach, citing a grandiloquent passage from Rousseau's *Émile*, or more precisely from that section of it titled 'The Profession of Faith of the Savoyard Vicar':

Show me another animal on earth that can make fire and admire the sun. What? I can observe and learn about other beings and their relationships, I can feel what order, beauty, virtue are, I can contemplate the universe,

---

41   Malthus 1986, p. 132.

raise myself to the hand that governs it; I can love good, do it, and I should compare myself to the beasts?[42]

Schopenhauer was already aware of the relationship between anthropo-centrism and the revolutionary proclamation of the rights of the human being. After the revolution of 1848, he quoted and expressed his approval for Gobineau's thesis, whereby human beings might well be distinct from other animal species but not because of their excellence; on the contrary, they were '*l'animal méchant par excellence*'. This type of polemical reversal of the usual anthropocentric hierarchy returned in Nietzsche, but in a different form, one that entailed no moral judgement: the spectacle of the animal 'tethered by the short leash [...] of the moment', and therefore 'neither melancholy nor bored', 'is hard on the human being to observe [...], because he boasts about the superiority of his humanity over animals and yet looks enviously upon their happiness – for the one and only thing that he desires is to live like an animal, neither bored nor in pain, and yet he desires this in vain' (HL, 1; I, 248 [87]).

The Jewish-Christian tradition was also called into question by Schopenhauer because of its cruelly exclusive anthropocentrism, which considered the human being as the only species worthy of attention and respect while reducing animals to 'simple "things", mere tools'.[43] In the course of his subsequent evolution, Nietzsche would reproach Descartes for having inspired the revolution with his 'rationalism', a rationalism that pushed the celebration of the human being as thinking subject to the point where animals were assimilated to simple machines. Yet rather than cite Hinduism and Buddhism, like Schopenhauer, the philologist-philosopher seemed to treasure the legacy of Greek culture and classical antiquity as a whole (*infra*, 21 §7 and 15 §5).

Shrewdly, he intuited that anthropocentrism, the delimitation of a restricted sacred space, is a precondition for the subsequent emergence of the discourse about the rights of the human being and only of the human being. And it was the critique of the human rights proclaimed by the French Revolution that stimulated the critique of anthropocentrism. Once the 'clever animal' was settled in that infinity without centre or points of reference mentioned in the 'fable', the critique of the hubris of reason found a new and fascinating fundament: it should in the meantime be evident to all 'just how pitiful, how insubstantial and transitory, how purposeless and arbitrary the human intellect looks within nature' (WL, 1, I, 875 [141]). Incidentally, this line of argument can

---

42   Taine 1899, Vol. 2, p. 32 (cf. Rousseau 1959 ff., Vol. 4, p. 582).

43   Schopenhauer 1976–82d, p. 691.

already be found in Malthus: 'Intellect rises from a speck, continues in vigour only for a certain period, and will not, perhaps, admit, while on earth, of above a certain number of impressions.'[44]

Yet Nietzsche's systematisation and radicalisation of these themes implied a qualitative leap. We are already familiar with the double movement by which the concept of human beings as such was deconstructed: on the one hand, it was dissolved into infinite irreducibly individual realities that it sought in vain to unify and homogenise in a single species, on the other hand, it was absorbed without residue into nature and placed on an equal footing with the other animal species. If the revolutionary theorisation of the rights of the human being set an equal sign within the human world and an unequal sign between it and the surrounding natural and animal world, Nietzsche did the exact opposite, emphasising the differences among human beings and the continuity between human beings and nature. The right to work, life, and happiness, in short, the claims that the labour movement was beginning to make its own, were contemptuously rejected, for the idea that human beings might occupy a privileged position in nature compared to that of the 'lowest worm' was denied (*infra*, 10 §3).

5   'Metaphysics of Genius' and Cultural Elitism

The discontinuity denied in the relationship between the human world and the animal and natural world re-emerged in radical form within the human species. Even as a student, Nietzsche emphasised the loneliness of the 'heroes of the spirit'. Separated from them by an impassable abyss was the *Dummkopf*, the 'fool', who, in his obtuse and almost animalistic pursuit of 'happiness', seemed descended from monkeys (B, I, 2, 84). Using different words, Malthus came to the same conclusion. After affirming the primacy in life of the 'pleasures of the intellect', he continued: '[H]ow am I to communicate this truth to a person who has scarcely ever felt intellectual pleasure? I may as well attempt to explain the nature and beauty of colours to a blind man. [...] There is no common measure between us.'[45]

Also to be found in Lagarde[46] and Wagner,[47] the celebration of genius or of the exceptional personality, as opposed to the mediocrity and vulgarity of

---

44   Malthus 1986, p. 133.
45   Malthus 1986, p. 92 f.
46   Lagarde 1937, p. 79.
47   Wagner 1910l, p. 46.

democratic massification, played an important role in Schopenhauer, who contrasted 'genius' or the 'great minds of all time' to the 'normal human being' or, worse still, the *Alltagskopf*, dull commonplace consciousness, the person of the street and everyday life. This was a recurring theme in the authors and circles Nietzsche frequented. In complete agreement with his friend, Rohde stressed that 'the promotion and elevation of genius' were the 'pinnacle' and 'purpose' of culture (B, II, 4, 622).

This thread of thought was so important that authors were sought beyond Germany and even beyond Europe who were capable of lending it additional authority and prestige. As early as 1864, Nietzsche drew attention to Emerson (B, I, 3, 23 and B, I, 2, 120), or rather, as he would say eight years later, to the 'excellent Emerson' (B, II, 3, 258). It is easy to understand the sympathetic interest in a writer who valued 'genius' so highly: 'Nature seems to exist for the excellent'; it was not by chance that 'all mythology opens with demigods'; the appearance of a 'genius', of a 'single great man', was sufficient to enable one to recover from the sight of an entire 'population of pygmies' or, even worse, of 'worthless and offensive members of society whose existence is a social pest'.[48]

Emerson was on friendly terms with Carlyle. Thanks to the latter, Overbeck believed he had been able to clarify for himself the 'task' that awaited him, namely the search for greatness and beauty (B, II, 4, 233). Rohde too looked with interest and sympathy on the English writer, this 'excellent human being, profound and enthusiastic', though weighed down by rhetoric (B, II, 4, 422). This author, who after 1848 took a stand against American abolitionism and European labour agitation, imagined to himself a British prime minister addressing beggars and vagabonds, especially Irish, in the following terms: 'Not "free" you, ... you palpably are fallen captive ... you are of the nature of slaves, or if you prefer the word, of nomadic [...] and vagabond servants that can find no master.' Well and good, someone had to provide for the mass, or rather the scattered herd, but they in turn were to submit to a harsh discipline from which they would not be allowed to escape: the disobedient would suffer the 'whip' and, if necessary, be shot.[49]

In quoting these passages, Engels said that 'the whip imagines it possesses genius'. While the ruling class was considered to be 'privy to genius', 'any oppressed class, the more deeply it is oppressed, the more is it excluded from genius'.[50] One could say that, in the domain of the process of secularisation,

---

48   Emerson 1983a, p. 615.
49   Carlyle 1983, pp. 49–58.
50   Marx and Engels 1975 ff., 10, pp. 309–10.

priviness to genius had replaced divine investiture as an element in the legitimation of rule.

Our thoughts turn to Nietzsche, who at the time spoke sympathetically of
the 'venerable Carlyle'. In Nietzsche's view, one had in any case to credit him
with the merit of having wished, albeit with confused motives, the 'victory'
of Germany, a country that, despite everything, represented 'the hope for an
emerging culture', called upon to put an end once and for all to the 'degenerate
and exhausted' culture of France (VII, 514 [93]). The convergence was all the
more effortless because, at the time, the category of genius had a somewhat
formal character and subsumed within itself, à la Schopenhauer, the figure of
he who 'yearns more profoundly for holiness because from his watchtower he
sees farther and more clearly than any other a human being', until he spotted,
beyond the 'negated will', 'the other shore of which the Hindus speak' (SE, 3, I,
358 [191]).

It is true Nietzsche later mercilessly flayed the English writer, whose moralism and persistent attachment to Christianity he lay bare. Even so, there
remained some elements of consonance: the unbridgeable distance between
the ordinary human being and the great personality, and thus the emphasis on
the celebration of hero or genius; and, as we shall see, the temptation, which
occasionally surfaced, to avert the socialist threat by militarising the workers
and 'vagabonds' (*infra*, 22 §5).

The celebration of genius was not confined to Germany. It could also be
found among leading exponents of liberalism elsewhere. John Stuart Mill held
up against the rising wave of levelling a vision of history that had analogies
with that of Carlyle, whom he reviewed benevolently not to say enthusiastically. Mill prided himself on having immediately praised Carlyle's 'epic poem'
about (or rather against) the French Revolution as 'one of those productions of
genius which are above all rules, and are a law to themselves', even before the
conventional critics had made themselves heard. This was not a purely literary
and aesthetic debate, for as Mill continued: 'The initiation of all wise or noble
things, comes and must come from individuals; generally at first from some
one individual. The honour and glory of the average man is that he is capable
of following that initiative.' It is true that the British liberal defended himself in
advance against the charge that he too was practising 'hero worship', but only
to provide a less threatening and more sugar-coated version that excluded the
right to violence and merely demanded for the human being of genius the freedom to 'show the way' to the masses.[51]

---

51   Mill 1972, p. 124.

So, we are dealing with a theme that had had considerable success at the European level. If this 'cultural elitism', as it is called,[52] began to take hold especially at the start of the second half of the nineteenth century, it already had at least one hundred years of history. In the second half of the eighteenth century, even before the outbreak of the French Revolution, there had emerged in the first German conservatism, in reaction to the struggle against feudal privilege to which the reformers aspired and which monarchic absolutism in some cases promoted, the celebration of 'genius', humiliated by the 'despotism' of the 'mediocre' and the prevalence, in the modern world, of 'general' and levelling rules.[53] Similarly, Rivarol had criticised monarchical absolutism for pursuing a levelling strategy that had humiliated the aristocracy and put 'works of genius' within 'reach of the rabble'.[54] Starting with the outbreak of the French Revolution, this strategy was blamed for trampling on 'genius' and lacking 'respect for great personalities'.[55]

The elaboration and diffusion of elitism were contemporaneous with the cultural crisis of the *ancien régime* and the development of the process of modern 'massification'. So, it is understandable that Marx pledged to fight it. *The German Ideology* started with Stirner. The latter polemicised against the levelling demands of the masses and the socialist movement, and contrasted the interchangeability of labour and ordinary individuals with the incomparability and uniqueness of a painter like Raphael.[56] Against the aspiration to establish a sort of insurmountable naturalistic barrier among human beings, Marx and Engels drew attention to the social and material conditions that made possible the emergence of these outstanding personalities of art and culture: 'The exclusive concentration of artistic talent in particular individuals, and its suppression in the broad mass which is bound up with this, is a consequence of division of labour'.[57]

Marx could already read the following in Smith:

> The difference of natural talents in different men is, in reality, much less than we are aware of; and the very different genius which appears to distinguish men of different professions, when grown up to maturity, is not upon many occasions so much the cause as the effect of the division of

---

52   Struve 1973, p. 13 ff.
53   Möser 1842, p. 21.
54   In Matteucci 1957, p. 263, fn. 68.
55   Gentz 1836–8, Vol. 2, p. 34.
56   Stirner, 1979, p. 281.
57   Marx and Engels 1975 ff., 5, p. 394.

labour. The difference between the most dissimilar characters, between a philosopher and a common street porter, for example, seems to arise not so much from nature as from habit, custom, and education.[58]

In this sense, the masses and the genius were two different faces of the same social reality, both of which moved in a space and environment historically and materially determined:

> Raphael as much as any other artist was determined by the technical advances in art made before him, by the organisation of society and the division of labour in his locality, and, finally, by the division of labour in all the countries with which his locality had intercourse. Whether an individual like Raphael succeeds in developing his talent depends wholly on demand, which in turn depends on the division of labour and the conditions of human culture resulting from it.[59]

The political significance of the celebration of the genius was not only obvious but sometimes even had an immediate value. At the time of the Restoration, intervening in the political and constitutional debate in France that preceded the launch of the *Charte*, the ex-Jacobin Görres drew attention to the uniquely 'liberal and generous' idea in the proposal for a hereditary Chamber of Peers, an idea that 'prevents the tumult of elections, promotes talent, makes genius and virtue permanent'.[60] In the young Nietzsche, we read this comment: 'Aversion to genius. The "social" human being. – Socialism' (VII, 259). 'Genius', previously promoted in the context of the French Revolution, was now set against the socialist revolution looming ominously on the horizon.

The Stirner criticised by Marx and Engels brings us in the vicinity of Nietzsche. In Nietzsche's youthful years, Haym attributed to romantic culture the merit of having demanded the rights of 'genial immediacy'. In elaborating on the theme of genius, Haym indicted not only the Enlightenment but Hegelian philosophy, which he accused of having inherited, along with its rationalism, all the shallowness of the Enlightenment:

> That which until now only scientific genius [*das wissenschaftliche Genie*] seemed able to accomplish, now appears all of a sudden as something that could be learned by anyone who studied the new logic. Like Bacon's

---

58   Smith 1981, p. 28 (Book 1, 2).
59   Marx and Engels 1975 ff., 5, p. 393.
60   In Losurdo 1997a, 2, § 9.

> Novum Organum, this logic claimed to be a universally applicable canon,
> a tool accessible to all of a livelier scientific knowledge, *ut ingenii viribus
> et excellentiae non multum relinquatur.*[61]

A clear opposition between the 'metaphysics of genius' and the 'philistine reason', said to preside over the Hegelian philosophy of history, was also established by Nietzsche, who thus once again took up a widespread theme with a long history. Naturally we are dealing here, yet again, with an extreme radicalisation, for the anti-democratic polemic was characterised by its clarity. To recognise the 'natural hierarchy in the realm of the intellect' (BA, 3, I, 699 [76–7]) meant to bow and to teach others to bow before the 'genius, the leader for all time' (BA, 1, I, 671 [41]). It is striking how bluntly and brutally Nietzsche asserted that 'every man, with his whole activity, is only dignified to the extent that he is a tool of genius, consciously or unconsciously' (CV, 3, I, 776 [172–3]). To want to provide education and freedom to those 'born to serve and to obey' blasphemed against the 'sacred hierarchy of nature'. They were to obey 'those few great and lonely figures of the period', who moulded and shaped to their liking the 'clay' of the masses (BA, 3, I, 698 [74–5]). 'The heroic' were 'the kind of people who alone matter' (FW, 292 [166]), and these heroes or 'geniuses' or 'great contemplating few, destined for the production of immortal works', were at an enormous distance from the 'stupid, dull masses, acting by instinct' (BA, 4, I, 722 [104]), whose existence lacked any autonomous meaning. Yes, only the 'genius' could give sense to the 'mechanical, lifeless bodies' of the 'crowd' (BA, 5, I, 751 [142]).

The newest element, however, was formed by the thesis that the entire organisation of society was to be inspired by the realisation that 'the production of genius [...] is the aim of all culture' (SE, 3; I 358 [190]). This produced the 'dreadful necessity of working for him, so that his procreation may be made possible' (BA, 1, I, 666 [34]), to reproduce and perpetuate the natural and immutable hierarchy that presided and had to continue to preside over the politico-social order. Unfortunately, modernity was defined by an opposite trend: 'The rights of genius are being democratised' (BA, 1, I, 666 [35]). The spread of educational institutions was to be placed within this context. It was promoted by 'zealous, yea, fanatical opponents of true culture, *i.e.* all those who hold fast to the aristocratic nature of the mind'. Committed to 'the emancipation of the masses from the mastery of the great few; they seek to overthrow the most sacred hierarchy in the kingdom of the intellect – the servitude of

---

61   Haym 1974, p. 327.

the masses, their submissive obedience, their instinct of loyalty to the rule of genius' (BA, 3; I, 698 [74]).

Only with Nietzsche did the 'metaphysics of genius' become the centre of a political programme of radical opposition to modernity and the subversive tendencies and massification associated with it. It was necessary to go back by a long and devastating path and to ensure that the natural and unbridgeable differences that existed among human beings were once again fully acknowledged by the division of society into 'castes'.

6   The 'Doric State' as Dictatorship in the Service of the Production of Genius

In this struggle against the stream the 'true Platonic republic', whose essence was 'the organisation of the state of genius', might offer a model (VII, 379). There could be no doubt that one had to recognise at least one merit in Plato. At the apex of the 'perfect state' he coveted stood genius, even if he did not understand this category in its general meaning, since he excluded 'artists of genius' from it, under the ruinous influence of the 'Socratic judgement' on art. Even so, this 'external, almost accidental gap' did not detract from the merit of having identified the 'connection between state and genius', of having understood that 'the actual aim of the state' lay in the generation and preparation of genius, in comparison with which everything else was a mere means (CV, 3, I, 776–7 [173]).

In the state taken here as a model, 'military genius', which was to be recognised 'as original founder of the state', played an essential role (CV, 3, I, 775 [172]). We were not to be fooled by that 'false gloss the moderns have spread over the origin and meaning of the state'. Its unique and decisive task was to render possible and defend a 'configuration of society' that revolved around the 'continuing, painful birth of those exalted men of culture in whose service everything else has to consume [verzehren] itself' (CV, 3; I, 769 [168]). The organisation of society, culture as such, and artistic creation 'rests on one terrible premise', on a 'horrifying, predatory aspect' (CV, 3, I, 767 [166]).

The foolish modern slogans, such as 'human dignity' and 'the dignity of work', mystified reality and impeded the forward movement of the chariot of culture. What sense did it make to speak of 'dignity' for the 'exhausting work [verzehrende Arbeit]' to which the masses were condemned, and what was the point of speaking of 'human dignity' for 'all the millions' whose conditions were characterised by a 'terrible predicament [furchtbare Noth]' and 'toil and moil [Arbeitsnoth]', in order to survive? For all its high-sounding rhetoric, the modern world also behaved 'in a thoroughly slave-like manner' (CV, 3, I, 764 [164]).

In their attempt to escape starvation and 'continue to vegetate at any cost', most people agreed to submit to work and conditions of life that were ultimately servile (VII, 336–7).

This powerful construction was not without elements of fragility. The ruling classes could retreat in horror at the sight of the enormous potential for pain, of 'the cruelty we found at the heart of every culture'. In such a case, 'the cry of compassion' and 'the urge for justice, for equal sharing of the pain' would 'tear down the walls of culture'. Martial education helped to overcome these weaknesses, and a strong military organisation prevented the 'revolt of the oppressed masses' (CV, 3, I, 768 [167]). More for reasons of domestic than of international politics, war and the 'military castes, from which there arises the construction of a "war-like society" in the shape of a pyramid on the broadest possible base: a slave-like bottom stratum', provided 'the archetype of the state' (CV, 3, I, 775 [172]).

Together with the 'military castes', an 'aeropagus for justice of the spirit' and 'actual educational authorities' with exceptional powers were called upon to discipline society (VII, 385). Nietzsche's formulations have sometimes been interpreted as the theorisation of a 'pedagogical dictatorship'. Yet this category is misleading. It can appear appropriate in the case of an elite that considers its rule as something temporary, destined to become superfluous once the masses have raised themselves to its level. But, here, we are dealing with a completely different perspective, which starts out presuming the gap is unbridgeable. The dictatorship of genius is destined to last forever and to ensure that no one can offend against 'the order of castes nor against the sequence of classes of rank' (WL, I, 882 [147]), to which end it imposes a strict social control that acts through both the institution of slavery and war. In this sense, Apollo was 'the just god who consecrates and purifies the state'. He, 'as at the beginning of the Iliad, [...] shoots his arrows at mules and dogs. Then he actually hits people and, everywhere, pyres with corpses blaze' (CV, 3, I, 774 [171–2]).

It was the 'Doric state', the 'cruel and ruthless State' that we already know and that was founded in the 'Doric vision of the world'. This vision was now to be taken up again and re-actualised by Germany: 'great geniuses' were to be considered as 'tried and true leaders and guides [Führer und Wegweiser] of this real German spirit' (BA, 4, I, 723 [105]). The authentic culture called upon to assert itself on the ruins of civilization had to be characterised by 'pre-established harmony' between leader and led [Führer und Geführtem] (BA, 5, I, 752 [140]). Although cultural elitism was widely diffused across Europe and the West, in Germany it had strikingly Caesaristic features.

CHAPTER 3

Socratism and 'Present-Day Judaism'

1   Aryan 'Tragic Profundity' and the 'Despicable Jewish Phrase'

We have spoken about why Nietzsche preferred the myth of the eternal and necessary tragedy of Prometheus to the historical and accidental fall of Adam and Eve. But, in expounding the reasons, *The Birth of Tragedy* took an unexpected turn:

> Originally, the legend of Prometheus belonged to the entire community of Aryan peoples and documented their talent for the profound and the tragic; indeed, it is not unlikely that this myth is as significant for the Aryan character [*arisches Wesen*] as the myth of the Fall is for the Semitic character, and that the relationship between the two myths is like that between brother and sister.
>
> GT, 9, I, 68–9 [49]

Here, the comparison between the myth of Prometheus and the biblical myth of original sin was presented as one between the Aryan and the Semite: the manly courage of the former, able to confront reality even in its most terrible aspects, was contrasted with the womanly cowardice of the latter. The Aryan had a frank and direct way of thinking and arguing, he was 'reflective [*beschaulich*]', in the sense that he knew how to reflect on and see [*schauen*] reality, without drawing between it and himself a veil of cowardly self-deceptions and sophisms. The Semite, on the other hand, sought to remove by chicanery and artifice [*wegdeuteln*] that which was disturbing or terrible in reality. It goes without saying: the 'Aryan peoples' had more talent for 'the profound and the tragic' (GT, 9, I, 68–70 [48–51]). Although the Aryan/Semitic dichotomy and the associated criticism or denigration of Judaism figured strongly in the culture of the time, in *The Birth of Tragedy*, it seemed to make only one, isolated appearance.

Not so in the correspondence. There, the angry anti-Judaism or the Judeophobia of the young student, who placed an advertisement in the *Leipziger Tagblatt* seeking accommodation in a 'non-commercial area' of Leipzig (B, I, 2, 123), to avoid Jews, found full and furious expression.[1] In a letter to the family

---

1   Hayman has pointed to it (1980, p. 78).

on 22 April 1866, he said how happy he was at having 'finally' found a restaurant where he could enjoy a meal without having to endure the sight of 'Jewish ugly mugs [*Judenfratzen*]', and, again with reference to Jews, of 'disgusting soulless apes and other merchants' (B, I, 2, 125). Things were even worse in the theatre, at least when it came to attending the performance of Meyerbeer's *Afrikan-erin* (Meyerbeer was a musician of Jewish origin mocked by Wagner): one saw 'Jews and cronies of Jews [*Juden und Judengenossen*] wherever one looks' (B, I, 2, 127–8).

The Judeophobia was interspersed with expressions of contempt for blacks:

> I also saw the *Afrikanerin* (by the way, send me clean linen): the music is bad, the people look repulsive, and at the end of the piece one strongly believes in the descent of human beings from apes.
>
> B, I, 2, 132

But let us concentrate on the polemic against the Jews. Generally, biograph-ers emphasise the stark contrast that would emerge later between the anti-Semitism of Nietzsche's sister Elisabeth and the philosopher's quite different attitude. But, at this point, the roles were reversed: it was the student who adopted a radically anti-Jewish tone that one would seek in vain among other members of his family. The personal encounter with Wagner was yet to come: it would lead to a strengthening of trends already in motion, for the great musi-cian would buttress them with theoretical motivations that, moreover, took a fascinating artistic and musical form. An autobiographical sketch dating from the summer of 1867 to the spring of 1868, in which Nietzsche referred contemp-tuously to 'Jewish Berlin' (KGA, I, 4, 509), took things from bad to worse.

Anyone committed to reconstructing the intellectual biography of such a fascinating author cannot help but ask: is it only the previously quoted page from *The Birth of Tragedy* that voices the Judeophobic themes Nietz-sche developed after his years at university, that he had absorbed by reading Schopenhauer and Wagner, and that he continued to cultivate thanks to his frequent visits to the revered musician and his admired companion and wife? The principal theme of that page is anticipated in a letter Deussen sent Nietz-sche in August 1866: an abyss separated the 'Indogerman, who thinks in a clear way', from the 'Semite' and the 'Oriental', incapable of that (B, I, 3, 125). Nietz-sche's notebooks also contrasted the authentic and tragic Hellas to Judaism, as well as to modernity. Unlike the Greeks, who showed 'moderation' in this regard too, 'the Jewish religion has an unspeakable terror of death, and the main goal of its prayers – is a long life' (VII, 106); yes, 'the Jew clings to life with incredible tenacity' (VII, 102). 'For the Jews of the Old Testament, the most terrible threat is not eternal torment but complete destruction'; 'not to be is the greatest of evils' (VII, 140–1). Ultimately, we were dealing with a religion that aimed only at 'well-being upon earth' (VII, 119), that had promoted and continued to promote the destructive pursuit of happiness. Because Judaism made the earthly world the place of the realisation of its exalted hopes, it expressed the same optimism manifested in the movements and upheavals of revolution. The necessary conclusion: to defend culture against the subversion that threatened it also meant 'to attack the despicable Jewish phrase of heaven on earth' (VII, 121).

The denunciation of Jewish optimism was widespread in European culture of the time: think, for example, of Kierkegaard, who also voiced his disgust for Jewish optimism, 'the most intensified lust for life that has ever attached itself to life'.[2] On the other hand, this theme was also present, though in a positive valuation, in Strauss, whom Nietzsche would later savagely criticise. At the end of the nineteenth century, it could also be found in a prominent French Jew. The latter identified 'eudemonism' as the fundamental merit of the 'philosophy of the Jew', who sought a 'sweet' life, not plagued by misfortune and injustice but rich in 'worldly pleasures'.[3]

But, to grasp the attitude of the author of *The Birth of Tragedy*, one must of course bear in mind above all else the influence exerted on him by Schopenhauer and Wagner. In the former, the condemnation of 'optimistic Judaism' (or of its 'variant, Islam') was constantly present.[4] By his very 'optimism', Spinoza showed himself to be a Jew: yes, 'the Jews are all more serene than other nations'.[5] Schopenhauer's polemic was directed above all at the Old Testament, characterised by a banally optimistic conception of life, which proceeded from the idea of a God who created a world from nothing, a world that, given its origin, could not but have a fundamentally positive value and was therefore a suitable place for the realisation of the wish for happiness. As for Wagner, he was in no doubt that the 'superficial optimists by definition' were 'the sons of Abraham, full of beautiful hopes'.[6] Similar views could be found in correspondents of Nietzsche, now professor of classical philology at Basel: in a letter to him, Malwida von Meysenbug denounced the 'colossal optimism' of the French, which 'is in no way inferior to that of the Jews' (B, II, 4, 219).

Unaware of the tragic dimension of existence, the exponents of 'optimism' succumbed to a vacuous and superficial 'serenity'. Even before the publication

---

2   Kierkegaard 1962 ff., Vol. 5, pp. 194, 201 f.
3   Lazare 1969, p. 152 f.
4   Schopenhauer 1976–82b, p. 569.
5   Schopenhauer 1971, p. 108 f.
6   Wagner 19100, p. 256.

of *The Birth of Tragedy*, Wagner declared that talk of so-called 'Greek serenity' was an expression of the tendency, to be found in Jewish music and culture, to transform Hellas into a 'neo-Hellenic synagogue' – perhaps this was a reference above all to Heine, criticised by Wagner at the end of his *Judaism in Music*.[7] So not only optimism in general but also the banally optimistic and serene interpretation of classical Greece led back to Judaism. We are dealing with a text (*Über das Dirigieren*) that must have had a big influence on Nietzsche. In a letter to Gersdorff dated 11 March 1870, he announced the publication of this 'small paper' which, because of its importance, could be compared with Schopenhauer's essay *On Philosophy in the Universities* (B, II, 1, 105), The latter, not by chance, harshly denounced optimism and blamed it on the persisting influence of 'Judaism'.

In truth, the relationship between master and disciple or between musician and philologist-philosopher was not one-way. In a note written in the winter of 1869–70, Nietzsche observed that Winckelmann's vision of Hellas represented the terrible 'flattening' of a world far more profound and tragic than its superficial interpreter. Nor was it merely an error of perspective, which one could not in any case overlook: 'One had the image of Roman-universal Hellenism, Alexandrianism.' All this was true, but in the modern triumph of this view much more obtained: 'Beauty and flatness in alliance, even necessarily. Scandalous theory! Judea' (VII, 81).

Both the denunciation of 'optimism' and that of pseudo-Greek but in reality modern 'serenity' united the party of the tragic worldview. In a letter full of venomously anti-Jewish allusions, Cosima mocked supposed 'Greek serenity' and those who claimed to be 'tranquil' and 'serene like the Greeks [*griechisch Heiteren*]'. She particularly attacked a jeweller who, by his looks, evoked 'Judea' even from a distance and was 'no problematic nature': for him, 'all is harmonious' (B, II, 2, 159–60). And when Gersdorff gave free rein to his contempt for the 'man of serenity [*Heiterkeitsmensch*]', he not only connected this figure with the flatness of the 'present time' but also with Judaism, which apparently celebrated its triumphs in Berlin (B, II, 2, 461).

Optimism, serenity, Judaism and modern civilisation tended to form a unitary and repugnant whole. This is a point Wagner insisted on, but his disciples thought and felt in the same way, and they included, at the time, Nietzsche, who also played a leading role in this school. It is he that converted Gersdorff to love and worship the master, and in the course of this conversion, he not only invited him to read the musician's theoretical texts but emphatically warned

---

7   Wagner 1910b, p. 84f.

him about the polemic going on with the Jewish circles. In a letter presumably written in early March 1870, Gersdorff thanked him for having 'warmly recommended' reading *Opera and Drama.* He added: 'Up to now, I have only heard the gossip and insults published in the Judaized [*verjüdelt*] press about Your Friend [...]. *Judaism in Music* has completely opened my eyes' (B, II, 2, 163–4). Nietzsche's response was immediate: he was happy that their friendship now appeared to have been further strengthened by a common admiration for a personality so great but at the same time so opposed; 'it is not easy and requires a vigorous manly courage not to allow oneself to be bewildered by the terrible yelling', the yelling of the 'opposing party', in whose ranks – the letter stresses – 'our Jews' distinguished themselves. It is they that, having placed themselves at the head of 'most people of our modern age [*Jetztzeit*]', rejected with horror both Schopenhauer's 'asceticism and denial of the will' and 'the incredible seriousness and German depth in Wagner's vision of the world and art, as it gushes forth from every note' (B, II, 1, 105).

Nietzsche completely convinced Gersdorff. The latter, who in the meantime, thanks to the mediation of his friend, had been able to attend a performance of the composer and come into direct contact with him, emphasised in a letter to Nietzsche dated 4 April 1870 that he had fully understood 'the wretchedness [*Nichtswürdigkeit*] of Judaism'; faced with the struggle of 'vulgarity against genius', one had to take a clear and unequivocal stand, without allowing oneself to be influenced by the boundless 'anger of Judaism' (B, II, 2, 188 and 192).

As we have seen, Nietzsche denounced the 'counter-party' of the tragic worldview. In the eyes of his friends, he seemed to be the leader of the party gathering around Wagner, pledging to defend him even in the controversy unleashed by his declaration of war on the noxious presence of 'Judaism' both 'in music' – the title of his pamphlet – and, more generally, in culture and political and sociopolitical life as a whole. When Nietzsche told Rohde about his aspiration to occupy the chair of philosophy that had become available in Basel, Rohde encouraged him: even Schopenhauer would have 'smiled' at the rise of one of his disciples who 'will tell the world the truth and drive the Jews and those circumcised in spirit back to their synagogue' (B, II, 2, 332).

There can no longer be any doubt: by this time, not only Wagner was of the opinion that 'our entire civilization is a barbaric-Jewish mishmash'.[8] For the young Nietzsche too, praising the musician as Schopenhauer's 'great spiritual brother' (B, II, 1, 8), the denunciation of civilisation and modernity was, at the same time, the denunciation of the shallow and banausic character of Judaism.

---

8   Wagner 1910p, p. 268.

Such is the case at least in the correspondence and the notebooks that paved the way to *The Birth of Tragedy*. What about the text Nietzsche presented to the press?

2   Socratism and the Jewish Press in the Struggle against Germanness

Between the notebooks and *The Birth of Tragedy* lie a series of lectures most of which ended up in the book as actually published. One is of particular interest, that of 1 February 1870, *Socrates and Tragedy*. Wagner received the text at once, read it to Cosima, and then wrote to the author, expressing his complete agreement and, at the same time, deep concern. Would Nietzsche not end up with a 'broken neck'? Even those 'initiated in my ideas', wrote the musician, would not be pleased by the excessive severity shown towards the 'divine errors' of great personalities of Hellas. But above all, how would the broad 'public' react to the 'surprisingly modern way' in which Socrates was treated? 'You will receive absolution only if no one understands anything of the same.' The fact remained that the lecture caused a 'fright' and commotion in Tribschen, especially in Cosima's case (B, II, 2, 137–8).

Two days later, Cosima confirmed this. After reiterating the general need for caution, her letter added a recommendation that shed light on the identity of the enemies lying in wait:

> Do not name the Jews, especially not *en passant*. Later, if you want to engage in this terrible struggle, in God's name, but not at the start, so that not everything on your path turns into confusion and entanglement. I hope you do not misunderstand me. You will know how much I agree, from the depths of my soul, with your statements, but not now, and not in that way.
>
> B, II, 2, 140

So, the lecture was read in Tribschen in a decidedly anti-Jewish key. At this point, it is worth reading it again, and in the version that stirred in Wagner and his companion feelings of both admiration and anxiety. Above all the conclusion attracted their attention:

> Is music drama really dead, dead for good? Should the German really not be allowed to put anything alongside that vanished work of art of the past other than 'great opera', much in the same way as the ape used to appear next to Hercules? This is the most serious question of our art, and who-

ever, as a German, does not understand the seriousness of this question has fallen victim to the Socratism of our days, which undoubtedly cannot produce martyrs nor speak the language of the 'wisest among the Greeks' and certainly blusters [like the historical Socrates] about not knowing anything, but really knows nothing. This Socratism is the Jewish press: I say nothing more.

ST, I, 549 and XIV, 101

Corresponding to the dichotomy between Germans and Jews was that between Greek tragedy, now reborn on German soil, and modern opera, synonymous with the optimistic and banausic view of life and, not by accident, propagated by the Jewish press, which thus sought to achieve in the present the same destruction of tragedy and the tragic vision of life that Socrates, in his time, represented. Moreover, without bothering to put on display the affected modesty of the Greek philosopher, contemporary Judaism did not hide the presumption and arrogance of its enlightenment.

One can understand the enthusiasm in Wagner's household. Cosima discovered in Nietzsche's text tones not only dear to her but that made her feel 'at home' (B, II, 2, 138). Richard looked forward to a fruitful 'division of labour' that would allow him and the philologist to weave into a single thread their strivings towards a common goal: 'You could free me of a good part, even an entire half, of my mission. While you may perhaps entirely follow your own mission' (B, II, 2, 145–6). If only *Socrates and Tragedy* could be turned into a broader and more coherent work, it could represent the *pendant* at the historical and philological level of *Judaism in Music* and other works by Wagner dedicated to ridding German culture and essence of any Jewish and Old Testament influence.

Intertwined with these confident and pugnacious plans for the future were concerns about the present. The Socratic 'fanatics of logic', said Nietzsche in his lecture, 'are as unbearable as wasps' (ST, I, 541). Here, however, Cosima made the 'motherly' recommendation not to stir up 'the wasps' nest [*Wespennest*]' of Jewish circles and power prematurely (B, II, 2, 140). Most worrying was the conclusion: it took to task directly, without further explanation, and thus with a degree of clumsiness, the 'Jewish press', which a few years later became a focus of the anti-Semitic polemic.[9] Nietzsche was quick to replace the word, and in the new version it was 'the press today' that represented 'Socratism'. This change was particularly effortless, since in the eyes of his friends in Tribschen, practically nothing has been changed. According to Wagner, it was to be univer-

---

9   Cf. Boehlich 1965, *passim*.

sally acknowledged that 'all the newspapers in Europe are almost exclusively in the hands of the Jews',[10] and 'Jewish journalism' was a highly disturbing power.[11] This was also Nietzsche's view: according to a note written in early 1874, the Jews 'possess most of the money and own most of the newspapers in Germany today' (VII, 766 [324]).

Not only on this point did the young professor in Basel welcome Cosima's authoritative advice. In telling his friend Deussen about his lecture, he observed:

> Part of it has caused anger and hatred. A clash is inevitable. On the main issue I have already learned to set aside every consideration: compassionate and condescending to the individual, we must be as stiff as the ancient Roman virtue in expressing our worldview.
> B, II, 1, 98–9

So, in Tribschen, they were right: certain themes were explosive; certain circles of people lay in wait. That did not mean one should beat a cowardly retreat. At most, a certain verbal caution might be in order. In a letter sent a few days earlier to his friend Rohde, after mentioning the lecture, Nietzsche added:

> Thanks to it, the link with my friends in Tribschen has become closer. For them, I am hope on the march. Even Richard Wagner gave me to understand in the most touching way the mission [*Bestimmung*] he sees foreshadowed in me. All this is a source of great anxiety. You know how Ritschl expressed himself in my regard. But I will not allow myself to be tempted: I have no literary ambitions whatsoever, and I do not need to follow dominant models, because I do not aspire to brilliant and famous positions. When the time comes, however, I want to express myself in the most serious and frank way possible.
> B, II, 1, 95

At this point, we can pause to take stock. Nietzsche had become aware of the dangers inherent in his new intellectual journey, but, far from giving up the fight, took upon himself the 'mission' entrusted to him by Richard Wagner, while accepting the advisability of caution: rather than provoke an immediate scandal in order to achieve celebrity, it was better to remain firm on the

10   Wagner 1911, p. 554.
11   Wagner 1910m, pp. 56, 58.

'main issue' while, at the same time, exercising a certain self-censorship in the expectation of being able to express oneself later with greater frankness.

In this spirit, Nietzsche worked on his *Birth of Tragedy*, by now taking shape. On the eve of its publication, Judeophobia seemed to reach its peak, evidenced by the brusque rejection of a request by his sister: 'How can you expect from me that I order a book from a scandalous Jewish antiquarian?' (B, II, 1, 262). The question arises, what traces did the Judeophobia of the correspondence, the manuscript notes, and *Socrates and Tragedy* leave behind in the work brought out shortly afterwards by Wagner's publisher and on Wagner's recommendation, and whose cover was graced with the model of a Wagner text?

One must ask whether the link between Socratism and the Jewish press (or the press of today), the underlying theme of the lecture that had both excited and alarmed his friends in Tribschen, really had disappeared. In fact, several months after the lecture, a note identified the 'Judaism of our days' as an essential manifestation of 'Socratism', 'hostile or indifferent to art' (VII, 99). *The Birth of Tragedy* had numerous references to the calamitous role Socratism played in the German press (GT, 22, I, 143–4 [107]). It is hard to view it as harmless if we think of the context and, above all, if we bear in mind Cosima's invitation to self-censorship and Nietzsche's resolve to heed it.

But this is not the main point. We know that Nietzsche saw Schopenhauer as a great interpreter of 'German Hellenism', synonymous with authentic culture. Whence the danger of debasement and degeneration? A letter to Wagner sheds light on this point: 'I have you and Schopenhauer to thank if up to now I have remained faithful to the Germanic seriousness of life, to a deepened contemplation of this enigmatic and problematic existence.' This 'more serious and soulful worldview', however, ran the risk of being spoiled by a 'clamant Judaism' (B, II, 1, 9). Let us now read the Basel lecture of 1 February 1870:

'From the infinitely deepened point of view of Germanic consciousness, that Socratism seems like a completely absurd world' (ST, I, 541). The Germanism-Judaism dichotomy coincided with the Socratism-Germanism dichotomy. It could not be otherwise: Socratism was synonymous with Judaism, as evidenced by the conclusion, subsequently amended, that identified and denounced the 'Jewish press' as the mouthpiece of the 'Socratism of our day'.

The Germanism-Socratism dichotomy was part of the deep structure of *The Birth of Tragedy*: 'From the Dionysiac ground of the German spirit a power has risen up which has nothing in common with the original conditions [*Urbedingungen*] of Socratic culture' (GT, 19, I, 127 [94]). The reference was not, of course, to Judaism, but did Socratism, which was the explicit subject, have nothing more to do with Judaism? That would be surprising: in that case, the published text would completely contradict the notebooks. Here we find formulated the thesis that 'Socratism of our time' was not only a force hostile to art in general but also 'without sympathy for the future of German art'. It had no 'sense of fatherland but only of state' (VII, 13). It was separated by an abyss from the authentic Greeks, characterised by the 'most natural instincts for the homeland [*Heimatsinstinkte*]' (GT, 21, I, 132 [98]). So, Jews could respect the laws of the country in which they lived, but still they were alien to the nation. Not by chance were they the people 'without a homeland [*heimatslos*]' *par excellence*! We know the decisive role *The Birth of Tragedy* attributed to Socrates in the destruction of tragedy. However, a preparatory note written in the winter of 1869–70 reads: 'Annihilation of Greek culture by the Jewish world' (VII, 83). Should the tragic death of Hellas be blamed on Judaism or on Socratism? There is no problem, for the two terms were indissolubly joined.

One even gets the impression that not only an elective affinity linked the gravedigger of authentic Hellenism with the Jewish world. We were dealing with a figure striking not only for his inherently anti-Hellenic worldview but also for his 'bizarrely attractive external ugliness' (ST, I, 541). This was not a mere detail: 'It is significant that Socrates is the first great Greek to be ugly' (ST, I, 545). This reminds one of the 'Jewish ugly mugs' Nietzsche, as a university student, sought to avoid. Even in the summer of 1877, Rohde, in a letter to his friend in Basel, expressed his disgust at the 'repulsive Semitic face' that generally characterised these 'bow-legged' Jews (B, II, 6, 1, 595–6). In the background, naturally, stood Wagner, according to whom Jewish 'physiognomies' in general did not give a 'good impression'.[12] In any case, Jews were revealed by their very 'appearance' to be 'unpleasantly alien' with respect to German and European nationality.[13] In Nietzsche's eyes, no less 'unpleasantly alien' with respect to the Greeks was Socrates, with 'his bulging eyes, his swollen lips, his sagging belly' (ST, I, 544). Later, the Greek philosopher would be explicitly stamped as a Jew. Nietzsche came to this conclusion because of Socrates's physical 'ugliness', a sign of a 'hybrid [*gekreuzten*] development, inhibited by crossing [*Kreuzung*]' (*infra*, 15 § 2 and 19 § 1). But even then, in these early years, one has the distinct impression of a figure alien in every respect to the authentic Hellas.

That Socratism continued to refer to Judaism was also confirmed by the at first sight strange reactions of Nietzsche and his friends to the polemics unleashed by *The Birth of Tragedy*. Nietzsche called Wilamowitz, the author of one of the reviews, 'a youngster suffering from Jewish arrogance' (B, II, 3,

---

12   Wagner 1911, p. 203.
13   Wagner 1910b, p. 69.

30). So far, we are simply dealing with a banal and generic stereotype.[14] More interesting is the judgement on Ritschl. As we know, he considered himself too 'Alexandrian' to support the thesis of his pupil or ex-pupil (B, II, 2, 541), who a few months later complained to his friend Rohde about the 'Jewish-Roman essay' his former teacher had sent him (B, II, 3, 181). Perhaps this description contained a malicious reference to the Jewish origin of Ritschl's wife, which Nietzsche had mentioned a few years earlier (KGA, I, 4, 519).

Let us now consider Rohde's point of view. In a letter dated 5 June 1872, he saw the capital of the Reich, where capitalism was in full spate, with the notable participation of Jewish finance, and where Wilamowitz had launched his attack on *The Birth of Tragedy* (and the tragic worldview), as a city characterised by 'the most repulsive Jewish opulence [*widerwärtigste Judenüppigkeit*]' (B, II, 4, 11). This Judeophobic or anti-Semitic theme, already present (as we have seen) in Nietzsche the student and commonplace in publications of the day, was now closely tied to the critique of modernity. This emerged clearly from two successive letters from Rohde:

> Faced with this Berlin, I feel a real repugnance. It is as if all the most horrible elements of modern civilization had united in a great tumour to allow the world to understand what really constitutes this civilization.

It was 'the bustle of a civilized anthill' (B, II, 4, 77–8), the 'high tide of vulgarity' (B, II, 4, 117). It was true, added Gersdorff, that Berlin was a horrible 'Jewish' city: a possible alternative to which was offered by 'Wagner and all those great men [who] have no point in common with the spirit of the "present age"' (B, II, 2, 461).

By now it is clear. While optimism was synonymous with Judaism and the tragic vision of life referred primarily to the Aryan peoples, those who rejected it were infected by the lack of creativity of both Judaism and modernity.

3   Judaism in Music and in *The Birth of Tragedy*

What is the role of anti-Judaism or Judeophobia in *The Birth of Tragedy*? When we read that Socratic existence is 'detached from the soil of home [*losgelöst von dem heimischen Boden*], unbridled in the wilderness of thought, morals, and action' (GT, 23, I, 148 [110]), we cannot but think of Wagner and his character-

---

14   Cf., e.g., Treitschke 1965b, p. 43 and Dühring 1881b, p. 88.

isation of the Jews 'as an ethnic group without ties to the soil [*Bodenlos*]'[15] and with the typical 'sobriety of someone without soil [*bodenlose Nüchternheit*]'.[16]

In turn, Nietzsche described the Socratic human being as follows:

> [C]onsider the rule-less wandering of artistic fantasy, unbridled by an indigenous myth; think of a culture which has no secure and sacred place of origin and which is condemned to exhaust every possibility and to seek meagre nourishment from all other cultures.
>
> GT, 23, I, 145–6 [108–9]

The Socratic human being, 'mythless man [...] stands there, surrounded by every past there has ever been, eternally hungry, scraping and digging in a search for roots, even if he has to dig for them in the most distant antiquities' (GT, 23, I, 146 [109]). Again, one thinks of Wagner and his denunciation of the 'ratiocinative intellectuality of the upper strata of Judaism', completely devoid of 'roots'.[17] Burdened by an irremediably vanished past, the wandering Jew could not recognise as his new home any of the countries in which he set himself up, so, in the end, he became an element in the dissolution of all the cultural traditions with which he came in contact, which is why he embodied the 'relentless demon of negation'.[18] In this sense, Judaism or Socratism, to use the language of *The Birth of Tragedy*, was synonymous with Enlightenment as the destroyer of myth. Here, then, we have 'abstract man, without guidance from myth, abstract education, abstract morality, abstract law, the abstract state' (GT, 23, I, 145 [108]).

Wagner never let off talking about the Jew's 'cold indifference'[19] or the 'inner incapacity for life'.[20] With no real mother tongue and hopelessly alien to the soil and the people amid whom he lived, he was 'hardly able to express his feelings and his visions artistically'.[21] He could at most become a 'thinker', never a true 'poet'.[22] Thus we are brought back to *The Birth of Tragedy*: Socrates was a 'theoretical man' and a declared 'opponent of the tragic art' (GT, 17, I, 115 [85] and GT 13 [65]; I, 89). Insofar as he was a 'poet of aesthetic Socratism', Euripides played the part of 'the first sober [*nüchtern*]' poet, committed to denouncing the '"drunken" poets' (GT, 12 [64]; I, 87).

---

15   Wagner 1910b, p. 71.
16   Wagner 1910b, p. 85.
17   Wagner 1910b, p. 77.
18   Wagner 1910b, p. 85.
19   Wagner 1910b, p. 71.
20   Wagner 1910b, p. 84.
21   Wagner 1910b, p. 72.
22   Wagner 1910b, p. 74.

This is the *Nüchternheit* already denounced by Wagner, who took his denunciation even further, adding a fresh count to the indictment. The same objective situation that prevented the Jew from being a true artist favoured his one-sided intellectual development:

> The true poet, whatever the artistic genre in which he starts writing poetry, receives his stimuli always and only from the true, loving contemplation of spontaneous [*uwillkürlich*] life, the life that manifests itself to him only in the people. Where does the cultured Jew find these people?[23]

The Jew was alien to the 'historical community' in which he lived, for 'only those who grow unconsciously [*unbewusst*] in this community can partake of its creations'.[24] Artistic creation presupposed full and spontaneous identification with a given people and a culture. To use the language of *The Birth of Tragedy*, the influence of 'logical Socratism' was 'disintegrative [of] the instincts' (GT 13, I, 91 [67]), looking with hostility at and rendering suspect norms and models of life followed 'only by instinct' (GT, 13; I, 89 [66]). Art was thus condemned by 'aesthetic Socratism', whose 'principle [was that] "[E]verything must be conscious [*verständig*] in order to be beautiful"' (GT, 12, I, 85 [62]). But this, according to Wagner, was precisely Judaism's standpoint: the limited 'capacity for musical perception of the educated Jew' allowed him to appreciate 'only that which appears comprehensible to the intellect [*verständlich*]'; the deeper 'popular [*volkstümlich*] and artistic dimension' remained closed to him.[25]

Detached from the people and from its deepest feelings, reduced to intellectualistic exercise, in Jews not only art but culture as such, 'learned and bought [*bezahlte*] culture, [...] can serve only as a luxury'. On the other hand – insisted Wagner – the weight of Judaism had meant that 'our modern arts and even music' had been reduced to 'luxury' articles or performances.[26] As the *Foreword to Richard Wagner* at the start of *The Birth of Tragedy* declared, one could not expect understanding or sympathy on the part of those 'incapable of thinking of art as anything more than an amusing sideshow, a readily dispensable jingling of fool's bells in the face of the "gravity of existence"' (GT, Preface, I, 24 [14]).

Together with the intellectualism, and bound up with it, Jews were marked according to Wagner by their banausic and mercantile view of life, sealing their

---

23   Wagner 1910b, p. 75.
24   Wagner 1910b, p. 71.
25   Ibid.
26   Wagner 1910b, p. 74.

aesthetic frigidity: 'Their eyes are always occupied with things much more practical' than art.[27] But Socratism too, according to Nietzsche, was wrong in that it negatively contrasted the tragic art not just to 'reason' but also to 'what is useful' (GT, 14: I, 92 [68]). Because of his concern to 'defend his actions with reasons and counter-reasons', the hero in Euripidean tragedy seemed to become unhappy merely as a result of 'errors of calculation'; the result was not 'sympathy' but an involuntary 'comic' effect, and the way was thus opened to 'the newer comedy with its continuous triumph of guile and cunning' (ST, I, 547). According to Wagner, even the best exponents of Jewish music failed to 'produce in us the profound effect that grips the heart and soul', and this could not be otherwise, given its intrinsic 'characteristic of coldness, indifference, and even triviality and ridiculousness'.[28]

Irredeemably marked by their intellectualism and lacking an organic relationship with the language, culture, sufferings and joys and fate of the country in which they lived, Jews were forced to express themselves in an 'aping language' and could only produce an imitative music, like 'parrots'. *The Birth of Tragedy* seemed to contrast these 'stupid birds', as Wagner called them,[29] to 'the Dionysiac bird', which showed the German people the way back to itself and to the reconquest of tragedy and of the tragic worldview (GT, 23; I, 149 [111]).

It is well known that Meyerbeer was, even more so than Mendelssohn, the chief target of Wagner's polemic. The second lecture, *On the Future of Our Educational Institutions*, referred explicitly to him. It described him as an expression of that 'cosmopolitan aggregate' (heavily influenced by the 'fundamentally and thoroughly un-German civilisation of France', and strongly represented in the 'press') of which the country, triumphantly emerged from war, had to rid itself once and for all (BA, 2, I, 690 [66]). On the other hand, Meyerbeer was not explicitly mentioned in *The Birth of Tragedy*. Yet the German composer of Jewish origin or the disciple of Rossini, who made use of an Italian librettist, was infected, in Heine's judgement, by 'Italian sensuality' and gaiety,[30] and celebrated his triumphs in the Paris that emerged from the July Revolution. In this sense, Meyerbeer was clearly also a target of the denunciation in *The Birth of Tragedy* of Latin operas, optimistic and inherently subversive.

To understand this, let us return to Wagner's attack: 'The Jew speaks the language of the nation among which he lives from generation to generation, but he speaks it as a foreigner'; even if his 'speech' was clear, his artistic inability

27   Wagner 1910b, p. 72 f.
28   Wagner 1910b, p. 79.
29   Wagner 1910b, p. 75.
30   Heine 1969–78, Vol. 3, p. 338.

was disastrously manifested in 'song', this 'speech excited by extreme passion'.[31] For Nietzsche, similarly, those who 'do not have music as their mother-tongue' were irredeemably excluded from an understanding of tragedy. Only those who 'have a direct affinity with music, who were born of its womb, so to speak, and who relate to things almost exclusively via unconscious [*unbewusst*] musical relationships', had access to the tragic myth (GT, 21, I, 135 [100]). Not so Jewish musicians, who – as we saw in Wagner – did not and could not have a 'spontaneous', 'unconscious', organic relationship with the people among whom they dwelled. Lacking true communion with the 'object',[32] they were interested only in 'how', in the outer form, and not in the content, that which was 'specific, necessary and real'.[33] But one could not produce art and aesthetic emotion if one remained locked in the cage of intellectualistic formalism.

To finish off Meyerbeer for once and for all, Wagner did not hesitate to draft in Heine, himself a Jew, yet still, according to Wagner, forced to recognise the artistic worthlessness of his 'famous musical colleagues of the same stock [*Stammgenossen*]'.[34] Heine's critical assessment of a certain musician (of Jewish origin) was read by the German composer as an involuntary admission and confirmation of the inability of Judaism as such to produce true music. Nietzsche did more or less the same. It was Heine who drew attention to the 'political significance' of Meyerbeer's operas:[35] in the France that emerged from the July Revolution, the enthusiasm for the definitive driving out of the Bourbons explained the extraordinary success of a musician who 'glows for the most sacred interests of humanity and forthrightly confesses his worship of heroes of the revolution'.[36] *The Birth of Tragedy* insisted, as we know, on the complicity of opera, modern subversion and Socratism (Judaism). It was more the 'longing for serenity [*Heiterkeit*]' than 'serenity' itself (Heine wryly observed) that most profoundly infused Meyerbeer's opera.[37] This was a key word in Wagner's polemic and especially in Nietzsche's, for whom 'serenity', 'optimism', and detachment from the tragic vision of life deeply marked Judaism and the development of the revolution. The cult of serenity, continued Heine, was the foundation of the 'supremacy of harmony' that characterised Meyerbeer's music,[38]

---

31   Wagner 1910b, pp. 70, 72.
32   Wagner 1910b, p. 78.
33   Wagner 1910b, p. 74.
34   Wagner 1910b, p. 85.
35   Heine 1969–78, Vol. 3, p. 150.
36   Heine 1969–78, Vol. 3, p. 341.
37   Heine 1969–78, Vol. 3, p. 343.
38   Heine 1969–78, Vol. 3, p. 335.

for its heroes 'become angry in harmony, exult in harmony, sob in harmony'.[39] The obvious contrast was with the 'joyful feeling of dissonance' in Dionysian music (and Wagner), the 'pleasurable sensation of dissonance in music' and the 'disharmonious' in the sense *The Birth of Tragedy* spoke of it (GT, 24, I, 152 [113–14]). From Wagner and Nietzsche's point of view, there could no longer be any doubt: the Jewish composer and Judaism as such pointed to hated civilisation and modernity.

4   Dionysian Germany and the 'Treacherous Dwarfs'

Wagner insisted that Judaism formed an 'essence [*Wesen*]' alien to Germany,[40] so it was easy to understand the German people's 'spontaneous' and 'instinctive repugnance',[41] its 'deepest revulsion at the Jewish essence'.[42] *The Birth of Tragedy* also repeatedly called on Germany to rediscover its true essence and free itself from an intrusive and noxious presence, and thus to end the long, 'painful' period 'when the German genius lived in the service of treacherous dwarfs [*tückische Zwerge*], estranged from hearth and home' (GT, 24; I, 154 [115]). Nietzsche would later return to his youthful work and write that 'its nuance is that it is German-anti-Christian'. To confirm this, he explained the passage quoted as an allusion to 'the priests'. So, according to this retrospective reading, the object of the denunciation was the 'transplanting into the German heart of a profoundly anti-German myth, the Christian one', which represented 'actual *German destiny*' (XIII, 227). This thesis was repeated in *Ecce Homo* (*The Birth of Tragedy*, 1). Are such statements credible, or was Nietzsche deceiving the reader (or, more properly, himself)?

    This self-interpretation is scarcely convincing, because the denunciation of the 'treacherous dwarfs' so alien to the true Germany did not prevent him in *The Birth of Tragedy* from citing Luther, the German chorales and Bach as fundamental moments in the emergence of the German people's tragic 'essence'. A contemporary text celebrated the 'wonderful and stirring times of the Reformation' (BA, 4, I, 730 [114]). Protestantism was interpreted and celebrated as a moment in the recovery of German identity: it was a matter of reappropriating 'the inner heart of the German Reformation, German music, and German philosophy' (BA, 3, I, 710 [89]). Around 1872, the later frontal struggle against

---

Christianity had not yet delineated itself. In the texts, the notebooks, and the correspondence of this period a number of distinctions were asserted: one thinks of the highly positive judgement on 'early Christianity' or the Gospel of John (*supra*, 1 §10 and 2).

The self-interpretation would still not compel even if 'priests' meant only the Catholic clergy and if the expression 'German-anti-Christian' were replaced by 'German-anti-Catholic'. The notebooks of these years recognised the work of the Jesuits, credited with having promoted 'ambition and competition in education' (VII, 394). On the other hand, if the 'treacherous dwarfs' referred only to the Catholic Church, it would be hard to understand the emphatic call on Germany, the whole of Germany, not only those parts of it with a strong Catholic presence, to rid itself of a foreign presence that threatened the culture of the German people as such.

Moreover, Christianity as a whole appeared for Nietzsche in these years to be something far more profound and metaphysical (in the positive sense the term then had) than the philistine and banausic modernity of Strauss and other authors, engaged in spreading the secular and scientific view of life. Finally, one should not forget the mistrust and hostility with which the philosopher regarded the *Kulturkampf*, which after all had directed a fierce polemic against Rome and the 'priests' (*infra*, 7 §2).

If there is still any doubt as to whether the malignant allusion in *The Birth of Tragedy* was aimed at the Jews, another passage must finally dispel it: once awakened, authentic Germany would 'slay dragons, destroy the treacherous dwarfs, and awaken Brünhilde – and not even Wotan's spear itself will be able to bar its path' (GT, 24, I, 154 [115]). It is easy to see through the reference to Alberich, Mime, and Hagen and to the Wagnerian rabble of dwarfs that in the *Nibelungenring* symbolised the pernicious merchant spirit attributed to Judaism. All three belonged, in Wagner's tetralogy, to a 'type [*Art*]' that was not the 'type' of Siegfried,[43] the fearless hero that symbolised Germany. These 'dwarfs' were motivated only by 'greed'[44] and interested only in wealth and power. They were stateless, without ties to the 'homeland' and the 'mother's womb',[45] they thought, acted, even laughed 'treacherously [*tückisch*]',[46] like the 'treacherous dwarfs' of *The Birth of Tragedy*. Apart from the adjective *tückisch*, Wagner employed a number of other synonyms: the repulsive 'false dwarf',[47] 'treach-

---

43   Siegfried, 1315 and 1779.
44   Rheingold, 1038.
45   Siegfried, 602–5.
46   Siegfried, 1181–2.
47   Siegried, 2190.

erous [*treulos*]', 'hypocritical',[48] 'obstinate and cold',[49] 'sly' and 'mischievous',[50] who relied on 'cunning', even 'tenacious cunning', to surround and strike at his enemies,[51] the 'foul dwarf',[52] the 'bad dwarf'.[53]

Against this figure, inscribed and stamped with all the stereotypes of Judeophobia, was set that of Siegfried. The 'light-eyed boy' represented the best of the Germanic:[54] a hero who fearlessly confronted and killed the dragon, and who, according to *The Birth of Tragedy*, loved nature and the 'fresh forest'[55] and expressed a vision of the world that, with Nietzsche, we could call tragic and Dionysian: 'Blithe in body / I sing of love / blessed in torment / I weave my song / only those who long can grasp its sense.' Both Siegfried and Brünhilde stress: 'One and all / shining love / laughing death.'[56] Only the followers of a banally optimistic view of life could pursue an ideal of 'serenity' that sought to separate joy from pain and from the negativity of existence. The Germanism/Judaism antithesis of the *Nibelungenring* was configured in *The Birth of Tragedy* as the antithesis of (Jewish) Socratism and the Dionysian and tragic spirit, which Germany was to find a way of inheriting from pre-Socratic Greece. Just as Wagner in his tetralogy sang of the desired end of the Jewish contamination that Germany had suffered in its own Olympus (starting with Wotan),[57] so Nietzsche hoped that the country that had emerged victorious from the war would rediscover its Dionysian essence and rid itself of all foreign elements.

Even the details are revealing. The 'German spirit' Nietzsche summoned to destroy the 'treacherous dwarfs' reminds one of Siegfried, who destroyed the treacherous (Jewish) dwarf Mime with his sword; and Siegfried's description of Mime's repulsive features[58] calls to mind Nietzsche's description of Socrates. Finally: after thundering against the 'treacherous dwarfs', *The Birth of Tragedy* throws the reader a look of understanding: 'You understand the word.' It is the conclusion of the section, and it immediately brings to mind the conclusion of *Socrates and Tragedy*, the original version of which reads: 'This Socratism is the Jewish press: I say not a word more.'

---

48   Siegfried, 1733 and 1735.
49   Götterdämmerung, 511.
50   Siegfried, 637.
51   Siegfried, 1390 and 1871.
52   Siegfried, 1909.
53   Siegfried, 1927 and Götterdämmerung, 1769.
54   Siegfried, 1578.
55   Siegfried, 1449.
56   Siegfried, 1944–8, 2736–8 and 2758–60.
57   Rose 1992, p. 68; cf. also Gutman 1971, p. 233.
58   Siegfried, 1459–64.

This is confirmed, finally, by the very interpretation *Ecce Homo* provided of *The Birth of Tragedy*. It was credited with having resisted Socrates's charm and 'any moral idiosyncrasy' and, instead, with having recognised 'aesthetic values' as the 'only values', denied *en bloc* by Christianity (EH, *The Birth of Tragedy*, 1 and 2 [107–8]). Indifference to aesthetic values was, of course, also attributed by the young Nietzsche, under Wagner's influence, to Judaism. If, in the early Basel years, Socrates was Jewish or 'Judaized [*verjüdelt*]', because he profaned and destroyed the enchanted world of Greek tragedy and art with his moralism, later the Jews as such represented the moral people in the purest sense of the word (*infra*, 15 §2).

On another occasion, instead of 'treacherous dwarfs', *The Birth of Tragedy* spoke of the 'German spirit' as 'tyrannized for too long by forms introduced from outside by a vast invading force' that dominated and perverted it, a spirit Nietzsche once again called upon to 'return to itself, a blissful reunion with its own being'. In this case, the foreign element from which it was to rid itself is 'Latin civilization' (GT, 19; I, 128–9 [94–5]). There can be no doubt that the immediate reference was to France, resoundingly defeated by Dionysian Germany, or a Germany that was about to regain its Dionysian essence. But one should not lose sight of the fact that the land of enlightenment, optimism and civilisation referred to 'Judea'. This was true not only of Wagner, who declared at the end of his polemic against 'Judaism in Music' that Judaism was the concentrated expression of odious 'modern civilization'.[59] Particularly significant was Wagner's description, a year before his death, of the German musician Renan, whose pervasive 'optimism' showed him to be a Jew; on the other hand, he was marked by the 'elegance and narrow-mindedness' typical of the French, a worldview that looked only to the comforts and spectacular aspects of worldly existence.[60] We have already mentioned Nietzsche's denunciation of 'French-Jewish "elegance"' and of the assimilation, on the part of Malwida von Meysenbug, of French and Jews, on the grounds of the 'colossal optimism' common to both. A provisional index of *The Birth of Tragedy* explicitly ranged 'Judaism' alongside 'France' (VII, 104). Not only civilisation but optimism united these two terms. Already in Schopenhauer's analysis, optimism referred to the land of endless revolutionary upheavals, all inspired by the insane determination to create institutions that ensured the earthly happiness of all, and thus to give concrete form to the ideal that lay at the heart of Judaism.[61] Treitschke

---

59   Wagner 1910b, p. 85.
60   C. Wagner 1976–82, Vol. 2, p. 879.
61   Schopenhauer 1876–82c, Vol. 4, p. 236.

denounced 'French-Jewish radicalism' in similar terms.[62] In a culture committed to celebrating Germanness as opposed to civilisation and revolution,
French and Jews tended to be equated, also in Nietzsche.

Insofar as the 'treacherous dwarfs' had anything in common with Christianity, they could be synonymous with what Schopenhauer denounced as
Judaised Christianity, or with what Wagner later described as 'the Semitic-Latin
church'.[63] Clearly, the young Nietzsche put a positive valuation on the Gospel
of John, in which Christianity tended to detach itself from its Jewish origins in
order to draw closer to Greece.

If, in France, it had associated itself intimately with the national and popular
culture and was practically one with it, the Judaism synonymous with civilisation remained, fortunately, a largely alien body in Germany. So only there could
the desired tragic and Dionysian regeneration find its starting-point:

> One would be bound to despair of our German character, too, if it had
> already become so inextricably entangled in its culture, indeed entirely
> at one with it, as is horrifyingly evident in the case of civilized France;
> the very thing which was France's great advantage for a long time, and
> the cause of its vast superiority, namely the identity of people and cul-
> ture, should now, as we contemplate the consequences, make us thank
> our good fortune that this questionable culture of ours still has nothing
> in common with the noble core of our national character.

Despite its influence on music, cultural life in general and the press in particular, Jewish intellectuality continued to be profoundly alien to the German
people, since it had not yet been able to attack its 'magnificent, inwardly sound,
ancient power', 'which indeed powerfully moves only in extraordinary times,
then return to dream waiting for a future revival' (GT, 23, I, 146–7 [109]).

5   Alexandrianism, Judaism and the 'Jewish-Roman' World

On closer inspection, the link between Judaism and the Roman world was an
old phenomenon. It coincided with the crisis of authentic Hellenism, overwhelmed on the one hand by the spread of Judaism and on the other by the
invasion of the Roman army and Roman power. For Nietzsche, there could be

---

62   Treitschke 1981, Vol. 4, p. 486.
63   Wagner 1910r, p. 280.

no doubt: the end of tragic Hellenism was the 'victory of the Jewish world over the weakened will of Greek culture', and 'Judea' referred ultimately to 'Roman-universal Hellenism' and 'Alexandrianism' (VII, 80–1). That is why the 'Alexandrian' Ritschl moved, in the eyes of the author of *The Birth of Tragedy*, within the ambit of a 'Jewish-Roman' vision.

The historical context to which Nietzsche referred can be explained by a great contemporary historian's reconstruction of Judaism's encounter with Hellenism: according to Arnold Toynbee, this 'was the most portentous single event in Hellenistic history'. Once Rome conquered Greece, the penetration of Greek culture into Rome proved irresistible. But this Hellas that, in the West, was 'conquering' at the cultural level was forced in the East to come to terms 'with an unbending Judea by adopting a Hellenized version of Judaea's fantastical religion'. Thus took place '[t]he stormy meeting and eventual mating of Hellenism with Judaism'.[64] This paved the way for the spread in the Greco-Roman world of the most varied Jewish and oriental sects, and for the advent of Christianity. The event described here was dated by Toynbee to the second century BC, but Nietzsche tended to date it further back, and to identify in Socrates the start of the 'decadence' that had resulted in the advent of Hellenistic or 'Jewish-Roman' society.

This tendency can also be observed in other authors of the time. Published in the same year as *The Birth of Tragedy*, Strauss's *The Old and the New Faith* spoke of the 'Jewish-Alexandrian philosophy of religion' (although he put a very different value on it), and linked Socrates and Plato with the 'Jews' of 'the final books of the Old Testament'. In both cases, we saw a belief in 'rewards and punishments in the future world'.[65] In the words of Burckhardt, whom Nietzsche followed closely at the time: it was the moment at which the Greeks and Romans, unable to renew their religion and culture, 'end up *ad hoc* relying on Jews (Christians)'.[66] This thesis must have made a strong impression on the young professor in Basel, as is clear from a letter to him from Cosima Wagner: 'I remember that J. Burckhardt told you that Plato took a lot from the Jews' (B, II, 6/1, 16). Therein lay the catastrophe of Alexandrianism. Nietzsche emphasised that Jewish culture, along with Egyptian and Indian culture, had exerted a very early influence on Hellenic philosophy, even if that did not mean that 'in Greece philosophy was simply imported' (PHG, 1, I, 806).

But, with Alexandrianism, there occurred a qualitative leap and a new and radically negative situation. The fourth *Unfashionable Observation* referred crit-

---

64   Toynbee 1959, p. 177 f.
65   Strauss 1872, pp. 41, 125.
66   Burckhardt 1978a, p. 32.

ically to it. If Alexander the Great had produced 'the Hellenization of the world, and to make this possible, the orientalization of Hellenism', a counter-movement now loomed on the horizon: 'The earth, which up to this point was sufficiently Orientalized, now yearns once more for Hellenization'. It is as though 'the pendulum of history is once again swinging back'; but it was not a matter of stopping, in the course of this counter-movement, at the 'Greek-Alexandrian world'. One had to proceed to the recovery of authentic Hellenism: to that end, there was now a need for 'a series of counter-Alexanders'. Nietzsche concluded: 'I recognize in Wagner such a counter-Alexander' (WB, 4, I, 446–7 [274]). It is significant that the turning point in the historical process of overcoming Alexandrianism and civilisation was individuated in the author engaged in the struggle against 'Judaism in Music' and the pseudo-culture of modernity. On closer inspection, the 'orientalization of Hellenism' and the world was in fact their calamitous Judaisation.

We are in the year 1876. In May, Nietzsche received a letter denouncing the 'Jewish vermin with their hooked noses' as a 'race hostile to culture' (B, II, 6, 1, 334). The sender was the conductor Carl Fuchs, who remained on good terms with the philosopher until the end and who, by expressing himself in this way, believed himself to be consonant with him. So, at least until 1876, Nietzsche was at ease in an environment saturated with anti-Jewish poison. The fourth *Unfashionable Observation* denounced a disturbing fact: those 'who traffic in money' (a branch of the economy that, as we shall see immediately, had fallen into 'particular hands') had become 'the dominant power in the soul of modern humanity, the group most coveted' (WB, 6, I, 462 [287]). Art and theatre were now subject to the 'brutal greed for profit on the part of owners' (WB, 4, I, 448 [275]). This was the explanation for Meyerbeer's 'great victories', achieved by an 'extensive, artificially spun web of influences of every sort', which was how to 'become a master in this field' (WB, 8, I, 474 [298]). On the opposite side, Wagner, committed to defending the purity of the German language and of an authentically popular and national art, suffered the 'hostility and malice [*Tücke*]' – we are back with the 'treacherous dwarfs' – of circles 'furiously opposed' to the great Bayreuth initiative, which they rightly saw as 'one of their most profound defeats' (WB, 4, I, 450 [277]).

Cosima's invitation to caution and self-censorship perhaps suggest that it is necessary for us to read the texts that precede the 'enlightenment' turning point against this background. When, in the Basel lectures, we encounter the assertion that '[i]n the newspaper the peculiar educational aims of the present culminate' and the vulgarity of modernity was expressed with particular clarity (BA, 1, I, 671 [41]), we must remember that, for Nietzsche in these years, as for Wagner, journalism was ultimately synonymous with Judaism. 'Genius'

was contrasted with the empty intellectuality of modern civilisation, but this
genius could only unfold when it 'has been brought up and come to maturity in
the tender care of the culture of a people'. '[W]ithout this sheltering home, the
genius will not, generally speaking, be able to rise to the height of his eternal
flight', according to the lecture *On the Future of Our Educational Institutions* (BA,
3, I, 700 [76]). Again, we are led back to a by now familiar polemical theme:
stateless and always forced to speak in an acquired tongue, the Jew was incapable, according to Wagner, of true genius and artistic creativity: one could not
'really write poetry in a foreign language'.[67]

Apart from the lack of a mother tongue, it was intellectualism that irredeemably held Jews back from true artistic creation and genius in general. Wagner
was a relentless critic of the 'dialectical Jews' jargon' and of the artificial, even
if 'elegant', dialectic to which the musician's Jewish enemies resorted (*infra*,
6 §2). Nietzsche, for his part, not only repeatedly denounced the role of the
dialectic ('an element peculiar to Socratism') and the 'superfetation of logic'
in the destruction of tragedy (ST, I, 545–6; VII, 12–13), but linked the dialectic
with the 'Socratism of our time' and the 'press'. Moreover, 'the dialectic is the
press' (VII, 13), and the press was, of course, Judaism. Nor should we forget
that the dialectic was synonymous with 'optimism' (GT, 14: I, 94–5 [69–70]) or
with the 'insatiable greed [*Gier*] of optimistic knowledge' (GT, 15, I, 102 [75]).
As if intellectualism and optimism were not enough, we now have 'greed' and
'insatiability'. Once again, we are led back to Judaism or, more accurately, to
anti-Jewish stereotypes.

We can now better understand the analysis developed by *The Birth of
Tragedy* and the notes that preceded and prepared the way for it. The Dionysian
element intervened in tragic Hellas 'lest this Apolline tendency should cause
form to freeze into Egyptian stiffness and coldness' (9, I, 70 [51]), and only in this
way could authentic Hellenism stave off 'Egyptianizing Hellenism' (VII, 46). We
could not but relate this category to statements of following years that spoke of
the 'refined Egyptianism' of the Jews (M, 72 [53]) or of the 'Jews corrupted by
Egyptian captivity' (X, 242). On the other hand, Socrates and Plato were infected by 'Egyptianism', for they were ultimately Jews (*infra*, 15 §2). 'Egyptianizing
Hellenism' was the Judaising Hellenism that finally triumphed with Socrates:
the dialectic and the 'superfetation of logic' killed tragedy and art.

In these years, Wagner and Schopenhauer were the two authors Nietzsche
followed. From Schopenhauer he took his 'hatred of the Jews' (FW, 99 [97]), as
he later mentioned in the *Gay Science*. In these circumstances, it is not surpris-

67   Wagner 1910b, p. 71.

ing that the early work negatively compared the Semitic version of original sin with the Aryan. This was not an isolated impulse. When we read that 'the festive procession of Dionysos [leads] from India to Greece' (GT, 20, I, 132 [98]) and the return of Germany to its essence and its Dionysian vocation was the return to the 'mythical home [*mythische Heimat*]' (GT, 24, I, 154 [115]), we tend to think of another author who exerted an overwhelming influence on Nietzsche in those years. When Schopenhauer praised the 'peoples of the Japhetic language family', the descendants of the mythical Japhet mentioned in the Bible, he called on them to remember their roots, which could be traced back to India. That had to be the starting point, as the discovery of Sanskrit showed, for a 'better understanding of Greek and Latin', the heritage and pride of the West. Germany and the West were, also on a cultural and religious level, to exploit this rediscovered linguistic unity and head back towards the 'sacred religions of the homeland [*Heimat*]', to the 'original religion of the homeland [*heimatliche Urreligion*]'.[68] This would bring to an end the disastrous interlude of a 'Judaized West',[69] or, to quote Wagner and the young Nietzsche, of a Germany polluted by 'treacherous dwarfs' wholly alien to it.

Immediately after the publication of *The Birth of Tragedy*, Rohde was worried: the book could hardly hope to achieve success in the 'synagogue gathering' of the literary reviews; or even in the 'Alexandrian gathering' of the 'specialist philological magazines' (B, II, 2, 502). The immediate allusion was to Alexandrian culture, but one should not forget that this, in turn, referred to the influence of Judaism in the Hellenistic period and, in particular, in the ancient Egyptian city. Significantly, a few years later, during the dispute on anti-Semitism, Mommsen would undertake to defend 'Jewish-Alexandrian literature' against Treitschke's attacks.[70]

6   On the Threshold of a Conspiracy Theory

We have seen how, after Tribschen's urging of caution in regard to the 'Jewish press', Nietzsche said he would wait for the right moment to express himself freely. In at least one of the *Prefaces*, not intended for the public and, not by accident, dedicated to Cosima Wagner, the path of self-censorship seems to have been basically abandoned. *The Greek State* linked the phenomena of the

---

68   Schopenhauer 1976–82c, Vol. 4, p. 236; Schopenhauer 1976–82c, Vol. 5, pp. 503, 347, 269; Schopenhauer 1976–82d, p. 638.
69   Schopenhauer 1976–82c, Vol. 5, p. 263.
70   Mommsen 1965, p. 214.

decadence of the modern world with the agitation and manoeuvres of particular people, who as a result of their 'birth' stood outside the nation. This clearly referred to the Jews: intent upon material enjoyment and the accumulation of wealth, they aimed primarily at achieving 'security' and wished, within each community and internationally, for a political organisation that conformed with their ideal and their supreme interest. So they wished to avoid danger and war, in order to build a world consonant with their banausic and mercantile nature (CV, 3, I, 772–3 [170]).

Let us dwell for a moment on this indictment. These were the years in which feelings of horror about the Paris Commune merged with the denunciation of internationalism and the ideal of perpetual peace. The revolutionary government in Paris had 'decided that the Victory Column on the Place Vendôme, which had been cast from captured guns by Napoleon after the war of 1809, should be demolished as a symbol of chauvinism and incitement to national hatred'.[71] Perhaps *The Greek State* was referring to this when it denounced the illusions and vulgarity of those (the demolishers) who aspired to 'make a successful attack on them, and therefore war in general, extremely unlikely' (CV, 3, I, 773 [171]).

Even before 1871, the International, through Marx, had called for a struggle for a 'new society ... whose international rule will be peace, because its national ruler will be everywhere the same – Labour'.[72] A whole series of conferences had been held on this theme. One had taken place in 1869 in Basel, where Nietzsche had arrived a few months earlier, and another in Lausanne in 1867.[73] These initiatives were apparently very successful. Strauss referred ironically to the 'famous Lausanne Peace Congress',[74] and he also polemicised against the Commune, the International and the ideal of perpetual peace. To want to abolish war was no less quixotic than to fight for the 'abolition of thunderstorms': 'Just as electricity will always accumulate in clouds, so too from time to time war material will accumulate in peoples.'[75] This statement was in a text Nietzsche would later polemicise against. But, on this point, the two authors were as one. The 'dreadful clouds of war of peoples', the 'thunder and flashes of lightning', were also (according to *The Greek State*) the precondition for society to 'germinate and turn green everywhere, so that it can let the radiant blossoms of genius sprout forth as soon as warmer days come' (CV, 3; I, 772 [170]).

---

71   Marx and Engels 1975 ff., 27, pp. 184–5.
72   Marx and Engels 1975 ff., 23, p. 221. Cf. Sautet 1981, pp. 77–93.
73   Montinari 1999, p. 54.
74   Strauss 1872, p. 260.
75   Strauss 1872, p. 259.

According to Strauss, perpetual peace was only a synonym for vulgar and alarming spiritual decadence:

> What on the other hand do today's preachers of the fraternization of peoples want? They want, above all, an equalization [Ausgleichung] of the material conditions of human existence, of the means for life and enjoyment; the spiritual element is a lesser matter and should serve primarily to procure those means of enjoyment.[76]

In this sense, according to Nietzsche, 'the egoism of the masses or their representatives' (CV, 3, I, 773 [171]) nurtured a horror of war. Strauss argued similarly. He launched a fierce attack on the workers' International: it wants 'the big nation states' to 'dissolve into heaps of small allied social democracies', 'among which the diversity of language and nationality would no longer be a barrier, a cause of conflict.'[77] But despite the noble feelings that the supposed 'cosmopolite' put on display, he was in truth a vulgar 'egoist': so the international socialist and labour movement was not only politically dangerous and subversive but it is also devoid of all moral dignity.[78] On this point too, he and Nietzsche thought alike. These were the years in which, as Marx noted, the dominant ideology, rendered anxious and fearful by the International, declared it 'the great problem of all civilized governments to weed it out'.[79]

At a certain point, however, their paths began to diverge. Together with the 'red' International, Strauss also took aim at the 'black' of the Catholic Church and the Jesuits. Nietzsche did not join in this polemic. He was sceptical of or hostile to from the very beginning the Kulturkampf and Bismarck's policy of favouring republican trends in France, designed to increase the defeated country's international isolation (infra, 7 § 2). As is clear from the positive reference to the 'monarchical instincts of the people', Nietzsche must at the time have viewed with sympathy the prospect of a Bourbonic restoration, which seemed to be looming on the other side of the Rhine in the immediate aftermath of the war and the defeat.

But that is not the most important difference. In The Greek State, the egoistic and banausic cosmopolitan, with his vulgarly hedonistic and mercantile view of life, acquired an ethno-religious connotation and thus tended to take on the

---

76   Strauss 1872, p. 264.
77   Strauss 1872, p, 262.
78   Strauss 1872, pp. 262–5.
79   Marx and Engels 1975 ff., 22, p. 354.

features of the Jew. According to Nietzsche, a quite specific circle of people with special characteristics wanted to banish war and its associated tragic vision of life:

> I cannot help seeing those truly international, homeless, financial recluses as really those whose fear stands behind these movements, who, with their natural lack of state instinct, have learnt to misuse politics as an instrument of the stock exchange, and state and society as an apparatus for their own enrichment.
>
> CV, 3, I, 774 [171]

The 'red' International of which Strauss spoke seemed in the Nietzsche of these years to have become a Jewish International, synonymous with an uprooted and stateless finance committed to avoiding tensions and clashes among the various European powers. What interest could such an 'International', which by definition ignored state and national frontiers, have in conflict? With a play on words and in reference to a theme commonplace in the culture and journalism of the time, Wagner had noted that 'the creditor of kings' had conquered not only economic but also political power, and become the 'king of creditors', supplanting the various national monarchies and unifying them under a supranational Jewish sceptre, so that now the Christians of the various countries had to fight for their 'emancipation from the Jews'.[80] A foremost researcher of anti-Semitism has noted that 'the Rothschilds did everything to avoid unnecessary bloodshed and slayings' and that 'peace was the bank's great slogan'. But not everyone was happy with the 'peace of the Rothschilds or *pax judaica*'. Certainly not an angry anti-Semite by the name of Toussenel, who warned as follows: 'And let us not thank the Jew for the peace he bestows on us. If he had an interest in war, there would be war.'[81]

According to Nietzsche, for this cosmopolitan finance, intimately linked with the centres of power in the various countries, abhorrence of war was functional to the smooth running of their businesses. The Jews saw in the state a mere 'tool'. In this way, they had a clear advantage over other citizens, who were far more inhibited in their behaviour because of their distance from this unscrupulous and instrumental view. The result was obvious: given the premise, 'it is practically inevitable that such men [the Jews] should win great influence over the state', which compounded their preponderance in the eco-

---

80   Wagner 1910b, p. 68.
81   Poliakov 1968, p. 356f.

nomy (CV, 3, I, 772–4 [170]). This was not only to be explained by the influence of Wagner and his denunciation of the 'usury' that allowed Jews to engage in unscrupulously accumulating money.[82] Other readings also had an influence. For example, in a note written in the summer or autumn of 1873 we read: 'The path along which the blindness of recent generations is driving us is one at whose conclusion, in the true words of Herr von Stein, "the Jews will be the ruling class, the farmer a rogue, and the craftsman a bungler: where everything will have disintegrated and only the sword will rule"' (VII, 673 [237]). So, it was time for a remedy.

Nietzsche was clearly polemicising against the granting of political rights, sanctioned by the Reich in 1871. Decades earlier, Schopenhauer had compared the Jews, members of 'an alien oriental people', with 'resident aliens' and argued that they should be accorded 'civil rights [*bürgerliche Rechte*]', like all foreigners, but definitely not 'political rights [*Staatsrechte*]'.[83] The young Nietzsche seemed to be moving in the same direction when, after having denounced the Jewish press, he took aim at Jewish finance, another classic *topos* of anti-Jewish journalism. A few years later, again in the course of the anti-Semitic polemic, Treitschke indicted not only the 'homeless international journalists' but 'the cosmopolitan financial powers' of the Jewish world.[84] *The Greek State*, after arguing that the Jews were alien to the German nation and had won enormous power, denounced the 'fact that the modern money economy has fallen into strange hands' and was controlled by 'a self-seeking, stateless money aristocracy'. The consequences were catastrophic at all levels: 'I view all social evils, including the inevitable decline of the arts, as either sprouting from that root or enmeshed with it' (CV, 3, I, 774 [171]). The first part of this declaration calls to mind a theme commonplace in anti-Semitic publications of the time, which tended to equate the social question with the Jewish question, i.e., to interpret it as the result of the greed and economic dominance attributed to the Jews (*infra*, 18 §7). When Nietzsche went on to refer to the decline of art, it is obvious that he was directly under the influence of Wagner, who lamented the 'complete victory of Judaism at all levels'.[85]

Sometimes, however, Nietzsche seemed to go even further. 'The widest dissemination of the liberal-optimistic world view' and 'revolutionary ideas' were not unconnected with the influence and machinations of the Jews. The individuals mentioned above were said to be actively engaged in slowly dissolving

---

82   Wagner 1910b, p. 73.
83   Schopenhauer 1976–82c, Vol. 5, p. 312.
84   Treitschke 1965c, p. 79.
85   Wagner 1910e, p. 257.

'the monarchical instincts of the people', in order to 'wrest the decision over war and peace away from the individual rulers' and even to wrest political power as such to themselves (CV, 3, I, 773–4 [171]). We are on the threshold of a conspiracy theory. This threshold was perhaps crossed by the draft version of *The Greek State*, which denounced the 'utilization' and 'the conscious dissemination of revolutionary ideas' by a wicked financial aristocracy acting in the shadows (KGA, III, 5/2, 1068). These were the years in which Wagner blamed 'agitators of non-German stock' for the democratic and revolutionary movement in Germany,[86] while Dühring made fun of the 'Marxist tribe of Jewified Social Democrats'[87] and said that even Lassalle had not overcome 'the innate habits and inclinations of his race'.[88] The young Nietzsche, familiar with conspiracy theory through his readings on the French Revolution (*infra*, 28, §2), was clearly influenced by this climate.

---

86   Wagner 1910l, p. 50.
87   Dühring 1881a, p. 55.
88   Dühring 1871, p. 559.

CHAPTER 4

The Founding of the Second Reich, and Conflicting Myths of Origin

1   In Search of Hellenism and a *volkstümlich* Germanness

The identification with the Second Reich and with the pathos of Germanness that accompanied its foundation was at this point undeniable. The meaning of the recent war, and of war in general, lay primarily in the reconsolidation of community in the ethical and spiritual sense:

> [I]n the excitement of which at least so much becomes clear, that the state is not founded on fear of the war-demon, as a protective measure for egoistic individuals, but instead produces from within itself an ethical momentum in the love for fatherland and prince, indicating a much loftier designation.
>
> CV, 3, I, 774 [171]

It was not only a case of the resumption of the classic *topos* that saw in war the antidote to the danger of particularistic and individualistic fragmentation. Nietzsche cherished the hope, or illusion, that the rebirth of tragedy and the assertion or reassertion of the Dionysian essence of the German people would make it possible to overcome the lacerations of modernity, in order to rebuild an organic society like the Greek or like the one he believed he could project onto ancient Greece. That is precisely why Wagner was an obligatory point of reference: he recognised that the only artist hitherto was 'the poetizing common people'. Still referring to the great musician, Nietzsche continued:

> Modern art is a luxury; he comprehended this just as thoroughly as he did the corollary that it will stand and fall with the rights of this luxury society. In just the same way as this luxury society knew how to exploit its power in the most hardhearted and clever way in order to render those who are powerless, the common people [*Volk*], ever more subservient, abject, and less populist [*unvolksthümlich*] and to transform them into modern 'workers'.

This laceration was all the deeper because myth and art were taken from the people. Both were degraded to the level of specialised 'modern arts' reserved for luxurious consumption and the pleasure of the few (WB, 8, I, 475 [299–300]), now separated from the community that was to nourish them and for which they were not to be destined, and therefore 'isolated and stunted' (WB, 1, I, 433 [261]).

It is important to explain that the object of celebration had nothing in common with the 'masses', which could only be tolerable or useful insofar as they provided a stimulus or raw material for the creations of higher beings (*supra*, 2 § 5 and below, chap. 6 § 5). The influence of Wagner, also of the opinion that 'the popular element [*das Volkstümliche*] has always been the source from which flow all the arts', is unmistakable. With an eye above all to countries beyond Germany, the musician described the advent of modernity: 'One had no need of the *people* but of the *mass*, the material residue of the people from whom the spirit of life has been sucked.'[1]

Behind Wagner lay an ideology of earlier vintage. If France had not forgotten the memory of its 'folk songs', said Arnim at the beginning of the century, there would perhaps have been no revolution: it had been nurtured by the drying up of traditions, sagas and legends, unanimous artistic expressions that bestowed unity and vitality on the people.[2] Fortunately, the ruinous effects of Enlightenment thinking, which disenchanted the community and tore it apart, were felt less in Germany, where one could therefore hope for a quite different development and future. Starting with the struggle against Thermidorian and Napoleonic expansionism, experienced and transfigured as a unanimous rising against the land of the Enlightenment, revolution and a rapacious campaign of conquest, the hope or myth arose of a German special way or *Sonderweg*, a hope or myth that became all the stronger the more the foreign preponderance and military occupation made felt the need for national unity. These were the years in which Fichte, even if for some time he had hoped that the army of the new France would aid the victory of the revolution in Germany, not only called for the internal and thus secondary contradictions of the nation German to be put aside but attributed their emergence to the spiteful manoeuvres of external foes:

It is true that often, in ancient as well as in modern times, the arts of seduction and moral corruption of the vanquished have been successfully used

---

1   Wagner 1910c, pp. 266, 270.
2   Arnim 1978, p. 701 f.; cf. Losurdo 1997a, 1, § 6.

as a means of domination. With lying fictions, with an artificial confusion of concepts and language, the princes are vilified among the people and vice versa, merely in order to reign more easily over the divisions.[3]

According to Fichte, the princes and the people in Germany had already succeeded during the Reformation, after initial misunderstandings stirred up by external enemies, in joining together in a struggle based on solidarity. It was no coincidence that Protestantism had never triumphed in the Latin countries, and had even been rejected as subversive: 'It seems that only where there is German thoroughness among the rulers and German good-heartedness in the people can this doctrine be in accord with authority.'[4] In a 'people with a living language', culture had spread through all walks of life: among peoples tied to a 'dead' language, culture was a game of the intellect and more or less a fashionable refinement, for in that case 'the educated classes are separated from the people and use them only as a blind tool to carry out their plans.'[5] German intellectuals, because of their eagerness to appear refined, uncritically absorbed or mimicked this culture, and 'want artificially to open the abyss that arose spontaneously abroad between the higher estates and the people'.[6] It was a fact that the culture of the Enlightenment, which had originated on the other side of the Rhine, with a diffusion limited to court circles and intellectual layers and without the backing of a strong middle class, certainly had not become a national and popular culture on German soil, unlike in France; rather, it had the effect of stimulating a cosmopolitanism that was at times superficial and alien to the life and problems of the nation and the people, a cosmopolitanism that was oriented towards the metropolis of an empire that oppressed Germany too.

This explains Fichte's resort to an ideology that, in denouncing the disruption and uprooting caused by the Enlightenment, summoned intellectuals to become an organic part of the people struggling against the army of occupation. 'If we remain German, we do not distance ourselves from the people that understands us and considers us like them; if, on the other hand, we take refuge with the latter [France], the people will not understand us and will see other natures in us.' Under the pressure of the objective situation, which put on the agenda the need to isolate the invaders, the distance between France and Germany was raised to the level of a fact of nature, like the insurmountable

---

3   Fichte 1971, Vol. 7, p. 277.
4   Fichte 1971, Vol. 7, pp. 349, 351.
5   Fichte 1971, Vol. 7, p. 327.
6   Ibid.

difference between the 'artificial and studied' character of the one people and the 'natural and spontaneous' character of the other.[7]

It was at this point, as has been observed, that '*Volk*' acquired a far more pregnant meaning than its equivalent in other languages; it denoted 'a group of people bound by a transcendent 'essence' […], at one with the most secret nature of the human being and the constitutive source of his creativity, of his deepest feelings, of his individuality, of his communion with other members of the *Volk*'.[8]

To lend even greater force and clarity to this view, a new term was introduced, *Volksthum* ('popular community'), whose meaning was explained thus by F.L. Jahn, who used it for the first time:

It was that which

> there is in common in a population, its intimate essence, its feeling and life, its power of regeneration, its ability to reproduce. As a result, there prevails in all the members of the people a common [*volkstümliches*] thought and feeling, love and hate, joy and sorrow, suffering and acting, sacrifice and enjoyment, hope and nostalgia, presentiment and faith. In this way each single member of the people enters into a multiple and many-sided relationship with all the others in a united community, without that member's freedom and autonomy being cancelled – on the contrary, it is precisely on that account further strengthened.[9]

The ideology that was dominant during the struggle against Napoleon I never really fell into oblivion and gained new vitality and relevance as the reconstruction of German national unity gradually advanced. The conditions now existed for the founding of the new Reich on truly *volkstümlich* foundations. Even before the war against Napoleon III, Nietzsche, speaking of Homer's Greece but with his eye constantly on Wagner's Germany, raised a hymn to the 'wonderful capacity of the soul of the people [*Volksseele*]' to 'infuse in the form of the personality the circumstances of custom and faith' (HKP, 255). It was in this context that artistic production belonged: 'The thought of a popular poetry [*Volksdichtung*] has something intoxicating, one senses the broad, powerful unfolding of a popular [*volksthümlich*] character with a sense of artistic well-being' (HKP, 258). Very different and far more miserable was the poetry 'that has not grown

---

7   Ibid.
8   Mosse 1979, p. 10; Mosse 1966, p. 4.
9   In Martini 1963, p. 339.

in the field of popular feeling [*volksthümliche Empfindungen*], but can be traced to a non-popular [*unvolksthümlich*] creator and first sees the light in a non-popular [*unvolksthümlich*] atmosphere, for example in a study by a scholar' (HKP, 261).

After the victory against France, Nietzsche expressed the 'hope of a national culture still to come', marked by 'the authenticity and immediacy of German feeling [*Empfindung*]', the 'unity of national feeling [*Volksempfinden*]', a robust and uncontaminated 'instinct of the people [*Instinct des Volkes*]' (HL, 4, I, 277–8 [114]). It was necessary, and at long last possible, to heal and overcome the lacerations of modernity: 'The more degenerate the Will is, the more everything fragments into individual elements; the more selfish and arbitrary the development of the individual, the weaker is the organism which it serves' (DW, 1, I, 557–8 [123]).

The *Volksthum* or 'popular community' here celebrated had nothing to do with the popular masses: it was even their complete antithesis. It was conceived in opposition not to the elites of wealth and power but to all that was 'alien' to the national soul, beginning with the revolutionary and subversive ideologies imported from abroad that sought to undermine the close unity that had to be so jealously guarded. It was no coincidence that this celebration went hand in hand with the denunciation of those (the socialists)[10] who called for 'the founding of the peaceful sovereignty of the people [*Volksstaat*] upon reason, education, and justice [*Gerechtigkeit*]' (BA, 4, I, 729 [112]). *The Birth of Tragedy* similarly celebrated the 'youthfully fresh, linguistically creative mass of people [*Volksmenge*]' (GT, 6, I, 50 [35]) while waging a polemic against an interpretation of Greek tragedy that saw the choir as a 'constitutional popular assembly [*Volksvertretung*]' (GT, 7, I, 53 [37]).

The Birth of Tragedy translated into 'Dionysiac' language the ideal of an organic community that had emerged in the struggle against the land of Enlightenment and revolution. The new Germany that had overcome the lacerations of modernity was called upon to follow a *Sonderweg*, which would lead it back to ancient Greece: '[E]very period which was rich in the production of folk songs [*Volkslieder*] was agitated by Dionysiac currents, since these are always to be regarded as the precondition of folk song and as the hidden ground from which it springs.' This was true also of Germany, as evidenced by *Des Knaben Wunderhorn* (GT, 6, I, 48 [33–4]), a collection of popular songs and poems published by leading representatives of German romanticism (Brentano, Arnim,

---

10   'Die Sozialdemokratie fordert den Volksstaat', Stöcker 1891a, p. 13.

the Brothers Grimm and Görres), once again in the course of the struggle against the French occupation and for the recovery of Germany's roots, identity, and soul.

This goal continued to be central to the concerns of the young Nietzsche:

> Anyone who wants to aspire to and promote the culture of a people should aspire to and promote this higher unity and work for the destruction of modern cultivatedness [*Gebildetheit*] in favor of a true cultivation. Such a person should dare to reflect on how the health of a people undermined by history can be restored, how it can rediscover its instincts and with them its honesty.
>
> HL, 4, I, 274–5 [111–112]

At the time, Nietzsche viewed Greece as the model of a closely united and fused community. Although marked by a splendid flowering of art and culture, the Renaissance could hardly be said to have aroused much enthusiasm. One fragment from the spring-summer of 1875 denounced it in bitter terms, for its 'terrible' *unvolksthümlich* character, its alienation and separation from the people (VIII, 69). The merit of Wagner's art was that it put aside 'the language of the culture of a caste' and thus overcame 'the distinction between cultivated or uncultivated'. In so doing, he stood out from all those who, 'in the refinement and unfruitfulness of their cultivation [...] are thoroughly unpopulist [*unvolksthümlich*]'. Wagner's art transported us beyond 'the portrayal of the most unpopulist [*unvolksthümlich*] riddle' that was Goethe's *Faust* and took a stance 'in opposition to the entire culture of the Renaissance, which up to now has enveloped us modern human beings in its light and its shadow' (WB, 10, I, 502–3 [324–5]). That was why Wagner's art was of such decisive importance at the political level for the new Germany, after its victory in the Battle of Sedan and its defeat of the country that, more than any other, represented the decadence and fragmentation of modern civilisation.

2   Greeks, Christians, Germans and Indo-Europeans

But this vision of the Second Reich as a Germanic regeneration of original Hellenism had to confront and grapple with other mutually opposing views. The founding of a large nation state and the struggles and movements that preceded and prepared the way for it were typically accompanied by the elaboration of myths of origin designed to underpin its legitimacy, grandeur and even 'mission'. This was not a phenomenon peculiar or unique to Germany, and it would make no historical sense to project the shadow of the Third Reich onto this celebration of Germany's past and future. A similar debate and similar ideological themes arose in Italy in the Risorgimento: Gioberti sought its remote origins among the mythical Pelasgians, while others favoured the ancient Romans and 'Scipio's helmet'. Even the most democratic currents were no stranger to the idea of a 'mission', and called, with Mazzini, for a Third Rome, the Rome of the people, to take the place of the Rome of the popes and emperors. After all, there had never been any lack of people focusing primarily on the Christian-Catholic legacy, who thus spun an ideological theme and myth of origin that clearly contradicted the appeal to the pagan and imperial Rome that persecuted the Christians.

While Catholicism remained on the margins of the Italian Risorgimento, the Protestant churches were much more active in 1813 and in 1870 in the struggle against Napoleon I and Napoleon III. So, the dilemma for Germany was acute: was one to look to Arminius, chieftain of the Germanic Cherusci, or to Luther? Kleist wrote a play about the leader of the resistance to Varus and the Romans, and Fichte also paid him much attention and respect. On the other hand, the struggle against France, dechristianised by the revolution and secularised by urban and industrial development, tended to be overtly religious and Christian in tone: 'The [German] soldier should be a Christian', warned Arndt, who even wrote a catechism for the fighters, in Biblical style.[11]

Even during the confrontation with Napoleon III, the so-called 'German war theology' issued a call to arms against the land of 'Godlessness' and 'immorality' and in defence of 'German uprightness' and 'Christian truthfulness'.[12] Marx commented ironically: 'And thus, at last, came out the true character of the war, ordained by Providence as a chastisement of godless and debauched France by pious and moral Germany!'.[13] Immediately after the founding of the Second Reich, in the same year *The Birth of Tragedy* appeared, Constantin Frantz, a man of high repute, made an impassioned plea to his fellow citizens not to lose or abandon the traditions of the 'pious German nation'.[14] This brings us back to Wagner, who referred to Frantz several times and with great warmth. Cosima would later explicitly praise the 'Christian-Germanic profession of artistic faith' in the music of her famous consort.[15] So here was a first myth of origin, the Christian-Germanic. It found its most complete expression in a

---

11   Cf. Losurdo 1997a, 2, §12.
12   Hammer 1971, pp. 53 and 184.
13   Marx and Engels 1975 ff., 22, p. 353.
14   Frantz 1970, p. 2.
15   In Zelinsky 1983, p. 8.

ballad by Emanuel Geibel, who imagined a German standing guard at the foot of the Cross of Christ on Golgotha.[16]

However, the most exalted Germanomaniacs were unable to identify with this myth. They were passionately committed to reclaiming a pure, authentic Germanness, uncontaminated either by the ideas of the Enlightenment and revolution that accompanied the invading armies of Louis XIV and Napoleon, or by Christianity, also introduced by force of arms, by Charlemagne, or by the Latin culture imposed by the legions of imperial Rome. Such were the characteristics of the purely Germanic myth of origin. This was the context in which we must view Friedrich Schlegel's polemic against those who saw the triumph of Christianity in Germany as a defeat for the 'religion of the fatherland' and who mourned the disappearance of the 'theology of the ancient Germans'.[17]

Mostly, however, the ideology that presided over the wars against France sought to combine the Christian-Germanic and the purely Germanic myths of origin, celebrating Arminius and Luther as protagonists of a national resistance against an eternal and eternally corrupt Rome (and Latinity), which finally took shape in Napoleon I and Napoleon III. Protestant Christianity thus tended to represent a kind of national religion in Germany. One can already find this dialectic in Arndt, who called upon the Christian soldier to lead a 'great and holy German war' in the name of a 'German God',[18] a dialectic that acquired clear contours in an author like Lagarde, who explicitly theorised a 'German religion', a 'national German religion', on more or less Christian foundations.[19]

The Indo-Europeans erupted forcefully into this debate. These were the years in which 'Aryan' mythology began to spread. We saw how Schopenhauer emphasised not only the linguistic but also the cultural unity of the 'Japhetic' or Indo-European race, which excluded Jews (and, occasionally, the Jewish elements of Christianity), while embracing the Greeks and Germans. Thus were laid the foundations of the Aryan-Germanic or Aryan-Greco-Germanic myth of origin.

After a broad reconstruction of the mythological and ideological debate that preceded and accompanied the founding of the Second Reich, we can now examine how Nietzsche was located in it. In his early years in Basel, he sometimes seemed to feel the magic or influence of the Christian-Germanic myth of origin, evident from the references in *The Birth of Tragedy* to the Reformation and Protestant choral music. The lecture *On The Future of Our Educational*

---

16   In Faulhaber 1934, p. 123.
17   Cf. Losurdo 1997a, 1, §7.
18   Cf. Losurdo 1997a, 2, §12.
19   Cf. Losurdo 1997a, 2, §12.

Institutions made it crystal clear: the 'true German spirit [...] speaks to us so
wondrously from the inner heart of the German Reformation, German music,
and German philosophy' (BA, 3, I, 710 [89]).

3   Nietzsche and the Greco-Germanic Myth of Origin

But the magic did not last long, and was from the beginning neutralised by
a twofold criticism of Christianity: the one already noted, which contrasted
it to classical antiquity, and another that involved the Germans. Excited by
the atmosphere of patriotic enthusiasm and chauvinism, the young Nietzsche
too seemed to be searching for a national religion, and looked on Christianity
with suspicion, as a singularly 'unnational religion' (VII, 128). A few years later,
between late 1876 and early 1877, he wrote:

> The Germans, originally of that extraordinary compactness and robust-
> ness that Tacitus, the greatest admirer of their health, describes, were
> not only wounded by the inoculation of Roman culture but almost bled
> dry: customs, religion, freedom, language were stripped from them to the
> greatest extent possible; they did not succumb, but that they are a deeply
> suffering nation they have shown by their soulful relationship to music.
> No people has as many lacerations as the Germans.

It is true that he immediately added that 'for this reason they are better pre-
disposed to any kind of freedom of the spirit' (VIII, 364–5). The fact remains,
however, that even on the eve of *Human, All Too Human*, Nietzsche sometimes
sensed the fascination of the Germany of Tacitus. According to *Mixed Opinions
and Maxims*, the inoculation, now no longer of Roman culture but of Christianity, had been a sort of 'poison' 'for young, fresh barbarian peoples' and had
brought about their 'fundamental weakening'. Yes, 'implanting the doctrine of
sinfulness and damnation into the heroic, childish, bestial soul of the ancient
Germans, for example, means nothing other than poisoning them' (VM, 224
[97]). The introduction of Christianity, a religion radically alien to Germanness,
whose 'monotheism' severely limited the 'poetic explanation of the world', was
a catastrophe:

> Our national gods and our feelings for them have received a changeling:
> we dedicate to it all those feelings. The end of religion arrives when
> one's national gods are made to disappear. This has brought about a ter-
> rible suffering in art. An enormous effort on the part of the German

essence to shake off this foreign and anti-national yoke, and it has succeeded. The breath of India is what remains: because it has affinity with
us.

VII, 99–100

With this last observation, we are back with the Aryan-Germanic myth of origin. That *The Birth of Tragedy* was not insensitive to its fascination is shown
by its author's preference for the Aryan over the Semitic version of original
sin. However, Nietzsche fixed his attention primarily on Hellas and the Greco-
Roman world as a whole. His lecture on Homer in 1869 already made clear
that it was a question of detaching 'so-called "classical" antiquity' (HKP, 249)
from among the 'series of antiquities' and raising it to a prominent position.
The 'ideals of antiquity' that one had to once again know how to actualise
in the struggle against modernity were precisely those of classical antiquity
(HKP, 252), with its 'eternally unrealized models' (HKP, 258). The catastrophe
of the modern world, according to the third *Unfashionable Observation*, resided
precisely in the fact that 'classical antiquity has become one antiquity among
others, and no longer strikes us as either classical or exemplary' (SE, 8, I, 424
[253]).

So, it is not hard to understand the harsh polemic against those who claimed
to have 'found among the honest Indogermans a form of religion purer than
the polytheistic one of the Greeks'. Those who believed in this way to have
attained a more original form forgot one essential fact: 'The way to the beginnings leads everywhere to barbarism.' It was senseless to oppose to the ravages
of the Enlightenment and civilisation peoples who had not yet achieved culture
in the actual sense: one was not to lose sight of the fact that 'hatred of knowledge' barbarised no less than the 'uncontrolled drive for knowledge' (PHG, 1, I,
807). In other words, one could not set against the 'Enlightenment' of Socrates
and Alexandrian-Roman civilisation the crudeness of Arminius. On the other
hand, according to a fragment from the same period, 'Buddhists lack art' (VII,
104), art that represented the most beautiful outcome of culture and was the
main claim to glory of Hellenism.

As for Christianity, it could sometimes be useful or effective in the struggle
against the further subversion that threatened culture, but it ultimately played
a positive role only to the extent that it contributed 'against its own will' to
'help make the "world" of antiquity immortal'. In this way, it transmitted to the
'degenerate, aged cultures and peoples' something of the Greco-Roman legacy;
they suffered no serious injury as a result but rather obtained a 'balm' for their
senility (VM, 224 [96–7]). This point of view is also represented in Nietzsche's
later development. In August–September 1885, he wrote:

One wishes to go *back*, through the fathers of the church to the Greeks; [...] one also enjoys the end of antiquity, Christianity, as a gateway to antiquity, as a good fragment of the ancient world itself, as a sparkling mosaic of ancient concepts and value judgements.

XI, 679

So, there was room neither for the Christian-Germanic myth of origin nor for an Aryan-Germanic version of it, which skipped over Greece and classical antiquity in general and claimed to link Arminius directly to the earliest conquerors of India. As for the ancient Germans, even if they were sometimes contrasted to the anti-nature of Christianity, as healthy and untouched nature, they still could not, because of their modest cultural development, constitute a privileged point of reference, and even less so an alternative, to classical antiquity and, above all, to Greece. In this case too, as already in the case of the Indo-germans, Nietzsche could have said, 'there is no art'. All that remained was the Greco-Germanic myth of origin. Not just Aeschylus but Heraclitus seemed to come back to life in Wagner: his 'overpowering symphonic intellect [...] continuously reproduces concord out of this conflict' and the 'vortex of oppositions', and his music 'taken as a whole is a likeness of the world in the sense in which it was conceived by the great Ephesian philosopher, as a harmony that discord produces out of itself, as the union of justice and strife' (WB, 9, I, 494 [316]).

But there is in Nietzsche, from the very beginning, an oscillation between references to Greece and to the Greco-Roman world. With an eye to France, *The Birth of Tragedy* took an unambiguously Greek and uncompromisingly anti-Roman stand, but *On the Future of Our Educational Institutions* painted a more varied picture. Certainly, Nietzsche was deeply convinced of the link between tragic Hellenism and rediscovered authentic Germanness. On the other hand, when the Basel lectures contrasted classical antiquity to modern devastation, they ended up paying Rome a sort of tribute. Thus 'the great earnestness with which the Greek and the Roman regarded and treated his language, from his youth onwards' was emphasised (BA, 2, I, 682 [55–6]). Above all, one had to ensure that 'a teacher of classical culture did not confuse his Greeks and Romans with the other peoples, the barbarians, [and did not] put Greek and Latin on a level with other languages' (BA, 3, I, 704 [82]). In the later Nietzsche, the dichotomy between Greece and Rome, which played such an important role in *The Birth of Tragedy*, faded and was replaced by the opposition between classical antiquity and modernity (and the Jewish-Christian tradition).

One point remains: even if one was not in any way to confuse Germans and Indo-Europeans with decadent and corrupt Roman civilisation, which brought forth the Enlightenment and was accused of insensitivity to artistic beauty and of generating constant subversion and revolution (blamed for the fire in the Louvre), they still fell short of the splendid culture produced by classical antiquity and especially by Greece. There could be no doubt: the Greco-Germanic (and, subsequently, Greco-Roman-Germanic) myth of origin assumed in Nietzsche a special clarity and emphasis.

4   Imitation of France and Germany's Abdication of its Mission

This myth, experienced with such extraordinary intensity, could certainly not be content with Germany's military triumph. No, a new, more ambitious and harder task awaited the Second Reich, which had become the hegemonic power in continental Europe:

> The German will be able to appear worthy of honour and as a bringer of salvation in the eyes of other nations if he can show that he is frightening and yet through the exertion of his highest and noblest artistic and cultural energies wishes it to be forgotten that he was frightening.
>
>   MD, I, 896

Before the 'tribunal of eternal justice' the Greek state could stand 'proudly and calmly', convinced of its justification. The potential for violence and suffering that this implied dissipated immediately in the face of Greek culture, the 'magnificently blossoming woman' that the Greek state led by the hand. It was true, 'For this Helen, he waged those wars – what grey-bearded judge would condemn this?' (CV, 3, I, 772 [169]). But to which Helen could the Second Reich appeal, in order to give legitimacy to the wars that had preceded its birth and the powerful military apparatus with which it continued to surround itself?

Unfortunately, the Battle of Sedan had not led to the start of a new period of great culture and art. Rather, the opposite had happened:

> Since the last war with France many things in Germany have changed or shifted, and it is obvious that we have also brought home with us some new wishes with regard to German culture. For many, that war was the first trip into the more elegant half of the world; what better way for the victor to appear unprejudiced than by not disdaining to learn some culture from those he has vanquished! Craftspeople, in particular, are constantly being encouraged to compete with our cultivated neighbor; the German house is to be furnished and decorated in a way similar to the

French house; by means of an academy founded along the lines of the
French model, even the German language is supposed to acquire 'sound
taste' and rid itself of the dubious influence exerted upon it by Goethe –
according to a recent pronouncement by the Berlin academician Dubois-
Reymond.

> SE, 6, I, 390 [221]

Here we seem to have a repetition, though with the roles reversed, of what Hor-
ace described in his time. Now it was no longer *Grecia capta* that conquered
Rome in the cultural field, but *Roma capta*, represented by those 'new Romans',
the French, that dragged a resurrected Greece, that should have been Germany,
onto the downward path of civilisation. The disappointment was bitter, and
with it began the polemic against those who were content with or enthusiastic
about what had already been achieved. The first target was Strauss. He seemed
to think that military and cultural pre-eminence coincided, thus forgetting that
'a great victory is a great danger' and losing sight of the fact that the victory at
Sedan could turn 'into a total defeat: into the defeat – indeed, the extirpation –
of the German spirit for the sake of the "German Reich"' (DS, 1, I, 159–60 [5]).

These statements are often cited in support of interpretations of the first
Unfashionable Observation as a polemic against chauvinism. It is true Nietzsche
had already expressed himself in regard to the Second Reich with a ruthlessness
and severity completely lacking at the time in the national liberals, but that is
only half the story. The other half is disappointment at the lack of a 'victory
of German culture' that one might have expected. In fact, 'French culture sub-
sists as heretofore, and [...] we Germans are just as dependent on it as we were
heretofore' (DS, 1, I, 160 [6]).

At this time, and right up until the 'enlightenment' turn, Nietzsche accuses
Strauss and the national-liberal party of having forgotten authentic Germanness and its due mission:

> I am often seized by the suspicion that the German is now anxious to
> escape those ancient obligations imposed upon him by his wonderful tal-
> ent, his peculiar natural inclination for seriousness and profundity. For
> once he would prefer to play the role of the buffoon or the ape; he would
> prefer to learn those arts and manners that make life entertaining. But I
> can conceive of no greater insult to the German spirit than to treat it as
> though it were so much wax, so that one day it might be able to be mol-
> ded into the shape of elegance. And if it is unfortunately true that a large
> proportion of Germans would like to be shaped and formed in this man-
> ner, then until they have finally listened to us we should not cease to tell

them: 'That ancient German spirit no longer dwells in you. To be sure, it is hard, harsh, and resistant, but it is made of the most precious material, one with which only the greatest sculptors are permitted to work, because they alone are worthy of it'.

SE, 6, I, 391 [222]

The more clearly modernity projected its shadow onto the Second Reich, the harder things became for those who wished to remain faithful to the deepest and truest nature of Germanness: '[H]e is pained and insulted by their inveterate pleasure in the false and counterfeit, in the badly imitated, in the translation of good foreign things into bad native ones' (SE, 6, I, 393 [223]). So, even if it made no sense to despise what was French, one was never to forget even for a moment that Germany's path and task were quite different. Unfortunately, 'the last war and the personal comparison with the French hardly seems to have called forth any loftier aspirations' than the slavish imitation of French civilisation: the victorious country borrowed from its victim 'those arts and manners [*Artigkeiten*] that make life entertaining' (SE, 6, I, 391 [222]).

Starting with the end of the war, a new slogan took hold among the winners: ' 'We have to learn from the French' – but what? 'Elegance'!' And so Strauss aspired in vain to 'Renan's elegance' (VII, 804 [359]). But this was just one example: '[E]ven the elegant German scholar has already been invented – and we can certainly expect that everything that up to now refused to submit to that law of elegance – German music, tragedy, and philosophy – will now be written off as un-German' (SE, 6, I, 390–1 [221]). 'Jewish-French elegance', denounced immediately after the Paris Commune, now found followers in Germany too.

This is a betrayal against which Schopenhauer's 'coarse and slightly bearlike soul' had already warned, when he 'teaches us not so much to mourn as to scorn the smoothness and courtly grace of good French writers' (SE, 2, I, 347 [180]). Nietzsche concluded his polemic as follows: 'I sense that the German culture in whose future one thereby expresses faith – a culture of wealth, of polish, and of genteel dissimulation – is the most hostile antithesis to that German culture in which I have faith' (SE, 6, I, 392 [223]). *The Birth of Tragedy* and contemporary writings had stressed that the Greeks had not been 'such practical, falsely serene, prosaic and schoolmasterly men as the learned Philistine of our days would seem to imagine' (PHG, 1, I, 805). Unfortunately, this seemed to be the path that the new Germany was taking. However, even though conditions had changed and unforeseen difficulties had arisen, the Greco-Germanic myth of origin continued to inspire the philologist and philosopher.

That Nietzsche's disaffection with developments in the Second Reich in no way meant a break with the myth of the superior and tragic 'German essence' is shown by the fact that the first *Unfashionable Observation* felt compelled to turn to the political authorities and warn against the danger represented by Strauss and the national liberals. He thought the trend they represented compromised the independence and survival of the 'German spirit', and – he added – 'who knows whether once this has occurred we will still be able to accomplish anything with what remains of the German body!' Already, 'we can only be surprised' that this trend 'had so little power to inhibit the development of these principles that have contributed to our great military success'. Perhaps because this trend 'considered it more advantageous, *in this instance*, to demonstrate its subservience to these other principles'. I italicise a phrase clearly designed to cast a shadow of suspicion. This much is certain, Nietzsche concluded: if 'allowed to grow and thrive', the tendency to practicism and the abandoning of the new Germany's cultural mission will eventually endanger 'its political existence and military power' (DS, 1; I, 160).

It was time to react decisively. The third *Unfashionable Observation* quoted Wagner: 'The German is angular and awkward when he affects polish, but he is sublime and superior to everyone when he catches fire.' An equally significant comment followed: '[E]legant people have good reason to beware of this German fire, for otherwise it might devour them some day, along with all their puppets and idols made of wax' (SE, 6, I, 391–2 [222]). Unlike Greece, to which it should have been the heir, the Second Reich led no Helen 'by the hand', but Nietzsche's invocation of this splendid figure did not mean, at least for the time being, that he was calling into question the military power that, for better or worse, had defeated the country of the revolution; just as his harsh criticism of political developments in the new Germany was in no way, at least for that moment, a renunciation of the idea of the mission it had been called upon to carry out.

5   Social Conflict and the National-Liberal Recovery of the 'Old Faith'

The clash with Strauss concerned not the opposition between a pan-European view and Germanic narrowness but two opposing visions of Germanness, and it was undoubtedly Nietzsche's that was more emphatic, as emerges clearly from his impassioned appeal to guard jealously the authenticity and originality of the German essence. Precisely this explains the incipient break with the Second Reich, its mediocrity by now clear to all. Where was the coveted national *volksthümlich* culture, which should have served at one and the same time to preserve true Germanness and recover tragic Hellenism? The expectation that military triumph might once again reinvigorate the struggle against civilisation and modernity was becoming ever less realistic: 'But for me it becomes ever more doubtful – and since the war, more improbable with each passing day – that it will be possible to channel German courageousness in this new direction, for I see how everyone is convinced that such a battle and such courage are no longer necessary' (DS, 1, I, 161 [7]).

Strauss, on the other hand, felt at ease in the new political reality created by the success of the Prussian army, precisely because it was not charged with renewing the world and reversing the course of history. The advent of modernity was greeted with goodwill and enthusiasm. The myth and the old faith were about to vanish. That did not mean that humanity would sink into emptiness and desolation. The moment of edification and rising up above everyday life was now no longer produced by the yearning to escape to a world beyond but by the enjoyment of humanity's greatest artistic and cultural productions, in which sense one could say that an absolute spirit reminiscent of Hegel took the place of religious edification. In a polemic whose end effect, objectively, struck at Nietzsche, Strauss pointed out that it made no sense to set art and *otium* against the banausic, utilitarian view of life. Without the 'acquisitive impulse [*Erwerbstrieb*]' and the subsequent development of social wealth, there would be no leisure, and 'without leisure there could be neither science nor art'.[20] He argued it was futile and tiresome to lament the past; better to continue with courage and confidence along the new road of the 'modern scientific world-view', destined to become, despite initial difficulties, 'the world road of the future'.[21]

These opinions met with suspicion or even outright hostility on the part not only of Nietzsche but also of national-liberal circles. How to explain the reaction of the latter? According to Engels's analysis developed at the end of the nineteenth century, the terror aroused by the workers' revolt in June 1848 and the Paris Commune drove the European bourgeoisie to distance itself from the more radical forms of criticism of the religious tradition and even to make a display of an affected deference to that tradition:

> [O]ne by one, the scoffers turned pious in outward behaviour, spoke with respect of the Church, its dogmas and rites, and even conformed with the latter as far as could not be helped. French bourgeois dined *maigre* on Fridays, and German ones sat out long Protestant sermons in their pews on Sundays.[22]

---

20   Strauss 1872, p. 64.
21   Strauss 1872, p. 373 f.
22   Marx and Engels 1975 ff., 27, p. 300.

According to Engels, all this was an attempt to use 'moral means', and above all religion, to contain the menacing rise of the labour movement (ibid.).

Does this explanation convince? Let us see how Treitschke polemicised against Strauss. According to Treitschke, Strauss might well be an 'acute theologian', but he had no idea of the 'essence of religion', and did realise it was rooted in 'an innate and indestructible impulse of our soul'. Above all, he lost sight of the crucial question: 'All theological criticism is as nothing when set against the practical duties of the pastor of souls, who has to comfort the weary and the afflicted.'[23] Haym expressed himself in similar terms: unaware of the 'dark powers of sentiment', the left Hegelian lacked the necessary 'tolerance in the face of the faith in miracles and fables and the superstitions of the multitude'.[24] Moreover, Strauss clearly lacked the *bon ton*: 'In the distinguished classes, one has tacitly agreed never to touch certain particularly important religious issues.' It could well be, admitted the historian, that this attitude was not entirely 'sincere'; on the other hand, conflicts about religion left a bad taste, while all 'free men' by now agreed 'religious truths are truths of sentiment', not amenable to refutation at the rational level.[25]

So it is easy to see why the general reaction to Strauss was one of hostility and annoyance. It is true that, with an eye to the Paris Commune, he seemed to want to tone down the polemic:

'It is not our intent to destroy any church, since we know that for many people a church is still a need. [...] I did not want and do not want to upset any contentment, any faith.' Now, above all, when a new wave of revolutionary upheavals had revealed the 'horrors' of which the 'socialist plague' was capable,[26] it was perhaps a good thing that the masses remained attached to the 'old faith'. On the other hand, Strauss clearly rejected the compromise suggested by the national liberals and sharply denounced it as untenable: 'The entire life and strivings of all the civilized nations of our time are based on a worldview diametrically opposed to the worldview of Jesus.'[27] Bearing in mind the 'inevitable dissolution of the old'[28] and proceeding gradually and with all due caution, it was therefore a question of spreading, also among the masses, the 'modern worldview, the result of hard-earned and long-term natural and historical

---

23   Treitschke 1981, Vol. 4, p. 489 f.
24   Haym 1861, p. 309; on Haym as author of the review cf. Westphal 1964, p. 322.
25   Treitschke 1886, p. 25 f.
26   Strauss 1872, pp. 8–10, 277.
27   Strauss 1872, p. 75.
28   Strauss 1872, p. 8.

inquiry'.[29] The separation of laity and initiates was bound to be overcome by modern historical development. Those who wished to hold on to it, though conferring on it a more secular form than in Catholicism, were implicitly accused of inconsistency or reserve: 'If we want to talk as honest and upright people, we must profess: we are no longer Christians.'[30]

The Old and the New Faith thus broke a taboo whose political and social significance was further clarified in Treitschke's polemic against Feuerbach. As a last step in his evolution, Feuerbach had joined Social Democracy, the party that, in the eyes of the historian (to a certain extent official) of Wilhelminian Germany, could be blamed for promoting 'sacrilege' as a professional activity, as well as (needless to say) 'incitement' of the masses.[31] This subversion was legitimised by Feuerbach's philosophy: for him, 'the whole, wonderful history of the church, which has filled so many centuries with spirit and life, was just some horrible sickness; and since no human being can live without faith, the radical atheist had no alternative but to believe in the state, in the authentic human being, who can achieve perfection only in the form of the republic'.[32] But the author of *The Old and the New Faith* expressed himself in precisely the same words as were so harshly criticised here; he asked, in a rather radical tone, 'what should a particular association like the church further serve, alongside the state, school, science and art in which we all have a part'?[33] Unlike Feuerbach, Strauss made no profession of republican faith, but would his devaluation of the religious dimension in favour of the secular and political one not pave the way for republicans and socialists?

6   The Young Nietzsche, the Struggle against 'Secularisation' and the Defence of the 'Old Faith'

When intervening in the polemic against Strauss, Nietzsche took up positions not unlike those of the national liberals. In the Pforta years, he had already expressed a clear and strong political concern: 'Great upheavals lie ahead, once the mass has understood that the whole of Christianity is founded on hypotheses' (FG, 433). *The Birth of Tragedy* continued to voice deep respect for

29   Strauss 1872, p. 10.
30   Strauss 1872, p. 94.
31   Treitschke 1878, p. 9.
32   Treitschke 1981, Vol. 4, p. 487.
33   Strauss 1872, p. 7.

Christianity. It was, in any case, clearly preferable to the view of Hellenism and paganism treasured by Heine, who to some extent took his bearings by some manifestations of the Hellenic world:

> This appearance of 'Greek cheerfulness' was what so outraged profound and fierce natures in the first four centuries of Christianity. It seemed to them that this womanish flight from all that was grave and frightening, this cowardly contentment with comfortable pleasure, was not simply despicable, but was the true anti-Christian attitude of mind.
>
> GT, 11; I, 78 [56–7]

At least in the polemic against 'comfortable pleasure', *The Birth of Tragedy* endorsed Christian concerns. Had not Heine specified as a precondition for communism a revival of the optimistic worldview, which he had attributed to the Greeks, who serenely and unreservedly recognised themselves and sought fulfilment in the earthly life? The worldview developed by Strauss was not much different, even though he was not fully aware of the political implications of his discourse.

If Nietzsche and the national liberals criticised the author of *The Old and the New Faith* so harshly, they perhaps knew or intuited something of the sympathetic echo his criticism of Christianity had found in the labour movement. Together with Feuerbach's texts, *The Life of Jesus* also circulated 'among proletarians' and even in some 'communist clubs'. This criticism of theology was read alongside the manifesto in which Proudhon denounced property as theft, confirming the fact, already pointed out by Heine, that the dissolution of the hope of heavenly consolation had as its 'natural consequence' the spread of communism. Moreover, Nietzsche explicitly criticised Strauss for reproducing, albeit in a 'ridiculously banal dilution', the 'strong words' of the French early socialist or anarchist (VII, 588).

Even more determinedly, *The Old and the New Faith* sought to block any escape from or evasion of the mundane world. Far from being 'contemptible', this mortal world was revealed 'rather as the true field of human labour, as the totality of the ends of human striving'. True, 'some workers' still adhered through 'habit' to the old faith, but they were by now just a 'shadow' destined to vanish.[34] We have already spoken of the 'critique of the vale of tears' in Marx (*supra*, 1 §9). This theme was also clearly present in Strauss. Despite its merits

---

34   Strauss 1872, p. 75 f.

in respect of valorising marriage and work, for him the Reformation had had a fundamental limit: 'The earth remained a vale of tears, people's eyes were on the future heavenly splendour.' While the 'deification of suffering' symbolised by the Christian cross was still a treasured theme for Luther, it was wholly alien to 'today's humanity, which rejoices in life and activity'.[35] The new faith summoned people to 'a truly human, moral and therefore happy life'.[36] These ethics were those of Hegel and the Young Hegelians, who saw in the realisation of a political community of *citoyens* an end to the vale of tears and the curse of original sin. In this sense, Ruge, who also reflected on the future of religion, had set against obsolete Christianity the new 'religion of ethics', which was also the 'religion of this mortal world'.[37] These positions, which had won broad support in the years before the Revolution of 1848, now appeared suspect and odious in the eyes of Nietzsche and the national liberals.

As a student, Nietzsche must have agreed at least to some extent with the contents of the letter sent to him in June 1866 by Paul Deussen, who thought that Strauss's *Life of Jesus* was unable to explain 'the most enigmatic apparition in history' (B, I, 3, 95). And the young professor of classical philology must also have been convinced by parts of the letter sent to him in September 1872 by his friend Rohde, likening Berlin ravaged by civilisation to what the 'great whore' Rome was in the eyes of the early Christians. True enough, their faith, 'however stupid', was nevertheless 'something great and uplifting' (B, II, 4, 78). So Christianity, even if it had declined ruinously since Greco-Roman antiquity, could still act as a restraint, however insecure and provisional, on the most repulsive and disturbing aspects of modernity.

In the first *Unfashionable Observation*, religious arguments are defended no less clearly than by the generality of national-liberal writers. The 'angry invectives against Christianity' (VII, 595 [165]) were firmly rejected: 'Strauss thought he could destroy Christianity by proving it is full of myths. But the essence of religion consists precisely in the possession of freedom and in the power to create myths' (VII, 587 [157]). There can be no doubt the author of *The Old and New Faith* remained deaf to the 'eternalising powers of art and religion' (HL, 10, I, 330 [164]). Unfortunately, 'he has ignored the best part of Christianity, the great recluses and saints – in short, its genius'; he 'constantly takes Christianity, art, in their most trivial and crude democratic form and then refutes them' (VII, 587–8 [157–8]). The denunciation of Strauss's 'true form of impiety' was final and conclusive (VII, 504 [84]).

---

35   Strauss 1872, pp. 82, 93.
36   Strauss 1872, p. 12.
37   Ruge 1847–8, p. 246.

This explains the sympathetic interest and even enthusiasm that the first *Unfashionable Observation* caused in some religious circles. Certainly, no believer could have evoked more heartfeltly the catastrophic consequences of the 'sad atheist twilight' of Holbach's eighteenth-century materialism: 'The ground appears strewn with ashes, all stars extinguished; every withered tree, every ravaged field, cries out to him: Barren! Lost! Here spring will never come again' (DS, 7, I, 200 [44]).

In the same tone, the third *Unfashionable Observation* described the consequences of the secularisation of the modern world:

> The floodwaters of religion are receding and leaving behind swamps or stagnant pools; nations are once again drawing away from each other in the most hostile manner and long to massacre each other. The various fields of learning, pursued without moderation and with an attitude of blind laissez-faire, are dissecting and dissolving all firm beliefs; the educated classes and states are being swept away by a grandly contemptible money economy. Never has the world been more worldly, never has it been poorer in love and goodness. [...] Everything stands in the service of approaching barbarism, contemporary art and science included.
>
> SE, 4, I, 366 [198]

'Complete secularization [*völlige Verweltlichung*]' was synonymous with 'a subordination of culture, considered as a means, to gain and earthly happiness crudely understood' (VII, 243). Here, we are back at a central theme of *The Birth of Tragedy*. The search for earthly happiness pushed the slaves all the more easily to rise in revolt, for the existing order had been demythologised and desecrated and so was no longer able to put up any kind of resistance to the assault by plans for transformation or destruction. The 'lay mentality' of art and life and the associated 'cheerful optimism of the theoretical human being' (GT, 19, I, 124 [91]) stimulated the hope that it was possible, through politics, to change the world and cause individuals to be satisfied with their worldly existence. What a pitiful illusion:

> Any philosophy that believes that the problem of existence can be altered or solved by a political event is a sham or pseudophilosophy [*Spass- und Afterphilosophie*]. Many states have been founded since the beginning of the world; this is an old story. How could a political innovation possibly be sufficient to make human beings once and for all contented dwellers on this earth?
>
> SE, 4, I, 365 [197]

But pitiful or not, the illusion continued to have devastating consequences. 'Philosophy has become worldly [*verweltlicht*]', Marx confidently announced in 1843, and he called upon it to join in the struggle for the overthrow of the *ancien régime*.[38] For that very reason, on the opposite side the 'deification of worldliness' was the target of Kierkegaard's polemic.[39] As late as 1881, Nietzsche was still explaining 'political madness', revolutionary agitation and 'socialism' by 'secularisation [*Verweltlichung*]' or 'belief in the world and beating from the mind concepts such as "beyond" and "hidden world"' (IX, 504). However, the tone had certainly changed by the time of *The Birth of Tragedy* and the *Unfashionable Observations*. Against the then ongoing process of 'secularisation' (and massification and disintegration) he unhesitatingly set Christianity: it 'is certainly one of the purest manifestations of that drive for culture, and especially for that drive for the ever-renewed production of the saint' (SE, 6, I, 389 [220]). So, one can understand the polemic against those who 'have forfeited the last remnant not only of their philosophical, but also of their religious sensibilities' (SE, 4, I, 365 [197]), and the condemnation of a philosophy of the universities that was harmful, also because of the crisis that it could bring about among 'young theologians' (SE, 8, I, 423 [252]).

The attitude of the 'young theologians' presented us with a problem of a more general sort: 'The educated classes are no longer lighthouses or havens in these agitated seas of secularization [*Verweltlichung*]; they themselves become more agitated, mindless, and loveless with each passing day' (SE, 4, I, 366 [198]). The intellectuals, won by now for the ideology of secularisation and the pursuit of earthly happiness, themselves became instruments of subversion. One had to stem this tide: 'A class of elementary school teachers is wholly bad. The education of children is the duty of parents and the community, the main task is to preserve tradition' (VII, 385).

The denunciation of Strauss, the prototype of the 'schoolmaster', was all the clearer (VII, 588 [158]). Not for nothing was he negatively compared to Renan, who, far from adopting a tone of radical criticism towards Christianity, seemed to be engaged in an apologetics of a new sort, able to do without the dogmatics: 'It was impertinent of Strauss to offer the German people a biography of Jesus as a pendant to Renan's much better biography' (VII, 587 [157]).

---

38   Marx and Engels 1975 ff., 1, p. 195.
39   Kierkegaard 1962 ff., Vol. 3, p. 3.

7   'Secularisation' and Crisis of Myths of Origin

So, driven by political and social fears, the trend towards reclaiming Christianity or the 'old faith' was widespread in the Second Reich. This was the picture
Engels painted. However, it requires completion. The devastation caused by
Socratic rationalism and 'secularisation' (notes *The Birth of Tragedy*) affected
the life and very identity of a nation:

> And a people – or, for that matter, a human being – only has value to
> the extent that it is able to put the stamp of the eternal on its experi-
> ences; for in doing so it sheds, one might say, its worldliness [*entweltlicht*]
> and reveals its unconscious, inner conviction that time is relative and
> that the true meaning of life is metaphysical. The opposite of this occurs
> when a people begins to understand itself historically and to demolish
> the metaphysical buttresses surrounding it; this is usually accompanied
> by a decided growth in worldliness [*Verweltlichung*] and a break with the
> unconscious metaphysics of its previous existence, with all the ethical
> consequences this entails.
>
>   GT, 23, I, 148 [110]

The decline of myth marked the end of tragic Hellenism, but it could also destroy the hope of the new Germany to assume the legacy of tragic Hellenism.
This was yet another reason to oppose all forms of radical critique of religion
and the celebration of modernity. In distancing themselves so clearly from a
radically secular view of life, the national liberals, and with them Nietzsche,
had an eye not only on the social question but also on international politics:
they felt the need to legitimise the mission or primacy they attribute to Germany.

In the debate about the identity of the Second Reich, Strauss's contribution was significant, for he took a critical distance from and had no part in the
myths of origin of that time. 'Classical antiquity does not exist for him', Nietzsche would later observe, in a tone of harsh reproach (VII, 591 [161]). In relation
to Greece, *The Old and the New Faith* emphasised that its 'republics', by virtue
of the slavery that marked them, were actually 'exclusive aristocracies', happily
overcome by the development of modernity.[40] If there was a period of classical
antiquity that is sympathetic to Strauss, it was that the author of *The Birth of*

---

40   Strauss 1872, p. 267.

Tragedy hated. The idea of brotherhood among all people finally began to assert itself in the Alexandrian period and with 'Hellenism': the 'nobler spirits among the Greeks and Romans' strove to overcome provincial and national boundaries in order to merge in the 'universal Roman Empire', in which direction Jews of the diaspora, scattered 'in all countries', also moved.[41] Here, the birth of the West could be located: in the Alexandrian period, Jewish monotheism, with its 'tribal and national god', met, clashed and merged with the 'universal god' theorised by the Greeks after overcoming the 'multitude of Olympian gods'.[42]

In this way, the elements that constituted the Greco-Germanic myth of origin were surrendered. In *The Old and New Faith* there was not even room for the celebration of the German Middle Ages and the Middle Ages in general, which were rather subjected to a merciless Enlightenment-style critique. There was even less room for Wagner's *Nibelungen* mythology, which was not even included in the pantheon of German music the final chapter of the book dealt with. One should add that Strauss also talked ruthlessly about Protestantism: in his eyes, the thesis that the Reformation had brought about a rigorous philological and historical analysis, which was still valid, of the Scriptures was a myth.[43] More generally, Luther was proud of his achievement in unleashing an attack on the Catholic Church, but despite that he was still far removed from the most advanced outcomes of modernity; he was an integral part of medieval tradition, even though he had helped to plunge it into crisis.

In addition to his radical laicism and modernism, Strauss dealt a heavy blow at the Christian-Germanic myth of origin, by distancing himself clearly from the general celebration of Luther as a German national hero. In the wake of Hegel, the Reformation was seen as an essential moment in world history: the gulf, explicitly declared in Catholicism, between initiates and the secular, between the powerful hierarchy, dispenser of the sacred, and the mass, compelled to obedience, continued to manifest itself, though in weaker form, even in Protestantism, and was only overcome with the advent of modernity and the modern idea of equality.[44]

We have already spoken of Strauss's positive view of the Hellenistic world. Striking was his sympathetic reading of Judaism, which followed a continuous line right up to the preaching of the Gospel and therefore refuted any attempt to dejudaise Christianity. And so we reach the final point. In Strauss,

41   Strauss 1872, pp. 83–5.
42   Strauss 1872, p. 106.
43   Strauss 1872, p. 90 f.
44   Strauss 1872, p. 6.

we find none of the Aryan pathos common to the various myths of origin, the Greco-Germanic, the Germanic, and sometimes even the Christian-Germanic. So, one should note that 'our European nations are mixed peoples'.[45] The 'highly developed nations on the spiritual and ethical level'[46] could claim superiority over the colonial world, but for the rest there was no point in trying to establish a hierarchy between 'Aryans' and 'Semites'. In reconstructing the 'first development of moral characteristics', *The Old and the New Faith* referred in an undifferentiated way to both, and even started out from the Mosaic Decalogue.[47] Those who praised the Aryan origins of the West certainly had to take note of the fact that the India they so highly exalted was marked by a 'rigid caste system' and an odious 'caste segregation'.[48]

More generally speaking, Strauss's worldview was in substantial contradiction with the theory of *Sonderweg*, of Germany's unique mission. True, it was not without the occasional modest concession to the idea, widespread in culture and political journalism at the time, also in Nietzsche, of the 'seriousness' of the German people.[49] However, the theme was profoundly reinterpreted: it was now a matter of the seriousness and radicalism with which Germany had succeeded in challenging the medieval theological tradition and in playing a leading role in the struggle for modernity and freedom of thought, to the affirmation of which other European countries had also effectively contributed.

Here, as elsewhere, the merits of the German people were not claimed as exclusive. Even if the Reformation had played a pioneering role in overcoming medieval 'asceticism', it had been able to reach that height only by taking advantage of the 'way of thinking of antiquity present in humanism'.[50] Like humanism, the Enlightenment also had taken as its reference a European framework. After starting in Britain, the movement of 'freethinkers' developed particularly strongly in France. But Germany formed the culmination of that process. The 'seriousness' of Reimarus corresponded to the irony of Voltaire, and though it was perhaps less brilliant, it was nevertheless more systematic and penetrating. It was thanks only to the work of Reimarus that the entire 'Christian system of faith' had been shown to be 'false and full of contradic-

---

45   Strauss 1872, p. 263.
46   Strauss 1872, p. 226.
47   Strauss 1872, p. 233.
48   Strauss 1872, p. 59f.
49   Strauss 1872, pp. 35, 37.
50   Strauss 1872, p. 255.

tions', untenable from the point of view of reason and also from that of the 'bringing of humanity to moral perfection'. In this sense, 'Germany, not France, became the cradle of rationalism'.[51] The German nation could claim a leading role for itself only to the extent that it endorsed and further deepened the achievements of European historical development. It could also boast of having, in Goethe, 'Darwin's precursor', and, in Kant, Laplace's precursor;[52] but once again, the progress of science and of the scientific worldview had to be placed in a framework other than the narrowly national.

Against this background, the various myths of origin, which vied with and polemicised against one another as they sought to snatch from the baptismal font the nation-state that had emerged from the victory at Sedan, appeared quiet inconsistent. So, it was easier to understand Nietzsche's criticism of the author of *The Old and the New Faith*: 'He plays at being a great popular writer: false notion of popularity' (vii, 591 [161]). Popularity, synonymous with the spreading among the masses of the hated modernity, was implicitly contrasted with *Volksthümlichkeit*, united and cemented by myth, granted the task of restoring tragic Hellenism in the shape of the German nation.

Strauss called upon his compatriots to embrace modernity to the hilt. The polemical response of *The Old and the New Faith* to the condemnation of the moral world by Schopenhauer, Nietzsche and Wagner was that 'we modern people [*Wir Heutigen*]' were to rally together.[53] While scathingly criticising Strauss's secularist and modernist manifesto, Nietzsche, despite his proclamation of its 'untimeliness', was substantially in consonance with the German culture of his time. The circles of Protestant orthodoxy declared themselves satisfied: 'The evangelical church newspaper is said to have enjoyed my Straussiade' (B, ii, 3, 193), Nietzsche told Gersdorff, in reply to a letter from Naumburg in which his friend had informed him that the first *Unfashionable Observation* has found 'diligent, excited and grateful readers' in some Protestant and military circles (B, ii, 4, 362). As for the national liberals, they could forgive Strauss neither his secular radicalism, which exposed the masses to the influence of the socialistic free-thinkers and the contagion of subversion, nor his modernist radicalism, which robbed the ancient gods of Germanic, Indo-European or Greek mythology of their sacred or even merely poetic aura; for this mythology had been called upon by the dominant culture to transform reality and the 'mission' of the Second Reich.

---

51   Strauss 1872, pp. 35–7.
52   Strauss 1872, pp. 182, 184.
53   Strauss 1872, p. 15 f.

Paradoxically, Strauss was more 'untimely', and well aware of the fact. He saw himself as the exponent and spokesperson of that 'thinking minority' committed to really settling accounts with the old faith,[54] did not want to 'go with the stream' and did not hesitate to defy the wrath of those who 'swim with the current of the culture of the time'.[55]

---

54   Strauss 1872, p. 7.
55   Strauss 1872, pp. 276, 178.

CHAPTER 5

From the 'Judaism' of Socrates to the 'Judaism' of Strauss

1   Myths of Origin and Anti-Semitism

Despite their radical differences, the myths of origin that accompanied the founding of the Second Reich had one thing in common: both had a more or less strained relationship and were engaged in a more or less acknowledged polemic with Judaism. The Germanomaniacs, who praised Germany's Christian mission and morale, tended to dejudaise Christianity, in order to turn it into a sort of national Germanic religion. As for the Aryan myth of origin, the implied contrast to Semitism was immediately evident. The magnificent culture of ancient Greece or of the ancient world as a whole, which could in no way be confused with the backwardness and barbarism of Judea, which was Asiatic and in rebellion against Greece and Rome, also pointed to great communities of the Indo-European peoples. Precisely because of their shared anti-Semitism, the Aryan-Germanic or Aryan-Greco-Germanic myths of origin were easily combined with the Germanic and even with the Germanic-Christian one: it was enough to deny or cast doubts – as Wagner did – on Jesus's membership of the Jewish people.[1]

From the point of view of those who followed these various myths, this was one more reason to look with deep suspicion and hostility at the historical and ideological platform elaborated by Strauss. We have seen there was no trace in him of Aryan (and anti-Jewish) pathos. Moreover, he had already developed a sympathetic interpretation of Judaism in his *Life of Jesus*: far from wanting to dejudaise, as Schopenhauer and Wagner did, he stressed the continuity between the Old and New Testaments. At least initially, 'Jesus remained faithful to the ancestral law [*väterliches Gesetz*]', and his manifestations of respect could not be explained as mere 'accommodation'. He even seemed to 'share the antipathy of his fellow-countrypeople towards the pagans'. In any case, he did not envisage 'overthrowing the ancient religious constitution of his people' and had no intention of going beyond the scope of his national community, as

---

1   Wagner 1910n, p. 232.

shown in particular by Matthew, the 'Judaizing author of the first Gospel'. One should add that even 'after the first Pentecost', the Apostles 'adhered strictly to Jewish law'. In confirmation of this, Strauss repeatedly referred to *Wolfenbüttel's Fragments of the Anonymous Author*, published by Lessing, the author labelled by Judeophobes and anti-Semites an elective Jew or a Jew *tout court*.[2] Later, after the publication of the first volume of *Life of Jesus*, when Strauss was depicted by zealots of Christian orthodoxy as a sort of second Judas, he did not hesitate to remind people of the 'proud memory' of the story of Lessing, who, as editor of the *Fragments*, was accused at the time of having been handsomely financed by the 'Jews of Amsterdam'.[3]

As in the *Life of Jesus*, Strauss also tried in *The Old and the New Faith* to refute some of the anti-Jewish or anti-Semitic themes common in German culture at the time. Wagner, like Schopenhauer before him, accused Judaism of ignoring the suffering of animals, often sacrificed in honour of Yahweh; but Strauss said animal sacrifices were a big advance on the human sacrifices of previous religious traditions, whereas the Christian idea of the sacrificial death of the Son of God might be seen to represent a frightening regression.[4] For those seeking a national Germanic religion, Christianity had to be purged of all trace of Judaism, also in regard of the particularism and exclusivism that marked the latter; but Strauss pointed out that even before Jesus, the theme of 'brotherhood among all people' could be found in Rabbi Hillel.[5]

However, for Nietzsche's polemic, other points mattered more. If *The Birth of Tragedy* privileged the Aryan version of original sin over the Semitic, *The Old and the New Faith*, in comparing the Jewish and Christian interpretations of the biblical story, reached an opposite conclusion: the former sought only to 'explain why people are so miserable, so unhappy', the latter to 'explain why people are so wicked, so sinful'. Only now, in the context of the religion that had triumphed in the West and among the Aryan peoples, did historically determined human misery and unhappiness receive moral and theological consecration and the seal of eternity; in this way, the Christian dogma of original sin sanctioned the perpetual 'damnation of all mankind'.[6] Because it was founded in the cancelling of the principle of individual responsibility, it condemned to

---

2   Strauss 1835–6, Vol. 1, pp. 496–504.
3   Strauss 1835–6, Vol. 2, p. vii.
4   Strauss 1872, p. 27.
5   Strauss 1872, p. 83.
6   Strauss 1872, p. 23.

eternal hellfire even the most remote posterity and 'innocent children, as long as they died unbaptized': all this deeply offended 'both reason and the feeling of justice'.[7]

With the preaching of the Gospel, the escape from the mundane and from the body became obsessive. It was not by chance that Jews and Judaising Christians still believed in the 'resurrection of the flesh', but this 'materialism' fell away during the subsequent evolution of the Church, with the preponderance of 'spiritualists', who saw paradise as a place where only a soul clearly and definitively separated from the body experienced bliss.[8] A 'fanatical world-denying trait' ran deep in Christianity as well as in Buddhism. At least in regard to the affirmation of the claims of body and worldly existence, the Old Testament was clearly superior to the New. Strauss contrasted 'Jewish and pagan optimism' to the Christian theme of the vale of tears.[9]

From the point of view of Wagner and Nietzsche, who at this point were joined in a seemingly indestructible friendship, pagan optimism was spurious, an invention or projection of modernity, while the optimism of the Jewish religion was authentic, and precisely that was the mark of its vulgarity and infamy. And so we come to the crucial point. The author of *The Old and the New Faith* did not stop at conferring a positive connotation on the category of 'optimism' and 'Jewish optimism'. Rather, he critically stressed the aristocratic gesture to which Schopenhauer's pessimistic profession of faith led: 'For him optimism is in all cases the standpoint of superficiality and triviality, while all the deeper and more distinguished [*distinguirt*] spirits cleave, like he, to the point of view of pessimism.'[10]

Strauss was not wrong to find a contradiction, of the sort that we would today call performative, in the attitude of those who set out with great dedication and energy to persuade others that all was vain. There was more satisfaction (and narcissistic enjoyment) in the distinguished gesture by which one professed pessimism than in the optimism so furiously denounced. In arguing more or less in these terms, Strauss drew strength from Hegel's pungent observation: 'There are many people who are unhappy [*unglückselig*], i.e., blessed [*selig*] in their misery [*Unglück*], they need unhappiness, they are dissatisfied with happiness, and therefore criticize when things go well'; because of this hypochondria, 'all objectivity' becomes 'vain', for the subject 'enjoys only this vanity

7   Strauss 1872, p. 23 f.
8   Strauss 1872, p. 32 f.
9   Strauss 1872, p. 61 f.
10   Strauss 1872, p. 145.

in himself'.[11] Nietzsche's reaction was so violent because the aristocratic gesture of Schopenhauer, the master of pessimism, was also that of his own youthful years.

Strauss did not sufficiently understand that the agitated application of the theme of pessimism, of seriousness, and of the tragic vision of life was the distinguished aristocratic gesture not just of individuals but of Germany as a whole, especially in contrast to France. And he understood even less that, in both cases, this distinguished gesture was chiefly aimed at 'Jewish optimism', which *The Old and New Faith* had quietly celebrated.

But was this celebration not suspect? After branding Renan a Jew because, as we know, of his 'optimism', Wagner went on to say it was an optimism 'entirely worthy of Strauss'. Renan 'could only be a Jew', the musician continued, since his entire historical reconstruction led ultimately to the 'celebration of Judaism'.[12] This argument could doubtless also be used against the author of the *Life of Jesus*: as one of Cosima's diary entries for the summer of 1878 suggests, Wagner seemed to attribute a Jewish descent to him too.[13]

2   Strauss, Judaism and the Threat to German Language and Identity

In preparatory drafts for the first *Unfashionable Observation*, we find a comment about Strauss that gives cause for thought: 'Somebody once said to me: You, Sir, are a Jew, and as such you don't have a complete mastery of German' (VII, 589 [159]). We have already seen that, in the young Nietzsche, the dichotomy between tragic Hellenism/modernity or pessimism/optimism tended to coincide not only with the Germany/France dichotomy but also with the Germanic/Jewish or Aryan/Semitic one. With his critique of pessimism and his explicit adherence to 'Jewish optimism', Strauss betrayed disturbing elective affinities, but were they really only elective? To grasp the full implication of this speculation, one should remember that many German Jews had surnames denoting birds. Take, for example, Gans (= 'goose'), another of Hegel's disciples. Was this also true of Strauss, the 'ostrich', the 'prodigy' about whom *Ecce Homo* (EH, *Unfashionable Observations*, 2 [113]) made fun, of the author whose first name, David, points explicitly to a central figure in Jewish history and religion?

---

11   Hegel 1973 f., *Vorlesungen über Rechtsphilosophie*, Vol. 4, p. 643 (cf. Losurdo 1997a, 10, §1).
12   C. Wagner 1977, p. 879.
13   C. Wagner 1977, p. 141.

In his later, ever harsher polemic against Wagner, Nietzsche made a similar insinuation: was his stepfather (actually perhaps his natural father) not Geyer (= 'vulture')? Well, 'a vulture is almost an eagle [*ein Geyer ist beinahe schon ein Adler*]': both names supposedly betrayed a Jewish ancestry. Hence the question: 'Was Wagner even German?' (WA, note to *Postscript* [255]).[14] Or did his veins flow with the blood of the race he considered hopelessly alien and hostile to the Germanness of which he posed as champion? According to some malicious fragments, the doubts seemed more than justified: '[C]ould Wagner be a Semite?' (VIII, 500 [309]).

In insinuating that Strauss's bad German was a sign of his Jewish alienation from the people among whom he lived, the young Nietzsche broached a theme that would play an important role in the debate about anti-Semitism in following years, but was already central to Wagner's anti-Jewish campaign. Wagner appealed to people to defend the German language against the contaminations disfiguring it and threatening its purity, beauty and identity, and in so doing tried to finish off Meyerbeer: 'As a Jew, he did not have a mother tongue that had grown inextricably interwoven with the innermost part of his being'; hence 'his indifference to the spirit of any language'.[15]

Well beyond Meyerbeer (who, unlike many of his fellow Jews, refused to convert because, thanks to an inheritance, he had no need of the business card of baptism to become part of the good society),[16] Wagner's campaign attacked other personalities that professed to be Christian and German but were suspected of being linked, by natural or elective affinity, to the Jewish world. Such was the case with Eduard Devrient, a theatre director and author of a book in memory of Felix Mendelssohn-Bartholdy, the great musician of Jewish origin. Wagner subjected this text to harsh criticism, which focused almost exclusively on language and grammar: it was a 'style without dignity'; the German language was 'neglected and deformed', it was 'mangled', to the extent that it required a harsh response.[17] This 'hack German [*Handlangerdeutsch*]' or 'coachmen's German [*Kutscherdeutsch*]' could not be tolerated. In a reconstruction of his meeting with the 'young Jew' Mendelssohn and in his memoirs, he accused Devrient of using 'Jewish German [*Judendeutsch*]',[18] and, as was well known, Jews always spoke like foreigners the language of the country in which they lived. Wagner concluded by sounding the alarm: the degeneration of 'our Ger-

14   Cf. Poliakov 1968, p. 441 f.
15   Wagner 1910c, p. 293 f.
16   Poliakov 1968, p. 282.
17   Wagner 1910d, p. 227.
18   Wagner 1910d, pp. 229, 231, 238.

man language' endangered the identity of Germany and its people: 'Fatherland, mother tongue: woe to those who become orphans.'[19]

The danger was so serious it required all-round vigilance. In his essay *Judaism in Music*, republished in 1869, Wagner added a few toxic pages about 'a writer of Jewish origin, full of talent and spirit who seems as if grown into the most particular life of the German people [*Volksleben*]' but who lacked the courage to dissociate himself from the campaign of slander and hatred unleashed by the international Jewish community against him, Wagner. So, even in this case, the link with Germany was not, when it came down to it, decisive.[20] The reference was to Berthold Auerbach: speaking in his defence, Laube (a member of Young Germany) said that he was actually 'a passionate German': his personality showed clearly how untenable was the argument of those who 'want to exclude the Jews from our national community'.[21]

Let us now look at the first *Unfashionable Observation*:

> I remember reading Berthold Auerbach's appeal 'To the German People', in which every expression was un-German, wrongheaded, and false, and which in general was comparable to a soulless word mosaic held together with international syntax; not to mention the shamelessly scribbled German used by Eduard Devrient in his memorial to Mendelssohn.
>
> DS, II, I, 222 [65]

This utterance was clearly in line with Wagner's campaign, echoed in a letter from Cosima to Nietzsche in which Auerbach, despite his poem in honour of those who died for Germany, was deemed alien to the 'German essence' (B, II, 2, 240). Like Cosima in her diary,[22] Nietzsche in his notes expressed his contempt for Laube (VII, 504), for coming to Auerbach's defence.

In discussing Wagner's comments about Meyerbeer (who, as a Jew, supposedly had no mother tongue), a historian of anti-Semitism explains the malignant effect and radiating power of the slogan that 'a Jew, when he speaks German, lies'.[23] This was exactly Nietzsche's argument, as we have seen. At the time, he seemed fully to support the campaign of the 'Master' (as he called him

---

19   Wagner 1910p, p. 272.

20   Wagner 1910e, p. 258 f.

21   Laube 1845–7, Vol. 9, p. 374. Auerbach as the recipient of the letter of 2 September 1841, in which Moses Hess talked enthusiastically about his meeting with Marx, 'my idol', 'the only true living philosopher'; cf. Poliakov 1968, 419, fn. 3.

22   Rose 1992, p. 201, fn. 12.

23   Poliakov 1968, p. 449.

in the correspondence) against the German Jews, or, more precisely, against Jews pretending to be Germans. In a notebook we read:

> Where Heine and Hegel have both had an influence – as, for example, in the case of Auerbach (even if not directly) – and, in addition, due to national reasons a natural foreignness enters the German language, the result is a jargon that is deplorable in every word, every phrase.
>
> VII, 598 [167–8]

'International syntax' and disfigurement of the German language were a tell-tale sign of the 'national' and 'natural' alienness of those who spoke or wrote that way. Just like Wagner for Devrient, so too Nietzsche for Strauss made a meticulous list of the improprieties of language and style, of errors of syntax, of sentences in which there was a 'displacement of the adverb', the 'construction is false', or the author went so far as to 'to mix up the prepositions' (DS, 12, I, 229, 235 and 230 [71 and 76]); all cases, at least, in which the German language had been intolerably distorted. In both texts compared here, we find a list that adds up to an indictment of those criticised at the political and even the ethnic level.

Nietzsche had learned Wagner's lesson so well that he was later able to apply it effortlessly against Wagner himself. In the fourth *Unfashionable Observation*, he declared that, precisely because of his great love for the German language, 'Wagner suffered more than any other German from its degeneration and debilitation, that is, from the manifold losses and mutilations of its forms' (WB, 9, I, 486 [310]) After the break, however, when he questioned the Germanic ancestry of his former 'master' and even emphasised Wagner's 'affinity with rather than difference from the Hebrew element' (IX, 597), Nietzsche again backed up his assertion with a linguistic analysis: one was not to 'conceal the fact that Wagner's style itself suffers rather seriously from all those ulcers and tumours' (FW, 99 [97]), even though he had condemned them in the Jew Devrient.

But let us return to the attack on Strauss in the first *Unfashionable Observation*:

> For anyone who has sinned against the German language has profaned the mystery of all our Germanness; it alone has been preserved over the entire course of that mixing and changing of nationalities and customs, and with it, as though by means of metaphysical magic, the German spirit. It along guarantees as well the future of this spirit, provided it does not perish at the hands of the profligate present.
>
> DS, 12, I, 228 [71]

The draft makes it even clearer. Here it is in full:

> German customs, German social life, German institutions and agencies –
> everything has a foreign tinge to it and looks like an incompetent imit-
> ation, whereby it even has been forgotten that it is an imitation at all:
> everywhere, originality out of forgetfulness. In this time of distress I seek
> my comfort in the German language, which is for the time being truly the
> only thing that has been spared all the intermingling of nationalities and
> the changing times and customs. [...] This is precisely the reason why we
> must select the strictest warders to watch over this unifying language that
> guarantees our future Germanness.
>
> VII, 582–3 [153–4]

So 'the intermingling of nationalities and customs' mentioned in the printed
text was to be understood as 'the mixture of nationalities and the change of
times and customs'. In the course of its complex history, the German people had
managed to keep its language basically pure, despite the penetration of individuals and ethnic groups alien to it. The identity of the country was primarily
entrusted mainly to its language, and those who polluted it were guilty of a
murderous assault on Germany's unity and identity.

Here there emerges a pathos of Germanness even more exalted than in *The
Birth of Tragedy*. Except that by now no few of the previously cherished hopes
had been dispelled. True, the German essence continued to be celebrated, but
this celebration was no longer conjugated in the present but in an increasingly
problematic future: 'The German essence does not yet even exist, it must first
come into being; at some time or other it must be born, so that it can above all
be visible and honest with itself. But every birth is painful and violent' (VII, 687
[250]).

The main battlefield for the conquest of the German essence seemed at
this time to be language. It was in this context that the repeated and relentless accusations against 'Strauss the language tamer' (DS, 12, I, 241 [81]), this
'stylistic pachiderm' (DS, 12, I, 235 [76]), should be understood. And just as Wagner fulminated against the German of the 'hacks' and 'coachmen', so Nietzsche
denounced the 'shoddy jargon [of the riff-raff] [*Lumpen-Jargon*]' (DS, 12, I, 235
and 230 [70 and 76]). In his indictment, the great musician built up towards
a crescendo culminating in the charge that Devrient lacked any 'sense [*Sinn*]
for the most elementary rules of grammatical correctness' and therefore resorted to a 'Jews' German'.[24] Similarly, for Nietzsche, 'Straussian German' (SD, 12;

---

24   Wagner 1910d, p. 238.

I, 236 [77]) was characterised by the 'lack of linguistic sensitivity [*Mangel an Sprachgefühl*]' (DS, 12; I, 229 [71]).

The same implication about Strauss's allegedly Jewish origins also appeared, although less clearly formulated than in the preparatory draft, in the printed text, in the form of a series of malignant allusions that depicted the author of *The Old and New Faith* with copious stereotypes promoted by the anti-Jewish and anti-Semitic press. For example, the attachment to the world of money and speculation, together with indifference to true spiritual values: anyone who, like Strauss, 'prefers to use such vulgar mercantile language to express things that are scarcely vulgar' (DS, 12, I, 233 [74]), 'tortures [himself] trying to draw [his] metaphors from the railroad, the telegraph, the steam engine, the stock market' (DS, 11, I, 223 [66]). The full import of these statements becomes clear if one compares them with those delivered by Treitschke a few years later during his campaign against German Jewry, which he accused of 'attempting to introduce into literature the market clamour of the business world and, into the sanctuary of our language, the barbarous jargon of the stock market'.[25]

Nietzsche's characterisation of Strauss also touched on his supposed miserliness and deceitfulness: an author who did not hesitate to perpetrate 'despicable violence' on the German language merely in order to 'spare us or cheat us out of a sentence' (SD, 12; I, 231 [73]). Then there was his parasitism: 'The Straussian philistine dwells in the works of our great poets and composers like a maggot that lives by destroying, admires by consuming, and worships by digesting' (DS, 6, I, 188 [32]). Finally, his hypocrisy and servility: Strauss posed as a fervent patriot, but, in reality, he did not support Germany's cause in an honourable way, from within the bosom of the national community, but rather displayed a 'lack of backbone where the status quo in Germany is concerned' (DS, 6; I, 191 [36]). There was also the suggestion of uncleanliness: the author of *The Old and the New Faith* belonged to a 'scribbling riffraff [*Sudler-Gesindel*]' (DS, 12, I, 231 [73]) or to a bunch of dirty 'ink smearers [*Tintenklexer*]' (DS, 12; I, 233 [75]). Had not Wagner already talked about the 'extremely filthy' appearance generally typical of Jews?[26]

And finally: that Strauss took Lessing as a model was massively and ridiculously overreaching (SD, 9.10; I, 216–7 [59]). Moreover, the very model was questionable, for here was an author with an 'overly subtle, excessively supple, and – if I may say so – rather un-German style' (SE, 2, I, 347–8 [181]). Not only Strauss but even Lessing was under suspicion of being alien to authentic Germanness.

---

25   Treitschke 1965c, p. 85.
26   Wagner 1911, p. 494.

3   'Jewish International' and 'Aesthetic International'

One must not forget that Judeophobia played an important role among the authors that enthused Nietzsche in those years (Schopenhauer, Wagner, Lagarde) and was frequently to be found in his correspondence. On 10 July 1874, replying to three letters from Nietzsche (in one of which he was addressed as 'dearest good friend' (B, II, 3, 237)), Gersdorff wished him a happy and healthy holiday in the mountains and the woods, 'where there is fresh air, so-called ozone, and no Jews, or as Lagarde would say, in a hotel free of Jewish essence [*judainfrei*]' (B, II, 4, 512). While not directly addressing these comments, the recipient of the letter replied with an expression of joy, all the greater because he was able to observe 'an identical state of mind' (B, II, 3, 246).

Gersdorff's comment was in reference to a text[27] that, when it appeared, immediately aroused the sympathetic interest of Nietzsche, who, while not identifying with it directly, warmly recommended it to Rohde, and said he would also send a copy to Cosima Wagner (B, II, 3, 121 and 145). Cosima's reaction was particularly significant. In an effort to dejudaise Christianity and pave the way for a 'German national religion', Lagarde focused his criticism on Paul. Cosima objected as follows: 'I do not understand his blows against Paul as opposed to residents of Jerusalem, who after all were three times more Jewish than Paul himself' (B, II, 4, 452). Whatever the case, Judaism was still synonymous with contamination; the only problem was to identify its principal vehicle.

The tenor of the myths of origin that attended the founding of the Second Reich and were designed to safeguard Germany's authenticity and purity certainly did nothing to mitigate the potential for Judeophobia that, as we have seen, animated Nietzsche's circle of friends and correspondents. In a letter to Nietzsche, Romundt warned against the 'evil eye of the Jews [*Judenpech*] to which one is exposed on entering into a relationship with people of that race' (B, II, 4, 85). Gersdorff too considered any relationship with 'a people completely devoid of *pudor*' as thankless (B, II, 4, 234).

There is little point in dwelling on Wagner's statements or outbursts. Suffice it to say that Gersdorff, in the presence of a Jewish 'physiognomy', in company where a 'poisonous Jewish snake' lurked with its 'bite', thought it appropriate to avoid any talk of the musician (B, II, 4, 234–5), whose hatred of the Jews was only too well known. But one should not forget that Nietzsche was, at the time, pursuing the idea of 'organizing a Swiss Wagner association' (B, II, 3, 120),

---

27   Lagarde 1937, p. 68.

and it was to these cultural and political circles that Cosima was alluding when she spoke of the 'great enthusiasm' aroused 'in the German Reich' by the book against Strauss (B, II, 4, 209).

Among the most enthusiastic readers of the first *Unfashionable Observation* was Hans von Bülow, who on 29 August 1873 wrote to Nietzsche:

> Yesterday I received your excellent tirade against the Philistine David and I read it carefully from start to finish, with true enjoyment. [...] Your description of the cultivated Philistine, the Maecenas of culture devoid of style, is an authentic, manly speech-action, worthy of the author of *The Birth of Tragedy*. Écr[asez] l'Int[ernationale] should be written by a present-day Voltaire. The aesthetic Internationale is for us an opponent far more odious than those of the black or red bandits.
>
> B, II, 4, 288

Strauss was already talking about the 'red' International of the socialist and labour movement, and the 'black' one of the Catholic Church.[28] Now they were joined by a third, in a direct and unambiguous reference to Judaism. Its members included the 'Philistine David', whose identity, thus defined, was unmistakeable. The denunciation of the 'Jewish International' was in no way an isolated event. The same category was used explicitly by Lagarde,[29] who sometimes preferred to speak of the 'grey International', in a reference to the grey Jewish eminences that, from the shadows, controlled and manipulated the centres of power.[30] In the publications of the period, the expression 'golden International' was also used, an obvious allusion to Jewish wealth and Jewish finance.[31] But why, in a letter of congratulation to Nietzsche, speak instead of an 'aesthetic International'?

The first to use this term was Cosima's first husband. Still on good terms with his ex-wife, he was certainly not unaware of Richard Wagner's denunciation of mercantile predominance in *Judaism in Music*. An unfortunate situation had come about, which had led 'in our time to public taste in art falling into the business hands of Jews'; the sacred sweat of 'the suffering genius of two millennia' had become 'artistic merchandise' in the Jew. In this sense, one could speak of the 'Judaization of modern art,'[32] or – to quote Hans von Bülow – of

---

28   Strauss 1872, p. 264 f.
29   Lagarde 1937, p. 295.
30   Lagarde 1937, p. 338 ff.
31   In Cobet 1973, p. 171.
32   Wagner 1910b, p. 68.

the 'aesthetic International', which choked and vulgarised art, aesthetic judgement and the public taste.

A leading member of this International, through either natural or elective affinity, was the author of *The Old and the New Faith*. Of that, Nietzsche too had little doubt. In both the first *Unfashionable Observation* and the preparatory drafts, he constantly referred to him as 'David Strauss', leaving out the second name, Friedrich, which might have obscured his target's alleged Jewish origin. What made the author of *The Old and the New Faith* particularly repugnant was his 'shameless philistine optimism' (DS, 6, I, 191 [36]). We already know from *The Birth of Tragedy* that optimism was entirely alien to the German essence and connoted with a world antithetically opposed to and in struggle with German authenticity. Here we were dealing with a faith that was not only optimistic but 'shamelessly' so. It completely lacked a sense of shame, a lack according to Gersdorff typical of Judaism.

So, it is easy to understand why Strauss saw the Christian view of an afterlife as woolly and unsustainable: '[T]he heaven of the new believer has to be a heaven on earth' (DS, 4, I, 178 [23]). We are reminded of the fragment quoted above, in which Nietzsche undertook to attack the 'despicable Hebrew phrase that speaks of heaven on earth' (*supra*, 3 §1). This theme was also popular with Wagner, who noted in connection with the Jews' apparent religious fervour:

> Truly, he [the Jew] has no religion, but only faith in certain promises of his god that do not extend in any way, as in all true religion, to a life beyond this real life, but merely and precisely to this present earthly life.[33]

Nietzsche, in turn, made fun of the 'new, comfortable, and agreeable highway to the Straussian paradise' (DS, 3, I, 176 [21]) and of Strauss's 'crudest sort of realism' (DS, 6, I, 190 [35]): 'Thus at bottom the new faith has less to do with a new faith than it does with modern science, and as such it is not a religion at all' (DS, 9, I, 211 [54]). Dühring would later make a similar argument. For him, Strauss 'sounds Jewish not only because of his first name' but also because of his intention to dissolve 'religious faith' in a mishmash of 'vulgar natural science and edification'.[34]

Up to now, Nietzsche's indictment had been clear and explicit, but, at this point the text, unexpectedly, continues as follows: 'Now if Strauss nevertheless claims to have religion, then its grounding principles must lie beyond the realm

---

33   Wagner 1910p, p. 271.
34   Dühring 1897, p. 16.

of modern science' (DS, 9; I, 211 [54]). What were the other sorts of grounds to which Nietzsche referred here? The allusive language gives cause for thought. It recalls the conclusion of *Socrates and Tragedy*, which evoked the danger posed by the 'Jewish press', as well as the passage in *The Birth of Tragedy* warning against the 'treacherous dwarfs'.

Let us continue our reading of the first *Unfashionable Observation* and its polemic against Strauss's philistinism. 'How is it possible that a type such as the cultivated philistine could have emerged [*entstehen*] at all and, once he had emerged [*falls er entstand*], could ascend to the seat of supreme judge over all German cultural problems?' (DS, 2, I, 167 [12]). Once again, we are faced with surprising forms of expression that, because of their allusiveness, obscure more than they clarify. What does the first question mean? It seems to suggest that the figure of the cultivated philistine referred to a remote past rather than to something recent. After receiving *Socrates and Tragedy*, Romundt observed in a letter to Nietzsche that in Nietzsche's lecture Socratism was a sort of 'eternal sickness' (B, II, 2, 176). This 'ewige Krankheit' now assumed the form of philistinism, and both configurations referred to Judaism.

Now the meaning of the second question becomes clearer: what processes had enabled this already old figure of the cultivated philistine to accumulate enough power to lay down the law in the artistic field? Here, there is an echo of the criticism we saw a moment ago in Wagner, that Judaism controlled 'the public taste in art'. But Nietzsche pressed on with his questions, all of them more or less allusive: how could people achieve a position of pre-eminence who only in a moment of delirium could claim to 'own' something fundamentally alien to them, that is, 'genuine originary German culture' (DS, 2; I, 167 [13])? The 'great heroic figures' produced by it seemed, confronted by the squalor of the present, to ask a reproachful question of the German nation: 'Is there a soil [...] that is so pure, so pristine, of such virginal sanctity that the German spirit might erect its house upon it and upon no other?' (DS, 2, I, 167 [12–13]). The first *Unfashionable Observation* was obsessively concerned with the loss of purity and the contamination not only of the 'spirit' but also of German 'soil.'

In Germany, a chasm separated reality from 'this contented, even triumphant faith' that Germany already had a 'genuine culture', able to shape the entire life of the nation in a unified and coherent way. The contrast should have been sensational and clear to all, and yet it was as if an obscure but thereby all the more effective prohibition stopped people realising it: 'How is this possible? What force is so powerful that it can dictate such an "ought not"? What species [*Gattung*] of a human being must have risen to power in Germany that they are able to forbid, or at least prevent the expression of, such strong and simple feelings?' (DS, 2, I, 164–5 [10]).

Rather than a human type in the purely psychological sense of the word, a *Gattung* or species or perhaps even a specific race seemed to exercise power in Germany, at least where public discourse about art and culture was concerned. The analogies with Wagner's denunciation of Jewish predominance are obvious. But Nietzsche answered his own question as follows: 'Let me call this power, this species [*Gattung*] of a human being, by its name – they are the *cultivated philistines*' (DS, 2, I, 164–5 [10]). So, would it therefore be misplaced to seek in this passage an allusion, however vague, to Judaism?

4   Superficial Culture [*Gebildetheit*] and Judaism

First, one should note that the philistine was marked by a superficial and artificial *Gebildetheit*. This category played an important part in Wagner's polemic against Judaism in music and in culture in general. Alien to the German people, reluctant to do 'hard, real work', of the sort to which those who grew up 'from below' were accustomed, and incapable of developing their own culture from an organic tie with a specific people, the Jews imposed themselves from the outside and from above. To achieve this result, if the banker contributed his capital, the Jewish musicians or intellectuals contributed their *Gebildetheit*, their capital consisting of a smattering of acquired knowledge.[35] Nietzsche, in turn, charged them with the 'misuse' of culture and 'the selfishness of the money-makers', for whom culture was ultimately synonymous with gain, calculating thought and 'earthly happiness': the target continued to be Judaism, judged according to the stereotypes with which we are already familiar and targeted with the caution that Cosima Wagner had at one point recommended. This is further confirmed by the observation that these 'moneymakers' maintained 'there exists a necessary alliance between "intelligence and property", between "wealth and culture"' (SE, 6, I, 387–8 [218–19]). The identity of these people is clarified once and for all by a fragment written a few years later: 'aristocracy of the spirit is a favourite motto of the Jews' (*infra*, 10 § 4). For those who held such a worldview, 'spirit' and 'culture' were a function only of social advance and the accumulation of capital. In a letter written shortly after the publication of the first *Unfashionable Observation*, Nietzsche expressed his utter contempt for 'the restless Jewish culture mob [*unruhige Bildungs-Juden-Pöbel*]' (B, II, 3, 194–5).

This capital, whether financial or 'cultural', had, in any case, no intimate relationship with the life of the subject and its deepest spirituality. Wagner was

---

35   Wagner 1910g, p. 313.

outraged by the fact that 'this empty cultivatedness arrogates to itself a judgement on the spirit and meaning of our wonderful music'.[36] Nietzsche was no less shocked by Strauss's claim to act as judge of realities that were unknown and alien to him: unfortunately, 'he [is] permitted to make the sign of the cross in public over the greatest and purest products of Germanic genius, as if they were godless obscenities' (DS, 5, I, 187 [32]).

According to Wagner, Jewish *Gebildetheit* was marked by flatness, commitment to 'a beautiful, calm clarity', and mistrust of anything in art and culture that was not 'harmless'. Whether intellectual or properly financial, Jewish capital aimed in all cases merely at achieving comfort and therefore liquidated as 'excesses and exaggerations' everything 'extreme, divine and demonic'.[37] In Nietzsche's eyes, this was exactly how Strauss proceeded: when he happened on the author of *The World as Will and Representation*, he 'reviles him, accuses him of absurdities, blasphemies, and infamies, and even pronounces the judgement that Schopenhauer is out of his mind' (DS, 6, I, 189 [34]).

Ultimately, *Gebildetheit* was part of a group of terms and neologisms that, starting in the period of the wars against Napoleon, emerged in the polemic against subversive or stateless intellectuals, often identified with Jewish intellectuals, a culture branded as rootless and uprooting. In this regard, Treitschke and Bismarck spoke of 'intellectualism [*Überbildung*]' (*supra*, 2 §1). But we find terms like *Verbildung* and *Verbildetheit* in the writings of this and that author and even in dictionaries. It was a pseudo-culture hostile to the 'powers that govern life' or, in the words of Dühring, who explicitly targeted Jews, a culture alien to the 'original, healthy instincts of the people'.[38] Bearers of this deviation were the 'so-called intellectuals [*sogennante Gebildeten*]' or the 'degenerate intellectuals', of whom Treitschke and Dühring spoke, always in the context of a more or less explicit hostility to the Jews.[39]

For Wagner, *Gebildetheit* was synonymous with *Afterbildung*, artificial and spurious culture, trite and imitative knowledge, without vital breath.[40] Alien to the language, life, art and culture of the people among whom they settled, Jews could only 'parrot that language [*nachsprechen*], imitate that art [*nachkünsteln*]', and thus they could only produce *Afterbildung*.[41] This latter category also made its appearance in Nietzsche, who condemned the false and artificial

---

36   Wagner 1910g, p. 314.
37   Ibid.
38   In Cobet 1973, pp. 111, 29; Dühring 1881b, pp. 45, 65, 87.
39   In Cobet 1973, p. 204; Dühring 1881b, p. 3.
40   Wagner 1910g, p. 314.
41   Wagner 1910b, p. 71.

culture along with the *Afterschulen* or pseudo-schools that transmitted it (VII, 268). This puts the *Afterphilologie* of which Rohde accused Wilamowitz in a new light, for Wilamowitz was, as we know, not by accident called a Judais-ing author, unable to understand either the German tragic vision of life or the creativity and originality expressed in *The Birth of Tragedy*. In a letter dated October 1872, after saying how happy he was to see Wilamowitz unmasked as a master of *Afterphilologie*, Gersdorff set the depth of Wagner's reflections on music and art in general against the superficiality of the modern exponents of a 'pseudo-aesthetics [*Afterästhetiker*]', who engaged in defaming or isolating the great musician, in cahoots with 'reform-Jewish national-liberal' journalistic circles (B, II, 4, 107–8).

If we look further back, we come across Schopenhauer's harsh criticism of 'Hegelian pseudo-wisdom [*Afterweisheit*]'.[42] It is interesting to note that this judgement appeared in a text linking the basic themes of Hegel's philosophy with Judaism (*infra*, 6 § 2). Nietzsche's condemnation of *Afterkultur* (VII, 805) and of *Spass- und Afterphilosophie*, the culture and philosophy of excess and artificiality associated with the apologists of modernity (SE, 4, I, 365 [197]), was also not unconnected with the anti-Jewish polemic, which ran deep through the writings of the early period.

5   Philistinism and Judaism

In seeking to remove all that was great and disturbing from art, culture and life, *Gebildetheit* (noted Wagner) is 'in wise accord with the Philistine of our time'.[43] So even the central category of the first *Unfashionable Observation* can already be found in the thinking of the musician, where it resonated with Judeophobic tones. Even earlier, Schopenhauer spoke with contempt of the Apostles of that 'Jewish demagogue' Jesus (*supra*, 1 § 11) as the 'twelve Philistines of Jerusalem'.[44] In late nineteenth-century Europe, the polemic against the commercial view of life, which led to vulgarisation and massification, jointly targeted 'Jews and philistines', all of whom were foes of both the warrior and the artist.[45]

How does Nietzsche fit into this context? While he denounced the 'Socrat-ism' of the 'Jewish press', the above cited Basel lecture noted that the hero of Euripides's tragedy, strongly influenced by Socrates, was a 'dialectician', imbued

---

42   Schopenhauer 1976–82c, Vol. 4, p. 179.
43   Wagner 1910g, p. 314.
44   Schopenhauer 1971, p. 44.
45   Mayer 1984, pp. 287, 291.

with a culture 'optimistic from the depths of its being', and a 'herald of triviality and moral philistinism [*Philisterei*]' (ST, I, 546–7). So this philistinism was closely linked with Socratism and optimism, both of which referred to Judaism. The 'death of tragedy' was decreed by the triumph of a worldview that had 'philistine existence [*Philisterdasein*]' as its ideal (VII, 40).

In a note titled 'Against David Strauss' written a couple of years later, Nietzsche said: 'The philistrious [*philiströs*] impotence of this cultivation [*Bildung*]. Resignation and affected cheerfulness. Without any feeling [*gefühllos*] for what is German' (VII, 586 [156]). Philistinism not only tended towards optimism ('artificial serenity') and 'resignation' (accommodation to modern civilisation, which celebrated its triumphs above all in France), but was synonymous with that which was alien to Germanness. Once again, we are brought back to the anti-Jewish polemic, above all because the main channels for the dissemination of this philistine *Bildung* were 'newspapers' and 'journals' (DS, 11, I, 222 [63]), the press, where the presence of Judaism was felt more strongly than ever.

The agreement with Wagner, who believed that common to *Gebildetheit*, philistinism and Judaism was the search for a 'clear, transparent serenity' that was 'tritely' content with existence and did not allow itself to be in any way disturbed by 'that which is serious and terrible in existence',[46] is clear to see. Nietzsche's reproach of Strauss was not so very different: 'He behaves like the proudest idler upon whom fortune [*Glück*] ever smiled, as if existence were something hopeless and questionable' (DS, 8, I, 202 [46]).

Rohde dispelled any remaining doubt about the anti-Jewish components of the critique of philistinism. After making the connection, as we have seen, between the author of the savage review of *The Birth of Tragedy* with the repellent Jewish civilisation and opulence of Berlin, he later, in a letter dated 1 November 1872, called him a 'gaping philistine [*gaffender Philister*]' (B, II, 4, 115).

The link between Judaism and philistinism is also confirmed by the history of the latter term. The first *Unfashionable Observation* mentions it: 'The word "philistine", as is well known, is drawn from the vocabulary of university students' (DS, 2, I, 165 [10–11]). We are referred to the period of the struggle against the Napoleonic occupation: secret patriotic societies spread across the country, excluding 'philistines' as well as Jews, even baptised ones; both groups were accused or suspected of seeking an accommodation with the occupiers, for the sake of a quiet life or because of ideological and political complicity, due to a common banausic view of life and a lack of ideals. '"Jews, Frenchmen and

---

46   Wagner 1910g, p. 314f.

Philistines" were seen then as representatives of the Enlightenment' and its inherent superficiality. The observation belongs to Hannah Arendt, referring in particular to Brentano,[47] an author Nietzsche knew and appreciated (IX, 600). In his youth, he had also read Menzel (*infra*, 28 §2), who formulated his indictment of the 'liberal philistine' or the 'self-righteous philistine' as follows: indifferent and perhaps even sympathetic to the 'foreign occupation' of Napoleon and imbued with 'the cosmopolitanism of the Enlightenment', he tried to 'imitate French liberalism'; 'in the name of culture [*Bildung*]', everything Christian and German was hated, and everywhere one 'serves alien idols and pays court to false prophets'. The links with 'Freemasonry' and even Judaism were obvious: not for nothing was he inspired by the 'little Jew Heine'. Menzel found one of the incarnations of this repugnant figure in Strauss.[48]

In the struggle to shake off Napoleon's military yoke, the *Burschenschaften*, student associations and corporations, played an important role: according to Brentano, the 'student', insofar as he was immersed in 'research of the eternal, of science or of God' and a 'worshipper of ideas', was the radical opposite of the 'philistine', shut away like a snail in the shell of the banality of his everyday life. This is the antithesis between *Burschenthum* and *Philisterthum*.[49] We saw how one of the lectures *On the Future of Our Educational Institutions* praised the *Burschenschaft*. Now, the first *Unfashionable Observation* settled accounts with Strauss, 'a true philistine with a cramped, dried-up soul' (DS, 10, I, 216 [59]). The anti-philistine polemic took as it target not only the Jews but also the masses, considered crude and vulgar.[50] To some extent, Strauss also belonged to the masses, for he was part (according to Nietzsche) of the 'class of scholarly laborers [*gelehrter Arbeiterstand*]' (DS, 8, I, 205 [49]), a 'cultivated philistine'.

Later, looking back at the first *Unfashionable Observation*, Nietzsche would write: '[M]y essay introduced the term "cultural philistine [*Bildungsphilister*]" into the German language' (EH, *Unfashionable Observations*, 2 [112–13]). In fact, it had already been used three years earlier, by Rudolf Haym, in his reconstruction of the polemic of the romantics and of Tieck in particular against the shallowness and banausic attitude of Enlightenment intellectuals.[51] But Nietzsche seemed not to know about this text, so one can assume he coined the term independently. Behind him stood in the first place Wagner, for whom the fig-

---

47   Arendt 1959, p. 120.

48   Menzel 1869, pp. 240–7.

49   Losurdo 1997a, 8, §1.

50   Losurdo 1997a, 8, §1.

51   Cf. Rickert 1920, p. 58 f., fn. 2; in 1867 the first edition of *Kapital* polemicised against the '*gebildeten Philister*' who were seeking to prettify the reality of capitalism.

ure of the 'cultured Jew'[52] tended to coincide with that of the 'philistine of our time', with whom we are already familiar. On the other hand, mockery of the 'cultured Jew' was commonplace in anti-Semitic polemics.[53] Infected in Wagner's eyes with philistinism, *der gebildete Jude* sought desperately to distinguish himself from 'his lower-class fellow-believers', on whom the stamp of vulgarity was most clearly imprinted;[54] in Nietzsche, the 'cultured Jew' became *der gebildete Philister* or, more often, *der Bildungsphilister*, the 'cultured philistine', who in vain affected a cultural superiority over the masses, of which he was actually an integral part.

There can be no doubt about the continuity of the Judeophobic tone. The campaign against philistinism seemed to be defined in the first *Unfashionable Observation* as a national liberation struggle:

> Should it be possible for the Germans to mobilize to raise that calm and tenacious courage, which they opposed to the pathetic and sudden impetuosity of the French, against their own inner enemy, against that extremely ambiguous and unquestionably no-native 'cultivatedness' [*Gebildetheit*] which, in a perilous misunderstanding, in present-day Germany is called culture [*Kultur*], then all hope for a truly genuine German cultivation, the opposite of that cultivatedness, would not be in vain.
>
> DS, 1, I, 160–1 [6–7]

The victory at Sedan did not put an end to the struggle 'for the German spirit' (DS, 1, I, 162 [6]). The alien element from which liberation was to be sought in order to gain or regain authenticity was undoubtedly Judaism. The first *Unfashionable Observation* was on a line of continuity with *The Birth of Tragedy*, which called upon Germany to shake off the weight of the 'treacherous dwarf'.

This was a constant concern of the young Nietzsche before the 'Enlightenment' turn. According to a note of the autumn of 1869: 'One of Richard Wagner's Jewish enemies had announced in a letter the advent of a new Germanness, Jewish Germanness' (VII, 25). That was a prospect that, four years later, continued to agitate the author of the first *Unfashionable Observation*. He still felt the influence and appeal of Wagner, and in 1873 drew up *An Appeal to the Germans* that called on the nation to regain its German originality and authenticity: 'The people need, now more than ever, to be purified and consecrated by the sublime magic and terror of authentic German art' and 'popular [*volksthümlich*]

---

52   Wagner 1910b, p. 73.
53   Cf. Boehlich 1965, p. 97.
54   Wagner 1910b, p. 73.

drama' (MD, I, 893–6). Here, too, the reference was to *Volksthum*, to which Jews were not only alien but for which they constituted an element of contamination.

As Nietzsche himself recognised, it was a case of an appeal 'in favour of Bayreuth' (B, II, 3, 165), that is, in favour of an initiative and a circle marked, beyond a common love of music, by a political programme meeting with resistance and difficulties. 'We "Wagnerians"', said Rohde, are forced to engage in a struggle that sometimes seems hopeless (B, II, 4, 78). It was a fight in which Nietzsche fully participated. Even before that, annoyed that a newspaper had placed him among 'Wagner's literary lackeys', he had voiced his satisfaction at seeing that his friend Rohde also stood by his side (B, II, 3, 72). The fourth *Unfashionable Observation* was also intended as a clear statement of support not only for the great musician but also for the 'Bayreuth Festival', the 'event at Bayreuth', an extraordinary 'enterprise such as that of Bayreuth'; one was to be able to look with 'great insight' at the 'event at Bayreuth', without being confused by the 'very unmagical lantern of our jeering journalists' (WB, 1, I, 432–4 [260–1]), by that rather 'Socratic' and rather 'Jewish' press, which had all along remained a constant target, ever since the period of gestation of *The Birth of Tragedy*.

6   Judeophobia, Anti-Semitism and Theoretical and Artistic Surplus in Nietzsche and Wagner

So, must we dismiss the writings of Nietzsche's pre-'Enlightenment' period as a series of anti-Semitic pamphlets? There is no doubt that, in them, German culture is viewed through the lens of the anti-Semitic Wagner. This is not merely because of the opinions expressed about Meyerbeer or Strauss or Heine. After all, Heine emphasised Meyerbeer's link with the 'young, generous, cosmopolitan [*weltfrei*] Germany of a new generation',[55] Young Germany, which the Judeophobes or anti-Semites contemptuously defined as Young Palestine.[56] Beyond this or that representative of it, the young Nietzsche condemned Young Germany in a language that gives food for thought: we are, he said, dealing with a 'degenerate literary art' whose perhaps most significant exponent, Gutzkov, was 'a degenerate man of culture [*entarteter Bildungsmensch*]' (BA, 5, I, 746– 7 [135]). Moreover, the young Nietzsche aired quite a few of the themes that

---

55   Heine 1969–78, Vol. 3, p. 339.
56   Poliakov 1968, p. 416.

would subsequently stoke up the anti-Semitic polemic. However, when this polemic broke out in November 1879, on the occasion of an article by Treitschke warning of the danger posed to Germany by an influential and inassimilable Judaism, the philosopher had already broken from his earlier positions.

But we are now discussing the writings of his early period. Were they anti-Semitic pamphlets? First of all, we must distinguish between racial anti-Semitism in the real sense, whose practices of exclusion and oppression allow no escape, being supposedly nature-given, and, on the one hand, Judeophobia (an attitude of insuperable hostility to the Jewish cultural and religious tradition, which fuels discrimination, more or less radical, at the political or social level, or at both) and anti-Judaism (a critical attitude that does not call into question Jews' civil and political equality).[57] The Judaism of *The Birth of Tragedy* is not defined in racial terms. In the letter of 1870 cited above, in which Nietzsche commented ironically about 'our "Jews"', one cannot but notice the quotation marks. He added, addressing his friend Gersdorff: 'You know how far this concept reaches.' Remaining within the same circle of friends, we have seen how Rohde aimed his barbs primarily at the 'circumcized in spirit'. So, in this case, as the philosopher's subsequent evolution confirms, it would be better to speak of Judeophobia than of anti-Semitism; or, more accurately, of anti-Judaism bordering on Judeophobia, perhaps with the refusal to grant German Jews full civil and political equality (*supra*, 3 § 6).

Wagner, on the other hand, stood from the very start on the grounds of Judeophobia. In a certain sense, his pamphlet itself was a sort of reversal of the boast of Disraeli, the British statesman of Jewish origin, who claimed an overwhelming hegemony for the 'Jewish' race even in the musical field (*infra*, chap. 18 §1). Wagner's polemic was aimed at Judaism as such, and seemed to go as far as to demand the disemancipation of the German Jews, as reflected in his scornful comments on 'equal rights' and the 'emancipation of the Jews', an 'abstract principle' propagated by a 'liberalism' fundamentally alien to the people.[58] So it was clearly a case of Judeophobia, always on the verge of over-flowing into actual anti-Semitism. It is true that Wagner distinguished between 'Judaism' in the proper sense and 'Judaism in music', understood in a spiritual and ideal-typical sense.[59] The 'repugnance [*Abneigung*]' or 'revulsion [*Widerwillen*]' in respect of 'Jewish essence' arose 'from the deepest intimacy', it was 'natural', 'instinctual', 'spontaneous [*unwillkürlich*]' and irresistible. It was a sentimental and perhaps physiological reaction, felt by individuals but also with

---

57   Losurdo 1999.
58   Wagner 1910b, p. 67.
59   Wagner 1910b, p. 84.

a communal dimension, it was a 'popular [*volkstümlich*] revulsion', felt also by the very people who said they wanted to emancipate the Jews.[60] Evidently, this Judeophobia had a strong ethnic and naturalistic component. On the one hand, Wagner gave expression to a violent assimilationism, directing the Jews to commit cultural 'self-destruction';[61] on the other hand, he himself cast doubt on the possibility of a real integration and fusion, as shown by his observation that the equation of Jews and Germans in Germany reminded him of Mexico, where blacks were allowed to pass for white or to acquire the same rights as whites, after filling up a bureaucratic form in however slapdash a way.[62] In a conversation in April 1873, the musician opposed mixed marriages, arguing that 'blond German blood' would be subjected to the 'corrosive' effect of Jewish blood.[63]

Nietzsche was present at that conversation, and one can say he distanced himself all the more clearly from his previous Judeophobia as the naturalistic and Judeophobic crudity of Wagner's substantial anti-Semitism became ever more evident. One might add that the young professor's anti-Judaism or Judeophobia certainly played a significant role in the denunciation of modernity, but through a series of filters. In this sense, Cosima's advice to be careful about what he said may have had a positive effect: far from remaining confined to the verbal level, the self-censorship led to a kind of sublimation and transcendence of immediacy, in the sense that the merciless analysis of modernity became to a certain extent autonomous of the Judeophobic themes that accompanied it. For example, there can be no doubt that the critique of a culture reduced to mass-journalism fed on Judeophobic themes, but one cannot deny the fascination and freshness of an analysis of modernity as 'a homogeneous group of people who seem to have conspired to take control of the modern human being's hours of idleness and meditation – that is, of his "cultured" moments – and to drug him by means of the printed word' (DS, 1, I, 161 [7]).

Anti-Judaism and Judeophobia probably also played a role in the critique of the haste and excitement of the modern intellectual and of Strauss. Wagner repeatedly criticised 'the busy and restless Jewish spirit',[64] 'the customary restlessness of the Jews',[65] the 'precipitation' that in the case of Eduard Devrient was in full harmony with his terrible German.[66] Yet Nietzsche's denunciation of

60   Wagner 1910b, pp. 66 f., 76.
61   Wagner 1910b, p. 85.
62   Wagner 1910p, p. 265.
63   C. Wagner 1976–82, Vol. 2, p. 667.
64   Wagner 1910e, p. 256.
65   Wagner 1911, p. 387.
66   Wagner 1910d, p. 226.

the intellectual reduced by haste and excitement to the level of an 'exhausted laborer' who thereby forfeited every critical faculty remains instructive: 'The most obvious question does not even occur to our scholars: What is the purpose of their labor, their frantic pace, their painful frenzy?' (DS, 8, I, 202–3 [46–7]).

Some analyses identify surplus not only in the Judeophobia but also in the author's openly reactionary intentions. A similar point can be made about Wagner: the relationship between Wagner's prose writings and his operas is mirrored in that between Nietzsche's letters and notebooks on the one hand and *The Birth of Tragedy*, the lectures *On the Future of Our Educational Institutions* and the first *Unfashionable Observation* on the other.

PART 2

Nietzsche in His Time:
Four Successive Approaches to the
Critique of Revolution

∴

Infamous profanation of a well-meant word, 'liberalism'.

VII, 355

• • •

[W]e are by no means 'liberal'; we are not working for 'progress'; [...] we contemplate the necessity for new orders as well as for a new slavery – for every strengthening and enhancement of the human type also involves a new kind of enslavement.

FW, 377 [241]

• • •

My terrible 'antidemocratism'.

B, III, 3, 58

• • •

The term 'aristocratic radicalism' that you use is very good. Let it be said without offending anyone, it is the most intelligent word I've read so far about myself.

B, III, 5, 206

• • •

[W]e cannot help being revolutionaries.

EH, Why I am so clever, 5 [92]

• •
•

CHAPTER 6

The 'Solitary Rebel' Breaks with Tradition and the 'Popular Community'

1   Prussia's 'Popular Enlightenment' as Betrayal of the 'True German Spirit'

In the early 1870s, no cloud seemed to trouble the horizon of hopes opened up by Sedan. Its realisation was in no way deferred to a remote and problematic future but it could already be located in the 'entrails of the present', so it was safe 'to promise a future victory to an already existing cultural tendency'. Naturally, it was important not to underestimate the obstacles and resistances. And yet – Nietzsche continued – this trend towards the tragic and Hellenic regeneration of Germany 'will be victorious, [...] because it has the strongest and mightiest of all allies in nature herself' (BA, Introduction, 1, 645–6 [10–15]). 'Despair' in the face of the vulgarity of the present made no sense: '[I]ts time is over; its days are counted' (BA, 2, 1, 673 [44]).

And, yet, none other than Prussia, the hegemon state of the Second Reich, was staging a drama that very soon raised disturbing questions: 'Why does the State require that surplus of educational institutions, of teachers? Why this education of the masses [*Volksbildung und Volksaufklärung*] on such an extended scale?' (BA, 3, 1, 710 [89]). There was a senseless proliferation of higher schools. Subordinated as it was to the professions, or rather to the 'so-called' professions (BA, 1, 1, 663 [49]), culture became a means of social mobility and social ascension: hence the rush for education and qualifications.

Even the army was affected: the desire to make one's way up the military hierarchy contributed to 'the universal congestion of all Prussian public schools, and the urgent and continual need for new ones' (BA, 3; 1, 707 [86]). Naturally, the spread of education also made possible a broader and better qualified military cadre. And, so, a situation came about in which the conditions of Prussian schools were 'admired by, meditated upon, and occasionally imitated by other States' (BA, 3, 1, 708–9 [88]); but this precisely confirmed the danger. Even the tiny island of 'military genius' (*supra*, 2 § 6) ran the risk of being swamped by the tide of modernity. In fact, Adam Smith had highlighted the link between modernisation (including military modernisation) and the spread of education. An illiterate could never be a good soldier, for he could neither understand his country's 'great and extensive interests' nor manage to 'defend his country in times of war'.[1] This was yet another reason – according to the great British economist – why the state should intervene actively to promote the spread of elementary education.[2] Wedded to the archaic ideal of 'military genius', Nietzsche criticised not militarism but the process of massification (and to a certain extent of democratisation) also taking place in military life. At this level too, the devastating consequences of the tendency towards the spread of education in order to have the 'greatest possible number of intelligent officials' could be felt (VII, 243).

Beyond the fact of general vulgarisation loomed an even greater threat. If everything came to depend on educational achievement, 'privilege' could no longer be justified (VII, 243). Viewing culture as a means to social advancement and well-being led not to a lessening but to an intensification of conflict: '[T]here arises the great and awful danger that at some time or other the great masses may overleap the middle classes and spring headlong into this earthly bliss. That is what is now called "the social question"' (BA, 1, I, 668 [37]). Once again, there came the spectre of a slaves' revolt, evoked earlier by *The Birth of Tragedy*, against the 'injustice' to which the slaves believed the deprivation of earthly happiness subjected them.

Nietzsche concluded: 'Universal education [*allgemeine Bildung*] is merely a preparatory stage of communism.' By accepting or suffering the 'dogma' of 'universal education', the Second Reich, and Prussia in particular, were promoting and strengthening a movement aimed at ditching 'great individuals', who would now be called upon to 'stand in the queue', so as to promote only 'servants of the masses' or, more properly, 'servants of a party' – a massification that gave further impetus to the socialist party (VII, 243–4).

So, a sort of *coup de théâtre* happened. Far from keeping its promise of the tragic regeneration of Europe, the Second Reich now seemed to embody 'scientific Socratism' and 'popular enlightenment'. It thus came to be seen 'to have a menacing and dangerous consequence for the true German spirit' (BA, 3, I, 707 [85]). Let us return to Nietzsche's initial question: why was Prussia promoting such a senseless expansion of the school system and, thereby, such a dangerous view of culture? Sadly, the answer it elicited left less and less room for doubt:

> Because the true [*echt*] German spirit is hated, because the aristocratic nature of true culture is feared, because the people endeavour in this way

---

1 Smith 1981, p. 782 (Book 5, 1, part 3, art. 2).
2 Smith 1981, p. 787 f. (Book 5, 1, part 3, art. 2).

to drive single great individuals into self-exile, so that the claims of the masses to education may be, so to speak, planted down and carefully tended, in order that the many [*Vielen*] may in this way endeavour to escape the rigid and strict discipline of the few great leaders, so that the masses may be persuaded that they can easily find the path for themselves – following the guiding star of the State!

BA, 3, I, 710 [89]

Behind this mistrust of and hostility towards Prussia lay a long tradition, which had frequently seen Prussia as the embodiment of the Enlightenment: nowhere in the world had the French ideas found as many followers as in Prussia, declared Gentz at the end of 1803. And, three years later, Friedrich Schlegel emphasised that 'no German government' so resembled the French as did the Prussian. The horrific bureaucracy was described by Adam Müller as a hotbed of 'Jacobins from above', particularly rampant 'in German state administrations [*Staatsadministrationen*]'. Shortly after the revolution of 1848, even Bismarck denounced the 'inclination of a large part of the Prussian bureaucracy towards levelling and centralization' and even towards 'red democracy', since public functionaries ended up unmasking themselves as 'royally Prussian court Jacobins'.

Nietzsche's disappointment at and resentment of the policy actually adopted by Germany after Sedan were part of this tradition. With a Reichstag elected by universal (male) suffrage busy spreading mass education everywhere, Germany offered no alternative to modernity, at either the political or the cultural level. Rather, one could not imagine anywhere a more complete and shameful abdication of the mission to struggle against civilisation and resist subversion. It was the defeat of the 'true German spirit', which now 'drags out an isolated, debased, and degraded existence' (BA, 4, I, 725 [108]).

2   The Germanic Myth of Origin and the Condemnation of Hegel

The tutelary deity of the capillary spread of education, of the multiplication of schools, of the redoubling of efforts to get at every level the largest possible number of intelligent functionaries, was Hegel: among his most prominent disciples was Lassalle, who, not by accident, had come out explicitly in favour of communism (VII, 243). The settling of accounts with the Prussia of 'popular enlightenment' and of 'scientific Socratism' was also a settling of accounts with Hegel. *On the Future of Our Educational Institutions* energetically condemned the Hegelian category of morality, or the view of the state as an 'absolutely complete ethical organism' (BA, 3, I, 711 [90]): this 'exaggerated concept of the state' (VII, 412) and this 'apotheosis of the state' were hopelessly in contradiction with the '"true German spirit"' (BA, 3, I, 708–10 [87]).

This harsh verdict was fully in accordance with the orientation prevalent at the time in German national-liberal circles: towards Hegel, one could feel only 'mistrust', 'aversion', 'repugnance', all the more so since, as a result of the exhilarating experience of victory against France and the founding of the Second Reich (according to Haym in the journal *Grenzboten*, with which Nietzsche was also familiar[3]), 'We have learned the true meaning of the universal, to which we would not wish, as in the Hegelian system, to see the individual sacrificed'. The target of this controversy was in the first place the Hegelian category of morality, considered alien – also by Dilthey – to the Germanic spirit:[4] in it one heard the echo of the Rousseauian and Jacobin ideals of the *citoyen* and of the demand for state intervention in the economic and social sphere, which had left a deep and devastating stamp on France's political and cultural tradition. For this reason, Treitschke established a dual contrast: on the one hand, the 'concepts of freedom of the Germans, who put a constant emphasis on the absolute right of personality', on the other, the Hegelian pathos of morality; on the one hand, an 'individualistic people' like the German, on the other, the French people, whose 'hereditary sickness' was represented by the 'omnipotence of the state in welfare matters'.[5]

These interventions by Treitschke, Haym and Dilthey date from the 1860s or from 1870 and 1872, the period of Nietzsche's formation and of the genesis and definitive elaboration of *The Birth of Tragedy* and the lectures *On the Future of Our Educational Institutions*. But, for a more direct reference to his spiritual world, we can better look to what Haym had written in the late 1850s, to explain his condemnation of Hegelian philosophy and especially of the category of morality:

> It was not the most noble and correct political views that had grown in the soil of the French Revolution. They stood in contradiction to the protestant-Germanic principle of the free personality. They stood in contradiction to the Greek ideal of the beautiful consonance of the natural and the spiritual.[6]

---

3   Haym 1927, p. 484.
4   Dilthey 1914–36, p. 71.
5   Treitschke 1886, p. 6; Treitschke 1865, p. 208 f.; later Treitschke would criticise the 'deification of the state' (1897–98, Vol. 1, 32).
6   Haym 1974, p. 262; cf. Losurdo 1997a, ch. 3, §1.

Against the French cycle of revolution and its claim to build a political community that could achieve earthly happiness for everyone the young Nietzsche too set not just Hellenism reinterpreted in a tragic key but a Germany that included among its merits the fact that it was the land of the Reformation, of Luther and the Protestant chorales. The Franco-Prussian war coincided with the hundredth anniversary of the birth of Hegel. The defeat of the country he admired was also an opportunity to expel the philosopher from authentic Germany. Nietzsche explicitly referred to the anniversary. In a letter to his friend Gersdorff on 7 November 1870, he described the enthusiasm Burckhardt had aroused in him, adding: 'In today's lesson he treated Hegel's philosophy of history in a way certainly worthy of the jubilee' (B, II, 1, 155–6).

There can be no doubt that the étatism for which Hegel was criticised was alien to the German essence. But did it refer only to France and the revolutionary tradition? We have already mentioned the link between the 'apotheosis of the state', optimism and Judaism established by Schopenhauer, who said in private conversation: '*Les Juifs! maudits soient-ils! Ils sont pires encore que les hégéliens!*'[7] And when Schopenhauer, in *Parerga and Paralipomena*, contemptuously conflated the 'synagogues and the lecture rooms of the Faculty of Philosophy',[8] he was naturally thinking primarily of the influence long exercised in Germany by the philosopher he hated most.

Beyond étatism and the associated optimism, what rendered Hegelian philosophy suspect was its legitimation of modernity. According to Wagner, who never tired of railing at the 'liberal-modern Jews'[9] and the 'victory of the modern Jewish world',[10] Judaism and modernity were one and the same thing. To quote another author followed closely by Nietzsche in these years, Lagarde said the Jewish people identified more than any other with 'modern culture'.[11] Hegelian philosophy also seemed to relate to Judaism from another angle: by sanctioning the legitimacy of modernity and *Jetztzeit*, it expressed, according to Schopenhauer, 'the tritest philistinism' not to say the 'apotheosis of philistinism'.[12] For the rest, Hegel had already been branded a 'philistine' by authors and movements with Judeophobic tendencies in the period of the anti-Napoleonic resistance.[13]

---

7   Schopenhauer 1971, p. 331.
8   Schopenhauer 1976–82c, Vol. 5, p. 443.
9   Wagner 1910m, p. 60.
10 Wagner 1910m, p. 58.
11 Lagarde 1937, p. 365.
12 Schopenhauer 1976–82c, Vol. 4, pp. 213, 190, 183.
13 Cf. Losurdo 1997a, 8, §1.

In circles influenced by Germanomania and animated by the pathos of Germanness, an elective affinity at least seemed an unlikely explanation for Hegel's Judaism. By elevating the state to an 'end in itself' and arguing that people achieved 'spiritual reality [...] only through the state', Hegel (according to Lagarde) showed himself to be so alien to the 'German essence' as to arouse the most disturbing doubts. He had admired Napoleon, and he in turn enjoyed the protection of 'apostates' of Germanness; among his best-known disciples was an Eduard Gans, who – a clear allusion to Gans's Jewish origins – could 'understand nothing of the German stock [*Art*]'.[14]

Nietzsche did not go so far. Yet it is significant that in his youth he not merely condemned Hegel for his 'tritely optimistic view of the world' (VII, 595 [165]) but counted him among the 'misfortunes of emerging German culture' and linked him again and again with Heine, who at the time was probably Hegel's best-known disciple of Jewish origin (VII, 504, 595, 598 and 600–1 [84, 165–7]). Symptomatic, moreover, was his characterisation of the poet: he 'destroys the feelings for a unified stylistic tone and is infatuated with the motley mixture of colors characteristic of the clown's outfit. [...] [H]e is a virtuoso who has mastered every kind of style in order to jumble them together' (VII, 595 [164]). At least at the cultural level, Heine's stateless nature was evident: he was incapable of agreeing seriously with any content, since he was alien to the people and the country in which he lived. In this sense, Treitschke talked of 'virtuoso formal talent', but he described it as 'soulless' and identified therein an essential element of the fortunately short-lived 'irruption of Judaism' into German literature.[15] We have already seen how Nietzsche emphasised the disastrous combined effect of Heine and Hegel on authors who, for 'national reasons', as Jews, were alien to the 'German language' (*supra*, 5 § 2). One might say that 'the Hegelians and their crippled progeny' were 'the vilest of all the corrupters of German' (DS, 12, I, 228 [70]). Nietzsche was perhaps alluding to Lassalle's Jewish origins when he observed that the disciple of Hegel, when engaged in stoking up the discontent of the masses and in encouraging them to raise ever more demands, believed that it was the 'rich wastrel' rather than the 'poor Lazarus' that deserved to be carried by the angels into 'Abraham's bosom' (VII, 243). If Strauss's Jewishness was beyond all doubt, the shadow of suspicion of affinity (in this case merely elective) with Judaism also touched on his teacher or ex-teacher. Whatever the case, in these years, Nietzsche also saw Hegel and his school, defined in a strongly anti-Jewish or Judeophobic way, as alien to the German essence.

---

14   Lagarde 1937, p. 376 f.
15   Treitschke 1981, Vol. 3, pp. 711, 714.

This is further confirmed by another aspect of the ideological and political controversy of these years. The condemnation of the 'Jewish dialectic' and
of 'Jewish dialecticians' and their destructive and subversive intellectualism
played a central role in the campaign against German Jewry.[16] Needless to say,
the dialectic led straight to Hegel. Treitschke attributed to Heine a 'sharp Jewish intellect nurtured in the school of Hegel'.[17] Similarly, Dühring accused the
poet of having learned Hegel's 'bad abstruse philosophy', which reminded one
a bit of the 'sophistry' so dear to Jewish intellectuals; moreover, socialism was
propagated in Germany by people 'circumcised in the manner of the Jews' who
wore 'Hegel's threadbare cast-offs'.[18] Wagner, for his part, not only condemned
the 'dialectical jargon of the Jews [*dialektisches Judenjargon*]'[19] but pointed out
that, as part of the 'Jewish agitation'[20] against him, the most insidious attack
was launched by 'a connoisseur of the Hegelian dialectic' who took pains 'prettily' to disguise his 'Jewish ancestry' and, just as 'prettily' and 'elegantly', to give
'a dialectical form' or a 'dialectic colouring' to his clichés.[21] Hegelianism and
Judaism were said to be closely united in the artificial intellectualism that distorted reality and natural feelings.

These themes resonated in Nietzsche, albeit in a mediated and so to say
sublimated way: the Socratic (and Hegelian) dialectic was synonymous with
(Judaising) optimism, and was particularly valued by the 'theoretical human
being', whose 'cheerfulness' and 'cheerful optimism' were at ease in a world,
like the Alexandrian, steeped in Jewish culture (GT, 17 [85] and 19 [91], I, 115
and 124). Because of his arid rationalism, irredeemably deaf to 'myth', the 'theoretical human being' was not only alien to the 'people' but its 'antithesis' (WB,
9, I, 485 [309]). Once again, the contrast between Germanness and Socratism
(Judaism) made its appearance. But one was not to forget that Socrates was
only 'the archetype and progenitor' of the theoretical human being (GT, 18, I,
116 [86]), and this figure lived on in Hegel and his school and in all those who did
not understand or who resisted the tragic worldview. In the eyes of his friend
Gersdorff, the 'theoretical human being' was Wilamowitz, who with his 'dialectic à la Lessing' and his attack on *The Birth of Tragedy* had by then entered
the ranks of 'Berlin's literary Judaism' (B, II, 4, 9–10).

---

16   In Boehlich 1965, pp. 105, 113, 122, 167.
17   Treitschke 1981, Vol. 3, p. 711.
18   In Cobet 1973, pp. 119, 81, 65.
19   Wagner 1910e, p. 255.
20   Wagner 1910e, pp. 249, 254.
21   Wagner 1910e, p. 243.

3   Delegitimisation of Modernity and Diagnosis of the 'Historical
       Sickness'

The picture presented by Prussia of 'popular enlightenment', of universal education and Hegelian morality, was discouraging. And yet, given these phenomena were radically alien to the true German spirit, there was still room for
hope. After all, 'nature' could sooner or later ensure Germany's tragic and Greek
regeneration. And in fact, there was no shortage of confident declarations. The
'eternal purpose of nature' and its 'sacred hierarchy' were in the process of
reasserting their rights and the 'necessary law of nature', 'the concentration of
education for the few' (thus excluding the vast majority of humans, born, as we
know, to 'serve' and 'obey') (BA, Introduction, I, 647 [13]). The renewed victory
of nature and of its inherent aristocratism would coincide with the victory of
tendencies 'as completely German as they are rich in promises for the future'
(BA, Introduction, I, 647 [13]).

Except that, far from vanishing, artificial and unnatural democratic social
engineering (with its accompanying hallucinations like 'human dignity' and
the 'dignity of labour'), this anti-Hellenic and anti-Germanic worldview, was
increasingly successful in imposing itself in the very country born or reborn
to a new life on the wave of the struggle against the ideas of 1789. There was
no longer anything that could ensure the defeat of modernity, which had on
its side, if not nature, then two thousand years of history that risked becoming
second nature.

By now the chasm that separated Nietzsche from Burke's school, from those
who, in opposition to the revolutionary upheavals, celebrated the placid and
tranquil course of peaceful tradition, is plain to see. A comparison with Taine
can help. Following in the footsteps of the British statesman, and in a polemic
against the Enlightenment, the French historian tenderly described the *ancien
régime*, which was based on 'timeless custom' and at the same time recognised
the inheritability of property and Christianity's role in society. 'And what legit-
imates this religion? Above all, a tradition of eighteen centuries, an immense
number of past and concordant witnesses, the enduring faith of the sixty previous generations.'[22] But it was precisely this long historical period under the sign
of Christianity and modernity that Nietzsche sought to call into question. That
is why the second *Unfashionable Observation*, in taking aim at the authors that
celebrated modernity and tried to show it was irreversible, ended up turning
against the arguments prized by Taine (and Burke):

---

22   Taine 1899, Vol. 2, p. 3.

For what is it about a couple of millennia (or, expressed in different terms, the time period of 34 consecutive human lives at 60 years apiece) that permits us to speak of humanity's 'youth' at the beginning of such a period, and of its 'old age' at the end!

HL, 8, I, 303-4 [138-9]

Traditionalism might well suit the lazy defenders of the good old days, but not those who wished to call into question two thousand years of history, reactualising and proposing for the future a past that only conformists and the servile could consider vanished once and for all. On the other hand, the liquidation of modernity here invoked could hardly be imagined on the basis of a banal scheme of development, even if the development were in a backward direction. On the contrary, a radical break was needed: by producing something 'thoroughly new' in comparison with the Second Reich, Wagner could 'well arouse the indignation of all those who swear by the doctrine of gradual development as though it were some kind of moral law' (WB, 1; I, 433 [261]). The great musician's artistic activity, which had revived Greek tragedy after an interminable silence, could be a model or stimulus for political action. Far from signifying a yielding to a dream world or an impotent yearning, evoking the fascinating reality of ancient Greece called attention to a still present possibility and therefore looked to the future: 'That work of art of the future is not at all a splendid but illusory mirage; what we hope for from the future has already been a reality, in a past more than two thousand years away from us' (GMD, I, 532).

The defeat of the land of revolution and civilisation seemed to have created a new and favourable situation: 'We still may hope for a revival of Greek antiquity of which our fathers have not even dreamed', he wrote from Basel on 14 July 1871, to Richard Meister, president of the Leipzig Philological Society. The serious study of classical antiquity had nothing to do with dead scholasticism: 'Do not think that we should be satisfied with parched and arid pastures, like starving cattle' (B, II, 1, 210). No, declared a contemporary piece: 'If philology is not to be mere craft or hypocrisy, it is not possible to continue to live with it in the old environment.' A new direction was needed: 'The Greek philosophers are our model' (VII, 155). Greece as a whole could and was to serve as a source of inspiration: its antique division into 'castes' could 'midwife the birth of genius' and thus perform a 'supreme and difficult task' (VII, 413).

But, to confer credibility on a project as ambitious as Nietzsche's, it was not enough to denounce the intrinsically 'servile' nature of the 'apologists of history' (HL, 8, I, 310 [145]), and the irredeemably 'philistine', i.e., banausic and plebeian, character of the rationality on which they claimed to base themselves. It was necessary to problematise and deconstruct the categories of history and reason. Nietzsche was well aware of this. After first reducing 'so-called world history' to a 'proud metaphor' (*supra*, 1 §19), he took aim at the 'religion of historical power' (HL, 8, I, 309 [144]). One was to settle accounts with the 'enormous historical need of dissatisfied modern culture' that, in the name of reason and history, called for accommodation to the present and its legitimation (GT, 23, I, 145–6 [109]). It was necessary to put an end to the 'excess of history' (HL, 8, I, 305 [91]) and even to 'historical cultivation' as such (HL, 8, I, 303 [118]), to a 'historical sensibility [that] makes its servants passive and retrospective', reducing them to 'epigones' (HL, 8, I 305 and 307 [140–2]). It was necessary to heal oneself of this devastating 'historical sickness' (HL, 10, I, 329 [163]), which injected human beings with the lethal conviction that it would be futile and senseless to pursue new and great prospects aimed at asking radical questions of the present. As a result of the administering of this 'opiate' (WB, 3, I, 445 [272]), together with boldness of thought and project there also disappeared the stimulus to action and, ultimately, to life. 'Historical culture is really a kind of congenital grayness, and it stands to reason that those who bear its sign at birth must arrive at the instinctive belief in the *old age of humanity*' (HL, 8, I, 303 [138]).

Smitten by the 'historical sickness', modern humans were born old and forced from the outset to lead a senile existence without prospects. There were no longer any attempts to sow 'the seeds of the new, to engage in daring experiments, to desire freely, [...] each flight into the unknown [is opposed]' (HL, 8, I, 304 [139]). The fact was, 'the historical sensibility, when it rules *uncontrolled* and is allowed to realize all its consequences, uproots the future' (HL, 7, I, 295 [131]). The future thus glimpsed was a revival of classical antiquity, which the moderns wrongly held, in the name of two thousand years of history, for dead and buried.

4   From the 'Christian' Critique of the Philosophy of History to the
        Critique of the Philosophy of History as Secularised Christianity

Compared with this radical settling of accounts with modernity, the intentions and perspectives of Strauss, also critical of the revolution, appeared mediocre. However, he was content with very little: 'A few pious wishes, the repeal of universal suffrage, retention of the death penalty, limiting the right to strike and the introduction of *Nathan* and *Hermann und Dorothea* in primary schools.' The fact was, for him 'all that is given' could be considered 'more or less rational' (VII, 596–7).

Clearly, to recognise and counteract 'the perversity of contemporary human nature', to eradicate 'the severely twisted and deformed human nature of our age' (SE, 7, I, 407 [237]), to react energetically to 'bad modern habituation' (GMD, I, 518), to be aware of the fact that 'our entire modern world by no means appears to be so solid and permanent that one could prophesy an eternal life for its concept of culture' (SE, 6, I, 401 [231]), in short, to mount a radical challenge to a two-thousand year-old historical cycle that had started with Socrates, was naturally impossible without first coming to terms with the Hegelian thesis of the rationality of the real and of the historical process.

This thesis was widely denounced in the conservative and reactionary culture of the nineteenth century. This culture could certainly not agree with Hegel's assertion that 'world history is a product of eternal reason and reason determined its great revolutions'. According to this view, argued Stahl, an eminent exponent of conservatism, 'modern times would be far superior to the Middle Ages'. Or – according to another critic – one would be forced, in accordance with the 'spirit of the time', to bow down to a 'one-sided preference for so-called *material interests*' and even to Saint-Simonism (and socialism).[23]

Naturally, Nietzsche was less concerned about the delegitimisation of the Middle Ages than about that of Greece, which he took as a model. The thesis of the rationality of the real – as the lectures *On the Future of Our Educational Institutions* have already asserted – was committed to transfiguring an odious and repulsive modernity, to 'bringing the irrational to "rationality" and "reason" and making black look like white' (BA, 5; I, 742 [129]). True, the modern world was the result of a long historical process, it had swept aside all the obstacles that blocked or slowed its rise. But 'greatness ought not to depend on success' (HL, 9; I, 321 [155]), and only a slave could surrender to the 'naked admiration of success' and 'the idolatry of the factual' (HL, 8, I, 309 [143]). Later, Nietzsche would write that 'success has always been the greatest liar' (NW; The Psychologist Has a Word, 1 [278]).

Lagarde, who was also disappointed by the democratic and modern orientations ascribed to the Second Reich, complained in similar terms that 'the Zeus of the modern Pantheon is success'.[24] Frantz, concerned above all by the advance of secularisation and the 'pagan' turn taken by Germany, which had thus surrendered its pious Christian traditions and descended into the shallows of a vulgar and repulsive modernity, noted bitterly that the national liberals had replaced 'justification by faith' with 'justification by success'.[25] Nietzsche

---

23   Losurdo 1997a, 8, § 3.
24   Lagarde 1937, p. 363.
25   Frantz 1970, p. 46.

seemed to some extent to be criticising him when he wrote that the tendency to elevate the 'state' to the 'highest aim of humanity' indicated 'a relapse not so much into paganism as into stupidity' (SE, 4, I, 365 [197]).

At least for a moment, the second *Unfashionable Observation* did not hesitate to refer to Christianity in its polemic against the Hegelian philosophy of history:

> The purest and most sincere adherents of Christianity have always tended to question and impede, rather than to promote, its worldly success, its so-called 'historical power', for they were accustomed to placing themselves outside 'the world', and they paid no attention to the 'process of the Christian idea.' This explains why they have for the most part remained unknown to and unnamed by history. Expressed in Christian terms: The devil is the ruler of the world, and hence the lord of success and progress.
>
> HL, 9, I, 321 [155]

This passage seemed to echo Burckhardt: 'Christian doctrine teaches that the prince of this world is Satan. There is nothing more anti-Christian than to promise virtue a lasting dominion, a material divine reward on earth.'[26] Unfortunately, observed the second *Unfashionable Observation*, modernity, 'our age', boasting of itself as 'the last possible age', acted as if it had been 'authorized to pass the Last Judgement on the entire past – a judgement that Christian belief certainly does not expect to come from humanity itself, but instead from the "Son of Man"' (HL, 8, I, 304 [139]). On another occasion, Nietzsche invoked against the 'idolatry of the factual' not Christianity but 'morality', which required one to swim 'against the historical tide' and always kept in mind the distinction between being and having to be (HL, 8, I, 310–1 [145]).

How to explain the appeal to morality on the part of an author whose philosophy was about to become synonymous with immoralism? The polemical target was a viewpoint, derived from politics or the philosophy of history, that claimed to justify philosophically the cancelling of the democratic 'rights of genius' consummated in the modern world by forgetting that, given the rarity of genius, few 'have a right to live [*Recht zu leben*]'. According to the young Nietzsche, the fact 'that many still live and that those few no longer live is nothing but a brutal truth, that is, an incorrigible stupidity, a tactless "That's just the way it is [*es ist einmal so*]"', as opposed to morality that says: "It should not be this way [*es sollte nicht so sein*]." 'Yes, as opposed to morality!' (HL, 8, I, 310–1 [145]).

---

26   Burckhardt 1978a, p. 191.

The continuity between the reference to Christianity and to morality, both polemically invoked against a philosophy of history that wished to justify the world that had emerged from the revolution, is evident. But suddenly we come up against a quite different thesis, that the legitimation of modernity and the assertion of its irrevocability would, ultimately, amount to 'a disguised Christian theodicy' (WB, 3, I, 445 [272]). Ranke had criticised the idea of progress precisely by referring to the theodicy: a God that favoured one generation to the detriment of another, less advanced and less successful, would be allowing 'injustice' to hold sway, for 'every era is in immediate relationship with God and its value lies not in what flows from it, but in its very existence, its singularity'.[27] From generation to generation, human beings were called upon to address the same existential problems, to live lives marked by finitude, pain and death. Nietzsche spoke praisingly of the great historian (*infra*, 28 §2), but he struck out in a quite different direction and began to criticise the philosophy of history that legitimised modernity and revolution, no longer in the name of Christianity, but, to the contrary, because he believed that philosophy was unable to cast off the religious tradition behind it. We were dealing, according to Nietzsche, with a superficially secularised version of the 'Christian-theological conception, inherited from the Middle Ages', which saw in the advent of Christianity the fullness of the times [*plenitudo temporum*] and therefore considered the historical process to have been basically completed. 'In this sense, we still live in the Middle Ages and history is still a disguised theology' (HL, 8, I, 304–5 [140]).

We have before us a new and fascinating chapter in the ideological struggle that developed above all after 1789 and had its centre in Germany. Polemicising against the theorists of the reaction and turning against them the theological arguments and themes they themselves used, Hegel accused them of 'atheism of the moral world': To denounce the modern world *en gros* would end in denying the presence of the divine in human affairs, so that the moral-political world seemed '*gottverlassen*', abandoned by God, and thus unable to embody true spiritual values.[28] On the other hand, the second *Unfashionable Observation* now turned against the followers of the revolution the ideology they themselves professed: in spite of their rebellious and iconoclastic posing, they were affected by the same theological worldview they claimed to contest and eliminate.

---

27   Ranke 1980, p. 7.
28   Hegel 1969–79, Vol. 7, p. 16.

5   Philosophy of History, Modernity and Massification

And yet, despite this turn in Nietzsche's manner of arguing, the target remained
the same. With and in modernity now triumphed 'that form of history [...] that
takes the great drives of the masses to be what is important and paramount in
history, and that views all great men as their clearest expression, as if they were
bubbles that become visible on the surface of the flood' (HL, 9, I, 320 [154]).
By this time, it had become customary to 'write history from the standpoint of
the *masses* and scrutinize history for those laws that can be derived from the
necessities of these masses, that is, for those laws that govern the movement of
society's lower strata, its loam and clay'. In this way, the philosophy of history
distorted the natural order, the natural aristocracy:

> Only in three respects does it seem to me that the masses are deserving
> of notice: first, as faded copies of great men printed on poor paper with
> worn-out plates; second as resistance to the great; and finally, as tools of
> the great. With regard to everything else, they can go to the devil and stat-
> istics.
>
> HL, 9, I, 319–20 [154]

Naturally, this truth sounded untimely or unfashionable. But to bow to the
'power of history' meant bowing 'as mechanically as a Chinese puppet to every
power – regardless of whether it is a government, a public opinion, or a numerical majority' (HL, 8, I, 309 [143]). The adverb Nietzsche used here, *chinesenhaft*,
was particularly significant. In later years, the Chinese came for him to symbolise the humble and servile worker, eager to please, the new type of slaves the
masters needed. So much was clear: to recognise the *fait accompli* of civilisation and modernity was an attitude typical of servants, not masters. The thesis
of the rationality of the real and the historical process was precisely the cult
of the numerical majority that found its expression in democracy and in the
growing presence and pressure of the masses and servants. The latter, whose
numerical weight was already felt at the strictly political level, ended up obtain-
ing a valuable and unacceptable recognition also at the level of the philosophy
of history, thanks to a view that ruled out in advance any pretension to withdraw behind the results of the modern world.

It was necessary to overcome the 'historical sickness' so that the 'great individuals' who formed 'the apexes of the intellectual pyramid' could escape the
buffeting of 'universal history [*das Drängen und Stossen der Weltgeschichte*] or
stride through it almost like a ghost passing through a dense gathering' (BA, 4, I,
722–3 [104]). The philosophy of history and even the idea of world history were

synonymous with massification, because it dissolved individual genius into an amorphous mass, an undifferentiated humanity, which became the subject of the historical process or progress.

Nietzsche tirelessly proclaimed his untimeliness, but he was airing themes widely present in the culture of the time. Take, for example, Ranke. According to Ranke, the concept of progress was not 'applicable to productions of genius in art, poetry, science and the state'.[29] Yes, 'there is much in human life, and it is perhaps that which is most significant to which it is not possible to apply the concept of progress'.[30] Here, too, we hear once more a protest against the massification implicit in the idea of progress and the philosophy of history:

> For genius does not depend on the concept of humanity, it has an imme-diate tie to the divine, from which it takes its origin. One would discredit an individual manifestation if one sought to trap it within its epoch; it is based on it but does not merge with it.[31]

The idea of progress was a misconstruing of the creative power of genius, now itself subjected to the anonymity of the historical process, a process that, because of its objectivity and irreversibility, even exceptional individuality could not escape. What happened to genius when, on the basis of the progress that developed from one generation to the next, the basest of human beings, the dwarf, could ride on the shoulders of the giant and see further than the giant himself? Voicing concerns similar to those of Ranke, Lagarde also accused the Hegelian philosophy of spirit and history of failing to recognise the value of the great personality and therefore of being permeated by the 'will of the masses [*Massenwillen*]'.[32] But, independently of this or that author, it was the constellation created in reaction to the past experience of the irresistibility, real or apparent, of the revolutionary tide that convinced its opponents of the need to struggle against the current. In an encyclopaedia published during Nietzsche's formative years, Gentz committed himself to the struggle 'against the wind and waves', and 'the revolutionary fanaticism of the time'.[33]

Such a view of life and history was seen as an essential element in the massification and coarsening of the contemporary world denounced by many authoritative and troubled voices. Think, for example, of Schopenhauer, who,

---

29   Ranke 1980, p. 10 f.
30   Ranke 1975, Vol. 4, p. 256.
31   Ibid.
32   Lagarde 1937, p. 376.
33   Haym 1854, p. 330, division a.

in the same period as Ranke, also offered a radical critique of the idea of progress. He contrasted it to the unchangeable aristocratic reality of nature, which at a hectic pace and in rich profusion 'mass-produced' ordinary people, while only sparingly, and in exceptional circumstances, allowing true individuality and genius to blossom (*infra*, 21 §3). The problem with the idea of progress, and of any historicism, was that it joined together and rendered shallow such different and conflicting realities. In this way, we can now better understand Nietzsche, who, from the very outset, set the 'rights of genius' and the 'metaphysics of genius' against the historical consciousness that had taken shape in European culture.

6   Philosophy of History, Élitism and the Return of Anthropocentrism

As we have seen, the human rights proclaimed by the French Revolution were also denounced as anthropocentrism. But, now, the celebration of the rights of genius led to an even more emphatic anthropocentrism than that criticised. After describing the 'senseless suffering' of animal life, a spectacle that 'arouses profound indignation', the third *Unfashionable Observation* went on to say that 'all of nature presses on toward the human being': in this way it could 'achieve its salvation from animal existence', where 'existence holds before itself a mirror in which life no longer appears senseless but appears, rather, in its metaphysical meaningfulness'. But to what sort of person does this refer? In other words: '[W]here does the animal cease, where does the human being begin! That a human being who is nature's sole concern!' Most of humanity, for most of its life, did not actually transcend 'the horizon of the animal', it simply 'desires with more awareness what the animal craves out of blind instinct': at this stage, 'all this is a continuation of animality'; and so at this stage nature did not yet find its metaphysical justification (SE, 5, I, 377–8 [209–10]).

> The human beings towards which all of nature opens a passage for salvation are [...] those true human beings, those no-longer-animals, the philosophers, artists, and saints; with their appearance and by means of their appearance, nature, which never leaps, takes its only leap; and it is a leap of joy, for it feels that for the first time it has arrived at its goal.
>
> SE, 5, I, 380 [211]

The moments of the Schopenhauerian overcoming of the will to live were here recuperated as diverse manifestations of the figure of genius, which alone could give sense and meaning to life.

Referring to Goethe, Nietzsche did not hesitate to rehabilitate the *causa finalis*: '[A]ll of nature presses and drives onward for its own salvation' to 'the ultimate and supreme becoming' (SE, 5, I, 382 [213–14]). Far from weakening this view, the encounter with Darwinism seemed to further strengthen it:

> How gladly we would apply to society and its aims a lesson that can be derived from the observation of every single species of animal and plant life, namely, that the only thing that matters is the superior individual specimen, the more unusual, more powerful, more complex, more fruit-ful specimen – how gladly, that is, if inculcated delusions about the aim of society did not put up stubborn resistance! In fact, it is easy to under-stand that the goal of any species' [*Art*] evolution is that point at which it reaches its limit and begins the transition to a higher species [*Art*]; its goal is not a large number of specimens and their well-being, nor is it those specimens that are the last to evolve. On the contrary, its goal is precisely those seemingly scattered and random existences that arise here and there under favorable conditions. And it should be just as easy to understand the demand that because humanity is capable of attaining consciousness of its aim, it must search out and produce those favorable conditions in which those great, redeeming human beings can come into being.
>
> SE, 6, I, 384 [215]

The worldview (and philosophy of history) expounded here should have been obvious and normal, except that it was tenaciously contested from two quite different points of view. On the one hand were those (the radical-democratic currents and the socialist movement) for whom 'the ultimate aim is supposed to lie in the happiness of all or of the majority'. Others (the nationalists and admirers of the Reich), on the other hand, claimed to find that purpose 'in the development of great communities [*grosser Gemeinwesen*]' (SE, 6, I, 384 [215]).

Naturally, Nietzsche was not rejecting the idea of sacrifice, nor was he cri-ticising the holism implicit in the view that demanded the sacrifice of spe-cific individuals in the name of a being considered superior. Indeed, we have even observed that the third *Unfashionable Observation* sang the praises of the 'powerful community [*Gemeinsamkeit*]', ultimately the cosmic order, that aimed to produce genius regardless of the potential for pain it entailed (*supra*, 1 §14). And the passage just quoted also confirmed that it was always a ques-tion of choosing between sacrifice and sacrifice. From the point of view of the philosophy of history, imposed along with modernity, '[i]t seems absurd that one human being should exist for the sake of another human being', rather than 'for the sake of all others, or at least for as many as possible'. But Nietzsche, directly addressing the individual as such, argued that the problem could be formulated as follows: 'How can your life, the life of the individual, obtain the highest value, the deepest significance? How is it least wasted?' The response was immediate: '[O]nly by living for the benefit of the rarest and most valuable specimens, not for the benefit of the majority, that is, for the benefit of those who, taken as individuals, are the least valuable specimens' (SE, 6, I, 384–5 [215–16]). Only when young people realised this were they placed 'within the circle of *culture*' and 'profess' to it. They were to nourish 'the innermost conviction of encountering almost everywhere nature in its need, in the way it presses onward toward the human being' (SE, 6, I, 385 [216–17]). It was by 'deeds' that those who were by now militants on the part of education and culture were to undertake to ensure that 'the unconscious purposiveness of nature', its 'dark drive', becomes 'aware', in order to achieve that 'supreme goal' that is 'the production of genius' (SE, 6, I, 386–7 [217–18]). But working for genius meant committing oneself to the struggle against the modern world's mass society. Schopenhauer's great merit was described as follows:

> He well knew that there were higher and purer things on this earth to discover and achieve than such a fashionable life, and that anyone who knows and evaluates existence only in this ugly guise does it grave injustice. No, genius itself is now called upon to hear whether this, the supreme fruit of life, can perhaps justify life as such. The marvelous, creative human being is supposed to answer the question: 'Do *you* affirm this existence from the bottom of your heart? Are you willing to be its advocate, its savior? For all it takes is one simple 'Yes!' from your mouth – and life, now facing such grave accusations, will be set free.'
>
> SE, 3, I, 363 [195]

Here, the cosmodicy, the inner justification of the cosmos, led to the celebration of genius: only the production of these exceptional individuals made it possible to reject the accusations against life that in the course of later developments were seen as an expression of nihilism.

The dichotomy of the natural and the artificial, already used to legitimise slavery and condemn as arbitrary and inherently violent any attempt to question it, was now used to assert the natural character of the vision that affirmed the supreme right of genius. To want to abolish slavery or undermine the absolute superiority of genius was an arbitrary act of social engineering against which was set a social engineering that was to some extent natural, one that enabled privileged individuals to behave like sculptors, chiselling away at the masses as if at a worthless raw material:

> A people acquires in its geniuses the actual right to exist, its justification; the mass does not produce the individual, on the contrary, it resists it. The mass is a block of stone hard to hew: a massive effort is needed on the part of individuals to make something of it that has a human semblance.
>
> VII, 244

Compared to the production of genius, common humanity and its history ('[t]he tremendous mobility of human beings on the great earthly desert, their founding of cities and states, their waging of wars', etc)., everything upon which the Hegelian philosophy of history had sought to confer sense, was devoid of intrinsic meaning, as a mere extension of the animal world (SE, 5, I, 378 [210]). So it was a question not of eliminating the philosophy of history as such but of replacing a tendentially democratic philosophy of history with a harshly aristocratic one: 'Humanity should work ceaselessly toward producing great individuals – this and only this should be its task' (SE, 6, I, 383–4 [215]). On the one hand, the Hegelian philosophy of history, centred on the idea of progress and now become an instrument for the legitimation of democracy and socialism, was attacked as 'theology in disguise'; on the other, Nietzsche, in a language replete with theological and teleological echoes, indicated the production of a few exceptional individuals as the 'redemption' of nature and the ultimate cause of the natural and historical process.

7 Cult of Tradition and Pathos of Counterrevolutionary Action

If one set against the hubris of reason the role of instinct and unconscious wisdom, transmitted quietly across the generations, one celebrated not revolutionary rupture but tradition and an attitude of reverence and piety towards institutions and relationships consecrated over the centuries. This was Burke's attitude. When, in 1799, Novalis, a great admirer of the British Whigs, described the clash then taking place at the European level between revolution and counterrevolution, he described the former inter alia as 'the taste for what is new and young', as 'casual contact among all citizens' and 'pride in principles universally valid for all human beings [menschliche Allgemeingültigkeit]', and the latter as 'reverence for the past, attachment to the historical constitution [geschichtliche Verfassung], love for monuments to the ancestors and the ancient glorious nation [*Staatsfamilie*]'.³⁴ Later, Savigny would treasure Walter Scott's 'loving eye for historical circumstances and objects'.³⁵ He too set 'purely rational' concepts with a claim to 'universality' against 'historical sense' and 'history', both summoned to perform the 'sacred' task of serving as a barrier to the ruinous wave first of the Enlightenment and then of the French Revolution.³⁶

Here, too, Nietzsche was not short of themes that referred, either directly or indirectly, to Burke. The grandiloquence of the British statesman gave way to tones that sang in a more subdued yet perhaps more seductive way: '[T]he contentment the tree feels with its roots, the happiness of knowing that one's existence is not formed arbitrarily and by chance, but that instead it grows as the blossom and the fruit of a past that is its inheritance and that thereby excuses, indeed, justifies its existence' (HL, 3, I, 266 [104]).

One could appreciate the denunciation of the journalistic slickness and violence with which language was treated: one was not to lose sight of the fact that it 'is an heirloom that is handed down from one's ancestors and that one bequeaths to one's descendants, something that one should honor as one would honor something holy and inestimable and sacrosanct' (DS, 12, I, 235 [76]). The same went for 'our educational institutions'; they 'link us with the past of our people, and are such a sacred and venerable legacy' that the 'numerous alterations which have been introduced into these institutions within recent years' were inadmissible and calamitous (BA, Introduction, I, 645 [9]). The 'mythical home' *The Birth of Tragedy* set against a culture without a 'secure and sacred place of origin' (GT, 23, I, 146 [109]) could also help to defuse social conflict:

> How could history serve life better than by binding even less-favored generations and populations to their native land and native customs, helping them settle in, and preventing them from straying into foreign lands in search of better things for whose possession they then compete in battle [*wetteifernd zu kämpfen*]? At times what ties individuals, as it were, to these companions and surroundings, to these tiresome habits, to these barren mountain ridges, seems to be obstinacy and imprudence – but it is an imprudence of the healthiest sort, one that benefits the totality.
>
> HL, 3, I, 266 [103–4]

---

34   Novalis 1978, p. 748.
35   In Stoll 1929, p. 279 (Letter to Jacob Grimm of 24 December 1821).
36   Savigny 1967, pp. 115–17.

In this sense, Burkean themes were resumed, with an eye not so much to the French Revolution as to the 'social question' and the socialist movement.

On the other hand, the tradition of thought that began with the British statesman was seen to be inadequate and of no real use for the immense task Nietzsche now set himself, 'freeing modern man from the curse of modernity' (BA, 4, I, 713 [92]). Centuries and millennia of history had again to be called into question, and that could certainly not happen under the signboard of a lazy cult of tradition. That was not the way in which the urgently needed counter-revolutionary activism could be called into being. The view of history of Burke and the German school of history

> understands only how to *preserve* life, not how to create it; therefore, it always underestimates those things that are in the process of becoming because it has no divining instinct. [...] Thus, antiquarian history impedes the powerful resolve [*Entschluss*] for the new, it lames the person of action, who as person of action, must always offend certain acts of piety.
>
> HL, 3, I, 268 [106]

At this point, the cult of tradition was shown to be not just inappropriate but even counterproductive and paralysing: 'The fact that something has grown old gives rise to the demand that it be immortal'; it is something to which 'an old custom, a religious belief, an inherited political privilege' could cling (HL, 3, I, 268–9 [106]). The examples were neither imaginary nor random. After the victory in the war against Austria at the time of the founding of the North German Confederation, Prussia had annexed some German states and abolished the small local dynasties, also in order to give continuity and spatial compactness to its territories: this in clear violation of the principle of legitimacy and of the 'rights consecrated by traditions and ideas'.[37] To accept Burke's and the historical school's view would mean casting a heavy shadow of suspicion onto the Second Reich, with which Nietzsche still identified at the time: he had, as we know, greeted the Prussian victory and the Prussian policy of 1866 with enthusiasm. And, as regarded religious faith, *The Birth of Tragedy* was already longing nostalgically for the situation before the advent of Christianity.

While the view of history of Burke and the German school delegitimised a Germany that seemed to embody the hopes of a revival of tragic Hellenism, it also ran the risk of sanctioning and fossilising a situation intolerable in Nietzsche's eyes:

---

37   Schieder 1979, p. 176 f.

The antiquarian sensibility of a human being, of a civic community, of an entire people always has an extremely limited field of vision. [...] This always brings with it one immediate danger: ultimately, anything ancient and past that enters into this field of vision is simply regarded as venerable, and everything that fails to welcome the ancient with reverence – in other words, whatever is new and in the process of becoming – is met with hostility and rejected.

In this way, 'antiquarian history' did not achieve the goal it had set itself: 'When the historical sense no longer conserves but rather mummifies [life], then beginning at its crown and moving down to its roots, the tree gradually dies an unnatural death – and eventually the roots themselves commonly perish' (HL, 3, I, 267–8 [104–5]).

In any case, the antiquarian view of history proved to be awkward and clumsy, definitely inferior to the view of history of the French revolutionaries, who (as *The Gay Science* later emphasised) 'seized Roman antiquity' (FW, 83 [82]) and thus gained nourishment and vigour, even though this operation seemed highly questionable in terms of philological and historiographical rigour. Inspired by a past transfigured and reinterpreted in the struggle against the *ancien régime* and revered as a monument and imperishable warning for later generations, the Jacobins were able in the present day to engage in vigorous action, however mad and criminal:

> Monumental history deceives by means of analogies: with seductive similarities it arouses rashness in those who are courageous and fanaticism in those who are inspired; and if one imagines this history in the hands and heads of talented egoists and wicked fanatics, then empires will be destroyed, princes murdered, wars and revolutions incited.
>
> HL, 2, I, 262–3 [100]

A view of history was therefore needed that summoned to action all those who wished once again to call into question the long and relentless revolutionary cycle. If 'antiquarian history' was able only to promote a cowardly traditionalism, any action aimed at countering the revolutionary use of monumental history could not do without the contribution of critical history. Only the latter could lead to an awareness of the fact that 'the existence of certain things – for example, a privilege, a caste, or a dynasty – really is' unjust and therefore deserved to be destroyed: and so 'its past is viewed critically, when we take a knife [*Messer*] to its roots, when we cruelly trample on all forms of piety' (HL, 3, I, 270 [107]). The difference with traditionalism now becomes apparent.

According to Savigny, historical sense had a 'sacred [...] duty', to warn against the temptation to treat existing political reality with a 'surgical scalpel [*wundär-ztliches Messer*]', which would inevitably risk cutting into 'healthy flesh'.[38]

Significantly, the image of the 'knife' or 'scalpel' was also found in the young Marx, who used this image to say 'criticism' should not restrict itself to being an *anatomisches Messer*, a knife used to dissect reality analytically, but should at the same time be a 'weapon' with which to change reality.[39] Traditionalist immobilism was challenged by two markedly different theories of action, as was immediately evident from Nietzsche's statements. To cut through the roots of institutions that in the meantime had come to be seen as unjust meant questioning 'what is innate and acquired a long time'. However, it was impossible to avoid the challenge. 'But here and there a victory is nonetheless achieved', and as a result the new becomes 'a new habit, a new instinct, a second nature', even a 'first nature' (HL, 3, I, 270 [107–8]). To introduce a new 'habit' and a new 'nature', vigorous action was obviously required.

The struggle against revolution could no longer be carried out while bowing reverently before institutions consecrated by tradition. Like the enemies he intended to fight, Nietzsche also realised the urgent need for action: 'To be sure, we need history; but our need for it is different from that of the pampered idler in the garden of knowledge' (HL, Preface, I, 245 [85]). Beyond historical knowledge, the critique applied to the figure of the pure scientist as such: in his muted world, 'suffering' was 'actually something irrelevant and incomprehensible, which was to say, at most just another problem'. Yes, 'scholarship sees only problems of knowledge', but against this merely theoretical and contemplative attitude it was necessary to stress that 'cold, pure, inconsequential knowledge' (SE, 6, I, 393–4 [224–5]) was despicable, because it was incapable of turning into action.

8   'Schopenhauer's Human Being' as Antagonist of 'Rousseau's Human Being' and of Revolution

So, Nietzsche's strong reservations about 'Goethe's human being' become easy to understand. Although Goethe had the merit of not having allowed himself to be carried away by the revolutionary wave, he nevertheless had a serious limitation: 'He is not the active human being', he was a 'contemplative human being

---

38   Savigny 1967, pp. 115–17.
39   Marx and Engels 1975 ff., 1, p. 159.

in the grand style' and could easily become a 'philistine'. We were dealing with a figure of little use in the struggle against revolution: at best, he could serve as 'a conserving and conciliatory force [...] – but one exposed to the danger, as I have said, of degenerating into a philistine, just as Rousseau's human being can easily become a Catilinarian', this 'threatening power' (SE, 4, I, 369–71 [202–3]) that inspired and drove the upheavals ravaging Europe. But one could not rely on 'Goethe's human being' for a transformation of society, for the longed-for revival of tragic Hellenism.

'Schopenhauer's human being' was quite another thing. Although animated by a passion for knowledge, he was no lover of 'pure knowledge' (SE, 3, 352 and 360 [192]). He was 'far removed from the cold and contemptible neutrality of the so-called scholarly human being'; he never lost sight of the relationship between knowledge and real life; he was 'always sacrificing himself as the first victim of recognized truth'; he not only displayed 'courage' but took up the burden and responsibilities of a 'heroic life' (SE, 4, I, 372–3 [204]).

It might, at first sight, seem strange that the third *Unfashionable Observation*, in evoking the figure of a supporter of the counterrevolution, drew its inspiration from the theorist of *noluntas* as the supreme goal to be pursued. Let us try to reconstruct Nietzsche's reasoning. In his eyes, Schopenhauer, who had passed through Kant's school and studied his distinction between essence and appearance, had first and foremost the merit of having problematised existence, thereby rendering more difficult philistine contentment and immediate identification with the present. By '[i]nciting contempt for his age' (VII, 807 [362]) and refusing to be seduced in any way by anything 'fashionable', 'from his earliest youth [he] struggled against that false, vain, and unworthy mother, his age, and by banishing her from himself, as it were, he purified and healed his own being and recovered all the health and purity that were properly his' (SE, 3, I, 362 [194–5]).

But Schopenhauer's greatness and above all his strength emerged particularly clearly from a comparison with Kleist, similarly wrapped in a 'cloud of melancholy', the sign of the seriousness and depth of noble souls (SE, 3, I, 354 [187]) and of all those 'who do not feel that they are citizens of this time' (SE, 1, I, 339 [173]) and who refused to adapt to a mediocre or repugnant reality. In the poet, however, the Kantian thesis of the unknowability of things in themselves [*an sich*] evoked that 'shattering and despair of all truth' that then led to his suicide (SE, 3, I, 355 [188]). Schopenhauer, on the other hand, knew how to avail himself of Kant's anti-philistine teaching without succumbing to the mortal 'danger' implicit in his philosophy (SE, 3, I, 354 [187]). He did not remain a prisoner of the 'sullen and irksome reflection' of reality (SE, 4, I, 372 [204]), and, for that very reason, he was the one 'who guides us out of the cave of skeptical disgruntlement or of critical renunciation up to the heights of tragic contemplation' (SE, 3, I, 356 [188–9]).

The impulse to action emanating from this philosophy was all the stronger when '[a] happy life is impossible' and 'the highest thing that a human being could attain is a heroic life', in the service of a great end (SE, 4, I, 373 [204]). Thus there emerges the figure of a human being that, having foresworn all vain 'hope to earthly happiness', indignantly rejected 'every enfeeblement of existence' (VII, 794 [349]), and did not flinch from going the whole way: 'His own courage destroys his earthly happiness' (SE, 4, I, 372–3 [204]). Yes, this human being was summoned by Schopenhauer to 'extinguish his individual will [*Eigenwillen*]' (SE, 4, I, 371 [203]). But this was in no way a call to inaction. On the contrary: by renouncing any attachment to one's own obstinate and narcissistic ego, one could devote oneself fully and with abandon to the great end to be pursued. In conclusion, the third *Unfashionable Observation*, without taking fright at the theme of *noluntas* and the rejection of politics or allowing itself to be misled by it, interpreted Schopenhauer as the philosopher who, with his potent demythologisation of modernity, could definitely give an active, energetic, and politically effective answer to the challenge of revolution.

Schopenhauer's courage was already manifest at the level of cognition. He is 'the genius of heroic truthfulness' (VII, 803 [358]). By disdaining half measures and exhibiting an 'unbending and rugged manliness' (SE, 7, I, 408 [238]), he unhesitatingly called the existing order as a whole into question. In this sense, 'anyone who wanted to live in a Schopenhauerian manner would probably resemble Mephistopheles more than he would Faust – at least to myopic modern eyes, which always see in negation the mark of evil' (SE, 4, I, 371–2 [203]). Engaged in a long struggle against subversion and entrusted with an immense and thankless task, Schopenhauer's human being

> must be hostile to the human beings whom he loves, to the institutions from whose womb he has sprung; he cannot spare either human beings or things, even though he suffers with them in their injuries; he will be mistaken for, and long considered to be, the ally of powers that he abhors; due to the human limitations of his insight, he will necessarily be unjust, no matter how hard he strives for justice.
>
> SE, 4, I, 372–3 [204]

Nietzsche tried to warn against superficial correspondences. A few years earlier, Rosenkranz had criticised the 'Mephistophelean interpretation' of revolutionary Hegel-interpreters, in whose eyes 'all that arises deserves to perish [*alles was*

entsteht, werth ist, zu Grunde zu gehen], and it would therefore be better if nothing arose'.[40] Later, Engels saw the final outcome of the dialectic precisely in the
assertion that 'all that exists deserves to perish [*alles was besteht, wert ist, dass es
zugrunde geht*]'.[41] To judge by Nietzsche's reading, however, for Schopenhauer,
the scope of the negation seemed more limited: 'All existence that can be negated deserves to be negated' (SE, 4, I, 372 [203]). But, elsewhere, he attributed
to Schopenhauer the merit of having dared to see that in the modern world
'nothing deserves to be shown any mercy' and '[E]verything is incomplete and
rotten' (VII, 803–4 [358]).

So, the real difference lay elsewhere. It is true that, in Schopenhauer too,
there was a 'dissolving, destroying aspiration', but, despite superficial analogies,
he had nothing to do with subversion: he was 'a liberating destroyer in his age'
(VII, 803–4 [358]). Nietzsche began to explain that the sort of human being
he thought necessary should not shrink back from the 'frightful decisions' of
which Rousseau's human being was capable (*infra*, 7 § 8). 'It is necessary for us
to get really angry for once' (SE, 4, I, 371 [201–3]). The clear way in which the
third *Unfashionable Observation* took its distance from 'Goethe's human being'
reminds one of the *Phenomenology of the Spirit*'s critical analysis of the 'beautiful soul', of 'conscience':

> It lacks the force of externalization, the force to make itself into a thing
> and to endure being. It lives in dread of staining through action and exist-
> ence the splendour of its interiority; and in order to preserve the purity of
> its heart, it flees contact with reality. [...] It may well preserve itself in its
> purity, for it does not act.[42]

Similarly, in Nietzsche's eyes, Goethe's human being had this big disadvantage: '[H]e hates all violence, every sudden leap – but that means, every action'
(SE, 4, I, 370 [202]). The heroic human being, on the other hand, far from
clinging narcissistically to his moral purity, 'disdains his own prosperity or
hardship, his own virtues and vices, and in general the measuring of things
according to his own standard' (SE, 4; I, 375 [206]), so he clashed with the
philistines for whom 'the preservation of their insufficiencies and lies [...] is
a duty of humankind' (SE, 4, I, 371 [203]). If Hegel, in his critique of the 'beautiful soul', was seeking to legitimise the French Revolution, Nietzsche, by taking

---

40   Savigny 1967, pp. 115–17.
41   Marx and Engels 1975 ff., 26, p. 358.
42   Hegel 1969–79, Vol. 3, pp. 483, 487.

his distance from 'Goethe's human being', was aiming to construct a militant alternative to 'Rousseau's human being' and to revolution.

9   Two Intellectual Types: The 'Deferential Bum' and the 'Solitary Rebel'

Where could one hope that 'Schopenhauer's human being' would become established? The lectures *On the Future of Our Educational Institutions* identified grammar-school youth as a possible force through which to realise the intended programme of radically anti-modern and anti-democratic revolt. Restored to its true meaning and vocation, the grammar school would inculcate 'upon young men [...] obedience to the sceptre of genius' (BA, 2, I, 680 [54]) and teach and promote 'obedience and submission to the discipline of genius' (BA, 4, I, 730 [114]). Now, however, it was necessary to acknowledge the reality of the spread of education and of the subjection of the grammar school to 'popular enlightenment'. So, on which circles was one to pin one's hopes?

Certainly not on professors of philosophy or, more generally, government officials, valued by Hegel but hated by Schopenhauer, even before Nietzsche. It was not the 'heroism of truthfulness' that inspired the thoughts and feelings of this social layer: 'Truth is served if it is capable of leading directly to a higher income and a higher position, or at least capable of winning the favor of those who have bread and honor to confer' (SE, 6, I, 398 [206, 228]). Even if immune to careerism in the actual sense of the word, these bureaucrats still tended to 'recognize something higher than the truth – the state' (SE, 8, I, 415 [244]), an institution the pillar of modern subversion and massification. The denunciation applied not only to Hegel: 'Kant was respectful and obsequious [...] in his treatment of the state' (SE, 8, I, 414 [243]).

Apart from servility and sheepishness, the figure of the functionary was also negatively characterised by a narrowness of horizon and professional routinism. The state 'forces those it has selected to take up residence in a specific place, among specific people, and for a specific activity; they are supposed to teach, every day and at fixed hours, each and every student that seeks instruction' (SE, 8, I, 416). On the other hand, the smooth and even comfortable insertion into the division of labour led to a dulling of intellectual capabilities and interests: various kinds of 'compilers' and 'commentators' were busier than ever, but they 'study and carry out research in a single field for the simple reason that it never occurs to them that there might be other fields'. Far from being a merit, '[t]heir diligence has something of the monstrous stupidity of gravity'.

They immersed themselves in research and reading, simply in order to suppress every problem and every attempt at clarification:

> Whereas the true thinker longs for nothing more than leisure, the common scholar [*Gelehrte*] flees from it because he does not know what to do with it. He finds his comfort in books: that means, he listens to other people thinking and thereby manages to keep himself entertained throughout the long day.
>
> SE, 6, I, 397 [228]

So far, Nietzsche's polemic had taken the fascinating form of a demand for the totality, freedom and boldness of intellectual inquiry: 'Let philosophers go on proliferating wildly, deny them any hope of employment or assimilation in civil occupations' (SE, 8, I, 422). But, while condemning the philosophy professors as servile and submissive, Nietzsche gave the political authority advice that seemed to go in a different and opposite direction: 'Since the state can have no other interest in the university than having it educate submissive and useful citizens, it should have misgivings about putting this submissiveness, this usefulness, into question by demanding from its young men that they be examined in philosophy.' The encounter with this discipline encouraged 'reckless and restless youths' to 'become acquainted with forbidden books' and to 'criticize their teachers' (SE, 8, I, 423 [251–2]). This theme was widespread in liberal or conservative culture of the time. Nietzsche shared the judgement of the 'unscrupulous English' Bagehot, who voiced his contempt for a 'deductive philosophy' that consisted of 'abstract principles' and ruinous 'abstractions' (SE, 8, I, 420 [249]).

So the main theme of the third *Unfashionable Observation* was not the dichotomy of impartiality versus servility or of seeking the whole versus professional idiocy. In this case, even the contrast between classical antiquity and modernity did not help, even if Nietzsche did refer to it: 'Today [...] the state makes it possible for at least a number of people to *live* from philosophy by being able to make it into a breadwinning occupation. By contrast, the ancient sages of Greece were not salaried' (SE, 8, I, 413–14). Schopenhauer belonged on a line of continuity with the 'ancient sages'. He was never oppressed by 'any of the vulgar necessities of life' and was thus able to live 'in keeping with his motto *vitam impendere vero*' (SE, 7; I, 411 [240]).

On closer inspection, the contrast between ancient and modern was shown to be that between two different social figures of modernity. On the one hand, Schopenhauer, who could enjoy the 'freer air of a large trading house' (SE, 7, I, 409 [239]), on the other, the scholar by profession [*Gelehrte*], who 'by nature is unfruitful – a consequence of the process that produces him!' (SE, 6, I, 399 [230]). Birth and social position weighed on the latter like a curse. We were dealing with 'a "deferential bum [*rücksichtsvoller Lump*]", greedy for honor and position, circumspect and pliable, obsequious to influential people and his superiors' (SE, 7, I, 411 [240–1]). The condemnation of the abstractness and congenital subversion of intellectuals without a fortune was a recurring theme of the critique of revolution, and Nietzsche's position must be viewed in the same context. Mocking the servility and intellectual ponderousness of the philosopher-functionary was not incompatible with denouncing the subversive potential of the 'abstract' culture of young and often uprooted people: these were two counts in the same indictment, which still targeted the class of intellectuals by profession, tied to labour and the ideology of labour and participating more or less actively and more or less consciously in modern subversion.

But what could one set against all that? Nietzsche was still inching his way forward. The opposite of the 'common intellectual' was sometimes the 'true thinker', sometimes the 'philalethes' (VII, 803–4), sometimes the 'genius', sometimes the 'free spirit', who 'takes a stand as a genius against the weakness of the age' (VII, 807), in short, as we shall soon see, 'the solitary rebel'. One thing is clear: this figure, however characterised, was given a demanding and exciting task that went well beyond the cultural:

> 'Beware', says Emerson, 'when the great God lets loose a thinker on this planet. Then all things are at risk. It is as when a conflagration has broken out in a city, and no man knows what is safe, or where it will end'. [...] A new degree of culture would instantly revolutionize the entire system of human pursuits.
>
> SE, 8; I, 426 [254–5]

The two camps in the struggle are clearly delineated. Against German Social Democracy and the parties of modern subversion, which had stamped even their organisational structure with the seal of massification, were to stand up all those 'banished' by the dominant ideology because of their refusal to bow to the spirit of the age. They were the 'solitary rebels [*Widerspänstigen und Einsamen*] – all those who look to higher, more distant goals', goals other than their careers and accommodation to the present (SE, 6, I, 402 [232]).

In conclusion: 'There are three images of the human being that our modern age has set up, one after the other.' The first, the one that inspired and promoted revolutions, 'possesses the greatest fire' and 'is assured of attaining the greatest popular effect [*populärste Wirkung*]'. To this passion, capable of inspiring a sweeping mass movement, the second image would certainly be unable to offer any resistance, for it was 'made for only a few, for those who are contemplative thinkers in the grand style', and lacked the ability to influence the 'masses'. It was necessary to look elsewhere. Hence the third image. Clearly distinguished from the 'contemplative' image, it sought to influence reality, engage in action; it 'demands as its beholders the most active human beings [*die thätigsten Menschen*]', but without mixing with or contaminating itself through contact with the 'masses', in which respect it also differed clearly from the first image (SE, 4, I, 369 [200–1]).

10   Schopenhauer, Wagner and 'Consecration' for the 'Battle'

One cannot ignore Nietzsche's militant language and tone. In his private notes, he even attacked Burckhardt, whom he counted among 'the degenerate forms of the Schopenhauerian human being' (VII, 795 [350]). As Nietzsche had said in a letter to his friend Gersdorff a few years earlier, the Basel historian had, in the course of 'confidential walks', spoken of Schopenhauer as 'our philosopher'; but, in public, he tended, 'if not to falsify the truth, [...] to keep it quiet' (B, II, 1, 155). He was completely void of 'heroic truthfulness', the most essential quality of 'Schopenhauer's human being'.

It is true that the third *Unfashionable Observation* attributed to the philosopher cited as a model the merit of having denounced the *furor politicus*, but this polemic was itself eminently political, since, as we shall see (*infra*, 9 §2), its target was the growing democratisation and massification of society. To counteract and throw back this trend, one was to strive towards a goal that fell within the field of the 'possible': 'upheaval in our educational system' (SE, 7, I, 404 [234]). One was to do away with a school and university system capable of producing or reproducing 'either scholars [*Gelehrte*], or state officials, or moneymakers, or cultivated philistines, or finally, as is usually the case, a combination of all four' (SE, 6, I, 401 [231]). It was a matter of creating the conditions for the 'genius' or 'solitary rebel', an intellectual of a completely different sort, able to stand up to the modern intellectual. To achieve success, the struggle against modernity and subversion had to be able to unfold over time and was not to exhaust itself in the actions of a single exceptional personality. Admittedly, Schopenhauer's merits were great, but for the '[c]ontinuation of his work [...]' it is necessary to educate [*Erziehung*] a generation of philalethes' (VII, 803–4 [358]), or, to be precise, several generations: '[S]ome generation or other must begin the battle in which a future generation will someday be victorious' (SE, 6, I, 402 [232]). The meaning of the title of the third *Unfashionable Observation*, 'Schopenhauer as Educator', is now starting to become clearer.

But how 'will they be educated [*erzogen*]', this series of generations (VII, 804 [358])? Here is the answer: 'How the Persians were educated: to shoot with a bow and to tell the truth' (VII, 795 [350]). That is to say, the philaletes, the 'true friends' of philosophy, were at the same time to be warriors, who 'prove through their actions that love of truth is something terrible and powerful' (SE, 8; I, 427 [255]).

Between *The Birth of Tragedy* and *Unfashionable Observations*, a number of important changes have come about. The previous denunciation of the the-oretical human being had focused on its claim to be able both to penetrate and transform reality, but, now, the 'criticistic' theme, which persisted and is even radicalised to the extreme, was interwoven with a passionate pathos of action. This explains the clear distancing from Kant. Previously, he was raised by virtue of his 'criticism' into the pantheon of authors who promised the tra-gic rebirth of Germany. This more problematic and sensitive conception of knowledge had, on the one hand, the merit of contesting the theoretical and practical optimism of revolution, but, on the other hand, it had the serious drawback of leading to renunciation and despair, as the tragic story of Kleist shows. This was a philosophy that can be a vehicle for 'corrosive and disin-tegrating skepticism and relativism' (SE, 3, I, 355 [188]). *The Birth of Tragedy* placed Kant in the vicinity of Schopenhauer, but, now, the two authors were kept strictly apart, even on the grounds of their social position: they referred to two intellectual layers that played a quite different and even antithetical polit-ical role.

And so to the second point. *The Birth of Tragedy* identified the start of the destructive development of modernity and the West in the 'theoretical human being' and in the plebeian Socrates, seen as the predecessor of the *philosophe* of revolutionary engagement. Now the 'theoretical human being', still under attack, was synonymous with the '*Lumpen*' (SE, 7, I, 411 [240]) and became the expression of a culture destructive of and hostile to life. But, against this sub-version, which presented itself at the social level in the form of a plebeian mob and at the cultural level with the characteristics of a terrible 'abstraction', was set no longer the member of a 'popular' community respectful of the sacred-ness of myth and tradition but a figure far more modern and pugnacious, able to ride the tiger of modernity at the level of both knowledge and action. This was the 'genius' or, more precisely, the 'solitary rebel': even before it happened in 'actions', the conflict with the intellectuals and the rascals had already started in 'ways of thinking'. '[G]eniuses and scholars [*Gelehrte*] have always been at odds with each other': 'The latter seek to kill nature, to dissect and understand it; the former seek to augment nature with new living nature' (SE, 6, I, 399–400 [230]).

Needless to say, this defence and multiplication of life demanded, under the historically given conditions, an attitude of frontal opposition. A radicalism of denial seemed to underlie both the revolutionary critique and action on the one hand and the metacritique and countermovement, which were supposed to stop them and throw them back, on the other. But one was not to lose sight of the essential: '[T]here is a kind of negating and destroying that is nothing other than the outpouring of that powerful longing for sanctification and salvation, and Schopenhauer appeared among us desanctified [*entheiligt*] and truly secularized [*verweltlicht*] human beings' (SE, 4, I, 372 [203]). The terms used here are highly significant. Having settled accounts with the Enlightenment and with the process of secularisation of culture and society, Schopenhauer represented an alternative to revolution, one quite different from the recourse to religion and to a nostalgic and inactive traditionalism.

The other tutelary god of the struggle against modernity was, of course, Wagner. Around him were gathered forces to which one could not not pay attention: independent intellectuals, often wealthy, who had nothing to do with the figure of the 'deferential bum'. We are already familiar with Nietzsche's appeal in 'favour of Bayreuth' (*supra*, 5 §5). The fourth *Unfashionable Observation* and fragments contemporary with it clarify in unequivocal terms its political significance:

> For us, Bayreuth signifies the morning consecration on the day of battle. One could do us no greater injustice than to assume that for us it is a matter of art alone, as if it were to function as a medicine or narcotic [*Heil-und Betäubungsmittel*] with which we could cure ourselves of all other miserable conditions.
>
> WB, 4, I, 451 [277–8]

One could and was to start out from art if one sought to realise such an ambitious project, which encompassed the whole of reality. On its ground, the vanguard of the movement could form, summoned as protagonists of the coming radical upheaval:

> Art has now become so powerful in the blood of some people that it also determines their relations with the surrounding world. That is a revolution, what is now taking place in Bayreuth, the constitution of a new power that is far from seeing itself as merely aesthetic.
>
> VIII, 248

The anti-modern and anti-democratic 'revolution' here predicted could not, as we know, appeal to intellectuals in the service of the state but only to 'solitary rebels'. Nietzsche was ready to draw all the consequences, also at the personal level. He seemed ill at ease with his membership of a social group he deeply despised. In criticising Kant as 'respectful [*rücksichtsvoll*]' towards authority, like the 'bum', Nietzsche added something very significant: 'as we scholars [*wir Gelehrte*] tend to be' (SE, 8; I, 414 [243]). A few years later, sickness would help him solve this problem, by removing him once and for all from the university and forcing him to live off a small annuity.

The 'Solitary Rebel' Becomes an 'Enlightener'

1   The *Gründerjahre*, Nietzsche's Disenchantment, and the Banishing of the Spectres of Greece

As we have seen, after his initial enthusiasm, Nietzsche became steadily more disappointed and embittered as a result of Germany's abdication of the task of combating modern civilisation and of the tragic and Hellenic mission entrusted to Germany. In a sense, even the most emphatic and unrealistic expectations were intertwined from the very start with doubts, but, for some time, these doubts were neutralised or held in check by the hope for change, by the expectation that different political and cultural trends might win the upper hand in Berlin. But the reality was evident for all to see: as the growing number of educational institutions showed with great clarity, the process of massification was forging ahead with particular impetuosity in Prussia and in Germany. The crisis of the political and theoretical platform of *The Birth of Tragedy* became ever graver, until it eventually exploded.

In *Human, All Too Human*, Nietzsche was forced to acknowledge that it was a waste of time to seek to establish differentiations in the German and European political panorama: as far as the Second Reich was concerned, national liberals and socialists ended up resembling one another (MA, 480 [261]); it was painfully true that a 'demagogic character and an intention of influencing the masses is common to all political parties today' (MA, 438 [236]) – and to all the countries of Europe. Later, retracing his earlier path, Nietzsche wrote: 'I have not allowed myself to be deceived by the splendid emergence of the German Empire. When I wrote my *Zarathustra*, I took as background a situation in Europe through which in Germany too the same frightful and dirty agitation of parties reigns that we find today in France' (XI, 425). In fact, this awareness can already be found in *Human, All Too Human*. Modernity and massification left no escape, any more so than the vulgarity of capitalist accumulation, which had already been criticised by large parts of public opinion, with an eye primarily or exclusively on countries other than Germany.

Nietzsche viewed the Second Reich, which, for him, had in the meantime become a sort of hiding place for modern and subversive ideas, with a contempt and hatred all the deeper given his previous exalted hopes in the regenerating mission of the country he had hailed as the new Greece. One is reminded of Marx's comments about France as it had emerged from the revolution: its protagonists 'performed the task of their time in Roman costume and with Roman phrases, the task of unchaining and setting up modern bourgeois society'; however, once the 'new social formation [was] established, the antediluvian Colossi disappeared and with them resurrected Romanity – the Brutuses, Gracchi, Publicolas, the tribunes, the senators, and Caesar himself'. All the ancient reminiscences were inevitably swept away by the compact concreteness of capitalist society and of the new theory committed to expressing the new reality. The bourgeoisie, '[w]holly absorbed in the production of wealth and in peaceful competitive struggle, [...] no longer comprehended that ghosts from the days of Rome had watched over its cradle'.[1]

More or less the same thing happened in Germany. The Greco-Germanic myth of origin, which, in competition with other myths, had spurred on the struggle against the France of Napoleon I and Napoleon III and strongly influenced the founding of the Second Reich, turned out to be an embarrassment once it had fulfilled its task. Each in his own way, both Wagner and Nietzsche had enthusiastically taken it over. But the former reacted to the new situation by giving autonomous form to the properly Germanic theme and then proceeding to an ever more emphatic celebration of a people called upon to rediscover its origins and its purity, in opposition to both Judaism and Romanism, and, more generally, to the modern and mercantile worldview. As for the latter, in his case the crisis of the Greco-Germanic myth of origin implied a radical break with respect to the beliefs and hopes of the past, and necessitated not just a deepened re-reading of modern and even ancient history but a rethinking of the philosophical and political categories used in the previous interpretation.

2   Taking One's Distance from Germanomania and the Break with the German National Liberals

In *Human, All Too Human*, one no longer finds any trace of the hopes Nietzsche had previously vested in *authentic* German culture and the *authentic* German spirit. His criticism of domestic policy was now linked to his perhaps even more severe criticism of international politics. Far from forming a bulwark against subversion, Germany actively promoted it in neighbouring and rival countries, on the basis of petty chauvinistic calculations that completely lost sight of the main issue. Without explicitly naming him, Nietzsche criticised Bismarck for his ruthless and unscrupulous efforts to weaken and

---

1 Marx and Engels 1975 ff., 11, p. 104.

isolate France. Bismarck was trying to encourage Catholicism in the defeated country, which he wanted to weaken further still; he wanted it to become 'the hearth and home of the Catholic Church', to avert the danger of an alliance with Orthodox Russia: the Catholic Church 'would in fact much rather be allied with the Turks' than with the schismatics (MA, 453 [244]). The promotion of an 'artificial Catholicism' on the other side of the Rhine (MA, 475 [257]) rendered ridiculous the anti-Catholic and anti-obscurantist pathos of the *Kulturkampf.*

Nietzsche had, several years earlier, already expressed strong reservations about this movement. True, he had granted it might come about that '[i]n some countries the fear of religious oppression is so general, and the dread of its results so marked, that people in all classes of society long for culture [*Bildung*]'. He said it was understandable that the state encouraged these trends, but it was not to forget that this was nevertheless a 'desperate remedy' (BA, 1, I, 668–9 [39]). By resorting to the indiscriminate spread of education, in the eyes of Nietzsche synonymous with massification and even communism, the remedy was likely to be worse than the sickness. The international politics of the Second Reich, which did not hesitate to promote the 'blurring of millions of brains in another State', now shed a new and disturbing light on the *Kulturkampf*. The fact was that Bismarck, thanks to the 'Catholicizing [of] France' he promoted, could pose as standard bearer in the struggle against the ultramontane danger (MA, 453 [244]). So we were no longer dealing with a 'remedy', however 'desperate', for a real evil, since, in reality, the very sickness was an invention or result of unscrupulous and cynical manoeuvres. The statesman generally celebrated as a great leader was shown in reality to be, in the title of the aphorism quoted here, *Der Steuermann der Leidenschaften*, 'the helmsman of the passions', and moreover of the most vulgar and least enlightened passions, those of chauvinism and religion (MA, 453 [244]).

But Bismarck's ruthlessness and duplicity did not stop here. While encouraging clerical circles, on the other hand, he 'supports the republican form of government in a neighboring state – *le désordre organisé*, as Mérimée said – solely because it assumes that this government will make the people weaker, more disunited, and less capable of war' (MA, 453 [244]). But (Nietzsche observed in a subsequently deleted supplement) 'this mentality may be useful to the prosperity of a state: it is hostile and harmful to the prosperity of culture as such [*allgemeine Kultur*]' (XIV, 147). The hopes for Germany's and Europe's Greek and tragic regeneration had now been definitively dashed by Bismarck's inexorable 'Machiavellianism' and his 'so-called *"Realpolitik"*' (FW, 357 [217]). In this respect, too, the Second Reich was synonymous with subversion and destruction.

And all this took place in the name of a blind chauvinism now the main target of Nietzsche's polemic. He looked anxiously at the continuing and renewed worsening of tensions between France and Germany. In 1875, Bismarck had initiated a press campaign that puffed up a supposed French danger and created a scare in public opinion and European governments about the possibility of a new war. 'Is war in the offing? [*Ist Krieg in Sicht?*]', ran the title of an article in a Berlin newspaper (*Post*) inspired by the Chancellor. The London *Times*, in an article with the equally telling title 'A French Scare', spoke of an artificially created panic caused by an alleged French threat.[2] Not even Nietzsche believed in this threat: three years later, he would denounce 'artificial nationalism' along with 'artificial Catholicism' (MA, 475 [257]).

But even though this feared and insidiously staged clash did not actually take place, the situation was anything but reassuring. Would Europe go the way of Hellas? Nietzsche had already, a few years earlier, expressed his opinion on the role played by internal conflict in determining the Greek catastrophe: 'This bloody jealousy of one town for another, one party for another, this murderous greed of those petty wars, the tiger-like triumph over the corpse of the slain enemy', the fact that the Greeks had not hesitated to 'sink its teeth into its own flesh', this *agon* without limits or any sense of proportion had produced a splendid culture, but had also brought about its early end (CV, 3, I, 771 [169]). Would Europe too commit suicide by civil war?

> But just as the Greeks wallowed in Greek blood, so do the Europeans today in European blood. [...] The crude patriotism of the Romans is today, when quite different and higher tasks than *patria* and *honor* stand before us, either something dishonest or a sign of backwardness.
>
> MA, 442 [239]

Greece was now compared to Europe, whose unity and peace were to be preserved, and no longer to Germany, which now evoked the disquieting shadow of exclusivity and the cold calculations of Rome's *Realpolitik*. One should also not forget that Nietzsche, although a volunteer in the Franco-Prussian War, immediately regretted and denounced the 'current German war of conquest' when the plans for the annexation of Alsace-Lorraine first emerged (B, II, 1, 164).

We have seen (above, chap. 1 § 8) that, immediately after the trauma of the Paris Commune, the philosopher had called for the 'international hydra head' to be struck off. It is true that, for Nietzsche, the latter showed its repulsive

---

2   Eyck 1976, p. 207 f.; cf. Röhl 1993, p. 275.

and threatening aspect above all in the land ravaged by incessant revolutionary upheavals. However, the coming battle, according to the same letter, went far 'beyond the struggle among nations'. In this perspective, the chauvinistic agitation of the German national liberals was undoubtedly devastating: they threatened to bring about a new outbreak of the conflict with Germany's neighbour and to cause Europe and what remained of the aristocracy and the leading layers to bleed to death in fratricidal strife, and to put a slaves' revolt back on the agenda.

The break with the ideology of the liberal-national movement was by now apparent. During the polemic against Strauss, Nietzsche had already refused to interpret the Franco-Prussian War as a clash of two different cultures (DS, 1, I, 159–60 [5–6]). It is true that, in the years of *The Birth of Tragedy*, he himself had agreed with this interpretation, but with one important modification. Yes, Germany was heir to tragic Hellenism, which represented genuine culture as against the banausic neo-Latin civilisation; but it could live up to its great heritage and mission only on condition that it forcefully rejected the 'autochthonous presumption' (PHG, 1, I, 807):

> Nothing is more foolish than to attribute to the Greeks an autochthonous culture: rather, they have absorbed every culture that lived among other peoples; they have come so far precisely because they have been able to throw the spear further from where another people had abandoned it. They are worthy of admiration in the art of learning fruitfully: and as they have done, so we too *should* learn from our neighbours, looking at life, not at erudite knowledge, and using everything that has been learned as a support on which to raise oneself up high and higher than the neighbour.
>
> PHG, 1, I, 806

Unfortunately, this philological and political warning had had no effect. Now Nietzsche hoped in Europe for the advent of radically new relations under the sign of cooperation and unity: 'The isolation of nations works consciously or unconsciously against this goal by engendering *national* animosities, yet the process of mixing goes forward slowly nonetheless, despite those occasional counter-currents.' Rather than hinder this process through chauvinistic agitation, Germany would have done better to encourage it: '[W]e should simply present ourselves fearlessly as *good Europeans* and in our actions work for the melting together of nations: a process that the Germans' ancient, proven trait of being the *interpreters and intermediaries between peoples* makes them able to assist' (MA, 475 [257–8]).

Despite the evident break with the liberal-national movement, one should not lose sight in these statements of the thin thread of continuity that continues to bind them to the ideology of *Freiheitskriege*, which Nietzsche had previously followed. When Arndt in 1813 contrasted the Germans to the Romans (actually the French), he had directed a significant appeal to his fellow countrymen: 'Be different from the Romans [...]: they never wanted to enter into a peace without territorial gain. You however should show your greatness through justice and moderation.'[3] Nietzsche, who now took this rejection of expansionism seriously, went even further, rejecting all forms of chauvinism and exalted parochialism. Together with the policy of the Second Reich, he also denounced the Germanomaniacal narrowness of culture during the anti-Napoleonic resistance.

It was a narrowness that expressed itself also in an obstinate attachment to an allegedly authentic German fashion, a tendency, however, which, luckily, despite all the warnings of the Germanomaniacs, was on the wane (WS, 215 [244–7]). To fully understand this point, one should bear in mind that, starting with the struggle against Napoleon I, the desire to differentiate oneself from France even with regard to fashion was widespread: whence the promotion, for example, of a 'national dress' for German women and, more generally, of a Spartan simplicity that disdained the trinketry and frills of a vain and dissolute people like the French. This aspiration retained its vitality over a long period, at least to judge by the sarcasm of Gans, Ruge, Heine, and the Hegelian school in general, which resumed a polemical theme of the master, who had been amused by the Germanomaniacs' wish to take over from the 'tailors' by inventing 'traditional German clothes [*altdeutsche Kleider*]'.[4] On the other hand, even in 1872, the abovementioned Frantz argued against those who, infected by Parisian fashion, wanted to 'abolish our ancient, simple Germanness'.[5] And even Wagner complained that 'the Parisian fashion journal' had suggested or dictated to German woman 'how they should dress'.[6]

Traces of this ideology can even be found in the early Nietzsche. In reference to the young Germans that had risen up against Napoleon, the fifth lecture *On the Future of Our Educational Institutions* celebrated 'the noble simplicity' that set them apart 'both in dress and habits' (BA, 5, I, 749 [138]) and compared them positively with the 'luxury' and 'fashion' chased after by modernity (VII, 243). The first serious doubts about this emerged in the second *Unfashionable Obser-*

---

3   Arndt 1963, p. 104.
4   Cf. Losurdo 1997a, p. 9 §6.
5   Frantz 1970, p. 217.
6   Wagner 1910f, p. 116.

vation, which made fun of a trend quite common at the time in Germany: 'A piece of clothing whose invention does not require any ingenuity and whose design does not cost any time – in other words, something borrowed from a foreign country and carelessly copied – is immediately regarded by the German as a contribution to German national dress [*deutsche Tracht*]' (HL, 4, I, 276 [112]). But, starting with *Human, All Too Human*, the tone turned much harsher: talk about fashion was ridiculed as 'national vanity', as an idle affectation made ridiculous by the fact that 'there has *never* been a costume that designated the German as German' (WS, 215 [246]).

In the meantime, the hopeful conversations in the Wagner household about the 'German essence' and the educational institutions that were to restore it to vitality gave way to discussions and acknowledgements marked by an increasing 'disgruntlement' with developments in the Second Reich, to which his friend Overbeck later bore testimony.[7] A cycle now closed, as the harsh polemic against the former teacher unequivocally revealed: 'How good bad music and bad reasons sound when one marches off after an enemy' (M, 557 [276]).

3   Critique of Chauvinism and the Beginning of the 'Enlightenment'

The critique of chauvinism and of Germanomania led, at a more strictly philosophical level, to taking a stand in favour of the Enlightenment, which proved to be the only way of counteracting Bismarck's policy of obscurantism planned from above and the chauvinistic excitement and blinding that were starting to spread across Europe: it was clear that 'science and nationalist feeling are contradictions. [...] [A]ll higher culture can only damage itself now by surrounding itself with a national picket fence' (VIII, 572 [381]). A variant, later dropped, of *The Wanderer and His Shadow* added: 'One thinks back on the homeland as the seat of stupidity and violence' (XIV, 197).

The break with the Germanomaniacs was also a break with the myth of German simplicity and the cult of the soil: 'Wherever ignorance, uncleanliness and superstition are still in vogue, wherever commerce is crippled, agriculture impoverished, and the priesthood powerful, we still find *national costumes*' (WS, 215 [244]). There was more morality in the development of trade and commerce, which brought people together, broke down borders, and did away with xenophobia, than in the Christian commandments or Kant's categorical imper-

---

7   Overbeck 1994–5b, p. 269.

ative: 'If with the word "moral" one thinks of superior utility, ecumenical aims, then *trade* contains more morality than a life' lived according to the precepts of Jesus or Kant. The commandment to love one's neighbour had not prevented the history of Christianity from being 'chock full of violence and bloodshed' (VIII, 460–1). Once again, Enlightenment tones resonated, both in the configuration of the countryside as a place of (religious and national) obscurantism and in the denunciation of the potential, typical of Christianity, for fanaticism and intolerance.

Even before the philosophy of the Enlightenment of the eighteenth century, the Middle Ages had been rocked by humanism and the Renaissance. In this sense, three names were inscribed on the 'flag of the Enlightenment', 'Petrarch, Erasmus, Voltaire' (MA, 26 [36]), as well as the names of the French moralists, who together 'form an important link in the great, ongoing chain of the Renaissance': in praise of their texts, one could say that, 'written in Greek, they would also have been understood by the Greeks' (WS, 214 [243–4]).

The history of Germany had to be relocated within the context of this general history. It now found itself at a disadvantage compared to Italy and France, the neo-Latin world targeted by *The Birth of Tragedy*; it no longer represented the culture that confronted civilisation but the countryside, which loped laboriously in the city's wake. Together with plebeian passions, the urban-rural conflict also played an important role in the analysis of the Reformation. On the one hand, the 'northern [*Nordische*] strength and stubbornness' of Luther, a peasant; on the other, the magnificent urban culture of the Renaissance. In short, the 'German Reformation' was

> an energetic protest of the spiritually backward, who were by no means sated with the medieval worldview and sensed the signs of its dissolution, the exceptional flattening and superficializing of religious life. [...] The great task of the Renaissance could not be brought to completion, the protest of a German nature that had meanwhile remained backward (whereas in the Middle Ages it had sense enough to seek salvation by climbing over the Alps again and again) hindered this.
>
> MA, 237 [163]

Set against the Reformation, this 'kind of redoubling of the medieval spirit at a time when it was no longer accompanied by a good conscience' (FW, 35 [54]), the 'German Reformation', was the 'Italian Renaissance', interpreted in an Enlightenment key, since it was marked by an endeavour to achieve the 'liberation of thought', by 'disdain for authorities', and by 'enthusiasm for science and the scientific past of humanity' (MA, 237 [163]). In the great encounter, it was in peasant and medieval Germany that the centre of obscurantist reaction lay:

> Luther's Reformation, for example, testifies to the fact that in his century, all stirrings of the spirit of freedom were still uncertain, delicate, youthful; science could not yet raise its head. Indeed, the entire Renaissance appears like an early spring that almost gets snowed under again.
>
> MA, 26 [35]

The Reformation was synonymous not only with backwardness but also with fanaticism and intolerance. Nietzsche lamented that Luther, unlike Huss, had not ended up burned: '[A]nd the Enlightenment would probably have dawned somewhat earlier and with a more beautiful luster than we can now conceive' (MA, 237 [164]).

So Nietzsche insisted on the Nordic and Germanic character of the Reformation. Now, the value judgement had been completely reversed, in comparison with that of *The Birth of Tragedy*. The fact that Christianity had, at least in some respects, struck deeper roots among the 'northern nations' was to the detriment of the latter. Catholicism now showed up better than Protestantism. It was widely spread, particularly across southern Europe, and still retained an element of 'religious paganism' (VM, 97 [43]). To be Germanic (or Nordic) and Protestant was no longer a good thing, it was no longer synonymous with a serious and tragic view of life, but with the Christian and barbaric Middle Ages. Not only Luther was overwhelmed. Bach, celebrated in *The Birth of Tragedy* as an essential moment in the revival of the Dionysian spirit in 'German music' (GT, 19, I, 127 [94]), was now radically reinterpreted: in him 'there is still too much crude Christianity, crude Germanness, crude scholasticism'; the weight of the Middle Ages could still be felt (WS, 149 [216]).

4   The Deconstruction of the Christian-Germanic Myth of Origin

'Raw Christianity' and 'raw Germanism' were the two constituent elements of the Christian-Germanic myth of origin that stoked up Germany's mounting chauvinist passion. Here, the demystifying quality of Nietzsche's analysis becomes clearer than ever. In his eyes, the national liberals were parading an ideology untenable on historical grounds and doubly hypocritical: they were Germanomaniacs and 'Cristianeers' (VM, 92 [41]), i.e., they spoke devotedly and contritely both of the Germans and of Jesus Christ (and of course of Luther), while 'the nation creases its face in Germanic and Christian ways'. In this, they had a dual aim: '[W]e demand Germanness out of imperial-political concern' in order to legitimise the world role assigned to the Second Reich, 'and Christianness out of social anxiety', in the hope of promoting resignation among the masses (VM, 299 [116]). But the Christian-Germanic myth of origin stood in stark contrast to actual history:

> To affirm that the German was prefigured and predestined for Christianity would require a fair amount of nerve. Not only is the opposite true, but it is self-evidently so. How could the invention of two prominent Jews, Jesus and Saul, the two most Jewish Jews that have perhaps ever existed, be better adapted to the Germans than to other people?
>
> IX, 80

Christianity had Jewish roots, and, with its 'vicinity, everywhere perceptible, to the desert', Jewish religion was very different from the Germanic, which pointed instead to the 'wild forest' (IX, 80). To realise the unsustainability of the mythological construction that governed the domestic and international politics of the Second Reich, a philological observation sufficed:

> The 'Germans': this originally meant 'heathen'; that is what the Goths after their conversion named the great mass of their unbaptized kindred tribes, in accordance with their translation of the Septuagint. [...] It would still be possible for the Germans to turn the term of abuse for them into a name of honour by becoming the first un-Christian nation in Europe.
>
> FW, 146 [129]

If the Germans had a mission, it was surely not to represent and spread a religion they had embraced late and with such marked reluctance that it had left a mark on the very term used to designate them. True, they had later claimed to be the privileged interpreters of the new religion, but the zeal of the neophyte led to some nasty surprises: 'But the oddest thing is: those who exerted themselves the most to preserve and conserve Christianity have become its best destroyers – the Germans' (FW, 358 [221]). Luther had launched the Reformation in the name of defending the purity of original Christianity, but what had been the real result of his action?

> He surrendered the holy books to everyone – thus they finally ended up in the hands of the philologists, who are the destroyers of every faith that rests on books. [...] He gave back to the priest sexual intercourse with a

woman; but three-quarters of the reverence of which the people, especially the women of the people, are capable rests on the faith that a person
who is an exception in this regard will be an exception in other regards as
well.

FW, 358 [222]

The Christian-Germanic myth of origin loved to present pious and God-fearing
Germany as the champion of the Reformation, the providential bulwark
against the destructive influence of France, debauched, atheistic and enlightened – except that it was Luther who had eventually set in motion the process
of secularisation.

Christomaniacs and Germanomaniacs liked to set themselves against not
just the French (and Romans) but also the Jews. Again, the absurdity of their
mythological and ideological constructions was strikingly apparent. They
ignored or suppressed the historical grounds in which the religion they so passionately professed was rooted. Wagner constantly railed against the Jews, 'to
whom he is unable to do justice even in their greatest deed; after all, the Jews are
the inventors of Christianity' (FW, 99 [97]). There was even an amusing paradox: 'Sin is a Jewish feeling and a Jewish invention; and given that this is the
background of all Christian morality, Christianity can be said to have aimed
at "Judaizing [verjüdeln]" the whole world' (FW, 135 [124]). That is to say, the
Germanomaniacs, with their Christian missionary zeal, applied themselves to
spreading a culture and a spirituality they claimed to despise.

Nor did the provocation stop here. It also directly affected Germany's national hero, often celebrated as the champion of a heroic resistance against
oppression by the Roman Empire. After observing that Judaism, Christianity
and Islam were three creations of Semitism (and thus indirectly ridiculing the
thesis or hypothesis, also dear to Wagner, of the Aryan or in any case non-
Jewish Jesus), Nietzsche proposed this internal differentiation: 'The subtlest
trick, which gives Christianity an advantage over other religions, is a word: it
spoke of *love*. Thus it became the *lyrical* religion (whereas both of the other
creations that the Semitic peoples gave the world were heroic-epic religions)'
(VM, 95 [42]). But, if this was so, then clearly 'what was best in the souls of
Luther and his kindred' was to be found in the 'great Jewish-heroic disposition'
(VM, 171 [72]). So, the Reformation's resistance to Rome had been inspired not
so much by Christianity as by its Jewish heritage.

Finally, Wagner, the point of reference for the fanatics of the Christian-
Germanic myth of origin, might take from Schopenhauer his 'hatred of the
Jews', but he also took from him other themes that had nothing to do with
Christianity: both the philosopher and the musician tried to conceive of Chris-

tianity 'as a seed of Buddhism that has drifted far and to prepare a Buddhistic age for Europe, with an *occasional* reconciliation with Catholic-Christian formulas and sentiments' (FW, 99 [97]).

Even if one disregarded the myth's historical and philological absurdity, it had to be added that the ancient Germans could hardly serve as a model. There was not only the basic contradiction between Christianity, with its Jewish origins, and Germanness: in the confrontation between these two elements it was the one hated by the Germanomaniacs that emerged victorious. Even if they expressed an unacceptable ideology (the feeling of sin, an enhanced ethnocentrism, etc)., the ancient Jews had achieved a level of cultural development far further advanced than that of the ancient Germans: the 'highest moral subtlety, sharpened by the intellect of a rabbi', as against the 'barbaric intellect' of a people still wearing bearskins. Overall, the German was 'indolent, but warlike and greedy for plunder'; he 'has not got beyond the mediocre, authentic religion of a redskin', and had not stopped 'sacrificing human beings on sacrificial stones' (IX, 80). The latter observation was also a polemical poke at the Christian-Germanic zealots: was not the charge of ritual murder a recurring theme in their anti-Semitic propaganda?

5   The Re-interpretation of the History of Germany: Condemnations
       and Rehabilitations

The more radical and explicit the condemnation of Christianity and Germanomania, the more severe and merciless became the judgement on Germany. The shadow of Luther, the peasant who, in the last analysis, rose up in defence of the Christian Middle Ages and of the nation oppressed by Rome-Babylon (the city branded as dissolute and pagan), seemed to lie across the history of Germany as a whole.

Inextricably entwined with Gallophobia, Protestant zeal and the Protestant cult of the soil and of a mythical simplicity of customs played an essential role in the anti-Napoleonic wars, which now, in a reversal of earlier positions, had become an object of ridicule. The cycle, which stretched from 1813 to 1871, ended with Wagner's music, which was deeply imbued with the 'pleasure in everything *nativist, nationalist or primeval* [*Wesen und Urwesen*]' and 'leads the last of all reactionary military campaigns against the spirit of the Enlightenment' (VM, 171 [73]). In this scathing critique, Nietzsche distanced himself from his recent past, when he himself had been a fanatical supporter of the most original possible essence of Germanness, that had to be rid of its alien Roman and Jewish encrustments. Now, however, the philosopher observed polemically: '[W]e will immediately revise the theoretical question: What *is* German?' – that is the title of an essay by Wagner[8] – 'with a counter-question: What is *now* German?' (VM, 323 [125]).

In light of the historical consciousness acquired in the meantime, the 'gods' and 'heroes' that animated the 'traditional sagas [*altheimische Sagen*]', so treasured by the musician and the party that surrounded him, were 'strange [*fremdartig*]' to modern Germany (VM, 171 [73]). They pointed to a remote world it would have been absurd to try to resurrect. Since the aura of timelessness that surrounded them had now vanished, the different 'essences' could no longer be rigidly set against one another: 'What are called national differences are usually different gradations of culture, on which the one people stands earlier and the other later. *Main thesis*' (XIV, 180).

We have seen how the lectures *On the Future of Our Educational Institutions* celebrated both German philosophy and the 'German soldier' (*supra*, 1 §5). Paradoxically, we encounter this same stereotype, though with an opposite value judgement, among those dismayed by the defeat of France. One thinks of Carducci, who exclaimed with reference to the Franco-Prussian War: 'But the iron and the bronze is in the tyrants' hands; / and Kant sharpens with his Pure / Reason the cold priming needle of the Prussian rifle.'[9] One would now say, following the condemnation of the chauvinism of the Second Reich, that the fallen 'soldier' also took down with him the great figures of German culture and Germany itself. In an aphorism written in the autumn of 1878 Nietzsche transcribed a scathing motto by Wieland: 'I cannot recall ever having heard the word German used for honor's sake' (VIII, 572–3 [382]).

Together with the anti-Napoleonic wars, Schiller too was harshly condemned. He was the author beloved of the young people of the *Freiheitskriege* and of the *Burschenschaftler* who feasted on the memories of those years and battles. They saw prefigured in Wilhelm Tell's oath their own sacred duty to oppose Napoleon I and Napoleon III: 'We want to be free like our fathers [...] / Let no emergency or danger separate us';[10] or they identified, as Nietzsche himself recalled, with the revolt of the 'robbers' against the 'tyrants' (BA, 4, I, 748 [137]). Schiller had also become the symbol of the struggle against philistinism, the hero of the rejection of a worldview incapable of understanding the 'dreams of youth', and which as a result – thus

---

8   Wagner 1910l.
9   *Per il LXXVIII Anniversario della proclamazione della Repubblica Francese*, vv. 17–20 (Carducci, 1964, p. 96).
10   *Wilhelm Tell*, Act Two, Scene Two.

Schelling, citing *Don Carlos* – was synonymous with the 'wisdom of the dust' that 'reviles enthusiasm, the daughter of heaven'.[11]

The young Nietzsche had fully shared this Germanomaniac and anti-philistine view. In celebration of 'Germanically conceived nature' (not to be confused with 'ordinary empirical' nature and even less so with that of Rousseau's *Émile*), he had referred to the 'great Schiller's Walk [*Spaziergang*]' (VII, 302). Now, however, he expressed himself in bitterly ironic terms about the poet and playwright, who aroused the enthusiasm of young people only because of 'their pleasure in the jangle of moral sayings (which tends to vanish in one's thirties)' (VM, 170 [71]). According to Nietzsche, this grandiloquence weighed heavily on Schiller's thought and prose: he was 'in every respect a model for how one should *not* treat scientific questions of aesthetics and morality' (WS, 123 [208]).

The moral declamation was proof of the all-pervasive influence the Reformation and Christianity continued to exercise, centuries later. German culture was revealed as poor and still fundamentally hypocritical, compared with the Italian Renaissance and the French Enlightenment. To be more exact, Kant had emphasised the limits of reason in order to 'pave the way for *faith*', and therefore belonged among the 'obscurantists'; he was the expression of a 'most refined and dangerous obscurantism, indeed, the most dangerous of all' (VM, 27 [22]). In this sense, he was a 'half-theological assault upon Helvétius', 'in Germany the most abused of all the good moralists and good humans' (WS, 216 [248]). Nietzsche set his sights on the author who allowed back in through the window of moral postulates the metaphysical content apparently kicked out of the door of pure reason: unfortunately, 'old Kant, who helped himself to [*erschlichen*] the "thing in itself" – another very ridiculous thing! – [...] was punished for this when the "categorical imperative" crept into [*beschlichen*] his heart and made him stray back to "God", "soul", "freedom", "immortality", like a fox who strays back into his cage. Yet it had been his strength and cleverness that had broken open the cage!' (FW, 335 [188]).

The settling of accounts with Wagner's Judeophobia and Kant's recuperation of metaphysics could not but have a profound effect on the picture of the philosopher Nietzsche had previously acknowledged and revered as his master. True, there remained a debt of gratitude: 'The Schopenhauerian human being drove me to skepticism toward everything respected, exalted, defended. [...] Via this *by-way*, I reached the *heights* with the freshest winds' (VIII, 500 [309]). Also, quite apart from the theory, there was the teaching of an author who

---

11   Schelling 1856–61, Vol. 13, p. 28; *Don Carlos*, Act Four, Scene 21.

'lived and died "as a Voltairean"' (FW, 99 [95]). Yet this enlightenment revealed itself as timid and inconsistent. After all, Schopenhauer was 'only too obedient a student of the scientific teachers of his time, all of whom paid homage to Romanticism and had abjured the spirit of the Enlightenment'. This explained the attempt to attribute a certain significance to religion, 'out of consideration for the understanding of the masses'. Perhaps it had been a mistake that should have been attributed more to the historical and cultural context than to Schopenhauer himself: '[B]orn into our present time, he would not possibly have been able to speak of the *sensus allegoricus* of religion; he would instead have honored truth, as he generally did', and would have declared himself explicitly for atheism (MA, 110 [87–8]).

And yet, despite this acknowledgement, Nietzsche's settling of accounts with his former teacher was unequivocal. After going over to the 'Enlightenment', he could not restrict himself to liquidating the credo, the content of the faith of positive religion. It was possible to observe how 'free spirits really take offense only at the dogmas, but are very familiar with the magic of religious sensation', which led to 'a [fruitless] theology calling itself free' (MA, 131–2 [99–100]). Although formulated specifically in regard to Schleiermacher, this critique also applied to the philosopher that had striven to discover oriental religions and bring about Christianity's anti-Pelagian regeneration. So, one was not to be taken in by his flirting with Voltaire: '[T]he whole medieval Christian way of viewing the world and perceiving humanity could once again celebrate its resurrection in Schopenhauer's teaching, despite the long-since achieved annihilation of all Christian dogmas.' It was true there was 'a strong ring of science in his teaching, but this does not master it; instead, the old, well-known "metaphysical need" does so' (MA, 26 [35]).

So, there was also a reversal of the value judgement for the term 'metaphysics'. Nietzsche now looked back on the years behind him as a 'metaphysical period' that, happily, he had now transcended (*infra*, 10 §1). He was no longer one and no longer wanted to be one of those 'metaphysicians of finer and coarser grain', those 'veil-making philosophers and world-obscurers' (VM, 10 [16]). Germany continued to be the metaphysical country *par excellence*, but that meant only that it was obscurantist and hopelessly backward.

The harsh critique of previously celebrated authors went hand in hand with some significant rehabilitations, above all that of Goethe. *The Birth of Tragedy* had excluded him from the pantheon of authors summoned to revive tragic Hellenism on German soil. He was to a certain extent drawn into the polemic against the serene and purely Apollonian picture of Hellas: even he had not managed to force the 'enchanted gateway leading into the Hellenic magic mountain', to 'penetrate to the essential core of Hellenism and to create a lasting bond of love between German and Greek culture' (GT, 20, I, 131 and 129 [96–8]). This criticism continued to peep from the third *Unfashionable Observation*, which emphasised the inclination towards philistinism of 'Goethe's human being' (*supra*, 6 § 8).

Now, however, the radical reinterpretation of the history of Germany threw a completely new light on Goethe, the author often accused of paganism and detachment or hostility to the national anti-Napoleonic resistance, and therefore far removed from both Christomania and Germanomania. In 1808–9, Friedrich Schlegel had denounced him as alien to the 'German spirit' and not unlike Voltaire. From the opposite side, Heine had attributed to him the merit of having declared war on 'German neo-Christian-patriotic art' and thus of having shooed away 'the ghosts of the Middle Ages'.[12] At this point, Nietzsche's meeting with Goethe became somehow obligatory. Goethe could be likened to Spinoza (VM, 408 [144]), and thus reached a sidereal height compared to the fanatics of the Christian-Germanic myth of origin. In any case, 'If we leave aside Goethe's writings and especially Goethe's conversations with Eckermann, the best German book that exists', indeed, 'the highest point of German humanity', 'what really remains of German prose literature that would deserve being read again and again?' (VIII, 603 [412] and WS, 109 [203]).

The totality of condemnations (clearly in the majority) and rehabilitations did not aim to build a new pantheon for Germany (as a nation with a special mission) – to replace, as it were, the one previously raised by *The Birth of Tragedy*. Now, the great personalities of German culture referred to Europe rather than to their country of origin: 'The Germans did not need *Goethe*, hence they do not know how to make any use of him either' (WS, 107 [202]); 'Goethe is in the history of the German people an episode without consequences' (WS, 125 [209]). His greatness lay in the fact that he belonged in 'a higher order of literatures than the one constituted by "national literatures"' (WS, 125 [209]). Something similar could be said of Lessing: he 'possesses a genuinely French virtue and is really the one who, as a writer, schooled himself most zealously among the French: he knows how to set up and arrange his things in the display window' (WS, 103 [201]). Even the celebration of Voltaire had a polemical significance in regard to the Germanomaniacs. As the *Preussische Jahrbücher* observed, he is the 'first and most powerful organizer of the doctrine of the providential preponderance of France'.[13]

---

12   Losurdo 1997a, p. 4, § 5.

13   Grimm 1871, p. 5.

In conclusion: it was no longer Germany but Europe that was compared to Greece; but if one could nominate a single European country as heir to that beautiful era, then it was, if anything, France. The 'European books' *par excellence* were those of Montaigne, La Rochefoucauld, La Bruyère, Fontenelle, Vauvenargues and Chamfort. They 'raise themselves above the changes in national taste', so they represented continuity with Hellas and classical antiquity in general (WS, 214 [243]).

6   Europe, Asia and (Reinterpreted) Greece

The Enlightenment also rose above provincialisms and national conflicts. It was the cultural and political epoch in which Voltaire spoke of Europe as 'a kind of great republic divided into different states'[14] or in which Vattel defined 'modern Europe as a sort of republic whose members, independent but bound by common interest, come together to maintain order and freedom'.[15] The pathos of Europe also led the struggle against revolutionary France, denounced for breaking the unity of the European community with its unprecedented political experiments. Referring to the teachings of the great Swiss jurist, and transcribing some significant passages, Burke declared that the other European countries could not remain indifferent and inert in the face of this crime.[16] The new regime was 'in contradiction to the whole tenor of the public law of Europe', and therefore this 'evil in the heart of Europe must be extirpated from that centre', to avoid contamination.[17] This was also the view of Gentz, who proclaimed the right of the 'European republic' to intervene in the individual countries that made it up.[18] Lord Castlereagh talked explicitly about a 'Commonwealth of Europe' – he was the colleague and friend of Metternich, who, together with him, worked out a new political order for Europe after the defeat of Napoleon and, ultimately, of the French Revolution. This was also the position of the Austrian Chancellor, who – as has been observed – saw Europe 'as a homeland' and also expressed 'a typical eighteenth-century Europeism', stating 'precepts completely identical with those formulated in the midst of the Enlightenment'.[19]

---

14   Voltaire 1906, p. 10 (ch. 2); cf. on this point Chabod 1989, p. 116 f.
15   Vattel 1916, Vol. 2, p. 39 f.
16   Burke 1826, Vol. 7, pp. 201–15 and esp. p. 211 (Burke transcribes passages from Vattel).
17   Burke 1826, Vol. 7, pp. 99 and 114.
18   Gentz 1836–8, Vol. 2, p. 195.
19   Chabod 1989, p. 131 f.

It is in this tradition, on this side of the nation of revolutionary memory (*infra*, 26 §6), that one must place Nietzsche, who was now obliged to ask a fundamental question: where were Europe's real roots? The Greek point of reference continued to be unavoidable, but how the picture had in the meantime changed! Far from symbolising mythical wisdom, which unfortunately had been desecrated and dissipated by the enlightenment of Socrates and modernity, as we know from *The Birth of Tragedy*, this culture now attracted the attention and respect of all, because it represented the flowering of the first great epoch of enlightenment: it was the 'exceptional Greeks who created *science*!' Therein lay their claim to glory: 'Whoever tells their story, tells the most heroic history of the human spirit' (VM, 221 [93]). We were dealing with a paradox. Hellas continued to be celebrated, but now the motivation was quite different and even opposite.

On the basis of this re-interpretation, the antithesis between Greece and Rome also fell away, even though Nietzsche may perhaps have continued to look with particular favour on the former. The celebration of the Renaissance as 'the golden age of this millennium' seemed to allude to tragic Hellenism as the golden age of the first millennium BC (MA, 237 [163]). The Reformation had been wrong to oppose such a world, which no longer represented the 'reawakening of Alexandrian-Roman antiquity' previously scorned as spurious (*supra*, 1 §9) but the true resumption of classical antiquity as a whole: the Reformation was no longer, as it were, a precursor of a return to tragic Hellenism but rather a belated clinging to the Middle Ages.

But it was not enough to know that Luther has nothing to do with Dionysus, as *The Birth of Tragedy* still claimed. The rethinking had to go much deeper: it was the very idea of a return to Dionysian Hellenism that had to be discarded: 'For ancient culture has its greatness and excellence behind it, and a historical education forces one to concede that it can never become fresh again; it requires an intolerable stupidity or an equally insufferable fancifulness to deny this' (MA, 24 [34]). Symptomatic of the radical nature of the change that had taken place was the now generally positive meaning of the term 'modern', as shown, for example, by the critical judgement on Bach, who had wrongly stopped 'at the threshold of European (modern) music', looking 'back from here toward the Middle Ages' (WS, 149 [216]).

So, it was not a question of returning to Greece but rather of taking possession of its legacy, which lay primarily in the *logos*, the ability to communicate and argue in rational terms. It was precisely by assimilating this heritage that Europe had acquired 'the scientific sense' that positively distinguished it from Asia (MA, 265 [181]).

'[R]eason and Science, the *supreme* powers of man', – as Goethe, at least, judges. – The great naturalist von Baer finds the superiority of all Europeans in comparison to Asians in the capacity that the former develop in school to be able to provide reasons for what they believe, something that the latter are wholly incapable of doing. Europe has been schooled in logical and critical thinking; Asia still does not know how to distinguish between truth and fiction and is not aware whether its convictions stem from personal observation and rule-governed thinking or from fantasies. – Reason in the schools has made Europe into Europe: in the Middle Ages, it was on the way to becoming once again a part and an appendage of Asia – hence to forfeiting the scientific sense that it owed to the Greeks.

> MA, 265 [181]

The dichotomy, typical of the 'romantic' period, between culture and civilisation, which coincided to a large extent with the dichotomy between Germanness and Romanism (and Judaism), was now supplanted by the opposition between a Europe raised to the level of a scientific and rational worldview and unenlightened Asia:

[I]t is Homer's feat to have freed the Greeks from Asiatic pomp and stupor and to have attained clarity of architecture on a large and small scale. [...] Because it is Greek to strive toward the light from an almost inborn twilight. [...] Simplicity, suppleness, sobriety were *wrung out* of the popular hereditary disposition, not given to it – the danger of a relapse into the Asiatic hovers constantly over the Greeks, and in fact it did come over them from time to time like a dark, overflowing flood of mystical impulses, elementary savagery and gloom. We see them go under, we see Europe, as it were, washed away, flooded over – for Europe was at that time very small – but always they return to the light, good swimmers and divers that they are, the people of Odysseus.

> VM, 219 [91]

In this sense, there was no lack of continuity with respect to the 'metaphysical' phase. The struggle between Greece and Asia continued to saturate the history of the West. In *The Birth of Tragedy*, the Dionysian, meaning the Orient, played a positive role only insofar as it was kept under control. It represented the moment of the swallowing of the individual will, which, forgetting itself, took upon itself the terrible burden of suffering in the name of the creation of art and culture. While Dionysus weakened or did away with the will of individuals to sacrifice themselves for art and culture, Apollo, by contrast, imposed the social discipline and hierarchy that were the foundation of culture and of the development of the few individual geniuses.

The control function of the Apollonian now became the control function of reason. All this pointed once again to Greece and Europe. Greece continued to be a model: 'They allowed for a moderate discharge of what was evil and questionable, of the regressively bestial as well as the barbaric, pre-Greek and Asiatic elements that still lived at the basis of Greek nature, and did not strive for their complete annihilation.' This was the 'truly pagan' (VM, 220 [91–2]), it constituted the greatness of a culture unfortunately destroyed by Christianity.

7   Enlightenment, Judaism and the Unity of Europe

The deconstruction of the Christian-Germanic myth of origin had already undermined Judeophobia, as one of its constitutive elements. The new interest in the Enlightenment led in the same direction. In the eyes of its opponents, Judaism embodied the worst of this current of thought. The Jewish intelligentsia, according to one of its anti-Semitic detractors, denounced all discrimination, real or imaginary, as unworthy of the 'enlightened nineteenth century', a century in which 'the world is ruled by free spirits.'[20] The Jewish intelligentsia, thundered Treitschke, continued to desecrate and mock Christianity, precisely under the flag of the philosophy of the Enlightenment.[21]

Nietzsche's writings of the 'enlightened' period date immediately from the years following the international crisis of 1875 and the anti-Semitism polemic. This polemic was officially inaugurated by an aggressive article by Treitschke in November 1879 but had already been anticipated a few years earlier by a few minor interventions, whose authors, in discussing the identity of the new Germany, denounced the role of Jewish finance in the speculatory wave that followed the founding of the Second Reich and the start of industrialisation. The German historian's campaign had been inspired primarily by his chauvinism and his national and military worries, at a time when the resumption of the war with France was, or appeared to be, on the agenda. Could an ethnic and religious group that struggled to assimilate and whose members, or some of them at least, still saw themselves as a distinct and separate nation, and moreover one 'chosen' by God, profess true patriotic loyalty?[22] On the other hand, did not

---

20   Otto Glagau in Claussen 1987, p. 99.
21   In Boehlich 1965, p. 10.
22   In Boehlich 1965, p. 38 ff.

the anti-Christian polemic and the spread of a 'mixed Jewish-German culture'[23] in itself constitute a serious danger, in that it harmed Germany's Christian identity (and the myth of origin to which it entrusted the legitimation of its imperial ambitions)?

Human, All Too Human hit the mark when observing that 'the whole problem of the Jews' was the result of the splitting of Europe into hostile nations and became acute 'the more these nations come to behave nationalistically again' (MA, 475 [258]). It was no surprise that Judeophobia and anti-Semitism boomed in France after the Sedan defeat. Yet one more ground to put an end to the competing chauvinisms and advance towards the merging of the various European nations (MA, 475 [258]).

To achieve this, it was necessary to break with the cult of tradition, attachment to the soil, and, ultimately, nationalism à la Burke. Nietzsche's polemic in the 'romantic' period against 'the abstract European, who imitates everything and does it badly', was in some ways inspired by this ideology (VII, 593 [163]). Now the perspective seemed to have changed: 'With regard for the future, the enormous prospect of ecumenical human goals that spanned the entire inhabited earth' (VM, 179 [78]), although it also had to be acknowledged that this ecumenism did not, as we shall see, go beyond the limits of Europe and the Occident.

Admittedly, even the earlier Nietzsche, who had identified more strongly with Germany and the German 'essence' and stressed more emphatically that a 'womb' was needed for the full unfolding of genius, had added that genius has, 'so to speak, only a metaphysical source, a metaphysical home' (BA, 3, I, 699 [76]). Particularly significant was the picture the third *Unfashionable Observation* painted of Schopenhauer: as a youngster he had travelled much 'in foreign countries'. This was an obligatory path for 'someone destined to know human beings, not books, and to revere truth, not governments'. Indeed, Schopenhauer 'lived no differently in England, France, and Italy than he did at home, and he felt no small affinity with the spirit of Spain. On the whole he did not consider it an honor to have been born a German' (SE, 7, I, 408–9 [238]). And, yet, we also find other accents in the third *Unfashionable Observation* in which the pathos of the German essence continued to reverberate. In *Human, All Too Human*, however, the European perspective prevailed. Complaining about the Enlightenment's role in the fall of the *ancien régime*, Taine noted that its champions 'emphasize diversity, contradiction, the antagonism of fundamental customs, which in each reality are all equally consecrated by tradition'.[24] But, for Niet-

---

23   In Boehlich 1965, p. 8.
24   Taine 1899, Vol. 2, p. 18.

zsche, awakened from the 'metaphysical' dream, this was precisely the great merit of the Enlightenment, which was therefore also essential for the construction of the new European identity:

> The less that people are constrained by tradition, the greater the inner agitation of their motives becomes, and the greater in turn their outward restlessness, the intermingling of peoples, the polyphony of their exertions. Who still feels any strict compulsion to tie himself and his descendants to his particular place?
>
> MA, 23 [33]

The previous regret for the vanishing of the 'myth of the fatherland' had given way to the celebration of mobility, exchange, encounters, crossings:

> Commerce and industry, the circulation of books and letters, the commonality of all high culture [*Kultur*], rapid changes of place and of scenery, the present nomadic existence of all those who do not own land – these conditions are inevitably bringing along with them a weakening and finally a destruction of nations, at least of the European ones: so that as a consequence of these changes and the continual crossbreeding that they occasion, a mixed race, the European, must come into being.
>
> MA, 475 [257]

Given this new philosophical and political horizon, there was no longer any place for the denunciation of Jews as stateless and incurably cosmopolitan, the traditional theme of the anti-Jewish polemic, found both in *The Birth of Tragedy*, dedicated to Wagner, and in one of the five 'prefaces' to *The Greek State*, which at the time had been sent to the musician's partner and consort (*supra*, 3 §4 and 6). If it was now a matter of constructing the new figure of the European, Jews were clearly its incarnation or anticipation: they were not tied to the land, which the laws of the 'Christian' states had long prevented them from owning; they were uprooted, they were nomads. The characteristics traditionally attributed to Jews by anti-Semitic and Judeophobic publications were taken up again, but with an opposite value judgement, which gave the discourse a tone not only profaning but highly provocative in respect of the dominant ideology.

Because of their constant travelling, Jews were of necessity polyglots, in this sense, they had no mother tongue to which they were bound by nature, once and for all. This was another traditional theme of the Judeophobes and anti-

Semites, which Nietzsche himself, following Wagner, had, as we have seen, also shared. But now a profound rethinking came about:

> The peoples that produced the greatest stylists, the Greeks and the French, did not learn any foreign languages. – But because human intercourse is inevitably becoming ever more cosmopolitan, and a good tradesman in London, for example, now has to make himself understood in writing and in speech in eight languages, the learning of many languages is admittedly a necessary *evil*: but one that will eventually reach an extreme and force humanity to find a cure for it: and in some far-off future there will be a new language for everyone, at first as a commercial language, then as the language of spiritual commerce generally, just as certainly as there will one day be air travel.
>
> MA, 267 [183]

If spatial distances were shrunk by the development of technology, a new common language would emerge and do away with difficulties of communication, at least for the European and Western élite. In the meantime, polyglots could play a valuable mediating role. The fusion of European peoples was to be promoted not only by modern industry and the intensification of trade and cultural exchange but also by the 'nomadic existence' of the modern world and, in particular, of the non-landowners, more inclined to mobility. In conclusion: 'As soon as it is no longer a matter of conserving nations, but instead of engendering the strongest possible European racial mixture, the Jew is just as usable and desirable an ingredient as the remains of any other nation' (MA, 475 [258]).

In addition to the Jews, other national remnants, not actually specified, also played a positive role. This was probably a reference to the Huguenots, exiled to Germany from France after the Edict of Nantes, about whom *The Dawn* spoke with great warmth: '[H]eretofore there has never existed a more beautiful union of militant and industrious disposition, of more refined customs and Christian severity' (M, 192 [137]). Treitschke also talked about the Huguenots, but in order to contrast them with the Jews, who, unlike the former, had not felt the need to 'Germanize' and to integrate into their new homeland.[25]

For Nietzsche, however, Jews and Huguenots were equally called upon to serve as bridges between the different countries, primarily France and Germany. With its call for a 'European mixed race', *Human, All Too Human* seemed to anticipate a central theme of the anti-Semitism debate. In his *History of*

---

25   In Boehlich 1965, p. 44 f.

Rome, Mommsen identified Judaism as 'an effective ferment of cosmopolitanism and national decomposition'. Treitschke mischievously quoted this thesis
to show how fully justified were the concerns he had expressed regarding the
role of the Jews.[26] Mommsen responded by reinterpreting and updating his
own analysis: just as they had contributed to the mixing of the different peoples
of the Roman Empire, so too the Jews could become 'an element in the decomposition of the various tribes (Germans, Slavs, etc). that now belong to the
Second Reich, and thereby strengthen rather than weaken its unity'.[27] The Nietzsche of the 'enlightenment' period went even further, identifying in Jewish
cosmopolitanism an essential moment in the process of fusion of the European
peoples he hoped will come about.

But the Jews not only stood for the future of Europe, they also embodied its
best legacy, the tradition of critical thinking and tolerance that had started in
Greece and classical antiquity and, having survived a perilous age of theological
fanaticisms and hatreds, finally reached the age of the Enlightenment:

> [I]n the darkest periods of the Middle Ages, when a band of Asiatic clouds
> hung heavily over Europe, it was the Jewish freethinkers [*Freidenker*],
> scholars, and physicians who held fast to the banner of enlightenment
> and of spiritual independence while under the harshest personal pressure
> and defended Europe against Asia; it is not least thanks to their efforts
> that a more natural, rational, and in any case unmythical explanation of
> the world could once again emerge triumphant and the ring of culture
> that now unites us with the enlightenment of Greek and Roman antiquity
> remained unbroken.
>
> MA, 475 [258]

Once again, what Nietzsche said must have sounded provocative for Wagner
and the dominant culture as a whole. Not only Lagarde thought the Jew not
just any 'alien' but a 'Semite' and therefore an 'Asiatic'.[28] This was also the view
of Marr, who towards the end of the nineteenth century proudly called himself the 'patriarch of anti-Semitism', lending a positive connotation to a term
presumably coined in Jewish circles with an obviously critical meaning.[29] For
Treitschke, Jews who were reluctant to assimilate fully or who refused to do
so were incorrigible 'Orientals', and it was because of this oriental feature or

---

26   In Boehlich 1965, p. 209 f.
27   In Boehlich 1965, p. 217.
28   Lagarde 1937, p. 292.
29   Cf. Zimmermann 1986, pp. 89 and 168 f., fn. 108 and Ferrari Zumbini 2001, p. 215 f.

component that 'the Occidentals' anti-Jewish hatred'[30] had already emerged in ancient Rome and there was a 'gap between Occidental and Semitic essence'.[31]

But, for Nietzsche, Europe and the Occident were represented by Judaism, which had inherited the reason and science of the Greek world. It was rather the religion of which Germany claimed to be the privileged interpreter that pointed to the Orient: 'If Christianity has done everything to orientalize the Occident, then Judaism has helped in an essential way to occidentalize it once again' (MA, 475 [258]). Christian asceticism was also Oriental: the Jews, however, were 'a people who held and hold firmly onto life – like the Greeks' (M, 72 [53]). There had been a radical reversal of positions in the years since *The Birth of Tragedy*, when Nietzsche contrasted the superficial 'optimism' of the Jews and their vulgar attachment to earthly things with the 'pessimism' of Hellenism and Christianity.

And yet, in *Human, All Too Human*, we find an utterance in seemingly striking contradiction with that analysis and, if anything, on a line of continuity with the early Judeophobia. The 'youthful stock-exchange Jew' is denounced as 'perhaps the most repulsive invention of the whole human species' (MA, 475 [258]). This can be read as a reference to the role, real or pathologically exaggerated by dominant ideology, played by 'Jewish finance' at the time of speculation after the founding of the Reich, during the stormy and unscrupulous capitalist development of the *Gründerjahre* (FW, 357 [217–21]). This was a recurring theme of the polemic against Judaism: 'its centre is the stock market' and it embodied 'the arrogant greed' and 'fraud' of those years.[32] How can we explain the presence of this polemical theme in the 'enlightened' Nietzsche? It looks as if the philosopher wanted, on the one hand, to distance himself from the prevailing Judeophobia and anti-Semitism and, on the other, to assure people he too had no sympathy for a type as revolting as the unscrupulous speculator.

Or perhaps it was precisely the new pan-European perspective that brought to light the disturbing role of 'Jewish finance'. When, in the spring of 1875, certain parts of the press (behind which one rightly suspects the presence of the Chancellor) spread alarming rumours about an imminent war with France, Bismarck, invited by Wilhelm I to provide an explanation, blamed it all on Rothschild's speculation on the stock exchange.[33] If Nietzsche had severely criticised cosmopolitanism and the philistine pacifism of Jewish finance in

---

30   In Boehlich 1965, pp. 12, 37.
31   In Boehlich 1965, p. 12.
32   Thus Otto Glagau in Claussen 1987, p. 106, and Treitschke 1965a, p. 9.
33   Eyck 1976, p. 206.

The Greek State, now, in a reversal of positions, he seemed at least in part to echo the contrary charge. It was 'above all the interests of certain princely dynasties and of certain commercial and social classes' that stood in the way of the merging of the European peoples (MA, 475 [257]). Jewish finance was also mentioned here, albeit in a subordinate role, connected with money; it stood to benefit from an international crisis and from the growing need on the part of each state to feed its war machine. However, the main responsibility lay with dynastic ambitions and interests (the Franco-Prussian War had been provoked by the emergence of a Hohenzollern candidature for the Spanish throne). In any case, '[E]very nation, every person has unpleasant, even dangerous qualities; it is cruel to demand that the Jew should be an exception'. There was no justification for 'the literary incivility of leading Jews to the slaughterhouse as scapegoats for every possible public and personal misfortune' (MA, 475 [258]).

8   Voltaire against Rousseau: Reinterpretation and Rehabilitation of the Enlightenment

Nietzsche finally dropped the myth of German authenticity when he gave the Enlightenment the task of combating chauvinistic obscurantism, which by favouring the 'international Hydra' had poisoned relations among the European countries. But was this hydra not, in its turn, encouraged by a philosophy that has stimulated the devastating cycle that had begun in 1789? *The Greek State* blamed the 'liberal and optimistic vision of the world', a harbinger of disasters, on the 'doctrines of the French Enlightenment and the French Revolution' (*supra*, 1 § 8). This link now became problematic and unsustainable. It was a question of 'purifying' the Enlightenment of the 'revolutionary substance' with which Rousseau and the French Revolution, which had wrapped itself in the Enlightenment's 'transfiguring halo', had infused it. This mystification was to be exposed:

> [T]he Enlightenment, which is so fundamentally alien to that entity and which, left to itself, would have passed through the clouds as quietly as a gleam of light, satisfied for a long time simply with transforming individuals: so that it would only very slowly have transformed the customs and institutions of peoples as well. But now, tied to a violent and abrupt entity, the Enlightenment itself became violent and abrupt.
>
> WS, 221 [250]

It was necessary to do away with this improper 'mixture', in order to 'smother the revolution in its birth, to undo its having happened' (WS, 221 [250]). So, the reference to Voltaire must have come in useful: he 'was one of the last of those people who could combine in themselves the highest freedom of the spirit and an absolutely unrevolutionary disposition without being inconsistent and cowardly'. Only when this model had been forgotten would the 'fever of revolution' be let loose, together with the continuing 'restlessness' of the 'modern spirit' with 'its hatred of moderation and restraint' (MA, 221 [149]).

In this sense, Nietzsche had not modified the programme set out in previous years. To begin with, the reference to the Enlightenment was definitely not to be separated from the warning of the dangers contained in it, as the wrong uses to which it was put in the revolution already showed. So, the target of the polemic remained the same: the 'great revolutionary movement', which continued to be inspired by Rousseau (WS, 221 [250]). Rousseau had been the target, as we know, of *The Birth of Tragedy*, whose denunciation of him was reaffirmed in the *Unfashionable Observations*: '[I]n the instances of all socialist upheavals and tremors, it is always Rousseau's human being that is doing the shaking, like old Typhon beneath Mount Etna'; hence it 'exerted a force that incited and still incites to violent revolutions'. One was dealing with a 'threatening power' (SE, 4, I, 369 [201]). *Human, All Too Human* made a similar argument, by again identifying and branding this author so dear to the Jacobins as the point of reference for those who 'ardently and eloquently demand the overthrow of all social order' (MA, 463 [448]).

Along with the accused, the charge against him also remained unchanged. We are already familiar with the polemic launched in *The Birth of Tragedy* against *Émile* and the myth of the good human being. 'Rousseau's human being', reiterated the third *Unfashionable Observation*, 'calls out in his time of need to "holy nature"', which was once again transfigured by an optimism empty and catastrophic, to justify his 'frightful decisions': through them, he hoped to achieve a new social and political order in which there was no longer any place for 'arrogant classes', 'merciless wealth', and other troubles brought about by the institutions and 'bad education' (SE, 4, I, 369 [201]). In *Human, All Too Human*, it was Rousseau who 'believes in the marvelous, primordial, but as it were stifled goodness of human nature, and which ascribes all the blame for this stifling to the institutions of culture embodied in society, state, and education'; and so the 'overthrow of all social order' was the prerequisite for building 'the most splendid temple of a beautified humanity'. The 'optimistic spirit of revolution' and its ensuing horrors took this vision of humankind and the world as their starting point (MA, 463 [248–9]).

But where, then, were the new elements in Nietzsche's development? On closer inspection, Rousseau's belief [*Glaube*] was a 'superstition [*Aberglaube*]', his theories were 'passionate follies [*leidenschaftliche Thorheiten*]', follies that stood out, negatively, only because of the fervour or fury with which they were announced to the world. His supporters were 'political and social visionaries [*Phantasten*]': the theory of revolution they followed was a 'delusion [*Wahn*]' (MA, 463 [248–9]). It was 'fanatical [*fanatisch*]', and engendered a movement that brought in its wake all that was 'half-crazed [*Halbverrücktes*]', 'especially sentimental [*Sentimentales*] and self-intoxicating [*sich-selbst-Berauschendes*]' (WS, 221 [250]). So, we were dealing with those phenomena of superstition, popular credulity and fanaticism, against which the Enlightenment had directed its criticism.

Why, then, should one confuse Voltaire with Rousseau and equate the clear gaze and cool reason of the former with the mad theory of revolution, which had its starting point with the latter? With his 'moderate nature' and his inclination towards 'organizing, purifying, and reconstructing', Voltaire was Rousseau's most lucid and implacable critic. Rousseau was the victim not primarily of a misunderstanding but of a mystification: '[H]e has for a long time frightened off the spirit of the enlightenment and progressive [*fortschreitend*] development', which had nothing to do with the upheavals announced and provoked by the dreamers of a radically new world. Against the latter it was possible and necessary to shout '*Écrasez l'infâme!*' (MA, 463 [248–9]), a motto created by Voltaire and used by him against religious fanaticism. The same motto could be used in the struggle against both Christianity and socialism, both marked by a superstitious conviction and a moral and missionary fanaticism. Against them, the Enlightenment could serve as an effective antidote, while, at the same time, mocking the Germanomaniacal and Lutheran bigotry of Germany's national liberals.

This attitude can be likened to that of Flaubert, who, also in these years, said in this regard:

> That's what we've arrived at – absolute clericalism. This is the result of the democratic bestiality! If one had continued along the great path blazed by Voltaire, instead of taking the neo-Catholic and Gothic one, the path of fraternity, with Jean-Jacques, one would not have reached this point.[34]

---

34   Flaubert 1912, p. 346 (letter to Jules Duplan, 18 December 1867).

Nietzsche too set about dissecting the philosophy of the eighteenth century, and in so doing took advantage of the teaching of Schopenhauer, who sharply criticised the revolution but hailed Voltaire as a 'great human being', to be placed among the 'heroes, these ornaments and benefactors of humanity'.[35] So the Voltaire of the enlightened Nietzsche was very different from that of Taine, for whom Voltaire led 'the philosophical army' that participated in the 'great expedition' against the *ancien régime*.[36] On the opposite side, this was also the view of Heine, to quote another author with whom Nietzsche was also familiar. One might say he too, with his corrosive spirit and desire to break apart the *ancien régime* that still resisted in Germany, wanted to emphasise the political efficacy of this attitude:

> Before the Revolution [...] Christianity had formed an indissoluble bond with the *ancien régime*. The latter could not be destroyed as long as the former continued to exert its influence on the multitude. Voltaire's keen ridicule was needed ere Sanson [executioner in Paris during the Revolution] could let his axe descend.[37]

The Voltaire prized in *Human, All Too Human* was, on the other hand, the philosopher according to whom everything was lost once the people intervened: '[Q]uand la populace se mêle de raisonner, tout est perdu.' He could therefore inspire the struggle against democracy and the denunciation of an epoch imbued with a pervasively 'demagogic character' (MA, 438 [236]). Nietzsche, who, as we know, had called for the crushing of the 'international hydra-head' immediately after the Paris Commune, received a letter two years later animated by the same concerns. In the face of the new fanaticism, the classic slogan ('*Écrasez l'infâme!*') was to yield to a new one: '"*Écr[asez] l'Int[ernationale]*", a modern-day Voltaire should write' (B, II, 4, 288).

Here, then, was the new Voltaire, violently criticising fanaticism, blind belief, and exalted adherence to one or the other idea: 'The Middle Ages are the age of the greatest passions. [...] [W]hen an individual became impassioned, the streaming rapids of his heart and soul had to be more powerful, the eddies more chaotic, the plunge more profound than ever before' (WS, 222 [250–1]). The discussion focused on the historical period criticised by the actual Voltaire. However, Nietzsche's gaze was at the same time directed towards the

---

35 Schopenhauer 1976–82b, p. 749 and Schopenhauer 1976–82e, p. 336; but the quotations could be multiplied.
36 Taine 1899, Vol. 2, p. 17.
37 Heine 1969–78, Vol. 3, p. 515.

revolutionary movement: not for nothing did this aphorism immediately follow that targeting the revolutionary movement.

One might say that Nietzsche the 'Enlightener' was committed to denouncing symptoms of 'superstition' and 'nonsense' not just among the masses but
also, and even more so, among revolutionary intellectuals:

> Clever people [*geistreiche Leute*] may *learn* as much as they please about
> the results of science: we can always tell from their conversation, and
> especially from the hypotheses it contains, that they lack the scientific
> spirit: they do not have the instinctive distrust for misguided ways of
> thinking that has sunk its roots into the soul of every scientific person as
> a result of lengthy training. It is sufficient for them to find any hypothesis
> whatsoever about something, and then they are all on fire for it and think
> that takes care of it. What it really means for them to have an opinion is:
> to be fanatical about it and henceforth to set their heart upon it as a con-
> viction. When something is unexplained, they become ardent for the first
> idea to occur to them that looks like an explanation for it: from which,
> especially in the field of politics, the most awful consequences continu-
> ally ensue.
>
> MA, 635 [300]

But what was 'blind or shortsighted "conviction"' if not another name for
'belief'? (MA, 636 [301]). For the sake of their beliefs, the revolutionaries were
ready to endure the same sacrifices as Christians for their own faith. Christianity openly flaunted its 'illicit finding that "what is strongly believed is true"';
however, 'even if one suffers tortures and death for one's faith, one does not
in any way demonstrate the truth but merely the intensity of the faith in what
one believes to be true' (VIII, 417). Rather, the intensity of faith should generate
suspicion in people possessed of clear reason: 'I have not gotten to know any
human being with convictions who did not soon arouse irony in me' (VIII, 504
[313]).

The presumption of possessing 'absolute truth' had had a dire effect on 'all
religious sectarians and "orthodox"' and had inspired 'all the scenes of cruel
persecution of the heretics of every kind'. All faiths (from Christianity to democracy and socialism) shared this fault:

'The presupposition of every believer of every persuasion was that he *could*
not be refuted; if the objections proved extremely strong, it still remained
possible for him to malign reason and perhaps even to plant the '*credo quia
absurdum est*' as the banner of the most extreme fanaticism' (MA, 630 [297]).
So, it was necessary to denounce the 'blind madness' of those who gave their

heart 'to a prince, a party, a woman'. 'Enthusiastic devotion' (meaning in particular religious fanaticism) was fraught with danger, as was 'wrath' and 'inflamed vengefulness' (meaning primarily revolutionary political fanaticism) (MA, 629 [295]).

The Birth of Tragedy had condemned the Socratic Enlightenment, which aimed to identify and denounce the lack of reasonableness and the 'power of madness [*Macht des Wahns*]' in the wisdom of tradition and in everything it was unable to understand (*supra*, Chap. 2 §1). Now, however, according to a fragment from the 'enlightened' period, one was to be able to smile at 'political madness [*Wahn*]', just like 'contemporaries at the religious madness [*Wahn*] of years gone by' (IX, 504).

9   Nietzsche and the Anti-revolutionary Enlightenment

When Nietzsche likened the revolutionary movement to a phenomenon of religious fanaticism, he was building on a long-established tradition. Let us read the indictment developed by Gentz of those that expected to be redeemed by the revolution and wanted to 'begin a new chronology for the whole human race':[38] 'The whim of a church that uniquely brings salvation' that had been driven from the specific terrain of 'religion' made its ill-omened reappearance in the field of 'politics', as a result of the action of revolutionaries who promised a colossal 'rebirth' by virtue of which the world would be freed of its burden of misery and instead experience the uninterrupted reign of 'freedom and equality'. 'The despotic synod of Paris, supported internally by its courts of the Inquisition and externally by thousands of volunteer missionaries', advanced the claim to be the sole means of the world's salvation and redemption.[39]

If Nietzsche, as we have seen, warned against believing in the 'absolute truth' typical of religious and political fanaticism, Gentz mocked the 'dream of a blissful omniscience' in which the revolutionaries indulged, these missionaries, as it were, who saw themselves as the custodians of sacred knowledge and a sacred task. In the struggle against 'political fanaticism' and 'religious fanaticism', *Indifferentismus* was called into play, an attitude of critical detachment sceptical of the saving truths proclaimed by religious and political prophets.[40] Metternich's adviser never tired of calling on people to struggle against the 'fanaticism [*Schwärmerei*]' of protagonists and followers of the French Revolution. This

---

38   Gentz 1800, p. 120.
39   Gentz 1836–8, Vol. 1, pp. 15–17.
40   Gentz 1836–8, Vol. 2, p. 27.

Schwärmerei was 'one of the most terrible sicknesses' that could afflict a people, and it had its 'twin sister' in 'religious fanaticism [*Religionsschwärmerei*]'.[41] It was a kind of contagion spread by the 'fanatical worshippers of freedom', the 'visionary [*schwärmerisch*] heads'.[42] These themes have something Voltairean about them.

One should not forget that there was a trend in Enlightenment philosophy or influenced by it that, far from welcoming the French Revolution, actively joined in its denunciation. It was precisely in these cultural and political circles that the Voltaire-Rousseau antithesis arose. In Germany, at the start of the century, a book appeared written by a French emigrant, Mounier, keen to rebut the thesis of a direct line of continuity from the philosophy of the Enlightenment to the Revolution and Jacobinism. According to Mounier, Rousseau, with his 'dark and chimeric dreams' and his ideal of 'despotic or absolute democracy', had provided the Jacobins with arguments or suggestions.[43] But neither Voltaire nor the true philosophy of the Enlightenment could be suspected of complicity in or indulgence of 'anarchy', the 'flatterers of the masses' or, worse, the 'fanaticism of the masses'. Real *philosophes* had nothing to do with the theories and practices of those who, because of 'theological disputes' rather than for political reasons, massacred one another and who, through their claim to spread their doctrines weapons in hand, in the last analysis, followed the example of Muhammad.[44] For all his faults, one was not to forget that Voltaire had 'smitten down superstition and intolerance' in all its forms.[45]

But it was above all Mallet du Pan (a patrician who was part of Voltaire's circle of friends, and who particularly appreciated the latter's tirades against the *canaille*[46]) that established an antithesis between moderate philosophers of the Enlightenment and Rousseau, 'the man who has made an enemy of the majority of philosophers in Paris' and 'become the prophet of revolutionary France'.[47] Those who, in denouncing the Revolution, equated Rousseau with the *philosophes* had failed to take this into account. What a colossal blunder! 'One should have set this terrible deserter against them, instead of taking him up into one's own ranks and then fighting him with *capucinades*.'[48] These were words that could well have expressed the new attitude adopted by Nietzsche,

---

41   Gentz 1836–8, Vol. 2, pp. 4 and 27.
42   Gentz 1836–8, Vol. 2, pp. 29 and 52.
43   Mounier 1801, pp. 19 and 119.
44   Mounier 1801, pp. 126, 118 f. and 131.
45   Mounier 1801, p. 18.
46   Gay 1965, p. 262 f.
47   In Matteucci 1957, p. 371.
48   In Matteucci 1957, p. 129.

who had stopped denouncing the philosophical and cultural period before the outbreak of the French Revolution *en bloc*, a denunciation that had resorted not to *capucinades* but to arguments that reflected the influence of traditionalism.

Count Rivarol saw himself as a disciple of Voltaire, and contrasted the latter's demystifying *bon mots* to the fanaticism and madness of the mob. Nietzsche, who mentioned him a few times, seemed to like him, particularly since he was a 'virtuoso of the word', to use Sainte-Beuve's definition.[49] Nietzsche might have drawn other information about the anti-revolutionary Enlightenment from the works of historians of the French Revolution, who played an important role in his formation (*infra*, 28 §2). Finally, he might have read Mallet du Pan's harsh criticism of the *Social Contract*, quoted in Taine: this work, 'which broke up society, was the Koran of the demagogues of 1789, the Jacobins of 1790, the Republicans of 1791 and of the most horrific madmen'.[50] Yet, when the French historian repeated this denunciation, he extended it to the 'philosophy of the eighteenth century' as a whole. It 'looks like a religion, the Puritanism of the seventeenth century, the Mohammedanism of the seventh century'. The commonalities were obvious: 'The same leap of faith, hope and enthusiasm, the same spirit of propaganda and domination, the same rigidity and intolerance, the same ambition to recreate the human being and to model all human life according to a predetermined type.'[51] Nietzsche, however, having left behind the attitude adopted in *The Birth of Tragedy*, was concerned to make a clear distinction between Voltaire on the one hand and Rousseau and the actual Enlightenment on the other.

It was much easier to talk of the anti-revolutionary function of the philosophy of the Enlightenment given that revolution itself sometimes adopted a religious language. The proclamation in the wake of the February Revolution of 1848 abolishing slavery in the colonies condemned slavery because it contradicted the 'republican *Dogma: Liberté, Egalité, Fraternité*'.[52] Later, Marx quoted a non-communist French writer he liked for whom the Communards and the socialists were 'fanatics' in the good sense of the word. Moreover, according to Renan, the Enlightenment and the French Revolution had raised the freedom of the individual to the level of a 'new faith of humanity [*foi nouvelle de l'humanité*]' – a thesis that attracted Burckhardt's attention.[53]

---

49   In Matteucci 1957, p. 263.
50   In Taine 1899, Vol. 2, p. 181.
51   Taine 1899, Vol. 2, p. 2.
52   Wallon 1974a, p. clxv.
53   In Burckhardt 1978b, p. 234.

So, Nietzsche's attitude is easy to understand. However, his stance in favour of the Enlightenment was far from unambiguous and unconditional. The *Volksaufklärung* (popular Enlightenment) denounced in the Basel lectures was certainly not rehabilitated. In this case, too, one can see an analogy with the anti-revolutionary Enlightenment, which, to quote Mallet, for example, argued that 'the *lumières*, by multiplying, have become the weapon both of evil and of good'.[54] Not for nothing the widely quoted aphorism in *Human, All Too Human*, which called on the Enlightenment to support the struggle against the revolution, bore the title 'The Danger of Enlightenment', a danger that, beyond the manoeuvres of the ideologues and protagonists of the revolution, seemed also to be the result of an internal dialectic. One could well denounce the instrumental nature of the reference by the fanatics of subversion to this school of thought: 'But now, tied to a violent and abrupt entity, the Enlightenment itself became violent and abrupt' (ws, 221 [250]). Nietzsche emphasised the beneficially ideological nature of religion: it defused social conflict by imparting 'a calming, patient, trusting attitude to the multitude', all the more impressive 'in times of loss, deprivation, fear, or distrust' or at the onset of 'famines, economic crises, wars' (MA, 472 [251]). Even regardless of crises, 'the Christian religion is very useful for such people, for in this case, servility [*Servilität*] takes on the appearance of a Christian virtue and is amazingly embellished' (MA, 115 [95]). This recommendation of religion (and obedience) for the servant confirmed Nietzsche's continuing hostility towards any form of 'popular enlightenment'.

The anti-revolutionary Enlightenment that developed between France, French-speaking Switzerland and Germany – this is why Gentz is sometimes called 'a German Mallet du Pan'[55] – on the one hand, distinguished Voltaire from Rousseau and, on the other hand, denounced both the author of the *Social Contract* and German idealism. Mallet du Pan expressed himself rather severely about the 'learned mishmash of the German doctors', these 'incorrigible philosophers' full 'of dogmatic rage'.[56] The 'enlightened' Nietzsche also joined in condemning both Kant and Rousseau, for both were still entangled in the net of fanaticism and theologism. The theme of German idealism as a theoretical counterpart to the French Revolution, found in Hegel, Fichte, and Heine,[57] also emerged, albeit with a negative value judgement, both in the utterances of certain exponents of the anti-revolutionary Enlightenment and in Nietzsche.

---

54   In Matteucci 1957, p. 129.
55   Baxa 1966, Vol. 1, p. 311 (Gentz himself reports this in a letter to Adam Müller of 22 September 1807).
56   In Matteucci 1957, p. 375.
57   Losurdo 1997a, p. 4, §2.

Regarding the latter, the turn was unmistakeable. The prolonged confrontation with France had given a powerful impetus to the tendency to reduce
national traditions to stereotypes and to oppose the one to the other. Nietzsche himself had been part of this tendency, and represented the dichotomy between the tragic vision of life and superficial optimism as a conflict
between two irreconcilable essences, the Germanic and the Roman (infected
by Judaism). Some doubts in this regard had already appeared in the third
Unfashionable Observation, which described Goethe's *Faust* as 'the supreme
and boldest likeness of Rousseau's human being' (SE, 4, I, 369–70 [201–2]).
But it was mainly the writings of his 'Enlightenment' period that drew attention to the influence of French culture, and especially of Rousseau, on German soil. The subversive philosopher *par excellence* had left a deep mark not
only on Kant but also on Schiller and Beethoven (WS, 216 [247–8]), not to
mention Goethe, whom we have already mentioned. The claim that the modern revolutionary sickness was alien to Germany could not but be meaningless.

'Only "German youth [*der deutsche Jüngling*]"' (WS, 216 [248]), the *Bursche*,
the member of the *Burschenschaft* and the mythical hero of the anti-
Napoleonic resistance, fell for this naïveté: blinded by Gallophobia, he had
forgotten the numerous ties to French culture. The lectures *On the Future
of Our Educational Institutions* put forward a quite different point of view
in this regard. The last lecture, almost as a conclusion, celebrated both the
Burschenschaft as a whole and the *Jüngling* engaged in the struggle against
(primarily French) 'un-German barbarism' (*supra*, 1 § 5). Now, Nietzsche clearly
distanced himself from that ideology. Not only had the sickness of subversion
also affected German culture, but, because of the decisive presence of Kant,
deeply influenced by Rousseau, purging the Enlightenment of revolutionary
contamination was in its case more difficult than ever.

10   The 'Wandering' Philosopher

Nietzsche was well aware of the caesura in his evolution. One of the aphorisms
with which *The Dawn* concluded seemed to be addressed to Wagner, attempting to understand his reasons but at the same time urging him not to lose sight
of those of his former disciple:

> Sorrow breaks the heart of those who live to see the very person they love
> most turn their back on their opinion, their faith – this belongs to the
> tragedy that free spirits *create* – of which they sometimes are also *aware*!

Then, like Odysseus, they too at some point have to descend to the dead to alleviate their grief and soothe their tenderness.

M, 562 [278]

However, the philosopher seemed to be addressing himself when he observed:

Not to be stuck to any person, not even somebody we love best – every person is a prison and a corner. Not to be stuck in any homeland, even the neediest and most oppressed – it is not as hard to tear your heart away from a victorious homeland.

JGB, 41 [39]

From the very beginning, the philologist-philosopher had also shown himself to be a great moralist, and as a moralist he mocked those for whom lack of questions and doubts was evidence of the rigour and irrefutability of their doctrines:

It is a consummate sign of the excellence of a theory if its originator has no misgivings about it for *forty* years; but I maintain that there has not yet been any philosopher who has not eventually looked down upon the philosophy he invented in his youth with disdain – or at least with suspicion.

MA, 253 [173]

It was true, Nietzsche conceded, that there had been a turning point in his thinking, but was it really equivalent to inconsistency? 'You contradict today what you taught yesterday.' – 'But there again, yesterday is not today' (IX, 598). It was not just a personal matter: 'The snake that does not shed its skin perishes. So too with spirits who are prevented from changing their opinions; they cease to be spirit' (M, 573 [281]). To the friends who called on him to go back to basics and again write 'a Nietzschean book',[58] he seemed to answer: 'I do not have the talent for being loyal and, what is worse, not even the vanity to seem to be' (VIII, 501 [310]). 'Loyalty' and swearing loyalty were of no value (MA, 629 [295]), contrary to what the Germanomaniacs believed – that loyalty was a fundamental element in the list of German virtues:

Are we are obliged to be true to our errors, even after we have seen that we are doing damage to our higher self as a result of this loyalty? – No, there

---

58   Ross 1984, p. 527.

is no law, no obligation of this kind; we *must* be traitors, act unfaithfully, forsake our ideals again and again.

MA, 629 [295]

Personal experience was another proof of the narrow-mindedness and provincialism of the Germanomaniac ideology. With its uncritical celebration of 'loyalty', it became a sort of dungeon for the individual, whose development and maturation it sought to block:

> Anyone who has not made his way through various convictions, but has instead remained attached to the belief in whose net he first became entangled, is at all events a representative of *backward* cultures precisely because of this constancy. [...] he is hard, injudicious, unteachable, without gentleness, always suspicious, an unscrupulous person.
>
> MA, 632 [298]

Metamorphosis was a general law, or, at least, a general law of the most advanced societies, founded on mobility rather than on superstitious attachment to ideologies handed down from generation to generation. To the critics of his alleged inconsistency and disloyalty, who in reality had shown by their arguments that they had grasped nothing of his innermost nature, Nietzsche responded:

> We are misidentified – for we ourselves keep growing, changing, shedding old hides; we still shed our skins every spring; we become increasingly younger, more future-oriented, taller, stronger; we drive our roots ever more powerfully into the depths.
>
> FW, 371 [236]

This is why Nietzsche identified with the wanderer: 'Anyone who has come even part of the way to the freedom of reason cannot feel himself to be anything other than a wanderer upon the earth – though not a traveler *toward* some final goal: for that does not exist.' He 'dare not attach his heart too firmly to any individual thing; he must have something wandering [*etwas Wanderndes*] within himself that finds its pleasure in change and ephemerality' (MA, 638 [302]).

The figure of the wanderer seemed like a reference to the Wandering Jew, evoked in harshly critical terms by Wagner at the end of his essay *Judaism in Music*. Nietzsche too later spoke of the 'nomadic life' of the eternal Jew or 'the wandering Jew' (JGB, 251 [142], WA, 3 [237–8]) and Zarathustra was defined as a 'wanderer' who could have been taken for an 'Eternal Jew', except he was neither 'Jew' nor 'eternal' (Za, IV, Shadow [220–1]).

Nietzsche's new commitment to the Enlightenment led increasingly to proud and defiant challenges to various cultural and political circles, including his friends, with whom he now broke: 'Fate bestows on us the greatest distinction when it has let us fight for a time on our opponents' side. Thus we are predestined for a great victory' (FW, 323 [181]). Now his insistence on the right to change his opinion became a gesture of distinction: a painful spiritual evolution was an integral part of the coming into being of a 'seeker after knowledge' (FW, 296 [168]), the inevitable Odyssey, indeed, the 'tragic Prometheia of all those who know' (FW, 300 [170]). Certainly, 'being able to stand contradiction is a high sign of culture', a characteristic of the 'higher human being' (FW, 297 [169]), even of the 'genius' (WA, 3 [238]).

Here, the great moralist seemed to give way to the theorist of élitism, or rather, the two closely intertwined. A change had taken place with respect to the years of *The Birth of Tragedy*. There was no longer any room for the gesture of distinction constituted by celebrating the 'depth' of the 'Germanic' essence as against fatuous Roman and Jewish optimism. Now, on the contrary, Nietzsche mocked the 'extravagance of German frills and profundity' that could be found in Kant and in particular in the *Critique of Pure Reason* (JGB, 11 [12]). The distinction was to be sought and located at most in the excellence of the European human being as a whole. The same law governs the development of civilisations and of individuals: ceaseless becoming constituted the greatness and the enduring youth of Europe, as against the 'enduring spirit', the immobility and senescence of a culture like China's (*infra*, 9 §5).

11 Nietzsche in the School of Strauss

The radical nature of Nietzsche's turn did not escape his contemporaries, starting with Wagner, who drew attention to the (fatal) influence exerted on the young Nietzsche, still in search of a way, by Rée and Burckhardt.[59] There can be no doubt that the relationship of respect and friendship with the brilliant Jewish intellectual had helped to undermine Nietzsche's previous Judeophobia. The same could be said of the second encounter. Its effect probably went beyond what Richard and Cosima Wagner thought. They mainly criticised the warmth with which the Basel historian talked about the Renaissance and the

---

59   Ross 1984, p. 522 f.; Janz 1981, Vol. 2, p. 99.

'arrogant, coldly contemptuous tone' with which he dismissed the mythology of the Germanic Middle Ages.[60]

And there is more. Burckhardt's unforgiving criticism of the beginnings of the Second Reich must have contributed to making ridiculous, even in Nietzsche's eyes, the new Germany's posing as hero of the struggle against 'civilisation' or at least as an alternative to modern massification and vulgarity. In fact, noted the Basel historian, one was witnessing an 'uninterrupted, extraordinary growth in acquisitiveness', together with the associated speculation and fraud. 'The so-called "best heads" turn to business'; 'spiritual production in art and science must take great pains to avoid sinking to the level of a mere branch of the metropolitan economy, to be independent of advertising and sensationalism'. There seemed to be no longer any room for genuine culture: 'Must everything become mere business, like in America?'[61]

Beyond the German context, the analysis of the situation in Europe as a whole shaped *Human, All Too Human*. 'The sense of power and the sense of democracy are mostly undivided', noted Burckhardt,[62] thus opening up for Nietzsche a new perspective with which to interpret Bismarck's foreign policy and, beyond that, the fundamental trends of modernity. Had not the introduction of universal suffrage accompanied, stimulated and consecrated the founding of the Second Reich? And did not the expansion of the military go hand in hand, as the lectures *On the Future of Our Educational Institutions* had already observed, with the access of new layers to education and the prospect of social mobility, i.e., a further massification and democratisation of society?

Moreover, it is very likely that the influencing was mutual. When Burckhardt underlined the 'optimism' of the French Revolution and of industrial society or the increasingly heavy shadow the 'daily press' cast on culture,[63] we are reminded of the heartfelt complaints of the young colleague of the Basel historian.

But were Rée and Burckhardt the only influences? It is true that Nietzsche himself suggested as much. However, perhaps this was a case of suppression. In the first edition of *Human, All Too Human*, in 1878, Nietzsche seized on the occasion of the centenary of the death of Voltaire to pay tribute 'to one of the greatest liberators of the spirit'. But before starting work on his criticism of Strauss, he made only one general and polemical reference to the French philosopher of the Enlightenment: 'Voltaire even recited his poems so pathetically

60   C. Wagner 1977, pp. 589, 837.
61   Burckhardt 1978a, p. 148 f.
62   Burckhardt 1978a, p. 149.
63   Burckhardt 1978a, p. 149 f.

monotonously' (VII, 318). There can be no doubt that the first real opportunity to come to grips with the great Enlightenment thinker came with his reading of Strauss's *Old and New Faith*. Here was an interpretation of the philosophy of the Enlightenment that, while ignoring (or denying) its contribution to the ideological preparation of the French Revolution, emphasised and celebrated the aspect of the struggle against the ascetic, visionary and intolerant spirit of the Middle Ages. True, positive judgements of the anti-dogmatic potential of the Enlightenment could already be found in Schopenhauer. These, however, called not on the Enlightenment to act as a barrier against the revolutionary tide but on a Christianity purged of Judaism and Pelagianism and replete with ascetic themes – an attitude, from the standpoint of the enlightened Nietzsche, too fixated on the Middle Ages.

However, one should not forget that, in *The Birth of Tragedy*, Voltaire's human being and Rousseau's human being seemed to merge into one: Socratism suffered at the theoretical and the practical level from hubris, it sought to penetrate the deepest recesses of reality in order to transform and subvert them radically. The picture was already beginning to change with the third *Unfashionable Observation*: meanwhile, the clash with Strauss had taken place. Now, 'Rousseau's human being' seemed to acquire a particular physiognomy, but it is significant that in sketching this portrait Nietzsche kept in sight the danger of 'atomic [...] revolution', the danger posed by the advent of 'the age of atomic chaos'. The cohesive strength of the Church, which in the Middle Ages was, according to Nietzsche, able to hold 'inimical forces' together, had gone missing (SE, 4, I, 368–9 [199]). It seems that the atomistic revolution, whose main figure in some respects was Voltaire's human being, continued to be the prerequisite for the violent upheavals in which Rousseau's human being engaged. The two figures no longer identified, but the violent actions of the latter nevertheless still presupposed the former's solvent critique.

Only with *Human, All Too Human* did Voltaire's human being become the antithesis of Rousseau's human being, with an attitude not unlike that of Strauss, who contrasted the great philosopher of the Enlightenment with both the Middle Ages and the 'socialist plague'. But Nietzsche took other suggestions and ideas from *The Old and New Faith*. One can even imagine that reading Strauss played a part in the choice of the very title of the book, which marked the philosopher's turning point. For Strauss himself noted that Reimarus had, 'in the entire course of the biblical story, [...] found nothing divine but all the more that was human [*um so mehr Menschliches*], in the worst sense of the term'.[64]

---

64   Strauss 1872, p. 36.

But we should direct our attention above all to the resemblances important for analysing Christianity. To begin with, it is worth noting that its origin could be located much more clearly and disturbingly in the Orient than in Judaism: think, for example (said Strauss), of the Eucharist, which referred to the 'ugly oriental trope of drinking the blood and eating the flesh of a human being'.[65] Behind the 'Christian doctrine of reconciliation', on the basis of which the catastrophic consequences of original sin were overcome by Christ's sacrifice, lay the practice of scapegoating, 'by which raw peoples thought they could appease their gods'.[66] Even before *Human, All Too Human*, Strauss had already pictured Christianity as far more oriental than Judaism!

The Old and New Faith also seems to anticipate some fundamental themes of Nietzsche's mature period. In Strauss's eyes, socialism was on a line of continuity with Christianity, a religion steeped in ill-will and hostility towards 'property' and wealth as such. In a clear reference to the parable of Lazarus and the rich man, Strauss observed: 'In the Gospels, the rich man is bound for hell, if only because he spends his days magnificently and joyfully, without our experiencing any injustice at his hand.'[67] Precisely because it was inspired by class hatred, the faith of the poor, on the other hand, aimed, at least in the years of early Christianity, not at 'our present spiritualistic world' but at something more concrete and material, 'the expectation of heaven on earth'.[68] This reminds one of the *Antichrist*, which saw in the Judgement Day, when the rich were punished and the poor rewarded, a kind of socialist revolution deferred in time.

Driven by resentment of wealth and power, Jewish-Christian morality was anything but politically harmless, as Nietzsche would later note. It was rather the instrument of struggle of a mob that lived in an 'absurdly unpolitical community'. Even though he used a language that at first sight seemed far removed from earthly conflicts, Jesus was to be considered a 'political criminal', who would today merit the banishment to Siberia reserved for Russian nihilists (*infra*, 15 §2). To understand the genesis of Christianity, said *The Old and New Faith*, one had to start with the situation of the Jews in the Roman Empire, which could be likened to that 'of today's Poles under Russia'. Given the balance of power, there was room for neither an armed uprising with any hope of success nor for 'the peaceful activities of citizens': the 'closing of all worldly

---

65   Strauss 1872, p. 91.
66   Strauss 1872, p. 27.
67   Strauss 1872, p. 63.
68   Strauss 1872, p. 74.

ways' thus lent every political aspiration 'a visionary turn'.[69] And yet, the political dimension of Christianity emerged clearly, with all its implicit charge of violence, in the 'belief in the devil' and the condemnation to hell of all opponents – even the innocent, to whom fate had denied the possibility of baptism and salvation.[70]

Nor can one neglect Strauss's influence with regard to another essential theme, that of nihilism. Here, it is not so important that Strauss used Nietzsche's categories and terms even before Nietzsche did. More suggestive is another element: far from functioning as an uplifting condemnation of atheism, the charge of 'nihilism' in no way spared the dominant religion in Germany and in the West, and was instead aimed primarily at Christianity, as well as Buddhism. Both religions explicitly invited people to despise life and reality as a whole, to strive for 'nothingness or the kingdom of heaven': nihilism was precisely the 'visionary world-denying' attitude, the 'rejection of everything earthly'.[71] The definition of this gloomy torment reminds one unmistakably of the Nietzsche of later years, while the writings of the pre-'Enlightenment' period were characterised by the negative value given to 'secularization', against which 'art' but also 'religion' were set (*supra*, 4 § 6).

But let us return to Strauss, for whom the Middle Ages, marked out by Christianity, were a period of history marked by 'contempt for the world'.[72] Insofar as Schopenhauer took over and emphatically developed this Buddhist and Christian 'pessimism', he remained a prisoner of the 'old Christian religious world view'.[73] To that extent, he too was infected by nihilism. Nietzsche would also use this analysis, when he broke with his former teacher.

The flight from the world had something crazy about it: *The Old and New Faith* talks about 'delusional belief [*Wahnglauben*]' in relation to the early Christian belief in the resurrection of Jesus, while Luther, who condemned monastic asceticism and the 'useless mortifications of the flesh', was said to display 'the healthiest humanity'.[74] The contempt was most clearly exhibited in the first *Unfashionable Observation*: Strauss was so banausic and philistine that he denounced the philosophy of Schopenhauer and his *noluntas* as 'unhealthy and unprofitable' (DS, 6, I, 192 [16]), and described Jesus as 'a fanatic who in our day and age would scarcely escape the madhouse' (DS, 7, I, 193 [38]). This

---

69   Strauss 1872, p. 65 f.
70   Strauss 1872, pp. 22–4.
71   Strauss 1872, pp. 61 f., 74.
72   Strauss 1872, p. 81.
73   Strauss 1872, pp. 61 f., 147.
74   Strauss 1872, pp. 73, 82.

criticism was similar to Treitschke's, who, as we know, was also outraged by the reduction of religion to a kind of 'sickness'. And yet this category and the psychopathological approach would later play an important role in Nietzsche's diagnosis of Christianity during his 'Enlightenment' period.

Nietzsche might also have found useful ideas regarding the analysis and history of moral sentiments in Strauss, even before doing so in Rée. He might have read in the mercilessly criticised book that 'justice' depended on 'the thriving of the group' as perceived and valued by 'members of the herd' as a whole. Thus 'within each tribe there gradually emerged first customs, then laws, and finally a doctrine of ethical duties'.[75] Far from being dictated by norms that transcended time and space or by a categorical imperative, morality thus referred to human history and prehistory, and even the history and prehistory of the 'higher animals': in this history and prehistory, one could trace the 'beginnings of moral sentiment', manifested 'in connection with their social impulses'.[76]

In formulating this argument, *The Old and New Faith* based itself on Darwin. The first *Unfashionable Observation* expressed disdain for the English naturalist and his followers in Germany, beginning with Strauss, about whom Nietzsche joked: 'Although he is timid when speaking of faith, his mouth becomes round and full when citing the greatest benefactor of modern humanity, Darwin: then he not only demands faith in the new Messiah, but also in himself, the new apostle' (DS, 9, I, 212 [55]). But then, as we will see, *Human, All Too Human* started by emphasising the connection between 'historical philosophy' and 'natural sciences', i.e., by inserting human history into the history of nature. In so doing, Nietzsche based himself on Darwin, whom he had got to know by way of Strauss.

Strauss drew attention to the anticipations evolutionary theory had experienced in Germany. *The Gay Science* proceeded similarly, even though it no longer referred to Kant or Laplace but to Hegel, who 'dared to teach species concepts develop out of each other'; in this sense, 'without Hegel there could be no Darwin' (FW, 357 [218]). Here, one might essay a more general observation. Polemicising against all forms of chauvinism and setting out from a European point of view, *The Old and New Faith* stressed that several countries had promoted a rationalistic and secularised vision of the world as opposed to a medieval one. And now let us see how Nietzsche interpreted Schopenhauer in his polemic against the Germanomaniacs: '[U]nconditional and honest atheism is simply the presupposition of his way of putting the problem',

---

75   Strauss 1872, p. 232 f.
76   Strauss 1872, p. 207.

but, far from being an exclusively German title to fame, 'the triumph of scientific atheism – is a pan-European event in which all races had their share
and for which all deserve credit and honour': here we could proclaim 'a victory of the European conscience won finally and with great difficulty' (FW, 357
[218–19]).

Finally, a problem. How to explain this passage, at the fall of the ancient
world, from paganism to Christianity, from a religion attached to the land and
the body to an emphatically spiritualistic and ascetic religion? The first *Unfashionable Observation* observed:

> Strauss does not know how to explain the entirely dreadful serious im-
> pulse toward self-denial and the pursuit of ascetic sanctification charac-
> teristic of the first centuries of Christianity other than as a reaction of
> disgust and nausea against the excess in every kind of sexual enjoyment
> practiced during the foregoing age.
>
> DS, 6; I, 193 [37]

Actually, Heine, who at the time counted among the 'misfortunes of emerging
German culture' (VII, 504 [165]) and was repeatedly placed side by side with
Strauss, argued in more or less the same way (VII, 600–1). He said, for example:

> We by no means deny the benefits which the Christian-Catholic theories
> effected in Europe. They are needed as a wholesome reaction against the
> terrible colossal materialism which was developed in the Roman Empire,
> and threatened the annihilation of all the intellectual grandeur of man-
> kind. Just as the licentious memoirs of the last century form the *pièces
> justificatives* of the French Revolution; just as the reign of terror seems
> a necessary medicine when one is familiar with the confessions of the
> French nobility since the regency; so the wholesomeness of ascetic spir-
> ituality becomes manifest when we read Petronius or Apuleius, books
> which may be considered as *pièces justificatives* of Christianity. The flesh
> had become so insolent in this Roman world that Christian discipline was
> needed to chasten it. After the banquet of a Trimalkion, a hunger-cure,
> such as Christianity, was required.[77]

This passage is worth quoting in full, since it provides a key to understanding the bitterness of Nietzsche's polemic. To him, the partial justification of

---

77   Heine 1969–78, Vol. 3, p. 362 f.

Christianity as a spiritualistic reaction to the debauchery of the Roman aristocracy sounded like a partial justification of Jacobin morality, which had similarly developed in the wake of the struggle against the libertine opulence of a nobility in decline. We will see later that the theme of spiritualistic reaction represented by Christianity also made an appearance in Nietzsche. But with one fundamental difference, especially by comparison with Heine. Despite the explicit condemnation of an ascetic and 'Nazarene' vision of life, the *ancien régime*, both that of pagan and imperial Rome and that swept away by the French Revolution, continued to cut a poor figure in the eyes of the poet and disciple of Hegel. In Nietzsche, the opposite was true: however severe his judgement of the Roman or French nobility, the fact remained that it had been overthrown by political and social movements that aggravated and accelerated the process of decay (*infra*, 30 §1).

12   Biography, Psychology and History in the 'Enlightenment' Turn

So, in reconstructing Nietzsche's evolution, one should not neglect his meetings and reading, including his polemical reading. But is this sufficient to explain the turn? According to a diary entry by Cosima Wagner on 21 February 1880, Wagner was unable to come to terms with the apostasy of his former disciple and his provocative behaviour: 'One can give up wrong inclinations, like mine for Feuerbach, but one should not insult them.'[78] This disappointment is a serious problem for interpreters: how is this radical change to be explained? Had he met someone or read something that overwhelmed him? A significant testimony by Malwida von Meysenbug says Nietzsche had come into contact by way of Rée with the French moralists, whose aphoristic style he then adopted.[79] In fact, as early as the Christmas of 1870, Nietzsche had received, as a gift, the complete works of Montaigne – ironically, from Wagner (B, II, 1, 172), against whom he would later use them. So, the reading in question took a slow hold over a long period of time and became intertwined with much other reading, especially the Greek and Roman classics, which were perhaps quieter and less conspicuous. In other words, it was not a sudden illumination as a result of a cultural or personal encounter.

  Nor can psychology provide a decisive key to explaining the turn, although Wagner thought it did: 'Simply to free himself from me, he indulges any platit-

---

78   C. Wagner 1976–82, Vol. 2, p. 494.
79   Meysenbug 1902, p. 24f.

ude.'[80] Even though some biographies seem at least in part to confirm this view, in reality it does not lead very far.[81] At best it might help to explain some polemical catchword or allusion or, more generally, the provocative way in which Nietzsche usually presented his new theses, but not their content.

Equally questionable is the polemical explanation that the former disciple himself gave of the admiration or veneration he had long felt for his former 'master': young men 'decide so unsubtly and so unselectively for this or that cause', what attracted them 'is the sight of the zeal surrounding a cause and, so to speak, the sight of the burning match – not the cause itself'. 'The subtler seducers' took advantage of this: they 'disregard justifying their cause' or adducing 'reasons' and instead appeal to youthful fervour (FW, 38 [55]). It was in this context that Nietzsche placed his previous Judeophobia: 'Please forgive the fact that, during a short and risky stay in a badly infected region, I did not completely escape this illness' (JGB, 251 [141]). In fact, however, both his Judeophobia and his Germanomania long preceded his meeting with Wagner: after all, it was Cosima who advised caution in relation to the Jewish question and who sought, in vain, to dissuade the young professor of classical philology from abandoning teaching in order to join the Prussian army as a volunteer.[82]

Rather than absolutise this or that text, this or that biographical episode, this or that psychological trait, one should focus on Nietzsche's manner of philosophising. One cannot escape the permanent presence and weight of history and reality. How could he remain indifferent to events that in his eyes, and not without reason, seemed to be a historical turning point? The land of thinkers and poets now stood at the forefront of capitalist development; it had posed as a standard bearer in the struggle against the revolution and now it promoted revolution in the defeated country; it had presented itself as the antidote to modernity and now it was giving full expression to that same modernity, and in its most repugnant form: the acquisitive pursuit of wealth and unbridled industrial and commercial activism, universal suffrage, compulsory education, and the weight of the unions and the socialist movement. If the 'metaphysical' Nietzsche was anxious to draw the historical and philosophical balance-sheet of the rise of Prussia and its clash with the land of revolution and the Commune, the Nietzsche of the 'Enlightenment' had in the first place to settle accounts with the degeneration and levelling of the Second Reich. Authors like Treitschke and Wagner could repress their earlier hopes, content themselves with

---

80   C. Wagner 1976–82, Vol. 2, p. 517.
81   Janz 1981, Vol. 2, p. 99.
82   C. Wagner 1976–82, Vol. 1, p. 267 f.

the political-military victory, and otherwise pretend nothing had happened, in the hope of becoming the official historian or official musician of imperial Germany.

Nietzsche's philosophical rigour and intellectual honesty ruled this out. A couple of years before the war, Wagner had denounced in grandiloquent tones the 'materialistic civilization', 'the most degrading materialism', 'the deepest depravity', the immorality, the debauchery of France.[83] At the start of the war, Treitschke had expressed the wish in a clear polemic aimed at the enemy beyond the Rhine: 'May German customs return to their old seriousness, to old-fashioned integrity, and may the virtues of domestic simplicity, still alive in the great mass of our people, gain new respect even in the circles of the financial aristocracy'.[84]

To the extent that the Gallophobic declamations had any meaning, we can define them, purged of the orgy of value judgements that accompanied and smothered them, as follows: since France had left behind the Enlightenment and the process of de-Christianisation driven forward by the French Revolution and was marked by a clear hegemony of the city and urban culture, it was decidedly more secularised than Germany and had customs and modes of living that had broken or are breaking with hearth and home. But, during the *Gründerjahre*, this opposition had lost all credibility. Now not only Nietzsche believed one should stop deceiving oneself. The stock exchange and speculation were everywhere dominant and unchallenged. The champions of the military victory followed with redoubled zeal in the footsteps of defeated France. One can even say that Germany, which had arrived later than other countries at the goal of capitalist development, exhibited a special vulgarity and arrogance. It was behaviour typical of the 'upstart', undistinguished either by 'morality' or 'intelligence'.[85] This harsh judgement was delivered by an author until then filled with a fervent belief in the 'universal and international mission of the German nation' and now forced to admit its frightening fall from Christianity into 'a new paganism'.[86]

Nietzsche's analysis and disappointment were similar, but they started from a very different myth of origin, which was moreover even more unrealistic than the Christian-Germanic one. Certain critical analyses of capitalism from *Human, All Too Human* and contemporaneous notes took particular aim at the *Gründerjahre*. They criticised the 'superstition about property' and the associ-

---

83   Wagner 1910i, p. 30f.
84   In Fenske 1977, p. 426; cf. Losurdo 1997a, ch. 3, §12.
85   Frantz 1970, pp. 216f., 221.
86   Frantz 1970, pp. v, 22 and 216. Frantz is cited very positively by Wagner 1910l, p. 53.

ated inability to 'make […] use of free time'. Worse still, wealth 'is often the result of spiritual inferiority', so it could only encourage 'immoral covetousness of the others', demagoguery and socialist agitation. These were phenomena that 'after the war' become widely evident, as Nietzsche emphasised, in bold type (VIII, 550–1 [357–8]).

Undeterred by the development of the Second Reich, Treitschke was still able to pay homage to this extraordinary and unique people, on account of its 'German loyalty', 'piety' and sense of 'justice'.[87] And Wagner was not far behind. But his former disciple, now busy ridiculing the myth of 'German virtue' constantly set by the champions of the struggle against France against their enemies' debauchery, did not follow him along this path of self-deception: 'At that time, people grew accustomed to demanding that virtue be understood to go along with the word "German" – and we have not completely unlearned this even today' (WS, 216 [248]). The title of another aphorism stressed that '[v]irtue was not discovered by the Germans' (VM, 298 [116]). And again: 'To the bad taste of the Germans I add: virtuous Germanomania, which has history against it and deserves to have shame against it' (XI, 498).

Even Nietzsche, as we know, had believed implicitly and passionately in the absolute peculiarity and regenerative mission of German culture. But now the process of levelling under the sign of modernity and capitalist development was inexorable and undeniable. Wagner could still continue to pronounce his faith in the regeneration of 'historical humanity' by Germany.[88] On the eve of the war, he had called on his country to bring 'salvation [*Heil*]',[89] and he repeated this theme imperturbably, for decades, as if nothing had changed. No less emphatic was Treitschke, who, in 1888, on the occasion of Wilhelm II's accession to the throne, celebrated the 'German century' and quoted verses from Emanuel Geibel, which had become famous in the climate of rampant chauvinism: in this context, he voiced the hope that the world might recover its health thanks once again to the 'German essence'.[90] Although Lagarde was disappointed by certain developments, he too continued to believe that the Germans 'have a mission for all nations of the earth'.[91]

Nietzsche must have also dealt with Geibel, both when he was a passionate admirer of the 'German essence' (XIV, 104]) and at the time of his break with Germanomania (B, II, 6/2, 907 and 957). *Human, All Too Human* respon-

87   In Fenske 1978, p. 416.
88   Wagner 1910o, p. 263.
89   Wagner 1910i, p. 49.
90   In Fenske 1978, p. 416 f.
91   Lagarde 1937, p. 449 f.

ded to the permanent propaganda of the idea of a mission by mercilessly dissecting Germany's history and ideologies. The gulf between the reality of the Second Reich and the myths of origin that had accompanied its founding was unbridgeable. The changes that had taken place at the political and social level were a powerful incentive to go far beyond the doubts and uncertainties that had begun fairly early to emerge. It is time to realise that the ideological platform of *The Birth of Tragedy* and the *Unfashionable Observations* had become unsustainable: with its simultaneous references to Dionysus and to the theorist of the denial of the will to live, to classical antiquity and Luther; with its celebration of Germany as heir both to tragic Hellenism and the Reformation; with its homage to *Volksthum* but also the élitist gesture with which the *Burschenschaftler* dismissed the Philistines and ordinary consciousness; finally, with the invocation of an organic community (the *Volksthum*) that, however, was founded on slavery, to which a social layer that was not only rebellious but ultimately constituted by uncivilised barbarians had inevitably to be subjected.

CHAPTER 8

From Anti-revolutionary 'Enlightenment' to the Encounter with the Great Moralists

1   Distrust of Moral Sentiments and Delegitimisation of the Appeal to 'Social Justice'

We have seen how *The Birth of Tragedy*, on the basis of the Paris Commune, evoked the terrible danger posed to culture by a 'barbaric slave class' that experienced its living conditions as 'unjust'. As one of the lectures *On the Future of Our Educational Institutions* declared, it was the advocates of revolution and of the 'people's state' that waved the flag of 'justice' (*supra*, 4 §1). Nietzsche did not fail to notice that the socialist movement of the time was strongly oriented towards demands for 'justice' and appeals to morality and conscience. 'No unjust law will be admitted in the code of the new moral world', said Robert Owen, in a naïve and passionate summary of his political and ideal programme.[1] *Dream of Justice* is the title of a book that a contemporary researcher dedicated to Weitling, an important representative of early German socialism.[2] Yes, 'property is an injustice', added Becker, another representative of the same movement,[3] – or 'theft', to quote the better-known Proudhon.[4] The moral pathos of this discourse was clear and explicit. Owen spoke of the 'base spirit' of the existing order,[5] and Weitling called to arms the League of the Just (or of Justice) (*Bund der Gerechten* or *der Gerechtigkeit*).[6]

This was the political organisation Nietzsche alluded to in developing his polemic against 'our anarchists': '[H]ow morally they evince in order to convince! They even go so far as to end up calling themselves "the good and the just [*die Guten und Gerechten*]"'. Even before the anarchists and socialists, Rousseau, this 'tarantula of morality', had struck a similar pose: '[H]e too held in the very depths of his soul the idea of moral fanaticism whose executor yet another disciple of Rousseau's, namely Robespierre, felt and confesses himself to be, when he longed', in his speech of 7 June 1794, to '*fonder sur la terre l'empire de la sagesse, de la justice et de la vertu*' (M, Preface, 3 [4]).

---

1   In Bravo 1973, p. 211.
2   Joho 1958.
3   Becker 1844, p. 1.
4   Proudhon 1926.
5   In Bravo 1973, p. 206.
6   In Bravo 1976, p. 293.

Nietzsche felt the need to develop this analysis further, in 1886, in the Preface to *The Dawn*, in order to clarify the political dimension of the discourse it contained. But it was already evident in the 'enlightened' period. Why was 'the reanimation of moral observation' now again necessary? And why could humanity not be spared 'the gruesome sight of the psychological dissecting table and its knives and forceps'? The answer came at once: 'For what rules here is the science that inquires about the origin and history of the so-called moral sensations and that as it advances has to pose and to solve complicated sociological problems' (MA, 37 [45]). The sort of problems it involved was clarified in a further aphorism criticising socialism. It was a political movement that 'prepares itself in secret for a rule of terror'. So what was its strategy? It 'pounds the word "justice" like a nail into the heads of the half-educated masses in order to rob them completely of their understanding (after this understanding has already suffered a great deal from their partial education)': in this way, the conditions ripened for violence and insurrection (MA, 473 [256]).

At the philosophical, historical and psychological level, Nietzsche now undertook a critical analysis of moral conscience with which to oppose the Jacobin-socialist tradition, the persistent and relentless revolutionary agitation. We have seen how Nietzsche had denounced, from the very start, the subversive implications of the Rousseauian theme of original goodness: this front was maintained even during the 'enlightened' period. If, in *The Birth of Tragedy*, Nietzsche confuted rationalist optimism by referring to the myth of original sin in Aryan or Semitic form, now he called upon psychological research to refute 'a certain blind faith in the goodness of human nature' (MA, 36 [44]). The 'socialists' with 'their fatuous optimism of the "good human being"' were 'ridiculous' (XI, 245). They were loudly contradicted by those who were really familiar with the human mind. 'The overall result of all moralists' was unequivocal: 'Man is evil, a beast of prey' (XI, 36).

After his transformation from critic of the Enlightenment and defender of myth into a philosopher of the 'Enlightenment', Nietzsche became an implacable opponent not only of revolutionary religion or pseudo-religion but of emphatic moral sentiments. In these years, he seemed to pay particularly close attention to Taine, as the ordering of his books shows (B, II, 5, 307 and 355). Taine, in reconstructing the ideological preparation of the French Revolution, stressed the important role played by Rousseau's moral pathos: 'Up to now the dominant institutions were accused only of being annoying and unreasonable; now they are also accused of being unjust and corrupting.' The attack on the *ancien régime* thus reached a higher and much more dangerous level: 'One is indignant [*on s'indigne*]', and this feeling 'opens up a breach beyond the salons and through to the suffering and coarse mass to which no one has so far turned and whose dull resentment finds for the first time a mouthpiece'.[7] Nietzsche too voiced his concern at the spread of 'a feeling of indignation [*Empörung*]' among the European 'workers' (VIII, 481–2) and condemned, with particular regard to the Russian revolutionary movement, the 'anarchism of exasperation [*Entrüstungs-Anarchismus*]' (FW, 347 [205]). He pursued this theme to the end: 'the socialist' appeals to 'beautiful indignation [*schöne Entrüstung*]' when he 'demands "justice", "law", "equality of rights"' (XIII, 233); but to allow oneself to be infected by the 'absurd spectacle of moral indignation [*moralische Entrüstung*] [...] is an unmistakable sign that a philosopher has lost his philosophical sense of humor' (JGB, 25 [27]).

The 'destructive instincts' of the masses, according to Taine, find their 'herald [*héraut*]' in moral pathos.[8] And Nietzsche, in turn, condemned 'the heralds [*Herolde*] of the sympathetic affections', keen to remedy the pain they identify or imagine everywhere (M, 174 [127]).

Unfortunately, the French historian continued, the moralistic criticism of the *ancien régime* had also spread in the meantime to the salons, among the nobles, who 'feel frustrated by the distribution of offices and favours', and among the courtiers, 'who retain only the crumbs, while all the bigger morsels were reserved for the favourites of the small inner circle of intimates'. So it was that 'Epicurean malcontents' became 'philanthropists' and also started to mouth the 'beautiful' and 'big words such as freedom, justice, public welfare, human dignity'. Even though one remained part of a privileged class, why deny oneself this intellectual pleasure, which appeared to cost nothing and would, if anything, lend a touch of excitement to an otherwise idle day?[9] Although Nietzsche's analysis was more subtle, it was not without resemblances to that just cited. Let us take a 'malformed' scion of the upper classes: '[T]hrough inheritance, he is deprived even of the last comfort, "the blessings of work", self-forgetfulness in "daily labour"'; his reading now only fed his 'will to revenge'. So, what did he need in order to put on display 'the appearance of superiority' over society and even over existence, from which he now felt rejected, and against which he sought 'revenge'? The answer was not hard to fathom: 'Always morality; you can bet on that. Always big moral words. Always the boom-boom of justice, wisdom, holiness, virtue.' In conclusion: 'Morality – where do you suppose that it finds its most dangerous and insidious advocates?' (FW, 359 [223–4]).

The question is rhetorical, but the answer had already been provided by Taine, who summed up the situation in France on the eve of the collapse of the

7   Taine 1899, Vol. 2, p. 34 f.
8   Taine 1899, Vol. 2, p. 35.
9   Taine 1899, Vol. 2, p. 132.

ancien régime as follows: 'Never was seen in a salon such a display of general phrases and beautiful words.'[10] One of the champions of the French Revolution, Sieyès, had even earlier come to the same conclusion, although he put an opposite value judgement on it, when commenting on an at first sight surprising fact – 'the most important defenders of *justice* and *humanity*' were even more likely to come from the 'two privileged classes' than from the Third Estate.[11]

Was this a phenomenon confined to the French Revolution, or was it likely to be repeated, in different ways, in the new wave of upheavals (desired or feared, depending on one's point of view) looming on the horizon? A fragment written in the summer of 1878 noted with concern the 'socialist range of ideas' among the 'upper classes' (VIII, 522 [330]). According to the *Communist Manifesto*, just as, 'at an earlier period, a section of the nobility went over to the bourgeoisie, so now a portion of the bourgeoisie goes over to the proletariat'.[12] *The Gay Science* seemed to reach a similar conclusion:

> When I think of the desire to do something, how it continually tickles and goads the millions of young Europeans who cannot endure boredom and themselves, I realize that they must have a yearning to suffer something in order to make their suffering a likely reason for action, for deeds. Neediness is needed! Hence the clamour of the politicians; hence the many false, fictitious, exaggerated 'emergencies' of all kinds and the blind readiness to believe in them.
>
> FW, 56 [64]

According to Marx, 'a portion of the bourgeois ideologists, who have raised themselves to the level of comprehending theoretically the historical movement as a whole', would side with the socialist revolution.[13] Sieyès argued similarly, when he explained the passage to the Third Estate of eminent members of the nobility and clergy: 'The enlightenment of public morality manifests itself first among men who are in the best position to understand wider social relations.'[14]

Nietzsche, however, denied any rationality to the phenomenon of members of the upper classes siding with the subversives. Far from being enlightened,

---

10   Taine 1899, Vol. 2, p. 133.
11   Sieyès 1985b, p. 143 f.
12   Marx and Engels 1975 ff., 6, p. 494.
13   Marx and Engels 1975 ff., 6, p. 494.
14   Sieyès 1985b, p. 144.

such defectors were victims of emotional turbidity. It was a case of 'the feel-ing of distress': 'They do not know what to do with themselves – and so they paint the unhappiness of others on the wall' (FW, 56 [65]). The skilful appeal to compassion on the part of the subaltern classes blended with the deserters' individual failure:

> The 'religion of compassion' to which one would like to convert us – oh, we know these hysterical little men and women well enough who today need just this religion as a veil and finery. We are no humanitarians; we should never dare to allow ourselves to speak of 'our love of humanity' – our type is not actor enough for that! Or not Saint-Simonist enough; not French enough.
>
> FW, 377 [242]

While the subversive wave swelled dangerously, the appeal to moral indigna-tion (noted Taine) stimulated the self-conceit of those who made use of it: 'Personal pleasure is not enough, he also needs the peace of conscience and the tenderness of the heart.' In this regard, the hymn Émile struck up in praise of moral conscience is instructive: 'Conscience! Divine instinct, celestial and immortal voice, certain guide of an ignorant and limited yet intelligent and free being, infallible judge of good and evil, which makes humans like God, it is you who determine the excellence of his nature.'[15]

The French historian emphasised the at once repulsive and devastating linking of moral pathos and narcissism. Nietzsche too insisted on this point, adding:

> Compassion is the most agreeable feeling for those who have little pride and no prospect of great conquests; for them, easy prey – and that is what those who suffer are – is something enchanting. Compassion is praised as the virtue of prostitutes.
>
> FW, 13 [39]

Even more than an expression of narcissism, the display of compassion was offensive and repugnant:

> It is the essence of the feeling of compassion that it strips the suffering of what is truly personal: our 'benefactors' diminish our worth and our will

---

15   Taine 1899, Vol. 2, p. 33.

more than our enemies do. In most cases of beneficence toward those in distress there is something offensive in the intellectual frivolity with which the one who feels compassion.

FW, 338 [191]

Taine called for 'a critic and a psychologist' to investigate in depth the psychology and psychopathology of revolution, starting from the 'singular clinical case' of Rousseau: 'In spite of the extravagances, bad deeds, and crimes, he maintained to the last a delicate and deep sensitivity, humanity, compassion, the gift of tears, the ability to love, passion for justice, religious sentiment and enthusiasm.'[16] The fact was, observed Burckhardt, 'virtuous feelings rather than virtues' inspired this 'plebeian' – 'the warmth of his soul was only apparent'.[17] The Rousseau enigma was the enigma of revolution as such.

The figure of the 'critic' and 'psychologist' evoked by Taine seemed to take shape in Nietzsche, who later credited the French historian with having achieved important results in the interpretation of the 'painful history of the modern soul' (*infra*, 28 §2). In so doing, Nietzsche emphasised the difficulty of the task in hand. It was primarily a case of overcoming 'an ingrained antipathy to the dissection of human actions, a sort of shamefulness in regard to the nakedness of the soul' (MA, 36 [44]). Dreamers of great transformations in the name of justice found it easier to surrender to the comfortable belief in the nobility of their own moral sentiments: 'a spectator who is governed not by the spirit of science, but by humanitarianism, finally curses an art that seems to plant a sense of diminishment and suspicion [*Verdächtigung*] in the souls of human beings' (MA, 36 [45]).

Social and political conflict thus tended to be configured, in cultural terms, as a conflict between naïve moral enthusiasm and mature scientific knowledge. By overcoming resistances and doubts that sought to block or hinder it, merciless psychological dissection could discover what was 'human and all too human' (MA, 37 [46]). It was not enough simply to destroy the myth of the original 'goodness' of a human being; one was also to be able to identify 'the black bull's-eye of human nature' (MA, 36 [45]) in moral and religious zeal in favour of those who suffered. '[T]he man of science must distrust all higher feelings', hitherto considered sacred and untouchable (M, 33 [29]).

This denunciation, too, was in no way general: in his struggle against injustice, Owen appealed to the 'spirit of benevolence, trust and affection that

---

16   Taine 1899, Vol. 2, p. 30.
17   Burckhardt 1978b, p. 398.

pervades the whole of humanity'.[18] This point of view was expressed with particular eloquence by Lamennais, who stressed that emancipation could succeed only on two conditions:

> A complete, selfless readiness to sacrifice oneself to the common cause, a
> deep feeling for justice, loved both in and for itself. Without this, everyone,
> thinking only of himself, becomes isolated and rots in his own egoism;
> without this, personal interest, limited and unfeeling, completely incom-
> patible with the spirit of sacrifice, suffocates in the depths of the soul the
> generous movements, the firm and holy resolutions, divides, abases and
> drives onto the steep slope of brutal desires.[19]

The protest against a system that looked with indifference or coldness on the
sufferings it brought about was here expressed, somewhat naïvely, in the celebration of the warmth of sympathetic feelings, the *élan* that should overcome the barriers that separate person from person. Engels also made fun of
this 'trivial and foolish sentimentality', and believed that he could give a more
mature expression to social protest.[20] Nietzsche's attitude was, of course, different, for he intended to rid the world not only of sentimentality but also of
the political and social movement that in his opinion it expressed: 'Economy of
goodness is the dream of the rashest utopians' (MA, 48 [53]); '[t]he sage must
resist those excessive desires for unintelligent goodness' (MA, 235 [161]).

2   Plebeian Pressure, Moral Sentiments and 'Moral Enlightenment'

Two sentiments that played a central part in early-socialist political discourse
required analysis: compassion, and a sense of justice in relation to the polarisation of wealth and poverty. As for the second, one was least to allow oneself
to be fooled by its appearance. After all, if one looked closely, only the evil Eris,
of whom Hesiod spoke, felt discomfort and resentment at 'every way in which
someone else attains eminence above the ordinary mass', and tried to remedy
it by a general downward flattening (WS, 29 [171]). On the one hand, the beggar
or the subversive claimed to be inspired by love for all people and the desire
for universal happiness, but on the other hand, and in reality, he rejoiced at the
mishaps that might befall a member of the upper classes: 'the harm that occurs

---

18   In Bravo, 1973, p. 211.
19   In Bravo 1973, p. 377.
20   Marx and Engels 1955 ff., 22, p. 453.

to someone else makes that person equal to the first'. As the psychological analysis proceeded, the love of equality in the name of justice was unmasked as
envy, and this in turn assumed the repulsive features of *Schadenfreude*, which
came about as a result not so much of self-affirmation as of the misfortunes of
superior people (WS, 27 [169]).

To the feeling of envy of the lower classes against the ruling classes corresponded the feeling of compassion the latter often experienced in regard of
those who suffered adversely. *The Greek State* had already warned of the devastating consequences 'the cry of compassion' and the consequent demand for a
less unequal and 'juster' distribution of the burden of pain and suffering could
have (*supra*, 2 §6). But now the feeling of compassion was being called into
question, not so much for extrinsic reasons (the need, whatever the cost, to
save culture) as for intrinsic reasons. Nietzsche again wielded his scalpel. Meanwhile, it was to be noted that '[t]here are cases where sympathy is stronger than
the actual suffering' (MA, 46 [52]). We shall see there was a happiness that consisted of 'resignation' or, in Tocqueville's definition, a 'vegetative' (*infra*, 13 §3).
This was not taken into account by the beautiful souls of the upper classes, who
allowed themselves to be morbidly moved by the spectacle of misery:

> There are people who become hypochondriac out of compassion and
> concern for another person; the resulting form of sympathy is nothing
> other than a sickness. So, too, there is a Christian hypochondria that
> attacks those solitary, religiously motivated people who constantly keep
> the suffering and death of Christ before their eyes.
>
> MA, 47 [53]

Nothing had been resolved, one had merely lost contact with reality. 'Compassion' was synonymous with 'doubl[ing]' these woes (JGB, 30 [31]). But another
aspect was especially important. This feeling was anything but natural and
spontaneous, it was stimulated from outside and struck through into the upper
classes with the help of a wave of pressure from below:

> Live in contact with the sick and mentally depressed and ask yourself
> whether eloquent complaining and whimpering or making a display of
> misfortune do not basically pursue the aim of giving pain to those who
> are present: the pity that those people then express is a comfort for the
> weak and suffering insofar as they recognize by this that they at least still
> have one power despite all their weakness: the power to give pain. The
> unfortunate person gains a sort of pleasure in this feeling of superiority,
> which the display of pity brings to his awareness; his imagination ascends,

he is still important enough to cause pain to the world. Thus, the thirst for pity is a thirst for self-enjoyment, to be earned at the expense of his fellow human beings; it shows the person in complete disregard of his own dear self.

MA, 50 [54]

One is struck by the eminently political character of the analysis of the feeling of both envy and compassion. In both cases, the initiative came from the subaltern classes: the wretched who wanted to bridge the gap to the superior people by dragging them down violently, to bring everything into an equal state of mediocrity and meanness, or by causing them to bow down out of a feeling of compassion. In this sense, '[i]n the gilded sheath of compassion there is sometimes stuck the dagger of envy' (VM, 377 [138]). Both the feelings here analysed were expressions of a movement or a process that strove to destroy all greatness and realise a general flattening. If the ruling classes were not to abdicate their role, they had to refuse to be infected by compassion: they were to follow the advice of La Rochefoucauld, who said 'leave that to the common people' who 'are not governed by reason' (MA, 50 [54]).

So, one can understand Nietzsche's meeting with the great French moralists: there is a need for 'humanity's examiners' (VM, 5 [14]). But, to legitimise further what will later come to be called 'a school for suspicion [*Verdacht*]' (MA, Preface, 1 [5]), Nietzsche did not hesitate to invoke Christianity: 'Christianity and La Rochefoucauld are useful when they cast suspicion on the motives of human actions: for the assumption of the fundamental injustice of any action, any judgement, has a great influence on the fact that human beings free themselves from the excessively violent impulses of liberty' (VIII, 319).

The revolutionary that set against the injustice of society the excellence of his moral intentions had to be injected with a healthy sense of doubt. Any contribution in this direction was positive: 'Wherever somebody is speaking "badly" of people – and not even wickedly [*ohne Entrüstung*] – this is where the lover of knowledge should listen with subtle and studious attention' (JGB, 26 [28]).

So, it was necessary to destroy the naïve faith in the excellence of moral sentiments that resulted in plans to change the world. And yet this work of destruction was not to pave the way for moral indignation, which could turn out to be a weapon of the revolutionaries: 'The angry man' could sink his teeth into 'himself' but also into 'society' (JGB, 26 [28]). Against all these things, it was necessary to demand a clear 'moral enlightenment' (FW, 5 [33]). And, once again, to achieve this result, the dominant religion in the West could play a role: 'Christianity, too, has made a great contribution to enlightenment: it taught moral skepticism; [...] it annihilated in every single man the faith in his "virtues"'. Of course, it is today necessary to proceed further, applying 'this same scepticism also to all religious states and procedures, such as sin, repentance, grace, sanctification' (FW, 122 [117–18]).

Compared with *The Birth of Tragedy* and its denunciation of Socrates's 'Enlightenment', a reversal of positions seems to have occurred. Now Nietzsche apparently even identified with the Greek philosopher he had previously attacked: 'Like Socrates about wise humans, so I about moral ones' (VIII, 555 [362]), which meant: just as Socrates exposed the fallacy of knowledge, so Nietzsche exposed the fallacy of moral purity and excellence. And yet elements of continuity shone forth. If *The Birth of Tragedy* took aim at the hubris of reason, which intended to put the world 'back into joint' (*supra*, 1 §19), the writings of the 'Enlightenment' period were equally committed to delegitimising revolutionary action, whose roots were now located in the hubris of moral conscience.

If they could count on Christianity, 'moral enlightenment' and 'scepticism' consigned a personality like Mazzini to the ranks of their 'opponents' (FW, 5 [33]). This was even truer of Luther. In the battle with the Catholic Church, Luther represented 'the noble scepticism, that luxury of scepticism and tolerance which every victorious, self-confident power permits itself' (FW, 358 [222]). While Luther and Mazzini, naturally each in his own way, expressed the belief in the good human being of the revolution, thus chiming with Rousseau (XIV, 274–5), the 'school of suspicion' seemed to find a first vague anticipation precisely in the millennial institution attacked by the fanatical monk: 'The entire Roman Church rests on a Southern distrust [*Argwohn*] of human nature' (FW, 350 [208]), even on 'a Southern suspicion [*Verdacht*] against nature, man, and spirit' (FW, 358 [221–2]). On the opposite side:

> Protestantism is, to be sure, an uprising in favour of the upright, the guileless, the shallow (the North has always been more good-natured and superficial than the South); but it is the French Revolution that finally and ceremoniously handed over the sceptre to the 'good people' (to the sheep, the donkey, the goose, and everything that is incurably shallow and loudmouthed and ripe for the madhouse of 'modern ideas').
>
> FW, 350 [208–9]

The conflict between 'moral enlightenment' or the 'school of suspicion' and distrust on the one hand and moral enthusiasm and belief in the 'good human being' on the other was not only political, for the subjects of this political conflict also had a clear social connotation:

[I]n all cardinal questions of power Luther was dangerously short-sighted, superficial, incautious – mainly as a man of the common people who lacked any inheritance from a ruling caste and instinct for power.

FW, 358 [222]

In preaching the universal priesthood of all believers and in promoting such an insane egalitarianism, 'abysmal hatred of "the higher human beings"' and the dominion of 'the higher human beings' as conceived by the Church found its expression. Luther 'himself brought about within the ecclesiastical social order what in relation to the civil social order he attacked so intolerantly – a "peasants' rebellion"' (FW, 358 [222–3]).

3   The 'Saint' and the Revolutionary 'Martyr': Altruism and Narcissism

Compassion and the demand for justice appealed to altruism and presupposed the reality of 'unegotistical' states. More carefully analysed, these turned out in reality to be determined by self-love or the love by a person of 'some part of himself', to which he was prepared to sacrifice 'some other part of himself' (MA, 57 [59]). This also applied to the 'saint'. 'Human, all too human' even went for saints. 'Certain people [...] have so great a need to exercise their passion for power and domination that, because other objects are lacking or because they have always proved unsuccessful otherwise, they finally hit upon the expedient of tyrannizing certain parts of their own nature, sections or stages of themselves, as it were' (MA, 137 [105]).

It was true, of course, that altruism or the belief in altruism could become terribly consequential and not flinch back from the ultimate sacrifice, thus apparently leaving no more room for doubt. In fact, the 'suspicion' continued even in this case to be admissible and inevitable:

[E]ven if we stake our lives, as martyrs do for their church, it is a sacrifice made for our desire for power or for the preservation of our feeling of power. He who feels 'I am in possession of the truth' – how many possessions does he not renounce in order to save this feeling! What would he not throw overboard in order to stay 'on top' – that is, above the others who lack 'the truth'!

FW, 13 [39]

In this regard, a parable (of sorts) from *Human, All Too Human* is interesting. It is the story of a 'martyr against his will', an activist who remained loyal to the party even unto death:

[T]hey used him to perform any service, they obtained anything from him, because he was more afraid of the bad opinion of his associates than of death; he was a pitiful weak soul. They recognized this, and on the basis of it made him a hero and finally even a martyr. Although the coward always said No inside, his lips always said Yes, even on the scaffold as he died for the views of his party: for beside him stood one of his old comrades, whose word and glance tyrannized him so thoroughly that he really did suffer his death in the most respectable way and has since then been celebrated as a martyr of great character.

MA, 73 [65]

Nietzsche immediately struck back against this celebration with an ironic counterpoint: 'We will seldom go wrong if we trace extreme actions back to vanity, middling ones to habit, and petty ones to fear' (MA, 74 [65]). Once the martyrs' haloes, on closer examination, dim, their followers became ridiculous: 'the disciple of a martyr suffers more than the martyr' (MA, 582 [279]).

But one thing remained disturbing, and full of dangers for society: 'Every party that knows how to give itself the air of a patient sufferer draws the hearts of good-natured people toward it and thereby gains for itself the air of being good-natured, to its greatest advantage' (VM, 294 [115]). One thinks at once of the Russian revolutionaries (the 'nihilists'), those new 'believers', also ready for 'martyrdom' (FW, 347 [205]), or German Social Democracy, exposed in those years to harsh repression and even so standing firm, thanks to the dedication of its activists: yes, commented *The Dawn*, even 'views' were subordinated to the party, and '[i]n the service of such morality there exists today all manner of sacrifice, overcoming of the self, and martyrdom' (M, 183 [131]).

It was a sacrifice that also seemed to throw a favourable light on the party on whose behalf it had happened. And, again, Nietzsche's ironic counterpoint rings out: 'But we basically mean that if someone sincerely believed in something and fought and died for his belief, it really would be awfully unfair if it was actually only an error that inspired him.' It would be enough to look at history to become aware of the absurdity of such an attitude, and yet we continue to not want to 'concede that all those things that people in earlier centuries defended by sacrificing their happiness and lives were nothing but errors' (MA, 53 [56–7]).

These were the years in which both Renan and Engels, each from a different starting point, compared the 'first Christian communities' and the local branches of the Working Men's International (*infra*, 15 §3). The comparison also featured in Nietzsche's work, though he used it to 'render suspect' and delegitimise the figure of the 'martyr' revolutionary, together with that of the saint and the religious prophet.

In his determination to refute the myth of 'so-called unegotistical actions' at all levels (MA, 37 [45]), Nietzsche also studied the erotic tie: 'Human beings have always misunderstood love – they believe themselves here to be selfless', and did not perceive the 'strong antagonism' that exists in love and 'marriage' as in any other reality (IX, 579 and 558); surprisingly, despite the 'savage avidness of possession' and the 'injustice' that mark 'sexual love', it had been transfigured to the point that 'the concept has been derived from it of love as opposed to selfishness, while it is perhaps the most single-minded expression of selfishness'. It is worth noting here that this analysis too was inspired by political motives. For the aphorism continued: 'Here it is evidently the have-nots and the yearning ones [*Nichtsbezitzende und Begehrende*] who have formed the linguistic usage – there have probably always been too many of them' (FW, 14 [40]). They like to quote a trinity that to a certain extent paraphrases that of the French Revolution: ' "Freedom", "Justice" and "Love"!!!' (XII, 419).

If we pass from the lover to the scientist and the intellectual, the result is no different: 'Even the instinct for knowledge is a superior instinct of property' (IX, 459). Here, Nietzsche defined his general task as follows: 'To describe the history of the feeling of the ego: and to show that, even in altruism, the key thing is the desire to possess' (IX, 450). In conclusion, egoism had to be recognised as an inescapable reality: 'The whole concept of "unegotistical action" gets scattered to the winds when rigorously investigated. [...] How would the ego be capable of acting without ego?' (MA, 133 [101–2]).

Both the saint of religion and the martyr of revolution were prepared to assert their sincerity and sacrifice themselves for their faith. And it was true, of course, that '[n]o power can maintain itself if none but hypocrites represent it' (MA, 55 [57]). Both were honourable, but they were not therefore any better than the conscious liar: 'The visionary [*Phantast*] denies the truth to himself, the liar only to others' (VM, 6 [15]). On closer psychological examination, the honesty of the religious or revolutionary visionary was revealed as a more radical lie, which became thus radical by systematically repressing all the doubt and temptation of real honesty. The 'founders of religions' differed from the 'great deceivers' in that they never emerged from the 'state of self-delusion'; if, despite everything, doubt arose in them, it was immediately rejected and blamed on the deceptions and seductions of the 'evil antagonist' (MA, 52 [56]). Yes, '[h]onesty is the great temptress of all fanatics' (M, 511 [252]).

The 'critic' and 'psychologist' invoked by Taine thus exposed the visionary and religious soul as such and the moral pathos that filled and gladdened it.

4   History, Science and Morality

The blow that psychological dissection inflicted on the naïve or narcissistic
enjoyment of moral sentiments was also one of the 'hammer blows of historical knowledge' (MA, 37 [46]). Reconstruction of the psychological genesis
was entwined with the reconstruction of the historical genesis. The discourses
about the 'abuse of history' seemed remote. Now *Human, All Too Human* pointed to the 'lack of historical sensibility' as an 'original failing' of all philosophers
and intellectuals of the period (MA, 2 [16]). There had been a reversal of roles,
but the target remained the same: it continued to be the modernity that had
resulted from a revolution and a repugnant distortion, and to call into question the 'present-day human beings' from whom, unfortunately, '[a]ll philosophers have the common failing that they start' (MA, 2 [16]). They 'do not
want to learn that humanity has come to be, that even the faculty of cognition has come to be'. In fact, '[E]verything [...] has come to be; there are no
eternal facts' (MA, 2 [16–17]). This applied primarily to morality and 'moral sentiments', which, now that they were subject to historical investigation (MA, 35 ff.
[43–4]), lost their aura of absoluteness: in this way, the claims of those who
challenged the social order in the name of 'justice' and unchallengeable ethical standards were rendered ridiculous. They had not yet learned 'the virtue
of modesty', the necessary consequence of 'historical philosophizing' (MA, 2
[17]).
      After Darwin, whose writings Nietzsche read in this period, talking about
history was also talking about the history of nature, which for its part referred
to science: 'Historical philosophy [...] can no longer be thought of as separate
from natural science, the youngest of all philosophical methods' (MA, 1 [15]).
      In light of these new insights, Kant became basically obsolete. His entire
criticism was designed only to make his ghostly 'moral realm' 'unassailable',
invulnerable by comparison with reason, whose limits were emphasised (and
expanded) instrumentally and in advance:

> In the face of nature and history, in the face of the fundamental immor-
> ality of nature and history, Kant was, like every good German from way
> back, a pessimist: he believed in morality, not because it is manifested in
> nature and history; rather, he believed in spite of the fact that nature and
> history constantly contradict it.

In this sense, Kant's attitude was not much different from Luther's. Both were
deaf to the objections of reason and science. Indeed, they reacted to them by
clinging even more firmly to their beliefs: '*Credo* quia *absurdum est*' (M, Preface,

3 [4]). Criticised for his poorly disguised theologism, Kant was at the same time lined up alongside Rousseau because of his 'moral fanaticism' and its subversive implications (M, Preface, 3 [4]). *The Gay Science* confirmed:

> [R]evolutionary politicians, socialists, preachers of repentance with or without Christianity: [...] they all speak of 'duties', and indeed always of duties with an unconditional character – without such duties they would have no right to their great pathos; they know that quite well! So they reach for moral philosophies that preach some categorical imperative, or they ingest a goodly piece of religion, as Mazzini did, for example.
>
> FW, 5 [33]

Morality, already problematised by the psychological dissection of the so-called higher feelings, was now plunged further into crisis by the reference to nature and science. Darwin had opened up new possibilities for the critique of revolutionary ideology. The discovery of evolution from animal species to humans further confirmed that humans as such did not exist: anthropological nominalism, which in *On Truth and Lies in a Nonmoral Sense* was developed, as it were, at the spatial level (each leaf differs from all other leaves), could now be diachronically extended. The history of 'human development' allowed one to refute a point of view common to 'all philosophers': 'Involuntarily, they allow "the human being" to hover before their eyes as an *aeterna veritas*, something that remains the same through all turmoil, a secure measure for things.' It was the continuing inability to emancipate oneself from 'teleology', which 'is built upon speaking of the human being of the last four millennia as something *eternal*, toward which all the things of the world have from their beginning naturally been directed' (MA, 2 [16–17]).

The critique of anthropocentrism (and human rights as such) now became much easier: it was possible to locate and destroy the teleological and theological presuppositions of revolutionary theory. The claim to happiness for all was ultimately advanced in the name of justice and morality. But how did morality differ from 'astrology'? '[I]t believes that the starry heaven revolves around the fate of human beings; the moral person, however, presupposes that whatever lies closest to his heart must also be the essence and heart of things' (MA, 4 [18]). Morality was a form of primitivism: in the eyes of the animist, the 'mechanism' that brought into play 'laws' rather than physical 'moral acts of will and choice' in the interpretation of nature, was 'a slander against God' (FW, 59 [70]). It was necessary to free oneself once and for all from a worldview so radically alien to the development of the sciences:

Philosophy divided itself from science when it posed the question: what is that knowledge of the world and of life by which human beings will live most happily? This occurred in the Socratic schools: by keeping their eye upon *happiness*, they tied up the veins of scientific inquiry – and do so to this day.

MA, 7 [19]

Clearly, the starting point was the same as that of *The Birth of Tragedy*: the idea of happiness could now be confuted at the 'scientific' level, by emphasising the anthropocentric presumption and the groundlessness and epistemological pointlessness of talking about human rights.

The science of Nietzsche as a philosopher of the 'Enlightenment' had nothing to do with the sort of science valued by positivism à la Comte, pervaded by a claim to be able to solve finally and in a concrete and positive way the problems of humanity addressed in such a vapid and metaphysical way by the grandiose proclamations of the revolutionaries about human rights. Through its claim, positivism itself was shown to have been affected by emphatic anthropocentrism and was therefore, from Nietzsche's point of view, no less anti-scientific than the revolutionary discourse it intended to refute.

The reference to science and nature now served to dismiss and make ridiculous the demand for equality:

If one understands how the sense of equity and justice [*Billigkeit und Gerechtigkeit*] arises, one must contradict the socialists when they make justice [*Gerechtigkeit*] their principle. In the state of nature the following proposition does not hold: 'What is good for one is just also for the other'.

VIII, 482

Moreover, the idea of equality was also affected by primitivism and an expression of an untenable worldview:

The belief that *identical things* exist has been handed down to human beings from the period of lower organisms (experience trained in the highest science is what first contradicts this proposition). From the very beginning, the primal belief of everything organic has perhaps even been that all the rest of the world is single and immobile.

MA, 18 [29]

5   Morality and Revolution

The role assigned to history in the 'Enlightenment' period demonstrates a new radical turn in Nietzsche's evolution: we have seen how the second *Unfashionable Observation* set 'morality' against the Hegelian philosophy of history (*supra*, 6 §5). Now, the 'history of moral sentiments' indicated that the widespread moral pathos, far from pointing to a timeless categorical imperative, was simply the '[m]oral fashion of a commercial society' (M, 174 [127]), a society that, having forgotten the war, flinched back like a coward from the harshness of reality. However, there was one clear element of continuity. Even if Nietzsche's arguments were not always mutually compatible, he nevertheless strove consistently to delegitimise the revolutionary movement, by contesting first the foundation that referred to the objectivity of the historical process and to the philosophy of history and then the foundation that appealed to moral sentiments and norms. We find the same approach in his re-interpretation of the Enlightenment and of historical consciousness: it was a matter of tearing both the one and the other from the deadly embrace of revolution and massification.

It is in this context that Nietzsche's encounter with the great moralists should be placed. Sometimes it has been taken as an indication of the philosopher's political innocence, as if the political interests and passions evident and explicit in the earlier writings had completely and mysteriously disappeared. In fact, the merciless critical analysis of moral sentiments continued, with a constant eye on social conflict and the threat of socialism. Nietzsche's evolution reveals an internal coherence and consistency. If the second *Unfashionable Observation* attacked the philosophy of history to which the revolutionary movement appealed, the writings of the Enlightenment period criticised and dissected the appeal to morality, which still characterised the movement (or sectors of it).

A clever utilisation of the moralists could help to carry out this second enterprise. Schopenhauer was of little use in this context, since he liked to set against the modern philistine the figure of the ascetic and the saint: but now it was precisely a question of unmasking the 'martyrs' and 'saints' of the socialist movement. Burke and his followers on German soil were of no avail: they tirelessly called on people in the name of morality and religion to respect the established order, and warned against the catastrophic consequences of the arrogance of reason. The agitators in this case appealed not to reason but to warm feelings, moral indignation and moral passions. A particularly effective way of countering them was to 'say a cold sarcastic word against those who become angry' (XIV, 128).

It was not even necessary, in the first place, to cite authors and texts that directly and explicitly condemned the French Revolution and the Paris Commune or the proliferation of schools and the introduction of universal suffrage. Their teachings continued to work in the background; but now that the political and social conflict had also been detected in a sphere apparently remote from it, it was useful and even necessary to quote authors and texts that were at first sight unpolitical but, on closer inspection, turned out to be the only way of getting access to that sphere. To delegitimise the preachers of social justice, the subtle and insidious critiques of moral life proved to be of greater use than indictments of the French Revolution and socialist subversion.

In the political and social conflict going on at the European level, the revolutionaries and the wretched were undoubtedly at an advantage because of their appeal to morality. So, the target of the psychological dissection of moral sentiments was clear. The problematic encounter with the great moralists was no less unpolitical than that with classical philology. If one was addressing not just the present or the immediate past but more than two thousand years of history, the reference to classical antiquity dramatically delegitimised and diminished modernity as a short-lived phenomenon that only a philosophy of history that was parochial and reduced to immediacy could claim to transfigure as the *plenitudo temporum*. More or less the same was true of the encounter with the great moralists. In place of the depth of historical time was the depth of conscience: once this level, invisible to the eye of the banal observer, was attained, the claim to absolutise or take seriously the noble moral sentiments that barely rippled the surface of consciousness was made to seem ridiculous.

From this moment on, the critical analysis of moral sentiments was inextricably bound up with political discourse. We have already mentioned the 'moral tarantula' attached to Rousseau, Robespierre's teacher. *Zarathustra* devoted a particularly passionate sermon to denouncing and unmasking 'tarantulas'. They posed as 'preachers of equality' and agitated under the slogan of 'justice', but, in reality, they cherished a desire for 'revenge' against the best. Yes, they resembled the 'inspired [*Begeisterte*]', but it was not the 'heart' or noble sentiments that inspired them, but 'envy' or 'revenge' (Za, II, On the Tarantulas [76–7]).

Two fragments from April–June 1885 are significant. The first criticised 'socialism', because it 'very naïvely' based itself on the highest values of 'goodness' (as well as of 'truth' and 'beauty'); more or less the same went for anarchism, although 'in a more brutal way' (XI, 480). The second fragment stressed that the 'good' formed the 'background of the democratic socialist movement' (XI, 487), the revolutionary German Social-Democratic Party. Later, *Twilight of the Idols* would observe that the socialist feminist George Sand 'comes from Rousseau', from whom she had taken over 'the herd ambition to have generous feelings' (GD, 6 [194]). Clearly both fell into the category of 'the merciful who are blissful in their pitying: they lack too much in shame' (Za, II, On the Pitying [67]).

Nietzsche took particular aim at the 'teaching of sympathetic affects and of compassion' expressed by many different authors (Mill, Comte, Schopenhauer), but which arose at the 'time of the French Revolution' and continued to resonate ominously in 'all socialist systems' (M, 132 [99–100]). From the 'Enlightenment' period onwards, the philosopher never tired of reaffirming the need to be wary of the 'so-called "selfless" drives, the whole phenomenon of "neighbour love"' (EH, Why Am I So Wise, 4 [79]). The critique of morality and Christianity continued to be developed with an eye constantly turned towards the revolutionary movement, the 'levellers' and their slogans about 'equality and equal rights' (JGB, 44 [40]), and 'compassion [*Mitgefühl*] for all sufferers' (XI, 478). Countering 'socialist pity [*socialistisches Mitleid*]' (JGB, 21 [22]) was an essential aspect of the struggle against subversion. Nietzsche insisted on this theme to the very end: 'My problem with people who pity is that [...] pity quickly begins to smell of the mob. [...] I consider the overcoming of pity a noble virtue' (EH, Why Am I So Wise, 4 [79]).

One could and had to come to a general conclusion regarding morality. While encouraging 'the common human being', it 'treats as enemies those who hold power, the violent, the "masters"', as well as the 'rulers' and '*their will to power*' (XII, 214), so subversion was 'common to all *morality* and *revolution*' (XIII, 444). Revolutionary 'political theory', 'morally speaking', demanded 'equal rights for all' (WA, 7 [245]).

Nietzsche was not the only one to link criticism of the democratic and socialist movement with the psychological dissection of moral sentiments, though he did so more radically and profoundly than any other. We have already mentioned Taine and Burckhardt. Let us now take a look at Germany. Paul Rée, Nietzsche's friend and interlocutor during the 'Enlightenment' period, also linked political discourse and analysis of moral sentiments. Communism would only become plausible and even within reach if everyone really loved their neighbour; but it was 'the error of the communist to consider human beings good while they are bad'.[21] He lacked a sense of reality. '"He does not know human beings", i.e., he considers them good.'[22] Along with the myth of original human goodness, that of altruism was also dispatched: 'The benefactor imagines that the beneficiary, delighted by him, exclaims "What a wonderfully good human

---

21   Rée 1877, p. 16.
22   Rée 2004, p. 67.

being", and he sheds tears on the greatness of his own goodness.'[23] Rée's little book had as its motto a saying of Gobineau, which, as we know, had already been quoted by Schopenhauer: *L'homme est l'animal méchant par excellence.*' On the other hand, for Nietzsche of the 'Enlightenment' period, Schopenhauer could only be saved to the extent that he showed 'a moralist's genius', with his 'great connoisseurship about human and all-too-human things' (VM, 33 [25]).

The political significance of the debate about moral sentiments did not escape contemporaries: 'In many modern demands for justice one hears a note of plebeian envy and hatred', wrote Brandes, when introducing and approving of Nietzsche's analysis.[24] Later, when the conscious life of the philosopher had already come to an end, a representative of social Darwinism noted, with reference to him, that democracy and socialism, by resorting to 'Christian moral chatter' and 'humanitarian exhilaration', boasted about their 'consciousness of moral right' and were thus able to lend 'an ethical glow' to their demands.[25] On the opposite side, in Mehring's eyes, Nietzsche was wrong to raise 'justice' to the 'principle of the socialists', for he concentrated on the utopian and sentimental currents and ignores 'scientific socialism'.[26] In fact, moral outrage was in no way alien to Marx and Engels. In any case, right or wrong, Mehring's critical contribution confirmed the eminently political character of the polemic carried out by the 'moralist' Nietzsche.

In the twentieth century, speaking of Kant and the tradition of Kantian socialism, Bloch wrote: 'Socialism is what has been sought in vain for so long under the name of morality.'[27] It seems that Nietzsche had anticipated this approach, when in his condemnation he linked moral discourse, socialism and democracy.

6   Expanding the Range of Social Conflict and Encountering the Moralists: 'Good Conscience', 'Enchantment' and the 'Evil Eye'

For the more intelligent critics of revolution, the traditional explanation of reactionary journalists, that revolution was the work of a handful of conspirators and villains, was not only weak at the historiographical level but unacceptable above all because of its populist and anti-élitist political implications:

---

23   Rée 2004, p. 68.
24   Brandes 2004, p. 75.
25   Tille 1893, pp. 85, 89.
26   Mehring 1961 ff., Vol. 13, p. 169.
27   Bloch 1973, p. 640.

for this explanation ended up from an objective point of view celebrating the health of the nation as a whole, as opposed to the immorality of a small intellectual and political élite. According to Mallet du Pan, in reality it was 'almost the entire nation that embraced the Revolution, embraced it with the stupidity of a dreamer, with the delirium of madness and the delusion of enthusiasm'. It was, at least for some time, a case of collective 'deplorable enchantment'. Quite apart from sheer force, the revolution had managed to deploy an irresistible seductiveness. It had the support of 'all the fake opinion-mongers, the energy of enthusiasm, the enchantment of pen and word, the passions that have the greatest hold on the human heart.' So, the counterrevolution had to learn this lesson: 'When a new doctrine captures people's spirits, one must beware of using only violence against it, for cannons never shot feelings to death.'[28]

There are resemblances to this analysis in the observations of an author who leads back into Nietzsche's immediate vicinity. Burckhardt emphasised the role played in the revolutionary process by 'virtuous feelings', 'pathos', the 'general need for emotion', which spread rapidly in the face of a 'general disposition to infection'.[29]

The realisation that feelings, passions and mass emotions could be devastatingly effective in major historical crises led inevitably to a revaluation of reason, as is clear from the following passage from *The Gay Science*: 'The Greeks are indescribably logical and simple in all their thought; at least in their long good age they never wearied of this, as so often do the French' (FW, 82 [82]). The various revolutionary explosions that marked the history of France were moments of the obfuscation of reason, moments in which the country denied its best traditions of rational rigour and love of clarity. It is impressive to see how Nietzsche denounced 'Wagner's hatred of science' (FW, 99 [97]) and set '[us] others, [us] reason-thirsty ones', against the musician and his party (FW, 319 [180]). Had not the Basel lectures strongly condemned the socialists for demanding a 'people's state' in the name not only of 'justice' but of 'reason' (*supra*, 4 §1)? There can be no doubt that the role assigned to reason had changed radically, even if the target of the criticism remained unchanged.

To the extent that the anti-revolutionary Enlightenment really wished to combat the feelings and passions that had nourished the protest movements and mass movements in France, it had to see itself as 'moral enlightenment', in Nietzsche's language. It was precisely at this point that the encounter with the great moralists took place. Not surprisingly, Rivarol, a merciless critic of

---

28   In Matteucci 1957, pp. 380, 278 f.
29   Burckhardt 1978b, p. 397 f.

revolution, was juxtaposed to Fontenelle (VIII, 594 [403]) or Chamfort (XI, 20). But how was one to explain the fact that the latter had himself succumbed to the magic of the slogans of 1789?

> That someone who knew humanity and the masses as well as Chamfort still joined the masses and did not stand aside in philosophical renunci-ation and defence, I can only explain as follows: one instinct in him was stronger than his wisdom and was never satisfied: his hatred of all nobility of blood.

A plebeian 'instinct for revenge harking back to his boyhood', perhaps due to his mother, must have played a pernicious role (FW, 95 [91]). When a great moralist allowed himself to be infected by revolutionary madness, he too had to undergo 'suspicion' and psychological dissection. The main concern was the critique of revolution: the utilisation of the moralists' lesson was subordinated to this goal.

The revolutionaries and the wretched succeeded in conferring recognition and efficacy on their struggle for equality by appealing to a sense of justice and posing as interpreters of a higher morality. They procured for themselves the 'good conscience [*gutes Gewissen*]' that was necessary for the 'evil game that they are to play' (MA, 473 [256]). The greatest danger to society came from those who 'have the faith and the good conscience of disinterestedness' (MA, 454 [245]). Calling forth a feeling of compassion in the upper classes, at the same time the revolutionaries undermined their capacity for resistance, gnawed away by feelings of remorse or at least of discomfort. It was the 'enchantment [*Bezauberung*]' of morality: 'From time immemorial, morality has been well skilled in every devilry of the art of persuasion'; '[s]he succeeds, often with a single glance, in laming the critical will, even in luring it over to her own side' (M, Preface, 3 [2–3]). Morality allowed the malformed to cast a sort of 'evil eye' on the well-formed, and it was this malignant procedure that had to be pre-vented and neutralised (*infra*, 29 §4). So, political passion had by no means vanished. On the contrary, the lesson of the moralists could be used to achieve a significant expansion of the field of social conflict, which could now be detec-ted in feelings, moods, and attitudes hitherto thought to be politically neutral or indifferent.

It is understandable that Nietzsche looked to the past in a search for preced-ents for his attitude. And yet, in referring to the moralists, there was an element of distortion. Whereas emphasising the black soul in people served in the case of Montaigne to destroy the good conscience of the *conquistadores*, in Nietz-sche it was directed at the good conscience of the revolutionary and socialist movement. For Montaigne, the critique of anthropocentrism was closely linked to the denunciation of the ethnocentrism of the Europe of the conquests and the wars of religion; in Nietzsche's case, this criticism was instead linked to the denunciation of the Europe of revolutions and the proclamation of human rights. It is no accident that the years of the encounter with the great moralists were also the years in which he most emphatically manifested his European self-consciousness. One should add that anti-dogmatism and scepticism also played a different role in the two cases: only Nietzsche used them to ridicule the aspirations to and dreams of redemption on the part of the subaltern classes or colonial peoples.

One last point. The encounter with the great moralists was merely one moment in the course of a rapid evolution during which the various intellectual experiments that accompanied each stage are thoroughly thought through but nevertheless quickly discarded. The historical-psychological genealogy served to dismantle the moral worldview, to pave the way for what would later be called the 'innocence of becoming'.

CHAPTER 9

Between German National Liberalism and European Liberalism

1   Representative Organs, Universal Suffrage and Partitocracy

So far, we have concentrated on Nietzsche's philosophical development, so his actual political development has remained in the shadows. We have talked of his profession of faith in national liberalism in 1866 (*supra*, 1 § 6), but what happened in the following years? At first sight, Nietzsche seemed to denounce liberalism. In reality, he treated this cultural and political current with a fundamental ambiguity. As we already know from *The Greek State*, the 'liberal world view' coincided with the 'optimistic world view', which underlay the French Revolution and the cycle of upheavals to which it gave rise (*supra*, 3 § 7). The critical judgement mainly concerned a certain philosophy of history, the ideology of progress, that could not but nourish the illusions and therefore the striving for change and the slaves' revolt. It is in this sense that Nietzsche was polemicising against those so-called 'Liberals' (the inverted commas in the text are significant) who, in their democratic zeal, had ended up being taken in tow by the 'Socialists' and 'Communists' (CV, 3, I, 767–8 [166]).

On the other hand, the draft preface, then unpublished, to *The Birth of Tragedy* denounced the 'infamous profanation of a well-meant word, "liberalism"' (VII, 355). Nietzsche here seemed to pose as a champion of genuine liberalism, the liberalism that held true to the tragic vision of the world without being overwhelmed by the destructive tide of optimism. This is why, in arguing against the liberals of his day, Nietzsche sometimes used inverted commas, as if to emphasise the spurious character of their liberalism. Or he spoke scornfully of the 'so-called liberals [*sogenannte Liberalen*]', who were scandalised by the fact that Schopenhauer 'bequeathed his estate to relatives of Prussian soldiers, who died in 1848 in defense of maintaining law and order'. In fact, by acting in this way, he was being perfectly consistent with the genuinely liberal inspiration of his philosophy:

> As is well known, he believed that the only purpose of the state was to provide protection from internal enemies, protection from external enemies, and protection from the protectors, and that to ascribe to the

state any purpose other than protection could easily endanger its true purpose.

SE, 7, I, 409 [238]

With the consolidation of the French Third Republic, which by now had brought the slaves' revolt under control, the anguish and horror aroused by the Paris Commune had faded, and Nietzsche's positions became even closer to those of European liberalism. He believed the extension of suffrage and democracy could serve as a means of stabilisation and control:

> It seems that the democratization of Europe is a link in the chain of the immense *prophylactic measures* that are the idea of the modern age by which we distinguish ourselves from the Middle Ages. Now is the age of cyclopic buildings! Finally, there is certainty about the foundations, so that the entire future can build upon them without *danger*! Impossible henceforth for the fields of culture ever again to be destroyed overnight by wild and senseless mountain waters! Stone dams and protective walls against barbarians, against plagues, against *physical and spiritual enslavement*.
>
> WS, 275 [265–6]

The recourse to popular legitimacy could well serve to banish the danger of uprisings and slave wars. A similar argument was made at the time by a leading French politician. Appealing in the autumn of 1877 to moderate and conservative public opinion, to get their support for the Third Republic based on universal (male) suffrage, Gambetta said: 'How can you fail to understand that if universal suffrage functions in the fullness of its sovereignty, revolution is no longer possible, since it can no longer be attempted?' It no longer had any legitimacy or any chance, 'once France has spoken', and spoken with all the authority that came from a massive investiture from below.

But the important thing was, for Nietzsche, that means and ends not be confused. Democracy was not an end in itself, and it was likely and desirable that it was not so for those who claimed to be inspired by it:

> [W]e should not count it too harshly against the workers of the present if they loudly decree that the wall and the trellis *are* already the purpose aim and the final goal; because nobody yet sees the gardener and the fruit-trees *for the sake of which* the trellis exists.
>
> WS, 275 [266]

On another occasion, the philosopher was less sure of the effectiveness of the means and proposed this or that remedy for a situation he felt was intolerable: 'It is ridiculous when a society of people who have nothing decrees the abolition of the right of inheritance' (MA, 436 [235]). This is reminiscent of a similar formulation by Marx, though under an opposite sign, according to which bourgeois democracy could be brought to fulfilment only 'when the have-nots become the legislators of the haves'.[1] When Marx wrote this in *On the Jewish Question*, the census restrictions in France and Britain were still in force, and continued to be so in Britain even when Nietzsche made his statement. Which, in any case, continued as follows: '[A]nd it is no less ridiculous when people without children engage in the practical work of making laws for a country – they do not in fact have enough ballast in their ship to be able to sail safely into the ocean of the future' (MA, 436 [235]). This basic idea was repeated in a later aphorism:

> If a man has no sons, he does not have the full right to participate in discussions about what any affair of state requires. We must ourselves, along with other people, have risked what is dearest to us; only this binds us firmly to the state; we must have the happiness of our posterity in view, hence, first and foremost have posterity, in order to take the proper, natural interest in institutions and in their alteration.
>
> MA, 455 [245]

It is true that in another variant, later dropped, he referred to Pericles's 'funeral oration' (XIV, 147), presumably the passage where the Athenian statesman, in connection with the war and the city's security needs, said: 'For it is not possible for men to counsel anything fair or just if they are not at risk by staking their sons equally.'[2] But here, allusions originating in contemporary reality and political debate were even more effective than the model of ancient Greece. On both sides of the Rhine, proposals for reform and changes in the electoral system were commonplace. For example, Renan,[3] an author who liked to count himself among the 'enlightened liberals', called for the privileging of married men with children.[4]

Against the dangers of democracy, Nietzsche proposed the introduction of a tiered electoral system. This was an idea Tocqueville had already suggested.

---

1   Marx and Engels 1975 ff., 3, pp. 146–74.
2   Thucydides, 1998, p. 96.
3   Renan 1947 ff., Vol. 1, p. 387.
4   Renan, 1947 ff., Vol. 1, p. 443.

For Tocqueville, the US Senate owed its excellence to the fact that it was not the direct result of an election; this was an idea to which Renan strove to give new relevance after the experience of the Paris Commune.[5] According to Nietzsche, one was to start with a group of 'the honest and trustworthy people of a country, those of them who were also masters and experts in some field', and then make 'a narrower vote' from them. Within the legislature thus constituted, 'only the votes and judgements of the most specialized experts' would decide, so that 'the law would proceed from the understanding of those who understand the best' (VM, 318 [122]).

Up to this point, we remain on quite traditional ground. Even in France, there were those who fought for the primacy of 'educated men' and 'scientists' over 'unintelligent citizens without education'. Although by way of a different voting mechanism that conferred multiple votes on the more educated and more responsible, even John Stuart Mill hoped to secure control over representative bodies for the intelligent and competent.[6] For a while, Nietzsche himself entertained the idea of the plural vote, though to the benefit not of the more intelligent, as in the British liberal model, but to 'fathers who bring many males into the world'! (XIII, 495). Apart from this latter point, which chimed with the obsession with 'eugenics' that marked out the final years of Nietzsche's life (infra, 19 §1), we are not that far removed from the world of German and European liberalism.

But Nietzsche of the 'Enlightenment' further clarified his thinking. Rather than the extension of suffrage or parliament, he took as his target what today one might call the partitocracy. In the notes and drafts for the lectures On the Future of Our Educational Institutions, he expressed distaste for the 'party throng' (XIV, 106). But now, that distaste took a more explicitly political form: 'At present, parties vote'. It was they that disdained the principle of competence and 'the belief in the supreme utility of science and of those with knowledge', turning every vote in parliament into a 'party-vote'. So 'let our watchword be: "More respect for those with knowledge! And down with all parties"' (VM, 318 [122]). The first draft of this aphorism put it even more emphatically: 'Abolish the parties in the parliament. Whoever is not competent shall abstain from voting. The inner morality of truth implies this' (XIV, 180). Representative bodies were useful, but it was important to free them from suffocating embrace and control. For Nietzsche, this programme was in perfect harmony with his 'Enlightenment' and his struggle against fanaticism. One had to take a stand

---

5   Ibid.
6   Huard 1991, p. 108; Losurdo 1993, 1, § 6–7.

against an institution, the party, that sought to turn each member into an 'unconditional supporter' (VM, 305 [118]).

Just as during the years of *The Birth of Tragedy*, even now his gaze continued to turn towards Social Democracy, which, unlike the parties of bourgeois opinion, because of the persecution it had suffered and its wish to transform society radically, tended to take the form of a sort of counter-state, and so could not but appeal to a sense of compactness, discipline and solidarity on the part of its activists.

Here, too, Nietzsche proved that he was able to understand, and often to anticipate, the mood of the time. Later, Haym would thunder against the 'partitocracy [*Parteiwesen*]', always with an eye to a party that, with its 'incitement of the masses against the propertied classes', represented a 'threat of destruction for any social order'. To neutralise the power of Social Democracy, it might be necessary to take a step backwards from universal suffrage.[7] For Nietzsche, too, universal suffrage was not irrevocable; indeed, the phenomenon of electoral abstention already required or implied its revocation. This was a fundamental contradiction: could one extend suffrage to all citizens even if all citizens did not agree? Universal suffrage could be legitimised only by the '*unanimity of all*'; the phenomenon of electoral abstention was enough to plunge it into crisis (WS, 276 [266]).

Haym formulated his position in the context of a sympathetic evocation of Baumgarten, the author of an essay (*German Liberalism. A Self-Criticism*)[8] that called on this cultural and political current to purge itself of its democratic incrustation and, on that basis, to become immediately successful. Liberalism developed in the course of a sharp polemic against what Treitschke contemptuously called the 'ideas of 89'.[9] Nietzsche belonged on this terrain. One should not forget that his declaration of adherence to 'liberal' and 'national-liberal' principles happened in the same year as the publication of the essay of 'self-criticism'.

As for the mistrust of and hostility towards universal suffrage, one should bear in mind that although universal suffrage was already established in France and Germany (where it is restricted, however, to elections to the Reichstag), it had not yet taken hold in Britain. Had Bismarck demonstrated wisdom and balance in bringing about such a drastic enlargement of the electorate? This question was also asked by Strauss, who contrasted the example of liberal Britain with that of the Second Reich: 'From time to time the census is lowered for

---

7   Haym 1903b, p. 627.
8   Baumgarten 1974.
9   Treitschke 1981, Vol. 1, p. 118.

parliamentary elections, but it would occur to no English statesman to abolish it.' This was a country that had the merit of standing up to democratic demagogy: together with the demand for universal suffrage, it also unhesitatingly rejected that for the abolition of the death penalty, which, in Germany, had become a serious issue.[10]

Nietzsche of the 'Enlightenment' also seemed to look with sympathy on the classic country of the liberal tradition, where only house-owners had political rights. But his sympathy and admiration were more general: 'Today, without a doubt, it is at the head of all peoples in philosophy, in science, in history, in the field of discovery and in the dissemination of the culture', only in England was the 'individual' allowed 'a victorious and joyous isolation from public opinion' (VIII, 466). In this context, the partial rehabilitation of Schopenhauer could be understood: it was important to appreciate 'his sense for hard facts, his good will to clarity and reason, that so often makes him appear so English and so un-German' (FW, 99 [95]). Probably the anglophilia of these years also helps to explain the preference for Hume over Kant, 'verbose' in his manner of communicating and prone to dilute 'his thoughts, perhaps perfectly clear, so that they become ponderous and dark' (III, 446).

Beyond Britain, his sympathy seemed also to extend to the other classic country of the liberal tradition, as is clear from his contrast between 'Anglo-American sobriety [*Nüchternheit*] in the reconstruction of state and society' and 'French revolutionary enthusiasm [*Umsturz-Schwärmerei*]' (VM, 171 [73]).

2   From the Statism of the Greek Polis to Socialism: Nietzsche, Constant and Tocqueville

But it was not immediate political influences and his mistrust of or hostility towards universal suffrage that brought the Nietzsche of those years closer to liberal thinking of the period. Together with Constant, he strove to denounce the Jacobin ideal of widespread participation in public life. This was an ideal that resonated on the other bank of the Rhine. When Heinrich Heine described the climate of fervour and enthusiasm in the years before the revolution of 1848, he celebrated 'the great science of freedom' in politics, with the interest and participation in public life it entailed.[11] On the other hand, the third *Unfashionable Observation* said one of Schopenhauer's great merits was to have

---

10   Strauss 1872, p. 286.
11   Heine 1969–78, Vol. 2, p. 657.

denounced the '*furor politicus*'. Whoever was cured of this sickness 'will wisely refrain from reading the newspapers every day, and above all from serving in a party, although he will not hesitate for a single moment to take up his position if his fatherland is threatened by a real danger'. In any case, as for Constant, for Nietzsche policy was also the responsibility of a limited group of people: 'All states in which people other than politicians must concern themselves with politics are badly organized and deserve to perish from this abundance of politicians' (SE, 7, I, 409 [239]).

There were, of course, other resemblances too with the French liberal, whose attack on the Rousseauean-Jacobin tradition was well known: it was accused of confusing ancient freedom (based on the omnipotence of the social body that absorbed and swallowed the individual) and modern freedom (based on the independence of the individual from the social body). Nietzsche, who seems to have had a direct or indirect knowledge of Constant, whose basic thesis was widely echoed on German soil by authors like Treitschke and Haym,[12] seemed to intervene in this debate. It may appear paradoxical to seek traces of the polemic against the 'ancient freedom' in an author that, in the name of the celebration and transfiguration of, above all, Greece, delivered a relentless indictment of modernity. And yet Nietzsche's rejection of the condemnation of ancient slavery did not mean he took the polis as his model. According to Burckhardt, the era of the 'rule of the masses' started in Greece as early as the fifth century BC.[13] For Nietzsche, as for the historian, the polis referred to the period in which 'the rabble gained prominence in Greece' (JGB, 49 [47]). It was synonymous with the senseless claim of all citizens to participate in political decisions: '[H]istory knows of no other example of such an awesome release of the political urge, of such a complete sacrifice of all other interests in the service of this instinct towards the state' (CV, 3, I, 771 [169]). The 'insatiability of public life' (XIV, 106), which Nietzsche, with an eye to democracy and socialism, denounced in the modern world, had its antecedent in the Greek polis:

> Their almost religious love for their king was passed along by the Greeks to the polis when the monarchy came to an end. [...] [R]everence for the polis and the state became greater than reverence for princes had ever been. The Greeks are the *fools of the state* in ancient history – in modern history, these have been other peoples.
>
> WS, 232 [253]

---

12   Cf. Losurdo 1997a, 14, §2 and §11.
13   Burckhardt 1978a, p. 120.

Classical antiquity and Greece became a synonym for the swallowing of the individual by the body politic: this was Constant's theme, and it was also commonplace on German soil, while the reference to modern nations clearly targeted the country of unending revolutionary upheavals. In fact, although in a different context, 'Greeks and French' were mentioned together in *Human, All Too Human* (*supra*, 7 § 7).

Nietzsche had already begun to take up these themes in the Basel lectures. They confront us with an interesting debate about the expansion of the educational and state apparatus in Prussia. An interlocutor complained that some spoke of 'a form of State omnipotence which was attained only in antiquity'; there was a danger, he said, that a view would gain the upper hand that, as in antiquity, considered such a state to be 'the crowning glory and highest aim of human beings' (BA, 3, I, 708 [87]). But, at this point, a more authoritative interlocutor intervened, 'the philosopher' *par excellence*, who pointed out that 'the ancient State emphatically did not share the utilitarian point of view of recognising as culture only what was directly useful to the State itself' (BA, 3; I, 708–9 [87–8]). Nietzsche here seems to be fighting on two fronts. On the one hand, he wanted to make clear that the Prussia he hated, that of the intensive spread of education and schools (with the aim of strengthening the bureaucratic and military apparatus), had nothing to do with Greece, at least not with the real one. On the other hand, he was anxious to distinguish Hellas from the image projected on it by the Jacobins and the anti-Jacobin (and anti-socialist) polemic of European liberal culture:

> [T]he profound Greek had for the State that strong feeling of admiration and thankfulness which is so distasteful to modern men; because he clearly recognised not only that without such State protection [*Noth und Schutzanstalt*] the germs of his culture could not develop, but also that all his inimitable and perennial culture had flourished so luxuriantly under the wise and careful guardianship of the protection afforded by the State.
>
> BA, 3; I, 709 [88]

This restricted state was, unfortunately, overwhelmed by the polis, whose image in Nietzsche scarcely differed from that of the liberal culture of the time:

> Like every organizing political power, the Greek polis resisted and mistrusted the growth of culture; its powerful basic impulse manifested itself almost exclusively in efforts to cripple and obstruct it. [...] Culture therefore developed *despite* the polis. [...] We should not appeal to Pericles' panegyric as evidence to the contrary: for that is nothing more than a

grandly optimistic, deceptive image of the supposedly necessary connection between the polis and Athenian culture.

> MA, 474 [256–7]

Human, All Too Human was here distancing itself from a text in which Pericles
emphasised the central role and fruitful function of 'knowledge' and 'attention
to public affairs'. It was precisely herein that the primacy of Athens lay: 'We are
unique in considering the man who takes no part in these to be not apolitical
but useless.'[14]

The theme of Pericles's panegyric seems also to be present in Heine. In the
Vormärz years, when the democratic revolution began to loom on the horizon,
he insisted there was no conflict between the development of art and culture
on the one hand and political participation and passion on the other. This
was demonstrated by the examples of Athens and Florence: the artists 'did not
lead an egoistically isolated life of art, their idly poetizing souls hermetically
sealed against the great sorrows and joys of the time [...], they did not separate
their art from the politics of the day, they did work with pitiful private enthusiasm.'[15]

In Nietzsche's eyes, however, the levelling character of the polis found its
fullest expression in Plato: the philosopher who would have liked to ban art
from his ideal city was also 'the typical old socialist', not surprisingly busy 'at
the court of the Sicilian tyrants'. The fact was that socialism was always in close
proximity 'to every excessive manifestation of power' (MA, 473 [255]).

So, we come to another classic argument of liberal thought of the time. We
have already seen how the fourth *Unfashionable Observation* cited Schopenhauer to underline that the 'true purpose' of the state was very restricted.
Human, All Too Human reiterated:

> The state is a clever arrangement for the protection of individuals from
> one another: but if we push its refinement too far, we will finally weaken
> the individual, even dissolve him – and thus the original purpose of the
> State will be most thoroughly thwarted.
>
> MA, 235 [162]

In its mad claim to solve the social question politically, the democratic and
socialist movement issued the slogan 'as much government as possible'. Well,

---

14   Thucydides 1998, p. 93.
15   Heine 1969–78, Vol. 3, p. 72.

'soon the opposing cry presses forward with an even greater force: "as little government as possible"' (MA, 473 [256]).

Because of the pathological expansion of the state it promoted, 'socialism', far from being a real novelty, was actually 'the visionary younger brother of an almost decrepit despotism whose heir it wants to be', bringing an 'abundance of governmental power' to an even higher level (MA, 473 [255]). This calls to mind Tocqueville's *L'Ancien Régime et la Révolution* and the continuous line that stretched from monarchical absolutism to Jacobinism and socialism, under the ensign of statism and despotism. On the other hand, Nietzsche might have read about this continuity in Taine, for he too, with an explicit reference to Tocqueville, believed the entire history of France was seamlessly characterised by 'the unlimited dictatorship of the state'.[16] Or he might also have heard it from Burckhardt, who repeatedly returned to this theme.[17] Beyond them, Gobineau also clearly asserted the line of continuity from monarchical absolutism to revolutionary and above all Jacobin statism.[18]

Tocqueville also emphasised the affinities and secret complicity of socialism and Bonapartism. *Human, All Too Human* declared that socialism 'longs for (and under certain circumstances promotes) the powerful Caesarean state of this century [*den cäsarischen Gewaltstaat dieses Jahrhunderts*] because it would like to be its heir' (MA, 473 [255–6]). So, there is a clear identification of Nietzsche of the 'Enlightenment' period with the standpoint of the liberal movement, from which he borrowed language and important categories: socialism, with its project for a further expansion of the state, was far from representing a step forward, but instead had 'aspirations [that are] in the deepest sense reactionary' (MA, 473 [255]). To use Tocqueville's words, we were dealing with 'doctrines' that claimed to be 'new' but were actually 'quite old'.[19]

Socialism was a movement, said *Human, All Too Human*, that aimed expressly at the 'outright annihilation of the individual: this it perceives as an unjustified luxury of nature that it ought to improve into a purposeful *organ of the community* [*Gemeinwesen*]' (MA, 473 [255]). There was no longer any mention of the pathos of the unanimous *volksthümlich* community that had clearly marked Nietzsche's 'romantic' period. The target of the polemic continued to be the endless cycle of revolution, ending in socialism. However, it was no

---

16   Taine 1899, Vol. 2, pp. 65–7.
17   Burckhardt 1978a, p. 68 ff.
18   Gobineau 1917, p. 20 f.
19   Tocqueville 1864–67, Vol. 9, p. 570.

longer criticised as alien to the Germanic essence and the popular community. Now, the beneficial function of property and individual initiative was the main issue: if one favoured 'returning property to the community [*Gemeinde*] and making the individual into simply a temporary tenant, we thereby destroy the arable land'. One was not to lose sight of one essential fact: 'For people do not exhibit foresight and a sense of sacrifice toward anything that they only possess temporarily; they behave exploitatively toward it, like thieves or dissolute spendthrifts' (WS, 285 [273]).

This was precisely what old and modern socialism was determined not to understand: 'Plato's underlying utopian melody, which is still being sung today by the socialists, rests upon a deficient knowledge of human beings.' In fact, when he 'supposes that selfishness would be abolished with the abolition of property, he can be answered by saying that after deducting selfishness, from human beings at least, none of the four cardinal virtues will remain. [...] Without vanity and selfishness – what are the human virtues then?' (WS, 285 [273]).

3   Political Realism and Antiquitising Utopia

We have seen that Nietzsche's interest in politics was so strong that he did not disdain to pay close attention to the phenomenon of electoral abstention and the various projects of anti-democratic electoral engineering. It should, however, be added that this 'realism' was linked to the singular utopianism of a classical philologist who was at the same time an antiquitising philosopher. One example is particularly telling. After condemning as absurd the enjoyment of political rights by those without descendants, Nietzsche continued:

> But it seems just as nonsensical if someone who has chosen as his task the acquisition of the most universal knowledge and the appraisal of existence as a whole burdens himself with the personal considerations of family, sustenance, safety, or maintaining the respect of his wife and child. [...] So I, too, arrive at the proposition that in matters of the highest philosophical kind, anyone who is married is suspect.
>
> MA, 436 [235]

Clearly, at stake was not the observation of reality in Germany or Europe, but the reading of Plato's *Republic*!

This reading, and the transfigured image of classical antiquity, played an even clearer role in the therapy proposed as a solution to the social question.

On the one hand, in his condemnation of socialist utopianism, Nietzsche resorted to themes commonplace in the liberal culture of the time:

> May good reason preserve us from the belief that someday or other humanity will discover an ultimate, ideal order and that then happiness will shine down with constant intensity upon the people ordered in this way, like the sun in the tropics: [...] No golden age, no cloudless sky is allotted to these coming generations. [...] Nor will suprahuman goodness and justice stretch like an immobile rainbow over the fields of the future.
>
> WB, 11; I, 506 [327]

This was not a case of digging in behind a wall of blind conservatism. It was necessary 'with relentless courage to set about the *improvement of that aspect of the world recognized as being alterable*' (WB, 3, I, 445 [272]). This was a more flexible attitude than in *The Birth of Tragedy*, which, as we have seen, strove to demonstrate, against theoretical and practical optimism, that one could do nothing to 'change the eternal essence of things' (GT [40]). Now, on the contrary, the existence of an area of possible and necessary change was recognised. But it could be correctly identified and circumscribed only after 'the extent to which things possess an unalterable nature and form' (WB, 3, I, 445 [272]) had been clarified philosophically, only after the problem ignored or neglected by revolutionary and socialist utopianism, which pursued the illusion of a total palingenesis, had been resolved.

The same argument can be found in Tocqueville, according to whom the clear vision and reaffirmation of laws and social structures 'located outside the scope of revolutions' had to be set against the socialist dream of eliminating 'human misery' (*infra*, 20 § 8).

The necessary social reforms were not in contradiction with a policy, if necessary, of robust political repression. This went as much for the French liberal Tocqueville[20] as for Nietzsche. The latter, in particular, advanced arguments of penetrating modernity and ruthlessness influenced by considerations of *Realpolitik*:

> We can divide those who intend the overthrow of society into those who want to attain something for themselves and those who want to attain something for their children and grandchildren. The latter are the more dangerous, for they have the faith and the good conscience of disinter-

---

20   Cf. Losurdo 1993, 2, § 4.

estedness. The others can be bought off: the ruling elements of society are still rich and clever enough for that. The danger begins as soon as the goals become impersonal.

MA, 454 [244–5]

So, while the opportunists and careerists of the socialist movement could be corrupted and even, to a certain extent, co-opted by the existing order and power, the greater danger was represented by the disinterested elements, generously committed to building a bloc of forces capable of organising a revolutionary overthrow.

Up to this point, we are not far removed from the ideas of European liberalism. But, again, antiquitising utopia intervened. For Nietzsche addressed himself as follows to the privileged classes:

The only remedy against socialism that still remains in your power is: not to challenge it, that is, to live yourselves in a moderate and unpretentious way, to prevent as far as you can any excessive displays of wealth and to come to the aid of the state when it places severe taxes upon everything superfluous and seemingly luxurious.

VM, 304 [117]

The memory of the sumptuary laws of antiquity seemed to stimulate a positive attitude here to a sort of progressive taxation: so it ended by objectively calling into question the demand to minimise the state and its sphere of influence.

The fact is that Nietzsche was still greatly concerned about socialism, this 'public sickness', this 'plague' or 'scabies', that 'communicates itself faster and faster to the masses'. The privileged classes had to be prepared to make some sacrifices to avert the danger: 'You don't want this remedy? Then', urged the philosopher, 'you rich bourgeois who call yourselves "liberal", just admit to yourselves that it is your own heartfelt convictions that you find so frightening and threatening in the socialists: only the possession of property makes any difference between you and them.' This even gave rise to the paradox that the 'first seat and incubator' of socialism was precisely the wealthy bourgeoisie it wanted to eradicate (VM, 304 [117–18]). The ruling classes did not realise they were promoting a vision of the world (all in the name of accumulation) of which they themselves could be the victims. One was instead to aspire to stand out from the crowd, by avoiding 'every impersonal form of life' as 'vulgar and despicable' and by demonstrating 'a great new scorn, for example, of the rich, the officials and so on', and of all those infected by mediocrity and the herd mentality (IX, 444).

A fragment from the years of *The Birth of Tragedy* already linked 'socialism' with, among other things, 'coarseness of the spirit' and suggested the following rule: 'At a certain level of affluence, ostracism' (VII, 299). With the same danger in mind, a fragment from the 'Enlightenment' period declared 'it is absolutely imperative that superior intelligence gives it [wealth] direction' (IX, 472). That was the only way to contain or avert the danger of subversion. If, on the other hand, 'the higher classes of society' became coarse, 'then the socialist multitudes would be quite right to also seek to level the outward differences between themselves and the others, since they would already be inwardly level with one another in head and heart' (MA, 480 [262]).

More than the ruling classes as such, the target of criticism here was a wealth that strove to free itself completely from its political and social obligations:

> Only someone who has *spirit* should possess *property*: otherwise property is *dangerous to the common good.* The proprietor, that is, who does not understand how to make any use of the free time that his property could provide for him, will *continue* forever to strive for more property: this effort becomes his entertainment, his strategem in the battle with boredom.

He who had excessive wealth 'can adopt the mask of cultivation and art: he can *buy* masks'. This led, on account of the envy and resentment that such a spectacle aroused, to disastrous consequences 'among the poorer and less cultivated': 'for gilded coarseness and histrionic self-inflation in the supposed "enjoyment of culture" inspires in them the thought that "all depends on money" – while certainly something depends on money, but much more depends on the spirit' (VM, 310).

In criticising the tendency of wealth to become autonomous, Nietzsche looked not only to classical antiquity but also to the *ancien régime* overthrown by revolution. He contrasted the vulgarity of the new class with the finesse of the traditional aristocracy:

> What provides men and women of noble blood with an advantage over others and gives them an unquestionable right to be esteemed more highly are two arts that are augmented more and more by hereditary transmission: the art of being able to command and the art of proud obedience. – Now wherever commanding is part of daily affairs (as in the world of business and industry), there arises something similar to those 'noble bloodlines'.
>
> MA, 440 [238]

Unfortunately, an irreparable loss had already come about: the ruling classes of the modern world 'lack the aristocratic bearing in obedience' that for the old aristocracy was 'inherited from feudal conditions and that will no longer grow in our cultural climate' (MA, 440 [238]).

4   Nietzsche, European Liberalism and the Complaint about the Crisis of Culture

The 'Enlightenment' turn led perhaps to an attenuation of the criticism or condemnation of modernity, although it certainly did not put an end to it. Must we conclude, at least on this point, that Nietzsche drew a clear line between himself and European liberalism? Not so. Tocqueville expressed his concern at the prospect of a 'levelled society'[21] or a 'society of bees and beavers', consisting 'more of trained animals than of free and civilized men'.[22] These terms are reminiscent of Schopenhauer, who also used a 'bees' and 'beehive' metaphor,[23] or, to remain within the vicinity of Nietzsche, one might quote Burckhardt, who mentioned the 'beehive' as well as the 'anthill'.[24] Later, in *Zarathustra*, Nietzsche would go even further, branding the modern world as synonymous with 'rabble mishmash [*Pöbel-Mischmasch*]' and 'the detritus of swarming ants [*Ameisen-Kribbelkram*]' (Za, IV, On the Higher Man, 3 [233]). It is interesting to note that this metaphor also cropped up in democratic culture, but there it was used to denounce, with Heine, the attitude of the aristocracy and of the wealthy in general, who looked down with sovereign contempt on the mass of the desperate poor 'as if they were tiny ants [*Ameisen*]'.[25]

But let us focus on the resemblances between Nietzsche's critique of modernity and the liberal culture of his time. *Human, All Too Human* warned that the 'ideal state' the 'socialists' dreamt of would destroy 'the soil from which great intellect and any powerful individual grow', thus leaving room only for 'enfeebled individuals' (MA, 235 [161]). Unfortunately, for him, this process was already under way.

This was also John Stuart Mill's view: '[T]he general tendency of things throughout the world is to render mediocrity the ascendant power among

21   Tocqueville 1951 ff., Vol. 12, p. 37.
22   Tocqueville 1864–67, Vol. 9, p. 544.
23   Schopenhauer 1976–82c, Vol. 4, p. 190.
24   Burckhardt 1978b, p. 388.
25   Heine 1969–78, Vol. 2, p. 542.

mankind.' At least from this standpoint, modernity was a moment of undeniable decadence:

> In ancient history, in the middle ages, and in a diminishing degree through the long transition from feudality to the present time, the individual was a power in himself; and if he had either great talents or a high social position, he was a considerable power. At present individuals are lost in the crowd. In politics it is almost a triviality to say that public opinion now rules the world. The only power deserving the name is that of masses, and of governments while they make themselves the organ of the tendencies and instincts of masses.[26]

The British liberal cited the authority of Wilhelm von Humboldt, another author valued by Nietzsche, to warn against 'the process of continuous assimilation' that marked the modern world. This destroyed 'the freedom and variety of situations', making impossible the development of strong and original individualities.[27] Yes, agreed Tocqueville, 'we live in a time and in a democratic society where individuals, even the greatest, are nothing'.[28] Mill welcomed this diagnosis, though he thought it should be generalised. There was no doubt 'the Frenchmen of the present day resemble one another [much more] than did those even of the last generation', but '[t]he same remark might be made of Englishmen in a far greater degree'.[29] Tocqueville agreed: 'England has, like us, become sterile in great men.'[30] This had, in the meantime, become a universal destiny, that even the country he particularly admired could not escape:

> Why, as civilization spreads, do outstanding men become fewer? Why, when attainments are the lot of all, do great intellectual talents become rarer? Why, when there are no longer lower classes, are there no more upper classes? Why, when knowledge of how to rule reaches the masses, is there a lack of great abilities in the direction of society? America clearly poses these questions. But who can answer them?[31]

---

26   Mill 1972a, p. 123.
27   Mill 1965b, p. 225.
28   Tocqueville 1951 ff., Vol. 8, 2. Half Vol., p. 369.
29   Mill 1972a, p. 130.
30   Tocqueville 1951 ff., Vol. 8, 3. Half Vol., p. 273.
31   Tocqueville 1951 ff., Vol. 5, 1. Half Vol., p. 188.

With the advent of democracy, '[t]he nation, taken as a whole, will be less brilliant, less glorious, and perhaps less strong'.[32] Beyond this or that aspect, the impression of 'universal mediocrity' created dismay.[33] Burckhardt referred to this analysis of Renan's when denouncing the increasing 'coarsening' of the world.[34] Tocqueville, for his part, talked of 'universal diminution'.[35] Similar though more poetic was the language of Zarathustra: now the 'little people' ruled (Za, IV, On the Higher Man, 3 [233]); 'the earth has become small' and 'the time approaches when human beings will no longer give birth to a dancing star'; it was the time of the 'last human being, who makes everything small'; who was unable even to aspire to greatness, and so was worthy only of contempt (Za, Zarathustra's Prologue, 5 [9–10]). The horizon of modernity was marked by the pursuit of 'momentary utility' (VII, 243). The ideal of 'a good life for as many people as possible' seemed to gain ever more followers even outside the circle of 'socialists' that propagated it with particular persistence (MA, 235 [161]). Here is the picture Tocqueville drew of France as it had emerged from the July Revolution and particularly of Louis Philippe:

> He loved neither literature nor the arts, but he loved industry with a passion. His conversation [...] afforded one the delight that can be found in the pleasures of intelligence, once delicate and lofty sentiments have been eliminated. His intelligence was notable, but it was limited and hindered by a spirit that did not nourish any elevated or profound sentiments. He was enlightened, refined, flexible and resolute; he was interested exclusively in profit.[36]

By then, the only 'ruling passion' of all 'human activity' was 'industry'.[37] This was also the view of Burckhardt, who was similarly uncomfortable with the 'ruling industrialism'.[38] The great historian noted with displeasure the 'incessant extraordinary growth in acquisitiveness'. The United States announced and promoted a 'purely acquisitive world'; and, unfortunately, the present of America seemed to be the future of Europe, too.[39]

---

32 Tocqueville 1951 ff., Vol. 1, 1. Half Vol., p. 7 (DA, Introduction).
33 Renan 1947 ff., Vol. 1, p. 483.
34 Burckhardt 1978a, p. 143.
35 Tocqueville 1951 ff., Vol. 12, p. 31 f.
36 Tocqueville 1951 ff., Vol. 12, p. 31 f.
37 Tocqueville 1951 ff., Vol. 3, 2. Half Vol., p. 101.
38 Burckhardt 1978b, p. 258.
39 Burckhardt 1978a, pp. 148–50.

Was there an antidote to this rampant coarsening? Whereas Mill sought a remedy in artistic genius (*supra*, 2 §5), Tocqueville lamented that 'in the century in which we live', 'the hunger [...] for greatness' could find nourishment only in reading Plutarch and in classical antiquity.[40] This attitude resembled that of Burckhardt and leads us back, above all, to Nietzsche.

Against the mediocrity and vulgarity of the modern world, religion could also help. This is rather clear in the case of Tocqueville. Hence his nostalgia for an era in which 'material enjoyments' were not the sole concern: there were not 'only interests, but also convictions'.[41] The American example showed so: 'His passions, his wants, his education, and everything about him seem to unite in drawing the native of the United States earthward: his religion alone bids him turn, from time to time, a transient and distracted glance to heaven.'[42]

As we have seen, in his polemic against Strauss even Nietzsche set the seriousness of the religious problematic against the coarseness of the vision of the philistine and mercantile worldview. While acknowledging 'a certain constraint of the intellect' implicit in 'religious feeling', *Human, All Too Human* continued to acknowledge 'the astonishing effects' that unfolded on the 'engendering of the genius'. And yet, even if one glossed over other considerations, it made no sense to abandon oneself to nostalgia for a world irretrievably elapsed: religious feeling 'has had its time, and many fine things can never grow again because they were able to grow only from it' (MA, 234 [160]). And yet one had to say that this conclusion was not void of inner pain. Again, *The Dawn* emphasised 'the powerful beauty and refinement of the princes of the church', and then asked itself a disturbing question: 'with the end of all religions will *this* [...] be also carried to the grave? And is something higher not attainable, not even conceivable?' (M, 60 [44–5].)

5   The Mediocrity of the Modern World and the Spectre of European 'chinoiserie'

The reduction and vulgarisation of the world was advancing implacably: '[T]he most profound levelling down to mediocrity and *chinoiserie*' seemed destined to triumph in Europe too. Those who sought to eliminate inequalities, alleged injustices and conflicts in order to build 'a realm of justice and concord' took as their model, whether they were aware of it or not, a country located outside

---

40   Tocqueville 1951 ff., Vol. 15, 1. Half Vol., p. 97.
41   Tocqueville 1951 ff., Vol. 3, 2. Half Vol., p. 134.
42   Tocqueville 1951 ff., Vol. 1, 2. Half Vol., p. 43 (DA, 2. Book, 1. Part, 9).

Europe and the West and characterised by pathological rigidity and irreversible decay (FW, 377 [241]). The theme of China's stationariness was commonplace in European culture of the time. It could even be found in Herzen, according to whom this large Asian country 'falls asleep in a *semper idem*'.[43] But it was, above all, alive and present in liberal thought. One need only think of Tocqueville's interpretation and celebration of the first Opium War: 'So at last the mobility of Europe has come to grips with Chinese immobility!'[44] John Stuart Mill came to a similar conclusion during the second Opium War: the Chinese 'have become stationary, and if they are to be improved it must be by foreigners'.[45]

While the British liberal was writing this, a revolution was taking place in China, the Taiping Revolution, gigantic in size (many millions died) and ideologically radical. It broke with Confucian tradition and borrowed from Christianity the messianic expectation of a *novum* of justice and peace. Hundreds of thousands of insurgents preferred to commit suicide rather than surrender.[46] The intervention by Britain, the country from which Mill denounced China's thousands of years of immobility, contributed decisively to the defeat. Here we are dealing with a stereotype. The traditional ideology of colonial expansionism, founded in the need to spread civilisation, was hard to apply to China, whose culture was far older than Europe's. But it had, in the meantime, become mummified and lifeless, the conquerors and their ideologues seemed to reply.

Nietzsche shared this stereotyped view of China in the years of Western colonial expansion: 'the more severe revenge' was, of course, 'Chinese revenge' (FW, 69 [74]), and the sole 'passions' of this people were 'opium gambling women' (IX, 454). The most important point, however, was this: 'the Chinese mind' was 'the most important monument to the spirit of endurance' (IX, 541). Perhaps a little more attention would now be paid to the unrest and uprisings in China, often targeted at the military, economic and religious expansionism of the West. And yet, to judge by one of the fragments, it was merely a question of 'the muffled pressure of an unsatisfied release' (IX, 453), of an explosion that had no noticeable effect and did not change the overall picture. It remained a fact that, in China, people had stayed 'almost unchanged for millennia' (IX, 547). And it was precisely this rotting mummy that Western revolutionaries held up as a model: '[T]he socialists and state idolaters, with their measures for making life better and safer, might easily establish Chinese conditions and

43   Herzen 1852, p. 24.
44   Tocqueville 1951 ff., Vol. 4, 1. Half Vol., p. 58.
45   Mill 1972a, p. 129.
46   Chesneaux/Bastid 1969, p. 86.

a Chinese "happiness"', on the model of 'a country where large-scale discontentment and the capacity for change became extinct centuries ago' (FW, 24 [49]).

This theme was commonplace in European liberal culture at the time. Tocqueville criticised the 'economists' and Enlighteners, as main figures in the ideological preparation of the French Revolution, even more than he did the socialists. In pursuit of their ideal of 'absolute equality', 'socialism' and the 'omnipotence of the state', they looked admiringly to China: 'This stupid and barbaric government, which controls a handful of Europeans at will, seems to them to be the most perfect model, to be proposed to all the nations of the world.'[47]

According to Nietzsche, not only socialism but 'positive philosophy', with its obsessive wish to 'eliminate the anarchy of the spirits', seemed inspired by the land of lifeless immobility (IX, 453). In similar vein, though with a vaguer focus, John Stuart Mill criticised the Chinese:

> They have succeeded beyond all hope in what English philanthropists are so industriously working at – in making a people all alike, all governing their thoughts and conduct by the same maxims and rules; and these are the fruits. The modern *régime* of public opinion is, in an unorganized form, what the Chinese educational and political systems are in an organized; and unless individuality shall be able successfully to assert itself against this yoke, Europe, notwithstanding its noble antecedents and its professed Christianity, will tend to become another China.[48]

So, the superiority of the West was, at the same time, the superiority of Christianity. One would think that, at least here, the difference should be obvious, with respect to Nietzsche. But, in this case, not so, at least to judge by a fragment from the spring of 1880:

> Christianity, thanks to its Jewish characteristics, has conferred on Europeans that Jewish self-loathing, the representation of inner restlessness as human normality: hence the flight of the Europeans from themselves, hence their unprecedented activity; they stick their heads and hands everywhere.
>
> IX, 89

---

47   Tocqueville 1951 ff., Vol. 2, 1. Half Vol., p. 213 (AR, 3. Book, 3).
48   Mill 1972a, p. 129.

In Europe, needless to say, along with Christianity, 'the struggle against Christianity', as well as, more generally, 'the anarchy of opinions and the competition of sovereigns, peoples and merchants' (IX, 452), played a positive role. But all these contradictions were still the legacy of the intrinsic restlessness of the Jewish spirit, by now part of the identity of the West. As things stood, the history of colonial expansion was the epic of the 'European spirit', of its 'strength', principally internal, of its 'reckless curiosity and subtle agility' (JGB, 188 [78]). By way of Christianity, the West had inherited from the Jews 'that sublime accusing morality' and 'the fierce heroism that manifests itself both in their dedication to the God of hosts, as well as in self-loathing' (IX, 89). Only for that reason were 'Europeans' the 'first and ruling human beings of the earth' (IX, 23). Tocqueville also proceeded in the same way. After presenting the war as a clash between European 'mobility' and Chinese 'immobility', he continued:

> It is a great event, especially if one thinks that it is only the continuation, the last in a multitude of events of the same nature all of which are pushing the European race out of its home and are successively submitting all the other races to its empire or its influence. [...] It is the enslavement of four parts of the world by the fifth.[49]

Thus, we experienced the victory march of the Western principle of mobility. Naturally, there was always the danger that the vanquished China would overwhelm the Europe of the conquerors spiritually. With a reference to Tocqueville and his analysis of the disappearance of great personalities, John Stuart Mill came to this conclusion: Europe 'is decidedly advancing towards the Chinese ideal of making all people alike'. It was a process that seemed unstoppable: 'If resistance waits till life is reduced nearly to one uniform type, all deviations from that type will come to be considered impious, immoral, even monstrous and contrary to nature.'[50]

For Nietzsche, too, 'the Chinese believe great men to be a national calamity'. 'Individuals are signs of decadence' in their eyes; they were an element of disorder and in contradiction with the ideal of 'everlasting time' (IX, 552). Unlike China, Europe's greatness lay in its liveliness and 'intellectual irritability that approximates genius and that is in any case the mother of all genius' (FW, 24

---

49   Tocqueville 1951 ff., Vol. 6, 1. Half Vol., p. 58.
50   Mill 1972a, p. 130 f.

[49–50]). The 'unnatural' tendency to 'perpetuate the state', in accordance with the Chinese model, caused 'the decline of individuals and the sterility of the whole', while, on the other hand, 'the dissolution of customs, of society, is a condition in which the new egg or several eggs emerge – eggs (individuals) as the germs of new societies and unities' (IX, 551–2). Or, in the words of John Stuart Mill: 'What is it that has hitherto preserved Europe from this lot? What has made the European family of nations an improving, instead of a stationary portion of mankind? [...] Individuals, classes, nations, have been extremely unlike one another.'[51]

For both these authors, the massification then going on was a sort of sinicisation. Nietzsche was distinguished primarily by his radicalism:

> With the progress of civilization, the senses of human beings – the eyes, the ears – have become weaker, because fear has diminished and the intellect become refined. Perhaps with the increase in security finesse of the intellect will no longer be necessary: and will diminish: as in China!
>
> IX, 452

Even more so than an epochal historical change, this was a change that was to be evaluated with the eye of an anthropologist or ethnologist: the 'Chinese' was 'the uniform and fixed' human being who had therefore followed the development of 'the greater part of animal species' and thereby ceased to be a human being in the true sense of the word; for 'the human being still transforms itself – it is in the becoming' (IX, 458). It was criminal folly to take as one's model the 'intellectual slavery' and anthropological numbing long characteristic of the Chinese landscape.

6   Jews, Colonial Peoples and the Mob: Inclusion and Exclusion

Jews and Judaism were an integral part of the Europe here celebrated. They had made a major contribution to the construction of the identity of the culture that now dominated the globe. The Nietzsche of these years scorned Judeophobia and anti-Semitism and the cult of Germanic authenticity and praised the exchanges, encounters and mergings of cultures and peoples. But this is

---

51   Mill 1972a, p. 129 f.

only half the story. As often happens, inclusion and exclusion were linked and mutually conditioned one another:

> Here, where the concepts 'modern' and 'European' are almost identical, Europe is to be understood to embrace lands that stretch far beyond the geographical Europe, the small peninsula of Asia: America, in particular, belongs to it, insofar as it is the daughter-land of our culture. On the other hand, not even all of Europe falls under the cultural concept of 'Europe'; but instead, only those peoples and parts of peoples that have their common past among the Greeks, Romans, Jews and Christians.
>
> WS, 215 [247]

So, what was being praised was not so much Europe itself but the West, with Russia excluded and the United States fully included. Now there was no longer any talk of the 'terrible danger' posed by 'American political worry' (*supra*, 1 §8). Germany was no longer set as the land of true culture against the vulgar civilisation represented above all by France and the USA. The unity of the West, finally achieved by the overcoming of the barrier between Aryans and Semites and between Germanness and Latinness, rendered even sharper the opposition to the outside world of the barbarians. The pathos of the Enlightenment was joined here to the pathos of the West as the exclusive place of enlightenment and culture: 'The great achievement of humankind to date is that we need no longer be in constant fear of wild animals, barbarians, the gods, and our dreams' (M, 5 [9]).

As soon as the conflict between the great powers in Europe and between North and South in the USA had slackened off, the focus fell fully on colonial expansion and the conquest of the Far West. *The Dawn* was clearly referring to this when it on the one hand noted, without any particular emotion, the tragedy of the Indians ('the natives these days are quickly corrupted and then destroyed by "firewater"') and on the other hand called for 'swarming migrations of colonists' (M, 50 and 206 [40 and 154]).

The new dichotomy between the West and the barbarians, which took the place of the old one, allowed crossings and mergers between conquerors and conquered. In this context, the 'mixed-race' category had unequivocally negative connotations:

> What is customary are the mixed races in which one inevitably finds, along with disharmony in physical forms (when, for example, eyes and mouth do not go together) disharmonies in customs and value judge-

ments. (Livingstone heard someone remark: 'God created white and black people, the devil, however, created half-breeds.'). Mixed races are always simultaneously mixed cultures, mixed moralities as well: they are usually more evil, cruel and restless.

M, 272 [180-1]

These were the years in which the whites in the United States, after the end of the Civil War and the abolition of slavery, imposed or reinforced segregation and the prohibition of miscegenation, sexual and conjugal contamination between different races (*infra*, ch. 12 §2). Similar customs, laws and ideologies spread throughout the colonies as a result of European conquest. The Livingstone mentioned here was the author of a book published in German translation, significantly in Nietzsche's university town, that recounted trips and missions in South Africa,[52] where the Boers were no less determined than the white Americans to preserve their purity.

Naturally, this purity was to be understood not in an absolute sense but as the separation of races regarded as heterogeneous and incompatible with each other. This was also Nietzsche's point of view: 'There is in all likelihood no such thing as pure races but only races that have become pure and this only with extreme rarity. What is customary are the mixed [*gekreuzte*] [...] races. Purity is the last result of numberless conformities, absorptions and expulsions [*Auscheidungen*]' (M, 272 [180-1]). Nietzsche seemed to have in mind the USA, where the fusion between different ethnic groups (the melting pot) went hand in hand with the extinction of the Indians and the segregation of blacks. In this sense, the 'purity' and the strong sense of identity of 'race' or of the American people that were in the process of formation were the result of both 'absorptions' and 'eliminations'.

But how was the problem posed in the Old World? 'May Europe be relieved of a quarter of its inhabitants' so it ceased to be overpopulated; that was why emigration and colonisation were necessary (M, 206 [154]). But this was not yet enough. Disposing of the dross could be increased or accelerated by much more radical measures, not excluding physical elimination (*infra*, 19 §3-6). If a vacuum were to arise as a result, it could be filled by Chinese immigrants, used to being and expected to act as 'diligent ants', as a more or less servile labour force (M, 206 [155]). Overall, these processes were a 'progress toward purity'. Thanks to them, 'the strength present in a race is restricted more and more to particular selected functions, whereas before it had to deal with too

---

52   Livingstone 1858.

many things that often contradicted one another' (M, 272 [181]). The goal: a situation in which the separation of mutually incompatible races was at the same time an international division of labour, whereby the 'barbarians' would have to be forced to carry out 'compulsory labour' to the benefit of the peoples that embodied culture. In Europe, the Chinese would have to play a similar role to the blacks in America (*infra*, 12 § 3). Such a division of labour and such a 'restriction' might appear to be an 'impoverishment' and initially raise problems. 'In the end, however, if the process of purification [*Reinigung*] is successful, all the strength that was earlier expended on the battle of disharmonious qualities is now at the disposal of the entire organism: which is why races that have become purified have always grown stronger and more beautiful as well' (M, 272 [181]).

Once again, this was confirmed by the example of Greece: 'The Greeks provide us with the model of a race and a culture that has become pure: and it is to be hoped that one day Europe will also succeed in becoming a pure European race and culture' (M, 272 [181]). This was a society in which the strict division of labour and slavery permitted *otium* and the production of art and culture; on the other hand, the ruling class had no problem in strengthening itself by means of opportune co-optations. There was no longer any sense in the narrow horizons and provincialism of the Germanomaniacs and anti-Semites:

> If one thinks that the Greeks, with their exiguous tribes, found themselves on densely populated ground, among a race of Mongolian origin, found the coast settled by a fringe of Semitic colonies interspersed with Thracians – then one will understand how they were forced above all to preserve and constantly reproduce the superiority of quality; thus they worked their magic on the masses. The feeling of holding out on their own as superior beings in the midst of enemies far more numerous than they drove them to constant and extreme mental tension.
>
> VIII, 327

The 'pure race' was not so much a presupposition as a result. When Greece repulsed the Persians, it was able to assimilate the Semites, who did not constitute an element of contamination. In that way, Hellenism was recuperated and subsumed under Europe and the West, although it had previously been excluded *inter alia* because it represented the moment of contamination between Hellenism and Judaism. Similarly, with regard to Europe, 'mixed race' was not in contradiction with 'pure race'. The co-optation into the ruling class of assimilated Jews, who often occupied important positions in society, accompanied by drastic measures including purification by the mob and over-population in general – all that meant not contamination but a decisive step in the direction of purity. In conclusion:

> What then is Europe? – Greek culture grew out of Thracian, Phoenician elements, Hellenism Philhellenism of the Romans, their world empire Christian, Christianity the bearer of antique elements, from these elements scientific seeds finally sprout, from Philhellenism comes a *philosophers' realm*: as far as science is believed in, so far does Europe now stretch.
>
> VIII, 566 [373]

7   The Unity and the Peace of Europe and the Enduring Value of War

The same dialectic of inclusion and exclusion also manifested itself in relation to the problem of peace and war. If, in the years immediately after the victory at Sedan Nietzsche celebrated war indiscriminately, the picture changed considerably in the 'Enlightenment' period. He now looked with concern at France and the fate of Europe as a whole, and clearly condemned the chauvinistic agitation, arguing that 'the very existence of individual states (which are necessarily in an unending *bellum omnium contra omnes*) is an obstacle to culture'. So, a *Realpolitik* founded on the provoking of rivalry and national hatred was 'harmful for universal culture' (XIV, 147).

Against all this, Nietzsche hoped for, and perhaps saw on the horizon, 'a European union in which each individual people, delimited according to geographical expediency, will occupy the place and possess the privileges of a canton'. Once 'historical memories' had disappeared, whatever 'corrections of boundaries' might be necessary were not to come at the expense of the union as a whole. 'Then, for the first time', concluded the aphorism, '*foreign* politics will be inseparably connected to *domestic* politics: whereas now, the latter still run after their proud masters and gather in their pitiful little baskets the gleanings left over from what the former have harvested' (WS, 292 [276–7]). This was a transparent allusion to Bismarck, criticised for having subordinated everything to the pursuit of hegemony in Europe. The efforts to increase the number of educational institutions in Prussia also served this same end. Thanks to the 'master stroke of weaving the school and the army', it became easier to militarise the nation (VM, 320 [124]).

This was the context in which Nietzsche placed the Second Reich's rearmament policy. In theory, it was to serve to guarantee Germany's safety. But 'how many *wars* of aggression are launched for the sake of self-preservation!' (VIII, 602 [411]). This argument, which seemed so innocent, was actually itself an essential contribution to the preparation of war and even the criminalisation of the enemy. Invoking 'the morality that justifies self-defense [...] as its advocate' meant throwing suspicion on neighbouring and rival countries, nourishing hostile feelings and the longing for conquest, and, ultimately, accusing them of 'inhumanity'. Germany could take the initiative to break this vicious circle – it had emerged victorious and powerful from the war, so it could fell '[t]he tree of martial glories' without undermining its own security and prestige:

> And there may come a great day when a people distinguished by war and victory, and by the highest cultivation of military order and intelligence, and accustomed to offering the heaviest sacrifices to these things, voluntarily cries out: 'we are shattering the sword' – and smashes its entire military way of life.
>
> ws, 284 [271]

This sounds like the impassioned plea of a pacifist. However, the traditional theme of the celebration of war had by no means vanished:

> *War as a remedy.* – War can be recommended as a remedy for peoples that have grown feeble and wretched: especially if they absolutely want to continue living: for there also exists a cure, brutality, for the consumption that attacks peoples. Wanting to live forever and not being able to, however, are themselves already signs of the senility of sensation; the more fully and ably we live, the more quickly we are ready to give up our lives for a single good sensation. A people that lives and feels in this way has no need of war.
>
> ws, 187 [232]

How to resolve this contradiction? We find help in an aphorism from *The Wanderer and His Shadow*, which set out the following significant programme:

> [W]orking toward making everything good into a common good and everything freely available for those who are free, and finally, *preparing* for that still far-distant state of things where their great task falls into the hands of good Europeans: the direction and oversight of the entirety of world culture.
>
> ws, 87 [197]

The condemnation of intra-European national chauvinism went hand in hand with the recognition of Europe's planetary mission and of the colonial wars. There was absolutely no contradiction between these two things:

> [S]hrewdness created the law in order to put an end to feuds and *useless* wastefulness among similar powers. But they come to *just as definitive* an end, if one side has *become* decisively weaker than the other: then subjection enters in and the law *ceases to exist.*
>
> ws, 26 [169]

Such was the situation that had arisen between Europe (including the USA) and the rest of the world. Colonial expansion was all the more necessary because it would help solve the social question in the metropolis, whose excess population could find an outlet in the conquered territories (M, 206 [153–5]).

But Nietzsche was also thinking of other sorts of conflict. This is clear, for example, from his warning to Russia, 'the extended jaws of Asia, which would like to swallow up tiny Europe' (ws, 231 [253]). Finally, as we shall see, the philosopher devoted particular attention to what he called the 'socialist wars' (*infra*, 11 §7).

CHAPTER 10

The Poet of the 'People's Community', the 'Solitary Rebel', the Anti-revolutionary 'Enlightener' and the Theorist of 'Aristocratic Radicalism'

1   From 'Enlightenment' Turn to Immoralist Turn

Before analysing Nietzsche's further evolution, we should take a closer look at the significance of the passage from the first to the second stage. In reconstructing the history of the ideological struggle against the French Revolution, one scholar has summed up the difference between 'the Enlightener Mallet' and 'the proto-Romantic Burke' as follows: while Burke 'exalts the depths of the soul and the irrational elements of experience over the exaggerated ambitions of reason', Mallet 'sees in the irrational forces that dominate the masses the enemy against whom the struggle must be waged'.[1] The distinctive feature of Nietzsche's evolution was that he probed the strengths and weaknesses of the first position and then quickly switched to the second. In a fragment from the summer of 1878, after underlining the obvious and 'trivial' thesis that '*self-love* furnishes the *motives of all* our actions', he added: '[F]or a long time I knew nothing about it (metaphysical period)', with ignorance typical of 'visionary youths' (VIII, 556 [362–3]). So, after the 'metaphysical period', followed another, marked by the encounter with Voltaire and with great moralists and by 'moral Enlightenment' (*supra*, 8 § 2).

So, a break had taken place: at the political level, with Germanomania and Judeophobia, and at the philosophical level, with an ideological platform à la Burke. Nietzsche himself explained this point, when, in clearly autobiographical vein, he reconstructed the evolution of the 'free spirit', or rather, the spirit that had become free. It may be assumed he has had 'the decisive event for a spirit in whom the type "free spirit" is someday to reach a perfect ripeness and sweetness [as] a *great liberation* [*Loslösung*], and that it will previously have been all the more firmly bound [*gebunden*] and have seemed forever fettered to it corner and column'. They were 'human beings of a high and select kind' that felt with particular force their 'duties', becoming 'cords' from which it was very difficult to extricate oneself: 'that shyness and gentleness in the presence

---

1   Matteucci 1957, p. 282 f.

of everything long-venerated and worthy, that gratitude toward the soil from which they grew, toward the holy place where they learned to worship' (MA, Preface, 3 [7]).

One can almost hear Burke, in his polemic against the arrogance and dissolving action of reason in its Enlightenment and revolutionary forms, when he praised the higher community, handed down by the 'wisdom of our ancestors',[2] which combined and fused in an indissoluble unity 'our state, our hearths, our sepulchres, and our altars'.[3] Indeed, Nietzsche, with all his strength, adhered to this ideology, commonplace in German Romantic culture and subsequently also to be found in national-liberal circles. Later, he radically and suddenly distanced himself from it. His friends or ex-friends were surprised and, in some cases, outraged. The philosopher seemed to be responding to them in his description of the later evolution of those who for a while had clung passionately to the cult of the soil:

> The great liberation for people bound to this extent comes suddenly, like an earthquake: all at once the youthful soul is deeply shaken, torn loose, torn from its place – it does not itself understand what is happening. [...] [A]n intense, dangerous curiosity about an undisclosed world flames and flickers in all its senses. 'Better to die than to live *here*' – thus the imperious voice and temptation rings out: and this 'here', this 'feeling of being at home' is all that up until now it had loved!

A 'rebellious, capricious, volcanically thrusting desire for travel, foreign lands, alienation, coldness, sobriety, freezing' began. A 'roaming', like crossing a 'desert'. The old enthusiasms had died away, but no new ones have yet arisen; 'years of convalescence' were now needed (MA, Preface, 3–4 [7–9]).

In many ways, what was commonly defined as the period of 'Enlightenment' was an 'experiment', an interlude. Nietzsche seemed, at times, to be aware of this, during the period of his transition: 'When the masses begin to rage and reason grows dark, we do well, insofar as we are not completely certain about the health of our souls, to step under a doorway and to keep an eye on the weather' (VM, 303 [117]).

This aphorism also sounds autobiographical. The previous ideological platform, which seemed so accomplished, proved to be unsustainable. Another was needed, but in the meantime one could not limit oneself to a spectator's

---

2   Burke 1826, Vol. 3, p. 81.
3   Burke 1826, Vol. 5, p. 79 f.

role. The acute crisis to which *The Birth of Tragedy* referred is over, but the dangers that had arisen (as Nietzsche observed in late 1878) from 'this decade of national wars, of ultramontane martyrdom and socialist alarm' (VM, 171 [73]) had by no means been definitively overcome. Here, the two most worrying points of crisis were indicated: the growing unrest of the popular classes in Germany and the conflict with France, exacerbated by extremist Catholicism, which Bismarck, as we know, had instrumentally promoted. In both cases, we were dealing with excited and agitated movements:

> [S]houldn't we, the more spiritual human beings of an age that is visibly catching fire in more and more places, have to grasp all available means for quenching and cooling, so that we will remain at least as steady, harmless, and moderate as we are now, and will thus perhaps become useful at some point in serving this age as mirror and self-recollection?
>
> MA, 38 [47]

As in the past, every attempt at desertion continued to be condemned as irresponsible, but the engagement coincided in this case with a cool and calm reflection and was bound up with an appeal to refrain from frivolous enthusiasms. At the time of the hopes aroused by the founding of the Second Reich and the prospect, which at the time seemed real, of a Germanic revival of tragic Hellenism, Nietzsche expressed a passionate pathos of action and strongly criticised the historical consciousness that threatened to undermine it. With the collapse of old certainties, the pathos of action momentarily reappeared. After the political situation in France and Europe had stabilised, it was no longer so urgent to set a counterrevolutionary against revolutionary action. It was better to make the latter psychologically 'suspect' and to delegitimise its motives, in order to deprive it of its good conscience, and thus to inhibit and neutralise it. The writings of the 'Enlightenment' period called not for action but for abstention from over-hasty action. So, it is understandable that, retrospectively, Nietzsche characterised the period of 'Enlightenment' as a time of profound crisis: '[A]t the age of thirty-six I hit the low point in my vitality, I kept on living, but without being able to see three steps ahead of me' (EH, Why I am so wise, 1 [75]). It was a 'stretch of desert, exhaustion, loss of faith, icing-up in the midst of youth' (FW, Preface, 1 [4]).

So, Nietzsche himself emphasised the linking of continuity and discontinuity in his development, in which he distinguished three stages, the 'metaphysical', the stage of Enlightenment, and finally the stage that began with the end of the crossing of the desert. Regarding the transition from the first to the second, there can be no doubt: it is defined by *Human, All Too Human*. The transition from the second to the third stage, on the other hand, is harder to define. Lou Salomé dated it to *The Gay Science*.[4] We are in the year 1882. When Nietzsche republished it five years later with an additional fifth book, he drew attention to a passage in the final paragraph of the first edition he viewed as essential: '"Incipit tragoedia", we read at the end of this suspiciously innocent book' (FW, Preface, 1 [4]). The aphorism, which immediately preceded the epilogue to the second edition, concluded: after wanderings, 'shipwreck and damage', the 'argonauts of the ideal' saw take shape before their eyes 'an as yet undiscovered land the boundaries of which no one has yet surveyed, beyond all the lands and corners of the ideal heretofore'. With this conclusion, *The Gay Science* intended to announce the transition to a new phase: 'The destiny of the soul changes' (FW, 382 [246–7]).

As the title of the aphorism ('The great health') shows, the metaphor of the journey through the desert was linked with the metaphor of overcoming sickness or depression:

> 'Gay Science': this signifies the saturnalia of a mind that has patiently resisted a terrible, long pressure – [...] – and is now all of a sudden attacked by hope, by hope for health, by the *intoxication* of recovery [...] This entire book is really nothing but an amusement after long privation and powerlessness, the jubilation of returning strength.
>
> FW, Preface, 1 [3]

Now a clearer picture emerges of Nietzsche's own view of his evolution. With regard to the first phase, it was characterised by 'the taste for the unconditional' and the lack of the 'art of nuance' that 'characterize youth'. In the evaluation of 'people and things', there seemed to be room only for 'reverence' (and here one thinks immediately of the fascination exercised by Schopenhauer and Wagner), for 'wrath' and 'suspicion' (JGB, 31 [31–2]). In the latter case, Nietzsche was perhaps referring to the rather critical opinion expressed by *The Birth of Tragedy* in regard to Goethe or its denunciation of the Hellenistic-Roman age and, in particular, of Rome.

So, the disillusion was all the more painful:

> Later, after the young soul has been tortured by constant disappointments, it ends up turning suspiciously on itself. [...] How furious it is with itself now, how impatiently it tears itself apart, what revenge it exacts for

---

4   Andreas-Salomé 1983, p. 168.

having blinded itself for so long, as if its blindness had been voluntary! In this transitional state, we punish ourselves by distrusting our feelings, we torture our enthusiasm with doubts.

JGB, 31 [32]

Viewed in retrospect, the 'Enlightenment' was synonymous with drying out, with loss of perspective. That is why the surmounting of this second phase was greeted with shouts of joy: 'No! No longer with the bitterness and passion of the one who has torn himself away and must turn his unbelief into another faith, a goal, a martyrdom!' (FW, 346 [203]). In the light of this new awareness, 'Enlightenment' appeared at a superficial level as arid and bitter disillusion, but, on closer inspection, as a 'faith' that had not yet found itself or did not yet have the courage to commit to itself. Only after long suffering did 'a new end' begin to assume precise contours (FW, 382 [246]). Now followed the moment of 'a reawakened faith in a tomorrow and a day after tomorrow, of a sudden sense and anticipation of a future, of impending adventures, of reopened seas, of goals that are permitted and believed in again' (FW, Preface, 1 [3]). The crossing of the desert and the years of sickness and depression also meant leaving behind disillusion and 'unbelief', with the happy and definitive arrival at a new 'faith', or rather, a 'gay science'.

According to Nietzsche, the 'highest type of convalescence' that took place at the end of the second stage (of 'Enlightenment') simultaneously implied a 'return to myself': it was the end of the period of estrangement, with the return to his deepest and truest and never entirely lost self (EH, *Human, All Too Human*, 4 [119]). The term 'Enlightenment' was justified only in this perspective. This is how the dedication in *Human, All Too Human* must be read: 'Voltaire, in contrast to all subsequent writers, is, above all, a *grandseigneur* of the spirit: which is precisely what I am too. – The name "Voltaire" on one of my writings – that was true progress – towards myself.' Observed more carefully and in an opposite light, 'a certain spirituality of noble taste seems to be constantly fighting a more passionate current in order to stay on top' (EH, *Human, All Too Human*, 1 [116]), that current that was reined in and repressed during the 'Enlightenment' period, but which could now unfold freely.

Precisely because of the delay it had suffered and the tests it had had to undergo, the new faith that characterised the final phase of Nietzsche's development was more solid and mature, just as the 'new health' was shown to be a 'health that is stronger, craftier, tougher, bolder, and more cheerful than any previous health' (FW, 382 [246]). At this point, in some ways, Nietzsche's evolution became a model. Speaking to those he hoped to win over as his followers, he said: 'Are you now ready? You must have gone through every degree of scepticism and have bathed ecstatically in ice-cold currents'; only then, however, 'can there be a situation that no utopian has been able to imagine' (IX, 573). The crossing of the desert or the 'seas' (FW, 377 [243]), the 'Enlightenment', became a necessary and beneficial rite of passage.

The new world, barely glimpsed, was yet to be discovered, but in the meantime Nietzsche made one thing clear: it was 'over-rich in what is beautiful, strange, questionable', but also in what is *terrible, and divine*. Thus 'the tragedy begins.' There was no doubt that the 'Enlightenment' was behind us, and it is significant that the new phase began with the watchword of the tragic view of life that had already marked the 'metaphysical' phase. On the other hand, this new ideal, 'which will often enough appear inhuman', was the 'incarnate and involuntary parody' of the 'solemnity' with which the rules of morality were traditionally proclaimed (FW, 382 [247]). And that was when, as we know, *'incipit tragoedia'*, but also, at the same time, *'incipit parodia'*, the radical and unprecedented demythologisation of the values handed down and still observed, which in the meantime had been wrapped in 'great suspicion' (FW, Preface, 1 and 3 [6]). In this sense, something was nevertheless preserved from the preceding 'Enlightenment'. The tragic view of life that had already manifested itself in the 'romantic' period was now, after the demythologisation, the disillusion and the frostiness of the Enlighteners and the 'school of suspicion', confirmed in a more mature form: as 'great seriousness [*grosser Ernst*]', as opposed to the 'earthly seriousness [*Erden-Ernst*] heretofore' of moral philistinism (FW, 382 [247]).

2   Anti-socialist Laws, 'Practical Christianity' and Wilhelm I's 'Indecency'

What happened between 1879–80 and 1882, the year of publication of *The Gay Science*, the book in which, according to a declaration by its author, 'the fate of the soul turns'? Nietzsche's development did not hover in a vacuum or in germ-free space, but was clearly and consistently stimulated by developments in the political situation in Germany and Europe. The first phase had as a point of reference the horror and dismay aroused by the Paris Commune, as well as the enthusiasm and hopes that accompanied the founding of the Second Reich; the second and third phases corresponded on the one hand to the attenuation and vanishing of such hopes, and on the other to the gradual stabilisation of the political situation in Europe, which made the danger of a revolt of the 'barbaric class of slaves' ever less likely. *Mixed Opinions and Maxims* and *The Wanderer and His Shadow*, published in 1879 and 1880, still belonged fully to the 'Enlight-

enment' experiment, and Nietzsche rightly put them in the second edition of
Human, All Too Human, of which they were to some extent an integral part. But
in which historical and political context was the post-'Enlightenment' phase to
be placed?

It makes sense to search Nietzsche's texts for references to the conflicts and
debates of his time.

Especially interesting is an aphorism from *The Gay Science*: '*Work. –* How
close work and the worker are now even to the most leisurely among us! The
royal courtesy of the words "We are all workers!" would still have been a cynicism and an indecency under the reign of Louis XIV' (FW, 188 [139]). The
allusion was to the imperial message addressed by Wilhelm I on 17 November
1881, to the Reichstag, when, on Bismarck's advice, he launched an incisive programme of social reform, as even a relentless critic of the Chancellor finally
recognised. According to Franz Mehring, it was a question of 'promoting the
positive well-being of the workers', by launching the 'law on insurance against
accidents' and thus ensuring a measure of state support for 'those affected by
an inability to work due to old age or invalidity' and by stimulating the development of cooperatives 'under the protection of the state'.[5] And all this in the
name of the dignity of labour, in which all participated, from the factory worker
to the sovereign.

One can understand Nietzsche's horror. The official celebration of labour
and the defamation of *otium* led to a major state intervention in the economy and an expansion of the state apparatus. *Human, All Too Human* had
warned against this tendency to socialism, which in this way revealed its despotic face. In *The Dawn* and the corresponding fragments, the familiar watchword once more rang out: 'As little state as possible!' (M, 179, cf. also IX, 294
[129]). And yet, there was a fundamental change. This watchword was no longer
used exclusively to polemicise against the socialist movement but also with
an eye to trends at the governmental level in Europe, and especially in Germany:

> I know what will destroy these states, the *non plus ultra* of the state, which
> is that of the socialists; whose opponent I am, I hate it already in the
> present state. [...] The great laments about human misery do not move
> me, they do not induce me to participate in that lament.
>
>   IX, 294

---

5   Mehring 1898, p. 447.

The polemic against the ideal of the social state, which was becoming ever more commonplace and even beginning to take on concrete form in some instances, was harsh and unrelenting. Now the emperor had joined in the contemptible 'glorification of "work"' (M, 173 [126]). Hence the impulse to 'transform the state into Providence in the good and bad sense'. However, according to Nietzsche, this 'prodigious intent to grate off all the rough and sharp edges on life', the ideal of 'common security', had started 'on the way to turn humanity into sand' (M, 174 and 179 [127 and 130]).

The Dawn called on German and European workers to take the road of colonial adventure rather than seek protection and salvation in state intervention (M, 206 [153–5]). Naturally, colonial wars led to a big expansion of the military and state apparatus, but it was not this that worried Nietzsche, but rather the demands of the popular and socialist movement for state intervention in the economy and social issues.

In his polemic against the social state, a state just beginning to take off, Nietzsche did not hesitate to resume the arguments of liberal and conservative culture and journalism, which saw the Church as a place of beneficence and charity.[6] *The Gay Science* welcomed 'non-public health care' on the part of the priest (FW, 351 [209]). Certainly, this classic argument took on new nuances in Nietzsche's hands. Compared to the state, as a place of massification, the Church as a whole was far superior and far more capable of resisting the mounting plebeian contagion:

> Let us not forget in the end what a church is, specifically as opposed to any 'state'. A church is above all a structure for ruling that secures the highest rank to the more spiritual human beings and that believes in the power of spirituality to the extent of forbidding itself the use of all cruder instruments of force; and on that score alone the Church is under all circumstances a nobler institution than the state.
>
> FW, 358 [223]

And this distinction became even more evident when compared with the more or less hypocritical obeisances of Wilhelm I to the plebeian defence of labour and Bismarck's concessions to the labour movement. Rather than chase after the impossible solution to an imaginary social question, one was to take note, said Nietzsche, of reality: 'Here it is simply the law of need [*Noth*] operating: one wants to live and has to sell oneself, but one despises those who exploit

---

6   Losurdo 1992, 10, §5.

this need and buy the worker [*Arbeiter*]' (FW, 40 [56]). The continuing anticapitalist polemic was proof that the working class, despite repeated concessions,
had not been to the slightest degree integrated, and rather continued to behave
malevolently and hostilely towards those who provided its employment and
livelihood.

3   From Critique of the Social State to Critique of the 'Representative
       Constitution'

When Nietzsche warned that the workers were impossible to please and condemned Bismarck's programme as both ineffectual and ruinous, he was arguing
along lines similar to those of the conservatives or liberals of a conservative
bent. At the time, the Chancellor was being forced to defend himself against
the charge of striving for a social programme under the sign of the 'providential' and 'all-powerful state'. Bismarck's supporters responded by arguing that
that was not the issue, that the real issue was the need to start thinking about a
'reconciliation of the workers with the state': this problem had been ignored by
the extremist theorists of *laissez faire*, by the 'clique of Manchester politicians,
ruthless representatives of the money-bag', who wanted to reduce the state to
the mere role of a police in the service of the propertied classes.[7]

But the reforms undertaken by the government went beyond 'socialism' and
marked the start of a capitulation to 'communism', according to the thunder-
ous objection of a member of parliament during a debate.[8] Nietzsche joined in
this polemic, radicalising it in extreme ways. His condemnation of Bismarck's
proposed social compromise became ever more bitter, culminating in its most
complete and radical form in *Twilight of the Idols*. Nietzsche denounced as folly
the theorising of an alleged 'labour question'. Clearly, the hope was somehow
to buy off the workers by demonstrating solicitude about their problems and
claims. But the truth was:

> The workers are doing far too well not to ask for more, little by little
> and with diminishing modesty. At the end of the day they have the
> great number in their favour. [...] Workers were enlisted for the milit-
> ary, they were given the right to organize [*Coalitions-Recht*], the polit-

7   Bismarck n.d., pp. 337–41.
8   Eugen Richter in Fenske 1978, p. 280.

ical right to vote: is it any wonder that workers today feel their existence to be desperate [*Nothstand*] (expressed morally – to be an injustice
[*Unrecht*]).

GD, 40, cf. XIII, 30 [215–16]

The emergency legislation against the socialists, against a workers' party on the
road to revolution or at least the road to an overall challenge to the existing
social order, was inadequate. Rather, it was necessary to deny the workers political and trade union rights. Whatever political party they belonged to, they were
members of an enemy class ready to engage in insurrection: it was suicidal to
recruit workers for military service and teach them to use weapons. Moreover,
they had also to be denied the right to education: for how could one educate as
a master someone destined to work as a slave? The ideal would be to develop
into a 'group [*Stand*]' 'modest and self-sufficient types, Chinese types', a kind of
caste without social mobility and tending to reproduce itself hereditarily (GD,
40 [216]).

It is true that Bismarck responded to the charge of communism by arguing
that he drew his inspiration from 'practical Christianity' or a Christianity put
into practice; Wilhelm I expressed himself similarly in his message to the Reichstag.[9] But for Nietzsche, this did not sound at all reassuring. For he was beginning to spot a substantial convergence between two, at first sight opposing,
currents, Christianity and socialism. Subversion posed a big threat and seemed
to encounter no significant resistance. After the disappearance or lessening of
the fears created by the Paris Commune, the situation had once more become
alarming. Bismarck's concessions or yielding did not seem to have appeased
the German Social-Democratic Party or made it more amenable. The Congress
of the preceding year (1880), held in Switzerland to escape persecution under
the anti-socialist legislation brought in by the Iron Chancellor, had not only
expressed 'its sympathy for the liberation struggle of the Russian nihilists' but
had modified the Gotha programme to the effect that 'the party would strive
towards its ends by *any* means and no longer simply by any legal means'.[10]
A similar process of radicalisation was happening in France, where, in the
same year, Jules Guesde's *L'Égalité* abandoned its previous subtitle of 'socialist republican newspaper' and proclaimed itself a 'collectivist revolutionary
organ'.[11] As for Russia, on 28 February 1881, a terrorist organisation, after several
failed attempts and heavy losses (waves of arrests and executions), succeeded

---

9   In Fenske 1978, p. 281; Mehring 1898, p. 447 f.
10   Mehring 1898, p. 430 f.
11   Mayeur 1973, p. 98.

in carrying out the 'death sentence' it had imposed on Alexander II. Even if Nietzsche's main focus was on Germany, he was not unaware of developments in European politics: an aphorism from the second edition of *The Gay Science* referred explicitly to 'Petersburg-style nihilism', which even led to 'martyrdom' (FW, 347 [205]).

The seriousness of the threat demanded an appropriate response. As the terrorist attacks on Wilhelm I demonstrated, the social conflict was escalating dramatically within Germany too. Taking his cue from this, Treitschke called on the authorities to crush the Social-Democratic conspiracy, to ban Social-Democratic speeches and writings, and to break the chain of the Social-Democratic 'newspapers': the necessary repression should not allow itself to be held up by a 'flabby and sentimental philanthropy'.[12] In the view of this national-liberal leader, it was a good idea to combine repression on the part of the state apparatus with repression emanating from civil society: 'Why do our great entrepreneurs not declare that they will not employ any workers who participate in Social-Democratic incitement?' 'Many organs of the bourgeois press' were demanding this, so that, as Mehring noted, they 'were able to publish long lists of companies that undertook not to give employment to Social Democrats'.[13] And yet, despite the climate of witch hunting, the emergency laws struggled to be passed by Parliament. This was confirmation, for Nietzsche, of the need to go beyond the 'representative constitution'.

Even in the 'Enlightenment' period, there were not just proposals to restrict or neutralise suffrage but more radical suggestions. An aphorism in *The Wanderer and His Shadow* aimed, in connection with the phenomenon of electoral abstention, to delegitimise universal (male) suffrage of the sort that applied to Reichstag elections (*supra*, 9 §1). But the preparatory draft of this same aphorism took an even more drastic position:

> If within a State that has a representative constitution a vote is taken, for example, to elect members of parliament, and fewer than half of those who have the right to vote take part in the election, then the representative constitution itself is rejected.
>
>   XIV, 198

Here the 'representative constitution' as such was called into question. After first dropping this idea, Nietzsche transformed it in subsequent years into an

---

12   Treitschke 1878, pp. 6–8.
13   Mehring 1898, p. 399.

explicit programme. His judgement on parliamentarism now turned contemptuous: it was homage to an obtuse 'herd', with 'the public permission to choose between five basic political opinions' (FW, 174 [136]). Even more radically, *Beyond Good and Evil* condemned 'all representative constitutions', in the final analysis, rule by the herd (JGB, 199).

It is interesting to note that this condemnation dated from the time of the emergence of the social state and from the period when, as a result, those deputies and groups in parliament that claimed to represent the needs of the populace could exercise a growing weight:

> Today, at a time when the state has a ridiculously bloated belly, there are in all fields and subjects, besides the actual workers themselves, also 'representatives', for example, besides the learned and the literati, besides the suffering [*leidende*] popular classes, there are also chattering and boastful 'do-no-goods' that 'represent' that suffering [*Leiden*], not to mention the politicians by profession, who are feeling fine, and 'represent' extreme misery [*Nothstände*] in Parliament.
>
> XI, 475

Nietzsche's conclusion was drastic: a system, a 'modern life' that, apart from everything else, was with its 'large number of intermediaries' and 'representatives' 'extremely expensive [*kostspielig*]', deserved a 'kick' (XI, 475). All this was made even more absurd by the fact that the ideal 'providential' state radically misunderstood human nature, whose mainspring was in no way the pursuit of security and material fulfilment:

> Not the bare necessities, not desire – no, the love of power is humanity's demon. You can give people everything – health, room, board, amusement – they are and remain unhappy and low-spirited: for the demon is waiting and waiting and wants to be satisfied.
>
> M, 262 [177]

Labour agitation was not driven by poverty and social malaise. Rather, it was a question of the malformed, the degenerate, the inwardly corrupt. From this moment on, Nietzsche never tired of harping on the theme of sickness and degeneration. Events seemed to prove him right. Take, for example, Mehring's portrait of the perpetrator of the first attack on Wilhelm I:

> Twenty years old but already a wreck of a human being, he bore the weals and wounds that bourgeois society tends to inflict on the wretches not

invited to its table. An illegitimate child, infected with hereditary syphilis, flogged as a pickpocket even as a child and put as a vagabond in a correctional institution. [...] Sick in mind and body, he did not possess the force of a revolutionary development, and fought like a cheat and idler against the hostile forces that had reduced his existence to a semi-bestial level.[14]

From Nietzsche's point of view, this confirmed the non-existence of the 'social question'. As *Thus Spoke Zarathustra* later observed, reality looked very different: 'Far too many are born: the state was invented for the superfluous!' or rather, the social state (Za, I, On the New Idol [35]). The reforms brought in by Bismarck not only promoted levelling and massification but could not even achieve the goals pursued by them, the integration of the labour movement into the existing order. So, in the face of absurd pretensions, one was to reaffirm a fundamental principle: 'There is no right either to existence or to work, or even to "happiness"; for the individual person is no different from the meanest worm' (XIII, 98).

4   '[W]e Cannot Help Being Revolutionaries'

At this point, we can try to understand better the overall meaning of Nietzsche's development as well as its various stages. In the first stage, which revolved around *The Birth of Tragedy*, his positions were not so very far removed from those of the German national liberals, as evidenced by his friendship with and devotion to Wagner and his admiration for Bismarck. This is also confirmed by his active participation in the transfiguration of Germany, indeed of the German 'essence', as the vanguard in the struggle against banausic 'civilization', 'levelling and Franco-Jewish "elegance"' and modern subversion. In the second stage, Nietzsche drew closer, in a certain sense, to the positions of conservative European liberalism, as shown, on the one hand, by his denunciation of Germanomania and, on the other, by his largely positive judgement of Britain, where universal (male) suffrage had not yet been implemented and liberal reforms had not yet swept away the elements of hierarchy and aristocracy of the *ancien régime*. In these two stages, the target of his condemnation was the increasing democratic contaminations of liberalism and parliamentary representation rather than liberalism and parliamentary representation as such:

---

14   Mehring 1898, p. 393.

hence the ambiguity of the value judgement made about liberalism and the attempt to distinguish between an authentic and inauthentic liberalism.

Now, however, the picture changed significantly:

> [W]e are by no means 'liberal'; we are not working for 'progress'; we don't need to plug our ears to the marketplace's sirens of the future: what they sing – 'equal rights', 'free society', 'no more masters and no servants' – has no allure for us.
>
> FW, 377 [241]

A new situation had arisen. Moreover, one had to take note of the fact that even liberalism tended to speak the language of subversion, for example, Sybel's ill-considered celebration of modernity and reckless campaign of denigration of the Middle Ages (*infra*, 17 §1). Worse: 'Liberalism: herd animalization, in other words' (GD, 38 [213]). It was inspired by the same egalitarian demagoguery and the same vision of life, under the sign of levelling and comfort for all, that characterised socialism.

Not only liberalism but conservatism too had become useless: '[W]e "conserve" nothing; neither do we want to return to any past' (FW, 377 [241]). What was the point of dwelling on an attitude of conservatism or striving for a restoration if the revolutionary cycle had been raging for centuries or even millennia? The conservatives based themselves on traditions that they loaded with big moral and religious significance, in an attempt to rescue them from the doubts and objections becoming rampant. But this was pointless and contrived: 'Here we have the great dishonesty of conservatives of all times – they are the add-on-liars' (FW, 29 [51]). Conservatism often struck a Christian tone. But when Church and religion could show themselves to be instrumentally useful in certain circumstances, 'we won't accept a state of affairs where some idiot is in charge' (EH, 5 [92]). The latter continued on the one hand to cling to a religion of whose subversive implications he was unaware, and on the other hand was entirely unequal to the challenge of the time.

Clearly, a new political 'party' was emerging that wanted to destroy the democratic and socialist movement but, in doing so, did not want in any way to be confused either with liberalism, which it accused of supporting or subordinating itself to this movement, or with conservatism, about whose empty posturing and hypocrisy it made a great fuss. And what then? A variant of the aphorism from *The Gay Science* cited above concluded explicitly that it was now necessary to 'discover unknown lands', 'new ideals, new realities, a new home!' (XIV, 276). A frontal struggle was needed against not only socialism and anarchism but also against the Second Reich, guilty, with Bismarck, of indulging the 'transition to mediocrity [*Vermittelmässigung*], democracy, and "modern ideas"' (GT, I, 20 [10]). Nietzsche aimed his polemic in particular at the concessions to the labour movement and the attempts to build a minimum of social state in the name of 'practical Christianity' and 'compassion' for the wretched or of vague ideas of 'justice', but now it also took liberalism and the 'representative constitution' as an important target.

5   The Shadow of Suspicion Falls on the Moralists

A political agenda as radical as this required a very different philosophical framework from that of 'moral enlightenment', whose task was more to undermine the 'good conscience' of revolutionary action than to create a basis for, and to stimulate, counterrevolutionary action. Even in *The Wanderer and His Shadow*, Nietzsche continued to feel the need to distance himself from immoralism:

> Moralists must now put up with being scolded as immoralists because they dissect morality. But anyone who wishes to do dissection will have to kill: only, however, in order that things might be better known, better judged, better lived; not in order that the whole world do dissection.
>
> ws, 19 [163]

And yet, little by little, the attitude taken by moralists began to seem inadequate. 'La Rochefoucauld is wrong only in this: he estimates the motives he deems to be the real ones lower than the other apparent ones: he basically still believes in the others, and takes his measure from them' (IX, 441–2). *De facto*, the moralists continued to pay homage to a morality they seemed so mercilessly to 'dissect':

> The moralists assumed as sacred and true the morality venerated by the people, and sought only to systematize it, they wrapped the robe of science around it. No moralist has dared investigate the origin: that had to do with God and his messenger! It was assumed that morality lived on disfigured in the mouth of the people, that it would need a 'purification'.
>
> IX, 127

If the moralists posed as defenders and restorers of true moral discourse, they ended up inheriting its contradictions and hypocrisies: 'Human beings act quite differently from what they say. Even moralists do. Why moralize? Be honest! The main thing is we cannot do otherwise! Every "why" is a charlatanry and a lie' (X, 282).

So, one can see why *Beyond Good and Evil* equated the 'old moralists [*Moralisten*]' with the 'preachers of morals [*Moralprediger*]': it was necessary and at the same time 'no small amusement' to 'keep a close eye on the cunning tricks' of both sets (JGB, 5 [8]). Later, reflecting on the 'long story' of his alienation from Wagner, Nietzsche would observe: 'If I were a moralist, who knows what I would call it! Self-overcoming, perhaps. – But a philosopher has no love for moralists ... or for pretty phrases ...' (WA, Preface [233]). Even moralists could be bombastic and self-satisfied, idealistic mystifiers of reality. So, in the end, the figure of the moralist identified with the figure of the idealist philosopher, rather than his antidote, as had previously been the case: 'Philosophers as moralists: they undermine the naturalism of morality' (XIII, 403).

After falling, thanks to the teachings of the moralists, on the pathos of the noble moral sentiments to which the revolutionary movement appealed, the shadow of suspicion now fell, and fell heavily, on the moralists themselves. Their line of reasoning tended to impede the 'good conscience' not only of revolutionary action but of action as such. One had to free oneself from a present that had become onerous. Only now could the field be free for counterrevolutionary action.

The crossing of the 'desert', accompanied by a disturbing and increasingly urgent question ('Can we not reverse all values? and is good perhaps evil?'), led finally to gaining the 'great liberation' (MA, Preface, 3 [8]). To clarify the meaning of this outcome, Nietzsche allowed a voice to speak to the free spirit (which in the meantime had acquired or was about to acquire the 'great health', and which had been called upon, from this hard-climbed peak, to embrace and enjoy the new horizon, but also to reflect on the path taken):

'You must learn how to grasp the *necessary* injustice in every For and Against, injustice as inseparable from life, life itself as *conditioned* by perspective and its injustice. Above all, you must see with your own eyes where injustice is always the greatest: namely, where life has developed in the smallest, narrowest, neediest, most preliminary ways and yet still cannot avoid taking *itself* as the purpose and measure of things and, out of love for its own preservation, secretly and meanly and ceaselessly crumbling away and putting into question all that is higher, greater, richer – you must see with your own eyes the problem of establishing *rank orderings* and how power and right and comprehensiveness of perspective grow up into the heights together. You must' – enough, the free spirit *knows* by now which 'you must' he has obeyed.

MA, Preface, 6 [11–12]

The goal consisted in overcoming the moral worldview, which furnished the revolutionary and socialist movement with so many weapons, but which also affected the moralists who previously delegitimised the good conscience of that movement, by exercising suspicion.

6   Hegel and Nietzsche: Two Opposing Critiques of the Moral Worldview

The moral worldview already began to be problematic in the 'Enlightenment' period. It was characterised by a basic contradiction:

> Loving and self-sacrificing people have an interest in the continued existence of egoists who are without love and incapable of self-sacrifice, and in order for the highest morality to be able to persist, it would really have to *force* immorality to exist (whereby it would admittedly negate itself).
>
> MA, 133 [102]

To be able to celebrate its absoluteness, the moral norm, which promoted altruism, was forced to presuppose the evil it never tired of denouncing. It is interesting to note that Hegel had similarly criticised the Christian commandment to love one's neighbour and help the poor: 'If poverty is to remain in order that the duty of helping the poor can be fulfilled, this maintenance of poverty forthwith means that the duty is not fulfilled.'[15]

This passage was commented on to great effect by a disciple of Hegel, Kuno Fischer, in his *History of Modern Philosophy*, with which Nietzsche was familiar:

> The greatest ethic requires: 'Help the poor.' However, real help means freeing them from poverty; and then, once poverty has ceased, the poor also cease and so does the duty to help them. If, however, for the love of alms the poor are allowed to persist, then, by allowing this poverty to persist, the duty [to actually help the poor, freeing them from poverty] is not [...] absolved.[16]

---

15   Hegel, 1975, p. 80.
16   Fischer 1911, p. 278.

The moral worldview suffered from a performative contradiction. It presupposed the existence and permanence of evil (of selfishness, poverty, etc.), and, at the same time, said it wanted to abolish it. This performative contradiction equated with narcissism: we were dealing with a type of human being primarily concerned with the enjoyment of his own interiority. One was not to allow oneself to be fooled by the self-denigration paraded by the moral subject. 'This shattering of oneself, this mockery of one's own nature, this *spernere se sperni* of which religions have made so much is really a very high degree of vanity', Nietzsche observed (MA, 137 [105]). On this point, Hegel expressed himself perhaps even more sharply, when he denounced the 'repugnant narcissism [*Eigensinn*]' that inspired the ascetic life of renunciation, committed exclusively to pursuing a 'wholly subjective' goal, a 'goal of the individual for himself', i.e., 'for the salvation of his soul, for his happiness.'[17] Brushing aside any linguistic taboos and cautions, Nietzsche even applied this criticism to the founder of Christianity, the God-human of the official religion: 'Jesus was a great egoist' (IX, 550).

After travelling for a while along a common route, the two philosophers struck out in radically opposite directions. For Hegel, criticising the moral worldview led to an affirmation of the need for a concrete ethical order capable of incorporating the moral needs of the subject – needs that, precisely on assuming the dimension of objectivity, proved their authenticity and ceased to be an instrument of narcissistic gratification. But, for Nietzsche, already on the point of going over to the positions of immoralism, the pathos of ethicality was no less suspect than the pathos of morality.

We have already seen how the loss of the individual in the process of the massification of the modern world was denounced in European liberal culture. It was a theme Nietzsche resumed, radicalised, and turned critically against not only democracy but also morality: 'In some epochs, the individual was higher, more frequent. They are the worse times: it became more visible; one dared more, one did more harm, but one lied less' (IX, 26). One could not struggle against and turn back the phenomenon of massification without calling into question the moral worldview. One had to be able to rehabilitate 'evil': 'What would have become of the human being without fear envy greed! It would no longer exist' (IX, 457). It was these passions and these alleged vices that stimulated innovation and prevented society's provincial entrenchment.

---

17   Hegel 1969–79, Vol. 14, p. 165 f.

At first glance, we are not so very far removed from Hegel. Hegel stressed the 'enormous power of the negative', and rejected an ideal of morality understood as aseptic purity, drawing attention to the fact that 'nothing great in the world has been accomplished without passion'.[18] Even Kant, when examining economic and social development, came to a positive evaluation of the 'pursuit of honour, pursuit of power, and pursuit of possessions', of struggle, and of 'resistance [*Widerstand*]', which 'awakens all man's powers and induces him to overcome his tendency to laziness'. When Kant shifted his attention from the subject to the objectivity of social relations and historical processes, he ended up returning to Mandeville's theme of the private vices that turned into virtues:

> Thanks be to nature, therefore, for the incompatibility, for the spiteful competitive vanity, for the insatiable desire to possess or even to dominate! For without them all the excellent natural predispositions in humanity would eternally slumber undeveloped. The human being wills concord; but nature knows better what is good for his species; it wills discord.[19]

So, we are dealing in these cases too with a kind of rehabilitation of evil. According to Kant and the liberal tradition, without evil that 'unsociable sociability' that is civil society would be unthinkable, as would the wonderful development of the productive forces that marks the modern bourgeois world. This aspect was also present in Hegel, who, however, insisted on another, even more important aspect: the mainspring that led to the realisation of ever more developed ethical organisms capable of giving an increasingly rich expression to mutual recognition among humans was the contradictions, the conflicts, the passions, the negativity as a whole. In this sense, it was necessary to distinguish the 'great world-historical passion' from passion that merely pursued particularistic ends.[20]

The rehabilitation of 'evil' had quite other characteristics in Nietzsche. He used a metaphor already present in Kant. Kant, as is well known, compared civil society to a forest:

> It is just the same with trees in a forest: each needs the others, since each in seeking to take the air and sunlight from others must strive upward, and

---

18   Hegel 1969–79, Vol. 12, p. 38.
19   Kant, 2009, p. 14.
20   Hegel 1969–79, Vol. 12, p. 55.

thereby each realizes a beautiful, straight stature, while those that live in isolated freedom put out branches at random and grow stunted, crooked, and twisted.[21]

And now let us read Nietzsche: 'Ask yourselves whether a tree which is supposed to grow to a proud height could do without bad weather and storms' (FW, 19 [43]). Here the tree is declined in the singular; the moment of its relationship with the other tree and of the stimulus, through competition, to mutual growth falls away. All that remains is the confrontation with the rigours of nature. Only those trees will survive and become more robust that pass the test: 'The poison from which the weaker nature perishes strengthens the strong man – and he does not call it poison.' Or, in other words, 'evil', which gives the aphorism its title, tests 'the lives of the best and the most fruitful people and peoples' (FW, 19 [43]).

It was not a matter of aspiring to 'a humanity that is beautiful, resting, nourished and thriving in every way'; this goal could also be achieved without 'evil', but it would have nothing to do with Nietzsche's goal, which he described as 'our best humanity'. Nietzsche clarified the meaning of this category in a further declaration: 'If one thinks of the richest human being, the most noble and fruitful, without evil – one is thinking of a contradiction. [...] A genius would have to suffer terribly, for all his fecundity wishes to feed selfishly off others, to dominate them, to suck them out, and so on' (IX, 457). It was a matter of understanding and justifying the sacrifice that culture demanded of a considerable mass of human beings, and even of the majority. Having first been identified in 'compassion', in 'noble sentiments', in appeals to 'justice', the danger of delegitimising such a sacrifice is now identified in morality as such. Nietzsche now annuled morality by developing the thesis of the irresponsibility of human action, the 'innocence of becoming'.

7   From Universal Guilt to the Innocence of Becoming

At first sight, a gap seems to have opened between this and Nietzsche's youthful adherence to the philosophy of Schopenhauer. Is not the author of *The World as Will and Representation* the theorist of guilt as inherent in human existence as such? Even so, Nietzsche now asserted the 'innocence of all existence [*Unschuld alles Daseins*]' (XIII, 426), the 'innocence of all actions [*Unschuld*

---

21   Kant 2009, p. 15.

aller Handlungen]' as well as all 'opinions' (M, 56 [44]), the 'innocence of becoming [*Unschuld des Werdens*]' (XII, 386, GD, 8 [182]). A complete reversal of positions seems to have taken place, but Nietzsche himself pointed out that the two seemingly opposite philosophical visions actually aimed at the same sociopolitical outcome:

> It is possible to turn worldly justice upside down – with the doctrine of everyone's complete lack of responsibility and innocence [*völlige Unverantwortlichkeit und Unschuld*]: and an attempt has already been made in the same direction, though on the basis of precisely the opposite doctrine of everyone's complete responsibility and guilt [*Verantwortlichkeit und Verschuldung*].
>
> WS, 81 [193]

It is true that, in the aphorism, the latter theory was attributed to the 'founder of Christianity', but it was a Christianity seen through the eyes of Schopenhauer, who not surprisingly stressed the central role that original sin, the 'profound guilt [*tiefe Verschuldung*]' of the human race by the very fact of existing [*durch sein Dasein selbst*], played in Christianity.[22] The fact remains that, in Nietzsche's eyes, even the doctrine of the inevitable and universal guilt or sinfulness of humankind could be read as an inexact and negative formulation of the thesis intended to exonerate everyone from an unbearable sense of guilt. On other occasions, Christianity was linked more directly with the thesis of irresponsibility and innocence, for Jesus 'took himself for the only begotten Son of God and therefore felt himself to be without sin'; in this way, he 'reached the same goal, a feeling of complete freedom from sin, of complete freedom from responsibility, that anyone at all can now acquire through science' (MA, 144 [113]).

In any case, in the 'Enlightenment' period, the tendency that later resulted in the affirmation of the innocence of becoming had already manifested itself: 'The complete irresponsibility of a human being for his behavior and his nature is the bitterest drop that the man of knowledge must swallow.' The sense of bitterness stemmed from a person's habit of 'seeing in responsibility and duty the attestation of nobility for his humanity'. But one had to be able to free oneself from this vanity too (MA, 107 [82–3]). To settle accounts with moral sentiments in a fundamental way, one could not stop halfway like the moralists. It was necessary, in the end, to recognise that '[t]he history of those sensations that

---

22   Schopenhauer 1967–82b, p. 802.

we use in order to attribute responsibility to someone, that is, of the so-called moral sensations', in short, 'the history of moral sensations is the history of an error' (MA, 39 [48]). So 'moral judgements' were meaningless: they could be equated with 'epidemics' or 'drugs' (IX, 483 and 481).

In the evocation of the coveted new world of innocence, the language of religion and the Enlightenment merged. On the horizon 'the sun of a new gospel' now rose: its 'rays' would realise a 'degree of self-enlightenment and self-liberation' unknown in the past. Now the hope was ripening that 'humanity can transform itself from a moral humanity into a wise humanity'. This was a new and exalting situation:

> All is necessary – so says the new knowledge: and this knowledge itself is necessity. All is innocence: and knowledge is the way to insight into this innocence. [...] The inherited habit of erroneously evaluating, loving, hating may still hold sway in us, but under the influence of increasing knowledge it will become weaker: the new habit of comprehending, not loving, not hating, overlooking, is gradually implanting itself in the same soil within us and will in some thousands of years perhaps be powerful enough to give humanity the strength to bring forth a wise, innocent human being (one conscious of his innocence) as regularly as it now brings forth – *as the necessary, preliminary stage to him, not his opposite* – human beings who are unwise, unjust, conscious of their guilt.
>
> MA, 107 [84]

Even people burdened by guilt were not guilty: their vision, their mistakes, their experience were a necessary stage on the road to self-redemption.

Nietzsche also referred to art to reinforce the thesis of innocence and irresponsibility. A person illuminated by the 'new knowledge' and transformed by the 'new gospel' had to 'stand before the actions of human beings, before his own actions' as one stood before a 'work of art' or a 'plant'. He was not to seek 'merits' there, of the sort that implied an imaginary freedom of will, but he could nevertheless 'admire the strength, beauty, and fullness of them' (MA, 107 [82]). Nietzsche set out a programme: 'My wish is that one works less and less with the moral balance and more and more with the aesthetic one, and that one finally experiences morality as the mark of arrested times and aesthetic incapacity' (XIV, 262).

At this point, another theme of a positivistic nature entered the discussion. Morality was ultimately an atavism, the residue of an age before scientific knowledge:

I want every day to unlearn more and more to weigh with the balance of morality; I want to take the emergence of a moral judgement as a sign that, in that moment, my nature is not in possession of its entire force and height and errs along the trail of its past, among the tombs, so to speak, of prehistory.

XIV, 262

Once the theological stage of humanity was overcome, the concept of moral norm and of 'sin' were, together with the concept of God, destined to become a 'child's toy and a child's pain' (JGB, 57 [51]).

Reflecting on the evolution behind it, the mature Nietzsche described the thesis of the innocence of becoming as the truth he had always sought, albeit along circuitous routes:

How long have I been trying to demonstrate the perfect *innocence* of becoming! And what strange ways I have taken in so doing! [...] And to what end is all this? Was it not to procure for myself the feeling of absolute irresponsibility [*völlige Unverantwortlichkeit*]?

XI, 553

In this context, the youthful adherence to the philosophy of Schopenhauer was recognised as a legitimate stage in the process of constructing a theory capable of fundamentally de-legitimising socialist protest and agitation. Schopenhauer cleared away the 'social question' by allowing the tormented to participate, thanks to the general unity created by compassion, in the 'guilt [*Schuld*]' of the tormentors. Nietzsche, on the other hand, eliminated the social question by shifting this 'generic' guilt onto the innocence of becoming.

The demand for 'justice' on the part of the rebellious slaves against which *The Birth of Tragedy* had already warned now found its most radical refutation. To speak of the 'profound injustice' of the social order means inventing responsibilities that did not exist, and moreover inventing them out of a rancour born of one's own failure (*infra*, 20 § 7). The 'innocence [*Unschuld*]' of that child that was reality allowed Nietzsche 'a sacred yes-saying' to life (Za, I. On the Three Metamorphoses [17]), but also to a social order that has hardened into nature; a yes to existing society, which Schopenhauer pronounced in an apparently more tortured but actually more hypocritical way, by means of compassion and the negation of the will to live.

8   Four Stages in Nietzsche's Development

The innocence of becoming was experienced as a liberating and exalting discovery, and cast its light also on the path already trodden. Starting from this outcome, in a sort of Nietzschean version of Hegel's phenomenology of spirit, the earlier stages through which consciousness had already passed also found their partial justification, to be regarded as successive attempts at and approximations to the central problem and its final solution. Now it was clear: it was necessary at the political level in its proper sense to face up to 'the problem of establishing *rank ordering*':

> Given that it is the problem of rank ordering that we can call our problem, we free spirits: only now, at the midday of our lives, do we understand how many preparations, detours, trials, temptations, disguises the problem required before it was permitted to rise up before us.
>
> MA, Preface, 6–7 [11–12]

At a more properly philosophical level, it was necessary to elevate oneself to awareness of the innocence of becoming. The previous writings and stages were now interpreted teleologically as moments in a tiring and sometimes tortuous journey towards the full understanding and assimilation of a worldview already implicitly present and active at the start: 'Aren't I always beginning over again and doing what I have always done, old immoralist and bird-catcher that I am – and speaking immorally, extramorally, "beyond good and evil"?' But then how to explain *The Birth of Tragedy* and the homage it rendered to Schopenhauer, who opposed his 'blind will to morality' to the will to live? In truth, this belonged among the things one had to 'forge and [...] invent'. One could, if one so wished, speak of 'counterfeiting', but it was still a counterfeiting functional to the manifestation of a higher 'truthfulness'; on the other hand, this deviation was the confirmation, to the shame of all moralists, of the tortuous way in which 'life' proceeded (MA, Preface, 1 [5–6]). Reread carefully, the early work spoke clearly enough: 'Against Schopenhauer and the moral interpretation of existence – I put above it the aesthetic interpretation', even though he did not go so far as to 'deny or change the moral one' (IX, 615).

This awkward combination was called into question in the course of subsequent developments. With *The Dawn*, Nietzsche declared, 'my campaign against morality begins' (EH, *The Dawn*, 1 [120]), a campaign 'to dig away at an ancient *trust* upon which, for the past few millennia, we philosophers have tended to build as if it were the securest of foundations: [...] I began to undermine our *trust in morality* (M, Preface, 2 [2]). In this way, a 'new morning' could break, long sought and finally found, in the 'revaluation of all values, in an escape from all moral values, in an affirmation and trust in everything that had been forbidden, despised, cursed until now' (EH, *The Dawn*, 1 [121]). The full understanding of this 'dawn' completed Nietzsche's development, and at the same time its significance was far more than that of a personal experience: 'Fulfilling itself in us is [...] *the self-sublation of morality*' (M, Preface, 4 [6]).

We can now look briefly at the route taken by the philosopher. As we have seen, he had spoken of three stages in his development: the 'metaphysical' stage, the stage of 'Enlightenment', and the 'immoralistic' stage. Regarding the first, it is helpful to introduce a further distinction. Using and radicalising the anti-revolutionary doctrine of Burke and German romanticism, *The Birth of Tragedy* denounced the devastating effects of the hubris of reason, whose beginnings it found on Greek soil. This theme left a clear trace in all the writings from the years before the 'Enlightenment' turn. In that sense, Nietzsche was right to speak of a 'metaphysical phase' as a whole. And yet, on the other hand, one was not to lose sight of the important innovations that already appeared in the second and third *Unfashionable Observation*. On a more strictly philosophical level, the critique of the purely antiquarian vision of history was also a critique of the ideological platform à la Burke, unable to establish and stimulate the urgent counterrevolutionary action for which 'Schopenhauer's human being' or the 'solitary rebel' took responsibility. At the more narrowly political level, this figure took the place of the member of the 'popular community' celebrated in the years of *The Birth of Tragedy*.

In *Human, All Too Human*, we see the emergence of an aristocratic 'Enlightenment' that mercilessly analysed the passions, illusions, and fanaticism of the revolutionary movement and dissected at the psychological level its moral watchwords. Finally, the fourth and last phase corresponded, at the political level, to 'aristocratic radicalism' (*infra*, 11 § 2), and, at the philosophical level, to immoralism, the affirmation of the innocence of becoming. The common thread and line of continuity could be found in the critique, not to say passionate denunciation, of the revolution and the mortal dangers it posed for culture. The protagonist of the struggle thus evoked and desired was firstly the member and poet of the 'popular community', against which the hubris of reason and of revolution set a suprahistorical myth. An entire people identified with and drew nourishment from this myth, a people that, thanks to the tragic worldview, had fused into a seamless unity, despite slavery and the burden of suffering that culture inevitably brought. Later, the 'solitary rebel' took the place of this figure: aware that he could no longer call on a 'popular community', which was irretrievably lost, he instead provocatively set his solitude against the massification produced by the revolution and modernity. He intended more than ever to oppose the revolution, but he was also aware he could learn something from it, starting with the refusal to entrust oneself lazily and inertly to tradition: the graduality of its unfolding had to be interrupted with a resolute deed fraught with risks and moral dilemmas. There then followed the figure of the aristocratic 'enlightener', who resorted *inter alia* to 'moral enlightenment' to pour scorn on the revolution's claim to appeal to reason and justice, and instead stressed how much there was in it that was coarse, superstitious, intolerant, fanatical and morbid. Finally, the radical aristocratic immoralist appeared on the scene, who, while subjecting the negative values and false ideals of the revolution and of modernity to suspicion and merciless demythologisation, at the same time preserved his zeal and enthusiasm for the new things he intended to achieve – and to achieve no longer as a 'solitary rebel' but in an organised form, by which he meant a 'party of life' or a still to be founded 'new party of life'.

So, what we have here is a linking of continuity and discontinuity. The first was, of course, represented by the condemnation of revolution. To understand the second, let us return to the theme of the rehabilitation and celebration of 'evil':

> The strongest and most evil spirits have so far done the most to advance humanity: [...] Mostly by force of arms, by toppling boundary stones, by violating pieties – but also by means of new religions and moralities! [...] What is new, however, is under all circumstances evil, being that which wants to conquer, to overthrow the old boundary stones and pieties; and only what is old is good! In every age the good men are those who bury the old thoughts deeply and make them bear fruit – the peasants of the spirit. But that land is eventually exhausted, and the ploughshare of evil must come time and again.
>
> FW, 4 [32]

Particularly significant was the fact that the term 'peasant' had become an insult. A reversal had taken place with respect to the preface to an unwritten book that described as 'elevating' the spectacle of the 'ethical relationship' of the 'serf' locked into his 'narrow existence' (*infra*, 14 §4). It is true that the discussion was directed not actually at the masters but at the serfs. Just as one turned to free spirits, and only to them, when declaring that 'being honest even in evil is better than losing oneself to the morality of tradition' (FW, 99 [98]). The fact remains that, in the pre-'Enlightenment' period, the charm of an ideology à la Burke was felt and one was not yet fully aware of the need for a double discourse to be directed at either slaves or masters, i.e., one was not yet fully aware of the 'rank ordering'.

After passing through the 'Enlightenment' stage, the critique and condemnation of revolution was now articulated on the terrain of 'reactionary modernism'.[23] The break with the cult of the soil was also a break with the cult of tradition. Nietzsche realised that, under the conditions of modernity, one could only oppose radical revolution by placing oneself on the same level as it. It is true, of course, that Zarathustra harshly criticised the 'great city' as a privileged place both of subversion and of mediocrity; but the alternative to it was not to be found in the impossible return to the soil but in colonial expansion: with its help, one could rid oneself of overpopulation and the pestilential stench of the malformed, while, at the same time, steeling the manly and martial virile virtues of the best (*infra*, 18 § 6 and 11 § 7).

Nietzsche himself drew attention to the big change in the last phase in comparison with the 'Enlightenment' period:

> If I had published my *Zarathustra* under a different name, 'Richard Wagner', for instance, the collective acuity of two hundred years would not have been enough to guess that the author of *Human, All Too Human* was the visionary (*Visionär*) of *Zarathustra*.
>
> EH, 4 [92]

The self-definition as formulated by Nietzsche in his late period is striking: 'Visionary'! Gone were the uncertainties and the basically defensive attitude of the 'Enlightenment' period. Now, he announced in inspired and confident tones the 'new knowledge' and 'new gospel' towards which he had previously been groping. The new truth, or, rather, the truth he had always striven towards and that had finally seen the light, was experienced as the conclusion of a long cycle, in whose course the terrible atavisms that weighed down on human existence, starting with the sense of guilt for sins imposed and instilled by the imaginary tyrant in the kingdom of heaven, were eliminated.

But, from the very element of discontinuity there again emerged a basic continuity, namely the critique and denunciation of revolution. Together with morality, the idea of equality was also an atavism: 'Through immense periods of time, the intellect produced nothing but errors; [...] for example: that there are enduring things; that there are identical things' (FW, 110 [110]). Now it was

---

23   On 'reactionary modernism', cf. Herf 1984 and Losurdo 1991, p. 5.

possible to recognise this primitive junk for what it was: 'Starting from the etymology and history of language, we consider all concepts as having become and
many as still becoming; and precisely in such a way that the most universal and
the falsest concepts must also be the oldest' (XI, 613).

Something of the previous 'Enlightenment' phase persisted. One example
was the denunciation of the 'illogical disposition', which 'is what first supplied
all the foundations for logic', to 'treat the similar as identical' (FW, 111 [112]),
to set an equals sign between people where there was a more or less vague
similarity. Even clearer was the persistence of 'positivism', as demonstrated for
example in the naturalistic configuration both of the idea of equality and of
the moral norm, both rejected because they did not correspond to any reality
or fact.

After the theological and revolutionary atavisms had been overcome, the
idea of irresponsibility and innocence was affirmed, with all its problematic
and disturbing features:

> What are the *profound transformations* that must derive from the *theories*
> according to which it is affirmed that there is no *God* that cares for us and
> there is no eternal moral law (atheistically-immoral humanity)? That we
> are *animals*? That our life is transitory? That we have no responsibility?
> The *wise man and the animal* will *approach* one another and produce a
> new *type*!
>
> IX, 461

CHAPTER 11

'Aristocratic Radicalism' and the 'New Party of Life'

1   The 'New Party of Life'

Towards the end of his conscious life, Nietzsche spoke of his intention to contribute to 'creating a party of life' (XIII, 638) or a 'new faction in favour of
life' (EH, *The Birth of Tragedy*, 4 [110]) charged with leading to the end the
struggle against subversion and modernity. The profile of the political 'party'
here invoked had been forming ever since the immoralistic turn. It had nothing to do with religious and political traditionalism, against which it even took
a polemical and demystifying stance. *Beyond Good and Evil* devoted an entire
chapter, the second, to the 'free spirit'. It concluded, however, with a warning
against a possible confusion between this figure and that of the 'free-thinker',
so highly valued by the most radical currents in the Enlightenment and now
also by the anarchist and socialist movement. The supporter of subversion
sometimes called himself a 'free spirit'. But one should not be fooled by the
similarities:

> In all the countries of Europe, and in America as well, there is now
> something that abuses this name: a very narrow, restricted, chained-up
> type of spirit whose inclinations are pretty much the opposite of our own
> intentions and instincts. [...] In a word (but a bad one): they belong to
> the levelers, these misnamed 'free spirits' – as eloquent and prolifically
> scribbling slaves of the democratic taste and its modern ideas.
>
>   JGB, 44 [40]

This was a case of terminological 'abuse' or false pretences, for these so-called
free spirits continued to demonstrate their 'servility', albeit a more 'refined' sort
than usual. When designing their projects for the transformation of society in
the name of justice, they proclaimed them to be 'principles of an unconditional "ought" to which one may openly submit and be seen to have submitted
without shame' (FW, 5 [33]). Despite the open-minded poses they adopted, they
were the heirs to clericalism and religious narrow-mindedness:

> The unsatisfied must have something to hang their hearts on: for example,
> God. Now that the latter is *not available*, many who in the past would have
> clung to God turn to *socialism* – or the *patria* (like Mazzini). A motive for

generous self-sacrifice, and in *public* (because it maintains discipline and cohesion, and creates courage!) must always exist!

IX, 591

Whether struggling for the democratic and national revolution or for socialist revolution, it was still a case of bigots and zealots in a new form. Here, then, was a first clear line of demarcation. On the one hand, we had a 'believer' who 'arrives at the basic conviction that he must be commanded', and, on the other, a person who 'takes leave of all faith and every wish for certainty' and so had the 'delight and power of self-determination'. This was the 'free spirit *par excellence*' (FW, 347 [205–6]).

It should also be borne in mind that moral pathos, the herd mentality and subalternity in regard to the philistine spirit of the time were all basically identical. With their watchwords about equality of rights and a compassion capable of embracing everyone regardless of difference of estate, the so-called free spirits or 'free thinkers' of anarchist and socialist mould distinguished themselves neither from the mass nor from the ruling ideology: 'What they want to strive for with all their might is the universal, green pasture happiness of the herd, with security, safety, contentment [*Behagen*], and an easier life for all' (JGB, 44 [41]).

We had before us 'slaves of the democratic taste' and 'people without solitude'. Things were quite different on the opposite side: 'Is it any wonder that we "free spirits" are not exactly the most communicative spirits?' If the former, like all those that had to do with the mass, were 'eloquent' and 'ridiculously superficial', the latter were distinguished by their depth and impenetrability. They had 'front and back souls whose ultimate aim is clear to nobody, with fore- and backgrounds that no foot can fully traverse, hidden under the cloak of light' (JGB, 44 [40–1]).

From the society they claimed to be fighting, the so-called free spirits inherited in reality the essential feature, the philistine view of life: 'they view suffering itself as something that needs to be *abolished*' (JGB, 44 [41]). The ideal of 'lack of pain' united '*socialists and politicians of all parties*', and they unanimously agreed to reject the more realistic and at the same time more alluring perspective, that of '*as much displeasure as possible* as the price for the growth of a bounty of refined pleasures and joys that hitherto have seldom been tasted' (FW, 12 [38]). This was the perspective pursued by genuine free spirits, well aware of the fecundity of 'harshness, violence, slavery, danger in the streets and in the heart', of 'everything evil, terrible, tyrannical, predatory, and snakelike in humanity'. These were the conditions under which 'the plant "human being"' grew in height and vigour, so that 'its life-will has had to be intensified to an unconditional power-will'. In their desire for peace and comfort, the so-called free spirits showed themselves to be fearful, while the genuine ones had to be 'ready for any risk' (JGB, 44 [41–2]), had to visit 'all the strange and questionable aspects of existence, everything banned by morality so far' (EH, Prologue, 3 [72]).

In conclusion, in breaking with all forms of conservatism, the new 'party' adopted the slogan of anti-conformism and the demythologisation of the dominant religious and political tradition. At the same time, it clearly distanced itself from a current that had already for some time been committed to this slogan, though to quite different ends. These were the years in which Büchner, president of the 'League of Freethinkers [*Freidenkerbund*]', was fighting for 'state old age and accident insurance', on the basis of a programme of progressive social reforms, even though, in the view of Mehring and revolutionary Social Democracy, this was in opposition to the 'autonomous movement of the proletariat'.[1] So one can appreciate the clear contrast between the *Freidenker*, who despite their apparently rebellious posturing on religious questions remained politically subordinate to the prevailing democratism and conformism, and the genuinely free spirits. In his later reconstruction of his own development, Nietzsche declared that ever since the first *Unfashionable Observation* he had felt the need to draw a line between himself and the political current of the 'free thinkers':

> Basically, I had put into practice one of Stendahl's maxims: he suggests entering society with a duel. And how I chose my opponent! The leading free spirit in Germany! ... In fact, the essay introduced an entirely new type of free-spiritedness: to this day, nothing is more foreign and unrelated to me than this whole European and American species of '*libres penseurs*'. Just with dyed-in-the-wool idiots and clowns of 'modern ideas', I find myself even more in conflict with representatives of this Anglo-American species than with any of their opponents. [...] I am the first immoralist.
>
> EH, 2 [114]

The new 'party', which rose on the ruins of conservatism and liberalism and on the basis of the experience of their pointlessness and detrition, had to wrench the flag of freedom and open-mindedness of spirit from the revolutionary movement, which it would set out to thwart and destroy. Precisely because of

---

1 Mehring 1961 ff., Vol. 13, pp. 133 and 137.

this task, resemblances might emerge between the two poles of the antithesis. The new 'party', or, as here defined, the 'aristocratism', had in common with 'anarchism' the complete rejection of the 'instinct' of bourgeois and philistine mediocrity (AC, 57 [59]). Going even further, Nietzsche declared: '[W]e cannot help being revolutionaries [*Revolutionäre*]' (EH, 5 [92]). As already announced in the preparatory notes for the third *Unfashionable Observation* (*supra*, 6 §9), the concern to tear from the socialist movement not only the flag of non-conformism and theoretical radicalism but also that of revolution became the essential mark of the new party.

2   'New Nobility' and 'New Slavery'

This was a case of a very singular revolution. Lest there be any doubt, Nietzsche immediately declared that the so-called free spirits he so hated 'are un-free and ridiculously superficial, particularly given their basic tendency to think that all human misery and wrongdoing [*Missrathen*] is caused by traditional social structures' (JGB, 44 [40–1]). Instead, one had to understand that it was nature as such that imposed an aristocratic order and condemned the mass of humans to a servile condition and a life of misery.

There can be no doubt that this conviction would remain with Nietzsche throughout the entire course of his development. Not even the 'Enlightenment' period was an exception: even *Human, All Too Human* reflected an interest in investigating the conditions of the formation and consolidation of a 'spiritual-bodily aristocracy' (MA, 243 [166]). But now the problem of the dominance of a 'good, healthy aristocracy' (JGB, 258 [152]) was a major concern, and its solution required repudiating half measures. So, when Brandes described Nietzsche's philosophy as 'aristocratic radicalism', Nietzsche promptly and enthusiastically accepted the definition, in a letter dated 2 December 1887 (B, III, 5, 206). The adjective and noun were interchangeable. 'Aristocratic radicalism' was an 'aristocratism' so radically committed to the struggle against 'the herd-animal ideal' (XIII, 65) that it could under no circumstances content itself with defending the existing order, itself saturated by a mercantile and plebeian worldview that had to be destroyed once and for all. On other occasions, Nietzsche professed such a consistent 'antidemocratism' as to appear 'terrible' in the eyes of his contemporaries (B, III, 3, 58). The polemic against 'this age of rabble and peasants' (B, III, 3, 65), against the 'democratic age' (B, III, 3, 32) and its 'freedom of press and impudence [*Press-und Freiheit-Frechheits*]' (B, III, 3, 62), remained constant.

The theoretical orientation of the new 'party' is now clear. We are dealing with an 'aristocratic radicalism' advocated in rebellious and even revolutionary tones, occasionally flirting with 'anarchism'. The more specifically political content shed further light on an aphorism from *The Gay Science*, which took a clear distance not only from liberalism and conservatism but also from the democratic and socialist movement:

> [W]e are delighted by all who love, as we do, danger, war, and adventure; who refuse to compromise, to be captured, to reconcile, to be castrated; we consider ourselves conquerors; we contemplate the necessity for new orders as well as for a new slavery – for every strengthening and enhancement of the human type also involves a new kind of enslavement – doesn't it?
>
> FW, 377 [241]

So, Nietzsche's rebellious stance wanted to call into question not only the existing social order but the entire historical cycle of the slave revolt. But how could this be achieved? This problem had already been confronted in another aphorism in *The Gay Science*, which we started to look at in the previous chapter and which attacked the social compromise proposed by Bismarck. But, here, Nietzsche did not merely criticise the Chancellor's policies but explicitly formulated an alternative. Initially, we encounter a familiar theme already highlighted in the title ('On the lack of noble style', *Vom Mangel der vornehmen Form*):

> Soldiers and leaders still have a far higher relation to one another than do workers and employers. So far at least, all cultures with a military basis are still high above so-called industrial culture: the latter in its present form is altogether the most vulgar form of existence that has ever been. [...] It is strange that submission to powerful, frightening, yes, terrifying persons, to tyrants and generals, is experienced to be not nearly as distressing as this submission to unknown and uninteresting persons, which is what all the greats of industry are: the worker usually sees in the employer only a cunning, bloodsucking dog of a man who speculates on all distress [*Noth*] and whose name, figure, manner, and reputation are completely indifferent to him. So far the manufacturers and large-scale commercial entrepreneurs have apparently been much too lacking in all the manners and signs [*Abzeichen*] of *higher race* that alone enable a *person* to become interesting; if they had the refinement [*Vornehmheit*] of noble breeding in their eye and gesture, there might not be any socialism of the masses.

So, socialism would not be defeated by the social reforms initiated by Bismarck, and less still by posing as apologists for labour. On the contrary, this demagoguery reinforced 'the notorious manufacturer's vulgarity with ruddy, plump hands', because it definitively eliminated all elements of outwardly visible distinction and hierarchy and thereby further undermined the respect and obedience of the masses:

> For the masses are basically prepared to submit to *any kind of slavery* provided that the superiors constantly legitimize themselves as higher, as *born* to command – through refined [*vornehme*] demeanour.
>
> FW, 40 [56–7]

Here, a new political programme was set out, one that looked beyond industrial society, but not in order to return to the soil. Also, it made no sense to nourish illusions in the enduring vitality of the traditional aristocracy, which vitality would have to reproduce itself in new forms. A 'higher form of aristocratism' was needed; to it belonged the 'future' (XII, 463). But, once the problem was solved, socialism could be liquidated and the popular masses thrown back so many centuries that they would accept 'slavery of every kind'.

The aristocratism Nietzsche professed did not have as its task the resuscitation of an agrarian society or one exclusively dominated by large landowners. It was meaningless to dream of turning the clock back to the time before industry and big industry. The task was rather to ensure industry was no longer led by a mercantile and vulgar class incapable of winning the respect of the mass of workers, but by an elite, an aristocracy, capable of investing its rule with greater legitimacy. Far from appealing to a community or similarity with the ruled, in accordance with Wilhelm I's slogan ('We are all workers'), the rulers now emphasised the insuperability and naturalness of the gap that separated them from the ruled – as if they wanted to form a new 'nobility of blood'.

The central problem was precisely the constitution of this estate. Moreover, the historical cycle of the slave revolt was in no way irreversible. There were plenty of encouraging symptoms of an inversion of this tendency: 'A layer of slaves is forming – we must make that an aristocracy also takes shape' (IX, 483). But 'how to organize the new nobility [*Adel*], as the estate that has power?' (IX, 445). To this question, a fragment from the spring–autumn of 1881 attempted an answer:

> Slavery is visible everywhere, although it does not want to admit this to itself; we must aspire to be everywhere, to know all its relations, to defend as well as possible all its opinions; only thus can we master and use it. Our being [*Wesen*] must remain hidden: like that of the Jesuits, who exercised a dictatorship in the general anarchy, but were introduced

as *tool* and *function*. What is our function, our mantle of slavery? Teaching? – Slavery must not be abolished, it is necessary. We merely want to ensure that such people emerge again and again *for whom* others work, so that this huge mass of political-commercial energy is not consumed in vain.

IX, 527

Not everything is obvious in these formulations. Some points, however, are immediately apparent: 1) the need for the maintenance of slavery for the purposes of the new nobility; 2) new and encouraging prospects opened up for this perspective if one was able to ride the tiger, shouting rebel and revolutionary slogans and, if necessary, throwing oneself without a moment's flinching into the subversive movement, to mix with the slaves and the slave revolt; 3) the need to act not in isolation but as an organised and quite specifically organised force.

Clearly, Nietzsche was speaking here as the member or leader of a party, and the organisational model to which he pointed was, significantly, the order of the Jesuits, celebrated by the culture of the Restoration as a valuable tool in the struggle against the subversive machinations of the Freemasons: according to Maistre, the revolution would have been 'impossible without the preliminary destruction on the part of the Jesuits'.[2] Perhaps Nietzsche was also thinking of the role played by the order in Paraguay and its ability on that occasion to impose discipline and compulsory labour. One thing was certain: the break with liberalism and conservatism had happened in terms not only of political content but also of organisation. This was the first theorisation of a party of struggle, one that had nothing in common with a bourgeois party of opinion: it aimed to be in a position to deal with the turmoil on the horizon.

3   Aristocratic Distinction and Social Apartheid

Whereas the 'free thinkers' with their socialistic orientation made common cause with a shapeless plebeian mass of which they were an integral part, the genuine free spirits, insofar as they were aristocratic, were marked primarily by the 'pathos of distance'. 'The rift between people, between classes [*Stand*], the myriad number of types, the will to be yourself, to stand out, what I call the

---

2   Maistre 1984, Vol. 8, p. 205.

pathos of distance, is characteristic of every strong age' (GD, 37 [21]), thus avoiding the contamination of 'the high-placed and the high-minded' by all that was 'lowly, low-minded, common and plebeian' (GM, I, 2 [11]).

Even as a student, in describing the aristocracy and identifying with its cause, Nietzsche had written: 'The nobleman must in all cases keep his distance from the rabble [a plebis commercio]' (DTM, 15, 59–60). This theme was now repeated with greater force than ever: 'Every choice [auserlesener] human being strives instinctively for a citadel and secrecy where he is rescued [erlöst] from the crowds, the many, the vast majority; where, as the exception, he can forget the human norm.' 'A person of higher taste' was to avoid 'bad company' and 'all company is bad company except with your equals' (JGB, 26 [27]). Or, more succinctly still: 'One must be very superficial, so that one never returns home full of remorse after having been with the common people' (VIII, 365). It was a matter of hygiene: 'Because solitude is a virtue for us, since it is a sublime inclination and impulse to cleanliness which shows that contact between people ("society") inevitably makes things unclean' (JGB, 284 [171]).

An aristocrat, a member of the 'higher ruling kind', was never to lose sight of or lessen the unbridgeable distance that separated him from the mob (GM, I, 2 [12]). This distance was not only spiritual. It was absolutely imperative 'that the healthy should remain separated from the sick, should even be spared the sight of the sick so that they do not confuse themselves with the sick'. And, most importantly, 'the sick should not make the healthy sick' (GM III, 14 [91])! One was to avoid not only the plebeians themselves but also the places they frequented: 'It usually stinks in places where the people eat and drink, even where they worship. You should not go to church if you want to breathe clean air.' The prohibition on commonality seemed to know no bounds: 'Books for the general public always smell foul: the stench of petty people clings to them' (JGB, 30 [31]). Zarathustra raised a song to the kind of social apartheid recommended here:

> And there is a life that the dregs of humanity do not drink! [...] Because this is our height and our home: we live in places too high and steep for the unclean and their thirsts. [...] Truly, no meals that the unclean can eat as well! They would think that they were feeding on fire and they would burn their mouths. Truly, we do not keep a home ready for the filthy! [...] And we want to live above them like strong winds; neighbours of eagles, neighbours of the snow, neighbours of the sun: this is the life of strong winds.
>
> Za, II, On the Rabble [74–6] EH, 8 [84]

The 'ordinary' or the 'little people' were so repugnant they aroused disgust even when one investigated them solely through thoughts. One was to 'banish from one's horizon all the lower steps of humanity! Or not want to see and hear them!' In this sense, the 'wise man' was marked by 'blindness' and 'deafness' (IX, 458). So one could say that genuine philosophy was 'a life lived freely in ice and high mountains' (EH, Prologue, 3 [72]). On the other hand, of course, the 'study of the average human being [...] is all a necessary part of the life story of every philosopher, perhaps the least pleasant, most foul-smelling part and the one richest in disappointments' (JGB, 26 [27]). If '[d]isgust with people, with "the dregs" of humanity, has always been my greatest danger', then it was precisely because it might suggest fleeing a battlefield that under no circumstances should be abandoned. Higher natures were not to indulge in a cult of abstract and cowardly purity – to do so would be synonymous with desertion. They were to face up to the contamination that was, as it were, implicit in the struggle, and could achieve 'redemption from disgust' as long as they inwardly reaffirmed the infinite distance that separated them from the mass (EH, 8 [83–4]).

The pathos of distance revealed itself not only on the spatial but also on the temporal plane. In the latter case, the separation and the abyss were created by the gaze directed to the future, which recoiled before the spectacle of the massified present: 'Some people are born posthumously' (EH, Why I write such good books, 1 [100]). One was never to lose sight of the fact that 'the greatest events and thoughts [...] are understood as never late.' And then: 'How many centuries does it take for a spirit to be comprehended?' (JGB, 285 [171]).

Temporal distance could also be created by setting one's gaze to the past. The motto of a true aristocrat read: 'My pride is, I have an origin' (IX, 642). Nietzsche also adopted this motto for himself, and constructed a personal genealogy that distanced him from Germany, from the place that, as we shall see (*infra*, 17 §1), had in the meantime become, for him, the main source of infection of modern massification: 'I was always taught to trace the origin of my blood and name to Polish nobles called Nïetzky' (IX, 681). This was no trivial matter: 'And this is where I come to the question of race. I am a pure-blooded Polish nobleman. [...] But I am a huge atavism, even as a Pole' (EH, 3 [77–8]).

Regardless of whether the pathos of distance and thus 'unfashionableness' or 'untimeliness' were articulated on a spatial or a temporal level and, in this latter case, with one's gaze fixed on the future or the past, at all events it was a hallmark of the genuine free spirit and aristocrat. This was a theme developed in particular in *Beyond Good and Evil*, about which *Ecce Homo* later observed:

The book is a school of the *gentilhomme*, taking the concept more spiritually and radically than it has ever been taken before. [...] All the things this age is proud of are viewed as conflicting with this type, almost as bad manners.

EH, *Beyond Good and Evil*, 2 [135]

In further confirmation of their distinction, 'noble' persons or those of a 'higher nature' all expressed their contempt for the utilitarian calculation that formed the sole horizon of ordinary humanity: 'The unreason or odd reason [*Unvernunft oder Quervernunft*] of passion is what the common type despises in the noble.' Someone outside the aristocratic circle who 'unflinchingly keeps sight of [his] advantage' failed to comprehend 'how anyone could, for example, risk health and honour for the sake of a passion for knowledge'. More generally, '[f]or common natures all noble, magnanimous feelings appear to be inexpedient and therefore initially incredible'. Yes, they 'are suspicious [*argwöhnisch*] of the noble person, as if he were furtively seeking his advantage' (FW, 3 [30–1]).

The moralist Nietzsche had asserted the 'school of suspicion' as against the 'higher feelings' to which the revolutionary movement appealed, waving the banner of social justice (*supra*, 8 §1 and 5). *The Dawn* argued that it was necessary to recognise that they were 'amalgamated [...] with madness and nonsense' (M, 33 [29]). But now it was merely the vulgar nature that denigrated as 'quite fantastic and arbitrary' the reasons given by 'the noble, magnanimous, and self-sacrificing person' (FW, 3 [31]). Nietzsche the moralist and Nietzsche of the 'Enlightenment' had set the Enlightenment against Christian and socialist beliefs; but now the aristocrat, whose 'reason pauses' 'in his best moments', and who 'reduce[s] the intellect to silence', was celebrated in opposition to the plebeian, for whom all these things seemed 'incomprehensible and impractical' (FW, 3 [31]).

In this sense, one can speak of Nietzsche's formalism: even if higher nature was at times defined by him in a radically different way, it was essentially to maintain the abyss that separated it from ordinary humanity. However, if we leave aside the period of 'Enlightenment', there is no doubt that the plebeian and vulgar person was exemplified by a calculating thought that knew nothing of greatness and was incapable of depth, looking instead exclusively for an absence of danger and for peace and quiet, comfort, and thus 'civilization'.

4   Aristocracy, Bourgeoisie and Intellectuals

Despite the transfiguration that initially rendered it unrecognisable, the figure of the longed for new nobility finally took specific political and social form. To reconstruct its features, I rely mainly on a few pages of notes written in May–July 1885 (XI, 543–5), which set out to answer the question: '*Was ist vornehm*', what were the characteristics of the distinguished and aristocratic individual? In the first place, 'the ability to be idle, the absolute conviction that a trade, in every sense, may not dishonour but will certainly degrade or depreciate [*entadeln*]' (XI, 543–4). Or, in other words, 'nobility is fecund in a big way, precisely because it has produced aristocratic customs, the most aristocratic of which is the ability to endure boredom' (IX, 453). To dispel all doubt, Nietzsche made it clear he was referring to 'nobility by birth' (XI, 543).

Moreover, 'diligence [*Arbeitsamkeit*]' was 'the indication of an ignoble [*unvornehm*] species [*Art*] of human being', even if it was 'a valuable and indispensable species of human being' (XII, 48). Doubtless. one was to 'highly honour' 'diligence [*Fleiss*]' in the 'bourgeois' sense, but still its role was clearly subordinate (XI, 544). So, even if nobility of blood claimed hegemony for itself, it would not aim to eliminate the capitalist bourgeoisie, as confirmed in particular by a fragment from the spring of 1888:

> One becomes a respectable [*anständig*] human being because one is a respectable human being, i.e., because one is born a capitalist of good instincts and prosperous conditions [*Capitalist guter Instinkte und gedeihlicher Verhältnisse*] … If one comes poor into the world, of parents that have squandered everything and saved nothing, then one is 'incorrigible', ripe for the penitentiary or the madhouse.
>
> XIII, 290

That the new nobility was not conceived as exclusive is shown by the fact that the term 'capitalist' was used synonymously with successful and being a member of the upper class. And yet Nietzsche seemed to want the capitalist in the actual sense of the word to give up all that was vulgar in his activities and to integrate more into the modes and ideology of the aristocracy. Such was the import of an aphorism from *The Gay Science* dedicated to the theme 'trade and nobility'. Of course, '[b]uying and selling are common by now, like the art of reading and writing'. And yet, things could change. Had that not happened with hunting? From an activity designed for subsistence, it became 'a thing of moods and luxury', and 'eventually it became a privilege and thereby lost its everyday and common character'. The same could happen with trade. 'Only then would trade become something exquisite [*Vornehmheit*], and the noble might enjoy trade as much as they hitherto enjoyed war and politics.' Conversely, politics 'could have changed completely. Even now it is ceasing to be the art of the nobleman, and it is quite possible that some day one will find it so base that, along with all political literature and journalism, one classifies it as a "prostitution of the spirit"' (FW, 31 [52–3]).

It was for the aristocracy, on the one hand, to take note of the fact that the political world was now marked by the plebeian character of parliament, universal suffrage and the advent of the masses; and, on the other hand, to recognise the aristocratic potential inherent in commerce. After much hesitation, Nietzsche called on the big capital engaged in the money business to become part of the dominant power bloc, on condition that it recognised the political and cultural hegemony of the nobility, by adopting the slogan *otium et bellum*, which was the motto of every true aristocracy. On this basis, as we shall see, not only a social but even a matrimonial fusion between Jewish finance and the traditional nobility was desirable. This was basically, according to the work of prominent historians, the situation in countries like Germany, Britain and Italy up to the First World War and the revolutions and upheavals that arose from it.[3] This ability of the *ancien régime* to absorb new life or survive in new forms was threatened by a social mobility and 'massification' stimulated by the rapid expansion of the capitalist economy and by the ever more impetuous growth of the labour and socialist movement. In view of the challenges and threats on the horizon, Nietzsche felt the need to emphasise that the dichotomy between the well-formed and the malformed, between 'capitalists of good instincts' and spendthrifts condemned to marginalisation, was transmitted from one generation to the next.

It is true that, while legitimising the ruling power bloc in the Second Reich, Nietzsche also violently criticised its 'Christian' ideology and attachment to parliamentary institutions. Regarding the first point, it is interesting to note a final detail that completed the description of the social bloc called on to rule. To be distinguished or aristocratic also meant 'delighting in princes and priests, because they keep alive at least *symbolically*, and on the whole also actually, even in evaluating the past, the belief in a diversity of human values, in other words in rank ordering' (XI, 544). So, to the extent that Nietzsche agreed to sanction the ruling bloc at the religious level too, the clergy and the higher clergy could be co-opted into it.

---

3 Mayer 1984, *passim*; cf., especially for Britain, Cannadine 1990, p. 19 ff.

The intellectuals, on the other hand, remained excluded. Nietzsche pointed out that the 'nobility of birth' he celebrated had nothing to do with the so-called aristocracy of the spirit:

'Aristocracy of the spirit' was a favourite motto among the Jews, dangerous because it risked giving prominence to 'artists', 'poets', and 'anyone who is a master of something', i.e., in the final analysis, to the intellectuals. When not inclined to 'demagoguery' and subversion, the latter deserved protection. But, Nietzsche added, in his capacity as a member and spokesperson of the new aristocratic 'party', 'we, as beings by nature superior to them, to those who simply know how to do something, to "merely productive" human beings, do not confuse ourselves with them' (XI, 543–4). A youthful fragment had already pointed out that '[t]here is an ethical aristocracy into which no one can gain entrance who was not already born into it and born for it' (VII, 809 [363]). Now one talked more explicitly of 'noble birth'. However, at least on one point, Bismarck deserved recognition: he was 'suspicious of intellectuals' (XI, 256).

Far from identifying with intellectuals, Nietzsche wanted to be the ideologue of the social bloc he wished for and transfigured: 'It seems to me that someone confers a very uncommon distinction on himself when he takes a book of mine in his hands. [...] It is an honour beyond compare to enter into this noble and delicate world' (EH, Why I write such good books, 1 and 3 [100 and 103]). An exclusive world: *Genealogy of Morals* 'has the good luck of being accessible to only the highest and most rigorous minds: nobody else has the ears for it' (WA, Epilogue, note [262]). The circle of readers was limited also because they needed not only to acquire a theoretical knowledge but also to undertake an action of decisive importance: 'the most select people will devote themselves to the greatest tasks of all' (EH, *The Birth of Tragedy*, 4 [111]).

5   From Cultural Elitism to Caesarism

We have seen how Nietzsche fundamentally denounced the 'representative constitution'. But with what could it be replaced? The more intolerable the present, the more passionate the call for change:

What a relief it is for these European herd animals, what a deliverance from an increasingly intolerable pressure, when, in spite of everything, someone appears who can issue unconditional commands; the impact of Napoleon's appearance is the last major piece of evidence for this: – the

history of Napoleon's impact is practically the history of the higher happiness attained by this whole century in its most worthwhile people and
moments.

JGB, 199 [87]

At first, Nietzsche blamed Caesarism on socialism, which he accused of promoting 'the powerful Caesarean state of this century' (*supra*, 9 § 2). Now, however, Caesarism was explicitly affirmed and celebrated. Yet it would be superficial to think that this represents a reversal of positions. The 'dictatorial Caesarean state' criticised in *Human, All Too Human* was the state to which Jacobins
and socialists aspired, one committed to achieving the happiness of all. The
Caesarism Nietzsche later invoked was designed to continue and intensify, by
different methods, the struggle against revolution and socialism.

When Nietzsche observed an emerging trend in the direction of the formation of a new type of political regime within the existing order, this was yet
more confirmation of the attention and focus with which he followed developments in the political situation in Germany and internationally. The representative bodies turned from being instruments of control and the limitation of
power into something radically different: 'Parliaments can be extremely useful for a strong and flexible statesman'; they seemed to present an element of
resistance, but in truth he could find 'support' in them and possibly 'offload
much responsibility' (XI, 456). This phenomenon manifested itself with particular clarity in Germany: 'Just as Frederick the Great constantly makes jokes
about the "féminisme" of the regency of the neighbouring states, so too does
Bismarck about "parliamentarism": it is a *new* means to do what one wishes'
(XI, 451).

These were the years in which Marx and Engels used the term Bonapartism
to characterise not only Napoleon III's regime but also the political reality of
the Second Reich, dominated by the Iron Chancellor. Nietzsche's analysis was
not dissimilar, although, in his case, the tone of satisfaction with which he
described the phenomenon was audible. Louis Napoleon himself, before he
became Napoleon III, wished for a regime in which the 'masses' and 'peoples'
could be 'dragged along by the influence of a great genius [who], similar to the
influence of divinity, is a fluid that spreads like electricity; it exalts the imagination, makes hearts throb, and enraptures, because it touches the soul rather
than persuades'. This irresistible charisma was a stabilising factor, it 'does not
disrupt society, but, on the contrary, reorders and reorganizes it': all were as if
subjugated to a superior personality and charm. At the end of the nineteenth
century, Le Bon maintained that culture was 'the work of a small minority of
higher minds, comparable to the tip of a pyramid', while the base was formed

by masses in the clutches of primitivism. But this was not a disadvantage but, rather, a prerequisite for the solution of the problem: 'The type of hero the masses love will always have the structure of a Caesar. The plume of his helmet seduces. His authority is respected and his sword strikes fear.' Even a leading member of the liberal tradition like Bagehot called for a charismatic leader who had 'an exceptional power in human relations' based on 'faith', 'enthusiasm' and 'trust', which he knew how to convey by 'appealing to some vague dream of glory'; the mass of people thus ended up acknowledging the 'action of a single will', and the 'command of a single man'.[4]

Nietzsche not only had Bagehot in his library but had read him. He was also familiar with Carlyle, who complained that democratic and levelling tendencies called into question every lordship or leadership or every Dux or Duke. Horrified by the revolution of 1848, the British writer sought shelter from the subversive upheavals no longer in the old society of aristocrats, 'lords' and notables, but in a new regime under a 'leader' or 'duce', thus evoking the image of a 'Real Captain', finally called upon to take the place of that 'Phantasm Captain' swept in by the unholy wave of 'universal democracy'.[5] In confirmation of his aristocratic radicalism and of the masters morality he theorised, Nietzsche adduced 'etymology' (the 'problems of origin' unfortunately concealed and suppressed by 'democratic prejudice') to show that the good/bad dichotomy originally contrasted the well-born and martial aristocrat to the vulgar and cowardly plebeian (GM, I, 4–5 [13]). Similarly, Carlyle felt the need to clarify his stance against democracy and in favour of a 'heroarchy' or 'hierarchy' in favour of a power that was somehow 'sacred' as against the bad government of the profane multitude: 'The duke means dux, leader; king is kon-ning, kanning, man that knows or cans.'[6]

But, while Bonapartist tendencies did not disrupt the parliamentary framework in countries with a more established liberal tradition or even in Germany, Nietzsche now looked beyond this. Yes, Bismarck could do more or less what he wanted with the representative institutions, but they were still marked by the stain of universal suffrage. Along with the Iron Chancellor, they were still an expression of the 'petty epoch of plebeian myopia' (XI, 353). And it was precisely this age to which an end had, once and for all, to be put:

On the whole, however, I would wish that the numerical idiocy and superstition of majorities does not become established in Germany as among

---

4   Cf. Losurdo 1993, 2, §2, §3 and §6.
5   Carlyle 1983, pp. 12 f., 31.
6   Carlyle 1934, p. 249.

the Latin races; and that in the end something *in politicis* is invented! There is little sense and great danger in letting the habit, still so brief and eradicable, of universal suffrage strike deeper roots, given its introduction was only a measure adopted at a time of necessity.

XI, 456–7

Again, Nietzsche's strong sense of history was confirmed. In Germany, representative institutions dated only from Bismarck's 'new era', and suffrage was even younger. Neither was the result of an acute social struggle: both were the products of tactical manoeuvres aimed at broadening the consensus necessary for achieving the unification of the country from above. Now the political scene had changed radically and the new situation that was emerging might render obsolete or superfluous the old remedy. One had however to be in a position to invent something new. The model was obvious: 'Great men like Caesar and Napoleon are living species! All other governing is imitation [*nachgemacht*]' (X, 282). This point of view was maintained to the end and reiterated in the most varied contexts: 'When I look for the highest formula for Shakespeare, the only thing I can find is the fact that he conceived the type of Caesar' (EH, 4 [91]).

The new perspective might be favoured precisely by the radicalisation of the socialist movement. The assassination attempts by the anarchists and the revolutionary movement in Germany and Russia also had a positive side: they shook the ground in which the usual philistinism was rooted, they paved the way for new experiments, they opened up new possibilities. True, they plunged the existing order into crisis, but not necessarily in the direction desired by the supporters and authors of the violence:

> Principle: Not the liberating releases, however violent they might be, caused most damage to humanity, but their inhibition. We need to eliminate bad temper, morbid feelings; but to do so one requires the courage to judge in a different and more favourable way the horror of the releases. Assassinations are better than subterranean hostility. Murders, wars, etc., overt violence, the evil of power should be called good: if, from now on, the evil of weakness is called evil.
>
> IX, 452–3

Unlike in the years of the encounter with the moralists, it was now no longer a question of throwing suspicion onto the higher moral sentiments of the socialists, but of using their violence to eliminate the moral worldview and break down the barriers that hindered an appropriate response to the situation. The

reference to the attacks on Wilhelm I was significant. While the dominant ideology shrieked with indignation and seethed with anger at the threat they posed
to the existing order, Nietzsche saw in the upheavals on the horizon the opportunity for a radical settling of accounts with modernity: 'We are entering the
age of anarchy: but this is also the age of the most spiritual and freest individuals. An immense spiritual energy is turning round.' The obstacles set up
by 'customs, morality, and so forth' were being torn down by the revolutionary
movement, which, with its violence, could objectively favour the advent of the
'age of genius' it hated (IX, 452).

In this sense, even the protagonists of the terrorist attacks were playing a
much more positive role than the petty-bourgeois clinging to peace and order:
'In lands where people are restrained and contained there nevertheless still
remain plenty of backsliding, unrestrained, and uncontained persons: at the
moment they are congregating in the socialist camps more than anywhere else.'
Were they come to power, they would impose a 'frightful discipline' and bind
others and themselves in 'iron chains' (M, 184 [131]). But this would be only
the beginning of a process with a quite different outcome: had not the French
Revolution ended by producing Napoleon I? Have not the upheavals of February and June 1848 resulted in the Bonapartism of Napoleon III? The 'great
upheavals' in the offing opened up 'good prospects': 'I hope that all the fundamental problems will come to light and that it will go well beyond the nonsense
of the New Testament' and the inability to act caused by uncertainty or the aestheticizing attitude of a 'Hamlet and Faust, the two "most modern men"' (XI,
155).

Even the intervention of the 'lower strata of the people' could produce positive results. Increasingly, new circumstances were arising 'in which the masses
are ready to risk their lives, their property, their conscience, their own virtue',
only to fulfil 'the need of the feeling of power', only 'as a victorious, capriciously
tyrannical nation to rule over other nations'. The reference to Napoleon and his
'grand politics' is, once again, transparent (M, 189 [133]). The outcome of these
upheavals was unclear, but they at least seemed to presage the end of the mercantile society and the philistinism associated with it: 'Socialism is a ferment
that announces a huge number of state experiments, and therefore also of the
state downfalls and new germs. The maturation of states today happens more
quickly; military violence is on the rise' (IX, 527).

This made the Caesarist perspective even more concrete: 'When "morals
decay"', the new figure of the 'individual' emerged, no longer tied to tradition and customary law: 'for the love of the newly discovered ego is now much
mightier than the love of the old, used-up, touted-to-death "fatherland"' (FW,
23 [48]). Now there was no longer any room for the sort of containment of

revolution envisioned by Burke and traditionalism in general. It was a situation full of difficulties but also of promises: along with individuals, 'those beings emerge for the first time who are called tyrants' and 'they are the precursors and as it were the precocious firstling instances of individuals' (FW, 23 [48]). This much had to be clear: not all had become individuals; 'their opposites, the herd people', were still present, and even formed the majority. They were the manoeuvre mass and the raw material for the individuals-tyrants, engaged in a struggle for power: 'Once decay has reached its peak along with the struggle of all sorts of tyrants, the Caesar always appears, the final tyrant who puts an end to the weary wrestling for sole rule by putting weariness to work for himself' (FW, 23 [48]).

6   Feminist Movement and 'Universal Uglification'

The settling of accounts with democracy was also the day of reckoning with the movement for female emancipation. Nietzsche was well aware that it was an integral part of the process of democratisation: 'Wherever the industrial spirit has won out over the military and aristocratic spirit, women are now striving for the economic and legal independence of a clerk' (JGB, 239 [128]). It was precisely in Germany, where the strongest socialist party was active, that the movement for the emancipation of women encountered particularly favourable conditions. This was confirmation, in Nietzsche's eyes, that it belonged among 'the worst developments in Europe's general trend towards increasing ugliness' (JGB, 232 [124]).

In the culture of the time, the comparison between women and the proletarian-slave was commonplace. In Engels, we find the argument that 'the modern individual family is based on the overt or covert domestic slavery of the woman'; in any case, 'in the family [the husband] is the bourgeois, the wife represents the proletariat'.[7] Nietzsche polemicised against the 'collect[ing] together, in an inept and indignant manner, [of] everything slavish and serflike that is and still is intrinsic to the position of women in the present social order' (JGB, 239 [129]). It was true that the position of women reminded one of the 'suffering of the lower orders', the 'work slaves [Arbeitssklaven] and prisoners' (GM III, 18 [100]); but slavery was a necessary condition for culture and its development.

---

7   Marx and Engels 1975 ff., 26, p. 181.

When woman rebelled and became a feminist, she nourished sentiments typical of the revolting slave:

> 'Emancipation of women' – that is the instinctive hatred of failed women [*missrathenen*], which is to say infertile women, against those who have turned out well. [...] Emancipated women are basically anarchists in the world of the 'eternal-feminine', people in bad shape whose bottom-most instinct is revenge.
>
> EH, 5 [106]

The characteristics Nietzsche attributed to women in the following lines reflected the conditions of his time, but he naturalised them and transfigured them *sub specie aeternitatis*:

'[W]hat would be rarer than a woman who really knew what science is? The best of them even nourish a secret disdain for it in their bosoms'; so 'there arises a not inconsiderable danger if politics and particular branches of science are entrusted to them (history, for example)' (MA, 416 [227]).

On the other hand: 'But she does not want truth: what does truth matter for a woman! Nothing is so utterly foreign, unfavorable, hostile for women from the very start than truth' (JGB, 232 [125]). After all, in truth woman was not even a 'thoughtful creature' (JGB, 234 [125]). Just like independent intellectual research, a strong and independent will was also alien to her:

> The passion of a woman, in its unconditional renunciation of her own rights, presupposes precisely that on the other side there is not an equal pathos, not an equal will to renunciation; for if both should renounce themselves from love. [...] Woman wants to be taken, adopted as a possession, wants to be absorbed in the concept 'possession', 'possessed'; consequently, she wants someone who takes, who does not himself give or give himself away; who on the contrary is supposed precisely to be made richer in 'himself' – through the increase in strength, happiness, and faith given him by the woman who gives herself.

It was a matter, according to Nietzsche, of an absolutely insuperable 'natural opposition [*Naturgegegensatz*]' (FW, 363 [228]), for '[t]he way of men is will; the way of women is willingness' (FW, 68 [73]). Naturalising historically determined social relations led, unsurprisingly, to stereotyping. Women were shallow and vain: one just had to look at her 'at the window of a fashion shop' (IX, 442); 'their great art is in lying, their highest concern is appearance and beauty' (JGB, 232 [125]). And again: with women, 'you never plumb their depths – they do not have any' (EH, 3 [141]); when they attended to literature, it was solely to attract attention (GD, 20 [158]).

The philosopher's polemic against the women's movement was so harsh that it led to his adoption of assertions of a disarming philistinism. Those who had been 'emancipated' were 'unsuccessful women' or 'those who do not have what it takes to have children' (EH, 5 [105]). More precisely, the 'emancipation of women' was promoted by 'women who do not manage to get husbands and children' or 'ugly women [who] require men to satisfy their drives' (XI, 513)!

Clearly, the desired aristocratic regeneration had at the same time to reaffirm the subordination of women. And, as in the case of the servant or slave, here too religion could be useful: 'a woman without piety' was 'absolutely repugnant or ludicrous to a profound and godless man' (JGB, 239 [129]). Even the authority of the church was invoked to attack the movement for women's emancipation: '[M]ale care and protection of women were at work when the church decreed: *mulier taceat in ecclesia.*' In the age of secularisation, this prohibition had to be recast in the manner of Napoleon: '*mulier taceat in politicis*'. The movement for female emancipation, which was steadily advancing, had to be opposed with the maxim '*mulier taceat de muliere*' (JGB, 232 [125]).

After all, there was no doubt what place men and women occupied in the social rank-ordering and the rank-ordering of values. The denunciation of Christianity as an unwarlike and plebeian religion was at the same time a denunciation of the 'religions of the lower mass of women, slaves and the non-aristocratic layers' (XIII, 116). In denouncing the lack of 'any nobility of demeanor and desire' in certain religious attitudes, such as in the case of Augustine, Nietzsche spoke of 'a womanly tenderness and lustfulness that pushes coyly and unsuspectingly towards a *unio mystica et physica*' (JGB, 50 [47]). On the other hand, when celebrating the rare 'women with lofty, heroic, royal souls, capable of and ready for grandiose retorts, resolutions, and sacrifices, capable of and ready for mastery over men', Nietzsche immediately hastened to add that in them 'the best of man aside from his sex has become an incarnate ideal' (FW, 70 [74]). The decadence of the modern world found its fullest expression in its 'moral sugariness and falsity, its innermost feminism' (GM III, 19 [102]), in the fact that 'Europe is, when all is said and done, a woman' (XI, 513). Overcoming this condition was synonymous with 'the masculinization of Europe' through the subjugation not only of the 'businessman' and the 'philistine' but also of 'woman' (FW, 362 [227]). It was a matter of averting the danger of the '*marasmus femininus*' that threatened Europe and of winning back the 'virile and warrior virtues' (XI, 587).

7   A 'New Warrior Age'

To understand the values of the new aristocracy, one had once again to go back to classical antiquity:

> A person of good family concealed the fact that he worked if need compelled him to work. The slave worked under the pressure of the feeling that he was doing something contemptible. [...] 'Nobility and honour are attached solely to *otium* and *bellum*' – that was the ancient prejudice!
>
> FW, 329 [184]

As we have seen, Nietzsche contemplated the prospect of the absorption of the commercial class into the traditional nobility. This, however, was 'repulsive' to the extent that the commercial class clings stubbornly to a calculating style of thought and to modern values and life-style (IX, 340). Nietzsche's contempt for the 'spirit of the market as a spirit of the age' knew no bounds (IX, 545). Nothing was more damaging for the fate of culture than a society wholly directed towards the pursuit of comfort, peace, and the absence of tensions and dangers. It followed that '[t]he greatest progress of the masses up till now has been the religious war, for it proves that the mass has begun to treat concepts with respect' (FW, 144 [128]). Yes, 'when one is divided by opinions and spills blood and there are sacrifices, culture rides high: opinions have become valuable goods' (IX, 556). To make a scandal about it in the name of tolerance was the height of narrow-mindedness: 'What is tolerance! And recognition of alien ideals! Whoever promotes with great depth and intensity his own ideals cannot believe in other ideals, cannot but judge them negatively – as ideals of inferior beings' (IX, 476–7).

An abyss now seemed to separate Nietzsche from his previous 'Enlightenment'. It even seemed like re-reading A.W. Schlegel, who thought 'religious wars [...] do greatest honour to humanity', because they were the 'strongest proof of the power of ideas'; for 'is not the tolerance of modern Europe nothing other than disguised indifference and the complacent celebration of enervation?'[8] The fact is that for Nietzsche 'a condition of wildness and individuals in struggle is, for the arts, better than excessive security' (IX, 337).

On the other hand, the celebration of war, far from vanishing in the 'Enlightenment' period, had already begun to take on particularly shrill and disturbing tones:

---

8 Cf. Losurdo 1997a, 9, 2.

[A] humanity as highly cultivated and therefore as inevitably exhausted as is the present European one requires not only wars, but the greatest and most terrible wars – and thus, temporary lapses into barbarism – if the means of culture are not to cost them their culture and their very existence.

MA, 477 [260]

War was called upon to give to exhausted peoples

that raw energy of the encampments, that deep, impersonal hatred, that murderer's cold-bloodedness accompanied by a good conscience, that shared, organizing ardor in the destruction of the enemy, that proud indifference toward great losses, toward our very existence and that of our friends, that muffled, earthquake-like shuddering of the soul.

MA, 477 [259]

So, there was nothing new in Nietzsche's profession in *The Gay Science* of a 'faith' in the manly regeneration of Europe by means of war (FW, 362 [227]). '[T]he secret for harvesting from existence the greatest fruitfulness and the greatest enjoyment is – to live dangerously! Build your cities on the slopes of Vesuvius! Send your ships into uncharted seas!' (FW, 283 [161]). This theme could also be found in the later writings: 'You give up the great life when you give up war', and you therefore inevitably remained a prisoner of the mediocrity and banality of modernity (GD, 3 [173]).

What was new in comparison with the 'Enlightenment' period was the confident expectation of a new era of wars, the conviction that the period of peace and the ideal of perpetual peace was now coming to an end: 'I welcome all the signs of a more virile, warlike age approaching that will above all restore honour to bravery!' There would be 'wars for the sake of thoughts and their consequences' (FW, 283 [160]). One was not to close one's eyes to the 'new, warlike age that we Europeans have obviously entered into' (JGB, 209 [102]).

What wars did he mean? The question must be asked, because the denunciation of German or, more generally, intra-European chauvinism already formulated in the writings of 'Enlightenment' period continued to be energetically maintained. The polemic against 'petty politics', which fed on the 'deadly hatreds' between European countries as well as on 'nationalism and racial hatred [*Rassenhass*]' and cultivated a 'mendacious racial self-admiration and obscenity' in Germany in particular was sharp and fascinating. Fortunately, '[a]mong Europeans today there is no lack of those who have a right to call themselves homeless in a distinctive and honourable sense'. And it was above all to them that *The Gay Science* wished to turn: 'In a word – and let this be our word of honour – we are good Europeans, the rich heirs of millennia of European spirit, with too many provisions but also too many obligations' (FW, 377 [241–2]).

So, what were the wars that were on the horizon? These were the years in which Western colonial expansion was advancing ever more vehemently. In Germany, too, the participation of the country in the competition taking place among the great powers was ever more noisily demanded. One manifestation of this mood was the foundation of the Deutscher Kolonialverein in 1882, the same year that saw the occupation of Egypt by Britain and the publication of *The Gay Science*. The more manly and martial period already hailed in the first edition acquired more precise contours in the second: there Nietzsche expressed the hope that, by building on the lessons of Napoleon, 'one Europe' would become 'mistress of the earth' (FW, 362 [267]).

Even in the 'Enlightenment' period, the philosopher looked with undoubted sympathy at the forward march of the expansionist West, among whose positive results belonged the end to the fear of 'barbarians' as well as of 'wild animals' (above, 9 §6). This process was particularly welcome because it could serve to defuse social conflict in the capitalist metropolis. In this respect, Nietzsche appealed to the German and European workers in general. Instead of becoming a 'slave of the state' as a result of the extension of state intervention in the economy, or worse still, 'a slave of the party of insurrection' and dupes of socialist propaganda, they would do better to take a different route:

> Better to emigrate, to seek in wild and fresh parts of the world to become *master*, and above all master of myself: to keep moving from place to place as long as any sign of slavery whatsoever still beckons to me; not to avoid adventure and war and, if worst should come to worst, to be ready for death: only no more of this indecent servitude, only no more of this growing sour and venomous and conspiratorial.
>
> M, 206 [154]

The emigration here recommended was of a warlike nature, it was the colonial expansion growing sectors of public opinion were calling for in Germany in this period. In 1879, two years before the publication of *The Dawn*, voices had been raised calling for the conquest of territories overseas as the main way of eradicating 'poisonous plants of socialist subversion' at home. In that way, 'overseas German master nations [*deutsche Herrennationen*]' could perhaps be created.[9]

---

9   In Wehler 1985, p. 143 f.

Here one is reminded of the 'sign of slavery' of which Nietzsche spoke. Thanks to these 'swarming migrations of colonists', *The Dawn* continued, Europe would cease to be 'overpopulated' and 'brooding in itself' because of the presence of 'workers' who were 'grumpy, irritable, and addicted to pleasure'. In conclusion: 'what inside the homeland began to degenerate into dangerous ill humor and criminal tendencies, will, outside, take on a wild, beautiful naturalness and will be called heroism' (M, 206 [154–5]). A similar conclusion was reached by the publicist quoted above, who credited colonisation with promoting 'the mass export of revolutionary explosives' and putting an end to 'socialist fermentation in the heads of our [...] propertyless masses'.[10]

And yet, fears were mixed in among the hopes. A subsequently deleted supplement to Aphorism 477 of *Human, All Too Human*, which, as is well known, celebrated the purifying virtues of war, talked of the 'socialist [...] wars', 'terrible' wars, which had to be confronted energetically: 'In order not to die of weakness, it is necessary to become barbarians' (XIV, 148). In this analysis of the political situation Nietzsche was also not isolated. Speaking one year after *Human, All Too Human*, the above-mentioned publicist commented: 'We live in the truest sense of the word on a volcano'. Social tension was gradually increasing and 'the hundredth anniversary of the French Revolution' might see the Second Reich submerged 'in a sea of blood'.[11]

In the following years, the assassination campaigns in Germany and Russia and the general radicalisation of the socialist and anarchist movement seemed to confirm that it was impossible to deal with the protest of the subaltern classes peacefully: 'social wars' were the order of the day (IX, 546). At the international level, further upheavals were to be expected, which, beyond the colonies, also tended to envelop the great powers. Nietzsche's gaze was directed towards Russia, already described in *The Wanderer and His Shadow* as 'the extended jaws of Asia, which would like to swallow up tiny Europe' (*supra*, 9 §7).

We were at the start of 1880. In October of the previous year, Germany had sealed an alliance with Austria, also in response to the pressure, perceived as threatening, of Russia. Alexander II, disappointed and frustrated by the outcome of the Congress of Berlin, which, on the initiative above all of Britain, had blocked the advance of his country in the Balkans and in the direction of the Straits, had sent a severe letter, little short of an ultimatum (the so-called 'slap letter'), to Wilhelm I. The danger (according to Bismarck in a letter to the

---

10   In Wehler 1985, p. 144.
11   In Wehler 1985, p. 143.

German Kaiser) of 'a barbaric attack' seemed to have become real.[12] In the following years, the tension did not slacken. In 1885–6, when a new crisis hit the Balkans, it seemed once again to become acute.[13] Perhaps the analysis in *Beyond Good and Evil* should be seen in this context. While the European countries often looked enfeebled, 'the force of will' continued to manifest itself impetuously 'in that vast intermediary zone where Europe, as it were, flows back into Asia: in Russia', which seemed to be exerting pressure in all directions:

> More than just Indian wars and Asian intrigues might be needed to relieve Europe of its greatest danger – inner rebellions might be needed as well, the dispersion of the empire into small bodies, and, above all, the introduction of parliamentary nonsense, added to which would be the requirement that every man read his newspaper over breakfast.
>
> JGB, 208 [101]

To prevent misunderstandings, Nietzsche immediately made clear that his preferences were in the opposite direction, but he stressed it was a matter of confronting a real danger. Against Russia, he proposed a *Realpolitik* similar to that put into effect by Bismarck against France and denounced in *Human, All Too Human*: to weaken the enemy country, it could be useful to promote political institutions within it capable of causing it to weaken or disintegrate. The 'increase in the threat Russia poses' was not just a danger but an opportunity. In the face of this challenge, Europe might feel compelled to choose

> to become equally threatening and, specifically, to acquire a single will by means of a new caste that would rule over Europe, a long, terrible will of its own, that could give itself millennia-long goals: – so that the long, spun-out comedy of Europe's petty provincialism and its dynastic as well as democratic fragmentation of the will could finally come to an end. The time for petty politics is over: the next century will bring the struggle for the domination of the earth – the compulsion to great politics.
>
> JGB, 208 [102]

In conclusion, one can say the following: Nietzsche's denunciation of chauvinism within Western Europe, far from being an act of homage to the ideal of peace, was of a piece with his scorn for the 'French Revolution, which aimed at

---

12   In Fenske 1978, p. 237.
13   Treue 1958, p. 612 f.

the 'brotherhood' of peoples and a general, blooming exchange of hearts'. It was to Napoleon's credit that he had swept away this stupidity and rubbish. Thanks to him, '*man* in Europe [has] become the master over the businessman and the philistine' and perhaps of feminine sentimentality, and so had defeated 'civilization', which he hated with all his might, thus confirming that he was 'one of the greatest continuators of the Renaissance' (FW, 362 [227]). 'The instinct of every civilized society' tended towards safety, comfort, peace, and the 'taming' of human beings, to a condition in which those 'great human beings' that were the essential aim of every true 'culture' appeared superfluous or impossible. In this sense, there was an 'abysmal antagonism' between civilisation and culture (XIII, 485–6).

As in the years of *The Birth of Tragedy*, Nietzsche's target continued to be 'civilization', but now its antidote was no longer in Germany, as heir to tragic Hellenism, but in Europe, which was resuming the Napoleonic programme of internal unity and domination of the land:

> [A] few warlike centuries, incomparable to any other in history, are likely to follow in succession – in short, that we have entered the classic age of war, of sophisticated yet popular war on the largest scale (in terms of weapons, talents, discipline); all coming ages will look back on this kind of war with envy and deep respect as something perfect.
>
> FW, 362 [227]

PART 3

Nietzsche in His Time:
Theory and Practice of Aristocratic Radicalism

..

[I]f you want slaves, then it is stupid to train them to be masters.

GD, 40 [216]

• • •

Who should be master of the earth? This is the refrain of my practical philosophy.

XI, 76

• • •

No study seems to me more essential than the laws of breeding.

XI, 480

• • •

Annihilation of the decadent races.

XI, 69

• • •

Annihilation of those that have turned out badly – for that, one must free oneself from contemporary morality.

XI, 75

• • •

Acquire that enormous energy of greatness in order, on the one hand by breeding and on the other by annihilating millions of those that have turned out badly, to shape the future human being and not to perish because of the pain that one creates and that is of a like one has never seen before.

XI, 98

• • •

Anyone who "explains" an author's passage "more profoundly" than it was meant has not explained the author, but *obscured* him.

WS, 17 [161]

• •
•

CHAPTER 12

Slavery in the United States and in the Colonies and the Struggle between Abolitionists and Anti-abolitionists

1 The Chariot of Culture and Slavery

As we have already seen, the theorist of aristocratic radicalism pointed to the need for a 'new slavery'. Even while writing *The Birth of Tragedy*, Nietzsche tirelessly asserted that slavery was inseparable from culture. Towards the end of his conscious life, he stated: '[I]f you want slaves, then it is stupid to train them to be masters' (XIII, 30, cf. GD, 40 [216]). To give them an education meant only to whip up a slave revolt, with catastrophic consequences. At bottom, it was in the interest not only of culture as a whole but also that of the slaves themselves that they did not become unadapted to the condition they suffered and had to suffer. This culture could be likened to a 'a victor dripping with blood, who, in his triumphal procession, drags the vanquished along, chained to his carriage as slaves', slaves that under normal conditions were blinded by a 'charitable power' that stopped them from becoming aware of the chains that held them captive (CV, 3, I, 768–9 [167]). The ideologues that strove to proclaim foolish programmes of general emancipation were the cruellest enemies of those they claimed to favour: 'If a slave in prison dreams of being free and released from servitude, who will be so hard-hearted as to wake him and tell him he is only dreaming?' (B, I, 2, 229).

So, slavery is a troublesome presence that is as if suppressed in the philosophical historiography and boundless literature about Nietzsche. It is understandable that, in the case of an author so fascinating and often viewed as a theorist of individualism, interpreters tend to consider this obsessively recurring theme as a paradox or an innocent and charming metaphor. On the other hand, what is 'truth' if not 'a mobile army of metaphors' (*supra*, 2 § 3)?

And yet one must not lose sight of the historical context. Nietzsche's beginnings fell in a period in which slavery was abolished in the United States and serfdom in Russia. In the following years, while forms of slavery or semi-slavery persisted in both countries, the debate on these issues at the international level was intense. Britain, which abolished slavery in its colonies in 1833, proceeded in the 1870s and 1880s to institute a naval blockade of the East African coast to prevent the continuing slave trade, above all in the direction of Brazil, which did not abolish slavery and the slave trade until 1888 – the year in which Nietzsche's conscious life drew to a close. It is also worth remembering that the entire historical period was notable for resolutions and treaties, like the one signed by Britain and Zanzibar in 1873, prohibiting the slave trade,[1] while in 1874 new states were founded or new settlements established on the coast of East Africa for former slaves, often at the instigation of Christian missions.[2] Finally, in 1884–5 in Berlin, the International Congo Conference delineated the spheres of influence in Africa of the colonial powers, which jointly undertook, not without a strong element of hypocrisy, to combat slavery. As the French Prime Minister Jules Ferry noted, the moral duty 'to fight the slave trade, this terrible traffic, and slavery, this infamy', was finally translated 'into positive law, into an obligation sanctioned by the signatures of all governments.'[3]

The debate also enveloped Prussia and Germany, at the highest political level, and not just because the conference was hosted in Berlin. It seems that at the outbreak of the American Civil War Bismarck had shown that he 'felt some sympathy for the people of the southern United States', even though he would have preferred a more humane treatment for blacks.[4] Similar sympathies were widespread in the officer corps: a reception they organised in July 1864 for officers of the Confederacy led to a protest by the Union and to an embarrassed denial or distancing on the part of the Prussian government.[5] The controversy did not end with the Civil War, but developed further with regard to the colonies. On 30 September 1890, shortly after his removal from office as Chancellor, Bismarck inspired an article in the *Hamburger Nachrichten* in which he distinguished between the slavery, cruel but now disappeared, in the southern United States, and the still existing slavery in the Muslim states, where the slave was basically a 'servant family member [*dienender Hausgenosse*]', well treated and content with his or her lot.[6] Wilhelm II, on the other hand, became the target of Nietzsche's polemic and sarcasm, in which the philosopher criticised the Kaiser's enthusiastic engagement in the struggle for the liberation of the 'black domestic slaves [*Hausknechte*]' (*infra*, 17 §3).

The debate also extended to the study of antiquity: in 1848 Henri Wallon published his *Histoire de l'esclavage dans l'antiquité*. In the long preface (a book within a book) he came out firmly in favour of the abolition of slavery in the

1   Renault 1971, Vol. 1, p. 89.
2   Hammer 1978, pp. 155, 295 f.; Warneck 1889, p. 36 f.
3   In Girardet 1983, p. 104.
4   Stolberg-Wernigerode 1933, pp. 60 f., 74.
5   Lutz 1911, p. 51.
6   Stolberg-Wernigerode 1933, p. 75.

French colonies, as decided by the republic that had emerged from the February Revolution. The second edition of the book by the *Secrétaire perpétuel de l'Académie des Inscriptions et Belles-Lettres* followed in 1879, the last year in which Nietzsche taught classical philology in Basel.

The involvement of the philologists is easy to understand. Wallon noted, in opposing the abolition of slavery in the French colonies, that 'the supporters of the *status quo* appeal to antiquity'.[7] In the United States, too, the anti-abolitionist polemic repeatedly hailed the wonderful flowering of ancient Greece, unthinkable without the presence of that charitable institution so hateful to the wretched ideologues that lack all sense of reality. A significant pronouncement was attributed to John Calhoun, the best-known theorist of Southern slavery: 'That if he could find a Negro who knew Greek syntax, he would then believe that the Negro was a human being and should be treated as a man.'[8] Aristotle's *Politics* was a constant point of reference not only for Calhoun but also for Fitzhugh, another leading theorist of slavery. More generally, in the years before the Civil War the study of Latin and Greek classics was central to the curriculum of schools and universities in the South.[9] Chateaubriand, with whose literary writings Nietzsche was familiar, reported on the debate that took place in the North American republic: 'A Virginia representative has championed the cause of ancient freedom and in so doing pointed to the existence of slavery as a result of paganism and used it to polemicize against a representative from Massachusetts who defended the cause of modern freedom without slaves, as brought about by Christianity.'[10]

These arguments in defence of slavery were not unlike those later found in Nietzsche. Anti-abolitionist propaganda sometimes pointed, as an alternative to or in combination with classical antiquity, to Paul of Tarsus and his letter to Philemon, the fugitive slave invited to return to his master.[11] But the young Nietzsche also credited 'primitive Christianity' with not having taken exception to the institution of slavery (*supra*, 1 § 10). Not many years before, eminent Christian conservatives (for example, Otto von Gerlach) had come out publicly in favour of the secessionists, said to have risen up in defence of an institution sanctified not only by 'nature' but by 'revelation'.[12]

---

7   Wallon 1974b, p. iv and Wallon 1974a, p. xxxiii.
8   Crummel 1897.
9   Harrington 1989.
10   Chateaubriand 1973, Vol. 1, p. 328; Chateaubriand is often cited in the posthumous fragments.
11   Stolberg-Wernigerode 1933, p. 62.
12   Lutz 1911, pp. 50, 63 f. and Bowman 1993, p. 23.

Even in the mature Nietzsche one finds this fragment: 'survival of lapsed ideals (e.g., slavery in Augustine)' (XII, 27). Now, however, the philosopher-philologist had taken note of the churches' role in the abolitionist struggle, a role highly significant and even hegemonic in certain settings (particularly in Britain and the United States).[13] Abolitionism in these two countries was the most frequent target of his polemic. He did not even spare *Uncle Tom's Cabin*, the famous abolitionist novel (XI, 61), whose author (Harriet Beecher-Stowe) could be seen as a clear embodiment of American puritanism: 'The daughter of a pastor, the wife of another pastor, with brothers and sons who were also pastors, she always lived in a religious atmosphere. She was born among religious beliefs, and the language of sermons shaped her childish stammering.'[14]

On the Catholic side, the Holy See bestowed a form of official recognition on a text that appeared in its first edition in 1876, crediting Christianity with the disappearance of ancient slavery.[15] Just over ten years after that, the Catholic Church, through Cardinal Lavigerie, led the campaign or crusade to abolish slavery in the colonies, even managing to involve Germany, thus rousing Nietzsche to sarcasm and indignation (*infra*, 17 §3). If the mature Nietzsche connected Christianity and slave revolt and even found in Paul of Tarsus a fierce servile and plebeian *ressentiment*, that too cannot be seen apart from events of *his* time.

In France, however, the abolitionist movement received its impulse from the revolution. In saying that, it should be noted, however, that the *cahiers de doléance* that at the time of the convocation of the Estates General criticised the slave trade and the institution of slavery often originated with the clergy.[16] Within the abolitionist movement, the figure of Abbé Grégoire took a prominent place. Revolutionary France first granted honorary citizenship to the Anglican clergyman Wilhelm Wilberforce, described as 'the most zealous and the most eloquent defender of negroes',[17] and later, with the Jacobins, carried out the emancipation of the slaves in the colonies. After Napoleon revoked this, the democratic socialist movement took the lead in the struggle for the final abolition of slavery in the colonies, and it is not by chance that this goal was achieved with the February Revolution. These events also found an echo in

---

13   Hammer 1978, *passim.*
14   Parrington 1954, p. 363.
15   Allard 1974; the text is preceded by a letter to the author of *Secrétaire de Sa Sainteté Pie IX pour les lettres latines.*
16   Blackburn 1990, p. 172.
17   Godechot 1956, p. 133 f.

Nietzsche's thinking. This is clear, for example, from his interpretation of Christianity, French Revolution and socialism as the three stages in the slave revolt. The Napoleon the philosopher treasured was the man who came to power brandishing the slogan of the end of the revolution and who, three years later, in 1802, enacted the law whose first article stated: in the colonies 'slavery will be maintained in accordance with the laws and regulations in force before 1789'.[18] In the parliamentary debates, no few politicians wanted to go to the 'school of the ancients' and put an end to the 'badly hidden philanthropy' that had originated with the French Revolution.[19] On the opposite side, to quote an author known to Nietzsche, Herzen denounced Napoleon as the 'restorer of slavery'.[20]

If this was the historical frame, a metaphorical interpretation of slavery seems rather problematic. Nietzsche would rekindle this 'metaphor' at a time when slavery was a very tangible reality and at the centre of gigantic struggles and a passionate debate that also draws in philosophers, writers and antiquarians.

2   Nietzsche, Slavery and the Anti-abolitionist Polemic

In Germany, it was no different. Let us focus on authors Nietzsche knew and valued. A novella by Kleist (*Betrothal in Santo Domingo*), set at the beginning of the nineteenth century, described the slave revolt in bleak colours: rash measures by the French Revolution unleashed a 'general frenzy of revenge' and the 'madness of freedom' led in reality to the 'slaughter of the whites'. The debate about slavery was closely linked with that about the French Revolution and the colonial question. In 1829, in his conversations with Eckermann, Goethe made fun of the 'declamations against the slave trade' in which England was indulging. He said it was putting on a display of 'moral maxims' but in reality it was unscrupulously and cynically pursuing its own 'mercantilist' and colonial interests. That is why, at the Congress of Vienna, it clashed with the Portuguese delegate, who pointed out he had not come to listen to lectures on 'moral principles' or to attend sessions of a 'universal court'. The conclusion: 'While the Germans torment themselves with solving philosophical problems, the English, with their great practical sense, deride us and conquer the world.'[21]

---

18   In Césaire 1961, p. 291 f.
19   In Césaire 1961, pp. 285 and 287 f.
20   Herzen 1871, p. 63.
21   Eckermann 1981, p. 347 f. (talk of 1 September 1829).

Speaking a few years later about this same problem, Schopenhauer instead praised the 'generous British nation' for its campaign against slavery and the slave trade.[22] The debate continued over the years and decades to come. Articles by anti-abolitionists continued to echo the arguments already seen in Goethe and the polemic against the 'hypocrisy' of the British, who in the 1870s and 1880s mounted naval blockades off the coast of East Africa to stop the slave trade.[23] This is the historical context in which we must view Nietzsche's statement that to oppose the unquestionable 'fact' of slavery and its necessity was hypocritical, or rather, to use his own term, 'damned English-European *cant*' (XI, 72–3).

The anti-abolitionist stance is clear, and with regard not only to the colonies but also to the American Civil War. One should bear in mind the argument that defenders of slavery used against the abolitionists: the condition of free workers was no better than that of slaves. In these years, a whole literature blossomed in which factory labour was compared with slave labour on the plantations, and wage slavery, described in implacably harsh tones, with actual slavery, described in mystified terms as if immersed in an atmosphere of patriarchal moderation: even in the titles 'English serfdom' was contrasted with 'American slavery', the 'hireling' with the 'slave'.[24]

This theme was naturally echoed in the anti-abolitionist press in Germany. Here are some of the most significant contributions: 'In Surinam, if an owner wished to impose on his female slaves just one-sixth of the daily labour [that male and female factory workers in Europe and the United States are forced to do], he would immediately forfeit the right to keep slaves on account of demanding excessive labour.'[25] The 'white slavery' in the British factories was, according to this argument, far more ruthless than the generally paternal and benevolent slavery in force on the plantations of the southern states of the United States.[26]

Even Kleist, an author with whose work the adolescent Nietzsche was already quite familiar (A, 43), wrote immediately after the Civil War that the fate of the black slaves in the United States was more acceptable and dignified than that of white workers in England.[27] An aphorism in *Human, All Too Human*

22   Schopenhauer 1976–82d, p. 763.
23   Cf. Lémonon 1971, p. 161; Hammer 1978, p. 296.
24   Parrington 1954, pp. 57–103; of the debate in France and the USA, cf. Canfora 1980, pp. 23–30.
25   Duttenhofer 1855, p. 70.
26   Bensen 1965, pp. 428–30.
27   Kleist 1973.

titled 'Slaves and workers' made a not dissimilar point: everyone desired the 'abolition of slavery'; however, one had to admit that 'slaves live more securely and happily in every respect than the modern worker [*Arbeiter*]' and 'the work [*Arbeit*] of slaves involves very little work compared with that of the worker' (MA, 457 [246]).

Nietzsche began his academic research with a study on Theognis: this work, deeply permeated by the issue of slavery, coincided with the years of the Civil War. The philologist cited the verse of the Greek poet: 'The slave never holds his head erect, / his neck is always bent and bowed. / From a squill will come no rose or hyacinth, / of a slave a free child is never born' (DTM, 15, 57). He argued it was stupid and criminal to wish to change the order of nature. Again, he quoted Theognis and identified with him: 'By teaching you will never make a bad one good' (DTM, 15, 59). It is hard to believe there is no relationship between the worldview outlined here and the huge clash happening at the same time in the United States. On at least one occasion, Nietzsche argued for the relevance of his analysis: as a further demonstration of the importance of wealth for the development of a class devoted exclusively to 'culture' and the 'liberal arts', he explicitly cited the events unfolding before his eyes, in 'our days [*nostris temporibus*]' (DTM, 15, 59).

In any case, when we read of the Greek poet's contempt for 'the noble blood contaminated by intermarriage with new people' (DTM, 3, 29), we are reminded of miscegenation in the sense against which theorists of slavery or white supremacy warned. The term was coined by juxtaposing Latin *miscere* and *genus*, at the end of 1863,[28] precisely the period in which Nietzsche was busy not only with Theognis but also with the United States and 'religious conditions' in that country (KZD, 18–31). When, twenty years later, Nietzsche returned to the Greek poet, defined and celebrated as the 'mouthpiece' of the aristocracy, and the underlying opposition of his youthful essay between *agathos* (the 'good' and noble slave owner) and *kakos* (primarily the 'bad' and despicable slave), he translated *kakos* by *malus* but also by *niger*. On the other hand, the *Genealogy of Morals* associated *malus* with *melas*; so *kakos* was identified because of skin and hair colour with the representative of a race different from and opposite to the 'blond race which had become dominant', the Aryan 'conquering race' (GM, I, 5 [14]). Here it occurs to us that, across the Atlantic, the spectre of miscegenation is also the spectre of *melaeukation*. Although this second term is much less happily chosen than the first – champions of purity do not always possess the classical culture of their leaders – it was coined simul-

---

28   Wood 1968, p. 53 ff.

taneously with it, again by the same authors and circles, and obtained this time by borrowing and combining the Greek *melas* (black) and *leukas* (white).[29]

There can be no doubt, in any case, that the young philologist looked with great interest at the United States. This is confirmed by the lecture he gave in mid-March 1865 on the 'religious conditions' of Germans in North America. In the meantime, the Southerners had almost been defeated (the formal surrender took place on 9 April), so it is understandable that nothing was said about a war already over. Yet this lecture is important for its references to the political situation. This particularly applies to the contempt expressed for the German democrats that had emigrated to America after the failure of the revolution of 1848 (KZD, 24–5) and were now to the fore of the press campaign for the abolition of slavery.[30] Here, one should not lose sight of the fact that, at certain times, the German press reported daily on this abolitionist activity.[31]

Let us now look at the correspondence. When, in December 1867, Carl von Gersdorff wrote to tell his friend Nietzsche that 'capital and labour are struggling against each other in France, in England, in America, among us', it is not difficult to hear an echo of the Civil War ended two years earlier (apart from the Civil War, which resulted in the emancipation of the slaves, the United States seemed to be immune from acute social conflict) (B, I, 3, 224). A few years later – in the meantime, *The Birth of Tragedy* had appeared – Rohde emphasised 'the profound upheaval that the abolition of slavery must have caused in all conditions and goals of cultural life'. In this case too, the topic of conversation was not the distant past. Despite the references to classical antiquity, the main issue was the present. Hellas pursued as its supreme goal the creation of 'genius' and did so with the necessary 'harshness and cruelty'; now, along with the latter, the 'most noble fruits' of that splendid culture had also vanished (B, II, 4, 622–4). Rohde's letter was addressed to both Nietzsche and Overbeck. The historian of Christianity, in his turn, noted in 1875 in his research on slavery the 'vanishing from our lives of a piece of antiquity'.[32] Again, this was a reference to the conflict that had ended ten years previously. On the other hand, Nietzsche, at least since the 'Enlightenment' period, had shown great though polemical

---

29   Wood 1968, p. 54.
30   Particularly significant is the figure of Friedrich Kapps, Feuerbach's friend and correspondent: a book by him about slavery and the struggles that preceded the Civil War (*Die Sklavenfrage in den Vereinigten Staaten, geschichtlich entwickelt*, Göttingen-New York 1854), was praised in *Preussische Jahrbücher* I, 1858, p. 475.
31   Lutz 1911, p. 47.
32   Overbeck 1994–5a, p. 144.

interest not only in Dühring but also in Carey (VIII, 587 [396]), authors whose work was full of references to the slave trade, the problem of slavery and the Civil War, that still 'mighty' event that marked the end of the influence, even beyond the United States, of 'Southern slavery'.[33]

Let us now return to the fragment that polemicised against the author of *Uncle Tom's Cabin*: Nietzsche emphasised here the critical role of suffering and of compassion for the suffering in the movements of revolt (XI, 61). This subject was central particularly to the *Genealogy of Morals*:

> Now, when suffering is always the first of the arguments marshalled against life, as its most questionable feature, it is salutary to remember the times when people made the opposite assessment, because they could not do without making people suffer and saw first-rate magic in it, a veritable seductive lure to life. Perhaps pain – I say this to comfort the squeamish – did not hurt as much then as it does now; at least, a doctor would be justified in assuming this, if he had treated a Negro (taken as a representative for primeval man) for serious internal inflammations which would drive the European with the stoutest constitution to distraction; – they do not do that to Negroes. (The curve of human capacity for pain actually does seem to sink dramatically and almost precipitously beyond the first ten thousand or ten million of the cultural elite.)
>
> GM, II, 7 [43–4]

Abolitionist publications in these years covered in great detail the inhuman suffering inflicted on black slaves by their masters. In response, a large body of 'medical' literature attributed to blacks not only a lesser intelligence but a greater ability to endure pain. One doctor, Carus, noted that 'the development of delicacy and sensitivity in the skin' was far more pronounced in whites.[34] Among the young Nietzsche's notes was a transcript of another paper by Carus and of two texts by Lorenz Oken (KGA, I, 4, 576), a naturalist who was part of the same circle as Carus[35] and exchanged opinions with him on these issues.[36] Wagner also believed that 'the capacity for conscious pain' was particularly developed in the 'white race':[37] however strong the 'suffering', among

---

33   Dühring 1871, p. 373 and *passim*; Dühring 1871 had a lot to say about Henry Charles Carey, author of *The Slave Trade* (1853).
34   Carus 1849, p. 21.
35   Cf. Schnabel on 'natural philosophy' and the 'romantic doctors' (1954, pp. 172–99).
36   Carus 1849, pp. 13 and 104, fn. 14.
37   Wagner 1910r, p. 281.

the 'lower natures' it did not reach full self-consciousness, because they were
to a certain extent protected by the inadequacy of their intellectual development.[38]

Even the representation of blacks as 'prehistoric people' was less general
than appears at first sight. This again brings us back to the anti-abolitionists,
who distinguished between 'peoples that have a history and peoples whose
history so far is a blank page': blacks stood outside the historical 'human species'.[39] Gobineau devoted a section of his book to the thesis that 'only the white
peoples have history'.[40]

3   Between Reintroduction of Classical Slavery and 'New Slavery'

Was Nietzsche really thinking of reintroducing actual slavery in Europe?
Today's interpreter often forgets that claims about the permanent validity
and actuality of this institution have long dominated Western history. In England in the seventeenth and eighteenth centuries, a philosopher as famous as
Hutcheson hoped to reintroduce slavery as a remedy for the scourge of vagabondage. As the case of Andrew Fletcher, 'a Scottish prophet of Enlightenment'
of the late seventeenth century, demonstrated, one could simultaneously be
a 'champion of freedom' and a 'champion of slavery' for the idle and incorrigible mob.[41] It was precisely against such views that Hume was arguing when
he pungently observed: 'Some passionate admirers of the ancients, and zealous
partisans of civil liberty [...] cannot forbear regretting the loss of this institution', meaning slavery.[42]

In France, we can read in Montesquieu: 'One can daily hear it said that it
would be good if we had slaves.'[43] Here, the target was principally Melon. But,
in the French context, the most significant author was, without doubt, Linguet,
who, also in the eighteenth century, never tired of reiterating the indissolubil-
ity of the link between slavery and culture, in accents reminiscent of Nietzsche:
'Most of the human race' was forced to act as an 'instrument', as 'artificial arms

38   Wagner 1910r, p. 277.
39   Duttenhofer 1855, p. 17.
40   Gobineau 1983, p. 623 ff. (Book 4, 1).
41   Morgan 1975, p. 324d; Davis 1966, pp. 405–10 (on Hutcheson); on Fletcher and his efforts
      to turn the 'beggars' into 'slaves', see Marx in *Capital* (cf. Marx and Engels 1955 ff., pp. 23,
      750, fn. 197).
42   Hume 1971, p. 786.
43   Montesquieu 1949–51, p. 497 (Book 15, 9).

and legs' in the service of those who developed culture and art; the suffering that resulted was the price of culture.[44]

This chapter of history by no means ended with the eighteenth century. In analysing the 'bloody legislation against vagabondage', Marx stressed that in Britain labour relations essentially of a slave type continued to exist deep into the nineteenth century. But attention must naturally focus primarily on the United States. For the purposes of a comparison with Nietzsche, of particular importance were those authors that, rather than focus their arguments on the racial destiny of the blacks, formulated a more general thesis: 'In all social systems there must be a class to do the menial duties, to perform the drudgery of life.' Thus argued one of those theorists of the South keen to 'recommend slavery as an answer to the European social problem'.[45] The most prominent and best-known exponent of this school of thought was Fitzhugh, according to whom 'slavery represents the correct relationship between every sort of labor and capital'.[46]

In Europe, Proudhon polemicised against the French journalist and politician Granier de Cassagnac, who died in 1880. According to Cassagnac, one was not to suppress slavery, this 'institution anterior and superior to society', but socialism, guilty of poisoning minds with the dream of an impossible emancipation of labour.[47] One was to admit reality: humanity was inevitably divided into a *'race libre'* and a *'race esclavage'*. The above-mentioned Wallon, angry about the 'philosophy of slavery', also opposed this vision of the world.[48]

The text Proudhon criticised was immediately translated into German.[49] However, voices were also raised on German soil that independently expressed a similar orientation. In *Vormärz*, a liberal distanced himself vehemently from the 'advice, admittedly more intimated than clearly pronounced, of those who would seek help against the impending danger (an unsolved and acute social problem) in the introduction of a formal *slavery of factory workers*'.[50] Such proposals were sometimes made by compassionate people horrified by the spectacle in these years of capitalist industrialisation. After pointing out that the worker's condition was far worse than the slave's, Lamennais added: 'In truth

---

44   Linguet 1984, pp. 444, 438 and 457 (Book 5, chs 1, 2, and 4).
45   In Genovese 1995b, p. 93; Genovese 1995a, p. 39.
46   In Genovese 1978, p. 139.
47   Proudhon 1858, p. 266.
48   Wallon 1974a, pp. xxvi, xxxiii and *passim*.
49   Cassagnac 1977.
50   Mohl 1981, p. 91.

I am not surprised that some who consider only the material aspect of things and view the present separately from the future lament, in our famous culture, ancient slavery.'[51]

Carlyle characterised the Irish as 'blacks' and, at the same time, justified the enslavement of Afro-Americans in America.[52] In his writings, one can find themes familiar to the reader of Nietzsche:

> I have come to the sad conclusion that Slavery, whether established by law, or by law abrogated, exists very extensively in this world, in and out of the West Indies; and, in fact, that you cannot abolish slavery by act of parliament, but can only abolish the name of it, which is very little![53]

Whether one was talking of slaves or of 'wage slaves for life' or of '*adscripti glebae*', it was still slavery.[54] It was an institution that belonged to the natural order: 'It is the slavery of the strong to the weak; of the great and noble-minded to the small and mean! The slavery of Wisdom to Folly'; on the other hand, the supposed emancipations were both precondition and result of devastating 'anarchistic-constitutional epochs'.[55]

A few decades later, Langbehn, as his biographer noted, hoped for 'the reintroduction of slavery' in order to enable the 'superior races' to devote themselves without hindrance to 'free occupations', art and culture, a goal that could be achieved only by clashing with the Church and promoting 'a Greco-German sovereign manliness.'[56] Not surprisingly, Langbehn was a great admirer of Nietzsche ...

After the end of the Civil War, Nietzsche was well aware of the difficulty or impossibility of reintroducing slavery in the strict sense of the word in Europe and the West, especially since the development of modernity and socialist agitation had put an end to the beneficent blinding of those chained to the chariot of culture. It was necessary to take cognisance of the new situation: 'Indeed in the European states the culture of the worker and of the employer is often so close that continuing to demand from the workers gruelling mechanical labour evokes a feeling of indignation.' A wide and ever growing space had opened up

---

51   In Bravo 1973, p. 91.
52   Carlyle 1983, pp. 463–5.
53   Carlyle 1983, p. 439.
54   Carlyle 1983, pp. 464 and 466.
55   Carlyle 1983, p. 439. At the end of the nineteenth century these comments were repeated by Anthony James Froude, an admirer of Carlyle and of British imperialism.
56   Nissen 1926, p. 37.

for agitation by the 'socialists' who 'make justice their principle'. Certainly, it was necessary to oppose this agitation also on the theoretical plane. One should not hesitate to proclaim a truth that has become uncomfortable in the modern world, that 'human rights do not exist' (VIII, 482). Since 'the socialists want the complete overthrow of society, they appeal to power', and so ended up in contradiction with the moral principles they invoked. It might well be necessary to press these arguments, but with them alone one would not be able to eliminate socialist agitation once and for all. So, what was to be done?

> If the need for and the refinement of a superior culture penetrates the working class, it can no longer do that work without suffering disproportionately. A worker thus developed aspires to *otium* and does not ask for a lightening of labour but for liberation from it, i.e., to impose its burden on another. One could perhaps think of satisfying his desires and massively introducing barbaric Asian and African populations, so that the civilized world continues to use the services of the uncivilized world, and thus non-culture would be considered precisely to be a sort of *corvée*.
>
> VIII, 481–2

So, it would be good 'to bring in the *Chinese* at that point: and they would bring along the ways of thinking and living that are suitable for diligent ants' (M. 206 [155]). The 'barbarian peoples from Asia and Africa' could also be sought in their places of origin by workers fleeing the slave labour that had in the meantime become problematic in Europe. In short: either turn the European working class into something of 'Chinese type' (GD, 40 [216]), a 'worker-*chinoiserie* [*Arbeiter-Chinesenthum*]' (XIII, 30), or the Chinese and the other barbarian peoples had, as a result of colonisation or immigration, to form the menial and working class of Europe and the civilised world.

Once again, this was not a metaphor. A similar position could be found in the utterances of Renan:

> Nature has made a race of workers, the Chinese race, who have wonderful manual dexterity and almost no sense of honor; govern them with justice, levying from them, in return for such a government, an ample allowance for the conquering race, and they will be satisfied; a race of tillers of the soil, the Negro; treat him with kindness and humanity, and all will be as it should; a race of masters and soldiers, the European race. Reduce this noble race to working in the *ergastulum* like Negros and Chinese, and they rebel. In Europe every rebel is, more or less, a soldier who has missed his calling, a creature made for the heroic life, before whom you are setting a

task that is contrary to his race – a poor worker, too good a soldier. But the life at which our workers rebel would make a Chinese or a fellah happy, as they are not military creatures in the least. Let each one do what he is made for, and all will be well.[57]

It should be added that Nietzsche's and Renan's proposals and suggestions were by no means the lonely fruit of purely abstract and bookish speculation: these were the years in which, for example, the American railway companies began building a line destined to consolidate the conquest of the Far West by importing more than 10,000 'coolies [labourers]' from China.[58] The Civil War was over. As Engels noted in a comment on Marx's *Poverty of Philosophy*, an attempt was under way to substitute for open black slavery, by that time formally abolished, the 'disguised slavery of Indian and Chinese coolies'. In this same period, 20,000 Egyptian fellaheen were used as slaves or semi-slaves to construct the Suez Canal, and many lost their lives.[59] This was the full picture of the 'barbarian peoples from Asia and Africa' of which Nietzsche spoke. We conclude with a comment by Lamennais:

> Ancient slavery, modified only in its forms, and modified to the disadvantage of the slave, yet actually subsists in the midst of modern societies, even those the most advanced; but it is there in contradiction to both the idea and the feeling of a right henceforth steadfastly homed in the reason of the public, in the universal conscience.[60]

Nietzsche's concern was precisely to eliminate this 'idea' and this 'feeling'.

4   Labour and *servitus* in the Liberal Tradition

When Nietzsche made fun of the new 'dignity' attributed to labour and asserted that, in any healthy culture, labour was synonymous with vulgarity and servitude, he took classical antiquity as his point of reference. In fact, we are dealing with themes that remained vitally important well after the decline of the Greco-Roman world and even of the Middle Ages. Let us interrogate the

---

57 Renan 1947 ff., Vol. 1, p. 390 f.
58 Nevins/Commager 1943, p. 338.
59 Sombart 1987, Vol. 3, p. 327. Lesseps, who built the Suez Canal, is referred to in a letter from Nietzsche written after the start of his madness (B III/5, 578).
60 In Bravo 1973, p. 384.

liberal tradition, starting with Grotius, for whom slavery was a fully legitimate institution. One of its sources was martial law. The victor guaranteed the life of the vanquished, who offered in exchange labour and lifelong services. As a relationship, it was essentially no different from that established between masters and 'those who, under constraint of poverty, have sold themselves into slavery'.[61] An aphorism in *Human, All Too Human* spoke in similar terms: 'The enemy gains an advantage from [...] preservation [of the loser]. – To this extent, there are even rights between slaves and masters, that is, precisely to the extent that the possession of the slave is useful and important for his master' (MA, 93 [71]).

But let us return to Grotius. For him, both wage labour and slavery had a contractual basis: master and slave, or prisoner and victor, agreed to lifetime subsistence in exchange for services. On the other hand, the work itself was subsumed under the category of *servitus*: slavery in the proper sense of the word was 'the vilest kind of subjection' and the most complete, it was *servitus perfecta*, as distinct from the *servitus imperfecta* of serfs and also of *mercenarii* or wage labourers.[62]

Locke's point of view was not much different. While viewing slavery in the colonies as uncontroversial and obvious, the British liberal philosopher spoke in the following terms about wages in the capitalist metropolis: 'A freeman makes himself a servant to another.' As is evident, labour itself continued to be subsumed under the category of *servitus*: in fact, the agreement put the wage worker 'into the family of his master, and under the ordinary discipline thereof', even if that discipline was very different from the 'absolute and unconditional dominion' of the master that characterised slavery and defined 'the perfect condition of slavery'.[63] We are back with Grotius's division into *servitus perfecta* and *servitus imperfecta*. To speak in this context of free labour would be an oxymoron, for freedom and labour were, as with Nietzsche, seen as antithetical.

With regard to the celebration of *otium* (the reverse of the contempt for the curse of slave labour), we see not only the after-effects of classical antiquity, to which Nietzsche explicitly referred, but also the liberal tradition. For example, Benjamin Constant justified the exclusion of non-owners from political rights as follows: *otium* and 'ease [*loisir*]' were 'indispensable for the acquisition of culture and correct judgement', and 'only property guarantees this ease, only ownership enables people to exercise their political rights'. But did this class

---

61   Grotius 1913, p. 544 (Book 3, 14, § 2).
62   Grotius 1913, p. 158 ff. (Book 2, 5, § 27 and § 30).
63   Locke 1970, pp. 157 f. and 128 (II, § 85 and § 24); on this point, cf. Losurdo 1992, 12, § 3.

that through its labour ensured the *otium* of the owners so they could exercise their political rights not remind one of the slaves of classical antiquity? No, replied Constant, 'here it is not a case of the distinctions that in ancient times separated slaves from free men'.[64] The theorist of liberalism rejected in advance the equation that Nietzsche, with greater ruthlessness, dared make explicit. And yet there is an undeniable element of continuity between the passionate glorifier of classical antiquity and polemicist against the modern world and the theorist of the superiority of modern over ancient liberty.

In Britain, one can also consider the case of Mandeville. Although he praised the harmony that resulted in bourgeois society from the various and opposing egoisms and private vices, he quietly noted that 'all the comforts of life', the 'civilized condition', depended on the 'hard and dirty labour' provided by the poor and 'the children of the poor' (rather than an open class, it was a sort of hereditary caste of pariahs). It is true that the condition of the workers was different from the actual slavery existing in the colonies,[65] but the distinction was sometimes evanescent: Mandeville himself acknowledged that 'the Hardships and Fatigues of War that are personally suffer'd, fall upon them that bear the Brunt of every Thing, the meanest Indigent Part of the Nation, the working slaving People'.[66]

Locke also described the development of wealth and culture as the result of the anonymous and brutalising hardship suffered by those Nietzsche called the 'blind moles of culture' (CV, 3, I, 770 [168]): for the British liberal, it was the workers who had to struggle for 'bare subsistence' and so never had 'time or opportunity to raise their thoughts above that'. Like Nietzsche's 'moles', the workers of whom Locke spoke did not and could not have a truly rational life, 'It is not to be expected that a human being who drudges on all his life in a laborious trade, should be more knowing in the variety of things done in the world than a packhorse, who is driven constantly forwards and backwards in a narrow lane and dirty road, only to market, should be skilled in the geography of the country'.[67] Although Locke praised labour with regard to the relationship between people and nature, in society, in the relationship between people and social classes, *otium* continued to be the precondition for culture and even for a truly human life.

If, for Nietzsche, the 'mole' was 'the slave' *tout-court*, for Locke, 'the greatest part of mankind who are given up to labour [...] are enslaved to the neces-

---

64   Constant 1957, p. 1146 f.
65   Mandeville 1924, p. 311.
66   Mandeville 1924, p. 119.
67   Locke 1963b, p. 160 (IV, XX, 2).

sity of their mean condition'.[68] This meant, in the second case, that this kind of 'slavery' was imposed not by a social class but by an objective condition. Mandeville and Locke took pains to distinguish modern wage labour from actual slavery (which they continued to take as given) in the colonies; Constant rejected the accusation that he wanted to equate manual workers with helots. Burke, on the other hand, did not hesitate to lump wage labour together with a set of occupations that were 'mercenary' and 'servile'.[69] Not without reason, Burke's translator and German disciple rendered the second term by *sklavisch* (slavish).[70] The figure of the worker tended once again to be confused with that of the slave. Moreover, Burke readily took over the distinction, typical for classical antiquity, between different work tools, and subsumed the wage labourer under the category of *instrumentum vocale*.[71] The English Whig did not mention the Roman scholar Varro, from whom the definition clearly derived,[72] but Nietzsche knew classical antiquity too well not to know that the *instrumentum vocale* was none other than the slave.

Behind Varro, of course, stood Aristotle. No less a person than Sieyès, the author of the most famous revolutionary manifesto of the French Revolution, demonstrated the influence of the great Greek philosopher when he contrasted 'a small, really small, number of free and thinking heads' with the 'greatest part of people' defined, especially in his private notes written before 1789, as 'labour machines [*machines de travail*]', 'work tools [*instruments de labeur*]', 'human instruments of production [*instruments humains de la production*]', or even 'two-legged instruments [*instruments bipèdes*]'.[73] These categories can also be found in Nietzsche, who himself defined wage labourers as 'intelligent machines' (AC, 57 [59]) or 'transmission tools' (XII, 491–2). But, in his case, the reference to classical antiquity was conscious: the expressions used refer directly to the Aristotelian definition of a slave as an 'instrument of action [*pratikon*]' used to transmit movement to those 'instruments of production [*organa poietika*]', i.e., the spools for whose operation the social figure of the slave is indispensable.[74]

We are already familiar with Nietzsche's violent polemic against a spread of education that would ultimately undermine the necessary subordination of

---

68   Locke 1963b, p. 159 (IV, XX, 2).
69   Burke 1826, Vol. 5, p. 105 f.
70   Gentz 1967, p. 91 f.
71   Burke 1826, Vol. 7, p. 383.
72   Varro, De re rustica, I, 17.
73   Sieyès 1985d, 236; Sieyès 1985c, pp. 75 and 81.
74   Aristotle, Politics, 1253b33–1254a8.

the sacrificial victims of culture. This theme too is found throughout the history of modern thought. For Necker, 'education is forbidden to all men born without property'; it would be a disaster if they were to develop 'the ability to reflect on the origin of ranks', of 'property', and of 'institutions'; one should not lose sight of the fact that 'inequality of knowledge' is 'necessary for the maintenance of all social inequalities'; to question 'the blinding of the people' and encourage 'the growth of enlightenment' among them would shake the social order.[75] This point was dealt with by Mandeville, with his usual ruthlessness:

> The Welfare and Felicity therefore of every State and Kingdom, require that the Knowledge of the Working Poor should be confin'd within the Verge of their Occupations, and never extended (as to things visible) beyond what relates to their Calling. The more a Shepherd, a Plowman or any other Peasant knows of the World, and the things that are Foreign to his Labour or Employment, the less fit he'll be to go through the Fatigues and Hardships of it with Chearfulness and Content.

The fact that one was forced to 'spend astronomical sums' to recruit workers for humble and tiresome occupations showed that 'the People of the meanest Rank know too much to be serviceable to us'.[76] Nietzsche had been able to read a critical discussion of this theme in Kant's *Critique of Judgement*:

> Skill cannot be developed in the human race except by means of inequality among men; for the great majority provide the necessities of life, as it were, mechanically, without requiring any art in particular, for the convenience and leisure of others who work at the less necessary elements of culture, science and art. In an oppressed condition they have hard work and little enjoyment, although much of the culture of the higher classes gradually spreads to them. Yet with the progress of this culture (the height of which is called luxury, reached when the propensity to what can be done without begins to be injurious to what is indispensable), their calamities increase equally in two directions, on the one hand through violence from without, on the other hand through internal discontent; but still this splendid misery is bound up with the development of the

---

75   Necker 1970–1, Vol. 1, p. 130 f. (this too is a passage that *Theories of Surplus Value* mentions: cf. Marx and Engels 1955 ff., 26, 1, p. 280 f).

76   Mandeville 1924, p. 302.

natural capacities of the human race, and the purpose of nature itself, although not our purpose, is thus attained.[77]

It was true that the hard work of the masses continued to be the precondition for *otium* and culture. But, unlike in the tradition we have examined up to now, by now this was no longer an indisputable and insuperable given: 1) the reality of oppression that the majority experienced was beginning to emerge into the open; 2) the privileged minority was being criticised for its 'insatiability' and for sacrificing to their own 'luxury' the vital needs of the working masses; and 3) this linking of poverty and hard work on the one hand and wealth and *otium* on the other was no longer understood as culture as such but as a much more ambiguous 'gilded misery [*glänzendes Elend*]'. Nietzsche was well aware of this, and, with specific reference to the *Critique of Judgement* (§ 65 note), criticised Kant for having seen 'in the French Revolution the transition from the inorganic to the organic form of the state' (AC 11 [10]). The attainment of the 'organic' form implied recognition of the intrinsic dignity of every human being, leading necessarily to an end to the 'instrumental' status accorded to the greater part of humanity. Kant identified so minimally with the *otium* of the privileged minority that in his *Lectures on Pedagogy* he strongly insisted on the importance, indeed the centrality, of labour: the school must somehow 'accustom the child to work'.[78]

5   The American Civil War, the Debate on the Role of Labour and the Special Nature of Germany

So, the nature of Nietzsche's polemic is clear. The radicalism and ruthlessness of his views were also influenced by the peculiarities of the situation in Germany. The apologetic preoccupations beginning to emerge in the more advanced European countries in the wake of the French Revolution and the industrial revolution manifested themselves only later in Germany. In France, especially after the workers' rising of June 1848, the liberal tradition seemed to bid farewell to the previous celebration of *otium*. Guizot raised a hymn to labour that oozed hypocrisy: 'The glory of modern civilization consists in recognizing and highlighting the moral and social importance of labour, and restoring to it the appropriate respect and status.' This labour was not that provided by wage-

---

77   Kant 1900 ff., Vol. 5, p. 432.
78   Kant 1900 ff., Vol. 9, p. 470 f.

dependent labourers: it was 'everywhere in this world'; it could be defined as the infinite 'variety of tasks and human missions'. Such a broad category could now embrace the condition of those social classes that, before the menacing emergence of the social question and the labour movement, boasted of their spotless purity with respect to material production.

Guizot had no difficulty in clarifying the ideological meaning of his utterances: it was a question of ensuring that 'the word labour' could no longer be a 'war cry' against the privileged layers. So it was an attempt to use this watchword to exactly opposite ends and against those who had first used it, and thus to take aim at the 'unintelligent, lazy, licentious workers'.[79] The targets, implicit or explicit, were the revolutionary workers, who, instead of working, had taken up political vagabondage. Reconstructing the eve of the workers' revolt of June 1848, Tocqueville looked with apprehension and disgust at the 'fearsome idlers' that surrounded the National Assembly.[80] *Oisif*, the term used by Saint-Simon to denounce the parasitical classes that lived off the labour of others, was now turned against revolutionary workers and 'demagogues' in general. Similarly, in Britain, Spencer thundered against the 'idlers' that disguised their parasitism by alleging a lack of available jobs.[81] Praising *otium* and representing work as a curse the subaltern lower classes could not escape was now perceived as outdated and even downright dangerous, for it was likely to heighten worker resentment and class conflict.

But there were times when the coherence of the new discourse started to crack. For example, Tocqueville emphasised the folly of searching for a 'remedy against the *hereditary and incurable disease* of poverty and *labour*'. We seem to hear tones of Nietzsche. On the other hand, when Nietzsche himself polemicised against the 'life of the idler [*Faulenzerleben*]' to which the theorists of Greek 'serenity' supposedly aspired (*supra*, 2 §2:01 §13), he seemed to take on tones of Tocqueville or Guizot. However, the occasional cracks in the consistency of the two different discourses should not cause us to lose sight of a fundamental difference. In Germany, where social conflict was less acute, the hypocritical apologetics of labour made a far later appearance. The celebration of *loisir*, of which Constant was so fond, which had vanished in France, resonated more than ever in the writings of Schopenhauer and Nietzsche, who continued to identify in *otium* the prerequisites for the full development of the intellectual faculties and of culture as such. When Wilhelm I also found it

---

79   Guizot 1849, p. 38 ff.
80   Tocqueville 1951 ff., Vol. 12, p. 131.
81   Spencer 1981, p. 32.

necessary, on the model of Guizot, to pay his respects to labour, Nietzsche did not hesitate to denounce the Kaiser's scandalous 'indecency' (*supra*, 10 §2).

But there was another peculiarity in Germany's historical and ideological development, beyond the widespread sympathy the 'southern Confederacy' enjoyed among student associations and, above all, 'much of the Prussian nobility and many army officers' during the Civil War.[82] Even in Britain, there was certainly no lack of conservatives that thought similarly.[83] While Bismarck, as we know, had some sympathy for the secessionists, Disraeli talked in rather harsh terms about the abolitionist movement.[84] The special nature of the debate in Germany and especially in Prussia lay elsewhere. Although developed from opposite points of view and with different value judgements, the comparison between the large plantations of the southern United States and the large estates of the Junkers, between black slavery and the serfdom that marked the history of Prussia and continued to exist to some extent when the Civil War broke out, is compelling. It is understandable that the Prussian nobility tended to identify with the rebels across the Atlantic. On the opposing side, a radical democrat who had participated in the Revolution of 1848, gone to prison, and spent a few years in the United States published a book in 1863 with a chapter titled, significantly, 'The Southern Plantation Owner, or the Cotton Baron of the New World'.[85] Almost three decades later, another journalist confirmed that the wealth and prosperity of the masters resulted in both cases from 'the forced labour of the unfree [*Zwangsarbeit von Unfreien*]'.[86]

On the basis of this comparison too, the main point of contention of the Civil War was found not in the fate of the black slaves but in the conditions of labour as such: Lincoln was a champion of 'free labour [*freie Arbeit*]', declared the Berlin workers' associations on the occasion of the assassination of the President of the United States.[87] If the anti-abolitionist press stressed that 'the bonded [*hörig*] Negro shares in this case the fate of the serving classes [*dienende Classen*] throughout the civilized world',[88] an article in the *Preussische Jahrbücher* criticised the fact that, for its defenders, 'slavery is the natural condition of the working classes, regardless of colour', while 'free labour' should be viewed as a 'failed experiment of modern society'.[89] The reality of the

---

82   Stolberg-Wernigerode 1933, p. 60 f.
83   Cf. Marx and Engels 1955 ff., pp. 23, 270 fn. and Mill 1965b, p. 267.
84   In E. Williams 1990, p. 195.
85   Griesinger 1863, p. 64 ff. Cf. Bowman 1993, p. 27.
86   Knapp 1891, p. 57.
87   Stolberg-Wernigerode 1933, p. 76 f.
88   Duttenhofer 1855, p. 73.
89   Rieffer 1858, p. 300 f.

Confederacy and the discourse of its ideologues were based on the supposition of the 'identity of labour and servitude'.[90]

The 'identity' thesis, at first rejected in Prussia, eventually took hold there too. Treitschke wrote: 'The masses will always remain the masses. No culture without servants [*Dienstboten*]'; 'millions must work on the land, or with iron or wood, so that a few thousand can study, paint or write poetry'.[91] In a similar vein, Nietzsche wrote: 'The misery of men living a life of toil has to be increased to make the production of the world of art possible for a small number of Olympian men' (CV, 3, I, 767 [166]). Both the philosopher and the historian set 'natural aristocracy' against egalitarian imaginings:[92] the rebellion against the necessity of things and the demands of culture was driven only by 'envy and greed'[93] or by the resentment on which Nietzsche insisted.

While, across the Atlantic, the war still raged, a fervent Christian abolitionist wrote that what was at stake is universal in character, namely the 'honour and dignity of labour'. *Ehre und Würde der Arbeit*: this was the watchword Nietzsche attacked, and against which he set the idea of slavery as an indispensable pre-condition of culture, as demonstrated in the first place by classical antiquity. The fervent Christian abolitionist attacked the secessionists of the Confederacy precisely for striving for the 'helotization of the workers' on an international scale, thus reproducing in the modern world the degradation to which labour was subjected in the ancient world.[94]

We are back with Nietzsche, who constantly stressed the superiority of classical antiquity. Fortunately, 'the aristocratic feeling that work is disgraceful [*Arbeit schändet*]' survived even in the modern world, though admittedly in small circles (JGB, 58 [51]). But was this not the worldview of the Junkers as well as of the owners of large plantations in the southern United States? As the radical-democratic writer mentioned above remarked, both were guided in their 'way of thinking and living' by one fundamental principle: 'Let others work on my behalf, for labour on one's own behalf dishonours [*selbstarbeit schändet*]'. The 'working class [*Arbeiterstand*]', which included slaves and servants indiscriminately, stood facing the 'exclusive gentleman', who made sure that he was and remained 'distinguished [*vornehm*]'.[95]

---

90   Rieffer 1858, p. 302.
91   Treitschke 1897–8, Vol. 1, p. 50 f.
92   Treitschke 1897–8, Vol. 1, p. 61.
93   In Iggers 1973, p. 181.
94   Thus V.A. Huber, quoted in Cronholm 1958, p. 87 f.
95   Griesinger 1863, p. 71.

This observation was confirmed by Tocqueville, at least as far as the ruling class in the southern United States was concerned: the highest value was 'oisiveté', otium, while 'labour is mixed up with the idea of slavery'.[96] A chasm separated the world of otium and culture from that of labour and servitude: 'Under threat of heavy punishment, it is forbidden to teach slaves to read and write.'[97] But similar concerns were expressed by the Junkers: 'Who will hire a servant [Knecht] that has become clever [klug] in school?'[98] Again, we are brought back to Nietzsche. It is true that during the 'Enlightenment' period he pointed to the edifying example of Diogenes, 'for a time a slave and a tutor' (MA, 457 [246]), or Epictetus, at the same time slave and master of the art of living, who knew how to accept his situation, without surrendering to the expectations and hopes of the Christian slaves (M, 546 [268–9]). However, the basic orientation remained the same: labour was synonymous with servitude, and, whether ancient or modern, servants or slaves were to be excluded from any form of education so they did not cherish illusions or claims suitable only for the masters.

6   Otium and Labour: Freedom and Slavery of the Ancients and the Moderns

The bloody clash in the United States sparked a debate about the role of labour, which, at the same time, was a new querelle of the ancients and the moderns. Nietzsche seemed to intervene in an original and provocative way in the debate started by Constant about ancient and modern freedom.

It is in this context that the thesis belonged that slavery was an indispensable basis not only of Greek culture but of culture as such. While the French liberal placed both the Jacobins and the lovers of classical antiquity on the same level, as enemies of modern liberty, Nietzsche denounced communists, socialists and 'their descendants, the white race of "Liberals"', as supporters of modernity united by their hatred for 'classical antiquity' (CV, 3, 1, 767–8 [166–7]). When speaking of 'socialists' and 'communists', the author of The Greek State, quoted here, was thinking principally of Lassalle. Lassalle indeed mocked the naïve transfiguration of classical antiquity by 'this people that, if it were to be transported today to Greece, could be used at most as the lowest slaves or helots, and would be really amazed to experience at their own cost an example of Attic

---

96   Tocqueville 1951ff., Vol. 1, half-vol. 1, pp. 392 and 362 (DA, Book 1, pt. 2, 10).
97   Tocqueville 1951ff., Vol. 1, half-vol. 1, p. 377 (DA, Book 1, pt. 2, 10).
98   Marwitz 1965, p. 143.

urbanity'.[99] On the other hand, the liberals targeted by Nietzsche were those who celebrated modern as opposed to ancient freedom and sharply criticised all forms of slavery: in this way, far from countering the Jacobin and socialist tide, they instead ended up swelling it and further fuelling a slave revolt that, as the Paris Commune had shown, continued to rage.

Once again, the discrepancy in the ideological development of the two countries becomes manifest: while, on one side of the Rhine, the Jacobins appealed to the polis in order to build the community of *citoyens* on the ruins of the *ancien régime*, on the other, in Germany, there developed a neoclassicism of a very different kind: in 1793, Wilhelm von Humboldt, an author whom Nietzsche, driven by his thirst for 'universal culture', already knew and appreciated in his teens (A, 73), noted that the institution of slavery, although 'unjust and barbaric' (*supra*, 1 §1), had nevertheless led to the exemption of free men from labour and the 'one-sided exercise of body and spirit', thus making possible the unfolding of the magnificent epoch of classical Greece.[100] A few years later, Schelling regretted 'the decline of the most noble humanity that had ever flowered',[101] the 'most beautiful flowering of humanity';[102] yet this sorrowful lamentation was part of a denunciation of the modern world and of 'so-called bourgeois freedom [*bürgerliche Freiheit*]', viewed and despised as the most 'turbid mixing of slavery with freedom'.[103]

In the France shaken by revolution, the reference to classical antiquity signified the celebration of the *agora* and of the unanimous participation of citizens in public life. The situation was quite different in Germany, where the *ancien régime* still ruled unchallenged and culture was the only field open to the activity of intellectuals. There, classical antiquity was synonymous with *scholè* and magnificent culture, and that is because it had not reached that intellectual division of labour that characterised the destructive decadence of the modern world.

With the eruption of the revolution of 1848 on both banks of the Rhine, the ideological non-synchronism between the two countries seemed to lessen somewhat. Just as Constant in France criticised Rousseau and the Jacobins, so Haym in Germany, also in the name of modern freedom, started liquidating Hegel, also accused of being heavily influenced by the Greek model, and

---

99   Lassalle 1864, p. 2 f. Quoted by Carl von Gersdorff, who requested Nietzsche to read this text (letter of 15 February 1868, in B I/3, 229).

100 Humboldt 1903–36b, p. 271 (§26).

101 Schelling 1856–61, Vol. 3, p. 604.

102 Schelling 1856–61, Vol. 5, p. 225.

103 Schelling 1856–61, Vol. 5, p. 314.

whose stress on the ethical and the political was by then seen as irreconcilable 'with the needs of today's reality and consciousness'. If, for Constant, the
primacy of wealth over political power was fundamental to modern freedom,
for Haym the modern state could not start from an 'abstract universal', i.e., from
a project of community, as in Rousseau and Hegel, but should rather be limited
to the political legitimation of the articulation of civil society into classes or
estates [*ständisch*], and therefore of existing social relations.[104] In either case,
one would ultimately have to stop praising the ancient polis, which not only
evoked memories of the community of *citoyens* of the Jacobins, but, worse still,
with its emphasis on the political and thus on the implicit disavowal of the
centrality and insuperability of the figure and sphere of the bourgeois, even
seemed to evoke the spectre of communism.[105]

However, there remained a fundamental difference between the two countries, highlighted by the comments Schelling addressed to the German people
after the revolution of 1848:

> Let yourselves be called an unpolitical people because most of you de-
> mand to be ruled rather ... than to rule, because you devote your leisure,
> spirit and inclination to other things and look for greater happiness than
> that or returning each year to political quarrels.[106]

For Constant, *otium* was the political prerequisite for modern freedom, for a
government capable of ensuring modern freedom, by rescuing it from the illusion of mass participation in public life and the 'infantile' passions of those
without property; in Germany, which had not yet been able to shake off the
burden of monarchical absolutism, Schelling saw *otium* as coincident with
the quiet acceptance of being governed, with the undisturbed enjoyment not
only of private property but above all of an inner spiritual life. But there was
more. The French liberal recuperated *otium* without consciously referring to
classical antiquity, and even in the course of a fierce polemic against ancient
freedom. Schelling, however, referred explicitly to Aristotle, with whom Germans agreed 'that the primary function of the state is to guarantee *otium* to
the best'. While the French liberal ridiculed the antiquitising political pathos
of the Jacobins and denounced slavery in the Graeco-Roman world, Schelling,
in condemning the illusions and utopias of the revolutionary movement, did
not hesitate to quote Aristotle as the theorist of the natural character of slavery:

---

104   Haym 1974, pp. 26, 377 f., 389 f.
105   Cf. Losurdo 1993a, esp. 1, § 4–6 and 2, § 1–2.
106   Schelling 1856–61, Vol. 11, p. 549.

'The one avails to be a slave, the other to be a master.' The *Philosophy of Mythology* cited this passage from *Politics* to demonstrate that 'there can be no sort of order that does not entail *from birth onwards* a distinction between ruler and ruled'.[107] At least as far as Europe was concerned, ancient slavery testified in favour of absolute monarchy, while actual slavery was conceivable only for blacks.[108]

We find the same contempt for politics and the same celebration of *otium* in Schopenhauer: economic 'independence', detachment from material concerns and from labour and profession, continued to be necessary conditions for 'true philosophizing', indeed for all true culture. It was not to be directed towards the exercise of a profession in civil life, and much less towards engagement in political life. The error, even the crime, of Hegel was precisely to have injected young people with 'the most vulgar, most philistine, basest way of thinking', to have extinguished any 'impetus towards something noble' and to have absolutised 'material interests, to which political interests also belong'.[109]

In expressing his contempt for labour and profession, Schopenhauer cited Theognis,[110] the author who would later become particularly important for Nietzsche. For the latter, the earlier ambiguities were resolved. In his struggle against the revolution, Schelling cited the authority of both Aristotle and Paul of Tarsus to remind the forgetful of the natural inequality between rulers and ruled, and even between masters and slaves. Nietzsche, on the other hand, after overcoming his early uncertainties, had slave revolt start with Christianity, or rather the Jewish-Christian tradition. In the second place, he invoked Greece, but Greece before the emergence of the polis, when it is not yet infected by the sickness of democracy and its splendid culture was based on the undisputed existence of slavery. Schopenhauer, who indicted the representatives of German classical philosophy for lacking material 'independence' and being remote from the ideal of *otium*, excluded the author of the *Critique of Pure Reason* from this judgement, for reasons of self-interest, for *The World as Will and Representation* made numerous references to the latter work. Quite a different view was taken in *Beyond Good and Evil*, which placed Kant, along with Hegel, among the 'philosophical scientific laborers', as opposed to the 'genuine philosophers' (JGB, 211 [105]). Nietzsche had no problem in sniffing out the banausic and plebeian elements in an author who mocked the 'distinguished tone' of the aristocratic idlers (*infra*, 22 §2).

---

107   Schelling 1856–61, Vol. 1, pp. 549, 530 and fn.
108   Schelling 1856–61, Vol. 11, pp. 514–15; see Lukács 1954, p. 144.
109   Schopenhauer 1976–82c, Vol. 4, pp. 238, 205 and 213.
110   Schopenhauer 1976–82c, Vol. 4, pp. 184 and 237 f.

SLAVERY IN THE UNITED STATES AND IN THE COLONIES   409

Now the picture is clear. In the modern world, labour and the ideology of labour had become generally contagious, with a frightening decadence by comparison with classical antiquity, which, freed from all Jacobin encrustations, became uniquely synonymous with slavery in all its forms and articulations: for Nietzsche, the 'slave class' proper to Greece and classical antiquity was to continue to exist, albeit in new forms, in the modern proletariat, if the destruction of culture was to be avoided. If, previously, political and social subversion had been blamed for assuming antiquitising hues, it was now accused of denying the legacy and lessons of classical antiquity. Constant reproached the Jacobins with having forgotten slavery as the foundation of the ancient freedom they so admired; the radical aristocrat reminded the French liberals of how many antiquitising elements there were in the view that only separation from labour guarantees the enjoyment of civil rights.

7   Marx, Nietzsche and 'Extra Work'

As in the ancient world, so too in the modern: the *otium* of the best, or of the ruling class, was founded, as Nietzsche noted with his customary ruthlessness, on the 'extra work [*Mehrarbeit*]' of slaves or servants of all kinds (CV, 3; I, 767 [166]). This category also had a long history. In the twelfth century, Tocqueville observed, the Third Estate had not yet formed, and the situation could therefore be described as follows: on the one hand were 'those who cultivated the land without owning it', on the other 'those who owned land without cultivating it'.[111] In fact, this situation continued to exist centuries later, at least according to Taine: in the *ancien régime* we had a 'class that, tied to the soil, hungers for sixty generations in order to feed the other classes'.[112] This is particularly confirmed by the picture painted by La Bruyère: human beings or perhaps 'wild animals' with a human appearance lived in 'caves' on 'black bread, water and roots' and thus 'save the others the trouble of sowing, working and harvesting, in order to live'.[113] Montesquieu, for his part, had no difficulty in identifying the source of the luxury (and, ultimately, of culture) in the 'labour of others [*travail d'autrui*]'.[114] Immediately before Nietzsche, Schopenhauer located the basis of the *otium* of the few, and the development of culture as such, in the 'overloading with work' of a great mass of workers, slaves and semi-slaves.

---

111   Tocqueville 1951 ff., Vol. 16, p. 121.
112   Taine 1899, Vol. 2, p. 61.
113   Taine 1899, Vol. 2, p. 199 f.
114   Montesquieu 1949–51, p. 332 (book 7, 1).

Nietzsche was more precise. In speaking of 'extra work', he used the same language as Marx, according to whom the extortion of 'extra work [*Mehrarbeit*]' or 'surplus value [*Mehrwert*]' was not the natural and insuperable foundation of culture as such, but rather of a society based on class exploitation. One could say the debate about labour reached its extreme logical consequence in Germany and, more precisely, in the two opposed theoretical and political projects of Nietzsche and Marx. Both agreed to view ancient society and capitalist society together: both based themselves on the 'extra work' that the beneficiaries of *otium* heaped upon their servants. Although, while imposing an opposite value judgement, Nietzsche would have had no difficulty in subscribing to this analysis of Marx: 'Modern nations have been able only to disguise slavery in their own countries, but they have imposed it without disguise upon the New World.'[115]

The two knew nothing about each other. However, Nietzsche criticised Marx's theses, although he encountered them only in partial, schematic and often distorted form, in Dühring. The latter expressed his sympathy for the 'oppressed elements of society' and his commitment to the struggle against 'social injustice',[116] along with 'economic systems based on the pedestal of slavery, whether ancient or modern or colonial-American', condemned the 'semi-free wage labour' of the modern world, which was, in fact, a kind of slavery,[117] and denounced 'slavery in the narrow sense and the broad sense [*eigentliche und uneigentliche Sklaverei*]'.[118] Here, too, the critical analysis dealt simultaneously with the United States of the Civil War and Europe of the industrial revolution, the capitalist metropolis and the colonies, the modern world and the ancient world. But, in his attempt to secure the emancipation of labour as such, Dühring (said Nietzsche) showed himself to be an 'anarchist' (JGB, 204 [94]), since he called into question the very foundations of all social order and culture in general.

Marx, who did not know Nietzsche, was nevertheless familiar with Linguet, a French eighteenth-century writer who demonstrated some clear resemblances to the German philosopher. Linguet saw slavery as a permanent precondition for culture, so that the use of 'softer' names changed nothing in the nature of the thing. '*The essence of society* ... consists in freeing the rich man from labour, giving him new organs, untiring members, which take upon themselves

---

115   Marx and Engels 1975 ff., 6, p. 168.
116   Dühring 1871, p. 385.
117   Dühring 1873, p. 16.
118   Dühring 1871, p. 400.

all the laborious operations the fruits of which he is to appropriate.'[119] Marx considered the French author to be at the same time 'reactionary', because of his nostalgia for the institution of slavery, and brilliant, because he effectively unmasked the dominant ideology, revealing the persistent reality of slavery and surplus value. Had he known Nietzsche, he would have ranked him alongside Linguet, among those modern authors that dared to pronounce without simulation the secret of capitalist accumulation (the inviolable taboo of vulgar apologetics), without hiding the extent to which modern wage labour also contained elements of slavery.

8   Race of Masters and Race of Servants: Boulainvilliers, Gobineau, Nietzsche

But precisely because Nietzsche, who always kept the model of classical antiquity in mind, always emphasised the identity of labour and servitude, there was little room in his thinking for racial slavery as such: slavery was primarily the result of an objective and unavoidable need of culture and, in itself, had little to do with skin colour. Similar positions emerged across the Atlantic during the debate before the Civil War. Although Fitzhugh, in his polemic against the abolitionists, defended the subjugation of blacks, he criticised the idea of confining the justification of slavery to them, for one read of no Negro slavery 'in ancient times'. For historical reasons or reasons of expediency, the population of African origin was certainly the most suitable reservoir for the provision of the slave labour culture needed; for the rest, slavery, 'black or white', was right and necessary.[120] A not dissimilar point of view was held by Nietzsche, who, although looking chiefly at the colonial world as a source of forced labour, did not exclude the promotion of a 'worker-*chinoiserie*' in the heart of Europe.

It is true that the master/slave dichotomy in the *Genealogy of Morals* corresponds to the dichotomy between the Aryan 'blond race which is dominant', and 'the dark-skinned, dark-haired native inhabitants' of non-Aryan origin (GM, I, 5 [14]), but this should not lead one to hasty conclusions. For the philosopher, the principal contradiction was not that between nations and ethnic groups but between masters and servants, the well-formed and the malformed. This tendency was already present in the text on Theognis. The Greek poet summed

---

119   Quoted in Marx and Engels 1975 ff., 31, p. 243.
120   Fitzhugh 1854, pp. 98 and 225.

up the decadence, not to say the degeneration, of Megara and its aristocracy as follows: 'Wealth confounded the race [*genos*]'. And the young philologist and student commented: 'It happened that, by now, the nobles no longer separated themselves from the rabble, but sought riches by contracting mutual marriages, while the plebeians could in this way aspire to nobility and even achieve it' (DTM, 16; 61).

To clarify this point, we can start with Boulainvilliers, who in the early eighteenth century interpreted the conflict between the aristocracy and the Third Estate as one between the conquering Franks and the conquered Gallo-Romans. Strongly contested by the theorists and followers of the French Revolution, Boulainvilliers's theories become 'politically effective only among emigrants'.[121] In fact, the same interpretation can be found in Montlosier. Nietzsche quoted and clearly subscribed to the thesis of this 'emigrant', as he calls him, according to whom 1789 was nothing other than the uprising of a 'slave race', the defeated Gallo-Romans, generously spared by their conquerors, the Franks (XII, 412). As is well known, Thierry endorsed this thesis, but he steered it in an opposite political direction, i.e. he celebrated the revolt of the Third Estate as a struggle for emancipation and freedom whose protagonists were an enslaved and oppressed class or race.[122] He identified with the 'losers' and praised the cause of the 'sons of the vanquished', which he also saw as his cause.[123] So one can appreciate the rebuke Nietzsche addressed to the French historian: that his 'history' was permeated by 'compassion for all those who suffer, who have turned out badly' (XII, 558), in which sense Thierry represented 'the popular uprising in science itself' (XIII, 199). Nietzsche expanded Montlosier's interpretation of the French Revolution and applied it to the situation in Europe after the Paris Commune: so the attempt at 'the radical mixing of classes [*Stände*] and *consequently* of races' was denounced (JGB, 208). The racialisation of the sociopolitical conflict was, at least where Europe was concerned, transversal, in the sense that it ran through and rent apart each national community by opposing masters and servants, the well-formed and the malformed, aristocrats and the rabble (*infra*, § 25 5).

And yet Boulainvilliers's dichotomy, which legitimised the servitude of the Gallo-Romans, could not be fully supported by Nietzsche, for whom the decline of classical antiquity was precisely a decisive moment in plebeian and anti-aristocratic subversion. The dichotomy was therefore reformulated with a view

---

121   Arendt 1966, p. 163.
122   Cf. Omodeo 1974, pp. 278–309.
123   In Poliakov 1987, p. 43.

to the Aryan irruption into India, where caste continued to be centrally important. We can now understand the role of Aryan mythology in Nietzsche. Already
present in *The Birth of Tragedy*, it reappeared with even greater force in the
final phase of his development. However, unlike in the case of the anti-Semitic
writers and currents, here Aryan was not set against Jewish: it was synonymous with noble and aristocratic, just as anti-Aryan was synonymous with plebeian and vulgar. One might say that Nietzsche, following the spread of Aryan
mythology, plunged and rinsed in the Ganges the interpretation of social conflict suggested by Boulainvilliers: Aryans took the place of Franks, and Gallo-
Romans were replaced by 'the sudra, a race of servants; probably an inferior
breed of people, found in the territory in which those Aryans settled' (XIII,
396).

The new dichotomy, which took the place of Boulainvilliers's, now had the
advantage of being valid not just in relation to a particular country but internationally. Moreover, it could subsume the ancient Greeks and Romans into the
dominant race. The result was a unified framework at the spatial and temporal
level. The Code of Manu, this 'absolutely Aryan product', influenced Plato, the
theorist of caste (B, III, 5, 325). On the other hand, the beginning of the slave
revolt long preceded the uprising of French plebeians against the aristocracy:
Christianity was 'the revaluation of all Aryan values, the victory of Chandala
values, the gospel preached to the poor and the base, the general revolt of
the downtrodden, the miserable, the malformed, the failures, against anyone
with 'breeding', – the eternal vengeance of the Chandala as a religion of love'
(GD, 4 [185]). Now Christian values had again to be revalued in order to repel
the Chandala and ensure the triumph of 'Aryan humanity'. So, the ideal was
proclaimed of a society divided into castes. To separate them and keep them
separate, strict barriers and ruthless measures were required against anyone
who dared to harm them. Thus, we are led back to the ban on miscegenation
in the southern United States, now reformulated in terms not of racial but of
social apartheid.

The influence of Gobineau, who praised the Aryan invaders of India that
subjugated and decimated the 'aboriginal races' belonging to the 'black type',
is evident.[124] 'Proud of its extraction' and attached to the 'idea of nobility', the
victor and conqueror took care not to disappear in the 'crowd': he kept well at
bay from himself 'the poor, prisoners, slaves, in a word, mestizos and beings of
inferior extraction'.[125] Gobineau described with satisfaction the violence ven-

---

124   Gobineau 1983, p. 480 (Book 3, 1).
125   Gobineau 1983, pp. 672, 986 (Book 4, 3 and 6. Book, 3).

ted on those who violated the banning of miscegenation and on their off-spring, the Chandala: 'But one could say that expulsion, and even death, were small sufferings' in comparison to the fate to which 'the unfortunate offspring of [...] prohibited unions were condemned'.[126] Nietzsche was also happy with the drastic measures used in caste society against 'the unbred people [*Nicht-Zucht-Mensch*], the human hodgepodge [*Mischmasch-Mensch*], the Chandala', or (quoting the Code of Manu) 'the fruits of adultery, incest and crime'. Yes, 'this system found it necessary to be terrible' (GD, 3 [184–5]). In similar terms, Gobineau observed: 'If one wishes to prevent the collapse of the system, [...] a vigorous remedy would be to cauterize the wound [of mixed marriages] on the social body as quickly as possible'; 'the category of Chandala arose in response to an implacable necessity of the institution'. The Chandala were considered and treated as sources of contamination: 'Any spring from which they drank was damned'.[127] As for Nietzsche, he spoke of the 'edict' according to which 'they cannot get their water from rivers or wells or ponds, but only from the entrances to swamps or from pits formed by animal footprints'. In this way, 'Aryan humanity' managed to preserve itself as 'pure and primordial'; the concept of purity, 'the concept of "pure blood", is anything but harmless' (GD, 3–4 [184–5]). 'To be hard here is synonymous with being "healthy": it is disgust in the face of degeneration' (XIII, 397). And Gobineau believed, still in relation to the Chandala: 'It was considered a disgrace to be in the vicinity of one of these wretched beings, a pollution' that had absolutely to be washed clean. Even so, one should not lose sight of the fundamental 'mildness of [Hindu] customs'.[128] *Twilight of the Idols* noted that it presupposed a type of person 'a hundred times gentler and more reasonable' than the Christian or the modern European (GD, 3 [184]).

Even though the author of the *Essai sur l'inégalité des races humaines* is explicitly mentioned only in a late letter (B, III, 5, 516), the essay's influence on Nietzsche had started several years earlier.[129] And that is easy to understand, for as Cassirer noted, perhaps no other modern writer was so deeply permeated by the feeling Nietzsche defined as 'pathos of distance'.[130] On the other hand, according to the French author, as a consequence of the mixing of blood and general bastardisation, no historically constituted nation could claim complete

126   Gobineau 1983, p. 528 (Book 3, 2).
127   Gobineau 1983, pp. 528, 530 (Book 3, 2).
128   Gobineau 1983, p. 528 (Book 3, 2).
129   Förster-Nietzsche 1895–1904, Vol. 2, p. 886; cf. Verrecchia 1986, p. 83 f.; 1978, p. 60 f. and Cancik 1997, p. 56.
130   Cassirer 2002, p. 306.

racial purity, so that, potentially at least, each country was rent transversally at the level of race and caste. In this sense, Gobineau resumed and reworked a tradition of thought that goes back to Boulainvilliers. So did Nietzsche, more or less: ancient slavery and Hindu caste society merged in the model of a 'new slavery', demanded by aristocratic radicalism.

CHAPTER 13

'Hierarchy', Great Chain of Being and Great Chain of Pain

1   The Chariot of Culture and Compassion for the Slaves

Why were slaves or members of the lower castes destined to suffer their fate without rebelling? The answer was clear: because that was the price of culture; moreover, 'the great majority' had no intrinsic value, they 'exist and are only *allowed* to exist to serve and to be of general utility' (JGB, 61 [55]). Awareness of the need for this sacrifice was dimmed by the feeling of compassion, which prevented one from looking with the necessary clarity and coolness at the sacrifice of the slave on the altar of the needs of culture. Once again, Nietzsche referred back to classical antiquity and Aristotle (IX, 128). However, it is not hard to see modern tradition behind this view. Mandeville denounced the 'Petty Reverence for the Poor' and considered that 'to be compassionate to excess where Reason forbids it, and the general Interest of the Society requires steadiness of Thought and Resolution, is an unpardonable Weakness'.[1] Compassion was the morbid absolutisation of the individual, which endangered the orderly unfolding of the universal. Burke not only condemned those who seek to 'excite compassion' but added that 'if we take pity on those who have to work so the world can exist, we are wasting our time with the condition of humanity'.[2]

The development of industrialisation and capitalist accumulation, together with its terrible human and social costs, clearly required a harder attitude towards the poor. In the words of Tawney, a prominent historian, in England in the mid-seventeenth century new doctrines came to the conclusion that 'severity is a duty and compassion a sin, since it simply perpetuated the bad circumstances'.[3] Almost two centuries later, the situation seemed not to have changed: 'Compassion has been has removed from hearts' while 'a stoic determination to renounce human solidarity [...] gained the dignity of a secular religion'.[4] So we can appreciate Malthus's position: compassion was, in some respects, blind and unthinking.[5]

---

1   Mandeville 1924, p. 311.
2   Burke 1826, Vol. 8, p. 368.
3   Tawney 1926, p. 267.
4   Polanyi 1957, p. 102.
5   Malthus 1826, p. 361 (Book 4, 10).

But it was above all Linguet, mentioned above, who leads us back towards Nietzsche. According to him, Rousseau's polemic against slavery was the typical discourse of 'compassionate hearts'. But 'the feeling of compassion was rightly a mere trifle in politics' and for politicians, aware of the fact that culture as such 'is based entirely on the annihilation of the rights of nature', in whose name Rousseau would have liked to see slavery banned. The legislator had to be able to be 'merciless'. If pity had free rein, along with slavery would be threatened the hierarchy on which social order necessarily rests: 'One needs ranks and distinctions in the world.'[6]

With Linguet, we are still in the period before 1789. During the radicalisation of the French Revolution, when the masses erupted onto the political scene and raised the curtain on the drama of their misery, the denunciation of compassion acquired new urgency. For Sade, 'far from being a virtue, it became a real vice [...], once it led to unsettling an inequality required by the laws of nature'.[7] In subsequent years, the debate about the revolution became a debate about the role of compassion. The *philosophes*, according to Mounier, had discredited the institution of slavery in the eyes of 'all men who do not have the heart of a tiger' and helped to undermine the *ancien régime* by recommending 'pity for the wretched'.[8]

Precisely this was the starting point for Tocqueville's critical analysis, according to which a morbid sensibility had contributed greatly to unleashing revolutionary passions:

> Towards the end of the century, when the particular language of Diderot and Rousseau has had time to spread and dissolve into the common language, the false sensibility that fills the books of these writers conquers even the administrators and even penetrates through to finance officials. A petty employee complains to the intendant of Paris that 'in the performance of his functions he often experiences a pain that is excruciating for a sensitive soul.'[9]

On the eve of the Civil War, abolitionist agitation and revolution was blamed by its opponents on the influence of 'French principles' and 'sentimental French

---

6   Linguet 1984, p. 459 f. (Book 5, 5).
7   Quoted in Horkheimer/Adorno 1947, p. 122 f. Hannah Arendt (1963) saw in 'compassion' the decisive cause of the 'degeneration' of the French Revolution.
8   Mounier 1801, p. 15.
9   Tocqueville 1951 ff., Vol. 2, half-vol. 1, p. 131 (AR, book, 6).

philosophy'.[10] So the debate about compassion accompanied and stimulated the entire revolutionary cycle. Whether it concerned the idea of happiness or the feeling (and ideology) of compassion, Nietzsche formulated his condemnation against the background of a precise historical balance sheet. Meanwhile, 'compassion' started to become the slogan not just of the socialist movement but also of authors and cultural circles in some way influenced by it. Such was the case, for example, of Giovanni Pascoli:

> Socialism! Without further arguments and facts, the rise of socialism would suffice to show that the kingdom of compassion is already far advanced. It is a phenomenon of altruism. [...] Oh gloomy apocalypse, I do not believe in you, because I believe in charity! That is the basis of my socialism: the sure and continuing increment of compassion in the hearts of men.[11]

This was the 'socialist compassion' mocked by Nietzsche (*supra*, 8 §5), and viewed with suspicion or hostility by critics of the revolution of all sorts. But, once again, the German philosopher was distinguished by his rigour. We have already seen how Tocqueville critically emphasised the role of eighteenth-century sentimentalism in the ideological preparation of the revolution. But, in another context, he assessed the feeling of compassion positively, seeing it as the common thread of progress or of the progressive construction of the unity of humankind. On the occasion of a popular revolt in Brittany in 1675, which had been repressed 'with unexampled cruelty', which Madame de Sévigné talked about in a letter to her daughter in a serene and almost amused tone, the French liberal commented that the noble lady 'had no clear idea of what it meant to suffer, if one was not an aristocrat'. In a rigidly hierarchical society, not even feelings could overcome the barriers of class or caste, and only in a democratic society, where the idea of equality had become dominant, would 'a general compassion for all members of the human species' begin to emerge.[12] The counterrevolution advocated by Nietzsche had to be able to question this outcome: if it were true 'that people have duties only towards their own kind', one must also realise 'that when it comes to creatures of a lower rank, to everything alien, people are allowed to act as they see fit or 'from the heart', and in any event, "beyond good and evil"'. And only at this level 'things like pity might have a place' (JGB, 260 [155]). The compassion

---

10   Calhoun 1992, p. 293; Merriam 1969, pp. 235 and 230.
11   Pascoli 1994, pp. 160 and 168.
12   Tocqueville 1951ff., Vol. 1, half-vol. 2, pp. 173–5 (DA, Book 2, pt. 3, 1).

here spoken of not only had no 'general' character but, far from annulling or reducing them, confirmed and further emphasised the differences between people.

Nietzsche's radicalism was understandable in light of the changes in the political situation. On the one hand, the sharpening, real or threatened, of social conflict in Germany and Europe led to calls for strong measures that should no longer be hindered by humanitarian and sentimental scruples. But compassion was condemned not only with an eye to the social question. Carlyle is a good example. He belonged without doubt to the tradition that condemned the new revolutionary trinity of 'philanthropy, emancipation and compassion for human misery'.[13] Also not so very far from this tradition was the assertion that, if one forgot the laws that governed the orderly functioning of culture, 'the universal Litany to Pity is a mere universal nuisance, and torpid blasphemy against the gods'.[14] However, one was not to lose sight of the fact that this discourse was closely intertwined, in Carlyle, with the defence of slavery and praise for the 'white European' and 'European heroism', with whose aid 'cannibals' and savages of all kinds were kept at bay.[15] So the new element was colonial expansionism, with the new brutality it entailed. Hence the polemic was directed not only against the revolutionary doctrine of natural law (for a black in the West Indies, 'the first "human right"' consisted in 'being forced to work'[16]) but also against 'sentimentalism' or 'Christian sentimentalism' and the sermons in 'the Gospels and the Talmud'.[17]

Together with the damning of the paralysing and perverse effects of the sense of compassion, Christianity or the Jewish-Christian tradition also ended up being called into question. In the framework of a historically and theoretically coherent discourse, this theme underwent a drastic radicalisation in Nietzsche:

> By and large, pity runs counter to the law of development, which is the law of selection. Pity preserves things that are ripe for decline, it defends things that have been disowned and condemned by life. [...] In the middle of our unhealthy modernity, nothing is less healthy than Christian pity.
>
> AC 7 [6–7]

---

13 Carlyle 1983, p. 66.
14 Carlyle 1983, p. 104.
15 Carlyle 1983, pp. 461 and 458 f.
16 Carlyle 1983, p. 435 f.
17 Carlyle 1983, pp. 428 and 440.

In this case, too, as we shall see, compassion was condemned with an eye to both the social conflict within the capitalist metropolis and colonial expansion. Both situations required a change at the ideological and moral level: 'Where lie your greatest dangers? In compassion' (FW, 271 [152]).

2   The Chariot of Culture and the Resentment of the Slaves

The feeling of discomfort with the universal laws of culture that inexorably required the chaining of the slaves was expressed among the upper classes as compassion, but in the lower as resentment. And just as compassion in the actual sense meant the beginning of the upper classes' abdication of the leadership role that accrued to them naturally on the victory-chariot of culture, resentment was the beginning of the slave revolt. Compassion and resentment were two moments in a crisis of culture that manifested itself both 'above' and 'below'. In that sense, too, Nietzsche revealed himself to be the end point of a long tradition that never ceased to denounce every protest against the existing order as a simple expression of envy and resentment: thus, social conflict lost its objective dimension and was traced back to the bad feelings of the lower classes or some of its inwardly corrupt representatives.

In Athenian democracy (wrote Ferguson) the poor, '[a]ctuated by envy, [...] were ready to banish from the state whomsoever was respectable and eminent in the superior order of citizens'. Envy and egalitarian passion expressed themselves in an inclination to downward levelling, with disastrous effects for culture: 'If the pretensions to equal justice and freedom should terminate in rendering every class equally servile and mercenary, we make a nation of helots, and have no free citizens.'[18]

The more the popular masses burst onto the political and social scene, the more urgent this accusation became. Burke warned against the dangers 'envy' and 'rapacity' represented, in the first place for big property and society as a whole.[19] In *Democracy in America*, having already experienced the workers' revolts in Lyon and the intensification of social conflict in the years of the July Monarchy, Tocqueville, with a clear reference to socialism, denounced the 'depraved taste for equality, which leads the weak to want to degrade the strong to their own level and leads people to prefer equality in slavery to inequality in freedom'.[20] These were people who 'eye up the immense space that separ-

18   Ferguson 1966, pp. 186–7 (pt. 2, 2).
19   Burke 1826, Vol. 5, p. 107.
20   Tocqueville 1951ff., Vol. 1, half-vol. 1, p. 53 (DA, Book 1, pt. 1, p. 3).

ates their vices and their misery from power and wealth, and who would heap rubble into this abyss in an attempt to close it'.[21]

But especially after June in Paris and even more so after the Paris Commune, the denunciation of envy and of the dismal feelings that underlay the socialist and proletarian agitation became, at the European level, a commonplace of culture and journalism of the sort that engaged in defending the existing social order. Lamartine conveyed his disdain for Marat and his egalitarian 'envy': 'L'égalité était sa fureur, parce que la supériorité était son martyre.'[22] In similar terms, Guizot pointed an accusing finger at the 'envious desire to debase all that is high' and at the 'need for revenge'.[23] If, in France, Renan called the revolutionary demand for equality a product of 'jealousy',[24] Bismarck in Germany called equality 'the chimeric daughter of envy and greed'[25] and in England Bagehot highlighted the role played in the Commune by 'envy which at all times and in all countries the desperate poor man feels of the happy rich man'.[26]

The target of all these accusations was the socialist movement, which Nietzsche also accused of making the workers 'jealous' and teaching them 'revenge' (AC, 57 [60]). Naturally, there were some innovations. The discourse lost its sociopolitical immediacy, while the denunciation moved from the moral to the psychological or psychopathological level: the impulse to revolution was to be found less in envy at the material wealth of the ruling classes than in the dull resentment that those who turned out badly felt for higher natures: the 'rancune of the great' poisoned European culture and society (EH, Thus Spoke Zarathustra, 5 [128]). But there was another element of novelty. The traditional critique of 'envy' was a call on the masses to be content with their lot; whereas the criticism of resentment was the polemical response to the frequent invocation by the organised revolutionary movement of the idea of justice and noble sentiments. That is to say, in the face of the revolutionary discourse of the critique and condemnation of the social order in the name of morality, Nietzsche's discourse appeared as a metacritique.

21   Tocqueville 195 ff., Vol. 1, half-vol. 1, p. 308 (DA, Book 1, pt. 2, p. 9).
22   Quoted in L. v. Stein 1959, Vol. 1, p. 294 f.
23   Guizot 1849, p. 9.
24   Renan 1947 ff., Vol. 1, p. 486.
25   In Herre 1983, p. 173.
26   Bagehot 1974c, p. 198.

3   Misery of the Poor and Responsibility and Boredom of the Rich

Resentment on the part of churls and the subaltern classes had no moral legitimacy and, moreover, no basis in reality. The fanatics of compassion had lost
sight of the fact that the ability to feel pain and suffering was not evenly distributed. It was well known that the more noble souls were more exposed and
vulnerable. This was the basic theme of Nietzsche's entire development, even
if it passed through different stages over time. As we already know, the 'cloud
of melancholy' always surrounded noble and higher natures, who, unlike the
philistines of every stripe, were unable to find fulfilment in their own time
and therefore constantly struggled with an inner unrest (*supra*, 6 §8). The
ordinary human being was unaware of this: 'The lower mass, with its scant
possession, will be dissatisfied by the sight of the rich, they believe the rich
is the happy one. The mass of slaves, who work, are overworked and rarely
rest, believes that the human being without physical work is the happy one'
(IX, 535). In fact: '[T]he duller the eye, the more extensive the good! Hence
the eternal cheerfulness of the common people and of children! Hence the
gloominess and grief – akin to a bad conscience – of the great thinkers' (FW,
53 [63]).
    This too was a theme with a long tradition. In Voltaire we read: 'All the poor
are not unhappy. The majority are born in that condition, and continual work
keeps them from feeling their fate too keenly.'[27] Mandeville had the following
to say in this regard:

> Besides that the things I called Hardships, neither seem nor are such to
> those who have been brought up to them, and know no better. There is
> not a more contented People among us, than those who work the hard-
> est, and are the least acquainted with the Pomp and Delicacies of the
> World.

On closer inspection, suffering was the exclusive and painful privilege of higher
souls and people of elevated status: '[T]he greater a Man's Knowledge and
Experience is in the World, the more exquisite the Delicacy of his Taste, and
the more consummate Judge he is of things in general, certainly the more difficult it will be to please him.' Let us compare the two extremes of the social
rank-ordering, on the one hand the 'meanest and most unciviliz'd Peasant' and

---

27   Voltaire 1834, p. 218.

the other 'the greatest king', and let us imagine one can observe the life of the other for a few days. Here is the result:

> Had the meanest and most unciviliz'd Peasant leave Incognito to observe the greatest King for a Fortnight; tho' he might pick out several Things he would like for himself, yet he would find a great many more, which, if the Monarch and he were to change Conditions, he would wish for his part to have immediately alter'd or redress'd, and which with Amazement he sees the King submit to.

On the other hand,

> And again if the Sovereign was to examine the Peasant in the same manner, his Labour would be insufferable, the Dirt and Squalor, his Diet and Amours, his Pastimes and Recreations would be all abominable; but then what Charms would he find in the other's Peace of Mind, the Calmness and Tranquillity of his Soul?[28]

So, there was no reason to question the social hierarchy: all could be content with their destiny, and this was particularly true of peasants and the poor in general, who had less to envy in the condition of the king than the king in that of the basest subject. The hardships and rags of a peasant or a shepherd hid greater happiness than the pomp of a king: this was a topos of modern thought that we can also find in Voltaire.[29] On that basis, Malthus reached a dramatic conclusion: 'Our feelings of compassion may be worked up to a higher pitch by a well-wrought scene in a play, or a fictitious tale in a novel, than by almost any events in real life.'[30] On the other hand, commented Nietzsche, 'one can also suffer from an excess' (FW, 14 [40]). Opulence and the exemption from having to earn a living did not guarantee happiness:

> There is a boredom of the most subtle and cultivated minds, for whom the best that the earth has to offer has become stale: accustomed to eating ever more highly sought-after food and disgusted by coarser fare, they are in danger of dying from hunger – for there is only a little of the very best things and sometimes it has become inaccessible or rock-hard, so that even good teeth can no longer bite it.
>
> VM, 369 [136–7]

---

28   Mandeville 1924, p. 315.
29   Voltaire 1991, p. 460 f.
30   Malthus 1826, p. 361 (Book 4, p. 10).

Even though this topos had a long history, it did not go unchallenged. Think, for example, of Diderot's polemic against Helvetius. To the latter's argument that 'boredom is a terrible evil, almost like misery', he answered: 'This is the reasoning of a rich man who has never worried about his lunch'; in reality, 'there are many layers in society that are worn down by exhaustion, that quickly run out of energy and shorten their lives, and whatever wage you assign to labour, you will prevent neither the frequency nor the justness of the workers' complaints'.[31]

But one should focus above all on two contributions. In criticising the ideology of the happiness of the poor, Rousseau spoke passionately against the callousness of the rich:

> He looks without pity on those wretches oppressed by uninterrupted labour, who barely earn a piece of hard black bread to prolong their misery. He does not find it strange that the product is in inverse proportion to the labour, and that a ruthless and debauched idler enriches himself through the sweat of a million wretches exhausted by fatigue and penury. That is their condition, he says, that is where they were born, habit makes everything equal and I am no happier under my sumptuous arches than a cowherd in his hut, or, he has to add, the ox in his stall.[32]

In his *Histoire philosophique et politique des Deux Indes*, Raynal-Diderot spoke similarly of 'the cruel sophistry with which the rich and great console themselves, as they fall asleep on the basis of the labour of the poor, close their hearts to their groans and divert their sensitivity from their vassals to their dogs and their horses'.[33] The reference to oxen or dogs and horses explains the anthropological nominalism on which this ideology was based: the poor were not truly subsumed under the category of human. In this sense, the rich behaved, in Rousseau's eyes, 'without mercy', that is, without the compassion that allowed one to subsume the vassal too under the human species.

This was a feeling that Nietzsche, with explicit reference to Rousseau, condemned precisely because of its 'realistic' assumption. Compassion was not only harmful and fateful, but also superfluous and misguided:

> One is deceived as the spectator of the suffering and deprivations of the lower strata of the people, because one inevitably takes as one's measure

---

31   Diderot 1994, p. 901.
32   Rousseau 1971, p. 330 f.
33   Raynal 1981, p. 263.

one's own sensibility, as if with one's highly and vulnerable brain one were placed in their condition. In truth, the suffering and deprivations increase with the growth in the culture of the individual; the lower layers are the most obtuse.

VIII, 481

Even actual physical pain seemed to be a privilege of the upper classes and of noble souls (*supra*, 12 § 2). In conclusion, from every point of view 'the caste of the idlers is the one that is more capable of suffering and does suffer more, its pleasure in existence is less, its task greater' (MA, 439 [237]).

In confirmation of its political dimension, this debate was conducted particularly intensely and passionately in the decades preceding the outbreak of the French Revolution. At the end of the eighteenth century, advocates of serfdom made extensive use of the argument that the supposed benefactors of the serfs exaggerated the serfs' suffering out of all proportion, confusing their own delicate sensibilities with the very different ones of peasants long accustomed to the harshness of life and of their condition.[34] In the nineteenth and twentieth centuries, the debate no longer concerned the serfs: instead, the workers were at its centre. A few years after the revolution of 1848, Gutzkow mocked the motto favoured by a 'well-known school' according to which 'for the rich, enjoyment is work, whereas for the poor, work is enjoyment'.[35] Dealing with the *Workers' Question*, Lange argued strongly against Leo's idea that the workers' 'horny skin' protected them against fatigue and suffering.[36] Later Kautsky ridiculed Schopenhauer's idea of the carefree serenity of the poor and of the hidden but all the more excruciating suffering of the rich.[37] Mehring then accused Nietzsche of having taken over Leo's 'horny skin' thesis, so brilliantly refuted by Lange.[38]

Finally, on the subject of the lack of susceptibility of the popular classes to pain as well as to the most delicate sentiments, here is a twentieth-century contribution. Talking of Paul Bourget, the writer Nietzsche ranked among those psychologists 'inquisitive and, at the same time, delicate' and to be found in great numbers in Paris in the late nineteenth century (EH, 3 [90]), Gramsci ironically observed that, for him, 'a woman needs 100,000 francs a year in interest to

---

34   Epstein 1976, pp. 205–7.
35   Gutzkow 1974, p. 300.
36   In Mehring 1961 ff., Vol. 13, p. 170.
37   Kautsky 1888, p. 103.
38   Mehring 1961 ff., Vol. 13, p. 170.

have a psychology'.[39] The Great Chain of Being saw in the philosophy of the seventeenth and eighteenth centuries all beings as placed in a strict rank-ordering in which a gradual and barely perceptible transition led from the higher animal species to human beings of lower nature.[40] This sublime and harmonious pyramid was also a Great Chain of Pain, or, to be more precise, of sensitivity to pain: the richness, distinction and fragility of one's inner life tended to correspond to the elevation of one's social position.

So, the philosopher-philologist was, in the first place, linked not to ancient thought but to a trend in modern and contemporary thought. Aristotle, moreover, formulated a thesis that seemed to be the exact antithesis of the topos just examined, i.e., that the slave and the philistine were incapable of happiness.[41] To admit that 'any random person, or a slave, might enjoy bodily pleasures no less than the best person' was to 'grant happiness to a slave, if he does not even have a share in his life'.[42] In fact, 'it is reasonable, then, that we do not speak of a cow or horse or any other animal as happy'.[43] But the contradiction between the two theses here compared is merely apparent: in either case, the philistine engaged in slave labour was excluded from a genuine spiritual life. The element of continuity was represented by the anthropological nominalism: if Aristotle seemed to assimilate the vassal to the ox because of his inability to achieve real happiness, reserved for men with *Arete*,[44] in one current of modern thought, as Rousseau noted, the vassal was equated with the ox due to his inability to experience spiritual pain, the privilege of noble souls.

Nietzsche also talked about the inability of the slave to rise to genuine happiness. In his eyes, it was not so much melancholy and pain that characterised the great souls as the extraordinary intensity of feelings in general: 'The higher the intellect, the greater the extent, dominion and degree of pain and pleasure' (IX, 567). The quest for truth or beauty implied a torment of which the worker immersed in corporal labour had not the slightest inkling. But one had to add that, in rare situations, the agony could turn into its opposite, a happiness whose intensity was unknown and inaccessible to normal people.

---

39   Gramsci 1975, p. 896.
40   Lovejoy 1961.
41   Aristotle 2002, 191, 1177a8–9; on the exclusion of philistines from happiness, cf. Eudemian Ethics, 1215a25–35, and Politics, 1329a20–4.
42   Aristotle 2002, 191, 1177a8–10.
43   Aristotle 2002, 15, 1099b32–3.
44   Aristotle 2002, 191, 1177a 10.

But don't disregard the fact that with this Homeric happiness in one's soul one is also more capable of suffering than any other creature under the sun! [...] As its owner, one becomes ever more refined in pain and eventually too refined; in the end, any slight discontentment and disgust was enough to spoil life for Homer. He had been unable to solve a silly little riddle posed to him by some young fishermen! Yes, the little riddles are the danger for those who are happiest!

FW, 302 [172]

So 'the higher human being always becomes at the same time happier and unhappier', for 'ever more baited hooks to attract his interest are cast his way; the things that stimulate him grow steadily in number, as do the kinds of things that please and displease him'. One wa not to lose sight of the Great Chain of the nobility of the soul, of sensitivity to pain and responsiveness to fine and deep feelings: 'Higher human beings distinguish themselves from the lower by seeing and hearing, and thoughtfully seeing and hearing, immeasurably more – and just this distinguishes human beings from animals, and the higher animals from the lower' (FW, 301 [170–1]).

If the vassal could achieve a certain happiness, noted Tocqueville with reference to the prerevolutionary society of the *ancien régime*, it was merely 'vegetative happiness [*bonheur végétatif*]'.[45] That the exclusion from spiritual life of the masses coarsened by labour was now equated with the absence of pain denoted the disappearance of the sure tranquillity with which classical antiquity viewed the division of society into masters and slaves; in the untiring reassurance of the happiness of the poor was revealed the modern bad conscience as well as the need for an ideology that repressed the negative and the potential for suffering entailed in the continuation of the master-slave relationship.

Nietzsche was consumed with longing for the ancient world, which was not ashamed of slavery and did not feel the need to hide it. But when even he spoke of the (vegetative) happiness of the slaves (in the times before their mass poisoning by socialist agitators through the dissemination of resentment), he showed he shared a thoroughly modern ideological need. For the rest, the continuity with respect to classical antiquity is evident. According to Nietzsche (and the modern tradition behind him), the slave should be satisfied with a dull and fundamentally subhuman happiness: the attempt to help the slave become aware of his condition was 'wicked' and cruel, because destined unnecessarily

45   Tocqueville 1951 ff., Vol. 16, p. 121.

to increase the suffering of the victims of culture. The compassion earlier condemned because it induced a pointless and troublesome sense of unease in the victors who steered the chariot of culture reappeared and was assigned an implicitly positive role, to the extent that it served not to question the shackling of the slaves to the triumphal chariot, i.e., that it facilitated the forward march of culture.

As for Aristotle, happiness in the actual sense of the word remained a prerogative of the upper classes. For that reason, the message of the Gospels revealed its subversive character in the fact that it wished to pave the way of the 'weak and the poor', the masses, to 'happiness'. If the 'lower layers', having been 'treated too philanthropically', then began to enjoy 'a happiness forbidden to them', the revolution, the slave revolt, was already under way (XIII, 178–9).

4   Schopenhauer and Nietzsche: Between 'tragic' Vision of Life and Relapse into Harmonisation

That Nietzsche took the ideological theme of the happiness or serenity of the poor in the first place from Schopenhauer's *The World as Will and Representation* is evident from a fragment from the spring of 1888: '"One is all the more unfortunate the more intelligent one is" – Schopenhauer' (XIII, 218). Rather than a direct quote, this was a passage transcribed by a French author (Féré),[46] whom we will meet again later. However, it confirms that European culture even beyond Germany in the second half of the nineteenth century ended up recognising its debt to Schopenhauer when, in its efforts to exorcise the spectre of the social question, it took to the field with this topos. According to Schopenhauer, 'the higher intellectual power' led precisely to a situation in which the upper classes, those apparently favoured by fortune, were in fact 'far more receptive to suffering than the more stupid could ever be'. If 'penury is the perpetual scourge of the people', for the upper classes it was 'boredom', 'against which the battle is just as tormenting as that against exigency'.[47] Nietzsche pointed out for his part that the aristocrat was called upon to deal with the serious problem of 'withstanding boredom' (*supra*, 11 § 4). Yes, 'the workers complain that they are worked too hard', but 'excessive activity', albeit spontaneous, not 'imposed from outside', also afflicted the 'wealthy classes', so the worker was not to believe that 'a banker lives today in a more enjoyable and

---

46   See on this point Lampl 1986, p. 251.
47   Schopenhauer 1976–82a, p. 430 f.

dignified way than he' (VIII, 335). In conclusion: 'Life becomes increasingly difficult the higher up you go, – it gets colder, there are more responsibilities. [...] For the mediocre, mediocrity is a happiness' (AC 57 [60]).

Both philosophers raised the ability to feel pain to a gesture of aristocratic distinction: 'He in whom genius lives suffers most.'[48] For both, the theme of the boredom of the privileged lost the critical charge it had had in the most advanced trends of the Enlightenment (and also in early socialism).[49]

And yet, there were also dissonances. After describing the condition of the workers in a bleak and seemingly heartfelt tone, as we shall see, Schopenhauer did not hesitate to affirm that the life and 'the labour of the proletarians' was 'a constant source of enjoyment; and that it is much more usual to see happy faces among the poor than among the rich is sure proof that it is used to good advantage'. True, it was an 'enjoyment' of a 'negative' kind, as 'freedom from some form of misery or need', but this did not affect the terms of the issue, especially since, for Schopenhauer, all enjoyment was 'negative.'[50]

We are dealing with a large number of ideological justifications that, in their redundancy, end up losing all coherence. On the one hand, the 'evil that in the name of slavery, or in the name of the proletariat, has always oppressed the great majority of the human race'[51] was exorcised thanks precisely to its eternal nature, i.e., because ostensibly it existed independently of the social and political order; on the other hand, this 'evil' was simply denied, in that it was hidden under the serene and smiling face of the proletariat. While, in the *World as Will and Representation*, it was possible to 'encounter at least as many happy faces among the poor as among the rich',[52] in *Parerga and Paralipomena*, their fates, as we have seen, were reversed, in favour of the poor, with the paradoxical consequence that now the thesis to be proved (that pain or joy were completely independent of 'change in external circumstances') was left reeling: to judge at least by *Parerga and Paralipomena*, it would have sufficed to spread poverty further in order to cause a certain number of rich to sink into this condition, and thus immediately to increase the number of 'happy' faces.

In Nietzsche, there was none of Schopenhauer's disarming philistinism. Even so, the tragic image of the triumphal chariot of culture, dripping with the blood of the slaves that supported it, sometimes seemed to give way to a more comforting picture, from which the suffering was either wholly absent or in

---

48   Schopenhauer 1976–82a, p. 426.

49   In Bravo 1973, p. 257.

50   Schopenhauer 1976–82c, Vol. 5, p. 698 f.

51   Schopenhauer 1976–82c, Vol. 5, p. 290.

52   Schopenhauer 1976–82a, p. 434.

which it was present only by virtue of an outside intervention by the socialists or other apostles, however disguised, of resentment and the spirit of revenge, who roused the slaves from their beneficent dream with shrill speeches. The oscillation or contradiction between two themes so hard to reconcile is evident: on the one hand, the suffering of the popular classes was so little concealed that one asserted the need to deepen it further simply in order to facilitate the forward march of culture, while, on the other, one did not hesitate to resume the topos of the slaves' non-suffering and even of their happiness or serenity, thus falling back into the harmonistic version of a certain modern tradition.

And yet there was a crucial point that continued to unite the two authors here compared with one another and bound both to a tradition strongly represented in modern thought: if, for Nietzsche, culture was the result of 'extra work', for Schopenhauer, it was the result, as we shall see in a moment, of the 'overwork [*Überarbeit*]' of the great majority to the benefit of the small minority that could and had to enjoy *otium*. And this relationship, far from being represented as a 'social question', was a natural, immutable given.

In this respect, we can distinguish three moments in the history of modern and contemporary thought. For Montesquieu, the category of extra work had absolutely no critical meaning, it was simply a statement of fact, with no real contestation. Marx, however, denounced the '*theft* of alien labour' as the secret of capitalist accumulation[53] and the characteristic that continued to unite slave society with bourgeois society, even though the latter tended to vaunt itself as the realisation of freedom. For Nietzsche, finally, the category of extra work appeared in the context of a discourse he meant as metacritical: political critique and moral indignation made no sense in the face of an inviolable natural order and culture, founded irrevocably in slave labour. It is worth noting, however, that, in terms of ideology and worldview, there was no return to the *status quo ante*. Extra work was no longer a matter of course; it was a truth one had to support against the illusions and progressive mystifications whose intrinsic cruelty could no longer be ignored.

---

53   Marx and Engels 1975 ff., 29, 91.

CHAPTER 14

The 'Uneducated Masses', the 'Freethinker' and the 'Free Spirit': Critique and Meta-critique of Ideology

1   Chains and Flowers: The Critique of Ideology between Marx and Nietzsche

Although for opposite reasons, the critique of ideology was an indispensable step for both Marx and Nietzsche: in this regard, they are often compared.[1] Even Nietzsche never ceased to emphasise what for him was an essential point: it was necessary to liquidate the 'conceptual hallucinations [*Begriffs-Hallucinationen*]' (CV, 3, I, 765 [165]), the 'nonsense [*Wahnvorstellung*]' (VII, 140), the 'means of consolation [*Trostmittel*]', the 'illusory images [*Wahnbilder*]', the so-called 'excellent notions' or 'lamentable expedients [*klägliche Nothbe-helfe*]' and 'deceptive, shining names [*trügerischen, glänzenden Namen*]' (VII, 336–7), the 'idols' (GD), that stopped one looking reality in the face, by hiding or transfiguring what was problematic and terrible in it. The resemblances between the two authors seem obvious, except that, in Marx, one can read a sort of advance warning against hasty assimilations or comparisons. Two fundamentally opposed types of critique of ideology must be distinguished: on the one hand, the revolutionary and progressive criticism, which 'has torn up the imaginary flowers from the chain not so that man shall wear the unadorned, bleak chain but so that he will shake off the chain and pluck the living flower'; and on the other, the criticism favoured by the defenders of the *ancien régime* and the historical school of law, which thought 'the *false flowers* have been plucked from the chains in order to wear *real chains* without any flowers'.[2]

The metaphor used here has a story behind it. 'Man is born free, and everywhere he is in chains', according to the famous opening of the *Social Contract*. Science and the arts then spread 'garlands of flowers' over the 'iron chains' of the political and social order to beautify it and make it more tolerable.[3] Locke

---

1   Ricœur (1965, p. 40 ff.; cf. 1969, p. 46) speaks of a 'school of suspicion' in relation to the Marx-Nietzsche-Freud triad, as is well known.

2   Marx and Engels 1975 ff., 3, p. 176, and 1, p. 205.

3   Rousseau 1959 ff., Vol. 3, p. 281.

had expressed himself in similar terms about the 'slavery' imposed by tyranny: 'Chains are but an ill wearing, how much care soever hath been taken to file and polish them.'[4]

This is why Marx described ideologies as *Schönredner* or *Gewissensbeschö-niger*, as if they were a kind of professional decorator charged with beautifying and hiding, with florally ornamenting, the harsh reality of the chains of social oppression. However, the mystifying embellishment that was ideology could be destroyed from opposite social and political standpoints. In arguing thus, Marx also built on the experience of the struggles since the French Revolution, in which, perhaps for the first time in history, three distinct social classes or blocs participated and clashed. For the new regime instituted following the collapse of the *ancien régime* was called into question both by the feudal aristocracy just overthrown and by the nascent working class and the popular masses, which continued to feel, and were, marginalised.

It is understandable that, in their defence of the *ancien régime*, the ideologists of feudal reaction tended to paint emerging bourgeois society in starkly realistic terms, thus drawing attention to the new but, for that reason, no less tolerable forms class rule was taking. Why should the plight of people forced to beg be seen as preferable to that of serfs or even slaves, who after all were ensured a living by their masters? According to Gustav Hugo, the new power holders and their ideologues criticised the violence, which was moreover rare and isolated, against slaves or serfs, but effortlessly ignored everything that 'the poor allow themselves to suffer' in the new conditions.[5] The young Marx pointed out in his polemic against this representative of the 'historical school of law' that this critique of bourgeois society was an indirect celebration of the *ancien régime*, of the plucking of 'flowers' in order to legitimise the 'chains' of serfdom, an institution still alive and kicking in Germany of the day.

Hugo's defence of slave labour in its various forms was explicit. It is useful to examine more closely the debate that developed in this regard to better understand how the critique of ideology could be conducted from two opposing points of view. For example, the term 'wage slavery', which recurred frequently in Marx, represented a denunciation of the dominant ideology and the chains wrapped around even 'free' workers, whose 'freedom' consisted in selling their labour-power on the capitalist market. However, the comparison between factory work and slave labour could also be found, in clearest terms, in Schopenhauer, who was anything but revolutionary: fundamentally, it was the

---

4 Locke 1970, p. 3 (I, §1).
5 Hugo 1819, p. 251f.

same fate, the same 'evil', according to *Parerga and Paralipomena*,[6] as that 'that always hangs over the majority of the human race, under the name of slavery or the proletariat'. Schopenhauer's description of capitalism was full of horrors and no way inferior to that of Marx's *Capital*. Here is how he described the condition of the workers: 'At the age of five years to enter a textile or some other factory, and from then on remain there daily, first ten, then twelve, and eventually fourteen hours, performing the same mechanical work', and all that in order barely to survive – how could one fail once again to think of 'Negro slavery'?[7]

Again and again, the 'three million European weavers' forced to 'vegetate, in hunger and in pain, in damp rooms or dismal factories'[8] were likened to 'Negro slaves.' The 'fundamental difference' between them was simply that 'the slaves owe their origin to violence, the poor to cunning'.[9] 'Cunning', which was the foundation of capitalist society and reduced an apparently free working class to conditions of terrible misery, was here exposed as nothing but a more subtle and refined form of 'violence'. One has the impression of confronting a relentless critique of social inequalities:

> Between serfdom as in Russia and landed property as in England, and generally between the serf and the tenant, cultivator, debtor, mortgage-holder, etc., the difference lies more in the form than in the substance. There is no essential difference if the peasant or the land from which he must live belongs to me, the bird or its feed, the fruit or the tree. [...] Poverty and slavery are thus only two forms, or one might almost say two names: two names for the same thing, the essence of which consists in the fact that the powers of a human being are for the most part not used for him himself but for others; from which what comes to him is partly overburdening with work [*Überladung mit Arbeit*], partly a meagre satisfaction of his needs.

But the conclusion was quite other than one might at first sight have expected. However atrocious the condition of the labouring masses, it was fated:

> As long as on the one hand there is luxury (and luxury is the essential condition for the existence of culture), on the other there must necessar-

---

6   Schopenhauer 1967–82c, Vol. 5, p. 290.
7   Schopenhauer 1976–82b, p. 740.
8   Schopenhauer 1976–82c, Vol. 5, p. 120 f.
9   Schopenhauer 1976–82c, Vol. 5, p. 291.

ily be excessive work [*übermässige Arbeit*] and a life of misery, whether it
be under the name of poverty or of slavery, of *proletarii* or of *servi*.[10]

The critique of the imaginary 'flowers' that adorned the workers' 'chains' ended
in legitimising the 'real chains' and their further strengthening. The harshness
with which relations of production within capitalist society were described was
aimed at destroying every hope of and every plan for their transformation: the
burden of misery and pain weighing down upon the human condition was
so heavy and above all so tenacious – it reappeared, always in new forms, in
changed historical situations – that it was crazy to hope for political and social
action, it would be absurd to expect anything from the transformation of institutions: 'The ceaseless efforts to banish suffering achieve nothing more than
changes in its form.'[11]

Under the influence of Schopenhauer, to whom he explicitly referred, the
early Nietzsche expressed himself in similar terms: against the superficial 'optimism' displayed above all by the socialist movement, 'our superior philosophy
teaches that wherever we turn, we always come up against absolute ruin, the
pure will to live, and here all palliatives are meaningless' (B, II, 1, 58). We have
seen how Schopenhauer and Nietzsche, in declaring 'overburdening with work'
or 'extra work' to be the basis of the culture, 'luxury' and *otium* of the best or
the richest, agreed, although from a very different political point of view, with
the Marxist thesis that 'extra work' was common to both slavery and capitalist society in general. So, it was typical of every society divided into classes
based on exploitation, or on the appropriation of the 'extra work' and the
'surplus value' extracted by a privileged minority. What distinguished 'socio-
economic formations, e.g., slave society from that of wage labour', was merely
the 'form' of the appropriation of extra work. Those who treated the appropriation of 'extra work' as a phenomenon exclusive to slave and feudal society
were engaged in a vulgar apologetics regarding capitalist relations of production.[12]

Even more important is that, in his writings, Nietzsche refuted the thesis,
cherished by the liberal tradition, of 'negative freedom'. How did the delivery
and appropriation of extra work happen? 'Slavishly subjected to life's necessity [*der Lebensnoth sklavisch unterworfen*]', 'the overwhelming majority' of
the population was forced to provide 'extra work' for the maintenance of the
'privileged class [*bevorzugte Klasse*]' (CV, 3, I, 767 [166]). It was only the hard

10   Schopenhauer 1976–82c, Vol. 5, pp. 288–91.
11   Schopenhauer 1976–82a, p. 432.
12   Marx and Engels 1955 ff., 23, p. 231 fn. 30.

THE 'UNEDUCATED MASSES', THE 'FREETHINKER' AND THE 'FREE SPIRIT'   435

necessity to escape hunger and starvation that forced the bulk of workers to endure a condition not unlike that of ancient slaves (*supra*, 2 §6). This was the wage slavery of which Marx spoke, and whose involuntary admission he was surprised to note even among representatives of the liberal tradition. *Capital* quoted in this regard Joseph Townsend, who welcomed the fact that the noisy and painful 'legal constraint to labour' had been replaced by the 'peaceable, silent, unremitted pressure of hunger', fear of death by starvation.[13] This ensured the necessary 'obedience' of the servant to his master, since for a 'disobedient servant' there was no 'punishment' more effective than dismissal and the 'hunger' that followed.[14] However, this did not prevent the British liberal parson from drawing a most edifying picture of his country: even the most wretched was a 'freeman', who provided a 'free service' on the basis of 'his own judgement', free of the 'constraint' to which the 'slave' was subjected.[15] For Nietzsche and Marx, on the other hand, this supposedly 'free human being' bore an impressive resemblance to a slave.

With an undeniable demystifying *élan*, Nietzsche identified factory workers as the modern slaves, but he immediately added that this mechanism was to be kept well oiled in the best interests of culture. He was no less committed than Marx to tearing away the veil with which the ruling ideology sought to disguise the reality of wage slavery. However, in his case, the destruction of the imaginary flowers resulted not only in the justification of wage slavery, as in that of Schopenhauer, but of slavery itself, which had persisted in the southern United States until the end of the Civil War and still existed, even vigorously so, in Africa and the colonial world in general.

Schopenhauer explicitly equated 'proletarian' and 'slave', but only in the first case were the chains of servitude insuperable. He mocked the attempts in any way to change the condition of the workers, but put his finest feelings on display in denouncing black slavery. Nietzsche overcame this contradiction, but the way out was perhaps suggested to him by Schopenhauer himself, who made a clear distinction between the 'wretched' plantation slaves in the southern United States and 'the slaves of the ancients, the *familia*, the *vernae*, a species [*Geschlecht*] satisfied and faithful to its master'.[16] For Nietzsche, too, ancient slavery seemed sometimes to take on the conciliatory face of Diogenes or Epictetus (*supra*, 12 §5). Now, however, ancient slavery was equated both with the condition of the workers and with modern slavery. The position thus

---

13   Townsend 1971, p. 23 f.
14   Townsend 1971, p. 26 f.
15   Townsend 1971, p. 24; on Townsend cf. Marx and Engels 1975 ff., 35, p. 640.
16   Schopenhauer 1976–82c, Vol. 5, p. 414.

reached was not only logically more stringent, but it was also fully immune to Schopenhauer's perhaps somewhat instrumentalising attitude: precisely in the country taken by European democrats as a model on account of its political institutions, the United States, where 'privileges of birth' had been abolished and 'pure abstract right' ruled, precisely there raged the barbarity of black slavery.[17]

2   Ideology as Legitimation of and Challenge to the Existing Social Order

The function performed by this illusory 'flower' of ideology was twofold and ambivalent. To the extent that it served to transfigure the real chains, to the extent that it acted in the framework of social oppression as consolation and opium, to the extent that it blocked the awareness of the oppressed class and paralysed its resistance, it played a conservative role in consolidating the chains: in this sense it was an integral part of a system of rule, and even its essential connective tissue. But precisely because it was meant to beautify and transfigure reality, social oppression, the ideological flower could not be immediately identified with it: it continued to represent an element of differentiation and, though illusory, of transcendence of that which existed.

Marx, who again and again emphasised ideology's conservative role, was also aware, on the other hand, of the restlessness and embarrassment the element of differentiation-transcendence in regard to that which existed could cause the ruling class. It was always possible someone would take the ideological embellishment seriously and demand its realisation. Thus, a complex dialectic developed, full of contradictions. The demands advanced on the basis of the claim or hope to realise in practice the ideological phrases with which the ruling class sought to beautify and consolidate its rule proved to be completely unrealistic. Was it not absurd to 'achieve the reorganisation of the world on a would-be new formula, which formula is no more than the theoretical expression of the real movement which exists and which is so well described by Ricardo'? The answer:

> [I]t is totally impossible to reconstitute society on the basis of what is merely an embellished shadow [*verschönerter Schatten*] of it. In propor-

---

17   Schopenhauer 1976–82c, Vol. 5, p. 299.

tion as this shadow takes on substance again, we perceive that this substance, far from being the transfiguration dreamt of, is the actual body of existing society.[18]

To fail to understand 'the necessary distinction between the real and ideal shape' of existing society was to 'undertake the superfluous business of once again realising the ideal expression itself, the clarified and reflected image emitted by reality as such'.[19]

But, however idealistic the attitude here criticised, which made the flower of ideology autonomous of the chain it was meant to transfigure and legitimise, however quixotic the wish to realise its ideological embellishment in the context of social reality, it was still disturbing for the ruling power. The differentiation-transcendence inherent in the ideology in respect of existence could become a contradiction, 'a certain opposition and hostility'. On the one hand was the ruling class, immersed in the daily management and practical implementation of the system of exploitation, which, in this sense, always remained with its feet on the ground; and on the other, the layers working to construct the ideology (of the flowers needed to embellish and conceal the chains), layers that for that very reason were inclined to take seriously the ideological phrases upon which those who actually ran the system of exploitation and rule looked with detachment, not to say contempt.[20]

So, the destruction of the ideological flowers by the ruling classes themselves was a moment of reaction or at least of sociopolitical retreat. 'Enthusiastic flowers' adorned the cradle of the bourgeoisie, but subsequently became 'faded'.[21] Having dropped the illusion of founding a community of *citoyens*, bourgeois society revealed itself unambiguously as the rule of wealth and capital. This process happened not only after the revolution of 1789 but also after that of 1848. When sociopolitical confrontation became more acute, the ruling class came to see the ideology meant to transfigure and legitimise its rule as an inconvenience. After the February Revolution of 1848, 'the emancipation of the workers, even as a phrase, became an unbearable danger for the new republic'; in the meantime, it had become necessary to suppress all 'formulas', all 'ideological trimmings', by means of 'force *sans phrase*', in order once and for all to create clarity and provide a conclusive definition of the capitalist system of 'subjugation of the proletariat', of the 'slavery of labour'.[22]

---

18   Marx and Engels 1975 ff., 6, pp. 123 and 144.
19   Marx and Engels 1975 ff., 29, p. 476.
20   Marx and Engels 1975 ff., 5, p. 60 f.
21   Marx and Engels 1975 ff., 4, p. 81.
22   Marx and Engels 1975 ff., 10, pp. 62–6 and 77, and 86.

After the revolution of 1848, Marx analysed the tendency of political economy to conceal the contradictions within an ostensibly superior 'harmony' as a symptom of the bourgeoisie's ideological decadence.[23] On the other hand, he criticised the tendency to destroy the harmonious illusion, to tear off the 'flowers' but only in order to make the naked 'chains' felt in all their hardness, as an even more brutal reactionary variant of the ideology of the ruling classes. Significant in this regard was his judgement on Malthus: 'As compared to the wretched bourgeois economists who preach harmony, Malthus' only merit lay in his pointed emphasis on the disharmonies', indeed he had 'emphasised, amplified and publicised [them]', though 'with complacent sacerdotal cynicism'. So, the impartiality was only apparent. The theorist of overpopulation 'affects ruthlessness; he takes a cynical pleasure in it and exaggerates his conclusions in so far as they are directed against the miserables, even beyond the point which would be scientifically justified from his point of view'.[24]

According to Marx, Malthus had none of the lucid objectivity and actual lack of regard of a scholar like Ricardo, who could seem 'cynical' only because he described bourgeois society and the condition of the workers without embellishing and legitimising it with the etiquette of 'a 'humanitarian' phraseology'. In Malthus, however, the apparent ruthlessness turned into its opposite, into 'an apology for the poverty of the producers'. When he tore the 'flowers' from the 'chains', in order to liquidate any even vague prospect of improvement for the working classes, he gave 'brutal expression to the brutal view taken by capital or by the exploiting classes in general'.[25]

Ideology, for Marx, was indeed the legitimisation and transfiguration of existing oppression, but also 'the fantastic realisation of the human essence'. In this sense, religion was 'at the same time the expression of real distress and also the protest against real distress'.[26] This element of protest, however timorous, against existence was the real target of the critique of ideology that looked exclusively at the 'flowers'. In Nietzsche's eyes, 'the dignity of labour is a modern delusion of the most stupid kind, it is a dream of slaves' (VII, 140). But, in this dream that was ideology, Marx criticised the illusoriness of the transcendence of existence, while Nietzsche, for his part, criticised the desire for transcendence to which this dream, however confused and unrealistic, gave expression.

---

23   Cf. the polemic against Bastiat, the theorist of 'economic harmonies', in Marx and Engels 1975 ff., 29, p. 476.
24   Marx and Engels 1975 ff., 31, p. 350.
25   Marx and Engels 1975 ff., 6, pp. 125; 28, 524; and 31, p. 349.
26   Marx and Engels 1975 ff., 3, p. 175.

Symptomatic were their opposed attitudes to Christianity. 'Christians', said Marx, 'are equal in heaven but unequal on earth', just as in bourgeois society 'the individual members of the nation are equal in the heaven of their political world, but unequal in the earthly existence of society'.[27] As an 'opium' and a consoling technique, heavenly equality confirmed or risked confirming worldly inequalities, the real target of Marx's critique. Nietzsche saw things very differently: even though the demand for equality was projected into a remote heavenly sphere, it represented a disastrous contradiction of worldly inequalities, which had to be accepted in eternity. Christianity, which Marx criticised as an instrument of sociopolitical conservatism and on account of its inability to distance itself in reality from the existing social order, was denounced by Nietzsche for its ideal and sometimes directly political proximity to egalitarian and socialist movements. In both cases, Christianity was the prototype of ideology. So, the opposite outcome that the critique of ideology assumed in the two authors becomes clear.

Again and again, the resemblances were at the same time moments of opposition. For Marx, the workers' condition was synonymous with 'economic slavery', 'disguised slavery [*verhüllte Sklaverei*]' or 'modern slavery', or, as we have just seen, 'labour slavery'.[28] In similar terms, Nietzsche spoke of 'factory servitude [*Fabrik-Sklaverei*]' and 'work slaves' (M, 206 [153] and GM, III, 18 [100]). While mocking the idea of the 'dignity of labour', Marx made fun of 'human rights' in capitalist society: 'And the first birthright of capital is equal exploitation of labour power by all capitalists'.[29] At first sight, it would seem that both men warned against the illusion that superficial reforms could have a fundamental impact on the reality of workers' slavery. In Marx, this was a well-known theme. But even Nietzsche wrote as follows about the workers' condition: 'To believe that higher payment could lift from them the *essence* of their misery, by which I mean their impersonal enslavement! Phooey!' (M, 206 [153]).

But here the convergence is transformed into a radical antagonism. From his observation of the essentially slave-like character of the workers' situation, Nietzsche inferred the pointlessness of any attempt at change. He not only called on the workers to ignore trade union demands but denounced the economic struggle, along with the political struggle of Social Democracy: 'To let oneself be talked into believing that through a heightening of this impersonality within the mechanical workings of a new society the disgrace of slavery

---

27   Marx and Engels 1975 ff., 3, p. 79.
28   Cf. Marx and Engels 1975 ff., 3, p. 420; 4, p. 474; 10, p. 59.
29   Marx and Engels 1975 ff., 35, p. 297.

could be turned into a virtue! Phooey!' (M, 206 [153]). Not only the slogan calling for the abolition of slavery was senseless: so too was the demand to damage
an institution so inexorably massive and compact. The only possible change
was that certain individuals and groups might escape the fate of subjugation
that continued to weigh on the majority of humanity. Hence the invitation to
German and European workers to join in the colonial adventure (*supra*, 11 §7).

Marx, on the other hand, invariably denounced the workers' conditions as
'wage slavery', but when the Civil War broke out, he called for the defence of the
'system of free labour' against the 'system of slavery'.[30] The sharp denunciation
of capitalist society did not lead to the reduction of wage labour to slave labour,
nor to the denunciation or undervaluing of the struggle to change, mitigate, or
limit 'wage slavery'.

The two critiques of ideology were antithetical not only at the immediately
political but also at the more strictly theoretical level. A process of double
historicisation confronted one of naturalisation. Unlike Nietzsche, Marx historicised the slave-worker equation, not only in the sense that he hypothesised and
predicted a social order very different from the existing one, but also because he
deemed it possible even within capitalist society to effect significant changes
in the workers' situation.

If one of the characteristics of ideological discourse is to hide negativity and
provide a rosy view of reality, it must be said that the attitude of Nietzsche and
Schopenhauer was ambiguous. On the one hand, they rejected edifying depic-
tions and laid bare the terrible reality of workers' conditions in that period,
while, on the other, they used a dual technique to conceal or neutralise that
negativity. In the first place, one was not to forget that the ability to suffer, or to
suffer spiritually and deeply, is above all a characteristic of the upper classes.
Although not denied, the sufferings of the lower classes thus lost the sting that
might call the existing social order into question. Above all: immersed as it was
in a bath of eternity and inevitability, the charge of negativity was defused.

The critique of ideology seemed to reach its peak when it directed 'a cold
malice against 'beautiful words' as well as 'beautiful feelings', against 'a prattle
of feelings', against the '"higher hoax" or, if you would prefer, "idealism"'. But
then, this 'unconditional will not to be fooled' was synonymous with 'realists'
culture', with 'courage in the face of reality', with the acceptance of the immutable reality of slavery, the division of humankind into masters and slaves (GD,
1–2 [224–6]). If there was a truly critical element in this view, it took aim at
the dreams, illusions, mystifications, self-deceptions, deliriums and hallucina-

---

30   Marx and Engels 1975 ff., 35, p. 542.

tions of those who would in one way or another change or attack the 'sacred order of nature'. It was not the ruling class being criticised but *homo ideologicus*. Against him was set the 'tropical human being', who, rather than dream of transcending the reality of hierarchy and struggle, was able to recognise and enjoy himself as a 'beast of prey' in the manner of Cesare Borgia (JGB, 197 [85]).

So, the juxtaposition of two different and antithetical criticisms of ideology was superficial and unsustainable. In a sense, Nietzsche's approach was condemned in advance by Engels, when he took to task the entrenched and explicitly conservative positions of certain British business circles and politicians. To workers calling for a reduction in the working day, they seemed to respond:

> 'You, working men, are slaves, and shall remain slaves, because only by your slavery can we increase our wealth and comforts; because we, the ruling class of this country, cannot continue to rule without you being slaves'.[31]

We have seen how Engels, in criticising Carlyle's theory of genius, commented ironically on the claim of the 'whip' to be a 'genius' (*supra*, 2 § 5). The young Marx presented a variant of the metaphor when he spoke of the 'knout' legitimised by the historical school of law as 'time-honoured, ancestral, historical'.[32] To a certain extent availing itself of Enlightenment doctrine, the historical school of law made a great show to all and sundry of a 'ruthless method' and adopted a sceptical rather than a fideistic stance (*infra*, 16 § 4). The result was paradoxical. A critique of ideology that destroyed the 'flowers', the attempts to legitimate the oppression and violence perpetrated by the ruling class, was transformed into an ideology that treated this violence and this oppression as if it did not even need to seek legitimation. One might say that Nietzsche conferred rigour and consistency on the procedure criticised by Marx in Hugo.

3   Direct Violence and Form of Universality

In analysing the two opposing types of critique of ideology, I started from the French Revolution. And yet, to clarify Nietzsche's attitude, one would have to

---

31   Marx and Engels 1975 ff., 10, p. 272.
32   Marx and Engels 1975 ff., 3, p. 177.

go much further back. One could even go as far back as Thrasymachus, who, according to Plato, defined 'justice' as 'that which is to the advantage of the existing power'.[33] Even if the demystifying potential seems in theory to affect every form of government, its actual political target was in the first place democracy: 'Each type of government enacts laws that are in its own interest, a democracy democratic laws, a tyranny tyrannical ones and so on'.[34] Democracy could claim no special legitimacy: the power of the *demos* was unmasked as resting, like other forms of government, on the violence it too claimed to want to overcome in the name of a higher sociopolitical organisation based on greater 'justice'. It was not for nothing that Thrasymachus ended up formulating a sort of 'manifesto of the oligarchic party' and propagating a 'return to *patrios politeia*',[35] to the constitution of the good old days, when oligarchical power was accepted as an evident and natural fact, without being challenged in the name of democracy or 'justice'. The initial impartiality with which one viewed any form of government made way in reality for an 'indirect apologetics'[36] for the aristocratic regime. The 'flowers' of the ideology of 'justice' had been plucked simply to confirm the need for 'chains'; power had been exposed as violence simply in order to present oligarchical violence as a form of power that, if not better, was certainly no worse than the rest. In this case, the critique of ideology was the reaction of those who invoked the principle of *tu quoque*, and, in invoking it, destroyed the form of universality both for themselves and for their opponents. Even the higher idealities they invoked to legitimise their position were an ideological veneer.

This aspect was also well represented in Nietzsche, who, from the very beginning was committed to disarming the revolutionary and socialist movement by neutralising its reference to 'justice' and higher moral sentiments. But especially illuminating was the comparison with Callicles, who said the following in Plato's *Gorgias*:

> If you ask me, the people who put laws – conventions – into place are the weak, the many. It is with an eye to themselves and their own advantage that they put the laws in place, praise the things they praise, and blame the things they blame. [...] For themselves, I imagine they are well pleased if they can have an equal share, given their inferiority. This is why, by convention, this is said to be unjust and disgraceful – trying to get the better

---

33   Plato, The Republic, 78.
34   Plato, The Republic, 78.
35   Thus Untersteiner (1954, p. 24).
36   On 'indirect apologetics' cf. Lukács 1954, p. 164.

of the many – and they call it acting unjustly. In my view, however, nature itself shows clearly what is just – for the better man to have more than the worse, and the more powerful more than the less powerful. It is evident in many areas that this is how things are, both in the animal world and among humans, in whole cities and races – that justice has been adjusted to be precisely this – the stronger ruling over, and getting the better of, the weaker.[37]

The norm, whether juridical or moral, gives the form of universality to contents and interests that are or may be merely special. And so, on the basis of this norm or system of norms, one can contest the illusory or mystifying character of the universality or the form of universality. Insofar as a system of power or rule assumes the form of universality, it achieves a legitimation that consolidates it. On the other hand, the form is never nothing, but always represents a concession on the part of the ruling class and a constraint on its action: as a result, its rule is in a certain sense constricted. From this point of view, said Hegel in polemic with Haller, whose position was similar to that of Callicles, the denial of universality was nothing more than the celebration of 'contingent natural violence'.[38]

In fact, Callicles, an 'Athenian aristocrat [...], a typical representative of his social class', counted among the 'natures that worshipped force'.[39] It is interesting to see in this case too categories and metaphors emerged that usually characterise the discourse of the critique of ideology: it was a question of freeing oneself from the 'fetters', from the 'spells', from the 'charms' of a mystifying 'equality' theorised and imposed by the weakest.[40] And so we reach the central question. In the ideological struggle, the weakest seized the initiative, propagating a mystifying 'universality' that in theory should transcend the conflict but, in reality, served only to keep a tight rein on the strongest.

This was also Nietzsche's point of view: since the weak person needed to avoid direct confrontation, he 'conceals himself in the communal generality of the concept "human being"' (M, 26 [24]). In the early writings, he emphasised that '*in modern times* the slave establishes the representations' (VII, 337). But, as the long duration of the decay became slowly apparent to Nietzsche, he dated the ideological initiative of the plebeians and the malformed ever further back,

---

37   Plato 2010, 57–8, Gorgias, 483b–d.
38   Hegel 1969–79, Vol. 7, p. 403 (*Grundlinien der Philosophie des Rechts*, § 258 A, fn).
39   Jaeger 1934, Vol. 1, pp. 410 and 404.
40   Plato 2010, 59, Gorgias, 484a.

until it eventually came to encompass the entire history of the West, beginning with Judaism, that first and devastating slave revolt in the name of moral universality.

Committed to denouncing the illusory character of universality in the context of a society based on class oppression, Marx focused on the role of the ruling classes in the construction of ideological discourse. In continuity with Christian discourse, the concept of *égalité* that had emerged from the French Revolution ended up concealing or legitimising the reality of exploitation and domination. And yet, this idea of equality was something great, it expressed 'the unity of human essence, for man's consciousness of his species and his attitude towards his species, for the practical identity of man with man, i.e., for the social or human relation of man to man'.[41] It represented 'a progress of history',[42] a concession, however partial, forced on the ruling classes. In this sense, Marx also recognised the role of the lower classes in the construction of ideological discourse. But it is precisely this content celebrated by Marx that attracted harsh criticism from Nietzsche, who saw in it the confirmation of the continuity of the slave revolt and of the ideological initiative deployed by slaves ever since Christianity, and indeed, since post-exilic Judaism.

4   From National-Liberal Reticence to the Duplicity of Aristocratic Radicalism

If Marx criticised religion as the 'opium of the people', as the dulling and neutralising of social protest and thereby an instrument of the consolidation of the existing order, on the other side we find a critique of ideology that combined its radical atheism with a recommendation of religion for the masses. Schopenhauer's attitude is significant. At first he seemed to embrace fully the results of the critique by Enlightenment thinkers of 'obscurantism', defined as 'a sin, if not perhaps against the holy spirit, then certainly against the human spirit', an unforgivable sin, in any case, that should be punished with implacable contempt, even *post mortum*, for those who caused it.[43] On the other hand, the memory of Voltaire, of the great thinkers of the Enlightenment and of

---

41   Marx and Engels 1975 ff., 4, p. 39.
42   Marx and Engels 1975 ff., 3, p. 465.
43   Schopenhauer 1976–82b, pp. 671–72 and 750; the consequences of this contempt are borne by authors like Adam Müller and Friedrich Schlegel.

all those who had distinguished themselves in the struggle against 'obscurantism' was to remain an object of veneration.[44]

However, the dialogue *On Religion*, which opened with a tribute to the courage of the truth of Bruno and Vanini, delivered by a participant in the dialogue, Philalethes,[45] closed with Demopheles's warning against the politically ruinous effects of the critique of religion: one had to take care not to encourage 'ochlocracy and anarchy [...], the sworn enemy of every legal order, of all civilization and all humanity'.[46] In a letter, Schopenhauer declared emphatically that he did not in any way identify only with Philalethes, who, as his name suggests, embodied the disinterested love of truth, consistent and open-minded theoretical research, but that he also shared the concerns of Demopheles, who represented awareness of the need not to undermine popular religiosity, the possible dam against the 'ochlocratic', anarchist and socialist tide.[47]

The same Schopenhauer that, with an eye to the past, celebrated Voltaire and the Enlightenment, now, in the present, supported and even demanded the dismissal of the materialists Büchner and Moleschott from their teaching posts: in a language that reveals a surprising concern for religious orthodoxy, he contemptuously consigned them to the ranks of 'heterodox teachers', also in consideration of the link between their materialism and their 'taking part in politics [*Politisieren*]'.[48]

The critique of religion and of ideology was not to penetrate through to the masses: this point of view was explicitly formulated by the young Nietzsche, who had already demonstrated its demystifying potential. However, this did not prevent him from praising the 'wholesome unconsciousness', the 'sound sleep' into which the people had sunk, and where it was good that they should stay (BA, 3, I, 699 [75]).

In the wake of industrialisation and the development of the labour movement, the urban masses began to break away from traditional ideology and to formulate new demands from a position culturally as well as politically independent of the old ruling classes. Against this, the young Nietzsche set nostalgia for a peasant world still dominated in the last analysis by serfdom

---

44   Schopenhauer 1976–82b, p. 749.
45   Schopenhauer 1976–82c, Vol. 5, p. 384.
46   Schopenhauer 1976–82c, Vol. 5, p. 424; Lukács (1954, p. 175) has already pointed to the significance of this conclusion.
47   Schopenhauer 1929–33, Vol. 2, p. 76 (letter to Julius Frauenstädt, 30 October 1851).
48   Schopenhauer 1929–33, Vol. 2, pp. 394 and 480 (letter to Julius Frauenstädt, 15 July 1855 and 28 March 1856).

and an unproblematic loyalty to the Junkers, devoid of all critical stimuli regarding traditional religion and ideology:

> What an elevating effect on us is produced by the sight of medieval serfs [*Hörigen*], whose legal and ethical relationship with their superior was internally sturdy and sensitive, whose narrow existence was profoundly cocooned – how elevating – and how reproachful!
>
> CV, 3, I, 769 [168]

Within these social relationships, 'the servitude [*Dienstbarkeit*] of the masses, their submissive obedience, their instinct of loyalty to the rule of genius' were guaranteed by the persistence of the 'religious instinct', the 'mythological images'. The 'loyalty' of the people to 'its customs, privileges, native soil, and language' as well as to its religion had not yet been affected by the demystifying intrusion of education or, worse still, of the appeal to 'emancipation' (BA, 3, I, 698–9 [74–5]).

Right up to the end, the echo of nostalgia for a world threatened or overwhelmed by modern subversion continued to reverberate in Nietzsche: 'There are no longer any poor to work the fields. Education destroys the *race* of workers and consequently agriculture' (XIII, 123). Another fragment lamented the disappearance of 'inalienable landed property', to which had corresponded, at the cultural and ideological level, the 'veneration of elders'; now, with the 'fragmentation of land ownership', 'a newspaper takes the place of daily prayers' (XI, 68–9).

The crime of the socialist and revolutionary movement lay primarily in its efforts to undermine this world and render it impossible: the polemic against the '[i]ll-fated seducers who have destroyed the slave's state of innocence with the fruit of the tree of knowledge' was unrelenting (CV, 3, I, 765–6 [165]). Along with education, new needs were injected: 'To have no needs is for the people the greatest misfortune, Lassalle once declared. Hence the workers' educational associations, whose aim has often been explained to me as the production of needs' (VII, 243)

Here, to create needs meant nothing other than to disturb the dull and sleepy peace created for the slaves by the ideological opium, despite the suffering caused by the chains. It meant introducing an alien element of reflection and division into this immediate and unproblematic identification with the existing social order and with a painful and wretched destiny. The blame lay with the 'socialist rabble' that 'undermine[d] workers' instincts and pleasures, their feelings of modesty [*Genügsamkeit*] about their little existences' (AC, 57 [60]), that had destroyed the conditions that made it possible to be 'poor, cheerful, and a slave', and that had irrevocably plunged into crisis the 'voluntary, idyllic poverty' with which the worker-slaves were content before socialist propaganda awakened 'mad hopes' in them (M, 206 [153–4]). It was the mark of infamy of contemporary society as a whole to have made impossible 'modest and self-sufficient [*selbstgenügsam*] types', capable of accepting calmly and as a matter of course their natural destiny, which was now experienced as 'desperate [*Notstand*]' and an 'injustice' and thus rejected (GD, 40 [216]). Despite all this, religion could and was to be recommended, so long as it was able to teach slaves to worship 'resignation and meekness' as 'the godhead', as something sacred, so long as it was able to convince them there was 'no reason to take life too seriously and certainly no reason to complain' (M, 92 [66]).

However, it should be added that Nietzsche, despite his disappointment at the vanishing of a world of pious peasant simplicity, not only did not identify with it but came to see it, at least in the years of his maturity, as the complete antithesis to his own worldview. There was no trace of the indecision present in Schopenhauer, who still wavered between Philalethes (said to embody the pure love of truth) and Demopheles; or of the ambiguity and hypocrisy implicit in the very name of Demopheles, as if the decision to exclude the people from the critique of religion was dictated by love of the people. As we shall see later, sometimes a reference was still made to 'general utility' (the need to avoid disturbing the cultural order), but, for the rest, it was a question of openly proclaiming that it was in the interests of the 'masters' to recommend religion to the 'vassals'. The difference was that now two opposing moral discourses were consciously directed towards the two social classes or 'races'. The former were called upon to free themselves from the shackles resulting from Christianity so that they could fully develop their will and their inclination to give orders; and these characteristics were also measured by the ability to preach to the lower classes the values of humility and resignation.

While Schopenhauer admitted that he did not want to identify unilaterally with Philalethes, Nietzsche, in a note written in the spring–summer of 1875, said he was 'not on the side of Demopheles' (VIII, 46). But that did not mean that he would be prepared to surmount the exclusion clauses implicit in his critique of ideology. On the contrary, they were reinforced by a wholly new radicalism. This attitude was definitely quite different from that mocked by Engels, i.e., an obsequious revering of the official religion, of the sort typical of the national liberals. The latter had so internalised the rule of reticence and self-censorship that they dared not even think about a real criticism of Christianity, let alone utter one in public. Indeed, they continued to praise its greatness in measured and devout tones, even if they then added with a sigh that the development of culture and science had undermined previous certainties –

certainties that nevertheless remained available to and, thankfully, continued to be effective among the lower classes.

Nietzsche, on the other hand, all along enounced the rule of duplicity. After upbraiding primary-school teachers for undermining the imperious necessity of ensuring that children continue to be educated in accordance with 'tradition' (*supra*, 4 § 6), he added in a note written in the winter of 1871–2: 'At the top, the vision must be magnificently free. The two are in excellent accord' (VII, 385).

Schopenhauer's mistake was, essentially, not to have moved on from the national-liberal standpoint: he had attributed to religion a *'sensus allegoricus'* and failed to understand that 'never yet has a religion, either indirectly or directly, either as dogma or as allegory, contained a truth' (MA, 110 [88]). This indulgent attitude towards religion encouraged and perpetuated prejudices, awkwardness and hesitations among the ruling classes that they should have actually been able to shake off. This was the main task. It was no longer a question of merely keeping the masses in the dark about the results of the critique of religion. Certainly, 'let Zarathustra not speak to the people' (Za, Zarathustra's Prologue, 9 [14]). But this was not all and is not even the main thing. It was necessary to become fully aware that the discourse reserved for the ruling classes is one thing, and that directed towards the subaltern classes another: 'We must distinguish strictly here between A and B' (XIII, 448).

5   Religions as 'Means of Breeding and Education' in the Hands of the Ruling Classes

While there were no problems about which discourse to direct towards B, to the well-formed, to those called upon to belong to the ruling class, there were some doubts about that to be directed towards A, the malformed, the menials. Was religion really capable of invoking a 'sound sleep' in them, as the survival of culture required? In the West, at least, Christianity was doubtless suffering from the same sickness that in theory it was supposed to eradicate. Plebeian resentment was strongly felt:

> Whether you attribute your bad situation to other people or to yourself (socialists take the former strategy and Christians, for instance, take the latter), it does not really make any difference. What is common to both (we can also say what is *unworthy*) is that somebody is supposedly to blame for your suffering – basically, that sufferers are prescribing themselves the honey of revenge for their suffering.
>
>   GD, 34 [208–9]

However, at the specifically political level, the Christian churches always succeeded in diverting *ressentiment* in the intimate sense and thus preventing a new wave of the slave revolt that had had its first act in the preaching of the gospel. If they were already incapable of preventing the emergence of *ressentiment* in the slave (a reference that now included the wage slave), the churches could at least channel this feeling in such a way as to make it politically and socially harmless:

> 'I suffer: someone or other must be guilty' – and every sick sheep thinks the same. But his shepherd, the ascetic priest, says to him, 'Quite right, my sheep! Somebody must be to blame: but you yourself are this somebody, you yourself alone are to blame for it, you yourself alone are to blame for yourself'. ... That is bold enough, wrong enough: but at least one thing has been achieved by it, the direction of *ressentiment* is, as I said – *changed.*
>
> GM, III, 15 [94]

An important result has been achieved: the socialist illusion and lie that 'by changing institutions happiness on earth is increased' was destroyed (VIII, 482). At this point, it was permissible and even obligatory to raise a song of praise to the figure of the priest:

> Here reigns a great necessity: drainages and their clean, cleansing waters are needed also for the spiritual refuse; swift streams of love are needed, and strong, humble, pure hearts who prepare and sacrifice themselves for such an office of non-public health care – for it is a sacrifice; a priest is and remains a human sacrifice ... The people see such sacrificed, subdued, serious persons of 'faith' as wise, that is, as having become knowing, as certain' in relation to their own uncertainty; and who would want to deprive them of this word and of their awe?
>
> FW, 351 [209]

But this reverence was not to overflow, drawing in and infecting even the ruling class, the successful, the 'philosophers' in the best sense of the word: in this circle, 'a priest, too, is considered to be one of "the people" and not a knower, primarily because philosophers do not themselves believe in "men of knowledge" and already smell "the people" in this belief and superstition' (FW, 351 [210]).

It was important never to lose sight of the distinction between A and B. In the first case, 'Christianity appears still to be necessary'. To be sure, it was not called upon to provide a cure; on the contrary, in certain circumstances, its point 'is to make sick, useful for breaking the spirit of rebellion and roughness', so that the 'rabble and the beast' could be immobilised by a sort of 'straitjacket'. When imposing gruelling 'penances' on the Chandala, the Brahmins were well aware that 'in the struggle against the beast making it sick is often the only way to make it weak'. In the case of B, however, religion and especially Christianity was a 'symptom of the sickness' that had definitely to be healed in the interests of the individual and society as a whole (XIII, 448–9).

The rule of 'duplicity' had to be applied: 'We immoralists and anti-Christians think that we benefit from the existence of the church' (GD, 3 [173]); it was 'in the instinct of those who rule (whether individuals or classes) to patronize and exalt the virtues thanks to which those who are subjected are made manageable and submissive.' In this sense, 'the "masters" too can become Christians' (XII, 568).

So, the problem was not to make a positive or negative judgement about different religions in general, but to ensure that the ruling class could exert social and political control: if religions, instead of acting as 'means for breeding and education [*Züchtungs-und Erziehungsmittel*]' of the masses, became autonomous and wanted to be 'the ultimate goal instead of a means alongside other means', the consequences were disastrous (JGB, 62 [55]).

But, once the aristocrats had been able to take control, religion became a vital means of countering subversion and realising the values of aristocratic radicalism:

> For people who are strong, independent, prepared, and predestined for command, people who come to embody the reason and art [*Kunst*] of a governing race, religion is an additional means of overcoming resistances, of being able to rule [*herrschen*]. It binds the ruler together with the ruled, giving and handing the consciences of the ruled over to the rulers – which is to say: handing over their hidden and most interior aspect, and one which would very much like to escape obedience.
>
> JGB, 61 [54]

It is interesting to note that religion was defined here in terms not dissimilar to those we find in Marx. Religion was the illusory community, the mystified universality that concealed domination and oppression. But it was precisely this element that attracted Nietzsche's attention. On the one hand, the illusion of community acted as an opium, as we already know: on the other, it allowed total control of the people of a sort no police force could guarantee. At this point, new and promising perspectives of social engineering opened up:

The philosopher as we understand him, we free spirits –, as the man with the most comprehensive responsibility, whose conscience bears the weight of the overall development of humanity [*Gesammt-Entwicklung des Menschen*], this philosopher will make use of religion for his breeding and education work [*Züchtungs- und Erziehungswerke*], just as he will make use of the prevailing political and economic situation.

JGB, 61 [54]

By the conscious and ruthless employment of the instrument of religion, the 'ruling race' shaped itself and became ever more capable and ever worthier to exercise its rule over those called to serve it and whose existence had no intrinsic value. To them

religion gives [...] an invaluable sense of contentment with their situation and type; it puts their hearts greatly at ease, it glorifies their obedience, it gives them (and those like them) one more happiness and one more sorrow, it transfigures and improves them, it provides something of a justification for everything commonplace, for all the lowliness, for the whole half-bestial poverty of their souls.

Despite the enormous burden of pain that their condition inevitably entailed, religion succeeded in keeping tied to life these servants called upon to sacrifice themselves for the cause of culture and, therefore, for 'general utility [*allgemeines Nützen*]':

Religion, and the meaning religion gives to life, spreads sunshine over such eternally tormented [*geplagt*] people and makes them bearable even to themselves. [...] Perhaps there is nothing more venerable about Christianity and Buddhism than their art of teaching even the lowliest [*den Niedrigsten anzulehren*] to use piety in order to situate themselves in an illusory higher order of things, and in so doing stay satisfied with the actual order, in which their lives are hard enough (in which precisely this hardness is necessary!)

JGB, 61 [55]

It was important, however, to bear in mind one essential point: depending on the 'type [*Art*] of person' involved, 'the influence that can be exerted over selection and breeding [*der auslesende, züchtende Einfluss*]' exerted by religion 'is always just as destructive [*zerstörend*] as it is creative and formative' (JGB, 61 [54]). This aphorism from *Beyond Good and Evil* did not dwell further on this aspect of selection and decimation as well as of destruction. It simply argued, by way of suggestion, that certain people, as we know, 'have a right to exist' only insofar as they were obedient 'servants' and ready to sacrifice themselves for the 'general utility'. Towards the end of his conscious life, Nietzsche became more explicit: he accused Christianity of having given a reason to survive to a rabble that no longer had any meaning from the point of view of 'general utility' (*infra*, 19 § 4).

The perspectives for social engineering opened up by the unscrupulous employment of religion had, at the same time, a eugenic dimension.

6   The City, the Newspaper and the Plebeians

The 'duplicity' of this specific critique of ideology is further confirmed by the bitter polemic Nietzsche directed not only at the access of the masses to education but also at the spread of the press, political interest and political particip- ation: the advance of 'general education', 'reading the newspapers', and 'taking part in politics' were three aspects of a single process of massification (JGB, 239 [129]).

In this theme too, as in many others of Nietzsche's philosophy, people have claimed to find proof of his rejection of the philistine accommodation to exist- ence, of his rebellious spirit, of his 'untimeliness'.[49] In reality, for the moment in which it fell, this polemical position was absolutely 'actual'. These were the years in which Wagner warned against the devastating effects of newspapers on the 'spirit of the people'[50] and Treitschke lamented the influence Social Demo- cracy was able to exert on the masses 'by demonstrating the power of its press', and argued its 'bureaucracy' could proliferate only on the basis of 'proceeds from the sale of its newspapers [*Zeitungseinnahme*]'.[51] On the opposite side, Engels, in an essay that, among other things, polemicised against the national- liberal historian, praised the socialist workers who 'have read newspapers to a far greater extent and far more regularly'.[52] With an eye to the press and the socialist opposition in general, Bismarck thundered against the 'journalist rabble [*Zeitungspöbel*]'[53] and went so far as 'to call the press and newspapers "weapons of *The Antichrist*"'.[54]

---

49   E.g. Negri 1978, p. 29.
50   Wagner 1910f, p. 116.
51   Treitschke 1878, p. 6f.
52   Marx and Engels 1975ff., 24, p. 458.
53   Bismarck n.d., Vol. 2, p. 342.
54   The observation is by Croce 1965, p. 219.

In these years, the conviction spread, at the European level, that 'the press and newspapers', if disseminated among the 'people', contributed to 'enhance the feeling of its own woes and the desire to free itself from them'.[55] So it was the partisans of 'social revolution' that made unscrupulous use of 'the means of modern education' and 'newspapers'.[56] That is why Kierkegaard blamed newspapers for 'dredging up all the pitifulness that no state can any longer master'; the daily press 'is and remains the evil principle in the present-day world'. One had to put an end to this incitement of the masses: 'For society, prohibitionist laws against newspapers are much more necessary than against alcohol'; there should be no delay in 'prohibiting the newspapers'.[57]

This was thus the topos of a culture engaged in criticism of revolution. We can find this in Comte, who in 1844 denounced the 'newspapers' as a main vehicle for the spread of 'metaphysical' and revolutionary 'contagion' 'among the lower classes'.[58] We can find it, in Italy, in *Civiltà Cattolica*, which in 1850 raged against 'journalism' and explicitly denounced the land of unending political upheavals; and not for nothing, for journalism, 'an instrument of permanent agitation among peoples', was nothing other than the 'pernicious legacy of revolutionary France'.[59] The condemnation from the Catholic side was officially confirmed, in 1878, in an encyclical of Leo XIII. This encyclical denounced socialists and communists and their doctrines, which they 'spread among the people by means of a large number of gazettes'.[60]

This recurring charge captured an essential truth about the issue. In Taine, Nietzsche may have read the summary that d'Argenson, a careful observer of the period, had written concerning the gathering of the storm in revolutionary France: 'Fifty years ago the public had no interest in news of the state. Today, everyone reads his *Gazette de Paris*, even in the provinces.'[61] In Germany, the Fronde or the struggle against the *ancien régime* had been constantly followed ever since the start of the French Revolution by an attentive and sympathetic readership. One can observe this phenomenon in the case of writers as diverse as Kant, Hegel, Heine, Ruge and Marx.[62] The latter, in the years before the outbreak of the revolution of 1848, accused academic and particularly German

---

55   Gioberti 1969, Vol. 1, p. 99.

56   Luthardt 1967, p. 157 f.

57   Kierkegaard 1962 ff., Vol. 2, p. 137 f.

58   Comte 1985, p. 98.

59   In Lerda 1976, p. 233.

60   In Giordani 1956, p. 29 (Quod apostolici muneris).

61   Taine 1899, Vol. 2, p. 145.

62   Cf. Losurdo 2001, 5, § 1 and Losurdo 1997a, 9, § 4.

philosophy of staying aloof from political reality and the problems and passions reflected in the newspapers:

> Philosophy, especially German philosophy, has an urge for isolation, for systematic seclusion, for dispassionate self-examination which from the start places it in estranged contrast to the quick-witted and alive-to-events newspapers, whose only delight is in information. [...] True to its nature, philosophy has never taken the first step towards exchanging the ascetic frock of the priest for the light, conventional garb of the newspapers.[63]

On the eve of the revolution, in Prussia – according to Friedrich Kapp, a friend and follower of Feuerbach – 'newspapers are generally devoured'.[64]

On the other side, Schelling, the spellbound spectator of the revolution and street battles in Berlin, denounced newspapers and 'bad journalists' for 'inciting' the masses.[65] A few months later, from a place of vantage, as the Assembly met in Frankfurt to decide on the future of Germany, Schopenhauer deplored the dark times 'for no one any longer opens a book, worthless newspapers having usurped the monopoly of being read'.[66] Another witness to these events, unprecedented for Germany, was the adolescent Nietzsche: in Naumburg, where he lived at the time with his family, newspapers were springing up like mushrooms,[67] but their effects were certainly not positive: 'The immense February Revolution in Paris spread with devastating speed', and around the slogan 'Liberty, Equality, Fraternity', civil war raged (A, 15).

Regardless of its content, a newspaper was an instrument of massification and plebeian subversion. We can find this observation in another author, the likewise apparently 'unpolitical' Kierkegaard: 'The entire essential form of this communication is a deception', in the sense that it promoted the coarsening and massification typical of the modern world: 'Everything the newspaper communicates [...] it communicates as if it were always the crowd, the majority, etc. that knows.'[68] In this regard, the Danish philosopher expressed himself in almost Nietzschean terms: a newspaper that wanted 'to be aristocratic and at

63   Marx and Engels 1975 ff., 1, p. 195.
64   In Wehler 1969, p. 51.
65   In Plitt 1869–70, Vol. 3, p. 211.
66   Schopenhauer 1929–33, Vol. 1, p. 635 (letter of 28 January 1849 to Johann G. von Quandt).
67   Ross 1984, p. 24.
68   Kierkegaard 1962 ff., Vol. 2, p. 137.

the same time to be a newspaper' made itself ridiculous; no, 'to be an aristocrat among journalists is like being an aristocrat among tramps'.[69]

Nietzsche provided the most radical and coherent expression of this view. It was not just a question of stopping socialist agitation. True, he invited the workers not to listen 'to the newspaper', those 'socialist pied pipers' (M, 206 [154]). But, along with socialism, the entire 'parliamentary nonsense' was to be liquidated, whose integral components were the 'newspaper' and its eager readers (JGB, 208). Moreover, it was precisely this 'nonsense' that paved the way to socialism: 'parliamentarism' and 'the press [*Zeitungswesen*]' were 'the means by which the herd-animal becomes master' (XI, 480).

The 'newspaper' was an essential component of the 'culture of big cities' (XIII, 93), where democratic and plebeian subversion was most virulent. No wonder, then, despite his radical critique of ideology, Nietzsche seemed to deplore the urbanisation process that drew the masses away from their previous life in the shadow of the village steeple. In the modern world, as we already know, newspapers had unfortunately 'taken the place of the daily prayers'. This view of the newspaper as a secular alternative to the sacred texts of religion can, of course, already be found in Hegel in Jena: in two aphorisms he likened the 'early morning reading the newspapers' to 'a kind of realistic blessing' and, significantly, tied this comparison to an explicit polemic against those who had 'lost religion' and therefore demanded that philosophy 'edify' and thus 'take the place of the parish priest'.[70] But, in this context, it is even better to quote Stendhal: on the eve of the July revolution he pointed to the 'fear' that the mere 'proximity of the Paris newspapers' caused the 'petty tyrants', and in *Le rouge et le noir* he asked: 'Can the newspaper ever replace the parish priest?'[71] This is a novel Nietzsche read with enthusiasm (B, III, 5, 27–8), and whose author he called a 'friend' (XI, 254).

The philosopher seemed to take over from the French writer the same dichotomy, but he reversed its value judgement. For the masses, life in the shadow of the village steeple was to be recommended. The denunciation of the press was the other side of the celebration of the torpor of the popular strata, of the celebration of the beneficial character of ideological opium.

---

69   Ibid.
70   Hegel 1969–79, 2. Bd., p. 547 f.
71   Stendhal 1973, pp. 227, 189 (2. Book, 1 and Book 1, 2, ch. 9).

7 'Free Spirits' *versus* 'Freethinkers'

The mature Nietzsche was no less aware than Marx of the fundamental opposition between the two types of critique of ideology, even though, obviously, he formulated it differently. Two seemingly similar but, in reality, antithetical figures now stood face to face: the 'free spirit' and the 'freethinker'. With particular clarity a note written in the summer of 1885 observed: the so-called 'freethinkers' might even adopt acceptable positions on the subject of 'souls' and 'denial of God', but this was not the main thing: because they were part of the 'democratic movement' and the 'levellers', raising 'all human beings to their degree of spiritual "freedom"' (XI, 557–8), in reality they occupied positions antithetical to those of genuine free spirits.

What distinguished the critique of ideology of the 'free spirit' from that of the 'freethinker' was the rejection of the idea that a community of reason could embrace all people:

> There are books that have inverse values for soul and for health, depending on whether they are used by the lower [*niedere*] souls and lowlier life-forces, or by the higher and more powerful ones. In the first case, these books are dangerous and cause deterioration and dissolution; in the second case, they are the heralds' calls that summon the most courageous to their courage.
>
> JGB, 30 [31]

A variant of this aphorism first denounced the terrible smell of plebeian sweat in the churches and then continued: 'But there are few that have the right to "pure air": those that would not be ruined by the pure air. That in order to refute the suspicion that I would want to invite "freethinkers" into my gardens' (XIV, 352).

Nietzsche was not immediately aware of this antithesis. In *Human, All Too Human*, the term *Freidenker* still had a positive connotation (*supra*, 7 §7), which it then lost once and for all. However, even at that point, the truly free spirit was characterised by an awareness of the need for a strict delineation of the ambit within which the critique of ideology should be developed. But under what conditions was such a delineation possible? Only as long as there was a gulf between a 'multitude still short of maturity [*unmündige Menge*]' on one hand, and the power that stepped up as its 'guardian', on the other. In such a case, 'the ruling people and classes are enlightened about the advantages that religion provides for them and consequently feel to a certain degree superior to it, insofar as they are using it as a means: which is why free-spiritedness [*Freigeisterei*] has its origin here' (MA 472 [252]).

Nietzsche's starting point was that of the liberal tradition before any democratic contamination: the uneducated masses had to be denied not just political rights but also the right to education and, *a fortiori*, to enlightenment by the critique of ideology. But what would happen, Nietzsche already asked in *Human, All Too Human*, with the advent of democracy? 'In this case, the government can only take the same position toward religion as that taken by the people' so that 'enlightenment' ended up investing even the 'representatives' of the people and the 'utilization and exploitation of the religious drives and consolations for government purposes will not be quite as easy'. So, even during the 'enlightenment' period, the demand for duplicity went hand in hand with the struggle against 'modern democracy', which was 'the historical form of the decline of the state' (MA, 472 [252–4]).

Stressing the need for religion and therefore ideology for the subaltern layers, Nietzsche quoted Voltaire: *'Pour la "canaille" un Dieu rémunerateur et vengeur'* (XII, 447). Were the positions of the two philosophers regarding duplicity the same? In reality, the French philosopher of the Enlightenment was a sincere follower of theism, which he regarded as beneficial at every level of social life, given it could contain both the anarchism of the rabble and 'the unbridled greed for power of the atheist prince'.[72] In any case, Voltaire considered hell necessary to keep the 'rogues' in check and to guarantee social order, so as to punish or prevent 'hidden crimes'. At the same time, he did not hesitate to declare that 'reason penetrates France more and more every day, in the shops of the merchants as in the palaces of the lords', so it was impossible to prevent the ripening of the fruits of reason.[73] While the community of reason was at first tendentially negated because of the danger represented by the mob, it was reaffirmed with an eye to the needs of the anti-feudal struggle.

Nietzsche, however, condemned the community of reason as inherently subversive: 'We rebelled against the *revolution* ... We have emancipated ourselves from the fear of *raison*, from the spectre of the eighteenth century' (XII, 514). Along with the ideal of a community of *citoyens*, the ideal of a community of reason continued to live in the Marxist critique of ideology. Marx could have subscribed to this declaration by Diderot: 'Ignorance is the legacy of the slave and of the savage. Education gives people their dignity, and the slave immediately feels he was not born for servitude.' Of course, for Marx, the process of emancipation from false consciousness was more complex and difficult than that from illiteracy. Ideology had a stronger social 'density' and greater

---

72   Mason 1981, p. 116.

73   Voltaire 1834, p. 364 (*Dictionnaire philosophique, enfer* entry) and Voltaire 1989, p. 131.

anchoredness than ignorance. But Marx held fast to the pathos of the universality of reason, the foundation of the pathos of emancipation. If Nietzsche denounced the spread of education among the masses because it could undermine culture and the rule of the masters, Marx could have countered with Condorcet's crucial question: 'What right would the mighty and the enlightened have to condemn another class of people to ignorance, so that they work for them without cease?'[74]

In demystifying Christianity in the face of those classes called upon to rule, Nietzsche pointed to the plebeian and subversive origins of the Gospel. As we shall soon see, his analysis on no few points resembled that of Engels and Kautsky and sharply contradicted official ideology, which denounced Social Democracy and tried to outlaw it in the name of the defence of Christianity. However, this very worldly analysis of Christianity was aimed at the political education of the ruling class in order to strengthen its rule, not to undermine it. The critique of ideology was not only exclusively directed at the ruling class, but it aimed explicitly to teach it that it would be absurd and dangerous to encourage or tolerate the spread within the subaltern classes of a culture capable of bringing them to consciousness.

Throughout his evolution, Nietzsche directed his critique of ideology at the ruling classes, so they would become aware of the need for the hardness of the chains and not allow themselves to be moved by the fate of the slaves: to indulge in flattering but empty slogans, the imaginary flowers of ideology could be an element only of weakness and uncertainty. The lack of awareness regarding the hardness of the chains was a sign in the ruling classes of ignorance and decadence, while among the oppressed classes it was highly 'beneficial'. If Marx stood in the first place on the side of the 'losers', called upon to recognise the chains that oppressed them in order to be able to break them, Nietzsche turned towards the 'winners' and revealed to them a truth of which they, in their own interest and that of the culture in which they exercised their hegemony, had to be aware, but which was to remain unknown to the vanquished. Nietzsche's critique of ideology, which denounced official hypocrisy only to replace it with a loudly proclaimed and unprincipled duplicity, continued to be set against that of Marx.

---

74   The quotes from Diderot and Condorcet are by way of Moravia 1986, pp. 321 and 328.

CHAPTER 15

From the Critique of the French Revolution to the Critique of the Jewish-Christian Revolution

1 Revolutionary Crisis and Acceleration of Historical Time

Nietzsche began his critique of revolution and modernity with the anti-democratic reaction that developed in Europe and Germany as a result of the June days of 1848 and the Paris Commune, and in doing so went well beyond the German national liberals. Therein lay his aristocratic radicalism. When did the ruinous cycle still devastating the West begin? The great historical crises and epochal caesurae required a different perception of time from that that obtained in periods of normality. The extraordinary character of the upheavals led to the division of the entire history of the country or humanity as a whole into just two epochs, the one the champions of the revolution sought to close and the one they sought to open. This tendency also manifested itself, differently, among those who took a more cautious and moderate stance. The chronological sequence underwent a dramatic acceleration. In 1795, after Thermidor, Boissy d'Anglas declared that the previous six years of revolution weighed in reality like six centuries.[1] Moreover, the Jacobins, with their hostility to culture and art, with their 'barbaric vandalism', were responsible for having 'regressed the human spirit by many centuries'.[2] Whether towards the future or the past, the vertiginous acceleration of change and historical time led to a shrinking of temporal distances. In the same year, another Thermidorian, Lanjuinais, demanded the abolition of Article 1 of the Jacobin Constitution, which declared 'common happiness' as 'the goal of society'. His motivation was as follows: 'Two thousand years ago, 288 kinds of happiness were counted; we certainly cannot hope to define it better today.'[3] Instead of in months and years, time apparently had to be measured in centuries and even millennia.

With the radicalisation of the French Revolution, and especially after the June days of 1848 and the Paris Commune, the liberal and conservative press likened the revolutionaries to the barbarians that had stormed the Roman empire and culture. On the opposite side, in mirror image, Marx, outraged by

---

1   In Bosc 2000, p. 125.
2   In Baczko 1989, p. 292.
3   In Bosc 2000, p. 609.

the bloodbath carried out against the Communards, argued: 'To find a parallel for the conduct of Thiers and his bloodhounds we must go back to the times of Sulla and the two Triumvirates of Rome. The same wholesale slaughter in cold blood; the same disregard, in massacre, of age and sex'.[4] The unprecedented nature of the events one was witnessing, the extraordinary or unique character one attributed to them, led in both cases to a drastic compression of temporal distances.

The later attempts to draw up a balance sheet did not confine themselves to immediate circumstances but sought the roots of the present, relatively weak or strong, in a more or a less remote past. A radicalisation took place in which the analysis and the denunciation ended up embracing and calling into question an ever more extended period of time. How to explain the end-less revolutionary cycle destroying France and Europe? The obvious culprits were thought to be Voltaire and Rousseau, but were they solely responsible? In the culture of the Restoration the argument emerged, especially in Catholic circles, that one had to go back to the Reformation or the more radical currents arising from it; the revolt was said to have begun with the Lutheran demand for 'the freedom of a Christian' and free access to the sacred text, with an exagger-ated individualism that could lead only to the de-legitimisation of authority as such.

And how to explain the extraordinary concentration of power under the Jacobin Terror? Tocqueville formulated the thesis of the continuity of absolut-ism and statism in France from the *ancien régime* through to Bonapartism and socialism. Moreover, even the abolition of feudal privilege had a long history. It was a process that began well before the collapse of the *ancien régime*, 'seven hundred years ago', with the active participation of the kings, who, indeed, 'proved to be the most active and tenacious levellers'.[5]

In the Second Reich, the historical balance sheet of the French revolutionary cycle was linked with the problem of the construction of national identity. Was Germany in the struggle against Napoleon I and Napoleon III the heir to Luther, to Charlemagne or to Arminius? That centuries or millennia of history were being questioned led to a further shrinking of temporal distances. Had rampant individualism contributed to the catastrophe in France? In an extreme radic-alisation of this theme, Schopenhauer denounced any worldview that, in los-ing sight of the essence of reality (the will to live innate in every person and indeed in every living being, uniting all in a state and fate that knows no distinc-

---

4   Marx and Engels 1975 ff., 22, p. 349.
5   Tocqueville 1951 ff., Vol. 1, p. 2 (Démocratie en Amérique, Introduction).

tions), went no further than surface appearances, the superficial domain characterised by the *principium individuationis*.

Other writers evaluating the causes of the revolutionary catastrophe put the blame on the idea of earthly happiness. Renan did this, but he stopped, essentially, at the Enlightenment in his search for the origins of this devastating endeavour. Again, Schopenhauer turned out to be much more radical, for he cast the shadow of suspicion if not on Christianity itself then at least on the impure Christianity of Pelagius, contaminated by Old Testament optimism. Many journalists denounced the arrogance of the intellectuals among the revolutionaries, boasting of their rationality, placing themselves at the centre of the universe, and claiming to shape it to their own liking. But should one confine oneself, in this context, to bringing into play the figure of the *philosophe*, or should one, in Schopenhauer's words, include the 'occidental, Judaized despiser of animals and idolater of reason' in the denunciation?[6] Authors like Burke and Tocqueville denounced the revolutionaries' social engineering, their wish to indulge in rushed or mad experiments on the vile body of society (*supra*, 2 § 2). But was not this attitude justified by the Old Testament account of creation and an idea of God that, according to the biblical story, gave human beings absolute power over the natural and animal world? Against the pathos of action, which devastatingly characterised the revolt against the existing order, was set the *noluntas*, which found its highest expression in ancient oriental religions, thus destined to call into question the long cycle of modern subversion.

By branding the Old Testament as the earliest point of origin of the revolutionary sickness, Schopenhauer was able to expel from the real Germany and the authentic West a religion and worldview alien to them. The same tendency can be found in Wagner, though undignified by any philosophy. According to him, the French Revolution could triumph only because art had reduced itself to a matter for specialists and dealers and become separated from the 'people'. In that way, the people was degraded to a 'mass' ready for every adventure and rebellion (above, 4 § 1). To remedy this situation once and for all, it was necessary to eliminate the 'anti-artistic demon of *two unhappy millennia*' and to settle accounts with a people that was deeply permeated with a traders' spirit and, despite 'having a *two-thousand-year* relation with European nations', had refused to renounce its oriental identity.[7] According to Wagner, for art, for knowledge and for awareness of the limits of knowledge, it was necessary to

---

6 Schopenhauer 1976–82d, p. 776.
7 Wagner 1910b, pp. 68 and 71.

cherish the lesson of Kant and Schopenhauer and thus reconnect with the reality and doctrines of ancient Greece and put an end to a '*two-thousand-year*' ill-starred oblivion.[8]

I italicised the references to a historical cycle of two thousand years to draw attention to the resemblances between Wagner and Nietzsche. The thesis of the long duration of the crisis of culture accompanied Nietzsche throughout all the stages of his development. At grammar school in Pforta, he confronted 'the doubt that humankind might for two thousand years have been misled by a chimera' (FG, 433). Subsequently, as a young philologist, he talked about the actuality of a cultural epoch that had flowered in all its glory 'more than two thousand years in the past'; immediately afterwards, as a philosopher, he pledged to liquidate a philosophy of history according to which the 'few thousand years' of decadence that followed were to be seen as irreversible (*supra*, 6 §3). Despite his indignation, Wilamowitz was right when he accused the author of *The Birth of Tragedy* of wanting to deny 'the development of the millennia'.[9] Even on the immediate eve of the onset of his mental derangement, Nietzsche formulated the rhetorical question: 'What in the end are these two millennia?' (XIII, 641) What he meant was: why did people insist on accommodating to the terrible interruption that had begun with the decline of the magnificent culture of ancient Greece; a culture based on an open recognition of the need for slave labour for the majority of people?

The more Nietzsche radicalised the critique of modernity, the more he insisted it was necessary to swim against the current not only of the worldview but also of the 'taste of two millennia' (GM, III, 22 [107]); one way or another, it was necessary to 'assassinate two thousand years of anti-nature and desecration of humanity' (EH, *The Birth of Tragedy*, 4 [110]) or a 'few thousand years' of history, or, more precisely, of degeneration (GM, III, 20 [104]). He intended to drive forward this campaign by way of *Zarathustra*, 'a voice that spans millennia', a book that represented hope for humanity and a prospect of healing, and therefore 'the greatest gift it has ever received' (EH, 4 [72]).

To accept as obvious the prevailing morality without realising this obviousness was the result of a long history and a long struggle, to confine oneself to the present or to the short term, as the moderns did, meant to be deprived of 'knowledge and [...] will to know the past', and therefore of authentic 'instinct for history' (GM, II, 4 [39]): 'But you don't understand that? You don't have eyes

---

8   Wagner 1910p, p. 264.
9   Wilamowitz-Möllendorff 1989b, p. 134.

for something that needed two millennia to achieve victory? ... There is nothing surprising about that: all long things are difficult to see, to see round' (GM,
I, 8 [18]).

2   From the French Revolution to the Reformation, from the
        Reformation to the Christian and Jewish 'Priestly Agitators'

So when and how had this 'thing', this history, begun? Nietzsche did not argue
deductively; he began, as always, from the cycle of subversion still unfolding
before his eyes, to start from there his search for its first beginnings. To clarify
his approach, one might mention another important intervention in the debate
sparked by the French Revolution. According to Chateaubriand, behind it lay
the Reformation. This was a classic theme of the Catholic culture of the Restoration, but which now underwent a new development. In connection with the
role of the Puritans in Britain in the upheavals of the seventeenth century, the
French writer observed: 'A spark of the fire lit under Charles I falls on America in
1636 (emigration of the Puritans), envelops it in 1755, and comes back across the
ocean in 1789 to devastate Europe once again.'[10] An authoritative contemporary historian has seen in this formulation an anticipation of the thesis, which
he supports, of a 'single Western revolution' on both shores of the Atlantic.[11]
In fact, Chateaubriand's ambition went much further. He did not stop at the
Reformation but believed that the concatenation could, in a sense, embrace the
revolutions of all times, 'so it would be strictly correct to say the first revolution
of the globe has produced in our days that of France'.[12]

    In a sense, the programme here vaguely sketched found its coherent realisa-
tion in Nietzsche. To begin with, the thesis of the single Western revolution
starting with the Reformation was present also, in radicalised form, in him.
Without it, the Peasants' Revolt in Germany and the Puritan Revolution in Britain were unthinkable. Nietzsche spoke of the Reformation as a 'German and
English' plebeian movement (GM, I, 16 [33]), with explicit reference, regarding
England, to Cromwell and the 'Levellers' (JGB, 44 [40]). Those religious dissid-
ents then left Britain and played an important role in America, not just in the
War of Independence: 'a race of former Puritans' were at the forefront of the
abolitionist agitation and revolution decades later (JGB, 228 [119]).

---

10   Chateaubriand 1978, p. 147, fn. F.
11   Godechot 1984, p. 139.
12   Chateaubriand 1978, p. 253.

One can already see here the novelty of Nietzsche, who viewed the revolutionary cycle that started with the Reformation as a social struggle: from the revolt of the serfs in Germany through the slave revolt in France to the emancipation of the Afro-American slaves on the wave of the Civil War. But the most important novelty naturally lay elsewhere. Could one accuse Luther while leaving Christianity to one side? If the German national liberals, celebrating Protestant Germany in opposition to perpetually subversive France, were not credible, then the Catholic ideologues of the Restoration, who denounced the Reformation as the starting point of the revolutionary wave but then said the Christianity in which Luther sought his inspiration was a dam, were equally not credible.

No, in searching for the origins of the slave revolt, one was not to stop midway. It had already flared up in the Christian Middle Ages, as the recurrent emergence of pauperistic movements and especially the figure of Francis of Assisi, who struggled 'in the name of poverty' against the 'hierarchy', showed (XIII, 183 and 196). Even Renan, who showed the Christian tradition great respect and veneration, was forced to recognise the hatred of wealth that exuded from the writings of the early Christians. One was to call the 'Church Fathers' by their real name: they were 'Christian agitators' (GM III, 22 [107]).

It was no accident that 'the socialists appeal to Christian instincts' (XIII, 424). So, in seeking the origins of the French revolutionary cycle, it was necessary to go back from the Reformation to the Gospel. In the 'concept of the *equality of souls before God*' could be seen 'the prototype of all theories of *equal rights*', theories that had then found political expression in the French Revolution and the socialist movement:

> Humanity was first taught in religion to stutter about the principle of equality, later it was turned into a morality. So it is no wonder that the human being ends up taking it seriously, taking it *practically*, i.e., politically, democratically, socialistically, with the pessimism of indignation.
>   XIII, 424

Even the Jacobin Terror was, in a way, already implicit in the Gospel: '[I]t is Christian value judgements these revolutions are translating into blood and crimes!' (AC 43 [40]). Writers like Burke, Tocqueville and Taine stripped the Enlightenment of its sheen of innocence when they denounced the seeds of the later inexorable revolutionary violence in their drawing-room conversations and seemingly innocuous maxims. In a similar way, Nietzsche argued in regard to Christianity: 'But when Christians condemn, libel, and denigrate the "world", they are motivated by the same instinct that moves the socialist worker to condemn, libel, and denigrate *society*.' The reference to the beyond seemed harmless and even edifying. In reality one had to ask, 'what is a beyond for, if not to denigrate the here and now?' (GD, 34 [209]). And what was this radical denigration of the here and now if not the declaration of an 'instinct of hatred for reality' (AC, 27 [27]) and against those who wished to stay true to reality and the earth? Read carefully, Christian discourse was shown to be the preliminary and radical delegitimisation of a world against which, later, revolutionary violence was unleashed: was this not the dialectic that had brought down the *ancien régime* in France? One was not to be fooled by the spiritual and uplifting appearance of what Jesus said: 'In the New Testament, especially in the Gospels', one could hear 'an indirect form of the most abysmal fury of denigration and destructive anger' (XII, 381).

The Enlightenment mocked the *ancien régime*, but even primitive Christianity acted subversively by demonstrating its 'disbelief in higher people' and questioning the 'hierarchy'. In this way, a revolt developed 'against the Jewish church, [...] against the social hierarchy – *not* against its corruption, but rather against caste, privilege, order, formula' (AC 27 [25]). These were trends and themes that recurred later in the Reformation, but the violent fury of the Peasants' Revolt took as its reference point not only Luther, as the Catholic ideologues of the Restoration claimed, but also Jesus. Jesus belonged among the 'levellers [*Gleichmacher*]' (XII, 380); on closer inspection, he was a 'holy anarchist who calls out to the lowly people, the outcasts and the "sinners", the Chandala within Judaism, telling them to protest against the dominant order – with a speech that (if the Gospels are to be trusted) would get you banished to Siberia even today.' He 'was a political criminal, to the extent that political criminals were possible in an *absurdly apolitical* society' (AC 27 [25]). Perhaps one had to go even further. Let us consider Jesus's preaching: 'If someone had said only a hundredth part of it, he would deserve, as an anarchist, to die' (XII, 381).

But Judaism, against which Jesus and above all Paul rebelled, was itself the result of a slavish degeneration and contamination. Pre-exilic Judaism was quite another thing:

> Originally, particularly in the time of the kings, Israel had a *correct*, which is to say natural, relation to all things. Its Yahweh expressed a consciousness of power, Israel's joy in itself and hope for itself: Yahweh allows people to expect victory and salvation, he allowed people to trust that nature would provide what they needed – above all, rain. Yahweh is the god of Israel and *consequently* the god of justice: the logic of every people that wields power with a good conscience.
>
> AC 25 [22]

The turning point was defeat and the Babylonian exile: in these circumstances, a ruinous revolution developed; its protagonists were the 'priestly agitators' that, for the first time, advanced the idea of a 'moral world order' and subjected even the concept of Yahweh to a radical transformation. They 'now interpret all happiness as a reward, all unhappiness as a punishment for disobeying God, for "sins" ' (AC 25 [22]). At this point, morality underwent a process of autonomisation, denaturalisation and superfetation, it was 'not the expression of the conditions of a people's life and growth any more, not its most basic instinct of life any more, but instead something abstract, an opponent of life'. The failed and the malformed recognised themselves in this denial of life. In their moral zeal, they tried in every way possible to strike at and poison those that experienced their lives and strength with joy (AC, 25 [22]). The Jewish prophets were primarily responsible for the 'slave revolt in morality'. They 'melted together "rich", "godless", "evil", "violent", "sensual" and for the first time coined an insult out of the word "world" ' (JGB, 195 [84]). Full of resentment, they never hesitated to invoke the 'Last Judgement' and a terrible revenge against their enemies (XIII, 158).

Unfortunately, not even Greco-Roman antiquity had remained immune to subversion. In drawing up a balance-sheet of the French Revolution, Constant attacked the Jacobin view of classical antiquity and, to a certain extent, classical antiquity as such, which, with its model of political democracy open to the active participation of all citizens, had inspired radicalism and the misdeeds of the Jacobins. In his turn, Burckhardt noted that the 'rule of the masses' had made its first appearance in Greece in the fifth century BC. But only Nietzsche made a connection between political development and philosophical and religious development. With the decline of authentic Hellas and the emergence of 'veneration for the polis' and an absolutist 'political urge' and 'instinct towards the state' (*supra*, 9 § 2), 'the rabble became preponderant in Greece' at every level: '[R]eligion became overgrown with fear as well, and Christianity was on the horizon' (JGB, 49 [47]).

In Greek philosophy, the worm of devaluation and denigration of the here and now wriggled into view, with reference to an imaginary transcendence or to the world of ideas and with the first emergence of a moral vision of the world. A consequential turning point had been reached: it was necessary to read 'Greek philosophy from Socrates onwards as a symptom of sickness, and therefore as a preparation of Christianity' (XII, 202); at bottom, Christianity was nothing more than a form of 'Platonism for the "people" ' (JGB, Preface [4]).

So, in Nietzsche's reconstruction, the endless cycle of subversion and revolution started, on the one hand, from the Jewish-Christian tradition (the 'Christian agitators' and, before that, the Jewish 'priestly agitators'), and, on the other hand, from Socratic-Platonic philosophy. Was there a connection between these two currents? We have seen how Plato's philosophy was tinged with Christianity; moreover, both the Greek philosopher and the Jewish prophets proved to be 'ungrateful' and unfair to the tradition upon which they rested (XIII, 168). But that was not all. In both Greek decadence and Socrates but also among the Jews one could see the dialectic and its irony, this 'plebeian *ressenti-ment*', at work (GD, 7 [164]). That was also true of the moral vision of the world: 'When Socrates and Plato took the side of virtue and justice, they were Jews and nothing but' (XIII, 331). Yes, Plato, this embodiment of 'anti-paganism' and anticipation of Christianity, was an 'anti-Hellene and Semite by instinct' (XIII, 114); starting with him, 'philosophy is under the rule of morality' (XII, 259), the moral vision of the world that referred primarily to Judaism.

On closer inspection, one was dealing here with something more than an analogy or an elective affinity among decadents: 'Plato perhaps learned from the Jews' (XIII, 264). One could even guess where the meeting happened: 'Plato, the great bridge of corruption, who was the first to want to misunderstand nature in morality, [...] had already been rendered Jewishly hypocritical (in Egypt?)' (XII, 580). The fact was, Socrates' and Plato's worldview exuded 'Egypti-city' (GD, 1 [167]).

The negative influence of Judaism was felt not only in the Greek but also in the Roman world. Classical antiquity, over which the Jewish-Christian religion had triumphed, was a Rome that had lost its authenticity, a 'Judaized Rome', already deeply steeped in Judaism, infected by an alien and hostile presence. A clear antithesis ran through the deep structure of the history of the West, and it could be summarised as follows: 'Rome against Judea, Judea against Rome.' After winning a decisive victory, initially by way of Jewish infiltration and sub-jugation of the ancient world (with the Jewish-Christian revolution), later with the Reformation and the French Revolution (GM, I, 16 [32]), Judea went on to inspire the socialist movement, which, with its dreams of social palingenesis, did nothing other than take up and propagate 'the despicable Jewish phrase of *heaven* on earth' (*supra*, 3 §1).

If, starting out from the present subversion, one followed history back, it was possible to reconstruct a unique gigantic revolutionary cycle extending over more than two millennia. The programme announced by Chateaubriand had now become a well argued and documented historical balance sheet. One could say that, at every stage in his development, Nietzsche was committed to deepening and enriching the analysis of that gigantic revolution that had devastated and was still devastating the West. The continuity was clear and obvious: just as in *The Birth of Tragedy*, so too now the starting point of the catastrophe was located in Hellenism and Alexandrinism strongly influenced by Judaism and was now in the process of accepting Christianity. Except that now 'Judaized Rome' had already been inwardly overcome by the slave revolt and was clearly distinct from authentic and imperial Rome. Whatever the case, 'the slaves' revolt in morality begins with the Jews: a revolt which has two thousand years of history behind it and which has only been lost sight of because – it was victorious' (GM, I, 7 [18]).

This gigantic cycle, this unique revolution, which spanned the entire history of the West, revolved around one single conflict: it was always masters and slaves that confronted one another. It was no longer a question of setting *noluntas* against the revolutionary pathos of action or of denouncing individualism in the name of a compassion that embraced all living creatures and overcame the *principium individuationis*. Arguing in this way, Schopenhauer had only showed he himself had been infected by slavish values or negative values. It was not even a question of reconstructing the idea of happiness as, following Schopenhauer, *The Birth of Tragedy* did, starting out from a Judaised Socratism. The critique of this idea could also be recuperated, but only within a much broader historical and conceptual context, one that at all levels took the struggle between masters and slaves as its central point. The slave revolt occurred firstly on moral-religious and later on more directly political terrain.

After placing the start of the realisation of *égalité* 'seven hundred years before', Tocqueville emphasised the significance of the Reformation ('Protestantism holds that all men are equally able to find the way to Heaven') and, even before that, of Christianity as such:

> Soon, however, the political power of the clergy was founded and began to increase: the clergy opened their ranks to all classes, to the poor and the rich, the commoner and the noble; through the church, equality penetrates into the government, and he who as a serf must have vegetated in perpetual bondage took his place as a priest in the midst of nobles, and not infrequently above the heads of kings.

From that he concluded:

> In pursuing the pages of our history, we shall scarcely meet with a single great event, in the lapse of seven hundred years, which has turned to the advantage of equality. [...] Whithersoever we turn our eyes we shall witness the same continual revolution throughout the whole of Christendom.[13]

---

13   Tocqueville 1955, pp. 5 and 44 (Démocratie en Amérique, Introduction).

The picture Nietzsche painted was more dramatic and less evolutionistic: there were counter-tendencies (the Renaissance, Napoleon, etc).; the value judgement was obviously different and opposed. But, for the rest, his point of view could be summarised as follows: for more than two millennia it was always the same revolution that continued throughout the Jewish-Christian world.

Once the revolution had been reconstructed across its entire timeframe, it could also be liquidated with regard to the chronology it imposed. So much was clear: what was to be abolished was not the chronology introduced by Jacobinism during a single stage of the long revolutionary cycle, but the one that marked the actual start of the cycle. *The Antichrist* concluded by announcing the 'year one' of a new post-Christian era, instituted with the cancelling of '1888' years of the old and 'false chronology'.

3   Christianity and Revolution

The German national liberals were timid and inconsistent when recommending Christianity as an antidote to the spreading sickness of subversion. Above all, they came too late. They had not noticed that citing the preaching of the Gospel and primitive Christianity had, in the meantime, become not only a topos but also a weapon of struggle of the early socialist movement and circles sympathetic to it.

Unlike Schopenhauer, even the young and even the adolescent Nietzsche seemed to have grappled at some depth with the French Revolution (*infra*, 28 § 2). In its course, there was no lack of attempts to justify in the name of Christianity the most radical plans for social transformation. In the polemic against the restriction of political rights on the basis of the Census, also supported by Abbot Grégoire, Camille Desmoulins addressed the 'despicable priests':

> [D]o you not see that your own God would not have been eligible? Jesus Christ, of whom you make a God in the pulpit, in the tribune you have just relegated to the rabble! And you wish me to respect you, you, the priests of a *proletarian* God, who was not even an *active citizen*! Respect, you yourselves, the poverty He ennobled![14]

In this way, through multiple channels, the theme of a proletarian Christ started to spread, one that would later play a major role in the early socialist movement.

---

14   Aulard 1913, p. 199.

It was a theme that, with some variations and in the context of a critical judgement, emerged also in Hegel, according to whom an element of 'sansculotterie' was already present in Christianity and in Christ, as Hegel's undifferentiated polemic against 'all that exists' in political and social life showed.[15]

In Heine, an author familiar to him, Nietzsche was able to establish that the French Revolution was also praised by two important historians, like Michelet and Quinet, who also displayed 'deepest sympathy for Christianity'.[16] With regard to the first, the philosopher expressed himself with hate-filled clarity (*infra*, 28 §2). It is not surprising that he linked him with the novelist Victor Hugo, that 'flatterer of the people, who speaks with the voice of an evangelist to all the lowly, the oppressed, the deformed, the lame' (XI, 602). Christian inspiration was no antidote to sentimental and intellectual complicity with Terror.

After the theme of original sin became overshadowed, tendencies began to develop in Christianity that were influenced by a progressive mythology. This was the case, for example, with Lamennais, of whom Nietzsche made fleeting mention in his later years (XII, 259). But perhaps even as a young a man he had been able to read in Heine how the 'Republican-Catholic doctrines of a Lamennais, who planted the Jacobin cap on the cross', were circulating in France.[17]

The French abbot, who called for a struggle against 'modern slavery', saw in the perpetuation of this ancient institution in barely transformed guise proof of a tragic failure: 'Eighteen centuries of Christianity have elapsed, and we still live under the pagan system'; 'we still use a pagan solution to the social problem, the slavery of the ancient nations, only softened and disguised under other names and in other forms'.[18] Against this situation, which he considered intolerable, Lamennais went so far as to invoke a 'Spartacus of modern slaves'.[19]

Although non-believers, some representatives of the early socialist movement fervently quoted the Gospels and even declared, with Weitling, that the militant engaged in the struggle for material equality 'is a Christian, is a communist'.[20] Outside or on the margins of the churches the 'new Christianity' of Saint-Simon began to spread. The latter strove to re-adopt and reinterpret in its true sense 'the divine part of the Christian religion'. In doing so, he talked

---

15   Hegel 1978, pp. 619 and 639.
16   Heine 1969–78, Vol. 5, p. 489.
17   Heine 1969–78, Vol. 3, p. 351.
18   Lamennais 1978, pp. 173 and 161.
19   Lamennais 1978, p. 172.
20   Weitling 1845, p. 72.

about the 'first Christian doctrine' and the early church, which 'taught that society should recognise as legitimate only those institutions meant to improve the life of the poorest class'. In its new and definitive form, Christianity was called upon to stimulate the constant 'progress' of the 'human species', in order to ensure the happiness of all.[21]

Heine included Saint-Simon among those 'great socialists' by whom 'the world has been enriched, enhanced with a treasure trove of ideas that open new worlds of pleasure and happiness'.[22] Saint-Simon's school could be regarded as 'the last religion'.[23] Grown on the trunk of Christianity, the 'invisible church of the Saint-Simonians' was reminiscent of the 'Christian Church before Constantine'.[24] With an *élan* still Christian and religious, the Saint-Simonians fought for 'the divine rights of the human being' and the 'material happiness of peoples'[25] and propagated their faith in 'progress' as 'natural law'[26] and divine law. It is easy to see why Saint-Simon, because of the tradition that lay behind him, was targeted by *The Antichrist*, which placed him, along with Savonarola, Luther, Rousseau and Robespierre, among the 'fanatics' that characterised the ruinous cycle of modernity (AC, 54 [54]). It is worth noting the prevalence, in this group, of followers of Christianity, new or old: for Nietzsche, it was a religion that influenced even those revolutionaries who did not make explicit reference to it.

In Renan, Nietzsche might have read: 'If you want to get an idea of the first Christian communities, take a look at the local section of the International Working Men's Association.' Engels took a similar position when, towards the end of the nineteenth century, in a series of articles and letters, he tried to reconstruct the origins of Christianity: 'The history of early Christianity has notable points of resemblance with the modern working-class movement ... Christianity, like every great revolutionary movement, was made by the masses.' One analogy is immediately obvious: 'What kind of people were the first Christians recruited from? Mainly from the "labouring and burdened", the members of the lowest strata', principally among slaves. Similarly, the socialist movement was based among wage slaves and factory workers.[27] These were the outcasts, the malformed, of whom Nietzsche spoke, but regarding socialism, he referred

---

21   Saint-Simon 2003, pp. 3, 7, 77, 91.
22   Heine 1969–78, Vol. 5, p. 503.
23   Heine 1969–78, Vol. 3, p. 540.
24   Heine 1969–78, Vol. 3, p. 317.
25   Heine 1969–78, Vol. 3, p. 570.
26   Heine 1969–78, Vol. 3, p. 177.
27   Marx and Engels 1975 ff., 26, p. 113; 27, p. 460.

less to the proletariat than to the lumpenproletariat, i.e., to a class that, from Marx and Engels's point of view, often ended up as a manoeuvreable mass of the reactionaries.

At the end of the nineteenth century, even the Social-Democratic Party likened itself to the early Christian community: 'It is now, almost to the year, sixteen centuries since a dangerous party of overthrow was likewise active in the Roman empire'; the fierce persecutions of Diocletian and the Roman ruling classes could prevent its final victory; so too it would be, according to Engels, with the socialist movement.[28] Extinguishing the Christian 'false chronology' would also be to deal a blow at the revolutionary movement's philosophy of history.

4   Denunciation of the Revolution, Critique of 'Hope' and Critique of the Unilinear View of Time

The interminable revolutionary cycle still raging in the West could be effectively combated and driven back without confuting once and for all the ideology that nurtured it. We are already familiar with a central theme of this ideology: the moral worldview that, in its various forms, denigrated nature and the natural order on which rested a society and a culture worthy of the name and, with this, denigrated and delegitimised the natural aristocracy, the successful, the best. However, this theme did not exhaust the revolutionary ideology and was not sufficient to explain its vitality and dangerousness. To be able to stimulate revolt and concrete revolutionary action, the moral denigration of the world and of nature and the appeal to 'justice' had to be combined with a further theme, that of the expectation of a different and better world.

The continuity that linked socialism with Christianity and, before that, with the Jewish prophethood, was defined by the messianic expectation of change and, therefore, the concept of time: 'The Christian lives in hope' and with him 'the great multitude of slaves.' Against them, *The Dawn* set Epictetus, the slave who relied on his inner 'valour' to endure or accept his external condition. He 'does not hope', but 'believes rigorously in reason' (M, 546 [269]). Clearly, hope, in its Christian or socialist form, was synonymous with superstition. One therefore understands why, on several occasions. the posthumous fragments announced a book with a highly telling title: 'The new enlightenment. Preparation for a philosophy of the eternal return' (XI, 228 and 346). In its new and

---

28   Marx and Engels 1975 ff., 27, p. 523.

more radical form, the 'Enlightenment' combatted messianic and revolutionary superstition, liquidating the unilinear view of time that underlay it.

A breakthrough had been made by comparison with the third *Unfashionable Observation*. Here, the pressing need to found a theory of counterrevolutionary action led to the emphasising of the inescapability of decision and choice. It was inescapable because it happened in an always determined and unique historical and temporal context: 'At bottom, every human being knows perfectly well that he lives in the world just once, as a *unicum*, and that no coincidence, regardless how strange, will ever for a second time concoct out of this amazingly variegated diversity the unity that he is' (SE, 1, I, 337 [171]). The gesture of aristocratic distinction also went in the same direction. The uniqueness of the individual and of the exceptional individual found its confirmation in the uniqueness of every moment and therefore in the irreversibility of time. To become aware of this could provide a foundation for the struggle against modern levelling and massification: '[O]ur curious existence in precisely this Now gives us the strongest encouragement to live according to our standards and laws: the inexplicable fact that we live precisely today and yet had the infinity of time in which to come into being, that we possess nothing but this brief today in which to show why and to what purpose we have come into being precisely at this moment' (SE, 1, I, 339 [173]).

But was not this view of time in danger of favouring the revolutionary movement? The socialists, according to Schopenhauer, exploited the idea of the transience of time and of earthly life to win the masses to their programme and push them into political action: '*Gaudeamus igitur!*'; '*edite, bibite, post mortem nulla voluptas*' (*supra*, 1 § 9). On this point, Nietzsche still seemed in the spring and summer of 1881 to agree with his former teacher. '*Belief in the world*' characterised revolutionary agitation:

> *Its aim is the welfare of the fleeting individual*: so socialism is its fruit, that is: the fleeting individuals want to gain *happiness* through socialization, they have no reason to wait, like people with eternal souls, of eternal duration and the prospect of future improvements.
>
> IX, 504–5

The expressions I italicise clarify the continuity with which Nietzsche, ever since *The Birth of Tragedy*, denounced the 'belief in the earthly happiness of all' as the basic inspiration of the revolutionary cycle, or rather, of the revolutionary sickness (*supra*, 1 § 3). Except that now against this sickness was set a far more radical antidote: 'My doctrine says: your task is to live in such a way that you must want to live again – you will in any case!' (IX, 505).

Here I am quoting a preparatory draft of *The Gay Science*, the work that at the end of the first edition formulated, for the first time and somewhat hesitantly, the thesis of the eternal return of the same. The political and even pedagogical motivation that inspired it is obvious and sometimes even explicitly formulated: 'Even if the cyclical repetition is merely a likelihood or possibility, the mere thought of a possibility can shake or transform us. [...] How the possibility of eternal damnation has worked!' (IX, 523–4). While setting against the moral worldview the thesis of the innocence of becoming, Nietzsche refuted the unilinear concept of time (the other essential component of the revolutionary ideology) with the thesis of the eternal return of the same.

A fragment from the spring–autumn of 1881 leads back to the starting point of *The Birth of Tragedy*:

> Why did Alexandrian culture perish? It did not succeed, despite all its useful discoveries and its pleasure in gaining knowledge of this world, in conferring on this world, this life, the supreme importance; the afterlife remained more important! To learn something new on this point is still today the main task: perhaps if metaphysics were to attribute to this life the maximum weight – according to my theory!
>
> IX, 515

The difference is that, set against the ruinous cycle that had overwhelmed Alexandrian culture and the ancient world as such was no longer the denunciation of the devastating effects of the Enlightenment and Socratic rationalism but, instead, the reference to a 'new Enlightenment'.

Even if this came about in the first instance as a result of ethical and political considerations, Nietzsche did not forego bestowing 'scientific' dignity on his new doctrine: 'Let us beware of thinking that the world eternally creates new things' (FW, 109 [110]). In fact, 'infinitely becoming new is a contradiction, it would presuppose an infinitely growing force', but it remained unclear whence it would grow: 'Whence to nourish itself, whence the excess with which to nourish itself!' (IX, 525). One must therefore start from the assumption of 'a determined force', however great it might be. If 'eternal', it would necessarily incur a repetition. This was the inevitable result of the encounter between a finite mass, or rather 'force', and an infinite temporal dimension. It followed: 'There are no infinitely new changes, but the circulation of a determined number of changes is continually repeated: the activity is eternal, the number of products and situations finite.' Naturally, one could deny the assumption of the eternity of force and assume it 'is only active from a given point in time and, in turn, will cease to be so' (IX, 558–9). But this would mean, ultimately, regressing to creationism: 'Whoever does not believe in a circular process of the universe must believe in a wilful God' (IX, 561).

Since the unilinear concept of time was intrinsically linked to Jewish-Christian theology and far from obvious and obligatory, it proved to be unsustainable. On the other hand, Nietzsche noted in the second *Unfashionable Observation*, 'the origin of historical cultivation [...] *must* itself, in turn, be understood historically' (HL, 8, I, 306 [141]). To put it in logical terms, Nietzsche employed a self-reflexive argument: historical consciousness was itself subject to the transience of historical events; having emerged in time, the unilinear concept of time was itself destined to disappear. Moreover, 'the doctrine of the "eternal return"', the unconditional and infinitely repeated circulation of all things, 'Zarathustra's doctrine', was itself a return. It was present in Heraclitus or '[a]t least the Stoics have traces of it, and they inherited almost all of their fundamental ideas from Heraclitus' (EH, *The Birth of Tragedy*, 3 [110]).

Beyond the direct reference to a particular author, we are led back to the world and the view of time swept away by anthropocentrism and Jewish-Christian messianism. From this point of view, it is interesting to re-read the arguments of Celsus in his polemic against Christianity:

> Neither has the visible world been given to men, but each particular thing both comes into existence and perishes for the sake of the whole according to the process of change from one thing to another of which I spoke earlier [...] The world is uncreated and indestructible, and only things on earth are subject to floods and conflagrations, and not all of them meet with these catastrophes at the same time. [...] And neither good nor bad can increase among mortals. [...] God has no need to have a new reformation. [...] Even if something seems to you to be evil, it is not yet clear whether it really is evil; for you do not know what is expedient either for you or for someone else or for the universe.[29]

In an effort to relativise two millennia of history, Nietzsche switched from denouncing the damage of history to life to a radical historicisation of knowledge. This historicisation finally grasped the feeling of hope, the unilinear concept of time, first relativised by showing its historical and social origins (the delirious illusions and claims of the rejected in the Jewish-Christian world) and finally dispatched by affirming the eternal return of the same.

---

29   Celsus 1953, 238–47, Alethes logos IV, p. 69 f.

In this way, one can see why Nietzsche represented 'the doctrine of the eternal return as a hammer in the hand of the most powerful' (XI, 295). In a long-term perspective, this doctrine was the right response of the ruling classes to the challenge of the malformed. Let us see when and how the unilinear concept of time was affirmed. While Rome ruled unchallenged, 'any other future seemed foreclosed, all things were arranged as if forever'. But now the world began to be calumniated. Rome was depicted as if it were already destined to decline because of its inner decay:

> [I]t avenged itself on Rome by installing a new future for itself, a future moreover – Rome had managed to transform everything into *its* prehistory and *its* present – in comparison to which Rome no longer seemed to be most important; it avenged itself on Rome by dreaming of a last *judgement* – and the crucified Jew as the symbol of salvation was the deepest mockery of the magnificent Roman praetors in the provinces, for now they appeared as the symbol of perdition and of a 'world' ripe for destruction.
>
> M, 71 [52]

The doctrine of the eternal return was then configured as the counter-revenge of the ruling classes, who now derided the hopes and illusions of the subaltern classes.

5   Doctrine of the Eternal Return and Liquidation of Anthropocentrism (from Judaism to the French Revolution)

In addition to the concept of unilinear time, the Jewish-Christian tradition was characterised by its foppish anthropocentrism, alien to classical antiquity and other extra-European cultures. Here, too, a clear line of continuity led from Judaism to the incessant subversion of modernity. After making its first appearance in a 'boundlessly ambitious little people', anthropocentrism then played a central role in a crudely ethnocentric form in Jesus and Saul: 'Both believed that the fate of every person and of all ages, in the past and in the future, along with the fate of the earth, the sun and the stars, depended on a matter of Jews: this belief is the Jewish *non plus ultra*' (IX, 80). In this way, an extravagant soteriology was elaborated in which the whole of reality and universal history were bent to the needs of emancipation and redemption of an insignificant riff-raff: 'What right have people to make such a fuss about their little failings, like these pious little men do? No cock is going to crow over it; still less,

God.' Instead, in the Old and especially the New Testament, every miserable wretch claimed to be the object of attention of the entire universal order and its creator: '[P]eople like that regurgitating their most personal affairs, stupidities, sorrows and lingering worries, as if the in-itself of things were duty-bound to concern itself with all that' (GM III, 22 [108]).

Again, Nietzsche's polemic leads us back to the world overwhelmed by the victory of the unilinear concept of time and messianism. The denunciation of anthropocentrism can also be found in Celsus's polemic against Christians and, more generally, against Jewish-Christian circles. They were blamed for asserting 'God made all things for the sake of human beings, rather than also for the sake of speechless animals; natural phenomena are made in no greater degree for human beings than for plants, trees, herbs, and thorn bushes'. Mocking the biblical story according to which God entrusted to humans the subjugation of nature and the animal world, Celsus observed: 'God gave us the ability to catch wild beasts and to make use of them, we will say that it is likely that before the existence of cities and arts and the formation of societies of this kind, and before there were weapons and nets, men were captured and eaten by wild beasts and it was very rare for beasts to be caught by men.'[30]

Just like the secularisation of the idea of equality, so too the secularisation of the anthropocentric view flowed into the upheavals of the French Revolution. With its theory of human rights, it not only placed the human world at the centre of the universe but, within that world, attributed even to the most mediocre and miserable beings the centrality and dignity of having their purpose in themselves. However, that 'alleged spider of purpose and ethics' was just another name for the good old God (GM III, 9 [82]); it was precisely the main thread of the progressive and revolutionary belief in a process tending to make the world a place of happiness for all and universal harmony. We see at work the same concept of time that seems to have achieved or is about to achieve its ultimate goal, its *plenitudo*: '[T]he "Last Judgement" is [...] the revolution that the socialist worker is waiting for, only a bit further off' (GD, 34 [209]).

An eminent contemporary historian has pointed out that the concept of unilinear time and 'Judeo-Christian messianism' plays an important role in bringing about, even outside Europe, revolutionary fermentations alien to other religions like Hinduism and Buddhism.[31] Nietzsche lived at a time when the United States experienced both its Civil War and the 'abolitionist revolution' (which sometimes took the form of a crusade to eliminate the sin of slavery

---

30   Celsus 1953, 246, Alethes logos IV, 74f and IV, 79a.
31   Hobsbawm 1959, p. 57 and *passim*; cf. also Marx and Engels 1955 ff., 22, p. 450, fn.

and build a new world in which the ideals of Christian were brought into play) and when Europe witnessed the Paris Commune and the development of the socialist movement. In Asia, and more specifically in China, the Taiping movement led a revolution and subsequently attempts to build a 'Heavenly Kingdom of Peace' also deeply influenced, as is well known, by Christian messianism.[32]

So, it is understandable that, in the years immediately following 1789, the critique of revolution took aim in particular at the expectation of the Novum and the anthropocentric view that underlay it. Chateaubriand tried to prove that the innovations promised or pursued by the French Revolution 'can be found almost verbatim in the history of the ancient Greeks'. There was nothing new under the sun: it was a 'important truth' that one should never lose sight of; 'the human being [...] repeats himself incessantly, he moves in a circle from which he tries in vain to escape'.[33] More frequently, the criticism of revolutionary messianism and the idea of progress as such went hand in hand with taking one's distance from Christianity. Schopenhauer's reference to religious traditions centred on the doctrine of reincarnation and, ultimately, the rejection of the unilinear concept of time can also be placed in this same context.

Even when the doctrine of the eternal return was not explicitly formulated, it appeared in anti-revolutionary culture in the form of an aspiration. Lapouge invoked 'the testimony of science against the utopia of progress'. He argued that astronomy destroyed not only anthropocentrism ('the history of our planet is merely a special case of the general history of the stars') but also the illusions pursued by revolutionaries and reformers: 'Incessantly, in a mechanical way, astral life is born, flowers, dies, and is reborn without anyone being able to capture a tendency to progress in its immense cycles.'[34] Gumplowicz ventured even closer to the theory of eternal return when he insisted on the 'cyclical course of social development'.[35] Here too, the polemic was directed against political movements that promised miraculous renovations. In reality, 'there is neither progress nor regression throughout the entire course of the natural process of history, except individually, in discrete periods of this eternal cycle'.[36] On the opposite side, Kautsky accused the ideologues of the ruling classes of being incapable of understanding not only progress but historical change as

32   Cf. Spence 1998.
33   Chateaubriand 1978, p. 432.
34   Lapouge 1896, p. 446f.
35   Gumplowicz 1885, p. 219.
36   Gumplowicz 1883, p. 351f.

such: 'The whole of history looks like a cycle that always returns into itself, an eternal repetition of the same struggles in which only the costumes change, without humanity making any headway.'[37]

Clearly, even with regard to the affirmation of the eternal return of the same (a doctrine that seemed a long way from common sense), Nietzsche was not really isolated. Occasionally, his view has been compared with that of Blanqui who, imprisoned by Thiers, also embraced the 'astronomical hypothesis' of the eternal return. In this case, however, the affinity is only apparent. For the French revolutionary, the repetition unfolded not only in infinite time but also in endless space, and it involved endless variants in the passage from one world to the next: 'Perhaps the British have lost the Battle of Waterloo many times on globes where their enemies have not committed the mistakes to which Napoleon was fated.'[38] How that can be reconciled with the affirmation of the repetition of the same is hard to understand, but the political and psychological meaning of it all did not escape Blanqui's contemporaries. One reviewer noted: 'It is not difficult to guess the hidden thoughts of a man whose life has been a series of defeats and falls. He does not accept the denial of the events, the verdict of people; his mind, which could not celebrate his triumphs here, dreams of them elsewhere, and not among the seraphim and archangels, but among people of flesh and blood, animated by our passions', and even if the worlds are distant from our earth. So, we are dealing with writing by a defeated revolutionary who had fallen into crisis yet was still sufficiently pugnacious to reject surrender, but who was driven by the situation in which he found himself to 'melancholy' thoughts and to the search for grounds of consolation.[39]

Quite different was the case of Nietzsche, who in formulating his doctrine of the eternal return of the same radicalised a theme widely found in the anti-revolutionary culture, though sometimes only *in nuce*. Now the negation of the unilinear concept of time reached its perfection, by targeting, quite apart from socialism, the very idea of social mobility:

> He to whom striving gives the supreme feeling, let him strive; he to whom rest gives the supreme feeling, let him rest; he to whom obedience gives the supreme feeling, let him obey. Only let him be aware of what gives him the supreme feeling, and not recoil from any means! At stake is eternity!
>
> IX, 505

---

37   Kautsky 1908, p. ix.
38   Blanqui 1973, p. 156.
39   In Blanqui 1973, p. 180 (*Le Temps*, 5 March 1872).

Thus, a further element of novelty emerges. The philosopher, who already had the great moralists behind him and was himself a great moralist, conferred a fascinating form of lived wisdom on a political programme that would like to make permanent and natural the division of labour and the division into social castes. He directed his gaze towards Europe of the Middle Ages, when the professions and trades were fixed and predetermined:

> But there are contrary ages, the truly democratic ones, in which people unlearn this faith and a certain audacious faith and opposite viewpoint moves steadily into the foreground – the Athenian faith that first became noticeable in the Periclean age; the American faith which is increasingly becoming the European faith as well, where the individual is convinced he can do just about anything and is up to playing any role; and everyone experiments with himself, improvises, experiments again, enjoys experimenting, where all nature ends and becomes art ... When the Greeks had fully accepted this faith in roles – the faith of artists, if you will – they underwent, as is well known, step by step an odd metamorphosis that is not in every respect worthy of imitation: they really became actors.
>
> FW, 356 [215–16]

Again, the denunciation of the adverse effects of social mobility, from the Greeks to the Americans, took on tones derived from a familiarity with the great moralists, resorting to arguments that referred more to the process of formation of the individual personality than to sociopolitical reality. The same went for the thesis of eternal return. To adopt it and own it meant breaking with anthropocentric megalomania, recognising and feeling oneself as part of the whole: 'The eternal hourglass of existence is turned over again and again, and you with it, speck of dust!' (FW, 341 [194]). To accept the human and social condition in which one found oneself was in no way a sign of anything but mediocrity:

> My formula for human greatness is *amor fati*: that you do not want anything to be different, not forwards, not backwards, not for all eternity. Not just to tolerate necessity, still less to conceal it – all idealism is hypocrisy towards necessity –, but to love it.
>
> EH, because they are so smart, 10 [99]

Yes, one should beware of indulging in evasion and empty fantasies, one should accept reality and joyfully recognise oneself in it: '*Amor fati*: let that be my love from now on!' (FW, 276 [157]). To be gloomy about life was a modern sick-

ness: 'The Greeks, to be sure, prayed: "Everything beautiful twice and thrice!"'
(FW, 339 [193]). To be more precise, it was a matter of adopting a positive attitude towards reality as such, without suppressing its tragic aspects, a matter
of willing 'the eternal recurrence of war and peace' (FW, 285 [162]), of ridding
the world once and for all of the nihilism implicit in religious or revolutionary transcendence: 'The thought of eternal return [is] the highest possible
formula of affirmation.' To say that was to proclaim a truth that brooked no
replies: no 'objection to existence, not even to its eternal return' (EH, *Thus
Spoke Zarathustra*, 1 and 6 [123 and 131]). The 'demon' that whispered of the
doctrine of the eternal return assumed ever more seductive tones: '[H]ow well
disposed would you have to become to yourself and to life to long for nothing
more fervently than for this ultimate eternal confirmation and seal?' (FW, 341
[194–5]).

'Saying yes' had to drive one 'to the point of justification, to the point of
salvation, even for everything past'. Denying or regretting nothing, the individual recognised himself in every single moment and action of his existence,
thereby transforming 'all "it was" into "that is what I willed!"' (EH, *Thus Spoke
Zarathustra*, 8 [133]). Nietzsche also submitted himself to this exercise in the
redemption of the past, by re-interpreting the previous stages in his development in the light of the joyful awareness, now acquired, of the eternal return
of the same:

> Anyone like me, who has tried for a long time and with some enigmatic
> desire, to think pessimism through to its depths and to deliver it from
> the half-Christian, half-German narrowness and naïveté with which it
> has finally presented itself to this century, namely in the form of the
> Schopenhauerian philosophy; anyone who has ever really looked with an
> Asiatic and supra-Asiatic eye into and down at the most world-negating
> [*weltverneinendst*] [...] [A]nyone who has done these things (and perhaps
> precisely by doing these things) will have inadvertently opened his eyes
> to the inverse ideal: to the ideal of the most high-spirited, vital, world-
> affirming individual, who has learned not just to accept and go along
> with what was and what is, but who wants it again just as it was and is
> through all eternity, insatiably shouting *da capo* not just to himself but
> to the whole play and performance, and not just to a performance, but
> rather, fundamentally, to the one who needs precisely this performance –
> and makes it necessary: because again and again he needs himself – and
> makes himself necessary. – What? and that wouldn't be – *circulus vitiosus
> deus*?
>
> JGB, 56 [50–1]

The cosmodicy, affirmed and pursued from the very beginning, now assumed its most complete form, justified not only by the world but also by each single step in the development and life of the theorist of the cosmodicy. We have seen how Nietzsche struck Enlightenment tones in the polemic against the unilinear concept of time and the expectations and hopes linked to it. But the language he used to proclaim the doctrine of the eternal return was clearly religious: it aimed at not only the justification but the 'redemption' of reality as a whole (EH, *Thus Spoke Zarathustra*, 8 [133]). At first, Nietzsche seemed, on taking the initial steps towards the affirmation of an eternal return, to reserve this fate only for those who believed in this doctrine: 'Those who do not believe in it must eventually become extinct, by their nature! Only those who hold their existence to be eternally repeatable will remain; but among them will be a condition that no utopian has been able to imagine' (IX, 573). The utopia in point was that of liberation from the burden of morality by affirming the innocence of becoming: a utopia that, according to a not unusual dialectic, also in the light of later historical experience, tended to be realised as dystopia.

6   Aristocratic Radicalism and Renewed Expulsion of Judaism to Asia

In the period of aristocratic radicalism, Nietzsche's judgement regarding (post-exilic) Judaism sharpened. He accused it of having stoked up and of continuing to stoke up revolution by furnishing it with both constituent elements of the ideology that inspired it, the moral worldview and the unilinear concept of time. It is now clear that Nietzsche, with regard to the judgement on Judaism, had taken a new turn since the 'Enlightenment' phase. We have seen how the writings of the 'Enlightenment' period interpreted Judaism in opposition to the orientalising Christian fideism as rationalistic, and celebrated it as an essential element of European identity. But this attitude was destined to enter suddenly into crisis. Regarding Christianity, there was a clear and firm element of continuity, at least starting from the fourth *Unfashionable Observation*, which, towards the end of the 'metaphysical' phase, contemptuously defined it as a 'bit of Oriental antiquity' (WB, 4, I, 446 [273]). From now on, this evaluation remained constant. There was 'something Oriental' in the attitude of complacent prostration before a god, an authority, with the thought that 'whom the Lord loveth he chasteneth' (M, 75 [55]). It was a case of an oppressive ruler whose wishes one sought to fulfil in all circumstances and before whom one had to kneel down and humble oneself, all the while confessing one's own unworthiness and sinfulness. 'Given such great power, he's more likely to pardon a guilty person than to admit that someone in his presence might be in the right': so thought the Christian of his oriental tyrant in heaven (M, 74 [54]). Yes, a God who threatened terrible revenge against those who did not 'believe in him' or did not believe in his 'love' was 'too oriental' (FW, 141 [127]).

However, one could not ignore the origins of Christianity, 'derived from Judaism and nothing else' (IX, 93); 'Salvation comes from the Jews' was the slogan launched by the new religion in the Roman Empire (IX, 52). Because of this connection, the opposition between Christianity and Judaism became untenable, whether or not it was declined in a judeophobic sense, as in the 'metaphysical' period, or in a judeophilic sense, as in the 'Enlightenment' period, in order to emphasise that Christianity, rather than Judaism, was alien to the West. Now it was monotheism as such that had something oriental about it, with its cult of an omnipotent and perfect God that humiliated and crushed human beings with the infinite distance and superiority it brought to bear on them.

The connective elements between Judaism and Christianity became clearer once one confronted both with the world they overthrew or lay waste. Already in *Human, All Too Human* we read:

> The Greeks did not see the Homeric gods above them as masters and themselves beneath as slaves, as did the Jews. They saw, as it were, only the mirror image of the most successful specimens of their own caste, hence an ideal, not an antithesis of their being. They feel related to each other, there exists an interest on both sides, a sort of *simmachia*. [...] By contrast, Christianity crushed and shattered human beings completely and sank them as if into slimy depths: then suddenly, in the feeling of complete depravity, the gleam of a divine pity could shine in.
>
> MA, 114 [94]

With the start of the final stage of Nietzsche's development, the Jewish-Christian tradition as a whole was clearly set against Hellenism and, more generally, classical antiquity. Despotism was intrinsic to a religion at whose centre sat enthroned a God that saw a *crimen lesae maiestatis divinae* in sin and in the slightest offence against the sovereignty emanating from him, and the same went for the idea of sin and the moral worldview (FW, 135 [124]). But to indict the moral worldview meant primarily calling into question Judaism and a people that embodied 'moral genius' (FW, 136 [125]), the people 'who invented sin' (FW, 138 [126]) and was the first to be 'able to invent the holy God and sin against him' (IX, 80). Thus appeared on the stage of history 'Jewish feeling, to which everything natural is indignity itself' (FW, 135 [125]), and began its devastating spread. Unlike the Greeks, Paul and the Jews aimed at 'the annihilation of the passions' (FW, 139 [126]), and so placed themselves in a wrong and disturbed relationship with nature.

The historical balance-sheet, which can be found despite some contradictions in *Human, All Too Human*, was now reversed. The Jewish-Christian tradition not only presented a unity but at the historical level the former was the decisive element, and tended to absorb the latter. When the 'founder of Christianity' posed as a 'judge' and at the same time claimed to be an 'object of love', he showed that he 'lacked delicacy of feeling in this regard, being a Jew' (FW, 140 [127]).

From this point of view, Christianity with its sense of sin was more the carrier of a sickness that referred primarily to Judaism. Against Jewish-Christian despotism, the religion of classical antiquity stood out as a bright world of freedom:

> But above and outside oneself, in a distant overworld, one got to see a plurality of norms: one god was not the denial of or anathema to another god! Here for the first time one allows oneself individuals; here one first honours the rights of individuals. The invention of gods, heroes, and overmen [*Übermenschen*] of all kinds, as well as deviant or inferior forms of humanoid life [*Neben- und Untermenschen*], dwarfs, fairies, centaurs, satyrs, demons, and devils, was the invaluable preliminary exercise for the justification of the egoism and sovereignty of the individual: the freedom that one conceded to a god in his relation to other gods one finally gave to oneself in relation to laws, customs, and neighbours. Monotheism, in contrast, this rigid consequence of the teachings of a normal human type – that is, the belief in a normal god next to whom there are only false pseudo-gods – was perhaps the greatest danger to humanity so far. [...] In polytheism the free-spiritedness and many-spiritedness of humanity received preliminary form.
>
> FW, 143 [128]

Sadly, this world of freedom had failed to achieve victory. The defeat of Hellas and classical antiquity had led to human beings' humiliation and denigration:

> The Jews, to the extent that they have despised human beings and at the same time found them to be bad and despicable, have shaped their god more purely and remotely than any other people: they nourished him with all the good and noble things that grow in the human breast.
>
> IX, 656

It is as if one were reading Feuerbach and Marx. But, in reality, the differences were profound. One would misunderstand the historical balance-sheet drawn up by Nietzsche if one were to ignore the fact that, in his eyes, the Jewish-Christian tradition, though admittedly synonymous with despotism, meant also, and above all, egalitarian levelling. In the philosopher's analysis, these were two sides of the same coin. Christianity set out to 'teach the complete unworthiness, sinfulness, and contemptibility of humanity so loudly that contempt for our fellow human beings is no longer possible' (MA, 117 [95]). Precisely because this religious tradition posited an infinite distance between God and a human being, it erased any distance and any difference between one human being and another. In political terms, while monotheism asserted man's absolute subjugation to the one almighty God, it flattened people as a whole to the basest rabble, thus delegitimising every aristocratic order. In this sense, 'the Jews take a pleasure in their divine monarch and the holy which is similar to that which the French nobility took in Louis XIV', after he had surrendered all his 'power and sovereignty' (FW, 136 [125–6]). The levelling despotism of absolute monarchy (which humbled the nobility and robbed it of any real power, thus anticipating the work of the French Revolution) was prefigured in the theological god of the Jewish-Christian tradition.

Oriental despotism, denounced by Montesquieu and other liberal writers, was now discovered in the heart of Europe. Burckhardt had already denounced this 'monster more Mongolian and Western, which is called Louis XIV'.[40] But Nietzsche introduced two fundamental innovations to this theme. First, those who accused the Orient were referred on to Judaism: in their faith, the Jews 'have behaved like Asian peoples against their princes, crawling submissively and full of fear' (IX, 89). It was a culture alien to the West, with regard not only to its values but also to geography: 'Jesus Christ was possible only in a Jewish landscape – I mean one over which the gloomy and sublime thunder clouds of the wrathful Jehovah hovered continually' (FW, 137 [126]). This observation could already be found in Renan. But in Nietzsche, the desert, beyond its geographical significance, was a metaphor for levelling, which resulted from the absence or destruction of any greatness or nobility. By promoting massification, the religion that had emerged from the desert reduced 'humanity' to 'sand' (*supra*, 10 § 2).

And so we reach the second point. The interpretation and denunciation of oriental despotism and the Jewish-Christian tradition developed out of the conflict between plebeians and aristocrats or servants and masters. The slavish

---

'prostrating' by Christians was 'oriental: not noble' (XI, 130). With the decline of
the ancient world a vision had triumphed that could only horrify a Greek. He
would say: 'Maybe slaves feel that way' (FW, 135 [124]). In fact, it was a case of
an attitude 'not European and not noble' (M, 75 [55]). 'This was the revenge of
the Orient, the deep Orient, this was the revenge of the oriental slave on Rome'
(JGB, 46 [44]). In a nutshell:

> As a great plebeian movement of the Roman Empire, Christianity is the
> uprising of the bad, the uneducated, the oppressed, the sick, the mad, the
> poor, the slaves, the old wives, the cowardly men, in short, of all those who
> would have had grounds for suicide but not the courage for it.
>
> IX, 52

The idea of sin, which because of the humiliation it entailed was odious to every
noble spirit, became for those whose lives had turned out badly an instrument
of political struggle precisely against the aristocracy. The collapse of classical
antiquity and the advent of detested modernity were marked by the victory of
the 'crucified Jew' over pagan Rome: revenge was taken on this aristocratic society 'by compressing Rome, "world", and "sin" into one sentiment' and propagating the idea of the end of this sinful world (M, 71 [52]).

Like every plebeian movement, the Jewish-Christian one was characterised
by fideism and fanaticism:

> The intensity of the Jewish and Christian faith was contemptible in the
> eyes of the Romans; it was the Jew in Christ that above all demanded faith.
> Cultivated people of that time, before whom all philosophical systems
> were at loggerheads, found this claim to faith to be unbearable. *'Credat
> Judaeus Apella* [Horace]'.
>
> IX, 76

Fideism and fanaticism referred in turn to the Orient, which represented a
world alien to true culture and the West: the 'oriental slave' that undermined
the ancient world was full of hatred for a superior culture characterised by an
attitude of detachment and the tolerance of different faiths (JGB, 46 [44]). In
the exclusive and total faith of the slave, of Jewish origin or indoctrinated by
Christianity and Judaism, on the other hand, one observed an 'oriental ecstacy'
(JGB, 50 [47]).

7   The Struggle against the Jewish-Christian Tradition and the
        Reconquest of the West

The harshness of the judgement on Judaism is undeniable. Is this a case of
a return of old national-liberal Judeophobia or the beginning of actual anti-
Semitism? In fact, the new elements are clear and obvious. Think only of the
denunciation of Luther and the Reformation, celebrated in *The Birth of Tragedy*
as an expression of the revival of tragic Hellenism in Germany. Most important
of all, the turning point in the history of the West was now identified in the
decline not of Hellas, whose heir Germany was, but rather of the Roman Empire
and of classical antiquity as a whole. The Jewish-Christian and the Greco-
Roman world stood opposite one another. In this context, Judaism referred not
to the enemies of Germany and to the Romans, the 'Franco-Jewish' world, but
to the rabble, to the long cycle of subversion that affected the West as a whole,
including the Latin countries and France, which sometimes called itself the
'new Rome' and was sometimes branded as such.

It is true, of course, that *The Birth of Tragedy* and contemporary notes had
already emphasised the plebeian character and tendential 'Judaism' of Socrates. However, these impulses were designed to characterise the basically plebeian and Jewish tendencies of the enemies of Germany, which Germany, as
a bulwark in the struggle against the revolution, was called upon to eliminate. In conclusion, we can say that Judaism now acquired a new position.
If, in the years of *The Birth of Tragedy*, it was inserted into the ambit of a
national and horizontal conflict, now it was seen within a social conflict that
tore through both the Greco-Roman world and modern Europe. While, in the
years of *The Birth of Tragedy*, Nietzsche set figures in the history of Christianity
and Christian-Protestant culture, for example Luther and Bach, against Socratism and Judaising Alexandrinism, now the denunciation of Judaism melted
together with that of Christianity, whose inextricably Jewish roots had already
been clarified in the polemic against supporters of the Christian-Germanic
myth of origin. Significantly, despite the general condemnation of Christianity in its various denominations, Catholicism was judged with less severity:
here 'the Roman element has come to predominate', while 'the Jewish element' predominated in the Protestantism of the Germans, 'further away from
the Romans' for geographical reasons (IX, 93). 'The whole of Protestantism is
devoid of any southern *delicatezza*', and therefore expressed with particular
clarity the 'oriental' soul and the 'slave' attitude (JGB, 50 [47]). The weight of
Old Testament culture was felt much more strongly in it than in Catholicism.

The separation from the 'metaphysical' period is therefore evident. In
another respect, however, it is undeniable that, precisely in this period, Niet-

zsche resumed a central theme, though in a new form. Now Europe as a whole and not just Germany as distinct from other European countries was called upon to rid itself of the alien presence that was still Judaism: 'Europe has allowed an excess of oriental morality to luxuriate in itself, as felt and invented by the Jews' (IX, 88–9). Judaisation was at the same time a phenomenon of Asianisation: 'Morality, an Asian invention. We depend on Asia' (IX, 26). Unless it overcame this dependence, Europe would be unable to recuperate the Greek heritage and rediscover itself. Unfortunately, the 'Judaising' that had developed with the spread of Christianity was deeply rooted:

> The extent to which this has succeeded in Europe is best brought out by how alien Greek antiquity – a world without feelings of sin – strikes our sensibility as being, despite all the good will expended by entire generations and many excellent individuals to approach and incorporate this world.
>
> FW, 135 [124]

The process of Judaisation was especially advanced in Germany:

> In our schools, Jewish history is taught as sacred history. Abraham is more for us than any other person of Greek or German history: and what we experience in the Psalms of David is different from what reading Pindar or Petrarch arouses in us, as different as home from abroad. Being drawn in this way to products of an Asian, very remote and eccentric race, [...] is the strongest moral after-effect of Christianity, which addressed not peoples but human beings, and therefore aroused no suspicion when it put into the hands of human beings of the Indo-Germanic race the religious book of a Semitic people.
>
> IX, 21–2

Should we speak in this regard of Judeophobia or even anti-Semitism? Wilhelm Marr, the 'patriarch of anti-Semitism', with whom we are already familiar, explained the reasons for his attitude as follows: 'The racial difference between Germans [*Germanen*] and Orientals is too big';[41] to avert the mortal danger facing culture, 'we need to de-Asianize the world'.[42] The analogies with Nietzsche seem obvious.

---

41   Marr 1862, p. 54.
42   In Zimmermann 1986, p. 68.

But, in fact, Nietzsche's attitude was different. As we have seen, the writings of the 'Enlightenment' period favourably stressed Judaism's role in decomposing or weakening the national element in Europe. In later years too, he viewed the spread of Jewish or Jewish-Christian religion far beyond its region of as an extremely positive factor: 'Today's feeling for the Bible is the greatest victory over the limitations of race and the conceit that everyone should actually consider valuable only what his grandfather and his grandfather's grandfather said and did.'

But then the fragment quoted went on to denounce the clamorous revenge achieved by narrow-mindedness and provincial entrenchment: so strong had the identification between Europe and Judaism become 'that he who now wants to take a free and objective position with regard to the history of the Jews must take great pains to rid himself of an excessive closeness and familiarity, and to again experience the Jewish element as alien'. In general, the 'European' made 'Jewish morality' and culture his own, and even felt them to be his own, and considered them far superior to all other cultures in the history of the world (IX, 22–3). In this way, provincialism and ethnocentrism paradoxically coincided with subjugation to a foreign model, whose importation led to catastrophic consequences in the West:

> Christianity has moreover managed to cause to appear in Europe negative models [*Gegentypen*] of purely oriental type, the anchorite and the monk, as representatives of a superior life; in so doing, it has pronounced a wrong critique about all the rest of life, and has rendered the Greek element impossible in Europe.
>
> IX, 89

The main danger for the degeneration of European and Western identity came from Judaism (and its Christian offshoot). So, we are dealing with an anti-Judaism that was certainly no less radical than that of Marr. Especially since, in leafing through the fragments, we come across the condemnation of the 'slavishness of today's Jew, even of the German' (XI, 130). Even so, one cannot speak of anti-Semitism, for Nietzsche's discourse moved at the cultural rather than the racial level. Nor can his position be confused with that of a Judeophobia that demanded the dissolution of Judaism in a Christian-Germanic identity, which from the point of view of the philosopher was in the first place mythical and in any case no less repugnant than Jewish identity.

Rather, Nietzsche was resuming a debate that had a long history in German culture. To Klopstock, who mocked Grecomania and asked, polemically, 'So is Achaia the Teutons' fatherland?', the young Hegel responded with a no less

polemical question, 'So is Judea the Teutons' fatherland?'[43] Hegel then sought
to overcome the dilemma by calling on Germany to recognise itself in modernity and in a philosophy of history understood as the history of the progressive
realisation of freedom for all, in a world-historical happening of emancipation,
in which Greek and Christian (and, indirectly, Jewish) heritage intermingled.
For Nietzsche, on the other hand, the victory of Judaism and Christianity over
the ancient world marked the beginning of the catastrophe of the slave revolt
and modern massification, as well as the degeneration of both Germany and
Europe.

---

43   Cf. Losurdo 1997a, 1, § 3.

CHAPTER 16

The Long Cycle of Revolution and the Curse of Nihilism

1   Three Waves of 'Nihilism'

The long cycle of revolution was also the long cycle of nihilism. Even if this category played a central role in the mature Nietzsche, it appeared relatively late in his writings, although, in a certain sense, he had come across it relatively early. As a student, he read immediately after its publication Haym's essay on Schopenhauer, in which the latter was sharply criticised for his 'nihilism'.[1] It is easy to understand the young reader's 'alienation [*Verstimmtheit*]' (B, I, 2, 128), for, at the time, he was a fervent follower of the philosopher revered as the opponent of 'optimism'. A more important encounter with this category was the fierce attack in the first *Unfashionable Observation* on Strauss, who had criticised, alongside Buddhism and Christianity, the 'nihilism' inherent in Schopenhauer's celebration of *noluntas* and Nirvana (*supra*, 7 §11). A few years later, Nietzsche read Dühring's *The Value of Life*, just as polemically as he had read *The Old and the New Faith*. The fact remains that he was forced to deal with a new diagnosis of nihilism. Even if, unlike Strauss, he did not use the term, Dühring tirelessly attacked Christianity on account of its 'flight into the hereafter or into nothingness', which he saw as the inevitable outcome of a religion founded on the thesis of the 'world's radical sinfulness and ruin'.[2] It was a 'doctrine inimical to life', full of 'views inimical to life' that lead to 'self-flagellation and self-mutilation, the destruction of natural impulses', 'the destruction of human beings as nature created them', 'castigation and torture of all life'.[3] Along with Christianity, Buddhism could also be counted among the Asian 'religions that castigate nature', that, in the final analysis, raised nothingness to the ideal, although presenting it each time differently. Unfortunately, this worldview had found new expression in Schopenhauer with his 'metaphysics hostile to life', his 'mystical cult of nothingness', his 'religiously metaphysically embellished adoration of nothingness'.[4] It was a case of

---

1   Haym 1903a, p. 273.
2   Dühring 1875, pp. 351, 354.
3   Dühring 1881a, p. 3 ff.
4   Dühring 1881a, pp. 7, 16.

a 'new cult of nothingness' that continued to bring forth proselytes and victims, as the case of Wagner showed.[5]

On 10 March 1881, Nietzsche's friend and disciple Köselitz (better known as Peter Gast) told him that his Enlightenment turn was regarded by Edouard Schure, an Alsatian admirer of Wagner, as an expression of 'repugnant nihilism [*nihilisme écoeuré*]', or – as the author of the letter translated it – of 'heartbreaking [*herzbrecherisch*] nihilism' (B, III, 2, 144). Nietzsche replied with a play on words: he wanted to listen to his friend's music to achieve the 'health' he felt he needed: 'It has penetrated a bit too deeply into my heart [*Herz*], this "heartbreaking [*herzbrecherisch*]" nihilism' (B, III, 1, 68).

So, the first encounters with the category and diagnosis of nihilism saw the teacher or teachers of Nietzsche's youthful years or Nietzsche himself under attack. However, the accusation took on distinctly differing and even contrary meanings from case to case. If Schopenhauer and Wagner had, in the eyes of the Enlighteners Strauss and Dühring, been infected by nihilism because of their negation of the will to live, a few years later, after his turn towards the Enlightenment, Nietzsche seemed to the circle around Wagner also to have fallen prey to it: after losing the love, enthusiasm, hopes, and convictions *The Birth of Tragedy* had promoted and accompanied, 'our poor friend', noted Cosima, was in an 'inconsolable position'.[6]

In the same year in which Nietzsche received Köselitz's letter, the fatal attack on Alexander II on 28 February 1881 drew the attention of a broad public to the threat posed by nihilism in Russia. At the time it happened, the debate on nihilism in Germany coalesced with that on the programme of social reforms promoted by Bismarck and the laws that continued to hit the socialists. A few weeks after the Tsar's death, Bebel, speaking at the Reichstag, said that only reforms could rein in 'international socialism and international nihilism' and repressive violence would certainly not do so.[7]

When, in the second edition of *The Gay Science*, Nietzsche analysed the phenomenon of 'nihilism', he referred to Petersburg and the Russian revolutionary movement (FW, 347 [205]). Right until the end, Nietzsche never stopped denouncing the presence of nihilism in the different variants of the revolution, the beginnings of which, as we know, were thrust back into an ever remoter past. However, that did not mean the significance of the category or diagnosis of nihilism in the case of Strauss, Dühring or the Wagner circle had disappeared.

---

5   Dühring 1881a, p. 18.
6   C. Wagner 1977, p. 431.
7   In Fenske 1978, p. 285.

To clarify the reasons for this polysemy, one must take a step back and enquire into the history of the category of nihilism. Leaving aside a few cases that referred more specifically to the prehistory of the term or terms, one can say that 'nihilism' and 'nihilist' emerged in the main European languages and entered the political-philosophical debate during the ideological conflicts that erupted in the wake of the struggle to overthrow the *ancien régime*. On the eve of the French Revolution, a disturbing new figure, that of the '*nihiliste*' or '*rienniste*', appeared in the writings of Louis-Sébastien Mercier[8] and Joseph De Maistre. If the latter denounced the scourge of 'Riénisme', which in its fury attacked all that is most sacred,[9] Anacharsis Cloots, a noble emigrant of German origin and an enthusiastic revolutionary, celebrated as '*nihiliste*' the 'republic of human rights', which laid bare the 'nothingness of cults' and of 'all the rituals' that did not belong to reason and the 'free human race'.[10] In Germany, the country most directly affected by the French Revolution, authors like Jacobi and Baader sounded the alarm about the dangers of 'nihilism'.

The second stage and the further geographical widening of the debate on nihilism coincided with the new wave of struggles against the *ancien régime*. In Italy, shortly before the revolution of 1848, Gioberti and Rosmini in particular attacked the '*nullismo*' (or 'absolute *nullismo*') or the '*nichilismo*' of Hegel and his school,[11] while on the opposite side Bertrando Spaventa repelled the charge of '*nullismo*' aimed at his teacher.[12] Above all, in Europe, the apocalyptic denunciation of nihilism by Donoso Cortés found a wide echo, a nihilism that after the upheavals and devastation of 1848 that it had produced threatened, together with socialism, the final ruin of culture as such.

Finally, the third wave was represented by Russia. While dissatisfaction and unrest were beginning to spread more and more and not long afterwards led to the abolition of serfdom, there emerged not only in the novels of Turgenev but also in actual social reality a movement determined to carry through to the end the struggle against tsarism and the *ancien régime*, a movement that was branded as nihilist by its opponents but wore with pride this badge meant as derogatory.

---

8   Venturi 1969–87, Vol. 4, half-vol. 1, p. 419; Volpi 1996, p. 23.
9   Maistre 1984, Vol. 8, p. 316, fn. 1.
10   Cloots 1980, Vol. 3, pp. 713 f., 717.
11   Gioberti 1938–42a, p. 326; Gioberti 1938–42b, Vol. 17, pp. 12 f. and 24, and Vol. 18, p. 223; Rosmini.
12   Spaventa 1972a, p. 619.

The revolutionary movement in Russia allied closely with the socialist movement that developed and spread in Western Europe after the Paris Commune. The theme of nihilism became central in philosophy (Nietzsche), literature (Turgenev and Dostoevsky), even in politics. In calling for a struggle to the bitter end against the nihilists, 'murderers in thought if not in action', Bismarck pointed in the direction of Russia but turned his gaze to Germany, where the devastating effects of *Überbildung*, a deracinated and deracinating intellectualism, a culture able only to 'stimulate envy and hatred of all that is eminent and happy', were equally to be felt.[13]

While the nihilism debate manifested itself most violently in the countries most affected by revolutionary agitation, it scarcely touched Britain, where it seemed to catch on only among academics.[14]

The third wave was the decisive one, also because it is far from having ebbed. Nowadays, the historical balance-sheet of the twentieth century, of the contemporary age, even of modernity as such, tends to be seen as that of the scourge of nihilism and its more or less remote origins. If one pursues this research retrogressively, it turns out that medieval theological and philosophical thought was already debating themes that resemble or remind one of the present problematic. Since God was the creator out of nothing of the totality of creation, people asked whether this totality was set to return to nothingness in a divine act of *annihilatio* that was the *pendant* and conclusion of the act of *creatio*. Even the accusation of *nihilianismus*, addressed to those suspected of reducing the basic truths of theology to 'nothing' and thus bearing responsibility for the terrible *annihilatio* of the building of Christianity as a whole, put in an appearance.[15]

With the link between the categories of everything and nothing it reveals, this prehistory provides an important key to addressing a decisive preliminary question: why did the charge of 'nihilism' force its way into the political debate, over and beyond the theological debate, at around the time of the French Revolution?

2   'Total Revolution' and Political, 'Metaphysical' and 'Poetic' Nihilism

There was one initial trait that clearly distinguished this revolution from the previous ones, which, although very different from one another, had in com-

---

13   Bismarck n.d., Vol. 3, p. 50.
14   Goudsblom 1960, pt. 1, p. 1.
15   Riedel 1978, p. 375 f.

mon the fact that they presented an ideological platform more or less rich in references to religion. This was true, of course, of the Protestant Reformation and Müntzer's anti-feudal revolution, of the puritan revolution in England, but also of the Glorious Revolution (whose Bill of Rights thanked 'God Almighty' for 'delivering this kingdom from popery and arbitrary power') and even of the revolution of the British colonies in America, whose proclamation of independence appealed not only to 'natural' law but also to 'divine' law as well as to the will of the 'Creator'. The French Revolution, on the other hand, came up with a secular programme, and in the course of its development clashed with the Church and even gave rise to atheistic currents, which for their part had already played a significant role in the Enlightenment, which had prepared the rupture of 1789 ideologically.

Political radicalism was linked to religious radicalism, so it is easy to understand why Burke and Gentz denounced the French Revolution as 'total revolution'.[16] Sieyès, who accused the Jacobins of wanting not a 'ré-publique' but a 'ré-total', was partly in agreement with this view.[17] The outcome of a political movement that rejected the social order and the ideal and moral patrimony of humanity root and branch was, of necessity, nothingness. Even if not literally, the category of nihilism had already emerged in one way or another, as demonstrated by the further formulation of the charge against the French Revolution, which, according to Gentz, 'completely [gänzlich] abandons the area of particular rights and declares everything is allowed [alles für erlaubt erklärt]'.[18] So a view was attributed to the protagonists and ideologues of 'total revolution' that was typical of the nihilistic negative heroes of Dostoevsky, who believed that 'if God does not exist, everything is permitted'.

The novels of the great Russian writers of the nineteenth century also clearly demonstrated the link between the conceptual pair everything/nothing and recourse to the category of nihilism. Bazarov, the main figure in Turgenev's *Fathers and Sons*, said the essence of nihilism, whose follower he wanted to be, was to 'condemn things' and 'smash things'.[19] In his turn, Dostoevsky blamed the nihilists for acting 'so that everything fails', and for aiming at 'universal destruction.'[20]

It is interesting to see how the category of nihilism slowly and laboriously spread. After a stay in a Berlin shaken by the revolution of 1848, Donoso Cortés

---

16   Burke 1826, Vol. 7, p. 9; Gentz 1836–8, Vol. 2, p. 43.
17   In Bastid 1939, p. 17 f.
18   Gentz 1800, p. 116.
19   Turgenev 1999, pp. 58 and 61.
20   Dostoyevsky 1994, p. 544.

applied the opposition so valued by the late Schelling between positive philosophy and negative philosophy. In November of the same year, the Spanish author wrote:

> Demagogy is an absolute negation: the negation of the government in the political field, the negation of the family in the domestic field, the negation of property in the economic field, the negation of God in the religious field, the negation of good in the moral field. Demagogy is not just any evil, it is the epitome of evil, it is not just in error, it is in absolute error, it is not just a crime, it is crime in the most terrible and extensive meaning of the word.[21]

Nothingness as the essence of the phenomenon Donoso Cortés later called nihilism was the result of the '*negación absoluta*' of total revolution, that 'universal [...] catastrophe'.[22]

The same conceptual dialectic manifested itself as early as the late eighteenth century in Germany, this time more with reference to the philosophical or philosophical-religious debate than to the political debate in the strict sense. In 1796, a critic of Kant and transcendental idealism, Jenisch, maintained that the thesis of the 'total [*gänzlich*], absolute unreality of human knowledge of things in themselves' inevitably produced '*the most manifest atheism and nihilism*'.[23] Although by a different path, Jacobi reached the same conclusion: above all in Fichte transcendental idealism led with unprecedentedly 'destructive force' to 'nihilism'.[24] This was the fatal outcome of a philosophy that extinguished the in-itself, the world as a whole, and that apart from 'mere subjectivity' allowed only the nothingness of 'logical phantasms' to exist.[25]

Taking stock of the situation, in 1828 the German Krug distinguished 'social or political and religious nihilists' from 'philosophical or metaphysical nihilists': the former (bear in mind the close intertwining of the theological and political dimensions of the conflict in those years) were 'many more' than the latter[26] and were a political movement that agitated in the newspapers, in cafes, in party branches, in the squares; the latter were philosophers that moved only within academic circles.

---

21   Donoso Cortés 1946a, p. 184.
22   Donoso Cortés 1946b, p. 192 f.
23   In Pöggeler 1974, p. 336 f.
24   Jacobi 1980, p. 19.
25   Jacobi 1980, p. 108.
26   Krug 1969, p. 83.

This distinction was not implausible. Let us consider the first meaning of the category in question. For Maistre, who attributed to Bossuet the warning against this final and inevitable goal of Protestantism, 'riénisme' was synonymous with 'déisme'. Baader, who wanted to make a precise distinction between two strands arising from Christianity, expressed himself similarly, albeit with greater caution: the pietistic and mystical were to be treated with respect, whereas the trend that resulted in 'destructive scientific nihilism' was to be resolutely combated.[27] The link was clear between the religious and the political negation: as mother of the revolution, the Reformation was also the mother (or grandmother) of nihilism, to which revolution led. This was the 'social or political and religious' nihilism of which Krug spoke.

Yet the border between the two nihilisms was tenuous. To begin with, 'philosophical and metaphysical' nihilism was less innocuous than it might at first sight seem: God himself was part of the realm of in itself, removed to an unattainable distance by the idealism of Kant and Fichte and, in that sense, reduced to nothing. Above all rose the question: was there a relationship between the two nihilisms, the one that had originated in France from the struggle between the *ancien régime* and the one inherent in the system of the two German thinkers? It is worth bearing in mind that, even before 1789, the author of the *Critique of Pure Reason* described his transcendental turn as a 'Copernican Revolution'. Later, Fichte saw in his philosophy, condemned as idealistic and nihilistic by Jacobi, the theoretical expression of the revolution then going on in France. While the revolution tore away the 'outer chains' and dissolved a sociopolitical order consecrated by centuries of history, Fichte's doctrine did not intend to be any less radical: it pledged to liberate the subject 'from the chains of things in themselves, from outside influence', thereby breaking with 'all rooted prejudices'.[28] But it was precisely this total negation that defined the nihilism blamed on the French Revolution by its critics. So, they tended to view 'metaphysical' nihilists and politico-religious nihilists as one and the same. While the former elaborated a strange and unprecedented system of philosophy that caused to disappear or called into question all that was most sacred, the latter opened a declared and frontal assault on the current system of church and state.

To these two types of 'nihilist' one must add a third, the 'poetic nihilists' of which Jean Paul spoke.[29] In this case, too, nihilism was defined as 'egotism', the dissolution, or rather the annihilation, of objectivity and the totality of reality,

27   Baader 1963, p. 74.
28   Fichte 1967, Vol. 1, p. 449.
29   Jean Paul 1879, p. 25 f.

a destruction whose protagonist was this time not the politician or the philosopher but the poet. Or the protagonist might, according to Friedrich Schlegel, also be the author of a witty remark that,[30] with its corrosive attitude, appeared to annul or damage the objectivity of reality and of values.

3   Possible Attitudes towards Nihilism

Regarding the phenomenon of 'nihilism', three or four different attitudes were possible. One could accuse one's opponent of nihilism, and the opponent could reject the accusation and even return it. When Rosenkranz defended his teacher, he pointed out that 'idealism' *only* 'became nihilism in certain currents';[31] one should speak of nihilism at most with regard to a severe critic of Hegel, namely, Stirner.[32] Ultimately, this was the attitude of Hegel himself, who seemed to want to reject in advance the charges that would later be levelled at him. Jacobi expressed his horror at the 'nihilism' he claimed to see in Fichte's idealism,[33] but he failed to realise that he suffered from the same 'metaphysics of subjectivity' of which he accused the author he was criticising.[34] Jacobi and the Romantics developed a narcissistic dissolution in the subject of all objectivity, including ethical objectivity, 'ethics and the law'.[35] For Hegel, it was his opponents that gave expression to an 'atheism of the ethical world' and thereby adopted a nihilistic or tendentially nihilistic attitude.[36] In this sense, Bertrando Spaventa accused the critics of Hegelianism of 'political atheism'.[37]

In another respect, a positive evaluation of 'nihilism' began to emerge in Hegel. Despite Jacobi's reproach, a system like Fichte's, which defined the ego from the point of view of its opposition to the non-ego, was not really capable of abstracting from the non-ego and thinking 'absolute nothingness', and so incapable of fulfilling the 'task of nihilism', the philosophical task of 'pure thinking'.[38]

The distinction between positive and negative meaning was clearer in the case of Herzen. The Russian revolutionary warmly welcomed nihilism as syn-

---

30   Volpi 1996, p. 15 f.
31   Rosenkranz 1862, Vol. 1, p. 133.
32   Rosenkranz 1854, p. 133.
33   Hegel 1969–79, Vol. 2, p. 410.
34   Hegel 1969–79, Vol. 2, p. 430.
35   Hegel 1969–79, Vol. 2, p. 384.
36   Hegel 1969–79, Vol. 7, p. 16.
37   Spaventa 1972b, p. 785.
38   Hegel 1969–79, Vol. 2, p. 410.

onymous with unprejudiced critical rationalism and commitment to transforming the world without allowing oneself to be intimidated by the authorities. This unprejudiced rationalism seemed to be the heir to Hegel's 'pure
thinking', the ability to abstract from the object, which was then primarily existing sociopolitical objectivity. If, on the other hand, one understood nihilism
as sterile scepticism, despair that led to inaction, things changed radically. To
Turgenev and the main character of his novel, according to whom 'there were
first Hegelians, now nihilists', Herzen, an admirer of Hegel, replied by criticising
the author of *Fathers and Sons* and the philosopher Turgenev particularly valued, Schopenhauer.[39]

The theorisation of nihilism in a positive sense already implied that the one
accused of nihilism could assume and make his own, in a gesture of defiance,
the originally offensive characterisation. Such was the case with the main figure in Turgenev's novel, who proudly declared: 'A nihilist is a man who doesn't
acknowledge any authorities, who doesn't accept a single principle on faith,
no matter how much that principle may be surrounded by respect.'[40] This is
how the nihilistic movement itself and some important representatives of the
revolutionary movement (Bakunin) conducted themselves. In a sense, the category of nihilism had a similar history to that of *gueux*, originally a derogatory
term that became a battle-cry of the Dutch rebels against Philip II.

Finally, a third possible approach remains to be examined, which could be
illustrated by the career of Heinrich von Kleist. Even if he did not use the term,
he provided an effective description of the nihilistic influence on him of the
critical thesis of Kant, that the subject could never attain the thing in itself. In
this way, the subject was compelled to remain alone with itself. 'The thought
that on this earth we know nothing, absolutely nothing, of the truth' was tormenting. The dissolution of objectivity in its totality flowed into the domain of
nothingness. Along with objectivity, the 'sanctuary of my soul' and the meaning
of life were 'shaken': 'My sole and highest goal has vanished, now I have none.
[...] I seek a new goal towards which my mind, gay and engaged, could again
stride. But I find none.' The result of this state of mind was 'anguish', 'nausea'.
The loss of sense was radical:

> Since this conviction, that in this world no truth is to be found, appeared
> before my soul, I have no longer touched any book. I have walked around
> my room doing nothing, I have sat at the open window, I have gone out

---

39   Walicki 1996, p. liif; Turgenyev 1999, p. 28.
40   Turgenev 1999, p. 26.

into the open, an inner restlessness drove me recently into big and small cafes, I have gone to plays and concerts to distract myself, and I have even committed a stupidity, to numb myself. [...] One morning I wanted to *force myself to work*, but an inner revulsion overcame my will. I felt an inexpressible desire to cry.[41]

A worldview that banished the thing in itself (and truth and values in their deepest sense) caused the 'goal', 'the answer to the question "why?"', to vanish, and thus ended in nihilism as defined by Nietzsche (xii, 350). In conclusion, the loss of (natural, axiological or sociopolitical) objectivity could be deplored in one's opponents, proudly affirmed in the form of a challenge, happily lived as an expression of freedom and painfully experienced in one's own skin. And so, we arrive at three figures: the antagonist of nihilism, the nihilistic rebel, the victim of nihilism.

4   Nihilistic Rebelliousness as Critique and Meta-critique

In reality, the second figure embraces two quite different figures. To understand this, it helps to bear in mind Stirner's polemic against the protagonists of the French Revolution and their admirers and imitators in the years leading up to 1848. Despite the upheavals whose protagonists they were or would have liked to be, they continued to fit into a tradition of 'popery [*Pfaffentum*]', of adherence to ideals or 'sacred and holy interests';[42] animated by the belief that they could realise a beautiful 'paradise of freedom', they moved 'in the religious field, in the region of the sacred', and merely 'proclaimed a new religion'.[43] This was also the view of Ruge, who, in his polemic against socialism, set the philosophy of Stirner against that of Feuerbach, attributing to Stirner the merit of having given up the 'theology of humanism, which has its monks, its priests, its fanatics, its Robespierres, just like the old religion of the ascetics'.[44] Feuerbach's 'humanism' was the destructive and, in that sense, nihilistic critique of the 'old religion of the ascetics' and of transcendence.[45] However, since this same humanism was now characterised as a new and no less dangerous 'theology',

---

41   In Losurdo 1997a, 10, § 4.
42   Stirner 1981, p. 83; cf. Marx and Engels 1955 ff., 3, p. 161 f.
43   Stirner 1981, p. 83; cf. Marx and Engels 1955 ff., 3, p. 161 f.
44   Stirner 1981, pp. 176, 207 and 268.
45   Ruge 1886, Vol. 1, p. 389 (letter to Karl Nauwerck, 21 December 1844).

it was subjected to a metacritique that directed its project of a complete and nihilistic nullification more at the new than at the old theology.

Revolutionary enthusiasm was answered by a mocking counter-melody. Against the demystification was set a meta-demystification, against the critique a metacritique that strove to emphasise how much there was of religious content in the revolutionaries' attitude. To be able to overthrow an order experienced as unjust and intolerable, the revolutionaries were forced, on the one hand, to demystify the ideology that legitimised existing sociopolitical relations and, on the other, to appeal to moral indignation, enthusiasm for the new society to be constructed, commitment and solidarity in the struggle, the spirit of self-sacrifice, a series of values that became the target of the nihilistic metacritique. So, one can appreciate Sade's irony ('*Français, encore un effort ...*') with respect of his fellow citizens, engaged in a difficult and tiring task not only to build new institutions but also to assert new values. The sceptical and rebellious aristocrat, inclined to dig a deep gulf between himself and the plebeians (who because of the 'baseness' of their origin were likened to 'animals' or to 'weak and chained beings, there only for our pleasure'), had therefore to despise more harshly than any other 'this type of fraternity sanctified by religion [...] that can have been imagined only by the weak'.[46]

To the careless observer, critical and metacritical demystification seemed to represent identical or contiguous attitudes. For Rosenkranz, both Proudhon and Stirner expressed a 'social radicalism'.[47] In reality, things were very different. The theorist of the 'unique' pointed out to the French revolutionary that denounced bourgeois property as 'theft' that his moral indignation presupposed the 'papist perspective' that theft was 'a *crime* or, at least, a misdemeanour'.[48] Now the critique sought also or in the first place to dissolve the values underlying that perspective, and it was especially in polemic against those values that Stirner ended his book with a gesture of pride and defiance: 'I founded my cause on nothing.' The negation had been further radicalised, but in the course of that radicalisation, it ended up taking the form of a negation of the negation of the existing order. When Proudhon declared property as theft, he radically disputed legal institutions that were thousands of years old as well as the ideas they upheld: in that way, he was a nihilist in the eyes of upholders of the dominant ideology. Property was theft – so what?, replied Stirner. In response to the passionate seriousness of the revolution-

---

46   Sade 1998, pp. 8, 11.
47   Rosenkranz 1854, p. 132.
48   Stirner 1981, p. 84.

ary rebel came the mocking calm of the metacritic, who, in this way, carried out a radical nihilistic negation not only of ruling ideas but also and above all of revolutionary ideology. The latter could dispense with the weapon of moral indignation, so now it had to deal not only with the bigoted defence of the established order but also with witty irony. In this sense, Friedrich Schlegel was right when he said nihilism was implicit in irony, in witty observation.

One can understand the revolutionaries' embarrassment at this attitude. The need Herzen felt to distinguish between nihilism in the positive and the negative sense corresponded, in the final analysis, to the distinction between critical demystification, which resulted in a commitment to building a new society, and metacritical demystification, whose main target was precisely this commitment. Operating on the terrain of historical reconstruction, Marx had no difficulty in ridiculing the interpretation of the French Revolution and the socialist movement as a fundamentally religious affair: those struggles appeared as a mere story of 'the sacred' to an author (Stirner) for whom their 'material foundation [...]' had remained sacred, i.e., alien'. To subsume Innocent III and Robespierre, Saint-Just and Gregory VII under the category of 'popery [*Pfaffentum*]' meant to submerge historical analysis in a night in which all cats were gray. However, the problem of the basis of the values revolutionaries professed remained unresolved.

This difficulty did not escape the young Marx, who, as we have seen, had distinguished two opposed types of critique of ideology. The second, which destroyed the illusory flowers of ideology to perpetuate and strengthen the real chains of oppression, he saw as exemplified in Gustav Hugo. Hugo demystified the reassuring and harmonious image of capitalist society and stressed that the poor (and modern workers) were even worse off than the serf and slave. However, he was interested in legitimising slavery in the actual sense of the word rather than in challenging the workers' conditions (Marx's 'wage slavery'). Justifying the chains was in this case not an expression of loyalty towards existing ideology and social relations but rather a 'method' just as 'ruthless [*rücksichtslos*]' as that of the revolutionaries. But this ruthlessness took aim in the 'flowers' or in current values not so much at the moment of transfiguration and legitimation of the chains as at the illusory and mystifying element of transcendence they embodied; along with the 'false flowers' of the *ancien régime*, this critique of ideology assailed also, and indeed primarily, the values that were to or could preside over the destruction of its chains and the building of a new society. The result was clear: '[T]he *eighteenth-century scepticism* in regard to the *rationality of what exists* appears as *scepticism* in regard to the *existence of rationality*'; the critique '*no longer sees anything rational in the pos-*

itive, but only *in order no longer to see anything positive in the rational.*[49] Acting more consistently than the 'other Enlighteners' as a 'complete sceptic', Hugo arrived at a justification of slavery that, precisely because of its 'ruthlessness', was especially hard to attack. Sociopolitical conservatism was now not the outcome of closure against criticism but of a recourse to metacritique.

The preoccupation already apparent in the early writings persisted in Marx's later development. That is why he criticised as 'cretinous cynicism' the scornful and demystifying tones Proudhon struck against the national aspirations of the peoples of Poland and Hungary.[50] In that case too, the ruthlessness served to legitimise the chains imposed by the Tsarist Empire on oppressed nations.

The distinction between the two opposing types of critique of ideology also emerged in the traditions of thought that began with Marx or were at least inspired by him. Gramsci stressed that one could adopt either of two irreconcilable critical attitudes towards the ideals that arose from the French Revolution: on the one hand, 'a passionately "positive", creative, progressive sarcasm', which questioned only the 'immediate form, connected to a particular "transitory" world', of those ideals; on the other hand, a 'sarcasm of the "right"', which is rarely passionate but always "negative", sceptical and destructive, not only in regard to the contingent form but also to the human content of those feelings and beliefs'.[51] Also significant was the contribution of Trotsky, who, with reference to Nietzsche, analysed the dialectic that led to the critique of ideology and the demystifying potential that flowed eventually into a 'frank cynicism' (see below, 24, § 2).

Horkheimer and Adorno made more or less the same arguments. In *Dialektik der Aufklärung*, which was the dialectic of enlightenment but also the dialectic of the critique of ideology, of the process of disillusionment and disenchantment of the modern world, there was definitely an important impulse towards liberation but also 'the germ of that regression that today can be found everywhere'. As a distant follower of the historical school of law against which Marx railed, even Nazism did not hesitate to strike up 'Enlightenment' tones, in denouncing as prejudice or mystification every universal value, in subjecting to the critique of ideology not just Christianity but also liberalism, democracy, socialism, viewed as secularised versions of Christianity.[52]

'Enlightenment' that confirmed the chains, 'cretinous cynicism', 'open cynicism', 'sceptical and destructive sarcasm' were the different forms of nihilistic

---

49   Marx and Engels 1975 ff., 1, p. 205.
50   Marx and Engels 1955 ff., 16, p. 31.
51   Gramsci 1975, p. 2300.
52   Losurdo 1991, 7, § 3.

rebelliousness in the metacritical sense from which Marxism had to take its distance, though perhaps without ever really confronting it. The disquieting guest that nihilism was for Nietzsche was presented in the revolutionary movement and the Marxist tradition in the guise of the crafty Enlightener that, with his 'cynical' or 'sceptical and destructive' sarcasm, mocked every plan for the transformation of society and the breaking of the chains.

5   Unease, Charm and the Curse of Nihilism in Nietzsche

Nietzsche's uniqueness lay primarily in the fact that, within him, all possible different attitudes towards nihilism, as listed above, coexisted. Even more than a disquieting guest, he was the 'most disquieting [*unheimlichste*] of all guests' (XII, 125). What were the preconditions, at the historical and sociological level, for its spread? 'The beginning of nihilism was detachment, the break with the soil; it began with a sense of disorientation [*unheimisch*], it ended in a sense of disquiet [*unheimlich*]' (XIII, 144). The blurring of boundaries between states and cultures marked the start of a process of crisis and dissolution. A European now appeared on the horizon, an 'excessively curious, multiform, softened, a cosmopolitan chaos of feelings and cultures' (XIII, 17). Confused and lost, he seemed to move in a sort of global supermarket of cultures, ideas, beliefs. He had by now lost all ties to any given system of values; in reality, he was no longer alive to any value, only to the lack of value and of meaning. 'Softened', he practised a 'cosmopolitan tasting' of everything as well as of the opposite of everything; 'historicism' and the wish to '*tout comprendre*' (XII, 410), which he flaunted, served only to disguise the inner emptiness and the inner distance from any value. To the dissolution of ontological objectivity criticised by von Kleist (whose careful reader Nietzsche was) was now joined the dissolution of the sociological objectivity of values, which, more than ever, floated in nothingness.

This led to the 'horizon of the infinite': recognised values, certainties, points of reference, had disappeared. It was a new, unknown situation, which could turn out to be terribly disquieting: 'There is nothing more awesome than infinity' (FW, 124 [119]). Yes, 'since Copernicus, the human being unrolls from the centre towards the x' (XII, 127). The loss of the centre was further aggravated by the death of God. The 'madman' who had dared to kill him described the consequences of his gesture:

> What were we doing when we unchained this earth from its sun? Where is it moving to now? Where are we moving to? Away from all suns? Are we

not continually falling? And backwards, sidewards, forwards, in all directions? Is there still an up and a down? Aren't we straying as though through an infinite nothing?

FW, 125 [119–20]

Yet the blows dealt by the nihilistic tide to certainties at the same time struck the terrible constraints consecrated by a millenary tradition. The feeling of unease and even anxiety began to intertwine with a fascinating experience: 'We have forsaken the land and gone to sea! We have destroyed the bridge behind us – more so, we have demolished the land behind us!' Ahead, there opened a disquieting space for a new and immense freedom. It would be abdicatory and futile to want to turn back: 'Woe, when homesickness for the land overcomes you, as if there had been more freedom there – and there is no more "land"'' (FW, 124 [119]).

Only now, after the loss of the centre and the death of God, could the individual truly step forth:

> [F]or the longest period of humanity's existence there was nothing more frightful than feeling alone [einzeln]. To be alone [allein], to experience things by oneself [einzeln], to neither obey nor rule, to represent an individual [ein Individuum bedeuten] – that was no pleasure back then, but a punishment; one was sentenced 'to be an individual' [Individuum].
>
> FW, 117 [115]

The victim of nihilism gradually gave way to the nihilistic rebel. While the third *Unfashionable Observation* shows that Nietzsche was still impressed by von Kleist, the victim of nihilism who had been unable to bear the consequences of the confusion caused by Kant's Copernican Revolution, *The Gay Science* allowed the fool who dared to kill God to proceed as follows: 'There was never a greater deed – and whoever is born after us will on account of this deed belong to a higher history than all history up to now!' (FW, 125 [120]). The one who spoke thus was the nihilistic rebel, who unmasked and indicted all current values and celebrated with accents of sweet seduction liberation from the terrible leaden weights that had weighed down on the West ever since the preaching of the Gospel. For two millennia, his joy of living had been as if dulled and poisoned. In the moral conscience, and even in Kant's categorical imperative, a terrible legacy of theological fury and 'cruelty' continued to express itself and submit to merciless vivisection the inner life of the subject, tormenting him with the damning of the flesh and the torture of remorse and self-flagellation. Moreover, the sense of sin was at one with the herd instinct that prevented the development of truly autonomous and complete individuality. Against all that, Nietzsche praised 'Goethe's paganism with a good conscience' (FW, 357 [217]), and did so while breaking radically with 'moralistic, old-maidish Germany' (WA, 3 [238]).

In the rehabilitation of the flesh seen thus far, there were no major differences with the tradition of thought that led from the left Hegelians to Marx. However, the negation of inherited values was now interlaced with the metacritique of revolutionary negation, which even became the prime target of demystification. We are already familiar with the polemic against the 'conceptual hallucinations' that sought to call into question the slavery on which culture inevitably rested; so together with these slogans, the demand for the 'abolition of slavery' as such was already devoid of meaning (MA, 457 [246]). Just as the figure of the nihilistic rebel in the critical sense corresponded to that of the 'freethinker', so the figure of the nihilistic rebel in the metacritical sense corresponded to that of the 'free spirit': in spite of superficial similarities, the latter saw his main opponent precisely in the 'freethinker' (see above, 14, §7). If de Sade was the counterpoint to the French Revolution and Stirner to Vormärz, then Nietzsche was the counterpoint to the incessant French revolutionary cycle and the socialist movement: the 'Petersburg-style nihilism' that courageously challenged the Tsarist regime was actually a *'faith in unbelief'* to the point of martyrdom'; it was a manifestation of the 'need for faith', for new believers (FW, 347 [205]).

The victim of nihilism had by now turned into a rebel, who, in his radicality, completed the nihilistic rebellion in its dual critical and metacritical form. He proudly and explicitly acknowledged his own 'extreme nihilism'. True, there was no ontological objectivity to guarantee values; however, the dissolution of objectivity was in no way the dissolution of values. It was much more a question of carrying out a sort of Copernican revolution at the axiological level: the successful individual 'sets the value of things'. To this 'value' there corresponded no reality, no thing or value in itself, 'only a symptom of force on the part of the imposers of value [*Werth-Ansetzer*]' (XII, 351–2), who in this way could assert their power and will to power. Thus we see an 'active nihilism' at work, which was 'a sign of strength', of the *'increased power of the spirit'*. The individual that had turned out well became aware of the loss of meaning and value of the 'goals hitherto' (XII, 350) – not, however, to give in to despair, but confidently to affirm the values he himself set and to do so in the knowledge that he was the only one able to set them: 'To that extent, nihilism, as the *denial* of a real world, of a *being*, could be a divine way of thinking' (XII, 354).

The further appeal (and ambiguity) of Nietzsche resided in the fact that, for him, critical rebellion and metacritical rebellion were closely intertwined.

Christianity was subjected to devastating criticism by both the critical rebel demanding the emancipation of the flesh and the metacritical rebel that mercilessly demystified all the themes this religion founded in the belief in the equality of souls could historically have delivered to the plebeian and slave revolts. The link was particularly indissoluble because the values of the revolutionary movement had also flowed into the fateful tradition imposed during the previous two millennia, although the movement now adopted a negative and defiant attitude. Nietzsche now systematised and radicalised the ideas already observed in Stirner, who subsumed both Christianity and revolution under the category of 'popery', both characterised by a spirit of sacrifice and renunciation as well as the abdication of individual autonomy, which is why he treated them as chapters of one and the same pernicious religious and political history.

Apart from the systematisation and radicalisation of already existing themes, a new one came into view. Not only did the revolutionary movement proceed in the wake of 'popery', but both the one and the other embodied values that were not merely nullities but rather the nothingness that emptied the all, swallowing and annulling the meaning of earth and life. On closer inspection, the different chapters of this fateful story were as many chapters in the history of nihilism. In both the Jewish-Christian tradition and the revolutionary movement, a concept of time held that devalued the present and the worldly as an unbearable vale of tears, and aspired to a future, a wholly other, in reality synonymous with nothingness. Waiting for the final judgement and waiting for the future society promised by the revolution expressed, in scarcely different forms, the self-same denial of earthly life with its limits and conflicts, with its deep, insurmountable, but profitable contradictions. These two sorts of nihilism were indicted by Zarathustra in his counter-speech against the Christian and socialist beatitudes:

> I beseech you, my brothers, remain faithful to the earth and do not believe those who speak to you of extraterrestrial hopes! They are mixers of poisons whether they know it or not. They are despisers of life, dying off and self-poisoned, of whom the earth is weary: so let them fade away!
>
> Za, Zarathustra's Prologue, 3 [6]

The nihilism here denounced was not 'active' and 'divine'. It was the 'passive [*passivisch*] nihilism' (XII, 351), the 'tired [*müde*] nihilism' (XII, 351) of those who proved, by their escape from the vale of tears or from the world of 'exploitation' and 'oppression', from the inequalities, rank-ordering, slavery in its various forms, they were tired of life and the world. The 'Christian nihilistic values' (XIII, 220) were perpetuated in the thought and action of the 'systematists of

socialism': to want a political change that removed the negative from existence ('vice, sickness, crime, prostitution, *misery*') meant nothing less than 'condemning *life*' (XIII, 256).

From Nietzsche's point of view, both Turgenev's 'sons' and his 'fathers' were
nihilists: they represented two phases of a single gigantic subversive cycle. By
setting Christianity against revolution, the 'fathers' failed to realise that it was
precisely the egalitarianism of the Gospels that lay at the roots of the slave
revolt, in the meantime threatening to destroy everything. The 'sons', struggling
against the existing order in the name of socialist utopia, failed to notice they
were moving in the wake of Christianity, with its denunciation of the world of
life and its preaching of nothingness.

We have seen in Nietzsche the passage from the victim of nihilism to the
nihilistic rebel. Now the 'active' nihilistic rebel became the great antagonist of
a scourge that had to be investigated and confronted in all its breadth and from
the point of view of its deepest and remotest origins.

6   Total Revolution, Attack on the 'Great Economy of the Whole' and Nihilism

Even if this denunciation of nihilism was unprecedentedly radical, there were
nevertheless elements of continuity with the preceding tradition. When equating 'the socialist, the anarchist, the nihilist' (XIII, 233), when referring to
'anarchism and nihilism' (XII, 410) or the Russian subversive movement (FW,
347 [205]), Nietzsche seemed to proceed in a similar way to Baader or Donoso
Cortés. The nihilists were still revolutionaries and nihilism was still synonymous with revolution, but now this total revolution displayed roots that pointed
to a very remote past. The two Catholic interpreters of the counterrevolution
dated back to the Reformation the start of the destructive revolutionary development that resulted in nihilism. That Luther should be lined up with Rousseau
(the key author for understanding the process of the plebeian and Jacobin radicalisation of the French Revolution) went for Nietzsche without saying. But
what lay behind the Reformation (and the Peasants' Revolt)? Even the Spanish
Catholic emphasised that the revolutionary movements took their bearings in
a sense from Christianity:

> Since that, there is no revolution that [is not founded in] [...] heresy,
> they are all fundamentally heretical. See, if not, how they all establish
> and legitimize themselves with words and maxims taken from the gos-
> pel. The *Sansculotism* of the first French Revolution sought its historic

antecedents and titles of nobility in the humble nakedness of the meek Lamb; nor are there wanting those who recognised the Messiah in Marat, and called Robespierre his apostle. From the revolution of 1830 sprang the Saint-Simonian doctrine, whose mystic extravagances formed, I know not what new gospel emended and improved. From the revolution of 1848 sprang impetuously and copiously all the Socialistic doctrines expressed in evangelical words.[53]

As Donoso Cortés himself recognised, the revolutionary and nihilist movement, throughout its entire cycle, drew inspiration from 'words of the Gospel'. So, according to Nietzsche, that had to be the starting point from which to reconstruct the course of the revolution and of nihilism in its entirety.

Between Catholics and Protestants, it came to a heated exchange of accusations. Stöcker told Leo XIII, who saw the source of those 'associated pestilences' that were 'communism, socialism, nihilism, hideous evils and practically the death of civil society'[54] in the 'heresy' of the Reformation, that in fact the Catholic countries were the privileged site of the revolution and therefore of nihilistic negation.[55] Moreover, no few Jewish authors identified and denounced Christianity as such as the disaster's point of origin. The Catholics accused Luther of having undermined the principle of authority: but had not Jesus or Paul of Tarsus already called into question or demystified the divine Mosaic law? On closer inspection, Paul of Tarsus revealed a fundamental 'anarchism' and his teachings could well be likened to those of Pierre-Joseph Proudhon.[56] As for Jesus, with his 'will to die', he showed clear signs of 'decadence'. The apologists of Christianity accused the Jews of a stubborn attachment to earthly life and therefore a substantial neglect of man's other-worldly destination, but this same charge, according to apologists of Judaism, demonstrated precisely Christians' contempt for the world and the earth, the preference for death over life. According to some observers, the Jewish criticism of Christianity thus struck tones occasionally reminiscent of Nietzsche.[57] There does not seem to have been any direct influence in one direction or the other. The fact remains that, from Nietzsche's point of view, this critique was a confirmation of the fact that Christianity was an integral part of two thousand years of subversive

---

53 Cortés, 1874, p. 267.
54 In Giordani 1956, p. 78 (Enzyklika Diuturnum of 29 July 1881).
55 Stöcker 1890, p. 449.
56 Fleischmann 1970, pp. 98, 151 ff., 143.
57 Fleischmann 1970, pp. 38, 153.

and nihilistic development. A line of continuity led from the Gospels to Russian nihilism and socialist agitation.

As we know, it is possible and necessary to go even further back in the search for the origins of the revolution. But this also means going even further back in search of the origins of nihilism. In Judaism, prophets and 'priestly agitators' had already been at work venting their hatred on power, wealth, rank-ordering, and, in the final analysis, life, thus giving expression to an anarchic and subversive nihilism. If we bear in mind that Plato and Socrates, insofar as they set against real life the world of ideas and of alleged moral values, showed themselves to be Christians *ante litteram* and even Jews, the picture is complete. Contrary to the beliefs of Baader and Donoso Cortés, one could limit oneself to emphasising the line of continuity from Luther to Rousseau: the cycle of total negation had already begun with Jesus and Socrates (Plato's teacher). Thus, we come to the 'four great democrats [Socrates, Christ, Luther and Rousseau]' (XII, 348), who were also the four great nihilists, protagonists of the various waves of total revolution and the preaching of nothingness. All, in one way or another, could be traced back to the Jewish-Christian tradition. The nihilistic catastrophe of the West thus began with the collapse of classical antiquity or of the Greco-Roman *ancien régime*.

By virtue of its radical subversive potential, Christianity was synonymous with 'world negation' (XII, 120), it was 'the attempt to conquer the world; that is, to negate it' (XII, 119). Morality was the insidious and treacherous weapon of this nihilistic subversion, which, along with wealth, rank-ordering and power, negated life itself. Nietzsche harped tirelessly on this: 'Insofar as we believe in morality, we *condemn* existence', '*moral judgements of value are condemnations, negations, morality is to turn one's backs on the will to exist*' (XII, 571).

On the other hand, 'Christian value judgements persist everywhere in socialist and positivistic systems. There is a need for a *critique of Christian morality*' (XII, 126). This critique, supposed once and for all to destroy the nihilism of more than two millennia of history, was decisive for the salvation of life. It was a question of doing away once and for all with the 'negation of the world' inherent in the 'moral interpretation of the world' (XII, 120); yes, 'with the moral interpretation, the world is unbearable' (XII, 119). Morality and religion, for Donoso Cortés and Baader the antidote to nihilism, turned out to be an essential moment in, indeed the actual starting point of, the catastrophe of the West. Here one should not forget: not only the total negation that was the foundation of the French Revolution but even the Terror was already implicit in the Gospels (*supra*, 15 § 2).

Just as the subject, the protagonist of the nihilistic total revolution that had raged for two millennia in the West, had greatly expanded, so too its target. The totality of culture and society was a mortal danger. When the 'natural course of development' was blocked or reversed, the triumph of 'anti-nature [*Unnatur*]' made its appearance (XIII, 470). In this case too, we can detect a continuity with respect to a tradition of thought that accused the French Revolution of wanting to trample underfoot 'nature', or, in Schopenhauer's words, the 'aristocracy of nature'.[58]

At other times, instead of 'nature', Nietzsche spoke of life. 'The morality of Christianity' lay on him like a terrible threat, 'the capital crime against life' (XIII, 417). It was necessary to realise that 'the most powerful instincts of life, those most fraught with future, have up to now been *slandered*, so that a curse weighs upon life' (XII, 430). By virtue of its egalitarianism and its spirit of compassion, which blocked the selection and expulsion of waste and poisoned and thus rendered impossible the healthy development of the social and vital organism, 'the altruism of Christianity is a *life-threatening* [*lebensgefährlich*] conception' (XIII, 219), even a 'crime against life' (XIII, 471). 'Nature' and 'life' – we will see how Nietzsche referred to the 'species' and the 'great economy of everything' – were different names for the totality of reality, beset by the nihilistic total revolution begun in Palestine and still persisting in all its devastating fury.

7   Total Negation, Nihilism and Madness

The revolutionaries and socialists were accused by their enemies not only of being nihilists but of being insane. The negation of the Whole, which was nihilism, was beyond doubt an expression of madness. Donoso Cortés spoke not only of nihilism but also of madness in relation to 'rationalism'[59] and even more so to subversion: '[A] human being, purified interiorly, cannot be the agent of disturbance; and the agents of disturbance, by the very fact of being so, declare that they are not interiorly purified.'[60]

Behind the accusation of madness lay a story similar to that behind the charge of nihilism. The exponents of the heretical currents, who in the political and social sphere frequently cherished subversive hopes, were accused by Thomas Aquinas of being driven by an *aliqua phantastica illusion*[61] – at the time a synonym for a heterodoxy dictated by the 'flesh', for sin and mad-

---

58   Schopenhauer 1976–82c, Vol. IV, p. 218.
59   Donoso Cortés 1946d, p. 606.
60   Cortés 1874, p. 197.
61   Thomas von Aquin, Summa Theologiae 2, 2, q. 11, art. 1, ad tertium.

ness. This intertwining of meanings also returned in Luther's polemic against Müntzer and his followers: they were branded not only as heretics, rebels and murderers but also as 'seditious [*aufrüherisch*] prophets', 'mad prophets [*tolle Propheten*]' who worked up the 'mad rabble [*tolle Pöbel*]', 'visionaries [*Schwärmerer, Geister, Schwarmgeister*]'.[62] Insofar as Müntzer wanted by way of abolishing serfdom to make all people equal and to turn the spiritual kingdom of Christ into an earthly and external kingdom, he was both a madman who wanted to achieve something impossible and a heretic and a false prophet who radically distorted the Christian message.

The madness of which the revolutionaries were accused continued to be laden with religious meanings in the case of Schelling. He set authentic Christian and Pauline eschatology, which emphasised the transience of this world, against the 'apocalyptic fantasizing [*Schwärmerei*]' of democracy, or worse still, the 'fantasizings [*Schwärmereien*] of communism'.[63] The denunciation of *Schwärmerei* or fanaticism, which Enlightenment thinkers and Kant and Fichte aimed at 'obscurantism', religious intolerance and the *ancien régime*, was now primarily aimed at the revolutionaries, with their heresy of the total regeneration of the world.

This was also Nietzsche's starting point, although he identified in Christianity the source of the 'fantastic [*schwärmerisch*] ideals' the revolutionaries espoused (M, 377 [209]). But the term was used only by way of exception. This language thick with religious echoes was gradually replaced by another, which at least at first sight was significantly different. The polemic was now aimed at the 'enthusiasts [*Begeisterten*]' (Za, II, On the Tarantulas), the 'fanatics [*Fanatiker*]', these 'sick spirits' or 'conceptual epileptics' (AC, 54 [54]). Now the categories were derived primarily from psychiatry. Moreover, the psychopathological approach was taken by many critics of revolution, from Burke by way of Constant and Tocqueville to Taine. There can be no doubt that, for Nietzsche, the revolution began long before 1789 and that the mad people in this interminable total subversion were all nihilists.

As the theoretical *pendant* of the French Revolution or, to use Friedrich Schlegel's words, the 'negative politics'[64] deduced from pure reason, the 'negative philosophy' (to use Schelling's expression) attracted the same accusations: since it was 'artificial',[65] it repelled every 'inwardly healthy person'.[66] When

---

62   Luther 1883 ff., Vol. 18, pp. 296, 301, 311, 316 and 319 and Vol. 23, p. 70 ff.
63   Schelling 1856–61, Vol. 11, p. 552; Maximilian II. King of Bavaria, and Schelling 1890, p. 277 f.
64   Schlegel 1963, p. 575.
65   Schelling 1972, p. 100.
66   Schelling 1972, p. 80.

Rosmini emphasised the logic of total 'annulment' that was the foundation of the Hegelian dialectic (which reduced being to an 'absolute negative'), he denounced it, because it was, at the same time, affected by 'nihilism' and 'hallucination'.[67] According to Radowitz (an intimate of the King of Prussia, Friedrich Wilhelm IV), the subversion of the revolutionary intellectuals was an expression not only of 'nihilism' but also of 'pure egotism' and was alien to 'normal common sense'.[68] The 'pure egotism' or attachment to the 'empty concept' with the consequent loss of a sense of reality that Prussian conservatism criticised in the Hegelian school – all that is reminiscent of Jacobi's criticism of Fichte, whom he accused of extreme subjectivism and nihilism.[69] The latter was later ranked by Constant among the 'mad' followers of Robespierre,[70] which meant, as we know, among Jacobins infected by 'delirium'.

According Donoso Cortés, to profess pantheism or atheism was the sign of a party plunged into the darkness of 'political paganism', of satanism, nihilism, madness, and ultimately 'death', to which the Spanish Catholic likened revolution.[71] The dichotomy all/nothing here took the form of life/death, above all in the sense of the theology of salvation. Dostoevsky proceeded similarly, as shown by the words he put in the mouth of a defector from nihilism: 'I'm running from a delirium, from a feverish dream, running to seek Russia', a symbol of orthodoxy and of the desired Christian (and Slavophile) regeneration of the world,[72] 'an end to the old delirium, disgrace, and carrion!'[73]

The accusation of madness, like that of nihilism, gradually detached itself from that of atheism and heresy. According to Burke, the rampant madness could be traced back to the terrifying 'abstraction' of the French Revolution, that total revolution that set out to negate everything. In Turgenev's novel, a representative of the generation of the fathers addressed the nihilists as follows: 'Let's wait and see how you get on in a vacuum, in airless space'.[74] In the analysis of the genesis of nihilistic and revolutionary madness, the denunciation of 'abstractness' was at first linked with that of heresy and atheism, and then gradually replaced it. No less a figure than Dostoevsky wrote that the nihilists were characterised by 'a total ignorance of reality, a terrible abstractness,

---

67   Rosmini 1840–57a, pp. 135, 139 and Rosmini 1840–57b, pp. lvi and xlviii.
68   Radowitz 1851, pp. 320, 328.
69   Losurdo 1997a, 13, § 5.
70   Losurdo 1996, 2, §1.
71   Donoso Cortés 1946c, p. 212; Donoso Cortés 1946b, p. 191.
72   Dostoyevsky 1994, p. 748.
73   Dostoyevsky 1994, p. 594.
74   Turgenev 1999, p. 27.

a dull and deformed one-sidedness of development'.[75] In the wake of Taine, Cochin pointed out that Enlightenment thinking and revolutionary thinking, dominated by abstractness, was 'poor in intuition, wholly divorced from reality [...], oriented towards the void',[76] and for that reason led to 'the negation of every belief [...], the negation of every rule', and thus to the 'nihilism' of which the philosophers themselves boasted.[77]

In Nietzsche's case, the criticism of the abstractness of revolutionary theory once again underwent an extreme radicalisation. Like total revolution, total abstractness had by no means made its first appearance in 1789: Judaism and the agitation of the Jewish priests had already led to the subjection of morality to a process of autonomisation, denaturalisation and superfetation, to the point where it lost all connection to life and became terrifyingly 'abstract' (*supra*, 15 §2). The 'attack of delirium' received a further decisive impulse from Christianity (XII, 119), committed, as we know, to a mad 'negation of the world'. The life/death dichotomy present in the writings of Donoso Cortés returned in Nietzsche, but the 'party of life' he called into being for the struggle against nihilism (EH, *The Birth of Tragedy*, 4 [110–11]) not only had no Christian theological foundation but acted in opposition to a cycle of madness and death that had started precisely with the Jewish-Christian tradition.

8   A Polemical Category

We can now summarise the elements of continuity and novelty of this historical balance-sheet compared to the previous anti-'nihilistic' tradition. A very large part of this tradition, even the official religion of the West, was now to accused of nihilism. So, a clear distance separated Nietzsche from the dominant ideology: yet there was continuity, in the sense that, in both cases, nihilism was denounced as a product of total revolution, even though this total revolution was very differently in each case.

A paradoxical situation had arisen. From Nietzsche's point of view, Baader, Donoso Cortés and Dostoevsky were nihilists on account of their fervent Christianity, but he, in his turn, would also be synonymous with nihilism in its most repulsive form in the eyes of the three Christian authors, by virtue of his atheism and immorality. Even where there was agreement about denouncing an opponent as a nihilist, the reasons given were often irreconcilable. According

---

75   Dostoyevsky 1994, p. 673.
76   Cochin 1979, p. 79.
77   Cochin 1978, p. 13.

to Haym, Schopenhauer was infected by 'professed nihilism', because he was basically atheistic and indifferent to the political and religious life of the new Germany.[78] For the mature Nietzsche, Schopenhauer was a nihilist because of his enduring ties to Buddhism and Christianity (and thus, indirectly, to the revolutionary cycle that began with the latter), and for Herzen, finally, he was a nihilist because of the passivity and inaction he recommended in regard to existing society.

Even if one considers the different authors and cultural environments separately, it becomes apparent that each linked the charge of nihilism with other accusations, whose compatibility with it was at the very least problematic. Diehard opponents of revolutionary France denounced its ideologues and leaders sometimes as nihilists (and atheists), sometimes as suffering, more or less, from religious fanaticism. Leading the assault on the nihilism of the revolutionaries was Friedrich Schlegel, who published articles in *Concordia* denouncing them as visionaries mystically awaiting the 'advent of Messianic times'.[79] This accusation lay, as we know, at the centre of Gentz's indictment (*supra*, 7 §9).

From this one can conclude: the accusation of atheism and nihilism either alternated or linked with that of religious fanaticism. Were these two charges reconcilable? From the point of view of Donoso Cortés (as well as of that of Baader and Maistre), given that the Reformation was a 'grand heresy' that represented 'a mortal danger for society' and a first manifestation of nihilism,[80] one could well accuse an opponent at the same time of nihilism and religious fanaticism, provided nihilism was taken as a synonym for a doctrine that threatened the survival of the Church and Christianity (the totality of values, the whole, from the point of view of a devout Catholic).

Nietzsche went far further back, and saw nihilism as arising not from a heresy that distorted and perverted 'authentic' Christianity but precisely from Christianity, or rather the Jewish-Christian tradition, as such. In that case too, the accusation of religious (Jewish-Christian) fanaticism was not incompatible with that of nihilism (now synonymous with the negation of the totality of living values embodied in paganism). The fact remains that this was a category under which the most different authors with the most different motivations could be subsumed and through which one writer could excommunicate and stigmatise another.

---

78   Haym 1903a, p. 273.
79   Bucholtz 1967, p. 239, fn.
80   Donoso Cortés 1946e, p. 501.

Nietzsche was aware of the problem, so he drew some essential distinctions. But even if one focuses only on 'passive' nihilism, it is clear that under this category, as under that of Stirner's 'popery', belonged not only Buddhists and Christians but also revolutionaries and – one must now add – all those who, having lost every belief, painfully felt the loss of the meaning of life. To counter Marx's criticism of Stirner (all cats are gray in the dark), one would need to bring in another distinction, perhaps implicit in Nietzsche but that refers in the first place to Hegel. One could say the Christian and the revolutionary were nihilists in themselves but not for themselves, they had not yet become aware of the nothingness that inhabited their values. But, for Nietzsche, it was often precisely the subjective dimension, the painful experience of the lack of value and meaning of existence, that defined nihilism. Even if meaning of existence meant meaning of *earthly* existence, the category of nihilism itself could apply at most to the Christian and the Buddhist but not to the revolutionary, who in his critique of the theme of the valley of tears was in perfect agreement with the author of *The Antichrist*.

Was Fichte a nihilist? In fact he was a philosopher with many of the traits of a missionary (think of his obsessive recourse to the theme of *Bestimmung*) and even of a priest (for it is more or less in that capacity, as a '*weltlicher Staatsredner*' or '*Feldprediger*', that he proposed participating in the anti-Napoleonic wars), but a priest who intended to fulfil his mission in this world, by contributing at first to the cause of the French Revolution and later to the struggle against the Napoleonic occupation and Bonaparte's betrayal of the ideals of the French Revolution.[81] The German philosopher was the opposite of nihilism, if by that one meant the vanishing of the meaning of life. More or less the same went for Cloots. Far more apt in his case than the category of nihilism was that of 'armed missionary' pinned on him by Robespierre, when the latter attempted to denounce the inconsistencies and dangers involved in the plans for the universal export of the French Revolution, and its ideas and values.

As for the Russian nihilist movement, it has rightly been observed:

> It was not hard to discover at once that the word was ill-chosen. If there were people that believed blindly, violently in their ideas, it was precisely the 'nihilists.' Their positivistic and materialist faith could be accused of fanaticism, of a youthful lack of critical spirit, but certainly not of indifference.

---

81   Fichte 1971, Vol. 7, p. 507; Fichte 1967, Vol. 2, p. 600 f. (letter to Georg H.L. Nicolovius of
       April 1813).

Even contemporaries realised that 'this was a "meaningless term, less able than any other to characterize the younger generation, in which one could discern all kinds of "isms", but certainly not nihilism"'.[82] Bazarov, the nihilist *par excellence* in Turgenev's novel, wanted to regenerate society by overcoming 'bad education'; he died of typhus, which he contracted while voluntarily taking care of a peasant, a representative of that class oppressed and despised by the aristocracy, but from which the young revolutionary hoped for 'a new epoch in history'.[83]

At best, the category of nihilism could be of some use in understanding the figures of the victim of nihilism or of the nihilistic rebel in the metacritical sense, and that meant, on the one hand, authors like Kleist and, on the other, authors like de Sade, Stirner or Nietzsche himself: in the latter case, critical and revolutionary negation was joined by metacritical negation, which brought forth something similar to a void of values and meaning. And yet we must not lose sight of the problematic that continued to exist even here: the exalted affirmation of the individual (or of the individual that rose above the herd) and of his superiority to every norm could also be an expression of cynicism, though only with difficulty could it be identified with nothingness. It was Nietzsche himself who in this affirmation praised the antithesis of the preaching of nothingness, this time not as a metacritical rebel but as an antagonist of nihilism.

To write a history of nihilism is like trying to write a history of heresy or immorality: heresy and immorality compared to what, compared to what norm? Nihilism too can be defined only in relation to something else, as the negation of a set of institutions, ideas and values that in the eyes of those who fully identify with them represent the totality. If we want to rediscover the ground beneath our feet, we must return to the historical and political genesis of the category of nihilism. The critique of nihilism cannot be separated from the critique of revolution, and it is precisely the extreme diversity in the interpretations of the revolutionary cycle that explains the extreme diversity in the interpretations of nihilism. It is the theorist of aristocratic radicalism that undertook the analysis of this scourge in the same far-reaching manner as the diagnosis of revolutionary sickness.

---

82   Venturi 1972, Vol. 2, p. 215. On Robespierre as a critic of Cloots, cf. Losurdo 1996, 3, § 4.
83   Turgenev 1999, p. 214.

9   At the Source of Nihilism: Ruling Classes or Subaltern Classes?

In confirmation of the polemical nature of the category of nihilism, one final reflection is helpful. We have seen how Dühring denounced Christianity because of its deadly hostility to life and nature, using expressions not unlike those later used by Nietzsche, who in the meantime had read Dühring's *Value of Life*. However, there is a fundamental difference. In Dühring's eyes, Christian nihilism was rooted ultimately in the profligacy and decadence of the ruling classes of the Roman Empire: 'Debauchery produces repugnance', 'the cult of nothingness of decrepitude'.[84] Even if he proceeded differently, even a prominent leader of German Social Democracy like Bebel ended up blaming on the ruling classes 'the destruction of the flesh' of Christianity: it was a polemical and extremist reaction to the 'bestial materialism that held sway among the rich and powerful of the Roman Empire'.[85]

This way of reasoning can also be found in Dühring. However, he went further, affirming that a substantial vein of nihilism could be identified in the history of the ruling classes well beyond the collapse of the Roman Empire. In the wake of the struggle against the French Revolution, he argued, 'tendencies hostile to life' had again emerged. One only had to think of Malthus, who 'like a real priest found sin in natural sexual increase'.[86] It was on the same counterrevolutionary wave that the 'heavenly sanctification of nothingness [*Nichtsverhimmelung*]' developed, which so appealed to Wagner and, before him, Schopenhauer. A nihilistic tendency could, said Dühring, even be found in social Darwinism: to 'found one's own existence on the destruction of the lives of others' meant to undermine coexistence between people and thus to promote a 'life-compromising corruption'.[87] Ultimately, nihilism constantly referred to the ruling classes: driven by their dissipation, they sometimes even lost the taste and pleasure of participating in the 'banquet of life', from which however they wanted at any rate to exclude the mass of the population.[88] So it was the affluent and ruling classes that gave expression to a partial or total nihilism, that compromised the reproduction of life and life as such, and with it the species and culture.

The contrast with Nietzsche could not be starker. If Dühring identified and denounced in the egoism, greed and depravity of the affluent and ruling classes

---

84   Dühring 1881a, pp. 7, 12.
85   Bebel 1964, p. 83.
86   Dühring 1881a, pp. 20, 22.
87   Dühring 1881a, pp. 17, 25.
88   Dühring 1881a, pp. 59, 23.

the origins of the doctrine that was 'hostile not just to the people but also to life',[89] for Nietzsche nihilism arose from the resentment and rancour of the wretched and the malformed, who along with wealth, power and rank-ordering challenged and negated life itself.

---

89   Dühring 1881a, p. 22.

CHAPTER 17

The Late Nietzsche and the Longed-for Coup against the 'Social Monarchy' of Wilhelm II and Stöcker

1   Germany as a Hotbed of Revolutionary Contagion

In the West, there raged a subversive and nihilistic devastation whose end was not discernible; but where was its epicentre? After the 'Enlightenment' phase, Nietzsche felt growing resentment and hostility towards Germany, which, as he put it in a letter to a friend written on 24 February 1887, had become 'a real school of stupefaction over the last fifteen years' (B, III, 5, 31). It was time to put an end to the mystifications: '"German Spirit": a *contradictio in adjecto* for eighteen years now' (GD, 23 [159]). If we go back over the period here specified, we come to the founding of the Second Reich, or, more precisely, to the bitter disappointments that soon intervened after the emphatic hopes and enthusiasm on the eve of and during the actual founding of the new state, this '*Reichs*-worm', gave way to a new perception of its real nature (WA, Second postscript [258]).

How can one explain such a devastating judgement? The Germany Nietzsche criticised was at the forefront regarding compulsory education and the diffusion of education, which for him, as we know, was synonymous with 'communism'. Germany was the country with the strongest trade-union and feminist movement, and where the workers' party was deeply rooted and close-meshed; the country in which Bismarck, after introducing universal (male) suffrage for elections to the Reichstag, something still unknown at the time in England, sought to forestall a revolution from below by promoting one from above, which introduced the first vague elements of a system of social security. These were the years in which Marx formulated the thesis that 'the centre of gravity of the labour movement in Western Europe' had shifted from France to Germany. Engels agreed: the vanguard role played by France until the terrible repression of the Paris Commune had now been transferred to Germany, the 'central sector of the socialist movement' at the international level, and not only for reasons of numerical strength and organisational efficiency: the German workers demonstrated an exemplary 'theoretical sense' and a revolutionary rigour.

This was a thesis echoed in the early twentieth century by Lenin, especially as the socialist movement in Germany had succeeded in overcoming the 'difficult test of the emergency laws'. Because of its compactness and militancy, under conditions of legality and illegality, Social Democracy as it existed in the Second Reich represented a model: 'Take the Germans. [...] But the Germans only smile with contempt at these demagogic attempts to set the "masses" against the "leaders". [...] Look at the Germans. [...] They understand perfectly.' Again in 1909, Trotsky contrasted Russia, which passively bore backwardness and Asiatic despotism, to Germany, shaken by revolutionary stirrings, 'where socialist workers consistently recognise themselves as participants in world politics and keep a watchful eye on events in the Balkans and on debates in the German Reichstag', where the strongest and best organised socialist party in Europe and the world constantly made its voice heard.[1]

Even beyond the cultural and political circles identified with Marx, Germany's image was no different. While Herzen in the mid-nineteenth century praised the Hegelian dialectic as the 'algebra of revolution',[2] in Italy, Cavour, with an eye to that same current of thought, warned of a disturbing phenomenon: 'We see today many communists emerging from the German universities.'[3] An alarm cry that crossed the Atlantic and reached the United States, where a prominent theorist of slavery maintained that 'Germany is full of communists'.[4] Mehring agreed, and asserted at the end of the nineteenth century, from the other side of the barricades: 'The struggle for the emancipation of the modern working class is the most glorious and greatest liberation struggle known to history, and the fact that Social Democracy is in the vanguard of this struggle redeems centuries of German shame.'[5] Starting with the Paris Commune and right through until the outbreak of World War I and the chauvinist betrayal of which German Social Democracy was accused, it was to Germany that the eyes and hopes of the revolutionary workers' and European Marxist-inspired movement were primarily turned.

These fervent expectations were the reverse side of the fearful anxiety and growing revulsion with which Nietzsche regarded developments in the Second Reich. The turn to the 'Enlightenment' period was precisely occasioned by the perception that the state that had its baptism in a brilliant military victory, far from being the bulwark of civilisation against modern subversion, was actually its epicentre: the Germans 'will [...] one day have a riot'; '[t]he Ger-

---

1   Trotsky 1971, p. 53.
2   Cf. Herzen 1950, p. 579.
3   Cavour 1970, p. 12 f.
4   Fitzhugh 1854, p. 44.
5   Mehring 1898, p. 548.

man Socialist is the most dangerous one, because he is driven by no *particular* need' (VM, 324 [127]), only an ideology, the 'theoretical sense' praised by Engels.

In the wake of the deep disappointment caused by the triumph of reaction after the revolutionary storm of 1848, Engels sought to inject new courage into the revolutionary movement by inviting it to rediscover its glorious past: 'The German people, too, have their revolutionary tradition'.[6] This was demonstrated in particular by three central moments, the last of which, in order of time, was classical German philosophy, which formed the theoretical *pendant* of the French Revolution, and of which only the 'workers' movement' could therefore be the 'heir'.

After the traumatic experience of the massification and modern vulgarity of the Second Reich, Nietzsche too was concerned to trace the origins of the disaster. That is why he denounced the 'two fateful farces, the revolution and Kantian philosophy, the practice of revolutionary reason and the revolution of "practical" reason' (XIII, 444). Thus he outlined a historical balance-sheet that, leaving aside its different and opposing value judgement, had significant resemblances to Engels's.

We have already seen how Nietzsche stressed the profound influence on Kant of Rousseau, the plebeian intellectual and scoundrel *par excellence*, not surprisingly beloved by the Jacobins, and we also know of the relationship Nietzsche established between revolution and socialism, on the one hand, and moral pathos, moral indignation towards life and its inequalities and conflicts, on the other (*supra*, 8 §1). Unfortunately, not only the philosophical epoch that began with Kant was laden with plebeian and subversive moods. Take, for example, German music:

> Today German music is, more than any other, the music of Europe only
> because it alone has given expression to the transformation that Europe
> underwent through the Revolution: only German composers know how
> to lend expression to animated masses of people; how to create that
> enormous artificial noise that doesn't even have to be very loud – whereas
> for example Italian opera knows only choruses of servants or soldiers, but
> not 'people'. Moreover, in all German music one can hear a deep bour-
> geois envy of nobility, especially of *esprit* and *élégance* as expressions of a
> courtly, knightly, old, self-assured society, as expressions of a courtly soci-
> ety, chivalrous, old, sure of herself.

---

6   Marx and Engels 1975 ff., 10, p. 399.

We were dealing with a chapter of a history by no means over: 'Consider finally whether the ever more widely reaching contempt for melody and the atrophy of the melodic sense among Germans can be understood as a demo-cratic boorishness and after-effect of the Revolution' (FW, 103 [100–1]). Obvi-ously, Nietzsche was fully aware of the radical change that had taken place in comparison with *The Birth of Tragedy*. That is why he criticised himself for hav-ing, in his time, transfigured 'the latest German music', putting 'hopes to things where there was nothing to hope for, where everything pointed all too clearly to an end!' (GT, 6 [10]).

The criticism of the plebeian and socialist contagion in Germany was aimed particularly at the author of the *Critique of Practical Reason*, who 'discovered yet another faculty, a moral faculty'; despite '*real-politisch*' posturing, the Germans showed themselves to be 'basically piety-craving' (JGB, 11 [12–3]). In the final analysis, they were admirers of 'moral world order' (EH, The Case of Wagner, 2 [139]). Precisely for that reason, they were particularly deaf to the psycholo-gical investigation that brought to light how murky the demand for justice and the moral slogans of the subversive and plebeian movements could be: 'I hold it against the Germans that they are wrong about Kant' and do not understand that his philosophy is not characterised by 'intellectual integrity' (GD, 16 [200]). The ability to delve deeply and penetrate was completely alien to the Germans. Zarathustra was 'the first psychologist of the good' (EH, 5 [147]), and it was no accident that he was not listened to in Germany. That is precisely why *Nietz-sche contra Wagner* was 'an essay for psychologists but not for Germans' (NW, Preface [265]). And so:

> The 'German spirit' is my bad air: I have trouble breathing when I am around the instinctive uncleanliness *in psychologicis* that is revealed in a German's every word, every expression. They never went through a sev-enteenth century of hard self-examination as the French did [...] – they have not produced a psychologist to this day. But psychology is almost the measure of the cleanliness or uncleanliness of a race.
>
> EH, 3 [141]

Nietzsche concluded: '[T]he Germans are canaille', they were egalitarians *par excellence* (EH, 4 [142]). As further confirmed by Germany's role in the anti-Napoleonic wars, the Germans, with their appeal to the masses and the unity without distinctions of the people, were profoundly influenced by the French Revolution, though they claimed in general to be struggling against it. And, again, there emerged the analogy and (regarding the value judgement) the con-trast with Engels, who saw the beginning of the bourgeois revolution and the collapse of the *ancien régime* in Germany precisely in the anti-Napoleonic wars. When Nietzsche interpreted these as an essential moment in modern subversion, he increased the dose, for he saw the confrontation as one between a fanaticised mass, often mobilised by Christian slogans, and a deeply secular hero (Napoleon) who had the merit of having defeated the hydra of revolution and restored slavery in the colonies and of invoking imperial and pagan Rome.

If we went further back, we encounter the Reformation and the Peasants' Revolt, which according to Engels struck the first blow at the *ancien régime* and the power of the feudal aristocracy: the latter were attacked by people singing a 'triumphal hymn imbued with confidence in victory which became the Marseillaise of the sixteenth century'.[7] Nietzsche's view was not dissimilar, though as usual it carried a different and opposed value judgement. Who if not Luther had given a new vitality to Christianity, and in its most plebeian form, saving it from the euthanasia that the Renaissance and the return of classical antiquity were preparing for it? '[A]t a moment when a higher order of values, the noble, life-affirming values, the values that guarantee the future, had triumphed; [and] had triumphed, moreover, at the very spot where the opposing values reside, the values of decline' (EH, 2 [140]), when paganism was about to ascend even to the See of Rome, at that moment the fanaticism of the German monk, with his preaching and moralising and his appeal to plebeian resentment against the Roman aristocracy and the lords of the splendid culture of the Renaissance, ruined everything.

The three moments (the Protestant Reformation and the associated Peasants' Revolt, the anti-Napoleonic uprising and *levée en masse*, and German idealism) that, for Engels, marked Germany's revolutionary tradition took the form for Nietzsche of three stages in the democratic and subversive sickness that had long been devastating the country.

But one could go even further back. On several occasions, Engels made an analogy between early Christianity and revolutionary Social Democracy. So did Nietzsche, though he found in the analogy yet another reason to denounce Germany. The country that, with Luther, had saved Christianity from the pagan reconquest of the Renaissance was responsible for having contributed, more than one thousand years earlier, to the triumph of the new religion, plebeian and subversive, over classical antiquity.

---

7   Marx and Engels 1975 ff., 25, p. 319.

Europe would not have been christianized at all had not the culture of the old world of the South gradually been barbarized through an excessive admixture of Germanic barbarian blood and its cultural superiority lost.

FW, 149 [130–1]

Even before the South, naturally and happily pagan, had been Christianised, the Germans had made a decisive contribution to the defeat of Rome and the rank-ordering it represented: '[I]n relation to the *imperium romanum* they are the bearers of freedom' (EH, 2 [139]). One should not wonder at the role played by Germany. Its people had always been to the fore when it came to falsifying reality and moralising about it at any price. It was certainly the master of *credo quia absurdum*, an attitude that, 'to every true Mediterranean, is a sin against the spirit' (M, Preface, 3 [4]). Even before the modern Germans, 'the Germans are "the moral world order" in history' (EH, 2 [139]). One tends to think here of the Jews, the moral people *par excellence* and thus the privileged protagonists of a long-lasting subversion. So it is easy to see why the Germans were particularly indifferent to Nietzsche, 'the first upright spirit' that dared to question four thousand years of Jewish-Christian 'counterfeiting' (*infra*, 29 §12).

In the history of Germany, a clear line of continuity led from early Christianity to Luther, to the not only 'teutomaniacal' but also 'Christomaniacal' uprising against Napoleon, to Kant's moralism, the theoretical pendant of the French Revolution and of socialism. At this point, Germany tended practically to blend with the cycle of modern subversion, which had developed in the wake of Christianity or the Jewish-Christian tradition. We have just seen that 'the German levels [*stellt gleich*]'; but we must not forget that it was in 'Christ' that the 'herd' manifested to an outstanding extent its 'instinct in favour of the levellers [*Gleichmacher*]' and its hatred 'of rank-ordering' (XII, 379–80).

Moreover, unlike in other countries, in Germany it was hard for any alternative to the democratic and plebeian drift to acquire shape. Britain had the merit, in the form of Galton, of having drawn attention to physiology and eugenics (*infra*, 19 §1), in sharp contrast to stubborn German 'idealism' and the associated democratic superstition, according to the which everything depended on the environment and upbringing. With regard to France, it was enough to compare Tocqueville and Taine with Sybel. The latter came off quite badly because of his indulgence of the French Revolution. Take, for example, this passage from Sybel's work, which Nietzsche read in French translation: 'It is in the feudal regime and not in its fall that the egoism, greed, violence and cruelty that led to the terrors of the massacres of September originated.' Nietzsche commented as follows on these 'superb thoughts', as he sarcastically called them: 'I believe that [such an attitude] feels and knows itself to be "liberalism"'; but he described as repugnant 'such a hatred displayed against the entire social order of the Middle Ages' (B, III, 5, 28). The German historian strove, even to the point of obsession, to put the blame for the crimes of revolutionary ideology and the French Revolution on the social system it had challenged and overthrown.

From his own point of view, Nietzsche was no doubt right. As has been pointed out, Sybel welcomed 'the anti-feudal trait of 1789' and, in analysing the French Revolution, he sharply denounced Jacobinism, as was customary for liberal conservatives, but without damning it *en bloc* or with the intention of questioning all its outcomes. Above all, the German historian sought to understand the upheavals in France, by paying due attention to the 'socio-historical dimension'.[8] Much more than social history, Nietzsche was concerned to bring psychopathology, criminal psychology and even the psychology of the 'hereditary criminal' into play. So he was closer to Taine and even to Tocqueville, who was also strongly committed to the psychopathological diagnosis in particular of Jacobinism. Even with regard to historiography, German culture showed itself to be the culture most powerfully infected by modern ideas.

2   Between Friedrich III and Wilhelm II

In the last years and months of his conscious life, Nietzsche had the impression of witnessing a dramatic acceleration of Germany's democratic and plebeian drift. This was the eve of the founding of the Second International, or the 'renewal of the International on an extended and expanded scale'. Thus commented Mehring, emphasising the leading role of German Social Democracy, now about to take over 'the leadership of the international labour movement'.[9] The party seemed to be going through a good period: 'Almost every month saw the emergence of new workers' newspapers', while more and more theoretical works by prominent intellectuals appear. Social-Democratic culture spread more and more energetically across the most diverse layers of the population: in the capital of the Reich there appeared 'the *Berlin Workers' Library*, a periodic series of popular pamphlets, in which Clara Zetkin makes herself known as the most gifted champion of German women workers by way of an excellent discussion of the women's question'. And that is not all: 'In literature too, new shoots sprouted. [...] Then came the party almanacs. [...] The creative ardour

---

8   Seier 1973, p. 142 f.
9   Mehring 1898, pp. 527, 514.

of spring thus animated the working class', especially when 'a general strike movement' led to the awakening 'to class consciousness of vast sections of the proletariat not yet touched by the labour movement'.[10]

The founding of the Second International was also 'the centenary of the Great French Revolution': its memory seemed to further stimulate the other revolution, which according to Mehring was maturing; in both cases, 'a historical necessity is accomplished with inexorable force'. The protagonist of this new historical era could only be the workers' party, advancing in Germany from victory to victory, with 'no power in the world' able to stop it.[11] 'In no other country are social-democratic principles so prevalent, so deeply rooted', lamented Stöcker in 1887–8, the years in which Nietzsche's anti-German tirade was shrillest. This was proved by the election results,[12] more and more disturbing, or – from Engels' point of view – more and more encouraging, so much so as to encourage the hope of a peaceful rise to power by the labour and socialist movement. The latter made masterful use of 'universal suffrage'; 'the hand of the state' was as if 'paralysed'; the ruling classes had 'exhausted all their expedients – uselessly, pointlessly, unsuccessfully'; their 'impotence' was clear for all to see.[13]

Nietzsche too began to believe (and to fear) that the ruling classes in Germany were no longer in a position to resist the political and ideological offensive of the revolution, all the more so because, at precisely this time, an acute political and even dynastic crisis was starting up. While the long reign of Wilhelm I, by then in his nineties, dragged on, the signs of the deadly sickness devouring the crown prince became apparent, so that he seemed destined to cede to his young, ambitious and inexperienced son, already at odds with his mother (the daughter of Queen Victoria of England) and also with Bismarck. This was a struggle of three 'parties', grouped around the ailing crown prince and his wife, his young son and the old Chancellor.

Before analysing the different political and ideological platforms, we should first note that Nietzsche had the opportunity to follow the crisis, for he seemed to have access to first-hand information.[14] In a letter to his mother dated 5 March 1888 about the intrigues developing around the crown prince he wrote: 'By chance I am very well informed, too well, about the *intima intimissima* of this horrible story' (B, III, 5, 269). Two weeks later, again in a letter to his mother

---

10   Mehring 1898, p. 528 f.
11   Mehring 1898, pp. 526, 548.
12   Stöcker 1890, p. 161.
13   Marx and Engels 1975 ff., 27, p. 514.
14   Treitschke 1978, p. 415.

(B, III, 5, 273), he recounted some very interesting details: next to him at table was 'Baroness Plänckner, *née* Seckendorff', thus a relative of Count Seckendorff, chief master of ceremonies at court and on good terms as acquaintance and patient with 'Privy Councillor von Bergmann', one of the doctors treating the crown prince, who at the time was trying to recuperate on the Ligurian coast not far from Nice, where Nietzsche was to be found. The letter concludes: 'So I am very well informed about the events in Sanremo. I even had in my hands sheets written by the Crown Prince a few days before his departure [for Berlin, where, after the death of Wilhelm I, he ascended the throne as Friedrich III]'.[15]

So, Nietzsche was able to follow the struggles, intrigues and rumours that developed one after the other in the period between the death of Wilhelm I through the agony and the brief reign of Friedrich III to the first acts of government of Wilhelm II, a period that coincided with the philosopher's lapse into madness. In the first of his two letters to his mother quoted above, Nietzsche reacted as follows to these events:

> The news from Sanremo is not at all reassuring. This system of lies and the arbitrary distortion of facts, which this Englishwoman carries on from month to month in league with an inept English doctor, has outraged even foreigners, not to mention the German doctors, the imperial family and Bismarck.
>
> B, III, 5, 269

The English doctor, strongly opposed to the emergency surgery recommended by his German colleague, had made a very reassuring diagnosis, which was readily accepted by Princess Victoria – presumably not only for sentimental reasons but perhaps also out of a Machiavellian calculation: if the heir to the throne Wilhelm I, although seriously ill, rejected the invitations to abdicate coming in from all sides, he would at least have the time to make adequate arrangements for his wife.

At the time, the philosopher's judgement did not differ from that of Treitschke, who also, soon after Wilhelm II's accession to the throne, expressed his distaste for the 'deceitful manoeuvres of the English doctor' and his circle. Nietzsche stuck to his criticism in a subsequent letter to his mother dated 20 March 1888. Friedrich III had been on the Hohenzollern throne for a few days. When Nietzsche reported that he had access to confidential information thanks to his neighbour at table, he added she was a relative of 'Count Seckendorff', who, 'as

---

15   Röhl 1993, pp. 715–34.

is well known, is the "right hand" – and a little more – of the new Empress' (B, III, 5, 273). This allusion to her extramarital affairs, conducted while the shadow of death fell ever deeper across the new emperor, certainly cast no favourable light on the Empress from London. But nor did the new Emperor cut a particularly good figure: his opponents accused him of being too influenced by his wife and thus by circles and interests alien or potentially hostile to Germany.

Quite a different picture emerges from a letter of 20 June 1888, shortly after the end of the 99 days of the reign of Friedrich III: 'The Emperor's death has moved me: after all, he was a small flickering light of free thought, the last hope for Germany. Now Stöcker's regime begins – I draw the consequence, and I already know that now my *Will to Power* will be immediately confiscated in Germany' (B, III, 5, 338–9). The criticism was directed more at the court preacher than at the Emperor, who was nevertheless accused of maintaining compromising relations with Stöcker.

In this case too, Nietzsche proved well informed. On 28 November 1887, a meeting under Stöcker's direction took place in the home of Count and General Waldersee (later Chief of Staff of the Army) in support of the 'Berliner Stadtmission', the 'Berlin Mission (on behalf of the poor)': Prince Wilhelm had not only participated personally but had also delivered a short speech in which he expressed his admiration for the court preacher's 'Christian-social thinking'. There was a big row and scandal. Even Bismarck had expressed himself in harsh terms in a long letter to Prince Wilhelm: it was unacceptable that a member of the royal family should be identified with a political party, especially such a controversial and discredited one.

As we already know from the letter of 20 June 1888 quoted above, this was essentially also Nietzsche's view. But, in a later letter, dated 14 September 1888, he seemed to introduce an element of caution:

> This young emperor gradually presents himself more favourably than might have been expected – he recently expressed himself in sharply anti-Semitic terms and has now publicly expressed his deep gratitude to the two (Bennigsen and Baron von Douglas) who, tactfully and at the right moment, removed him from the compromising company of Stöcker and co. I am told that even his behaviour towards his mother is a hundred times more considerate than partisan passion in Germany and England might desire.
>
> B, III, 5, 433–4

Two days later, on 16 September, the caution seemed even to have given way to complete identification: 'I like our young German Emperor more and more:

almost every week he takes a step to show that he wants to be confused neither with the *Kreuzzeitung* nor with [Stöcker's] "anti-Semitism"' (B, III, 5, 439).

As is clear from the reference to the press and various people, Nietzsche was talking about concrete events. The 'Baron v. Douglas' mentioned in the letter of 14 September had been elevated by Wilhelm II three weeks earlier, on 20 August, to the rank of count. In any case, it was someone who expressed a very different orientation and political line from that of Stöcker. This was dramatically confirmed by the speech Count Hugo von Douglas gave later, on 4 October 1888, and which was immediately given great publicity and widely promoted from above. This text (*What We Can Expect from Our Emperor*) advocated the 'strengthening and consolidation of the monarchical principle' in an obvious polemic against the 'democratic parties and parties that steer towards democratic goals' that would have liked to reduce the emperor to 'a merely representative figure'.[16] The contrast with Stöcker was unmistakeable: the latter, as we shall see, did not hesitate to appeal to the French Revolution and even to demand 'political and social democracy'.

But back to Nietzsche. His confident expectation of Wilhelm II, following on from his initial doubts and misgivings, was short-lived. A letter from early December 1888 ranked the 'German Emperor' among the *braune Idioten* (B, III, 5, 501). We all know what an idiot is. But what did he mean by 'brown'? And what had happened that was so important, in the period from September to December, to bring about such a harsh judgement?

3   The Emancipation of the 'Black Domestic Slaves' and Wilhelm II, the 'Brown Idiot'

While seeking materials that would allow an answer to this question, I came across a specific charge in *Ecce Homo*, which Nietzsche began writing in mid-October: 'The German emperor makes deals with the Pope, as if the Pope did not represent a deadly hostility to life!' (EH, 10 [98]). In fact, in September 1888, on the occasion of his trip to Rome, Wilhelm II had visited and paid homage to Pope Leo XIII, the pope who, a few years later, with the encyclical *Rerum Novarum* and his attention paid to the social question, presented himself as the true defender of the legitimate claims of the peasants and workers, in an attempt to extend the influence of the Catholic Church among the masses in competition with the Second International.

---

16   Röhl 2001, pp. 32–6.

But this meeting is not sufficient to explain Nietzsche's polemic. At another point in *Ecce Homo*, one finds a new, more precise indictment: '[R]ight now the German emperor calls it his "Christian duty" to free the slaves in Africa' (EH, 3 [141]). A question arises: is there a relationship between the polemical remarks? They came at a time when the abolitionist campaign launched in Europe, from Paris, by Cardinal Charles Lavigerie received a loud echo: the European and Christian great powers in Africa were being called upon during their expansion in Africa to promote the liberation of black slaves from the inferno they inhabited. Officially supported by the Holy See, this campaign seemed particularly successful in Germany. On 26 October 1888, in response to a papal brief of a few days earlier, the semi-official *Norddeutsche Allgemeine Zeitung* wrote: 'The magnanimous action of the supreme head of the Catholic Church, motivated by a sublime Christian love of humanity, allows us to hope that it will not remain isolated, but, on the contrary, will find in the hearts of others a strong resonance and a fruitful imitation.'[17]

While Germany, on the one hand, 'wants to liberate black domestic slaves for love of the slaves' (XIII, 643), on the other hand, through its chauvinistic agitation under Wilhelm II, it unleashed a bitter polemic against France that went so far as almost to seek to exclude France from the ranks of civilised countries. Nietzsche could not suppress his indignation: 'The *Norddeutsche Zeitung* [...] see[s] the French as "barbarians", – personally, I look for the "*dark* continent", the place where "the slaves" should be freed, in the vicinity of north Germans' (NW, [273]). These were the years in which Bismarck denounced the French, incurably infected by the herd spirit and inveterate enemies of the country of culture *par excellence*, as follows: they were 'thirty million docile kaffirs, each lacking in quality and value'.[18] Significantly, Nietzsche particularly targeted the newspaper that was to the fore in supporting the Christian-Catholic abolitionist campaign. For him, on closer inspection, the country of Wilhelm II referred precisely to Africa, the 'dark continent'. Now we know why Wilhelm II was included among the *braune Idioten*. In the United States, the 'democrats' of the South, determined to defend first slavery and then white supremacy, similarly called the anti-slavery republicans campaigning for abolitionism and racial equality 'black republicans'.

The fact was, returning to Germany, that Bismarck and Wilhelm II were among the strongest (and least prejudiced) supporters of Cardinal Lavigerie: if abolitionist and Christian slogans helped the Chancellor to gain the support

17 *Norddeutsche Allgemeine Zeitung*, 26 October 1888, no. 507.
18 In Herre 1983, p. 167.

in the Reichstag of the Catholic Zentrum party,[19] they could also be particularly useful in a country that arrived late among the colonial powers. All this did not fail to arouse suspicion at the international level. A former French diplomat wrote as follows in a book published in 1889: 'The great German Chancellor has sent a letter to the Holy Father supporting the work of a Frenchman who seems to forget the interests of his country in the name of a vague humanitarian idea.' Evidently, opinion regarding Cardinal Lavigerie was lukewarm if not hostile.[20] From Nietzsche's point of view, France had the merit of appearing less pious and Christian than Germany. It is in this context that one should understand the insults hurled against the 'bigot' leading the Second Reich and trying in vain to disguise himself in the 'scarlet' of a hussar's uniform (EH, 5 [92–3]). This explains the furious polemic against the 'scarlet idiots [*scharlachne Idioten*]' (B, III, 5, 565–6) or the 'purple idiots [*gepurpurten Idioten*]' (XIII, 641) that ruled in Berlin. If the noun referred unequivocally to the 'idiot on the cross' that was Christ (XIII, 644), the two adjectives seemed to suggest that, under the disguise of the uniform of a hussar, lurked a cardinal's purple like that worn by Lavigerie. Both were inspired by 'deadly hostility to life': 'dynastic institution' and 'institution priestly' seemed in Germany to become one (XIII, 645): in polemic against the Second Reich, which in the meantime had become synonymous with Christianity, Nietzsche declared himself 'anti-German and anti-Christian *par excellence*' (B, III, 5, 537).

At the end of his development, the philosopher seemed to be returning to his starting point: he had begun, with an eye to the workers of the Paris Commune, by warning against the terrible danger of a 'barbaric slave class' in revolt; now, instead of among the workers of France, this danger seemed to be materialising in an ill-starred Christian court that hoisted and waved the flag of the emancipation of black slaves.

The abolitionist campaign sometimes took the form of a crusade against the Muslim world, accused of promoting or encouraging the black slave trade in Africa.[21] This was one more theme that aroused Nietzsche's indignation; after stressing the 'noble [...] masculine instincts' of this world, he issued a decidedly provocative slogan: 'War to the death against Rome! Peace, friendship with Islam' (AC, 60 [63–4]).

By now, the picture was clear: 'The Germans are too stupid and too base for the height of my spirit' (B, III, 5, 543). They were unable to understand aristo-

19   Wehler 1985, p. 363.
20   Renault 1971, Vol. 2, p. 222 f.
21   Renault 1971, Vol. 2, p. 368 f.

cratic radicalism. The modern and democratic devastation that had found its chosen place in Germany was now dramatically accelerated with the ascent to the throne of a Christian and abolitionist emperor, a 'purple' or 'brown' idiot.

4   The 'Social Monarchy' of Stöcker and Wilhelm II and the Counterrevolution Hoped for by Bismarck

But not just international politics explains Nietzsche's turn and his unspeakable hatred for Wilhelm II. In *Twilight of the Idols* we read: 'The tired worker with his slow breath' was a typical figure 'in this age of work (and the "Reich"!)' (GD, 30 [206]). There was not only no place in the Second Reich for *otium* (MA, Preface, 8 [13]), but the frenzy and glorification of labour had infected the very Crown. We are already familiar with the irony and contempt with which the philosopher treated Wilhelm I's attempt to present himself as a 'worker' like any other (*supra*, 10 § 2). But his grandson Wilhelm II, who before ascending to the throne had looked sympathetically on Stöcker's 'Christian socialist' project, was even more radical, and had prompted a wave of indignation that swelled as a result of Bismarck's attitude. In two letters to the Chancellor, Prince Wilhelm took a small step back and gave an assurance that he did not wish to identify with the party of the court preacher, but at the same time he reiterated his commitment, inspired by '"Christian love" of the "poorer classes of our people"', to the 'lower strata of workers in the population'.[22]

After his coronation, Wilhelm II showed himself to be determined to take action to mediate in the conflicts of the day, 'breaking all precedent' – writes an American historian – 'the Kaiser allowed a deputation of strikers to come to the palace to present their demands for an eight-hour day'. Not content with this, two days later, he asked the mine owners to maintain the 'closest possible contact' with their employees, without ever forgetting the right of the latter to share in some way in the fruits of their labour. Motivated primarily by the desire to gain popularity, he was perhaps also moved by 'some small trace of Christian responsibility' when he outlined a reform programme 'to protect workers' and the abolition of Sunday work and other measures concerning women and children. In this way, Wilhelm II actually won 'considerable popularity with the working class', and was even hailed as 'the workers' King' during his visits to 'the more destitute quarters of Berlin'.[23]

---

22   In Bismarck 1919, pp. 586 f., 598.
23   Cecil 1989, Vol. 1, p. 133 ff.

So, one can appreciate Nietzsche's feelings of horror: the king of the 'black house slaves' in Africa was, at the same time, 'king of workers' in Germany. Drawing a line of continuity from Wilhelm I to Wilhelm II, the philosopher observed that 'the cursed dynasty' of the Hohenzollerns was always waving the flag of the 'blessing of labour' (XIII, 645).

As Mehring said, it was at this moment that 'the clarion call of social monarchy rang from all official towers'.[24] This was Stöcker's slogan. He summed up his political project in a paper that appeared in 1891, shortly after Nietzsche's descent into madness, and which, significantly, bore the title 'Social Democracy and Social Monarchy'. After expressing his pleasure at the lifting in the meantime of the anti-socialist legislation, the court preacher pronounced in favour of 'political and social democracy'[25] Regarding the first point, he gave a positive assessment of constitutional monarchy and condemned 'Caesarism [perhaps a polemical allusion to Bismarck]' and welcomed the advent of 'universal, equal and direct suffrage' and the 'legal and civic equality' resulting from the French Revolution. With regard to the second point, he defined the real socialism he aimed to promote and that, unlike 'vulgar communism', respected the 'freedom of personality' as the 'aspiration to lead to victory also in the economic field the world-historical movement for equality'.[26] Against the 'state of the people' desired or threatened by Social Democracy, Stöcker set the idea of a 'social state' realised and directed by a 'social monarchy' inspired by Christianity.[27] If social Darwinism tended to assert the validity of the laws of the 'animal world' 'for us human beings and Christians', if the liberals of the Manchester School could remain indifferent to the drama of mass misery, the same was not true of the 'conscience of Christendom':[28] even though it firmly rejected revolution and violence, 'Christianity is social like no other system of thought in the world'.[29]

These themes were again taken up and further developed by Stöcker in other interventions. The world-historical movement for the realisation of equality could not ignore the male/female relationship. In countering extreme exploitation in the workplace, women should not hesitate to form 'unions [*Koalitionen*]' and to carry out 'agitations' and 'strikes': 'To improve their conditions, women workers must form their associations exactly like the men, otherwise they will

---

24   Mehring 1898, p. 523 f.
25   Stöcker 1891a, pp. 17, 26, 21.
26   Stöcker 1891a, pp. 25, 18.
27   Stöcker 1891a, 13, 19.
28   Stöcker 1891a, 10 f.
29   Stöcker 1891a, 16.

make no progress.'[30] Women should, under all circumstances, have the right to education and jobs, starting with the medical profession. Stöcker seemed not even to exclude the ordination of women. He saw the United States as a model (albeit one difficult for Germany to follow) of the 'full emancipation' of women and their 'full equality with men'. Whatever the case, the movement for the emancipation of women was 'a stream [...] that is completely unstoppable'.[31]

The social reforms proposed and advocated here are embedded in a Christian-social philosophy of history. A society whose motto was *Noblesse oblige!* had made the transition to one whose motto was *Richesse oblige!* But even this order 'challenges God and, rightly, men'.[32] After it had set in motion the process whereby 'slavery is abolished', Christianity inspired authentic socialism, this 'idea that moves the world' and that was called upon to achieve the 'equalization of economic inequalities'.[33] At the more strictly political level, just as absolute monarchy had given way to constitutional monarchy, so too the 'absolute employers' had as it were become 'constitutional' by agreeing to 'discuss with their workers the factory order and social care'. Prussia and Germany had set out on this road, and entered its vanguard, when abolishing serfdom in the struggle against Napoleon. With his message of 1881, Wilhelm I had ruled that 'the working classes' had the right not to alms but to 'organised state aid'; so Wilhelm II not only reprised and further enriched the legacy of his grandfather, but, from Berlin, sought to call into being an 'international' movement for the implementation of the measures necessary to protect workers.[34]

It is for just such a philosophy of history that Bismarck reprimanded the young emperor: he was accused of wanting to promote the 'emancipation of the workers', in emulation of his ancestors who had emancipated the peasants; but this attitude was dictated by the incessant quest for 'popularity among the masses of the population', whose outcome could only be to spread suspicion and alarm among 'all the propertied classes'.[35] The former Chancellor did not hide his contempt for the 'so-called workers' protection law', which he said was less for the 'protection of workers [*Arbeiterschutz*]' than for the 'coercion of workers [*Arbeiterzwang*]', who were forced from above to 'work less'. The 'limitation by law of women's and children's work and Sunday working' not only met

---

30   Stöcker 1891b, 7; Stöcker 1899, 45.
31   Stöcker 1899, 48 f.
32   Stöcker 1891b, 12.
33   Stöcker 1891a, 16 ff.
34   Stöcker 1891a, 22 f.
35   Bismarck 1919, 623; Bismarck n.d., Vol. 2, 567.

with the well-founded hostility of the world of industry but also violated 'the worker's independence, in his employment and his rights as head of the family'. The worker would certainly not be 'grateful' for such restrictions and impositions, and the only ones to benefit would be the socialist 'agitators' who sought to pass on the costs of this unfortunate law to the employers, by demanding a reduction in working hours but not in wages. All this would only further fuel 'the growing expectations and insatiable greed of the socialist classes'.[36]

It is easy to see why Bismarck, in the letter to Prince Wilhelm, warned of the danger posed by Stöcker. Stöcker expressed his amazement and disappointment at the fact that, after having introduced social legislation, Bismarck was now leading the opposition to the further development of that legislation being promoted by the grandson of Wilhelm I: according to the court preacher, a 'soundly socialist attitude' had given way in the case of the Chancellor to a 'vision fundamentally of the Manchester School'.[37] Was this analysis well founded? Actually, Stöcker himself gave the main reason for Bismarck's change of heart when he interpreted the social legislation passed or to be passed as recognition of the fact that 'the working classes have a legitimate right to state aid'. In so doing, he inserted that recognition into a framework of philosophy of history according to which the constitutional limitations on the power of proprietors should logically correspond to the constitutional limitations on the power of the monarch.[38] This went well beyond that minimum support graciously granted from above, as prescribed by the Christian love and 'practical Christianity' of which Bismarck spoke in 1881.

Now, however, the Chancellor noticed the smell of revolution: 'Priests can do a lot of harm and be of little help; the countries most devoted to the clergy are the most revolutionary.' From a position of weakness one must make no concessions to a subversive movement menacingly on the rise. Rather than watch while the monarchy decays, a king should be ready to 'die sword in hand as he struggles for his rights on the steps of the throne'. In any case, 'there are times of liberalism and times of reaction, and even of rule by violence [Gewaltherrschaft]'. That was a kind of call for pre-emptive civil war. And for those who had not yet understood, the Iron Chancellor recalled the slogan of the counterrevolution in 1848: 'Against democrats only soldiers are of use [Gegen Demokraten helfen nur Soldaten]'.[39]

---

36   Bismarck 1919, 617 f., 621.
37   Stöcker 1890, 181.
38   Stöcker 1891a, 23.
39   Bismarck 1919, 593, 595.

Far from wanting to weaken or abolish the anti-socialist law, Bismarck demanded its indefinite extension and a further crack down. If necessary, he was even ready to proclaim martial law and to break any resistance in Parliament by a sort of coup. He formulated the thesis that 'Social Democracy implies for the monarchy and the state a more acute danger of war than the current international situation and should therefore be considered by the state not as a matter of law but as a matter of internal war and force.'[40] Clarity on this point was essential: 'The social question cannot be resolved with rose water, blood and iron are what is needed'; 'ultimately, the socialist question is [...] a military question'.[41]

These were not just words. Bismarck aimed to break the miners' strike by sending in the army with orders to open fire: the bloodshed and the resulting unrest would then create an opportunity to proclaim a state of emergency and proceed to a final reckoning with Social Democracy, without the hindrance of constitutional scruples. In any case, the 'agitators', the leaders and activists of the Socialist Party, should be deprived of the right to vote and to stand in elections and should even be expelled from the country.[42] As a contemporary witness observed, the Chancellor wanted to pose as the 'sole saviour' of the 'propertied classes'.[43] At the end of his analysis of the irresistible rise of Social Democracy in Germany, Engels exposed the inclination of the ruling classes to make their own the motto of Odilon Barrot: 'La legalité nous tue, legality is the death of us'.[44] Bismarck arrived at this conviction in the last months of his rule.

Here it is interesting to note the objective consonance of the programme developed by the Iron Chancellor on the eve of his defeat with Nietzsche's ideas. As we have seen (supra, 10 § 3), an aphorism in the Twilight of the Idols complained that the workers had been granted political rights. Bismarck now intended to challenge them. Furthermore, Nietzsche denounced 'the right of trade-union association [Coalitions-Recht]', theorised and defended by Stöcker. The court preacher was hated not only by the philosopher but also by the Chancellor, who had now resolved to crush strikes and labour unrest manu militari. Even regardless of his further plans for a more radical turn, the final phase of Bismarck's time in government was marked by frenzied attacks on the trade-union movement and the 'right of trade-union association'.[45] The recourse to

40   Bismarck 1919, 611.
41   Bismarck n.d., Vol. 2, 564 and Vol. 3, 71.
42   Röhl 2001, 298–302 and 329–31; Gall 1980, 690–700.
43   Gall 1980, 696.
44   Marx and Engels 1975 ff., 27, 522.
45   Mehring 1898, 504.

drastic measures was all the more necessary if it proved impossible through
the use of concessions to appease 'the insatiable greed of the socialist classes'.
This was also the standpoint of Nietzsche, for whom the worker took advantage of every concession to 'make more and more immoderate demands'. This
was no longer a case of excessive material demands though: the workers now
experienced their situation as 'unjust and, to change it, were prepared to use
violence and stage uprisings'. Thus concluded the aphorism from *Twilight of the
Idols* cited here, but this is also the conclusion of the Iron Chancellor, according to whom the threat of Social Democracy could be averted only by force. It
was necessary to dispense with the 'humanitarian sentimentality [*Humanitäts-
dusel*]' that had even infected Wilhelm II. It was a dream to imagine that one
could 'make contented people of the workers by legislative measures', and not
even a pleasant one, for 'universal satisfaction' would bring with it the end of all
'ambition', all effort and energy, and the triumph of 'stagnation'.[46] The struggle
against the social state thus took on tones we can call Nietzschean.

5   'Anti-German League' and Coup against Wilhelm II

During the last months of the philosopher's conscious life, the contradictions of
the Second Reich approached breaking point. The internal crisis and the international crisis became linked. While the reign of Wilhelm I extended beyond all
expectations, a crown prince (the future Friedrich III) was preparing to ascend
the throne who, because of the sickness that was consuming him, was in no
position to carry out his functions. According to Bismarck, his wife, the crown
princess, 'influences and dominates him completely'.[47] Under such conditions,
would it not be she, the daughter of Britain's Victoria, who would ultimately
take control of the throne of the Hohenzollerns? Through her behaviour, 'the
Englishwoman', as she was disparagingly called by her opponents,[48] justified
the gravest suspicions. At first, she made light of the heir to the throne's sickness. When it became clear things were hopeless, she strove with all her might
to prevent the abdication proposed by many. Once she had become Empress,
she justified the leading political role she wished to play with the strangest
statements: if her mother could run a world empire from London, there was
no reason why she could not direct a mere European state from Berlin![49]

---

46   In Cecil 1989, Vol. 1, 135 f. and Bismarck n.d., Vol. 3, 53.
47   Bismarck n.d., Vol. 2, 424.
48   For this definition, cf. Mehring 1898, 523.
49   On the latter point, cf. Cecil 1989, Vol. 1, 113.

In such circumstances, Field Marshal Waldersee, very close to the future Wilhelm II, not only spoke of 'violent struggles' but went so far in his diary as to toy with the idea of a coup.[50] This seemed to be the best solution, especially since the international situation was fraught with danger. Beyond the Rhine, the growing popularity of General Boulanger demonstrated the power of revanchism in France, which seemed about to enter into an anti-German alliance with Russia. The danger of war on two fronts loomed. Perhaps a pre-emptive strike was required: one could then profit from the 'internal disorder' or the 'upheavals in France or Russia' that were appearing on the horizon or could easily be provoked from outside: this was the plan or temptation especially of Field Marshal Waldersee.[51]

Nietzsche closely monitored developments. From Nice, on 1 January 1887, after reporting the arrival that had already happened or was expected to happen of leading members of the Russian imperial family, he added: 'The last season before the war – everyone is saying so' (B, III, 5, 4). The philosopher limited himself to registering the crisis, without taking sides. However, a subsequent letter dated 12 February harshly criticised Germany, and Nietzsche complained that, under Bismarck's leadership, the country 'is working with feverish virtue on its rearmament and has in all respects the appearance of a hedgehog determined to be a hero' (B, III, 5, 249). But there was not yet any unambiguous and exclusive condemnation of the Second Reich. The philosopher still seemed to be uncertain in the letter (already quoted) of 14 September 1888, which praised Wilhelm II for adopting an attitude towards his mother (the daughter of Victoria) that was 'one hundred times more considerate than the partisan passion in Germany and England might wish'. At the time, the chauvinism from which it was necessary to take one's distance was no less manifest in London than in Berlin.

But, just a few weeks later, the judgement on the new emperor became so sharp it extended to the entire Hohenzollern dynasty. A note immediately before the collapse of 3 January 1889 reproached Berlin's 'Christian band' on two counts: on the one hand it had adopted a position in favour of 'black slaves', and on the other it was 'sowing the cursed dragon's teeth of nationalism among the peoples [of Europe]', pursuing an unscrupulous policy of expansion that stretched back to 'the days of Friedrich the Great Thief' (XIII, 643). On the first point there could be no doubt. The commitment of Wilhelm II, in the name of Christianity, to the abolition of slavery in Africa, as well as the improvement

---

50   In Röhl 1993, 615.
51   In Röhl 1993, 603.

of the condition of the masses in Germany, could not but arouse Nietzsche's indignation. The new emperor referred to Friedrich the Great and his thesis that the king was the first servant of the state.[52] That a great military leader could acknowledge the ideology of labour confirmed the victory of that ideology at the Berlin court. Nietzsche had expressed his admiration for the great general (*infra*, 21 § 6), but now Friedrich II, precisely because of his victorious battles and conquests, became 'the Great Thief'.

And, so, we come to the second aspect. The denunciation of the chauvinistic agitation then rising in Europe was now directed primarily and almost exclusively against the Second Reich, and this denunciation threw negative light backwards onto Friedrich II. Germany was not only preparing for war, but was doing so on the basis of highly disturbing plans. Obsessed with the danger of a war on two fronts, Waldersee thought it possible or necessary, above all in a campaign against Tsarist Russia, to work on the Catholic clergy, possibly with the help of a suitable 'directive coming from Rome', to spark a rising in Poland.[53] In his 'Enlightenment' period, Nietzsche had already denounced the tactics adopted by Bismarck to weaken France (the encouragement of radical left currents, to exacerbate internal disorder in the country and isolate it internationally). In the meantime, he had also given up his previous Russophobia (which had led him suggest a Realpolitik in regard of the Tsarist Empire similar to the one he had criticised in the Chancellor, in respect of France) (*supra*, 7 § 2 and 11 § 7). Now, after the pan-European option had taken on a clearer form and become more radical, he could not but be appalled by the increasing lack of scruples of the Second Reich's foreign policy. Now more than ever, Germany focused on rivalry with neighbouring countries rather than on the issue that in the philosopher's eyes was truly decisive: the conflict that set the European elite, the master race as a whole, against the socialist rabble and the barbarians in the colonies. Due above all to the actions of the German leaders, a revolutionary conflict was looming in Europe that thus spread subversion in the enemy camp. Indeed, the war planned and advocated by Waldersee,[54] but also by other members of the general staff, would lead several decades later to the swelling of a gigantic revolutionary wave.

Ultimately, it was the spectre of revolution that anguished Nietzsche, who issued a lucid warning about the danger represented by mass armies and the arming of the people. His admiration for the aristocratic warrior was undiminished, but the warrior was about to be superseded by the socially and politically

52   Röhl 2001, 31.
53   Röhl 1993, 609 f.
54   Ritter 1960, Vol. 2, 139 f.

very different figure of the conscript that evoked the spectre of the armed slave (*infra*, 22 §5). The danger was great. How could it be averted?

In his opposition to the policy of concessions and social reforms proposed by Wilhelm II, the Chancellor developed a manoeuvre with an international dimension: while the ambitious Emperor placed himself at the head of the crusade for the 'abolition of slavery' in the colonies and, similarly, sought to promote an international campaign that, in the name of Christian values, called attention to the hardships suffered by the workers in Europe, Bismarck, to the contrary, was trying to push 'the German and foreign governments' to take a stand against Wilhelm II's initiative in favour of 'workers' protection'.[55]

The idea of a coup, at first secretly nurtured in Berlin by Waldersee, with Queen Victoria's daughter in mind, and then by Bismarck, against Social Democracy, took on the shape in France of a real prospect, in the throes of the severe crisis provoked by General Boulanger's Bonapartist ambitions. Nietzsche not only seemed to be aware of these manoeuvres but clearly hoped for their success, as the correspondence shows: 'I think I'll need Victor Bonaparte as Emperor of France' (B, III, 5, 569). Nietzsche imagined for himself a new Bonapartist leader, who would put an end to the Third Republic and the long revolutionary cycle from which it had sprung, and who could perhaps also play an important role in the struggle against the subversion so prevalent in Germany.

This was the context of Nietzsche's appeal to the 'European courts' to unite in 'an anti-German league' (B, III, 5, 551). By now presenting itself as the champion of 'worker' subversion and of Christian, humanitarian and nationalistic subversion, Germany posed a serious threat to Europe and to culture as such. This threat had to be averted once and for all. Since the victory over France, Bismarck had worried about the *cauchemar des coalitions*; now this nightmare was to take shape in a 'league' conceived on the model of the coalitions formed against revolutionary France and revived by the doctrine and practice of the Holy Alliance. Except that the target was now Wilhelm II's Second Reich, which in the meantime had proved to be the most dangerous source of revolutionary infection.

But it was not enough simply to rely on wisdom and what remained in neighbouring countries of the aristocratic spirit. It was necessary to act decisively in Germany itself. In several letters, the last written by him, Nietzsche pursued the hope that somehow a process would be set in motion that would eventually lead to the removal, capture and even shooting of Wilhelm II (B, III, 5, 551

---

55   Treue 1958, 644; Röhl 2001, 298–301 and 329 ff.

and 568 etc). There can be no doubt: the philosopher's conscious life was coming to an end. However, rather than dismiss these thoughts *en bloc* as senseless, one should seek method in the incipient madness. The tangle of contradictions with which, at that moment, the Second Reich is struggling led Nietzsche to play with the idea of a coup that would put an end not only to the reign of the sort of Christian-socialist Emperor that was Wilhelm II but also to a long subversive cycle that began with Christianity and even to Christianity itself.

The philosopher also wondered about the sociopolitical bloc that might be able to carry out the desired anti-Christian and anti-socialist counterrevolution. A long passage of the draft of a letter to Brandes from early January 1888 is worth quoting in detail:

> Since it is a matter of a mortal blow [*Vernichtungsschlag*] against Christianity, it is clear that the only international power that has an instinctive interest in the annihilation [*Vernichtung*] of Christianity is the Jews: it is an instinctive enmity, not the 'imaginary' sort of the 'free spirits' and the socialists – I don't give a damn about free spirits. So we must be able to count on all decisive powers of this race in Europe and America; in addition, such a movement has the necessary big capital. Here is the only naturally prepared ground for the greatest and most decisive war in history: the rest of the followers can be considered only after the blow is struck. This new power, which will be formed here, could in the blink of an eye be the first world power: assuming that initially the ruling classes take a stand in favour of Christianity, they will be threatened by the axe to the roots insofar as all strong and vital individuals will necessarily break from them. You don't need to be a psychologist to know that, on such an occasion, all the spiritually sick races will feel Christianity to be the faith of the rulers and thus take a position in favour of the lie. The result is that, at this point, the dynamite will blow up every military organization, every Constitution, so the enemy front will be disjointed and unprepared for war. All in all, we will have on our side the officers by virtue of their instincts: that it is highly dishonourable, cowardly and impure to be a Christian, this judgement will inevitably result from a reading of my *Antichrist*. [...] With regard to the German emperor, I know how to deal with these *braune Idioten*; this is pitted against a successful official.
>
> B, III, 5, 500–1

So the success of the coup would depend on the support of the two forces that in Nietzsche's eyes were anti-Christian par excellence. Here is the first: 'If I ask who are my natural allies, they are above all the officers; with military instincts in one's body one cannot be Christian – otherwise one would be false as a Christian and false as a soldier' (XIII, 642). Should the officers still be inhibited or hesitant about attacking a religion that was the antipode of their sound warrior instincts, they could boost their awareness and energy by reading *The Antichrist*. Seen in this context, the feverish activity in which Nietzsche engaged in order to complete the texts he was planning acquires further significance: it was a matter of strengthening the 'party of life' theoretically as well, so it would be equal to the decisive tests ahead.

But, along with the officer corps, Jewish big capital was also to play a major role. Here one detects an echo of the conflict that was developing between Wilhelm II's 'social' programme and the interests and resistance of big business: the circles influenced by Christianity were the least reliable; their religion on the one hand summoned them to obedience to constituted authority and, on the other, made them receptive to the pauperist ideology flaunted by Wilhelm II. Big Jewish capital, however, was doubly anti-Christian: it referred, on the one hand, to an essential component of the aristocratic world and, on the other, to a culture and community that for nearly two millennia had been forced to come to terms with Christianity, to a people whose indomitable warrior spirit was reflected in the history recorded in the pre-exilic parts of the Old Testament. That is why Nietzsche insisted forcefully: 'For my international movement I need the whole of big Jewish capital' (B, III, 5, 515). Had not the Jews observed with sympathy Julian's efforts to put an end to Christianity?[56] Now, a millennium and a half later, they were being called upon to play a central role in the struggle against Wilhelm II, a sort of Constantine in Christian-socialist form.

6   Big Jewish Capital, Prussian 'Aristocratic Officers' and Eugenic Cross-breeding

It should immediately be pointed out that Nietzsche spoke with respect and even admiration only of the Jewish capitalists. And the Jewish capitalist or financier deserved respect and admiration only to the extent that he detached himself from anything in Judaism that might link him to the mob and subversion: 'I wish more and more they come to power in Europe, so that they lose the characteristics (i.e., no longer need them) by virtue of which they have so far affirmed themselves as oppressed' (B, III, 5, 82). Through their participation in power, the upper classes of Judaism could finally abandon every remnant of

---

56   Cf. Gager 1985, 94 f.

resentment and messianism and make a valuable contribution to the struggle against subversion. In *Beyond Good and Evil* we read:

> Religion tempts and urges them to take the path to higher spirituality and try out feelings of great self-overcoming, of silence, and of solitude. Asceticism and Puritanism are almost indispensable means of educating and ennobling a race that wants to gain control over its origins among the rabble, and work its way up to eventual rule.
>
> JGB, 61 [55]

The big Jewish families passed on not only wealth, refinement of manners, love of the arts, and the power and capacity to rule and rule oneself, but also a vision of life and a sense of space and time that went far beyond 'petty politics', with its provincial narrowness and mean-spirited hatreds. These big families knew no national and state borders and, from the height of their centuries-old existence and experience, could look down complacently on the daily squabbles that ripple the surface of political life. So they were an integral and prominent part of the 'new nobility' and the pan-European elite Nietzsche sought; but they were all those things under the condition they shook off once and for all the plebeian dust that marked the greater part of the history of Judaism.

Happy that his philosophy had been described by Brandes as 'aristocratic radicalism', Nietzsche commented to Peter Gast: 'That is well said and received. Ah, these Jews' (B, III, 5, 213). Such a happy definition suggests that the best and most successful Jews, among whom Nietzsche placed Brandes, evinced a certain affinity with the cause of 'aristocratic radicalism' and the philosophy able to express it. The struggle against the mob could not dispense with the contribution of Western Jews, at least of those integrated into the society, culture and values of Europe in its most emphatic and authentic sense: having risen to very exalted positions, many were an integral part of that master class that, in exercising its mastery, should not let itself be paralysed by short-sighted and disastrous quarrels.

The gravity of the subversive and revolutionary challenge forced the ruling elites towards unity. While Stöcker complained that capitalists of Jewish origin tended to fuse with the big Prussian landowners, either because they controlled an increasingly important part of the land or because they were more and more able, thanks to their financial power, to acquire aristocratic titles,[57] the late Nietzsche, to the contrary, greeted this process with enthusiasm, having

---

57   Stöcker 1890, 481f.

overcome his earlier mistrust and hostility. The process could be further con-
solidated and rendered irreversible if an interlacing of the families of the two
decisive components of the aristocratic camp could be furthered. The 'problem
of the merging of the European aristocracy, or rather of the Prussian Junkers,
with Jewesses', should be resolved once and for all (XI, 569). This 'recipe' can
be summarised as follows: 'Christian stallions, Jewish mares' (XIV, 370). Such
a marriage politics would serve not only to reduce tensions within the upper
classes. It was a eugenics programme in the real sense of the word, aiming to
'add into, *breed into* [*hinzuzüchten*] the hereditary art of commanding and of
obeying', which were 'classic features of the Mark [of Brandenburg] these days',
the Jews' 'genius of fortune and fortitude' (JGB, 251 [143]). The struggle against
modernity and democracy could not dispense with the qualities and skills of
the Junkers, but the latter could only remain a significant force if they succeeded in facing the economic challenges of the new era:

> The Germans must breed [*züchten*] a ruling class: I confess that the Jews
> have inherent qualities that are essential ingredients for a race that should
> conduct a global policy. The sense for money must be learned, inherited,
> and inherited a thousand times: even now the Jew can still vie with the
> Americans.
>
> XI, 457

It should be added that the Jews, apart from money and the sense for money,
would also bring along a more important dowry, 'some spirit and spiritedness,
which are in very short supply' in a body characterised by soldiery crudeness
and provincial narrowness (JGB, 251 [143]). The Jews would also have much to
gain: because they had never been a 'ruling caste' even 'in their fatherland', they
were not able to 'represent power'. This was something to take note of:

> Their eye does not convince, their tongue easily runs too quickly and
> becomes entangled, their anger does not achieve the deep and honour-
> able leonine roar, their stomach cannot deal with carousals, their head
> with strong wines – their arms and legs do not permit them proud pas-
> sions (in their hands there often twitch I know not what memories); and
> even the way a Jew mounts a horse [...] is not without its difficulties, and
> shows that Jews have never been a knightly race.
>
> XI, 568

We know that 'nobility of form' is essential for commanding respect and awe
from the people. Unfortunately, the Jewish financiers retained some repre-

hensible habits. They tended to 'be fond of ensconcing themselves parasitic-
ally in places'. What is more,

> [t]he habit of expending much spirit and perseverance spending for min-
> imal gain has worn a fatal furrow in their character: so that even the most
> respected financiers in the Jewish money market are unable to refrain,
> when circumstances allow, from extending their fingers cold-bloodedly
> to petty defraudations that would cause a Prussian financier to blush.
> XI, 569

But, for the late Nietzsche, these disadvantages could be overcome by social
fusing and eugenic cross-breeding of the two essential components of the 'ruling class' to be 'bred'.

We can now look back once again over Nietzsche's development in this
regard. In the early writings, he had branded the stateless and Jewish moneyed
aristocracy as the originator of subversion and even of revolutionary conspiracy (see above, chap. 3, § 5–6). In *Human, All Too Human*, despite everything,
he condemned the young Stock Exchange Jew as 'the most disgusting invention of the human race ever' (see above, chap. 7, § 7). Finally, even in the fourth
part of *Thus Spoke Zarathustra* he called on the traditional landed aristocracy to
keep its distance from Jewish finance (see below, 18, § 5). And yet, the process of
rethinking had already begun. The greater the danger of plebeian subversion,
the more urgent the search for a social bloc capable of stemming and reversing
it. Especially after *Beyond Good and Evil*, Nietzsche ended up recommending
the merger of the Prussian aristocracy with Jewish finance: only in that way
could one solve an essential problem for the formation and consolidation of a
caste of masters equal to the situation – the problem, namely, of how to link the
representation of the power and the nobility of form with the force of money
and the breadth of horizons.

7   'Aristocratic Radicalism' and the Party of Friedrich III

Solving this problem was particularly urgent, because Wilhelm II's Christian-
socialist turn put the master caste and culture as such in mortal danger. Bismarck too was decidedly hostile to this turn, but Nietzsche was unaware of
this. So, his sharp denunciation of both the Court and the Chancellor was
understandable. After initially oscillating in his judgement of Wilhelm II and
Friedrich III himself (think of the criticism of the latter's wife), the philosopher
finally came out in favour of the party that its opponents had branded as anti-

national and pro-British, but which today's Nietzsche interpreters present in a liberal and progressive light.

In analysing this party, one should focus primarily on the person of Victoria, wife of the Crown Prince (later Friedrich III) and daughter of the British Victoria. Despite the new position that she had acquired after her marriage on 25 January 1858, even decades later the wife of the designated heir to the Hohenzollern throne defined herself as 'an Englishwoman, a Briton born to freedom'. Britain's first task was to 'civilize other countries'; its strength was 'a blessing for humanity', so (she concluded) 'I am very proud of all else regarding my country'. To her young son she addressed the following words: 'But unfortunately I can accept neither that the form of government is first-rate nor the development of your trade and of agriculture or of social conditions, even in art you cannot beat the others – and you are backward in many, many things in which civilized modern nations must be perfect if they cherish the thought of being a leader for the others.'

In vain the tutor to the future emperor warned against '*insisting* on English superiority'.[58] Victoria was the offspring of the most distinguished dynasty, which ruled the industrially most developed and militarily most powerful country in the world, and she never missed an opportunity to emphasise Germany's backwardness. Immediately after the marriage, she expressed her disappointment at the modesty and mediocrity of her new accommodation, informing Bismarck that there were more silver plates in Birmingham alone that in the whole of Prussia. Many years later, she was moved by the fate of a diplomat who had lost his hat while on his way to visit her: 'Poor Sir Edward! And in a country like this, he could not even buy a new one.'[59] It is true that Germany was developing apace, but it remained a plebeian upstart affected by vulgarity, as demonstrated by the phenomenon of 'wildly rampant communism'; it would take years to eradicate the 'wild doctrines' to which the happy island wss basically immune.[60] The social legislation promoted by Bismarck in 1881 confirmed her worst fears: 'If he can carry out his plans successfully, Germany will one day fall victim to communism', the Crown Princess told her mother in a letter.[61] The Chancellor, for his part, had the circle of the Crown Prince and the pro-British party in mind when he denounced the 'clique of politicians of the Manchester School, representatives of the ruthless moneybags', who cried foul at any state intervention in the economy. As Bismarck

58   In Röhl 1993, 282 f.
59   Balfour 1964, 66.
60   In Röhl 1993, 278.
61   In Röhl 1993, 409.

observed in 1881, they were incapable of seeing beyond 'their share companies' and the performance of their shares on the Stock Exchange, so they hoped for the death of Wilhelm I, at the time already eighty, and the ascension to the throne of the Crown Prince (later Friedrich III), to dispense once and for all with social legislation that in their eyes reeked of socialism or communism.[62]

For the daughter of Queen Victoria, the civilising mission of what she continued to consider *her* country did not stop at the borders of Germany. No less harsh were her judgements on Russia and France. With regard to the former, it was enough to read the novels of Dostoevsky: 'disgusting and horrible, but [...] as true as a photograph'; 'Thank God I do not have to live in Russia.' As for the latter, 'How small Paris seems to one who comes from London! How narrow is the Seine River as against the Thames, and the view of the Palace of Westminster is so much more impressive than that of Notre Dame.' Needless to say, Berlin came off even worse: a mere 'cage'.[63] The entire European continent was regarded with condescension or contempt. Having landed in England, along with her husband, in the vain hope of his recovery, the Crown Princess said: 'We are really happy to be on the side of the English Channel that for me will always be the right one.'[64]

If one compares the chauvinism of the future Wilhelm II and that of his mother, hers was probably at the time the greater; whatever the case, the British chauvinism of the one confronted the German chauvinism of the other. This antagonism, which would later play a decisive role in the outbreak of the First World War, had already become apparent several years earlier in the fraught relationship between the daughter of Queen Victoria and the future Wilhelm II; the European and worldwide tragedy of 1914–18 had a tragicomic prologue in the Court in Berlin within the prince's family.

However, regarding domestic politics, it is hard to deny that the project, promoted by Wilhelm II under the influence of Stöcker, to overcome the anti-socialist legislation and develop 'workers' protection' was more balanced and forward-looking than Bismarck's plans for an anti-socialist and anti-democratic coup. Speaking of Wilhelm II, a Social-Democratic writer of the time who was an implacable critic of the Hohenzollern dynasty could not hide his appreciation. The young emperor had 'not remained untouched by the historical developments' and challenges of his time:

---

62   Bismarck n.d., Vol. 2, 339 and 364.
63   In Röhl 1993, 652.
64   In Röhl 1993, 652.

He was not averse to the view, which the clearest minds of the ruling classes were increasingly induced to hold, that it was precisely in the urgent interests of these classes to abolish the law against the socialists and improve workers' legal protection. The fact that he himself could not take a step without being surrounded by a swarm of spies meant that when he learned about it from a Social-Democratic speech in parliament he personally took against the anti-socialist law.[65]

Even when the 'party of the Kronprinz', later Friedrich III, opposed the reactionary decisiveness of the late Bismarck, it was indifferent to the social question. Not surprisingly, its 'basic pillars' were primarily 'the big ship-owners and big traders', alarmed by Wilhelm II's plans for social reform.[66]

The *History of German Social Democracy* quoted here was published by Mehring in 1897–8. The Boxer Rebellion and the Emperor's truculent speech to the German troops preparing to choke it in blood still lay ahead; above all, the First World War was still a long way in the distance. This explains the balanced judgement we have just seen, confirmed by modern-day historiography. About Bismarck, the American historian already quoted several times points out that he 'was not prepared to accommodate himself to Wilhelm's progressive views on the labor question'.[67] With regard to Friedrich III, a British historian comes to the following conclusion: 'He intended to rule with and for the bourgeoisie and is thrown into perplexity by the more and more rapid emergence of the workers; his formulae do not cover this situation.'[68] According to a German historian, Wilhelm II had distinguished himself both from his predecessor and from his Chancellor, and voices a widely held public view when he sought 'a compromise, albeit partial, with the working class and the forces representing it' as the only way to avert 'catastrophe' and 'political and social upheavals'.[69]

This was a compromise Nietzsche decisively rejected. After an interlude of uncertainties and oscillations, he took the side of 'the unforgettable Friedrich III' (XIII, 643 and 646), and angrily denounced the arbitrary arrest of Heinrich Geffcken for 'treason'. The latter was close to the widow of the late emperor. The widow was suspected in turn of wanting to ship to England the many documents left by her husband, which she considered her private property. The philosopher thus took a strong stand in favour of the pro-British party, the party

---

65   Mehring 1898, 530.
66   Mehring 1898, 476.
67   Cecil 1989, Vol. 1, 149, and more generally 147–70.
68   Balfour 1964, 94.
69   Gall 1980, 689.

that, as early as 1881, had joined with Princess Victoria in thundering against the communist threat represented by Bismarck and Wilhelm I's timid programme of 'practical Christianity'.

Admiration for the aristocratic island, which had been spared excessive democratisation and massification, and with respect to which the German Chancellor is the mere 'consorte of a *parvenu*' (XIII, 646), was widespread in these years. Nietzsche's attitude was not dissimilar to that taken by the followers of 'aristocratic radicalism', whose interpreter he wished to be. In the light of these considerations, there can be no doubt that the 'anti-German league' and the coup of which the philosopher dreamed were reactionary, as was the already mentioned eugenics project, clearly aimed at saving and strengthening the social bloc of the *ancien régime*.

'Anti-Anti-Semitism' and the Extension to Christians and 'Anti-Semites' of the Anti-socialist Laws

1 Anti-Jewish Polemic of the Christians and Anti-Christian Polemic of the Jews

But how then to explain the desire to neutralise and even to 'get rid of' and 'shoot all the anti-Semites', along with 'Wilhelm II, Bismarck and Stöcker'? In reality, this list is incomplete and, in its incompleteness, likely to be misleading. There is another famous personality that Nietzsche, already in the throes of madness, would have loved to hit: I 'throw the Pope in gaol' (B, III, 5, 572, 575 and 579). As we know, Leo XIII, the object of Nietzsche's anger, had, by way of Cardinal Lavigerie, promoted the campaign for the release of 'black slaves': two years later, with *Rerum Novarum*, he would seek a relationship with the labour movement, but he had already taken the first steps in this direction as early as 1878. The encyclical *Quod apostolic muneris* warned against the danger that 'the greatest part of humanity could fall back into the most abject condition of slaves, which was long in use among the unbelievers', and warned the 'rich' that 'if they do not come to the aid of the poor, they would be punished with eternal torments'.[1] Regarding Wilhelm II, we already know Nietzsche particularly hated the policy, inspired by Stöcker, of compromising with the Social Democrats, from whom the emperor had already borrowed the plebeian ideology of the abolition of slavery and the glorification of labour, of workers, and of 'starvelings'. Hence the insults against the 'herd-race *par excellence*', the German 'stupid race' (B, III, 5, 568–9), led by 'idiots in purple' or 'brown idiots'. The words 'idiot' and 'stupid' referred unambiguously to the figure of Jesus. The target of Nietzsche's wrath was not anti-Semitism, as is commonly maintained, but a Christian-social project against which he pronounced an implacable indictment that *also* included the charge of anti-Semitism.

This indictment was obviously aimed in the first place at Stöcker. Up to now, we have seen the sympathetic face of the court preacher, his engagement as a social reformer. Now we must also explore his hateful face, his virulent attack

---

1 In Giordani 1956, 36.

on Judaism. They are two sides of the same coin, but so are the anti-Jewish polemic of Christian circles and the anti-Christian polemic of Jewish circles, who had gained emancipation and no longer needed, as in the Middle Ages, to suffer in silence the sermons and accusations of their opponents, but were now determined to 'lay bare' the real and repulsive nature of that heresy of Judaism that had become the dominant religion in the West.[2]

Particularly in Germany, the 'Jewish press' and journalists in the 1870s and 1880s set going 'with great zeal and often with an aggressive and provocative spirit' a campaign whose target was 'the impure and inconsistent monotheism of Christianity', indeed its essential 'paganism', which 'repels modern human beings'. In order to render 'many traditions of the New Testament' ridiculous, they did not flinch from resorting to 'abusive and disparaging language'.[3] The scornful treatment, traditional in Talmudic literature, of Mary's virginity and the real identity of the Holy Ghost now underwent a new development. Having turned its back on monotheism, Christianity invented a mediator between human beings and God: the Son. But then the Madonna intervened, to intercede on behalf of sinners and thus mediate with Jesus: after the Virgin Mother would it be the turn of an equally heavenly grandmother?[4]

In this campaign, the eminent historian Graetz, sharply criticised by Treitschke and defined by the liberal circles of German Jewry, not by accident, as 'a Stöcker of the synagogue', played a prominent role.[5] Thus there arose a lively exchange of charges and counter-charges. Was Christianity the last and definitive revelation, or was it truer to say: '*Israel is called upon to bring salvation to the entire world, and the time is near, for the cross is crumbling and the crescent fading*'? Was the Christian people or the people of Israel 'God's favoured'? Which of the two religions had contributed more to the development of tolerance and the overcoming of the Middle Ages and which was better placed to resist the wave of secularisation and materialism? And, with regard to the history of religious persecution, could one really reduce the whole history of Christianity, from the time of its separation from Judaism, to a '*river of blood*'? Could one really support the argument that 'Christians alone are guilty, Israel alone is innocent'? Or, in order to draw a correct historical balance-sheet, was one to take into account the bloody anti-Christian persecutions in which Jews indulged on the rare occasions when they held power (for example, in Yemen in the sixth century) and the cooperation they offered Islam when it was fight-

---

2   Fleischmann 1970.
3   Tal 1975, 209 ff.
4   Fleischmann 1970, 119 f.
5   Bamberger 1965, 153.

ing and threatening Christendom? The measures to introduce a minimum of social security for the working classes were inspired, according to Bismarck, by Christianity; but, said the Jews, was the idea of social justice not already present, and centrally, in the Old Testament? Did the odious figure of Shylock find its expression in Judaism or rather in Christianity, as Graetz maintained, despite Treitschke's indignation?[6] In fact, countered Stöcker, 'in Berlin and in all the places where Judaism has become rich and powerful, Nathan the Wise has given way to Shylock'.[7]

The theological and theological-political controversy became intertwined with the national one: given the fervent adherence of Treitschke, Stöcker and many others to the Germanic-Christian myth of origin, the anti-Christian polemic ended up including Germany too. Thus Graetz emphasised 'the narrowness of the German essence' and criticised the Germans as the 'inventors of serfdom, of the feudal aristocracy and of the vulgar servile spirit', obviously arousing Treitschke's outrage.[8] The latter charged the Jews with 'arrogance', as evidenced *inter alia* by their refusal to assimilate, and even with 'stubborn contempt for the German goyim'. Graetz replied by provocatively inviting him to take Disraeli to task, who had praised the Jews as a 'pure' and even as a 'superior race [that] should never be destroyed or absorbed by an inferior'.[9]

Disraeli also claimed hegemony for the Jews in the musical field: 'Musical Europe is ours. [...] Almost every great composer, skilled musician, almost every voice that ravishes you with its transporting strains, springs from our tribes'; in this regard, he named Meyerbeer, Mendelssohn and Rossini, all of 'Jewish race', all shining examples of 'Jewish genius'.[10] But whatever the response and Wagner's retort, with which we are already familiar, it caused lasting outrage among Judeophobes and anti-Semites, who cited this bragging as further evidence of the 'arrogance' of the 'chosen people'.

The exchange of accusations between Christians and Jews, or between defenders of the Christian-German myth of origin (with the claim for a special mission for Germany as champion of Christianity) and defenders of the myth of the divine election of the Jewish people, occasionally, took grotesque forms. Was gunpowder invented by a German or a Jew? And was it really true

---

6   In Treitschke 1965b, 40; Graetz 1965b, 49.
7   Stöcker 1890, 481.
8   In Treitschke 1965b, 41.
9   Treitschke 1965a, 8 f.; Graetz 1965a, 31.
10   Disraeli 1982, 222 (Book 4, 15).; cf. Vincent 1990, 30 f.

that *'the splendour of Germany is dissolved in the Jews'*?[11] In this section, I have italicised the statements Stöcker took from Jewish publications and that particularly enraged him. On the other hand, he had no difficulty in paying warm and repeated homage to the Old Testament. 'What is true in socialism' was already present in 'Mosaic law': by means of the 'prohibition on interest', labour was 'protected from exploitation'; if one bore in mind other rules, such as the obligation to observe a weekly day of rest, one could only conclude that what we had here was the 'Magna Carta of all workers and oppressed'. A line of continuity led from Moses to the passionate denunciation of wealth by the prophets.[12]

So how should one judge Stöcker's position as a whole? It must be kept clearly distinct, for example, from that of Dühring, who made the 'Jewish question' a matter of race that could certainly not be remedied by baptism or conversion to a religion, Christianity, that was itself deeply and irreparably Jewish. The court preacher took a very different stance. As has been observed, he 'even took a firm stand against radical anti-Semitism'.[13] It is not by chance that he was frequently criticised, sharply, in the columns of *Antisemitische Correspondenz*. He was described as a very useful 'lightning rod' for the Jews[14] by Wilhelm Marr, who continued his polemic as follows: 'If your point of view is the right one, then we completely give up all anti-Semitism and found an abstract "Society for the Conversion of the Jews" and, through baptism, turn them all into "Christian socialists".' 'Shem rejoices' at this attitude, how could he not? He had already come to the following conclusion: 'If there were no Stöcker, we would have to invent one'.[15] Nietzsche hated the court preacher, but there was not much difference between the one and the other in the eyes of the genuine (racial) anti-Semites. By nurturing the illusion that the upper layer of the Jews could be assimilated into the German community, the author of *Beyond Good and Evil* was shown to be 'a dogmatist as stubborn as those pastors who want to cure the Jews by baptism', noted Thomas Frey (pseudonym of Theodor Fritsch), with heavy irony.[16]

Just as Stöcker had nothing in common with anti-Christian anti-Semites like Dühring, so too he had little or nothing in common with the anti-Semites of Christian inspiration like Wagner, who were committed to demonstrating

---

11   Cf. Stöcker 1890, 361–7, 386 and 395.
12   Stöcker 1890, 185–8.
13   Broszat 1952, 35.
14   *ASC*, no. 1, 6.
15   *ASC*, no. 8, 5.
16   *ASC*, no. 20, 13.

Jesus's Aryan descent. In reference to the Jews, Stöcker did not hesitate to declare: 'We respect them as our fellow-citizens and love them as the people of the prophets and apostles from which came our Redeemer.'[17] Likewise, he had no difficulty in recognising the merits of Lassalle, as a forerunner of social monarchy, even though he emphasised the latter's Jewish ancestry.[18]

The activities of the court preacher in Berlin coincided roughly with the period in Europe, after the challenge posed by the development of democracy and the labour movement, in which Christianity sought to redefine itself in a democratic and social sense. Stöcker could thus be bracketed with the Italian Murri or those representatives of French 'social Catholicism' also struggling for a 'Christian democracy' and a 'Christian socialism', and therefore keen to 'restore Christian France'.[19] It was precisely here that the Judeophobic or anti-Jewish temptation of the Christian socials lurked: in an effort to absolve Christianity of responsibility for the social question and of the accusations of the labour movement, they put the blame for mass misery on the de-Christianisation of society or on its incomplete Christianisation. In Germany, when praising Christianity's struggle against the 'new form of slavery', Cardinal Ketteler denounced the 'liberals' as 'the new pagans'.[20] From Stöcker's point of view, the distance between paganism and Judaism was not so great. Obsessed by the idea of conversion and assimilation, he arrived at Judeophobia. That is to say, he demanded measures of negative discrimination against the Jews: in the judiciary, their numbers should not exceed their proportion of the overall population; it was time to deny them the right to teach in 'our elementary schools', so they were not in a position to undermine the 'Christian-Germanic spirit' of that institution.[21] Certainly, the Jews were to be treated in an 'absolutely humane' way, but as 'aliens', to whom the enjoyment of political rights should therefore not be granted.[22]

There can be no doubt that Stöcker's Judeophobia is odious, but it cannot be separated from his sincere and positive Christian-social commitment, of which it is the by-product and secondary aspect.

---

17   Stöcker 1890, 360.
18   Stöcker 1891a, 20.
19   Mayeur 1973, 195 f.
20   Ketteler 1864, 103, 111.
21   Stöcker 1890, 369.
22   Stöcker 1890, 482.

2   Stöcker and Disraeli: The Linking of Inclusion and Exclusion
        between Germany and Britain

The same goes for Nietzsche's radical counter-position. It too can only be
understood by taking into account the court preacher's whole political programme. He too was horrified by the Paris Commune, where 'bloody social
revolution' had made its terrible experiments, and he too warned strongly
against socialist 'agitators'.[23] But, whereas Nietzsche equated them with the
folk leaders of the religious movements, subsuming all under the category of
'visionaries' and 'fanatics', Stöcker insisted on making clear they were 'false
prophets' bent on inciting the masses against the existing order.[24] They accused
the Christians of promising 'change in heaven' while doing nothing about
hunger and starvation 'on earth'. But, the Protestant preacher told an audience of workers, 'what they promise you is exactly a change in an unforesee-
able future'.[25] So, we are again brought back to Nietzsche, who also equated
the expectation of a future society without exploitation and injustice with
an apocalyptic vision, except that, in his case, socialist revolution and the
final judgement, revolutionary apocalypse and Christian apocalypse, were ultimately one and the same thing. Stöcker, on the other hand, undertook to show
the 'respectable working class'[26] that the Christians, precisely because they
clearly distanced themselves from the apocalyptic dreams of worldly regeneration propagated by socialism, were able to promote and realise a concrete and
incisive programme of 'practical reforms' here on earth:

> The workers' existence must be protected. [...] Their invalids must also be
> cared for, their widows and orphans must have bread. I consider ensuring
> the workers' existence to be the most important and most necessary ele-
> ment in their situation. But beyond that, there are many wounds to heal.
> It is necessary to limit women's work, forbid Sunday work, create a labour
> law, and meet other such legitimate claims.

Overall, 'a peaceful organization of labour and of the workers' was needed.[27]
To demonstrate the feasibility of this programme, the court preacher pointed

---

23   Stöcker 1890, 4.
24   Stöcker 1890, 5.
25   Stöcker 1890, 4.
26   Stöcker 1890, 3. 1105 Stöcker 1890, 4f.
27   Stöcker 1890, 5.

out that 'the German Reich' had granted the workers 'universal suffrage on its own initiative'.[28] Stöcker had no problem adopting the slogans of the French Revolution ('liberty, equality, fraternity'), which, stripped of their revolutionary impact, were traced back to 'the Gospel of Christ'. Those who appealed to the Gospel were called upon to move from an 'abstract Christianity' that turned a blind eye to mass misery to a practical Christianity. Individual charity was not enough: 'If a class is oppressed, it is to the entire social class one should provide help'; 'the Kingdom of God is a social Kingdom. It belongs not just to the beyond but also to the here and now'.[29]

The 'new and revolutionary element' of this Christianity was unmistakable. It aspired to a kind of 'state socialism' that 'was aimed more against liberalism than against the Jews'.[30] There was a clear and explicit attempt on Stöcker's part to split the workers away from revolutionary democracy by appealing to the values of the fatherland and of Christianity, and thus to a sense of belonging to a community defined simultaneously in both national and religious terms. So, it was a question of integrating social layers susceptible to revolutionary agitation into a German-Christian community. This also explains the Judeophobia, the furious onslaught against a group suspect in both ethnic and religious terms, accused of being a 'people within the people, a state within the state, a race for itself among an alien race'.[31]

Stöcker's attitude or rather programme reveals the same dialectic and interlinking of inclusion/exclusion and emancipation/disemancipation observable in other European countries at about the same time. This goes particularly for Britain. The second Reform Bill, which, for the first time, extended political rights to a large part of the population, together with significant new social legislation (concerning factory labour, insanitary neighbourhoods and workers' housing) were introduced by the Conservative Disraeli, long active in countering the revolutionary moment by insisting on the dignity of 'labour' and that 'rich and poor' belonged to the same community – which was, needless to say, to be distinguished from the inferior races in territories gradually being conquered by this superior and triumphant community. Here, the inclusion/exclusion dialectic applies to the colonial peoples, not to Jews, and not because Disraeli was himself of Jewish origin and an admirer of the 'pure' and 'superior' race to which he belonged. Far weightier were two other factors: on the one hand, the reality of overseas expansion, on the other the Anglo-Saxon-

28   Stöcker 1890, 5.
29   In Broszat 1952, 29 f.
30   Broszat 1952, 29, 32.
31   Stöcker 1890, 367.

CHAPTER 18

Jewish myth of origin, which was deeply rooted in British (and American) tradition and which justified and praised this expansion in the name of the mission that befitted a country and a people heir to the Old Testament's 'chosen people'.[32]

In Germany, on the other hand, where a Christian-Germanic myth of origin prevailed and colonial expansion was still to come, the community into which the masses were to integrate was defined in opposition to Judaism. In the two countries here compared, it is evident how, under different conditions, two programmes were propagated and realised that were founded on an analogous dialectic of inclusion/exclusion or emancipation/disemancipation. Racist features can be found in the pronouncements of the British Prime Minister: one would seek in vain for his thesis that '[a]ll is race, there is no other truth' (*infra*, 20 § 2) in the thoughts of the court preacher. That is exactly why, in this case, it is necessary to speak of Judeophobia.

To properly assess Nietzsche's attitude, it is not enough to emphasise his opposition to Stöcker's 'anti-Semitism'. One must rather point out that he rejected all the measures of inclusion and exclusion proposed by Stöcker. A few months before he proposed shooting Stöcker, he criticised the court preacher for propagating the 'most hackneyed and odious thoughts', those of 'equal rights and suffrage' (XIII, 92–3). It goes without saying that, for Nietzsche, the idea of the social state was even more hackneyed and odious.

3   Germany, France, Russia and the Jews

It should be added that Nietzsche's anti-anti-Semitic polemic had one particular characteristic on which one should reflect. He always developed it with Germany in mind and never the two countries (France and Russia) where, in these years, the scourge raged most fiercely. Regarding France, the correspondence, we have seen, demonstrated an indirectly positive opinion about General Boulanger, around whom a sociopolitical bloc was forming that was certainly not immune to Judeophobia or anti-Semitism. But, in this case, the scant amount of information available played a role: Nietzsche's sympathy was above all for the movement's anti-parliamentary and Bonapartist direction.

One must, instead, focus on his attitude towards Russia. In the words of Engels in 1878, 'hatred of the Jews, which [Herr Dühring] carries to ridiculous

---

32   Losurdo 1993b, 2, §5, and 3, §9.

extremes and exhibits on every possible occasion', was very prevalent in Prussia but was above all 'specific to the region east of the Elbe'.[33] It was precisely in the Tsarist Empire, starting in 1881–2, that anti-Semitism assumed its most hateful forms, exploding in bloody pogroms and further fuelling a wave of emigration already stimulated by the need to escape poverty, and directed mainly towards the United States. However, a smaller stream also reached Germany.[34] Was Nietzsche unaware of the agitation by the 'Eastern European anti-Semites' mentioned by Engels in 1890? As we shall see shortly, his reference to 'Polish Jews' and the wave of Jewish immigration from the East would seem to suggest not. And that is not the only indication. The philosopher was not unfamiliar with the nihilist movement in Russia. He read Dostoyevsky, an author by no means free of Judeophobic traits. As for Germany, he closely followed a debate in which the most fanatical anti-Semites sometimes took the Tsarist Empire as a model. Such was the case with Marr,[35] but it was also true of *Antisemitische Correspondenz* as a whole. Almost every issue referred with enthusiasm to the growth in the 'mighty anti-Semitic current':[36] 'In Russia, the government proceeds increasingly energetically against Judaism and forces many of these dirty elements to emigrate';[37] 'fully aware of the Jewish peril, the Russian government continues in all fields to impose energetic restrictions on Judaism'.[38] When would the 'first circles' of German society resolve to follow suit?[39]

But it was precisely the late Nietzsche, the one most engaged in the polemic against German anti-Semitism, that spoke most warmly about Russia. When some twenty years earlier, in 1869, Wagner complained about the 'Jewish agitation' unleashed against him thanks to the Jewish control of the press in the various capitals of Western Europe, he had taken comfort in the exception represented by Russia: 'only in St Petersburg and Moscow' could the musician experience the 'miracle' of newspapers and a 'public' not yet incited against him by the 'Jewish community'. It is not by chance that these remarks were directed in an open letter to a Russian lady of high rank.[40] Now it was Nietzsche who compared the attention and sympathy for him in the Russian aristocracy

---

33 Marx and Engels 1975 ff., 25, 103.
34 Frankel 1981, 49–107.
35 Zimmermann 1986, 79, 88.
36 *ASC*, no. 13, 9.
37 *ASC*, no. 9, 1.
38 *ASC*, no. 17–18, 12.
39 *ASC*, no. 15, 10.
40 Wagner 1910e, 248 f.

to the silence and hostility surrounding his work in Germany. He was elated that his books were welcomed in aristocratic circles and by the 'gourmets of Russian society' (B, III, 5, 506), therefore far superior, culturally and politically, to the German nobility and public. St Petersburg was, he believed, a city where the theorist of aristocratic radicalism was understood and appreciated by numerous readers: '[N]othing but select intelligences and proven characters, educated to high positions and duties', even 'real geniuses' (EH, 2 [102]). Nietzsche felt an affinity only to 'the wittiest French and Russians' (B, III, 5, 70). In Nice, Nietzsche too seemed to await the arrival of the 'Russian Empress', and meanwhile he rejoiced in the presence of the 'heir to the Russian throne' (B, III, 5, 4), the future Nicholas II, no less zealously anti-Semitic than Wilhelm II.

In Nietzsche's eyes, the success his books and theses achieved in Russia was a symptom of something deeper. The philosopher who in his lifetime had been able to tolerate situations and environments perceived as almost unbearable saw in 'Russian fatalism', 'the fatalism without revolt', which immunised against resentment and possessed an 'excellent reasoning' within itself, something congenial: 'To accept yourself as a fate, not to want to "change" yourself – in situations like this, that is reason *par excellence*' (EH, 6 [81–2]).

One could even say Nietzsche adopted a theme circulating at the time in Slavophile circles: the Russians were 'a people that has not yet used its forces, like most European peoples, neither its force of will, nor that of its heart' (B, III, 5, 39). In *Beyond Good and Evil*, one still finds an oscillating and contradictory attitude towards Russia. On the one hand, the dismemberment of this still basically Asian power, which posed a serious threat to Europe, was seen as desirable; on the other hand, one senses the charm of a country still largely immune to the harmful influences of modernity, civilisation and parliamentarism rampant in the West. 'The disease of the will has spread unevenly across Europe. It appears greatest and most varied where the culture has been at home for the longest period of time'; if 'the will is most sick', especially 'in present-day France', there were signs in Germany and especially in Russia of increased vitality (JGB, 208 [101]).

A fragment from April–June 1885 went even further:

> It seems to me that among the Slavs, thanks to an absolute regime, inventive capacity and accumulation of willpower are at their greatest and most intact: and a German-Slavic world government is not among the most improbable hypothesis. The English are unable to overcome the consequences of their stubborn 'self-glorification'; as time goes by, more and more *homines novi* come to power, and finally women enter parliament.

> But politics is, in the end, also a question of heredity: none that starts as
> a private man becomes a person of infinite horizons.
>
> XI, 457

These were the years between the renewal of the Three Emperors' League (Germany, Russia, and Austria-Hungary) in 1881 and the Russian-German Reinsurance Treaty of 1887. Nietzsche must have looked with favour on this rapprochement between the two powers, as demonstrated by one of the points in the later indictment against Wilhelm II: he 'opens chasms between nations in the making [*werdende Nationen*]' (XIII, 644). In any case, Nietzsche still had big hopes of 'St Petersburg, where people guess things not guessed even in Paris', and where 'instinct' was perhaps less 'weakened' and 'European *décadence*' less developed (WA, 5). The 'need to see into the distance' without limiting oneself to the present linked the Tsar to Nietzsche's Zarathustra (EH, *Beyond Good and Evil*, 2 [135]).

Paradoxically, however, it also linked Tsarist Russia to Judaism. As a 'strong' and 'tenacious' race, the Jews did not 'need to feel ashamed in the face of "modern ideas"'; 'they change, if they change, only in the way the Russian empire makes its conquests (being an empire that has time and was not made yesterday)'. A similar sense of the accumulation of power over centuries, or millennia, belonged to this race *aere perennius* that was the Jews, because 'if they wanted (or if they were forced, as the anti-Semites seem to want), [they] could already be dominant, or indeed could quite literally have control over present-day Europe' (JGB, 251 [142]). Like the great families of the Russian aristocracy, the great families of Jewish finance were also marked by a continuity of wealth, power, culture and good manners that defied the centuries: neither the one sort nor the other was affected by that paralysis of the will raging across Western Europe.

4   Nietzsche and the Three Figures of Judaism

How can one reconcile the criticism of anti-Semitism in Germany with sympathy for Tsarist (and anti-Semitic) Russia? Nietzsche's attitude is less contradictory than might appear at first sight. In these years, Judaism was incarnated in three quite distinct social types: the proletarian and the petty artisan, who often swelled the migrant wave, the subversive intellectual (or the intellectual considered as such) and, finally, the capitalist. Regarding the first, in *Beyond Good and Evil*, Nietzsche called on people to face up to the fact that Germany 'has ample quantities of Jews', and is already struggling to 'cope [...] with even this number of "Jews"'. For better or worse, a rule was needed: 'Don't let in any more Jews! And lock the doors to the east in particular (even to Austria)!' (JGB, 251 [141–2]).

On this point, there was not much difference between him and Treitschke and Stöcker. Both opposed the immigration from the Russian Empire of Jews that, in the words of the court preacher, were often prey to 'wild enthusiasms',[41] revolutionary ideas dangerous for the established order. *The Antichrist* displayed boundless contempt for the *Ostjuden*:

> [Y]ou should put on gloves before taking up the New Testament. The presence of so much uncleanliness almost forces you to. We would not want to associate with the 'first Christians' any more than with Polish Jews: not that you would even need to raise any objections ... Neither of them smells good.
>
> AC, 46 [44]

Compared with Stöcker, who, in this case, argued in sociological and political terms, Nietzsche was far more drastic, with his clear allusion to the Schopenhauerian theme of the *foetor judaicus*.[42] But there was an even more important difference. The ragged Jews from Poland, who, according to the court preacher, were ready to fill the ranks of revolutionary socialism, were for the philosopher no less repulsive than the ragged Jews of Palestine, who, 'ready for any type of madhouse', swelled the ranks of Christian subversion, calling themselves 'the fair and the good' (AC, 44 [42]), as would socialists, anarchists and the 'League of the Righteous' later do (*supra*, 8 §1).

Treitschke set the 'Spanish Jewish stock' against the 'Polish Jewish stock', and argued that the latter, because of the deep 'scars of a centuries-old Christian tyranny', were, unlike the former, a long way from integrating themselves into 'Western' culture and customs. Unfortunately, Germany had to deal precisely with this second strain, alien to Europe.[43] Nietzsche argued similarly: 'Among the Portuguese and Moors the superior race of the Jew endures', while the oriental 'Jew of Prussia has to be a decadent and stunted species of Jew'; apart from the climate – and that is the sole addition to Treitschke's analysis – 'the closeness to ugly and oppressed Slavs' also exercised an influence (XI, 568–9).

For the theorist of aristocratic radicalism, the eastern Jew meant the rabble. Here, Nietzsche adopted an attitude not unlike that of the *Antisemitische Cor-*

41   Stöcker 1890, 363.
42   Schopenhauer 1976–82d, 786.
43   Treitschke 1965a, 8.

respondenz, which voiced its complete satisfaction with the attitude of the Tsarist government: 'The stringent measures against the foreign Jews, who trade in Poland, are multiplying'.[44] It was the same immigrants that were deported or expelled from Germany. Fritsch notes after Nietzsche's critical letter to him that at least on that point there was no disagreement between him and the philosopher: as *Beyond Good and Evil* recognises, on German soil there are already 'more than enough Jews'.[45]

Ultimately, the second figure in Judaism was also part of the rabble. Nietzsche's polemic against it was sometimes more strongly and sometimes more weakly expressed – it was at its weakest during the 'Enlightenment' period – but now it was becoming ever fiercer. If 'the sons of Protestant ministers' presupposed 'they will be believed', those who found themselves at odds with the dominant religion inevitably had a quite different attitude:

> A Jew, on the other hand, in keeping with the characteristic occupations and the past of his people, is not at all used to being believed. Consider Jewish scholars in this light: they all have a high regard for logic, that is for *compelling* agreement by force of reasons; they know that with logic, they are bound to win even when faced with class and race prejudices, where people do not willingly believe them. For nothing is more democratic than logic: it knows no regard for persons and takes even the crooked nose for straight.
>
>   FW, 348 [207]

Already the Jews were beginning to be identified as rationalist and revolutionary intellectuals *par excellence*. They 'have taught people to make finer distinctions, draw more rigorous conclusions, and to write more clearly and cleanly; their task is always to make a people "listen to *raison*"' (FW, 348 [207]). At this time – there was still an echo of the 'Enlightenment' – the value judgement was not unequivocally negative, even if distinctly critical tones could already be heard. The rebellious intellectual or artist is a kind of 'actor', especially if he came from the 'lower-class families who had to survive under fluctuating pressures and coercions, in deep dependency'. So, it was understandable that it is precisely the Jews that create 'a world-historical organization for the cultivation of actors, a veritable breeding ground for actors'; the Jew was a 'born literary man' and, as such, 'essentially an actor' (FW, 361 [225–6]). It is worth

---

44   *ASC*, no. 16, 7.

45   *ASC*, no. 20, 13.

noting this was also the opinion of Fritsch, according to whom 'staging comedies' was a sort of 'mission' for Jews: it was the 'only positive talent' at their disposal.[46]

What sort of comedy? The *Genealogy of Morals* clarified this in its polemic against intellectuals full of holy indignation regarding the existing social order. They want 'to *impersonate* [*darstellen*] "beautiful souls"', with 'the word justice continually in their mouth', to '*represent* superiority', playing their 'favourite role of 'righteous indignation'' and adopting 'spiteful, long-suffering looks'. In fact, they are 'vengeance-seekers disguised as judges' and ready to perform other 'masquerades of revenge' (GM III, 14 [90–1]). They do not shy away from 'temporarily humbling and abasing' themselves, only in order to hit out at and poison the aristocratic and the successful (GM, I, 10 [21]). In their 'inability to represent [*repräsentieren*] power', because of the servile relations that have permanently characterised their history, the Jews demonstrate 'play-acting' of a special kind: they are the 'actors' 'in a democratic age' (XI, 568–70). The people leading the slave revolt in the field of morality specialise in performing the comedy of moral indignation.

Jewish intellectuals were also said to be fond of playing out the slogan of 'aristocracy of the spirit' in polemic against the aristocracy of birth (*supra*, 11 §4), and here too they played a subversive role. The more reason and the dialectic became synonyms of revolution in the course of Nietzsche's development, the more Jewish intellectuals stepped forth as carriers of the democratic and socialist infection laying Europe waste. The founding father of these subversive intellectuals is Paul of Tarsus, in whom 'the priestly instinct of the Jews' (AC, 42 [38]) and the potential for resentment of a people that spearheaded the slave revolt with the sophisticated weapons of ideology and moral discourse found expression. In other cases, in reconstructing the history of the subversive intellectual, Nietzsche went back to Socrates, that '*roturier*', who turned the dialectic into a deadly weapon of war and revenge against the aristocracy. But precisely thus Socrates betrayed his non-Greek and ultimately Jewish origin: 'The Jew is dialectical, and so was Socrates. One has a terrible tool in one's hand: one confutes the adversary by compromising his reason – one subjects him to an interrogation, by making him defenceless – one leaves it to one's victim to prove that he is not an idiot' (XIV, 414).

So, the judgement on the first two figures of Judaism is highly negative. When *The Antichrist* equated Jesus with the Russian nihilists and revolutionaries and maintained, as we have seen, that a resurrected Jesus would be rightly deported

---

46   Fritsch 1893, 261f.

to Siberia, in practice it justified a treatment meted out to many Jews, who were tried as subversives and suspected of subversion more than any other ethno-religious group: it was in the first place – as the *Antisemitische Correspondenz* complained – Jews that filled the ranks of the nihilist movement.[47]

It should be added that Nietzsche never mentioned the Zionist movement, which, after a first vague appearance in the writings of Moses Hess, was start-ing to receive support mainly from the eastern Jews, interested in escaping both national oppression and poverty. The philosopher would presumably have viewed this movement with the same contempt he reserved for Germanomania (which for him was also doubly plebeian on account of its social base and its objectives), the more so, at least according to the writings of the 'Enlight-enment' period, because the Jews played a positive role only insofar as they constituted a 'national residue' (*supra*, 7 §7). Whatever the case, the Jews, who by now had put 'an end to the nomadic life' and abandoned the role of the 'wan-dering [eternal] Jew', should 'be carefully noted and accommodated', which was unfortunately not happening in Germany. However, the Jews were to be '[a]pproached selectively and with all due caution' (JGB, 251 [142]), i.e., while marginalising the two figures in which the plebeian element and modern sub-version found expression.

That Nietzsche developed a theory of social and eugenic crossing between the Prussian officer and Jewish finance did not put an end to the polemic against the other two types associated with Judaism. On the contrary: while, on the one hand, Nietzsche became increasingly bitter towards anti-Semites that resorted to socialist rhetoric or were suspected of being socialists, on the other he took an increasingly radical stand against Judaism and in particular the figure of the Jewish priest-intellectual, branded as the primary source of the slave revolt. Even in the *Genealogy of Morals*, which called, as we shall see, for the deportation of anti-Semites, he interpreted the entire history of the West as the history of a disaster that has occurred with the victory of Judea over Rome. In that sense, the Jews continued to be 'the most disastrous people in world history'. Their influence was felt everywhere: '[T]hey have left such a fals-ified humanity in their wake that even today Christians can think of themselves as anti-Jewish without understanding that they are the *ultimate conclusion of Judaism*' (AC, 24 [21]). Nietzsche ridiculed the anti-Semitic Christians, taunting them with the thought that their plebeian resentment and entire worldview made them an expression if not a tool of Judaism.

---

47 *ASC*, no. 22, 11.

5   Zarathustra, the Applause of the Anti-Semites, and Nietzsche's
      Indignation

So, the sympathetic echo that the airing of these themes caused in anti-Semitic circles is understandable. According to Joseph Paneth, a young Viennese physiologist of Jewish origin, Nietzsche told him in January 1884 of the repeated and urgent attempts by those circles to draw him over to their side (KGA, VII, 4/2, 18). Here are some passages from his correspondence: 'Of *Zarathustra* not even one hundred copies were sold (almost all of them to Wagnerians and anti-Semites!!)'; so the philosopher had to experience the 'joke' of being praised 'in an anthem with the terrible anarchist and poisonous snout Eugen Dühring' (B, III, 3, 117–18). The author of the 'joke' was a certain Paul Heinrich Widemann: 'His book ends completely with *Zarathustra* ideas, and on the last page Dühring and I appear in great solemnity and glory' (B, III, 3, 71). He was a rather persistent admirer: 'Herr Widemann told my mother he would like to spend a few years in my vicinity; I confess I have my reservations' (B, III, 3, 137). These reservations did not prevent him from corresponding amiably with the person in question: 'My dear friend, with your letter and by sending me your work you have done me no small honour, not to mention the last page, where you solemnly and festively granted the first public recognition to my son Zarathustra. I will never forget you did this' (B, III, 3, 74). Apart from Widemann, other important personalities in the anti-Semitic movement also showed a sympathetic interest in *Thus Spoke Zarathustra* and its author. Theodor Fritsch, the editor of *Antisemitische Correspondenz*, himself wrote to the philosopher in an attempt to win him to the cause. Meanwhile, he started sending Nietzsche the journal, usually 'sent only in private and to "trusted party comrades"'. The observation was by Nietzsche, in a letter to Overbeck of 24 March 1887, when he added: 'My name appears in almost every issue' of the magazine; there can be no doubt that *Thus Spoke Zarathustra* 'appeals to the anti-Semites' (B, III, 5, 48).

It is enough just to browse through the journal to realise the element of complacent exaggeration in that statement. However, there certainly was a degree of sympathetic interest among Judeophobes and anti-Semites. To explain this, we will try to read *Zarathustra* from their point of view. The decisive turning point in the history of the West was the victory of Judea over Rome, the fatal moment in which 'Rome sank to a whore and to a whorehouse too'. (This is the 'Judaized Rome' with which we are already familiar.) 'Rome's Caesar [sank] to beast, God himself – turned Jew!' (This refers to the conversion of Constantine to Christianity and thus ultimately Judaism.) So began a ruinous development that ended in the vulgarity and horrors of modernity: what prevailed was the '[r]abble mishmash: in it everything is jumbled together, saint and scoundrel and Junker and Jew and every beast from the ark of Noah' (Za, IV, Conversation with the Kings, 1 [197–9]).

The Junker/Jew dichotomy is striking. At the time, Nietzsche was far from advocating the matrimonial and eugenic fusion he later proposed as an antidote to the socialist threat and plebeian drift of Wilhelm II. So, the sympathetic attention of the anti-Semites is easy to understand. The turning point came with *Beyond Good and Evil*, with the recommended co-option of Jewish capital into the master race (see above, 17, § 6). Against the 'new nobility' whose arrival he invoked, Zarathustra set a despicable pseudo-aristocracy 'that you could buy like the shopkeepers and with shopkeepers' gold'. As the polemic against a 'spirit' that claimed to be 'holy' and was oriented towards 'promised lands' shows, the reference to the Jews is transparent: in reality, there (in Palestine), where from Jewish roots 'the worst of all trees grew, the cross' (a likewise Jewish religion), is 'nothing to *praise!*' (Za, III, On Old and New Tablets, 12 [162–3]).

Boundless is Zarathustra's disgust at 'the convicts of wealth who cull their advantage out of every dustpan, with cold eyes, horny thoughts; for this mob that stinks to high heaven, – for this gilded, fake rabble, whose fathers were pick-pockets or vultures or rag pickers' (Za, IV, The Voluntary Beggar [219]). We are already familiar with the theme of the *foetor judaicus*. The 'rag-collectors [*Lumpensammler*]', whose children or descendants were flush with money, remind one of the Jewish immigrants against whom Treitschke railed: they start out as 'young men striving to sell a pair of pants [*strebsam hosenverkaufende Jünglinge*]' only for their 'children and grandchildren' to end up 'dominating Germany's stock exchanges and newspapers'.[48] While the historian dwells mainly on diligence and the ability to work, Zarathustra talks of the swindles or profiteering these parvenus perpetrate on their victims, like 'vultures'. The term used here, *Aasvögel* (literally, carrion bird), is a synonym for *Geier*; on another occasion, Nietzsche pointed out that surnames designating types of bird, and in particular the surname *Geyer*, betrayed Jewish ancestry (*supra*, ch. 5 § 2).

The polemic against the Jewish merchants, alien to authentic nobility, played an important part in *Zarathustra*:

> Just look at these superfluous! They acquire riches and yet they become poorer. They want power and first of all the crowbar of power, much money – these impotent, impoverished ones [*Unvermögenden*]!
> Watch them scramble, these swift monkeys! [...]
> They all want to get to the throne, it is their madness. [...]

---

48   Treitschke 1965a, 7.

Mad all of them seem to me, and scrambling monkeys and overly aroused. Their idol smells foul to me, the cold monster: together they all smell foul to me, these idol worshipers.

My brothers, do you want to choke in the reek of their snouts and cravings? Smash the windows instead and leap into the open!

Za, I, On the New Idol [35]

The *foetor judaicus* stereotype was now joined by the charge that Jews used their wealth to control state power, which became their new idol. We already know the connection established by Schopenhauer between Judaism and the 'apotheosis of the state' (*supra*, 6 §2). This theme was now reinterpreted, in the culture of its time and in *Zarathustra*, to denounce the ruthless tendency of (Jewish) wealth to wrench power into its hands. One was not to be fooled by appearances. Real power was not exercised by the kings:

And I turned my back on the rulers when I saw what they call ruling today: haggling and bartering for power – with the rabble!

Among peoples of foreign tongues I lived, with my ears closed, so that the haggling of their tongue and their bartering for power would remain foreign to me.

Za, II, On the Rabble [75]

The second paragraph was an obvious reference to Jews, whom Nietzsche, following in Wagner's footsteps, had denounced in his youth for being alien to the German language and the German essence. Now, the indictment became more explicitly political. It expressed the unease of aristocratic radicalism at the fact that industrial and financial wealth are gaining the upper hand over the traditional classes of the *ancien régime*: 'Damned I also call those who must always wait – they offend my taste: all the publicans and grocers and kings and other shop- and countrykeepers' (Za, III, On the Spirit of Gravity, 2 [156]).

Quite apart from its financial weight, Judaism was also targeted because of its wide-reaching control over the press. The denunciation of the 'Jewish press' as a synonym for a destructive and subversive 'Socratism' dated back to the Basel years. Even though it had taken on new form, this theme had not disappeared: 'Just look at these superfluous! They are always sick, they vomit their gall and call it the newspaper' (Za, I, On the New Idol [35]). We are dealing with a 'writing rabble' or 'the power-, the scribble-, the pleasure-rabble [*Macht und Schreib- und Lust-Gesindel*]'. To Judaism, always going on about '"aristocracy of the spirit"' (*supra*, 11 §4), Zarathustra replies: 'Oh, I often grew weary of the spirit when I found even the rabble had wit!' (Za, II, On the Rabble [75]). 'Spirit' often characterised the 'actor', a figure that, as we know, tended to be embodied in Judaism: 'To overthrow – to him that means: to prove. To drive insane – to him that means: to convince' (Za, I, On the Flies of the Market Place [37]). And, again, we witness the denunciation of the subversive and destructive character of the Jewish dialectic.

Finally, Zarathustra took up the role of Judaism in the socialist and revolutionary movement. The accusation against the 'tarantulas', agitators that whipped up the resentment of the masses, seemed to involve Freemasons too: '[W]elcome, tarantula! On your back your triangle [*Dreieck*] and mark sits in black; and I know too what sits in your soul. Revenge sits in your soul.' By preaching vengeance, a 'people of bad kind and kin [*Volk und schlechter Art Abkunft*]' came into prominence (Za, II, On the Tarantulas [76–7]), a people that had always been the vehicle of plebeian resentment and rancour.

If we add to these Judeophobic attacks and insinuations the fact that *Zarathustra* mimics biblical language, the language of the book whose place it is supposed to take, it is in no way surprising that anti-Semitic circles were interested in it, sympathetic towards it, and sometimes even enthusiastic about it. Even after the philosopher had indignantly put them right, they continued to refer to *Zarathustra*.[49]

6   Zarathustra, the Ape and Dühring

Already in the third part of the book Nietzsche tried to distance himself, if not from anti-Semitism as such, then at least from anti-Semitism with socialist rhetoric. This was the polemic against 'Zarathustra's ape' or his 'grunting pig' (probably an allusion to Dühring). Yet, despite its harshness, this polemic did not deny resemblances. Zarathustra recognised this, and addressed his supposed disciple as follows: 'But your fool's words injure me, even where you are right!' The charge brought by the 'ape' against the 'big city' dominated by 'shopkeepers' was certainly not rejected by Zarathustra, who said in turn: 'I am nauseated too by this big city.' On closer inspection, the 'ape' seemed repeatedly to want to echo Zarathustra: '[H]e had memorized some of the phrasing and tone of Zarathustra's speaking and also liked to borrow from the treasure of his wisdom' (Za, III, On Passing By [140–2]).

We know that it is the 'vultures or rag pickers [*Lumpensammler*]' who had laid the foundations for the fortunes of today's merchants. And this is how the

---

49   Weichelt 1922, 249.

'ape' voiced his disgust with the 'big city': 'Do you not see the souls hanging like limp dirty rags? – And they even make newspapers out of these rags! [*Lumpen*]'. The ape also shared the contempt with which we are already familiar for the supposed 'aristocracy of the spirit': 'Do you not hear how the spirit here turned into wordplay? It vomits dirty dish-word water! – And they even make newspapers out of this dirty dish-word water' (once again, reference was made to the control of the press of which the Jews were accused). Those who ruled were the 'shopkeepers': in fact, 'the prince too still revolves around what is most earthly – and that is the gold of the shopkeepers'. So who were they? 'There is also much piety here and much devout spittle lick quaking and flatter cake baking before the God of Hosts' (the god of the Jewish national religion). At first sight, this god should not stand in opposition to the worldview of the warrior aristocracy. But this was merely an appearance: 'The God of Hosts is no God of gold bars; the prince proposes, but the shopkeeper – disposes!' (Za, III, On Passing By [141]). Zarathustra did not object to this repulsive representation of Judaism and the 'big city' – the reference is clearly to the capital of Prussia and the Reich,[50] to 'Jewish Berlin', which Nietzsche had already criticised in his youth (*supra*, 3 § 1–2); he confined himself, as we shall see, to accusing the ape of inconsistency in practice.

Even leaving aside *Thus Spoke Zarathustra*, there are obvious resemblances between Nietzsche and Dühring. Here, we will analyse the latter's indictment of Judaism. According to him, it was a monotheistic religion based on the 'despotism' of a jealous and monopolistic divinity that left no room for 'free men' and 'feelings of freedom'.[51] It was the oriental religion of a people that had experienced slavery in Egypt; a 'servile religion', 'the servile form of religion', which 'knows no free men' and 'feelings of freedom';[52] from this religion were derived the 'morality of vassals [*Knechtsmoral*]' and the 'servile spirit *par excellence*'.[53] But all that was inherited in every respect by Christianity, which was itself inherently Jewish. The 'oriental servile religiosity', born with Judaism, deeply permeated Christianity.[54] And so we have 'the old and the new Judaism, the Jewish and the Christian'.[55] There was no point in pursuing the hypothesis of Jesus's Aryan origin: even if it could not be excluded *a priori*, it was in any case

---

50   Weichelt 1922, 139.
51   Dühring 1881b, 30 f.
52   Dühring 1881b, 24, 30 f., 47.
53   Dühring 1881b, 24, 32.
54   Dühring 1875, 438 f.
55   Dühring 1897, 5.

irrelevant, and would not 'erase that which is essentially Jewish in the spirit of the person' and the religion he founded.[56]

Apart from servility, the 'Christianity that was a product of Judaism'[57] was characterised by a fundamental nihilism mixed up with a 'desire for revenge' that was often 'boundless' and 'the vilest cruelty' towards one's enemies: to grasp this, one need only read Dante's *Inferno*, with its condemnation of the supposed sinners to eternal torment; one should not be taken in by the Jewish 'hypocrisy of love for one's neighbour and compassion'.[58]

Throughout history, said Dühring, there had been attempts in the West to shake off this tragic burden. During the Renaissance and even in Tasso one sees how 'instead of dependence on Jewish Christianity one borrows ever more from classical antiquity'; then comes the unhappy re-emergence of 'Christianity churned up by the Reformation' with its 'Jewish essence'.[59] Now, a turning point had been reached: 'It was not enough merely to transform existing religion, [for] there always remained an element of Asianism'; one should have 'the strength to close down the old religious era'.[60] Since Christianity was essentially Judaism, the purification of Judaism, necessary in the West, as at the same time the purification of Christianity. It was a question of putting an end to 'two millennia of errors' – according to Fritsch and the *Antisemitische Correspondenz* (no. 8, 8, and no. 9, 1) – with a dating both Nietzsche and Dühring could easily put their names to.

Dühring too was now calling for the devotees of a religion founded on the enslavement and humiliation of the individual to be replaced by a 'free spirit',[61] defined as a person that had attained full maturity, a 'solid person' far from dogmatism in all its forms. He was aware that a closed theory free of doubts and 'problems' could not assume the legacy of religion. Unlike Lassalle and the socialists of Marxist inspiration, inspired by the certainty of a shining future, 'he certainly would not claim, foolishly, to have a monopoly on truth and to anticipate the future': 'It would need Jewish effrontery thus to sever the rights of future individuals and peoples.'[62] No wonder Widemann matched this text by Dühring to *Thus Spoke Zarathustra*, the 'profound gospel of the overman'.[63] And one can understand why Nietzsche, in one of his last letters, which toyed with

---

56   Dühring 1897, 22.
57   Dühring 1881a, 3.
58   Dühring 1897, 23 f., 42.
59   Dühring 1897, 45.
60   Dühring 1897, 260 f.
61   Dühring 1897, 5.
62   Dühring 1897, 265 f.
63   Widemann 1885, 239. The reference is to Dühring 1897.

the idea of coup against the social monarchy project attributed to Wilhelm II, was keen to distinguish the 'free spirit' he treasured from the one wrongly and instrumentally propagated by the socialists (*supra*, 17 §5).

A few years later, an authoritative Jewish historian of anti-Semitism also compared Nietzsche and Dühring, and subsumed both under the category of 'anti-Christian anti-Semitism', whose target was 'Jewish and Christian morality' (itself of Jewish origin) and the Jewish-Christian religious tradition as such.[64] In this regard, one should particularly cite an old friend like Overbeck, who in his memoirs went so far as to say of the philosopher: 'When he speaks frankly, the opinions he expresses about Jews go, in their severity, beyond any anti-Semitism. The foundation of his anti-Christianity is essentially anti-Semitic.'[65]

7   The 'Jewish Question' as 'Social Question' (Dühring) or the 'Social Question' as 'Jewish Question' (Nietzsche)

And yet, in spite of the real resemblances, even at the immediately ideological-political level, there were also huge differences between Nietzsche and Dühring. The ape's denunciation of the 'big city' as inconsistent in Zarathustra's eyes: 'Why have you lived so long near the swamp, that you yourself had to turn into a frog and a toad? [...] Why didn't you go into the woods? Or plow the earth? Isn't the sea full of green islands?' (Za, III, On Passing By [142]). The alternative to the corrupt and corrupting city was seen in a return to the land (of which the Jews seemed incapable) or in colonial expansion (the other form of return to the land). So, one can see why colonialism was praised as something opposed to the mercantile (and Jewish) spirit:

> Let the shopkeeper rule where all that is left to glitter – is shopkeepers' gold! The time of kings is no more; what calls itself a people today deserves no kings. Just look at how these peoples themselves do the same as the shopkeepers; they pluck themselves the tiniest advantage from any dustpan! They lie in wait for one another, they look in hate at one another – this they call 'good neighbors.' Oh happy distant time when a people said to themselves: 'I want to be ruler over peoples!'
> Za, III, On Old and New Tablets, 21 [168–9]

---

64   Lazare 1969 (1894), 124.
65   Overbeck 1906, 222.

With their petty rivalries and petty territorial disputes (e.g., Alsace-Lorraine), the European countries demonstrated the mercantile spirit typical of Judaism. But they should have instead embarked on vigorous overseas expansion. That is what the 'ape' failed to grasp. True, he could denounce the 'big city' as 'the big scum trap where all spumy crap spumes together!' (Za, III, On Passing By [141]), but he was unable to formulate an alternative. Berlin, seen as the Jewish city *par excellence* by the young Nietzsche and his circle of friends and permanently branded as such by Dühring, was also the capital of Social Democracy.[66] Instead of urging the surplus population 'to emigrate to wild and fresh parts of the world', socialists of all stripes preferred to fish in the turbid waters of the 'swamp' or 'sewer'. In this way, they revealed the same inability to create a relationship with the 'earth' and the 'forest' as that of which they accused the Jews. By deterring colonial expansion, the Dühringian and socialist ape ended up stimulating a senseless rivalry among the peoples of Europe, marked by a narrow-minded spirit of territorial accumulation, a mercantile spirit that ultimately pointed to Judaism.

But that was not yet all. We have seen how the ape indiscriminately denounced both the god of hosts and the god of merchants. Nietzsche's point of view was quite different. Although he too despised the mercantile spirit, which, like Dühring, he ascribed to Judaism, he had no difficulty in identifying with the Jewish ancestry of the rulers that, thanks to their national religion, conquered Canaan. And even the merchants' god aroused indignation only when he sought to subordinate to himself the god of hosts, thereby destroying the ancient and noble ideal of *otium et bellum*. The picture, however, changed radically when the god of merchants recognised the ideal primacy of the god of hosts, when, in political terms, the social and eugenic merger of Jewish finance and the 'aristocratic officer' led to the infusion of new blood and power into the class destined to combat the vulgarity and negative values of modernity, also by means of a vigorous programme of colonial expansion.

But Dühring referred precisely to the Canaan story to demonstrate not only the ruthless brutality but also, and above all, the national unreliability of the Jewish people, whose '*ultima ratio* [...] is power and dominion'.[67] Except that this charge sounded in Nietzsche's ears as the highest recognition: an acknowledgment that breeding the master race could not happen without the Jewish contribution.

---

66   Dühring 1881b, 6, 20.
67   Dühring 1881b, 33 f.

Summarising, one can say that, of the three figures of Judaism, Dühring most hated the one that, in his eyes, led from the pitiless conqueror of Canaan to the ruthless capitalist and financier that had conquered the stock exchange and the press in Berlin. This is the only figure Nietzsche admired, in the form of the conqueror of Canaan, and allowed as a possibility, in the form of the financier. The philosopher reserved his hatred in particular for the figure of the Jewish prophet, who unfortunately continued to manifest himself, now in the guise of a socialist agitator. The contrast with Dühring, who was, to a certain extent, indulgent precisely towards the prophets, whom be credited with having tried to carry out a self-criticism of the most odious aspects (boundless will to power) of Judaism,[68] is evident. Despite the resemblances, the contrast between the two personalities compared here again emerges quite clearly.

Dühring made a lapidary pronouncement: 'The Jewish question is itself a social question.'[69] Reversing that sentence, Nietzsche might have said: 'The social question is itself a Jewish question.' In the first case, it is a question of striking out at big Jewish capital to integrate the popular classes, by weakening or silencing their protests; in the second, of acknowledging that the so-called social question is a mere invention of the resentment and spirit of revenge stoked up by Judaism or the Jewish-Christian religious tradition. Nietzsche was far from wanting to hit the Jewish capitalists and financiers. Instead, especially in the last years of his conscious life, he was obsessed with the idea of co-opting them into the master race, and of doing so completely and irreversibly, not only at the sociopolitical but also at the eugenic level.

The strengthening of the ruling bloc would then pave the way for a general offensive against the insane demands of the popular classes and against the socialist movement. In the course of such an action, the other two figures of Judaism were not to be spared. Rather, the polemic and the struggle against those who through their agitation betrayed their 'Jewish' character was to be escalated.

8   Feudal Anti-Semitism, 'Anti-capitalist' Anti-Semitism and 'Feudal Socialism'

At this point, it is a good idea to re-read Nietzsche's polemic. A few years after the end of the conscious life of the philosopher, in 1894, Chancellor

---

68   Dühring 1881b, 26, 28.
69   Dühring 1881b, 154.

Caprivi, speaking in the Reichstag, observed that anti-Semitism 'is the germ of Social Democracy'. While criticising in particular 'anti-Semitism directed against capital [*Kapitalantisemitismus*]' and addressing representatives influenced by anti-Semitism, the Chancellor continued:

> People direct their hatred and aversion at capital as such; if the movement continues, you will not be able to limit it to Jewish capital – it will turn against capital as such! And so I say that your party has a link with the party of the extreme left side of this chamber.[70]

The target of Nietzsche's polemic was precisely the 'party of the extreme left' with its various and conflicting components. We have already mentioned the attack on Stöcker because of his stance in favour of universal and equal suffrage. Even those that really did merit the charge of anti-Semitism were condemned in the first place because they were infected in one way or the other by democratic or, worse still, socialist superstition. Bernhard Förster was an 'agitator' that, because of his egalitarian tendencies, was repugnant to Nietzsche's 'taste': 'I for myself am too aristocratically minded to put myself in this way on the same level, legal and social, as twenty peasant families: as he has it in his programme.' Moreover, this agitator was a vegetarian (B, III, 3, 54) and vegetarians, with their tendency to call the natural order and the struggle that marked it into question, were an expression of decadence (GM, III, 17 [95–9], and WA, 5 [241]). One should not forget that in a letter written in 1869, under Wagner's influence, Nietzsche had already associated 'vegetarian doctrine' with 'socialism' (see above, chap. 1, § 9). Nietzsche compared the effeminateness and eccentricity of the brother-in-law with the example of the decidedly 'carnivorous' English, whose colonial expansion had been more successful than that of any other 'race' (B, III, 3, 54). This argument about imperial ideology was widespread at the time and, as often happens in such circumstances, was even adopted by the victims themselves. In his autobiography, Gandhi said that, during his childhood and adolescence, there was a nursery rhyme, written by a poet, that went: 'Behold the mighty Englishman!/ He rules the Indian small/ Because being a meat eater/ He is five cubits tall.'[71]

---

70   Caprivi 1894, 192.

71   Gandhi 1969–2001, 106 f. Nowadays, it is the Hindu fundamentalists and chauvinists that make propaganda for a vegetarian diet, in order to restore the customs of the original and untouched Aryan population (Sengupta 2002); a similar ideological process may have taken place in the case of Hitler, who in his dinner conversations criticising meat-eating

Here were the charges Nietzsche levels against Dühring: he too was a 'poor devil of a screaming agitator' and, worse still, a 'poor communist' (XIV, 382); it was not by chance that he belonged among the 'defenders and supporters' of the 'Paris Commune' (XI, 586). And that was not all: he was a 'man of the rabble' (XI, 494), a 'proletarian' (X, 363), a 'poisonous and bilious ruffian'; among his followers, apart from 'the *species anarchistica* within the educated proletariat', there was not 'one decent person' (XIV, 422; GM, III, 26 [115]). More generally, one could say that 'the "unconscious" stretching out of long fingers, too long, the swallowing of other people's property, always seems to me more evident in every anti-Semitic than in any Jew' (XIII, 611). This reminds one of the denunciation of 'Weitling's thieving proletariat [*Weitlings stehlendes Proletariat*]', which constantly cropped up in Schelling[72] and the anti-socialist culture of the time, including that of Nietzsche: we have seen how he criticised the labour movement for not complying with the 'seventh commandment', enunciated by a respectable 'Jew of antiquity', which required that one should 'not steal' (*supra*, 1 §10).

Of course, Herr Dühring really was an anti-Semite. But the anti-Semitism targeted by Nietzsche referred precisely to the social protest that fuels socialism, to the mob or the '*canaille*' (XIII, 92 and B, III, 5, 218) that formed the revolution's social basis or manoeuvre mass. That 'socialism of fools' that, according to August Bebel (or, rather, the definition he made famous), was anti-Semitism[73] was denounced by Nietzsche with an attitude laden with contempt not only for the fools but most of all for socialism as such. One might even add that if, for the disciple and collaborator of Engels, stupidity consisted in expressing in a grotesque and barbaric fashion a social protest to which, nevertheless, it was necessary to give heed, for the theorist of aristocratic radicalism it resided precisely in this sympathetic attention to the subaltern classes: 'the social question is a consequence of *décadence*' (XIII, 265).

We now proceed to a closer comparison of Nietzsche's anti-anti-Semitism and that of the Social-Democratic circles. Engels noted that the anti-Semitic 'chorus ... is provided by those whom competition from big capital has ruined – the petty bourgeoisie, skilled craftsmen and small shop-keepers' crushed by the competition of big capital (not infrequently Jewish), and fascinated by anti-Semitism understood as a kind of 'feudal socialism', or 'the lesser nobility, the Junkers', who, in their profligacy, continued to live beyond their means and

---

sometimes cited alongside the arguments of apostles of good health the supposed eating habits of the soldiers of 'ancient Rome' (Hitler 1989, 241; 25 April 1942).

72   In Pareyson 1977, 645.

73   On the history of this formula, cf. Massara 1972, 105.

ended up indebted to Jewish capital. Warning against anti-Semitic and 'feudal socialism', Engels stressed the important contribution made by Jews to the anti-capitalist struggle, as demonstrated by the rise in Britain of 'strikes by Jewish workers', often 'the worst exploited and the most poverty-stricken', and by the prominent role played in the socialist movement by intellectuals like Lassalle, Bernstein and many others, 'people whom I am proud to call my friends'. Not to mention Marx, who 'was a full-blooded Jew'. Even Jewish capital did 'good work' to the extent that it undermined classes 'reactionary from top to bottom', like the petty bourgeoisie and, above all, the feudal aristocracy.[74] The latter was the main target of the Social Democrats' anti-anti-Semitic polemic. It was also the source, according to the *Communist Manifesto*, of the attempt to weaken and deflect the popular protest by projecting the mirage of 'feudal socialism'. Bebel made a similar argument. Noting the spread of anti-Semitism among 'officer circles', 'our Junkerdom' and the debt-laden 'feudal aristocracy', he commented: 'That does not, of course, prevent some of our noble born from trying to catch a Jewish goldfish, in order to use its money to put a fresh layer of gold-plating on the old coat of arms and save themselves from an existence that has become insecure.' The ironic allusion was to the efforts of noblemen and officers keen to retain their traditional opulence to marry a Jewess, as long as she was richly endowed, despite their Christian beliefs and Judeophobic convictions.[75]

This was precisely the marriage policy recommended by Nietzsche, well aware that anti-Semites could also be found in society's upper classes: 'It seems to me that the entire Prussian nobility is getting excited about them', he commented in a letter to Overbeck on 16 October 1885 (B, III, 3, 97). In this case, however, his judgement was far less severe. His indignation was targeted at quite other social and political circles: 'I've never experienced such an offence' as the 'combining of the names "Dühring" and "Zarathustra"' (B, III, 3, 120). Actually, Dühring's secular and anti-Christian anti-Semitism should have been more bearable to Nietzsche than the Junkers' Christian-inspired anti-Semitism or Judeophobia, but it was not. One would seek in vain in him a polemic against feudal anti-Semitism similar in its severity to that against 'anticapitalist' anti-Semitism. This explains the silence about Russia and even the admiration he expressed for that country's aristocracy.

In conclusion, Engels reached a positive, if more differentiated, judgement about all three figures of Judaism. Nietzsche, on the other hand, was hostile to the figure of the proletarian Jew and, above all, the subversive Jewish intel-

---

74 Marx and Engels 1955 ff., 22, 49 ff.
75 Bebel 1995, Vol. 3, 379 f.

lectual. As for the third type, the capitalist and financier, Engels attributed to him the objective merit of undermining the power and prestige of the aristocracy and the military, while Nietzsche hoped he might be able to contribute to the social and eugenic strengthening precisely of this class. To the anti-Semitic press, which sometimes represented him as a Jew, Engels replied: 'I'd as lief be a Jew as a 'Herr von'!'[76] The theorist of aristocratic radicalism could hardly have agreed, for he hated socialism even in its 'feudal' and 'stupid' form and held the Jewish intellectual primarily responsible for promoting this ruinous political movement.

9   Denunciation of Anticapitalist Anti-Semitism and Settlement of
       Accounts with the Socialists, the Christian-Socials and Subversives
       Generally

In Nietzsche, the characterisation of anti-Semitism and socialism were two peas in a pod: 'The anti-Semites do not forgive the Jews for having "spirit" – and money: anti-Semitism, a name of "those that turned out badly"' (XIII, 365). 'Those that turned out badly, the *décadents* of every sort', were forced to conceal their failure even from themselves, by hunting out the 'guilty ones', 'scapegoats': either 'the social order, or education and instruction, or the Jews, or the nobility, or those that turned out well of every kind', or even dear God (XIII, 423). However, anyone that beyond Stöcker or Dühring dared to question existing social relations 'invents responsibilities in order to gain a pleasurable feeling – revenge' (XIII, 423). Whether the protest against inequalities took as its target Jews or concrete sociopolitical relations, it was any case an expression of resentment and invented responsibilities that did not exist.

As with all those whose lives had turned out badly who joined the 'slave revolt in morality', in Dühring too we see 'an extravagance of disdainful moral attitudes'. He would like to stage a sort of 'last judgement' against life and history and claims 'that his drivel itself means justice' (XIV, 382). But even the wretched 'Jews', who invented Christianity, claimed to be 'the ultimate tribunal on everything else' (AC, 44 [42]). Even though they 'thirst to be hangmen', among anti-Semites and socialists of every stripe 'we find plenty of vengeance-seekers disguised as judges, with the word justice continually in their mouth like poisonous spittle', claiming to be 'good and just' (GM III, 14 [90]). In that way, they conducted themselves, once again, like Jews and 'Judeo-Christians',

---

76   Marx and Engels 1955 ff., 22, 51.

who also claimed to be 'the fair and the good' (AC 44 [42]). One essential point had to be borne in mind: 'The enraptured dictum, "love your enemy!" had to have been invented by the Jews, the best haters who have ever lived' (M, 377 [209]). But, in more or less the same way, socialists of every sort (including anti-Semites) hid under slogans proclaiming brotherhood, philanthropy and universal love their thirst for revenge against the powerful, the rich and those that had turned out well.

And, finally, Dühring was a 'puller of faces', just like those 'superficial, envious people, three quarters of them actors', that promote 'socialism' (XI, 586). But this was also true, as we have seen, of the subversive Jewish intellectual, that actor *par excellence* of moral indignation. Plebeian resentment and the subversive potential of those whose lives had turned out badly united the socialist agitator, the subversive Jew and ... the anti-Semite that spouted socialist rhetoric!

We know the anti-Semites themselves were numbered among those whose lives had turned out badly, but we should not forget that these losers, these 'bearers of oppressive and vindictive instincts', were 'the descendants of all European and non-European slavery, in particular of all pre-Aryan population' (GM, I, 11 [24]). Here, one inevitably thinks of the Jews, that pariah people *par excellence*, that had suffered centuries of subjugation ever since the Babylonian exile. In any case, in criticising the anti-Semites and those of every sort whose lives had turned out badly, Nietzsche did not hesitate to quote Aryan mythology, the mythology that was beginning to target the Jews. Energetic measures were needed: it was essential to free oneself from 'the disgusting spectacle of the failed, the stunted, the wasted away and the poisoned' (GM, I, 11 [24]). These were the same measures demanded against anti-Semites. While, in *Beyond Good and Evil*, Nietzsche still problematised the issue – 'it might be practical and appropriate to throw the anti-Semitic hooligans out of the country' (JGB, 251 [142]) – in the *Genealogy of Morals* he seemed no longer to have doubts. It was merely a question of seeing how many 'anti-Semites' and 'how many comedians of the Christian-moral ideal Europe would have to export for its air to smell cleaner' (GM III, 26 [118]). So the anti-Semites should share the fate of the subversives, who were, in many cases, of servile and non-Aryan origin and among whom there were certainly Jews. The reckoning of accounts with the anti-Semites paradoxically made the situation of the Jews themselves more dangerous and precarious.

On closer inspection, the radical measures against 'all anti-Semites' Nietzsche called for were actually an extension and tightening of the special laws put in place against the socialists and subversives. Apart from 'Stöcker' and his entourage of 'anti-Semites', one should deal severely with the 'priests' as such, all infected by 'criminal folly'. These were far from harmless. 'Let us not underestimate the priest', that 'vindictive and subtle animal'. No weakness was permissible in respect of the 'priestly institution that seeks with horrifying cunning to destroy from the very beginning' the best men, 'the strongest, those that have turned out best, the magnificent ones' (XIII, 645–6). Strong measures were required: 'Against the priest', Nietzsche wrote to Brandes at the beginning of December 1888, 'there is need not for arguments but only for prison' (B, III, 5, 502). This thesis was developed further in *The Antichrist*: 'Against the priest one has not arguments but prison [...] The priest is our Chandala – he should be outlawed, starved, driven into every kind of desert.' Apart from this figure, which was moreover 'the most vicious sort of human being', it was necessary to destroy, as we have seen, the 'priestly institution'. And so: 'He who eats at the same table as a priest, drive him out', the churches should be destroyed. It was necessary to take aim at the Christian as such, without distinguishing between Catholics and Protestants, or between Christians of a fundamentalist orientation and liberal and modernist Christians – if anything, the latter should be treated with greatest severity. Ultimately, it was a question of recognising the 'criminality of being Christian' and treating it accordingly (AC, Law against Christianity [67]).

The righteous indignation at Stöcker's Judeophobia should not cause one to lose sight of the highly disturbing nature of Nietzsche's 'anti-Semitism'. The 'law against Christianity' with which *The Antichrist* ended was an extension to Christians of legislation already in place against Social Democracy. The Social Democrats liked to compare their situation in the Second Reich with that of the persecuted Christians in the Roman Empire. This comparison was in a certain sense endorsed by Nietzsche, though with an opposite value judgement: one had to be able to see 'the cross as the mark of the most subterranean conspiracy that ever existed' (AC, 62 [66]), a conspiracy that continued to grow almost two millennia later in socialist and Christian-social circles.

The 'law against Christianity', dated '30 September 1888 of the false chronology', was further radicalized after the onset of madness. Nietzsche declared that one should not only arrest the pope but also shoot Stöcker and 'all anti-Semites', including Bismarck and Wilhelm II. Yet Bismarck was a declared enemy of the court preacher and had an excellent relationship with the Jewish banker Gerson von Bleichröder, whose advice no doubt also benefited his private finances.[77] But, for Nietzsche, Bismarck was to blame for having, in 1881, endorsed and promoted in the name of 'practical Christianity' the ideology of

---

77   Cecil 1989, Vol. 1, 141 f.

labour and the social legislation then experiencing a further, ruinous expansion under Wilhelm II. That is why the Chancellor was defined as 'the idiot among statesmen of all times', a term that once again had Christian connotations, with the 'idiot on the cross' pilloried a few lines later (XIII, 643–4).

A particular hatred was directed at the young emperor. He was not only, as we know, a 'brown idiot', but also a 'Christian in the uniform of a hussar [*cristlicher Husar von Kaiser*]' or 'the most wretched abortion [*Missgeburt*] of a human being that until now has ever come to power' (XIII, 643); the object of the denunciation was clearly not the hussar but the Christian, who as such as malformed, an abortion. With his aspiration to free the black slaves in Africa and the proletarians or white slaves in Germany, the young emperor was promoting a programme that he called Christian but should actually, in the eyes of the philosopher, more properly be called Christian socialist.

So the late Nietzsche aspired to an extreme radicalisation of the anti-socialist laws, which he thinks should be extended to Christian-socials, Christians as such and all those suspected of having Christian and socialist sympathies. In this same area 'all anti-Semites' belonged.

CHAPTER 19

'New Party of Life', Eugenics and 'Annihilation of Millions of Deformed'

1   Naturalisation of the Struggle and the Arrival at Eugenics

The pressure for a final reckoning of accounts came not only from developments in domestic and international politics but also from the gradual maturation of Nietzsche's convictions. In the course of his development, one can perceive a gradual accentuation of the tendency to understand history and conflict in a naturalistic way. In the years of *The Birth of Tragedy*, the philosopher already emphasised the partly physiological dimension of the degeneration embodied by Socrates, not coincidentally also ugly in face and body. But now we read in *Twilight of the Idols*:

> Socrates was descended from the lowest segment of society: Socrates was plebeian. We know, we can still see how ugly he was. But ugliness, an objection in itself, was almost a refutation for the Greeks. Was Socrates Greek at all? Often enough, ugliness is a sign of crossbreeding, of arrested development due to crossbreeding. In other cases it appears as a declining development. Anthropologists specializing in crime tell us that the typical criminal is ugly: monstrum infronte, monstrum in animo. But criminals are decadents. Was Socrates a typical criminal?
>
> GD, The Problem of Socrates, 3 [163]

The increasing significance of physiology brought with it a shift in culture: '[W]e must become physicists in order to be creators in this sense – while hitherto all valuations and ideals have been built on ignorance of physics or in contradiction to it' (FW, 335 [189]). Physics is here synonymous with physiology or with sciences that start from nature and the body. To neglect it was already a symptom of lack of honesty: 'So, long live physics! And even more long live what compels us to it – our honesty!' (FW, 335 [189]). In its turn, the lack of honesty implicit in the suppression of physics pointed beyond psychology and even more so ethics to a dimension that was, ultimately, physiological: 'The things that humanity used to think seriously about are not even realities, just figments of the imagination or, to put it more strongly, lies from the bad instincts of sick natures who were harmful in the deepest sense' (EH, 10 [98]).

It was necessary to put an end once and for all to 'ignorance *in physiologi-cis* – damned "idealism"'. To begin with, one should investigate 'the influence of climate on metabolism' (EH, 2 [88]). Even in the 'Enlightenment' period, the pagan 'southern innocence' (FW, Appendix, In the South [251]), which manifested itself above all in the 'luxury of the Renaissance', was set against 'Nordic flatheadedness', permeated by the moralism also to be found in Rousseau (XIV, 274).

But it was not sufficient to point to climate. One was not to forget nutrition:

> Another question interests me in a much different way: the question of nutrition; the 'salvation of humanity' is much more dependent on this question than on any theological oddity. We can formulate it in rough and ready terms: 'what do you yourself eat in order to achieve the maximum of strength, of virtu in the style of the Renaissance, of moraline-free virtue?'
>
> EH, 1 [85]

Diet seemed to play a decisive role in explaining world history (someone has talked in this regard of the 'sanctification of the nutrition question').[1] 'Thus the spread of Buddhism (not its origin) depends greatly on the Indians' excessive and almost exclusive diet of rice and the general enervation resulting from it.' On the other hand, the Christian gloom of the Germanic Middle Ages could not be understood apart from 'alcohol poisoning' (the 'noxious stove fumes in German living rooms' might also have played a role). One could say as a general rule: 'Wherever a deep dissatisfaction with existence comes to prevail, it is the after-effects of some great dietary mistake made by a people over a long time that are coming to light' (FW, 134 [124]).

Finally, inheritance: 'All good things are inherited: anything that is not inherited is imperfect, a beginning' (GD, 47 [220]). With his book *Hereditary Genius*, Francis Galton was described as having thrown light not only on the figure of the 'hereditary genius' but also on that of the 'hereditary criminal' and on the 'history of criminal families' (B, III, 5, 508). The British author seemed to figure in a fragment from October 1888, according to which 'the first questions of life' had only finally been taken seriously over the last '20 years' (XIII, 610). If we go back over those twenty years, we encounter the publication of the book just mentioned, whose first edition appeared in 1869. So one can appreciate the growing importance Nietzsche attributed to the themes of 'sickness' and of the

---

1 Bernoulli 1908, Vol. 2, 393.

physical and mental 'inclination to sickness' (transmitted hereditarily), 'hereditary weakness' and 'racial and family *décadence*', which he also interpreted as
a product of 'insufficient nutrition', 'erotic precocity' ('the curse especially of
the youth of France, especially Parisians') and 'alcoholism' (XIII, 250, 456, and
passim).

In putting an end to accursed 'idealism', it became necessary to discover
or rediscover the natural sciences ('from that point on, I pursued nothing
more than physiology, medicine, and the natural sciences', EH, *Human, All Too
Human*, 3 [118]). 'Physiology', 'statistics', 'the doctrine of health': thanks to the
'progress' they had achieved, 'our feeling for moral actions and judgements
could in future become incomprehensible' (XIV, 259).

Thus, Nietzsche appropriated the slogan 'nature and nurture', the subtitle of
a later book by Galton and widespread in the culture of the time.[2] The attention devoted to climate, nourishment, and hereditability led to the following
conclusion: 'No study seems to me more essential than the laws of breeding.'
It was a question of exploring and combating not only 'ways of living' but also
'counterproductive unions' (XI, 480). The problem of 'eugenics', the new 'science' invented precisely by Francis Galton (a cousin of Darwin), came up in
Nietzsche's letters to Overbeck and Strindberg – the latter, in turn, talked of the
significance of the genealogy of the 'criminal' sketched by Lombroso (B, III, 5,
347 and 508, and III, 6, 376).

The struggle against the ideas generated by the French Revolution and
against the labour and socialist movement's plans for social transformation had
led to the naturalisation of social conflict and the historical process. Now it
became possible to establish general laws that applied to both the human and
the animal world. For example, in both cases 'overabundant diets' and 'more
than their share of protection and care' could have negative or catastrophic
consequences. Decadence beckoned where stress, tension and 'hardness' were
completely lacking. Those who study the history of an 'aristocratic community'
(e.g., Venice or a Greek polis) were well aware of this, but so too were 'breeders'. Both groups had hit upon a fundamental truth: 'A species [*Art*] originates,
a type [*Typus*] grows sturdy and strong, in the long struggle with essentially
constant unfavorable conditions'; decadence and 'variations of the type', 'rich
in wonders and monstrosities (including monstrous vices)', were the result of
wrong 'breeding' (JGB, 262 [158]). We know that the aristocracy 'needs slavery,
whatever its form and whatever its name, as its foundation and condition': for
that very reason it needs 'a systematic, artificial and conscious breeding', of

---

2 Galton 1874.

both the master caste or race and of the servile caste or race; only thus could
the 'revolt of the slaves' or the 'conspiracy of the herd as a whole' be averted
(XII, 71–4).

2 Optimism/Pessimism; Being/Becoming, Reason/Art; Historical
   Consciousness/Supra-historical Myth; Sickness/Health

Starting from this new awareness of the importance of physiology, Nietzsche
went back over his previous development and critically analysed the dichotomies he had gradually formulated. He was concerned not only to interpret reality
but to act on it. Modern mediocrity and subversion, which he had diagnosed
and denounced ever since *The Birth of Tragedy*, were the constant targets of his
polemic. Could they really be seen as an expression of fatuous optimism, and
thus combated with the help of the optimism/pessimism dichotomy? In search
of new interpretive keys, in *The Gay Science* he stressed the substantial political
continuity of the struggle in which he had been engaged ever since his youth:

> It may be recalled, at least among my friends, that initially I approached
> the modern world with a few crude errors and over-estimations and, in
> any case, with hope. I understood – on the basis of who knows what
> personal experiences? – the philosophical pessimism of the nineteenth
> century as if it were a symptom of a higher force of thought, of more
> audacious courage, and of more victorious fullness of life than had char-
> acterized the eighteenth century, the age of Hume, Kant, Condillac, and
> the sensualists.
>
>   FW, 370 [234]

Similarly, Wagner's music was interpreted 'as the expression of a Dionysian
might of the German soul': 'I believed I heard in it the earthquake through
which some pent-up primordial force is finally released – indifferent about
whether it sets everything else which is called culture atremble' (FW, 370 [234]).
The desired 'Dionysian pessimism', ready to accept life and rejoice in it even in
its terrible conflicts, were unfortunately confused with the 'romantic pessimism', fearful, tearful and ultimately life-denying, that characterised Schopenhauer, Wagner and the nineteenth century in general.

The inadequacy and ambiguity of the dichotomy thus far used was demonstrated above all by a reading of Dühring. He simultaneously professed 'cosmic optimism' (the confidence of being able to act positively on the world
and realise 'justice' in it) and 'the pessimism of indignation [*Pessimismus der*

Entrüstung]' (the moral revolt against the countless injustices that prevented the majority of people from enjoying their right to a dignified life and happiness).[3] The 'pessimism of indignation [*Entrüstungs-Pessimismus*]' became one of the late Nietzsche's favourite targets. It was synonymous with the 'democratic' and 'socialist' view: yes, the 'pessimists of indignation [...] will make a mission out of sanctifying their filth in the name of "indignation"' (XIII, 424–6). 'Pessimism of indignation' even tended to become synonymous with 'anarchism of indignation' (*supra*, 8 §1). Whatever the case, the banner of pessimism could no longer be brandished at subversion, as happened in *The Birth of Tragedy*. So one can understand Nietzsche's conclusion: 'Out of a word arbitrary and casual in all respects, the word "pessimism", has come an abuse that is spreading like an epidemic: and thus the problem in which we live, that we are, has been neglected' (XIII, 398).

Thus, the dichotomy of being/becoming, 'far more obvious' and convincing, made its appearance. On the one hand, the 'desire for fixing, for immortalizing, for *being*', and on the other the 'desire for destruction, for change, for novelty, for future, for *becoming*' (FW, 370 [235]). In the years of *The Birth of Tragedy*, the 'metaphysics of art' was also the celebration of 'the artist's delight in Becoming', which found its magnificent expression in Hellas (GT, 9, I, 68 [49]). For that very reason, a philosopher like Parmenides, whose thinking fled 'into the rigid mortal stillness of the coldest and emptiest concept, of being', was fundamentally alien to Greece (PHG, 11, I, 844). Instead, Heraclitus expressed the essence of tragic Hellenism. Reality and life were revealed in their true meaning: 'A becoming and a passing, building and destroying, devoid of all moral imputation, in an eternally equal innocence' (PHG, 7, I, 830).

And, like pessimism, becoming too seemed for a while to find its chosen place in Germany, the heir also in this regard to tragic Hellenism. Even if immobilism was said to have had its fullest expression in Chinese society, it was certainly no stranger to the Latins. The aspiration to 'definitive ideal arrangements' and a 'justice' that lights up the earth like 'an immobile rainbow' was typical of revolutionaries (*supra*, 9 §3), and so pointed in particular to France and the 'optimism' that characterised its culture. Precisely because the German people embodied the idea of becoming, this utopia or dystopia of a condition of immobile perfection and perfect immobility was foreign to it. It 'always wants to reform and never to revolutionize', without ever losing the unrest, 'the noblest disquiet, that of the renewing deed': a further proof of that, according to the fourth *Unfashionable Observation*, was the music of Wagner, who had

---

3   Dühring 1875, 346 f.

once written: 'So the German is not revolutionary, but reformatory.'[4] Again, we can read in *The Gay Science*:

> We Germans are Hegelians even had there been no Hegel, insofar as we (as opposed to all Latins) instinctively attribute a deeper meaning and greater value to becoming and development than to what 'is'; we hardly believe in the justification of the concept 'being'.
>
> FW, 357 [218]

However, even this second dichotomy had its drawbacks. The exaltation of 'progress' or 'movement' could be significant and appropriate 'if one lives among the Egyptians', in societies, like the Egyptian (or Chinese), marked by immobilism. The situation in 'movable Europe' was quite different (M, 554 [275–6]). There, becoming can also be synonymous with lack of *otium* (MA, 285 [191–2]). To counter this tendency, one could again invoke Hellas. One might think of the Athenians: they were no strangers to the 'unprecedented activity' that characterised the Jewish-Christian tradition (*supra*, 9 §5); 'they felt like the most restless Greeks; but with respect to us, how calm they appear, how full of themselves and other good things' (IX, 89). Becoming could refer not only to lack of *otium* but also to surrender to the transience of the moment and to the current of the moment, with the renunciation of any higher purpose, any ambition to leave one's mark on history (SE, 4, I, 374–5 [172–3]).

In conclusion, not even the categories of becoming and being were an adequate key for the interpretation of the world and of worldviews. Each term of this dichotomous pair could have meanings very different from the other:

> The desire for destruction, for change and for becoming can be the expression of an overflowing energy pregnant with the future (my term for this is, as is known, 'Dionysian'); but it can also be the hatred of the ill-constituted [*Missrathenen*], deprived, and underprivileged one who destroys and must destroy because what exists, indeed all existence, all being, outrages and provokes him. To understand this feeling, take a close look at our anarchists.
>
> FW, 370 [235]

The idea of becoming could also nourish the mad hope for the freeing of slaves and the malformed, called to order and derided by the theory of the

---

4 Wagner 1910f, 85.

eternal return of the same. But 'the will to eternalize', the pathos of being, could also assume opposite meanings: 'It can be prompted, first, by gratitude and love', stimulating art that casts 'a Homeric light and splendour over all things'. However, the pathos of being could also be an expression of the torment of the malformed, who, with 'tyrannical will', would like to impose on the richness of reality the seal of a paralysing and levelling 'binding law and compulsion', thus taking 'revenge on all things' (FW, 370 [235–6]).

Nor did the other dichotomies Nietzsche experienced in the course of his development prove to be more appropriate: art and myth against Socratic rationalism? In fact, the writings of the 'enlightened' period denounced revolutionary and religious 'madness' also in the name of enlightenment and reason: it was the merit of the 'scientific person' to counter the tendency towards the 'supernatural' and the 'inexplicable' (MA, 136 [104]). Was the supra-historical myth really an antidote to a historical consciousness that sought to legitimise modernity? In fact, an essential element of modern subversion was a morality that, in its prescriptive fanaticism, ignored the history behind it. This was not a case of a reversal of positions. The various dichotomies acquired a unitary and coherent meaning if reinterpreted in the light of the dichotomy that marked the final phase in Nietzsche's development: on the one hand, the health inherent in the affirmation of life with its conflicts and its potential for negativity, on the other, the sickness of religious and revolutionary transcendence, which flinched before the potential for negativity and thereby negated and endangered life itself.

The Gay Science insists on this, when summarising the path that lies behind it:

> Every art, every philosophy can be considered a cure and aid in the service of growing, struggling life: they always presuppose suffering and sufferers. But there are two types of sufferers: first, those who suffer from a superabundance of life – they want a Dionysian art as well as a tragic outlook and insight into life; then, those who suffer from an impoverishment of life and seek quiet, stillness, calm seas, redemption from themselves through art and insight, or else intoxication, paroxysm, numbness, madness.
>
> FW, 370 [234]

From the height of this new perspective, the previous dichotomies could be grasped in their true meaning and reclaimed. So, pessimism could again be celebrated if by that was meant 'Dionysian pessimism', the antithesis of Schopenhauer's pessimism and his denial of the will to live. Becoming as once again, or still, a point of reference, on condition one did not lose sight of the fact that 'the eternal joy in becoming [...] includes even the eternal joy in negating'. The worldview founded in becoming and 'Dionysian pessimism' were one and the same thing. They both meant: 'The affirmation of passing away and destruction that is crucial for a Dionysian philosophy, saying yes to opposition and war, becoming along with a radical rejection of the very concept of "being"' (EH, *The Birth of Tragedy*, 3 [110]).

The critique of reason in *The Birth of Tragedy*, which accused 'Socratic optimism' and rationalism of having a 'corrosive' effect on life, could also be reclaimed (*supra*, 1 §16). *Ecce homo* continued to attribute to the youthful work the merit of 'the understanding of Socratism': Socrates was 'recognized for the first time as the instrument of Greek disintegration, as a typical *décadent*'; in opposing 'instinct', '"[r]ationality" at any price' appeared as 'dangerous, as a form of violence that undermines life' (EH, *The Birth of Tragedy*, 1 [108]). Yes, '[a]n instinct becomes weaker if it rationalizes itself: because the very act of rationalization represents a weakness' (WA, Postscript [255]). But this did not prevent the late Nietzsche, also in the name of science, from accusing all those who rejected the doctrine of the eternal return of regressing to a theistic and creationist view, a religious tradition hostile to life. Similarly, it was the merit of the second *Unfashionable Observation* to have understood how much 'danger [is] inherent in the way we conduct our scholarship, which gnaws away at life and poisons it', and in the science of history in particular, which celebrated modernity and blocked every action designed to challenge it (EH, *Unfashionable Observations*, 1 [112]). But, again, this did not stop the late Nietzsche broadening and sharpening historical consciousness to the point where even the unilinear concept of time was historicised and challenged (*supra*, 15 §4).

The pessimism/optimism dichotomy and the others gradually developed were incapable of grasping the essential problem: 'It is not a matter of who is right, the question is to determine in which part we find ourselves, that of the condemned, of the products of decadence ... In this case we judge nihilistically' (XIII, 398–9). And again: 'It is not at all a matter of the best or the worst of possible worlds: no or yes, that is here the question. The nihilistic instinct says no' (XIII, 528).

It was ultimately a choice between sickness and nihilism on the one hand and reaffirmation of life on the other, or, to put it in a more political language, between the subversion raging for two millennia and the party of life or aristocratic radicalism. Put religiously: '[H]e who suffers most and is poorest in life' would need 'a god who truly would be a god for the sick, a "saviour"' (FW, 370 [235]). Quite a different human being opted for the religion of Dionysus:

He who is richest in fullness of life, the Dionysian god and man, can allow himself not only the sight of what is terrible and questionable but also the terrible deed and every luxury of destruction, decomposition, negation; in his case, what is evil, nonsensical, and ugly almost seems acceptable because of an overflow in procreating, fertilizing forces capable of turning any desert into bountiful farmland.

> FW, 370 [234–5]

3   Birth Control, 'Castration' of the Malformed and Other Eugenic Measures

The stronger the conviction of the psychopathological and even physiological origins of the so-called 'social question' became, the more eugenics appeared as its true and definitive solution. Too much rubbish had accumulated in the European cities. Emigration to the colonies might help. But however useful and necessary it might be as a vent for 'old Europe, which is currently over-populated' (M, 206 [155]), it was not enough. So a policy to regulate marriage and procreation was to be devised. Malthus's fears took on fascinating tones in Zarathustra's mouth:

> You are young and wish for a child and marriage for yourself. But I ask you: are you a person who has a right to wish for a child? [...] [T]hat which the far-too-many call marriage, these superfluous ones – oh, what do I call that? Oh, this poverty of the soul by two! Oh, this filth of the soul by two! [...] Which child would not have reason to weep about its parents?
> Za, I, On Child and Marriage [52]

The problem of birth control, at least for certain strata of the population, was for Nietzsche so important it was treated in his work not only in theoretical terms but also in his historical reconstruction of the past: the Greeks 'promoted pederasty to preclude overpopulation (which generates impoverished, restless circles, and even within the nobility)' (IX, 514).

The philosopher dwelt extensively on this theme, especially in the last phase of his development. During the last few months of his conscious life, he came up with a number of prescriptions, some of them quite detailed. Having noted, disturbingly, that people of lower nature 'have the advantage of a compromising fertility' (XIII, 317), it was necessary to discourage celibacy among the healthy elements of the population by manipulating the burden of taxation and 'extending military service' and also by granting 'all sorts of benefits for the fathers' of large numbers of children (especially sons). To prevent the reproduction and proliferation of degenerates, one might think of introducing 'a medical report signed by the community authorities before every wedding, in which those engaged to be married and the doctors must answer several given questions ("family history")' (XIII, 495).

'Inappropriate unions' could be avoided simply by treating those guilty with 'contempt' and 'a declaration of dishonour'. It was 'wishful thinking' to believe that the 'sex drive' could be neutralised in this way in sick people or criminals; all the more so since it 'often exhibits a repugnant excitability in people of that sort whose lives have turned out badly.' Nor was it even sufficient to punish with 'loss of "freedom"' those that transgressed against eugenic norms. Prison sentences were certainly necessary, and should be severely threatened, and not only limited to those directly responsible. As we know, 'prison' was also necessary for the 'priest', who by preaching chastity to the healthy and compassion for those whose lives had turned out badly was the ideologue and agitator *par excellence* of the party of 'counter-nature' opposed to the 'party of life'. All these measures were useful and necessary, but other more radical ones were also needed. To stop criminals contributing to the creation of a 'race of criminality', one had to not flinch from 'castrating' them. That was exactly the way to deal with 'the chronic sick and neurasthenics of the third degree', with 'syphilitics': so it was a matter of preventing procreation 'in all cases in which a child would be a crime' (XII, 479; XIII, 401–2).

Did Nietzsche's eugenic policy stop here? Beyond Galton, the Greek model also influenced him: in Greece, 'religion did not preach morality, so on the whole customs were left free.' Slavery was not a problem: nor was 'the killing of the embryo, the elimination of the fruits of unfortunate coitus' (IX, 476). At least on this point, Nietzsche was in full accord with Plato and his urgent eugenic recommendations to keep 'pure' the 'race of the guardians' and also the polis, the human 'herd' in general, and not to allow the life of 'inwardly constantly sick bodies' to be both long and wretched.[5] Moreover, for this very reason, Galton enthusiastically praised classical Greece, where, 'thanks to a system of selection that is in part unconscious, a magnificent breed of human animals builds up'.[6] For the English naturalist as for the German philosopher, it was Christianity that had allowed this lesson to be forgotten.

How far could one go, now this religion contrary to nature was declining? Unfortunately, 'the earth is full of the superfluous, life is spoiled by the all too

5   Plato, Politeia 459e, 460c, 407 d–e.
6   Galton 1869, 340 f.

many. May they be lured from this life with the "eternal life!"' (Za, I, On the Preachers of Death [31]). Naturally, it would be better if the superfluous 'were never born.' However, they could take their leave as quickly as possible from a world that they, in their nihilism, could not appreciate and in which they were unable to recognise themselves. Zarathustra devotes almost an entire speech to this theme:[7]

> For some life fails [*missräth*]: a poisonous worm eats its way to their heart. Let them see to it that their dying succeeds all the more. Some never become sweet, they rot already in summer. It is cowardice that keeps them clinging to the branch. Far too many live and far too long they hang on their branches. Would that a storm came to shake all this rot and worm-food from the tree! Would that preachers of the *quick* death came! They would be the right storms and shakers of the trees of life for me! But I hear only preaching of the slow death and patience with all things 'earthly.' Indeed, you preach patience with earthly things? It is the earthly things that have too much patience with you, you slanderers!
>
> Za, I, On Free Death [53]

Rather than discourage or prevent the 'free death' of the malformed, of those unable to accept and enjoy earthly existence with its potential for joy and negativity, it should be consciously and actively promoted: 'Oh my brothers, am I perhaps cruel? But I say: if something is falling, one should also give it a push! [...] And whomever you cannot teach to fly, him you should teach – to fall faster!' (Za, III, On Old and New Tablets, 20 [168]).

4   'Free Death', 'Active Nihilism' and 'Nihilism of the Deed'

The late Nietzsche believed the historical conditions for the solution proposed by Zarathustra were maturing. The West was facing a turning point. Christianity was in crisis even among its followers and ex-followers, who apparently no longer gave credence to a faith shaken by the development of culture and modern society. Certainly, the convinced Christian was a nihilist 'in himself', but not 'for himself': he believed he was expressing the fullness of values without realising that, in the afterworld, this fullness was nothing. Western history was marked by the transition from nihilism in itself to nihilism for itself. Paradox-

---

7   On the 'suicide chapter', see Bernoulli 1908, Vol. 1, 405.

ically, this transition was facilitated and even imposed by what remains of a bloodless and dying religion. In the blood of Europeans, Christian moral education, which commanded truthfulness, was to some extent still present (XII, 125–6 and 571). After the ancient and deceptive certainties of faith and its surrogates had been lost, such truthfulness had to face nothingness, and recognise that it itself was nothingness. In this sense, 'European nihilism' was the 'necessary consequence of the ideals hitherto in force'. A terrible reality was there for all to see: 'absolute valuelessness' (XII, 339).

So far, 'human beings have done nothing but invent God, in order not to kill themselves' (XIII, 144), but God had in the meantime disappeared or was soon to disappear from human consciousness. 'Incomplete nihilism' had now turned into 'radical nihilism [radikaler Nihilismus]', or the 'last nihilism', marked by 'the conviction of the absolute unsustainability of existence' (XII, 571). And then what? The only concrete act to which the passive nihilist could rise was suicide, the 'act [Tat] of nihilism' par excellence (XIII, 222). This was 'nihilism of the deed [Nihilismus der Tat]' (XIII, 221). The vision of the earthly world as a vale of tears, the inability to accept worldly existence with its contradictions, should lead to the actual negation of life itself. During the decline of the ancient world, many of those whose lives had turned out badly and of the deformed were inclined to go to the very end. Christianity had stopped them, blocking them halfway:

> One cannot condemn Christianity enough for having devalued, through the idea of the immortality of the soul, such a great purifying nihilistic movement, which was perhaps on the way to having devalued it by the thought of the immortal private person as well as through the hope of resurrection: in short, always by abstaining from the nihilistic act, suicide ... It substituted slow suicide.
>
> XIII, 222

The dominant religion in the West had played a calamitous role, because 'instead of urging them on to death and self-destruction, it protects all the deformed and the sick and induces them to reproduce' (XIII, 222). But now a new situation had come about. The decline of morality meant also the abandonment of the moral condemnation of suicide, to which those whose lives had turned out badly and those who no longer saw any sense in living could now feel drawn. 'This is the European form of Buddhism, the no-doing [das Nein-Thun], after which the whole of existence has lost its "sense"' (XII, 216).

A point had been reached where the mortal crisis could finally turn into its opposite:

Morality protected *those whose lives had turned out badly* [*die Schlecht-weggekommenen*] from nihilism [radical and for itself] by attributing to *all* an infinite value, a metaphysical value. [...] *Assuming that belief in this morality perishes*, those whose lives have turned out badly would no longer have their consolation – *and would perish* [*zu Grunde gehen*]. *Perishing* [*zu Grunde-Gehen*] presents itself as *condemning oneself to death* [*sich-zu-Grunde-Richten*]. [...] *Symptoms* of this self-destruction of those whose lives have turned out badly: self-vivisection, poisoning, intoxication, romanticism, especially the instinctive compulsion to perform acts that turn the powerful into *mortal enemies* (– as if breeding one's executioners), the *will to destruction* as will of a still deeper instinct, the instinct of self-destruction, of *will into nothingness* [*Willens ins Nichts*].

XII, 215

We have already seen Zarathustra stress that 'the earth is tired' of the tired of life. The fragment quoted above reinforces the idea that the voluntary perishing of those whose lives had turned out badly and those who were tired of life was a kind of 'instinctive selection [*instinktives Auslesen*]' of what nature 'must destroy'. Assuming radical forms and passing from the in itself to the for itself, tired and passive nihilism suddenly acquired dignity and, by means of a suicidal act, brought to completion the very design of nature and the will to live of life itself. As the expression of a radical and self-conscious nihilism, the will to suicide and self-destruction was manifested in the most varied forms. The extreme rebellion of those whose lives had turned out badly could itself even be an indirect and deferred kind of suicide: 'nihilism as a symptom of the fact that those whose lives have turned out badly no longer have any consolation; that they destroy to be destroyed' (XII, 215–16).

But only an elite capable of breaking radically and definitively with the ruling values or negative values that had established themselves in the wake of the total nihilistic revolution that had raged in the West for two millennia could encourage those whose lives had turned out badly to move from whining passive nihilism to a more virile nihilism of the deed. The countermovement to this ruinous cycle was expressed initially in the 'attempts to escape nihilism without transvaluing those values'. But, in this way, one remained within the ambit of nihilism: an 'incomplete [*unvollständig*] nihilism' that, by stopping halfway, exacerbated the problem and ended up bringing about the 'opposite effect' (XII, 476). How could this situation be remedied? The destructive course of nihilism had to be followed through to the end so it could then be blocked and finally overcome. Only active nihilism, aware of its divine strength and will to power, could bring this about. What attitude was the extreme and active nihilist to take to the dramatic turn under way? It was the time of the 'decision' (XII, 120). Previously blocked by Christian morality and religion, now 'great crises of selection and purification' appeared on the horizon (XIII, 222), called into being by the radicalisation of passive nihilism, by its configuration as 'radical nihilism'. These crises were highly beneficial, and were to be under all circumstances supported and promoted:

> Nothing would be more useful and worthier of promotion than a consistent *nihilism of the deed* [*Nihilismus der Tat*]. As I understand them, all the phenomena of Christianity, of pessimism, say: 'We are ripe not to be, for us it is reasonable [*vernünftig*] not to be.' This language of 'reason [*Vernunft*]' would, in this case, also be the language of selective nature [*selektive Natur*].
>
> XIII, 221

Far from blocking the 'nihilism of the deed' to which those whose lives had turned out badly were now tending to turn, one was to do everything possible to promote it. So: 'By what sort of means would a strict form of the great contagious nihilism be achieved: a form of nihilism that with scientific conscientiousness would teach and put into practice voluntary death? (And *not* weakly vegetating with the prospect of a false post-existence)' (XIII, 222).

5 From the 'Elimination' of Beggars to the 'Annihilation' of the Malformed

Have we with the encouragement of 'free death' reached an insurmountable barrier? Among 'all the things that deserve to be taken seriously in life', alongside 'questions of nutrition, residence, spiritual diet', 'cleanliness, weather', *Ecce homo* also mentions 'treatment of the sick [*Krankenbehandlung*]'. The meaning of this expression, already in itself ambiguous, at once becomes clear in the context of the polemic that immediately follows: '[I]n the concept of the good person, the defence of everything weak, sick, badly formed, suffering from itself, everything that should be destroyed [*zu Grunde gehen soll*] –, defiance of the law of selection' (EH, Why I am a Destiny, 8 [150–1]). Moreover, to dispel any lingering doubts, Zarathustra says: 'One should not try to be a physician for the incurable' (Za, III, On Old and New Tablets, 17 [166]).

Again, we ask ourselves: have we now reached an insurmountable barrier? One understands Zarathustra's hesitation: 'I once asked, and almost choked on my question: What? Does life also require the rabble? Are poisoned wells and stinking fires and soiled dreams and maggots required in life's bread?' (Za, II, On the Rabble [75]). At the end of the 'Enlightenment' period, radical proposals were already beginning to appear in Nietzsche's pronouncements that went well beyond the usual eugenic remedies: 'One ought to do away with [*abschaffen*] beggars: for you feel annoyed giving to them and annoyed when you don't' (M, 185 [132]). One had to realise: 'The development of taste [...] feels the need to look at beautiful, joyful human beings.' And so: 'Let us seek out those that bring us joy, and foster them, and flee the rest – this is real morality!' (IX, 250). This was a period in which many in Europe were demanding a purge of the urban landscape. In Britain, the *Manchester Guardian* published a letter from a lady of fine feeling who lamented having to endure, even in the main streets of the city, the spectacle of 'swarms of beggars', including some with 'disgusting wounds and deformities'. A taxpayer surely had 'the right to be spared such disagreeable and impertinent molestations'. Engels was furious that the letter was 'published without comment as a perfectly natural, reasonable thing'.[8] Marx, for his part, pointed to the spread, since the time of Napoleon, of 'punitive institutions' for the poor and the sick, to free the public from the '*image dégoûtante des infirmités et de la honteuse misère*'.[9]

Despite a certain ambiguity, the programme announced by Nietzsche was doubtless more radical than that denounced by Marx and Engels, for it demanded much more than the mere segregation of those whose lives had turned out badly. To start with, one was to encourage them to commit suicide, but it was perhaps possible to go even further. If in them radical nihilism tends to assume the form of nihilism of the deed, then in strong spirits active nihilism, in practice breaking completely with traditional morality, became 'ecstatic nihilism'. It could 'inspire desire [*das Verlangen*] for the end in degenerates that wish to die', but could also serve as 'a hammer with which to smash and eliminate the degenerating and dying races, in order to make way for a new order of life' (XI, 547). We have seen how the young Nietzsche theorised a Dionysian and 'ecstatic' moment that with the absorption in a cosmic unity of the sacrificial victims of culture led to the forgetting of singularity. The supreme 'gratification of primordial unity [*höchsten Wonnebefriedigung des Ur-Einen*]' 'chisels the Dionysian world artist' into marble (*supra*, 1 §14 and 19). This was the overcoming of the *principium individuationis*, which now assumed a more compact shape, to the point of becoming synonymous with annihilation.

---

8   Marx and Engels 1975 ff., 4, 565.
9   Marx and Engels 1975 ff., 3, 196.

'Honesty towards us', says Nietzsche, already imposes a rigorous 'selection':

> To cause the lamentable ones, the deformed, the degenerate to die out
> must be the trend! Don't keep them going at all cost! [...] Always build on
> the natural instincts: 'Cause joy to those in whom we rejoice, suffering to
> those that irritate us.' We destroy wild animals, and we breed tame ones:
> This is a great instinct.
>
>   IX, 250–1

One was finally to become fully conscious of the meaning of life:

> Life – that is: continually shedding something that wants to die; Life –
> that is: being cruel and inexorable against anything that is growing weak
> and old in us, and not just in us. Life – therefore means: being devoid of
> respect for the dying, the wretched, the aged? Always being a murderer?
> And yet old Moses said: 'Thou shalt not kill'
>
>   FW, 26 [50]

But Nietzsche let Moses, the founder of the Jewish-Christian tradition that
dominates the West, answer a holy man that in a parable in *The Gay Science*, the
saint recommended killing a 'wretched, misshapen' newborn child, that which
'doesn't have life enough to die'; to those who thought the advice to kill the child
cruel, the saint responded: 'But is it not crueller to let it live?' (FW, 73 [76]).
    A few years later, Zarathustra invited the still hesitant free spirit not to allow
itself to be concerned by outdated 'old tablets': ' "Thou shalt not rob! Thou shalt
not kill!" – such words were once held holy. [...] Is there not in all life itself – robbing and killing? And for such words to have been called holy, was truth itself
not – killed?' (Za, III, On Old and New Tablets, 10 [161–2]). This theme returned
in a more radical form and with obsessive insistence in the notes from the last
months of Nietzsche's conscious life:

> The supreme law of life, first formulated by Zarathustra, requires that one
> have no compassion for all the dross and refuse of life, that one destroy all
> that which for ascending life is mere obstacle, poison, *conspiracy*, under-
> ground hostility, in a word Christianity ... It is immoral, and against nature
> in the deepest sense, to say 'Thou shalt not kill.'
>   The biblical prohibition 'Thou shalt not kill' is naïve in comparison
> to my prohibition on the *décadents*, 'Thou shalt not reproduce!' – it is
> something even worse ... In regard to the dross and refuse of life there is
> only one duty, to *destroy*; to be compassionate here, to want to preserve at

all cost, would be the highest form of immorality, actual counter-nature, deadly enmity to life itself.

XIII, 611–12

Ultimately, one was dealing with a sickness: 'The European disguises himself with morality because he has become a sick, sickly, maimed animal. [...] It is not the ferocity of the beast of prey that needs a moral disguise, but the herd animal with its deep mediocrity, fear, and boredom with itself' (FW, 352 [210]). To allow oneself to be overwhelmed by compassion and weakness was not only a dreadful mistake. Worse still: it was to be complicit in a 'conspiracy' that, beyond the social order, had as its target life itself.

The late Nietzsche insisted obsessively on the need to amputate the sick parts of the social organism. To resist the essential hygienic measures seemed to him ultimately criminal. Those that still had moral qualms should bear in mind this truth: 'To bring a child into the world in which one has no right to be is worse than taking a life' (XIII, 402). It is necessary to dwell for a moment on this passage: killing is not necessarily the most reprehensible act; the malformed, the subject of these remarks, do not have the right to procreate, and cannot even claim for themselves the right to life. Nietzsche is explicit: 'I do not even give the malformed the right' to live (XI, 102). And again: 'Annihilation of those that have turned out badly – for that, one must emancipate oneself from morality up to now' (XI, 75). One was not to allow oneself to be paralysed by meaningless scruples: 'The weak and the failures [*Missrathnen*] should perish. [...] And they should be helped to do this' (AC, 2 [4]); the necessary and beneficial 'attempts to assassinate two thousand years of anti-nature and desecration of humanity' led to 'the ruthless extermination of everything degenerate and parasitical' (EH, *The Birth of Tragedy*, 4 [110]). Nietzsche repeatedly used the word 'extermination [*Vernichtung*]'.[10]

Precisely because life was at stake and it was a matter of conquering 'counter-nature' and 'vice' in its basest form, the war on the horizon and indeed already under way was a total war: 'Merciless hardness' was essential. The 'great politics [...] inexorably puts an end to all that is degenerate and parasitical' (XIII, 638).

The programme set out here was of a radicalism without precedent in Galton or, obviously, in Plato. A fragment from the spring of 1884 gives the 'great men' that wanted to 'imprint their shape onto great communities' an important piece of advice:

---

10   Nolte points this out (1978, 617 and 1990, 193 f.); cf. also Taureck 1989, 34, 255.

Acquire that enormous energy of greatness in order, on the one hand by breeding and on the other by annihilating millions of those that have turned out badly, to shape the future human being and not to perish because of the pain that one creates and that is of a like one has never seen before.

XI, 98

'Millions of the deformed'! Nietzsche stretched the category of sickness frighteningly wide: 'To understand the mutual connection of all forms of corruption; and, in so doing, not to forget Christian corruption' and 'socialist-communist corruption (a consequence of the Christian)', and to draw the necessary conclusions: 'Here there can be no *covenants*: here we must destroy, annihilate, make war' (XIII, 220). And one was not to forget that a physiological defect underlay Christian and socialist 'counter-nature.'

But there were 'malformed peoples' as well as malformed individuals (XI, 102), or, as we have seen, 'degenerating and dying races'. In this case, too, Nietzsche was not for half measures: 'Annihilation of the decadent races' (XI, 69)! Needless to say, there were also useful races that culture needed to ensure *otium* for the best. What attitude should one take to them?

By what means should one treat raw peoples, and one can touch *in praxi* with one's hands the fact that the 'barbarity' of means is nothing arbitrary and random when, with all one's European pampering, one finds it necessary to remain, in the Congo or wherever, master over the barbarians.

XII, 471

The example given is significant. One year after the end of the philosopher's conscious life, Joseph Conrad travelled to Africa and the Congo and collected information and ideas that later took shape in *The Heart of Darkness*, with its descriptions of the horrors of colonial expansion and rule: think of the 'heads [of the rebels] drying on the stakes under [the slave-owner] Mr Kurtz's windows'.[11]

---

11   Conrad 1989, 97.

6   Eugenics, Utopia and Dystopia

Most interpreters tend to suppress the brutality of these assertions, which, in any case, are an expression of a spiritual climate quite widespread in these years. But to limit the analysis of nihilism in Nietzsche to the pages that describe it as a guest at once both fascinating and disquieting is to read him in an indulgently edifying key. The nihilist rebel whose writings contain a seductive and irresistible emancipatory charge after thousands of years of moralistic oppression cannot be separated from the antagonist of nihilism resolved to put an end in every possible way to a scourge that in his eyes threatened life itself. Nietzsche was aware of the extreme radicality of the vision that had matured in him and of the moral disquiet it was capable of provoking. He himself seemed to hesitate, as a comparison of two almost identical texts shows. We read the following in *The Gay Science*: the movement now taking place in Europe 'could easily confront coming generations with the terrible Either/Or: "Either abolish your venerations or – *yourselves!*" The latter would be nihilism; but would not the former also be – nihilism? That is *our* question mark' (FW, 346 [204]). A worldview that undermined life, the 'species', 'the largest economy of the Whole', was undoubtedly nihilistic; but did not a transvaluation so radical it could not flinch from destroying all that was degenerate in order to break decisively from the previous worldview itself run the risk of being affected by nihilism? A few years later, the question mark had disappeared: 'There dawns the antithesis of the world we worship and we live, which we are. What remains is to erase either our veneration, or ourselves. The latter is nihilism' (XII, 129). In *The Gay Science*, both alternatives were regarded with horror and as expressions of nihilism, even though the accent was placed on the danger of the obliteration of existence. In the second text, nihilism, important to overcome, was that which desired or suffered the obliteration of existence; the other, prepared to resort to extreme measures to save culture and existence itself, active ecstatic nihilism, was no longer nihilism in the proper sense, and already appeared to announce the overcoming of that scourge. This is confirmed by a fragment from the autumn of 1887: '"Nihilism" as an ideal of the supreme power of the spirit, of abundant life: part destructive, part ironic' (XII, 353). The quotation marks indicate that this destructive power, no longer held in check by the ruling values, was already beyond nihilism.

Certainly, the utterances that are not only disquieting but positively repugnant are linked to others that, at first sight, look reassuring and even seductive. This is the period in which the madness was already becoming evident. After the coup against Wilhelm II, which inevitably ended in brutality (the shooting of those principally responsible for the Christian-socialist subversion), a completely new phase seemed to open up, described and celebrated by Nietzsche in his notes and his correspondence in unusually utopian tones: 'If we win, we will have in our hands the government of the world, including world peace. We have transcended the boundaries of the absurd race, nation and estates [*Stände*]' (B, III, 5, 502). Together with provincial, chauvinist and racial hatreds, politics and even power as such seemed to vanish: 'The concept of politics is completely dissolved in a war of spirits, all centres of power have been blasted into the air' (B, III, 5, 503–4). But other letters reveal quite other perspectives: 'A couple of decades of world-historic crisis.' There would not just be 'wars' (B, III, 5, 515), but 'wars as there have never been' (B, III, 5, 504).

And so, utopia changes into dystopia. The wars looming on the horizon would not be 'between people and people' (XIII, 637). The language seems reassuring, but only in appearance. The 'annihilation of the decadent races' or the imposition of 'rule over the barbarians' (e.g., in the Congo) was aimed not at a 'people' but precisely at 'decadent races' or 'barbarians': neither the one nor the other could lay claim to the dignity of being a 'people', which fell only to Europeans. The wars invoked by Nietzsche on the threshold of his madness were also not 'between estates' (XIII, 637). Again, the language sounds reassuring. In fact, the eugenic preoccupation had become so obsessive by this time that even the traditional free zones were not spared: it was necessary to combat degeneration and sickness 'regardless of estate, rank and culture' (XIII, 402). History had demonstrated the catastrophic consequences to which 'degeneration of rulers and ruling estates' led: this dialectic had brought about the triumph of Christianity (XI, 102–3). A similar dialectic in Germany was paving the way to the advent of social Christianity: it was necessary to react with the energy the situation demanded. One was not even to stop before 'our upper estates' if they sided with the 'party for the lie' (meaning the Christian socialists): 'It is not their choice – they have to do it' (XIII, 637). So, they too, like the millions of malformed, were hopelessly burdened. They were people that, because of their social position, 'have been honoured as first so far'. But Nietzsche countered: '[T]hese supposedly "first" people to be people at all, – to my mind they are human waste, excrescences of sickness and vengeful instincts: they are nothing but disastrous, fundamentally incurable nonhumans who take revenge on life' (EH, Why am I so wise, 10 [98–9]). In this context, the desire to shoot even Wilhelm II grew in him. The category of the 'malformed' became ever more extensive, as did the eugenic war the 'party of life' was called upon to wage against them.

It was in the first place a question of asserting with greater strength the 'rank-ordering among human beings' and of respecting the 'infinitely long ladder of rank-ordering' that characterised the natural as well as the human world

(B, III, 5, 502). Regarding the latter, on the lowest level were the 'dross and refuse' (*infra*, 20 §4), those whose lives had turned out badly, the malformed, the 'Chandala' (AC, 58 and 60 [58 and 60]), the 'lowest classes, the underworld' of society (AC, 22 [18]), whose resentment against the best and against society grew the more their own physiological constitution rotted and putrefied. In this sense, rank-ordering was a ladder that also distinguished degrees of health and sickness. So it was 'a war that passes through all these absurd accidents of people, estate, race, occupation, education, schooling: a war as between rise and fall, will to life and thirst for revenge against life, probity and wicked mendacity' (XIII, 637). The 'new party of life' or the 'party of life' Nietzsche craved had to be 'strong enough for *big* politics' (XIII, 638), for 'big politics *par excellence*' (B, III, 5, 502), which had to focus on a eugenics programme of extreme radicalism.

It was necessary to be able to 'destroy with divine eye and undisturbed' (XII, 31). The state of mind here advocated seems to have already been achieved by Nietzsche, who, as the theorist and inspiration of the 'party of life' and of the 'big politics' advocated by it, did not hesitate to declare: 'There has never been a human being with greater right to destroy than I' (B, III, 5, 512). And yet: 'I am unable to rid myself of my happiness in times of terrible decisions' (XIII, 639).

PART 4

Beyond 'Metaphor' and 'Anticipation':
Nietzsche in
Comparative Perspective

∵

Together with his colleagues, he [the privileged one] considers himself a member of an exclusive order, a chosen nation in the nation.

SIEYÈS

• • •

[I]t makes us "God's elect".

FW, 379 [243]

• • •

The privileged even come to see themselves as a different human species.

SIEYÈS

• • •

What helps feed or nourish the higher type of human being must be almost poisonous to a very different and lesser type.

JGB, 30 [31]

• • •

As for the *human being*, I declare that I never met him in my life; if he exists, it is unknown to me.

MAISTRE

• • •

[T]he soul-superstition that still causes trouble as the superstition of the subject or I.

JGB, Preface [3]

• • •

The supernatural essence of the soul has served as starting point for the theory of human rights, prior and superior to nature and society.

VACHER DE LAPOUGE

• •
•

CHAPTER 20

'Metaphor', 'Anticipation' and 'Translatability of Languages'

1   'Metaphor' as Suppression and the Short Cut of 'Anticipation'

Often ignored or suppressed, the ever more frequent and insistent calls for '"barbarity" of means' against colonial peoples, for the 'annihilation of decadent races' and the 'annihilation of millions of malformed', confront us with a problem: is this the worldview of a prophet of the Third Reich? Naturally, there is no shortage of techniques of suppression. Does the philosopher insist obsessively on slavery as the unavoidable foundation of culture? Let no one dare to disturb the magic of the metaphor by vulgar historical references to the situation in the southern United States before the Civil War or the practice of forced labour in the colonies! So, must we assume that Nietzsche was wholly unaware of the debate that raged in his time and around him with reference to this specific institution? His apologists try to shield him from contamination by attributing to him an inability or a very limited capacity for discernment at the level of historical and political analysis. Thus, he is gratuitously suspected of having used slogans and 'metaphors' without being fully aware of their true meaning, unlike all his contemporaries.

Or take the topic of 'breeding [*Züchtung*]', which plays an ever more important role in Nietzsche. No need to worry, we are immediately reassured by a series of interpreters, 'this biologism is an allegory', the term is synonymous with 'self-discipline' or is to be understood in the 'moral sense'.[1] In reality, *Twilight of the Idols* says explicitly that 'the project of domesticating the human beast as well as the project of breeding a certain species of human being' are two 'zoological terms' that the 'priests do not know anything about' (GD, 'Improving' humanity, 2 [183]). Speaking of the 'transformation of the human being', Nietzsche observed:

> Why should we not do with human beings what the Chinese can do with trees – so they produce roses on one side, pears on the other? These natural processes of the breeding [*Züchtung*] of human beings, for

---

1   Vattimo 1983, 182; Kaufmann 1950, 269; Ottmann 1999, 263.

example, which have hitherto been exercised infinitely slowly and clumsily, could be taken in hand by human beings.

IX, 546–7

Moreover, how to explain the repeated references to Galton, for whom the problem of breeding played a central role? By favouring the begetting and propagation of the basest natures, the men of the Church were said to have acted as sadistic 'breeders', intent on producing a race of monstrous animals or men. That demanded a reaction: by 'judicious marriages over several consecutive generations' one could achieve also in the human case improvements similar to those obtained by breeding dogs or horses.[2] According to the hermeneuts in metaphorical key, Nietzsche had understood nothing of the British theorist of eugenics, despite the fact that he underlined his importance and recommended reading him; and he had also not noticed the polemic about the 'breeders of the human race' then raging throughout the West.[3] Once again, it is necessary to defend the philosopher against his defence advocates. He had understood Galton perfectly well: he called for a 'party of life' that in the first instance would campaign to realise a eugenics programme; he demanded the introduction of thorough checks before allowing a new marriage; with an eye to the malformed, he set the eugenic commandment 'Thou shalt not procreate' against the biblical commandment 'Thou shalt not kill' (*supra*, 19 §5). The necessary transition 'from genus [*Art*] to super-genus [*Über-Art*]' (Za, I, On the Bestowing Virtue, 1 [56]) entailed painful or even drastic measures. And for what should the call for the castration and even annihilation of the malformed and of 'decadent races' be a metaphor? And how can one explain that these supposed metaphors were widely present in the culture and press of the time, also among authors and 'scientists' not accustomed to using rhetorical speech?

No doubt is allowed in the enchanted world of metaphor, from which every possible disturbing element is relentlessly rubbed out. Thus, the celebration of war becomes 'Nietzsche's negation of the unity of being' or 'insistence on the conflict, chaos and interpretative character of everything';[4] it is merely a 'battle without gunpowder'.[5] And the 'socialist wars', these 'terrible' wars against the labour and socialist movement? And the wars by which Europe would become master of the earth (*supra*, 11 §7)? Those that interpret Nietzsche allegorically do not explain whether their reading of him also applies to his contemporar-

---

2   Galton 1869, 357 and 1.
3   Colajanni 1906, 13, fn. 3.
4   Vattimo 1983, 184, fn. 11.
5   Ottmann 1999, 264.

ies, who also tended to transfigure the colonial wars of the time as spiritual adventures. Making a complete abstraction of the second half of the nineteenth century, they prefer to evoke the figure of Jesus Christ, who after all also declared that he had come into the world to bring the 'sword' rather than 'peace' (Mt 10: 34).[6] He that invited us to turn the other cheek (Lk 6, 29) can thus be safely bracketed with the philosopher that branded as an 'idiot' the founder of an unwarlike and servile religion, who admired Alexander, Caesar and Napoleon and especially the latter's 'militarism' as a necessary 'cure' for the 'civilization' that was inwardly corrupt because of its attachment to peace and security and infected by Christianity (XIII, 273 and 427)!

In the hermeneutics here examined, history is not reconstructed or even interrogated. This is a reading that, in contrast to the black and white one sometimes attributed, with good reason, to Lukács, could be defined as tending towards pink, given that it shrinks from any investigation aimed at reconstructing the historico-political meaning of a philosophical proposition – as if to do so would risk an unbearable contamination and application of violence: once one enters the realm of philosophy or art, the conflicts that mark a historical period vanish and fall silent, as if by magic. A historiography of that sort is all the more remarkable when applied to a master of the school of suspicion that can track down political and social conflict not only, as we have seen, in the Gospels but also in the Socratic syllogism, in logic and in science as such (see below, 21, §1–2), in short, in all cultural phenomena, including apparently those that move in a completely rarefied sphere. It is now clear: to be able to appreciate Nietzsche as a great philosopher, one must first defend him against his apologists.

Lukács is absolutely right to refuse to read Nietzsche's glorification of slavery as an innocent and fascinating metaphor. Must we therefore conclude that Nietzsche was the prophet of the mass slave labour of the Third Reich? But in fact, as we have seen, the philosopher lived in a time wholly permeated by the debate about slavery and its abolition in the United States, Brazil and the colonies. It was also a time in which, despite abolitionism, mass slave labour spread ever more widely as a result of the West's colonial expansion. One might formulate the dilemma of those that have left behind the hermeneutics of metaphor and innocence in the following playful (but not too playful) terms: Nietzsche and the Third Reich or Nietzsche and the Second Reich (or the historical period and international context of the Second Reich)? Between the two interpretations pops up a Reich of differences, and no mean one. Of course, it is legitimate and proper to enquire about the continuity between the affirmation of the

---

6 Kaufmann 1950, 340.

eternity and fertility of slavery on the one hand and the glorification of the *Herrenrasse* on the other. But one must start primarily from the nineteenth century.

In the standard analyses of the theoretical preparation of the Third Reich there is a widespread tendency to isolate developments in Germany from those in Europe and the West. This makes it easier to abandon the long and difficult path of historical contextualiaation and to replace it with the short cut of the category of anticipation as opposed to that of historical context. When Lukács asks about the antecedents of the Nietzschean theme of the inevitable and beneficial character of slavery, he rightly draws attention to Schelling's *Philosophy of Mythology*: here we read 'an apologia for Negro slavery in Africa, tortuous in form but whose sense is quite clear'.[7] Should we see in Germany the privileged or exclusive place of the celebration of slavery, starting with Schelling and ending up by way of Nietzsche with the Third Reich? In fact, the declarations of the *Philosophy of Mythology*, to which Lukács refers in *The Destruction of Reason*, are contemporary with the debate in the United States before the outbreak of the Civil War. And Schelling was referring explicitly to the North American republic when he talked of the ultimately beneficial character of the 'export of Negroes [*Negerausfuhr*]' from Africa to America, where, despite the persistence of the chains, their conditions were better than at home.[8] Schopenhauer, however, raged precisely against black slavery in the United States. On the one hand, the substantial reality of slavery in the United States and in other forms in the colonies (at this time mostly British or French), on the other, the abolitionist stance of a philosopher that played a key role in Lukács's representation of the destruction of reason: all this shows it is not historically accurate to paint a picture that shows irrationalism on the one hand and the theoretical transfiguration of slavery on the other in Germany as proceeding hand in hand, until the complete destruction of reason and political community in the Third Reich.

Also, with regard to 'breeding', the alternative to its suppression does not lie in maintaining an unbroken line all the way up to Nazi racial hygiene. Especially since the author to whom Nietzsche referred was, as we know, an Englishman, and the 'science' he theorised was successful far beyond Germany and Europe.

One could also say, more generally, that there was no belligerent or Darwinian 'slogan' in Germany that could not also be found in Britain, Europe and the United States.[9] Intervening in the fiery polemic that developed during the

---

7   Lukács 1954, 179; cf. Schelling 1856–61, Vol. 11, 498–513.

8   Schelling 1856–61, Vol. 11, 513.

9   Ritter 1960, Vol. 2, 136.

First World War and the years immediately following, Max Weber answered those that put all the 'blame' on Germany by noting the strong presence in the United States of an 'ideology of war': at the beginning of the century, a famous American sociologist (Veblen) had formulated or supported the 'completely erroneous theory of the alleged natural necessity of a trade war'.[10] And Weber might have added that Veblen also made a subtle apologia for the 'dolichocephalic blond' race that supposedly embodied more than any other the warrior spirit, as well as scientific inventiveness and industrial efficiency.[11] For Aryan mythology celebrated its triumphs not only in Germany and Europe but even across the Atlantic: it is not difficult to identify in the United States counterparts of the Anglo-German Chamberlain.[12] Moreover, this mythology is not at all confined to ideologues: to take just one example, in 1902, Arthur MacArthur, the military governor of the Philippines, claimed for the United States the right to rule in the name of its membership of the 'magnificent Aryan people'.[13]

2   Ideological Nuremberg, Principle of *tu quoque* and Myth of the German *Sonderweg*

The tendency to burden Nietzsche with a sort of ideological Nuremberg began to manifest itself even before the advent of the Third Reich, starting with the First World War, and not only in Europe. We can see the philosopher's influence on the other side of the Atlantic, particularly on American social Darwinism. But as soon as the clash with Germany started to loom, it was brought into discredit at every level by judgements that were an integral part of actual military operations: 'With the help of the daily press, Nietzsche's name begins to take on a sinister meaning for the man in the street.' But this was true not only of Nietzsche.[14] The enemy country and its whole culture became the target of a campaign, or rather a crusade, that despite its indiscriminate character seemed ever more reasonable and justified under the looming shadow of the Third Reich. So ideological Nuremberg is the conclusion of a movement that stretches over decades.

Grotesque tones and accents can be found in the writings even of well-known contemporary historians. Mosse says, for example: 'What differentiated

---

10   Weber 1971, 495, 585; cf. Veblen 1904, 292 ff.
11   Veblen 1904, 396 f., fn. 1; 354, fn. 1.
12   Bracher 1982, 59.
13   In Karnow 1989, 171.
14   Hofstadter 1944–45, 170 f.

Germany of this period from other nations was a profound mood, a particular view of man and society which seems alien and even demonic to the western intellect' and this oriental barbarism, this satanic distance from the sacred site of Western culture, is said to have begun to emerge in the nineteenth century, perhaps even in the 'late eighteenth century', when 'German romanticism' and a ruinous essentialist and organicistic vision of the 'people [*Volk*]' took hold.[15] Against this view one can set that of Arnold Toynbee, who draws attention to the fact that fascism and Nazism 'have not been recent proselytes to our Western civilisation, but native-born members of our Western family'.[16] Moreover, it is Mosse, who stresses the influence that Disraeli and his argument that 'all is race' had on Langbehn, whom he counts among the masters of the ideological movement that culminates in Nazism.[17] Chamberlain refers to Disraeli's thesis, and reproaches the British statesman (and Judaism) for one-sidedly emphasising the theme of racial purity and thereby forgetting the positive role that the 'mixing of blood' can have among races of equal value and dignity.[18]

Examples of this 'circulation of ideas' from one country to the next could be multiplied.[19] It makes no sense to set a mysterious German 'essence' against a no less mysterious Western 'essence'. On this basis, without indulging in any way in the hermeneutics of allegory and innocence, it is possible to overcome once and for all the historiographical distortion that claims to bring Nietzsche into an *immediate* relationship with the Hitler regime, turning the anti-democratic reaction of the late nineteenth century, social Darwinism and Nazism into an entirely German affair.

Not even culture of Marxist inspiration has been able to resist the myth of an evil German *Sonderweg*. We shall see that Bloch characterised as unambiguously fascist the theory of the overman, which however also resonates, disquietingly, even within British culture (*infra*, 24 § 4). Lukács started *The Destruction of Reason* with an extensive preface on 'irrationalism as an international phenomenon in the imperialist period'. However, the task thus adumbrated was merely expressed and not really tackled. It is true that there is an explicit statement that 'German sociology, in its critique of democracy, frequently elaborates

15   Mosse 1979, 7, 10; Mosse 1966, 1, 4.
16   Toynbee 1952, 29.
17   Mosse 1979, 53; Mosse 1966, 44.
18   Chamberlain 1937, 322, 328.
19   On this category as well as on the temptations and danger of a naturalisation, cf. Losurdo 1997b, 6.

the results of the West adapting them to specifically German goals'.[20] Yet Lukács had to recognise that his representation, on the whole, 'save for a few interpolations, like Kierkegaard and Gobineau', was 'limited to German irrationalism'. In his defence, he asserted that 'only in extremely rare, isolated and episodic cases' had this 'international phenomenon' been as pervasive and consistent in other countries as in Germany.[21]

It is completely understandable that Lukács should have devoted special attention to the development of philosophy in Germany, whose weight in this field and in this period of time is beyond question. And yet, in a work claiming to go beyond the speculative contexts and to reconstruct the actual real historical processes, it is surprising to find neither the American Emerson nor the British Galton in the index. There is therefore a risk of understanding the Nietzschean theme of the celebration of genius and of the overman or of the necessity of eugenic intervention solely in relation to the looming Third Reich rather than comparing it *primarily* to similar themes circulating widely in European and American culture in the late nineteenth century. Even Disraeli is absent from the index: his reading of history was far more rigidly and unambiguously racial than the one for which Nietzsche can be reproached. Beyond this or that author, it is amazing that important historical facts such as slavery in America and in the colonies are absent from *The Destruction of Reason*: and again, the old and 'new' slavery invoked by Nietzsche runs the risk of becoming detached from its real historical context and being *immediately* linked to the forced labour imposed by the Third Reich on the 'colonial' peoples of Eastern Europe.

The fact is that Lukács sought to understand Nietzsche on the basis of a dubious historical balance sheet: 'Fascism is heir to the entire reactionary development of *Germany*. [...] National Socialism is a great appeal to the worst instincts of the *German* people.'[22] Must we start from the view that the horrors of the Third Reich are already inscribed in the reactionary and 'irrationalistic' drift of German culture? In fact, Germany's *ideological* framework in the second half of the nineteenth century is not so very different from that of other Western countries. To explain the rise of Nazism, one must therefore cite other factors that go beyond philosophical and cultural development: defeat in the First World War and the humiliation of Versailles; territorial contiguity with Soviet Russia and the particularly virulent campaign against Bolshevism or the Jewish-Bolshevik 'plot'; the devastating effects of the 1929 economic crisis; the need to

---

20   Lukács 1954, 26.
21   Lukács 1954, 15 f.
22   Lukács 1954, 566 f. (italicization by DL).

redouble one's efforts, and brutality, to catch up in the conquest of colonies and of 'Lebensraum', etc. The error in evaluation concerns the history of Germany as such more than it does Nietzsche.

Even if one wished to focus exclusively on ideological development, one would need to consider systematically which extra-German factors have contributed to the process of cultural barbarism that led to the Third Reich. We can find some pointers in this direction from a reading of Hannah Arendt, who points in particular to the British cultural (and political) tradition: in the second half of the nineteenth century, Galton was extremely successful with his theory of 'hereditary genius' and his thesis that '[a]ristocracy was held to be the natural outcome, not of politics, but of natural selection'; 'the English brand of race-thinking was almost obsessed with inheritance theories and their modern equivalent, eugenics'.[23] The idea of racial superiority led a theorist of imperialism to set the English 'superman' people against the rest of humanity or sub-humanity; and one should not forget that among the defenders of 'race' was not only Gobineau but Disraeli.[24] Moreover, at the start of the twentieth century, a British leftist liberal pointed out that in Britain, colonial expansion went hand in hand in theory and practice with paying tribute to the 'temple of Janus', with the condemnation of the 'ideas of '89', with the 'reaction against humanitarianism [...] now dismissed as sentimentality', and with the spread of the 'unadorned gospel of blood and iron'.[25] No less attention should be paid to the American theorists of the annihilation of the Indians and the 'final solution' of the black question.[26]

As is well known, the real Nuremberg, called upon to judge the crimes of the Third Reich, refused to allow the principle of tu quoque invoked by the accused. And under the circumstances, it is easy to see why. Essentially, it was a kind of revolutionary court instituted at the end of a world revolution (which, in Germany, had achieved victory from the outside). It had the legitimate and unavoidable task of passing sentence on the horrendous crimes to which Hitler's attempt at a global counterrevolution had given rise, extending from the colonisation of Eastern Europe (with the reintroduction of racial slavery in new forms) to the systematic annihilation of the bacillus of revolution, identified in the figure of the Jew. But today, decades later, to reject the principle of tu quoque also for ideological Nuremberg, which people insist on trying to stage, is unacceptable on the ethical plane and misleading at the level

---

23   Arendt 1966, 179 f., 176.
24   Arendt 1966, 180–83.
25   Hobhouse 1904, 28, 59, 61 f.
26   On these theories, cf. Losurdo 1998, 1.

of historiography. It is right to draw attention in the face of the hermeneutics of innocence to the statements in which Nietzsche craved the annihilation
of the 'decadent races' and a final settling of accounts with the Chandala and
the malformed of all sorts. However, before jumping to hasty and one-sided
conclusions, one should ask a preliminary question: do the above statements,
expressions and themes refer exclusively to Nietzsche and Germany or are they
also present in the culture and press of Europe and America in the second half
of the nineteenth century?

In other words, it is necessary to set the philosopher's discourse in its historical (Western and German) context. Only then can one raise the issue of
possible elements of continuity between this context and the subsequent ideology and practice of the Third Reich. Unfortunately, the Nuremberg judgement,
by dismissing the principle of *tu quoque*, continues to exercise a negative influence on philosophical and historical criticism. If one blames Lukács for focusing almost exclusively on 'irrationalistic' German culture, one can also blame
Arendt, who sets out to reconstruct an overall picture of the development of
imperialism, for passing over in almost total silence the social Darwinist currents, eugenic practices and genocidal efforts in the United States in the nineteenth and twentieth centuries.

Lukács in particular managed to see how much English and French (in
the progressive sense) there was in Hegel, but not how much English, French
and American (in the reactionary sense) there was in Nietzsche. The comparative analysis of ideological processes should help to close this gap. It is a
question of setting out from the critique of revolution and the processes of
democratisation and 'massification' it gave rise to: this critique, which accom-
panies the successive upheavals that had their epicentre in France, underwent an extreme radicalisation precisely at the time of Nietzsche's life and
thought.

3   'Untimeliness' and Aristocratic Gesture of Distinction

The comparative perspective is a constant element of this work, and now it
is a question of placing it at the centre of attention: numerous resemblances
will emerge, as well as a political radicalism, a theoretical rigour and psychological subtlety that bestow a special role and importance on the figure of Nietzsche. Yet this approach clashes immediately with the extreme 'untimeliness' or
unfashionability he always claimed for himself. In his eyes, this characteristic
defined the philosopher as such. The true thinker would 'overcome his age, to
become "timeless"', taking on 'the greatest challenge' to avoid being contamin-

ated by what was timely; he was to impose upon himself a 'profound alienation, a profoundly cold and sober attitude towards everything timely, time-bound' (WA, Preface [233]).

On the other hand, we have seen how Nietzsche constantly participated, with trepidation, in historical and political developments in Germany and Europe. Far from retreating into an inner world to avoid contamination by the outside world, he argued on several occasions against those intellectuals incapable of measuring up to reality. It is true there was nothing about him of the ideologue diligently seeking to justify and legitimise the immediate political choices and later turns of the Second Reich and therefore willing to give up his own theoretical independence. Nietzsche was proudly aware of the deep abyss that separated him from the mass of ideologues, and he believed he could explain his attitude by the category of 'untimeliness'.

But is this category really appropriate? Once again, the interpreter cannot merely reproduce the consciousness of the interpreted author. Let us look at Nietzsche's development. He came to philosophy on the wave of his enthusiasm for Schopenhauer. These were the years in which, after the failure of the Revolution of 1848, the German bourgeoisie decisively turned its back on Hegel and threw itself into the arms precisely of Schopenhauer.[27] At the outbreak of the Franco-Prussian War, the young professor of classical philology was among the volunteers; although he lived at the time in Basel, in neutral Switzerland, he was so borne along by national passion that he did not hesitate to abandon his professorial chair. A little later, *The Birth of Tragedy*, in spite of 'look[ing] very untimely', according to the author (EH, *The Birth of Tragedy*, 1 [108]), gave voice to the general enthusiasm that accompanied the founding of the Second Reich. In denouncing the destructive potential of the idea of happiness, it resumed a theme widespread in the culture of the time. Nietzsche himself displayed some uncertainty regarding the claim to 'untimeliness' of *The Birth of Tragedy*, 'this questionable book': '[T]he times in which it was written, and in spite of which it was written, [are] the turbulent period of the Franco-Prussian War of 1870–1.' Is the relationship to the climate of these years merely polemical? In fact, it was 'a book which has proved itself, by which I mean one which at least satisfied "the best of its time"', one steeped in 'premature hopes' in the 'German essence' and the 'erroneous morals applied to the most contemporary things [*auf Gegenwärtigstes*] with which I ruined my first book' (GT, An Attempt at Self-Criticism, 1, 2 and 6 [3, 10]).

---

27   Mehring 1961 ff., Vol. 13, 159.

With the attack on Strauss, 'untimeliness' became a sort of profession of faith to which Nietzsche held firm to the end, as evidenced in particular by *Expeditions of an Untimely Man*, which stands at the heart of *Twilight of the Idols*. But, as we have seen, at the time of the attack on Strauss's *The Old and the New Faith*, the author of the mocked text was much more critical of prevailing orientations than the mocker. The latter was substantially in accord with national-liberal circles, embarrassed or outraged by the declaration of war against the Christian Churches and by the attempt to raise to the level of official ideology in Germany a secular and materialistic worldview that was centred on the idea, dangerous and potentially subversive, of earthly happiness. The fact was the ideologues of the new Reich could tolerate neither political 'nor religious radicalism'. Hence their reaction, as described by Mehring:

> Like furies they rushed at Strauss, the Old Catholics and the Protestants to the fore, and even good old Nietzsche earned his stripes in this witch hunt, with the 'noise of a herd of pigs' that guaranteed the attacked man the sympathies of all decent people. Strauss himself, in an afterword to a new edition of his book, made reference to the Social-Democratic newspapers, which, while rejecting his political positions, were able to make an objective appreciation of his philosophical arguments, unlike the 'cultured' bourgeois press.[28]

In an attempt to rescue it from the suffocating embrace of orthodox circles, a sympathetic reviewer of the first *Unfashionable Observation* felt the need to make clear it was not motivated by *'furor theologicus'*.[29] But even if it was right to distinguish the author from the circles that applauded him, it remained a fact that Nietzsche was far from a voice in the wilderness. Some time earlier, Rudolf Haym, director of *Preussische Jahrbücher*, the semi-official organ of national-liberal culture and therefore of the dominant ideology, had directly attacked Hegel, accusing him of a clumsy attempt to secularise and rationalise religion 'under the rule of philosophy'.[30] The term used here, *Säkularisierung*, suggested Nietzsche, who also engaged in denouncing the 'secularization [*Verweltlichung*]' of culture that finds in Strauss its most repugnant expression and, outside Germany, was also Kierkegaard's polemical target (*supra*, 4 §7).

It is no less difficult to see the two essays dedicated to Schopenhauer and to Wagner as 'unfashionable' or 'untimely'. The musician was near or at the peak

---

28   Mehring 1961 ff., Vol. 13, 122.
29   Hillebrand 1892, 282.
30   Haym 1974, 402.

of his fame. As for the philosopher, recommended to the German nation as 'educator', Nietzsche himself stressed he was becoming the general centre of attention: in 'this feeble age', one would even say that Schopenhauer was served 'like a strange and pungent spice, a kind of metaphysical pepper, as it were': in any case, 'he gradually won renown and fame, and I believe that there are at present already more people who know his name than Hegel's' (SE, 7; I, 406 [236]). Admittedly, there had been a time in which 'the beautiful green crop of Hegelianism is growing in all the fields', but it was now irrevocably past, 'this harvest has been destroyed in a hailstorm' (SE, 8, I, 423 [252]). It was, at least to judge by a note of Nietzsche's from the spring of 1868, a process that had ended long before: 'Hegeliana and its collapse' (KGA, I, 4, 578).

Regarding *The Use and Abuse of History for Life*, the sympathetic reviewer whose acquaintance we have already made declared it a *zeitgemäss* text, timely, i.e., reflecting certain moods of the time. 'Herr Nietzsche speaks indeed in the name of an entire class of Germans and he speaks against an entire class of other Germans.'[31] The second *Unfashionable Observation* also had as its prime target Hegel and 'Hegeliana', although from a higher theoretical point of view. Hegel's bad name, which the essay by Nietzsche dedicated to Schopenhauer later emphasized, had already been noted immediately after the Revolution of 1848 by Haym: 'No one except for someone completely blind or retarded dares to say that this system continues to rule life and science as it ruled them in the past'; even disciples pathetically loyal to the teacher at most 'allow themselves the assertion that Hegel, in spite of everything, has "not been unfruitful" for the development of philosophy'.[32]

When the encounter with Schopenhauer and Wagner lost its magic and the hope vested in Germany's metaphysical mission gave way to disillusion, Nietzsche started to take an interest in certain strands of Enlightenment and positivistic thinking. Not even this change signified a break with the culture of the time. According to Haym's testimony, the failure of the Revolution of 1848 in Germany marked the beginning of the crisis of 'metaphysics'.[33] In the view of the eminent historian of ideas and prominent exponent of national liberalism, the experience had taught one to be 'a little more practical, a little more realistic and historical, and a little less dogmatic'.[34] On the other hand, in this period it was precisely the *Preussische Jahrbücher* that promoted and dissemin-

---

31   Hillebrand 1892, 300.
32   Haym 1974, 3–5.
33   Haym 1930, 134 (letter to Max Duncker of 30 March 1852).
34   Haym 1930, 142 (letter to Friedrich Theodor Vischer of 21 October 1857).

ated the thought of Comte.[35] Positivism was called upon precisely to liquidate revolutionary 'metaphysics', which in 1848 had found a wide and worrying echo also in Germany.

On a more strictly political level, the clear distancing from the politics of Bismarck, which Nietzsche considered as partly responsible for the subversive and plebeian drift, certainly in some respects strongly contradicted the dominant ideology. Yet, even here, the 'untimeliness' category seems unconvincing: the reality of the Second Reich was, in comparison with the hopes that had accompanied its founding, too mediocre; hence the aristocratic reaction sought refuge in the splendour of ancient Greece and even of ancient slavery, from the modern vulgarity that despite all promises and illusions prevailed in Germany (*infra*, 25 § 4).

Thus, a paradox arises. The more Nietzsche insisted on the 'untimeliness' of his radicalising positions, the more his readers highlighted the consonance of his discourse with the spirit of the age. For example, they likened him to Carlyle. Here is the philosopher's response: certain 'scholarly cattle [...] have even read into it the "cult of the hero" that I condemn so bitterly, the invention of that unknowing and involuntary counterfeiter Carlyle' (EH, Why I write such good books, 1 [101]). In fact, the distance between the German philosopher and the British writer was unbridgeable. From the point of view of the former, the latter espoused an exalted 'idealism' and, what is more, in its most odious, i.e., Christian or Christian-inspired form. The lecture series on hero worship ended with an eloquent plea to the public: 'God be with you!' The celebration of Plato ('Nature was to this man, what to the Thinker and Prophet it forever is, preternatural'[36]) was intertwined with that of Luther ('the bravest heart then living in this world', yes, 'the bravest, if also one of the humblest, peaceablest', who indignantly attacked 'Pagan Popeism' and dared 'tell all men that God's-world stood not on semblances but on realities; that Life was a truth, and not a lie!')[37] For Carlyle, the exceptional personality was defined above all by faith, which found its highest expression in Christianity: a religion that had its 'germ' precisely in 'Hero worship'; not for nothing 'the greatest of all Heroes is One – whom we do not name here!'[38]

Nietzsche was right to resist being confounded with a sort of bigot in genial getup. To emphasise the distance by means of a provocative gesture, the author of *Ecce homo* suggested one should 'look more like a Cesare Borgia than

---

35   Simon 1963, 238–63.
36   Carlyle 1934, 245.
37   Carlyle 1934, 364.
38   Carlyle 1934, 249.

a Parsifal'; in any case, Zarathustra had nothing to do with the "'idealistic' type of the higher sort of humanity, half 'saint', half 'genius'" (EH, Why I write such good books, 1 [101]). The judgement on 'England's worst writer', responsible among other things for ruining even Emerson's style through his influence, was severe and pitiless (VIII, 588 [397]). The distancing went much further than merely the aesthetic. In the eyes of Nietzsche, whose immoralism became ever more radical, Carlyle made the mistake of referring to heroes that were the embodiment of the 'highest moral values': in this way, he showed that he too belonged to the category of 'moral fanatics' and had therefore been smitten by the 'sickness' that marked modernity (XII, 358 and 560). Hence his 'yearning for a strong faith', and 'fury at people who are less naïve' (GD, *Expeditions of an Untimely Man*, 12 [198]). Constructed as 'symmetrical, soft-lined, undetermined', the great personality became a sort of saint to whom one had to offer 'praise' and 'incense' (M, 298 [187–8]). So, on closer inspection, hero worship was just a bland substitute for religion. In short, the British writer, this 'fatuous dolt', brought to expression the basic limits of his incurably Christian country (JGB, 252 [143]), and expressed them with great grandiloquence, with a 'garrulousness from an inner pleasure in noise and confusion of feelings' (FW, 97 [93]).

And yet the indignantly rejected approximation was not entirely unsubstantiated. True, the philosopher-philologist was right to mock a hero worship godfathered by a religion of the humble and poor in spirit. Even so, despite their differences, the two authors here compared had in common the aristocratic gesture of setting the great personality against common humanity. And that in the context of a polemic against democratic and levelling tendencies that was so harsh that it led in both cases to the justification or glorification of slavery (*supra*, 12 § 3). Of course, Nietzsche denounced Carlyle's Christian or Christian-inspired hero as an unconscious and unreflected oxymoron: only someone wholly lacking in historical sense and aristocratic instinct could give credence to a religion as plebeian as the Christian one. But the philosopher's way of arguing and his attitude were not synonymous with 'untimeliness' as such. Rather, what was 'untimely' was the ambition of conferring rigour and coherence on themes widespread in the culture of the time: if these themes were thought through in all their radicality and consistency, they ended up in hopeless conflict with the dominant ideology and religion that, despite everything, continued to be Christianity.

On the other hand, for Nietzsche, the celebration of 'untimeliness' did not always have an unequivocal meaning: the philosopher 'has to be the bad conscience of his age, – and that is why he needs to know it best' (WA, Preface [233]). This was certainly a polemical relationship that aimed to apply 'a vivisecting knife directly to the chest of the virtues of the age' (JGB, 212 [106]). Yet the relationship was unavoidable: 'Other people might be able to get along without Wagner: but a philosopher has no choice in the matter' (WA, Preface [233]): the musician and the ideologue had to be overcome and rejected if one were to achieve 'untimeliness'. So this was an 'untimeliness' that could not skip over the moment of mediation and that therefore consisted of rejecting certain tendencies of the time and giving expression to others.

Eventually, it was Nietzsche himself that, in a sense, ended up confirming the historicising interpretation of his thought that he had so indignantly rejected. In an autobiographical sketch from his youth, he described the Revolution of 1848 and the repugnance it aroused as the decisive and 'fateful' moment in his formation (A, 91). Critical interpreters of the philosopher contemporary with him proposed a similar contextualisation and periodisation. According to Duboc, 'the reactionary high tide of the fifties', which flowed from the failure of the revolution, swelled further with the 'ethical materialism' of the late nineteenth century: it 'cannot be doubted' that this was the context in which to place 'Nietzsche's "morality" of the overman'.[39] Here was an author with 'innumerable readers belonging to the upper classes of society'.[40] In similar terms Mehring, writing a few years before Nietzsche's death, put him, along with Schopenhauer and Hartmann, in the group of 'three fashionable philosophers that have obsessed the German bourgeoisie in the second half of this century'.[41] One should immediately point out Nietzsche's admirers also questioned his 'untimeliness': 'His ideal belongs to his time, but he was allowed to express it in all its purity.'[42]

These various interpretations, which for one reason or another emphasised the consonance of the theorist's 'untimeliness' with his age, might have been inaccurate or misleading. But, from the philosopher's point of view, they all had the disadvantage of undermining the claim of untimeliness as a gesture of aristocratic distinction. Ultimately, this was Overbeck's view. The friendly relationship and affection did not blind him, when he wrote as follows about Nietzsche:

Nietzsche was far from as reclusive as he seemed; he affected reclusiveness, rather than that he was actually reclusive or wanted to be reclusive. Neither from a historical angle nor retrospectively are any of his thoughts

39   Duboc 1896, 133, 117.
40   Duboc 1896, 124.
41   Mehring 1961 ff., Vol. 13, 167.
42   Tille 1895, 218.

essentially new and original. Similarly, the way in which he appropriates the common heritage of thoughts of the present time has nothing that is peculiar to him, when measured by these loans.[43]

This judgement was completely unacceptable, insofar as it failed to understand the philosopher's greatness and originality, his subtlety and psychological depth as well as his radicalism, at the level of historical reconstruction and theoretical consistency. But it has the merit of refuting a tenacious myth.

4   The 'Great Economy of the Whole' and the Costs of Compassion

Schopenhauer had already professed his 'untimeliness'. But let us take a look at *The World as Will and Representation*. The denouncing of the sexual instinct as an expression of an irrepressible will to live, the celebration of asceticism (and, in this context, even the ecclesiastical celibacy of the Catholic world), all that fell at a time in which Malthus identified sexual incontinence of the poor classes and overpopulation as the true cause of mass misery. While the British author refuted the idea of progress with the help of political economy and demography, the German philosopher liquidated it by an articulated metaphysical construction in which overpopulation and political economy played a subordinate role.

The concern at the heart of Malthus's work was clearly also present in Nietzsche (*supra*, 19 §3). Here too a consideration already raised about Schopenhauer proves true, that a theme of political economy was transformed and developed into a metaphysical theme in the transition from British to German culture. The overpopulation of which Malthus spoke now became the totality of the 'far too many [*Viel-zu-Vielen*]' or 'superfluous [*überflüssigen*]' against which Zarathustra never tired of railing (Za, I, On the New Idol, On Child and Marriage, On Free Death). The 'surplus [*Überschuss*] of failures [*Missrathenen*] and degenerates [*Entartend*], of the diseased and infirm, of those that necessarily suffer', manifested itself 'among humans as with every other type of animal' (JGB, 62 [55]). A 'law' of political economy was thus transformed into a general 'law' of the living world. This was a case of 'dross and waste materials [*Auswurf-und Verfall-Stoffe*]' (XIII, 87). Bentham too spoke of the population as 'dross': after an appropriate course of treatment in the workhouses, it could be turned

---

43   Overbeck 1906, 219.

into cash. The constant point of reference here was capitalist production.[44] For Nietzsche, the capitalist factory became a sort of factory of life; merging with biology, political economy was transformed into the 'economy of the preservation of the species' (FW, 1 [27]). And this economy could require that the malformed or dross was treated far more drastically than Bentham envisaged.

For the theorist of aristocratic radicalism, it was inevitable that the 'chariot' of culture continued to trample over and sacrifice countless individual lives. Burke's metaphor was not so very different: the 'great wheel of circulation' and the 'distribution' of riches meant hard work and sacrifice for many 'unhappy people'. If, for the German philosopher-philologist, the 'slaves' chained to the victors' chariot were to be sacrificed, for the British politician it was those that 'worked from dawn to dark in the innumerable servile, degrading, unseemly, unmanly, and often most unwholesome and pestiferous occupations, to which by the social economy so many wretches are inevitably doomed'.[45] Linguet expressed himself in similar terms when he said that the privations and sufferings of the slaves were as 'the dust raised by a carriage on a sandy path'.[46] It was always the sweat and blood of the sacrificial victims of culture that lubricated the workings of the 'chariot', 'wheel', 'carriage', or 'great machine' of which Malthus spoke – or of the 'great machine of society', which according to Jefferson was not to be put at risk by reckless public statements against the institution of slavery.[47] We are dealing with a metaphor that also appeared, implicitly, in Sieyès, according to whom 'the working classes of the advanced societies [...] are crushed under the weight of the needs of the whole society'.[48] Finally, the image of the 'chariot' and the 'triumphal march' already seen in Nietzsche also made an appearance in the writings of a leading figure in the imperial administration of British India, writing under the pseudonym of A. Carthill. He said of the fate of the colonial peoples: 'One must always feel sorry for those persons crushed by the triumphal car of progress.'[49]

When Burke stressed the inevitability of the sacrifice of countless servants and individuals, he referred not only to 'the great wheel of circulation' and 'distribution' but also to the 'economy of society'. Political economy had meanwhile penetrated the metaphors used to clarify and legitimise the capitalist

---

44   Bentham 1838–43, Vol. 8, 398 and Himmelfarb 1985, 80.
45   Burke 1826, Vol. 5, 291f.
46   Linguet 1984, 524 (Book 5, 19).
47   Malthus 1986, 75; on Jefferson cf. Jordan 1977, 435.
48   Sieyès 1985c, 73.
49   In Arendt 1966, 143, fn. On the other hand, Marx criticised bourgeois society by referring to the chariot of the Indian god Vishnu, by which believers allowed themselves to be crushed, as the 'Juggernaut of capital' (Marx and Engels 1975 ff., 35, 285).

system. 'The general bank and capital of nations and of the centuries' were, according to the British statesman, to be shielded against criticism and hasty and wasteful innovations.[50] The laws of nature were also laws of economics; and, on the other side of the Atlantic, Jefferson spoke of the 'economy of nature'.[51] Even more interesting in this context was Malthus's intervention. To demonstrate the thesis that poor individuals should complain about the improvidence of their parents rather than the alleged injustice of the social order, he cited both the 'laws of nature' and those of political economy, as well as the 'ethical world order'.[52]

Political economy, nature and morality tended to blend into one. One could say that this process came to an end with Nietzsche. The direct or indirect reference to political economy pervaded his entire thinking. We have seen how *Human, All Too Human* mocked the 'economy of goodness' of the 'rashest utopians', who would banish the negative from society and reality (*supra*, 8 §1). To this false 'economy', based on alleged moral sentiments, he opposed the true 'economy', which disdained to suppress or falsify reality. It was the 'entire economy of the world [*Gesammt-Haushalt der Welt*]' (XI, 699), the 'higher economy of culture' (XIII, 641), 'the overall economy of humankind' (JGB, 62 [56]), the 'great economy of the whole [*grosse Ökonomie des Ganzen*]' (EH, Why I am a destiny, 4 [146]).

In order to be able to judge the various worldviews and moral philosophies, it was necessary to bear this economy constantly in mind, for it embraced every aspect of reality:

> This is my endeavour, to have claimed for the first time a counter-reckoning! – to have asked: what unspeakable misery, what deterioration human beings have undergone, because altruism has been raised to an ideal, because selfishness was called evil and experienced as evil.
>
> IX, 571

What is more: 'To estimate [*abschätzen*] the value of any given type of person [*was ein Mensch Typus werth ist*] you need to work out how much it costs [*den Preis nachrechnen*] to maintain him' (EH, Why I am a destiny, 4 [146]). One was not to proceed abstractly but instead subject to rigorous 'evaluation [*Abschätzung*]' the 'ideals hitherto in force' (XII, 459). 'The good man' came out

---

50   Burke 1826, Vol. 5, 168.
51   Jefferson 1955, 53.
52   Malthus 1826, 345.

very badly from this 'counter-reckoning'. On balance, compassion played a cata-strophic role, for it prevented or hindered the necessary and beneficial sacrifice of those whose lives had turned out badly. The kind of human being celebrated by Christian morality and traditional morality was 'the most harmful [*schäd-lichst*] type of person because they exist at the expense of [*auf Kosten*] the truth as much as they exist at the expense of [*auf Kosten*] the future' (EH, Why I am a destiny, 4 [146–7]). For the economy of life and society, he was a debit item that it was absolutely necessary to get rid of: 'And whatever harm [*Schaden*] the evil may do, the harm of the good is the most harmful harm [*der Schaden der Guten ist schändlichste Schaden*]' (Za, III, On Old and New Tablets, 26 [171]). The advantage and the 'depth of the tragic artist' lay in the fact that he 'affirms the economy on a large scale [*Ökonomie im Grossen*], which justifies that which is terrible, evil, questionable and not only ... justifies' (XII, 557).

Regarding this overall economy of the real, it was necessary to be able to evaluate not only the different religions but also their different uses: '[T]here is a high and horrible price to pay when religions do not serve as means for breeding and education in the hands of a philosopher' (JGB, 62 [55]). Evid-ently, the reference was constantly to political economy. This also played a role in the condemnation of the parliamentary system and democratic society as 'extremely costly [*kostspielig*]' (*supra*, 10 §3). The new science that accompan-ied the development of the bourgeois world also played a part in the analysis of interiority: Nietzsche intended to investigate 'the entire economy of my soul and the balance' (FW, 338 [191]).

The scope of the new science was much wider than that of the old. Beyond the production and distribution of wealth, it also embraced morality, reality and life as such: 'I am attempting an economic [*ökonomisch*] justification of virtue' (XII, 459). This virtue was not to be understood in the moral sense, for as we know, it was the obvious and inevitable antithesis of the 'great economy of the whole'.

At least since 1789, the role of propertyless intellectuals has been at the centre of political and cultural debate. Nietzsche continued to intervene in this debate when he defined himself as '*grandseigneur* of the spirit', just like Voltaire (EH, *Human, All Too Human*, 1 [116]). Quite different was the case with Wagner: 'the "regal generosity"' generally attributed to him and also to Victor Hugo was revealed to be an illusion or cosmetic. Only '[a]s long as people are childish (and Wagnerian as well) will they even think of Wagner as rich, as the epitome of extravagance, as a big landowner [*Grossgrundbesitzer*] in the realm of tones'. Very soon, the admirers of the German musician and the French novelist were satisfied with much less. They appreciated them 'for the opposite reason, see-ing them as masters and models of economy [*Ökonomie*], as shrewd hosts', for '[n]obody comes close to them in officiating over a princely table at modest expense' (WA, 8 [248]). In Wagner, in particular, one could observe 'a technical economy [*technische Ökonomik*] that had no reason to be subtle' (WA, 9 [249]). In conclusion, the noble spirit, merely fraudulent in Wagner and Hugo, was a reality in Nietzsche.

5   Sociology and Psychopathology of the Intellectual Layers

As in the tradition that preceded him, in Nietzsche too the condemnation of the revolution was at the same time a denunciation of the fateful role played by propertyless intellectuals, of the 'scholars' infected by 'political delusions' (WB, 4, I, 450 [277]) and 'political fever' (WB, 3, I, 444 [271]). Their active participation in the growing vulgarisation and runaway massification of the modern world was not unrelated to their social origin. To the mediocre social position of the intellectuals corresponded the mediocrity of their horizon: 'It follows from the laws that govern rank-ordering [*Rangordnung*] that scholars, insofar as they belong to the intellectual middle class [*geistiger Mittelstand*], are not even allowed to catch sight of the truly great problems and question marks; moreover, their courage and eyes simply don't reach that far' (FW, 373 [238]).

The fact was that propertyless intellectuals were petty bourgeois, and ideologically and above all socially bordered on the popular masses (FW, 349 [207–8]). This explained the diffusion of the plebeian view of history, which put the masses rather than great personalities at the centre of attention: 'The German scholars, who invented the historical sense – the French are training in it now – make clear to everyone that they do not come from a dominant caste' (XI, 588).

So far, the attitude was not unlike that of French or English authors in their critique of the French Revolution. According to this view, propertyless intellectuals played a fateful role in the revolution, because they were prone simultaneously to abstraction and envy, and therefore, as Constant stressed, ready to elaborate ruinous 'chimerical theories'. In a similar vein, Burke denounced the '*gueux plumées*' and Maistre those he defined as the 'Pugachevs of the university', a reference to the protagonist of a huge peasant revolt in Russia a few decades earlier.[53] With the same contempt and betraying the same sociopolitical preoccupation, Schopenhauer spoke of the 'hungry literati'[54] and

---

53   Cf. Losurdo 1996, 2, §11.
54   Schopenhauer 1976–82c, Vol. 4, 213.

Nietzsche of the 'educated proletariat' (GM III, 26 [116]). If Burke denounced the 'swinish multitude',[55] Nietzsche described plebeian intellectuals as 'educated swine' (XII, 320). Because of their *ressentiment* against the upper classes and against wealth and power as such, and because of their dissatisfaction with their current conditions and their dreams of redeeming and regenerating themselves and society as a whole, propertyless intellectuals and those of modest social backgrounds tended to ally with the mob in its attack on property and the existing social order: they were in any case prominent protagonists of subversion at the level of ideas, even more so than at that of politics.

Understandably, Nietzsche saw the new figure of the plebeian intellectual embodied above all in Rousseau, plebeian on account both of his social origin and his ideological positions and particularly treasured by the Jacobins. In his speech on inequality, Voltaire had already commented: 'This is the philosophy of a beggar [*gueux*] that wants the rich to be robbed by the poor.'[56] One can see why Rousseau became for many the first and best of the *gueux plumées*. Constant accused him of having inspired with his 'tirades against wealth and even against property' the most brutal phase of the French Revolution, namely the social unrest of the disinherited masses and the Jacobin policy of intervention in the economy and the private sphere.[57] Similarly, Flaubert saw in the author of *The Social Contract* 'the progenitor of envious and tyrannical democracy'.[58] These themes also found support in Germany, so a contemporary and opponent of Hegel, Gustav Hugo, ranked Rousseau among the 'opponents of private property'.[59]

But it was above all Taine that took us back into the immediate vicinity of Nietzsche, whose school he claimed to have followed (*infra*, 28 §2). While the French historian denounced Rousseau on account of the 'rancour [*rancune*] of the poor plebeian' that oozed from his writings,[60] Nietzsche called him the 'person of rancour [*Ranküne-Mensch*]', who sought 'in the ruling classes the cause of his being miserable [*Miserabilität*]' (XII, 421), or a person of '*ressentiment*' (GD, *Expeditions of an Untimely Man*, 3 [193]). He was 'idealist and *canaille* rolled into one'. Up to now, we had been looking at a familiar discourse linking the mediocrity or social origin of an intellectual or a layer of intellec-

---

55   Burke 1826, Vol. 5, 154.
56   In Havens 1933, 15.
57   In Constant 1957, 1050 fn. and 1051.
58   Flaubert 1912, 343 (letter to Jules Michelet of 13 November 1867).
59   Hugo 1819, 28; Hugo adds in Diderot.
60   Taine 1899, Vol. 2, 40.

tuals with the exalted speeches about regeneration; in that sense, Rousseau was the 'first modern human being', the starting point of a cycle of agitations and upheavals still far from over (GD, *Expeditions of an Untimely Man*, 48 [221]).

Like the rest of the culture and journalism engaged in a critique of the French Revolution, in Nietzsche too the sociological analysis of the intellectual layers gave way, at a certain point, to psychopathological diagnosis. After denouncing in Rousseau the 'rancour of the poor plebeian', Taine went on to warn against the 'unique clinical case' represented by the Genevan philosopher.[61] The description, in a France 'drunk on the bad *eau de vie* of the *Social Contract*', of the contagion to which France was prey, not unlike the 'strange sickness one usually encounters in the poor quarters'[62] – here, at least, psychopathology was still linked to sociology – was transformed at a certain point into a condemnation of the 'alteration of the mental balance' of the Jacobins,[63] wherewith any remaining element of social analysis vanished. Similar considerations can apply to Burke, Constant or Tocqueville.[64]

The consonance between Nietzsche and the culture of his time is clear. But no less obvious and equally important are the new elements. After pointing out that 'the duality of idealist and *canaille*' could also be seen in the French Revolution, the aphorism from *Twilight of the Idols* continues: 'I do not really care about the bloody farce played out in this Revolution, its "immorality": what I hate is its Rousseauian morality.' Rousseau, 'this deformity of a person', 'needed moral "dignity" in order to stand the sight of himself'. And, in the name of morality, the revolution propagated the 'doctrine of equality', which 'seems as if justice itself is preaching here, while in fact it is the end of justice', since it claimed to even out realities actually separated by an abyss (GD, *Expeditions of an Untimely Man*, 48 [221–2]). Not only the claim to social equality, made especially by liberal authors, but also the claim to equality as such, and even the reference to an allegedly universal morality, itself pervaded by an egalitarian logic, was an expression both of plebeian rancour and exalted revolutionary utopianism.

So, the condemnation of the subversive intellectual could not stop halfway. It was a figure that had begun to emerge long before Rousseau and the French Revolution. One need think only of the Reformation. It 'also shares the blame

---

61   Taine 1899, Vol. 2, 30.
62   Taine 1899, Vol. 4, 261 f.
63   Taine 1899, Vol. 5, 21 ff.
64   Losurdo 1996, 2, §1.

for the degeneration of the modern scholar, for his lack of reverence, shame, and depth, for the whole naïve guilelessness and conventionality in matters of knowledge – in short for that plebeianism of the spirit that is peculiar to the last two centuries' (FW, 358 [223]).

While demanding a sort of universal priesthood, the Reformation called into question the distinction between initiated and uninitiated with regard to the interpretation of the sacred text, and saw the emergence of a lower clergy that polemicised at every level against the hierarchy. Take, for example, the pastors of the 'puritan revolution'. Nietzsche's insertion of the Reformation in the long cycle of subversion gave rise to a scandal in Protestant Germany, but it was not in itself a particularly new thesis: it could already be found, in more schematic and superficial forms, in Catholic circles of the Restoration. But Nietzsche did not stop here. It was not with Luther that the revolutionary cycle began but with Christianity, identified as the original source of the Jacobin Terror. On the other hand, the description of Paul of Tarsus seemed to lead back to Rousseau: he too showed signs of insanity or, more accurately, 'hallucination', as well as a huge rancour against those who had turned out well (*die Wohlgeratenen*) and the upper classes (AC, 42 [39]).

If we go even further back than Christianity and the 'Christian agitators', as Nietzsche calld the 'Fathers of the Church', we meet with the 'priestly agitators', with their disastrously 'abstract' morality (*supra*, 15 §2). Just as for the cycle of revolution, so too for the reconstruction of the history of the figure of the subversive intellectual one had to start out from post-exilic Judaism. Not just the religious tradition but also the intellectual tradition of the West was subjected to radical and ruthless interpretation. The abstractness, the pathology the liberal and reactionary traditions denounced in the revolutionary intellectuals, now became the pathology of a good number of philosophers.

> These old philosophers were heartless: philosophizing was always a kind of vampirism. When considering such figures, including even Spinoza, don't you feel something deeply enigmatic and strange? [...] In sum: all philosophical idealism until now was something like an illness.
>
> FW, 372 [237]

Looking back over the history of philosophy, one could and should proceed as far as Greek antiquity, and Plato. The abstractness that played such a fateful role in the revolutionary cycle was already manifest in him: it was 'Plato's invention of pure spirit and the Good in itself' (JGB, Preface [4]). Probably the Greek philosopher, like Spinoza, also harked back to Jewish roots, to the Jewish priests, this first and fateful figure of the abstract and subversive intellectual. With the terrible abstractness of which they displayed evidence, philosophers stood in a line of continuity with the figure of the priest. The moralists 'undermine the naturalism of morality' (*supra*, 10 § 5), but the basic fault of 'philosophers' was precisely to pose as 'moralists' (XIII, 403).

But if one so radically prolonged the cycle of subversion, the condemnation of the intellectual's fateful role extends also to the ideologues of the existing order and to this order itself. How could one explain the mean calculating thought that marked modernity?

> [T]he sons of all types of clerks and office workers [*Büreauschreibern*], whose main task was always to organize various different kinds of material, to compartmentalize and in general to schematize, when they become scholars, show a tendency to consider a problem practically solved when they have merely schematized it. [...] The talent for classifications, for tables of categories, reveals something: one pays the price for being the child of one's parents.
>
> FW, 348 [207]

One could similarly explain the success of a theory that purported to interpret reality and history on the basis of the 'struggle for existence', i.e., starting from a category that referred clearly to the problems and distress of the poorest layers of the population. If one thought about the 'origin of most naturalists', everything became clear:

> [T]hey belong to 'the people', their ancestors were poor and lowly folks who knew all too intimately the difficulty of scraping by. English Darwinism exudes something like the stuffy air of English overpopulation, like the small people's smell of indigence and overcrowding.
>
> FW, 349 [208]

Naturally, they were to strive to transcend their miserable 'human corner', in which case they would realise that 'in nature, it is not distress which rules, but rather abundance, squandering – even to the point of absurdity', and that 'the struggle for survival is only an exception'. But they were not able to overcome the limitations of their social background and reach the doctrine of *The Will to Power* (FW, 349 [208]).

More generally, there was a link between the social origin of intellectuals, who were mostly not of aristocratic descent, and the blind faith in rational and logical argumentation that knew no difference of caste and class and was therefore inherently democratic (FW, 348 [206–7]). Nietzsche seemed to want to reconstruct for intellectuals the 'family tree' of which Schopenhauer spoke in regard to criminals and rebels.[65] '[I]n a scientific treatise' one could almost always find

> the scholar's 'prehistory', his family, especially its occupations and crafts. Where the feeling, 'This is now proven; I am done with it', is expressed, it is usually the ancestor in the blood and instincts of the scholar who from his standpoint approves of 'the finished job' – faith in a proof is only the symptom of what in a hard-working family for ages has been considered 'good work'.
>
> FW, 348 [206–7]

From that one could conclude that, by intervening in the debate on the role of intellectuals raging since at least 1789, Nietzsche was taking up themes widely developed in the culture of the time but was clearly distinguished by his efforts to reconstruct the long, long history that lay behind the figure of the subversive intellectual. As with Burke, Constant and many other representatives of the liberal tradition, here too the absolute primacy of the propertied intellectual was maintained. However, the economic and sociological category now tended to be laden with additional meanings from the more properly cultural and moral sphere. On the opposite side, the plebeian intellectuals, full of *ressentiment*, the beggars of the pen and the academic Pugachevs of whom Burke and Maistre spoke, defined as Chandala, i.e., identified with a category that referred to extra-European countries and cultures. World history and culture were embraced in a unified vision, and this totality was inserted into an all-encompassing 'economy' of reality.

6   Revolution as Sickness, Degeneration and *décadence*

Like its promoters and protagonists, the revolution haunting Europe was a sickness. This was also the thesis of Comte, who invited people to step up against this 'chronic sickness', this 'insidious unrest', these 'deceptive hopes'.[66] Along with his diagnosis of the sickness, he also revealed a concern, like Nietzsche, that it might spread among the 'proletarians', especially given the state of 'continual excitement systematically directed towards passions related to their

---

65   Schopenhauer 1976–82b, 767, 666.
66   Comte 1985, 22, 94, 97.

social condition'.[67] The sickness that affected certain intellectuals engaged in 'sterile metaphysical agitation' that tended to take up 'all the aberrations that arise daily from our mental anarchy' might therefore – thanks in part to the ill-omened role of the 'newspapers' – turn into a 'metaphysical contagion'.[68]

In the lives of individuals and of peoples, the sickness in question consisted of a fixation on or a regression to a lower stage located in the 'mental, individual or collective development between childhood and manhood'.[69] This was also Nietzsche's view in his 'enlightenment' and 'positivistic' period: '[J]ust as even today people draw conclusions while dreaming, so for many millennia, humanity drew conclusions *while awake*' and, '[a]ccording to the tales of travellers, primitive people still behave the same today'. Yes, 'while we are dreaming, this primeval part of humanity continues to exercise itself in us, for it is the foundation upon which a higher reason is developed and is still developing in every human being: dreams take us back to the distant circumstances of human culture and give us the means for understanding them better' (MA, 13 [24]).

Le Bon argued similarly. According to him, revolution represented the 'triumph' of 'atavistic instincts', 'instincts of primitive barbarism', 'instincts of the ancestral wild', or the 'natural instincts transmitted to man from his primitive animality'.[70] Taine also argued in the same way, at least in the interpretation of the crowd psychologist Le Bon, who credited the French historian with having finally clarified the meaning and course of the revolution, starting from its regression to a 'wild primitive stage'.[71] So it was clear that the key to understanding revolutions was not sociology or political economy, and not even history.

Precisely because revolutions were not unleashed by objective contradictions, psychology or psychopathology were called upon to explain them. According to Le Bon, big historical crises very often confronted us with 'conflicts of psychological forces' that 'must be studied with methods derived from psychology'.[72] And here is Nietzsche: '[P]sychology is again the path to the fundamental problems'; it must 'again be recognized as queen of the sciences, and that the rest of the sciences exist to serve and prepare for it' (JGB, 23 [24]). According to Le Bon, Taine had the merit of 'extinguishing' the 'old prestige' of the traditional historiography of the French Revolution.[73] But Nietzsche too

---

67   Comte 1985, 90.
68   Comte 1985, 89, 98.
69   Comte 1985, 22.
70   Le Bon 1925, 56 f., 63.
71   Le Bon 1925, 113.
72   Le Bon 1925, VII.
73   Le Bon 1925, 112.

credited the French historian with explaining the upheavals in France by the passions and history of the 'modern soul' (*infra*, 28 §2). As for the German philosopher, so too for Le Bon there was no more effective way of liquidating an author than to demonstrate his lack of psychological penetration. Which was more or less what Le Bon does with Rousseau, 'a stranger to all psychology'.[74]

Starting from the assertion that the sickness as diagnosed was incurable, as confirmed by its periodic re-emergence, it was easy to slip from psychology to physiology. The same was true of Nietzsche: 'The means of comfort thought up by beggars and slaves are the thoughts of malnourished, tired or overexcited brains; that is the yardstick by which Christianity and the socialist visionary spirit [*Phantasterei*] should be judged' (IX, 66). But the tendency to give a physiological basis to psychopathological diagnosis was already present in *Human, All Too Human*. '[T]he daimon of Socrates is perhaps an ailment of the ear' (MA, 126 [97–8]), and in any case: 'With complete tranquillity we will leave to physiology and the developmental history of organisms and concepts the question of how our image of the world could differ so much from the disclosed essence of the world', once the irrational metaphysical fears had been vanquished (MA, 10 [21]).

This led us once again back to Comte. Not by accident, after the Revolution of 1848 and in polemical opposition to it, doctors joined the Société Positiviste, driven by a clear conviction that the revolutionary agitation, 'decomposition' and 'social sickness' then raging increasingly required an energetic 'medical intervention [*médication*]', as a challenge that could only be met by a 'regeneration of the medical art'.[75]

Arguing so, these doctors remained true to their teacher, according to whom 'the metaphysical aberrations of the last century' could be overcome once and for all only thanks to the 'fundamental subordination to biology' of 'positive sociology' and the development of 'brain physiology'.[76] And here is Nietzsche:

> We have to consider the people who are cruel nowadays as stages of *earlier cultures* that have remained behind. [...] They are backward human beings whose brains have not been very delicately and manifoldly developed due to some sort of accident in the process of heredity. They show us what we all were. [...] In our brains there must also be furrows and whorls

---

74   Le Bon 1925, 144.
75   In Larizza 1999, 426 f.
76   Comte 1969, 482, 539.

corresponding to that state of mind, just as reminders of our existence as
fishes should be ascertainable in the form of individual human organs.
MA, 43 [50]

In conclusion, we can summarise the resemblances that, despite everything,
linked Nietzsche with Comte and Le Bon. For a whole historical period, apart
from a few isolated and partial exceptions, revolution had been denounced
because of its irreligiosity and atheism. Now this accusation underwent a thoroughgoing reversal: revolution now became synonymous with messianism or
a theological-metaphysical stage. Whatever else, it was a symptom of sickness. Thus Comte, Nietzsche and Le Bon ended up perpetuating a tradition of
thought that saw in the upheavals in Paris the eruption of delirium or madness, of plague or smallpox, in any case of a sickness of the soul or body. It
was against this tradition that Hegel polemicised: the revolutionary crisis could
in no way be equated with 'an anomaly and a transitory morbid paroxysm', as
the theorists of the Restoration claimed; rather, objective contradictions underlay it; these formed 'the principle of all self-movement, which consists only in
an exhibition of it'.[77] If, in the historiography of the Restoration, the revolutionary 'sickness' was largely a metaphor, in the second half of the nineteenth
century, following developments in psychology, psychiatry, criminal anthropology and physiology, the metaphor gradually assumed the form of a 'scientific'
diagnosis.

Against this historical background we can better understand Nietzsche's
development. 'The barbaric slave class' posed a terrible threat to culture in
the years of *The Birth of Tragedy*, and then turned into reborn savages in the
'Enlightenment' period, to finally become the malformed and those whose lives
had turned out badly. Leading this mass inclined to revolt were the innerly
sick intellectuals. If continuity was expressed by means of the denunciation
of the revolutionary sickness, what changed was the diagnosis of this sickness
and the nature of the antidote. In the first and second phase, the so-called
'metaphysical' period, or rather the period the 'enlightened' Nietzsche called
'metaphysical', the revolutionary sickness was synonymous with the hypertrophy of reason and historical consciousness, so the antidote was represented by instinct, instinctive wisdom and super-historical myth. In the period
of 'Enlightenment', the revolutionary sickness was above all the *Schwärmerei*
in which the religious and political *Phantasten* or 'metaphysical and artistic'
people engaged, people that had not yet achieved the 'manliness' reached by

---

77   Hegel 1969–79, Vol. 6, 75 f.

the rest of humanity (MA, 3 [17]); they showed themselves to be infected by the primitivism typical of those left back in the 'distant circumstances of human culture' and at the level of 'primitive people' (MA, 13 [24]). Against all this, enlightenment and science had to be set. In the final phase, the revolutionaries were represented as the malformed and those whose lives had turned out badly; their ideology and their behaviour were explained by means not only of psychopathology but also of a physiological component, which sometimes seemed to be inherited (Nietzsche now spoke, not by accident, not only of delirium and hallucination but also of epilepsy).

So, the antidote was not to be sought in the liquidation of a nihilistic ideology; rather, measures were to be taken that provide for eugenic prophylaxis or even more drastic remedies. As well as Galton, the philosopher cited other prominent European personalities in the fields of medicine and eugenics, including Claude Bernard and Charles Féré (XIII, 250, 456 and *passim*); the latter played a leading role in the campaign to denounce and combat by all means, even the most brutal, the plague of 'degeneration'.[78] Nietzsche copied long passages from both Galton and Féré, so that his text, especially in the 'final biennium' of his conscious life, sometimes looks like a sort of 'palimpsest':[79] as soon as the first writing has been scraped off, the denunciations of 'degeneration' that deeply pervade European and western culture at the end of the nineteenth century come into view.

At each stage in Nietzsche's development, the revolutionary prophet had a distorted relationship to reality, and in his various configurations he presented himself in the first two phases as the 'fanatic of logic and the dialectic [Socrates]', later, in the 'Enlightenment' period, as a visionary, and finally as the nihilist unable to find his way in reality and life. The difference between the final period and the period of 'Enlightenment' lay above all in the recognition that a science was necessary that had nothing to do with that promoted by Comte, characterised by a progressive and humanitarian pathos. At best, Nietzsche looked to a science of the sort cherished by social Darwinism, though with one significant difference: now, he clearly stated that the evolution then happening would tend to result in the triumph of the malformed.

---

78   Pick 1989, 31 f.

79   Cf. Lampl 1986 (on Féré) and Haase 1989 (on Galton).

7   From the Innocence of Institutions to the 'Innocence of Becoming'

Revolutionary intellectuals and revolutionaries as such were inflicted by madness or an even worse sickness mainly because, in fleeing in horror from reality
and their dreams of social regeneration, they invented non-existent guilts and
responsibilities. For Malthus, it was pointless to blame 'human institutions' for
a poverty that was the 'necessary and inevitable result of the laws of nature'.[80]
Likewise Burke, for whom 'the laws of trade' revealed by political economy were
'laws of nature and consequently laws of God'.[81] In presenting the British Whig
to the German public, Gentz also stressed that the 'welfare of the peoples' was
not actually tied to given political institutions, to the 'form of government' and
to 'the state constitution'.[82] After the outbreak of the February Revolution, Tocqueville thought it had been infected by socialism, for in it were strongly represented the 'economic and political theories' that gave rise to the belief 'that
human misery is a product of laws and not of providence, and poverty could be
eradicated by changing the social order'.[83] Bagehot praised those classes that,
although unable to 'lead a life worthy of a human', did not allow themselves
to get caught up in the agitation and do not 'blame their misery on politics'.[84]
Unfortunately, according to Spencer, little by little, also on the other side of
the English Channel, the superstition was gradually spreading that entrusted
hope for change to 'effective institutions' and lost sight of the decisive role of
the individual.[85] While the protest of the masses that previously stood on the
margins of history and politics swelled, the culture of the period was keen to
emphasise the innocence of the social order. As the young Marx observed, the
state sought the causes of mass misery 'partly in nature, which is independent
of man, partly in private life, which is independent of the administration, and
partly in accidental circumstances, which depend on no one'.[86]
    In Germany, Schopenhauer thundered against the 'demagogues' that
blamed on 'governments, laws and public institutions' the 'misery inseparable
from human existence as such'.[87] This theme was also present in Nietzsche:
those that spoke of 'profound injustice' in the social order 'imagine *responsibil-*

---

80   Malthus 1986, 70.
81   Burke 1826, Vol. 7, 404; cf. Marx's polemic in Marx and Engels 1955 ff., 23, 788, fn.
82   Gentz 1836–8, Vol. 1, 9.
83   Tocqueville 1951 ff., Vol. 12, 92 ff., 84.
84   Bagehot 1974b, 380.
85   Spencer 1981, 69.
86   Marx and Engels 1975 ff., 1, 345.
87   Schopenhauer 1976–82c, Vol. v, 306; this theme also crops up in private conversations.

ities and forms *of will* that do not in any way exist'. No, 'one should not speak of an *injustice* in cases where there are no *prior conditions* for justice and injustice' (XIII, 73–4).

So far, there were no major differences from the liberal tradition. Even today, Hayek tirelessly repeats that it is absurd to speak of 'social' justice or injustice in the face of a state of affairs not the result of someone's 'conscious will'; for this state of affairs has not been 'deliberately brought about by men can possess neither intelligence nor virtue, nor justice, nor any other attribute of human values'.[88] The call for 'social justice' is in reality fed by 'envy' and 'rapacious instincts'.[89] Or, to quote Mises, it is resentment of the condition of those that have been most successful. It is precisely those whose lives have turned out badly that want to call the existing order into question in the name of vague and hypocritical ideals of justice: 'They sublimate their hatred into a philosophy, the philosophy of anti-capitalism, in order not to hear the voice within, telling them that personal failure can be attributed solely to their own fault.'[90]

Even the language recalls Nietzsche, to whom the author of a weighty monograph on the nefarious role of 'envy' or of *ressentiment* in society and in history even refers explicitly. The sociologist of whom I speak quotes at length, approvingly and with obvious satisfaction, the terrible attack in the *Genealogy of Morals* on those that display '*ressentiment*'.[91] They are 'worm-eaten physiological casualties', a 'whole, vibrating realm of subterranean revenge, inexhaustible and insatiable in its eruptions against the happy', only satisfied when they succeed 'in shoving their own misery, in fact all misery, on to the conscience of the happy: so that the latter eventually start to be ashamed of their happiness and perhaps say to one another: "It's a disgrace to be happy! There is too much misery!"' (GM III, 14 [91]).

Nor does the agreement with Nietzsche end here. Hayek regards Christianity with deep suspicion: 'A large section of the clergy of all Christian denominations' has borrowed from socialism the desire for 'social justice', so this ruinous slogan has become 'the distinguishing attribute of the good man, and the recognized sign of the possession of a moral conscience'. Unfortunately, '[t]here can be no doubt that moral and religious beliefs can destroy a civilization'. 'Sometimes saintly figures whose unselfishness is beyond question may become grave dangers to the values which the same people regard as unshakable.'[92] Again, it is

---

88   Hayek 1982, Vol. 2, 70 and Vol. 3, 136.
89   Hayek 1982, Vol. 2, 98.
90   Mises, 1956, 15.
91   Schoeck 1980, 207 f.
92   Hayek 1982, Vol. 2, 66 f.

as if we are hearing Nietzsche. The biggest significant difference is that Hayek lacks the great philosopher's courage and intellectual honesty. Not daring to openly proclaim his disgust for Christianity, he merely criticises the 'Christian Churches' of our time, contaminated by socialism, for replacing a promise of 'temporal' for 'divine justice'.[93] But, here too, the argument points to Nietzsche, who at least attributed to the Christian Church of his time the merit of seeking to divert proletarian *ressentiment* in order to render it politically and socially harmless. Those that suffer were persuaded to consider themselves guilty of and responsible for the misery they encounter (*supra*, 14 §5). The contemporary sociologist quoted above referred specifically to this passage from the *Genealogy of Morals* when he argued that the proper ordering of society presupposed one essential condition: if 'those who believe themselves to be disadvantaged' really want to find someone to blame, they should blame themselves.[94]

The theme of the innocence of institutions was already widely present in the liberal tradition, but Nietzsche subjected it to a further radicalisation. This happened not just in the sense that the polemic against those that wanted to bring an allegedly social issue into play became more violent: they wanted 'to get rid of bad weather – maybe out of pity for poor people' (EH, Why I am a destiny, 4 [146]). Even more important was the extension of the polemic. Not only the preachers of equality but also the advocates of peace invented non-existent responsibilities: since both groups were unable to find their way in reality, they reacted to this maladjustment by imagining those politically and morally blameworthy. On the other hand, they wanted to delete the negative from reality, in order to pursue the ideal of prosperity and comfort for all and forever, an approach not only unavailing but philistine.

And so, the target of the polemic widened even further. Schopenhauer, in mocking plans and dreams for the transformation or palingenesis of society, had already taken aim not only at those that expected progress from 'constitutions and laws' but also those that had set their hopes on 'steam engines and telegraphs' (*supra*, 1 §4). Similarly, the young Nietzsche found philistine 'optimism' not only in the revolutionary movement itself but also among 'political economists' that believed that, by means of 'as much production as possible', they could achieve 'as much happiness as possible' (VII, 378). Since 'liberal optimism' spread in the wake of the 'modern money economy' (VII, 346), to end the ruinous and persistent revolutionary drift it was necessary to liquidate the 'optimism of state and economic theories' as a whole (VII, 61). Entrusting

---

93   Hayek 1982, Vol. 2, 66.
94   Schoeck 1980, 208.

realisation of the dreams of regeneration to the development of the productive forces rather than to the victory of political and social revolution changed nothing, for we were still dealing with a philistine ideal. So one could understand the denunciation of the 'tartuffery of political economy' (XI, 285). As long as the hope remained that political economy could eliminate or significantly reduce poverty, the search for the responsibility for actually existing misery would never cease: if one did not blame political institutions for 'unjust' distribution of wealth, then one could at least blame them for its imperfect development. That is precisely why Nietzsche denounced 'economic optimism' to the very end (XII, 463).

Now, the thesis that institutions were not responsible spread to excess, taking in the human world as a whole, the historical process, and even the process of life in its entirety: this was the affirmation of 'everyone's complete lack of responsibility and innocence' (WS, 81 [193]), the innocence of becoming.

8   From Dismal Science to 'Gay Science'

To understand and legitimise the existing social order was, according to Malthus, a task of political economy, concerned with demonstrating the inevitable inadequacy of resources in relation to human needs and desires: 'It has appeared that from the inevitable laws of our nature, some human beings must suffer from want. These are the unhappy persons who, in the great lottery of life, have drawn a blank.'[95] The same argument and the same metaphor can be found in Nietzsche: 'Consolation for those that perish! Consider their passions as an unlucky lottery ticket. Observe how the greater part of shots must fail, that perishing is as useful as becoming. No remorse, suicide as that that abbreviates' (IX, 604). The difference between the two texts: the latter is more radical and brutal.

Malthus contrasted the 'melancholy tone' and 'dark colours' of human life with the glittering but deceptive revolutionary ideal of happiness.[96] Not dissimilar was the position of the young Nietzsche, who criticised the moderns for fantasising about a supposed 'value of existence [*Werth des Daseins*]' (WL, 1, 1, 876 [142]) that they wished to make happy for all. Let us dwell for a moment on the expression used here. Precisely on the basis of the emphatic affirmation of the 'value of life', Dühring wished to abolish the misery of the popular classes

---

95   Malthus 1986, 74.
96   Malthus 1986, 11.

to generalise 'the banquet of life'[97] that, according to Malthus, was reserved for the few. It was precisely as the science of the limited nature of resources and the resulting hardships that political economy became, for Carlyle, the dismal science.[98] For the mature Nietzsche, this vision was afflicted with philistinism: the air of sadness in which it was bathed was one of disappointment arising from the realisation that the ideal of comfort forever and for all was beyond reach. Moreover, the feelings of melancholy and resignation projected onto existence hindered the joyous and overflowing acceptance of life. One could and needed not resign oneself to this condition: 'Perhaps even laughter still has a future'; a 'gay science' was necessary, in which laughter 'formed an alliance with wisdom' (FW, 1 [27–8]).

When the laws of political economy were understood as laws of the 'great economy of the whole', their inevitability was further strengthened. But there was no reason for sadness, provided, of course, one left behind any form of philistinism or feminine weakness. Once one was aware of the unimputability of institutions regarding mass misery, of the innocence of becoming, one needed no longer refer to the limited nature of resources to overcome guilt complexes and feelings of guilt, and one could enjoy life to the full. 'Gay science [*fröhliche Wissenschaft*]' took the place of dismal science. Even if Nietzsche took this and the equivalent expressions (*gaya ciencia* and *gay saber*) from Herder, who was referring to the culture of Provence,[99] the problematic the philosopher thereby addressed referred to the debate about political economy and the social question going on at the time at the European level.

The new science also differed from the old with regard to the sociopolitical group it addressed. For Malthus, it was necessary to transmit the dismal science primarily to the popular classes; political economy was to become 'an object of popular education'. With its help, the poor would understand that the cause of their misery was to be found in stepmother nature or in their own individual improvidence.[100] This was also the view of Tocqueville, who considered it necessary to

> spread among the working classes [...] some of the most elementary and most certain notions of political economy to make them understand, for example, that which is permanent and necessary in the economic laws that govern the wage rate; for such laws, which are to a certain extent

---

97   Dühring 1881a, 23.
98   Carlyle 1983, 431, 571.
99   Herder 1978, 37.
100   Malthus 1826, 354, fn. (Book IV, 9).

divine, since they arise from the nature of men and the structure of society, stand outside of the scope of revolutions.[101]

'Gay science', on the other hand, addressed the 'master', to stop him giving in to 'morbid over-sensitivity and susceptibility to pain'. He was called upon to resist the 'cult of suffering' of the modern world, and not to be impressed by the 'excessive amount of complaining'. 'Gay science' opposed this 'latest type of bad taste', which raged among the popular masses and the intellectual 'enthusiasts' linked with them (JGB, 293 [174]). It was well aware of the social and human cost of the 'great economy of the whole' and culture, but it did not allow itself to be perturbed by it.

Compared with the end of the eighteenth century, when Malthus's essay had made its first appearance, the element of novelty lay in the development of the labour movement and of socialist or socialistic currents. The latter were no longer persuaded by the 'lottery' argument, but instead denounced the 'exploitation' that according to Marx was a necessary part of capitalist 'appropriation' of the workers' 'extra work'. And now let us read Nietzsche:

> [L]ife itself is essentially a process of appropriating, injuring, overpowering the alien and the weaker, oppressing, being harsh, imposing your own form, incorporating, and at least, the very least, exploiting, – but what is the point of always using words that have been stamped with slanderous intentions from time immemorial?
>
> JGB, 259 [153]

In rejecting the charges against the existing order, the German philosopher justified this position with a general law of life. And once again the transition was made from political economy to metaphysics:

> [T]hese days, people everywhere are lost in rapturous enthusiasms, even in scientific disguise, about a future state of society where 'the exploitative character' will fall away: – to my ears, that sounds as if someone is promising to invent a life that dispenses with all organic functions. 'Exploitation' does not belong to a corrupted or imperfect, primitive society: it belongs to the essence of being alive as a fundamental organic function; it is a result of genuine will to power, which is just the will of life.
>
> JGB, 259 [153]

---

101   Tocqueville 1951 ff., Vol. 16, 241.

In citing this, Mehring had no doubts: it was 'the philosophy of – capitalism', the worldview of 'exploiting capital'.[102] There is a limit to this judgement: the translation of an economic and political category into metaphysical terms leads to an (admittedly) partial disentanglement from the economic and political immediacy that must be taken into account. But present-day interpreters that tend to dissolve the questionable category into a rarefied aura with no relation to reality and sociopolitical conflicts are even further from the truth than Mehring. Not only Marx spoke of 'exploitation'. So did other authors well-known to Nietzsche. While Dühring spoke up for those excluded from 'the banquet of life' and commited himself to fighting 'the exploitation of the propertyless by the propertied,'[103] Heine attributed to the school of Saint-Simon the merit of having coined '*la belle formule*' of the '*exploitation de l'homme par l'homme*'.[104]

But, for Nietzsche, who, as we have seen, acknowledged the reality of 'extra work', there was no doubt: the socialist aspiration to overcome the real world of 'exploitation' and 'oppression', i.e., inequality, hierarchy, and slavery in its various forms, was on the same line as the Christian sermon condemning the vale of tears. We were dealing here with two different expressions of nihilism, of escape from the world of life (XIII, 220). And, again, like the category of 'exploitation', the criticism of this category was placed in a much wider context that transcended or wished to transcend economic and political immediacy.

---

102   Mehring 1961 ff., Vol. 13, 165, 160.
103   Dühring 1881a, 59, 23.
104   Heine 1969–78, Vol. 2, 677.

Politics and Epistemology between Liberalism and 'Aristocratic Radicalism'

1 Epistemology, Defence of the Individual and Critique of Revolution

The metaphysical 'translation' of the conflicts and political debates went hand in hand with their historical and theoretical deepening. At the centre of attention, together and interwoven with the social question, were the revolutionary cycle and the demands and hopes of redemption that fed it. This was as true for Nietzsche as for German and European culture of the time. It was on the basis of the critique of revolution that in his youth he adhered to the philosophy of Schopenhauer (the implacable enemy of 'optimism') and encountered Wagner and the national-liberal movement. But, in his critique, Nietzsche went far beyond the German National Liberals and the anti-democratic liberalism that spread in Europe in the wake of the reaction against the workers' revolt in June 1848 and the Paris Commune. It was a radicalism that manifested itself, even more so than in the immediate political positions taken, in an effort to liquidate the epistemology, historical vision and worldview underlying the revolutionary project.

It may be useful to start from Hegel, who interpreted the revolutionary cycle that marked the birth of the modern world as follows: after already having begun to take effect in the course of the American Revolution, 'the principle of the universality of the principles [*allgemeine Grundsätze*] was strengthened in the French people and brought forth the revolution there'.[1] Significantly, Tocqueville spoke in similar terms: for him, 'great, general ideas [...] announce the total subversion of the existing order'.[2] In the France of incessant revolutionary upheavals, 'the passion for general ideas' seemed to have become 'so rampant that every theme is enough to satisfy it'.[3] Despite the differences in value judgement, both Hegel and Tocqueville identified universality with revolution! This, as Hegel noted, was because the category of *Allgemeinheit* referred ultimately to the category of *égalité*.[4]

---

1 Hegel 1919–20, 920.
2 Tocqueville 1951 ff., Vol. 5, half-vol. 2, 39.
3 Tocqueville 1951 ff., Vol. 1, half-vol. 2, 21 (DA, Book 2, pt. 1, 3).
4 Hegel 1969–79, Vol. 2, 491.

One could say that, in these years, the political battle also tended to be conducted at an epistemological level. What sense did it have to speak of human rights as such? Did a reality correspond to the universal concept of human being? And what then was the status of universals? The critique of revolution implied the critique of universality. In some respects, Nietzsche's historical balance sheet presented itself as an extreme radicalisation of the balance sheet liberal and conservative circles formulated after the French Revolution. One sees this in the way in which, in the wake of the enormous impression made by the collapse of the *ancien régime* in France and during the workers' revolts in Lyons at the time of the July monarchy, which evoked the threat of a new and even more terrible revolutionary wave, Tocqueville summarised his epistemological-political programme:

> Everything that in our times raises up the idea of the individual is healthy. Everything that gives a separate existence to the species [*espèce*] and enlarges the notion of the type [*genre*] is dangerous. The *esprit* of our contemporaries turns by itself in this direction. The doctrine of the realists [*la doctrine des réalistes*], introduced to the political world, urges forward all the abuses of Démocratie; it is what facilitates despotism, centralization, contempt for individual rights, the doctrine of necessity, all the institutions and all the doctrines which permit the social body to trample men underfoot and which make the nation everything and the citizens nothing.[5]

On the other hand, Constant had already praised the categories of individuality, specificity and variety as opposed to the stuffy 'uniformity' of which the Jacobin and democratic movement was accused.[6] This thread of thought was widespread in Germany (think only of a great critic of the revolution like Adam Müller[7]) and was also manifest, in a different way, in the culture and press of North America, engaged in a defence of that 'peculiar institution', slavery, in the teeth of the standardising crusade of the abolitionists and the North.

Tocqueville's text is particularly interesting: (1) it establishes a relationship between the epistemological and the ethical-political sphere; (2) on this basis, it demonstrates that the revolutionary tradition that has developed out of Jacobinism applies the 'realism' of universals in the political field; and (3) it once

---

5   Tocqueville 1951 ff., Vol. 6, half-vol. 1, 52 f.
6   Constant 1957, 1014–20.
7   Losurdo 1992, 13, § 2.

again seeks to set nominalism at both the political and the epistemological level against the 'realistic' incorporation of the individual in 'species' and 'kind'.

This was also Nietzsche's programme. If Tocqueville defended *particular rights*', *Beyond Good and Evil* criticised modernity's 'opposition to any special claims, special rights, or privileges' (JGB, 202 [90]). If the French liberal blamed this trend for encouraging 'despotism' and 'centralization', Nietzsche, even more radically, maintained that 'opposition' to any 'special rights' actually meant opposition to 'any rights'. Just as for Tocqueville the 'social body' raised to the level of 'everything' swallowed up the individual, so for *Beyond Good and Evil* 'faith in the community as redeemer' fulfilled this role (JGB, 202 [91]). In arguing against the 'doctrine of the realists', the French liberal had in mind the pathos of the nation of revolutionary memory, and socialism. Nietzsche, for his part, put it this way: 'In general the tendency of socialism, like that of nationalism, is a reaction against becoming individual. One has difficulties with the ego, the immature, crazy ego: they want to put it back under the bell' (IX, 515). The only relevant difference is that, in the meantime, especially in Germany, 'nation' had become the watchword more of the chauvinists than of the revolutionaries.

We have seen how Tocqueville established a relationship between politics and epistemology. In similar terms, on German soil, Heinrich Leo explained the incessant upheavals and the emergence of the spectre of socialism on the other side of the Rhine by the 'realism' of the 'Roman-Celtic tendency', which tended to use 'abstract concepts as if they were realities'; it was a matter of countering this 'despotism of abstract concepts' by reaffirming the 'nominalism' of the 'Germanic tendency'.[8] Nietzsche professed himself a nominalist from the very start. *The Birth of Tragedy* referred explicitly to the medieval discussion about universals. Quoting with approval the view of Schopenhauer, it declared that 'concepts are the *universalia post rem*', to use 'the language of the scholastics'; the concrete is provided by 'what is perceptive, special, and individual', while 'the concepts contain only the forms, first of all abstracted from perception' (GT, 16, I, 106–7 [78]). Was this process of abstraction legitimate? In fact, 'nature knows neither forms nor concepts and hence no species [*keine Gattungen*]' (WL, I, 880 [145]). *Gattung*: this was the *genre* or *espèce* against which Tocqueville warned in his polemic against the 'doctrine of the realists' of the Jacobins and socialists. Nietzsche, on the other hand, took aim at the French Revolution itself and its proclamation of human rights in the name of a supposed 'human being as such' or 'absolute human

---

8   In Kraus 1894, 1017 (letter to Ludwig von Gerlach of 23 March 1861).

being' (CV, 3, I, 776 [172–3]), in the name of the 'bloodless abstraction "human being"', that 'common, pallid pale fiction' (M, 105 [72]).

At this point nominalism reaches its final consequences: not only the concept of human being but the concept as such leads to 'overlooking what is individual and real' and ends up equating 'non-equivalent actions [*Gleichsetzen des Nicht-Gleichen*]' (WL, I, 879–880 [145]). Since the 'justice' demanded by the democratic and plebeian movement was also based on a concept of the human being, it too made the absurd claim to 'make the unequal equal' (GD, *Expeditions of an Untimely Man*, 48 [222]). Together with the concept, the syllogism that subsumed the individual under the general concept and thereby showed it was inspired by the levelling fury of the most mediocre and base natures was also to be put on trial. There can be no doubt: the plebeian 'knife' was present in Socrates's 'syllogism' (GD, The Problem of Socrates, 7 [164]). He had committed the mistake too of making 'a tyrant' of reason (GD, The Problem of Socrates, 10 [165]), of absolutising the proof by means of concepts and reasoning: yet '[n]othing with real value needs to be proved first'. Here that which is egregious, excellent, out of the ordinary in higher natures does not belong (GD, The Problem of Socrates, 5 [164]). Reason homogenises and levels, it absorbs and incorporates the individual in the universal, just like revolution. Kant had already pointed out, though in the context of a positive value judgement, that the 'strict universality [*strenge Allgemeinheit*]' of reason excluded in advance 'any exception',[9] so it denied the 'particular right' and 'privilege' Nietzsche sought to defend at every level. That is why *Beyond Good and Evil* identified the inspirer of the catastrophe that would later befall France and Europe in the rationalist Descartes, a century earlier (*infra*, 21 § 7).

2   The Nominalist Polemic and the Nietzschean Critique of Liberal Inconsistency

Starting out from this extreme radicalisation of the anti-'realistic' polemic, Nietzsche viewed the national-liberal and liberal attitude as timid and inconsistent. Ultimately, this was the basis of the polemic against Strauss. For Nietzsche, Strauss was not even able to shake off the ideas that most immediately referred to the French Revolution, as demonstrated by the fact that, in his determination of morality, he continued to make use of the idea of 'species', a 'concept of the human being [under which] one can yoke together the most

---

9   Kant 1900 ff., Vol. 3, 28 f.

diverse and manifold things, from the Patagonian savage, for example, to Master Strauss' (DS, 7; I, 195 [39]). One was dealing here with a fundamental contradiction. Devoid of logical rigour and intellectual courage, the German National Liberal oscillated between nominalism and realism. On the one hand, he asserted the irreducibility of the individual to the species; on the other, he used the species to construct his morality:

> While Strauss certainly must assume that no two creatures are ever exactly the same, and that the human being's entire evolution, from the animal stage up to the height of the cultural philistine, depends on the law of individual differences, he nevertheless has no trouble whatsoever preaching the exact opposite: 'Act as though there were no individual differences!' Where in all this is there room for moral doctrine à la Strauss-Darwin; where, indeed, is there room for courage?
>
> DS, 7, I, 196 [40]

Nietzsche's later polemic against Renan had a similar significance. The French liberal despised the 'mass'[10] and defended 'multiplicity' and individuality,[11] but he too was completely inconsistent. He wanted 'to unite *la science* with *la noblesse*', not realising that '*la science* belongs with democracy' (GD, *Expeditions of an Untimely Man*, 2 [192]), that it 'is fundamentally democratic and anti-oligarchic'. So, Renan demonstrated an 'absolute lack of instinct' (XII, 349). Science, which is based on concepts themselves responsible for making the unequal equal and implies at the epistemological level the same tendency to levelling expressed by the idea of equality at the political level and by moral norms at the ethical level, could not call a halt to the forward march of democratisation and massification and the imminent slave revolt. It was a question of defending 'special right' not only against incorporation through 'community' but, as the same aphorism from *Beyond Good and Evil* makes clear, also against the 'morality of communal piety' (JGB, 202 [91]). Nietzsche's nominalist polemic now subsumed science, morality and the dominant religion in the West under the hated revolutionary and socialistic realism.

The struggle against the category of universality could not but also take aim at Christianity itself, which first formulated at the religious level those ideas of equality and of the human being as such later interpreted and propagated in political terms by the French Revolution: not by chance did churches

---

10   Renan 1947 ff., Vol. 1, 344.
11   Renan 1947 ff., Vol. 8, 146.

often engage in the abolitionist struggle that in Nietzsche's eyes was responsible for destroying or damaging beyond repair the indispensable foundation of society. Along with Christianity, morality, or at least Kantian morality, was also to be liquidated, for declined as it was in the singular, it was applied to human beings as such, formulated absolutely general norms and was founded in that category of universality that was the German counterpart of French *égalité*.

Nietzsche could also have asserted in regard to Tocqueville the charge of inconsistency and lack of intellectual courage made against Strauss and Renan. *Democracy in America* contains critical tones with regard to England, where the social distance was so great that masters and servants formed 'two opposing societies': one could say there were 'as many distinct humanities as there are classes', and so 'one loses sight of the general link that unites them all in the broad lap of the human species [*genre*]'.[12] The fact was that, in aristocratic societies, 'the poor man is, properly speaking, in no way a fellow human of the rich man; he is a being of another species [*espèce*]'.[13] So while, on the one hand, in the polemic against Jacobinism and socialism, Tocqueville demanded the reorganisation of the categories *espèce* and *genre*, on the other, he appealed to these categories to take their distance from aristocracy and reaction; in this way, conscious nominalism yielded to involuntary realism. The French liberal felt compelled to fight on two fronts: 'If the aristocratic nations use too few general ideas and often demonstrate a reckless contempt for them, it happens that democratic peoples, to the contrary, are always ready to misuse this sort of idea and to become excessively enthusiastic about them'.[14] To this 'centrism' at the political level corresponded a kind of centrism at the epistemological level: 'The merit of general ideas is that they allow the human spirit to make rapid judgements at the same time about a large number of objects; on the other hand, they provide only incomplete knowledge and always lose in exactitude what they gain in extent'.[15]

In his critique of revolution, Nietzsche, on the other hand, wanted to take the anti-'realistic' battle to extremes, on epistemological and political grounds, and, in doing so, ended up attacking even those timid and inconsistent nominalists that were the liberals and National Liberals.

---

12   Tocqueville 1951 ff., Vol. 1, half-vol. 2, 185, 21f. (DA, Book 2, pt. 3, 5 and Book 2, pt. 1, 3).
13   Tocqueville 1951 ff., Vol. 1, half-vol. 1, 222 (DA, Book 1, pt. 2, 5).
14   Tocqueville 1951 ff., Vol. 1, half-vol. 2, 24 (DA, Book 2, pt. 1, 3).
15   Tocqueville 1951 ff., Vol. 1, half-vol. 2, 20 (DA, Book 2, pt. 1, 3).

3   Schopenhauer's Oscillation between Nominalism and Realism and
       Nietzsche's Break

One can also place the break with Schopenhauer in this context. At first sight, the break seemed to contradict the dominant ideological climate in Europe, characterised by an individualistic and nominalistic pathos. The great theorist of compassion seemed to celebrate 'species [*Gattung*]', immobile and indifferent with regard to the fortunes, including birth and death, of its 'individuals'.[16] It was an ambit from which not only social conflict but even plurality as such vanished; the contradiction, even the difference, between rich and poor and between oppressor and oppressed dissolved, however shocking the social polarisation and however hard and pitiless the oppression: 'The tormentor and the tormented are one. The former errs in not feeling part of the torment, the latter in not participating in the guilt [*Schuld*]'.[17] However, the nominalistic pathos at the phenomenal level (the sphere of sociopolitical relations and conflicts) corresponded to the pathos of species at the noumenal level (the sphere of transcendence and forgetting of the political).

At the phenomenal level, Nietzsche and Schopenhauer were evidently close. If the former nominalistically dissolved the universal category of person, individual and human being, the latter similarly treated the category of human existence, for depending on the subject to which it referred, he accorded it a quite different meaning: 'A man has a *degree of existence* [*Dasein*] at least ten times higher than the other – in other words, exists [*da ist*] ten times as much.' If Nietzsche was ironical about subsuming the Patagonians under the concept of human being, Schopenhauer declared that the life of 'savages [*Wilden*]' is 'just *one* stage above monkeys perched on their trees'. And even if one confined oneself to Europe, 'the existence of the proletarian or slave, who lives from day to day without awareness, is clearly closer to the existence of animals, completely limited to the present, than our existence'.[18] To demonstrate the 'original diversity of spiritual forces' among human beings, Schopenhauer insisted that 'individual character' belonged only to higher human beings, while ordinary human beings were 'factory goods [*Fabrikware*]' and, like animals, completely absorbable into the species: '*Ce sont des espèces* [...]. The curse of vulgarity puts human beings on a par with the lower animals, by allowing them none but a generic nature, a generic form of existence'.[19] In this sense, there was a

---

16   Schopenhauer 1976–82b, 617.
17   Schopenhauer 1976–82a, 484.
18   Schopenhauer 1976–82c, Vol. 5, 698.
19   Schopenhauer 1976–82c, Vol. 5, 697, 701; Schopenhauer 1976–82a, 268.

correspondence between the ontological and epistemological levels, since 'the content and extent of the concepts are in an inverse proportional relationship'; the breadth of the concept was in proportion to its poverty: concepts could be ordered in a 'scale, a hierarchy, from the particular to the general: at the lower end almost there is almost scholastic realism, at the upper end, nominalism'.[20] The richer the reality, the less it could be grasped by general concepts. That is to say: the categories of species and kind could be used to describe the mass but not the outstanding or even brilliant individual.

Until now, species and kind had had an unequivocally negative meaning. Species being was gregarious being, the lower human being, the non-individual, the non-person, an integral part of the herd, and therefore 'realistically' ascertainable. But as soon as they demanded their right to happiness and participation in social wealth, these 'factory goods', the proletarians, were immediately invited to raise their gaze to the noumenal level: at this level, the special claims and rights were shown to be senseless and vulgarly selfish, for they were guilty of ignoring or trampling on the harmony and unity of the 'species' (a term that has now acquired emphatically positive connotations).

So, on the one hand, the privileges of the ruling elite were justified on the grounds of the outstanding individuality that was its members' due, thereby raising them above the mass and its incurably gregarious nature, 'vulgar and generic'; on the other hand, the privations and sufferings of this mass were substantially removed by the fact that their subjects were reabsorbed at the noumenal level into a species that also embraced members of the ruling elite: so the latter could not be criticised since they now no longer constituted an individuality distinct and separable from the mass. The reabsorption of the individual into the species at the noumenal level allowed at the phenomenal level the undisturbed unfolding of the most striking inequalities, which could not damage the metaphysical unity of the species. Noumenal realism (anti-nominalism) served as a justification for phenomenal nominalism, which developed without hindrance of any kind in the sociopolitical world.

Like the liberals and National Liberals, Schopenhauer must have seemed inconsistent in the eyes of the theorist of aristocratic radicalism. It is no accident that compassion was a main target of the polemic, for Nietzsche, thinking principally of Rousseau, had good reason to suspect it of subversion, given that, due to the 'realistic' vision of the human race it presupposed, it removed the distance between the masters and those whose lives had turned out badly. Admittedly, for Schopenhauer compassion, far from being an expression of

---

20   Schopenhauer 1976–82b, 87 f.

protest against the political and social order, had a directly apologetic function: it aimed to restore the unity of the species, but always on the basis of the irrelevance and intangibility of the inequalities that characterised the phenomenon, the sociopolitical semblance. Compassion made it possible to understand the unity of one's own existence with the 'existence of all living things', to destroy the *'difference* between me and everyone else', and to become conscious of the 'metaphysical identity of the will as a thing in itself despite the countless multiplicity of its manifestations'.[21]

Significantly, Schopenhauer was concerned to contrast 'compassion [*Mitleid*]' and 'envy [*Neid*]', which, just like Nietzsche's *ressentiment,* was a feeling full of 'poison' and 'hatred' towards those that were more fortunate or betterformed, and above all towards 'genius' and everything not mediocre. Envy was synonymous with the desire for revenge.[22] If the compassion celebrated by Schopenhauer implied overcoming the phenomenal dualism between 'the tormentor and the tormented', and even more so between the different social classes, envy as an object of condemnation led to the perpetuation and further intensification of this dualism, with the consequence that that species unity that constituted reality in its true and noumenal sense fell into oblivion.

Sooner or later, Nietzsche could not but find the underlying hypocrisy of this Schopenhauerian sermon unbearable, as well as the persistent 'species' tone that continued to resonate in this compassion, though reduced to an ideological tool to condemn envy and 'egoism' and to recommend 'resignation or denial of the will'.[23] Nietzsche could not help but be suspicious of a compassion that Schopenhauer did not hesitate to celebrate by citing Rousseau. The latter, however, precisely in the passages quoted by Schopenhauer, explicitly linked this feeling with the idea of *espèce humaine,*[24] and, in this case, the idea of species was in no way intended to skip over the sociopolitical 'phenomenon' but was entirely pervaded by the will to change it. So Nietzsche was quite right to identify in Rousseau a plebeian potential that then unfurled its effectiveness in the radicalisation of the French Revolution.

If, in *The Gay Science,* Nietzsche completed the break with his former teacher and the teacher's tortuous and almost self-ashamed anthropological nominalism, he stressed 'the nonsense about compassion and how, as the source of all morality, it enables one to make the break through the *principium individuationis*' (FW, 99 [95–6]). In comparison to *The Birth of Tragedy* and the

---

21   Schopenhauer 1976–82d, 811, 740; Schopenhauer 1976–82b, 771.

22   Schopenhauer 1976–82c, Vol. 5, 255–58.

23   Schopenhauer 1976–82a, 553.

24   Schopenhauer 1976–82d, 781–84; cf. Rousseau 1959 ff., Vol. 3, 155.

third *Unfashionable Observation*, a turn had come about: these two texts used Schopenhauerian compassion to theorise a Dionysian 'community' that wholly absorbed the individual and individual suffering and thus removed any ground for the protest of the slave or of culture's sacrificial victim (*supra*, 1 §14). This solution made possible the neutralisation of the social question, but at a high price: the affirmation of the 'improvable doctrine of the One Will' led to the 'negation of the individual' and therefore to an irremediable contradiction with the aristocratic radicalism Nietzsche now professed.

4   From Nominalism to Perspectivism

In the culture and press of the time, the nominalist critique of universal principles (and of universal human rights) often led to the glorification of the concrete and the immediate. From the 'Enlightenment' period onwards, Nietzsche became aware of the problematic and dangerous nature of this approach. The early socialist movement also stressed concreteness and immediacy. For example, Feuerbach, preparing to leave the Hegelian Left to join German Social Democracy: 'Where words end, there life begins', and life requires that 'the concrete, the real man' enjoy 'freedom and happiness'.[25] One should not close one's eyes to the immediacy and inescapability of material needs: if 'the human being is what he eats', it must not be forgotten that 'hunger parches head and heart'.[26] This theme can be found, formulated in more sharply political terms, in France. In his self-defence, Blanqui set against that 'abstract word' that was law (and the right to property) the 'cry of hunger of thousands of wretches' or 'the cry of anguish of a starving population'. How could 'people with a heart' remain 'indifferent' to these obvious 'sufferings'?[27] These attitudes were so widespread they were taken up by personalities remote from political engagement in the actual sense. Decades later, the poet Giovanni Pascoli argued his 'socialism' in the following terms: 'The kingdom of slavery, war, conquest, exploitation, i.e., of mere reason, is coming to an end.' One could no longer be indifferent to the suffering of others: 'The merely reasonable man has become sentimental.'[28]

It would seem the suffering of the masses, and the compassion and moral outrage they aroused, were incontrovertible: physical evidence and moral conscience blocked all escape from the 'social question'. But was this really so? 'In

25   Feuerbach 1966, 187, 192.
26   Feuerbach 1967, 229, 225.
27   In Bravo 1973, 137–39.
28   Pascoli 1994, 160, 168.

the socialist representation of the current "misery" I know not what prevails, the representers' incompetence or fanaticism or hypocrisy – but I always find a bit of all three' (XIV, 244). As we have seen, in *The Birth of Tragedy* the early Nietzsche denounced the destructive nature of the revolutionary and socialist demand to banish the tragic from the world and thus realise the earthly happiness of all; later, he used the teachings of the great moralists to question the innocence of moral sentiments and of the judgement damning the misery and suffering of the masses in the name of justice. Now, in the final phase of his development, he was concerned to problematise the very 'evidence' of pain.

There was no lack of attempts to do so in European culture of the time. Spencer not only served up the classic topos, with which we are already familiar, according to which 'classes engaged in strenuous occupations' revealed scant sensitivity to pain 'at the intellectual and emotional level' but also drew attention to the therapeutic character suffering assumed in certain circumstances, so the attempt to eliminate it at all costs led paradoxically to the liquidation of the remedy rather than of the evil.[29] But the efforts were disorganised. In this case, Nietzsche was not content to discuss and radicalise themes already widely disseminated. Rather, he succeeded in responding to an ideological need strongly felt in the culture and press engaged in criticising the labour and socialist movement.

Pain was in no sense the incontrovertible immediacy fabricated by the revolutionary movement, which wanted to abolish it by means of sociopolitical upheavals, for 'pain is a product of the brain' (IX, 565), just like the happiness demanded by the revolutionary movement: 'Measured intellectually, how full of error pleasure and pain are' (IX, 565). And it was not only the intellect that intervened: 'Without fantasy and memory, there would be neither pleasure nor pain' (IX, 556). On closer inspection, the alleged immediacy disappeared completely: 'Why does a cut finger hurt? In itself it does not hurt (even though it might feel "stimuli"); someone whose brain is chloroformed feels no "pain" in his finger' (IX, 559). Moreover, a general consideration applied:

> [W]e should use 'cause' and 'effect' only as pure concepts, which is to say as conventional fictions for the purpose of description and communication, not explanation. In the 'in-itself' there is nothing like 'causal association'. [...] There, the 'effect' does not follow 'from the cause', there is no rule of 'law'.
>
> JGB, 21 [21]

---

29   Spencer 1981, 397.

As for the pain, one was perhaps dealing more with a 'judgement about harm to a functioning organ, on the part of the unit that has the representations', than with a perception that arose infallibly as the effect of a cause in itself (IX, 559–60).

The unity and immediacy of perception gave way to the complexity and problematic nature of judgement:

> Observe how a pleasure arises, how many representations must come together! And, in the end, it is a one and the whole, and no longer wants to acknowledge itself as a plurality. So it could be with all pleasure, all pain! They are phenomena of the brain! But pluralities that we long ago assimilated and only now present themselves as wholes!
>
> IX, 559

One could even ask whether the perception of pain does not play a role in 'anger at wounding, and the feeling of revenge', ultimately *ressentiment* (IX, 560). This means that ideology, politics and history are relevant: 'Talk of pain and misfortune always strikes me as exaggerated, as if it were a matter of good manners to exaggerate here.' Narcissistic complacency, or the tendency 'to trickle sweets onto our bitternesses, especially onto the soul's bitternesses' (FW, 326 [182]), also played an important role. Socialist ideology and propaganda strongly emphasised that 'suffering is always the first of the arguments marshalled *against* life' and the burden of negativity, starting with slavery, it inevitably entailed (GM, II, 7 [43]); it was the 'contemporary moral fashion', which recommended 'eagle eyes for every distress and every suffering existing elsewhere!' (M, 174 [127]). Together with a history, it was also possible to construct a sociology of sensitivity to pain: it was clear that 'the curve of human tolerance to pain' varied greatly across cultures, peoples and social classes and was not the same for the black slave as for his white master, for the aristocrat and the plebeian (*supra*, 12 §2). Therefore: 'What does suffering and pleasure have to do with the actual event! They are a thing alongside, which does not penetrate deeply' (IX, 468).

So, the perception of pain was ultimately a historical and social construct. This rendered all the more problematic sympathetic identification with the pain of others, or, more precisely, with the pain one imagined or constructed in the subject with which one thought one was identifying. One can already read in *Human, All Too Human*: 'But what a difference always remains between a toothache and the pain (sympathy) that the sight of a toothache evokes?' (MA, 104 [80]). A twofold awareness had to take the place of the 'immediacy' of sympathy for the misery and hardships of the poor: in those classes, habit had

brought about a sort of numbness; with the advent of modernity, the sensitivity of the upper classes for the imagined suffering of the other had grown, but
this development was not without its pathological aspects.

On the other hand, even the direction of the feeling of compassion was
somewhat problematic. It could easily turn towards the author rather than the
victim of the action generally considered to be wicked: '[I]n any harm done
out of so-called malice, the degree of the pain engendered is unknown to us in
any case; but insofar as there is a pleasure along with the action (a feeling of
our own power, of our own strong stimulation), the action occurs in order to
preserve the well-being of the individual and thus falls under a point of view
similar to self-defense' (MA, 104 [80–1]).

The political significance of this epistemological revolution is clear and not
passed over in silence:

> The pillars of social order rest upon the foundation that everyone looks
> upon all that he is, does and strives for, upon his health or sickness, his
> poverty or prosperity, his honor or insignificance, with cheerfulness and
> thereby feels, 'I would not change places with anyone.' – Anyone that wants
> to help construct the order of society has only to implant in people's
> hearts this philosophy of cheerfully renouncing any change of place and
> being without envy.
>
> VM, 396 [142]

The 'levellers, these misnamed "free spirits"', stoked up the struggle against the
supposed sufferings of humanity: in fact, they revealed their emptiness, particularly their 'tendency to think that all human misery and wrongdoing [Miss-
rathen] is caused by traditional social structures: which lands truth [Wahrheit]
happily on its head!' (JGB, 44 [40–1]). The call for an end to the pain of others
and happiness for all had a subversive character – this theme is already present
in The Birth of Tragedy. The demand that Nietzsche had already denounced at
the actual political level because of the threat it posed to the future of culture
as such was now refuted at the epistemological level, with the help of the perspectivistic relativisation of pain and pleasure.

Again, it is clear that this course of action is not in itself new. Are we really
sure the fate of the poor and of the beggar fighting for survival is not preferable to that of the rich and powerful man overwhelmed by the weight of his
responsibility or plagued by boredom? This is a rhetorical question, a topos
with a long history, which also recurs in Nietzsche. The subaltern classes of
the ancien régime, doomed in the eyes of the compassionate revolutionary
to an unhappiness incompatible with a sense of justice, actually enjoyed a

'vegetative happiness' destroyed by the upheavals passionately invoked by a mistaken love of one's neighbour: thus Tocqueville seemed to argue. Rather than of 'vegetative happiness', Nietzsche sometimes spoke, in relation to the servants of the *ancien régime*, of 'serenity' and sometimes, more precisely, of a 'melancholy enclosure of their narrow existence'. Whatever the case, it was an 'uplifting' spectacle, a 'reproach' to modernity (*supra*, 13 §3 and 14 §4). But now one had become aware of the inevitable disappearance of this world: there was no longer any room for regret. The pain exhibited and exploited by the apostles of compassion, justice and subversion now had to be problematised differently, by questioning at the philosophical level the presumed immediacy of the perception of pain and the presumed objectivity of the cognitive process in general.

5   'Plebeianism' of Science, Perspectivism and Will to Power

The assertion that there was only one 'rightful interpretation of the world' was completely unfounded. Rather, a paradox emerged: the 'scientific' or rather 'mechanistical' interpretation of the world revealed itself, in its naïve certainties, to be 'one of the stupidest of all possible' such interpretations, a 'crudity' and an 'idiocy' (FW, 373 [238–9]). So far, perspectivism had taken aim at dogmatism and exclusivism. But now further considerations of a quite different sort intervened:

> Suppose one judged the value of a piece of music according to how much of it could be counted, calculated, and expressed in formulas – how absurd such a 'scientific' evaluation of music would be! What would one have comprehended, understood, recognized?
>
> FW, 373 [239]

Music was a kind of metaphor for life. One was not to lose sight of the 'ambiguous character' of existence (FW, 373 [239]), 'the perspectival character of existence' (FW, 374 [239]), 'the perspectival optics of life' (JGB, 11 [13]). One was not to 'demote existence [...] to an exercise in arithmetic [*Rechenknechts-Übung*] and an indoor diversion for mathematicians' (FW, 373 [238]). Now it was no longer a question of asserting the multiplicity of interpretations of the world. A choice was to be made, less between different interpretations of the world than between different ways of living, different existential options. This theme referred to German Romanticism, with its polemic against a worldview that rejected as obscure everything that went beyond 'tables and registers [*Tabellen und Register*]' and that was at ease only in an existence ruled by 'tables and statistics [*tabellarisch-statistisch*]' or by 'mechanical laws of the social order'. Behind the German Romantics stood Burke, with his contempt for the 'economists' and 'calculators' that together with the 'sophisters' had come to power in France in the wake of the collapse of the *ancien régime*.[30]

Clearly, there had been a shift in the discourse from the epistemological to the existential-political field. The target was patently political, and now constituted not only by the worldview but also by the order that had emerged from the French Revolution. This was confirmed by Nietzsche's further polemic against a worldview that 'permits counting, calculating, *weighing*, seeing, grasping, and nothing else' (FW, 373 [239]). After the idea of equality had been sharply criticised in political discourse, it was now discovered and rejected, with the help of perspectivism, within scientific discourse too. And the perspectivistic interpretation of scientific discourse was itself eminently political. It was accused of a political prejudice that led it to see regularities, norms and equalities in nature. The presumed 'conformity of nature to law' went hand in hand with presumed 'equality before the law'. In fact, it was 'a lovely case of ulterior motivation [that] serves once more to disguise the plebeian antagonism against all privilege and autocracy'. When physicists shouted 'hurray for the laws of nature!' they did the same as the anarchists, with their slogan '*Ni dieu, ni maître*.' The perspectivistic polemic against dogmatism took the form of and was now revealed to be a polemic against egalitarianism and anarchism, which, on closer inspection, was also seen to emerge in 'scientific' discourse. The so-called objective interpretation of the 'text' of nature was in fact 'only a naïve humanitarian correction and a distortion of meaning' with which physicists 'comfortably accommodate the democratic instincts of the modern soul', as evidenced primarily by the centrality given to the idea of equality (JGB, 22 [22]).

Nietzsche set the idea of equality in all its forms against an extreme nominalism. We have already seen how it developed at the spatial level (every thing was different from all others). Perspectivism led to its development also at the temporal level (every thing already became something else the next moment):

> The tree is each moment something new; the form is asserted by us because we cannot perceive the finest absolute movement: we add a mathematically average line to the absolute movement, indeed we invent lines and surfaces, because our intellect takes for granted the error: the

---

30   Losurdo 1997a, 3, § 3, and 9, § 1.

hypothesis of sameness and permanence, for we can see only that that
remains, and we can only remember what is similar (equal).

IX, 554

As soon as extreme nominalism unfolded at the temporal level, it became a
Heraclitism that, together with the idea of equality, undermined the idea of
'substance'. 'This faith in permanence, in substance, i.e., in its remaining equal
to itself' no longer had any foundation (IX, 570). One was dealing only with atavisms: 'At the beginning of all intellectual activity are the crudest assumptions
and inventions, for example, "equal", "thing", "remain"' (IX, 572). The critique of
the idea of substance was the critique of the idea of equality in the temporal
dimension it assumed in 'scientific' discourse.

Once the ideas of normativity, equality and substance had been problematised or refuted, it became possible to set 'an opposite intention and mode of
interpretation' against the democratic and plebeian interpretation of nature.
They were to be able to 'read from the same nature, and with reference to the
same set of appearances, a tyrannically ruthless and pitiless execution of power
claims', of the 'will to power' (JGB, 22 [22]).

The clearer the shift from the gnoseological to the existential-political level
becomes, the more evidently the perspectivism/dogmatism dichotomy was
replaced by the aristocratism/plebeianism dichotomy. And Nietzsche's position in this respect was unambiguous. Those that clung to the idea of substance
(and therefore of equality) did not understand that everything was always 'in
itself different', they denied or doubted the change that had occurred. But, said
Nietzsche, 'we must not transfer our scepticism into the essence' (IX, 554).

The roles were now reversed. The perspectivistic philosopher wanted to stick
to the 'in itself'; the plebeian vision of life, previously denounced for its dogmatism, its claim to represent its own interpretation as objectivity as such, was
now accused of projecting its own 'scepticism' onto the 'in itself' or onto the
'essence' of reality. The polemic against dogmatism had not disappeared, but
it appeared in quite a different light. Certainly, the 'philosophers of the future',
the 'upcoming philosophers', 'will not be dogmatists' (JGB, 42 [40]). But why?

It would offend their pride, as well as their taste, if their truth were a
truth for everyone (which has been the secret wish and hidden meaning
of all dogmatic aspirations so far). 'My judgement is my judgement: other
people don't have an obvious right to it too' – perhaps this is what such a
philosopher of the future will say. We must do away with the bad taste of
wanting to be in agreement with the majority.

JGB, 43 [40]

This rejection of 'dogmatism' represented the reaffirmation of the unbridge-ability of the abyss that separated higher from lower natures, the rejection of the community of reason and of the concept that – starting out from people's mutual recognition on the basis of their common dignity – can and does, for me, found a political community. Nietzsche was well aware of all this. His argumentation crossed over clearly and professedly from epistemology to practical philosophy. The 'in-itself' thrown into crisis by the anti-dogmatic and perspectivistic turn attacked the idea of 'pure spirit and the Good in itself', invented, as we know, by Plato even before Christianity. It was time to bring this devastating cycle to an end: '[T]alking about spirit and the Good like Plato did meant standing truth on its head and disowning even perspectivism, which is the fundamental condition of all life' (JGB, Preface [4]). In his perspectivistic radicalisation, 'critical philosophy' did not confine itself, as with Kant and the neo-Kantians, to attacking metaphysics but also targeted morality, which the latter looked upon as a shelter and safe haven in the storm caused by the criticistic destruction of metaphysics. Nietzsche contested not the content of a particular moral discourse but rather the possibility of a moral discourse capable of embracing all people:

> 'Good' is no longer good when it comes from your neighbor's mouth. And how could there ever be a 'common good'! The term is self-contradictory: whatever can be common will never have much value. In the end, it has to be as it is and has always been: great things are left for the great, abysses for the profound, delicacy and trembling for the subtle, and, all in all, everything rare for those that are rare themselves.
>
> JGB, 43 [40]

The aristocratism/plebeianism dichotomy was now so central that it absorbed the perspectivism/dogmatism dichotomy. Perspectivism was the due only of higher natures: the rabble could not rise to it. It was meaningless to believe

> that the people might come to understand something of that which is most remote from them, something of the great passion of the know-ledge-seeker that steadfastly lives, must live, in the thundercloud of the highest problems and the weightiest responsibilities (and thus in no way as an observer, outside, indifferent, secure, objective).
>
> FW, 351 [209]

After the shift from the gnoseological to the existential-political level, a further shift took place that led from the existential-political to the social level. Perspectivism was not only an existential option rather than the obligatory result of an epistemological deepening but a socially and politically conditioned or determined option pointing to a restricted and exclusive aristocracy. Even better: strictly speaking, one could no longer speak of options: if dogmatism was the inescapable mode of being of the plebeian, perspectivism was the inescapable mode of being of a truly aristocratic nature.

6   Three Political Projects, Three Epistemological Platforms: Mill, Lenin, Nietzsche

Between the mid-nineteenth and the early twentieth centuries, three great political projects emerged in Europe, each linked to a specific epistemology. In Britain, John Stuart Mill published in 1843 his *System of Logic, Ratiocinative and Inductive*. The author fully identified not only with the political institutions of Britain of the time but also with its international role. In the territories gradually conquered by the British Empire, in 'those backward states of society in which the race itself may be considered as in its nonage', culture spread as a result of the 'absolute obedience' of the subjugated peoples and the 'despotism', in this case 'legitimate', exercised by the big Western powers.[31] While, in general, colonial expansion served the cause of progress, for Mill the triumphal march of the British Empire was a quite special contribution to the success of 'universal peace' and 'generally friendly cooperation among nations'.[32] In this basically harmonious context, at the theoretical level there was only a place for quite specific problematisations and, at the practical level, for policy interventions aimed at particular and well-defined aspects of the existing order and existing international relations. *A System of Logic, Ratiocinative and Inductive* grounded science in an 'inference' that goes 'from particulars to particulars'.[33] Logic was nothing more than 'the common judge and arbiter of all particular investigations',[34] while sociology was the application to society as a whole of laws discovered by psychology and ethology (the science of 'character') in relation to the single individual: 'Next after the science of individual man, comes the science of man in society.'[35] On the other hand, a 'possible or desirable' social change presupposed an 'equivalent change of character' in individuals

---

31   Mill 1972a, 73.
32   Mill 1972b, 380.
33   Mill 1965c, Vol. 7, 186 ff. (Book 2, 3, §5).
34   Mill 1965c, Vol. 7, 10 (introduction, §5).
35   Mill 1965c, Vol. 8, 875 (Book 6, 6, §1).

in the various social classes,[36] and one of the first reforms to make was to be to guarantee the autonomy of the individual, and especially of exceptional individuals, in the face of advancing levelling and massification.

For sure, this was an epistemological and political platform Lenin would have to reject. Far from identifying with the existing order in Russia and the West and with the relations between the capitalist metropolis and the colonies, he called both radically into question. Colonial expansion, in Mill's eyes, particularly with regard to Britain's role, was a contribution to perpetual peace, but for Lenin, it led not only to the outbreak of terrible violence and massacres of subject peoples but also to the accumulation of flammable materials and the maturing of devastating conflicts even in the heart of Europe and the West. So, on the one hand, it was a question of shaking the quiet certainty of the masters of the world that represented culture and, on the other, of realising political interventions that went much further than those planned by the British liberal. Hence the use of the dialectic: 'Dialectics – as Hegel in his time explained – contains the element of relativism, of negation, of scepticism, but is not reducible to relativism.'[37] Lenin mocked the traditional opposition between 'civilized and advanced Europe' and 'backward' Asian, for in reality the roles could easily be reversed, as the title of a subsequent article made clear: 'Backward Europe and Advanced Asia'.[38] But this bitter irony aimed at stimulating actions not limited to particular aspects and details of the existing order and existing social relations.

Already, at the outbreak of the First World War, the Russian revolutionary felt the need to reflect on Hegel's *Science of Logic* to clarify for himself the conditions of revolutionary action he was hoping and preparing for. In this text, he sought confirmation not only of the objective character of contradictions but also of the need for a scientific analysis not limited to investigating this or that particularity of the existing order:

> Thought proceeding from the concrete to the abstract – provided it is correct [...] – does not get away from the truth but comes closer to it. [...] [All] scientific (that is, correct, serious, not absurd) abstractions reflect nature not only more deeply and correctly than living contemplation or notion but also more fully.[39]

---

36   Mill 1965b, 239.
37   Lenin 1975–, Vol. 14, 137.
38   Vol. 19, 99–100.
39   Lenin 1975–, Vol. 38, 171.

In Germany, after having passed through the 'metaphysical' and the 'Enlightenment' stage, Nietzsche thought he had finally found the epistemological platform, at the height of the 'aristocratic radicalism' he professed. Levelling and massification were no longer only a danger, as in Mill's analysis, but a terrible reality: instead of being the result of an objective and irreversible historical process, this reality was linked with the agitation and, even earlier, the distorted vision of individuals and layers internally and irredeemably defective. Perspectivism made it possible to solve a problem that had bothered Nietzsche ever since the second and third *Unfashionable Observation*. We have seen him denounce the inability of conservative or anti-revolutionary circles to oppose real and truly effective action to revolutionary action; and he had criticised Goethe's human being for not realising that in real life there was no place for actions protected from all violence and all forms of injustice.

Even before the actual act, the moment of choice, estimation and, ultimately, violence already lay in seeing and judging, which inevitably depended on 'perspective' and the 'injustice' related to it. However, that a perspective was in any case unavoidable did not mean that perspectives were all equivalent. To assess them in a differentiated and appropriate way, it was necessary to go back to the human and social reality at the root of each. On the one hand, life manifested and unfolded itself with its gushing and overwhelming power and wealth: on the other, the malformed crouch together in their petty *ressentiment* in a vile and twisted conspiracy, plotting their cowardly and wounded revenge on life. So, asserting the inescapability of 'perspective' and 'injustice' also asserted the inescapability of 'rank-ordering' (*supra*, 10 §5).

In contrast to Lenin, relativism was now everything. To presuppose an objective knowledge, a community of reason and concept, was a symptom of democratic and plebeian dogmatism; but to liquidate this dogmatism meant creating an unbridgeable gulf between aristocrats and plebeians, with the assertion (which brooked no doubts or objections given it refers to an inescapable 'nature') of the excellent character of the former and the inherently worthless and diseased character of the latter. In this sense, relativism, anti-'dogmatism' and perspectivism strengthened the proud and exclusivist self-consciousness as well as the capacity to act and fight of the true aristocrat, who indignantly rejected 'that enormous bloodsucker, the spider of scepticism'. This inert and cowardly scepticism was to be clearly distinguished from 'masculine scepticism', the 'scepticism of a bold masculinity, which is most closely related to the genius for war and conquest': it 'does not believe but does not die out on this account'; it was 'hard enough for evil and for good'. The rejection of the superstition of an objective knowledge and universal values by no means led to a hindering of the will to and capacity for action, but rather strengthend them: it was the ideology of aristocratic radicalism. This was demonstrated by the example of Frederick the Great, who had passed through the Enlightenment, disbelief and 'atheism' without his 'will', his will to power, being thereby 'shattered' (JGB, 209 [102–3]).

7   Perspectivism, Critique of Human Rights and Dissolution of the Subject

Attached as it was to the dogmatism of substance, the 'people' was not able to deconstruct the 'I think', the subject (JGB, 16 [16]). But those alien to the people had to understand that holding on to 'the opposition between subject and object', or to the 'soul-superstition', the 'superstition of the subject or I', meant remaining tangled up 'in the snares of grammar (of folk metaphysics)', a 'piece of folk superstition from time immemorial' that 'still causes trouble [*Unfug stiften*]' (FW, 354 [214] and JGB, Preface [3]). So, we were faced with a problem not purely philosophical. It was no accident that the metaphysics of the subject found its most emphatic expression in Descartes, who, as 'father of rationalism', was also 'grandfather of the Revolution' (JGB, 191 [81]). The pathos of 'I think' had created the preconditions for the construction of the subject as bearer of the inalienable rights proclaimed by the French Revolution, and it was to this subject that the socialist and anarchist agitation continued to refer.

By engaging in the deconstruction of the subject, ultimately Nietzsche resumed the programme of Maistre, who made an important critique of the various post-1789 constitutions. Although different from each other, in Maistre's view they all shared a fundamental error: however they defined the inalienable rights, they attributed them to a new and mysterious figure, the human being as such. However: 'In the world the *human being* does not exist. In my life I have seen Frenchmen, Italians, Russians, etc.; I also know, thanks to Montesquieu, *that one can be Persian*: but as for the *human being*, I declare that I never met him in my life; if he exists, it is unknown to me.'

The subject to which the proclamation of human rights that emerged from the French Revolution referred and to which the revolutionary press continued to appeal was imaginary. It was 'a pure abstraction.'[40] The young Nietzsche, who expressed himself even more strongly in denouncing the 'conceptual hallucinations' inherent in the claim to 'human dignity' and human rights as such, was already moving in this same direction (*supra*, 2 §4). But that was not

---

40   Maistre 1984, Vol. 1, 74 f.

the truly new element. The truly new element was that the central category of revolutionary discourse was now subjected to an unprecedentedly radical deconstruction. It was not just a question of affirming the irreducible singularity of every human being and every reality by highlighting the insurmountable differences that separated each from the next. One had to go even further, by deconstructing the category of human being as it were from within, whereby other singularities were not set against one singularity but singularity itself was dissolved in a multiplicity.

> The individual itself is a mistake. [...] But I distinguish: between the individual existing only in the imagination and the actual 'vital system' that each of us is; the two are merged into one, while the 'individual' is only a sum of sensations, judgements, conscious errors, a belief; a small fragment of the actual vital system or many fragments thought into one and imagined as one, a 'unity' that does not hold up.
>
> IX, 442–3

When Nietzsche brought 'I think' into the equation as an essential moment in the ideological preparation of the French Revolution, once again he was not isolated. According to Lichtenberg, an author he knew and valued, 'philosophy' and *cogito ergo sum* were the premise for the later 'echo of the cry "à la Bastille"'.[41] Moreover, the National Convention itself had decided on 2 October 1793 to transfer Descartes's ashes to the Pantheon.[42]

So one can appreciate the efforts of *Beyond Good and Evil* to deconstruct the 'I think' of Descartes and Kant: on closer inspection, this supposed 'immediate certainty' was actually a 'process' and the result of 'a whole set of bold claims', beginning with the assertion 'that *I* am the one that is thinking' and 'there is an "I"' (JGB, 16 [16–7]); in this way, 'the honest old I has disappeared' (JGB, 17 [18]).

Deconstructing the figure of the human being as such or of the subject, of the 'I think', also meant taking into account the religious tradition behind it. Before the idea of equality was articulated at the political level, it was declined in a Christian manner as equality of souls, so the idea of the subject and of man as such was prefigured in the Christian idea of the soul. Therefore, it was a matter of getting rid of the 'more disastrous atomism', the 'atomism of the soul' taught by Christianity, of 'the belief that the soul is something indestructible, eternal, indivisible, that it is a monad, an *atomon*'; only concepts like the 'mortal

---

41   Lichtenberg 1949, Vol. 1, 479.
42   Aulard 1977, 470.

soul' and the 'soul as subject-multiplicity' and the 'soul as a society constructed out of drives and affects' could 'have civil rights in the realm of science' (JGB, 12 [14]). Science, which Nietzsche criticised and deconstructed in so far as it implied the idea of equality (and substance), was now called upon for the definitive refutation of the idea of the subject (as bearer of the right to equality). The consistency of this argument was undeniable, but it was a wholly political consistency.

To say soul, subject, *cogito* and 'I think' also meant saying self-consciousness. Here was a new target of Nietzsche's critique:

> My idea is clearly that consciousness [*Bewusstsein*] actually belongs not to man's existence as an individual but rather to the community and herd – aspects of his nature; that accordingly, it is finely developed only in relation to its usefulness to community or herd.
>
> FW, 354 [213]

To understand better the meaning of this aphorism, it helps to confront it with a passage from Hegel's *Philosophy of Right*:

> It is part of education, of thinking as the consciousness [*Bewusstsein*] of the single in the form of *universality*, that the ego comes to be apprehended as a universal person [*Allgemeinheit*] in which all are identical. *A human being counts as a human being in virtue of his humanity alone*, not because he is a Jew, Catholic, Protestant, German, Italian, etc.[43]

Here a link was made between three categories: consciousness, universality and the human being as such. Like the pathos of the category of the human being as such, the pathos of the category of consciousness was also an expression of the universalistic tendency and so, in Nietzsche's eyes, of the tendency to levelling and massification brought about by the French Revolution. 'The world of which we can become conscious', of which the human being as such could become aware, was 'a world turned into generalities [*verallgemeinert*]', and this in turn was a 'debased [*vergemeinert*]' world. Turning things into 'generalities', 'generalization [*Generalisation*]', was synonymous with 'superficialization'; the subsumption into the species, the reduction to the species, entailed the liquidation of that which was individual and noble in it; the world then became 'shallow, thin, relatively stupid, general'. For, to reside at the level of conscious-

---

43   Hegel 1969–79, Vol. 7, 360 (§ 209 A).

ness, 'even with the best will in the world to understand ourselves as individually as possible', always meant residing at the dubious level of herd instinct: 'At bottom, all our actions are incomparably and utterly personal, unique, and boundlessly individual, there is no doubt; but as soon as we translate them into consciousness, they no longer seem to be ... This is what I consider to be true phenomenalism and perspectivism' (FW, 354 [213]).

The sphere of consciousness and of the conscious subject also referred to the 'intention' one assumed at the root of a given action. This attitude, which seemed almost obvious, was actually the result of modern subversion, which had broken with 'the last ten millennia' of history, during which 'the origin, not the consequence, [was] decisive for the value of an action', with 'a criterion' that was ultimately 'an unconscious after-effect of the dominance of aristocratic values and the belief in "origin"' (JGB, 32 [32–3]).

With modernity, on the other hand, the 'prejudice' had triumphed according to which 'intention', i.e., intellectual consciousness and moral conscience, decided the value of an action. But now a new turn was possible and necessary,

> on the threshold of a period that would be designated, negatively at first, as extra-moral, [a period in which] we immoralists, at least, suspect that the decisive value is conferred by what is specifically unintentional about an action, and that all its intentionality, everything about it that can be seen, known, or raised to 'conscious awareness', only belongs to its surface and skin – which, like every skin, reveals something but conceals even more.
>
> JGB, 32 [32–3]

In this way, besides recuperating the aristocratic value of origin, the new worldview also allowed one finally to overcome the concept of responsibility and guilt. What sense could that have once the subject to whose action it referred was no longer there? '[O]ur body is, after all, only a society constructed out of many souls' (JGB, 19 [18]). Like Descartes's 'I think', Schopenhauer's 'I want' also could and had to be deconstructed (JGB, 16 [16]). True, it was a long-standing prejudice, but that did not confer authority on it:

> That everything is a consequence of acts of will and can be explained in such a way and is not further explicable – is a belief savages share with Schopenhauer; this belief once ruled all human beings; to have it and preach it still in the nineteenth century, in the centre of Europe, was nothing more than an atavism.

It was necessary to overcome this atavistic prejudice and rise to the awareness that 'in every happening will plays no role' (IX, 589). On the other hand, it could be instructive to reflect on the history of a prejudice that had already been overcome: 'Although the shrewdest judges of the witches and even the witches themselves were convinced of the guilt of witchcraft, this guilt still did not exist'; but 'this is true of all guilt' (FW, 250 [249]). In the meantime, it was going in this direction: the intervention of circumstance in the evaluation of an action or crime was shown by the 'loss of our belief in the absolute responsibility of the person' (IX, 570–1).

Like the ideas of equality and substance, the idea of guilt was an atavism and a plebeian legacy: the 'well-turned-out person' was also characterised by the fact that he 'does not believe in "bad luck" or "guilt"'' (EH, Why I am so wise, 2 [77]). He gave expression to a worldview in which there was room neither for religious transcendence nor for revolutionary transcendence. It is

> an unreserved yea-saying even to suffering, even to guilt, even to everything questionable and strange about existence. [...] Nothing in existence should be excluded, nothing is dispensable – the aspects of existence condemned by Christians and other nihilists rank infinitely higher in the order of values than anything the instinct of decadence is able to approve, to call good.
>
> EH, *The Birth of Tragedy*, 2 [109]

8   The Dissolution of the Subject in Nietzsche and European Culture

The category of 'untimeliness' proved to be inconclusive or misleading also with regard to the theme of the dissolution of the subject. This theme was widespread in European culture of the time, and for understandable reasons. If human rights were solemnly proclaimed in 1789, the revolution of February 1848 abolished slavery in the French colonies, also in consideration of the fact that 'by destroying man's freewill, it suppresses the natural principle of right and duty'.[44] With an eye to wage slavery as well as colonial slavery, Lamennais wrote:

> The essence of slavery lies in the fact, as we have seen, that it destroys human personality, namely the freedom or natural sovereignty of man,

---

44   In Wallon 1974a, CLXV.

which makes a moral being of him, someone that is responsible for his acts and capable of virtue. Lowered to the level of the animal and even below that of the animal, he ceases to be a personal being, he is discharged from the rights of mankind, and consequently from every right and duty.[45]

In these years, the pathos of the human being and of the subject and of their dignity was a central theme of the struggle against ancient and modern slavery in its various forms. It was seen as an infamous institution because it 'suppresses the personality', trampled on 'the principle of consciousness, of personality', and reduced slaves to 'bodies [*somata*]'; it forgot the 'soul' that dwelt in them and humiliated the 'moral human being'; in that way, it claimed to destroy the 'will' and the 'inner power' of slaves, subordinating them wholly to the will of the master, who, as 'sovereign arbiter of what is right and wrong', thus usurped the role that is rightly that of 'God'.[46]

This is the historical and political context of Nietzsche's polemic against 'those deceitful concepts [...], the supporting concepts of morality – "soul", "spirit", "free will", "God"'; they ran the risk of 'the physiological ruin of humanity', by affirming the inviolability even of the hopelessly malformed and thereby blocking the necessary process of selection (EH, *Daybreak*, 2 [122]). Lapouge expressed himself in more or less the same terms: 'The supernatural essence of the soul has served as starting point for the theory of human rights, prior and superior to nature and society.' He viewed as disposable rubbish 'so-called human freedom', a further ominous remnant of the revolutionary years: fortunately, 'we are a long way from Rousseau's time'.[47]

In the second half of the nineteenth century, deconstruction of the subject, the critique of reason and the denunciation of revolution were all as one. This was the view, for example, of Theodule Ribot, a leading figure in France's conservative culture in these years: 'The person, the ego, the thinking subject, taken as a perfect unity', was in truth a fiction.[48] Citing Darwin, Galton emphasised a whole set of 'unconscious or barely conscious elements' were at work within human beings. Developments in science required a radical conclusion: 'Thus the word "Man", when rightly understood', became a noun of multitude, because he was 'composed of millions, perhaps billions of cells, each of which

---

45   Lamennais 1978, 161f.
46   Wallon 1974a, xxv.
47   Lapouge 1977, 509 and VIII.
48   In Pick 1989, 42.

possesses, in some sort an independent life.'[49] Taine brought in psychology as well as biology, and reached a similar conclusion:

> The simplest mental operation, a perception of the senses, a memory, a name, some judgement, are the result of the functioning of a complicated machine, the joint and concluding work of several million mechanisms that, like those of a clock, pull and push blindly, each for itself, each driven by its own strength and maintained in its function by balances and counterbalances.

The French historian added in a footnote: 'It is estimated that the number of brain cells (cortical layer) runs to twelve hundred million, and that of the fibres that connect them to four billion.'[50] After the critique of revolution had dissolved into a multiplicity of processes the subject that should have been the carrier of human rights, it hoisted 'reason' into the equation. While the revolution wrote reason on its banners, to establish the dignity of the human being as such and increase equality among human beings to the level of one of the 'truths already taken as self-evident', like the Declaration of Independence of the American colonies, in reality reason was merely the servant of passions and interests:

> Overtly or covertly, it is nothing other than a handy subaltern, a provoked domestic lawyer employed by the owners to defend their businesses: if they give way to him in public, it is merely through good manners. They have no problem in proclaiming it the legitimate sovereign; they never let any real, non-ephemeral authority have any influence on it, and under its nominal government they are the true rulers. These rulers of the human being are the temperament, physical need, animal instinct, hereditary prejudice, imagination: in general the dominant passion, most particularly the personal interest or the interest of family, caste, party.[51]

This theme can also be found in Barrès: 'Human reason is fettered' and 'there are no personal ideas'. According to him, rationalism ignored or suppressed an essential truth: 'We are not the masters of the thoughts that arise in us. They do not spring from our intelligence; instead, they constitute modes of reacting

---

49   Galton 1869, 363.
50   Taine 1899, Vol. 2, 56 f.
51   Taine 1899, Vol. 2, 59 f.

in which are transmitted very old physiological dispositions.'[52] Nietzsche too brought 'heredity' into his dissolution of the subject (JGB, 3 [7]). The target was clear, and common to both authors: Cartesian rationalism, the fateful fomenter of revolution.

Now let us look at Le Bon. The human being is led much more by instinct than by reason:

> The unconscious, which directs all actions of our inorganic life and the vast majority of the actions of our intellectual life, is to the conscious life of the spirit as the mass of the deep ocean to the waves rippling on the surface; if the incessant activity of the unconscious ceased, the human being could not live a single day.[53]

Similar themes can even be found in Spencer. He pointed to the impotence of the intellect and its subservience to the emotional sphere, as against the revolutionary fantasies of the regeneration of society through education or political action in general:

> Men are not rational beings, as commonly supposed. A man is a bundle of instincts, feelings, sentiments, which severally seek their gratification, and those which are in power get hold of reason and use it to their own ends, and exclude all other sentiments and feelings from power.[54]

The example adduced by Pareto to demonstrate this same thesis is illuminating: 'Many are not socialists because they have been persuaded by some reasoning: rather, they agree with such reasoning because they are socialists.'[55] Given the decisive weight of will, passion and interests in any kind of argumentation, the protest against mass misery was no more reasonable than the defence of privilege or of a society based on the polarisation of wealth and poverty.

Finally, the deconstruction of the subject went hand in hand with the denunciation of its anthropocentric vanity, as if the universe was there to revolve around the gratification of its desires and its demands for security, well-being and happiness. This is a claim whose absurdity was well demonstrated by Lapouge: 'Human beings are not a separate being', and in any case, 'their actions

---

52   In Girardet 1983, 186.
53   Le Bon 1920, 61 f.
54   In Duncan 1996, 366 (letter to J.A. Skilton of 10 January 1895).
55   Pareto 1974, 141.

are subject to the determinism of the universe.'[56] Here we are reminded of the polemic in *Beyond Good and Evil* against the thesis that the human being was 'the "measure of things"' (JGB, 3 [7]). Gumplowicz also mocked the 'boundless presumption of the individual',[57] with formulations reminiscent of Nietzsche's denunciation of human megalomania. There can be no doubt Nietzsche developed the idea of the dissolution of the subject with an incomparable finesse and mental penetration, thus displaying his extraordinary critical power: 'Who is it really that questions us here? What in us really wills the truth? [...] Which of us is Oedipus? Which one is the Sphinx?' (JGB, 1 [5]). It is an undoubtedly fascinating and fruitful attempt to get a glimpse of the human being as it were from outside and from above (*infra*, 29 § 3). The fact remains that the thesis of the dissolution of the subject was the counterpoint to the revolutionary proclamation of human rights; in this sense, Nietzsche was heir to Maistre, who was ironical about the category of the human being as such, and claimed never in his life to have met one.

---

56   Lapouge 1977, 511.
57   Gumplowicz 1885, 228.

CHAPTER 22

Otium et bellum: Aristocratic Distinction and the Struggle against Democracy

1   'Aristocratic Radicalism' and 'Great Conservative Reaction': Prussia, Russia and America

Nietzsche refused to identify with the interpretations of his contemporaries, so he was compelled to polemicise against the *Nationalzeitung*: a 'Prussian newspaper [...] [that sees] the book [*Thus Spoke Zarathustra*] as a "sign of the times"', as the 'true Junker philosophy that the *Kreuzzeitung* is not brave enough for' (EH, Why I write such good books, 1 [101–2]). Nietzsche's shocked tone was understandable. He could not identify with a social class that, as the title of its newspaper showed, was stubbornly attached to Christianity: 'Christian Junker' was an unaesthetic concept; it revealed an 'innocence among opposites' (an inability to grasp the contradiction), worse still, this '"good conscience" in lying, is really modern *par excellence*, it is almost definitive of modernity' (WA, Epilogue [262]).

But the reviewer definitely had a few reasons on his side. Authoritative historians of the time proceeded to make a comparative study of the Prussian Junkers, the slave owners of the plantations in the southern United States and the feudal nobility in Czarist Russia. Despite big differences, all three of these social classes, whose splendour and the splendour of the culture of which they were protagonists was more or less based on forced labour, also had features in common at the ideological level: the celebration of *otium* was linked as a gesture of aristocratic distinction to contempt for productive labour. Identification with a refined culture based on slave or semi-slave labour went hand in hand with the proud distancing from the massification of democratic and industrial society, which was advancing impetuously and irresistibly and claiming to have the wind of history in its sails. Finally, mockery of the idea of progress encouraged a further gesture of distinction, namely the proud claim of 'untimeliness' as well as the ability to swim against the general tide of the world's vulgarisation.[1] After their defeat, the ideologues of the southern slave owners posed as champions of the Lost Cause, champions of a Cause subdued by the great

---

1   Kolchin 1987, 157–61 and 177.

military and industrial power of the Union but no less noble for that.[2] In the middle of the Civil War, Fitzhugh wrote: 'Begin a great conservative reaction.'[3] Nietzsche identified himself similarly, in defining his philosophy as 'aristocratic radicalism'. In Russia too, at the end of the nineteenth century, there developed an aristocratic reaction that strove to turn back the development of the country by several centuries. People went so far as to 'arrest noblewomen for teaching peasant children how to read and write in their spare time'.[4] Although this chapter of history was probably not known to Nietzsche, it described a measure that fitted well with the aspirations and plans of his aristocratic radicalism.

Committed to a struggle they experienced as common to them, these three worlds flaunted an aristocratic cosmopolitanism: the Russian nobles despised not only the language but also '[m]ost of them were contemptuous of Russia, speaking French not Russian and spending more time in Nice and Biarritz than on their landed estates in the provinces'.[5] One need only read the novels of Turgenev, Dostoevsky and Tolstoy to notice how often, in conversations and entertainment, the Russian nobility used French. In Germany, it was different. True, Friedrich II spoke and wrote in French and surrounded himself with intellectuals from France, without hiding his contempt for German literature and culture. In an essay in 1780, written of course in French, he had even accused the German language of being incapable of producing good poetry and literature. This view was widely shared by the nobility. Its members addressed the *domestique* in German, but among themselves they resorted exclusively to French, thereby raising (as Herder pointed out) an insurmountable barrier against the 'popular classes'.[6] Herzen made the same observation about the Russian aristocracy: it was 'more cosmopolitan than the revolution'; far from having a national base, its rule rested precisely on the denial of the possibility of a national base, on the 'deep division [...] between the civilized classes and the peasants, between a very restricted elite and the vast majority of the population'.[7]

However, in Germany and especially in Prussia, the struggle against the expansionism first of Louis XIV and later of Napoleon had led necessarily to a rediscovery of the national language and even of the sense of a national community. At least during the most combustive moments of the uprising

---

2 Miller/Stout/Wilson 1998, *passim*.
3 In Woodward 1960, XXXVIII.
4 Figes 1996, 14, 53.
5 Figes 1996, 23.
6 Cf. Losurdo 1997a, 3, §5.
7 Herzen 1851, 160 ff.

against the French military occupation, cracks had started to appear in the barriers between the estates and castes: for that reason too, the mature Nietzsche expressed his hatred for the movement.

Finally, the three social worlds and classes compared here showed their greatest contempt for the expectations and hopes of the subaltern classes. Slaves and serfs strove to create an autonomous religious space that sometimes, most so in the southern United States, recalled the religions of the 'slaves of early Christianity'.[8] Moreover, not only the slaves but also the abolitionists themselves were filled with the crazy expectation of an 'approaching millennium', according to a theorist of the South.[9]

Against the credulity and fanaticism attributed to the slaves and their ideologues was set a mocking and demystifying attitude. In this sense, Fitzhugh, the most radical spokesperson of the culture committed to the defence of slavery, has been interpreted as an author of 'merciless and iconoclastic argumentation' or as 'the most logical reactionary of the South' and therefore as the main exponent of the so-called 'reactionary enlightenment'.[10] Without using this category, Herzen arrived in his analysis of the worldview of the Russian aristocracy at the same conclusion:

> In Petersburg the influence of the philosophy of the eighteenth century had a partly adverse effect. In France, the Encyclopaedists freed people from the old prejudices, they inspired the most elevated moral instincts and rendered them revolutionary. After Voltairean philosophy had broken the last ties that reined in a half-savage nature, it could oppose nothing to the ancient convictions and traditional moral duties. It armed the Russian with all the instruments of dialectic and irony, so that he could exonerate himself in his own eyes for the condition of bondage in which he found himself in relation to the ruler, and for his position as ruler with respect to the slave.[11]

Something similar happened in Germany. As Marx observed, a defender of slavery like Gustav Hugo did not hesitate to pose as a more consistent supporter of the Enlightenment than others that still dreamed naïvely of emancipation (*supra*, 14 § 2). This is the context in which we must place Nietzsche's 'Enlightenment', a constant feature of his thinking, well beyond the actual period of

---

8   Kolchin 1987, 222.
9   Fitzhugh 1960, 9.
10   Hartz 1955, 145 ff.; Woodward 1960, IX.
11   Herzen 1851, 47 f.

'Enlightenment'. Even towards the end of his conscious life, he described as 'visionary, sentimental, full of mysteries' and feminine the abolitionist morality that found its most significant expression in the figure of the female writer Beecher-Stowe (*infra*, 30 §5). A lucid, manly and sober worldview that did not indulge sentimental and feminine evasions and weaknesses did not shrink back from the slavery and mass sacrifice to which culture inevitably condemned the slaves and the vast majority of humanity.

I have stressed the enduring role of the aristocracy in Prussia, Russia and the southern United States. Nietzsche was in one way or another linked to all three of these worlds. As a young man, he compared Theognis, the spokesperson of the aristocracy and of slave society, to 'a finely educated and degenerate Junker with the passions of a Junker' (FS, III, 74). Even as an adolescent, he sympathised with Russia, which he fervently hoped would win the Crimean War (A, 20–1), and he continued to speak positively about this country, not yet completely contaminated by modern ideas, in the years and months preceding the end of his conscious life. The polemic against Beecher-Stowe was after all a denunciation of the abolitionist revolution that, along with slavery, extinguished a magnificent aristocratic culture.

In the United States too, the enemies of the Confederacy of the southern states give vent to nationalist tendencies: the protectionism of the Union was also aimed at developing a domestic industry that would let the country compete, economically and militarily, with the great European powers; beyond humanitarian indignation, the abolitionists were also moved by the ambition to hold up the United States as a model for other countries and other peoples. On the eve of the Civil War, Lincoln said of the institution of slavery: 'I hate it because it deprives our republican example of its just influence in the world.'[12] Decades earlier, the 'colonisation' movement, with the transfer of emancipated slaves to Africa, had been promoted by 'evangelicalism', but a 'nationalist evangelicalism', committed to spreading not just the Christian message but the influence and hegemony of the United States.[13]

However, these concerns meant nothing to the owners of the large plantations of the southern states, the watchful custodians of a refined lifestyle made possible by the enslavement of the blacks. The ideologues of that society were fully aware of this: not for nothing did the most ruthless among them go so far as to affirm the necessity of the institution of slavery even regardless of skin colour,[14] thus becoming theorists of a non-racial slavery, not unlike

---

12   In Bowen 1990, 88.
13   Fogel 1991, 461, fn. 43.
14   Bowman 1993, 13.

that of classical antiquity, which Nietzsche had in mind. With regard to Russia, one should not forget that the abolition of serfdom followed on defeat in the Crimean War: military recruitment on a large scale, necessary for competing with the other European powers, required that the central authority could also mobilise the serfs, up to then the exclusive 'property' of their masters. In that case too, national concerns played an important role in plunging into crisis an aristocratic world to which Nietzsche directed his attention and sympathy.

In the three ruling classes here compared, there was not even an idea of the nation, for this is divided up transversely into different and opposed 'races', in accordance with Boulainvilliers's model, taken up and reworked by Nietzsche and other exponents of the late nineteenth-century aristocratic reaction.

Even the crisis of the three different societies of which we speak has some analogies and a dynamic that makes one think of Nietzsche's analysis. Recent historians have traced the first cracks in the *ancien régime* in Russia to the spread of compassion, of 'guilt feelings' and 'bad conscience' among the upper classes, especially on account of the famine of 1891. This is seen as the beginning of the revolution: 'Everything has happened because of our own sin', 'there is only one remedy – by repentance, by changing our lives, and by destroying the walls between us and the people', wrote Tolstoy to a friend.[15] This same phenomenon can be observed in the United States: Calhoun polemicised against 'the rabid fanatics that regard slavery as a sin' and 'a crime – an offense against humanity'.[16] 'They regard themselves as implicated in the sin, and responsible for not suppressing it by the use of all and every means.'[17] In Germany, Cardinal Ketteler, despite joining the struggle against the socialist movement, strongly denounced the 'cruel' offence to 'true humanity' and the 'infanticide' implicit in child labour in the factories.[18] The language he used was reminiscent of Marx, who for his part resorted to biblical language to denounce 'the great Herodian child-stealing committed by capital'.[19]

Calhoun polemicised against the 'crusade' spirit of the abolitionists[20] that believed it was 'the most sacred obligation to use every effort to destroy' slavery.[21] In 1892, Tolstoy published an essay titled 'The Kingdom of God is Within

---

15   In Figes 1996, 160.
16   Calhoun 1992, 529.
17   Calhoun 1992, 582 f.
18   Ketteler 1967, 131.
19   Marx and Engels 1955 ff., 23, fn. 425.
20   Calhoun 1992, 528 f., 530 f., 469.
21   Calhoun 1992, 582.

You', [22] while in Prussia a leading representative of the Junkers mocked those that saw 'salvation [*Heil*]' in the abolition of hereditary servitude.[23]

It is understandable that the aristocracy in the three different countries often waged a polemic against the central authority, using liberal slogans. The Junkers, who represented an *'imperium in imperio'*, were mistrustful of a monarchical absolutism that did not let them transform their serfs into actual property, like the slaves in the southern United States.[24] Here Calhoun called for a struggle against an absolute power that wanted to remove the rights of the states and the slave owners.[25] In the face of a timid and partial emancipation of the serfs promoted or imposed from above, the Russian aristocracy was even ready to adopt 'liberal' attitudes, although without enthusiasm. The Junkers of prerevolutionary Prussia also saw themselves as 'liberals'.[26] Hence Bismarck claimed to have developed his 'revulsion at the rule of the bureaucracy' precisely because of his 'liberal sentiments of estate [*ständisch-liberale Stimmung*]'. That liberalism, he hastened to add, had to be clearly distinguished from 'Rhenish-French liberalism', inclined to incisive anti-feudal reforms from above and inspired by an oppressive and stifling state bureaucracy.[27] Regarding Nietzsche, one could speak of a 'liberalism' similar to that of the Junkers. It was also a fact that this liberalism quietly yielded to emergency legislation and Bonapartist temptations when faced with the socialist threat, just like the Iron Chancellor himself.

One can see in this sort of 'liberalism' a preventive warning against the dangers posed by the extension of the sphere of the state; but the same can be said of the ideologues of the slave-owning South. This thesis has been put forward not only by people explicitly claiming the heritage of the Confederation[28] but also by an eminent historian of Marxist provenance and with a Communist and Marxist past: 'The slave holders, however great their crimes against black people, mounted the first and only serious native-born critique of the totalitarian tendencies that have run wild' in the twentieth century.[29] Calhoun's polemic against 'absolute democracy', which would like to abolish the rights of the separate states and the slave owners,[30] is thus linked to today's denunciation of 'totalitarian democracy'. But the opposition in Russia of sectors of the

---

22   Figes 1996, 160.
23   Marwitz 1965, 134.
24   Bowman 1993, 18f.
25   Calhoun 1992, 120, 61.
26   Figes 1996, 47.
27   Bismarck 1919, 51f.
28   Weaver 1987, 78.
29   Genovese 1995a, 115.
30   Calhoun 1992, 120, 61.

aristocracy to measures intended, by abolishing serfdom, to strengthen the military apparatus and the potential for total mobilisation can be seen in the same context; as can Nietzsche, who sang the praises of slavery and was a relentless critic of the state, 'the coldest of all cold monsters' (Za, I, On the New Idol [34]). In all three countries, slavery and serfdom were abolished or greatly eroded as a result of a revolution from above. Its protagonist was the central state authority, which came up against the more or less trenchant opposition of the aristocratic class that was a beneficiary of those two institutions.

In the three different situations, this social class embodied the cruel truth, upon which Nietzsche tirelessly insisted, that slavery in its various forms was of the essence of culture. On the other hand, this class continued to profess a religion that, at least in Nietzsche's eyes, hopelessly contradicted the truth on which rested its own existence and success. In the expression 'Christian Junker', it was the adjective that horrified; and particularly because it was tied to a noun, to a social layer, that could have and should have put an end to Christian and socialist subversion. Again, Nietzsche's attitude was defined not so much by 'untimeliness' as by the attempt to lend rigour and consistency to a trend already under way.

2　Aristocratic 'Distinction' between the Late Eighteenth Century and the Late Nineteenth Century: Sieyès versus Nietzsche

This *ancien régime*, which appeared lively and vital, was the point of reference in the late nineteenth century in Europe and the West for the aristocratic reaction that lay such stress on the pathos of distinction and the distance between the nobility and the mob. In this case too, it is best to start with the struggle against the French Revolution. At the end of the eighteenth century, Burke warned against the devastating subversive threat to 'power, authority, and distinction'.[31] In the face of the tide of plebeian levelling, it was necessary to reaffirm that 'there are some distinctions to be kept in mind'.[32] While Gentz in his translation of the British statesman used other terms, Kant, who also knew Burke,[33] translated 'distinction' with the term later favoured by Nietzsche: a 'distinguished tone [*vornehmer Ton*]' was the hallmark of those that claimed to be custodians of a privileged knowledge inaccessible to ordinary mortals and not under the control of reason. In social terms, it was 'those that can *live off*

31　Burke 1826, Vol. 5, 106.
32　Burke 1826, Vol. 5, 105.
33　Losurdo 1983b, *passim*.

private means, meagre or abundant', without being 'forced to work for a living': 'in a word, all consider themselves distinguished to the extent that they believe they do not have to work', not even on the strictly conceptual and philosophical level: *beati possidentes*![34] For Kant, a distinguished tone was an essential element in the behaviour of the nobility and its ideologues.

In the same period, Mounier, who took a centrist stand, attacked the revanchism of the aristocrats, who set against 'the chimerical plans for absolute equality' the 'apologia of humiliating distinctions'.[35] On the other hand, Heine, starting from a democratic standpoint, condemned the attitude of the English aristocrat that threw 'an indifferently distinguished [*gleichgültig vornehm*] glance at the crowd [*Menschengewühl*] beneath him', that 'heap of inferior creatures whose joy and pain have nothing in common with his feelings – for above the rabble [*Menschengesindel*] stuck to the surface of the earth hovers England's nobility, like a being of a higher nature'.[36]

The necessary defence of 'distinction' against advancing massification and levelling was also part of the liberal tradition. For example, Tocqueville denounced the ideal pursued by the more radical thinkers of the Enlightenment as follows: 'No more hierarchies in society, no more *distinguished* classes, no more established ranks, but a people made up of individuals almost the same and entirely equal.'[37] Unfortunately, this model had by no means faded away: according to John Stuart Mill, a gradual levelling of the 'various social eminences' was happening; it was a process of constant 'assimilation', favoured by the spread of education. The result: 'Non-conformity' lost all social support, while the rule of the 'masses' imposed itself without opposition.[38] And, as is well known, Treitschke also praised the '*distinguished* classes' (*supra*, 4 § 5).

Needless to say, the celebration of 'distinction' was much more emphatic among representatives of the aristocratic reaction in the late nineteenth century: they committed themselves not only to slowing down or containing the process of democratisation and 'massification' but to rolling it back as much as possible. And again we see that Nietzsche greatly radicalised a tendency already present in the culture of his time: now the gulf that separated the upper classes of society from the rest of the population became unbridgeable. The dichotomy of plebeians and noblemen also took the form of a dichotomy of the profane and the initiated or of an opposition of 'the exoteric and the esoteric',

---

34 Kant 1900 ff., Vol. 8, 390, 395.
35 Mounier 1801, 5.
36 Heine 1969–79, Vol. 2, 542.
37 Tocqueville 1951 ff., Vol. 2, half-vol. 1, 213 (AR, Book 3, 3).
38 Mill 1972a, 130 f.

which could be found in all higher cultures, 'everywhere that people believed in an order of rank and not in equality and equal rights' (JGB, 30 [31]). The two extremes of the hierarchy not only could not recognise one another in a common knowledge but in truth could not even communicate with one another:

> Our highest insights must – and should! – sound like stupidities, or possibly crimes, when they come without permission to people whose ears have no affinity [*geartet*] for them and were not predestined for them. [...] What helps feed or nourish the higher type [*Art*] of the human being must be almost poisonous to a very different and lesser type. The virtues of a base human being could indicate vices and weaknesses in a philosopher. If a higher type [*hochgearteter*] of human being were to degenerate [*entartete*] and be destroyed, this very destruction could give him the qualities needed to make people honor him as a saint down in the lower realm where he has sunk.
>
> JGB, 30 [31]

As confirmation of the continuity of the ideological process starting with the struggle against the French Revolution, it is interesting to note that, in Sieyès, we can find a critique of positions taken nearly a century later by Nietzsche. The '*Art*' at the centre of the discourse of the theorist of aristocratic radicalism, declined in the plural and conjugated in a series of nouns and compound verbs, was the *espèce* on whose unity Sieyès insisted throughout his fierce attack on the aristocracy. 'The privileged even come to see themselves as a different human species', far above the 'little people [*gens de rien*]', i.e., common humanity. The representative of the Third Estate added that they did not hesitate to project themselves as 'a chosen [*choisie*] nation within the nation'.[39] As we shall see, Nietzsche called the aristocratic circle that he summoned to distinction 'God's elect' (*infra*, 28 § 6).

The characteristics the theorist of 'aristocratic radicalism' celebrated were just as many points in the French revolutionary's indictment. The latter accused the aristocrats of 'an involuntary movement of revulsion' when they happened to come into contact with ordinary people: 'The false sentiment of personal superiority was so important to the privileged that they would like to extend it to all their relations with other citizens. They are not in any way inclined *to mix*, to stand *alongside* them, to be *together* with them, etc. etc.'[40] What Sieyès

---

39   Sieyès 1985a, 99.
40   Sieyès 1985a, 100.

highlighted critically by way of italics Nietzsche told the members of the 'new nobility' to avoid at all costs.

But the resemblances between the two authors, naturally with opposing value judgements, go even further. We already know that the German philosopher praised the pride of the aristocrat that proclaimed before him and others: 'I have an origin.' This is an attitude the French revolutionary mocked a century earlier:

> In the old castles the privileged man cherishes greater respect for himself, he can stand for long periods in ecstasy before the portrait of his ancestors and become even more inebriated, at will, by the honour of being descended from people that lived in the thirteenth and fourteenth centuries; in fact, he does not suspect that such an advantage might be shared in common by all families. In his opinion, it is a characteristic peculiar to certain races.[41]

Let us return to Nietzsche. In *Beyond Good and Evil* he wrote:

> A profound reverence for age and origins, [...] a faith and a prejudice in favor of forefathers and against future generations is typical of the morality of the powerful. And when, conversely, people with 'modern ideas' believe almost instinctively in 'progress' and 'the future', and show a decreasing respect for age, this gives sufficient evidence of the ignoble origin of these 'ideas'.
>
> JGB, 260 [155]

And, again, one hears Sieyès' anticipatory sneer:

> What is a bourgeois in the face of a privileged noble? The latter has his eyes constantly fixed on the noble past. There he is aware of all his titles, all his strength, he lives off his ancestors. The bourgeois, on the other hand, whose eyes are permanently fixed on the ignoble present and the uncertain future, bears the one and prepares for the other with the resources of his industry. [...] Ah! Why can the privileged man not return to the past to enjoy his titles, his magnificence, and leave the present to a stupid nation in all its ignobility?[42]

---

41   Sieyès 1985a, 100.
42   Sieyès 1985a, 101.

In the course of his indictment and his political struggle against the *ancien régime*, Sieyès also took aim at the aristocracy's good manners:

> The privileged Frenchman is not polite because he believes he owes it to others, but because he believes he owes it to himself. He respects not the rights of others but himself, his own dignity. He would in no way wish to be confused, on account of his vulgar manners, with what he calls bad company. One could say that he fears that the object of his kindness might take him for a non-privileged person, as he is.[43]

As for Nietzsche, he characterized the aristocrat as 'pleasure in forms: taking under protection all that is formal, the belief that courtesy is one of the great virtues; distrust of all forms of letting oneself go'; for this concern for forms 'delimits, holds at a distance, protects against being mistaken for another' (XI, 543–4); the aristocrat could 'choose for company that mischievous and cheerful vice, politeness' (JGB, 284 [171]).

In conclusion, the world denounced by the French revolutionary returned a century later as a mark of the distinction of the new nobility, but with a series of distortions caused by the process of artificial rejuvenation. Even if Sieyès emphasised that the nobleman with his good manners was out only to confirm his own dignity and that of his estate, he nevertheless accorded him the ability to be polite with all. With Nietzsche, on the other hand, we detect a slipping and a fall in tone. According to him, the aristocrat should observe the following rules of life: 'The belief that one has duties only in respect of one's peers; in respect of others, one can behave as one pleases' (XI, 543).

This comparison of Sieyès's denunciation of aristocratic 'distinction' and Nietzsche's celebration of it, almost a century later, is made possible by a precise historical circumstance. After having made its appearance in the struggle against the French Revolution, the claim to 'distinction' made its reappearance, albeit with modifications, in the course of the aristocratic reaction.

3   *Ancien régime* and the Military Role of the Aristocracy

The watchword *otium et bellum*, which Nietzsche valued (FW, 329 [184]), also brings us back to this movement and this spiritual climate. *Otium et bellum* described and transfigured the conditions of the lives and the values of the

---

43   Sieyès 1985a, 102.

aristocracy in a large part of the West in the second half of the nineteenth century. While the aristocracy based its wealth and splendour on the possession of land and the labour of a farming population still burdened by the feudal legacy, it was called upon by tradition to occupy the higher ranks of the military. The master-servant relationship was reproduced in the army in the form of an officer/soldier relationship; for a long time, master and officer in Prussia retained the 'right to inflict corporal punishment' on serfs and soldiers.[44] More or less the same can be said of Russia.[45] In the latter case too, the beneficiary of *otium* was at the same time the protagonist of *bellum*, just as the mass of serfs and the children of serfs had to bear the burden of the *otium* and *bellum*.

On the eve of the First World War, 'it was the officer corps of the army, that perfect and majestic embodiment of Prussianified Germany, that represented the feudal element in its most distilled form, especially at the higher levels'.[46] This was true of the Second Reich, and not only of the Central Powers, but also of Britain. 'The officer corps of England's fighting services, notably in the top ranks, continued to be a highly exclusive body. By birth and training it was steeped in a gentlemanly code of service.'[47] And while enjoying their possessions and wealth, the aristocratic officers posed as 'chivalrous heroes', called upon to show 'spartan and stoic courage'.[48] Even if we cross the Atlantic, the picture does not change radically, at least in the South. The watchword *otium et bellum* was congenial not just to Prussian Junkers but also to the slave-owning aristocracy of the southern states. The latter decided to fight the Civil War in part to protect its 'special culture' and to avoid being reduced to the level of 'a nation of Yankee traders'.[49]

The celebration of war was also stimulated by colonial expansion and the hope, nourished by no few liberal writers, that it might provide an antidote to the vulgar hedonistic ideology in whose wake had followed democratic and socialist agitation. 'The masses want tranquillity and earnings', and thus peace, but the advantage of war was precisely that it undermined this philistine view of life, said Burckhardt, citing the saying of Heraclitus[50] of which Nietzsche too was fond: 'War is the father of all good things' (FW, 92 [90]). Renan attributed to the 'Germanic race' the merit of being 'dedicated to war and patriotism', so

---

44   Köselleck 1975, 641–46.
45   Figes 1996, 57.
46   Mayer 1981, 309.
47   Mayer 1981, 307.
48   Cannadine 1990, 74.
49   Thus an ideologue of the South (cited in Genovese 1998, 104). This is the world Mark Twain
       mocked (cf. Kiernan 1988, 312 f.).
50   Burckhardt 1978a, 150, 118 f.

it escaped the infection not only of democracy but also of 'bourgeois materialism, which asks for nothing more than the peaceful enjoyment of acquired wealth'.[51] That was precisely why Germany was spared the horrors of the Paris Commune. Tocqueville's view was not much different, as was clear from a letter written on the occasion of the international crisis of 1840, in which the French liberal, without hiding 'a certain satisfaction' at the looming showdown, confessed as follows to a dear friend: 'You know how I welcome *great events* and how fed up I am with our mediocre democratic and bourgeois *soup*.'[52] This was not just an occasional theme. *Democracy in America* was quite explicit: 'I do not mean to speak ill of war; war almost always opens the mind of a people and raises its soul.'[53] So we should not be surprised by his celebration of the Opium War, in which geopolitical considerations concerning the relentless forward march of the 'European race' (*supra*, 9 § 5) were interwoven with moral and aesthetic considerations on the role of war as an antidote to the danger of banality and the banausic qualities inherent in the modern world: 'So let us not speak too badly of our century and of ourselves; men are small, but events are great.'[54]

Crossing from France to Britain, we see there too the theme of the celebration of war as an antidote, in Carlyle's words, to the 'Gospel of Mammon' or, to quote a contemporary scholar, as 'an act of purification of the dominant materialism' was by no means absent. Sometimes, for example, in the case of Ruskin, the flourishing culture of ancient Greece and ancient Rome, the splendours of a world kept wide awake by a constant military tension, were cited to confirm the purifying function of war.[55]

In Britain, this attitude was by no means exclusive to authors and currents suspicious of or hostile to liberalism. The recipient of the letter in which Tocqueville praised the Opium War was the British liberal Reeve, who during the Crimean War, in correspondence with the French liberal, expressed himself even more grandiloquently:

> We live in a time in which we must be able to suffer and see suffering. The sword of war penetrates into our very marrow. But what a mighty influence this struggle exerts on the political and social body! What a union

---

51   Renan 1947 ff., Vol. 1, 332 f., 383.
52   Tocqueville 1951 ff., Vol. 8, half-vol. 1, 421 (letter to Gustave de Beaumont of 9 August 1840).
53   Tocqueville 1951 ff., Vol. 1, half-vol. 2, 274 (DA, Book 2, pt. 3, 2).
54   Tocqueville 1951 ff., Vol. 6, half-vol. 1, 58.
55   Barié 1953, 70, 79, 275; on the denunciation of the 'politics of Mammon' in Britain in the nineteenth century, cf. too Bodelsen 1968, 105, 115.

of sentiments and efforts it produces! What an awakening of those forces that are, after all, the greatness of a people. I gladly accept all the anguish and evils of war, for what it gives us on the moral and even more so on the political plane.[56]

The theme of war as an antidote to radical democracy and socialism, which played such an important role in Nietzsche and in Western culture between the nineteenth and twentieth centuries, already began to emerge in previous decades, in a society that was admittedly liberal, but where, on the one hand, remnants and memories of the *ancien régime* continued to survive and, on the other, everything was geared to colonial expansion. Once again, we must take as our starting point the struggles that unfolded in the wake of the French Revolution.

Against the mediocrity and vulgarity of the society of 'sophists, economists and accountants' that was emerging with the collapse of the *ancien régime* Burke set the 'glory' of 'the old chivalry' and the medieval warriors.[57] Some decades later, Nietzsche stressed that the *vornehme Krieger*, the 'noble warriors', formed an integral part of the aristocracy, of the 'distinguished' layers and individuals, set against the herd and the general levelling (AC, 57 [58]). This was also the opinion of Langbehn, citing a thesis of Moltke, the Prussian count and victor at Sedan, who declared the German army is the 'most distinguished [*vornehmst*] institution in the German Reich.'[58]

The specificity of the aristocratic reaction lay in the fact that the celebration of war coincided ever more clearly with that of the figure of the warrior. Warriors were part of the aristocracy in two respects. They embodied the opposition to feminine sentimentality, which wanted to remove the harshness of life and thereby destroy the sense of distance. They were part of it also because the hierarchy and spirit of sacrifice that war entailed put it at odds with the idea of gain and labour and thus with the mercantile spirit as well as with socialist discourse.

In praising *bellum*, Nietzsche sometimes stressed a contrast between Germans and British. The latter seemed to have 'renounced war', in which they resembled the Romans, who 'became rather tired of war' (MA, 477 [260]). This theme can also be traced to European culture, for example, to an author against whom Nietzsche otherwise waged a fierce polemic. According to Renan, the warrior character *par excellence* was represented by the 'Germanic element'. As the defeat at Sedan had shown, it had already been expunged from France,

56   In Tocqueville 1951 ff., Vol. 6, half-vol. 1, 150.
57   Burke 1826, Vol. 5, 149 f.
58   Langbehn 1922, 35.

so that this 'previously brilliant and warrior' nation had plunged to a level 'of mediocrity'. But the Germanic and warrior element was also about to be expunged from Britain, to be supplanted by a 'softer, more sympathetic, more human' spirit, which reminded the French writer of the decadence of the Roman Empire.[59]

This characterisation of Britain as vulgarly mercantile and pacifistic sounds rather strange. One could cite against Nietzsche (and Renan) a British liberal, Richard Cobden, who in the middle of the nineteenth century painted a very different picture of his country's military and foreign policy:

> We have been the most combative and aggressive community that has existed since the days of the Roman dominion. Since the revolution of 1688 we have expended more than fifteen hundred millions of money upon wars, not one of which has been upon our own shores, or in defence of our hearths and homes. [...] This pugnacious propensity has been invariably recognised by those that have studied our national character.[60]

To understand the particular emphasis with which German culture struck up its song of praise to the virtues of war, one must take two factors into account. It was not until the 1870s that Germany was able to construct itself as a unitary nation-state. After years of resistance and the armed uprising against Napoleon, the historical retardation was overcome by means of a series of wars (against Denmark, Austria and France) that could obviously not be conducted without creating a martial spirit in the country. Secondly, Britain, thanks to its European and worldwide hegemony, was more easily able than Germany to afford a 'pacifist' ideology, by presenting its colonial conquests as a contribution to the cause of peace. Not only John Stuart Mill, as we have already seen, but even an advocate of incessant wars of conquest like Rhodes was able to celebrate the global empire that he aspired to build as a precondition for the realisation of perpetual peace. So, Britain's relentless colonial expansion contributed on the one hand to a noble and disinterested cause and, on the other hand, allowed the country that was the protagonist of this triumphal march to become stronger and richer. In a nutshell, 'philanthropy + 5 per cent'.[61] But, for that very reason, for Nietzsche at least, in the last years of his conscious life, 'the English are the people of perfect cant', the people that personified moral

---

59   Renan 1947 ff., Vol. 1, 348–50.
60   In Pick 1993, 21.
61   In B. Williams 1921, 51 f.

hypocrisy and was inextricably tied to the merchant spirit (GD, *Expeditions of an Untimely Man*, 12 [198]).

4 *Otium et bellum*, 'War and Art'

The aristocracy, whose recovery the aristocratic reaction wanted, was in conflict with both the masses, who were becoming ever more restless, and a bourgeoisie that tended to undermine it. In arguing against those that would challenge the social and political function of the nobility, Burke declared that if, in establishing representative bodies, one absolutised the elective principle by 'abolishing hereditary titles and functions, levelling all social ranks', that would mean sanctioning the power of 'money',[62] with disastrous results at all levels: '*Nobility is a graceful ornament* to the *civil order*. It is the *Corinthian capital* of polished society'; in France or elsewhere, aristocrats stood out as 'for the greater part composed of men of high spirit, and of a delicate sense of honour; [...] with a good military tone; and reasonably tinctured with literature'.[63] Together with the 'glory' of 'ancient chivalry', beauty and art were called upon to oppose the coarsening and massification of the world.

Some decades later, in Germany, in calling for a struggle against democracy, Langbehn launched the slogan 'war and art'. This man saw himself as a 'disciple' of Nietzsche: and yes, his motto echoed *otium et bellum*, where *otium* was the indispensable condition for the emergence of culture and, in the first place, of art. This was shown particularly by the example of Greece. Burke too referred indirectly to Greece, with his mention of the 'Corinthian capital', and so did Langbehn: '"War and art" is a Greek, a German, an Aryan slogan.'[64] In Britain, also at the end of the nineteenth century, Ruskin declared: '[A]s peace is established or extended in Europe, the arts decline'; as an antidote to mediocrity and vulgarity, war was a powerful stimulus for art, and inextricably tied to it.[65] As regards Italy, in 1900 Trotsky drew attention to D'Annunzio (matched with Nietzsche) and his insistence on appealing primarily to 'poets', so they would act as a bulwark against democracy's levelling and massifying tendency by relying on their immediately obvious cultural and human excellence.[66]

---

62 Burke 1826, Vol. 7, 18 f.
63 Burke 1826, Vol. 5, 251, 254 f.
64 Langbehn 1922, 193.
65 In Pick 1993, 68 f.
66 Trotsky 1979, 118 f.

The courage of the warrior and the cult of beauty were two basic pillars of the gesture of aristocratic distinction. This is particularly clear in the case of Langbehn, who celebrated art and the 'artistic worldview' as synonymous with creativity, granted to very few, and thus with 'distinction' and 'aristocracy'. Here we were dealing with the most radical and, at the same time, most immediately evident refutation of the democratic superstition according to which the spread of education would lead to the development of culture. Art could not be learned, so it referred to nature, which was 'constructed in an aristocratic way'.[67] Far from being synonymous with an innocent occupation far above the human fray, art, as natural aristocracy, represented the most radical antithesis to socialism, which meant levelling and 'reversion to the principle of the herd'.[68] Precisely because it had as its reference nature, which was never static, art was in no way in contradiction with *polemos*. Because it rendered immediately visible the reality of a natural aristocracy and was intimately linked to *Concordia-discors* and *polemos*, art was a synonym for Langbehn with the domination the superior man, the great artist, exercised over the raw material formed by the mass and common humanity. To be political in the best sense of the term 'means being creative and being an artist'. So 'art is a task even higher' than politics, which it embraces within itself: 'All the higher spiritual forces gravitate around the concept of art, which represents the human being's authentic and perfect destination.'[69] Understood in this broad and pugnacious sense, art resembled Dante's 'Beatrix': it would lead the 'German' through the inferno of modern mediocrity onto 'purer heights'. Hopes of regeneration could be vested only in an 'artistic-political' (and military) 'activity' worthy of the name.[70]

The courage of the warrior and the cult of beauty made it possible to distinguish true aristocracy not just from the popular masses but also from the parvenus that saw wealth as a value in itself. Unlike the 'old wealth', noted Bagehot in Britain, the 'new wealth' or the 'plutocracy' had something 'coarse' about it.[71] This reminded one of the 'ruddy, plump hands' of which Nietzsche spoke in regard to the 'manufacturers' who, lacking any aura of superiority, were hardly distinguishable from their workers or servants (*supra*, 11 §2). Driven on by the frenzy of accumulation and labour, these 'convicts of wealth' were the 'gilded, fake rabble', scarcely to be distinguished from the mass of the starving: '[R]abble above, rabble below!' (Za, IV, The Voluntary Beggar [219]). In this way,

---

67   Langbehn 1922, 33–35, 59–61.
68   Langbehn 1922, 141.
69   Langbehn 1922, 225, 47.
70   Langbehn 1922, 107, 225.
71   Bagehot 1974a, 178 f.

'the actual purpose of all wealth is forgotten', for these '"rich" – they are the poorest' (x, 292).

Bagehot urged the 'new wealth' to make common cause with the 'old wealth' to avoid stoking up further discontent and protest among the popular masses.[72] To the extent that the 'plutocracy' refused to participate in the sociopolitical bloc here recommended, it became identified, even in America, with both crass materialism and subversion.[73] This was also Nietzsche's view, when he hoped for the social and eugenic merger of the layers called upon to stem the tide of vulgarity and modern degeneration.

5   The Warrior and the Soldier, War and Revolution

Otium et bellum, 'war and art', could be blended so harmoniously that Nietzsche was able to include the 'Prussian officer corps' among the art works he admired (XII, 118–9). It was the first line of defence in the struggle against the democratic and subversive threat: 'The future of German culture rests on the sons of Prussian officers' (XI, 569). Was not this, more than any other, the milieu that had expressed special sympathy for the cause of the slave-owning Confederation (*supra*, 12 § 5) and thereby shown that it understood the essential truth that slavery was the indispensable foundation of culture? In any case, even in his early years, Nietzsche praised 'military genius' as a 'cure' for the vulgarisation and massification of the modern world (*supra*, 2 § 6), and he continued right until the end to recommend 'the militarism, starting with Napoleon, that saw its natural enemy [*Feindin*] in civilization' (XIII, 427). In this sense, he expressed his joy at 'Europe's military development' (XI, 263).

Of course, it was necessary to point out that the object of praise here was the warrior and not the soldier. Zarathustra warned against confusing them: 'I see many soldiers: if only I saw many warriors! "Uni-form" one calls what they wear: if only what they conceal with it were not uni-form!' (Za, I, On War and Warriors [33]). The idea of a mass army implied an element of standardisation and the erosion of differences between social layers: Nietzsche identified in it a moment of crisis, at least potential, for the *ancien régime*, all the more so because of doubts about the loyalty of the mobilised mass. A fragment from the spring of 1884 had already noted that 'arming the people – is ultimately arming the mob' (XI, 71). Some four years later, the philosopher drew attention

---

72   Bagehot 1974a, 178 f.
73   Sumner 1992, 141–5.

once again to the grave dangers inherent in the new situation: the 'worker' had become 'fit for military service', and had at the same achieved 'the right of association' and 'the political right to vote', yet still he experienced his situation as an 'injustice'. The development of the mass army and what later would be called total mobilisation went hand in hand with the extension of political citizenship and the recognition of further rights for the popular classes. Nietzsche's attack focused on the second aspect of this link.

Outside Germany too, the celebration of the warrior effortlessly coexisted with a distrust or hostility towards the figure of the soldier. While Ruskin nostalgically evoked the old wars, which supposedly resembled knightly tournaments that consecrated the courage and nobility of the soul, he expressed his disappointment at wars in which victory was determined by machines or, worse still, 'the angriest mob'.[74]

And yet there was a period in which Nietzsche declared himself ready, under certain conditions, to accept the mass army and even general mobilisation. This is clear from a fragment written towards the end of his conscious life:

> No one demands more rigorously than I that everyone be a soldier: there is no other means to educate a whole people to the virtue of obeying and commanding, to cadence in behaviour and gesture, to cheerfulness and courage, to freedom of spirit – it is by far the most rational element of our education that everyone should be a soldier.
>
> XIII, 645

Even Zarathustra addressed the warrior as follows: 'Rebellion – that is the nobility of slaves. Let your nobility be obedience! Your commanding itself shall be obeying! To a good warrior "thou shalt" sounds nicer than "I will." And everything you hold dear you should first have commanded to you' (Za, I, On War and Warriors [34]). The discipline and hierarchy of army life was here explicitly recommended as an antidote to the spirit of revolt and agitation of the socialist and labour movement. In this case too, we are dealing with a pan-European theme. If Carlyle called on the mass of vagabonds to respect the orders of the master 'with manlike, soldierlike obedience and heartiness',[75] Nietzsche voiced the following hope: 'Workers should learn to experience in the same way as soldiers' (XII, 350).

But the fragment from the end of 1888 or early January of 1889 cited above contained a new element: 'Nor is there any other way to spread, beyond every

---

74   In Pick 1993, 72.
75   Carlyle 1983, 58; cf. Marx and Engels 1975 ff., 10, 301–310.

abyss of rank, spirit, duty, a manly reciprocal benevolence throughout the whole of a people' (XIII, 645). Starting above all with the First World War, the theme of the warrior community in the face of imminent danger and the threat of death became a central theme of war ideology. At least for a short while, concern about the worker 'fit for military service' yielded to the confident expectation that total mobilisation might open new perspectives for the social control of the masses.

Despite these oscillations and troubled reflections, one can say, overall, that in the late Nietzsche fear of the terrible dangers of subversion inherent in the growing chauvinist agitation and the consequent military mobilisation that marked the European scene in the late 1880s tended to predominate. It should be added that, with his fears and oscillations, the philosopher once again displayed his extraordinary empathy. The reasons for the cult of *bellum* in the aristocracy and the aristocratic reaction have been well explained by an eminent sociologist. If 'the machine' was a leveller, a vulgariser, militarism and war promised to bring back onto the agenda not only discipline but also a sense of hierarchy, courage and honour, in the last analysis, the values of the *ancien régime*.[76] And it is for that very reason that the call for war and possibly for a 'splendid little war' was so widespread in the reactionary culture of the time.[77] This theme was certainly not alien to Nietzsche, but he could also see or imagine the other side of the coin: the appeal to the people in arms, its mobilisation and rebellion, would actually unleash an unprecedented wave of revolution.

---

76   Veblen 1904, 358, 398 f.
77   Losurdo 1996, 3, § 3.

CHAPTER 23

Social Darwinism, Eugenics and Colonial Massacres

1   Selection and 'Counter-Selection'

The theme of *polemos*, *bellum*, war, *agon*, struggle was omnipresent in Nietzsche. However, in the eyes of the author of *Ecce Homo*, only the usual 'scholarly cattle' could link his thinking to Darwinism (EH, Why I write such good books, 1 [101]). Actually, reading Darwin was important in Nietzsche's development. The vision of life as '*agon*', which Nietzsche derived from classical antiquity, was now confirmed at the 'scientific' level: 'Now one has rediscovered struggle everywhere, and one talks of the struggle of cells, tissues, organs, organisms' (IX, 487). At long last, the view that sought to give credence to 'a false concept of harmony and peace as the most useful condition' had been refuted at every level. 'In reality, for something right to grow, a strong antagonism is needed *everywhere*' (IX, 558). The adverb I have italicised clearly expressed the desire not to confine simply to the realm of nature the discoveries and worldview of the great English naturalist. This was an essential aspect of social Darwinism.

Spencer condemned any state interference in the economy with the argument that we should not hinder the cosmic law that requires the elimination of the incapable and of those whose lives had turned out badly: 'Why the whole effort of nature is to get rid of [the weaker,] to clear the world of them, and make room for [the] better'? All human beings were subject to God's judgement: 'If they are sufficiently complete to live, they live, and it is well that they should live. If they are not sufficiently complete to live, they die, and it is best they die.'[1] In Sumner's eyes, the folly of socialism lay precisely in its claim to 'save individuals from the difficulties or hardships of the struggle for existence and the competition of life through the intervention of the "state"'.[2] But we are already familiar with Nietzsche's sarcastic view of the 'superfluous ones' that demanded to be saved by the state.

And yet, even in this case, the protest of the 'untimely' philosopher could take advantage of a fact: he denounced the economistic pettiness of the category 'struggle for existence', a merely specific, and plebeian, manifestation of the much wider phenomenon of the will to power; in any case, contrary to what

---

1   Spencer 1865, 414–5.
2   In Hofstadter 1944–45, 48.

the more naïve exponents of that school of thought believed, selection did not necessarily lead to the triumph of the best: '[W]ho can give any guarantee [...] that the conquering master race, that of the Aryans, is not physiologically being defeated as well?' (GM, I, 5 [15]).

Should we then conclude that Nietzsche was far removed from social Darwinism? In fact, in asking his worried question, he was far from alone. Eugenics arose and expressed itself precisely because of its anxiety about the selection in reverse underway: due to their fertility, the lower classes and the malformed were threatening to take over.[3] On the other side of the Atlantic, Sumner was wondering whether the 'survival of the fittest' would not soon become the 'survival of the unfittest'.[4] It was foolish and dangerous to allow oneself to be lulled into a consolatory view of the laws that govern evolution: 'Rattlesnakes may survive where horses perish ... or highly cultivated white men may die where Hottentots flourish.'[5] Unfortunately – added Lapouge – the 'Aryan genius' was in great difficulties; 'the race with slave-like features' was gaining the upper hand.[6] The devastating effects of demography were further accentuated by their combination with the spread of philanthropy. Referring to Nietzsche, in 1895 Ploetz warned against the danger of 'counter-selection' and the 'growth of counter-selection' promoted by the victory of the 'humanitarian idea of equal rights' and of the 'ideals of humanity and justice'.[7]

Sometimes, instead of 'counter-selection', people preferred to speak of 'regressive evolution'. Such was the title of a book published in Paris in 1897 (*L'évolution régressive*), quoted favourably by Vacher de Lapouge two years later. Lapouge, for his part, insisted: 'Selection often goes in the worst direction.'[8]

Unfortunately, a phenomenon like war, in itself beneficial, could also push in this same direction. This was something that had concerned Nietzsche ever since his 'enlightenment' period. It was the basis for the break with Bismarck and the National Liberals, accused of not realising that '[t]he greatest disadvantage of the conscript armies that are so highly extolled today consists in the fact that they squander some of the most highly civilized individuals'. Chauvinism and the wars in Europe and the West strongly promoted subversion, by exhausting the forces that should be used 'frugally and anxiously', 'since it

---

3   Galton 1869, 356 f.
4   Sumner 1992, 189 f.
5   Sumner 1992, 223.
6   Lapouge 1896, 67.
7   Ploetz 1895, 183 ff., 194 f.
8   Lapouge 1977, 502 f.

requires great stretches of time to create the conditions that might chance to produce such delicately organized brains!' (MA, 442 [239]).

This concern returned with redoubled intensity towards the end of the philosopher's conscious life: during wars and upheavals, the 'strong' were sacrificed: their numbers steadily decreased, while the 'weak have a tremendous instinct to spare themselves, to preserve themselves, to support each other reciprocally' (XIII, 219). The higher natures were endangered precisely because of their best features: courage, generosity, ambition, loyalty and the refusal to resort to subterfuge. 'The strong races decimate each other: war, hunger for power, adventure; their existence is costly, short, they wear themselves out. [...] They are wasteful races' (XIII, 369–70). There was even a danger of the 'extermination of the men that have turned out best' because of the senseless 'wars for the "fatherland"' in Europe. And 'in the midst of this *décadence*', the 'deformed, degenerate and impotent of all kinds' stepped up their pressure (XIII, 430–1). In such a dangerous situation, 'it is madness to put in front of the cannon such a flower of force and youth and power' (XIII, 645).

By comparison with the cabinet wars of the *ancien régime*, which traditionally almost exclusively affected only the plebeian mob, while the opposing leaderships engaged in a diplomatic-military ballet, a change had come about. Burckhardt still subscribed to Heinrich Leo's theory, that war was about to 'wipe out the scrofulous mob', or, as the Basel historian adds, the 'miserable, stunted lives [*jämmerlichen Notexistenzen*]'.[9] Now the picture had changed: think in particular of the Civil War, in which the aristocrats that embodied the ideal of *otium et bellum* Nietzsche so greatly valued were mown down, while the black population of the South largely stood on the side-lines. In the France of the Second Republic, the general rule permitting the exemption from military service of those able, thanks to their wealth and social position, to find a replacement was questioned[10] – despite the opposition of Tocqueville (who favoured maintaining the old privilege).

So much was clear. Nietzsche had not the slightest intention of condemning the *polemos*, *bellum* as such, as he explained on several occasions. Those that cited him also understood this well. War is 'one means in the struggle for existence', observes Ploetz: however, one must ensure it decimates the 'worst individuals' or the 'bad variants [*Varianten*]' of the population and not its best elements.[11] This theme too was widespread in the culture of the time. It was very clearly expressed by Pareto: 'War is a potent cause of the extinction of the

9   Burckhardt 1978a, 118f.
10   Jardin 1984, 396.
11   Ploetz 1895, 147.

warrior elite' and the aristocrats.[12] But it can be found, in more subtle form, even in Veblen.[13] When it was a question of denouncing the perverse effects of war and militarism from the point of view of selection, Lapouge waxed particularly eloquent: 'In modern nations, war and militarism are real scourges, whose final result is to weaken the race', since they reduced 'the chances of reproduction of the elite, while ensuring an enduring posterity for the dregs' of society. He concluded: 'Contemporary militarism not only exerts a dangerous selective influence on individuals but also compromises the future of Europe.'[14]

That is why the 'struggle for existence', even if it took the form of expressly violent conflict, by no means guaranteed the triumph of the best. According to Lapouge, one had to be careful not to confuse the theory of 'selection' with a theory of 'progress'.[15] In its naïve popular version, Darwinism was in danger of justifying the triumph of modernity, democracy and even socialism. In these years, there was no lack of thinkers that inferred from the British naturalist a belief in the natural necessity of a new society destined to take the place of capitalism, just as capitalism had taken the place of the *ancien régime*, again in accordance with the inexorable laws of evolution. Thanks to the 'nose' and 'instinct' of which he often and rightly boasted, Nietzsche was able to sense the danger of these ideological themes, and to warn against them. Apart from that, social Darwinism in its traditional form represented the recognition of that which existed,[16] so it could not satisfy an aristocratic radicalism committed to calling into question two thousand years of history. For the rest, Nietzsche clearly, unambiguously and insistently spoke out against a morality that, in the name of compassion, sought to block selection that might work to the disadvantage of those whose lives had turned out badly and of the malformed. So, his adherence to social Darwinism, the dominant ideology of the time, was clear and unmistakable.

As with the 'Christian Junker' then in vogue in Prussia and Carlyle's Christianising hero, so too with Darwinism it was always and only the possible modern and plebeian contamination or degeneration that was called into question. In this case too, we are dealing not so much with a distancing in the name of an 'untimeliness' so arrogant it rejected even a confrontation with the culture of its own time as with an effort to bring coherence and rigour to the undemocratic tendencies in it. While trying to adapt Christianity to social Darwinism,

---

12   Pareto 1974, 131 f.
13   Veblen 1904, 396 f., fn. 1.
14   Lapouge 1977, 230.
15   Lapouge 1977, 503.
16   Struve 1973, 47.

Spencer saw in altruism an ideal to be pursued. So, it is clear why Nietzsche felt such boundless contempt for the English liberal. In truth, he was a 'decadent', not unlike the 'socialists': 'he sees something desirable in the victory of altruism!' (GD, *Expeditions of an Untimely Man*, 37 [213]); he wished all men to become 'altruistic', so as to create a collectivity of 'herd animals', 'benevolent', 'good-natured' (EH, Why I am a destiny, 4 [146]).

2   Between Eugenics and Genocide: The West in the Late Nineteenth
        Century

At the end of his conscious life, referring to *The Use and Abuse of History for Life*, on whose untimeliness he continued to insist, Nietzsche observed: 'In this essay, the "historical sense" that this century is so proud of is recognized for the first time as a sickness, as a typical sign of decay' (EH, *The Untimely Ones*, 1 [112]). In fact, not historical sense but heredity and nature seemed to be the logo of the culture of the late nineteenth century, or at least of some of its essential components. In the same year as the second *Unfashionable Observation*, a book appeared whose subtitle proclaimed the central role of *Nature and Nurture (supra*, 19 §1).

At the time, 'eugenics' was highly popular, and not only in Europe. At the forefront of the practical implementation of the measures of this new 'science' was the United States. Under the pressure of a movement that developed at the end of the nineteenth century, between 1907 and 1915 thirteen American states passed laws requiring compulsory sterilisation, which applied, in conformity with the law of Indiana (the state that first moves in this direction), to 'habitual criminals, idiots, imbeciles and rapists'. There are even some that thought these measures inadequate, and held up sterilisation in the first place as a social prophylaxis that should apply to the poor and to habitual vagabonds, as well as, more generally, to the lower and tendentially criminal classes.[17] 'The Americans, practical people', became a model to follow in Europe.[18] As far as Germany was concerned, it is worth noting that a book published in 1913 took, as its title suggests, 'racial hygiene in the United States of North America' as its point of reference.[19]

The cultural and political atmosphere of the second half of the nineteenth century was full of the idea or the temptation to resort to 'eugenic' and other

---

17   Cf. A.E. Fink 1962, 188–210.
18   Lapouge 1977, 505.
19   Hoffmann 1913; cf. Kühl 1994 and Lifton 1988, 29 ff.

even more radical measures. Tocqueville hoped that it would finally be possible to get rid of the 'prison rabble' like rats, perhaps by means of a huge fire. Even if the French liberal was not necessarily thinking of 'genocide', as a later interpreter maintained,[20] his attitude to the 'prison rabble' was not so very different from Nietzsche's to the 'malformed'.

Le Bon was quite explicit. Sooner or later, it would be necessary to sweep away the 'immense pile of rubbish' that had accumulated on the other side of the Atlantic and that consisted of a mass of emigrant misfits 'lacking in energy and resources', the basis for the recruitment of 'a vast army of sectarians' that was more and more of a threat:

> The United States already presage the day in which we must enter into bloody battle against these multitudes and engage in pitiless struggles to exterminate them; struggles that will recall, though on a larger scale, the destruction of the barbarian hordes that Marius had to attack to save Roman civilization from their invasion.[21]

This reminds one of the 'annihilation of millions of the deformed' of which Nietzsche spoke. But it would be superficial and overhasty to turn the German and French authors into precursors of Nazism. In the same book in which he expressed himself with such brutality, Le Bon praised 'England, land of the free', and on other occasions he constantly took the Anglo-Saxon world as his model.[22]

It is in its attitude to the superfluous colonial populations that could not be used for more or less forced labour that 'eugenics' came dangerously close to genocide in the real sense. Karl Pearson, one of Britain's most enthusiastic and radical followers of the new 'science', hoped for a strong increase in the healthy population of the UK, but stressed that the forward march of culture implied inevitable 'hecatombs of inferior races'.[23] These were the years in which Emerson, though not with reference to eugenics, said wars, fires and natural disasters 'break up immovable routine, clear the ground of rotten races and dens of distemper, and open a fair field to new men'.[24] In turn, Carlyle coolly observed that 'the *black African, alone* of *wild men, can live among men civilized*': the

---

20   Perrot 1984, 38.
21   Le Bon 1920, 138.
22   Le Bon 1920, 389 and Le Bon 1928, *passim*.
23   In Brie 1928, 260.
24   Emerson 1983b, 1084.

others were condemned, by nature or by the forward march of culture, to 'anni-hilation'.[25] With equal indifference or rather with complete approval, Le Bon looked at the 'fatal removal' of the 'lower peoples, Indians, Australians, Tas-manians, etc.'[26] Similarly, Gumplowicz reported that in southern Africa 'the bushmen and the Hottentots' were often considered and treated not as human beings but as 'creatures [*Geschöpfe*]' that one could exterminate just like the game in the forest.[27] The 'Christian Boers' also behaved like that: religion and ideology proved powerless before an inexorable law of nature. Hartmann too spoke as if of a matter of course of the 'war of annihilation, based on natural necessity', that the superior white and 'Caucasian' race waged against the 'races left too far behind'.[28] The young Nietzsche had carefully read the book in which this statement appeared and even criticised it, but certainly not in relation to the thesis just quoted. Indeed, on this point, there must have been agreement, at least to judge by a letter in which Nietzsche praised Hartmann for joining in 'the ancient song of the Norns about the curse of existence' (B, II, 1, 73). The 'natural necessity' of the 'war of annihilation' against the colonial peoples and, of course, the starvation rampant in the big European cities were presumably part of this 'curse'.[29]

Nietzschean accents also seemed to resonate in Lombroso:

> And whoever has read the lives of the pioneers of Australia and America will realize that they were born criminals, pirates and murderers, used by humanity to conquer new worlds, who vented on savage tribes their need for action, struggle, bloodshed and novelties that would have created an enormous danger in the motherland.[30]

This reminds one of the analysis in the *Genealogy of Morals* of the 'blond beast': '[T]his hidden centre needs release from time to time, the beast must out again, must return to the wild' (GM, I, 11 [23]).

Just as in the treatment of the 'prison rabble' mentioned by Tocqueville, so too in the treatment of colonial peoples, social Darwinist ideas can be found in authors in one way or another part of the liberal tradition. Although he con-sidered himself a liberal, Renan had no doubt that the 'semi-savage races' were

---

25   Carlyle 1983, 436f.
26   Le Bon 1894, 46.
27   Gumplowicz 1883, 249.
28   Hartmann 1989, 518.
29   Hartmann 1989, 554.
30   Lombroso 1995, 646.

not part of the 'great Aryan-Semitic family', and that they were destined to be subjugated or exterminated.[31] Even Burckhardt seemed to think that the 'annihilation or subjugation of the weaker races' was part of the 'great economy of world history'.[32] In the view of Hobson, the British liberal, whose writings Lenin read, colonial expansion went hand in hand with 'the extermination of lower races' that 'were incapable of profitable exploitation by the superior white settlers'.[33]

Needless to say, there was no shortage among Nietzsche's contemporaries of critical and even outraged voices. To quote an author known to him (and close to Social Democracy), in 1865 Lange drew attention to the 'extermination' of the indigenous people in the United States, Australia and other parts of the world, as well as to all kinds of cruelty being inflicted by European conquerors on conquered peoples.[34] Similar anguished voices were raised among some sectors of the Christian world, troubled by the 'uninterrupted martyrdom' of the 'North American Indians' and the brutality of the theories that explicitly deny the 'right to exist' to 'savages'.[35] Let us consider the slogans that accompanied these positions: unity of the 'great human family', respect for the 'principles of humanity', which made it impossible to remain indifferent to the 'misery of suffering humanity'; refusal to equate the human world with the 'struggle for existence' in the animal world ('for we want a different nature for man than for animals.')[36] And, on the part of the Christian author, a reaffirmation of the 'value' of the 'individual soul even of the poorest and the most outcast', as well as a rejection of the argument that 'philanthropy' would impede the forward march of culture.[37] Such were the slogans and circles that Nietzsche despised and hated.

3   Social Conflict, Colonial Expansion, Critique of Compassion and Condemnation of Christianity

In confirmation of his 'untimeliness', Nietzsche subsumed '"sympathy with all sufferers"' among '[a]ll the things this age is proud of' and that he had the cour-

---

31   Renan 1947 ff., Vol. 8, 585.
32   Burckhardt 1978a, 190.
33   Hobson 1983, 253.
34   Lange 1975, 14.
35   Warneck 1879, 253, 193, fn. 141.
36   Lange 1975, 14 f., 7 ff., 12.
37   Warneck 1879, 125, 194, fn. 141.

age to protest against (EH, *Beyond Good and Evil*, 2 [135]). In fact, we are dealing with a recurrent theme of the anti-democratic reaction of the late nineteenth century.

We are already familiar with Treitschke's polemic against the 'lifeless and sentimental philanthropy' that hindered the repressive measures needed against Social Democracy. In Britain, the liberal-conservative Lecky also drew attention to the dangers inherent in 'sensitivity' and the great increase in philanthropy.[38] In similar terms, Spencer criticised the 'philanthropists' for their crusade against 'social suffering' and the sentimentality that led them to separate punishment from the bad behaviour that was its foundation.[39] An American disciple of Spencer, Sumner, mocked the 'sentimental philosophy' and the poets and sentimentalists who, in their utopias and fantasies, suppressed the 'struggle for existence'.[40] Even sharper, and one might say Nietzschean tones, echoed in the speeches of Pareto and Le Bon. Pareto says:

> If European societies were modelled on the ideal that ethicists uphold, one would go so far as to hinder selection, to systematically favour the weak, the vice-ridden, the idle, the ill adapted, the 'little and humble' people, as our philanthropists call them, at the expense of the strong, of the energetic, who form the elite, so that a new conquest by new 'barbarians' would not be at all impossible.[41]

Le Bon said he hoped 'a benevolent deity' would decide to 'destroy the deadly breed of philanthropists', so as to do away with the 'sick humanitarianism that has already brought about the bloodiest revolution history has ever seen'.[42]

This theme had already begun to circulate in the ideological struggle against the French Revolution, though in embryonic form and less strongly formulated. It suffices to think of De Sade and the ironic way in which he debunked compassion as 'the sin *par excellence*'.[43] On the other hand, we have already seen how Tocqueville emphasised the baleful role played by 'pity', said to have disarmed the French aristocracy, ideologically and even emotionally, in the face of the swelling revolutionary tide (*supra*, 1 § 4).

---

38   Lecky 1883–88, Vol. 6, 243.
39   Spencer 1981, 32, 34.
40   Sumner 1992, 187, 190 f.
41   Pareto 1974, 134.
42   Le Bon 1920, 459.
43   In Horkheimer/Adorno 1947, 122.

So, we can understand that a worldview was starting to form that, in Nietz-schean language, we might call immoral. Emerson, for whom war (as we have seen) had the job of sweeping away the 'rotten races' and the 'dens of distem-per', painted a significant and admiring portrait of Napoleon as the 'genius' of war that left 'sensitivity to women' and removed the barriers in the way of achieving his objectives; he did not allow himself in carrying out his actions to be held up by 'moral principles', but merely followed 'the eternal law of man and the world', not hesitating to sacrifice 'millions of people', 'not sparing of blood, and pitiless'.[44] This reminds one of the *Genealogy of Morals*, which celebrated Napoleon as a 'synthesis of *Unmensch* (brute) and *Übermensch* (overman)' (GM, I, 16 [33]). For Emerson, Napoleon was, along with Caesar and other generals, one of those 'great men' that the Philistines liked to call 'the scourge of God': but 'what indemnification is one great man for populations of *pygmies*!'[45]

So, one can understand the discomfort that began to spread in regard of Christianity. At least in his private conversations, Gobineau 'accuses the Gospel of having intervened on behalf of the poor and the oppressed', thus creating 'a religion of the poor, that is to say, of the masses', with which 'great personalit-ies' could not but clash. However, 'in a world of misery to prefer the poor to the rich, the poor in spirit to the wise, the sick to the person of good health is to commit a mistake of which a Hindu would never have been guilty'.[46]

These critical themes achieved a quite special importance in the second half of the nineteenth and the early twentieth century, in connection with, on the one hand, the growing threat of socialist revolution and, on the other, the devel-opment of colonial expansion. This led to the opening and extension of a space where, in Kipling's words, 'the *best is like the worst*' and '*there* aren't no Ten Commandments'. As Arendt noted, morality here became synonymous with philistinism:

Outside all social restraint and hypocrisy, against the backdrop of native life, the gentleman and the criminal felt not only the closeness of men who share the same color of skin, but the impact of a world of infinite pos-sibilities for crimes committed in the spirit of play, for the combination of horror and laughter, that is for the full realization of their own phantom-like existence. Native life lent these ghostlike events a seeming guarantee against all consequences because anyhow it looked to these men like a

---

44   Emerson 1983a, 732, 742–45.
45   Emerson 1983a, 625, 627.
46   In Lémonon 1971, 503 f.

mere play of shadows. A play of shadows, the dominant race could walk through unaffected and disregarded in the pursuit of its incomprehensible aims and needs.[47]

In certain cases, instead of challenging Christianity head on, people preferred to subject it to a more or less radical reinterpretation. Tocqueville highlighted the negative role played by 'pity' in the dissolution of the *ancien régime* and of the capacity of the ruling class to resist, so as to be able to denounce 'philanthropy' as 'anti-Christian', with an eye to the ongoing social unrest:[48] in its campaign for 'material improvements' in the condition of prisoners, it propagated a worldview inconsonant with spiritual and religious values.[49] This explanation, which Tocqueville used to justify the opposition between Christianity and philanthropy, is hardly persuasive. On another occasion, Tocqueville accused philanthropists of harbouring the naïve illusion they could win over even the most hardened criminal, even 'the most infamous being', to the side of 'virtue' and 'honour'.[50] So materialism was not the only motive behind the philanthropists' actions. Political calculation also played a role in Tocqueville's attack on them, waving the flag of the dominant religion.

Spencer, on the other hand, accused the Christians of his time of allowing themselves to be overwhelmed by blind compassion and adhering to the absurd view that 'there should be no suffering, and that society is to blame for that which exists'. In fact, we read in the New Testament: 'He *who does not work neither shall he eat.*' The 'idle' and the 'good for nothings' that wished to live at the expense of hard-working and decent people were given short shrift. In its true meaning, Christianity converged fully with 'that universal law of Nature under which life has reached its present height – the law that a creature not energetic enough to maintain itself must die'.[51] Here, the political calculus was sheer hypocrisy. Christianity was reinterpreted along social Darwinist lines: thus 'science' and the dominant religion were brought into full agreement. We are a long way from the ruthlessness and intellectual courage of Nietzsche, who in denouncing the negative effects of compassion took aim first at Christianity.

With an eye to colonial expansion and the race for world hegemony, certain Teutomaniac circles active in the Second Reich reinterpreted the figure of Jesus in an Aryan-Germanic sense, while in Great Britain Kipling, in mirror

---

47   Arendt 1966, 189 f.
48   In Perrot 1984, 38.
49   Tocqueville 1951 ff., Vol. 4, half-vol. 1, 136.
50   Tocqueville 1951 ff., Vol. 4, half-vol. 1, 197.
51   Spencer 1981, 32 f.

image, interpreted the dominant religion in the light above all of the Old Testament themes of the 'Lord God of the Battles' and the 'chosen people', which by then tended to mean the British.[52] The 'Lord God of the Battles' theme seemed to fascinate even Nietzsche. However, he had not passed in vain through the school of philology: he could take seriously neither Christian-Germanic mythology nor the attempt to unite as one the New and the Old Testaments, the figure of Jesus and the conqueror of Canaan!

4   Christianity, Socialism and 'Free Spirits': The Reversal of the Alliances

Beyond Nietzsche, there was no lack of voices at the end of the nineteenth century calling for a radical rendering of accounts with Christianity. According to Lapouge, 'the morality of Christianity' surely counted 'among the worst', since it 'sacrifices society to the individual', or, more precisely, to the malformed individual.[53] Fortunately, 'the sentimental idealist politics of Christianity is in the meantime dead', the very 'idea of morality' destined to be replaced by 'social hygiene'.[54]

Galton was particularly harsh towards Catholicism. Insofar as the church abandoned the terrain of 'natural morality' and of nature by persecuting and decimating the freest and boldest thinkers and people by means of the Inquisition, insofar as it required celibacy of the best and left the way open to the procreation and multiplication of the worst, insofar as (in a word) it completely abandoned the terrain of 'natural morality', it was implementing a terrible counter-selection and bringing about a catastrophic degeneration.[55] Now its sins would find it out. The development of science would make it clear to all that a deadly struggle for the future of culture lay ahead:

> When the desired fullness of information shall have been acquired, then and not till then, will be the fit moment to proclaim a 'Jehad', or Holy War, on customs and prejudices that weaken the physical and moral faculties of our race.[56]

---

52   Brie 1928, 227.
53   Lapouge 1977, 508.
54   Lapouge 1977, IX, 509.
55   Galton 1869, 357 f.
56   Galton 1907, 30; cf. Poliakov 1987, 333 f.

This reminds one of Nietzsche and his accusation that Christianity with its morality was guilty of a 'capital crime against life' (*supra*, 16 § 6). *The Antichrist* ends by calling for a '[w]ar to the death' against the 'vice' and 'anti-nature' represented by Christianity and its clergy. The preaching of 'chastity' was to be considered and treated as a crime, and 'the execrable location where Christianity brooded over its basilisk eggs should be razed to the ground' (AC, Law against Christianity [66–7]).

In respect of the need to preserve the culture and even the physical survival of the human species, the usual conflicts between European states proved to be absolutely petty-minded:

> Because when truth comes into conflict with the lies of millennia there will be tremors, a ripple of earthquakes, an upheaval of mountains and valleys such as no one has ever imagined. The concept of politics will have then merged entirely into a war of spirits, all power structures from the old society will have exploded – they are all based on lies: there will be wars such as the earth has never seen. Starting with me, the earth will know great politics.
>
> EH, Why I am a destiny, 1 [144]

Once the malignant role of Christianity in obstructing or blocking selection had become apparent, a sort of reversal of alliances came about. This, at least, was Lapouge's view. According to him, the development of the sciences and the theory of evolution and selection had created serious difficulties for the supporters of the democratic and socialist movement. So-called 'freethinkers' could not give up the theological and moral worldview upon which their political programme was ultimately based, they too were 'slaves' of 'theological doctrines'. Instead of radically calling themselves into question, they would perhaps end up explicitly re-embracing Christianity: 'Their psychology is that of the people that once prostrated themselves in the churches and had the heretics burned. [...] In the near future our children will observe this curious spectacle: the theorists of false modern democracy will be forced to take refuge in the citadel of clericalism.' Thus 'the alliance of the men of the Church and those of the Revolution will be tomorrow's fact'.[57] This led us back to Nietzsche's confrontation between the so-called 'freethinkers' and the genuine 'free spirits', the only ones able to liquidate Christian-socialist dogmatism.

---

57 Lapouge 1977, 513 f.

So, Christianity would be followed not by atheism, which the socialist or socialistic freethinkers so prized, but a new religion. Maybe (noted Lombroso) a contribution in that direction might come from the 'Anglo-Saxon', at the time at the head of the conquering races: in him 'religious fertility is not extinguished'.[58] In any case, according to Le Bon, the phase in which 'the heavens stand empty' was merely transitional; 'the birth of new gods' would mark the beginning of a 'new culture', which would have nothing more to do with the Christian deity and the values and negative values it embodied.[59] But it is *The Antichrist* that gives this expectation its most fascinating form: 'Almost two thousand years and not one new god!' (AC 19 [16]).

In conclusion, rather than base itself on the category of 'untimeliness', the interpretation of Nietzsche should try a different approach. Just as one can see in German idealism the epistemological and philosophical translation of the French Revolution, so in Schopenhauer and Nietzsche one can observe the epistemological and philosophical translation of the critique of the French Revolution. In both cases, this translation makes it possible to rise above immediacy and insert individual problems and the different aspects of each problem into a structured, coherent whole, an overall view of the world and of history – after all, we are dealing here with great philosophers.

Except that, especially with regard to Nietzsche, the hermeneutics that today predominate transfigure into pure metaphor and pure artistic expression the grandiose epistemological and philosophical translation of an eminently political discourse. This procedure collides precisely with the philosopher that is the object of transfiguration. Nietzsche even got angry about an interpretation of *Zarathustra* that benignly viewed it as 'a superior stylistic exercise' but invited its author to 'concern [him]self with content too'. The 'content' of which the reviewer felt the lack was, as Nietzsche immediately pointed out, unmistakably political: 'The word "overman", as a designation for a type that has the highest constitutional excellence, in contrast to "modern" people, to "good" people, to Christians and other nihilists' (EH, Why I write such good books, 1 [100–1]); that is to say, in opposition to the democratic and socialist movement as the culmination of the subversive development that has begun with the Gospel or Jewish prophetism. Zarathustra and the '"distinction" of the overman' (B, III, 1, 356) intervened to combat and denounce centuries of vulgarization and plebeian subversion.

---

58   Lombroso 1995, 523.
59   In Sternhell 1978, 15.

PART 5

Nietzsche and the Aristocratic Reaction in Two Historical Epochs

∵

Nationalism is the most ignoble aspect of the modern spirit
DRIEU LA ROCHELLE

• • •

Mussolini and Hitler, the two men who brought in a counter-movement against
nihilism, both learned from Nietzsche, though in essentially different ways
HEIDEGGER

• • •

Did Israel not reach the pinnacle of her sublime vengefulness via this very
'redeemer', this apparent opponent of and disperser of Israel?
GM, I, 8 [18]

• • •

Paul wanted the end, and consequently he wanted the means to it as well ...
What he did not believe himself is believed by the idiots he threw his doctrines to. – What he needed is power; with Paul, the priests wanted to return
to power, – he can only use ideas, doctrines, symbols that would tyrannize the
masses and form the herds.
AC 42 [39]

• •
•

Philosophers, Historians and Sociologists: The Conflict of Interpretations

1   Elisabeth's 'Conspiracy'

As we have seen, there is no shortage of unsettling and horrific passages in Nietzsche's writings. Although they can be linked in the first place to the spiritual climate of the late nineteenth century, it is not surprising leading ideologues of the Third Reich made reference to their author. A whole series of authoritative Nietzsche experts have indignantly rejected this claim to inheritance and have dragged in the philosopher's sister, accusing her of having invented or cleverly manipulated *The Will to Power* in order to transform it into one of the books that inspired the Third Reich and, even before that, the preparatory stages of protofascism and proto-Nazism. It is odd that, merely in order to prove the philosopher's political purity, people are prepared to elevate Elisabeth to the level of a world-historical personality. The results are paradoxical. As we shall see, one historian of the twentieth century has not hesitated to say that the Nazi genocide in Eastern Europe would hardly have occurred 'but for Nietzsche'! The statement is at least debatable, but it becomes positively hilarious in the light of the amendment suggested by proponents of the manipulation theory. The history of the twentieth century would have been quite different and much better but for ... Elisabeth! An intellectually rather mediocre woman thus becomes the inspiration of a political movement able not only to win and set in motion great masses of people but also to fascinate, at least for a while, leading representatives of European culture: *in principio* was Rasputin in a skirt!

At bottom, this interpretation leads to an unsustainable conspiracy theory. An interpreter describes the fateful role played by the philosopher's sister: 'By misquoting him out of context, she heavily implied anti-Semitism in his writings. In the 1930s, she aligned herself with Hitler and her Nazi friends that decided to utilize her brother.'[1] But *The Will to Power* first appeared when the future Führer was still a child, so it would seem Elisabeth played the main role in this plot and forged it long before the birth of the Nazi movement!

---

1   Santaniello 1994, 148.

The beauty of it is that, if we subject Elisabeth's Nietzsche biography to a careful reading and compare *The Will to Power* with the text of the *Posthumous Fragments*, we come to a conclusion directly opposite to that of the version now dominant. In the biography, one seeks in vain for the brother's letters, which exude a violent Judeophobia. And that is not all. When dealing with the Basel lecture *Socrates and Tragedy*, Elisabeth skipped over the conclusion, in which Nietzsche brought the 'Jewish press' into the equation; she reported the anxiety raised by the text of this lecture in Tribschen, but said nothing about the reason for it or about Richard and Cosima's invitation to the young professor not to engage lightly in a challenge to the Jewish community or to underestimate its power and vengefulness.[2] Elisabeth knew that, in the first phase of the philosopher's development, Socratism was actually synonymous with Judaism, but she warned against making too much of 'certain bitter words' pronounced by him about Judaism as 'the destroyer of the Greek conception of life'. The main thing was the clear rejection of anti-Semitism in all its forms, said the loving sister.[3]

And, according to her, that is primarily why Nietzsche broke with Wagner, without flinching from the consequent isolation:

> The noise of war and victory had coarsened our spiritual sense of hearing. [...] Wagner with his ideals (among them anti-Semitism) hypnotized the best of his time, and it was only them my brother needed for his new ideas. Now the spell is broken: the high-flying young minds of today are turning to new ideals, now they venerate Nietzsche.[4]

In this regard, the biography quotes an entire paragraph from *Nietzsche Contra Wagner* titled 'How I got rid of Wagner'. Let us read the beginning and the end: 'I cannot endure anything double-faced. Since Wagner had returned to Germany, he had condescended step by step to everything I despise – even to anti-Semitism. [...] I was always condemned to Germans.'[5] This passage is subtly self-justifying. It seems to suggest the future philosopher, at the time of his encounter with the musician, had nothing to do with the attitude that later led to the break. In fact, we know Wagner's and the young Nietzsche's

2 Förster-Nietzsche 1895–1904, Vol. 2, 20 f.
3 Förster-Nietzsche 1895–1904, Vol. 2, 501.
4 Förster-Nietzsche 1895–1904, Vol. 2, 317.
5 Förster-Nietzsche 1895–1904, Vol. 2, 322 f.; http://www.gutenberg.org/files/25012/25012-h/25012-h.html#toc7.

anti-Semitism or Judeophobia predated their meeting, and their relationship actually developed on the basis of this community of ideas.

Elisabeth had no difficulty in coming to the defence of her brother. Her biography did not seek to accommodate his image to the ideological needs of the movement that later became Nazism, but instead strove to represent Nietzsche as the champion of the struggle against Germanomania and anti-Semitism, as the 'good European' *par excellence*.[6] Basically speaking, that corresponds to the truth, though with a few distortions. These are exemplified by the silence about and the suppression of the early years, and by other small details: for example, Elisabeth insisted strongly on the Christian origin of the morality of *ressentiment*, but seemed to pass over in silence or to minimise Judaism's role.[7] It was not the 'anti-Semitic' sister but two others, a long-time friend of the philosopher and a prominent representative of Jewish culture in France, who spoke, well before the publication of *The Will to Power*, of an anti-Semitism disguised as 'anti-Christianity', or of an 'anti-Christian anti-Semitism' in Nietzsche (*supra*, 18 § 6). Obviously, apart from the value judgement, the interpretations of Lazare and Overbeck came closer to those favoured by early Nazis and pro-Nazis. We have already mentioned Nietzsche's contempt for Fritsch, but the latter, in maintaining that Christianity was inherently and irremediably Jewish in character, continued to refer to *The Antichrist*[8] and to use it and other of the philosopher's texts to denounce Jews as 'Chandala'.[9] Baeumler, for his part, emphasised that for Nietzsche 'Judaism and Christianity are basically the same thing'.[10]

Elisabeth was not content with emphasising her brother's rejection of anti-Semitism but even tried to place his thinking in a European and Western context, going clearly beyond Germany. For example, she linked his view of women as the mothers of as many as possible healthy children to the American President Theodore Roosevelt.[11] Above all, when highlighting and praising Nietzsche's aristocratism, she referred to Britain and the role the 'old nobility' continued to play in that country.[12] The biography drew a comparison between Germany and other European countries wholly to the detriment of the former: in Germany, intellectuals were most likely to come from the 'lower

---

6   Förster-Nietzsche 1895–1904, Vol. 2, 555.
7   Förster-Nietzsche 1895–1904, Vol. 2, 449.
8   Fritsch 1943, 265; on the history of this text, cf. Ferrari Zambini 2001, 971.
9   Fritsch 1911, 184–87.
10 Baeumler 1931a, 158 f.
11 Förster-Nietzsche 1895–1904, Vol. 2, 565 f.
12 Förster-Nietzsche 1895–1904, Vol. 2, 617.

classes' and to think more of 'earning a living' than of analysing the 'deepest problems of life'.[13] She maintained the victory at Sedan, which made the
Second Reich proud and thrilled it, had prevented people from becoming aware
of the significance of this problem: 'This brutally bragging German' was 'the
most repulsive spectacle Germany offers', she concluded, thus summarising her
brother's view, with which she was fully in agreement. The admiration and gratitude she expressed for Karl Hillebrand, for recognising Nietzsche's genius at
the time of the publication of *Human, All Too Human* and describing him as
'the last humane German', can also be understood in this context.[14] As should
be evident, there was no shadow in this reconstruction of Germanomania or
chauvinism.

In conclusion, Elisabeth not only left aside anti-Semitic interpretations, of
which there was no shortage even in the years of the philosopher's conscious
life (and which he immediately and disdainfully rejected), but also devoted
scant attention to social-Darwinian interpretations. A case in point is the work
of Alexander Tille, which does not even appear in Elisabeth's index. On the
other hand, Elisabeth quoted sympathetically and respectfully the contributions of Simmel and Vaihinger, two Jews! Space was also accorded to Alois
Riehl, who praised the 'aristocratic individualism' of Nietzsche as 'artist and
thinker'[15] – and for being in opposition to its 'time', which was 'collectivist' in
orientation.[16]

Reading her biography does not in any way confirm the legend of Elisabeth
as a forger in the service of the Third Reich, whose advent could not at the time
(ten years before the outbreak of the First World War) have been predicted even
by an extraordinarily gifted prophet. Nor is it confirmed by a reading of *The
Will to Power*. This is the work on the basis of which a pro-Nazi interpreter in
1936 accused Nietzsche of being pro-Semitic. He particularly had in mind the
sections dedicated to Heine, Offenbach, Mendelssohn, Rahel Varnhagen and
Jewish art and culture as a whole.[17] The denunciation even ended up including
Elisabeth herself, accused of sympathetically confirming her brother's philo-
Semitism: she had thanked Brandes and the other Jews that had admired the
philosopher during his conscious life; she had overstepped the limits of the permissible by calling 'as a witness for the correct interpretation of her brother's

---

13   Förster-Nietzsche 1895–1904, Vol. 2, 108 f.
14   Förster-Nietzsche 1895–1904, Vol. 2, 664.
15   Förster-Nietzsche 1895–1904, Vol. 2, 620–22, 569 f., 664; cf. Riehl 1920, 161.
16   Riehl 1920, 11.
17   Westernhagen 1936, 18–23; cf. WzM § 832–35.

doctrine' the 'Jew Georg Simmel'.[18] And it is true that Simmel was amply and favourably cited in the biography on account of his 'excellent' treatment of Nietzsche's 'aristocratic ideal'.[19] The accusation of philo-Semitism against Elisabeth later became one of anti-Semitism.

There can be no doubt that the text of *The Will to Power* is more an 'interpretation' than a 'fact'. Observers have rightly noted the tendency of its two publishers to soften the harshest parts. This applies particularly to the harsh statements about 'religion, church and Reich', but also to statements hostile to women.[20] We can better understand the spirit in which Elisabeth worked by looking at one particular small passage. At § 872 we read: 'The rights a human being takes for himself are proportional to the duties he imposes on himself, to the tasks he feels up to. The great majority have no right to exist, but are a misfortune for superior human beings.' In the corresponding passage in the *Posthumous Fragments*, the aphorism continues with an emphatic declaration: 'I do not even give the deformed the right [to exist – DL]. There are deformed peoples too' (XI, 102). In seeking to adhere as far as possible to her brother's theses, to which she wanted to raise a sort of monument, poor Elisabeth must have found embarrassing and excessive the idea that a whole people could or should be denied the right to exist. One can say what one likes about the work of Nietzsche's sister as biographer and editor, but one cannot say she rendered a service to the interpretation advanced several decades later by the Nazis. True, the biography insists, and rightly so, on the philosopher's implacable hostility to socialism, but not even that can be considered a favour to a movement calling itself 'National Socialist'.

Regarding the text of *The Will to Power*, there are no particularly relevant differences between it and the *Posthumous Fragments*, and it is a waste of time hunting for instances of manipulation and distortion capable of compromising the work of the interpreter.[21] One can even ask whether the liberties Elisabeth took were any greater than those taken by today's editors of *Socrates and Tragedy*: the paradox is that, in censoring the lecture's Judeophobic conclusion (see below, Appendix 1, § 1), they sail in the wake of the philosopher's sister they so despise.

---

18   Westernhagen 1936, 12, 74.
19   Förster-Nietzsche 1895–1904, Vol. 2, 660–62.
20   Fuchs 1998, 391 f.
21   Ferraris 1995, 614–17.

2   Nietzsche Interpretation before *The Will to Power*: Critique from the 'Left'

The peculiar mythological and ideological edifice built by the hermeneuts of innocence is particularly fragile, because, even before the publication of *The Will to Power*, the author's thinking triggered a debate that brought about some very disturbing scenarios. As early as 1884, an admirer of Nietzsche's, who has left us a sympathetic portrait of him, reported a conversation that is worth reflecting on. The philosopher explained his thesis that in order to make possible 'a few quite outstanding human beings' one must be able to be 'cruel' and not hesitate to 'suppress perhaps all else'. In its radicalism, the vision he had developed 'in relation to the problem of what is good and what is evil' could 'terrify', which is why he hesitated to communicate it completely; the fact remained that it was necessary to 'repress one's good inclinations, one's compassion, for the sake of a higher purpose'. Nietzsche's interlocutor argues, sensibly, that 'no one can rule over human beings in the same way as a cattle-breeder over his cattle' (KGA, VII, 4/2, 24).

The reference here is to *Thus Spoke Zarathustra* and the theory of the 'over-man'. Shortly after the appearance of *Beyond Good and Evil*, its first reviewer noted the book applied 'to humankind the power concept of nature', all the more disturbing because of the extreme cruelty of nature it emphasised:[22] that is to say, we were dealing with an extremely brutal social Darwinism. Similarly, in regard to *Beyond Good and Evil*, Rohde, in a letter to Overbeck dated 1 September 1886, expressed both anxiety and indignation:

> What's being said about the herd character of humanity today might be right – but how should one imagine to oneself what Nietzsche fantasizes about the cannibal morality that according to his philosophy should be imposed dictatorially? What sign of the times do these stilted berserkers of the future herald?[23]

What effect would such a philosophy have in the actual political arena? A book published in 1893 warned against the 'dangers' inherent in it, as the book's title shows. Its author, Ludwig Stein, likened Nietzsche to Gumplowicz and accused him of a 'brutal, despotic trait in which the wild instincts of the as yet untamed

---

22   Joseph Victor Widmann, in Janz 1981, Vol. 3, 260 f.
23   Overbeck/Rohde 1990, 109.

original human beast break through with elemental violence': this instinct 'would like to destroy the free individual life of all human beings so that the few geniuses, the "overmen", can indulge their cravings without restraint'.[24] In this same period, we can find a similar interpretation of the overman in Nordau.[25] The latter – it should not be forgotten he was of Jewish origin – also expressed his concern and indignation at the fact that in places Nietzsche attributed to the 'Jewish people' a 'plan' or a conspiracy to overthrow morality and the dominance of the masters (*infra*, 27 §3 and 5).

It is now time to focus on the reactions from the Left properly understood. In 1896, Julius Duboc, a disciple of Feuerbach sympathetic to Social Democracy, said Nietzsche's writings exuded the 'stench of fire and burning', a 'miasmatic air in which is immersed the rogues' aristocracy of his overmen.'[26] Even more significant is the warning that then follows: it was understandable that the denunciation of the 'slave revolt in morality' and the proclamation of the advent or return of the 'morality of the masters' was especially welcomed by the 'better social classes', but had they really understood the full extent of the philosophy that so enthused them?[27]

Had they realised Nietzsche was 'the enemy of compassion'?[28] The definition is Tönnies's. In 1897, Tönnies had launched a bitter polemic against the 'cult' of a philosopher that 'recommends destruction where care and conservation take place' and that railed against the disastrous consequences of the 'accumulation of sick and deformed individuals'. But where was he headed with his arguments, Tönnies asked. Was he perhaps demanding that 'those individuals [...] be annihilated', a method fundamentally alien even to the 'greatest savages'?[29] One thing was for sure: Nietzsche raised an insuperable barrier between 'overmen' and 'helots', and for the latter he demanded extraordinarily harsh measures. In this way, he was setting a dangerous trend that was spreading alarmingly:

> In the petty and big bourgeoisie of our time, nothing is more popular than to curse 'humanitarian spouting'. [...] The strong-arm tactics [...], the provocative, highly inhumane manner, still sadly flourish under the name

---

24   Stein 1893, 63 fn., 43 f.; cf. Duboc 1896, 144.
25   Nordau n.d., Vol. 2, 327 f.
26   Duboc 1896, 123.
27   Duboc 1896, 112, 124, 134.
28   Tönnies 1897, 92.
29   Tönnies 1897, 106 f.

of resoluteness among us Germans today, not only in military relations (which is to some extent inevitable) but also on the part of officials posing as masters. [...] The aristocratic Nietzsche books can serve above all as a mirror for our new nobility, simultaneously committed to preserving religion, namely Christianity, for the people.[30]

Of particular note are Franz Mehring's interventions in this debate. Mehring was a leading member of the German Social Democracy, and did not escape the spell of the author investigated by him, as both thinker and writer. He particularly appreciated the 'struggle against the dominant morality', a morality unable to keep up with capitalist development and now being challenged by brilliant thinking and fascinating prose.[31] The first *Unfashionable Observation* met, as we know (*supra*, 4 §7), with the enthusiasm of orthodox circles and the liberal bourgeoisie, inclined to duplicity in the religious domain. Mehring was aware of this, and yet for him there could be no doubt this polemic was intended to protect 'the most glorious traditions of German culture'.[32]

But although the engaged intellectual of the labour movement valued these important achievements, he could not ignore the 'banal hatred against the socialists' and 'Nietzsche's cursing of socialism'. Even if the struggle against the hypocrisy and puritanism of prevailing morality was brave and inspiring, it led to a 'morality of cruelty'.[33] This was not just a 'philosophy of capitalism' but one with particularly worrying characteristics: 'His view of history is of a brutal crudeness devoid of spirit, made all the more repulsive by the 'spirited' and sparkling style.'[34]

In terms of the socialist movement, Trotsky's contribution was also important. Writing in 1900, he denounced Nietzsche's 'ultra-aristocratic ideas': 'The social axis of his system [...] is the recognition of the privilege granted a few "chosen" to freely enjoy all the goods of existence.' One was not to be taken in by the fascinating formulations and rebellious posing: 'In appearance, what limitless radicalism, what a daring revolutionary idea.' In fact, Nietzsche was defined by a decidedly reactionary characteristic: 'His mouth foams at the word democracy.' His was an ultra-aristocratism that demonstrated several particularly sinister characteristics: he theorised '"supermen" freed of all social and

30   Tönnies 1897, 107.
31   Mehring 1961 ff., Vol. 13, 174.
32   Mehring 1961 ff., Vol. 13, 177.
33   Mehring 1961 ff., Vol. 13, 169, 180 f.
34   Mehring 1961 ff., Vol. 13, 165.

moral obligations', that did not hide their 'open cynicism' and were prepared for 'the elimination of all that might resemble "pity"'.[35]

Needless to say, there was no lack in German Social Democracy of views more sympathetic to Nietzsche.[36] However, this demonstrated not the non-political character of his thought but the complexity of the ideological struggle. Sociopolitical upheavals and processes of secularisation had led to the emergence of a thick layer of intellectuals that looked with suspicion or hostility at the role of the Christian churches. Would these people fall under the influence of the socialistic 'free-thinkers', that in criticising the churches as a relic of the past express their confidence in 'progress', or of the 'free spirit' of aristocratic sentiments, which mocked not only Christian faith but also the belief in progress? The theorists of aristocratic radicalism aimed consciously and explicitly to absorb and neutralise the figure of the freethinker into that of the free spirit, the latter skilfully conceived as metacritique of the former. The two discourses were mutually antagonistic, but stirred by similar themes. Both adopted a rebellious attitude to that which existed and targeted the same audience: it was not surprising that in this audience uncertainties and fluctuations arose, as well as changings of sides. That was the context, for example, in which to understand the Nietzscheanism of the young Mussolini.

At the end of the nineteenth century, a similar phenomenon to that in France on the eve of the Revolution occurred, but under a reversed sign: a century earlier, the culture of the Enlightenment widely penetrated aristocratic circles, which were, after all, its target. Some one hundred years later, Nietzsche succeeded on the basis of the demystifying potential of his writings in making inroads into sectors of the socialist movement, for which the philosopher naturally never tired of expressing his contempt and hatred. Plenty of historians, starting out from the observation that the philosophy of the Enlightenment had also spread through the ranks of the aristocracy, denied or minimised the opposition between this class and the Third Estate. So, more or less, did those interpreters that suppressed Nietzsche's furious anti-socialism because of the sympathy roused by certain parts in his thinking among authors or sectors of that movement. In reality, every concrete struggle for hegemony presupposed both a minimum of social proximity regarding the layers to be conquered (for otherwise there would be no rivalry and competition) and, at times, a

---

35   Trotsky 1979.
36   Vivarelli 1984.

minimum of ideological proximity between its protagonists, if both aspired to occupy space vacated by a declining ideology (at the end of the nineteenth century, the struggle on the basis of a common detachment from Christianity and traditional morality). If at first sight this minimum of social and ideological contiguity appeared as commonality and even affinity, a closer look revealed it to be an expression of antagonism.

3   The Nietzsche Interpretation before *The Will to Power*: Applause
       from the 'Right'

While, on the 'left', the main reaction was one of alarm and rejection (to which not even Nietzsche's acquaintances and friends were immune), on the 'right', recognition and applause became ever more frequent. And once again, this happened long before the publication of *The Will to Power*. As motto for his book and for his new 'science', Alfred Ploetz, a founding father of 'racial hygiene', chose an excerpt from *Thus Spoke Zarathustra*, in which Nietzsche hoped for the passage from 'species' to 'super-species' (*supra*, 20 §1).

In this context, Tille, already briefly mentioned, occupied an important place. He credited Nietzsche with having drawn all the consequences at the ethical and sociopolitical level from Darwin's theory, without allowing himself to be hindered by the English scientist's moral scruples. It is worth thinking about this interpretation. In fact, there was no lack of perplexity and unease in *The Descent of Man*:

> We civilised men, on the other hand, do our utmost to check the process of elimination; we build asylums for the imbecile, the maimed, and the sick; we institute poor-laws; and our medical men exert their utmost skill to save the life of every one to the last moment. There is reason to believe that vaccination has preserved thousands, who from a weak constitution would formerly have succumbed to small-pox. Thus the weak members of civilised societies propagate their kind. No one that has attended to the breeding of domestic animals will doubt that this must be highly injurious to the race of man. It is surprising how soon a want of care, or care wrongly directed, leads to the degeneration of a domestic race; but excepting in the case of man himself, hardly any one is so ignorant as to allow his worst animals to breed.

A further factor compounded the threat to the future of humanity: 'The finest *young* men are taken by the conscription or are enlisted', while those of weaker health stayed at home and were more likely to marry and have children. 'Hard reason' would perhaps suggest energetic remedies. But to silence the 'instinct of sympathy' would mean renouncing 'our most noble attribute': 'Hence we must bear without complaining the undoubtedly bad effects of the weak surviving and propagating their kind'; one could only hope that the weakest would refrain as much as possible from marrying.[37]

Darwin's hope became a fixed point in Galton's programme, which nevertheless betrayed residual moral scruples. Thus, at least, in Tille's eyes: 'Excision [*Ausscheidung*] of the worst seems to him to be too cruel, although the facts of evolution point directly to it; so a planned increase in the number of the fittest seems the better course.' The fact was that the 'morality of compassion', 'Christianity's morality of love for one's neighbour [*Nächstenmoral*]', had a negative effect on 'humanity [*Humanität*] and democracy'.[38] It was not easy to free oneself from the burden of the 'democratic Christian ideals of love for one's neighbour', the 'Christian-human-democratic ideals', 'Christian-human ethics'. By hindering the 'pitiless trampling underfoot' of the 'sick' and the 'failed [*Unterliegend*]', they prevented selection and the process of life.[39] And yet, as a result of later attempts and authors, there was a growing awareness that it was pointless to try to impose our 'petty morality [*unser Moralchen*]' on 'grand nature', and thus to watch inertly and even to encourage the multiplication of the 'crippled, the lame, the blind, the insane, the tubercular, the syphilitic'.[40] This realisation reached its pinnacle with Nietzsche. According to Tille, his thoughts could be summarised in a formula that was also an appeal: 'Beyond slave morality', which was 'the morality of Buddhism, Christianity, modern humanity'. Against all this stood the 'morality of the masters', so dear to 'ancient Hellenism', in which 'rising life' rather than 'physiological decay' found expression. It was necessary to realise that 'Christian-democratic culture is thereby a phenomenon of decline [*Niedergangserscheinung*]'.[41]

The 'Jewish-Christian tradition', the 'communism of the early Christians', Tille continued, lay at the root of this rotten or pseudo-culture. Jesus had been merely a 'rabbi', persecuted by the Roman administration on account of his 'communist activities'. Tille argued that with Jesus and with Paul of Tarsus there began that 'defamation of all that is healthy, joyful and vital' and the enunci-

---

37   Darwin 1984, 323 f.
38   Tille 1895, 111 f.
39   Tille 1895, 121, 196 f.
40   Tille 1895, 120.
41   Tille 1895, 210–12.

ation and spread of the 'senseless doctrine of the equality of all', now present
in particularly virulent form in the socialist movement properly understood.
This movement claimed to oppose the 'dominant superstition, Protestant or
Catholic', but is actually its heir, its 'child.' So it is a question of challenging
'almost two thousand years of history', and of once again asserting 'the impulse
for power [*Trieb zur Macht*]' against the 'instincts of the herd'.[42] A new era was,
he said, beginning: it was finally time to do away with the 'cult of the masses', the
myth of the 'so-called innate rights of man' and the 'abstraction' of 'humanity'
and the 'theory of respect for other members of humanity [*Mitmenschen*]', even
to be considered as one's 'brothers'; it made no sense to continue to indulge
in the farce of parliamentarism and of a political system, 'democracy', that, by
virtue of universal suffrage, gave power to the idiots and incompetents that
formed the majority of the population.[43]

According to Tille, it was wrong to stop halfway. Once cured of the 'hallucination of the famine fever', represented by a belief in the ideas of equality,
democracy and humanity, there was no choice other than to proceed with the
compulsory sterilisation of the dregs of the population.[44] Moreover, it would
be ridiculous and insane to shed tears over the fact that the 'North American
Indians' and the other 'savage tribes' are vanishing as a result of the irresistible
advance of 'higher races', in accordance with the law of nature that 'the superior
vanquishes the inferior'.[45]

Nietzsche, hailed by Lapouge as a 'selectionist' and likened to Ammon,[46]
even influenced social Darwinism outside Europe. Kidd, a British sociologist
very well known in the United States in the early twentieth century, identified
completely with Nietzsche's contempt for the socialist movement, which had
become very influential in Germany: it is the agitation of a 'servile population'
that took its 'slave morality' and a number of other themes from Christianity, themes that gained them sympathy for their cause and enabled them to
neutralise or paralyse the natural aristocracy. But not only socialism should be
indicted: 'What is our Western Liberalism at best? An augmented animal nature
of the herd? What is democracy? A declining type of the state in which the natural superior is enslaved by feelings of sympathy so that that which is proper
to him can be taken away from him.' Against all this, one should be able to set,

---

42   Tille 1893, 91 f., 191, 364.
43   Tille 1893, 80 f., 32, 191 f.
44   Tille 1893, 86, 138–41.
45   Tille 1893, 26 f.
46   Lapouge 1896, 470.

according to the German philosopher, a 'new table' of values and a regained firmness: 'In modern literature no man of international reputation except Nietzsche has yet dared to utter such thoughts so directly.'[47] This was a sign that we were at a turning point, the 'end of an epoch' and the beginning of a new, radically different one.[48] It hardly needs adding that *The Will to Power* played no role for Kidd either: the first edition had appeared a year earlier, but it was completely ignored.

4 From Elisabeth's 'Proto-Nazism' to Lukács' 'Objective Convergence' with the Nazi Ideologues

So, there is no way one can use the sister's manipulation to explain the social-Darwinist interpretation of Nietzsche that became popular in the nineteenth and twentieth centuries. One way out of the problem is to declare those 'many [...] European intellectuals' that 'at the turn of the century' saw in Nietzsche 'a kind of [reactionary] Messiah' were 'mentally deficient'.[49] But it is a vain and desperate enterprise to wish to re-immerse in a bath of political innocence the theorist of aristocratic radicalism by reverting to one of the most controversial and disturbing themes of his thinking, the psychopathological interpretation of social conflict, or, in this case, of the conflict of interpretations.

Lukács managed little better than the many European and also American 'mentally ill': his interpretation, said to have had 'negative effects [...]', especially within Marxism', coincided *de facto* with the Nazi one, the only difference being in its value judgement, which was of course the opposite.[50] The same accusation was levelled at the philosopher's sister. Both the theory of Elisabeth's 'proto-Nazism' and that of Lukács's objective convergence with the pro-Hitler ideologues proceed tacitly from the assumption that the debate about Nietzsche's political significance began in the years and with the movement immediately preceding the advent of Third Reich. It is as if, to take two examples, Rohde and Duboc had never warned of the dangers of glorifying 'cannibal morality' or of the 'aristocracy of rogues'!

Skipping over the debate at the turn of the century is all the more serious because in it there emerges an anticipatory critique of the hermeneutics of innocence that prevails today. The fascination Nietzsche induced led and leads

47   Kidd 1902, 128 f.
48   Kidd 1902, 1–29.
49   Montinari 1999, 128.
50   Vattimo 2000, 145.

some to believe that he is an author that could not be 'subject to logical under-standing but only to aesthetic enjoyment'.[51] Mehring emphatically rejected the artistic and metaphorical approach that aimed to remove as irrelevant and sac-rilegious any consideration of a historical-political character and sometimes even of a logical-conceptual character:

> One should not object that Nietzsche always took his distance from the capitalist machine, that in his own way he always fought honestly for the truth, that he wanted somehow to ascend to the highest summit of the spiritual spirit, that he felt at ease only amid the solitude of the high mountains and that for him every community [*Gemeinschaft*] with people is 'vulgar [*gemein*]'.[52]

All that is true, but it in no way guarantees immaculateness. One can rather speak of a paradox: 'A philosophy that wants to breathe only in the absolutely free ethereal heights and despises the conditions of real life tumbles back brusquely into matter at its most foul and repugnant.'[53] However fascinating such a philosophy might be, it ended up justifying exploitation and oppression, even in its most brutal form.

But why go so far afield? Let us put Mehring to one side and take an author like Brandes, who enjoyed Nietzsche's respect and sympathy and, in his turn, admired Nietzsche. In this case too, the radical and brutal nature of the philo-sopher's political programme emerged:

> For Nietzsche, the size of progress must be measured by the sacrifices it requires. Hygiene that keeps alive millions of the weak and useless, of people that would be better dead, does not for him constitute real pro-gress. A world of mediocre happiness secured for the greatest possible number of those wretched creatures we nowadays call human beings would not for him be true progress.[54]

According to Brandes, such a radical perspective was horrifying only for those that did not realise that the 'masses' must be considered either as 'bad copies, crudely made with poor material, of great personalities' or as 'tools' of the latter.

51 Mehring 1961ff., Vol. 13, 182f.
52 Mehring 1961ff., Vol. 13, 166.
53 Mehring 1961ff., Vol. 13, 166.
54 Brandes 2004, 77.

But, in his determination to undermine 'the respect modern historians cherish for the masses', Nietzsche nourished the desire to 'raise a race of higher spirits capable of seizing power' and pointed out that, in the past, aristocrats worthy of the name 'were no better to their enemies than unleashed beasts of prey'.[55] So how can one maintain that Lukács subscribes to the Nietzsche interpretation of Nazism, merely reversing the value judgement? If one really wishes to stick to the idea of an objective convergence, one could say he took over and reversed the value judgement of Brandes' interpretation, which derived from the circle around Nietzsche himself.

On the other hand, if one limits oneself to the period after the Second World War, one has to recognise that the Hungarian Marxist philosopher was by no means the only one to pose the problem of the relationship between Nietzsche and the Third Reich. While the World War was still in full swing, Croce for example wondered what connected Nietzsche (and other personalities of German culture) with 'the sinister events happening in the course of the nineteenth century and especially of the twentieth in his country and throughout the world'.[56]

But let us focus on Germany. In Bloch, for example, we find the thesis that the 'overman [...] is fascism as clear as day', and the celebration of 'the will to power' is very welcome to 'monopoly capital as well as to the imperialist war'.[57]

As is well known, Adorno was a fierce critic of *The Destruction of Reason*; on the other hand, however, both he and Horkheimer drew attention to the fateful passages in which Nietzsche passed a sort of death sentence on the 'weak' and the 'deformed', So much is clear: 'There are the weak and the strong, there are classes, races and nations that rule, and there are those that are inferior'; and later, fascism raised 'the cult of force to the level of a world-historical doctrine.'[58] Nor should we be taken in by the celebration of 'beauty': 'Just like Sade, Nietzsche also uses the testimony of the *ars poetica*' in support of political theses far from innocent and indeed decidedly disturbing.[59]

Regarding authors far removed from Lukács, one should not forget Thomas Mann, reluctantly compelled to recognise that the eugenic recommendations of the philosopher he loved had become part of the 'theory and practice of National Socialism.' In the same way, the condemnation of Christianity, by

---

55   Brandes 2004, 52 f., 35, 70.
56   Croce 1959, 72.
57   Bloch 1962, 344, 359, 362.
58   Horkheimer/Adorno 1947, 119–22.
59   Horkheimer/Adorno 1947, 122, 124.

its moral scruples said to block the necessary and beneficial 'annihilation of millions of deformed', had helped create a favourable ideological ground for Hitler's genocide.[60]

The authors cited here obviously represent different and opposed positions, but none seems to have subscribed to the hermeneutics of innocence that today rules the roost. In conclusion, to explain the social-Darwinist interpretation (with positive or negative value judgement) of Nietzsche, one can resort neither to the idea of spiteful manipulation by the sister, elevated to a brilliant though ruthless forerunner of a movement that would prevail decades later and in a completely different historical situation, nor to the clumsiness of an 'orthodox' Marxist interpreter, said to have confirmed the instrumental interpretation of the Hitlerite or pro-Hitler ideologues. On the one hand, one raises to the level of world-historical figures (in the negative sense) the protagonists of manipulation, while on the other hand this honour (in a distinctly positive sense) is reserved for himself by the scholar that from time to time announces his 'authentic' interpretation: had he lived just a few decades earlier, the Nazis would not have been able to take advantage of Nietzsche's power of seduction and would have found it hard to seize power or to carry their crimes through to the end.

In this way, decades of real history are effaced as falsifications of an 'authentic' history that unfortunately never happened. Thus, a question arises: was the disaster in Germany and elsewhere in Europe and across the Atlantic simply a huge misunderstanding?

5   Historical Reconstruction, Nietzsche's 'Self-Misunderstanding' and
        the Right to 'Deformation' on the Part of the Interpreter

Nowadays, anyone setting out to produce a new interpretation of Nietzsche must first confront a preliminary problem. It is not just a question of dealing with the many and conflicting interpretations. After all, the same goes for other major players in the history of thought. We can say with Hegel that a great human being condemns others to interpret (and reinterpret) him. But in Nietzsche's case we are faced with a special problem: how to explain the fact that basically non-political interpretation now widespread and dominant among philosophers corresponds to a very different interpretation on the part of his-

---

60   Mann 1986, 257, 253.

torians? The latter, who want to reconstruct not only the history of ideas but also and above all the political and social history of the second half of the nineteenth century and the first half of the twentieth century, run into Nietzsche and come to believe it is impossible to escape the discussion of the political significance of his philosophy. The historians in question can and do follow, in effect, the most varied political and ideological orientations, but overall they seem to share the conviction one expressed as follows: 'In this sense the new *Weltanschauung* was anything but innocent.'[61]

This point is stressed by the American scholar Arno J. Mayer, who explored the persistence of the *ancien régime* in Europe way beyond the French Revolution, right up to the outbreak of the First World War. But what does the author of *The Birth of Tragedy* or *The Gay Science* or *Thus Spoke Zarathustra* have to do with the fact that the monarchs and aristocrats, the big landowners and the members of the bureaucratic-military caste, stubbornly cling on to power? According to Mayer, in the second half of the nineteenth century an 'aristocratic reaction' emerged determined to oppose by all means the development of democracy, the rise of the socialist movement, the arrival on the political scene of the masses, and the mass parties and trade unions. They were concerned to block or roll back social and political processes they perceive to be a source and expression of massification, vulgarisation, decadence and degeneration:

> Nietzsche was the chief minstrel of this battle. Notwithstanding the purposely provocative contradictions and ellipses in his writing, his thought was coherently and consistently antiliberal, antidemocratic, and antisocialist, and it became more intensely so with the passage of time. [...] Nietzsche was prepared to enslave the rest of mankind in the pursuit of high culture, to which he assigned absolute priority. [...] Ultimately, though, Nietzsche looked for a caste of superiour masters to arrest and reserve the onrush of philistines and slaves by articulating and implementing the tranfigured visions and values of an imagined aristocratic past.[62]

So these were not the fantasies of an intellectual divorced from real life. After the worldview he elaborated had overcome the initial difficulties, it began to take hold on the elites. With the end of his conscious life, the philosopher of

---

61   Mayer 1981, 291.
62   Mayer 1981, 285, 286, 288.

untimeliness became increasingly timely, while the contradictions that later led to the outbreak of the First World War became ever sharper:

> Between 1890 and 1914 social Darwinist and Nietzschean formulas permeated the upper reaches of polity and society. Because of their anti-democratic, elitist, and combative inflection they were ideally suited to help the refractory elements of the ruling and governing classes raise up and intellectualize their deep-seated and ever watchful illiberalism. They provided the ideational ingredients for the transformation of unreflective traditionalism into a conscious and deliberate aristocratic reaction.[63]

Nietzsche not only bestowed an ideological and political consciousness on the layers seemingly overwhelmed by revolution and modernity, or stunned and bewildered, but also provided guidance about the methods to be used. The importance of the issues at stake and the severity of the encounter required a 'ruthlessness on the part of the elite', which was not to allow itself to be hindered by meaningless sentimentality and humanitarianism from finally realising that violence, oppression, the will to power was of the very essence of life, which was not to be tempered by 'sympathy, solidarity or kindness to the "slaves"'. In this sense, war was, for Nietzsche, a special opportunity 'for the aristocracy to show its power and superiority, its honour and heroic capacity for command'.[64]

Hobsbawm reached similar conclusions: insofar as Nietzsche reacted vigorously to the 'truths' of the nineteenth century and engaged in a relentless struggle against democracy, socialism and the 'suffocation of genius by mediocrity', he became the prophet of a selection 'destined to produce a new race of "superman" to dominate inferior human beings as man in nature dominates and exploits the brute creation', which is why he prophesied 'a war' that said 'yes to the barbarian in each of us, even to the beast within us'.[65] Let us now take a look at German historiography. Elias drew attention to the change that came about in Germany, above all after the victorious conclusion of the war with France. From Schiller's appeal to universal brotherhood in *Ode to Joy* (*Seid umschlungen Millionen*, 'Be embraced, oh millions'), set to music by Beethoven, there was a switch to 'Nietzsche's hymn to war and strength': here the enthusiasm and zeal with which the bourgeoisie adopted the 'warrior code'

---

63   Mayer 1981, 290.
64   Mayer 1981, 288 f.
65   Hobsbawm 1987, 252–3, 303; the quotation is from WzM § 127.

whose 'initial carriers were the nobles' found its highest expression. And therefore: 'What Nietzsche preached so angrily and loudly, as if it were something new and extraordinary, was, in essence, merely the reflected verbalization of a very old social strategy.'[66] Ritter reached not dissimilar conclusions: there could be no doubt that, in Germany, Nietzsche's philosophy, with its cult of the 'master-being of the indomitable will', with its celebration of the warrior's 'sure instincts' as opposed to calculating and cowardly intellect, with its contempt for 'humanitarian and pacifistic currents', had made an effective contribution to stimulating 'the "militarization" of the bourgeoisie' and preparing public opinion for the war.[67]

In one way or another, we are brought back to the 'aristocratic reaction' mentioned by Mayer or to the 'cultural elitism' spoken of by another historian and sociologist, Struve, with whom we are already familiar (*supra*, 2 §5). Widely diffused at the time, this elitism found in Nietzsche its 'extreme formulations': now 'the complete subordination of the masses to the elite' was being demanded. Those interpretations that seek to prove his political innocence or at least the emancipatory potential of his thinking by pointing to his anti-statist polemic appear naïve. In fact, the state he condemned stood for egalitarianism and massification. Its mistake was not to have 'resisted the demands of the masses' and to have set off along a disastrous 'basically democratic road'. Precisely because of his radicalism, Nietzsche could identify neither with the existing state nor with the then dominant version of social Darwinism, which proclaimed the inevitable victory of the best in the 'struggle for existence' and thereby led to the recognition of the status quo.[68]

Nolte certainly adopted very different political and ideological positions from those of the historians mentioned so far. Yet even he, throughout all the stages of his development, underlined Nietzsche's eminently political role. According to Nolte, the texts of his last conscious years carry an unequivocal call for the merciless destruction of all that is 'degenerate'. Because Nietzsche had decided to undertake a radical rendering of accounts with socialist agitation and with all those that threatened the orderly functioning of culture, he was the theorist of 'counter-destruction' whose task it was to confront the destruction with which the Marxist revolutionary movement threatened the ruling classes.[69] This thesis, whose partial legitimacy we will see later, is already found in Pareto. At the beginning of the twentieth century, Pareto had noted

---

66   Elias 1989, 154, 157 f.
67   Ritter 1960, Vol. 2, 136.
68   Struve 1973, 45, 47.
69   Cf. Nolte 1990.

that 'there is no reactionary, however radical, that would dare speak ill of the people-god'. Indeed, the anxiety went even further:

> The parties opposed to the 'bourgeoisie' constantly write in books, pamphlets and newspapers that they want to destroy, destroy it. Well, there is no bourgeois that dares, even in anger, even as a joke, to say: 'You say you want to destroy us? Come on, then. It's us that will destroy you.'

The only exception to this rule was 'a bizarre spirit like Nietzsche'.[70] This again brings us back to the 'aristocratic reaction', to which the analysis of another great sociologist also referred. Although Max Weber was deeply influenced by the great German philosopher, to the extent that he expressed his contempt for the 'herd' and the 'deformed', he nevertheless proposed that one should avoid exaggerating the Nietzschean theme of the 'aristocratic opposition' of the elite to the 'far too many'.[71] There can be no doubt: while it flourishes more than ever among philosophers, the hermeneutics of innocence leads a difficult life among historians and sociologists.

The picture does not change if we move from general history to the research of specific aspects. Take for example the history of the idea of 'degeneration'. This theme was widespread in European culture and the press at the time and employed in the struggle against the 'myth' of progress. Nietzsche, as has been observed, lent this theme the 'form of an extreme provocation'.[72] The reverse of the nightmare of 'degeneration' is the eugenic dream. So let us take a look at the history of the 'utopias of human breeding'. In this case too, the encounter with Nietzsche is inevitable. Hence a history of this important chapter in social Darwinism reaches the following conclusion:

> What a distance there is in spiritual level between the banal, crude and primitive attitude of Tille and that of the scintillating, sensitive and brilliant Nietzsche. Yet it is and remains shocking to observe the extent to which Tille can deduce conceptions and formulations from Nietzsche (and moreover with a real basis) in order to justify his relativistic, anti-human, brutal and ruthless doctrine of society. Thus National Socialism began its march.[73]

---

70   Pareto 1988, 1588–89 (§ 1712 and fn. 1).
71   Weber 1971, 285.
72   Pick 1989, 226.
73   Conrad–Martius 1955, 276.

These findings are borne out by recent historical research. Even a scholar that moves cautiously on ground alien to him, that of philosophical historiography, and clearly wants to avoid a critical confrontation with the hermeneutics of innocence is forced to acknowledge an essential point regarding Nietzsche interpretations: 'Much in his work can be interpreted in terms of racial hygiene.'[74] Other authors are even clearer: with his insistence on the 'degeneration' and 'physiological decline of European humanity', the philosopher must be placed 'in the context of the direct preparation of eugenics'. Indeed, in this context, he sadly occupies a privileged position: he represents the 'turning point' for the transition from the 'idea of selection' to 'anti-degenerative activism'. The reconstruction of the history behind Hitler's eugenic and genocidal practices cannot, in this view, ignore Nietzsche, who expressly and peremptorily demanded the 'suppression of the wretched, the deformed, the degenerate.'[75]

Evidently, not only 'aristocratic reaction' but also racial hygiene and, indirectly, the Third Reich cast its shadow on the philosopher's image. Here too, historians of widely differing orientations agree. For example, Mayer comments as follows about the process of the ideological preparation of Nazism:

> Friedrich Nietzsche was the most profound and lucid member of this deracinated intelligentsia, which also included Paul de Lagarde, Julius Langbehn, and Houston Stewart Chamberlain. Alienated from the contemporary world, these non-academic men of ideas railed against liberal democracy and industrial capitalism; against Marxism and organized labour; and against the philistine bourgeoisie and the culture of modernism.[76]

According to Nolte, the dialectic already apparent at the end of the nineteenth century of threats of destruction and counter-destruction was a sort of anticipation of the inexorable clash between communism and Nazism in the twentieth century. Thus, *The Antichrist* was a response to the *Communist Manifesto*, just as *Mein Kampf* took up the challenge of Lenin's *State and Revolution!* This interpretation is misleading and one-sided: it focuses exclusively on the conflict within the capitalist metropolis and does not take into account the role of colonial expansion and the crusade against 'barbarians' beyond or in the

---

74 Schmuhl 1992, 416, fn. 60.
75 Weingart/Kroll/Bayertz 1992, 66 and 72 (for the general picture); Burleigh/Wippermann 1991, 34f. (for the Hitler link).
76 Mayer 1988, 91.

West (think of the African-Americans or, for Britain, the Irish) in the spread of social-Darwinist theories in the late nineteenth century. The fact remains that, with Nolte, who in other respects engages in a sharp polemic against Mayer,[77] the shadow of the Third Reich becomes thicker and darker. Nietzsche now seems to be the theorist or indirect inspirer of Nazi genocide, even if Nolte, the most prominent exponent of historical revisionism, interprets this policy, not without a certain indulgence, as an annihilation that both contrasts with and replicates a previous annihilation (which he blames on the Bolsheviks).

Whatever the case, it is time to dispatch once and for all the myth that it is only Lukács's supposed Marxist dogmatism that has brought up the question of the Third Reich in relation to Nietzsche. Lichtheim criticised Lukács so harshly that he even sounds vulgar and insulting. However, his own judgement on Nietzsche's thinking was even sharper than that formulated in *The Destruction of Reason*, and as hard and cold as a tombstone: Nietzsche's tone

> was heady stuff. It took time for Nietzsche's 'transvaluation of values' to grip the minds of some Germans sufficiently to make Auschwitz possible. [...] Nietzsche's obsessional hatred of democracy, his exaltation of violence and his readiness to let the weak go to the wall, all became part of the Fascist creed. [...] The consequences were dramatic, for Nietzsche had provided a section of the intellectual elite with a Weltanschauung wholly consistent with Hitler's long-term aims. [...] It is not too much to say that but for Nietzsche the SS – Hitler's shock troops and the core of the whole movement – would have lacked the inspiration which enabled them to carry out their program of mass murder in Eastern Europe.[78]

The usual accusations against Lukács are petty and misleading. The clear distance between his approach and that of the supporters of today's innocence theory cannot be defined by the line that separates supposed dogmatists and self-proclaimed anti-dogmatists. To represent the conflict of interpretations according to such a scheme would itself be no less than dogmatism! At best, one should propose a different dichotomy or conceptual pair. No historian (and no sociologist) can afford the sublime gesture of Foucault, who, without troubling to distinguish between historical reconstruction and theoretical instrumentalisation, claimed the right to be allowed to 'deform' and 'ill use' Nietzsche's thought; or that of Vattimo, who cares so little about historical context and

77 The review of Mayer 1988 is in Nolte 1991.
78 Lichtheim, 1974, 185 f.

philological reconstruction that he wants to purge Nietzsche of his own 'self-misunderstandings' (*infra*, Appendix 1). In contrast to the 'pure' philosophers, who look only at the speculative connections and the further constructions they might be able to derive from them, historians and sociologists have sought to analyse an author with particular regard to his relations to sociopolitical movements. This is the context in which Lukács belongs. His methodology for interpreting Hegel in *The Young Hegel and the Problems of Capitalist Society*[79] is similar to the one he used for Nietzsche, when he situated him in the wake of *The Destruction of Reason*. As for the accusation of dogmatism or Manichaean-ism, it is worth thinking about something that at first sight might seem paradox-ical: Lukács (and Mayer and Hobsbawm) interpreted the German philosopher as the most brilliant of the many intellectuals that produced a cultural and ideological current that later flowed into the Nazi *movement*; while Lichtheim and Nolte and established a far more direct link between Nietzsche and the Nazi *regime* and its policy of genocide.

Even historians that speak of 'posthumous ideologisation' or polemicise against the unfortunate sister recognise Nietzsche's influence on the anti-democratic movements, on Chamberlain, on Rosenberg and even on Hitler, 'intoxicated by Wagner's and Nietzsche's tragic heroism' – the reference is clearly to Friedrich, not Elisabeth![80] Not surprisingly, Bracher sums up the meaning of his discourse as follows: 'The twentieth century was born under the sign of a long prepared battle of ideas that in consequence of extreme thinkers like Marx and Nietzsche now become directly operative also at the political level.'[81] This view seems to confirm Nolte's central thesis. Thus, we are brought back to an overtly political reading of Nietzsche, in further confirmation of the difficult life the hermeneutics of innocence leads outside the circle of 'pure' philosophers.

Should we blame historians and sociologists for venturing onto a terrain not their own? In fact, to paraphrase a famous saying, philosophy is too serious and important to be left to professional philosophers (it goes without saying that a similar argument can be made of history and professional historians or sociology and professional sociologists). However much a philosopher wishing to understand Nietzsche may search for 'pure' interpretations, he cannot help but wonder about the reasons behind a disturbing fact: 'The German National Socialists were merely the most fanatical among his admirers. Not a single Fas-cist – from Mussolini to Oswald Mosley [the British Fascist Leader] – escaped

---

79 Lukács 1948.
80 Bracher 1982, 33 f., 37, 208.
81 Bracher 1999, 678.

his pervasive influence.'[82] Even if the philosophers want to continue to be wary of historians, they should at least take note that, in 1936, Heidegger saluted in Mussolini and Hitler, the two men who 'brought in a counter-movement against nihilism', after 'both learned from Nietzsche, though in essentially different ways'.[83] They might also note that Heidegger, in the course of progressively distancing himself from the Third Reich, felt obliged to distance himself simultaneously from Nietzsche.

6   Philosophers and Historians or Anti-political Pathos as Medicine and Sickness

While historians interpret Nietzsche from their various and opposing cultural and political positions as a champion of 'aristocratic reaction', as prophet of eugenics and 'anti-degenerative activism', or as theorist of 'counter-destruction' and even as trailblazer for the final solution, today's dominant philosophical historiography is above all concerned with dividing equally between Elisabeth Förster and György Lukács responsibility for the 'manipulation' or 'misunderstanding' of the politically reactionary interpretation of Nietzsche. Rather than confront the approach shared, in different ways, by eminent historians, most philosophical historiography seems be engaged in discouraging it and discrediting it in advance.

In his analysis of 'aristocratic reaction', Mayer felt the need to thank the friends that have 'encouraged [him] not to let [himself] be intimidated by the canonical Nietzsche interpretations',[84] the innocence theory dominant in today's philosophical historiography. And, of course, it is true that the American historian showed intellectual courage in failing to heed the harsh warning implicit in the declaration of an authoritative Nietzsche interpreter, also from the United States, who argued that, in the studies focusing on the theoretical connection of the will to power to the reactionary currents of the nineteenth or twentieth century, Elisabeth's influence 'is still tremendous, even if unconscious'.[85] So it is important not to become a mouthpiece, even 'unconsciously', of this crazy forerunner of Nazism! Here what is delegitimised is not political interpretation as such but only a *certain* political interpretation (on the other

---

82   Lichtheim, 1974, 186.
83   Cf. Losurdo 1991, 5, § 2 (120, 229, fn. 44).
84   Mayer 1981, Foreword.
85   Kaufmann 1950, 4.

hand, there are abundant references to the philosopher's conflictual relationship with the Second Reich), but, in other cases, any interpretation of Nietzsche
that in any way raises political arguments or questions is targeted, as an expression of violence and profanity towards the philosopher:

> With utmost vigour, the attempts to drag Nietzsche into day-to-day polit-
> ics must be rejected. [...] However, that Nietzsche was misused for polit-
> ical purposes is not an argument against him, unless it can be shown that
> the disreputable political practice derived from a genuine understanding
> of his actual philosophy.[86]

No grounds are given for this imperious prohibition. Perhaps the thesis that
in *The Birth of Tragedy*, or starting from it, the thinker 'is able to see into the
heart of the world only with the eye of art'[87] can be understood as an attempt
at rationalisation. There can be no doubt that referring to art is the favoured
argument of all those that want to wash Nietzsche in a bath of political innocence.

So, we reach the saddest, or perhaps the most amusing, chapter in the
mutual incomprehension or failure to meet on the part of philosophers on the
one hand and historians, sociologists and politicians on the other. In the eyes
of the former, it would be absurd to want attribute a political meaning to an
author that has dedicated himself so passionately to art. The latter respond that
Nietzsche 'simultaneously extolled the aesthetic appeal of a highly developed
aristocratic culture and the brutality of aristocratic power politics'.[88] In any
case, the cult of beauty is not a synonym for innocence. Here is the contribution
of a historian that until recently has not intervened in the debate: according to
Mosse, we should not lose sight of the fact that the 'aestheticization of politics'
played a major role both in the aristocratic reaction and in the enthusiasm with
which, at least initially, the storm of fire and blood of the First World War was
greeted: 'Many German youths during the war carried Nietzsche in their ruck-
sacks, together with volumes of poetry.'[89] And they also took with them the
desire to escape a civilisation perceived as artificial and decadent, as opposed
to 'the love of adventure and the ideals of manhood', 'love of adventure, and
ideals of masculinity', the 'quest for the beauty of nature and manly beauty',

---

86   Fink 1993, 8.
87   Fink 1993, 17.
88   Mayer 1984, 284.
89   Mosse 1990, 59.

the cult of militant virility, in short, cultural and ideological baggage not unrelated to the author lovingly stored in the rucksack.[90]

Later, in 1918, in the framework of that tradition, Ernst Bertram, a follower of George, who would subsequently and not by chance become a Nazi, celebrated the 'artistic and vital' thinking of Nietzsche (and Heraclitus). The vision of reality as 'harmony in struggle', which also embraced the war and the 'annihilating' moment, and of justice 'as the eternal synthesis of vitally struggling injustices', had 'found its theoretical form in *The Will to Power* and its artistic and "musical" form in *Zarathustra*'. More precisely, he argued we were dealing with a thinking that tends to express itself 'poetically, musically', because in its essence it was intimately connected to art: it was both 'tragic music and yes-saying will to power'. On the other hand, Nietzsche himself had praised Wagner's 'overpowering symphonic intellect' that 'continuously reproduces concord out of this conflict' (WB, 9, I, 494 [316]) (*supra*, 4 §3).[91] We are already familiar with the line of continuity that leads from the Nietzschean ideal of *otium et bellum* to the slogan of 'war and art' propagated by the reaction at the end of the nineteenth century. An echo of this theme and tradition can also be heard in Hitler, who contrasted the celebration of the art of war to the hated 'mercantile-capitalist' society and mentality: unfortunately, the Second Reich was unable to accompany its own foundation with an artistic and cultural production equal to the occasion, so it was inferior to those epochs in which in both Germany and Europe 'the realizations of art corresponded to this spiritual greatness of human beings'.[92]

Hitler's formative years were characterised by the 'dreams of a great artist': he spent his youth in the beautiful art city of Vienna, passionately attending concerts and visiting galleries, and made a living by selling his paintings. He was a failed and marginalised artist, who, as a result of the experience of the massacres, enthusiasms, hatred and disillusionment of the First World War, set about realising his artistic ambitions in the guise of a demagogue.[93] As another eminent historian, Fest, notes, Hitler 'felt no doubt closer to Langbehn's "great art hero" than, for example, to Bismarck, in whom he, as is clear from many of his utterances, admired less the politician than the aesthetic phenomenon of the great man'; the Nazi leader 'wanted not only to be great in himself but great in the manner, style and temperament of an artist.'[94] His 'overman

---

90 Mosse 1990, 53, 55, 59f.
91 Bertram 1919, 100f.
92 Hitler 1935, 5; Hitler 1939a, 1.
93 Kershaw 1998, 22, 73; for the whole picture, chs 1–3.
94 Fest 1973, 525, 1034.

poses' were clearly aestheticizing, and a reference 'to the time of Gobineau, Wagner and Nietzsche'.[95]

Even as undisputed Führer, he not only continued to flaunt his 'love of art' but added: 'Against my will I have become a politician. [...] If another had been found, I would never have gone in for politics; I would have become an artist or philosopher.'[96] But that is not all. Hitler called on schools and teachers to commit themselves to 'arousing in human beings the instinct of beauty' and added: 'That was certainly the ideal in the Greek heyday'!'[97] As with the 'ancient Greeks, who were also Germanic', so too the greatness of the Germans lay among other things in their superior 'artistic sense'. This is further confirmed by the actual commitments of the Third Reich: 'I get more and more enthusiastic about the upgrading of Linz, and I know that if needs be it is the artist that reacts in me.'[98] When considering the problem of the succession, Hitler immediately excluded from the list of candidates those he calls 'unmusical people [*unmusische Menschen*]' and put in a prominent position Speer, who seemed to him, by virtue of his training as an architect, to be an 'artist', a 'genius', and 'a musical person'. Are these qualities of no particular importance for a statesman? Not in the view of the Führer, who thought even a 'general' could achieve nothing on the battlefield unless he was at the same time 'a musical person'.[99]

Together with his passion for art, his disdain for politics is frequently taken as evidence of the untenability of any interpretation of Nietzsche that goes beyond the enchanted sphere of culture. Yet as Fest emphasises, Hitler can and must be considered as the heir to an 'anti-political pathos' that deeply penetrated German cultural history. 'I became a politician against my will', he liked to say, and beyond the flirting, there is no doubt that at play here is an 'intellectual-aesthetic *ressentiment* of politics' and a well-defined cultural tradition. We must not lose sight either of Wagner's hatred for politics and his statement that 'a political person is repugnant'.[100]

But it is above all Nietzsche's more or less mediated actuality that makes it possible to translate the artistic and anti-political pathos into a reactionary political programme. Of particular interest in this context is a speech in which the Führer declared the 'dictatorship of genius'.[101] This formulation immedi-

95   Fest 1973, 732, 1035.
96   Hitler 1980, 234 (25–26 January 1942).
97   Hitler 1980, 312 (3 March 1942).
98   Hitler 1980, 232 (25–26 January 1942); Hitler 1989, 245–46 (27 April 1942).
99   Fest 1973, 526.
100   Fest 1973, 522, 526.
101   Fest 1973, 1034.

ately recalls the young Nietzsche, theorist of the 'metaphysics of genius' and art. This impression is further strengthened when we read in Hitler that 'geniuses of an extraordinary sort have no regard for normal humanity'. The mass, according to Fest, represented both for the philosopher and for the politician merely an object for the experiments and attempts with whose help nature produces superior people. Only the latter were equipped with meaning and dignity and able to act on the mass itself as a kind of raw material: 'Greatness simply legitimated everything.'[102]

Similar considerations apply to Mussolini. He too, in his socialist period, despised the amorphous and cowardly mass and pointed to the overman as 'Nietzsche's great creation'; he too celebrated the creativity of the subject, in a certain sense of the artist, as opposed to the merely 'quibbling' attitude and mechanical nature of calculations, balance sheets and figures.[103] As the Duce of fascism, he not only, by referring to Nietzsche, posed as 'a philosopher and prophet of war'[104] but would have liked to 'dominate the mass as an artist would'. This required not only aesthetic sensitivity but also energy: 'Does not the sculptor perhaps sometimes break the marble because it does not shape up in his hands precisely according to his initial vision?'[105]

Particularly with reference to Nietzsche's celebration of art and his anti-political pathos, 'purely' philosophical interpreters tend to present as a medicine that which in the analysis of historians is the very sickness. That produces yet more paradoxes. One might say the former have forgotten Benjamin's lesson, that the 'aestheticisation of politics' is a fundamental trait of fascism, while the latter remind themselves of it.[106]

7   A Selective Hermeneutics of Innocence: Nietzsche and Wagner

Let us return to the thesis that, leaving aside the value judgement, the interpretation of Nietzsche is identical in Nazism and for Lukács. We have already looked at the inconsistency of this thesis at the historical level; we must now reflect on its absurdity at the theoretical level. To demonstrate the untenability of the approach favoured by Vattimo, we need only attempt to apply it to another author, e.g., Wagner. In this case too, the interpreter has his back

---

102   Fest 1973, 732.
103   Nolte 1960, 306, 287.
104   Dino Grandi in De Felice 1981, 652.
105   Ludwig 2000, 97.
106   Fest 1973, 526.

to the wall: if he really wants to differentiate himself from the Nazis, he must recogniae that ... Wagner had nothing to do with anti-Semitism! According to this logic, today's interpreter would be justified in reckoning among the more or less remote ancestors of the Third Reich only those authors that the regime rejected in disgust!

In fact, the hermeneuts of innocence cannot think through and apply consistently the methodology they follow. On the one hand, they consider as politically irrelevant to Nietzsche the denunciation of democracy and the parliamentary system, the celebration of slavery and the theory that it is necessary to expel the 'waste materials' that hinder the orderly functioning of culture. On the other hand, with the same casualness, but with an entirely new note of severity, they identify the prophets of the Third Reich in this or that contemporary of Nietzsche with whom the philosopher had a polemical relationship. This does not only concern Wagner, the 'typical proto-Nazi'. The musician had read Renan with interest and sympathy,[107] and thus the fate of the latter is also marked. Unfortunately Todorov has already said that 'the portrait painted by Hitler of the Semites [...] owes much to Renan'.[108] But the followers of the hermeneutics of innocence (in relation to Nietzsche and only him) go much further: as a 'leading proponent of the Aryan myth', Renan was 'almost an official ideologue of the Third Reich'.[109] In actual fact, the French author ranked the Jews among the 'great civilized races' or the 'great Aryan-Semitic family'.[110] So far, we have been dealing with a view that shows certain resemblances with that of Nietzsche. Both authors shared a belief in the continuity between Judaism and Christianity, but only in Renan was it accompanied by a positive, even enthusiastic, value judgement: 'Christianity is the masterpiece of Judaism, its glory, the synthesis of its evolution. [...] Jesus is already fully contained in Isaiah.' So we can understand the indignation of Chamberlain – it would be quite possible to designate him as 'an almost official ideologue of the Third Reich' – at the 'enormity' of the affirmations and at the 'grandiloquent phrases of the free-thinker' Renan, that 'great friend of the Jews'.[111] According to Chamberlain, even when talking about the European nations and the idea of the nation in general, he revealed his 'inability' to understand the weight and real meaning of race in history.[112] It makes so little sense to see

---

107 Janz 1981, Vol. 2, 507 f.
108 Todorov 1989, 186.
109 Santaniello 1997, 22.
110 Renan 1947 ff., Vol. 8, 585.
111 Chamberlain 1937, 265, 383.
112 Chamberlain 1937, 344.

the French writer rather than Nietzsche as the true prophet of Hitler that the philosopher's most suspicious and hostile Nazi interpreters can think of no better way of demonstrating that he had essentially nothing to do with the Third Reich than to link him with none other than Renan![113] Needless to say, there are disturbing aspects of Renan: think of the theory of the right of the 'great civilized races' (which speak a 'Semitic or Indo-European language' and of which the Jews were part, albeit in a subordinate position) to subjugate or exterminate 'semi-savage races';[114] but this theme again leads us straight back to Nietzsche.

The arbitrarily discriminatory and selective character of the usual hermeneutics of innocence is particularly evident from a comparison of its treatment of Nietzsche and Wagner. The continuity scheme is not challenged as a whole but indignantly rejected in the case of Nietzsche while being all the more energetically and mechanically pushed onto Wagner. Such, for example, is the procedure followed by Montinari. While tirelessly denouncing the 'misunderstandings' and 'imposture' to which the philosopher fell victim, he seems without further ado to accept the thesis, formulated by a Nazi ideologue, that 'the true prophet' of the Third Reich was the musician.[115] Another authoritative exponent of the hermeneutics of innocence went even further, calling Wagner a 'proto-Nazi', even though he was more 'talented' than the others, particularly the philosopher's wretched family (sister and brother-in-law).[116]

In fact, both authors belonged to the pantheon of Hitler, who moreover, probably on the basis of a Nietzschean recollection, openly paid tribute to Bizet's *Carmen*.[117] On the other hand, it was not hard in these years to find intellectuals more or less close to the Nazi party that sided with Nietzsche against Wagner. In 1930, Baeumler praised the philosopher's struggle 'against Wagnerism, Christianity and bourgeois morality',[118] and speaking shortly after the start of the Third Reich, he said the 'Heil Hitler' greeting was an implied homage to Nietzsche![119]

Rosenberg used Nietzsche's violent polemic against the musician when he made a series of harsh criticisms of Wagner:

---

113   Steding 1938, 748.
114   Renan 1947 ff., Vol. 8, 581, 585 f.
115   Montinari 1999, 130 ff.; cf. Bataille 1973, 187.
116   Kaufmann 1950, 37.
117   Hitler 1980, 407 (13 March 1944).
118   Baeumler 1937a, 280.
119   Baeumler 1937b, 294.

The accompanying music absolutely destroys the expression of will and thought [...]; where a thought is to be transmitted, the orchestra stands in the way, as an obstacle [...]; the audience hears only loud inarticulate exclamations, it sees only hands raised without reason. This leads not to form but to chaos.[120]

When we then read that Wagner's work as a whole 'destroys the rhythm of the soul and hinders the expression and impression of motion [*den motorischen Ausdruck und Eindruck*]',[121] the echo of the 'physiological objections' raised by Nietzsche became even louder (*infra*, 29 § 9).

To prove Nietzsche had nothing at all and Wagner lots to do with Nazism, usually their very different attitudes to Judaism are cited. There is no doubt anti-Semitism formed a strong element of contradiction between the philosopher and the Third Reich. When Hitler raised the thesis of the semi-Aryan nature or race of Jesus, who had a Jewish mother but whose father was to be sought among the 'many descendants of Roman legionaries' that 'lived in Galilee',[122] we tend to think of Wagner and the tradition that lies behind him, but certainly not of Nietzsche, immune to such grotesque constructions, if only because of his robust philological and historical training.

But there is another side to the coin. The denunciation of Christianity as a plebeian and cowardly religion and of a two thousand-year historical cycle from Paul to Bolshevism played an essential role in Nazism. Wagner was to some extent immune to such themes, which were abundantly present in Nietzsche, because Wagner celebrated 'the miraculous effects of revelation',[123] i.e., because he continued to be tied to Christianity, although to a form of Christianity that he had artificially and dangerously stripped of its Judaism. The 'gospel of the lowly' of which the philosopher accused the musician (WA, Epilogue [261]) and also Renan (GD, *Expeditions of an Untimely Man*, 2 [192]) was hardly compatible with the ideology of the master race espoused by the Nazis.

So, one can juxtapose and contrast to an anti-Semitic line of continuity from Wagner to the Third Reich an anti-Christian and neo-pagan line of continuity from Nietzsche to the Third Reich. If anti-Semitism drove the Christian-Germanic Wagner to pursue a mythical non-Semitic origin for the founder of the religion to which he adhered and of which the Second Reich posed as mouthpiece, the permanent profession of Christian faith somehow immun-

---

120   Rosenberg 1937a, 429.
121   Rosenberg 1937a, 432.
122   Hitler 1980, 412 (30 November 1944).
123   C. Wagner 1882, 347.

ised him against the aesthetising cult of violence and war that spread at the end of the nineteenth century and was later inherited and radicalised by the Nazis. While Nietzsche, especially in his final phase, called for an end once and for all to the revolutionary and subversive movements and did not exclude the most radical means, Wagner denounced 'the repressive laws against the socialists', as an expression not only of indiscriminate violence but also of 'narrowness' of the spirit.[124] When Nietzsche praised eugenics well beyond the compulsory sterilisation of the 'malformed', he provided a theoretical foundation for the annihilation, in one way or another, of the 'decadent races'. Such thoughts were alien to Wagner, who, not surprisingly, remained bound to a religion that, in Nietzsche's eyes, was the plebeian and ignoble religion *par excellence*.

The nationalism disdainfully rejected by Nietzsche was only intra-European; this denunciation went hand in hand with the celebration of the expansionist forward march on a global scale of Europeans and of war as an expression of vitality and health. On the opposing side, Wagner's tireless hymn of praise for Germany and the Germans was not unequivocally synonymous with the exaltation of imperialism and warmongering. Indeed, in this regard, there was no lack of critical accents that, in these years, sounded definitely 'untimely'. A good example, in 1880, is *Religion and Art*: 'Spiritual culture continues to decline. Violence can civilize, but culture can blossom only on the ground of peace.'[125] Nietzsche's condemnation of 'civilisation' was aimed at the philistinism of security and the taming of the beast of prey, Wagner's at law and the 'victory of the fittest', the affirmation of the 'beast of prey' and its work of 'destruction and annihilation'.[126]

Not surprisingly, the musician was on very good terms with Frantz, who sharply criticised, from a Christian point of view, the militaristic intoxication of the Second Reich. Frantz published an essay in *Bayreuther Blätter* in March 1881 that even criticised the hero of the Blitzkrieg against France. Against Moltke's thesis, which denounced the ideal of perpetual peace as a dream, and one that was anything but beautiful, Frantz set the Ten Commandments, which forbade killing, and the maxims of the Gospel. Unfortunately, these lessons were suppressed by the 'military religion' that was spreading across Germany and meanwhile casting a worrying shadow across 'European culture' as a whole. To the apologists for war, who celebrated it as an antidote to materialism, Frantz

---

124   C. Wagner 1977, 98, 102.
125   Wagner 1910n, 234.
126   Wagner 1910n, 225, 227.

and the Wagnerian Review pointed out that war actually furthered this scourge and 'unleashes the beast in man'.[127]

Frantz's denunciation of the glorification of war in the name of Christianity found its polemical echo in Nietzsche's denunciation of the anti-war and anti-Aryan character of Christianity, an element undoubtedly taken over by the Third Reich.

8 Gobineau and Chamberlain in Light of the Hermeneutics of Innocence

We have spoken of the caprice and arbitrariness of the procedure followed by the hermeneutics of innocence. It must also be pointed out, however, that its consistent application would lead to a paradoxical outcome. Take, for example, a writer like Gobineau. His 'ideal of the fraternity of the European aristocracies' rendered him 'untimely' even at the end of the nineteenth century, at a time when the chauvinistic passions that eventually led to the First World War were on the rise.[128] On the other hand, his book about the natural and insurmountable inequality of the races was so deeply imbued with a tone of melancholy resignation in the face of the inexorable development of the process of the bastardisation of races and thereby the withering of culture that it could easily have borne the title *Sunset of the White Race* or, more exactly, *Sunset of the Superior White Race*. What could be further from the pugnacious tone and confident certainty of victory of Nazism? To this first element of differentiation, already highlighted by Lukács, one can add at least one more: disgusted by the subversive tide overwhelming every tradition and hierarchy in the West, Gobineau was loath to endorse its expansionist mission. Finally, one should not forget that the *Essai sur l'inégalité des races humaines* was, as we shall see shortly, celebrated above all in Britain.

Although Chamberlain distanced himself from Gobineau's 'pessimistic vision' or 'hallucinatory representation' of the inevitable deterioration of the purity of race and culture, he referred to him warmly, praising his 'brilliant work on the inequality of races, surprisingly rich in insights, later confirmed, and historical knowledge'.[129] At least with regard to this Anglo-German writer, there can be no doubt that he played an important role as *maître à penser* of Nazism. Goebbels spoke of him in particularly enthusiastic terms. When he visited him

---

127   Frantz 1881, 67 f.
128   Digeon 1959, 93 f.
129   Chamberlain 1937, 313 f.

on his sick-bed, he uttered a kind of prayer: 'Hail to thee, father of our spirits. Precursor, pioneer!'[130] In no less inspired terms, Chamberlain saw in Hitler a kind of saviour, and not only for Germany.[131] Even after the Nazi conquest of power and while he was feverishly engaged in the war he has unleashed, the Führer gratefully recalled the encouragement he had received from Chamberlain during the period of his imprisonment.[132]

So, in this case, at least, there should be no doubt. But let us try once again to bring the hermeneutics of innocence into the equation. It is true that the Germans [*Germanen*] were emphatically celebrated, but the Anglo-Saxon also belonged to them absolutely, as conquerors that had spread to every corner of the world: in the final analysis, *Germane* was synonymous with *homo europaeus*. Clearly, we are far removed from German chauvinism in the strict and exclusive sense. Indeed, on the grounds of the affirmation of European unity, Chamberlain went perhaps further than Nietzsche, for he even subsumed Slavs under the category of *Germane* and *homo europaeus*. The Slavs ere even credited, through their presence in Prussia and the consequent 'mixing of blood', with having made the country that later assumed hegemony in the German Reich more vital and creative. When he wrote that 'the German is the soul of our culture', he meant it only in this very wide sense. With an eye not only to Britain but to Russia, Chamberlain said proudly: 'Only Germans sit on the thrones of Europe.'[133] So even cultures and peoples later racialised as a chaotic mass of *Untermenschen* by the Nazis and the target of the Nazis' colonisation of Eastern Europe, with a massive killing of 'natives' and the substantial enslavement of the residual population, were regarded with sympathy. Here the Anglo-German writer was separated from the theory and practice of the Third Reich by an abyss.

In an attempt to free Gobineau from the Nazi embrace, a recent biographer of him stresses he was a 'bitter enemy of despotism' and praises his 'proud Aryan individualism, precisely that which Hitler has identified as the *punctum dolens* of the German people', which needed to be overcome and removed once and for all.[134] This argument applies even more to Chamberlain, for whom Germanicness [*Germanentum*] was completely irreconcilable with 'monarchical absolutism' and every worldview that sacrifices the 'single individual' on the

---

130   Goebbels 1991a, 247 (8 May 1926); cf. Reuth 1991, 74.
131   In Fest 1973, 259.
132   Hitler 1980, 224 (24–25 January 1942).
133   Chamberlain 1937, 305, 331f.
134   Castradori 1991, 201.

altar of collectivity.[135] Not surprisingly, Locke was the 'first to re-elaborate this new Germanic worldview';[136] and if one seeks even earlier precedents, they can be found in Ockham and before that in Duns Scotus, for whom 'the individual' represented the 'only reality.'[137] Moreover, if Gobineau praised the 'liberal traditions of the Aryans', that had long withstood this 'Canaanite monstrosity' of the idea of a 'fatherland',[138] Chamberlain himself, as has been noted, was a 'good citizen and liberal', for he 'raises the banner of individual freedom'.[139] If Langbehn is then inserted into this context, as most historians engaged in the reconstruction of the 'intellectual origins of the Third Reich' do,[140] we see that the profession of individualistic faith, even the celebration of the 'holy spirit – of individualism', the 'German principle of individualism', this 'fundamental and original motive power of all Germanicness', was even more strongly marked.[141]

Even with regard to anti-Semitism, it is difficult to regard as an advocate or precursor of the 'final solution' an author that claimed to want to distinguish between 'Jews of noble and Jews of less noble origin' and that at least credited the Jews, 'uniquely' among the 'Semites', with having 'contributed positively to our culture', starting with the important role they had played in preserving and transmitting the heritage of 'antiquity'.[142] This is an author that had insisted on making clear that the 'Jew is no enemy of Germanic culture and civilization' and warned precisely against 'the ridiculous and outrageous tendency to make the Jew the universal scapegoat for all the vices of our time'.[143]

So, should we conclude that the meeting, in this case not just ideological but actual, between Chamberlain and Hitler was merely the result of a misunderstanding, an illusion, of which both fall foul? If so, this illusion blinds not just the ideologues of Nazism but numerous contemporary historians who, in their efforts to reconstruct the genesis of the Third Reich, pay particular attention to the author of the *Foundations of the Nineteenth Century*. This is the paradoxical but inevitable outcome of a hermeneutics of innocence, once consistently thought through and applied.

---

135 Chamberlain 1937, 995, fn. 291.
136 Chamberlain 1937, 1088, fn.
137 Chamberlain 1937, 1035 f.
138 Gobineau 1983, 678 f., 681 (Book 4, 3).
139 Nolte 1963, 351.
140 Mosse 1979 and 1966, *passim*.
141 Langbehn 1922, 36, 210, 3.
142 Chamberlain 1937, 386, 304.
143 Chamberlain 1937, 18 f.

CHAPTER 25

Aristocratic Radicalism, Pan-European Elite and Anti-Semitism

1   Britain and 'the Way to Distinction'

Nietzsche's close connection with the aristocratic reaction of the late nineteenth century should by now be clear. And yet, today, the dominant trend is to use categories like 'anti-Germanicness' and 'anti-Semitism' to erect an insurmountable barrier between the philosopher on the one hand and the most reactionary currents of the Second Reich (not to mention the Third Reich) on the other.[1] There can be no doubt that Nietzsche called for 'a pan-European elite',[2] but he was by no means the only one to do so. Think of the pathos of *homo europaeus*, which, to name two examples, was in favour with Lombroso and above all with Lapouge, who saw in this figure the embodiment of 'Aryan' culture and the antithesis of the imminent barbarism.[3] This was also true, as we have seen, for Chamberlain. In this case, we can even cite the judgement of a faithful friend of Nietzsche. This is what Overbeck wrote about the author of *Foundations of the Nineteenth Century*: 'By Germans he means nothing other than "the whole world", the whole range of Slavo-Celtic-Germanic Europeans, defined as *Homo Europaeus albus, sanguineus* by Linnaeus.'[4] One should not forget that the European dynasties were all related to each other and met regularly at engagements, weddings and funerals: they prided themselves on being part of a family or a highly exclusive race. Defined by the most varied names (European, white, Nordic, Western, Aryan, etc)., they indicated culture as such. This is the situation Nietzsche described and ideologically transfigured.

If there was a country the aristocratic reaction of the late nineteenth century took as model, it was Britain. It is easy to understand why. France had been long ravaged by one revolution after the other, while after the collapse of the Paris Commune the Second Reich had been particularly exposed to socialist agitation. Apart from that, on both sides of the Rhine universal suffrage (for men) had been introduced, a contagion to which the happy isle had remained so far

---

1   Montinari 1999, 136 f.; cf. Bataille 2005, 221–29; Bataille 1973, 185–88.
2   Struve 1973, 43, fn.
3   On Lombroso cf. Teti 1993, 154; on Lapouge cf. Poliakov 1987, 305.
4   Overbeck 1994–95c, 233.

immune. Even Treitschke looked on with admiration and envy: after socialism had unfortunately migrated from its original 'French homeland' to Germany, it met precisely in Britain with an insurmountable obstacle. There 'common sense' and the 'political tact of a free people accustomed to struggle' left little room for 'social-democratic dreams': in any event, 'the valiant legal sense of the upper estates has always been the rock against which the blind faith of the misled masses has broken its horns'.[5]

Langbehn too looked across the English Channel when invoking an anti-democratic counteroffensive: 'Even today England is organized in part aristocratically'; it 'has not experienced the political success of the fourth estate'. Among the British, 'the healthy old aristocratism has not disappeared,'[6] so that they, as 'the most distinguished of all peoples', 'show the way forward to distinction [*Vornehmheit*] for the Germans as a whole'.[7] If we cross over from Germany to Austria, the picture does not change: in Vienna under the Habsburgs as described by Musil, the 'nobility', which was very proud, 'considered itself second only to the English'.[8] Gobineau too liked this model: in his eyes, Britain was 'the country in which the blood of its founders had undergone the slowest and least significant changes', and where, thanks precisely to this greater purity, 'institutions of the fourteenth and fifteenth centuries continue to form the basis of the social structure', together with 'remnants of Germanic customs'.[9] It is no accident that the essay devoted to denouncing all manifestations of the idea of *égalité* was dedicated to 'His Majesty King George V'. In France, Paul Bourget, an author known to and appreciated by Nietzsche, spoke with similar respect and admiration of 'aristocratic and monarchic England', in a text and with a judgement that would later become a reference point for Charles Maurras and Action Française.[10] For Lapouge, Britain seemed to be 'the advanced sentinel of Europe', the country in which there was no trace of exhaustion of the 'aristocratic caste' that had occurred in France.[11] The allure of the island was in these years so strong that not even Wilhelm II could escape it: in his veins too, he bragged, 'runs good, stubborn, unquenchable English blood'; 'I adore England', the emperor told Theodore Roosevelt.[12]

---

5   Treitschke 1879, 461f.
6   Langbehn 1922, 140.
7   Langbehn 1922, 213.
8   Musil 1952, 104.
9   Gobineau 1983, 179, 1013 (Book 1, 5, and Book 6, 3).
10   Cf. Girardet 1983, 168.
11   Lapouge 1896, 71, 76.
12   In Balfour 1964, 84.

Britain was a country that was at the forefront of colonial expansion and at the same time continued to be ruled by an aristocracy of extraordinary vitality. So the admiration it aroused among writers committed to or influenced by social Darwinism was understandable: 'The most energetic, restless and courageous people from all over Europe have, over the last ten or twelve generations, migrated to that great country and achieved their greatest success there', says Ploetz, who also cited Lombroso in support.[13] Contrary to current myths, Nietzsche was cooler: yes, he set the quite different colonialism of Britain against the presumptuous and plebeian colonialism of his brother-in-law, Bernhard Förster (*supra*, 18 §8), but otherwise he accused the British of having a shopkeeper's mentality and of being moral hypocrites. He also chided them for their insufficient frankness and ruthlessness, which prevents them from recognising the superior right of the 'blond beast' to conquest and violence.

2　　European Decadence and Germany's 'Backwardness'

If the philosopher subjected the Second Reich, and Germany after Luther, to pitiless criticism, his views on other countries were hardly more flattering. Let us leave the United States to one side: '[W]hat do I care about the pathetic drivel of American idiots and asses?' (EH, Why I am so clever, 4 [92]). He seemed to target Britain in particular. We have already seen that the main obstacle to a reaffirmation of slavery was 'damned English-European cant'. The English were 'the people of the perfect cant' (*supra*, 12 §2 and 22 §3), the people that represented 'moral hypocrisy' (XI, 523) and '"altruistic" morality' in its most concentrated form: this was a 'bad sign' and 'is true for the individual [and] even more true for peoples' (GD, *Expeditions of an Untimely Man*, 35 [209]).

And that is not all: 'The fundamental trend of English philosophy is the pursuit of comfort [*Comfortismus*]' (XI, 72), in the sense of happiness at its most philistine, 'happiness of the most', in the final analysis, 'English "happiness"' (XI, 523). The English embodied the mercantile and philistine view of life: 'People don't strive for happiness, only the English do' (GD, Judgements and arrows, 12 [157]). In reality, a 'free human being is a warrior'. As soon as one achieved authentic freedom, one had no choice other than to trample underfoot 'the miserable type of well-being that grocers, Christians, cows, females, Englishmen, and other democrats dream about' (GD, *Expeditions of an Untimely Man*, 38 [213]). Along with the love of risk, courage for thinking

---

13　Ploetz 1895, 135.

also seemed to have vanished. These 'moral little females' were even incapable of rising to the level of a real atheism:

> In England, every time you take one small step towards emancipation from theology you have to reinvent yourself as a moral fanatic in the most awe-inspiring way. That is the price you pay there. – For the rest of us, things are different. When you give up Christian faith, you pull the rug out from under your right to Christian morality as well.
>
> GD, *Expeditions of an Untimely Man*, 5 [193]

On this point, at least, Germany seemed superior. It is true the *Critique of Practical Reason* had appeared in Germany. Here too, Nietzsche's contempt was boundless: 'Kant: or *cant* as intelligible character' (GD, *Expeditions of an Untimely Man*, 1 [192]). Perhaps this aphorism was a play on the Scottish origin of the philosopher whom, by virtue of his cant, British nationality citizenship would have well suited. Whatever the case, on German soil there was more intellectual courage: an atheist had the courage to declare himself as such, quite unlike Carlyle, who 'is basically an English atheist who stakes his honour on not being one' (GD, Skirmishes of an untimely man, 12 [198]). What a difference from Schopenhauer, 'admitted and uncompromising atheist' (FW, 357 [219])! The fact was that in Britain one was dealing with a 'race of former Puritans' (*supra*, 15 §2), 'not a philosophical race', and moreover not a warrior 'race', a race known to 'firmly support Christianity'; 'they need its discipline', continued *Beyond Good and Evil*, 'to be "moralized" and in some sense humanized' (JGB, 252 [143]).

Even for an author well versed in hyperbole, the attack on England took on extraordinarily bitter tones. There was no doubt there was 'nothing more lamentable than the moralistic literature in today's Europe', but at the head in terms of shallowness and emptiness were 'the utilitarian English, plodding like cattle in the footsteps of Bentham, as he himself in the footsteps of Helvetius'; they were 'heavy herd animals of a troubled conscience', incapable of understanding the 'rank-ordering of human beings' (XI, 523–4). It was terrifying to see how quickly the process of massification and stultification of the herd induced by democracy was proceeding: in the 'famous case of Buckle; the plebeianism of the modern spirit, which began in England, broke out there once again on its native soil as violently as a volcano of mud' (GM, I, 4 [13]).

'English' became almost an insult. When he wanted to denounce Rée's banality and thus to destroy him, Nietzsche said he belonged among the 'English genealogists' of morality and that, in the last analysis, he was 'English' (GM, Preface, 4 [6]). The stereotype continued, though in weakened form, in the years of

The Birth of Tragedy, which celebrated German depth as against modern banality and superficiality. In fact, the great German thinkers (not just Schopenhauer, but also Kant, Schelling and Hegel) were invoked as judges of the emptiness of English pseudo-philosophy, which signified 'an attack on the philosophical spirit in general', 'a degradation and a depreciation in value', an 'English-mechanistic world-stupidification' (JGB, 252 [143]). Nietzsche identified with the praise lavished on him by Hillebrand, who hailed the first *Unfashionable Observation* as 'a real return of German seriousness and German passion in spiritual matters' (EH, *The Untimely Ones*, 2 [113]).

Beyond Spencer's Britain, the denunciation of positivism and of the spirit of 'altruism' and the herd mentality that pervadesd it also extended to Comte's France. Both authors were equally as '*décadents*' as the 'socialists':

> My objection to the whole discipline of sociology in England and France is that it has only experienced the decaying forms of society, and innocently uses its own instinct of decay as the norm for sociological value judgements. Declining life, the loss of all the forces of organization, which is to say separation, division, subordination, and domination, is formulated as an ideal in sociology.
>
> GD, *Expeditions of an Untimely Man*, 37 [213]

Above all, in the last years of his conscious life, Nietzsche spoke in ever sharper terms about France. He voiced contemptuous opinions not just about Rousseau, long his favourite target, due to his own permanent and consistent denunciation of the catastrophe of the French Revolution, but also about Victor Hugo, George Sand, Zola (or 'the joy of stinking'), the 'Parisian novelists' in general ('practicing psychology everywhere'), the Goncourt brothers (they 'make the worst job of it: they cannot put three sentences together without it hurting your eye, the psychologist's eye'), Sainte-Beuve, Baudelaire and Comte (GD, *Expeditions of an Untimely Man*, 1–7 [192–5]); not to mention Renan, treated by Nietzsche as the symptom of a degenerate process that went far beyond a single person. The author of the *Life of Jesus* was 'a spirit that enervates, [...] one more disaster for poor, sick, sick-willed France' (GD, *Expeditions of an Untimely Man*, 2 [192]).

This sickness went back to the French Revolution and the philosophy that lay behind it and continued to reveal a malevolent vitality. Take Sainte-Beuve, for example: 'Plebeian in the lowest instincts and related to Rousseau's *ressentiment*', 'revolutionary, but kept pretty much in check by fear', in him 'lies the hungering, howling, Rousseauian instinct for revenge'; '[n]othing manly; full of a petty rage against any manly sort of spirit. Drifting around, refined, curious, bored, inquisitive – a woman at heart with a female vindictiveness and female sensuality' (GD, *Expeditions of an Untimely Man*, 3 [192]).

The fateful presence of Rousseau could also be felt in George Sand, with her 'ambition to have generous feelings', which in reality are steeped in *ressentiment* and stoke up the plebeian revolt. This feminist and socialist writer was admired and even 'adored' by Renan (GD, *Expeditions of an Untimely Man*, 6 [194]). It was easy to see why. Despite his claim to be part of the 'aristocratism of the spirit', 'when faced with its counter-principle, the *évangile des humbles*, he falls down on his knees' (GD, *Expeditions of an Untimely Man*, 2 [192]). Here we had a sort of national defect. It also affected Comte, who apparently fed his 'religion of the heart' by reading the *Imitatio Christi*, a book that created feelings of 'physiological feeling of repulsion': to be able to tolerate and even appreciate it, one had to be 'French – or Wagnerian' (GD, *Expeditions of an Untimely Man*, 4 [193]); supporters of the German but at the same time repugnantly Catholicising musician found their elective homeland precisely in France.

By comparison with other European and Western countries, Germany came off relatively well. The pacifism of the English was despicable, but the French, with their cult, inherited from the revolution, of the human being as such and of brotherhood among nations, were no different: 'One really has to be afflicted with a Gallic excess of erotic irritability and enamoured impatience to approach humanity honestly with one's lust' (FW, 377 [242]). Fortunately, in Germany there were 'the most masculine virtues that can be found anywhere in Europe' (GD, What the Germans did not have, 1 [186]). We already know that the 'Latin races' embodied that 'numbers nonsense' and 'superstitious belief in majorities' that fortunately had not yet taken root in Germany (*supra*, 11 §5). The philosopher noted 'with pleasure' that the 'Mephistophelean nature' already manifested by Friedrich the Great (interpreter of the virtues of *bellum*) and by 'that much greater Friedrich, the Hohenstaufen Friedrich II' (who had the merit of having striven to emancipate himself from the straits of the Christian world) still lived (XI, 452).

A very significant fragment tried to identify and enumerate the most repulsive expressions of modernity: 'Authors that compromise once and for all those who, even today, read them with pleasure: Rousseau, Schiller, George Sand, Michelet, Buckle, Carlyle, the *imitatio*' (XIII, 189). Evidently, Germany had a modest presence on this list. Schiller was on it, but of the Germans of the day, all that can be said is that they 'can no longer bear the big, shining, glittering Schillerish words' worshipped by their 'grandfathers' (XI, 567).

In conclusion, it seemed to be precisely Germany that offered a minimum of resistance to the general subversive drift:

And this muted resistance to Wagner might not be the least of the signs that the German character still retains a degree of health, the trace of an instinct for harm and danger, in spite of the totalizing character of European decadence. This is a credit to us, it even gives us hope: France would not have this much health at its disposal any more. The Germans, historically the procrastinators [*Verzögerer*] *par excellence*, are the most backward of all civilized peoples [*zurückgebliebenste Culturvolk*] in Europe these days: this has its advantages, – it means that they are the youngest.

WA, Postscript [255]

This theme already emerged in Nietzsche when the enthusiasm of *The Birth of Tragedy* waned. 'Imperfection' marked the German people: 'What is German has not yet expressed itself with full clarity.' Precisely this situation left room for hope for the future despite all the mediocrity: 'The German essence does not yet even exist, it must first come into being; at some time or other it must be born, so that it can above all be visible and honest with itself. But every birth is painful and violent' (VII, 687 [250]). This hope never completely disappeared, for even on the brink of the onset of his madness, Nietzsche reckoned Germany among the 'becoming nations' (*supra*, 18 §3).

But that did not protect it from modernity: 'All of our political theories and constitutions (*very much including the 'Reich'*) are consequences, necessary results of the decline' (GD, *Expeditions of an Untimely Man*, 37 [212–13]). As is clear from my italics, it was not a question of negatively discriminating against Germany by comparison with the other European countries, but of spreading the illusion that the state that had emerged from its war against the land of revolution and of the Commune itself constituted a real alternative to modern subversion. Without allowing oneself to be constrained by patriotic indulgences, it was necessary to condemn and struggle against 'modern democracy (together with its hybrid forms [*sammt ihren Halbheiten*] like the "Reich") as the state's form of decline' (GD, *Expeditions of an Untimely Man*, 39 [214]). Even if Germany represented a less advanced stage of modern subversion and dissolution, it was still not right to have illusions or come to terms with a miserable present. It was a point on which Nietzsche felt the need to insist forcefully: the virulence of the polemic was aimed in general at the renegades, those guilty of a betrayal that could perhaps still be annulled. Hope had not yet vanished entirely.

3   Permanent Celebration of the German 'Essence' and Wagner's Exclusion from Authentic Germany

Gradually it became evident that the category of 'anti-Germanicness' was all too vague and inconsistent. Based on the unspoken assumption of a Germany always and forever malign, the polemic against the Second Reich or some of aspects of it would also imply a critique of the Third Reich. So to denounce Germany, which with the Reformation and the Peasants' War had contributed greatly to the overthrow of the aristocratic *ancien régime* – and, with Kant, Beethoven and the anti-Napoleonic risings, echoed themes of Rousseau and the French Revolution – would be to issue a warning against the Nazi regime, in reality pervaded by the idea of a crusade against the ideas of 1789 and the revolutionary cycle as a whole!

Let us try, instead, to interpret the polemic against the Second Reich starting from the category of 'aristocratic reaction'. This category has been asserted both by today's historians and by Nietzsche's contemporaries, and even by the philosopher himself, when proudly professing his 'aristocratic radicalism'. While Engels reacted to the triumph of reaction after 1848 by pledging to study Germany's revolutionary tradition, at least since the Peasants' War (*supra*, 17 §1), Nietzsche strove in the face of the democratic and subversive 'betrayal' of the Second Reich to construct an aristocratic tradition to set against plebeian degeneration.

On the one hand, the Germans had unfortunately invented the press, thus contributing to the massification of culture and society, while on the other hand it was their merit to have invented gunpowder, thereby discovering an antidote to the poison of mercantile society and calculating thought (JGB, Preface). Moreover, the polemic raging against Germany at the time did not prevent the philosopher from celebrating the 'Prussian officer corps' as a work of art and seeing the officers as his 'natural allies' (*supra*, 22 §5 and 17 §5). So, it was not a case of subjecting Germany as such to a withering judgement but of finding in it an alternative tradition to the misery of the present.

At the historical level, *Ecce Homo* set 'an atheist and hater of the church *comme il faut*, one of the people most closely related to me, the great Hohenstaufen emperor, Friedrich II' (EH, *Thus Spoke Zarathustra*, 4 [127]) against Christian or 'Christomaniac' personalities and trends (to borrow the mocking language of the 'Enlightenment' period), a historical personality, that is to say, that had the merit of having furthered aristocratic Islam rather than plebeian Christianity (AC, 60 [63]). Perhaps it was also in tribute to the name he bore that Nietzsche looked with such sympathy on 'the unforgettable German emperor Friedrich III' (EH, *Thus Spoke Zarathustra*, 1 [125]): he that disappeared with the velocity of a meteor seemed to be a sort of second Julian; after the death of Wilhelm I, he sat on the throne for only a few weeks, before opening the way, through his death, to the rise of Wilhelm II, who represented the lowest point of the Second Reich's Christian and Christomaniac drift.

Also at the strictly cultural level, the interpretation of German history, despite the profound disappointment and tone of resentful denunciation, turned out to be more ambiguous than at first sight seemed. Perhaps German philosophy was not unambiguously synonymous with modern subversion. *The Gay Science* had already emphasised, in relation to Hegel, 'his grandiose attempt [*grandioser Versuch*] to persuade us of the divinity of existence' (FW, 357 [219]). In that period, the value judgement was not unequivocally positive, for this attempt was made by appealing to 'historical sense' and with continuing formal tributes to the Christian God (FW, 357 [219]). Later, these elements of ambiguity seemed to vanish. The 'meaning of German philosophy' and of Hegel in particular was identified in the attempt to 'devise a pantheism in which evil, error and suffering are not experienced as arguments against divinity'. Even if the powers that be had exploited this in an attempt to legitimise a mediocre present rendered vulgar by modernity, it was still a 'great initiative [*grandiose Initiative*]' (XII, 113) that seemed to reprise the cosmodicy of the Hellenic world, thus putting an end to the wailing of the Christians and socialists in the face of the harshness of reality.

Goethe's personality must also be placed in this context. It is true the great poet did not progress beyond Winckelmann's point of view of and so 'did not understand the Greeks' (GD, What I owe to the ancients, 4 [227]). However, he was the only great European to experience 'disgust' in the face of the French Revolution and, in so doing, to carry out 'a magnificent attempt to overcome the eighteenth century by returning to nature', namely 'the naturalness of the Renaissance'. With his 'realism', Goethe had succeeded in recovering 'the entire expanse and wealth of naturalness', also that which was terrible in it, without stifling or suppressing it with idealistic and moralistic superimpositions and mystifications. In that sense, rejecting Christianity, he was able to express a 'belief' in life that could well be 'christened with the name Dionysus' (GD, *Expeditions of an Untimely Man*, 48–9 [222–3]). Again, we are led back to Hellas, which, despite everything, revealed its mysterious present and continued to reverberate in German history more than any other country.

This was a fact whose meaning needed be elicited: 'How come it was precisely the Germans that discovered Hellenism' (X, 646)? At this point, perhaps even Christianity itself, which played such an important role in the history of Germany, might have had a very different meaning from what at first sight seemed:

One wants to go back through the Fathers of the Church to the Greeks, from the North to the South, from formulas to forms; one still enjoys the end of antiquity, Christianity, as a gateway to antiquity, as a good piece of the ancient world itself, as a glittering mosaic of ancient concepts and ancient value judgements.

In this sense, German philosophy could also be interpreted as 'a piece of the Counter-Reformation, even the Renaissance, or at least the desire for Renaissance, the desire to advance further in the discovery of antiquity, the unearthing of ancient philosophy, especially the pre-Socratic, the most deeply buried Greek temple'. Thus the bitter denunciation turned into its opposite, into an exalted hope; or rather, the two aspects coexisted and intertwined, save that now, if the denunciation was conjugated in the present, the confident expectation looked to the future. This future was all the more compelling in that it was rooted in firm reality: 'Here lies (and always lay) my hope for the German essence!' (XI, 678–9).

Already present in a certain sense in Goethe and Hegel, the Dionysian vision of life and the cosmodicy acquired full consciousness in Nietzsche, who therefore could and should be considered – this was the philosopher's self-reflection – as the culmination of the Hellenic tendencies that imbued the history of German culture. This culmination was, on the one hand, the result of a positive movement in which the 'great initiative' and 'great attempt' of Hegel and Goethe were realised, and, on the other, the result of the negative movement of a relationship highly polemical and conflictual, but precisely for that reason extraordinarily fruitful and instructive, to the disastrous manifestations of modernity on German soil:

> I would not be possible without a race of contrary nature, without Germans, *these* Germans, without Bismarck, without 1848, without 'freedom wars', without Kant, even without Luther. [...] The great crimes of the Germans in the field of culture are justified in a higher economy of culture. [...] I want nothing else, not even retrospectively, – I was not allowed to want anything else. [...] *Amor fati*. Even Christianity becomes necessary: only the highest form, the most dangerous, the most seductive in the no to life demands its supreme affirmation: me.
>
> XIII, 641

Starting from this outcome, and the double movement, positive and negative, that led to it, it was possible to grasp the decisive and unique role played by Germany in the recovery of the tragic and authentically Greek vision of life: 'I justify the Germans, I alone'; the contrast is in some respects radical, but 'that is precisely the condition' for the fact that the raging of Christian nihilism on German soil was transformed into its opposite (XIII, 641). On closer inspection, even the disastrous manifestations of modernity on German soil were shown to be a *felix culpa*. Even if the process was far more complex and contradictory than imagined by *The Birth of Tragedy*, Germany once again took possession of the supreme legacy of Hellas and a position of absolute eminence over other countries.

How little sense it makes to contrast Nietzsche's 'anti-Germanness' to Wagner's Germanomania is also demonstrated by the fact that the philosopher tried to seal his attack on the musician by repeatedly and with different and sometimes contradictory formulations to expel him from the Germanic community. Above all: the musician, '[f]or half of his life, [...] believed in the Revolution as only a Frenchman could' (WA, 4 [239]). It was not just something that belonged to the past: 'Wagner's sensitivity is not characteristic of Germany' (XIII, 407). He 'belongs in the French movement' (XI, 63), an integral part of 'sick Paris' (B, III, 5, 518); 'his heroes, his Rienzi, Tannhäuser, Lohengrin, Tristan, Parsifal – they have blood in their veins, no doubt – but certainly no German blood!' (XIII, 407).

Moreover, it was enough simply to leaf through the musician's family album. The 'French Romantics' were among his 'next of kin' (XIII, 407), observed Nietzsche, in an obvious allusion to Cosima: the mother of the latter, Marie d'Agoult, had tried, perhaps on the model of George Sand, to be a writer in Paris, and had partly transmitted her literary ambitions to her daughter, who had also lived for a long time in France.[14] Worse still was Wagner's paternal ancestry, which for Nietzsche linked him to Judaism (above 5 §2). This biographical detail is not unimportant in cultural terms. One need only think of the 'emulation in respect of Meyerbeer', pursued 'by Meyerbeerian means.' The Jewish musician attacked by Wagner was, for Nietzsche, in reality his model: 'What's German about it?' (XIII, 408).

But what Wagner could never be forgiven was that he was a devotee of Christian-Catholic 'Rome': from this point of view, he was more than ever alien to the German essence, even to the 'German body [*Leib*]' (JGB, 256 [150] and NW, Wagner as Apostle of Chastity, 1 [274]). Responding on this point to the interpretation of Parsifal by his 'dear friend' Nietzsche, a well-meaning correspondent objected: 'I can find no trace of the faith of Rome, only pure Christianity, and this, for me and many German, is not yet anti-German' (B, III, 6, 108).

---

14   Gutman 1971, 303 ff.

Here the philosopher was accused of narrow-minded Teutomania, for wanting to expel from the true German essence a religion with which the great majority of the German population had long identified. This attempt at a chauvinistic excommunication of Christianity later became a constant theme of the most radical reactionary circles right through until the Third Reich. Rosenberg spoke contemptuously of German Catholics as 'the Roman centre party'.[15]

Ultimately, for Nietzsche, Wagner belonged to the enduring cycle of Jewish-Christian subversion, which then led to the upheavals in France: it was no accident he had had his recognition precisely in Paris, where the 'French socialists' were strongly present (JGB, 256 [150]). For half his life, Wagner had believed, 'like any ideologue of the revolution', that 'all the world's problems' could be overcome by changing 'laws' and 'institutions' and destroying the moral-political foundations upon which 'the old world, the old society' rested. Thus he 'set to music' 'optimism', thereby pursuing a 'socialist utopia' 'where "all will be well"' (WA, 4 [239–40]). At least as far as the young Wagner was concerned, Nietzsche's critique was not only formulated from an openly reactionary point of view but was infected by the philistinism of the ideology then prevalent in Germany and Europe: the musician had made the mistake of propagating or singing about 'free love' and the emancipation of women (WA, 4 [240]); he embodied all the values of *décadence*, namely 'an anarchy of the atom, disintegration of the will, "freedom of the individual", morally speaking, – or, expanded into a political theory, "equal rights for all"'. In short: 'Life, equal vitality, the vibration and exuberance of life pushed back into the smallest structures, all the rest impoverished of life' (WA, 7 [245]). It was only the encounter with Schopenhauer and his 'pessimism' that destroyed socialistic 'hope', but even that did not change the picture substantially (WA, 4 [240]). There then followed the 'big show of Christian pity' (WA, 6 [244]), a theme still linked to plebeian subversion and also found in Victor Hugo, an author deeply sympathetic to the popular and revolutionary movement (WA, 8 [247]). The French writer and the German musician 'signify the very same thing': both were synonymous with decline and the hegemony of the 'masses' (WA, 11 [253]).

A large distance separated Wagner from the 'German essence' that Nietzsche stubbornly hoped might perhaps one day, despite all the symptoms of degeneration, put a final end to the revolutionary cycle and pave the way to the rebirth of tragic Hellenism. Similarly, his glorification of the Hellenic essence in *The Birth of Tragedy* and in other texts from the period did not prevent him from excluding a large part of Greek culture (Euripides, Socrates, the Eleatics and

---

15   Rosenberg 1937b, 7.

Plato, not to mention the Hellenistic and Alexandrian world) as fundamentally alien to it. This analogy can be found even in the last phase of Nietzsche's conscious life. His views on Germany were not substantially more stringent than on Greece and classical antiquity as a whole: so one had to beware of 'saying yes to everything'; '[t]here are really very few ancient books that made much of a difference in my life; they do not include the most famous ones' (GD, What I owe to the ancients, 1 [224]). The critique of Hellas, although not new, now became at times merciless: Plato 'remains Europe's greatest *malheur*'; in Hellenistic philosophy, 'the falsification of reality by morality is present in all its splendour', and already one felt the devastating irruption of Christianity (B, III, 5, 9).

Apart from the sharpness of the criticism, the extent of its target was also new. Sometimes one has the impression that the target was Greece as a whole: 'These Greeks have much on their conscience, falsification was their true trade, the whole of European psychology suffers from Greek superficialities' (B, III, 5, 28). However, this did not stop Nietzsche announcing and hoping for the 'imminent return of the Greek spirit' (EH, *The Birth of Tragedy*, 4 [111]). He conceived and defined this spirit in opposition to the phenomena of degeneration or to a phenomenon that seems to be spreading ever more: 'Greek philosophy' was to be understood 'as the decadence of the Greek instinct' in the deepest and truest sense. So, there was no point in wanting to judge true Greece by its 'philosophers'; the latter 'really are the decadents of the Greek world, the counter-movement to the ancient, noble taste' (GD, What I owe to the ancients, 2–3 [225–6]). As in the earlier writings, so too on the eve of his spiritual collapse Nietzsche set against the central and ever broader aspects of visible Greece a Greek essence that was becoming ever more elusive and intangible. He treated Germany, too, in a not dissimilar manner.

4   Critique of the Second Reich and Aristocratic Reaction

This tendency can also be found in other authors. For Langbehn, faith in the future of Germany in no way contradicted harsh criticism of the Second Reich. It was a country of boundless vulgarity and 'extraordinarily averse to powerful spiritual individualities'.[16] According to Lagarde, in Germany 'despotism disguised as freedom' prevailed;[17] we were still far removed from culture in the

---

16   Langbehn 1922, 229.
17   Lagarde 1937, 282.

strong sense of the word: 'Universal education is the specifically German form of civilization', which was 'essentially semblance and deception'.[18] There was no trace of 'a new religion, much less of a German religion'.[19] As the widespread cult of the state and of Hegelian philosophy showed, what obtaind was 'idol worship'. Clearly, even the language is reminiscent of Nietzsche.[20] Hegel showed he was alien to the 'German essence [*Wesen*]' insofar as he promoted the 'horizontal extension' of knowledge at the expense of its depth and a 'universal education' synonymous with 'civilization', as well as a belief in the 'omnipotence of the state', said Lagarde.[21] Thanks to the disastrous actions of two Ministers, 'apostates' of Germanness,[22] Hegel in any case became the 'darling of the Prussian state'.[23]

Such a drastic judgement on the present naturally also necessitated a strict reinterpretation of the past, one that spared not even the national heroes: the 'so-called Reformation of 1518' – noted the contemptuous tone – was a foretaste of the French Revolution; both sprang from the 'naked greed of the have-nots'.[24] Lagarde even went so far as to denounce the Second Reich's 'incapacity for the future',[25] but without completely losing hope in the revival of the authentic Germany, which, even though constantly misunderstood and betrayed, would prove in the long run to be stronger than its degenerate children. This is why Lagarde was adopted by the ideological currents and political movement that later converged in Nazism. Moreover, Nietzsche's now hated sister and his even more hated brother-in-law now took a similar position, as is clear from Elisabeth's letter to the philosopher: 'On one point we agree wonderfully, that you see the "Reich" as so incredibly Chinese, quite anti-German' (B, III, 6, 147).

The denunciation of Germany's present and the pathos of the German essence in no way contradicted one another, but were two aspects of the aristocratic reaction of the late nineteenth century. In it participated forces and personalities with a more or less radical programme. They fought for the abolition of universal suffrage and the passing of more or less drastic anti-union and anti-socialist legislation, they observed with horror the spread of education, and they demanded measures to restore the political and social status of tradi-

---

18   Lagarde 1937, 85.
19   Lagarde 1937, 282.
20   Lagarde 1937, 141.
21   Lagarde 1937, 209, 85, 376.
22   Lagarde 1937, 377.
23   Lagarde 1937, 410.
24   Lagarde 1937, 282.
25   Lagarde 1937, 365.

tional elites; with Langbehn, they even maintained that slavery on the model of ancient Greece was still relevant (*supra*, 12 § 3).

5   Horizontal and Transversal Racialisation

But who was to be subject to servitude? Like some theorists of slavery in the southern United States, the philosopher-philologist, with the model of classical antiquity in mind, never identified fully and completely with the idea of racial slavery. Slavery was absolutely indispensable, for culture required an extreme division of labour: a considerable mass of people had to sacrifice itself to ensure the *otium* of those called upon to create art and culture. Naturally, one thought immediately of the colonial or semi-colonial peoples, but primarily for practical considerations. This was because these peoples have not yet been touched by socialist agitation and above all the ill-fated European and particularly Prussian-German practice of indiscriminately spreading education, which made the reproduction of a 'race' of slaves problematic or impossible. The fact remained that no country was without potential slaves, human raw material to be put at the disposal of superior human beings and their creations.

The constant element in Nietzsche's complex development was his tendency to racialise the lower classes. He denounced them successively as the 'barbaric slave class' in revolt, as a rabble constitutionally incapable of understanding and rendered frantic and delirious by the visionary spirit, by fanaticism and by *ressentiment*, as a set of work tools at the service of the ruling classes, as a 'semi-bestial' mob, as waste material or raw material for the artistic creations of a small minority, and as a mishmash of the malformed and those whose lives had turned out badly.

Arguing in this way, Nietzsche continued and radicalised a trend already clearly present in early liberalism. This, as we have seen (*supra*, 12 § 4), identified the wage labourer with an *instrumentum vocale* (Burke) or 'two-legged instrument' (Sieyès). A leading sociologist has compared the 'attitude towards the new industrial proletariat' developed in England between 1660 and 1760 with 'the behaviour of the less reputable of white colonists towards coloured labour'.[26] In fact, Locke said quite clearly that a wage worker was 'no more capable of reasoning than a perfect natural': neither the one nor the other reached the level of 'rational creatures and Christians'. And Sieyès wrote that 'a great nation is necessarily composed of *two peoples*', to a certain extent of

---

26   Tawney 1926, 269.

two different races of essentially different value, since on the one hand there were the real 'producers' or the 'leaders of production' and, on the other, the 'human instruments of production'; on the one hand, 'the intelligent people' or 'the honourable people [*gens honnêtes*]', on the other 'the workers, who only have passive strength' and are mere 'instruments of labour'. Although Mallet du Pan had a different political viewpoint, he too contrasted the honourable and moneyed people, the *honnêtes gens*, to the 'hungry mass of both sexes'.[27] Madame de Staël said more or less the same at the time of the Brumaire.[28]

The formulations sometimes lead us into Nietzsche's immediate vicinity. While Taine honoured the 'well-born and well-behaved [*nés bien, bien élevés*]',[29] across the Atlantic Alexander Hamilton and John Adams voiced similar opinions about 'the rich and well-born' that rose above the 'mass of the people', 'mechanical' and devoid of culture and 'liberal' education.[30] In the same way, Nietzsche contrasted those that 'have turned out well [*wohlgeraten*]' to the mob, and to the mass of those whose lives had turned out badly. While working intensively on his planned book *The Will to Power*, he said in a fragment written in the spring of 1888: 'This book is dedicated to those that have turned out well, those that do my heart well' (XIII, 432). *Ecce Homo* struck up a veritable hymn of praise to this figure of the 'well-turned-out' (EH, Why I am so wise, 2 [77]).

A great gulf separated the 'honourable people' or the 'well-turned-out' from those excluded from citizenship, who could therefore without further ado be likened to 'foreigners'. Even before Constant, this metaphor could already be found, in a certain sense, in Sieyès, for whom there was none in 'this giant mass of two-legged instruments' 'capable of entering into society' and forming part of the narrow circle of the truly 'civilized [*policés*]'.[31] Here, manual worker was synonymous not only with foreigner but also with those that stood outside culture, somehow members of an inferior race. It is significant that Locke had already used this same metaphor in respect of

> another sort of servants, which by a peculiar name we call slaves, who being captives taken in a just war, [... have] lost their estates; and being in the *state of slavery*, not capable of any property, cannot in that state be

27   Losurdo 1993b, 1, § 11 (on the general context); Guillemin 1958, 31 f., 41–3 (on Mallet du Pan).
28   In Guillemin 1958, 182 f. GM I, 5.
29   Taine 1899, Vol. 1, 290.
30   In Morison 1953, 259; Merriam 1969, 130, 132, 142.
31   Sieyès 1985c, 81.

considered as any part of *civil society*; the chief end whereof is the preservation of property.[32]

The tendency to racialise the subaltern classes within the capitalist metropolis diminished more and more in the wake of the political and social struggles waged by the victims of exclusion, and also thanks to the extraordinary ability to adapt that is the strength of the liberal tradition. However, far from vanishing completely, this trend persisted, and regularly cropped up again during particularly acute crises. Confronted with the spectacle of the eruption of the starving rabble onto the scene of political struggle and history, Rivarol observed: 'It is neither French nor English nor Spanish. The populace is always and in all countries the same, it is always cannibalistic, always man-eating.'[33] Mallet du Pan emitted a similar cry of alarm: 'The Huns and the Heruli, the Vandals and Goths, will come neither from the North nor from the Red Sea, they are among us.'[34] To the extent that the great critic of revolution became aware of this new and disquieting fact, the traditional conflicts between states seemed to him irrelevant or secondary. In this way he became, as has been observed, 'a European journalist', committed to 'establishing a new programme for Europe'.[35]

After June 1848, Marshal Bugeaud, who had already distinguished himself during the repression in Algeria, spoke as follows about the workers and insurgents that, though defeated and repressed, continued to show signs of restlessness: 'What brutal and ferocious beasts! How can God allow mothers to give birth to such as these! They are the real enemies, not the Russians or the Austrians.'[36] This view seems to be confirmed in 1871: in the face of the terror and dismay caused by the Paris Commune, the ruling classes of the two countries up to that point at war seemed to forget their differences and joined forces to extinguish the revolutionary conflagration threatening not just France but the whole of Europe. On 30 April 1871, Gustave Flaubert wrote to George Sand: ' "Ah, *thank God* the *Prussians* are there!" is the *universal cry of the bourgeois*.'[37] Although Renan was critical of the harsh peace conditions imposed by the victors, he conceded Prussia and its army a role in maintaining public order at the European level. According to an analysis in the *Figaro* of 3 January 1871, the struggle for hegemony seemed to have vanished, to make room for another,

---

32   Locke 1970, 158 (II, § 85).
33   In Matteucci 1957, 264.
34   In Matteucci 1957, 279.
35   Matteucci 1957, 243.
36   Moissonnier 2001, 67.
37   In Willard 2001, 71.

even more important one: 'Forces of good against forces of evil. Order against anarchy. [...] A crusade of culture against barbarism.'[38] On the occasion of particularly acute crises, a renewed and even more explicit racialisation of the lower classes was joined by a theory of international civil war, transcending national borders. In it the 'civil' European elites jointly confronted the threat posed by 'barbarians' within and without the West. Nietzsche too belongs in this context. He already believed, as we know, at the time of publication of *The Birth of Tragedy* that 'beyond the struggle between nations' an 'international hydra head' had risen up, which as 'the herald of quite different future struggles' sowed universal dismay.

6   Pan-European Elite and Co-optation of Big Jewish Capital

The pan-European elite praised by Nietzsche also included assimilated Jews, who occupied prominent positions. It is worth noting that Langbehn did the same, when he spoke in highly positive terms about Disraeli, aristocratic as both an Englishman and a Jew. When Langbehn cited Rembrandt as the teacher of the new and aristocratic Germany, he stressed that the great artist had shown a 'predilection for the Jews', while at the same time making choices: 'He stuck with the aristocratic Jews, not with the plebeian ones.' It was important to know the difference:

> Undeniably, a true and orthodox Jew has something aristocratic [*etwas Vornehmes*] about him; he belongs to the ancient ethical and spiritual aristocracy, from which most modern Jews have deviated; in this sense, Lord Beaconsfield [Disraeli] was half right when he proclaims them the oldest nobility in the world.[39]

It was by no means merely a vanished nobility restricted to the 'orthodox'. Even Rahel Varnhagen 'was an ethical, spiritual and even social aristocrat'.[40]

As we have seen, even Chamberlain bothered to distinguish between 'Jews of noble and Jews of less noble origin' (*supra*, 24 §8). But, in this context, the most interesting point concerns the author of the *Essai sur l'inégalité des races humaines*. His attitude is summed up, perhaps with some exaggeration, as follows: 'Regarding Jews, to whom Gobineau attributes a relatively unadulterated

---

38   In Willard 2001, 72.
39   Langbehn 1922, 36.
40   Langbehn 1922, 37.

Semitic blood, the description he makes of them might have been inspired by Disraeli; it ends up by bordering on a panegyric to this "chosen race."[41] The same can be said not only of Galton, who was British,[42] but also, naturally, of Lombroso and Gumplowicz, both of Jewish origin. The German social Darwinist Ploetz declared that 'in Judaism there is more Aryan than Semitic blood', and praised Jews and Aryans together as 'the best races': it was ultimately they that would decide the fate of culture.[43]

While co-opting the Jewish big bourgeoisie into the master race, Langbehn also denounced 'a relapse into the herd principle of savage tribes, characteristic of the most primitive stage of human existence', in Social Democracy and the egalitarian tendencies.[44] We are once again back with Nietzsche, who recommended a social and eugenic merger of Jewish capitalists and financiers with the race of the 'masters' and those that had turned out well, the pan-European elite, also in order to make the struggle against the slave rebellion more effective. Nietzsche was describing and praising a tendency, contested but nonetheless real, that manifested itself in Germany as part of the aristocratic reaction.

This explains both his silence on the persecutions of the Oriental Jews (subsumable under the category of serfs and the malformed) and his firm condemnation of anti-Semitism in Germany, which split the master class, sparked agitation against it in the German populace and above all replaced the master/servant contradiction with the German/Jew contradiction.

So the anti-Semites had recourse not to a transversal but to a horizontal racialisation that pitted Germans as a whole primarily against Jews. From Nietzsche's point of view, the contrast was so clear that it was precisely the anti-Semites that were to be racialised as Chandala, because they were an integral part of the socialist and anarchistic mob, the mass of the malformed, who had to be contained by eugenic or police measures, or by using even more radical methods. Anti-Semitism was also absurd and repellent because its invective against finance and the respectable professions and positions of power simply gave voice to the *ressentiment* of those whose lives had turned out badly against those that had turned out well, against the aristocracy, or what was left of it.

Nietzsche's polemic against anti-Semitic racism and its 'constant absurd falsifications and distortions of vague concepts like "Germanic", "Semitic", "Aryan", "Christian", "German"' was violent and unrelenting (B, III, 5, 51). If racism, as is sometimes thought, consists only of the naturalisation of nations

---

41   Poliakov 1987, 267.
42   Galton 1869, 4, 362.
43   Ploetz 1895, 139, 130, 89.
44   Langbehn 1922, 141.

and national differences, it would be hard to find an author further away from it than Nietzsche, at least in regard to Europe. The same went for Boulainvilliers. Both were far from wanting to naturalise the category of nation and even rejected the idea radically, because of its egalitarian implications and its presupposition of a community of citizens that, at least in theory, transcended the distinction between nobles and plebeians, between the few and the many.

Only thus can we understand the letter by Nietzsche cited above. The category 'Christian' belonged among the 'absurd falsifications and distortions' denounced by him only insofar as it was intended to contrast one country with others, one supposed 'nation' with other supposed 'nations', and in particular the pious Germany of Luther with the immoral France of the Enlightenment and of urban culture. For the rest, the philosopher used the category 'Christian' to characterise the plebeian movements as well as the values and negative values of the Chandala, as opposed to '*Aryan* values'. Here Nietzsche resorted to a category he had severely criticised in the letter just quoted. But there is no contradiction: it was misleading and absurd to want to praise the Aryan German 'nation' as a whole, while excluding or excommunicating the Jews from it because they were Semites; but it might well be illuminating to divide both the German and the Jewish community into Aryans and Chandala. And while it was senseless and disgraceful to exclude capitalists and financiers, in any case part of the master race, from Germany simply because they were Jews, it was legitimate and even obligatory to draw a clear line between true Hellenism and those plebeians and 'Jews' and early Christians like Socrates and Plato.

7   Aryan Mythology, Old and New Testament

Each of the two components of the social bloc Nietzsche wished to forge had its own religious ideology. And there can be no doubt that the philosopher preferred the Old Testament to the New. Should we read this as an anticipatory criticism of the crazed and bloodthirsty anti-Semitism of the Third Reich? First, it is worth noting that despite having ceased to be the God of the 'chosen people', 'the God of the "great numbers", the democrat among gods, did not become a proud, heathen god: he stays Jewish, he was still the cranny God, the God of all dark nooks and corners, of unhealthy districts the world over! His empire is as it ever was, an empire of the underworld, a hospital, a basement-kingdom, a ghetto-kingdom' (AC 17 [15]). The special contempt for the New Testament in no way spared Judaism.

On the other hand, what awakened Nietzsche's sympathetic interest was not the Old Testament as such but 'its older parts' (XIII, 380). There again, as we know, his contempt and hatred for the Jewish prophets, in his view primarily responsible for the subversive and nihilistic cycle raging in the West, was boundless. After leaving behind the denunciation of Jewish 'optimism' from the period of the *Birth of Tragedy*, starting with the writings of the 'Enlightenment' period Nietzsche attributed to pre-exilic Judaism the merit of a sense of the earthly and of reality, which brought it close to Hellenism and clearly distanced it from Christian asceticism (*supra*, 7 §7). The philosopher stuck with this theme to the end. So, because of the paganistic amorality with which he was reproached, Goethe had 'always scandalized [...] the Germans', steeped in Christianity, while 'his only real admirers were Jewish women' (WA, 3 [238]). Moreover, in the course of his venomous campaign against Judaism, Wagner nominated among the various Germanic virtues 'purity', 'chastity', separation from 'the corrupted world' (WA, 3 [237]).

However, the sense of the earthly and of reality that Nietzsche so valued had another less seductive and indeed highly disturbing side. The Jews were 'strong realists' before the later 'unnatural castration of a [national] god to a God of good'. They were well aware of a great truth: 'For what counts a God that knows no anger, revenge, envy, violence and perhaps even the dangerous *ardeurs* of destruction?' The characteristics of the God worshipped were also the characteristics of the people that worshipped him. Thus: 'What is with a people that does not know how to be terrible?' (XIII, 523).

The reference to the events in Canaan is clear. 'Respect' for the Old Testament was created above all by the presence of 'great human beings', the 'heroic landscape', the gestures of a 'people' that moved with 'the incomparable naïveté of the strong heart' (GM III, 22 [107]). Just as the Greeks were 'naïve' in their relationship to slavery and war, which often ended with the decimation and enslavement of the defeated (*supra*, 2 §1), so too a text that described without sentimentality and dismay the conquest of a city and the annihilation of its inhabitants was wonderfully 'naïve'. The religion of these 'bold realists' was not unlike the 'realists' culture' that finds its 'most perfect expression' in Thucydides (GD, What I owe the ancients, 2 [225–6]). In him, we could read the funeral oration in which Pericles praised 'with lasting monuments of our acts of harm and good' erected by Athens in the struggle against its enemies.[45] To the 'naïveté' of the heroes of the Old Testament corresponded the 'shocking cheerfulness and depth of delight in all destruction' that the *Genealogy of Morals* attributed to the Athenians (GM, I, 11 [23]). Together with Athens and Florence, Jerusalem was one of the places where even 'malice [*Bosheit*]' was part of 'happiness' (EH,

---

45   Thucydides 1998, Book II, Paragraph 41, 94.

Why I am so clever, 2 [88]). If Athens was associated with the fate of the Melians (massacred and enslaved in line with the law of the stronger)[46] and Florence with the culture of the Renaissance, produced by the 'beast of prey' Cesare Borgia (*supra*, 14 § 2), Jerusalem was associated here with the events in Canaan.

How pitiful compared to the protagonists of the Old Testament was the 'dull, tame, house pet' of the New Testament, with its 'proper, tender, musty stench of true believers [*Betbrüder*] and small souls [*Kleine-Seele*]' (JGB, 52 [48])! This comparison was not meant in an aesthetic sense. Nietzsche always read the sacred texts of the various religious traditions from a sociopolitical point of view. While the 'older parts' of the Old Testament (and of the Koran) revealed 'a yes-saying Semitic religion, spawn of the ruling classes', the New Testament was 'a no-saying Semitic religion, spawn of the oppressed classes' (XIII, 380). Here was the key to understanding the transition from a god with which a specific people, with its vitality and will to power, identified to one that was moralistic, universalistic and hostile to life. In Paul of Tarsus one witnessed the 'transvaluation of the concept "Jew": "race" is set aside' (XIII, 585). But what did that mean in sociopolitical terms?

According to the 'Christian theologians' and Renan, 'the development of the idea of God from the "God of Israel", the god of a people, to the Christian God, the epitome of all goodness', would be a decisive 'progress'. But, according to Nietzsche, this was vulgar apologetics. In reality, the moral god was the 'god of the physiologically retrograde, the weak', in whom in the meantime 'the will to power' in any form had vanished. They 'do not call themselves weak, they call themselves "the good." [...] There is no great mystery as to when, historically, the dualistic fiction of good and evil gods becomes possible. With the same instincts they use to reduce their god to "goodness in itself", the subjugated scratch out the good qualities from their conquerors' god. They take revenge by demonizing their masters' god' (AC 17 [14–15]). The transition from the Old Testament god to the Christian one was a decisive moment in the subversive cycle, in the class struggle waged by the slaves and plebeians.

Nietzsche proceeded similarly in his reading of the Old Testament. He observed two sharply contrasting themes: on the one hand, the hopes for emancipation on the part of a mass of slaves, first in Egypt and then in Babylon; on the other, the conquest of Canaan and the annihilation of its inhabitants, carried out by a people with a good conscience granted it by the election of God: on the one hand, the moral pathos of the 'slave revolt in morality', on the other, the will to power and the innocence of becoming. The first theme had played an

---

46   Thucydides 1998, Book V; cf. MA 92.

important role in many emancipatory movements: blacks oppressed by slavery and colonialism often identified with the Jews fleeing Egypt in search of a homeland and a promised land.[47] The Puritan settlers who, in America, seized the land from the Indians and then progressively erased them from the face of the earth identified, on the other hand, with the conquerors of Canaan.[48]

Nietzsche used angry words about the first theme, but talked warmly about the second. Precisely because, for him, racialisation was transversal, the dichotomous pair of well-formed/malformed [*Wohlgeratene/Missratene*] or noble/plebeian could easily be expressed with the dichotomous pair Aryan/Chandala and chosen people/Canaanites. While insisting on the need to erect an insurmountable barrier between masters and mob, Nietzsche had no difficulty in drawing from time to time on Aryan mythology, positivistic 'science' (now with the contrast between the healthy and the sick as well as degenerates of all kinds), or Old Testament mythology. True, he was sometimes ironic about the 'people chosen of all peoples' (JGB, 195 [84]) and pointed out that this proud self-consciousness did not exclusively characterise the Jews: 'Every people sees itself, at its height, as elected' (XIII, 524). But the most important aspect lay elsewhere. Nietzsche did not hesitate to apply the Old Testament theme in secularised form, to the conflict between the aristocracy and the rabble: 'Moreover, it makes us "God's elect [*die Auserwählten Gottes*]"' (FW, 379 [243]), 'the most select [*Auserwähltesten*]' (EH, *The Birth of Tragedy*, 4 [111]). Zarathustra put it eloquently: 'You lonely of today, you withdrawing ones, one day you shall be a people: from you that have chosen yourselves [*euch selber auswähltet*] a chosen people [*ein Volk auserwähltes*] shall grow and from them the overman' (Za, I, On the Bestowing Virtue, 2 [58]).

Nietzsche would have had no problem in reckoning the Old Testament representatives of the conquest of Canaan among the 'noble races' at whose centre 'we cannot fail to see the beast of prey, the magnificent blond beast avidly prowling round for spoil and victory' (GM, I, 11 [23]).

---

47   Lanternari 1960, 40–7; Appiah 1992, 19 and *passim*; Fredrickson 1995, 63 and *passim*.
48   Toynbee 1951–4, 211 f.

Culture in Search of Its Slaves: From the Late Nineteenth Century Anti-democratic Reaction to Nazism

1 Ideological Processes and Historical Time

As we know, Arno Mayer sees Nietzsche as part of the 'aristocratic reaction' of the late nineteenth century. I cited this interpretation to show the untenability of the hermeneutics of innocence, but now it requires further clarification and substantial corrections. Alongside, in competition and sometimes conflict with 'aristocratic reaction', there developed in this same period another anti-democratic trend, based on an authoritarian and regressive populism. One thinks of the figure of Boulanger in France and other similar attempts on the part of reaction to win a mass popular base by appealing to chauvinism (including intra-European chauvinism) and anti-Semitism or both. These two anti-democratic currents of the late nineteenth century had a lot in common (the social-Darwinian view, a positive evaluation of eugenics, enthusiasm for colonial expansion, the denunciation of subversive intellectuals as pathogenic). On the other hand, there was a clear opposition between the radical-aristocratic and the populist-reactionary tendencies. While the former continued, within each country, to build an impassable barrier between elite and 'barbaric slave class', the latter sought to integrate the popular classes in subaltern position into a comprehensive national community, defined above all in contrast to the 'barbarians' outside the country. Fritsch declared explicitly that anti-Semitism was 'an excellent lever for the awakening and strengthening of national consciousness', for a 'better appreciation of the *German essence*', for the 'strengthening of the feeling of belonging' and, more generally, for the 'political education of our people [*Volk*]' (*ASC*, no. 6, 12). Certainly, *Antisemitische Correspondenz* occasionally gave voice to extremely heterogeneous endeavours, by allowing anti-Semites and chauvinists to speak. In any case, it declared that it wanted to develop a 'mass agitation' and was even ready to learn from German Social Democracy, so that it could fight this 'organisation of the international Jewish league' on its own ground.[1] Having flirted at the time of *Birth of Tragedy*

---

1 *ASC* No. 20, 1 and no. 8, 2.

with reactionary populism and the rhetoric of the '*German essence*' and of *volksthümlich* authenticity (note how the language resembled Fritsch's), the mature Nietzsche was the theorist of aristocratic reaction or, rather, of 'aristocratic radicalism'. He had absolutely nothing to do with the second tendency, to which he responded with implacable hostility.

As far as Europe was concerned, Nietzsche could disdainfully reject horizontal racialisation, for he had already rent the nation into two different, opposing and rigidly hierarchical races. Certainly, he rejected both the deadly clash between the ruling classes of Western Europe and, *a fortiori*, the sacred patriotic union within each country that led to the erasure of the only distinction that really counted, that between masters and servants, the well-formed and the malformed, Aryans and Chandala. But the aristocratic circles in Europe in the late nineteenth century did not behave so very differently, for they were connected with one another by ties of kinship and saw each other as members of a family and a 'race' in whose veins the same blood flowed and whose roots lay deep in a remote past.

Nietzsche's life and the century in which it lay came to an end with the joint expedition of the great powers to suppress the Yihetuan movement, China's Boxer Rebellion. Despite numerous massacres perpetrated against the 'barbarians', the expedition was supported by its ideologists and by broad public opinion in the West – Lenin spoke in this context of the realisation of the '*dream of idealistic* politicians, the *United States of the civilized world*'.[2] The ruling classes of the time were mistaken, and so was Nietzsche. The Holy Alliance against the external and internal barbarians would soon prove to be an illusion, for the intensification of social conflict would not eliminate the geopolitical and colonial conflict. Rather, this conflict was further fuelled, for the ruling class of each country was under the illusion that it could reduce or redirect social conflict by heightening and taking advantage of imperialist rivalry to create an atmosphere of holy patriotic unity. But the full impact of these political, social and ideological processes was felt in a period of history that was not Nietzsche's.

The problem of the philosopher's individual relationship with the Third Reich, so often raised affirmatively or negatively, can now be radically reformulated: once one has established the philosopher's broad consonance with the aristocratic reaction of the late nineteenth century, it is necessary to analyse historically which social, political and ideological processes, by way of unforeseen twists and turns and catastrophes, could lead from this movement of

---

2 Lenin 1953–, Vol. 39, 684.

reaction to Nazism. In analysing these processes, one must not lose sight of the
fact that the points of departure and arrival were separated by the two epochal
breaks of the First World War and the October Revolution, which radically distinguished the historical time in which Nietzsche and his contemporaries lived
from the historical time that saw the triumph and defeat of Hitler and the Third
Reich.

Here a preliminary comment is in order. The movement of ideological preparation that lies behind every great historical crisis is always a mixture of
continuity and discontinuity. So much is indisputable: if one goes in search
of a school of thought or an author that implicitly contains within itself the
whole of Nazism or at least its overall worldview, so that from the first element
the second can be deduced *a priori*, clearly one is on a path to nowhere. But
it would be a serious mistake to conclude from the impossibility of connecting
the two elements by an analytical judgement *a priori* that there is absolutely no
mutual interaction between them. In that case, one might just as well abolish
the category of the ideological preparation of Nazism, or of any other regime
or political movement. It would be pointless to wonder about the 'intellectual origins of the Third Reich',[3] but also of the English, American, French and
Bolshevik revolutions. And yet it is a matter of questions and analyses of fundamental significance for both sociopolitical historiography and the history of
thought. Think, in particular, of the great debate sparked by the French Revolution or the French revolutionary cycle, which concerned the greatest thinkers,
including Nietzsche. The latter in no way rejected as nonsense the category of
ideological preparation, but subjected it to an extreme radicalisation: instead of
simply identifying Descartes as the 'father' of rationalism and the 'grandfather'
of the French Revolution, he went back thousands of years to bring the Jewish-
Christian tradition as a whole into the equation. Think of the thesis that a line of
continuity led from the prophetic and Christian cursing of wealth to the bloody
terror against the privileged unleashed by the Jacobins and revolutionaries in
general. And now compare the supreme audacity of this statement with the
fear and trembling that overcomes certain of today's interpreters when faced
with the problem of a possible relationship between the theory of the 'annihilation of millions of the malformed' and the 'annihilation of decadent races' on
the one hand and the eugenic and colonial politics of the Third Reich on the
other! Paradoxically, Nietzsche's apologists can drag him onto the dry land of
pure theory only on condition that they liquidate his entire philosophical and
historical approach. If they were then to think through consistently and in a

---

3 Mosse 1979 and 1966.

generalised way the methodology followed in this case, they would ultimately have to put an end to historical research as such.

On the other hand, it is only possible to assert the category of ideological preparation correctly by taking into account the heterogeneity of historical time and the resulting link between continuity and discontinuity. This also applies to 'minor' authors like Gobineau and Chamberlain. As we have seen, both paid tribute to the liberal tradition or to some of its aspects and writers, and this marked an important difference from Nazism. However, Gobineau's assertion of a radical inequality of the races is not insignificant. The only ones to deny this inequality, noted Chamberlain, chiming with Gobineau's thesis, were the 'vapid, venal and ignorant chatterboxes, slaves' souls born of the chaos of peoples, at home only in the primitive slime of characterlessness and lack of individuality'.[4] Even more significant is that, in the hierarchy of races, the Anglo-German author went so far in certain circumstances as to consider the destruction of the colonial peoples beneficial or inevitable. In Puerto Rico, the natives had been 'completely exterminated, and the result is a pure Indo-European population'; 'from the beginning to the present day, we see the Germans [to which the Anglo-Saxons engaged in hunting down the 'Redskins' also belong] slaughtering whole tribes and peoples or slowly killing them off by means of thoroughgoing demoralization, to make room for themselves'; even if these methods were extraordinarily cruel, culture benefited from them.[5]

Even so, the path that led to the ideology and above all the practice of the Third Reich was rather tortuous. The fact is, as Mosse observes, that '[E]xperiences rarely, if ever, turn out exactly as anticipated, and this is rarely true if the anticipation has gone on for a long time.'[6] More precisely, there is always a discrepancy between a movement and a political system on the one hand and its long and complex process of ideological preparation and gestation on the other. Neither Gobineau nor Chamberlain (at least when writing his infamous book) foresaw that reaffirming the principle of the inequality of races would lead to deadly battles between the 'higher', 'noble' races and, through the efforts of the Third Reich, reduce the Slavs of Eastern Europe to a colonial people. Nor did they yet know anything about the goal of building a 'German India' in a geopolitical space easier to incorporate and defend that the distant overseas possessions lost immediately after the outbreak of the First World War.

So, it would be a sheer waste of time to look for a line of ideological continuity that proceeded by virgin birth, independently of the upheavals caused

---

4 Chamberlain 1937, 304.

5 Chamberlain 1937, 339 fn. 1, 864.

6 Mosse 1966, 3.

by the actual historical process. Chamberlain was fully aware of this: immediately after the first cannon shots that convulsed Europe, hitherto thought of as an 'organic unity', inextricably tied by the common 'Germanic blood flowing in the veins of its peoples,'[7] the English author that married Wagner's daughter and in his own person seemed to embody this unity, was forced to make a choice: now he railed against a nation of merchants, envious of the greatness of the other people and resolved to suppress it by all means; now, on the opposite side, he celebrated the Germans as the only true and worthy 'Führer of the world'. Or, in other words: 'new goals and new methods for the new era!'[8]

As well as the heterogeneity of historical time, it is necessary to take into account the ideological contradictions and discrepancies that occur objectively during the development of a political movement. An example is the case of Nazism. It came to power with the slogan *Blut und Boden*, denouncing the big city as a place of uprooting and subversion; conquering new *Lebensraum* in the colonised East was also supposed to confer new vitality and youthfulness on a certain type of rural living and to thin out the urban centres and drain the water in which Jewish and communist agitators moved like fish (this theme can be found in *Mein Kampf*). And yet, by promoting and unleashing war, Hitler was forced to give further impetus to the process of militarisation, industrialisation and thus urbanisation. The demands of war also required the removal of women from the bucolic and *völkisch* idyll, thus making a mockery of the vision propagated by the ideologues of *Blut und Boden*. So, must we conclude that this slogan and the movement lying behind it had nothing to do with Nazism and the Third Reich? For that is how the hermeneuts of innocence proceed. In their eyes, the incongruity and contradiction between a worldview and the objective result that, in a concrete and determined historic space, that worldview helps to bring about demonstrate that the one has nothing to do with the other.

At the turn of the century, war was demanded by Nietzsche and by the press in Germany and far beyond, also in the name of the struggle against the vulgarisation and mercantile spirit of modern society, marked by the levelling of values and the standardisation of behaviour, thus more and more resembling a beehive or an anthill. But, under the specific conditions in which the First World War took place, it became synonymous with total mobilisation and regimentation and promoted a 'massification' unprecedented in history. In the decades leading up to the catastrophe, which began in 1914, the cult of danger and the warrior ethic were constantly contrasted with the demands of the labour and people's movement for a welfare state and the philistine ideal of comfort

7   Chamberlain 1937, 305.
8   Chamberlain 1914, 44–67, 36–43.

and security. However, in the course of endless war, opposing elites sought to secure the loyalty of the mobilised workers and peasants by enticements and sometimes astonishing promises, so laying the ground for the subsequent social demagogy of fascism and Nazism.

The slogans with which war was glorified at the turn of the century made fun of bourgeois and Christian sentimentality, considered to be in striking contradiction with the laws of nature; but, in the incredible conflagration that then followed, the need to give meaning to the death and sacrifice of millions of people and of youth in the flower of their lives led to a revitalisation of Christianity, as evidenced by the recourse to military chaplains, with a cult of the dead and the incessant preaching of a religion understood as *verbum crucis*. This is a central paradox of contemporary history. At the turn of the century, the militant and mass parties of the subaltern classes burst through onto the political stage. They clearly distinguished themselves from the traditional groups of aristocratic or bourgeois notables by their organisational structure and the spirit of struggle and solidarity that inspired their members. In declaring a crusade against this 'democratic herd', the cultural elitists and the aristocratic reaction used slogans imbued with an emphatic pathos of the individual. However, they encouraged political processes and movements that ended up not only making use of the mass army but also learning and borrowing something from the despised and hated enemy: thus the militant parties of the labour and popular movement were opposed by parties that reproduced the hated and despised massification and regimentation. This was the historical space in which authors such as Gobineau and Chamberlain belonged.

2   The Pathos of Europe from the Aristocratic Reaction to Nazism

The methodological criteria set out here must also be applied to the great philosophers. The attempt to exploit Nietzsche's Europe pathos to celebrate him as an antagonist of the Third Reich *ante litteram* is shockingly naïve from a historical point of view. We have seen, on this point, that he was far from isolated in the aristocratic reaction of the late nineteenth century. As for Nazism, it is definitely schematic to imagine that, from the very beginning and without oscillations or internal contradictions, it had been unequivocally marked by the glorification of Germany and its solitary opposition to the rest of the world. In reality, even on the eve of the outbreak of the Second World War, a direct witness of Nazism – someone from its very ranks – emphasised the 'pan-European' pathos of this movement, which, in the name of 'racial affinity', had long pursued the idea of an 'alliance of this block with England' and other countries with which it later came to blows.[9] Rosenberg struck up a hymn to the 'European human being', and Goebbels continued to intone it even while the European countries were engaged in a deadly struggle against one another.[10] The fact is the Third Reich continued to pose as a genuine representative of the culture and history of the 'European human being' and of the striving towards European unity. Particularly significant here is the figure of Himmler: he 'was always of the opinion that Europe should be ruled by a racial elite embodied in the ss, which should not be nationally bound'.[11]

One can understand nothing of the irresistible rise of Hitler without bearing in mind the geopolitical and ideological balance sheet he drew regarding the catastrophe of the First World War: he thought one had to put an end to the sort of wars of secession that had ravaged peoples of the superior culture; and reconstitute, by means of an appropriate delimitation of colonial and civilising spheres of influence, the unity of the Nordic peoples (Germany, Britain and, if necessary, the United States), in order to address jointly the barbarian threat posed by the revolt of the 'inferior races' and by the Bolshevik revolution, itself tied by racial or elective affinity to peoples of colour. The elimination of these threats would put an end once and for all to the subversive cycle that had long raged in the West, thus averting the danger of its decline and even paving the way for its revival and the overcoming of its sharp oppositions.[12]

Only in this way can we explain the fascination Hitler exercised at least for a while on intellectuals and philosophers even of the highest order. Heidegger, for example, sympathised with the Third Reich. He believed the new regime was committed, on the one hand, to promoting an 'understanding' between the peoples of Europe and, on the other, to denouncing and combating the endless cycle of nihilism, by furthering the 'countermovement' started by Nietzsche – it is no coincidence that in those years (1936/37) he still broadly identified with him.[13]

During the Second World War, there was no shortage of ideologues of the Third Reich calling on the peoples of the occupied countries to overcome the narrow-mindedness and provincialism of national conflicts and adopt the standpoint of 'one Europe', and in doing so they referred to Nietzsche. The Nietzsche thus cited was the philosopher that, by virtue of his celebration of Napoleon, was said to count among the 'greatest spiritual witnesses' of the

---

9   Rauschning 1938, 427.
10   Rosenberg 1935, 20, 24; Goebbels 1991a, 1867 (10 January 1943).
11   Arendt 1945, 20.
12   Losurdo 1996, 4, §6.
13   Cf. Losurdo 1995, 3, §8, and 5, §2.

pan-European idea.[14] Hitler too personally posed as a new Napoleon, after the triumph of his campaign in France, and lost no time in visiting the grave of the unifier of Europe and of 'a unique military genius'.[15]

These themes explain the success achieved by the Nazis even beyond Germany and among authors that supported the Third Reich because they believed in so doing they were being true to Nietzsche's European programme. Such was the case, for example, with Drieu La Rochelle. As has been noted, 'his internationalism is mixed with Nietzscheanism and a violent critique of modern culture'. The French writer expressed either in person or through the characters in his novels ideas that clearly betrayed Nietzsche's influence: it was necessary to be clear about the 'need for a European federation, which is only way to avoid the destruction of Europe by war'. Above all he believed: 'Nationalism is the most ignoble aspect of the modern spirit.' A novel by Drieu La Rochelle seemed to indicate even in the title (*Le jeune européen*) the presence of the German philosopher, committed to glorifying the figure of the 'good European'.[16] The same went for Brasillach and Hamsun, who, in the last analysis, joined the collaboration in the name of Europe.[17]

3   The Greco-Germanic Myth of Origin from the Second to the Third Reich

If Greece was the cradle of Europe, its 'sacred heart' was Germany, according to Heidegger.[18] This thesis was connected with a tradition of thought to which Nietzsche was no stranger. In distancing himself from the enthusiasm of the *Birth of Tragedy*, he described the development of the Second Reich as follows: it was the period in which 'the German spirit, which had recently shown the will to rule Europe and the strength to lead Europe, had abdicated, finally and definitively, and, using the pompous pretext of founding an empire, is in a process of transition to mediocrity, democracy, and "modern ideas"' (GT, An Attempt at Self-Criticism, 6 [10]). It was the 'abdication' that roused his indignation. In the bitterness of the denunciation, the echo of a special recognition of Germany's role in keeping the Greek heritage alive continued to resonate. Moreover, Nietzsche himself expressed the admiration in which he continued, well beyond the

---

14   In Opitz 1977, 836.
15   Hitler 1989, 195 (5 April 1942).
16   In Kunnas 1972, 197–202.
17   Kunnas 1972, 196, 232.
18   Cf. Losurdo 1995, 2, §7.

Birth of Tragedy, to hold the Prussian officer corps when he characterised it as 'cheerful speeches and hyper-Germania' (JGB, 251 [143]). As a whole, Germany had committed a shameful betrayal, but was it definitive?

The bitter disappointment caused by the development of the Second Reich and the 'Enlightenment' turn did not mean that the Greco-Germanic myth of origin, which played such an important role in the early writings, had disappeared. The theme, far from being abandoned, kept coming back in new and no less fascinating formulations, as is clear from this fragment of the summer of 1885:

> Maybe in a few centuries we will judge that all German philosophizing has its true dignity in being a gradual recovery of ancient ground, and that every claim to 'originality' sounds petty and ridiculous in relation to that higher claim of the Germans, to have mended the bond that seemed torn, the bond with the Greek, that thus far highest type of 'human being'.
>
> XI, 679

One might say, after the disappointments caused by the specific development of the Second Reich, that the Greco-Germanic myth of origin was conjugated in the future rather than the present tense, even if this future was at times very problematic. The permanent reference to the 'German essence' allowed one to tie the merciless criticism of Germany's present to the evocation of a future made all the more credible by the fact that tragic Hellenism was somehow already living, even if no longer in the Wagner of the *Birth of Tragedy* and the fourth *Unfashionable Observation* but in the very author of the evocation of this hope.

The fragment concludes thus:

> We will from day by day become more Greek – first, as is right in concepts and evaluations [...]: but one day, it is to be hoped, also with our body! Herein lies (and always did lie) my hope for the German essence.
>
> XI, 679

Heraclitus *redivivus*, who had taken shape in Nietzsche as the tragic and Dionysian philosopher *par excellence*, seemed to announce *Hellas redivivum*, destined to take shape in Germany, which would sooner or later be able, despite everything, to rise to the level of its essence and mission. Precisely because the philosopher-philologist was in a position to bestow on the Greco-Germanic myth of origin a form that was, in a certain sense, open, this myth continued to play an important and ill-fated role right up to the defeat of 1945.

Inserted into *The Will to Power*, the fragment just cited (§ 419) was recalled in 1918 by Ernst Bertram, to confirm Nietzsche's 'faith' in the German character's profound predestination to an 'inner Hellenization'.[19] Insofar as Germany or the 'German becoming' took heart from Heraclitus' lesson and set themselves against the shallow 'Latin realism of being', it was thanks to Nietzsche gain and confirm 'the most Greek of all the conceptions of the world': 'From the war of opposites arises all becoming' and 'the struggle continues for eternity.'[20]

Heidegger chose the first part of the fragment (and the corresponding paragraph from *The Will to Power*) as the motto for his lectures of the summer semester of 1931, two years before the Nazis' advent to power and the philosopher's own adherence to the new political regime.[21] Baeumler, after praising 'the Germanic-Hellenic foundation' of Nietzsche's philosophy as early as 1930,[22] concluded his essay on *Hellas and Germany* seven years later, by which time he had become an ideologue of the Third Reich, with a song of praise to the 'mysterious relationship' that bound the two countries and the two cultures, once again referring to Nietzsche and the fascinating fragment or paragraph.[23]

It must also be said that the Greco-Germanic myth of origin played an important role not only among intellectuals more or less close to Nazism but also in the leading circles of this political movement. Rosenberg, who saw himself as the movement's ideologue, located and celebrated the origins of Germanic culture in the 'ancient Hellenes', whose worldview (he emphasised, with an explicit nod to Nietzsche) was to be strictly distinguished from 'Hellenistic late-rationalism'.[24] No less emphatic was Hitler's reference to Greece, the cradle of 'Europe', the sacred space of the culture whose centre now lay in Germany.[25]

This does not mean that we should hasten to establish a line of continuity. However, it is worth taking note of the ideological and mythological materials by which Nazism was served. That Nietzsche played a central role in this context is confirmed by two important details. As we know, Nietzsche's invocation of authentic Hellenism, also conceived in opposition to Romanness, gradually gave way to an invocation of the Greco-Roman world as a whole, overrun by Jewish-Christian subversion. That is why Heidegger, towards the end of the Second World War, criticised the philosopher for having been inspired

---

19   Bertram 1919, 89 f., 84.
20   Bertram 1919, 66, 99.
21   Heidegger 1981, XI.
22   Baeumler 1937a, 253.
23   Baeumler 1937c, 309–11.
24   Rosenberg 1937a, 37 f.
25   Hitler 1980, 124 (2–3 November 1941).

not by Greece but by Rome. The glorification of Greece over Rome was clearly practised by intellectuals and personalities directly linked to Nazism.[26] Not so Hitler, who denounced Christianity for bringing about the 'end of a long reign, that of the beautiful clarity of the ancient world'.[27] Rome was in no way synonymous with decadence: 'Even today the Roman Empire still lacks its equals. To have succeeded in completely dominating the world! No empire has radiated such a unified culture!'[28] In this sense, Heidegger, who had begun to distance himself from the Third Reich, was right to accuse both Nazism and Nietzsche of having allowed themselves to be captivated by the Roman option.

There can no doubt that both in the Second and the Third Reich conflicting myths of origin existed simultaneously, but it is also true that Hitler preferred the myth of origin associated with the Greek and Roman world (including the Holy Roman Empire reconstituted by Charlemagne):

> There has been a lot of talk about the excavations undertaken in regions inhabited at one time by our ancestors. I am not at all enthusiastic about this. I cannot forget that at the same time as our ancestors were making their stone basins and clay jugs, which so excite our archaeologists, the Greeks were building the Acropolis.[29]

And Rosenberg, who occasionally demonstrated a measure of indulgence for the mythology of the ancient Germans, told the Führer it was not appropriate 'to call a hero like Charlemagne Karl the "Saxon killer"'.[30] The Nazi myth of origin of Europe went through various stages: Europe was identified successively with Greece, the Roman Empire, Charlemagne (true to the 'ancient idea' and heir to Caesarism) and the 'Holy Roman Empire of German Nations', and finally, in the twentieth century, with the Reich Germany was seeking to construct.[31] Again we come back to Nietzsche, who, far from sharing the Teutomaniacs' hatred for Charlemagne, appreciated in him the elements associated with classical antiquity and the 'Imperium Romanum' (VIII, 67–8 and XII, 341).

---

26   Cf. Losurdo 1995, 6, §2 and §3.
27   Hitler 1980, 150 (13 December 1941).
28   Hitler 1980, 125 (2–3 November 1941).
29   Hitler 1989, 426 (7 July 1942).
30   Hitler 1989, 166 (31 March 1942).
31   Hitler 1989, 165 f. (31 March 1942) and Hitler 1980, 124 (2–3 November 1941).

4   Total War, the Sacred Patriotic Union and the Crisis of Transversal Racism

That the transition from the reaction of the late nineteenth century to Nazism was discontinuous results not from the pathos of Europe or the Greco-Germanic myth of origin but from other factors. Let us return to Nietzsche's first social-Darwinist admirers. Tille quotes extensively from the aphorism from *Twilight of the Idols* that called for a humble and submissive 'Chinese-style' working class for Germany too (*supra*, 10 §3), and notes critically: 'The European worker is surely also a power factor. In its ranks there are numerous capable elements that feel the urge to rise to the role of masters, to become master beings [*Herrenmenschen*]. Why is Nietzsche so angry with them?'[32]

According to Tille, German and European workers were not to be confused with the members of 'inferior' races. The 'Indo-Germanic race' as a whole occupied a higher level in the natural hierarchy.[33] The German people in particular 'is the people of the social aristocracy, and thus called upon to be a leader of other peoples on the road to the future'.[34] Nietzsche's error lay in having 'thought only of the antithesis between rulers and ruled', while 'he has less heart for the battle of competition that peoples, tribes and races wage against each other, on a global scale'; but precisely this conflict was destined to dominate the European and world scene.[35]

Here, the opposition between transversal and horizontal racialisation (which also shaped the two basic trends of anti-democratic reaction in the late nineteenth century) was clearly manifested. Naturally, it would be wrong to interpret this picture in a schematic way. Tille recognised that elements of horizontal racialisation could also be found in Nietzsche: was it not he that insisted on breeding a unified master caste in Europe that would be able to dominate the world?[36] In fact, in the philosopher's view, there seemed to be no room for a master caste in the Chinese people, which, taken as a whole, was described as a more or less servile workforce. Between Europe and the 'decadent races' there was a relationship of master and serf.

On the other hand, elements of transversal racialisation could also be found in Tille. He too, citing both Galton and Nietzsche, pleaded for a vigorous eugenic intervention that, with the help of forced sterilisation and other such

---

32   Tille 1895, 236.
33   Tille 1893, 25.
34   Tille 1893, 109.
35   Tille 1895, 239–41.
36   Tille 1895, 239 f.

measures, should prevent in every culturally advanced society, and above all in Germany, the procreation of those whose lives had turned out badly and of waste elements.[37] Yet, despite these clarifications and reservations, a fundamental difference remained: for Europe at least, Nietzsche's rank-ordering in the first place set the 'race' of masters against the 'race' of servants. Tille argued quite differently: after denouncing the presence in the German Reich of 'aliens' (not just Slavs, but also French, Latvians and Danes), amounting to '8 per cent of the total population', he proposed their deportation – also with an eye to future wars and expansions, to leave room only for true Germans. Only in this way could Germany strengthen its ranks and homogeneity, and pave the way to a future continental empire.[38]

There could be no doubt there was no place in Nietzsche, as far as Germany and Europe were concerned, for the measures of ethnic cleansing advocated here. For this reason too, his admirer and critic accused him of adopting an attitude of detachment and estrangement from his own people. Transversal racialisation entered into a particularly serious crisis above all when the prospect of total war loomed: it was not easy to persuade the mass of soldiers to sacrifice their lives while, at the same time, constantly reminding them they were only servants and Chandala; clearly, the new situation required substantial concessions to the populist-authoritarian tendency.

It is interesting to note that this populist-authoritarian trend could also use and criticise Nietzsche from the point of view of a non-German imperialism. At the beginning of the twentieth century, a Scottish poet, John Davidson, referred enthusiastically to the overman theory only to criticise it for its generic, transversal character. Of Polish descent, as he himself acknowledged, and therefore with a racially mediocre genealogy, the author of *Thus Spoke Zarathustra* was unable to grasp a fundamental truth: 'The true overman is the Englishman, and the history of England is the history of his evolution.'[39]

Tille's critique of Nietzsche was similar to Chamberlain's of Gobineau. The latter's 'hopelessly pessimistic vision' of a general bastardisation, so that no country and no people could claim true racial purity, was a 'delusion'. So, the 'brilliant' theorist of the inequality of the races stopped at a transversal racialisation,[40] but imperialism needed a horizontal racialisation to rank countries and races hierarchically, a need met by Tille and Chamberlain in Germany and by Davidson in Britain.

---

37   Tille 1893, 87 f. and *passim*; Tille 1895, 231 and *passim*.
38   Tille 1893, 35.
39   Brie 1928, 268; cf. Arendt 1966, 180.
40   Chamberlain 1937, 313 f.

Tille's critique was later taken up by certain circles in the Third Reich: a leading ideologue criticised Nietzsche for glorifying an 'ideal of power' of dubious value and utility: it was *volklos*, it made no reference to the people, and instead excluded the people.[41] This manner of arguing must have been fairly widespread, for a year or two earlier Heidegger had felt the need to point out that the 'mass' targeted by Nietzsche referred to 'mediocre educated philistines' and not, for example, to 'the peasant and worker truly integrated into the world of his machines'.[42] In a similar way, Jaspers felt the need to exonerate Nietzsche from the charge that he was 'alienated from the people [*Volksfremdheit*]', by adapting the philosopher, in a certain sense, to the ideological needs of the moment: he had looked full of 'longing' at the 'actual people', located in the 'minority of masters called to the legislation by virtue of their creative essence'.[43] But precisely this elitism, rigorously declined even at the internal level, was in contradiction with the need imposed in the course of the second Thirty Years' War to mobilise the people as a homogeneous community against its enemies.

This was also the context of the polemic about Nietzsche and anti-Semitism that developed at the time of Hitler's seizure of power. Baeumler emphasised the philosopher's insistence on the inherently and irremediably Jewish character of Christianity, to support his view that Nietzsche's furious anti-Christian polemic was underpinned by an equally furious anti-Semitism. Other authors saw this as an 'artifice' and pointed to Nietzsche's clear preference for the (pre-exilic) Old Testament over the New Testament.[44] While Baeumler tried to make the Nietzschean master race consonant with the *Volk* (from which Jews were excluded), others pointed out that Nietzsche included part of the Jews in it, so they denounced the sadly transversal character of this master race.

5   Persistence of Aristocratic Reaction and Transversal Racialisation

Although it entered into serious crisis with the advent of total war, transversal racialisation did not vanish altogether. At the outbreak of the First World War, Peter Gast began singing songs of praise to the 'German sword'. But these themes of his master continued to resonate. Despite his patriotic fervour, this faithful disciple of Nietzsche shook his head 'at the absurdity of this war, at

41   Böhm 1938, 3; Steding (1938, 35, 54, 112) is on essentially the same wave-length.
42   Heidegger 1961, 146.
43   Jaspers 1936, 374 f.
44   Baeumler 1931a, 158 f.; Westernhagen 1936, 42 f.

the equation of the elect with the far too many in front of guns and cannons'. Although he described the war then in course as 'magnificent', he regretted the 'many men of culture and art destroyed' on either side.[45] Peter Gast would certainly have preferred a reckoning of accounts by the pan-European elite with the Chandala of all countries.

Transversal racialisation did not even disappear completely from the ideological horizon of fascism and Nazism, despite the need to appeal to the popular masses and enact total mobilisation in order to step up against overwhelming enemy forces. Between the two world wars, Ludendorff condemned the French Revolution as 'a massacre of unprecedented proportions directed against France's blond leading upper layer'.[46] While Nazism had to praise Germany's supreme right and – on the basis of a horizontal racialisation – appeal for the support of the entire people for its expansionist war, in denouncing revolution and subversion it continued to blame them on races foreign to true Aryan and Western culture. In France in 1789 and 1871, and in the German revolution of 1918, which marked the start of the Weimar Republic, an ethnic group had come out on top that had no connection to the higher 'type of ancient France' or of authentic Germany. Thus Rosenberg, basing himself not on Boulainvilliers, with whom he was probably unfamiliar, but on Lapouge.[47] The latter, under the influence of the eighteenth-century theorist of the aristocratic reaction, also undertook a transversal racialisation, to the point where it became a key to the whole of world history: in ancient Rome, 'civil wars' already depended on a 'mob' composed of the 'social underclass of all the surrounding peoples'. But, even in our case, added the French social Darwinist, 'racial matters simultaneously determined internal policy'.[48]

Even though the two forms of racialisation sought to fulfil different ideological demands, their coexistence was not unproblematic. The relationship became more conflictual the more the internal situation in Germany (and Italy) stabilised, albeit under a terrible reaction; but in anticipation and preparation of the imperialist war, horizontal racialisation became dominant or exclusive. This produced very interesting polemics. In this context, the most significant personality was an author that, despite being on excellent terms with Mussolini and certain circles of the Third Reich, was committed to criticising the two regimes 'from the point of view of the right',[49] i.e., from the

---

45   Podach 1932, 122 f.
46   E. Ludendorff 1928, 36.
47   Rosenberg 1937a, 638 f.
48   Lapouge 1896, 74 f.
49   Evola 1964, 96 (on relations with Mussolini).

standpoint of the 'aristocratic reaction' that found its expression in Nietzsche, though with some naturalistic limits.[50] This was the argument made by Julius Evola, who ultimately criticised fascism and Nazism for having abandoned transversal racialisation or having insufficiently borne it in mind. In the magnificent Imperial Germany evoked by *Mein Kampf*, 'to be a street-sweeper citizen of this country must be a higher honour than to be king in a foreign state'. Here is Evola's critical comment: 'In this, a precise degradation of the concept of race can be observed. According to traditional views, true race is manifested and realized only in the elites, in the aristocracies'.[51]

Apart from Nietzsche, a constant presence,[52] Evola referred to Gobineau: here, 'racism is essentially a manifestation of a noble instinct, an aristocratic reaction against times of democracy, egalitarianism and the rise of the masses'; that is why it had to be kept strictly apart from a racism that gave expression to '"socializing" and modernizing tendencies'.[53] Apart from horizontal racism, 'superstitious belief in the "fatherland" and the "nation" is also a veiled and tenacious residue of democratic impersonalism', synonymous with massification and levelling.[54] Like the category 'humanity', nation also reflected 'the democratic mentality'.[55] Evola was well acquainted with the revolutionary history that lay behind the idea of 'nation',[56] so he rejected with contempt 'the democratic myth of the nation' or 'a kind of nationalism that is simply a mask for Jacobinism'.[57] In contrast to this world and this ideology, he praised Metternich as 'the last "European"',[58] and pointed out: 'Nationalism and imperialism are two very different, not to say contradictory, things.'[59] That is to say, imperialism presupposed a hierarchy of people, which was negated by the idea of 'nation', at least in relation to a particular community.

Beyond the 'superstition' of the nation, it was also necessary to deal a final blow at the Jacobins and Hegel's 'God state',[60] the 'superstitious belief in and idolization of the "state"' that appealed to the 'levelled multitudes'.[61] The state

50   Evola 1995a, 47.
51   Evola 1995a, 283; cf. Hitler 1939b, 491.
52   Evola 1978, 64, 84, 126, 128.
53   Evola 1995a, 41, 90.
54   Evola 1978, 45.
55   Evola 1978, 50.
56   Evola 1995b, 67.
57   Evola 1995b, 120.
58   Evola 1995b, 354.
59   Evola 1978, 35.
60   Evola 1978, 153.
61   Evola 1978, 51 f.

itself was synonymous with levelling, for it subsumed both master and servant, as well as the aristocrat and the Chandala, under the figure of the citizen
subjected in theory to the equal rule of law. Precisely because Evola tirelessly
reaffirmed 'the value of the individual' and even denounced 'the decline in the
value of individuality in the West', he did not hesitate to profess a 'true liberalism' unfortunately betrayed by modern liberals with their concessions to the
superstition of the general legal norm, of the nation and of the state.[62] This did
not stop Evola expressing feelings of nostalgia for the world before the abolition
of slavery ('only a race of slaves can have willed the abolition of slavery') and for
'oriental castes'.[63] From his point of view, there was no contradiction, for only
individuals of a lower nature or, more precisely, labour machines completely
devoid of individuality were and should be sentenced to slavery and relegated
to the lower castes.

Precisely because he remained faithful to Nietzsche's model of transversal
racialisation, Evola was basically luke-warm about what he regarded as racial
anti-Semitism in the narrower sense. His denunciation not only of Judaism but
also of Christianity, on whose intrinsically and repugnantly Jewish character
he constantly harped, was certainly obsessive. On the whole, it was a tradition
guilty of having questioned the hierarchical order of nature: 'The hallucination
of another world and of a messianic solution that escapes from the present
is the need for an escape on the part of those whose lives have turned out
badly, the rejected, the damned, those incapable of accepting and willing their
reality'; this idea has been 'hatched within the Semitic race' and thanks to Christianity received a planetary affirmation.[64]

On the other hand, Evola seemed unenthusiastic about the myth of blood
in the strictly biological sense. When the Nuremberg laws of 1935 excluded
Jews from citizenship as 'foreigners', they made provision for exceptions for
Jews that had performed 'special merits for the Reich' and elevated them to the
status of *Ehrenarier*, 'honorary Aryans'. But, said Evola, this category 'should
have as a counterpart *Ehrenjuden*, "honorary Jews", to be applied to the many
who, though Aryans in race and body, are far less so in character and spirit'[65]
For Nietzsche's disciple, what really counted was transversal racialisation, the
contrast between masters and servants, aristocrats and Chandala.

---

62   Evola 1978, 61, 91, 39.
63   Evola 1978, 41, 30.
64   Evola 1978, 90.
65   Evola 1995a, 260.

6 From Boulainvilliers's Negation of the Idea of 'Nation' to Imperialist Chauvinism

Beyond Nietzsche and Gobineau, explicitly cited and praised, Evola's radical critique of the idea of nation is linked to a tradition that goes back ultimately to Boulainvilliers. According to the latter, the plebeians or Gallo-Romans were, properly speaking, not even 'subjects of the state in general'; only by virtue of the 'relations that their masters', and they alone, hae to the whole could they be considered as such.[66] The abyss between plebeians and nobles, between the defeated Gallo-Romans and the victorious Franks, was so deep it could be bridged neither by the nation nor by the state; so different were the two ethnic and social groups that they could never be part of a single community, nation or state. They were separated and set at odds with one another by 'a true and eternal difference.'[67]

The elaboration of the concept of nation was also a response to the transversal racism of the aristocratic reaction. The latter was rudely reminded that it was possible to 'drive back into the forests of Franconia all the families that dare advance the absurd claim to be descended from a lineage of conquerors and to have inherited their rights'.[68] The aristocrats were called upon to recognise once and for all that they had no right to place themselves above the community of citizens and the French nation, and ultimately would derive no advantage from doing so. Gobineau, on the other hand, followed Boulainvilliers, and never tired of ridiculing the 'fatherland' as a 'fictitious person', an 'abstraction' and a barbarian residue.[69] Unknown in the happy days of 'our feudal times' and the rule of the aristocracy, 'the term *"patrie"* [...] was rarely used; we first thought of it when the Gallo-Roman layers raised their heads again and played a role in politics'; yes, 'with their victory, patriotism again became a virtue'.[70]

At this point, the problem of a possible relationship between Nietzsche, who above all theorised transversal racialisation, and the Third Reich, which based itself above all on horizontal racialisation, could be reformulated thus: who was closer to Nazism, Sieyès, with his pathos of the revolutionary *nation* in struggle against the exclusivism and proud consciousness of the nobility of being masters, or Boulainvilliers and Gobineau, with their mockery of a category that sought to embrace in a higher unity two castes and 'races' separated by an

---

66   Boulainvilliers 1727, Vol. 1, 33 f.
67   Arendt 1966, 162.
68   Arendt 1966, 164.
69   Gobineau 1983, 678, 681 (Book 4, 3).
70   Gobineau 1983, 678 fn. 2 (Book 4, 3); cf. Arendt 1966, 173.

abyss? In fact, two quite different attitudes can be found in Sieyès. Looking towards the nobility and expressing his disdain for the claim of the 'privileged' to be a different and higher 'species' (SEe above, 22, §2), the French revolutionary praised the nation as 'a body of associates living under a shared law', in which 'he that possesses great wealth is not worth more than those that live off their daily wage', at least with regard to the enjoyment of 'rights' and 'protection of the person'.[71] Elsewhere, however, with an eye to the mass of the wretched, the theorist of the Third Estate not only divided the nation into 'two peoples' completely different from one another and arranged in a clear hierarchy (see above, 25, §5) but went even further: in the society towards which he strove, 'the production heads would be whites, while the auxiliary instruments of labour would be negroes'.[72] So who was closer to Nazism, Boulainvillers and Gobineau or Sieyès? And as for the latter, who was closer to Nazism: the leader of the battle against the aristocracy, who emphasised the unity of the French nation (and humankind), or the one that identified with the privileged fraction of the Third Estate and thus ended up reintroducing a transversal racialisation to the detriment of the lower classes that tendentially coincided with horizontal racialisation to the detriment of blacks? There can be no doubt Hitler succeeded in making use of the idea of the nation, even though in a rigidly naturalistic and racist sense, while Boulainvilliers, Gobineau and Nietzsche either had nothing to do with this idea or explicitly rejected and despised it. But it is also true that it would be impossible to understand anything of the horror of the Third Reich without taking into account the radical negation of the unity of humankind, its split into two sharply opposed components.

It is worth noting that, in reconstructing the prehistory of Nazism, two authors as different as Lukács and Arendt both referred primarily to Boulainvillers and the aristocratic reaction to the French Revolution.[73] Regarding Britain, already a major colonial power, in Burke one observed the transition from celebrating the natural superiority of the feudal aristocracy (ideology à la Boulainvilliers) to celebrating the superiority of the British people, elevated as a whole 'to the rank of aristocracy among the nations'.[74] So a transition took place from the transversal hierarchisation/racialisation of the aristocratic reaction to the horizontal hierarchisation/racialisation of imperialism.

---

71   Sieyès 1985b, 121; Sieyès 1985a, 105.
72   Sieyès 1985c, 75.
73   Lukács 1954, 526; Arendt 1966, 165.
74   Arendt 1966, 175f.

7   Division of Labour, Worker Chinoiserie and Racial Slavery

Here we have proof that transversal and horizontal racialisation, despite their differences and contradictions, were not separated by an impassable barrier. This becomes even clearer if one considers a leading social Darwinist and contemporary of Nietzsche. Gumplowicz also paid tribute to the 'heroic age, repeatedly praised and much admired', of India, when the Aryans, bearers of a superior culture, defeated the original population, forced them into the 'lowliest roles of slaves and the lowliest workers', and conferred stability and maturity on the caste-based society.[75] Up to then, races were only castes and the result of the naturalisation of the social division of labour.

But the original inhabitants of India had darker skin than their conquerors, so the victory of the Aryans was a victory of whites over the '"black" tribes', which could be likened to the victory of whites over 'Redskins' in America. At this point, the difference in skin colour became decisive; it fixed the 'unbridgeable gulf' between winners and losers, between the master race and the race of those destined to slavery or annihilation.[76] At this level, Aryan was still in no way opposed to Jewish. Rather, Gumplowicz, of Jewish origin, likened the eruption of the Aryans into India (and the expansion of the whites in America) to the conquest, '1000 years later', of Palestine by the 'tribes of Israel', with similar results.[77] The Aryan community was here ultimately synonymous with Western community, within which, according to Gumplowicz, Jews were also to be subsumed. Set against it were the colonial world and the world of the coloured people, to which in the meantime India too belonged, substantially equated with the dark-skinned people overwhelmed and subjected by the Aryan victors. Transversal racialisation had in practice already become horizontal racialisation, and no longer to the benefit of a single people or country but to that of the West as a whole.

One can describe the developments that led to the Third Reich as the transition from one sort of racialisation to another. For culture slaves were needed, but where could they be found? According to Nietzsche, European culture was at a crossroads: either it decided to turn the European working class into a 'type of Chinese', or the Chinese themselves (this people that brought with it a 'way of thinking and living that befits laborious ants') and other 'barbarian peoples from Asia and Africa' had to, as a result of colonisation or immigration, constitute the slave labour force Europe and the civilised world needed

75   Gumplowicz 1883, 292, 295.
76   Gumplowicz 1883, 292–4.
77   Gumplowicz 1883, 292, 295.

(*supra*, 12 §3). The first perspective was becoming increasingly difficult due to the spread of education and socialist agitation. However, Nietzsche never completely renounced it. Let us return to that aphorism in *Twilight of the Idols* that mocked the 'labour question', denounced as a disaster all the concessions won by the proletariat from the ruling class, and declared it necessary to exclude from education all those destined to serve as slaves (GD *Expeditions of an Untimely Man*, 40).

Obviously, one still flirted with the idea of some form of slavery in the heart of Germany. The picture changed greatly when the conflict between the imperialist great powers began to loom: each had to appeal to the loyalty and spirit of sacrifice of the masses to be able to face up to the trial of strength at the international level and conquer the colonial space to which each aspired.

Nazism spoke up clearly and unambiguously for racial slavery or semi-slavery, to which those peoples outside the sacred space of culture and destined to be a slave caste in the service of the Germanic (and Western) master race could and had to be subjected. The discontinuity is obvious. Far removed from Nietzsche's horizon is not only the perspective that the Western great powers turn against one another in the conquest of colonies and the struggle for hegemony, but also the perspective of a continental empire in Eastern Europe with the subjugation of its inhabitants, the 'natives', in the language of the Führer, in a state of racial slavery or semi-slavery.

Even so, the element of continuity must not be neglected. We have seen how Langbehn translated Nietzsche's '*bellum et otium*' as 'war and art'. Hitler wrote: 'Wars come and go, what remains are solely the values of Culture.'[78] But culture could not do without a social layer required to perform more or less forced labour: 'One of the most essential preconditions for the formation of higher cultures was the availability of inferior people.' The availability of human instruments of labour was so intrinsic to the existence and orderly functioning of culture that the recourse to them preceded even the domestication of animals.[79] In any case, even now there was still a need for a 'modern class of slaves',[80] and it was foolish and criminal to educate them. The Führer pointed out it was important not to allow the populations of occupied territories to develop 'a master consciousness': 'The opposite is necessary.'[81] The natives, said an SS boss, who had learned the lesson well, must adapt as docile instruments

---

78   In Fest 1973, 527.
79   Hitler 1939b, 323.
80   In Fest 1973, 928.
81   In Poliakov/Wulf 1978, 518.

of labour, as 'slaves in the service of our culture'.[82] The only education permissible for Poles, declared Governor-General Hans Frank, was to impress on them the certainty of their 'destiny' as slaves.[83] There can be no doubt: we are dealing here with an actual slogan of the colonial politics of the Third Reich. Himmler warned against compassion for those destined to work 'as slaves for our culture'.[84] According to Hitler, they could only be taught what was necessary to learn to understand and respect 'our leadership'.[85]

This representation of the relationship between culture and slavery cannot fail to remind one of Nietzsche, even if, in the transition from transversal to horizontal racialisation, the 'barbaric slave class' could no longer be sought within the German *people*. While maintaining the pathos of distance, the social apartheid theorised by the philosopher of aristocratic radicalism now became an explicitly racial apartheid:

> To this end, it is necessary to separate as far as possible the life of the Germans in the Eastern areas to be colonized from that of the native population. We Germans must refrain from frequenting inns defiled by the spittle of the natives. Let the Germans have their own guesthouses, access to which is forbidden to the native population.[86]

Naturally, the model of the measures used against blacks in the southern United States and in South Africa played a much more important role here than Nietzsche's theory, but one should not forget that his theory too was not uninfluenced by the historical apartheid relations of the late nineteenth century (*supra*, 11 § 3 and 12 § 2).

---

82   Thus the Reichsführer of the ss, in Jacobsen 1989, 141.
83   In Poliakov/Wulf 1978, 502.
84   In Conrad–Martius 1955, 267.
85   Hitler 1989, 454 (22 July 1942).
86   Hitler 1989, 435 (9 July 1942).

Transformations of Aryan Mythology, Condemnation of the Revolutionary Conspiracy and the Formation of Anti-Semitism

1   In Search of the True Aryan and Anti-Christian West

According to Nazi ideology, Jews were not and could not be part of the German people, regardless of their social position and political orientation. We know that not only Nietzsche but the aristocratic reaction as a whole distanced themselves more or less clearly from anti-Semitism and especially from its plebeian manifestations. But Lichtheim, who sees Nietzsche as one of the inspirers of the 'final solution', argues as follows: it is true that the philosopher hated anti-Semites and got particularly worked up about Christianity, but we must not lose sight of the fact that what he 'detested about Christianity was precisely its Jewish origins'; he scorned the 'vulgar anti-Semites of his day' only because 'they were not radical enough', they did not understand that, as Christians, they themselves were 'carriers of that Jewish infection' they claimed to want to struggle against. The conclusion: the strict line of continuity that begins with Nietzsche 'holds true for every aspect of National Socialism, including its murderous onslaught on the Jews'.[1]

So, would Nietzsche be a more consistent sort of anti-Semite? Even though this interpretation can cite the testimony of Overbeck, already mentioned, and even the analysis of a historian of anti-Semitism like Lazare, it does not convince. The tone in which the philosopher addressed the anti-Semites of his time was not pedagogical; he certainly did not invite them to make a mental effort, since he considered them utterly incapable of doing so, but simply to disappear from circulation. The feelings of contempt and hatred were unequivocal. The continuity idea is no more convincing than the 'allegorical' scheme.

It is worth, at this point, returning for a moment to the debate at the time of the founding of the Second Reich. We have spoken of the strong presence of the Christian-Germanic myth of origin, which, in opposition above all to the anti-Christian France of the Enlightenment and the Revolution, celebrated

---

1   Lichtheim 1974, 186.

Germany as the privileged interpreter of the dominant religion in Europe and the West. The irruption of Aryan mythology complicated the situation, by introducing an element of contradiction between the linguistic origin of Germany and of the West (which excluded the Semitic languages) and their religious origin (which referred essentially to the Jewish tradition). Teutomaniacs like Wagner solved the problem by inventing an Aryan Jesus and thus developing a Christian-Aryan-Germanic mythology. This had a certain influence on the *Birth of Tragedy*, which positively contrasted the Aryan version of original sin with the Semitic version and counted Luther among the prophets of the revival on German soil of tragic Hellenism.

But Nietzsche was already aware of the absurdity of this construction as early as the 'Enlightenment' period, and made it the target of an ever sharper polemic. The *Genealogy of Morals* was particularly scornful of the 'Christian-Aryan-Philistine' attitude (GM III, 26 [118]). However, simply to highlight Nietzsche's implacable hostility to the Christian-Germanic (or Christian-Germanic-Aryan) myth of origin of the Second Reich would be to utter only half the truth. The other half, ignored or repressed, is that the deconstruction of this myth at the same time stimulated the construction of a Greco-Germanic-Aryan myth of origin understood in an anti-Jewish and anti-Christian sense. We know the 'German calamity' began and coincided with the 'transplanting of a deeply anti-German myth, the Christian one' (*supra*, 3 §4). On the other hand, we must not lose sight of the fact that Christianity 'can be said to have aimed at "Judaizing" the whole world' (FW, 135 [124]). The late Nietzsche never tired of insisting on the Jewish character of Christianity. It 'it is not a counter-movement to the Jewish instinct, it is its natural consequence' (AC, 24 [20]), on closer inspection, 'a foul-smelling Judain of rabbinism and superstition' (AC, 56 [56]). The historical development of Yahweh was extraordinary:

> God used to have only his people, his 'chosen' people. But then he took up travelling, just as his people did, and after that he did not sit still until he was finally at home everywhere, the great cosmopolitan, – until he had 'the great numbers' and half the earth on his side. Nonetheless, the God of the 'great numbers', the democrat among gods, did not become a proud, heathen god: he stayed Jewish.
>
>   AC 17 [15]

It was thanks to Christianity that Judaism and the Jewish slave revolt in morality, which would otherwise have remained confined to a small people and a small corner of the earth, took on a planetary dimension:

Christianity, which has sprung from Jewish roots and can only be understood as a plant that has come from this soil, represents the counter-
movement to every morality of breeding, race, or privilege: – it is the anti-
Aryan religion *par excellence*: Christianity, the revaluation of all Aryan
values, the victory of Chandala values, the gospel preached to the poor
and the base, the general revolt of the downtrodden, the miserable, the
malformed, the failures, against anyone with 'breeding', – the eternal vengeance of the Chandala as a religion of love.

For Germany and the West, finding oneself meant liquidating the process of
Judaisation that had begun with the spread of Christianity; insofar as it shook
off this 'anti-Aryan religion *par excellence*', Aryan 'humanity' would regain its
authenticity and true vocation (GD, 'Improving' humanity, 4 [185]).

Against the two-thousand year-old cycle of subversion that had begun on
Jewish soil, Nietzsche set a tradition antithetical to it not only culturally and
politically but also 'racially'. In doing so, he drew above all on the model of caste
society set out in the Aryan Code of Manu:

Caste-order, the most supreme, domineering law, is just the sanction of a
natural order, natural lawfulness par excellence – chance and 'modern
ideas' have no sway over it. [...] Nature, not Manu, separates out predominantly spiritual people from people characterized by muscular and
temperamental strength from a third group of people that are not distinguished in either way, the mediocre, – the latter being the great number,
the first being the exceptions. [...] Caste-order, order of rank, is just a formula for the supreme law of life itself, splitting off into three types is
necessary for the preservation of society, to make the higher and highest
types possible, – unequal rights are the condition for any rights at all. – A
right is a privilege.

AC, 57 [59]

This hierarchically organised Aryan society smoothly reproduced the natural
order and opposed the subversion that soon set in, at least with the prophets in Judaism. The 'blond beast' gave another splendid account of itself in the
magnificent Hellenic culture (GM, I, 11 [23]). Still under the leaden heaviness
of Christianity (and, indirectly, of Judaism), Aryan culture struggled to rediscover itself. On the one side was the Church, in which '[i]n the early Middle
Ages the choicest specimens of the "blond beast" were hunted down everywhere', for example the 'Teuton nobles', to reduce them to a 'caricature' (GD,
'Improving' humanity, 2 [183]). On the other, a movement of resistance and
counter-offensive:

The medieval organization seems like a wonderful groping towards the reconquest of all those representations on which ancient Indian-Aryan society rested – but with pessimistic values rooted in the soil of racial *decadence*.

B, III, 5, 325

In this case too, by virtue of the transversal racialisation we have already discussed, the conflict was both social and 'racial': we witnessed the clash between the plebeian tendencies of a Christian (and Jewish) church and an Aryan aristocratic reaction. But the same happened even in Nietzsche's time. Subversion, begun with the Jewish prophets, now revealed its Jewish face in socialism, which with its 'will to deny life' was shown to be the fruit of 'deformed people and races' (XI, 586–7; WZM, 125).

The Aryan 'blond beast' was sometimes called the 'blond Germanic beast' (GM, I, 11 [23]), with reference not exclusively or particularly to the inhabitants of the Second Reich but to the peoples of the 'Indo-Germanic languages' (VIII, 453) or of the 'Indo-Germanic race' (IX, 22). However, even the present-day Germans, and the West as a whole, were called upon to shake off Christianity and Judaism, and thus to put an end to a long cycle of subversion and regain the aristocratic and Aryan culture from which they arose.

At the time of Hitler's seizure of power, a debate developed that, in a certain sense, was a continuation of that held at the time of the founding of the Second Reich. The *Deutsche Christen*, the 'German Christians', adapted Christianity to the needs of the Third Reich, citing the Protestant Reformation, interpreted in a nationalistic key, to theorise a Church merged with the German 'popular community' and founded on the basis of the 'recognition of the diversity of peoples and races as a God-willed order'.[2] In this way, they followed the Christian-Germanic-Aryan mythological tradition. Other circles, especially that gathered around Ludendorff and his second wife, criticised Christianity as a religion profoundly alien to the Germanic essence, and even to the Germanic race; moreover, it was a religion that with its humanitarian and moralising sermons rendered the German people 'helpless [*abwehrlos*]'.[3] In making this argument, the Ludendorffs referred expressly to Nietzsche, to his 'mighty shaking and rattling' of the Christian 'tree planted thousands of years ago'.[4] In fact, even the language was reminiscent of the philosopher: in the final analysis, the univer-

---

2   In Kupisch 1965, 256–58.
3   E. Ludendorff 1935, 17; M. Ludendorff 1931, 7–9.
4   M. Ludendorff 1931, 9.

sal spread of the Jewish Old Testament was the work of 'Christian churches'[5] that were inherently 'Semitic'; and eventually the Reformation showed itself to be a 'Hebrew revival of Christianity'.[6]

For fear of a frontal confrontation with the Christian churches, Nazism was sometimes reticent about the explicitly and violently anti-Christian stance of the Ludendorff circle. On the other hand, as we have seen, Hitler made concessions to Christian-Germanic-Aryan mythology when he resumed the theme of an Aryan or half-Aryan Jesus. But the main thing for the Nazis was a lasting de-Judaisation and de-Christianisation of Germany and Europe. Rosenberg began his *Myth of the Twentieth Century* with the glorification of the victorious irruption of the 'blond [*hell*] Aryans' into India, where they subjugated the 'native' 'dark skinned [*Dunklen*]' and brought about a 'caste-based order'. The second chapter of this glorious sequence talked of the 'Hellenes as Aryans', and there finally followed 'the colonization of the world by the Germanically defined West'.[7] The catastrophic moment in this epic was the penetration of 'late Roman, Christian, Jewish or Egyptian representations and values into the soul of the Germanic human being'.[8]

The link between the anti-Christian and the anti-Jewish polemic characterised the most violently anti-Christian circles of the Third Reich, who oriented themselves towards Nietzsche; but, for the latter, this struggle against the Jewish-Christian tradition went hand in hand with the struggle against anti-Semitism.

2   The Jews as a Chandala People and as a Priestly People

In his contemptuous response to Fritsch, to whom he returned the three issues of *Antisemitische Correspondenz*, the philosopher mocked the superficiality or extravagances of the anti-Semites 'in matters of morality and history' (B, III, 5, 51). Nietzsche intended to move on the terrain of history. It is true that in his eyes, the development of the slave revolt coincided substantially with the development of post-exilic Judaism. But to understand the reasons for this, one had to interrogate history more closely: 'Even in their fatherland, the Jews were not a dominant caste [...]', the Jews 'have never been a race of chivalry' (XI, 568). Nietzsche developed the analysis further in a fragment from the beginning of 1888, worth quoting at length:

---

5   E. Ludendorff 1934, 3–7.
6   E. Ludendorff 1934, 13.
7   Rosenberg 1937a, 28 f., 38.
8   Rosenberg 1937a, 40.

The Jews make the attempt to assert themselves after losing two castes, the warriors and the farmers.

They are in this sense the 'circumcised.'

– they have the priest – and then immediately the Chandala ...

Understandably, with them it comes to a break, an uprising of the Chandala: the origin of Christianity.

Since they knew only the warrior as their master, they brought into their religion hostility against the distinguished, the noble, the proud, against might, against the ruling estates: they are the pessimists of indignation.

Thus they created an important new position: the priest at the head of the Chandala – against the noble [*vornehm*] estates.

Christianity drew the ultimate consequences of this movement: in the Jewish priesthood too it perceived caste, the privileged, the noble –

It erased the priest –

Christ is the Chandala that rejects the priest ... The Chandala that redeems itself ...

This is why the French Revolution is the daughter, the continuator of Christianity ... by instinct it is against the Church, against the aristocrats, against the last privileges –

XIII, 396

For nearly all their history, the Jews had got to know the master caste only as hated alien occupiers. In the struggle against them, they tended to appeal without distinction to the mass, and in so doing they had lost or never gained the sense and pathos of distance. Because of the political and military defeat, the long years of exile, and slavery, the slave morality and *ressentiment* and hatred of the aristocratic classes and values had become second nature to this people. This analysis was subsequently picked up by Weber, according to whom 'Judaism has, since the Exile, been the religion of a civic "pariah people"'.[9] Neither Nietzsche nor Weber referred to nature or race, so it would be completely inappropriate and misleading to speak here of anti-Semitism.

However, Nietzsche went further. Already at the time of the exile, it was religion that drove the national resistance struggle of the Jew. So, the mass was led by the type of priest Nietzsche saw as the last remnant of the dominant caste. The priest was, in his turn, cast into doubt by Christianity, similarly permeated by the anti-aristocratic spirit of Judaism. Thus, the foundations for the Reform-

---

9   Weber 1972, 240.

ation and later for the French Revolution were laid. These too were stages in the slave revolt, constantly fuelled by the slave morality *par excellence*. The argumentation ran the constant risk of slipping into naturalism, because of both the long, millennial duration of the historical processes to which it referred and the psychopathological and even physiological components Nietzsche identified in the degeneration he denounced.

And yet, up to this moment, one continued to move on a historical plane. However dominant the figure of the priest in Judaism, it already existed earlier. The Manu Code talked of 'a kind of human being, the priestly, that feels itself to be the norm, the climax, the highest expression of humankind' (XIII, 439). It was from here that one had to start: 'The development of the priestly state of the Jews is not original: they have got to know the pattern in Babylon, the scheme is Aryan.' The 'Semitic spirit of the New Testament', of which 'one speaks a lot nowadays', was therefore simply the 'priest' spirit, and 'this kind of 'Semitism', i.e., the priest spirit', could already be found 'in the Aryan code of the purest race', where it was manifested even more strongly than elsewhere (XIII, 386). Here, the polemic against biological anti-Semitism was evident. Lazare was wrong to speak of an 'anti-Christian anti-Semitism', and Overbeck was even more wrong to assume an anti-Semitism disguised as anti-Christianity. A true anti-Semite would never have been able to pen or subscribe to the declaration found in a fragment of the first months of 1888: 'The Aryan influence has corrupted the whole world' (XIII, 440). Did Nietzsche change his mind about the excellence of 'Aryan humanity'? That is not the point. The judgement is contained in a sketch for a kind of world history of the pernicious figure of the priest or the intellectual-priest.

But it was precisely on this point of the anti-Jewish polemic that a fatal turn took place. Even if the priest had an Aryan past, he found his ideal standpoint and unique role in that place from which ruling castes were absent or had disappeared, namely Judea. And here, subversion already arose among the priests, rather than among the prophets. At first glance, this was merely a further, modest backwards projection of an endless revolutionary cycle. In reality, now it was no longer a historically determined Judaism, albeit one that stretched over a very long period of time, but, ultimately, Judaism as such. The development of subversion and of Judaism coincided perfectly. There was also another, no less consequential novelty. The social bloc of subversion was in no way homogeneously constituted by Chandala but now displayed a significant internal stratification. A crude mass, incapable of independent will, was steered by a very sophisticated ruling caste that found its expression in the figure of the priest.

3   Revolution as Plot and the Role of Jewish Priests

What was the relationship between the fanaticised mass and the top? In other words, to what extent did the latter truly identify with the beliefs and values or negative values it diffused across the base? They were unambiguously hostile to life, they embodied and propagated nihilism, they blocked the natural selection process of society as well as the amputation of the degenerate and sick parts. Thus, they encouraged infection and hastened the destruction of the whole. What was the logic behind an action so clearly nefarious? Can we really believe that the intellectual-priests were merely credulous? On closer inspection, it turned out that 'a theologian, a priest, a pope, is not only wrong, it is a lie, – and he is not free to lie out of "innocence" or "ignorance" any more. The priest knows as well as anyone that there is no "God" any more, that there is no such thing as "sin", or the "redeemer", – that "free will" and the "moral world order" are *lies*' (AC 38 [34]). We were never to lose sight of the fact that the 'priest' 'consciously' promoted nihilistic destruction (AC, 8 [8–9]). It was not a case of a devastating error but of despicable duplicity. Take the Gospels. A 'psychologist' that read them carefully would have noticed right away that they were 'the opposite of naïve corruption'; on the contrary, they were 'refinement *par excellence*, they are psychological corruption raised to an art' (AC, 44 [40–1]). Nietzsche insisted on this point to the last: '[W]hat the priests want is precisely the degeneration of the whole, of humanity: that is why they preserve degenerates – this is the price of ruling over them' (EH, *Daybreak*, 2 [122]).

The dissolution and denial deliberately pursued were not an end in itself. Even in this case the will to power took effect. Think of the personality that first gave dogmatic and institutional form to 'Christianity'. 'To take this Paul (whose homeland was the centre of the Stoic enlightenment) as sincere' would have been naïve or stupid. If we observed this person with the penetration and clarity of a 'psychologist', we would have reached a quite different conclusion:

> Paul wanted the end, and consequently he wanted the means to it as well ... What he did not believe himself was believed by the idiots he threw his doctrines to. – What he needed was power; with Paul, the priests wanted to return to power, – he can only use ideas, doctrines, symbols that would tyrannize the masses and form the herds. – What was the only thing that Mohammed would later borrow from Christianity? Paul's invention, his method of priestly tyranny, of forming the herds.
>
> AC 42 [39]

And thus Jesus, this 'idiot' devoid of political ability, who preached 'the superiority over every feeling of *ressentiment*', was transformed into a figure 'in revolt against the order' and subjected to a political project that exuded *ressentiment* and a will to power animated only by *ressentiment* (AC, 40 [36]). This 'counterfeiter' Paul 'epitomizes a type that is the antithesis of the "bringer of glad tidings", the genius in hatred, in the vision of hatred, in the merciless logic of hatred' (AC 42 [38]).

This was quite different from the picture given by the fragment from the beginning of 1888, quoted at the start of the previous section. Here Christianity was a revolution, the Chandala uprising against the priest, against what little remained of the ruling class in the Jewish world, which had already become thoroughly plebeian. In the *Antichrist*, on the other hand, manipulation and conspiracy took the place of revolution: the Chandala was no longer the enemy of the priest but his unwitting instrument. And yet, in this context, both the one and the other were members of the same Jewish community, although they played very different roles.

But, in other passages, the switch from revolution to conspiracy was matched by another even more serious or dangerous switch. After emphasising the intrinsically Jewish character of Christianity, the *Genealogy of Morals* continued:

> Did Israel not reach the pinnacle of her sublime vengefulness via this very 'redeemer', this apparent opponent of and disperser of Israel? Is it not part of a secret black art of a truly grand politics of revenge, a far-sighted, subterranean revenge, slow to grip and calculating, that Israel had to denounce her actual instrument of revenge before all the world as a mortal enemy and nail him to the cross so that 'all the world', namely all Israel's enemies, could safely nibble at this bait? [...] At least it is certain that *sub hoc signo* Israel, with its revenge and revaluation of all former values, has triumphed repeatedly over all other ideals, all nobler ideals.
>
> GM, I, 8 [18–19]

With Christianity, a religion emerged that, despite its novelty and apparent hostility to Jewish priests, was consciously used by the latter for purposes that could not be revealed. Here the main figure and victim of the plot referred to two different communities. It was no longer Paul manipulating Jesus, no longer the Jewish priest manipulating the idiotic Jew or the Chandala; here it was Israel as such that took revenge on the Gentiles or 'the whole world'. How was one to characterise a people with such special features? This was a problem Nietzsche struggled with. Starting with the defeat and exile, it was at all

events a Chandala-people. But even this definition was not entirely satisfactory. One was dealing with Chandala or those whose lives have turned out badly
of a particular type, with the 'rebels among those whose lives have turned out
badly' (XIII, 438). To be more precise, one was dealing with the instigators of
the rising, with the priest-ideologists of subversion. On another occasion, the
Jews appeared 'as a kind of Chandala race, which learns from its masters the
principles by which the priesthood becomes master and organizes a people'
(B, III, 5, 325). Although Nietzsche's thinking on this question underwent oscillations, thought experiments and corrections, the figure of the priest tended
to take an increasingly central part in the definition of Judaism. Israel was no
longer only the place where, for well-defined historical reasons, the priest had
achieved an eminence unknown elsewhere, but became more and more the
'priestly people' as such. This is confirmed by a further passage from the *Genealogy of Morals*:

> Nothing that has been done on earth against 'the noble', 'the mighty', 'the
> masters' and 'the rulers', is worth mentioning compared with what the
> Jews have done against them: the Jews, that priestly people, which in the
> last resort was able to gain satisfaction from its enemies and conquer-
> ors only through a radical revaluation of their values, that is, through
> an act of the most deliberate revenge [*durch einen Akt der geistigsten
> Rache*].
>
> GM, I, 7 [17]

Once the Jews had been configured as the priestly people, the conscious lying
and the dark will to power of priests became the conscious lying and dark will
to power of Jews. Now everything became clearer. First, one was to bear in
mind that the preaching of nothingness (i.e., of that which was beyond morality, of the 'ethical world order') was aimed at quenching an inordinate thirst
for power: 'Morality is the best way of leading people around by the nose!'
(AC 44 [41–2]). And again 'When theologians use the "conscience" [*Gewissen*]
of princes (*or* peoples –) to reach out for power [*Macht*], let us be very clear
about what is really taking place: the will to an end, the nihilistic will willing
power ...' (AC, 9 [8–9]). Second, one was not to lose sight of who it was that
preached morality and humility and put on the 'airs of modesty': it was 'the
most disastrous type of megalomania the world has ever seen', 'the highly conscious conceit of being chosen'. The latter expression obviously referred to the
Jews, explicitly named at the end of the paragraph: the secret directors of this
enactment of the religion of modesty, humility and resignation were priests or
'superlative little Jews', even if they claimed to be Christians (AC, 44 [42]).

We have seen that in interpreting Christianity, the category of revolution was replaced by the categories of manipulation and conspiracy; now the 'wicked conspiracy [*Verschwörung*] [...] of those that suffer against those that are successful and victorious' (GM III, 14 [90]) tended to become the conspiracy of the wretched and the Chandala, led by priest-ideologues. This also applied to the Reformation: by defeating the Renaissance, this plebeian movement had breathed new life into the 'new, Judaic Rome built over' the ancient pagan Rome, that 'ecumenical synagogue' that called itself Church (GM, I, 16 [33]). Similar considerations applied to the French Revolution, which sanctiond a further triumph of 'Judea' (*supra*, 15 § 2).

The representation of revolution as a conspiracy with more or less significant participation or leadership by Jews was widespread in the culture of the time. It seems this theme as reinterpreted and radicalised by Nietzsche, to make it valid for the entire revolutionary cycle, with an extreme emphasis of the role of the Jews. Far beyond the French Revolution, it was now the long cycle of subversion as a whole that practically coincided with an equally long cycle of Jewish conspiracy. The protagonist of a sort of archetypal plot was Paul, 'the Jew, the wandering Jew *par excellence*' (AC, 58 [61]), an 'appalling fraud' (AC, 45 [43]), who sprang into action with the 'logical cynicism of a Rabbi' (AC, 44 [40]). Here we come up against a dissembler of modesty and humility, actually motivated by an unquenchable thirst for power. But beyond this or that personality, it is worth reading the Bible:

> The pretence [*Selbstverstellung*] at 'holiness' is conducted with a talent bordering on genius (no book or person has ever come close), this counterfeiting of words and gestures as an art form is not some one-off, accidental talent, some exception of nature. It is part of the race. [...] [T]hat is not only tradition, it is endowment: only as endowment would it act like nature. (AC, 44 [41].)

Paul's modes of action were illuminating. They allowed us to draw a general conclusion:

> Looked at psychologically, Jews are the people with the toughest life force; when transplanted into impossible conditions they took sides with all the instincts of decadence, and they did this freely and out of the most profoundly shrewd sense of self-preservation – not because they were dominated by these instincts, but rather because they sensed that these instincts had a power that can be used to prevail against 'the world'. The Jews are the opposite of decadents: they had to *act* like decadents to the

point of illusion, they knew, with a *non plus ultra* of theatrical genius, how to put themselves at the forefront of all movements of decadence (– like the Christianity of *Paul* –) so they can make these movements into something stronger than any yes-saying defenders of life. For the type of person that wields power inside Judaism and Christianity, a *priestly* type, decadence is only a means: this type of person has a life interest in making humanity sick.

AC 24 [21]

At this point, the entire history of the West became an endless conspiracy: the ghettos of society, those whose lives had turned out badly, the outcasts, the sick incapable of self-will, were expertly manipulated by a race that considered itself chosen and, by virtue of its chosen status, had developed a boundless desire to dominate, to which end it was even ready to sacrifice the very existence of society.

4   Critique of Christianity, 'Jewish Nietzscheanism' and Nietzsche's Contribution to the Theory of the Jewish Conspiracy

We can now try to explain one of the paradoxes that mark Nietzsche's history of effects. On the one hand, substantial sectors of Jewish culture looked with interest and sympathy on a philosopher that so strongly denounced (plebeian) anti-Semitism and, at least in his later years, expressed his admiration for big Jewish capital. On more strictly cultural and religious grounds, Nietzsche's contrasting of the Old and New Testaments and, in particular, certain topics in his anti-Christian polemic could not but find a sympathetic echo: 'God gave his son to forgive sins, as a sacrifice. [...] The guilt sacrifice, and in fact in its most revolting, barbaric form, the sacrifice of the innocent for the sins of the guilty! What gruesome paganism [*schauderhaftes Heidenthum*]!' (AC, 41 [37]). On another occasion Nietzsche defined himself as a 'pagan' (XIII, 487); moreover, the *Antichrist* also spoke positively about paganism in a later aphorism: '[A] pagan is anyone who says yes to life' (AC, 55 [56]). But in the passage criticising the Christian scapegoat theme, the value judgement was reversed. The same is true of similar passages denouncing Paul as the great and calamitous theorist of 'a pagan doctrine of the mysteries' that needed a 'sacrificial victim', a 'bloody phantasmagoria (think of the "drinking of the blood" in the Eucharistic rites). Paul is the main figure of this fall or relapse into "full paganism", with an instinct for the needs of non-Jews', the Gentiles (XIII, 107–9). Nietzsche's description of triumphant Christianity as vulgar paganism seemed to echo a traditional

theme of Judaism's anti-Christian polemic. It is not impossible that this representation was influenced by the relations Nietzsche maintained throughout
his life with friends and acquaintances of Jewish origin (Rée, Paneth, Brandes).
If one adds to this the sympathetic reinterpretation of 'circumcision' among
Jews and Arabs as a warrior and virile rite (XIII, 112–3) as well as the assertion
of the 'relative rationality' of 'Judaism' and of the (Judaising) 'oldest Christianity' compared to Pauline Christianity, steeped in 'superstition' and the need for
'miracles' (XIII, 116–17) – if one bears all this in mind, it is understandable that
Nietzsche's philosophy was hailed as a healthy counterpoint to Christian apologetics, which for centuries had persecuted, stifled, and oppressed the Jews.
This incessant campaign of propaganda against and denigration of Judaism
left important traces even among those that refused to convert; and for an
understanding of the plummeting loss of self-esteem, Nietzsche again provided
important keys (*infra*, 30 § 4). In this way, a significant wave of 'Jewish Nietzscheanism' took shape.[10]

For the theorist of aristocratic radicalism, Christianity was in truth merely
a more advanced stage and therefore an even more repugnant manifestation
of the long cycle of subversion that at all events had originated with the Old
Testament (even if only with its post-exilic parts). And that was not yet all.

In anti-Semitic publications of the time, the Jews were the people *par excellence* of subversion, also because they challenged or erased the dividing line
between superior and inferior races, between masters and servants. When Marr
spoke to the Jews, this 'mongrel race [*Mischlingsvolk*]' of Egyptian and African
origin, he addressed them in these terms: 'That Negro blood also managed to
smuggle itself into your stock you will not deny.' As we have seen, for Nietzsche
in his final years, the Jews were a Chandala people: the Chandala was also, in a
way, a mongrel, being the child of a *sudra* or servant and a woman of the Brahmin caste. It is true the philosopher recommended the marital and eugenic
merging of the Jewish and Prussian-German elites. But this theme could be
found even in Marr, who exhorted not just the upper classes but Jews in general as follows: thanks to true 'emancipation', i.e., 'assimilation with your fellow
citizens in the West', which had to be total at all levels, cultural and religious as
well as eugenic and racial, you could achieve the 'ennoblement of your people,
which will remain untouched by Copts, Moors, Chaldeans, Babylonians, Assyr-
ians and Negro blood'.[11] To grasp the real difference between Nietzsche and
the patriarch of anti-Semitism, it is necessary to bear in mind once again the

---

10   Cf. Stegmaier/Krochmalnik 1997.
11   Marr 1862, 46, 51.

distinction between transversal and horizontal racialisation. In his efforts to draw a line between blacks and whites, between the West and the colonial peoples, Marr confronted the Jews in general with the threatening demand that they give up their history and identity in all respects. Nietzsche, on the other hand, emphasised the gulf between masters and servants, and called on the upper layers of Judaism to take a clear distance from all that was servile and ignoble in their history: if they consciously redefined themselves as masters, they could confidently and usefully appeal to the pages of the Old Testament that described and celebrated the conquest of Canaan; the important thing was they were tp break off all relations with the other two figures of Judaism, those connected with the slave revolt.

So, the opposition between the patriarch of anti-Semitism and the theorist of aristocratic radicalism clearly remained. However, when the late Nietzsche described Jews as a people of priests involved in an obscure and evil power plan and even capable of using Christians as a manoeuvre mass for the Judaisation of the world, decidedly disquieting tones are heard. No wonder Nordau, an interpreter of Jewish origin and a prominent figure in the nascent Zionist movement, writing at the end of the nineteenth century, was suspicious of these formulations. Where would a theory stop that saw in the presumed ideological and political triumph of 'Israel' or the 'Jewish people' the result of a 'plan', an operation 'planned, deliberate and lucidly executed', a Jewish 'act of revenge, knowing and intentional'?[12]

5   From the Revolution as Conspiracy to the Jew as Revolutionary Virus

Nordau's suspicions were not ungrounded. There can be no doubt the view he criticised in Nietzsche was eventually taken over and made absolute by the Nazis. Of course, this could only happen with grotesque adjustments and vulgarisations: the 'idiot' Jesus manipulated by Paul from within the same community had become the Aryan Jesus or at least semi-Aryan Jesus, manipulated by a character presented more as a bearer of Jewish blood than as a priest. And yet, it is worth thinking about the crime of which Hitler accused Paul: he used the preaching of Jesus, as we shall see in the next section, to enact an infamous slave revolt against the best, against the legitimate rulers. It follows: 'The religion fabricated by Paul, from then on is called Christianity, is

---

12   Nordau n.d., Vol. 2, 314, 320.

nothing more than communism!' On hearing this, Bormann, the Secretary, added with the Führer's consent: 'Everywhere the Jews have raised the populace against the ruling class. Everywhere they aroused discontent against existing conditions, because only from the seed of this discontent could harvest come.'[13]

Evidently there were not only the similarities with the late Nietzsche but full consonance between the two discourses. Is this a further confirmation of the approach I have already rejected, which looks for an immediate relationship between the philosopher and the Third Reich and draws a direct line of continuity from the one to the other? Such is not the issue. And not just because Nietzsche did not refer to blood and, as we have seen, traces a history of the sinister figure of the priest that, despite everything, went beyond the scope of Judaism. There is a deeper reason: the events described here, which must now be analysed further, took place not only within Germany.

One can start with a comment by Engels in 1851: 'The times of that superstition which attributed revolutions to the ill-will of a few agitators' are long gone.[14] In putting this argument, Engels was wrong or deceiving himself. The vision he thought dead and buried evinced a considerable and even enhanced vitality. In these years, more and more people accepted a psychopathological explanation or even diagnosis of revolution, together with the ensuing indictment of the abstract, visionary and neurotic intellectual as the real representative of the turmoil raging in the West. According to Burke, this intellectual was a vehicle of the ideological 'intoxication' on the other side of the English Channel.[15] In France, one revolution followed the other. Tocqueville identified the bearer of the 'revolutionary sickness', the 'permanent sickness', the 'virus of a new and unknown species' that continued to rage, in a handful of agitators: 'We are always dealing with the same men, although the circumstances change', with a sort of 'new race [race nouvelle]'.[16]

The term used here is significant. Also during this period, Schopenhauer was formulating the thesis that 'innate character' not only had its 'originality and unchangeability' but was also so hereditary that one could effortlessly reconstruct the 'family tree' of criminals and rebels.[17] One might say the French liberal was tempted to reconstruct the family tree of the subjects, of the bearers of the fatal revolutionary sickness: if one could reconstruct one for idiots, imbe-

13   Hitler 1980, 412 (30 November 1944).
14   Marx and Engels 1975 ff., 11, 5.
15   Burke 1926, Vol. 7, 135.
16   Tocqueville 1951 ff., Vol. 2, half-vol. 2, 348 f. and Vol. 13, half-vol. 2, 337.
17   Schopenhauer 1976–82b, 767, 666.

ciles and defectives of all kinds, why not also for these crazy and sick subversive intellectuals? Tocqueville's diagnosis could already be found in Constant: 'Cold in their delirium', subversive intellectuals, these *'jongleurs de sédition'*, undermined not only a given society but 'the very foundations of the social order'. They were 'beings of an unknown species [*êtres d'une espèce inconnue*]', they even formed a 'new race [*race nouvelle*]', a 'detestable race [*détestable race*]'.[18] In a crescendo, the psychopathological type of explanation tended to pass over onto the anthropological and racial plane (the shift from the category of *espèce* to that of race is symptomatic).

One can say that, since 1789, Western culture had been engaged in a breathless search: once one had equated revolution and above all the endless revolutionary cycle with a sickness, it is a question of identifying the social, anthropological and ethnic vehicle of its transmission, the pathogen that attacked a healthy social organism and prevents it from functioning properly and regularly. With regard to the ethnic characteristics of this transmitter, the Jews had naturally, as early as 1789, been the first to be suspected or accused: their religion, culture, history, 'nationality', their internal cohesion and international ramification, all pointed to their being the people of subversion. However, it is interesting to note that there was no lack of attempts to attribute the revolutionary virus to another ethnic group. Le Bon thundered against 'those neurotic, frantic, semi-alienated people living on the edge of madness', the misfit intellectuals 'ready for any revolution, whatever its leaders and purposes',[19] and he further pointed out that they could be found in particular 'among the Latin peoples': it was here, above all, that 'the Jacobins of all ages' could be found.[20] A few decades later, in 1925, a document of the US army, taking up a theme already long present in American ideology, saw 'mass psychology' as embodied in blacks: partly because of the 'reduced capacity of the skull', they were a hotbed of unrest, turmoil and frenzy.[21]

After various attempts and oscillations, the subversive race was eventually identified with the Jews. Even if Nietzsche was, basically, engaging in historical and social analysis, he played an essential role in identifying the Jew with *homo ideologicus* as such. In that respect, it is unimportant that he described rampant subversion as a process of 'intoxication', 'poisoning' and even 'blood-poisoning' (GM, I, 9 [19]). These are metaphors with which we are already familiar from the traditional liberal and conservative critique of revolution and revolutionary

18   In Guillemin 1958, 13 f., 84, 194; Constant 1988, 44.
19   Le Bon 1982, 83, 65; Le Bon 1928, 120, 77.
20   Le Bon 1982, 33 f.; Le Bon 1928, 39.
21   Daniels 1997, 127 f.

intellectuality; we have seen the former in Burke; the latter, with its variations, is not so very different from Tocqueville's metaphor of the virus, of the pathogen that attacks a healthy organism and endangers its condition. Only, now the bearer of this process of intoxication and poisoning, as a result of which 'everything is being made appreciably Jewish, Christian or plebeian', was to be found uniquely among the Jews (GM, I, 9 [19]).

According to the *Gay Science*, they were 'as it were a world-historical institution for breeding actors' that staged moral outrage to promote subversion (*supra*, 18 § 4). The writings of Nietzsche's last years and months went even further. 'That parasitical type of human, priests, who, with their morality, have lied themselves into the position of determining values, – that see Christian morality as their means of wielding power' referred above all to Jews (EH, Why I am a destiny, 7 [149]). The priest-ideologue, the *homo ideologicus*, artificially stimulated subversion to extend his rule: the mob in the struggle against the aristocrats was the manoeuvre mass of a sinister figure with a distinct ethnic basis. While rejecting biological anti-Semitism, Nietzsche made an essential contribution to the ethnicisation of the ideological virus, a process that later, in the Third Reich, experienced its tragic fulfilment.

Here too, the ideological process extends far beyond Germany. Regarding the *instrumentum vocale*, we have seen how it passed from a transversal racialisation, beyond the colonial peoples, that targeted the wretched and the malformed of all countries, to a horizontal racialisation that identified the slave caste or race in Eastern Europe. Similarly, in the case of *homo ideologicus*, it passed from a transversal racialisation that targeted an 'unknown species' and a 'new' and 'detestable' race that did not coincide with one nation or one particular ethnic group to a horizontal racialisation that uniquely identified the Jew as the virus or bacillus of the 'revolutionary sickness'. In both cases, despite the strong elements of discontinuity that always characterised an ideological process in the transition from one historical epoch to another, Nietzsche's influence was undeniable, although largely indirect.

6   Hitler and Rosenberg as Interpreters of Nietzsche and
       Nietzscheanism

At this point, it might be useful to examine more generally the role of Nietzscheanism in Nazism. One can go in search of aphorisms or isolated passages quoted in the guise of proverbs, for example, when Hitler, in November 1942, believing he had conquered Stalingrad despite the initial difficulties, referred to the 'word' of a 'great philosopher' and paraphrased Nietzsche: 'What does not kill us makes us stronger' (XII, 506).[22] Similarly, Goebbels, to justify his belief that brutality was not to allow itself to be hampered by 'grandiloquent phrases of civilization', by now 'vacuous and empty': 'What must fall, falls – and our only task is to give it a push.'[23] Clearly, this last sentence was a quote from *Zarathustra* (*supra*, 19 §3), a work of which the Nazi chief,[24] who bragged of reading Nietzsche 'until late at night',[25] was apparently fond.

Even though this sort of exploitation is not without interest politically, one should rather focus on the problem of Nietzsche's presence in Nazism by analysing the movement's worldview, with particular reference to two of its most important representatives, Rosenberg and Hitler, the ideologist or aspiring ideologist and the Führer of the Third Reich. How can one summarise their *Weltanschauung*?

The starting point must be the denunciation of the revolutionary cycle then rampant in the West, which threatened culture as such. When had 'nihilism', the 'proletarian-nihilistic political current', the enemy of all hierarchy and culture, started to spread?[26] One should begin by noting that not only the overall vision but even some significant details echoed and popularised Nietzsche. The argument was made that symptoms of decadence had already become manifest in Greece. If 'the great Theognis complains that money mixes the blood of the noble and the ignoble',[27] thus confirming the aristocracy of nature and the mythical element of life, the picture changed radically with 'late Hellenistic rationalism';[28] at this point, 'Socrates was able to preach the madness that virtue is teachable, teachable for all people.'[29] With the crisis of authentic Hellenism, 'slaves from all parts of the world cry out for "freedom"'.[30]

But the real catastrophe began with Christianity, or, more precisely, with Paul of Tarsus. Certainly, Jesus was sometimes called an Aryan or semi-Aryan (see above, 24, §7), hostile to 'Jewish egoism and materialism'[31] – a reprisal of themes favoured by Wagner. On the other hand a rhetorical question was asked in relation to Christianity that brought us back to Nietzsche: 'Do we need a

---

22   In Ruge/Schumann 1977, 129.
23   Goebbels 1991b, Vol. 2, 62 f.
24   Goebbels 1991a, 911.
25   Reuth 1991, 34 f., 65.
26   Rosenberg 1937a, 77, 71.
27   Rosenberg 1937a, 51.
28   Rosenberg 1937a, 37.
29   Rosenberg 1937a, 78.
30   Rosenberg 1937a, 51.
31   Hitler 1980, 412 f. (30 November 1944).

fairy tale invented by Jews? What interest can we have in the story of a few lousy Jews and epileptics?'[32] However, with Paul the doctrine of Jesus became 'the leading concept of the lesser races, of the slaves, of the oppressed, of those poor in money and goods, against the ruling class, against the superior race, against the oppressors'.[33] Now the new religion engaged itself and organised the 'incitement of the mob' and succeeded in mobilising 'an enormous mass of uprooted people', 'the underworld'.[34] They saw in Jesus the longed for 'leader and liberator of the slaves'; from here on, Paul began, with 'indomitable fanaticism', to set in motion the 'international world revolution against the Roman Empire'.[35]

Decadence was frightening not just at the political level but also at the actual cultural level. Even the meaning of life withered and degenerated. There could be no doubt that the 'philosophy' of classical antiquity was incomparably superior to the narrow-mindedness of Christianity: 'One thing is certain, if a Greek entered the Parthenon and saw Jupiter there: the divine image makes a different impression from that of a contorted Christ.'[36]

Thus, a disastrous cycle was set in motion. For Nietzsche, it led to the French Revolution and the socialist movement of his own time, but now it experienced a further extension. As a result of Christian or Jewish-Christian agitation, 'Rome was Bolshevized', or at least experienced the victory of a 'pre-Bolshevism'. A clear line of continuity led from 'Christianity' to 'communism'.[37] There could be no doubt: 'Pure Christianity [...] is naked Bolshevism in metaphysical dress'; nihilism thus reached its climax and announced 'the annihilation of humankind'.[38]

As an expression of nihilism, Christianity was synonymous with sickness and degeneration. It 'is an invention of sick brains'. It would be necessary sooner or later 'to put an end to it'.[39] Luckily, there were already promising signs of an imminent end to the cycle: it was 'the breakdown of Christianity that we are experiencing'; yes, 'the time in which we live will undoubtedly see the end of the Christian sickness'.[40] But it was not a question of replacing it with the atheism of the freethinkers or the Marxists: one was not to be 'purely negative',

---

32   Hitler 1980, 338 (11 August 1942).
33   Hitler 1980, 413 (30 November 1944).
34   Hitler 1980, 98, 150 (21 October 1941 and 13 December 1941).
35   Rosenberg 1937a, 74 f.
36   Hitler 1980, 98, 288 (21 October 1941 and 20–21 February 1942).
37   Hitler 1980, 98, 150, 413 (21 October, 13 December 1941 and 30 November 1944).
38   Hitler 1980, 152 (14 December 1941).
39   Hitler 1980, 150, 338 (13 December 1941 and 11 August 1942).
40   Hitler 1980, 297, 303 (26 and 27 February 1942).

like the 'Russians', in the course of the necessary 'struggle against the church'. Christianity was particularly pernicious because it objectively stimulated atheism: it qas 'an outrage against all that is divine'.[41]

If it is possible to eradicate subversion once and for all, it is also possible to recover the world overwhelmed by the religiously inspired slave revolt and modern decadence. Naturally, one was to take note of the difficulties of such an undertaking: 'Christianity has systematically undertaken to eliminate the spiritual labours of ancient culture. [...] We are perhaps almost entirely unfamiliar with the most precious spiritual treasures of mankind. Who can know what was in there?' It was also necessary to rewrite history, countering the falsifications of the victors, or rather of the momentary victors: 'It would be better to speak of "the traitor Constantine" and "Julian the faithful" instead of Constantine the Great and Julian the Apostate.'[42]

Since Christianity was 'a religion permeated with servile fervour [*Knechtseligkeit*]', contempt, and a nihilistic rage against the flesh and the world, it was much worse than the other great religions.[43] Unquestionably superior was Islam: 'The Arab era [...] was the golden age of Spain, the most cultured. Then came the era of persecution, which began again and again.'[44] Islamic culture brought about in Spain a splendid flowering of culture and a 'colossal chivalry', and was also 'something infinitely aristocratic [*vornehm*]'. Unfortunately, the victory of Charles Martel blocked the way to the penetration of Europe by a religion centred on the 'rewarding of heroism', and sealed the victory of Christianity and the 'Jewish world'.[45] This reminds one of Nietzsche's position in the *Antichrist*: 'In itself, there really should not be any choice between Islam and Christianity, any more than between Arabs and Jews' (AC, 60 [64]).

Hitler similarly appreciated Shintoism: 'The religion of the Japanese is first and foremost the worship of heroes.' Christians, on the other hand, honoured the saints, who 'lie on a bed of thorns instead of responding to the smile of beautiful girls'. The conclusion: 'There is something unhealthy about Christianity.'[46] As in Nietzsche, so too in the political movement that claimed to follow him the rehabilitation of the flesh and of the world was closely intertwined

41   Hitler 1980, 286, 150 (20–21 February 1942 and 13 December 1941).
42   Hitler 1980, 107, 236 (25 October 1941 and 27 January 1942).
43   Rosenberg 1937a, 76.
44   Hitler 1980, 323 (1 August 1942).
45   Hitler 1980, 370 (29 August 1942).
46   Hitler 1989, 210 (9 April 1942).

with the rehabilitation of the *polemos* as the essence of life. With a clear reference to Heraclitus, rebadged for the occasion as 'a great military philosopher', Hitler stressed that 'struggle and therefore war was the father of all things.'[47]

Nietzsche's presence in this worldview is undeniable. Hitler venerated him so unconditionally that he even resumed themes dating back to the period of the philosopher's 'Enlightenment'. It was not just a question of condemning the Inquisition and the witch-hunt: 'Near Wurzburg there are villages where literally all the women were burned.'[48] He also reprised themes that put Luther and the Reformation in a decidedly negative light: 'Basically, we should be grateful to the Jesuits. [...] In opposition to Luther's efforts to bring back the already secularized high clergy to mysticism, Jesuitism appealed to sensual joy!'[49]

This theme is further reinforced:

> I think I could have got on with the popes of the Renaissance. [...] A pope, even a criminal, who protects great artists and spreads beauty around himself is more likeable than a Protestant minister drinking at the poisoned source.[50]

The propaganda machine of the Third Reich was mostly devoted to celebrating the superiority of Nordic people. However, Hitler had no problem in appropriating Nietzsche's view that the North, with its unfavourable climate, was the elective homeland of the fanaticism and anti-nature of Christianity:

> Fanaticism is a matter of climate – for Protestantism too burned its witches at the stake. In Italy, there was none of that. Southerners treat the things of faith more lightly. Even the French behave in an easy-going way in church. With us, however, we risk being noticed if we don't kneel down.[51]

And further:

> We now have the misfortune to be tied to a religion that denies all the joys of the senses. In this regard, the hypocrisy of the Protestants is even

---

47   Hitler 1989, 491 (Adolf Hitler's secret speech of 30 May 1942).
48   Hitler 1980, 262 (3–4 February 1942).
49   Hitler 1980, 42 (21–22 July 1941).
50   Hitler 1980, 152 (14 December 1941).
51   Hitler 1980, 42 (21–22 July 1941).

worse than that of the Catholics. Each church reacts according to its own nature; but in this respect, Protestantism has the warmth of an iceberg.[52]

Even the details betray Nietzsche's influence. The representation of Pontius Pilate as 'a Roman so superior to the Jews around him racially and in terms of intelligence that he stood out like a rock in the midst of a heap of manure' echoes the *Antichrist* (*infra*, 28 § 4).[53] In *The Will to Power*, Hitler could read the following about the Christian heaven: 'Have you ever noticed that in heaven there are no interesting men? ... This, just to give a nod to the ladies, about the best place to find salvation' (WZM, § 871 = XIII, 72–3). In his dinner conversations, the Führer joked about there being only 'halleluiahs and nothing more than palm leaves, babies, and old people' in the other world so coveted by Christians.[54] In *The Will to Power* (§ 796 = XII, 118–19), Hitler could read about the glorification of 'works of art' as 'body, organization', the case not just with the 'Prussian officer corps' but also with the 'order of the Jesuits'. Again, when praising the SS: 'It was with Himmler that the SS became this extraordinary militia, devoted to an idea, faithful unto death. In Himmler I see our Ignatius of Loyola.'[55]

Still following Nietzsche or trying to echo his thinking, Hitler also stressed the catastrophic role the myth of good nature played in revolutionary upheavals. One was only to think of the Russians: 'This will to return to a state of nature is evident in their revolutions.' And these revolutions continued to mean 'nihilism'.[56]

Finally, Hitler repeated the accusations levelled by Nietzsche at the Communards. The behaviour attributed to them was inserted by Hitler into a millennial revolutionary-nihilistic cycle that had to be destroyed once and for all if civilisation, culture and art were to be saved: 'I am sure that Nero never burned Rome. It was the Christian-Bolsheviks, just like the Commune set fire to Paris in 1871 and the Communists burned down the Reichstag in 1933.'[57]

---

52   Hitler 1980, 149 (1–2 December 1941).
53   Hitler 1989, 422 (5 July 1942).
54   Hitler 1980, 150 (13 December 1941).
55   Hitler 1980, 169 (3–4 January 1942).
56   Hitler 1980, 39 (5 July 1941).
57   Hitler 1980, 107 (25 October 1941).

7   *Übermensch, Untermensch* and the Nominalistic Deconstruction of
     the Concept of Humanity

To put an end to egalitarian subversion, it was necessary to reaffirm 'the aristocratic underlying thought of nature', which requires the 'victory of the better
and stronger' and the 'subjugation of the worse and the weaker'.[58] Here we
come up against the recurring theme of social Darwinism, which goes far beyond Nietzsche or Germany. On the other hand, the fear that the worst, by taking
advantage of certain circumstances, could win the upper hand seemed to refer
particularly to Nietzsche. Since war required the sacrifice of the noblest, of
those that despised cowardice and flight, it could bring about a sort of selection in reverse. That is why immediate intervention was needed: 'If to offset
such losses I do not ruthlessly exterminate the mob, one day the situation could
become serious.'[59]

    It was not just a question of striking relentlessly at those dodging the war
effort. Selection in reverse also had to be blocked by ensuring that 'only those
physically healthy and racially unobjectionable can marry'.[60] The eugenic
measures Nietzsche, following Galton, recommended, and in harmony with
the thinking of a number of other authors, were included as part of a eugenics programme summarised as follows in *Mein Kampf*: A state attentive to the
laws of evolution and that did not allow itself to be impeded by false compassion

> must ensure that only those that are healthy produce children. [...] It
> must put the most modern medical instruments at the service of this
> realization. It must declare unfit for procreation all those visibly ill and
> hereditarily defective, and also put this into practice.[61]

In this case, an appeal to compassion was, more than ever, pointless. On the
other hand, this sentiment so often invoked wrongly referred to a human 'species', for the latter was constructed by means of artificially and violently bringing into line individuals and above all peoples separated from one another by
an abyss. The main target of the Nazi polemic was, together with the revolutionary cycle, the idea of a humanity as subject of a world history inspired by
a universal aspiration towards something better, all the more so if this pro-

---

58   Hitler 1939b, 421.
59   Hitler 1980, 349 (20 August 1942).
60   Hitler 1989, 240 (24 April 1942).
61   Hitler 1939b, 446 f.; cf. Lifton 1988, 29 f.

gress was understood in the sense of an increase in general well-being and material goods. Rosenberg's contempt for 'materialistic historicism [*materialistischer Historizismus*]'[62] was boundless, and he tirelessly mocked the 'sense of world history',[63] the 'dogma of a supposedly "general development of humankind"'.[64] The subject of this imaginary process, 'humanity', which had taken the place of God in the Jewish-Christian tradition, was mythical.[65] According to Rosenberg, a vision that sought to drown the particular value of individuals and races in 'the stream of supposed progress' had a dangerously egalitarian potential.[66] The transition from transversal to a predominantly horizontal racialisation is clear, and this too implies a significant difference from the theorist of aristocratic radicalism; but just as clear is the ability of the Nazis to capitalise on the nominalist deconstruction of the concept of the human being.

Finally, Nietzsche played an important role in the development of some central categories of Nazi ideological discourse. This is immediately evident with regard to the explicitly Nietzschean concepts of *Herren-Rasse* or *herrschaftliche Rasse* (XII, 426 and GM, I, 5 [14–15]; XIII, 18), attacked by contemporaries concerned about the serious political implications of this opposition of 'master race' and 'slave race'.[67] Far more complex is the history of another particularly pernicious category of Nazi ideological discourse, that of the *Untermensch*, which is hard to separate from that of *Übermensch*: they are constituents of a single conceptual dichotomy.

But this is a particularly enlightening example to demonstrate that the alternative to the hermeneutics of innocence cannot consist in identifying Nietzsche with the Third Reich. Its linguistic-ideological history is surprising and highly informative. Rosenberg expressed his admiration for the American Lothrop Stoddard, who first coined the category of *Untermensch* ('under man' in the original English). The term appeared as the subtitle of a book published in the United States in 1922 and translated into German three years later.[68] It should be added that the American author quoted here had the opportunity to study in Germany for a year and a half.[69] Both Stoddard and his Ger-

---

62   Rosenberg 1937a, 237.
63   Rosenberg 1937a, 675.
64   Rosenberg 1937a, 40.
65   Rosenberg 1937a, 127.
66   Rosenberg 1937a, 690.
67   Nordau n.d., Vol. 2, 311 and 313; Stein 1893, 73, 77.
68   Rosenberg 1937a, 214; Stoddard 1984.
69   Heise 1925, 4.

man translator appear to have heard of Nietzsche, at least superficially. That much is apparent from the polemic against the 'fetish' or the 'idol [*Götze*]' of 'democracy', the evocation of a 'new aristocracy' or a 'new nobility [*Neu-Adel*]', and the admiration for Theognis and his battle against marriages between the nobility and the common people.[70] Finally, it is clear from the tribute paid to Galton and eugenics, thanks to which it was now supposedly possible to block the procreation of the worst. However, the American author was concerned to distinguish the 'sterilization' he recommended (in the meantime, vasectomy had been invented) from the far more brutal 'castration'. And yet, in order to 'make impossible social breakdowns', an even more radical measure was to be considered, the 'elimination' of the sick or the irredeemably degenerate.[71] Just like Nietzsche, Stoddard too tasked the new science with making a powerful contribution to defending culture, by blocking the reproduction of the under man or *Untermensch* and favouring the development of a 'super race' or a 'super-species [*Überart*]' – here, the German translation borrowed a term already used by Zarathustra (*supra*, 20 §1). This figure of Nietzsche's (he as expressly cited) may have been 'splendid' but unfortunately rested on an extremely broad and indiscriminately 'servile' foundation.[72] Lothrop Stoddard inclined more to a transversal than to a horizontal racialisation, aimed domestically at the blacks and internationally at the colonial peoples and Russian-Bolshevik barbarians.

So, the differences from Nietzsche are clear. Nevertheless, the latter had, through his nominalist deconstruction of the concept of humanity and his theory of the 'overman', in certain respects inspired the theory of the *Untermensch*. On the history of the word, it may be interesting to note that it made its appearance at the end of the nineteenth century. In his polemic against Nietzsche, Nordau argued that, because of his claim to reduce the mass of people to simple tools and because of the brutality to which he gave vent, the *Übermensch* actually showed him to be an *Untermensch*.[73] The author of this criticism was known to Lothrop Stoddard,[74] who of course gave the term *Untermensch* a quite different meaning. This is confirmed by the complexity of the linguistic-ideological history and the unsustainability of a theory that seeks to explain Nazi ideology as a diabolically German *Sonderweg*. A key category of Nazi ideological discourse was elaborated by an American, in dialogue with Nietzsche

---

70   Stoddard 1984, 265, 237 ff., 36 f.
71   Stoddard 1984, 42, 249 and fn., 253.
72   Stoddard 1984, 262.
73   Nordau n.d., Vol. 2, 328.
74   Stoddard 1925, 85, fn.

but, at the same time, proud of having been eulogised by two presidents of the United States, Harding and Hoover.[75]

But this matter also confirms the lack of historical understanding of the usual hermeneutics of innocence. Let us return to Hitler. Even his language is significant: while Christianity honoured as 'saints' those that negated life,[76] now it was a question of restoring the natural aristocratic order and putting an end to this deadly inversion. Perhaps it is exaggerated to say, as a recent study on the Third Reich does, that Hitler used his stay in prison to carry out a 'systematic reading' of Nietzsche, among other authors.[77] However, it is worth noting that another recent and very authoritative study maintains the philosopher took first place on the Führer's reading list.[78] But here, I have sought, on the basis of the methodology already set out, to discover above all the sociopolitical history of certain ideological themes and the elements of continuity and discontinuity that characterise them, rather than concentrate on a direct interpretation of a relationship formed between two individual people.

8   'Anti-Germanism' and 'Anti-Semitism'

We have already seen how Chamberlain regarded the Slavs as members of the higher Germanic race. But that did not stop him later becoming amenable to a party that unleashed a war of extermination against the Slavic *Untermenschen* of Eastern Europe after coming to power. Although he counted the Jews among the 'best races', Ploetz had no particular difficulty in joining the Third Reich, the regime of the 'final solution'.[79] Even though Gobineau made fun of the idea of the 'fatherland' and sanf a sort of 'eulogy' to the Jews, he became a point of reference for a movement and a regime marked by exalted chauvinism and the infamy of the 'final solution'. If one explains the Nazis' employment of Nietzsche as a misunderstanding or manipulation, there is no reason why this explanation should not also apply to the authors cited above. In fact, there is no lack of scholars that think that, 'even more so than in the case Nietzsche, the history of Gobineau's impact is a history of his misunderstandings'.[80] But to apply the category of 'misunderstanding' to the history

---

75   Cf. Losurdo 1996, 4, §6.
76   Hitler 1989, 210 (20–21 February 1942).
77   Weissmann 1995, 43.
78   Kershaw 1998, 240.
79   Poliakov 1987, 335 f.
80   See 1994, 290.

of the impact of Gobineau, who believed unambiguously in the inequality of races and declared the 'black race' and other 'human tribes' to be incapable of 'civilization', is, objectively, to reduce the hermeneutics of innocence *ad absurdum*.[81]

For an overall balance, it is therefore better to return to the categories of 'anti-Germanism' and 'anti-Semitism' generally used to shield Nietzsche from a reactionary political interpretation. There can no doubt that we can find in him a denunciation of the fateful role played by Germans ever since Arminius and the crisis and collapse of the Roman Empire. For this reason, the philosopher was used and even 'annexed' at the end of the nineteenth and start of the twentieth century by French nationalists demanding *revanche* against an enemy intrinsically and irredeemably barbaric. This ideological climate even infected a significant interpreter like Andler. On the one hand, he used his more directly political, patriotic books to propagate a pan-Germanism supposedly lying in the remotest past, which had been '*always* present' in a nation that had '*always* gladly and emphatically glorified German strength'; on the other hand, in his monograph on Nietzsche, he veered towards an anti-German interpretation when stressing the philosopher's preference for the 'French moralists' and the 'French' nation, which unlike the German nation did not like to 'lie to itself'. It is no accident Andler dedicated this monograph to his disciples 'who died in the Great War for their country and for humanity'.[82] In view of the passions and hatreds aroused by the First World War, the chauvinistic excitement on both banks of the Rhine was understandable. But anyone that still unconsciously clings to the disturbing mythology of an eternal and eternally evil Germany, whose denunciation, from whatever perspective, would be welcome, would do well to bear in mind Simone Weil's warning: 'In this way racial prejudice, to which, however, they do not admit, conceals from them a very obvious truth – which is that what resembled Hitler's Germany two thousand years ago was not the Germans; it was Rome.'[83]

The *Antichrist* took aim at a theme dear to the liberal tradition when it mocked 'German historical scholarship', convinced 'that Rome was a despotism, that the inhabitants of Germania brought the spirit of freedom into the world' (AC 55 [55]). For example, Montesquieu, referring to Tacitus, believed the origin of free and representative government could be found in the 'forests'

81 Gobineau 1983, 186 (Book 1, 5).
82 Andler 1958, Vol. 1, 8, 107 f.; cf. Digeon 1959, 455–57 (on the whole picture) and Losurdo 1997a, 13, §13 and 14, §1 (on Andler's undifferentiated anti-German polemic).
83 Weil 1962, 96.

inhabited by the Germans.[84] In similar terms, Hume, also referring to Tacitus, declared that the 'government of the Germans', formed on the 'ruins of Rome' and its 'military despotism', had been 'extremely free.'[85] In this sense, one can speak of a 'philo-Germanism' in Montesquieu and Hume (and Tacitus) and an 'anti-Germanism' in Nietzsche; but no one would want to deduce from that statement that the two liberal writers and the Roman historian were closer to German reaction and Nazism than the author of the *Antichrist!* Moreover, one can even find traces of 'anti-Germanism' in Hitler. In March 1945, when the defeat of the Third Reich looms and the German people did not seem to be prepared to struggle with the prescribed heroism and self-sacrifice, the Führer passed a harsh judgement on Germany as such: 'only inferior beings' had survived, unable to resist the 'stronger Eastern peoples'; and it was to the latter that 'the future belongs'.[86] In conflict with its true warrior essence and infected by a philistine vision of life, Germany deserved no leniency.

On the other hand, as we have seen, Nietzsche denounced in the strongest terms the conversion of the Germans to Christianity, a religion totally alien to them and moreover linked to the hated Judea. Should we speak here of 'Germanism'? One must not confuse two different problems. There can be no doubt that the collapse of the Roman Empire, under the growing pressure of the Germans, represented for Nietzsche a catastrophe of culture, but a catastrophe no less serious in his eyes than the subsequent conversion of the Germans to Christianity, a religion completely alien to them and intrinsically Jewish. This is not a case of an oscillation between 'anti-Germanism' and 'philo-Germanism'. The collapse of the Roman Empire and the spread of Christianity were two essential stages in the long cycle of slave revolt: and in both cases, Nietzsche took the side of the 'masters'. This ideology was in no way in insurmountable contradiction with the ideology of Nazism that later developed: one must not lose sight of the fact that for Nietzsche, long before the conversion of the Germans, it was the collapse of the Roman Empire that represented the victory of 'Judea'. The stages of the slave revolt were so many stages in the triumph of the people of supreme *ressentiment*.

Finally, it is historically naïve, disconcerting so, to interpret Nietzsche's furious polemic against Wilhelm II as a prescient warning about the Third Reich. On closer inspection, it is clear that this denunciation of the German emperor as an 'idiot of colour', as a sort of Negroid, influenced by the cause of the emancipation of slaves and blacks and of the colonial peoples, radically turned

---

84   Montesquieu 1949–51, 407 (Book 11, § 6).
85   Hume 1983, Vol. 1, 160 f.
86   In Hillgruber 1982, 141.

things upside down. We are inclined, rather, to think of the language and insults the most chauvinistic circles used even before the Nazis seized power. France, which deployed colonial troops, was for Spengler a 'European-African' country.[87] Hitler borrowed this theme from the so-called 'conservative revolution' and radicalised it, when he denounced France as a 'Europe-African mulatto state'[88] or lamented the 'Negroid appearance' of Roosevelt's wife, whom he accused of maintaining relations with certain African-American circles.[89]

Equally devoid of historical sense is the invocation of the fantasisings of the late Nietzsche about having Wilhelm II shot as a champion of the emancipation of black slaves in support of the Nuremberg judgement against the leaders of the Third Reich for reintroducing slavery, above all in the case of the *Untermenschen* of Eastern Europe. It is an offence against logic to use the fact that the theorist of 'aristocratic radicalism' denounced Germany as a hotbed of revolutionary contagion to confirm the Nuremberg finding that Germany was a manifestation of an *ancien régime* that stubbornly clung to the idea of the natural inequality of people and races! Here too, we are inclined at most to think of the second great wave of anti-democratic reaction following defeat in the First World War. The polemic against the Weimar Republic and the hated democracy and modernity was based on revolutionary slogans. So, one can understand the reference to an author that during his struggle against the Second Reich and its 'worst' aspects had expressed himself in a similar way: the conservative revolution, which saw in Nietzsche its founding father or 'patriarch [*Erzvater*]', ended up,[90] through a process not without its contradictions, being taken over and absorbed by the Nazis. The accusation by Nietzsche that the emperor had flirted with Social Democracy brings to mind Hitler's polemic against Wilhelm II, who at the end of the First World War had committed the terrible crime of 'stretching out his hands in reconciliation to the leaders of Marxism', a movement that, by rejecting 'the aristocratic principle in nature', endangered the orderly functioning of culture and culture as such.[91]

Hardly more persuasive is the category of 'anti-anti-Semitism'. Once again, the inability of the hermeneuts of innocence to think through in general terms the methodology applied to Nietzsche becomes apparent. Should we add Gobineau to the ranks of the prophets of resistance to Hitler, since, as we have seen, he sang a eulogy to the Jews? Should we also add those theorists of

---

87   Spengler 1937, 88.
88   Hitler 1939b, 730.
89   Hitler 1989, 399 (1 July 1942).
90   Mohler 1989, supplementary Vol., 29 f.
91   Hitler 1939b, 225, 69.

black slavery that, as ultimate proof of the absolute and insuperable unsuitability of blacks (and the 'savage hordes' of 'gypsies') for culture, pointed to the extraordinary ability of the Jews to develop a great culture under extremely difficult conditions?[92] Whatever the case, Ploetz, already cited above, would not have gained entry to this noble assembly, because though he had generously co-opted the Jews into the superior races, he later became an authoritative exponent of Nazi racial hygiene.

As for Nietzsche, his hatred for Jewish intellectuals was so intense that he eventually ended up rehashing and further radicalising the conspiracy theory cherished by him in his youth. Let me be clear: this is not to turn the celebrated 'anti-anti-Semitism' into its opposite, for the philosopher remaind to the last aloof from biological racism. The real problem lies elsewhere. Like 'anti-Germanism', 'anti-anti-Semitism' was asserted quite abstractly, regardless of content. It is disarming when Deleuze cries out in joy: 'Little is more astonishing than Nietzsche's admiration for the kings of Israel and for the Old Testament.'[93] Nietzsche hated and despised the prophet, the priest and also the Jewish mob called into life by Christianity, and he repeatedly demanded that the biblical prohibition 'thou shalt not kill' be dropped as out-of-date and hostile to life. On the other hand, he praised the Old Testament story about the conquest of Canaan and the extermination of its inhabitants. It is this story that filled Simone Weil with horror. On closer inspection, the late Nietzsche with his glorification of the 'blond beast' was not so far removed from the Old Testament-Roman line, which according to this eminent Jewish philosopher (who in a certain sense inherited the prophetic tradition) had inspired the most terrible pages of Western history.

The method proposed here, to interpret the philosopher in a historical and political way and to view him as an integral part of a long tradition of critique of revolution, passing through the privileged moment of anti-democratic reaction of the late nineteenth century and finally ending up in Nazism, is in no way to consider the matter closed and to ignore the problem of his theoretical surplus. In interpreting Nietzsche, a peculiar ideological process has come about. The victorious West has suppressed the black pages of its history. Thus, the terrible statements about the 'annihilation of the malformed' or the 'annihilation of decadent races' have been brought into immediate association with the horrors of the Third Reich. To free the philosopher from the shadow that

---

92   Duttenhofer 1855, 17.
93   Deleuze 1962, 145. On the 'extravagant' character of this admiration cf. Aschheim 1997, 3–
       20.

the suppression casts on him, the hermeneuts of innocence can think of nothing better than to introduce a further suppression, which ignores or glosses over the most disturbing passages written by the philosopher or miraculously transforms them into a set of improbable metaphors. But proving the unreliability of the hermeneutics of innocence does not yet put an end to the debate. An understanding of Nietzsche's theoretical surplus, far from contradicting the historical contextualisation and political interpretation of his thought, actually presupposes it.

PART 6

In Nietzsche's Philosophical Laboratory

..

There is nothing more important than problems of morality.

XIV, 263

• • •

We are all wary of navel-gazers, on the grounds that self-observation is reckoned as a degenerate form of psychological genius.

XIII, 231

• • •

At bottom, you always teach history and, in this book, you have opened up some amazing historical perspectives.

BURCKHARDT to NIETZSCHE: B, III, 2, 288–9

• • •

Perhaps he would like to see me inherit his chair.

NIETZSCHE to LOU SALOMÉ, commenting on BURCKHARDT's letter: B, III, 1, 259

• • •

There is a stupid humility that is by no means rare, and those afflicted with it are altogether unfit to become votaries of knowledge. For as soon as a person of this type perceives something striking, he turns on his heel, as it were, and says to himself, "You have made a mistake! Where were your senses? This cannot be the truth!" And then, instead of looking and listening more keenly again, he runs away, as if intimidated, from the striking thing and tries to shake it from his mind as fast as possible.

FW, 25 [50]

• • •

What makes a human being original is that he sees something all others do not see.

IX, 591

• •
•

CHAPTER 28

A Philosopher *totus politicus*

1   The Unity of Nietzsche's Thought

Why must the denunciation and critique of revolution be the leading thread in interpreting Nietzsche? Because otherwise it is not possible to grasp the philosopher as a whole and to 'save' him. Should one see him as a theorist of a sharp and merciless critique of ideology that takes apart the myths of Germanism and anti-Semitism? Apart from other difficulties, this sort of interpretation would still result in the elimination of the early works, which, although extremely fascinating, echo the themes of Germanomania and Judeophobia commonplace in the culture of the time. Should one regard Nietzsche as a champion of the 'free spirit' and the theory of the rehabilitation of the flesh, as opposed to the asceticism of the Christian West? Again, one would have to make painful cuts and forego the disciple of Schopenhauer, who expressed his contempt for galloping 'secularization', sorrowfully evoked the catastrophic consequences of the 'sad atheist twilight' and defended against Strauss 'the best side of Christianity', that of the hermits and saints.

One would encounter similar difficulties if one were to take the critique of nihilism as the leading thread. As a fragment from the spring of 1888 observed, nihilism was expressed in the thesis that 'not to be is better than to be' and 'nothingness is supremely desirable' (XIII, 528). How could one forget that *The Birth of Tragedy* adopted Silenus's terrible motto ('The best thing is [...] not to be born, not to be, to be nothing')? On the other hand, the writings of the mature period reproached Christianity rather than nihilism for its fatal incompleteness, which led an innumerable mass of the wretched and the malformed to cling to life.

Those that would like to start out in their interpretation from the critique of reason and science would land up in great difficulties when it comes to explaining the 'Enlightenment' and the 'positivistic' pathos of certain writings that not only attempt to discover the errors and distortions but also the pathologies that lie at the basis of worldviews devoid of any sense of reality and tending to indulge in fantasies and visions. The late Nietzsche described in stinging terms how, for Wagner, patriotic-dynastic zeal combined with mythologies that that could clearly be called irrational: 'An approach to German princes, then obeisances before the emperor, the Reich, the army, and then before Christianity too' and 'imprecations against "science"' (XI, 250). If the term 'science' appears here in quotation marks, these tended to fall away when the philosopher spoke with great warmth and high hopes of Galton, the founder of eugenics.

An interpretation that makes everything revolve around the glorification of art would be least able to overcome the difficulties mentioned here. In this case, eager defence more than ever becomes cruel and arbitrary mutilation: as we shall see, Nietzsche aspired to Burckhardt's chair, and Burckhardt noticed the extraordinary richness of Nietzsche's reflections on history. Moreover, leading authors including Lukács and Habermas have deemed it appropriate and necessary to linger on Nietzsche's gnoseological and epistemological reflections.[1]

It is true that these reflections have to do with something ulterior, but this something is other than aesthetic contemplation. Nietzsche puts radical questions to the traditional theme of 'will to truth' and says of this unexplored 'problem' with justified pride: 'We were the first to ever see it, fix our gaze on it, risk it' (JGB, 1 [5]). The dogmatism that was accustomed to celebrate an imaginary good in itself entered once and for all into crisis: 'The fundamental belief of metaphysicians is the belief in oppositions of values' (JGB, 2 [6]), with an unambiguous distinction between good and evil, and therefore with the construction of a metaphysical world of objective moral values. Now this more or less camouflaged theological world was in ruins: the consequences for the understanding and construction of the human world were incalculable. We are brought back to the ethical-political sphere, to which the metacritique of critical philosophy also leads us. In his desperate attempt to rescue objectivity in the theoretical and ethical field, Kant first discovered 'the faculty for synthetic judgements *a priori*' and then a 'moral faculty' in human beings (JGB, 11 [12]). The second discovery was no less ridiculous than the first. Moral dogmatics followed the fate of metaphysical dogmatics: 'As soon as we deny absolute truth, we must abandon every absolute claim and retire to aesthetic judgements. [...] Reduction of morality to aesthetics!' (IX, 471). Now the appeals to 'justice', the claims to call into question the innocence of becoming, seemed unfounded and absurd.

While mocking '*l'art pour l'art*' (JGB, 208 [101]), Nietzsche praised art as a beneficial antidote to the universalism of morality and science: 'Science and democracy belong together (as Mr Renan likes to say) as surely as do art and "good society"' (XII, 347). A valuable contribution to the desired 'reversal of values', i.e., of the values of the herd, could be made by 'certain insatiably ambitious artists, struggling relentlessly and absolutely for the special rights of

---

1   Lukács 1954, 298–300, 305–307; Habermas 1968b, 237–261.

superior human beings and against the "herd animals", that employ the seductive means of art to put to sleep in the more elect spirits all the instincts of the
herd and precautions of the herd.' On the other hand, the great men, called
upon to put an end to the dogmas of the 'equality of rights' and 'compassion
for all that suffers' would have to demonstrate an 'artistic will [*Künstler-Willen*]
of the highest order' (xi, 581–2).

Art only played a role of the highest order when it reinforced rank-ordering.
One should not forget that 'for the Greeks, artistic creation falls just as much
under the concept of undignified work as any banausic handwork' (vii, 338).
But Hellas did not cease for that reason to be a magnificent model. The reference to art was an instrument of struggle of aristocratic radicalism and the
'party of life'. Particularly significant is a fragment that might date from the summer of 1886 and the spring of 1887: '[*N*]*oblesse*: what is beauty? Expression of he
that has been victorious and become master' (xii, 245). On the opposite side,
the condemnation of the 'demagogues in art – Hugo, Michelet, Sand, R. Wagner' was irrevocable (xi, 546). The artists infected by modernity were 'mentally
ill' and belonged among the 'criminals', 'anarchists' and 'Chandala', and those
whose lives had turned out badly (xiii, 504), all that was most repellent in the
world. In conclusion: 'Aesthetics is inextricably linked to these biological presuppositions: there is an aesthetic of decadence, there is a classical aesthetic, –
"beauty-in-itself" is a fantasy, like all of idealism' (wa, Epilogue [261]).

It would be just as fruitless to seek to understand the various aspects of Nietzsche's personality and evolutionary history listed up to now (and there are
more) on the basis of a psychological interpretation. That would, in this case,
be not only a mutilation but a reduction, as if the effort to embrace and understand reality in its totality and the drive to have an active effect on it were
extraneous to our author. Nietzsche despised the figure of the 'spoiled idler
in the garden of knowledge', and it is hard to see why the philosopher that so
effectively and ruthlessly sketched it should be ascribed to it, especially if these
gardens proved to be nothing more than a poor backyard marked by a boring
artistic and psychological monoculture. If the philosopher expressed his great
contempt for the 'navel-gazers', he strove hard, as we shall see, to construct
a psychophysiology in the face of which every cultural expression, however
seemingly pure, revealed the presence of an aristocratic or plebeian spirit and
even body.

Only by not suppressing the element that deeply permeates it, only by keeping permanently in mind the criticism and *militant* denunciation of revolution
and modernity, is it possible to grasp the unity of Nietzsche's thought and its
internal consistency. Its development embraced varying positions that proved
on closer inspection to be increasingly precise fine-tunings always designed

with the same aim, to criticise and denounce revolution and modernity. The philosopher that, at the end of his conscious life, dreamt of an anti-Christian and anti-socialist coup and worked frantically to finish the texts intended as the theoretical platform for the desired turn in world history had come to Basel full of enthusiasm at the success of Germany's process of unification. In his eyes, Germany was thus preparing to carry out its mission in Europe, against the land of revolution and civilisation:

> Politics is now the organ of thought in its totality. Events leave me stupefied. [...] Bismarck delights me enormously. Reading his speeches is, for me, like drinking a strong wine, and I try not to drink too quickly so I can long savour the taste.
>
> B, I, 2, 258

The young Nietzsche was also speaking of himself when he polemicised against the then current interpretations of a great philosopher of antiquity:

> Less than ever may we see in Plato a mere artist. [...] We err when we consider Plato to be a representative of the Greek artistic type: while this ability was among the more common, the specifically Platonic, i.e., dialectic-political, was something unique.
>
> KGA, II, 4, 14

And Nietzsche still seemed to be talking of himself when he criticised the reduction of Schopenhauer to 'a stupefying and exciting drug', 'a kind of metaphysical pepper': the third *Unfashionable Observation*, on the other hand, interpreted him as the theorist of 'Schopenhauer's human being', called upon to oppose and struggle against 'Rousseau's [and the revolution's] human being'. An equally unacceptable outcome would be achieved if one were to put psychology, pure speculation or philology in place of art. In this latter regard, one should think of the letter from the young Basel professor to Ritschl: 'Here a complete radicalism is needed, a real return to antiquity' (B, II, 1, 173), with the resumption of relations and institutions that had unfortunately disappeared from the modern world. From the very beginning, for Nietzsche even philology had a vital significance.

The philologist-philosopher not only paid constant attention to history but understood it as 'struggle of estates and classes [*Stände-und Klassenkampf*]' (XII, 493). This definition calls to mind the famous Marxist definition, even if the classes were ultimately schematically and sometimes naturalistically reduced, outside any concrete historical dialectic, to those of masters and

slaves. And yet, in his will and ability to interpret class conflict, however understood, even in morality, religion and science, in the Socratic 'syllogism', Nietzsche was, in a sense, even more radical and immediately political than Marx,
who, though with oscillations and contradictions, seemed to place science in a
sphere that at least partially transcended the conflict. In contrast to Nietzsche,
Marx's denunciation of false consciousness as a means of legitimising unac-
knowledged and unacknowledgeable interests went hand in hand with the
pathos of the objectivity of true scientific knowledge and with the celebration
of its emancipatory potential. For Nietzsche, however, there were no neutral
territories. As we know, even physics, with its theory of laws applicable to all,
was a reference to hated egalitarianism. Not even art was neutral. Marx could
express his admiration and amazement at the fact that, while clearly 'bound
up with certain forms of social development', Greek art and epic poetry 'still
give us aesthetic pleasure and are in certain respects regarded as a standard
and unattainable model'.[2] Political and social conflicts had no part in this analysis. Marx was not for nothing a disciple of Hegel: the doctrine of the absolute
spirit lived on. Not so for Nietzsche, who discovered in Euripides' tragedy a
sociopolitical conflict that, far from being concluded, continued to make its
presence felt in all its sharpness in the present. And, as for the Homeric poems,
they handed down to us the memory of a heroic and organic *volksthümlich*
community that at least in the first phase in our philosopher's development
represented a model (*supra*, 4 §1). Precisely because for Nietzsche historical
development in its entirety was traversed by a clash between masters and servants – a clash that lasted not just several thousand years but, ultimately, was
eternal, there was no artistic and cultural production that could be considered
immune to the presence and actuality of this clash.

2 Nietzsche and the Historians

The philosopher's commitment to reconstructing the millennial historical
cycle that led to the French Revolution and the threatening emergence of the
socialist movement, and the rigour with which he set about this task, should
be enough to disprove the myth that he was interested exclusively in art and
psychology. That history and historians played a central role in Nietzsche's
discourse is a barely studied aspect of his intellectual biography. In Pforta
the young schoolboy carefully read history texts and copied passages from

---

2   Marx and Engels 1975 ff., 28, 47.

them that he considered especially significant. His interest in and knowledge of history at the time was quite extraordinary. He was not only interested in Mommsen and Roman history but also paid close attention to historians or historical writers of the modern and contemporary era. He copied passages not only from German authors (Mundt, Menzel, Gervinus) but also from prominent European historians like Guizot and Macaulay (KGA, I, 2, 389–412 and 487–509).

In a letter to his sister written in November 1861, Nietzsche said he 'wishes' at Christmas to get books on the history of Germany, the Reformation and especially the French Revolution. Even though he was also interested in studying the history of the United States, he seemed above all eager to immerse himself in reading volumes on the upheavals begun in 1789: 'You must know that I am now very interested in history' (B, I, 1, 189). Not long afterwards, he announced he had changed his mind about the books he wanted, but only because the library in Pforta was very well stocked with publications on the subject closest to his heart (B, I, 1, 191). A couple of years later, still writing to his sister (and mother), he announced he was absorbed in Sybel's lectures (B, I, 2, 18). On the other hand, the correspondence of these years evinced a keen interest in the contributions of Treitschke, a prominent historian and politician (B, I, 2, 150 and 158). A programme of studies formulated in late 1869 and early 1870 gave first place to 'politics and history' (VII, 61).

Let us dwell for a moment on this dual concept: historical interest is at the same time eminently political. On the pages of history on which the texts were transcribed or the reader's reflections noted can be found the names not only of Napoleon, Metternich and Castlereagh (KGA, I, 2, 496–505) but also of leaders of the struggles that at this time were still far from concluded: Blanqui, Blanc, Ledru-Rollin, Cavaignac, i.e., leaders of the labour movement and the main figure in the bloody repression of the working-class revolt in Paris in June 1848. For the struggle between revolution and counterrevolution in France was of particular interest to Nietzsche. Hence the attention he devoted to Louis-Napoleon (Napoleon III): he was the 'genius' or the 'genius of power', who unhesitatingly resorted to 'force of arms' against the subversive machinations of a large number of deputies and brought about the final defeat of the 'socialists', 'republicans' and 'democrats' (KGA, I, 2, 357–62). This referred to the period between 1861 and 1862. Four or five years later, the French emperor who hindered the process of Germany's national unification became *Louis le diable* (see above, chap. 1, §6). The attention to social conflict combined with attention to the development of national and international politics.

The political interest was certainly never narrow. To understand the present, one must also be in a position to look backwards: this is what the young Nietzsche did, studying not only ancient history, already to a certain extent also for 'professional' reasons, but the 'worldview of the Catholic Middle Ages', the 'worldview of Protestant orthodoxy' and even the 'biblical worldview' (KGA, I, 4, 69–75). But looking to the past never really distracted from the present. Even when dealing with Theognis, the philologist (as we know) never lost sight of the Prussia of his time (*supra*, 22 §1). On the other hand, the study of such different historical periods and contexts did not lead to a loss of focus, for Nietzsche constantly sought to place individual peculiarities and details in a framework that made sense as a whole. A note made in the spring of 1868 documented his interest in Herder and his philosophy of history (KGA, I, 4, 573).

In the meantime, we are at the eve of his arrival in Basel. Nietzsche continued to show an interest in Mommsen, Niehbuhr, and Grote. But a new encounter was of particular importance. During the gestation of *The Birth of Tragedy*, its future author listend with such great interest to Burckhardt that he wrote to his friend Gersdorff: 'For the first time ever I take pleasure in a lecture.' The lecture even became a model for Nietzsche, who played with the idea of being able to do something similar at a later age (B, II, 1, 155). The chair of philology started to seem too narrow to the young professor, but one could say that to solve the problem, he thought more of the chair of history than the chair of philosophy.

The depth and intensity of his historical interests did not escape Burckhardt. When the latter received *The Gay Science*, he wrote to his former university colleague:

> What always intrigues me time and again is the question: how would it turn out if you taught history? At bottom, you always teach history and, in this book, you have opened up some amazing historical perspectives. But what I mean is: what if you were to shine on world history, *ex professo*, your shafts of light, and from the angles of illumination agreeable to you? How many things would be nicely turned upside down with respect to the current *consensus populorum*.
>
> B, III, 2, 288–9

And, after receiving *Beyond Good and Evil*, Burckhardt reinforced his point: 'What I especially appreciate in your work are the historical judgements and, in particular, your glances into time [...]: regarding democracy as the heir to Christianity' (B, III, 4, 221–2).

Far from being irritated by such judgements, which allotted him to an arena so alien to the pure philosophy, poetry and metaphor so highly praised by today's hermeneuts of innocence, Nietzsche as so flattered that, for a moment, he even seemed to entertain the idea of returning to university teaching, but this time as a historian. This is what he said in a letter to Lou Salomé about the first of the letters from Burckhardt quoted here: 'Perhaps he would like to see me inherit his chair' (B, III, 1, 259). In writing to his faithful disciple Peter Gast, all shadow of doubt seemed to have vanished: 'Jacob Burckhardt wants me to become "professor of world history." I enclose his letter' (B, III, 1, 263). The philosopher expressed similar sentiments in two subsequent letters to his friend Overbeck (B, III, 1, 354 and 496). To judge by the last, he even wanted to take concrete steps in preparation for such a prospect: 'For the last few months I have done "world history", and with delight, albeit with some terrible results.'

When he sent the great Basel historian *Beyond Good and Evil*, he attached a letter: 'I know no one that shares so many assumptions with me as you' (B, III, 3, 254). Naturally, one should not set too much store by what were sometimes mere expressions of politeness; but even the aforementioned letter to Lou Salomé points out that the Basel historian 'has a personality in some ways irresistible' (B, III, 1, 259).

Particularly important is that in a letter to Franz Overbeck dated 23 February 1887, Nietzsche claimed to have 'passed through the school of Tocqueville and Taine' (B, III, 5, 28), and engaged in a correspondence with the latter marked by mutual respect. Nietzsche attributed to him the merit of having been able to describe 'the tragic history of the modern soul' (B, III, 5, 76). Luther should be 'narrated' using the same methodology: putting aside both 'the sugary, deferential modesty of Protestant historians' and the 'moralistic simplicity of a country pastor' typical of Catholic historians, a 'real psychologist' should have showed him 'with the intrepidity of a Taine, from strength of soul and not from a shrewd indulgence toward strength' (GM, III, 19 [103]). Ultimately, Nietzsche put to use the link between psychological insight and historical accuracy, used by Taine to reconstruct the crisis of the *ancien régime* and the development of the French Revolution, to reconstruct the entire cycle since Luther or earlier still, starting with the preaching of the Gospels and even the agitation of the Jewish prophets.

The gallery of historians he counted among his teachers did not end there. After stressing the importance of Ritschl for his education – 'the only brilliant scholar I have ever come across' – Nietzsche added: 'I have absolutely no intention of underestimating my close compatriot, the clever Leopold von Ranke' (EH, Why I am so clever, 9 [98]). He had already read the latter with interest in the Basel years (B, II, 3, 193) and praised him as the 'born classical *advocatus* of every *causa fortior*' (GM III, 19 [103]). Burckhardt, Tocqueville, Taine, and Ranke: these great historians had in common the fact that each had engaged, in one way or another, in pitiless analysis of the French Revolution.

Like the teachers, so too the authors Nietzsche classed as antagonists were often historians. This applied first and foremost to Michelet, the repugnant 'plebeian' (XI, 588), analysed and experienced with great hatred. He was described as a sort of historiographical *pendant* to Victor Hugo. He too was 'a human being of compassion', with a sympathetic empathy for the masses. Except that 'in place of painterly eyes', the historian of the French Revolution revealed 'an admirable ability to reconstruct within himself the moods' of the crowd, which he described and with which he identified emotionally: 'When he reaches a certain degree of excitement, he is seized each time by a fit of the people's tribune, he knows from personal experience the rabid raging of the mob' (XI, 602–3).

Another polemical target was Buckle. After reading his *History of Civilisation in England*, Nietzsche wrote to Gast: 'Strange! It turns out Buckle is one of my strongest adversaries'; he was a 'democrat' (B, III, 5, 79). In this case too, the feeling of bitter hostility did not muddy the clarity of analysis. The work of the English historian had a central theme ('the hall of science is the temple of democracy') that fascinated its translator, Arnold Ruge, a leading exponent of the Hegelian Left.[3] Another exceptional personality of the democratic movement, Johann Jacoby,[4] who after a long period of courageous activism in the opposition finally joined German Social Democracy in 1872, was also attracted and fascinated by it.[5]

According to Nietzsche, Buckle's 'banal value judgements' found sympathy with Dühring and in various circles of the socialist movement (B, III, 5, 79). And, once again, the philosopher was right. The English historian exercised 'a great influence' on Wilhelm Liebknecht, one of the party's leading figures.[6] All this had to do not so much with Buckle's radical pacifism as with the great sympathy he seemed to display towards the masses, for he criticised the great German writers for expressing themselves in a 'dialect' incomprehensible to the lower classes.[7] Precisely because of his 'plebeianism of the spirit' (*supra*, 25 § 2), Nietzsche linked Buckle to Michelet, among others (XIII, 189).

In this case too, we are dealing with a profoundly 'democratic' philosophy of history, which derives 'geniuses' or 'great human beings' from the living environment (GD, Skirmishes of an untimely man, 44 [218]). That Buckle mocked the usual historiography for focusing on 'meaningless stories of kings, courts, diplomats, battles and sieges' struck a sympathetic note in German

---

3 Ruge 1886, Vol. 2 (letter to Br. Brückmann of 5 November 1864).
4 Jacoby 1978, 190 (letter to Fanny Lewald of 11 February 1862).
5 Cf. Silberner 1976, 492 f.
6 Mehring 1961 ff., Vol. 8, 80; cf. Mehring 1898, 333.
7 Mehring 1961 ff., Vol. 13, 43.

Social Democracy.[8] Nietzsche knew this passage and the thinking behind it, and commented as follows:

> What depths the inability of a plebeian agitator of the mob to clarify the concept of 'higher nature' plumbs are best exemplified by Buckle. The opinion he so passionately rejects – that 'great men', individuals, kings, statesmen, geniuses and generals are the levers and causes of all great movements – is instinctively misunderstood by him, for he assumes it asserts that the essence and value of such 'superior human beings' lies precisely in their ability to set masses in motion, in short, in its effect. But the 'higher nature' of the great man lies in being other, in incommensurability, in the distance of rank – not in some effect: even if he shakes the globe.
>
> XIII, 497–8

Nietzsche did not lose sight in subsequent years of Sybel and Treitschke, whom he had read in his youth. Yet the more radical his positions became, the more severe Nietzsche as with the two national-liberal writers: they now appeared as 'poor historians [with] thickly bandaged heads' (JGB, 251 [141]). In the early months of 1887, the philosopher reported he was busy reading 'Sybel's main work' (B, III, 5, 28): although strongly critical of the French Revolution, it seemed to draw the *ancien régime* too into its condemnation, which roused Nietzsche to indignation (*supra*, 17 §1).

To complete the picture of Nietzsche's interest in history and historians of the Revolution, one could cite 'the mediocre Thiers, elegant in the bad sense of the word' (XI, 588), who according to Nietzsche was too well-disposed towards the French Revolution and too reserved about Napoleon, and unable to comprehend Napoleon's greatness on account of his own lack of it (VII, 675–6); one could point as well to Montlosier and Thierry, from whom Nietzsche took over the somewhat racial interpretation of the clash between nobility and Third Estate. Finally, one should not forget the critical interest Lecky aroused, with his reconstructions of the history of Methodism, England and the origins and development of the Enlightenment.

There can be no doubt about the political meaning of Nietzsche's encounter with the great historians. Tocqueville and Taine, whom he valued, were summarily dismissed by Engels as authors 'deified by the philistine',[9] and it was

---

8   In Mehring 1961 ff., Vol. 7, 427.
9   Marx and Engels 1955 ff., 37, 154.

precisely Engels who seemed to show a certain interest in Buckle, even though he did not share the enthusiasm of other members of German Social Democracy.[10]

3 Continuity and Discontinuity: Genius, Free Spirits, Rank-Ordering and Overman

We can grasp the leading thread of Nietzsche's complex and tormented development only if we keep sight of the continuity and central role of the historical-political interest and aristocratic radicalism. 'Genius' was the watchword of the youthful 'metaphysical' period: the glorification of ancient Greece was primarily reverential homage to the 'supreme geniuses' it was able to produce (PHG, 1, I, 808). Unfortunately, all that vanished in the modern world: 'The carters have struck a labour contract and decreed genius superfluous' (HL, 7, I, 301). The enthusiastic encounter with Schopenhauer was also the discovery of the fascinating theme of the 'republic of geniuses' evoked by the latter. The possibility opened up of an interpretation of history quite different from the philistine and optimistic one, which aimed to ensure progress, education and happiness for all, submerging exceptional individuality in an anonymous mass. But Nietzsche described his own understanding of history: 'Through the desolate intervals of times past, one giant speaks to another giant, and this conversation between superior spirits [das hohe Geistergespräch] continues regardless of the dwarfs' petulant and shrill clamour' (PHG, 1; I, 808).

So, alongside the category of 'genius' and as its synonyms, the categories of 'giant' and 'supreme spirit' emerged. 'Free spirit', on the other hand, became the watchword of the 'Enlightenment' period. Hence the subtitle of *Human, All Too Human*, as we know, *A Book for Free Spirits*. This as not a caesura, not even terminologically. If we examine the genesis of *The Birth of Tragedy*, we see that one of the titles initially considered was *Tragedy and Free Spirits. Considerations on the Ethical-Political Significance of the Musical Drama* (VII, 97 and 103). Even now, 'free spirits' were set against the 'people' and especially the 'mass' (PHG, 19, I, 869–70).

In the 'Enlightenment' period, 'free spirits' were also 'good Europeans' [WS, 87], praised in contrast both to the chauvinists and the 'barbarians' and 'Asiatics' (*supra*, 7 § 6). Thus, the contrast between elite and mass was also asserted at the international level. The political significance of the free spirit, called upon

---

10   Marx and Engels 1955 ff., 33, 261, 275, 283, 289.

to overcome vacillation and weakness of purpose in the struggle against modernity, was clarified by Nietzsche as follows in the *Preface* to the new edition of *Human, All Too Human* in 1886:

> And so at one time, when I needed to do so, I invented for myself the 'free spirits' to whom this heavy-hearted, high-spirited book of the title *Human, All Too Human* is dedicated: such 'free spirits' do not and did not exist. [...] That such free spirits could someday exist, that our Europe will have this sort of lively and audacious companion among the sons of its tomorrows, physically and tangibly present. [...] I would be this very last person to doubt this. I see them coming already, slowly.
>
>   MA, Preface, 2 [6–7]

Enlightened rejection of religious superstition was certainly not enough to define a genuinely free spirit. Such a spirit had also to be able to assimilate the critique and demystification of democratic and egalitarian superstition and rise to a vision of the central problem, which was that of 'rank-ordering' (*supra*, ch. 10 §5 and 8). Rank-ordering found its highest expression in 'overman'. If *Human, All Too Human* pointed out that the state was 'in contradiction' with 'genius' (MA, 235), *Thus Spoke Zarathustra* stressed: 'There, where the state ends, only there begins the human being that is not superfluous', and only there can 'the rainbow and the bridges of the overman' be glimpsed (Za, I, On the New Idol [36]). The overman was to the human being as the human being was to the ape: in the modern human being there was still too much ape (Za, Zarathustra's Prologue, 3). This theme can be found, in confirmation of the basic continuity in Nietzsche's evolution, in slightly different form in the notes of his youth: 'According to Heraclitus: the cleverest philistine (human being) is, compared to the genius (God), an ape' (VII, 607).

It is true that, during the 'Enlightenment', there was no shortage of polemical digs at the 'superstition of genius' (MA, 164). Particularly biting in this regard was *Dawn*:

> No wonder an overestimation of half-disturbed, fantastical, fanatical, so-called persons of genius continues to spill over into our age; 'they have seen things that others do not see' – indeed! And this should incline us toward them more cautiously, but more credulously.
>
>   M, 66 [47]

Here one distances oneself from the theme, popular in these years, connecting genius with madness. Later, in Germany, it was claimed that Nietzsche's personality could be explained precisely by this link.[11] According to this view, genius was 'a divine special variant' of the 'sacred sickness', epilepsy.[12] Thus Lombroso, who also counted among the more or less half-mad geniuses the great religious reformers and the inspirers of religious-political movements with a popular and plebeian social base.[13] So it is clear why *Human, All Too Human*, while continuing to speak of 'genius', felt the need to issue a warning: it was 'a word that I ask you to understand without any mythological or religious flavor' (MA, 231 [159]); it in no way referred to those personalities later branded as 'holy epileptics' and 'visionaries' (XIII, 245).

On the other hand, the denunciation of the 'superstition of genius' was not in contradiction with the glorification of the 'great spirits' (MA, 164 [35]), rather of the 'oligarchs of the spirit – that exist in every age' (VIII, 472) or of the 'strong, round, secure minds that have a firm grip on themselves' (FW, 345 [202]), the 'chosen human being' with a 'higher nature', not to be confused with 'vulgar natures' (*supra*, 11 § 3).

Even though it is true that elitism was a fundamental and constant feature of Nietzsche's thought, we can distinguish the various stages in its evolution: the first two were concerned with the celebration of genius, and artistic genius in particular, the third celebrated the free and enlightened spirit, and the last celebrated the overman and rank-ordering.

The usual division into three, which depicts Nietzsche as passing from romantic to Enlightenment-style positivist and theorist of nihilism, or 'the metaphysics of the artist', the 'Enlightenment' and 'the destruction of the Western metaphysic',[14] do not do justice to him, even if they can find points of support in his declarations. The transition from romanticism to a culture as different as the Enlightenment and positivism or from the celebration of the metaphysics of the artist to enthusiasm for the enlightenment and science seems arbitrary; no less mysterious is the transition from the pathos of reason, the pride of the West, to the destruction of Western metaphysics. In other words, the consistency and rigour that marked Nietzsche's development are left out of the picture. Yet without these features, if we are only dealing with brilliant ideas, but ideas that lack real connections among themselves, we could hardly consider him a great philosopher.

On the other hand, only the political significance and political continuity outlined here would allow us to confer a specific meaning on the categories

---

11   Nordau n.d., Vol. 2, 301f.
12   Lombroso 1995, 579.
13   Cf. Frigessi 1995, 365.
14   Thus Fink 1993, 119 ff.

used in the usual reconstructions of Nietzsche's development. Should we speak of a first 'romantic' phase? Romanticism, or certain of its themes, seems to be implied by Fichte's celebration of the subject: he posits a parallel between the elimination of the unknowable thing in itself undertaken by his philosophy and the destruction of the shackles of feudalism by the French Revolution, between his own 'inner struggle' against secular 'prejudices' and the French nation's powerful 'effort' to gain 'political freedom'.[15] But this is not the romanticism of *The Birth of Tragedy*, which – in it impious claim to penetrate and transform the essence of reality – denounced the precondition for the never-ending and ruinous slave revolt. Should one speak of an 'Enlightenment' phase? Nietzsche himself warned against confusions, and said his 'enlightenment' had nothing to do with the attitude of those that, in the name of reason and the universality of reason, attacked the edifice of the *ancien régime* and wanted to make a clean sweep of the old 'prejudices', particularisms and privileges.

It is also not persuasive, in relation to the early years, to speak of a 'metaphysics of the artist', for this category can be used for no few exponents of German romanticism: think of the young Schelling, Novalis or Jean Paul. Moreover, we have seen that Nietzsche, even when paying homage to Wagner, was quick to make clear that he viewed music and art not as a 'medicine' or 'narcotic' but as a terrain on which to muster the forces necessary for the desired 'revolution' (*supra*, 6 §10).

The real meaning of the reference to art becomes clear when seen from the point of view of Nietzsche's cultural and political elitism. Only this thread of thought makes it possible to grasp the unity of Nietzsche's worldview and philosophy of history. It is exceptional individuality, however defined, that conferred meaning on what was usually called 'world history'; the mass of people could only constitute the raw material those individual used for their artistic creations in the narrow or broad sense. This ideological thread, which we already know from the period (wrongly) called 'romantic', was also present in the period (wrongly) called 'enlightened'. The 'perfect state' or the 'ideal state' or 'the ideal state' of which 'socialists' dreamt was definitely to be rejected, because in it 'enfeebled individuals' could find a place, while on the other hand those 'themes for poetry' that made art possible were lost (MA, 234–5 [161–61]).

The dichotomy already present in *The Birth of Tragedy* once again shows its face: art *contra* socialism. And once again, art is a worldview, a philosophy of history that sees in the mass of ordinary people a simple tool for the production of beauty and culture:

---

15   Fichte 1967, Vol. 1, 449.

So it is very much the question whether in those orderly conditions that socialism demands the same great results for humanity could ensue as those that ensued in the disorderly conditions of the past. Probably the great human being and great works only bloom in the freedom of the wild. But humanity has no purpose other than great human beings and great works.

VIII, 481

Only the 'appearance of the highest intellect' could determine 'the value or disvalue of life'. So, one had to start from here, to take the necessary steps towards making a judgement about ideologies and the political orders:

But under what circumstances will this highest intellect arise? It seems that those that promote human well-being as a whole currently set themselves goals quite other than the creation of this highest value-shaping intellect. One seeks to provide well-being for the greatest number possible; this well-being is understood moreover in a quite external way.

VIII, 365

The problem of the production of genius had now become the problem of the appearance of the highest intellect and already tended to be configured as the problem of the restoration of the rank-ordering and 'breeding' necessary for the affirmation of the higher type of human being. And again, as we shall see, the reference to art must be understood as the reference to the 'fundamental artistic phenomenon called "life"' (XI, 129), which required the pitiless use of the mass of people as raw material for the artistic creation meant to give meaning to society and life.

4   Continuity and Discontinuity: The 'Enlightenment' from Pilate to the *ancien régime*

Not even the 'Enlightenment' phase called cultural elitism into question. This elitism was a constant feature in Nietzsche, but one that, over time, found expression in various categories and watchwords. This 'enlightenment' was certainly not be taken to mean the confident expectation that the intensive diffusion of enlightened ideas would stimulate emancipation and progress. This attitude, which had played an important role in the ideological preparation of the French Revolution, continued to animate the early socialist movement: 'If the art of printing had been discovered earlier, and if the first Christians had all been able to read', wrote Weitling, Constantine would have found it hard to expunge the egalitarian *élan* from the teachings of the Gospel and transform the new religion into an instrument of conservatism. 'Since then a dark night has lain over the pure principles of Christianity', and, 'protected by darkness', the privileged were able to oppress the masses; 'but the night is beginning to lift'.[16] Other members of this movement, for example Owen, called for 'a new rational mentality' to replace the 'irrational' mentality of a society founded in the unhappiness of the masses; thanks to reason and its affirmation, it was possible to overcome 'individual and particular' criteria to assert 'universal' principles and rights.[17] Or, to quote a well-known author hated by Nietzsche, Dühring: it was necessary to eliminate the 'mummified ignorance and super-stition of the masses', in order to lay the basis for realising 'political justice' and the 'social, economic and financial organizations of the future'.[18]

One could say that, in *Human, All Too Human*, Nietzsche set against this 'Enlightenment' from below, which aimed to delegitimise and challenge the power of the ruling classes, an 'Enlightenment' from above, which scrutinised and mercilessly exposed the fanaticism, the credulity, all the weak elements of plebeian movements of revolt. So, this was a highly elitist Enlightenment that emphatically celebrated the decisive role of great personalities in history. They had been entrusted with the dissemination of authentic enlightenment, the promotion of reason and science in the struggle against fanaticism and the vis-ionary spirit that presided over the traditional religions and the revolutionary and socialist movement: 'The darkening of Europe may depend on whether five or six freer spirits remain true to themselves or not' (VIII, 338).

Rather than actually referring to a period and a particular historical move-ment, 'Enlightenment' in this sense tended to become an ideal-typical cat-egory. Nietzsche was aware of this. In projecting the *Aufklärung* into classical antiquity, it was no accident that *Beyond Good and Evil* set it in quotation marks. And the struggle power had to wage against a Christianity by then unstop-pable was described thus: on one side, the 'noble and frivolous tolerance' of Rome, which had at its centre 'never faith itself, but rather the freedom from faith', and, on the other, the 'slaves': they 'want the unconditional; they under-stand only tyranny, even in morality', and saw in the 'smiling nonchalance' of their masters an insult to their suffering: '"Enlightenment" is infuriating' (JGB, 46 [44–5]). Christianity prevailed in Rome and was able to overwhelm 'a skeptical, southern, free-spirited world, a world that has century-long struggles

---

16   Weitling 1845, 17.
17   In Bravo 1973, 218.
18   Dühring 1873, 563.

between schools of philosophy behind and inside it, not to mention the education in tolerance given by the *imperium Romanum*'; now came 'the gruesome appearance of a protracted suicide of reason – a tough, long-lived, worm-like reason that cannot be killed all at once and with a single stroke' (JGB, 46 [44]).

This was an Enlightenment with antiquitising features. Towards the end of his conscious life, Nietzsche referred to the 'noble Romans' that 'viewed Christianity as a *foeda superstitio*' (WA, Epilogue [262]). This was probably an echo of the *exitiabilis superstitio* of which Tacitus spoke,[19] or the 'new and pernicious superstition [*superstitio nova ac malefica*]' mentioned by Suetonius.[20] Whatever the case, it was not so much Voltaire as the Greek and Latin classics that were at work in the philosopher-philologist's background. When we read in the *Annals* that the 'contagion [*malum*]' from Judea spread even to Rome, where there was an urban mass ready to welcome 'every monstrosity and shame [*cuncta* [...] *atrocia aut pudenda*]',[21] we are reminded of Nietzsche's earlier description of the relentless spread of 'superstition', of 'passionate foolery', of the 'delusions [*Wahn*]' of Rousseau and revolution (*supra*, 7 § 8).

If this description was based, on the one hand, on a reading of Taine, on the other hand, it seemed to echo the pagan authors' polemic against the early Christians, who, as Celsus noted, were 'willing and able to convert only the fools, the ignoble, the deluded, the slaves, the little women and the small children'. They targeted a public that had little inclination for, or was decidedly unreceptive to, calm reasoning, in order to spread 'the most amazing stories'; it was no accident that they condemned as evil 'being educated and experienced in the best disciplines and being and looking intelligent'.[22] In debate, their weapon of choice was the 'absurd subterfuge' that sought to extricate itself from logical difficulties and the objections of opponents by referring to faith and God, for whom 'everything is possible'.[23] The Christians, Celsus added, subjected themselves and require other to subject themselves to 'an immediate faith', even an 'immediate and preventive faith', which eschewed 'any rational procedure that adheres to the truth' and attentive and calm discussion, the 'method of questions and answers' that Plato and the great pagan culture had so valued.[24]

---

19   Tacitus, Annals XV, 44.
20   Sueton, Vitae Caesarum: Nero, 16.
21   Tacitus, Annals XV, 44.
22   Celsus, Alethes logos III, 44, 49 and III, 55.
23   Celsus, Alethes logos V, 14.
24   Celsus, Alethes logos, VI, 7a and VI, 8.

Nietzsche was heir to this 'enlightenment'. It came up quite explicitly in *Human, All Too Human*: 'Many educated people still believe that the triumph of Christianity over Greek philosophy is proof of the greater truth of the former – although it was only the case that the coarser and more violent force triumphed over the more spiritual and delicate one.' This was confirmed by the fact that, with the passing of the Middle Ages, 'the awakening sciences have point by point attached themselves to Epicurus's philosophy, but have point by point rejected Christianity' (MA, 68 [63]).

Tacitus reported that Christ, the author and the person primarily responsible for the spread of superstition and contagion, was sentenced 'to execution on the orders of the procurator Pontius Pilate'.[25] In the *Antichrist*, Pilate represented 'science', whereas Jesus and Paul expressed 'faith', nothing more than 'a veto on science' (AC, 47 [46]). The first struggle between enlightenment, science and tolerance on the one hand and faith and fanaticism on the other began with the decline of the ancient world: on the one hand, Pilate, who declared he did not know what truth was, on the other Jesus, who claimed to be identical with it: 'The noble scorn of a Roman when faced with an unashamed mangling of the word "truth" gave the New Testament its only statement of any value, – its critique, even its annihilation: "What is truth!"' (AC 46 [45]). Nietzsche did not hide but even emphasised the conflict's social dimension. To the attitude of scepticism and tolerance of Rome's self-satisfied ruling class he contrasted the need for dogmatic certainties of the 'slave', inspired and excited by foolish ideas of emancipation.

Even in the later writings, Wagner, already criticised by Nietzsche for his Christianity and his links, which persisted well beyond the years of his youth, with socialism (*supra*, 25 § 3), was denounced at the same time as an expression of the 'blackest obscurantism', the 'deadly hatred of knowledge', the 'corruption of concepts', the abandonment of the terrain of 'knowledge' (WA, Postscript [256-7]). In him lived on the Christian dogmatism that, in various ways, had animated all slave revolts: '[Y]ou should and must believe.' Being scientific was a crime against 'everything highest and holiest' (WA, 3 [238]).

Like 'astrology', this 'dogmatists' philosophy' was also destined to be overcome in future centuries (JGB, Preface [3]). This comparison with astrology, with which, as we have seen (*supra*, 8 § 4), the demand for happiness for all was equated, is interesting. We are again brought back to the hopes and false expectations and certainties of the slaves, the wretched, the simple. And it is precisely in opposition to this world that Nietzsche celebrated the 'sceptics, [...]

---

25   Tacitus, Annals XV, 44.

the only respectable types among the philosophical tribes, tribes that generally talk out of both sides of their mouths (they would talk out of five sides if they could)!' (EH, Why I am so clever, 3 [90]).

So 'Enlightenment' ideas were not lacking even in the late Nietzsche, who attacked with particular violence reason, science, the syllogism, plebeian 'stabbing' and the potential for subversion contained in all that. On several occasions, fragments from the mid-1880s announced a book with a very significant title: *The New Enlightenment* [*Die neue Aufklärung*] (XI, 228 and 346; XII, 34). However, this was a very different Enlightenment from the 'old' one, which functioned 'in the sense of the democratic herd, the levelling [*Gleichmachung*] of all'. The 'new' one, on the other hand, which subjected morality to the demystifying scrutiny of enlightenment, 'wants to show the way to the ruling natures, in the sense that they are allowed to do what the herd-being is not' (XI, 295).

Moreover, one can find a defence of myth against the hubris of reason in the same works that flirt with Enlightenment. *Daybreak* launched a sort of appeal:

> Do not even dream of mocking the mythology of the Greeks because it is so little like your ponderous metaphysics! You ought to admire a person that held acute understanding in check at precisely this point and for a long time had enough tact to avoid the danger of scholasticism and of the crafty superstition!
>
> M, 85 [62]

Later, *The Gay Science*, in positively evaluating the role of the priest as 'sage' for the 'people', whose sense of 'veneration' was to be respected, stressed at the same time that 'philosophers' were not to bow to 'this belief and superstition' (FW, 351 [209–10]). The free spirit was to be able to emancipate itself from any 'superstition', but the indiscriminate spread of enlightenment would itself be a 'superstition', and perhaps the most destructive of all.

Saying goodbye to the 'metaphysical' stage did not call elitism into question, yet it represented a radical turn with regard to evaluating the Reformation. In this case too, only the political thread of the critique of revolution allows us to orient ourselves in the labyrinth of the interpretations of Luther Nietzsche successively developed. From being the point of reference for the Dionysian reconquest of Germany he became the obscurantist monk mocked by the writings of the 'Enlightenment' period, finally configured as the protagonist of subversion brought about by the Reformation and the Peasants' War and the privileged interpreter of Germany's incurably plebeian soul. Clearly, in the years of *The Birth of Tragedy*, when Nietzsche had high hopes for the new Germany, he was under the influence of the national-liberal interpretation of the time. This praised Luther as the champion of a great national uprising against Rome and all that was 'Roman', which signified both subversion and anti-metaphysical flatness. When the critique of revolution passed over into the 'Enlightenment' period, Luther, together with the other representatives of obscurantism and the visionary religious or revolutionary spirit, came under attack. The late Nietzsche seemed, though with a reversed value judgement, to finally agree with the interpretation of Luther spread on the 'Left'. Not only Engels and Lassalle but even, before them, the Hegelian Left and Hegel himself praised the Reformation, albeit in different ways, as the first blow against the *ancien régime*. Thus, they established a line of continuity that led by way of the Peasants' War to the French Revolution.[26] This theme was found not only among individual great intellectuals but also in broad sectors of the popular and socialist movement. One of its representatives put it this way: 'Europe sighed under the yoke of serfdom and spiritual slavery. Then came Luther and Münzer – and they were understood.'[27] For the post-'metaphysical' Nietzsche, this was confirmation that the hero of the Reformation was the disastrous representative of an essential stage in the slave revolt.

5   Continuity and Discontinuity: From the Neutralisation of the Theodicy of Suffering to the Celebration of the Theodicy of Happiness

A similar combination of continuity and discontinuity can also be found in Nietzsche's attitude to the slaves' demand for happiness, to the 'social question'. To clarify this point, it helps to mention two categories developed by Weber. In analysing the religious phenomenon, he distinguished between two fundamentally different ideal-typical attitudes. We have on the one hand the 'theodicy of suffering' of the religions of redemption: it takes root above all in the less privileged sections of society or in disadvantaged individuals, who present their suffering as a claim to merit in the light of their future liberation.[28] On the other hand, we have the 'theodicy of happiness', to which the ruling classes or at least those classes content with their social status and life in general refer:

---

26   Losurdo 1997a, 2, §10 and §12.
27   Becker 1844, 20; on the Reformation as revolution, cf. also Weitling 1845, 53 f.
28   Weber 1972, 241 f.; Weber 1985, 299–302.

The happy person is seldom concerned with the fact of the possession of happiness. Beyond that he has the need: also to have a *right* to it. He wants to be convinced he also 'deserves' it. And so he also wants to be able to believe: the less happy person gets what he deserves in not possessing the same happiness. Happiness wants to be 'legitimate.'[29]

The rejection of the theodicy of suffering is a constant in Nietzsche's work. *The Birth of Tragedy* tried to neutralise it by dismissing any hope of redemption of the slave with the argument that his condition was immutable. The youthful writing went further. It subscribed to and reinterpreted Schopenhauer's thesis, according to which, at noumenal level or the level of the Dionysian 'higher community', there was an identity 'of existing and being guilty' as well as of all human and living beings: so the opposition between masters and servants, between those called upon to guide the chariot of culture and those destined to be its sacrificial victims, was meaningless.

The 'Enlightenment' period proceeded to a different method of eliminating the theodicy of suffering. In these years, Nietzsche was quite close to European liberalism: who bore the heaviest load, the popular classes (whose sensitivity was dulled by daily toil and hardship) or the ruling classes (oppressed by the weight of responsibility and even boredom)? In *Human, All Too Human*, Nietzsche talked about what he called 'my utopia':

> In a better-ordered society, the hard labour and the exigencies of life would be assigned to the one that suffers least from them, that is, to those that are most insensible, and thus step-by-step upward to the one that is most sensitive to the highest, most sublimated species of suffering and that therefore still suffers even when his life has been made as easy as possible.
>
> MA, 462 [248]

This utopia envisioned a distribution of responsibilities in perfect correspondence to degrees of merit and spiritual distinction, as well as a distribution of toil and tribulations in inverse proportion to the capacity to suffer and the degree of sensitivity. This outcome could be achieved if one split society into two classes: on the one hand, 'the caste of forced labour', on the other 'the caste of free labour' or 'caste of idlers', the elite consisting of those 'capable of true leisure' and capable at the same time of suffering much more deeply than common natures (MA, 439 [p. 237]).

---

29   Weber 1972, 242.

A final provision might serve to make the picture even more harmonious and the utopia even more enticing:

> Now if it is even possible for some movement between the two castes to take place, so that the duller, less intelligent families and individuals from the upper caste can be doomed to the lower one and the freer people from the lower caste can in turn gain admission to the higher one: then a state has been reached beyond which only an open sea of indefinite wishes can be seen. – Thus the fading voice of days gone by speaks to us; but where are there still ears to hear it?
>
> MA, 439 [238]

In this way, the Christian theodicy of suffering was radically neutralised. There was not the slightest shadow of 'unjust' suffering, because the division of labour was carried out in strict compliance with the criteria of merit and sensitivity to pain. In fact, there was not even suffering in the actual sense: those inclined to feel it were exempted from toil and even from labour as such, while toil and labour were piled onto those by definition insensitive. The socialists' big mistake was to target 'the better, outwardly more favourably placed caste of society whose real task, the production of the highest cultural goods, makes their inner lives so much harder and more painful' (MA, 480 [262]).

But doubts about this construction began to emerge immediately. The aphorism just quoted, from *Human, All Too Human*, let slip that '[h]ow happiness gets divided is not an essential consideration when it is a matter of engendering a higher culture' (MA, 439 [237]). This was an indirect admission that unhappiness continued to exist and its distribution was so minimally harmonious that it could not be justified with reference to the merits and the degree of sensitivity of this or that individual but only by the requirements of a higher culture.

In the last phase of Nietzsche's development, the polemic against '*la religion de la souffrance humaine*' (JGB, 21 [22]), i.e., against Christianity and the 'theodicy of suffering' in all its forms, became increasingly violent. But the most important innovation lay elsewhere. Even if the harmonistic theme was present to the end, in the sense that the philosopher never gave up emphasising the burden of responsibility and suffering that weighed on the more noble and delicate souls (*supra*, 13 § 3), his thinking was now marked by the frank or brutal assertion that the forward march of culture in every case required sacrifices. Meanwhile, Nietzsche had also decided to give up the attempt, undertaken in *The Birth of Tragedy* and inspired by Schopenhauer, to defuse the charge of negativity by referring to a noumenal sphere beyond the *principium individuationis*. On the other hand, in the meantime the world in which slaves or servants could accept their status as natural had vanished. The socialist 'tarantulas' had achieved at least one result: they had poisoned with their *res-sentiment* the consciousness of the subjugated. But woe betide if they achieved their next goal: '[T]here could be no greater or more disastrous misunderstanding than for the happy, the successful, those powerful in body and soul to begin to doubt their right to happiness in this way' (GM III, 14 [91]).

To be able to repel the attack, the theodicy of happiness was to become even harder. In demanding a strict social apartheid, the *Genealogy of Morals* invited people not to allow themselves to be held back by meaningless scruples: 'Away with this disgraceful mollycoddling of feeling!' (GM III, 14 [91]). The requisite new theodicy of happiness was no longer the quiet enjoyment of power and wealth: it required a relentless struggle to eliminate the threats to it. The happiness Weber spoke of, which wanted to be 'legitimate', was now like an island in danger of being swamped by the surrounding ocean. Under these circumstances, the theodicy of happiness had to be aware of the extent of the evil it faced, as well as of the hardness the happy ones had to demonstrate to defend their legitimate 'right to happiness'. It was a tragic and Dionysian 'theodicy of happiness' that despite everything could reinforce the innocence of becoming, and that was called upon to lay aside once and for all the Christian-socialist theodicy of suffering.

6   The Philosopher, the Brahmin and the 'New Party of Life'

The philosopher so often interpreted metaphorically not only thought in deeply political terms but also asked himself which means were needed to achieve the stated objectives. Hence his desire to establish or encourage the establishment of a 'party of life' to realise 'big politics' (*supra*, §11 1st 7). It was marked among other things by its ability to 'pull out Christian and nihilistic values from all sides and fight them in every disguise ... From present-day sociology, for example, from present-day music, for example; from present-day pessimism (all forms of the Christian ideal of values)' (XIII, 220).

Nietzsche himself interpreted his thinking in political or ethical-political terms. The merit he ascribed to himself is not in the first place to have encouraged philological or aesthetic or psychological research. All that played a subordinate role. Even when, in the years of *The Birth of Tragedy*, he declared that 'becoming is not a moral phenomenon, but only an artistic phenomenon' (PHG, 19, I, 869), he took as his first polemical target the moral worldview that drove slave revolts against 'injustice'. This is confirmed by subsequent developments: 'Thus no one until now has examined the value of that most famous of all medicines called morality; and for that, one must begin by questioning it for once. Well then! Precisely that is our task' (FW, 345 [203]). It was a task whose meaning far transcended the realm of pure science or culture: 'The question of the origin of moral values is a question of the first rank for me because it determines the future of humanity' (EH, *Daybreak*, 2 [121]).

Solving this problem was a 'task', a 'mission', a 'destiny'. Nietzsche insisted on this throughout the entire course of his development. As a letter from the young professor to Rohde shows, in Basel he had already willingly assumed the 'mission [*Bestimmung*]' that Wagner 'sees foreshadowed in me' (*supra*, 3 §2). The later change in the content of the 'mission' does not mean the disappearance of this form of self-consciousness: 'Our mission has us at its disposal; even if we do not yet know it' (MA, Preface, 7). This theme returned insistently, although not always in the same words: 'Changing the estimations – is my task [*Aufgabe*]' (IX, 470). In addition to making clear – said the philosopher – 'the discrepancy between the greatness of my task [*Aufgabe*] and the smallness of my contemporaries' (EH, Prologue, 1 [71]), '[r]evaluing values might have required more abilities than have ever been combined in any one individual' (EH, Why I am so clever, 9 [97]). The empirical individual was the carrier of a destiny: '[A]n unspeakable responsibility rests on me. [...] I am carrying the destiny [*Schicksal*] of humanity on my shoulders' (EH, *The Case of Wagner*, 4 [143]). The title of a chapter of *Ecce Homo* says it all: 'Why I am a destiny [*Schicksal*]'. As Nietzsche explained, he felt a sense of 'responsibility for all the millennia to come' (EH, Why I am so clever, 10 [99]).

This shows 'how useless, how arbitrary my whole existence as a philologist seemed with respect to my task' (EH, *Human, All Too Human*, 3 [117]). Philology, art, psychology, and all other disciplines were nothing in comparison with 'world-historical tasks' (EH, *The Untimely Ones*, 3 [114]), or rather the tasks whose solution divided the history of humanity into two parts. To those interpreters that would like to put Nietzsche in a sphere remote from political conflict and closer to pure aesthetic contemplation or pure psychological research, one could say, in the words of the philosopher: 'There is nothing more important than problems of morality' (XIV, 263).

Even if Lou Salomé's interpretation was not free from contradictions, it nevertheless highlighted an essential aspect of Nietzsche's thought and personality: he 'seeks not to teach, but to convert'.[30] From the very start, he spoke as a follower and theorist of a worldview that went far beyond his person, as member or leader of a movement by no means confined to the academic field but

---

30   Andreas-Salomé 1970, 186.

engaged instead in intense political struggle. Already as a young student, in a letter to Rohde of 3 or 4 May 1868, he formulated this intention: 'To put at the disposal of our fellow-human beings our constellation of powers and views. [...] After all, we are not allowed to live for ourselves' (B, I, 2, 275).

This attitude accompanied the young student, the philologist, the philosopher to the end. It is perhaps helpful, even at the cost of some repetition, to review the most significant expressions encountered in this regard in the course of reconstructing Nietzsche's intellectual biography. Shortly after his arrival in Basel, he called for a 'struggle' without quarter: many would fall, but the important thing was that others were ready to take up the 'banner' (*supra*, 1 §17). He was no philologist motivated by the desire to reconstruct a chapter of history, in order to produce a nostalgic reference to the land of Aeschylus and the pre-Socratic philosophers, but an activist in search of a political model to set against modernity: 'Hellenism has for us the value saints have for Catholics' (VII, 18); 'what we hope for from the future was once already reality' (GMD, I, 532).

Similar considerations applied to his relationship with Wagner. Before the 'Enlightenment' period, Wagner was admired and held up to the public as the 'sublime' champion of a great cause that bears on the future of Germany and culture as such (GT, Preface [14]). A sort of army was to muster around the great musician: 'For us, Bayreuth means the morning consecration on the day of battle' (WB, 4, I, 451).

He distanced himself from those that stood apart from reality and the political struggle: 'Only the doer learns' (Za, IV, The Ugliest Human Being [216]). One had to take sides. If Strauss summoned those that identified with modernity ('We of Today', *Wir Heutigen*) (*supra*, 4 §7), Nietzsche appealed to the 'untimely', 'we posthumous ones' (FW, 365 [230]); '[w]e that are new, nameless, hard to understand; we premature births of an as yet unproved future'. One can understand now why Nietzsche, in defining his position, always used the plural: 'we argonauts of the ideal' (FW, 382 [246], EH, *Thus Spoke Zarathustra*, 2 [125]); 'we free spirits' (JGB, 44 [40], MA, Preface, 7, WA, Postscript), 'we immoralists' (JGB, 32 [117]), 'we immoralists and anti-Christians' (GD, Morality as anti-nature, 3 [173]), 'we pagans' (XIII, 487); 'we halcyon ones', followers of the *'gaya scienza'* (WA, 10 [253]).

Gradually, these slogans filled with a precise political content: 'We are no humanitarians', 'we contemplate the necessity for new orders as well as for a new slavery' (FW, 377 [241–2]). And precisely because the main contradiction was between masters and servants, we were 'homeless' 'good Europeans'; (FW, 377 [241–2]); 'our homeland', more accurately, our 'height', our endless distance from the mob (Za, II, On the Rabble [76], EH, Why am I so wise, 8 [84]). Looking down from this peak, the national enmities that plagued the European elites seemed petty and senseless. A break with the past was needed. The new anti-'humanitarian' and anti-democratic front then forming had nothing to do with traditional provincialism and chauvinism or with the clerically oriented conservatism with which it was often linked.

The members of the new 'party' were called upon to be proudly self-aware and to draw a clear line of demarcation, especially between themselves and the wretched and the 'rabble'. But it was not just the wretched that swelled the ranks of the democratic and socialist movement; intellectuals, artisans, etc., also joined. Aristocratic radicalism was to have no dealings with them, with 'merely "productive people"' (*supra*, 11 § 3–4). Ordinary humanity was mediocre and inwardly poor and empty, above all it was fearful and unable to think in large perspective, be adventurous, and take risks. What an abyss in relation to 'our taste', Nietzsche commented. We left all that 'to the many, the great majority! We, however, want to become who we are – human beings who are new, unique, incomparable, who give themselves laws, who create themselves!' (FW, 335 [189]).

While 'the noble method of valuation' draws a clear line with the mob, it strengthened the bond between members of the elite: '[W]e the noble, the good, the beautiful and the happy!' (GM, I, 10 [20]), we, the 'generous and rich in spirit' (FW, 378 [243]); 'we are artists of contempt', 'it makes us "God's elect"' (FW, 379 [243–4]); 'we *other ones* will proceed at once to the grand and sublime work of life' (XIII, 644).

Self-awareness gained or regained itself generated a pugnacious spirit of defiance: 'Let us whirl the dust in doses / into sickly people's noses, / let us shoo these sickly flies! / This whole coast we must unshackle / from their shrivel-breasted cackle, / from these courage-vacant eyes!' (FW, Appendix, To the Mistral, A Dance Song [259–60]). The critical dissolution of traditional dogmas and values in no way translated into an inert and cowardly scepticism (*supra*, 21 § 6).

The relationship Nietzsche established between himself and the 'party of life' he envisaged is clarified by a passage from *Beyond Good and Evil*, which asked about the possible role of 'individuals from [...] a noble lineage [*vornehme Herkunft*]' that tended, because of 'their high spirituality, towards a retiring and contemplative life, reserving for themselves only the finest sorts of rule (over exceptional young men or monks)'. They were a bit like 'the Brahmins', who 'assumed the power to appoint kings for the people, while they themselves kept and felt removed and outside, a people of higher, over-kingly tasks' (JGB 61 [54]). Later, Zarathustra became the point of reference for kings committed to the struggle against modern massification and devastation: 'With the sword of your words you strike through our hearts' thickest darkness. You discover our distress, for behold! We are on our way to find the higher man. [...] Again and again you pricked our ears and hearts with your sayings' (Za, IV, Conversation with the Kings, 1–2 [198–9]). Zarathustra-Nietzsche aspired to be the Brahmin of the 'party of life.'

7   'Linguistic Self-Discipline' *contra* 'Anarchy' and 'Linguistic Raggedness [*Sprachverlumpung*]'

Even aspects at first sight purely literary and aesthetic reveal a certain connection to political interest. In the meantime, the accuracy and elegance of prose are no strangers to the pedagogical intent: We know 'that whatever is well said is believed' (FW, 23 [48]). Anyone that wants to act on reality cannot simply appeal to reason: 'The more abstract the truth you want to teach, the more it needs to seduce the senses first.' It is not a matter of a purely external element: 'Style must prove that you believe in your thoughts, that you do not just think them but experience them.' In that sense, 'style must live', it must demonstrate that it is life: such were the recommendations in the sort of 'Ten Commandments' the philosopher sent to Lou Salomé in August 1882 (B, III, 1, 243–5). On the other hand, the addressee knew the writer 'wants to convince the whole person, he wants his words to submerge themselves in the soul and restitute its depths', because only thus could he achieve the goal to which he aspired, to convince and even, as we know, convert the reader.[31]

But the elegance and vigour of the prose, quite apart from their pedagogical effectiveness, had a deeper political significance. The stylistic mediocrity of modernity pointed up the absence of *otium* from a world that had forgotten the cultural foundation of slavery and celebrated the 'dignity of labour' even for intellectuals. The intellectual ended up reduced to the status of a journalist doing 'day labour [*Tagelöhnerei*]'; and just like the *Tagelöhner* [day labourer] proper (BA, 1, I, 670–1 [41]), the intellectual-journalist was also a 'slave of the day, chained to the present moment, and thirsting for something – ever thirsting!' (BA, 5, I, 747 [135]). Nietzsche had been pursuing this theme ever since the years of *The Birth of Tragedy*. Because of this unbridled productivity, there was no longer any place left for form and for taste for form:

'Rather do anything than nothing' – even this principle is a cord to strangle all culture and all higher taste. Just as all forms are visibly being

31   Andreas-Salomé 1970, 187.

destroyed by the haste of the workers, so, too, is the feeling for form itself,
the ear and eye for the melody of movements.

FW, 329 [183–4]

So, the attention to form, the 'goldsmith's art and connoisseurship of the word,
which has nothing but fine, cautious work to take care of and which achieves
nothing if it does not achieve it lento' (M, Preface, 5 [6–7]), was also an essential moment in Nietzsche's critique of modernity. In Germany it was preferable
'in future that Latin be spoken; for I am ashamed of a language so bungled and
vitiated' (BA, 2, I, 675 [47]). '[S]elf-discipline in [...] language', the invitation and
obligation to walk 'the thorny [road] of language' in order to give stylistically
appropriate expression to one's thoughts, all that as aimed at turning away even
more radically from the present, an object of 'physical loathing', now also criticised on the grounds of an 'aesthetic judgement' (BA, 2, I, 684 [48]) that was
simultaneously political.

Modern intellectuals seemed to want to appropriate the motto 'Primum
scribere, deinde philosophari' (FW, Seneca et hoc genus omne, 34 [17]). This attitude had devastating consequences:

> We think too fast, while on our way somewhere, while walking or in the
> midst of all sorts of business, even when thinking of the most serious
> things; we need little preparation, not even much silence: it is as if we
> carried around in our heads an unstoppable machine that keeps working
> even under the most unfavourable circumstances.

What an abyss separated this from classical antiquity and its habit of meditation: '[Y]es, one stood still for hours on the street once the thought "arrived" –
on one or two legs' (FW, 6 [34]). And to the seriousness and intensity of thought
there corresponded attention to and respect for form, as already demonstrated
by the 'great earnestness' accorded 'language' (supra, 4 § 3). Fortunately, something of this great legacy lived on in the scholar formed by the careful reading
and interpretation of the great Greek and Latin texts. First and foremost, the
philologist felt discomfort and repulsion in the face of the mess that was modern 'culture': 'For in the case of most scholarly works done by philosophers in
universities, the philologist feels that they are poorly written, without scientific
rigour and, for the most part, odiously dull' (SE, 8; I, 417). He that had truly
measured up to classical antiquity tended to be a 'teacher [...] of slow reading'. 'You end up writing slowly as well', in clear contrast to '[a]n age of "work"'
marked by 'unseemly and sweating overhaste': 'Philology is, namely, that venerable art that requires of its admirers one thing above all else: to go aside, to

take time, to become still, become slow', not 'that wants at once to be over and done with everything, even with every old and new book' (M, Preface, 5 [6–7]).

If form and content tended to blend into one, one could not separate philosophical content from a writing style that in its very shape emphasised the rejection of modern frenzy and vulgarity: 'The poverty of the language corresponds to the poverty of opinion: think of our literary journals' (VII, 830). 'But better writing means at the same time better thinking; to find things more and more worth communicating and really to be able to communicate them' (WS, 87). Nietzsche went out of his way to emphasise this theme:

> Now the good writer is distinguished not only by the force and conciseness of his sentence form: but one can guess, one can smell, if one has fine enough nostrils, that this writer constantly forces himself and practices, principally to establish, in a rigorous way, and make firmer his concepts (i.e., to combine his words with clear concepts): and until that happens, not to write.
>
> XI, 445–6

Familiarity with classical antiquity and a distance at least in theory from modernity had a positive effect: 'badly schooled and unphilosophical spirits' were those without a philological education to lend precision and clarity to categories and concepts and to sweep away the 'formless, floating splodges of concepts' (XI, 445).

Naturally, these passages also had an autobiographical meaning that at times became explicit: 'I am not one of those who think with a wet quill in hand' (FW, 93 [90]). The following passage reads like a confession: '[T]he great masters of prose have almost always also been poets, be it publicly or only in secret, in the 'closet'; and verily, one writes good prose only face to face with poetry!' (FW, 92 [90]). As the 'father of all good things, [...] war is also the father of good prose!' (FW, 92 [90]).

And yet, the loss of feeling for form and the struggle to recover it went far beyond this or that personality. Even regardless of classical antiquity, 'the mistrustful constraint in the communicability of thought, the discipline that thinkers imposed on themselves, thinking within certain guidelines imposed by the church or court or Aristotelian presuppositions', had been 'the means through which strength, reckless curiosity, and subtle agility have been bred into the European spirit' (JGB, 188 [78]).

The emergence and rise of the intellectual-journalist, at once eulogist and slave of the present, was a tragic symptom of decay and a turning point in history. In this figure were embodied 'all the faults of our public, literary, and artistic life, [...] hasty and vain production, the disgraceful manufacture of books; complete want of style; [...] the loss of every aesthetic canon; the voluptuousness of anarchy and chaos' (BA, 2. I, 681 [54]). Later, *Twilight of the Idols* would accuse Socrates, the champion of plebeian subversion, of 'chaos and anarchy of his instincts' (GD, The Problem of Socrates, 4 [163]). On the other hand, regarding the present, David Friedrich Strauss, the uncritical eulogist of modernity, to which he adhered with 'the shameless optimism of the philistine' (DS, 6; I, 191), was at the same time guilty of 'linguistic raggedness [*Sprach-Verlumpung*]' (MA, Preface to the second vol., 1 [3]).

'Anarchy', 'raggedness': the boundaries between aesthetic judgement and political judgement are transient. There can be no doubt that the denunciation of stylistic coarsening was also a denunciation of the political coarsening of modernity. Strauss's 'shoddy jargon' (*supra* 5.2) was the 'shoddy jargon of our noble "today"' (DS, 12, I, 235 [70, 60]), according to the first *Unfashionable Observation*, quoting Schopenhauer (DS, 11, I, 221). Superficiality of content and sloppy style were unmistakable symptoms of the emergence of a fateful social type, the plebeian intellectual: 'For the only form of culture that concerns the bloodshot eye and the numbed thought organ of this class of scholarly laborers is precisely that philistine culture whose gospel Strauss is preaching' (DS, 8, I, 205 [48–9]).

The main diet of this new social class was newspapers. We already know from the preparatory texts and versions of *The Birth of Tragedy* about the relationship between the shallow optimism of 'Socratism' and the then 'press' (*supra*, 3 §2). As for the reading of a German philistine like Strauss, 'without doubt, newspapers, and the magazines that go with them, constitute the bulk of what the German reads everyday' (DS, 11, I, 222 [64]). And it is from here that the 'mundane political discussions', naturally 'about marriage' and 'capital punishment', but above all about 'universal suffrage' and 'labour unrest' 'take their cue' (DS, 9, I, 215 [58]). Again, poverty of form coincided with that of content. This theme was resumed and radicalised in the following years:

> The greatest part by far of what is read is newspapers and suchlike. Look at our magazines, our learned journals: all those that write speak as if to an 'unselected audience', and let themselves go, or rather fall, on their armchairs. – It's worst for those that above all value hidden thoughts and, more than anything openly expressed in books, love the ellipses. – Freedom of the press ruins style, and eventually spirit. [...] 'Freedom of thought' ruins thinkers.
>
> XI, 440

On the basis of the unbreakable bond between form and content, the struggle for form – at least in the hopeful years of the foundation of the Second Reich – was configured as an immediately political struggle. One was to put an end, at least in Germany, to every 'modern carnival motley', often celebrated by intellectuals as 'the "modern as such"' (DS, 1, I, 163 [9]). 'We Germans commonly regard form as a convention, as a disguise and deception, and for this reason among us form, if not actually hated, is at any rate not loved' (HL, 4, I, 275 [112]). It was considered inessential and external, unlike 'content' and 'inwardness'; however, when separated from form, this 'inwardness' could have all sorts of qualities, though 'as a totality it remains weak because all the beautiful threads are not bound together as a strong knot' (HL, 4, I, 276 [113]). The political impotence of the Second Reich, its inability to keep the promises made at the time of its foundation, was also its stylistic impotence.

8 Aphorism, Essay and System

The central significance of political or ethical-political interest also explains the succession of literary and stylistic forms in Nietzsche's development. He began his philosophical career with two manifestoes of the 'party' or movement of the tragic vision of the world (*The Birth of Tragedy* and the lectures *On the Future of Our Educational Institutions*) and moved onto texts (the *Unfashionable Observations*) that aimed either to subject the most prominent representatives of the 'party' of modernity to a devastating theoretical and political critique or to analyse the authors and central points of the platform of the 'party' or anti-modern movement he was seeking to develop. Only when this platform entered into crisis, as a result of the obvious modern vulgarity of the Second Reich and the dwindling hope for Germany's tragic regeneration, did Nietzsche arrive at the aphorism. It allowed him the mobility needed at a time when old certainties had collapsed and no new ones emerged.

On the other hand, during the 'Enlightenment' period, deeper-lying trends reached maturity and their full expression. We shall see later that at the basis of Nietzsche's thought and philosophising lay a complex interdisciplinary combination and a conviction in the translatability of languages. In the passage from one language to another, translation was mediated by way of the attempt at psychological empathy, not by way of the systematic treatment of each individual discipline, which was obviously impossible. That is why Nietzsche resorted to the aphorism. This genre also attracted Nietzsche because of the rigorous linguistic self-discipline present from the beginning and to which, as we have seen, he attributed the philosophical significance of a distancing from the journalistic hustle and lack of leisure that characterised modernity in all its manifestations. In this sense, the aphorism was a trend already inherent in the manner and content of Nietzsche's philosophy. And, with the growing sense of isolation and 'untimeliness', it became gradually accentuated. One could make no impression by means of a new knowledge yet to be constructed on a madness hundreds of years old that had become common sense and pervaded every manifestation of cultural and political life: one could do so only with the hammer-blows of deadly aphorisms. For these were highly effective, pedagogically and politically: 'Finally, my brevity has yet another value: given the questions that occupy me, I must say many things briefly so that they will be heard even more briefly.' In order to influence even readers furthest from anti-democratic radicalism, 'my writings should inspire, elevate, and encourage them to be virtuous' (FW, 381 [245]).

The vision of philosophy as self-confession also led to the fragment. Starting out from the conviction that 'the will to a system is a lack of integrity', so one was to be wary of 'all systematizers' (GD, Judgements and arrows, 26 [159]), one could conclude that 'the most profound and inexhaustible books will probably always have something of the aphoristic and sudden character of Pascal's *Pensées*. The driving forces and evaluations are very much below the surface; what comes out of them is the effect' (XI, 522). But one was also not to lose sight of the political meaning of this priority accorded to psychology. What really mattered in a philosophy was not its systematic constructions and logical and speculative links but the noble or plebeian spirit expressed in it, the healthy and vital nature of those that had turned out well or the sick and troubled nature of those whose lives had turned out badly. To attribute too much importance to the chains of demonstration was already itself an indication of plebeianism, for by so doing one put at the centre not the egregious and exceptional personality but the commonality of the concept, and thus ultimately the herd.

In two fragments of the spring and summer of 1885, Nietzsche felt the need to reflect not only on the intellectual journey he had accomplished but also on the forms of expression he had used at each stage in his development. The philosopher likened his writings to 'nets cast' with the aim of winning others to his theoretical and political vision (*supra*, 1 § 17), and asked:

> Who to turn to? I made my longest attempt with that many-faceted and enigmatic human being through whose mind have perhaps passed more good and bad things about the soul than through that of any other human being of this century, with Richard Wagner. Later, I imagined I would 'seduce' German youth. [...] Later still, I made myself a language for manly and audacious heads and hearts waiting in some remote corner of the

earth for my strange things. Finally – but you will not believe at what 'finally' I arrived. Enough, I invented *Thus Spoke Zarathustra*.

XI, 507

The second fragment continues:

I do not write essays (*Abhandlungen*): essays are for donkeys and magazine readers. Speeches too! As a young man, I directed my 'unfashionable observations' to young people, to whom I spoke of my experiences and vows, to lure them into my labyrinth. [...] Well: so I no longer have any reason to be 'eloquent' in that old way; today, I would perhaps no longer be able to.

XI, 579

The continuity of the pedagogical-political concern remained, but found expression in ever changing literary forms. The attempt to influence the Wagnerian 'party' by means of *The Birth of Tragedy* and the *Five Prefaces* devoted (not by accident) to Cosima Wagner gave way to the *Unfashionable Observations*. The latter, on the model of the Basel lectures, seemed to take on the shape of 'speeches [*Reden*]', which tried to influence the 'youth' to join the struggle against modernity. This attempt proved futile, so there followed the appeal to 'manly and audacious heads and hearts', the lonely spirits that the aphorisms of the 'Enlightenment' period in particular addressed.

They were also the target of *Zarathustra*, but by recourse to a different genre: it was no longer, as Nietzsche observed in his letters, 'a collection of aphorisms' but 'poetry [*Dichtung*]', presented at the same time as a kind of 'fifth "gospel"' (B, III, 1, 326–7). He had meanwhile overcome the 'ice' of the 'Enlightenment' period, and this 'new health', this regained confidence in his own ability to intervene politically, was matched by a more aggressive literary form.

In the second of the above fragments, Nietzsche poured scorn on the essay genre. It was still two years to the publication of the *Genealogy of Morals*, made up precisely of three 'essays [*Abhandlungen*]'. The 'moral preachings' of *Thus Spoke Zarathustra* (B, III, 1, 321) were now replaced by a more organic reflection. On the other hand, in a letter written in 1883, Nietzsche had already expressed his satisfaction at 'the consistent compactness and coherence of the thoughts, even if not consciously and intentionally pursued, in the variegated mass of my recent books' (B, III, 1, 429). And, in 1885, he spoke of his 'books of aphorisms' as 'chains of thoughts' (XI, 579). So the prerequisites for the development of the systematic thinking soon to be realised were already in place: Nietzsche long toyed with the plan to elaborate his definitive work, *The Will to Power*, which had the task of organically shaping the theoretical and political platform of the 'party of life' and in which the aphorisms were connected to a logical sequence and supposed to take a form not unlike the propositions, corollaries, and scholia of Spinoza's *Ethics*.

How to Challenge Two Millennia of History – Anti-dogmatism, and Dogmatism of Aristocratic Radicalism

1   *Philosophia facta est quae philologia fuit*

To highlight the thoroughly political and consistently reactionary character of Nietzsche's thought is not at all to engage in reductionism and lose sight of its theoretical surplus. On the contrary, only with these in mind can it emerge in full force. To challenge two thousand years of history is, at first sight, a hopeless undertaking. It can only be attempted if one has the courage to question not only the apparent 'evidence' of the dominant ideology but also, and above all else, the political, epistemological, philosophical and scientific categories on which it is based. Aristocratic radicalism cannot go onto the attack against an enemy so deeply entrenched without arming itself in an appropriate manner at the theoretical level, without readying a mighty war machine; it cannot refute two thousand years of the 'lie' without problematising and redefining the concept of 'truth', together with everything else.

We have seen how the second *Untimely Observation* mocked the 'religion of historical power', which wanted to acknowledge as rational and irreversible the world as it had emerged from the French Revolution, modernity as such. But how specifically could one neutralise this religion and this power? Perhaps philologists were in a privileged position: they had not lost, indeed they were required to keep, the memory of a living, wonderful world in a time-span of barely '34 successive lives, each calculated at 60 years' (above, chap. 6 § 3). It was a past that was not too remote as long as one freed oneself from the superstition of the end of history and the dimension of the *longue durée*.

The college years and the semi-reclusion of Pforta and the subsequent time at university brought about in Nietzsche a positive identification with Greece, that 'real home of culture' (BA, 2, I, 686 [41]), celebrated and inwardly lived as an irremediable antithesis to the present: 'How wretched we moderns are compared to the Greeks and Romans' (SE, 2, I, 343). So, philology had the task, quoting Rohde, 'to keep awake and clear for senescent humanity the memory of the richest days of its happy youth'.[1]

---

1   Rohde 1989c, 109.

Thus was delineated a philology-philosophy animated by a strong political passion that, far from fixing on parliamentary matters in the narrower sense, experienced as petty and misleading, aimed instead to challenge the entire historical cycle of modernity. By making possible or encouraging the seductiveness of classical antiquity, a philological education provided essential weapons in the struggle against massification and modern egalitarianism. Nietzsche was fully aware of this: only the 'strongest souls', the 'souls that have turned out well', the 'strong and enterprising souls', those that could understand and accept 'a different, grander morality from that of today' and were ready to struggle or already were 'struggling relentlessly and absolutely for the special rights of superior human beings and against the "herd animal"' could experience 'the finest of all the seductions' or 'the finest and most effective of all the anti-democratic and anti-Christian' seductions (XI, 480 and 582–3). The final chapter of the *Twilight of the Idols*, 'What I owe the ancients', sounded like an indirect but solemn acknowledgement of his philological training.

Only by settling accounts with Christianity was it possible to challenge current moral and political ideas. And, once again, familiarity with the world and texts of classical antiquity proved to be valuable and decisive. Regarding the importance of philology in Nietzsche's intellectual formation, Deussen, a classmate from grammar school, gave an interesting example:

> Our Christian faith lasted to some extent until after the final exam. It was inadvertently undermined by the excellent historical-critical method with which the ancients were treated at Pforta, and which was then transferred automatically to the territory of the Bible.[2]

As early as 1862, while at school in Pforta, Nietzsche expressed the wish for 'a freer point of view, which would allow us to deliver an impartial judgement appropriate to its time on religion and Christianity' (FG, 431–2). Later, he noted that 'philologists' were 'the destroyers of every faith that rests on books' (FW, 358 [222]).

The explosive results and effects of this discipline went far beyond destroying the belief in the divine inspiration of a sacred text abstracted from the contingencies of history. The third *Unfashionable Observation* noted that 'the modern human being lives in this oscillation between Christianity and antiquity, between a fearful or lying Christianity of customs and an antiquitizing equally timid and self-conscious' (SE, 2, I, 345). Thus, Nietzsche began to

---

2 Deussen 1901, 4.

call into question a long tradition that lay at the roots of Western identity, that appealed both to classical antiquity and to Christianity, without realising the fundamental contradictions inherent in this genealogical construction. It was, he argues, now time to take note of the incompatibility of 'Christian feelings' and 'ancient taste' (JGB, 210 [104]).

Above all, Christian identity, the unity of the sacred text on which rested current orthodoxy in the West, was shown to be mythical. Nietzsche was boundlessly contemptuous of the 'philology of Christianity', which with its 'shameless arbitrariness of interpretation' had staged an 'unprecedented philological farce' around the Old Testament, raped and instrumentalised in prophecy of Christ to the extent that 'a philologist, on hearing of it, is caught halfway between wrath and laughter' (M, 84). A preparatory notice for *The Birth of Tragedy* had already observed: 'Well-being on earth is the religious tendency of Judaism. Christianity's lies in suffering. The contrast is enormous' (VII, 119). Nietzsche's anti-Judaism at around this time can be explained by Schopenhauer and Wagner's influence. Later, the hierarchisation of the two constituent parts of the Christian Bible was reversed. The thesis of their absolute incompatibility as retained:

> [T]his New Testament (which is a type of Rococo of taste in every respect) gets pasted together with the Old Testament to make a single book, a 'Bible', a 'book in itself': this is probably the greatest piece of temerity and 'sin against the spirit' that literary Europe has on its conscience.
>
> JGB, 52 [48]

The 'sin against the spirit' was primarily a sin against philology. Once philology was taken seriously, the political orthodoxy of the West, along with its religious orthodoxy, fell apart. The unitary tradition whose representative and heir the West claimed to be was actually composed of different and conflicting traditions.

To the watchful eye of the philologist, modernity revealed itself to be not only repulsive but untenable, precisely at the philological level. Reversing Seneca's saying, Nietzsche summed up the meaning of his fateful intellectual development from philologist to philosopher or to a philosopher radically critical of modernity as follows: *philosophia facta est quae philologia fuit* (HKP, 268). Obviously, the philology at issue here was not the usual one, marked by 'a micrological and sterile learning' (BA, 3, I, 706 [92]), not the discipline cultivated by 'philologists' that 'work perseveringly on a small screw' and are content to be master of 'this narrowest of fields', ignoring the 'remaining questions even of their own science', and of the whole of 'philosophy'; they were to be con-

sidered as mere 'factory workers in the service of science', completely subjected
to the intellectual division of labour and professional routine and unable to
acquire an overview of the whole (FS, III, 329).

The 'too soft [*zu weichlich*]' philologists, those that lacked the courage to
look the reality of classical antiquity in the eye and were therefore prone to
suppress everything in it that was in contradiction with the modern world,
could also not be taken into consideration. In this way, along with courage,
historical distance from the present was also lost. On the other hand, a great
scholar of the Homeric epics was not lacking in courage: 'That Friedrich August
Wolf has affirmed the necessity of slavery in the interests of culture is one of
the most powerful insights of my great predecessor' (VII, 156). This acknowledgement, expressed by Nietzsche while still professor of classical philology,
was repeated in following years: 'The best Germany has given is critical discipline'; in confirmation, he mentioned Friedrich August Wolf, together with a few
other authors (XI, 496), and reckoned him, alongside Lessing, Herder, Kant and
Niebuhr, to the 'beautiful audacious race' of the 'brave', capable of expressing
'a certain spiritual "militarism" and "Fridericianism"' (XIV, 362–3), which Nietzsche, as we know, recommended as an antidote to the soft taste of modernity.
So, a philology that was not 'soft' raised the question of the link between culture and slavery, forcing us to look at modernity not as something obvious but
as a frightening deviation.

2   Interpretation of the 'Text of Nature' and of the History and
Problematisation of the 'Obvious'

It is no accident that, in defining philosophising, Nietzsche resorted to categories clearly derived from philology. The world, reality as a whole, was a text that
had to be interpreted. It was Schopenhauer's merit to want to 'interpret [*deu-
ten*]' the 'picture of life'. Nature presented itself in 'big strokes', a necessary starting point for understanding 'our small writing' (IX, 463). Elsewhere, he spoke of
'interpreting the world [*Welt-Ausdeutung*]' (JGB, 20 [20]). In the final analysis,
'human understanding [...] is simply interpretation on the basis of us and our
needs' (XI, 624). Here, then, an 'old philologist' – as Nietzsche called himself –
'cannot help maliciously putting his finger on bad tricks of interpretation' (JGB,
22 [22]), criticising 'false interpretations [*Ausdeutungen*] of things' (XI, 501).
The analogy between philological precision and philosophical rigour was clear:

> In the same way a good philologist (and generally any scholar schooled in
> philology) is averse to wrong interpretations of texts (for example those

of Protestant preachers in the pulpits – which is why the educated classes no longer go to church), so too, and not just because of great 'virtue', 'honesty', etc., the counterfeiting of religious interpretation of all experiences goes against the grain.

XI, 435

Like nature, history seemed to take the form of a text. What, for example, was the French Revolution, if not a big text waiting to be interpreted (JGB, 38 [37])? The great importance of the philology model encouraged an anti-sensualistic epistemology that was aware of its own intrinsic problematic and rejected the illusion of immediacy and evidence: after all, reality, even that that appeared immediately to our senses, still had to be interpreted. Not for nothing did *Beyond Good and Evil*, a text that developed in particular detail the theory of philosophical systems and worldviews as 'interpretations' of the 'text' formed by nature and history, polemicised with particular force against the belief in an 'immediate certainty', this *'contradictio in adjecto'* (JGB, 16 [16]); the 'belief in immediate certainties [...] is a moral naïveté that does little credit to us philosophers' (JGB, 34 [34]). Even pleasure and pain, or rather, the feelings of pleasure and pain, were ultimately interpretations: to elevate them to the dignity of an immediate and incontrovertible fact was to surrender to 'superficiality' (*supra*, 21 § 4). Along with the supposed immediate certainties vanished the illusion that knowledge could be acquired without effort and rendered into undisputed common sense: ' "All truth is simple" – Isn't that a double lie?' (GD, Judgements and arrows, 4 [156]).

> Now it is beginning to dawn on maybe five or six brains that physics too is only an interpretation and arrangement of the world (according to ourselves! if I may say so) and not an explanation of the world.
>
> JGB, 14 [15]

The natural sciences were not only an interpretation of the world like all others, they were an interpretation formulated and asserted on the basis of preoccupations and choices not epistemological but aesthetic and political in character. They started out from the democratic and plebeian taste for flattening and homologising reality. Misunderstood and transfigured as a place of incontrovertible certainty, 'science' turned out in the end to be 'prejudice' (FW, 373 [238]).

3 The Philologist-Philosopher and the View from Outside and Above

Given the store he set by interpretation and thus by its inherent anti-dogmatic potential, philology too exerted a profound influence on the manner of Nietzsche's philosophising. Classical antiquity became a point of observation so remote, and so elevated, that it could critically overlook centuries, even more than two millennia, of Western history in its entirety. For that reason, it was able to unsettle the present, the more radically, the stronger the familiarity and identification with the past: 'antiquity', taken in its most profound sense, made it 'untimely' (VIII, 49), stressed the change and 'becoming' that marked the historical process, and awakened in respect of existing social and political reality that *thaumazein* that, in Aristotelian thinking, was the foundation of philosophising (VII, 387). Common consciousness 'feels in complete harmony with the present state of affairs and acquiesces in it as something granted or self-understood [*selbstverständliches*]' (BA, Introduction, I, 646 [11]). While classical philology destroyed the supposed immediate evidence and obviousness of modernity, it encouraged philosophical interrogation, that 'lasting kind of philosophical wonder, from which alone, as a fruitful soil, a deep and noble culture can grow forth' (BA, 5, I, 741 [128]).

In the face of the degrading spectacle of the modern world, philosophy 'must not only astonish, but terrify' (BA, 2, 673–4 [92]), with 'that humble feeling that we, when compared with such a world as it was, have no right to exist at all' (BA, 3, I, 701 [78]). In any case, estrangement from a present and a reality experienced for the most part as obvious and peaceful remained in need of no further explanation and interrogation. Nietzsche was well aware of the importance of philology for his philosophical formation. In the last years of his conscious life he again observed: 'Having been a philologist is not for nothing; perhaps you remain one ...'; this allows one to grow and express one's beliefs '[m]ore cold, more distant, shrewd, lofty' (M, Preface, 5 [6]).

So, to be authentic and radical, philosophical reflection had to be able to incorporate a view [*Blick*] from outside that was also a view from above: 'Error of errors! The familiar is what we are used to, and what we are used to is the most difficult to "know" – that is, to view as a problem, to see as strange, as distant, as "outside us"' (FW, 355 [215]). This statement can be compared with a famous passage from *The Phenomenology of the Mind*: 'Generally, the familiar, precisely because it is familiar, is not known.'[3] If, in Hegel, it was the dialectic that problematised concepts, so that they lost their fixity and apparent unam-

---

3 Hegel 1969–79, Vol. 3, 35.

biguity, in Nietzsche this role was taken over by the view, which also lost its apparent unambiguity: 'What makes a human being original is that he sees something all do not see' (IX, 591). But the novelty of the view is no 'fact' in the positivistic sense. For the novelty of the view to be able to emerge and unfold, one needed the courage to be able to detach oneself from apparently obvious and incontrovertible representations:

> There is a stupid humility that is by no means rare, and those afflicted with it are altogether unfit to become votaries of knowledge. For as soon as a person of this type perceives something striking, he turns on his heel, as it were, and says to himself, 'You have made a mistake! Where were your senses? This cannot be the truth!' And then, instead of looking and listening more keenly again, he runs away, as if intimidated, from the striking thing and tries to shake it from his mind as fast as possible.
>
> FW, 25 [50]

Nietzsche insisted forcefully on this point: 'Even the bravest among us only rarely has courage for what he really knows' (GD, Judgements and arrows, 2 [156]), 'because the forcefulness with which you approach truth is proportionate to the distance courage dares to advance' (EH, *The Birth of Tragedy*, 2 [109]). The philosopher was encouraged in his attempt to go 'out there, up there' by the imperative 'you must', perceived by us 'seekers of knowledge'. This was not a straightforward operation: 'One has to be very light to drive one's will to knowledge into such a distance and, as it were, beyond one's time; to create for oneself eyes to survey millennia and, moreover, clear skies in these eyes' (FW, 380 [244]). The philosopher, then, had to be able to exit mentally from the narrow circle of his city and his culture: 'In order to see our European morality for once as it looks from a distance, and to measure it up against other past or future moralities, one has to proceed like a wanderer.' A truly critical thinking and attitude required 'at least a point beyond our good and evil, a freedom from everything "European", by which I mean the sum of commanding value judgements that have become part of our flesh and blood' (FW, 380 [244]). It was a question of realising an enormous broadening of the field of observation: 'As humanity's spiritual vision [*Blick*] and insight grows stronger, the distance and, as it were, the space that surrounds us increases as well; our world gets more profound, and new stars, new riddles and images are constantly coming into view' (JGB, 57 [51]).

Nietzsche made this point again and again. The extraordinary strength of Bizet was summarised as follows: in him, 'the world surveyed as if from a mountain. – I have just defined the pathos of philosophy' (WA, 1 [235]). Even after distancing himself from Schopenhauer and the latter's admiration for religions now starting to be seen to be affected by nihilism, Nietzsche continued to attribute to his former teacher a fundamental merit: '[T]here are even moments when he sees with oriental eyes' (XI, 471). Strauss, on the other hand, seemed provincial: even while posing as a radical critic of Christianity, he not only made no effort to observe from the outside the cultural world in which he lived, but he was not even able to look beyond Christian Europe: 'He has completely forgotten that even today most of humanity is still Buddhist and not Christian. How can one automatically think, on using the words "old faith", of Christianity?' (DS, 9, I, 210).

If one delved back further, one could find something similar to what was observed in Schopenhauer in Leonardo, this Renaissance spirit, who, thanks to his distance from Europe and the Christian Middle Ages, succeeded in developing 'a supra-European' and 'truly supra-Christian vision' (XI, 470 and 512). One had to pay heed to these examples; one was to be able to observe with 'with an Asiatic and supra-Asiatic eye' (JGB, 56 [50]).

To produce the view from outside, philology linked up with other disciplines, starting with 'comparative ethnology' (MA, 133).[4] In addition to the ancient Greeks and Romans, Nietzsche referred to 'the ancient Germans' (X, 329) and the most diverse cultures and peoples: primitive peoples in general, the 'free-thinking Inca' (VII, 107), the 'Parsis' (VII, 106), the 'Indians' (IX, 605), the 'Negro' with his 'fetish' (IX, 422), the 'Tibetans' (FW, 128 [122]), the 'Wahanabi' (FW, 43 [58]), the 'Hottentots' (IX, 549), the 'Kamchadals' (M, 16), 'the Bogos' (GM III, 14 [91]), the 'Arabian sect of the Assua that one encounters in Algiers' (FW, 306 [174]), 'the Tonga islanders', 'the ancient cultural peoples of America', 'the Chinese', the 'Siamese', 'the Tupinamba', 'some inhabitant of the Fijian islands' (GT, 15, I, 100 [74], X, 325 and 329) and the 'South Sea islanders' (IX, 422), not to speak of the Jewish, Islamic, Buddhist and Hindu worlds, which were to be kept constantly in mind by the philologist-philosopher who, also in the wake of Schopenhauer, was deeply interested in the comparative study of world religions. Why should 'Jewish morality' (inherited by the West) be considered *a priori* superior to 'Arabic, Greek, Indian, Chinese' morality (IX, 22–3)?

One was never to lose sight of the fact that 'among different peoples moral valuations are necessarily different' (FW, 345 [203]). The 'demonstration of the reasons for the variety of moral climates ("why does the sun of one fundamental moral judgement and primary value-standard shine here – and another

---

4   Nietzsche turned his attention to this discipline especially after the break with the theoretical and political platform of the *Birth of Tragedy*; cf. Orsucci 1996.

one there?")' (FW, 7 [34]) was an integral part of philosophical questioning. Sometimes, peoples treated by classical philology were put alongside those surveyed by comparative ethnology, accentuating the effect of alienation with respect to modernity: 'Thus the Wahanabis have only two mortal sins', like the 'old Romans' (FW, 43 [58]).

Nietzsche was not the only one to link disciplines at first sight very different from one another. His friend Rohde, in *Psyche*, also expressed the 'fruitful interpenetration of the studies of anthropology and classical antiquity being carried out at the turn of the century', so that, as a distinguished reviewer[5] (Eduard Meyer) controversially noted, in order to clarify a magnificent chapter in the history of culture even the 'views of the American, African and Australian natural peoples' were cited.[6] Even if this approach was not entirely original, it bore its philosophical significance and strength only in Nietzsche. In fact, he could, for his part, have responded thus to Meyer's objection: 'Even "savages" are extremely evolved human beings if viewed in the very long term' (X, 333).

As Nietzsche stressed, the philosopher had to wander 'through the many subtle and crude moralities that have been dominant or that still dominate over the face of the earth' (JGB, 260 [153]). Only in this way could he achieve noteworthy results: '[T]he genuine problems involved in morality [...] only emerge from a comparison of many different moralities.' One had to break once and for all with a tradition of ethnocentrism and provincialism: the usual 'moral philosophers' 'were poorly informed (and not particularly eager to learn more) about peoples, ages, and histories' (JGB, 186 [75–6]). Linked to comparative ethnology was not only classical philology but historical research as such: 'Sense of history and of the geographic-climatic side by side' (XI, 481).

From here one can grasp the radical nature and magnitude of Nietzsche's philosophical interrogation. No doubt there is a tradition behind him. One author particularly dear to him, Montaigne, on the one hand referred to 'old customs', as the title of a chapter of his *Essais* shows, in order to call into question the tendency to 'have no other model or measure of perfection than one's own customs and usages'. On the other hand, he also referred to China, whose rich culture and history had taught him 'that the world is wider and more varied than the ancients or we ourselves were able to conceive'.[7]

To get to know a great non-European culture was like getting in touch with 'people from another planet'. As Leibniz emphasised, it was then 'impossible

---

5 Canfora 1986, 35.
6 Meyer 1895, 282.
7 Montaigne 2002, I, 446, III, 450; Montaigne 1965, Vol. 1, 423 (Book 1, 49, *Des coutumes anciennes*) and Vol. 3, 361 (Book 3, 13, *De l'expérience*).

that even a bare but exact description of their habits and customs would not give us important enlightenment that in my opinion would be far more useful than the knowledge of the rites and furnishings of the Greeks and Romans to which so many scholars devote themselves'.[8] But the opposition instituted here proved incorrect precisely in light of the intellectual course followed by Nietzsche, who encountered the 'other planet' on the basis of the studies Leibniz viewed with some disdain. It would seem that the alienation effect was even more radical in the attitude of an author who observed the present through the eyes of a Hellene of the sixth century BC or even earlier! On the other hand, we have seen Montaigne refer, in his critique of ethnocentrism, both to the ancient world and to the non-European world of his time. This observation could also be applied to the French eighteenth century as a whole. Taine, another author well known to Nietzsche, analysed with acuity the attitude of the *philosophes* when he criticised the 'great warlike enterprise' developed by the Enlightenment against the beliefs and certainties of the *ancien régime*:

> Montesquieu looks at France through the eyes of a Persian, and Voltaire, on his return from England, describes the English, an unknown species. Confronting dogma and the prevailing system of worship, accounts are given, either with open or with disguised irony, of the various Christian sects, the Anglicans, the Quakers, the Presbyterians, the Socinians, those of ancient or of remote people, the Greeks, Romans, Egyptians, Muslims, and Guebers, of the worshippers of Brahma, of the Chinese and of pure idolaters.[9]

To the authors cited here, one could add Rousseau: in his case, the alienation effect was achieved by recourse to the figure of the noble savage. The attitude of those who, 'under the pompous name of the study of man', in reality analysed and made absolute only 'people of their country' and their own political and cultural area, was ridiculed.[10] The fact remained that, while in the eighteenth century the French critique of ethnocentrism was in the first place a critique of the *ancien régime*, in Nietzsche it was the critique of the world that emerged from the French Revolution and modernity as such.

If, in the case of an author like Montesquieu, the view from outside was an amusing though genial intellectual experiment, in Nietzsche it was a hard-

---

8   In Widmaier 1990, 213 f. (letter of 18 August 1705 to Pater Antoine Verjus); cf. Gernet 1972, 454 f.

9   Taine 1899, Vol. 2, 17 f.

10   Rousseau 1959 ff., Vol. 3, 212 f.

won style of thought acquired while still an adolescent and experienced with an incomparable existential intensity. Connected to it was an extreme radicalism. Even Rousseau was far ahead of his contemporaries in his denunciation of ethnocentrism. Beyond the 'yoke of national prejudices', he wanted to problematise or place in question the 'civilized man [*homme civil*]' as such.[11] But Nietzsche went even further. He strove to place himself outside not only a given culture but the human being as such: 'We want to heal ourselves of the great fundamental stupidity of measuring everything by our own lights. [...] Also, exercise in seeing with the eyes of others, in seeing without reference to human relations, thus with detachment [*sachlich*]! To cure human megalomania [*Menschen-Grössenwahn*]' (IX, 444). Nietzsche struggled with all his might towards this goal: '[T]o want more than anything else an eye like Zarathustra's, an eye that looks out over the whole fact of humanity from a tremendous distance' (WA, Preface [233]). The seriousness of the philosophical interrogation required the view from outside to be radicalised to the extreme:

> If we cannot imagine beings different from human beings, everything remains small-town, petty-human. The invention of gods and heroes was inestimable. We need beings for comparison, even human beings wrongly interpreted, saints and heroes, are a powerful means.
>
> IX, 577

In this way, mythology and hagiography, useful to the extent that they also contributed to the development of a perspective that could transcend the human being as such, could be retrieved.

Ethology, 'natural history [*Thiergeschichte*]' (FW, 354 [212]) and 'zoology' (VII, 695) also worked in this direction. Even when not named explicitly, the presence of these disciplines can already be perceived in the youthful writings. Because Socrates forgot that the cognitive impulse was only a vital function, he absolutised it and thus made it dangerous and harmful for life itself. So, one was not to lose sight of the fact that recourse to the intellect was merely how human beings measured up in nature to physically stronger species (WL, 1, I, 876 [152]). In the same way, the superfetation of historical consciousness was combated: 'For every action forgetting is important', emphasised the second *Unfashionable Observation*, thereby referring to the fact that the 'herd' and the animal 'live unhistorically' (HL, 1, I, 250 and 249). In this same context belonged the definition of the human being as 'the as yet undefined animal' (XI, 125) or as

---

11   Rousseau 1959 ff., Vol. 3, 210.

'a multiform, mendacious, artificial, and untransparent animal' (JGB, 291 [173])
and even as a 'mad animal' (IX, 473), and the observation that, as far as pleasure
went we had inherited pleasurable sensations 'from animals' (MA, 98 [p. 75]),
and the human being was, ultimately, 'a herd animal' (VII, 695).

4   The Metacritical View

But what distinguishes Nietzsche and defines his power and appeal is above
all what one might call his metacritical view. To clarify this point, we quote a
passage from the third *Unfashionable Observation*: '[A]nd it is highly recommended that we finally begin to examine and analyse scholars, now that they
themselves have grown accustomed to laying bold hands upon and dissecting
everything in the world, no matter how venerable' (SE, 6, I, 394 [225]). In other
words, one should not shrink from dissecting the dissectors. The intellectuals,
and the 'science' they professed, were no more venerable than the objects they
had from time to time and investigated and desecrated.

The Birth of Tragedy was already committed to analysing the 'theoretical
human being', that 'enjoys and satisfies himself with the discarded veil, and
his desire finds its highest goal in a process of unveiling [*Enthüllung*] which he
achieves by his own efforts and which is always successful' (GT, 15, I, 98 [72–3]).
Subjected in turn to an investigation and revelation, the human being turned
out to be driven by theoretical motivations far more complex and far less pure
than the mere disinterested love of truth. In fact, 'the intellectual [*der Gelehrte*]
is made up of a complex mixture of different stimuli, he is a thoroughly impure
metal'. One had to be aware of the fact 'that it is not actually truth that is sought,
but the act of seeking itself, and the primary pleasure lies in slyly stalking, surrounding, and skilfully killing one's play' (SE, 6, I, 394–5 [225]).

Nietzsche problematised 'the will to truth', subjecting it to investigation, calling radically into question the status traditionally ascribed to it of an immediate and untranscendable given. What function did it exercise in life and what
place did it have in the long evolution of the human species? In a certain
sense, the criterion of self-reflection was asserted: did the will to truth establish
itself and was it able to legitimise and justify itself? Was the philosopher who
carried out this interrogation right to be proud of posing questions hitherto
unasked? When Nietzsche deconstructed the belief in the subject-matter animated solely by love of truth, he argued as follows:

> Just as the act of birth makes no difference to the overall course of hered-
> ity, neither is 'consciousness' opposed to instinct in any decisive sense –

most of a philosopher's conscious thought is secretly directed and forced
into determinate channels by the instincts. Even behind all logic and its
autocratic posturings stand valuations or, stated more clearly, physiological requirements for the preservation of a particular type of life.

JGB, 3 [7]

The first chapter of *Beyond Good and Evil*, whose title reads 'On the prejudices
of philosophers', belongs in this same context. After professing himself part of
the 'Enlightenment' and criticising, in the tradition of the *philosophes*, the prejudices of the people, Nietzsche associated himself with a point of view that
was so to speak one of meta-Enlightenment and criticised the prejudices to
which the *philosophes* had wrongly thought themselves immune. Even when
Descartes (like Kant and many others with him) proclaimed the *De omni-
bus dubitandum*, he continued to adhere to the dogmatics and metaphysics
of the subject (JGB, 2 [6]). From this, one could draw the general conclusion
that 'philosophers', despite their predilection for exhibiting a radical critical
attitude, were in reality 'hidden priests' (EH, *Daybreak*, 2 [122]). Their prejudices weighed no less than those they would have liked to bring to light and
denounce. Thus, for example, Schopenhauer, far from being immune to 'popular prejudice', adopted and exaggerated it (JGB, 19 [18]).

The metacritical view also sought to investigate 'the psychology of the psychologist' (XIII, 230), the 'superstition of the logicians' (JGB, 17 [17]), the history
of historical consciousness, the ideology of the critics of ideology. This same
attitude was also adopted in respect of morality and its theorists. Moral judgement expressed estimations of value regarding human actions, but now it was
a question of evaluating the very act of evaluation. After declaring himself an
'immoralist', Nietzsche continued: 'I am proud of having a word that pits me
against the whole of mankind. Nobody so far has felt Christian morality. [...]
that before me has climbed into the caves that spew out the poisoned breath of
this type of ideal – the ideal of slandering the world?' (EH, Why I am a destiny,
6 [148]). The metacritical view was also manifest in the invitation to despise
the unworthy despisers of the world. In early Christianity, 'psychology served
not only to make everything human seem suspicious, but also to slander, to fla-
gellate, to crucify'; one slandered human beings to 'make nature seem suspect
for them', eros, vitality, life as such (MA, 141 [109–10]). Now, this moral attitude
was made suspect: 'My writings have been called a school for suspicion, or even
contempt, but happily, for courage as well, and even for audacity'; 'In fact I do
not believe that anyone has ever looked into the world with as deep a suspicion' (MA, Preface, 1 [5]). Christian morality cast a sort of curse and 'evil eye' on
those that had turned out well (AC, 25 [22]), and Nietzsche responded to this

with what he called 'my "evil eye"' (GD, Preface [155]). The evil eye of the moral worldview was thus targeted by the evil eye or the meta-view of the immoralist and destroyer of idols.

The metacritical view was essential. Only the ability of a discipline to investigate itself with the methodology and criteria it asserted in regard to the objects it generally investigated, only this capacity for self-reflection conferred true cognitive dignity on the discipline. In this sense, Nietzsche could assert: 'Psychology did not exist until I appeared' (EH, Why I am a destiny, 6 [148]). Psychology actually began only when it was able to act as a 'psychology of psychology'.

5   Comparatistics – the Striving for Totality and the Translatability of Languages

Gradually, the intricate network of disciplines that serves as the foundation of Nietzsche's discourse starts to emerge. To the disciplines we have already encountered can be added several others he not only mentioned in passing but considered essential for the correct construction of philosophical discourse: we have already mentioned the importance attached to 'physics', 'physiology, medicine and natural sciences', 'statistics' and 'hygiene' (*supra*, 19 §1). There was also 'mathematics' (one of the 'branches of knowledge where weak personalities are useful', IX, 466), 'political economy [*Volkswirtschaft*]' (even in this seemingly so objective discipline one could sense the omnipresence of nihilism, XII, 127 and 130), 'criminalists' (who supposedly set an authoritative seal on the diagnosis of the decadent and sick nature of Plato's teacher, GD, The problem Socrates, 3 [163]), 'physiology and natural history' (supposed to confirm the role of the unconscious in human life) (FW, 354 [212]).

Not even sociology escaped Nietzsche's attention. It was perceived across the Atlantic, by Fitzhugh, and in Britain, by Mill (who spoke in this context of 'convenient barbarism'[12]) as novel. Nietzsche saw its emergence as yet more proof of the process of levelling and massification associated with modernity (GD, Skirmishes of an untimely man, 37 [112] and XIII, 220). After all, the most diverse and daring articulations of historical knowledge were supposed to remedy the 'lack of historical sense' that was 'the inherited defect of all philosophers' (*supra*, 8 §4 and 28 §2). Nietzsche's library was doubtless extremely diverse.

12   Mill 1965c, Vol. 8, 895 (Book 6, 9, §1); Fitzhugh 1854, v.

How could one master such a multiplicity of disciplines and the vast mass of material produced by them? Nietzsche polemicised fiercely against the intellectual who minutely and superstitiously tilled his field of specialisation and forgot the whole:

> Maybe we philosophers are all in a bad position regarding knowledge these days: science is growing, and the most scholarly of us are close to discovering that they know too little. But it would be even worse if things were different – if we knew too much; our task is and remains above all not to mistake ourselves for someone else. We are different from scholars. [...] It is not fat but the greatest possible suppleness and strength that a good dancer wants from his nourishment – and I wouldn't know what the spirit of a philosopher might more want to be than a good dancer.
>
> FW, 381 [246]

Nietzsche set the lightness and grace of the dancer against the 'beaver and ant spirit of the scholar' (XI, 590); in reality, 'the specialist is necessary, but he belongs to the class of tools' (XII, 62). In light of all this, Nietzsche saw giving up his profession and university chair as a fundamental turning point in his intellectual development and his life:

> At the same time, the illness gave me the right to change all my habits completely; it permitted, it required me to forget; it gave me the need to lie still, to be idle, to wait and be patient ... But that would certainly mean thinking! ... My eyes alone put an end to any bookworm behaviour, in plain language: philology: I was redeemed from the 'book', I did not read anything else for years – the greatest blessing I ever conferred on myself!
>
> EH, Human, All Too Human, 4 [118–19]

And yet, even before this sort of call of destiny, Nietzsche's philosophical discourse was marked by its tendency to draw on the most diverse disciplines. In *The Birth of Tragedy*, historical reconstruction and political denunciation were inextricably intertwined with the 'metaphysics of art' in its various expressions, with an epistemological analysis of the validity of universals, which Nietzsche developed under the influence of Schopenhauer, and with further considerations on the value, also cognitive, of instinct. In a contemporary text, linguistics, philology and physiology were called upon jointly to explain the origin of language: 'The stimulation of a nerve is first translated into an image: first metaphor! The image is then imitated by a sound: second metaphor!' (WL, 1, I, 879 [144]). The transition to 'Enlightenment' did not change the picture, for in fact this new phase even opened with the statement that philosophy could not do without history and 'historical sense' and 'historical philosophy' could not, for its part, be abstracted from 'natural science' (*supra*, 8 § 4).

Certainly, after giving up teaching, to which he had dedicated himself very professionally and conscientiously, the philosopher was freer to follow his vocation. But the problem remained of how to give shape and a unitary meaning to research nurtured by the most varied disciplines without falling into despised erudition.

The Birth of Tragedy deciphered the tragic vision of life in the sounds of the gripping music of Beethoven as well as the sounds and texts of the music of Wagner, in the subtle and rigorously scientific analyses of Kant and Schopenhauer, in the religious eloquence of Luther, and also in the philosophy, art, and way of life as such of pre-Socratic Greece. On the opposite side, the same ideational content (in this case, fatal optimism) could be found in the philosophy of Socrates, the tragedies of Euripides, Rousseau's pedagogic novel, the neo-Latin operas and the political movements of Jacobinism and socialism.

During the 'Enlightenment' phase too, the historical balance sheet under the sign of the *longue durée* continued to incorporate the most diverse expressions of cultural and political life. Beethoven was ranked with Rousseau: the great symphonies of the German composer were nothing more than the 'moralism of Beethoven in sounds' (WS, 216), so they expressed in musical language the philosophical and political content of the author that had presided over the radicalisation of the French Revolution. 'The older morality, notably Kant's, demands from the individual those actions that one desires from all people: that was a beautiful, naïve thing; as if everyone would immediately know which modes of action would benefit the whole of humanity, hence which actions would generally be desirable; it is a theory, like free trade, presupposing that a general harmony must result of itself according to innate laws of improvement' (MA, 25 [35]).

In Handel's music rang out the 'best in Luther and his kindred souls', i.e., '[t]he great Jewish-heroic disposition' of the Reformation, while in 'our newest German music', i.e., in Wagner, not only 'pleasure in everything nativist, nationalist or primeval' but also a 'certain Catholicism of feeling' was expressed, and in this sense Nietzsche was referring to a world destined for decline (VM, 171 [72 of vol. 4]).

Underlying Nietzsche's approach was what, in the words of an author far removed from him, we can call the 'translatability of languages'.[13] It was not

---

13   This category is derived from Gramsci, but he applies it more narrowly, for a comparison

only possible to compare the artistic forms of expression: Wagner was 'the Victor Hugo of music as a language' (WA, 8 [247]), just as Michelet was the Victor Hugo of historiography (*supra*, 28 § 2). But one was to add that art could also be compared with philosophy: we have seen at work in Bizet the view 'as if from a mountain', synonymous with 'the pathos of philosophy'. Nietzsche concluded 'that you become more of a philosopher, the more of a musician you become' (WA, 1 [235]).

The 'labyrinth' that is the modern soul could also be found in 'architecture' and especially in music. Here it emerged with particular clarity because the element of supervision and self-censorship of consciousness vanished or was reduced: 'In music, namely, people let themselves go, for they fancy no one can see them concealed amid their music' (M, 169 [124]). Overall, with regard to the understanding of modernity, the value or disvalue of equality and levelling was active both in the unending revolutionary cycle of the West and in the Socratic syllogism and the iron lawfulness affirmed by physics; 'the rising nihilism, theoretical and practical', the 'nihilistic trait', could be discovered not just in morality, religion, and philosophy but also in the 'natural sciences' as well as in certain tendencies in 'politics', 'political economy', 'history', 'art', and 'psychology' (XII, 129–30).

It was quite naïve to seek a content of thought only in philosophical or literary works in general. 'Everything that is thought, written, painted, composed, even built and sculpted' had to be included (FW 367 [231]). In fact, one could and had to go even further: 'That one can think in images, in sounds, there can be no doubt: but also in feelings of pressure' (XI, 644).

The translatability of languages was also the translatability and comparability of feelings:

> In those days souls swelled with drunkenness when the rigorous and sober play of concepts of generalization, refutation, limitation was practised – with that drunkenness with which perhaps the old great rigorous and sober contrapuntal composers were familiar.
>
> M, 544 [267]

Thus, with regard to Germany of the seventeenth and eighteenth centuries, 'the German Baroque of the churches and palaces is a close relative of our music –

---

of the French Revolution and German classical philosophy and, more generally, of politics and philosophy. Hence in the German edition of Gramsci's *Prison Notebooks* '*traducibilità dei linguaggi*' is rendered as '*Übersetzbarkeit der Kultursprachen* [translatability of languages of culture]'.

it gives rise in the realm of the eye to the same sort of enchantment and seduction that our music produces by means of another sense'; even the philosophy that was developing in this period, 'with its braid and spider webs of concepts, its malleability, melancholy, with its hidden infinity and mysticism, is part of our music and is a kind of baroque in the realm of philosophy' (XII, 69).

The key to this translatability of languages was precisely psychology, which allowed Nietzsche not only to compare the most diverse cultural expressions and, along with them, even the 'feelings of pressure', but also to step boldly beyond all boundaries of time and space. The role played by theology in the Middle Ages was now replaced by psychology, the true 'queen of the sciences' (JGB, 23 [23–4]).

6   'Reverse syllogism' and the View from Inside

Nietzsche defined his task with precision: it was a question of investigating from 'our psychological perspective' 'the entire history, so far experienced, of the soul and its not yet fully exhausted possibilities' (XII, 395). This new enterprise required a sustained and united effort; the psychologist needed 'fine hounds trained to be able to run forward in the history of the human soul'. And, in this sense, the philosopher defined himself as 'a born psychologist' (JGB, 45 [43]), or 'a born, inevitable psychologist and unriddler of souls' (JGB, 269 [164]).

Under investigation were not only individual personalities but also 'the Greeks' secret, deep-seated anxiety' (M, 156 [118]), or, to come to our time, 'the conscience [Gewissen] of today's European' (JGB, 201 [89]), or 'the basic instincts of our Europe's political intellectual social movement' (XII, 155). So, it is understandable that Nietzsche emphasised the radical novelty of his approach. A 'new psychologist' was needed (JGB, 12 [15]). The 'psychology' he practised had little or nothing to do with introspection: 'We psychologists of the future have little good will for self-observation', we 'are all wary of navel-gazers'. Of the 'great psychologist', it could be said he 'never seeks himself, has no eye, no interest, no curiosity for himself'. On closer inspection, the obsession of introspection was only a secularisation of a religious theme and concern. But 'we are no Pascal', said Nietzsche, 'we are not particularly interested in "healing the soul", in our own happiness, our own virtue' (XIII, 231). One had to beware of 'father-confessor psychology and Puritan psychology, two forms of psychological romanticism' (XII, 130).

One was to focus not on one's own inner life but on the authors, cultural and philosophical currents, and political and social movements under investigation, ultimately on the objectivity of the historical process in its various

manifestations and articulations. It was precisely here that 'psychology' intervened. Symptomatic is the judgement on Wagner delivered in the autumn of
1881: even before he formulated 'Christian thoughts [*Gedanken*]', he cherished
'Christian feelings [*Empfindungen*]' (IX, 591). So, it was a matter of proceeding
beyond the conceptual and conscious sphere to capture the feelings, love and
hatred, moral views, values and negative values that drove and characterised
the personalities, movements, cultures on which, from time to time, this new
'psychology' focused. After having conquered a position outside and higher
than his own cultural environment and even his own human condition, the
philosopher-psychologist should now have been able to grasp from within the
'valuations' of an author or historical movement: they 'reveal something about
the structure of his soul' (JGB, 268 [164]). The philosopher–psychologist had to
strive with all his might to perceive and understand this 'structure of the soul'.
Along with the requirement to view the world in which one lived from outside
and above, Nietzsche demanded that the world whose deeper meaning one
aspired to grasp should be considered from the inside out.

While reading *The World as Will and Representation*, said Nietzsche, 'I tried
to see through the book and imagine to myself the living human being' that
was its author (SE, 2, I, 350). Moreover, Schopenhauer followed the same procedure. His 'greatness' lay in the fact that he 'sets himself against the picture of
life as a whole, in order to interpret it as a whole'. This was a lesson not to be
forgotten. Unfortunately, not even 'the sharpest minds' could free themselves
from an approach that led nowhere: they endeavoured to investigate 'painstak-
ingly the colours with which this picture is painted; perhaps with the result that
it is a quite intricately woven cloth with colours on it that cannot be investigated chemically'. The same was true of interpreters that, in their analysis of a
philosophical system, focused on the details and so lost sight of the whole, the
true personality of the philosopher, his soul, his values, his worldview. Schopenhauer, on the other hand, was fully aware that 'one must divine [*errathen*] the
painter to understand the picture' (SE, 3, I, 356–7). With regard to philosophy,
'the only critique of a philosophy that is possible and that proves anything' was
that 'that checks whether one can live by it' (SE, 8, I, 417) and that grasped the
'meaning' of the 'life' (SE, 3, I, 357) that worked and expressed itself within it.

But how to achieve this? One had to know how to admit and incorporate
the 'attempts of scientific curiosity, of the coddled, experimental imagination
of psychologists and historians that easily anticipate a problem and seize it in
flight without knowing what it has caught' (FW, 345 [202]). 'Historical sense'
was then defined as 'the ability quickly to guess the rank order of the valuations
that a people, a society, an individual has lived by'. The 'divinatory instinct' (JGB,
224 [114]) enabled the historian-psychologist to grasp the object.

Of course, this 'divinatory instinct' presupposed an attempt at historicising. Unfortunately, the lack of 'historical sense' was widespread: '[M]ost moral philosophers represent only the currently dominant rank-ordering [...] – they are themselves dominated by the morality that teaches that what is current is eternally valid' (XI, 510). So they precluded for themselves an understanding of the ancient world and of the earthshaking novelty Christianity represented for it:

> Obtuse to all Christian terminology, modern people can no longer relate to the hideous superlative [*fühlen das nicht mehr nach Schauerlich-Super-lativistische*] found by an ancient taste [*antiker Geschmack*] in the para-doxical formula 'god on the cross'.
>
> JGB, 46 [44]

The work of historicising was not merely an intellectual process. The historian had also to be able to become a psychologist, in the sense that he had to be capable of reactualising in himself the ancients' way of seeing, hearing and evaluating; he had to be able to bring back to the surface that 'ancient taste' trampled underfoot and suppressed by almost two thousand years of Christianity. Only so could he succeed in grasping on the emotional level, in *nachfühlen*, the disaster that came about with the advent and triumph of the religion of the cross and slaves. Only thus could he 'reconstruct [*nachbilden*]' the past 'in itself'. That made 'historical sense' (XI, 509).

This *nachfühlen* and *nachbilden* meant, in the last analysis, an intensive empathising, without which classical antiquity in general and Hellas in particular remained a closed book: 'It seems the Greek world is a hundred times more hidden and alien than the intrusive nature of today's learned men might wish. If anything will ever be known here, it will certainly only be like knowing like' (XI, 424).

One could see why, despite everything, Goethe and Winckelmann foundered. Prisoners of modernity, they failed to penetrate the secret or sanctuary of a culture like that of the Greeks, at whose heart lay an acute awareness of the 'immutable rank-ordering and inequality of value between human being and human being'. An unbridgeable distance seemed to separate this world from modernity. Rather than approach it without adequate historical and mental preparation with a profane and desecrating eye, a period of silent and anxious waiting was preferable and perhaps even inevitable:

> This is the greatest depth, the great silence for all that is Greek – one does not know the Greeks as long as the hidden underground access remains

buried. The prying eyes of scholars will never see anything in these things, no matter how much scholarship they must employ in the service of those excavations –; even in the noble zeal of friends of antiquity like Goethe and Winckelmann there is here something unallowed, almost immodest.

XI, 681–2

An appropriate understanding of authentic Hellas presupposed a counter-movement or the beginning of a counter-movement against modernity. Above all, a view from outside and above was needed to 'overcome all things Christian by things supra-Christian'. But this was not enough. The efforts to free oneself from subalternity with respect to the present and modernity took the form of spiritual exercises: 'Wait and get ready, await the gush of new sources, prepare in solitude for alien voices and faces; wash from one's soul the fairground dust and clamour of this age and make it purer' (XI, 682). Even when Nietzsche expressed himself in the language of a devotee of authentic Hellas, he posed a real problem: the work of historicisation on the part of the interpreter had to grasp not only conceptual categories but also the world of feelings; for an adequate understanding of Hellenism and classical antiquity, it was necessary to understand them in their actual autonomy, abstracting from the 'obviousness' not only of conscious representations but also of the feelings of modernity.

In conclusion, with respect to the method of research proposed by Nietzsche, the traditional syllogism [*Schluss*] was replaced by an as yet unknown 'reverse syllogism [*Rückschluss*]':

[M]y vision grew keener for that most difficult and insidious [*schwierigst und verfänglichst*] form of backward inference with which the most mistakes are made – the inference from the work to the maker, from the ideal to the one that needs it, from every manner of valuation to the commanding need behind it.

FW, 370 [235]

The view from inside (the link between the psychological and the historical approach) enabled Nietzsche to achieve significant results, despite its problematic nature and the associated risk of arbitrariness. This was true, for example, of his subtle and insightful observations on the role of women, particularly in the abolitionist movement, also confirmed by historical research carried out in a more traditional way (*infra*, 30 § § 5–6).

7   'There are no Facts, Only Interpretations': Along with the 'Fact', the
     'Text' Disappears

Since the problematisation and historicisation of 'obviousness' are so radical
that they even involve the sphere of the emotions, the interpretation of history and of reality in general lose all semblance of immediacy and evidence.
The omnipresence of interpretation justifies a radical conclusion: 'There are
no facts, only interpretations' (XII, 315). So it is understandable why Foucault
believes he can conclude that for Nietzsche 'interpretation is always incomplete'.[14] But is that true?

Let us analyse this famous thesis. It entails an extreme expansion of the category of interpretation: it now embraces both discourses that strive to move
on the ground of logical and scientific argumentation, to preserve an inner
consistency and to refer to verifiable 'evidence', and discourses that move on
a radically different terrain and justify themselves by referring to the authority
of tradition or to the privileged revelation of this or that master. At least on one
point, however, one cannot but agree with Nietzsche: even the most rigorously
scientific theory is an 'interpretation', and it is based on other 'interpretations';
to seek after an elementary 'fact', completely free of theory and therefore of
'interpretation', would lead nowhere.

Lukács likens Nietzsche's perspectivism to the empiriocriticism criticised by
Lenin.[15] In refutation of idealistic fluctuations, Lenin cites among other things
the example of an incontrovertible and therefore 'eternal' truth he takes from
Engels's *Anti-Dühring*: Napoleon died on 5 May 1821. But even this is not a 'fact'.
Chronology, dating, the periodisation of time imply a complex 'interpretation'
that is not by chance expressed in different ways by the Christian calendar
(Julian or Gregorian) and the Jewish or Islamic calendars. So is Nietzsche's
thesis fully confirmed? Once a calendar is chosen, it is no longer possible to
ignore it or change it at will, according to momentary convenience and individual whim. That means that, in the context of the Gregorian 'interpretation'
of time, it is a 'fact' that Napoleon died on 5 May 1821. These considerations
can be reformulated in Kantian language. Since the Copernican revolution, we
know the role of the subject and therefore of 'interpretation' even in the natural
sciences. But it is important to distinguish between the transcendental subject and the empirical subject. The statement that Napoleon died on 5 May
1821 is the 'interpretation' of a transcendental subject that has carried out a

well-defined but rigorously structured periodisation of time. As part of this periodisation, any statement that Napoleon died in 1921 would be a (wrong) 'interpretation' by an empirical subject (e.g., a student unfamiliar with history).

In Nietzsche these distinctions are missing, which tends to mean the category of 'interpretation' turns into the night in which all cats are grey. This is a fundamental problem. Again and again, Nietzsche resorts to very general categories each of which covers a number of quite different phenomena. For example, the category of the will to power subsumes the actions of the saint as well as those of the criminal, and in this case the common subsumption is equivalent to a reductionism: it denies the possibility of any axiological hierarchisation of the different forms of behaviour. Just as everything is will to power, so too everything is cruelty:

> I concede only that cruelty now refines itself and that its older forms henceforth offend taste; but wounding and torturing with word and eye reaches its highest cultivation in times of corruption – it is now alone that malice and the delight in malice are born. People that live in an age of corruption are witty and slanderous; they know there are other kinds of murder than by dagger or assault.
>
> FW, 23 [47–8]

There seems to be no difference in value between sublimated cruelty (a joke or biting comment) and brutal violence inflicted on the body. The extreme expansion of the categories of cruelty and will to power makes it impossible to condemn even the most immediate and radical forms of cruelty and of the will to power.

Similarly, the exaggerated and undifferentiated generality of the category of 'interpretation' opens the door to arbitrariness. After the text has taken the place of a positivistic 'fact', the 'text' highlighted by the philosopher-philologist seems to vanish along with the fact: it is impossible to distinguish between different interpretations on the basis of their truth content. There is no problem in equating physical-mathematical 'interpretation' with the interpretation of reality through fairy-tales or fables. It is worth noting that there are Protestant fundamentalists that (although without explicitly mentioning the German philosopher) start out from the thesis that 'any judgement on the origin of life should be considered as theory and not as a fact'; so they demand equal time for evolution and the Old Testament in the teaching of natural sciences at school.[16]

---

16   Glanz 1999.

But even more interesting is the attitude of some of Nietzsche's followers. When Vattimo comes across the doctrine of the eternal return of the same, he feels a bit embarrassed. Here is how he gets out of the difficulty: it is true Nietzsche treats this doctrine as a scientific theory; however, at the same time, he advances the thesis that 'there are no facts, only interpretations', so theory is not and cannot be based in 'description' (and the philosopher is to some extent aware of this).[17] Here Vattimo, on the one hand, misunderstands one of Nietzsche's strong points and, on the other hand, inherits his weaknesses. Newton's theory of gravitation is also an 'interpretation', but that does not mean it is not based in 'description'. One can doubtless say Napoleon died on 5 May 1821, but that remains an 'interpretation'. For Nietzsche, the doctrine of the eternal return has, despite its pedagogic-moral efficacy, no value as truth and 'interpretation' other than that he attributes to Newton's theory (which, as we know, with its emphasis on general laws, also has a political significance). It is no accident that the philosopher not only undertakes to demonstrate the rigorously scientific character of his doctrine but even goes so far as to accuse of theologism those that attack it. Vattimo, on the other hand, uses the thesis that 'there are no facts, only interpretations' to 'tone down' certain and only certain aspects of Nietzsche's thought (for example, he certainly does not want to 'tone down' the positions taken against Germanomania and anti-Semitism). The same exaggerated extension of the category of 'interpretation' that enables American fundamentalists to equate qualitatively different discourses in an undifferentiated way enables Vattimo to deal variously and arbitrarily with different aspects of the philosopher's thought.

8   Sympathetic Empathy and the Elimination of Conceptual Mediation

While Nietzsche's critique and challenge on the one hand open the door to arbitrariness because of their extreme radicalism, on the other they end up turning into their opposites. To understand this dialectic, let us return to the 'reverse syllogism'. The attention he devotes to the whole, to the author's personality, to be grasped by a view from within, goes hand in hand with the undervaluing or denial of the conceptual dimension or, to use Nietzsche's contemptuous language, of the 'critique of words by means of other words'. Philosophers that, 'in building grand philosophies, immediately start thinking about

---

17   Vattimo 2000, 88.

where, academically, is the pro and contra, where is it permissible to dig, to doubt, to contradict' are, in his eyes, completely unproductive. They end up 'caught in conceptual webs', thus losing sight of the whole and suffering 'the fate of the unbridled dialecticians' (SE, 3, I, 356–7). Zarathustra celebrates the 'bold seekers, experimenters' that 'hate to guess [*erschliessen*] where [they] can discern [*errathen*]' (Za, III, On the Vision and the Riddle; EH, Why I write such good books, 3 [104]). The radicalisation of the role of courage in the knowledge process is now configured as the pure and simple elimination of the moment of conceptual mediation: between the soul of the interpreter and of the interpreted it comes to a positive relationship of empathy or of mutual radical repugnance. This is the meaning of 'guessing' or 'discerning [*errathen*]'. The chain of argumentation and reasoning, the search for inconsistencies and logical refutation, the categorical apparatus, the 'conceptual scholastics', the 'words', the consciously and explicitly formulated ideas, all that is basically worthless. And, for the interpreter, it all becomes even more insignificant, because it is already insignificant in the interpreted author:

> I have gradually come to realize what every great philosophy so far has been: a confession of faith on the part of its author, and a type of involuntary and unself-conscious memoir; in short, that the moral (or immoral) intentions in every philosophy constitute the true living seed from which the whole plant has always grown.
>
> JGB, 6 [8]

Paradoxically, we meet here with an attitude that bears some resemblance to that of the much despised Fichte:

> The choice of a philosophy depends on what you are as a human being: a philosophical system is not an inert furnishing you can use or not, at will, but is animated by the soul of the human being that has it. A character weak by nature, or weakened and bent by spiritual servitude, by refined luxury and frivolities, can never rise to idealism.[18]

An authoritative interpreter like Jaspers has no hesitation in placing Fichte alongside Nietzsche, since both theorists dissolve philosophical discourse in the plurality of the psychologies of worldviews.[19] In fact, a gulf separates the two authors. Fichte feels constrained to take cognisance of the fact that rational

---

18   Fichte 1971, Vol. 1, 434.
19   Jaspers 1985, 38.

refutation is powerless in the face of a dogmatist who refuses *a priori* to argue at the rational and conceptual level. From Fichte's point of view, it is precisely Nietzsche's attitude that is dogmatic, and Nietzsche, in his turn, would see such a devotion to 'conceptual scholastics' as the manifestation of a repulsive meaning of life and personality.

Nietzsche sets against the traditional method of reasoning – rational refutation – a real alternative method. In this sense, he has little or nothing to do with the usual 'dogmatist' targeted by Fichte. Sometimes, it may seem the 'reverse syllogism', based on the view from inside, does not work, in the sense that the relationship between the text and the beliefs expressed in it on the one hand and the author on the other is transient. But this would be a really revealing clue:

> It makes the most telling difference whether a thinker has a personal relationship to his problems and finds in them his destiny, his distress and his greatest happiness, or an 'impersonal' one, meaning he is only able to touch and grasp them with the antennae of cold, curious thought. In the latter case nothing will come of it, that much can be promised.
>
> FW, 345 [202]

The text under investigation in any case represents a self-confession. At this point, the problem of the multiplicity of disciplines Nietzsche needs to capture the 'soul' of the most varied authors and movements in the most varied cultures and historical periods is no longer insurmountable. How to master the enormous mass of material we face? That is impossible, but it is also unnecessary: 'We rarely read; but are none the worse on that account – and oh, how quickly we guess how someone has come to his ideas' (FW, 366 [230]).

Once one has reduced philosophy to more or less voluntary self-confession and laid bare the soul of an author, everything else becomes synonymous with redundancy, or worse, with artifice and deceit, with 'feigning scientificity' (XI, 522). For example: 'Thus Kant falsifies in his "morality"' and in his tiresome and Baroque system 'his intimate psychological tendency' (XI, 522).

Nietzsche's polemic refers not just to the author of the *Critique of Practical Reason* but also to the history of philosophy as such: 'What goads us into regarding all philosophers with an equal measure of mistrust and mockery is not that we are struck repeatedly by how innocent they are [...] but rather that there is not enough genuine honesty about them.' Even though 'they all make a huge, virtuous racket as soon as the problem of truthfulness is even remotely touched upon', they proceed in completely different ways when constructing their system:

They *all* act as if they had discovered and arrived at their genuine convictions through the self-development of a cold, pure, divinely insouciant dialectic. [...] [W]hile what essentially happens is that they take a conjecture, a whim, an 'inspiration' or, more typically, they take some fervent wish that they have sifted through and made properly abstract – and they defend it with rationalizations after the fact. They are all advocates that do not want to be seen as such; for the most part, in fact, they are sly spokesmen for prejudices that they christen as 'truths'.

JGB, 5 [7–8]

9   How to Orientate Oneself among the Interpretations: From Psychology to Physio-psychology

We have already seen the central role granted the 'rank-ordering of valuations'. But what in general prevents historians and philosophers from grasping its significance? The courageous interpreter, faced with a text (in the broad sense of the term), creates an immediate tie that consists either of positive empathy or of mutual radical repugnance. It is the 'reverse syllogism' with which we are already familiar. While *The Gay Science* warned of the pitfalls and dangers that lurk within it, that caution later seems to disappear. An unbridgeable gulf in the meantime separates the brave, capable of knowledge, from the fearful for whom lying is a way of life:

Knowledge, saying yes to reality, is just as necessary for the strong as cowardice and fleeing in the face of reality – which is to say the 'ideal' – is for the weak, who are inspired by weakness ... They are not free to know: decadents need lies, it is one of the conditions for their preservation.

EH, *The Birth of Tragedy*, 2 [109]

Here, a clear shift from psychology to psychopathology is apparent. The lack of courage points for its part to a deeper and more troubling element. We have three dichotomies: truth/error, courage/fearfulness, health/sickness. The second underlies the first and the third underlies the second. And so:

A psychologist knows few questions as attractive as that concerning the relation between health and philosophy. [...] For assuming that one is a person, one necessarily also has the philosophy of that person; but here there is a considerable difference. In some, it is their weaknesses that philosophize; in others, their riches and strengths. The former need their philosophy, be it as a prop, a sedative, medicine, redemption, elevation, or self-alienation; for the latter, it is only a beautiful luxury, in the best case the voluptuousness of a triumphant gratitude that eventually has to inscribe itself in cosmic capital letters on the heaven of concepts.

FW, Preface, 2 [4]

Sickness is elevated to the universal criterion of explanation: '[B]oth world religions, Buddhism and Christianity, may have owed their origin and especially their sudden spread to a tremendous sickening of the will. And that is actually what happened' (FW, 347 [206]).

Not only is there a shift from psychology to psychopathology, but mental illness itself tends to point ever more clearly to a physiological dimension or foundation. In other cases, the explanation is even more crudely naturalistic: 'It is symptomatic that certain philosophers, such as the consumptive Spinoza, took and indeed had to take just the so-called self-preservation instinct to be decisive – they were simply people in distress' (FW, 349 [208]).

And thus, from psychology to psychopathology and from psychopathology to physiology. After reading the *Confessions* of St Augustine, Nietzsche wrote in a letter to Overbeck (31 March 1885) that 'this book', although full of 'psychological falsehoods' and with a 'philosophical value equal to zero', had the advantage that in it 'one sees into Christianity's bowels [*in den Bauch*]'. This is not just a metaphor, for immediately afterwards the philosopher adds: 'I stand there with the curiosity of a physician and physiologist'. 'Psychological falseness' was, in the final analysis, a physiological falsehood or corruption (B, III, 3, 34).

If there is still a degree of ambiguity, it disappears quickly. There is one theme Nietzsche repeats again and again: 'Cramped intestines [*das geklemmte Eingeweide*] betray themselves' (FW, 366 [230]); 'all prejudices come from the intestines [*Eingeweide*]' (EH, Why I am so clever, 1 [87]). That too is the interiority within which one must locate oneself to be able to express a correct value judgement about people, movements and cultures:

> The sensitivity of my instinct for cleanliness is perfectly uncanny, and I can physiologically perceive the presence or – what am I saying? – the very centre, the 'intestines', of every soul [*das Innerlichste, die 'Eingeweide' jeder Seele*] – I can smell it ... This sensitivity gives me psychological antennae to feel and get hold of every secret: I notice the abundant, hidden dirt at the bottom of so many characters (*the result of bad blood, perhaps*, but whitewashed by education) almost as soon as I come into contact with it.
>
> EH, Why I am so wise, 8 [83]

One was never to lose sight of the physiological dimension of decadence. It was disgusting and nauseating to have to endure the proximity or even the approach of 'something failed [*etwas Missrathenem*]', to have to 'smell [*riechen*] the bowels of a failed soul' (GM, I, 12 [25]). Even leaving aside physical presence, a decadent literary or musical text provoked reactions of repugnance that went far beyond the strictly psychological:

> My objections to Wagner's music are physiological objections: why disguise them with aesthetic formulas? My 'fact [*Thatsache*]' is that I stop breathing easily once this music starts affecting me; that my foot immediately gets angry at it and revolts. [...] [B]ut doesn't my stomach protest, too? My heart? My circulation? My intestines [*mein Eingeweide*]? Do I not unnoticeably grow hoarse as I listen?
>
> FW, 368 [232]

On the other hand, those sick in body were even more surely excluded than those sick in soul from the noble and aristocratic world of Nietzsche's books. These were two inextricably intertwined aspects of one and the same reality:

> Any infirmity of the soul will permanently disqualify you – even dyspepsia: you do not need nerves, you need a joyful stomach. Not just poverty, the stale air of a soul will bar you from them too, and cowardice, uncleanliness, secret vengefulness of the intestines [*in den Eingeweiden*] even more so: one word from me will drive all your bad instincts into your face. [...] Completely depraved 'spirits', the 'beautiful souls', that are liars through and through, have no idea how even to approach these books.
>
> EH, Why I write such good books, 3 [103]

The emphasis on the physio-psychological dimension of the discourse not only restricts or annuls the space for communication but ends up rendering the refutation seemingly meaningless: 'Anyone who does not just understand the word "Dionysian" but understands himself in the word "Dionysian" does not need to refute Plato or Christianity or Schopenhauer – he smells the decay [*Verwesung*]' (EH, The Birth of Tragedy, 2 [109]). 'A philosopher will have to wash his hands after dealing with "the case of Wagner" for so long. – I will give my thoughts on what is modern' (WA, Epilogue [260–1]). The transition repeatedly announced or invoked by Nietzsche to the 'great health' was once again more than a mere metaphor:

I am still waiting for a philosophical physician in the exceptional sense of the term – someone who has set himself the task of pursuing the problem of the total health of a people, time, race or of humanity – to summon the courage at last to push my suspicion to its limit and risk the proposition: what is at stake in all philosophizing hitherto is not at all 'truth' but rather something else – let us say health, future, growth, power, life.

FW, Preface, 2 [6]

Logical refutation was replaced by hygienic and prophylactic measures, and this prophylaxis could also take a police form: once Christianity was defined as 'unnatural', the healthy nature had to preclude contamination, which did not exclude custodial measures even for 'priests' (*supra*, 18 § 9).

10   Two Radically Different Types of Mask

Nietzsche explicitly declared himself the initiator of 'a genuine physio-psychology' (JGB, 23 [23]). From the psyche it was necessary to descend to an even deeper layer: 'Opinions themselves are merely the form of expression known to us of a physiological process'; erroneous opinions 'are great sicknesses transmitted across many generations, finally healing physiologically and thus dying out'; and one was not to forget that 'there are individual and super-individual sicknesses' (IX, 473). Moreover, it was absurd to think the different moral systems could be thought of independently of the body of which they were the expression:

Today we can no longer think of moral apart from physiological degeneration: the first is merely a syndrome of the second; one is necessarily bad, as one is necessarily sick. [...] Vice is not the cause, it is the effect. Vice is a conceptual delimitation, somewhat arbitrary, to summarize certain consequences of physiological degeneration.

XIII, 290

Value judgements 'have value only as symptoms', symptoms of the body as well as of the soul, symptoms of the health or insanity of those that expressed them. Socrates and Plato could be evaluated positively only by other sick people. The precondition for such an attitude is that they were 'in physiological agreement' about something (GD, The problem of Socrates, 2 [162]). One had to understand once and for all: 'There is a physiological disaster at the bottom of all so-called "beautiful souls"' (EH, Why I write such good books, 5 [105]). More generally, to understand the kind of person with whom you were dealing, 'you first need to be clear about what he presupposes physiologically' (EH, *Thus Spoke Zarathustra*, 2 [125]). The oscillation of the contemporary Western world between Christianity and the recovery of a pagan and tragic worldview gave expression not only to a clash of cultures: 'Biologically, modern people represent a contradiction of values', but this meant that 'physiologically considered, we are false'; we were dealing with the combination and confrontation of two mutually incompatible natures, a healthy and a sick nature (WA, Epilogue [262]).

At this point, physiology becomes the decisive element in understanding the different spheres of culture, whether of 'aesthetics' or of the 'sphere of so-called moral values'. Regarding the latter, the 'morality of Christian notions of value' was rooted 'in soil infected to its depths', so it as irreducibly antithetical to the 'morality of masters', based on 'will to power as the principle of life'. Now not only the conflict of values appeared as a conflict between health and sickness, but, more importantly, both health and sickness found their theoretical expression *immediately and necessarily* in a corresponding worldview:

> Both of these opposing forms in the optics of value are necessary: they are ways of seeing that cannot be approached with reasons and refutations. You do not refute Christianity, you do not refute an eye disease. It was the climax of scholarly idiocy to fight pessimism as if it were a philosophy. The concepts 'true' and 'not true' do not seem to me to have any meaning for optics.
>
> WA, Epilogue [261]

There was no room for argumentation and refutation, since the theories and concepts referred to a deeper sphere from which they were deterministically derived and in which their meaning was resolved completely and without residue. Nietzsche continued to talk until the end about science, but this had nothing to do with a community of concept with which everyone could potentially identify. Science was synonymous with health, just as superstition was synonymous with sickness, while psychology was the ability to detect the presence of health and sickness: 'I have a subtler sense of smell for the signs of ascent and decline than anyone has ever had' (EH, Why I am so wise, 1 [75]).

Because the subject tended to conceal itself, it is all the more necessary to go beyond the level of consciousness and explicit declarations: 'How can anyone believe a philosopher has ever expressed his opinions in books?' (XIV, 374). In fact, '[o]ne does not only wish to be understood when one writes; one wishes just as surely *not* to be understood' (FW, 381 [245]). This was just the point: '[D]on't people write books precisely to keep what they hide to themselves?

[...] Every philosophy conceals a philosophy too: every opinion is also a hiding place, every word is also a mask' (JGB, 289 [173]). And then, for the interpreter it was necessary to 'look behind the masks' (XI, 481).

We are dealing with an undoubtedly fascinating theme, which not by chance has attracted exceptional interpreters.[20] Moreover, it is beyond dispute that Nietzsche contributed to the development of depth psychology and psychoanalysis.

On the other hand, the political significance of the theme of the mask and of depth has seldom been explored. Actually, we are dealing with two radically different types of mask. On the one side, it is a question of penetrating to a deep dimension, protected by silence, repression and disguises, of those interested in obscuring, concealing, or repressing their sickness. On the other side looms a fundamentally different type of mask:

> A man with something profound in his shame [...] instinctively needs speech in order to be silent and concealed, and is tireless in evading communication – wants and encourages a mask of himself to wander around, in his place, through the hearts and heads of his friends. [...] Every profound spirit needs a mask: what's more, a mask is constantly growing around every profound spirit, thanks to the consistently false (which is to say shallow) interpretation of every word, every step, every sign of life he displays.
>
> JGB, 40 [38–9]

If the malformed were inevitably banished to the realm of sickness and the lie (with regard to themselves rather than to others), aristocratic natures wished to avoid all chance of contact with and contamination by the rabble, including the intellectual and history-writing rabble:

> The historians today want too much and sin in all cases against good taste: they rush to penetrate into the souls of human beings to whose rank and society they do not belong. For example, what does a jumpy and sweaty plebeian like Michelet have to do with Napoleon! It makes no difference whether he hates him or loves him: because he sweats, he does not belong in his vicinity.
>
> XI, 588

---

20   Cf. Vattimo 1983.

There could be no doubt: '[E]very profound spirit needs a mask' (JGB, 40 [38]); indeed, 'the higher the nature, the more a human being needs incognito' (XI, 543). Superior people were well aware of this: 'We know that we are hard to know, and we have every reason to provide ourselves with foregrounds' (XI, 545). The superior human being, who suffered much more than the common and vulgar human being, 'needs all kinds of disguises to protect itself from the touch of intrusive and pitying hands' (JGB, 270 [166]). The Great Chain of Being manifested itself as the Great Chain of the need for disguise, after having been the Great Chain of sensitivity to pain.

Even if the two types of mask had an opposite meaning, they jointly brought about one outcome: the impossibility of communication between human beings of superior and inferior nature.

11   Psychology and Ethnology of Worldviews

The analysis of the history of ideas and political and ideological conflicts leads to the construction of psychological and anthropological typologies. Let us return to *The Birth of Tragedy*. Socrates represented 'the archetype of a form of existence unknown before him, the archetype of the theoretical human being; our next task is to understand the significance and goal of this human type' (GT, 15, I, 98 [72]). More exactly, he 'is the archetype of the theoretical optimist' (GT, 15, I, 100 [74]). So to the 'theoretical human being', the 'Socratic human being' (GT, 20, I, 132 [95–8]), or 'abstract human being' that represented 'abstract education, abstract morality, abstract law, the abstract state' (GT, 23, I, 145 [108]), was contrasted the 'tragic human being' (GT, 18, I, 119 [88]). We were therefore dealing with the 'eternal struggle between the theoretical and the tragic views of the world' (GT, 17, I, 111 [82]); facing each other, without the possibility of mediation, were 'two different forms of existence' (GT, 19, I, 128 [95]). The third *Unfashionable Observation* introduced a new typology that distinguished, as we have seen, between 'Rousseau's human being', the basis of 'every socialist shaking and quaking', 'Goethe's human being', immune to subversive infatuations but prone to philistinism, and, finally, 'Schopenhauer's human being', the only one really able to confront and overcome the challenge posed by revolution (*supra*, 6 §8–9).

The psychology (and physio-psychology) of worldviews tended to supplant rather than merely accompany the history of ideas or even history as such. Moreover, it seemed at times to be articulated on a national basis, and so ran the risk of lapsing into national stereotypes. Thus, the German essence was called upon during the years of *The Birth of Tragedy* to discard the 'Latin' (GT, 23, I, 149

[111]), or better still, the 'essence of neo-Latin' (BA, 2, I, 690), also more or less
frozen in time, in order to recover its intrinsic and only superficially dimmed
'Dionysiac capacity' (GT, 24, I, 153 [114]).

So, it is understandable that Nietzsche, from the point of view of such a
psychology-ethnology of worldviews, suspected Socrates and Strauss of being
alien to the Greek or German essence, in order to allocate both to the Jewish world (supra, 3 § 2–4 and 15 § 2). This manner of reasoning did not vanish
with the end of the 'metaphysical' and romantic phase. *Beyond Good and Evil*
developed a consideration of a general character: philosophising

> is not nearly as much a discovery as it is a recognition, remembrance, a
> returning and homecoming into a distant, primordial, total economy of
> the soul [*uralten Gesammt-Haushalt der Seele*], from which each concept
> once grew: – to this extent, philosophizing is a type of atavism of the
> highest order. The strange family resemblance of all Indian, Greek, and
> German philosophizing speaks for itself clearly enough. Where there are
> linguistic affinities, then because of the common philosophy of gram-
> mar (I mean: due to the unconscious domination and direction through
> similar grammatical functions), it is obvious that everything lies ready
> from the very start for a similar development and sequence of philosoph-
> ical systems; on the other hand, the way seems as good as blocked for
> certain other possibilities of interpreting the world [*Welt-Ausdeutung*].
> Philosophers of the Ural-Altaic language group (where the concept of the
> subject is the most poorly developed) are more likely to 'see the world'
> differently, and to be found on paths different from those taken by the
> Indo-Germans or Muslims.
>
> JGB, 20 [20]

This theory reminds one of Renan, who in this same period preferred to speak
of 'linguistic races' rather than of 'anthropological races',[21] so that, for example,
the Semitic languages were 'the organs of a monotheist race', the 'religious
race *par excellence*'.[22] On the other hand, there were peoples that by virtue of
their language (which was alien or resistant to 'revolutions') were 'doomed to
immobility'.[23]

But, in Nietzsche, one finds a further naturalistic rigidification: '[T]he spell of
particular grammatical functions is in the last analysis the spell of *physiological*

---

21   Renan 1947 ff., Vol. 8, 1224.
22   Renan 1947 ff., Vol. 8, 97.
23   Renan 1947 ff., Vol. 8, 162; cf. Olender 1989, 4.

value judgements and racial conditioning' (JGB, 20 [20–1]). Since the different worldviews were ultimately founded in physiology – the philosopher emphasised this point with italics – they were unable to communicate with each other: 'The hardest thing to translate from one language into another is the tempo of its style, which is grounded in the character of the race, or – to be more physiological – in the average tempo of its "metabolism"' (JGB, 28 [29]). The translatability of languages applied only to the multiple manifestations of one and the same culture but not to relations between different cultures.

This articulation of worldviews according to their ethnic and physiological basis had serious implications: unable to communicate with each other, they remained immobile and permanently hierarchical, and in such a way that the peoples whose expression they were were also hierarchised. 'Individuals', 'classes [Stände]' or 'even whole races' could give expression to a worldview hostile to nature and life (FW, Preface, 2 [5]). Perhaps here was an allusion to the Jews, elsewhere repeatedly branded as the incarnation of the anti-aristocratic and anti-natural moral worldview.

12   Reappearance of the 'Text' and Its Transformation into a 'Fact'

The shift from psychology to physio-psychology in the interpretation of individuals as well as of peoples and 'races' led to a paradoxical outcome. We have seen the text too vanish along with the 'fact', but now the text not only reappeared but tended to be configured as an inescapable objectivity and evidence. Against idealistic mystifications, Nietzsche called for recognition and respect for 'the terrible basic text of homo natura'. So one had to 'translate humanity back into nature; to gain control of the many vain and fanciful interpretations and incidental meanings that have been scribbled and drawn over that eternal basic text of homo natura so far' (JGB, 230 [123]). In light of this approach, it was not only 'the "miracles" [that] are just errors of interpretation' and 'a lack of philology' (JGB, 47 [46]). Morality too was an arbitrary superimposition on the text of nature. The distinction between the interpretations now appeared to be so easy that their plurality tended to vanish: now 'moral and religious interpretation' of the world had become 'impossible for us'. It was necessary to affirm a completely different 'new interpretation' (XI, 633): 'the aesthetic interpretation' (IX, 615) or the 'dynamic interpretation of the world' (XI, 565), based on joyous recognition of the reality of the will to power and the innocence of becoming.

This new, more valid interpretation, indeed the only truly valid one, had to embrace 'every happening' (XI, 619 and 629); together with the 'moral interpretation of all facts of nature', 'the moral interpretation of our actions' was also to be condemned (XI, 501). In this way the transition from nature to history came about. In interpreting the French Revolution, Kant and no few of his contemporaries proceeded arbitrarily. Instead of respecting the text in its autonomy, they projected moral concerns and hopes onto it that are completely alien to it. In 'that gruesome and (on close consideration) pointless farce [...] noble and enthusiastic [*edlen und schwärmerischen*] spectators across Europe have, from a distance, interpreted their own indignations and enthusiasms into it, and for so long and with such passion that the text has finally disappeared under the interpretation' (JGB, 38 [37]).

The evidence of the text formed by reality was so incontrovertible that the interpretations that ignored or misunderstood were to be viewed not just as errors but as forgeries:

> Anyone who 'explains' an author's passage 'more profoundly' than it was meant has not explained the author, but *obscured* him. That is the way our metaphysicians deal with the text of nature; even worse. For to adduce their profound explanations, they often adjust the text accordingly: i.e., they corrupt it.
>
> WS, 17 [161]

In the end, the text of reality even seemed to assume a physical dimension. As we have seen, the aphorism of *The Gay Science* polemicised against the 'prejudice' of scientists that would have liked to claim sole and exclusive validity for their mathematical and calculative interpretation of the world. But the conclusion of the argument was that this claim was 'a crudity and naïveté, assuming it is not a mental illness, an idiocy' (FW, 373 [239]). The problematic, which consisted in conceiving the relationship between world and worldview on the model of the relationship between text and interpreter-philologist, turned into its opposite. The soul apprehended by 'guessing' referred, for its part, to the body: 'Behind the highest value judgements that have hitherto guided the history of thought are concealed misunderstandings [*Missverständnisse*] of the physical constitution – of individuals or classes or even whole races' (FW, Preface, 2 [5]). We are dealing here with a subjective rather than an objective genitive: in the last analysis, it was the sick body that misunderstood itself. The philological model, the category of interpretation, continued to be present, but its meaning had undergone a complete reversal: 'Every philosophy that ranks peace above war' is 'no more than an interpretation of the body and a misunderstanding of the body'. One could rightly ask 'whether it was not illness that inspired the philosopher'; one should not allow oneself to be misled by the 'unconscious disguise of physiological needs under the cloaks of the objective, ideal, purely spiritual' (FW, Preface, 2 [5]). Even more so than the soul, the system or the conceptual mediation hid the body and the sickness of the body, which was tp be brought to light and unmasked by this new 'psychology' and physio-psychology.

In conclusion, anti-sensualistic epistemology, implicit in the philological approach, entered into contradiction with the profession of sensualistic faith that, on the political and moral level, Nietzsche set against Platonism, Christianity and socialism. In its various configurations, 'idealism' abandoned the terrain of actual objectivity to chase a fantasy world of religious and political ideals and evasions, moral demands and recriminations, a world that could only be the result of insanity, sickness and corruption of the body. On closer and deeper inspection, it turned out that a wrong proposition or misinterpretation was physiologically and pathologically conditioned and determined. The sceptical attitude, as opposed to what was celebrated as 'the security of measures of value', was now decidedly suspect: 'But we are no sceptics – we still believe in a rank-ordering of people and problems' (XI, 529). Now there seemed to be no longer any room for doubt: 'Skepticism is the most spiritual expression of a certain complex physiological condition which in layman's terms is called weak nerves or a sickly constitution' (JGB, 208 [100]).

This explains the singular contradiction whereby, on one and the same page, one finds the thesis that 'good and evil are only interpretations and in no way a fact', so that it is now time to free oneself from the 'rooted compulsion to interpret morally' and, immediately after that, the reproach that the moral interpretation neglects 'the fundamental fact', i.e., the 'contradiction between 'becoming more moral' and the elevation and strengthening of the type human being' (XII, 131–2). On the other hand, one could set against Nietzsche's harsh call to follow the 'eternal basic text of *homo natura*' his own polemic against the Stoics' claim to live 'according to nature'. In fact, nature was 'indifference itself as power'. So 'how could you live according to this indifference? Living – isn't that wanting specifically to be something other than this nature? Isn't living assessing, preferring, being unfair, being limited, wanting to be different?' *Beyond Good and Evil* continues: 'Your pride wants to dictate and annex your morals and ideals onto nature' (JGB, 9 [10]). But does Nietzsche not proceed similarly, when he confines himself simply to replacing the 'moral interpretation of the world' with a 'dynamic world interpretation', raised to the level of an incontrovertible 'fact'?

Even if Nietzsche employed the category of sickness more and more often over the years, it was a trait that marked all stages of his development. The germs of this type of interpretation can already be found in *The Birth of Tragedy*, where Socrates was seen as the expression of a sick vision of life, a gloomy psychology. In him (and in Euripides) a philosophy disruptive of myth and the existing social order went hand in hand with the 'progressive [...] atrophying [*Verkümmerung*]' of 'physical and spiritual energies'; 'the old, sturdy, Marathonian toughness of body and soul' had now vanished (GT, 13, I, 88 [64]). That 'profound delusion [*tiefsinnige Wahnvorstellung*]' according to which thought could penetrate 'down into the deepest abysses of being, and that it was capable, not simply of understanding existence, but even of correcting it' 'first appeared in the person of Socrates' (GT, 15, I, 99 [73]). 'At present, however, science, spurred on by its powerful delusion [*Wahn*], is hurrying unstoppably to its limits' and to the point of foundering (GT, 15, I, 101 [75]).

The writings and notes written contemporaneously with *The Birth of Tragedy* confirm not only the thesis of 'mania [*Wahn*]' and 'hallucination [*Wahnvorstellung*]' (VII, 134 and 132), but further develop the indictment, more and more clearly shown to be a diagnosis without hope: even in his physical appearance, Socrates was 'a quite abnormal person'; moreover, he was marked by a 'one-sided intellect' hostile to the healthy 'instinct' and by a 'huge will' and he lived in 'an absurd and inverted world' (ST, I, 541–2).

The theme can also easily be found in the 'Enlightenment' period. When Socrates dignified what was perhaps a banal 'earache' as a 'demon' he was guilty of a 'false interpretation' of a pathological symptom: the saint behaved in a similar way in relation to his 'visions' and his 'states of sickness' (MA, 126).

In this way, an exalted pathos of truth erupts into Nietzsche's discourse, a pathos that sets the 'truth' and its 'revelation' against the millennia of erroneous and sick interpretations of the text of nature. The language of the philologist gives way to the language of the prophet. The latter thus celebrates the unprecedented turning point represented by his Zarathustra: 'Until then, you do not know what height, what depth really is; you know even less what truth is. Not a single moment of this revelation of truth has been anticipated or hinted at by any of the greatest people' (EH, *Thus Spoke Zarathustra*, 6 [130]).

We have seen Nietzsche set the noble enlightenment and scepticism of Pilate against the claim of the visionary and fanatic to represent and embody truth. Yet here the philosopher ended up assuming the attitude of Jesus rather than of the procurator he admired:

> But my truth is terrible: because lies have been called truth so far. – Revaluation of all values: that is my formula for an act of humanity's highest self-examination, an act that has become flesh and genius in me. My lot would have it that I am the first decent human being, that I know myself to be opposing the hypocrisy of millennia ... I was the first to dis-

cover the truth because I was the first to see – to smell – lies for what they are ... My genius is in my nostrils. [...] [A]ll hope had disappeared until I came along.

EH, Why I am a destiny, 1 [144]

So exalted was the pathos of truth that Nietzsche went so far as to define himself as 'the first honest spirit in the history of spirit, the spirit in which truth comes to pass judgement over four thousand years of counterfeit' (EH, *The Case of Wagner*, 3 [141]), the counterfeit of the long and ruinous cycle in which had raged the error or, more precisely, the Jewish-Christian delirium. And precisely because the health/sickness dichotomy takes the place of the truth/error dichotomy, Nietzsche can now formulate the thesis that 'perhaps sick thinkers are in the majority in the history of philosophy' (FW, Preface, 2 [4–5]).

13   'Reverse syllogism', 'Soul Atomism' and Omnipresence of the Will to Power

The 'reverse syllogism' was to seek to understand the 'soul atomism' of an author or a movement, but what was the essential element of this atomism? We already know that the cultivation of one's own interiority favoured by the 'old psychologists' was quite alien to the 'new psychologist'. But there is a further element of differentiation. In its new form, psychology had the task of 'putting an end to the superstition that until now has grown around the idea of the soul with an almost tropical luxuriance' (JGB, 12 [14]).

It was a question of breaking with the religious and moral tradition that had weighed down on psychology and prevented it from becoming aware of the real problems, even before developing appropriate responses: 'scientific curiosity' had been inhibited (FW, 345 [202]). Insofar as 'psychology' decided finally to overcome a millennial inhibition about 'daring to go into depths' and really reading the depths of the human being and its 'soul', it took on a new and unprecedented form:

To grasp psychology as morphology and the doctrine of the development of the will to power, which is what I have done – nobody has ever come close to this, not even in thought: this, of course, to the extent that we are permitted to regard what has been written so far as a symptom of what has not been said until now.

JGB, 23 [23]

'The power of moral prejudice' was now broken, even if it 'has deeply affected the most spiritual world, which seems like the coldest world, the one most likely to be devoid of any presuppositions'. Once its 'harmful, hindering, dazzling, and distorting' pervasiveness had been neutralised (JGB, 23 [23]), one could finally perceive the reality of the will to power. This also worked in moral discourse and in the moral attitude that tried to hide or deny it. But the will to power could manifest itself in radically different ways. Let us examine them:

> How poisonous, how cunning, how bad you become in every long war that cannot be waged out in the open! How personal you become when you have been afraid for a long time, keeping your eye on enemies, on possible enemies! These outcasts of society (the long-persecuted, the badly harassed, as well as those forced to become hermits, the Spinozas or Giordano Brunos): they may work under a spiritual guise, and might not even know what they are doing, but they will always end up subtly seeking vengeance and mixing their poisons (just try digging up the foundation of Spinoza's ethics and theology!)
>
> JGB, 25 [26-7]

The universality of the reality of the will to power did not in any way imply the equivalence of its different manifestations. Their hierarchisation was the key to judging personalities and movements. To the extent that it was possible to distinguish between the different forms, the superior form was the will to power that was not disguised and was expressed with the greatest sincerity. At first glance, the moral value of sincerity was the key criterion, but sincerity here was synonymous with the immediacy with which the body expressed itself and this in turn was synonymous with health. As we know, every worldview, every philosophy, even every aesthetic was an expression of psychophysical subjectivity; and yet there was subjectivity and subjectivity, there was the body and no body, the healthy body and the sick body.

Far from being 'infinite', as Foucault would like, the game and the comparison of interpretations come to a very abrupt conclusion. The 'altruistic manner of evaluation' was an expression of the 'instinct of having turned out badly'. It was without a doubt an 'interpretation', but 'the very use of interpretations of this sort is a symptom of decadence [*Verfall*]'. As well as psychic, the decadence spoken of here also had a physiological dimension; it denoted 'the lack of great feelings of power (in the muscles, nerves, centres of movement)' (XIII, 232). Like cruelty and the will to power, egoism was also manifested in a convoluted and distorted way in so-called altruism, which again referred to a nature malformed in all respects. What Nietzsche explicitly asserted regarding egoism ('egoism is worth as much as the one that has it is physiologically worth') could also be said of interpretation: its value corresponded to the physiological value of the one that carried it out. The interpretation to be rejected pointed not so much to a mistake as to a sickness, and moreover an incurable one. Here the sceptical demystifier became a dogmatic positivist. This also had consequences at the practical level. Since there could be no real argumentation or communication between a healthy and a sick body, between health and sickness, it would be naïve to seek to refute the egoism of the physiologically ailing individual. 'Whether in the case of individuals or entire decaying stunted popular layers, [...] the suppression of that egoism' is necessary that 'sometimes expresses itself absurdly, morbidly, rebelliously' (XIII, 231–2).

Foucault's claim that Nietzsche's later madness could be interpreted as a metaphor for the defeat inherent in the infinite and infinitely complex task of interpretation[24] is bad literature.

14   'Sickness', 'Bad Faith' and the Impossibility of Self-Reflection

Nietzsche drew ever more obsessively in the course of his development on the category of degeneration to explain conflict and history. But, in doing so, he forfeited the opportunity for self-reflection, the capacity of an author to apply to his own discourse and to himself the criteria for interpretation and critique he enunciates for the discourses of others. He never tired of repeating that his antagonists, and only they, were sick:

> All questions of politics, of social organization, of education are shown up as forgeries at a very basic level when the most harmful people are taken for great human beings. [...] When I compare myself with people that have been honoured as first so far, then the difference is palpable.

On the one hand, we have beings stricken by an incurable 'sickness' and become one with it, and on the other:

> I want to be the opposite of all this: it is my privilege to have the finest sense for all signs of healthy instincts. I do not have any sickly features; even in times of widespread illness I do not get sick; you won't find a single trace of fanaticism [*Fanatismus*] in my character.
>
> EH, Why I am so clever, 10 [99]

---

24   Foucault 1967, 188 f.

The philosopher defined his thinking and himself in opposition to the rampant sickness of religion and subversion: 'It is not a "prophet" speaking here, not one of those awful amalgams of sickness and will to power known as founders of religions' (EH, Prologue, 4 [72]); '[t]hese are not the words of some fanatic, nothing is being "preached" here, nobody is demanding that you believe' (EH, Prologue, 4 [73]).

Yet from the point of view of the religious person, the atheist had a mutilated (or self-mutilated) humanity that prevented him from grasping the sacred. The accusation of sickness bounced from one to the other precisely because both employed a category that permitted no self-reflection. On the other hand, *The Gay Science* discovered in the dying Socrates the indirect yet fatal confession that finally unmasked him: '[L]ife is a disease' (FW, 340 [194]). It would be easy for the purposes of comparison to cite the clear declarations in which Nietzsche indulged in moments of the most acute suffering. Bedridden by a 'most violent attack', he made a painful confession to Lou Salomé on 25 August 1882: 'I despise life' (B, III, 1, 245).

Towards the end of the nineteenth century, some of Nietzsche's 'devotees' praised his 'psycho-physiological' or 'psychophysical intuition', understood as the ability to 'eavesdrop and spy on all the secret processes and nooks' and then to proceed back to the psychological and physiological characteristics of the personality or movement under investigation.[25] Not for nothing Nordau took over from Nietzsche and the culture of the time the category of 'degeneration', to use it against him. The conclusion is highly significant: 'So the degenerate must succumb, for they can neither adapt to the conditions of nature and society nor assert themselves in the struggle for existence against the healthy.' Ultimately, those also inadequate 'organically' were destined to be swept away: 'They become hysterical and neurasthenic, they produce degenerates, and therewith ends their stock.'[26] Apart from optimism, on the basis of which the victory of the best and the healthiest would seemed to be guaranteed, such was Nietzsche's picture.

Lou Salomé argued similarly in her Nietzsche biography: 'He basically thought for himself alone, he wrote for himself, because he described only himself, he turned his own self into thoughts'; so it was futile to search for a 'theoretical importance' that went beyond the philosopher's inner wealth and 'intimate force'.[27] Despite the accolades this biography has received, it not only does not do justice to the writer that is its subject but it absolutises his weakest

25   This is mocked in Nordau n.d., Vol. 2, 367.
26   Nordau n.d., Vol. 2, 527 f.
27   Andreas-Salomé 1983, 29 ff.

side. The interpretation is moreover self-contradictory, since, as we have seen (*supra*, 28 § 6), Lou Salomé herself emphasised the desire for conversion that had inspired Nietzsche.

So, the philosopher's sister was right to reject this interpretation:

> Mrs Andreas' basic ideas about my brother are quite wrong, indeed the contrary is true. In particular, by seeking to reduce the core of his character and development to purely pathological causes, she sets the truth on its head and shows that she has not the least sensitivity to his real personality. The effect of this false representation is obvious: in fact, with this idea Mrs Andreas meets up with a current of the age, which would explain every spiritual greatness pathologically.[28]

Even if the criticism is one-sided and generously spares the brother, Elisabeth reveals in her rejection of psychological and biographical reductionism a greater philosophical subtlety than Lou and even, in this concrete and limited case, than Friedrich. The latter continues, a century after his death, to stand at the centre of philosophical debate, because he proposed ideas and suggestions that, whatever their psychological genesis, have a validity that goes far beyond the sphere of 'self-confession'. Moreover, Lou herself underlined, once again contradicting herself, 'the presence, in Nietzsche, of an unreserved striving for knowledge, which as it were constitutes the unifying force of his whole being'; the philosopher 'abandons himself to this god of knowledge that is his'.[29]

In confirmation of her criticism, Elisabeth recalled the letter of February 1888 in which her brother complained about the lack of reviews and critical discussions of his books; instead, 'now they muddle by with the words "eccentric", "pathological", "psychiatric"' (B, III, 5, 248).[30] In reality, this statement indicates a serious problem. While, on the one hand, he never tired of interpreting the positions of his opponents psychopathologically, on the other hand he tried to explain that this interpretation did not apply to himself. The author of *Ecce Homo* at first emphasised that the dialectic, as 'the case of Socrates' had already shown, was a 'symptom of *décadence*', and then continued:

> All pathological intellectual disturbances, even that half-stunned condition that follows a fever, have been completely alien to me to this day, and I have had to learn about their nature and frequency through study.

---

28   Förster-Nietzsche 1895–1904, Vol. 2, VII.
29   Andreas-Salomé 1970, 187.
30   Förster-Nietzsche 1895–1904, Vol. 2, VIIf.

My blood flows slowly. Nobody has ever detected a fever in me. A doctor who treated me for a long time as a neurological patient finally said: 'No! The problem is not your nerves, I am the one that is nervous.' Any sort of local degeneration simply cannot be proven; there is no organic cause for stomach pain, however profound the weakness of my gastric system may be as the result of a state of complete exhaustion. Even the eye-aches that sometimes come dangerously close to blindness are just the effect, not the cause: so that with every increase in vital energy, my visual acuity increases as well.

EH, Why I am so wise, 1 [75–6]

Since the sickness lacked an organic base and was only the result of exhaustion, in Nietzsche's case it had played only a positive role. It had granted him a certain familiarity with '*décadence*', yet without him being really affected by it (EH, Why I am so wise, 1): 'As *summa summarum* I was healthy; as a niche, as a speciality, I was decadent.' This (he argued) was an ideal condition for describing the scourge of decadence and degeneration with greater penetration and a greater resolve to combat it (EH, Why I am so wise, 2 [76]).

It is worth thinking about this insistence on the part of the late Nietzsche that the sickness that attacked his opponents and antagonists was apparently not present in him. It confirms that there was no longer any room for self-reflection; and if self-reflection is a prerequisite for any genuinely critical, non-dogmatic theory,[31] it must be said that the late Nietzsche was decidedly dogmatic.

We arrive at the same outcome if we analyse another category favoured by Nietzsche. We already know that, in his eyes, the priest propagated lies, and was fully aware of doing so. Here, the dichotomy between truth and error was so evident as to be perfectly clear to the priest (as well as to all those professional liars that were the enemies of the party of life). The struggle to the end against the priest, 'this professional negater, slanderer, poisoner of life' was absolutely necessary if one wanted 'an answer to the question: What is *truth*? *Truth* has already been turned on its head when someone that consciously champions nothingness and negation passes for the representative of "*truth*"' (AC, 8 [8]). It is worth noting the term 'truth' appears three times here, but Nietzsche uses quotation marks only when referring to his opponents. Here the philosopher expresses himself not so much like the Pilate he admires (*Quid est veritas?*) but like the Jesus he despises (*ego sum veritas*). And, in fact, in a letter dated 18 Octo-

---

31   Cf. Habermas 1968a; Ferry/Renaut 1985, 225 f.

ber 1888, he described himself as a 'genius of the truth' – in contrast to Wagner, the 'genius of lies' (B, III, 5, 452).

It is true the lie here spoken of sometimes had a wider meaning than usual:

> I call lies not wanting to see what you see, not wanting to see it the way you do: it makes no difference whether the lies take place in front of witnesses. The most common lie is the one you tell yourself; lying to other people is a relatively exceptional case. – Now, this not wanting to see what you see, this not wanting to see the way you do, is almost the first condition for being partisan in any sense of the term: the partisan [*Parteimensch*] will necessarily turn into a liar.
>
> AC, 55 [55]

The widening of the concept of the lie made things even worse, and not only because the field of the liars targeted became wider. Now the truth/falsehood dichotomy or the truth/'truth' dichotomy became the partisan/non-partisan dichotomy. So, the criterion of self-reflection went missing even in a naïve sense: as if Nietzsche had not repeatedly stepped up as leader or ideologue of the party of life!

The more or less conscious liar, however, was radically incapable of grasping and expressing the truth, for he was inwardly and irredeemably rotten. And again, the tendency to trace the conflict back to the dishonesty of the opponent or even to his nature, even his physiology, collapsed the space for communication. As Nietzsche himself explicitly recognised: 'I consider anyone that disagrees with me about this [the triumph of '*décadence* morality'] to be infected ... But everyone disagrees with me. For a physiologist, this sort of value contrast leaves no doubts' (EH, *Daybreak*, 2 [122]).

CHAPTER 30

From Suprahistorical Myth to the Opening of New Perspectives for Historical Research

1   Counterrevolutionary Hatred and the Highlighting of 'Reactionary' Aspects of the Revolutionary Process

Aristocratic radicalism does not keep, cannot keep, its anti-dogmatic promises. But even so its powerful theoretical endeavour is not without results. Its critical and demystifying *élan* challenges many certainties and shatters many commonplaces. It is possible to understand this only if one does not lose sight of the reactionary coherence of aristocratic radicalism. One can ignore and suppress the condemnation of liberalism, democracy and equal rights or reinterpret all this more or less metaphorically. The result is very unfavourable for Nietzsche. The philosopher who, in professing his aristocratism and thereby bringing into play a new and original reading of the two-thousand-year cycle of revolution raging in the West, sustaining this reading with a constant confrontation with the great historians of his time, that philosopher was not even taken into consideration. Instead, he was granted the dubious honour of being immersed in a rarefied aura where there was room for neither history nor politics. But as soon as we try to take aristocratic radicalism seriously, we see it is capable of developing an analysis of the problems, difficulties and dilemmas of the revolutionary project that is certainly merciless but all the more instructive, not just for professional historians but even for revolutionaries, who despite everything do not intend to renounce the perspective of the emancipation of the subaltern classes and peoples.

Since the subaltern classes live in restricted material circumstances, if only to survive they must develop what Adam Smith call 'austere morality', characterised by the glorification of labour and sacrifice, distrust of and hostility towards luxury and sexual and spiritual freedom, and the 'liberal morality' of the ruling classes.[1] Nietzsche saw this 'austere morality' full of envy and frustration in action in the plebeian movements of revolt, from Jesus to Luther and from Rousseau to the socialists.

Against each stage in the development of the revolution, Nietzsche set the greater cultural richness and mental agility of the *ancien régime* that had been

---

1   Smith 1981, 794 (Book 5, 1, pt. 3, art. 3).

overthrown again and again. So, Rousseau cuts a worse figure than Voltaire and Montaigne, and the same goes, but even more so, for Luther in relation to Erasmus and the Renaissance, let alone for Jesus in relation to the authors of classical antiquity:

> Even during the era of Græco-Roman splendour, which was also a splendour of books, in the face of an ancient world of writings that had not yet succumbed to decay and ruin, at a time when you could still read a few books we would nowadays give half of whole literatures to possess, the simplicity and vanity of Christian agitators – we call them Church Fathers – dared to decree: 'we have our own classical literature, we don't need that of the Greeks', and so saying, they proudly pointed to books of legends, letters of the apostles and apologetic little tracts, rather similar to the way the English 'Salvation Army' today fights Shakespeare and other 'heathens' with similar literature.
>
> GM III, 22 [107]

We know that, even within the Jewish world, Christianity represented a moment of subversion. And, once again, the *ancien régime* sparkles, the world of masters and warriors, first thrown into crisis by the preachings of the prophets and then overwhelmed by Christianity. Compared to this world, the 'New Testament' (not by chance put between inverted commas by Nietzsche) is something entirely different: here the 'little provincial people', suffering from a manic obsession with their own sins and peccadilloes, get excited (GM, III, 22 [108]). The upper classes give way to the common people – throughout, Nietzsche subjected the historical processes to a social analysis – and with the lower classes, a cramped and mediocre world asserts itself: the hostility towards the comfort and luxury of the ruling classes is also a hostility towards the culture they express; in addition, there is the '[c]ontempt for sexuality, making it unclean with the concept of "uncleanliness"', and the preaching of 'chastity', this 'public incitement to anti-nature' (AC, Law against Christianity [67]).

In his own way, Nietzsche hit the mark. We have already seen him denounce Robespierre's pathos of 'virtue' (*supra*, 8 §1); but historians know that similar trends have also emerged during other revolutions, and not just in that defined as 'Puritan.' The tendency to 'organised asceticism' and the 'crusade against the customary vices' were not absent even from the American Revolution, although there social protest on the part of subaltern classes played a lesser role.[2] On the

---

2 Brinton 1953, 209 f.

eve of the abolitionist revolution, which after all coincided with the American Civil War, exponents of abolitionism criticised the South for being an 'erotic society' given to sexual licentiousness; this licentiousness could unleash itself without restraint thanks to the institution of slavery that obstinately persisted.[3]

To understand Nietzsche's attitude better, it is helpful to venture a few comparisons. Marx and Engels severely criticised the claim to give 'Christian asceticism' a 'Socialist tinge';[4] the same went for the 'universal asceticism' preached by movements that, under the influence of the conditions of shortage in which their social base lived, often expressed their anticapitalist rebellion in reactionary forms and content.[5] But there was no room for such distinctions in Nietzsche, who drew a firm line of continuity between Christian and socialist asceticism, thereby destroying both.

The bigoted virtuousness that in Nietzsche's eyes was typical of revolutionary movements was bound up with their herd mentality. The tendency to 'austere morality', already stimulated by the plebeian social base, was further strengthened by the crises these movements faced, when only self-denial and the spirit of unity could save them from repression and ensure their chances of survival and success. But, as we know, Nietzsche's analysis slipped continuously from the historical-social to the psychological and psychopathological level: 'The "person of faith" does not belong to himself, he can only be a means, he needs to be used up, he needs someone to use him up. [...] Every type of faith is an expression of self-abnegation, of self-alienation' (AC, 54 [54]).

And so we come to the fideism and fanaticism of which revolutionary movements are accused. In fact, striving for a radical renewal of society seems to imply a kind of faith in a better future. To set in motion the forces necessary for the desired change, a project for a different society must give expression to a strong moral tension and, to some extent, a missionary *élan*. While scepticism suits the ruling class, or rather, suits above all its more balanced and enlightened members, it would condemn the subaltern classes to resignation or helplessness. Disinclined to make distinctions or offer justifications, Nietzsche set against people of 'faith' those sceptics that were 'strong spirits' (AC, 54 [53–4]). A line of continuity led from the *ego sum veritas* of Jesus and the *credo quia absurdum* of Tertullian to the socialist movement's belief in social palingenesis. Yet the anti-dogmatism of the ruling classes praised here may not go so far as to weaken their ability to act decisively at the political level: in this case, it was precisely Nietzsche who despised a scepticism that could

---

3 Fogel 1991, 327.
4 Marx and Engels 1975 ff., 6, 508.
5 Marx and Engels 1975 ff., 6, 514.

inhibit or paralyse an energetic response to the permanent plebeian challenge to the hierarchical order (*supra*, 21 § 6). On the one hand, pagan and aristocratic Rome, not yet affected by cowardly scepticism, had no scruples about drowning in blood the dreams of emancipation and uprisings of the zealots, while on the other hand it mocked in the figure of Pilate the dogmatic and fanatical strife agitating the Jewish populace.

Again, a comparison helps. When looking sympathetically at the early Christian preaching and community, Engels had no illusions about how irrational and even regressive it was. However, he added: 'The question to be solved, then, is how it came about that the masses in the Roman Empire preferred this nonsense – which was preached, into the bargain, by slaves and oppressed – to all other religions'.[6] As is clear from the opposition, with which we are already familiar, of the sceptical 'aristocrat' to the 'slave' that desires certainties and absolute truths, even in Nietzsche the politico-social dimension of the conflict ended up in a certain sense revealing itself; but the psychological or psychopathological characterisation prevailed.

The attitude here taken by the philosopher ended up drawing attention to a fundamental weakness of the Enlightenment. At the end of the eighteenth century, Friedrich II of Prussia took advantage of the anti-Catholic sentiments of the Enlightenment to justify the annexation of Polish territories, by presenting it as a contribution to the spread of the Enlightenment and the defence of the cause of tolerance. In a letter to him, d'Alembert praised the 'charming verses' of the enlightened sovereign, who by means of his happy joining of 'imagination' and 'reason' made a mockery of the Poles and the 'Blessed Virgin Mary' to whom they entrusted their naïve hopes of 'liberation'.[7] In an effort to discredit the national aspirations of the Polish people, emphasis was put on the religious forms, often naïve, in which they were expressed. Nietzsche's 'Enlightenment' was no different: he denounced the endless revolutionary cycle ravaging the West as a kind of tidal wave of fundamentalism and obscurantism.

As Marx and Engels observed in *The Communist Manifesto*, the as yet immature protest of the subaltern classes practised a 'social levelling in its crudest form' alongside 'universal asceticism'.[8] But 'crude egalitarianism', fuelled by *ressentiment*, began according to Nietzsche with Christianity, and marks all revolutionary movements. How to explain the gloomy picture the Gospels painted of the Pharisees and scribes? 'In the end, they are people of privilege: this was enough, the Chandala hatred did not need any other reason',

---

6 Marx and Engels 1975 ff., 24, 428.
7 Frédéric II Roi de Prusse 1791, 169 f. (letter of 3 March 1772).
8 Marx and Engels 1975 ff., 6, 514.

and the Christian was 'a rebel against all privilege from out of their most basic instincts, – they live, they keep fighting for "equal rights"' (AC 46 [45]).

Once again, Nietzsche grasped a real problem of the dialectic of revolution, a problem that continues to assert itself even in the context of 'scientific socialism' as theorised by the authors of the *Communist Manifesto*. Mao Zedong was not the only one to struggle against 'absolute egalitarianism': with its pettiness, its feelings of envy and, one might even say, its *ressentiment* (when the Red Army took up quarters, 'equality was demanded in the allotment of billets, and the Headquarters would be abused for occupying larger rooms'), it was an expression of narrow social relations, the 'product of a handicraft and small peasant economy',[9] and obstructed or prevented the formation of the social bloc necessary for overthrowing the *ancien régime*. On the one hand, this supports Nietzsche's analysis, but on the other hand it refutes it. It is impossible to make a revolution exclusively on the basis of *ressentiment*: the revolution's success requires a policy of alliances, and this means in its turn preventing envy towards social strata contiguous to or immediately above the revolutionary core classes, strata that are also the natural target of this feeling. Contrary to the theory of aristocratic radicalism and the assumption already commonplace in the tradition of liberal thought, *ressentiment* is an instrument of reaction that aims to divert social protest onto false targets, to fragment the subaltern classes into countless corporate branches. This is why Gramsci saw in the cathartic 'moment' the 'starting point for the entire philosophy of praxis' and revolutionary theory.[10] One should not forget that this reflection in the *Prison Notebooks* was formulated at the same time as in Germany the Nazis were stirring up the resentment and envy of the most backward sections of the people against intellectuals, especially revolutionary intellectuals, and diverting against the Jews the frustration of the masses impoverished by war and economic crisis.

Nietzsche was unable to recognise the significance of the 'cathartic moment' in great revolutions. Instead, he sought to highlight and absolutise the dismal ballast of frustrations, envy and even regressive tendencies that every revolutionary process brings. At this point, it would be easy to quote polemically what Marx had to say: 'The abstract enmity between sense and spirit is necessary so long as the human feeling for nature, the human sense of nature, and therefore also the natural sense of man, are not yet produced by man's own labour'.[11] Austere morality has its basis on the one hand in the insufficient development

---

9   Mao Tse-tung 1967, 111.
10   Gramsci 1975, 1244.
11   Marx and Engels 1975 ff., 3, 312.

of the productive forces and on the other in a social system that, as Nietzsche explicitly explained, rests on the surplus labour and toil of a mass sacrificed on the altar of culture. Similarly, one could set against his praise of the *ancien régime* overthrown by revolution Freud's comment about the beginning of Christianity: 'In *some respects the new religion meant* a cultural *regression* as compared with the *older*, Jewish *one*, as regularly happens when a new mass of people, of a lower level, break their way in or are given admission.'[12] Or Nietzsche could be contrasted with Gramsci, who, despite pronouncing himself for the 'new order', was fully aware that the 'swan song' of the *ancien régime* could sometimes be 'wondrously splendid'.[13]

All this is true, but it in no way invalidates the important perceptions contained in Nietzsche's analysis. Current historical research confirms a 'cultural counter-revolution in sexual mores' whose protagonist is Christianity.[14] But this is not the most interesting thing. Starting with the great upheavals of the modern world, a comparative study of revolutions has developed whose prevailing tendency favours the negative isolation of the French Revolution (and the Bolshevik Revolution). On the other hand, more mature works seek to reconstruct a phenomenology of revolutionary processes that identifies, beyond the obvious differences, the common traits that link to one another revolutions as different as the Puritan and the Bolshevik. Nietzsche went even further and started with the preachings of the New Testament, the mother of all revolutions. Certainly, he was concerned to destroy the two thousand-year Western revolutionary cycle by denouncing the 'reactionary' traits that manifest themselves as a whole and at each separate stage. Nevertheless, the demystifying potential of this ambitious comparative study remains intact. It suffices to ponder the following example. To the cries of horror that also echoed in *The Birth of Tragedy* in reaction to the destruction of art works blamed on the Paris Commune, Marx responded:

> If the acts of the Paris working men were vandalism, it was the vandalism of defence in despair, not the vandalism of triumph, like that which the Christians perpetrated upon the really priceless art treasures of heathen antiquity; and even that vandalism has been justified by the historian as an unavoidable and comparatively trifling concomitant to the Titanic struggle between a new society arising and an old one breaking down.[15]

---

12   Freud 1964, 88.
13   Gramsci 1975, 733.
14   Seccombe 1992, 72.
15   Marx and Engels 1975 ff., 22, 351.

Again, we come up against a comparative study of revolutions that does not spare Christianity, to which the dominant ideology refers. Instead, Marx and Nietzsche emphasise, each in his own way, the iconoclastic tendencies present in the different revolutions, including the Christian or Protestant.

2 Radicalisation of Historical Consciousness and *longue durée*

Nietzsche began his philosophical career arguing that the 'enormous historical need of dissatisfied modern culture' led, as a result of the consequent 'accumulation of countless other cultures', to 'the loss of myth, the loss of a mythical home, a mythical, maternal womb' (GT, 23; I, 146 [109]). The indictment of historical consciousness that started with *The Birth of Tragedy* was further developed, as we know, in the second *Unfashionable Observation*, in which he recommended 'the unhistorical and the suprahistorical' as 'natural antidotes to the suffocation of life by the historical' (HL, 10; I, 330–1).

This theoretical platform quickly entered into crisis. Already by the time of the third *Unfashionable Observation*, he believed 'the engagement with history by past or alien peoples was precious', especially 'for the philosopher who wants to give a fair judgement on all of human history'; he 'must estimate his own time in respect of its difference from others' (SE, 3, I, 361).

But the turning point becomes especially apparent with the start of the 'Enlightenment' period. The struggle against modernity was now conducted with reference not to suprahistorical myth but with the 'hammer blow of historical knowledge', which shattered ideas that, despite their emergence in time, present themselves as self-evident and natural (*supra*, 8 § 4). An entire chapter of *Human, All Too Human* is devoted to reconstructing the 'history of moral sentiments'.

These feelings and, more generally, the emotional sphere became the privileged object of historical research:

> So far, all that has given colour to existence still lacks a history: where could you find a history of love, of avarice, of envy, of conscience, of piety, of cruelty? Even a comparative history of law or even of punishment is so far lacking entirely.
> FW, 7 [34]

This aphorism from *The Gay Science* represents a sort of anticipation of the current development of historical research, which is no longer interested in political events in the narrower sense but also explores private life, feelings, mentalities, and collective emotions: the aura of immobile naturalness and eternity that seems to envelop certain themes is dispelled. Hence the need to design a 'history of cruelty; of dissimulation; of bloodlust'. The latter must be reconstructed in its various forms: it can also be expressed 'in the killing off of opinions, in passing judgement on works, persons, peoples, past'; at bottom, 'the judge is a sublime hangman' (IX, 477). Every expression of life and even of death, or the perception of death, becomes the object of history: 'our 'death' is a completely different death' from that in the past (FW, 152 [132]).

In his determination to investigate not this or that individual political event but the collective feelings and emotions that govern sociopolitical conflict, Nietzsche greatly broadened the scope of historical investigation. After his energetic denunciation of the 'harm of history', before succumbing to the seduction of the 'eternal return of the same', Nietzsche actually extended and radicalised historical consciousness and historical research, which now, together with the 'capacities for knowledge' (MA, 2) and the 'emergence of morality' (GM I, 1 [10]), included numerous other fields. Now various other fields were called upon to contribute to the promotion of knowledge of social reality: the 'history of ethical systems', as distinct from the 'history of origins of these feelings and valuations' (FW, 345 [202]); the 'history of narcotics' (FW, 86 [87]); the 'history of taste' (IX, 481); 'etymology' and the history of words, 'concepts', and the 'history of human language' (XI, 613–4); and the 'history of women' (FW, 361 [226]).

To the extent that the attention of the historian does not stop at the relentless daily pursuit of political events, the times of history and of historical change lengthen. Through battles and wars, the balance of power between states constantly changes, political geography is continuously rewritten, governments and dynasties follow one another in quick succession. But this does not change the modes of production. Already present in Marx, the perspective of the *longue durée* took on even greater prominence in Nietzsche, who called for research into aspects of culture and human behaviour whose changes could be perceived only in the very long term, even longer than those that govern the succession of modes of production: 'We measure the effects on the basis of individuals, at most on the basis of centuries' (IX, 458).

3   'Struggle of Estates and Classes' and Interpretation of the Religious
       Phenomenon

We have seen how Nietzsche energetically insisted on the line of continuity from Christian to socialist messianism. At first sight, this interpretation would seem to have triumphed in today's culture. But only at first sight. It is true that countless authors and books summarily dismiss the philosophy of Marx and Engels and, more generally, the aspiration to a world not torn by class antagonisms or not subject to the law of the strongest, especially in international relations, as a resurrection, in superficially secularised form, of Christian eschatology. Yet this is not Nietzsche's point of view, and it would be a great injustice to attribute it to him. To do so is to fail to grasp his originality and strength. To denounce revolutionary messianism is certainly nothing new. We already saw it in Gentz (*supra*, 7 § 9). It can also be found in Schelling, for whom not only socialists were guilty of indulging in an 'apocalyptic fantasy' but all those who, in pursuit of their amazing projects to transform political institutions in a constitutional and democratic sense, forgot that 'the true *politeia* is only in heaven'.[16] It can be found in Gobineau, who after Sedan had no difficulty in mocking the view of 1789 as 'the year of salvation' for France and the world.[17] In this context, several other authors could also be cited (beyond Germany, one thinks of Donoso Cortés): but none dared interpret Christianity and the Jewish-Christian tradition in a sociopolitical sense, as Nietzsche did.

In him, instead of a rewriting of the history of socialist movements as sacred history, we find on the contrary a sociopolitical reading of religious movements. While, for Löwith and many others, Marx's theory, 'historical materialism, is the history of salvation expressed in the language of political economy',[18] for Nietzsche, as well as for the Marxist Kautsky, Christianity or the Jewish-Christian tradition are an essential chapter in the history of slave revolt expressed in the language of religion. While, for Löwith, Marx's work is 'animated by an eschatological faith from the first to last proposition',[19] for Nietzsche, Jewish-Christian eschatology is animated through and through by strong social protest and even by an implacable class hatred. Far from reducing the revolutionary project to apocalyptic literature, the author of *Twilight of the Idols* discovered the presence of social protest and the aspiration to revolution even in this literature, and particularly in the Christian awaiting of the final judgement. Marx and Engels, and authors influenced by them, argued similarly. Even if Christianity promised the slaves an emancipation realised only at the end of the historical world, it would nevertheless be overhasty, warned Engels, to interpret this theme as a mere evasion. It is true that the 'thousand-year empire' comes only after death, but it takes 'the here and now' as its reference and is 'described in

16   Schelling 1856–61, Vol. 11, 552 and Vol. 7, 461 f.
17   Gobineau 1917, 19.
18   Löwith 1961, 48.
19   Löwith 1961, 48.

earthly colours'. One could argue that the labour movement and radical Christianity are at least different in their attitude towards violence. But that was
not Engels's view. He said with particular reference to the Apocalypse: 'So here
there is no mention of a "religion of love", of "love your enemies, bless them that
curse you", etc. Here undiluted revenge is preached, sound, honest revenge on
the persecutors of the Christians'.[20]

Just a few years later, Kautsky, editor of the magazine *Die neue Zeit*, in which
Engels had published the above-mentioned article, even went so far as to say in
his comprehensive reconstruction of the origins of Christianity that 'the *class
hatred* of the modern proletariat has almost never reached the fanatical form
of that of the Christian'. Especially in the Gospel of Luke Kautsky saw 'a fierce
class hatred of the rich'. This emerges particularly from the Lazarus parable:

> The rich man goes to hell and the poor man to Abraham's bosom, and
> not because the rich man was a sinner and the poor man was just: noth-
> ing is said about that. The rich man is damned just because he was rich.
> Abraham says to him: 'Remember that thou in thy lifetime receivedst thy
> good things, and likewise Lazarus evil things: but now he is comforted,
> and thou art tormented.' The thirst of the oppressed for *vengeance* gloats
> in this image of the future.[21]

I emphasise with italics Engels's and Kautsky's use of the terms 'revenge' and
'class hatred'. They are categories that play a central role in Nietzsche's analysis:
'[T]he Apocalypse of John' is 'the wildest of all outbursts ever written which
revenge has on its conscience' (GM, I, 16 [32]); Christianity as such embodies
'the bacillus of *revenge*' (XIII, 425), while in the Gospels one notes a 'hatred' not
only furious but expressed in 'the most dishonest forms', since it is disguised as
loving and uplifting speech (XII, 381). In reality, the Gospels express the feelings
of a 'poor rabble of hypocrites' that creeps around directing against its opponents and enemies the 'curse', the threat of eternal damnation and of the most
terrible torments (XII, 577–8).

While Nietzsche, in his harsh condemnation, did not distinguish between
the Gospels, Kautsky here believed he had detected a fundamental contradiction or ambiguity. As proof, he compared the two different versions of the
Beatitudes in Luke and Matthew. While Luke has 'Blessed are you that are *poor*,
for yours is the kingdom of God', Matthew has 'Blessed are the poor in spirit,

---

20   Marx and Engels 1975 ff., 27, 462.
21   Kautsky 1908, 34 ff.

for theirs is the kingdom of heaven'. While Luke has 'Blessed are you that are *hungry* now, for you shall be satisfied', Matthew has 'Blessed are those that *hunger and thirst for righteousness*, for they shall be satisfied'. Luke's demands are deprived of their material content by Matthew and spiritualised. The latter, not by chance, drops the cursing of the rich, which in Luke is the counterpart of the beatification of the poor: 'But woe to you that are rich, for you have received your consolation. Woe to you that are satiated now, for you shall hunger.' From this synoptic comparison, concluded Kautsky, the 'cunning revisionism' of Matthew is clearly evident: he seeks to purge Luke's discourse of its worldly and material dimension, reinterpreting it in a purely personal way.[22] Nietzsche, however, opted for an overall interpretation: the Gospels were the banner 'of the poor, the hungry, the weeping, the hated, the outcast, those of ill repute', that took to struggling against, damning and discrediting 'the rich, the satiated, the serene, the learned, the respected' (XII, 577). That the distinction made by Kautsky was here absent is understandable: independently of the reference to hunger and thirst in their materiality, Nietzsche was concerned to identify the 'struggle of estates and classes' even in the spiritually most rarefied discourse, even in the seemingly most generic denunciation of power, wealth, and culture as such.

4   Expanding the Range of Social Conflict and the Role of Psychology

We here encounter one of the most compelling strengths of the teachings of Nietzsche, who was rightly proud of his finesse and psychological penetration. As we have seen, especially after his encounter with the great moralists he decisively broadened the scope of the conflict. This could be waged with weapons far more subtle and insidious than usual in explicit political discourse. It was a question of creating for oneself and the camp to which one belonged the 'good conscience' of standing on the side (in moral terms) of the righteous or the inevitable (in terms of the philosophy of history). At the same time, one sought to 'paralyze the critical will' of one's opponents, not only by logically refuting their arguments but above all by injecting them with a feeling of remorse and guilt or with doubt and resignation and thus depriving them of all power by means of a sort of 'spell'. We have seen how Nietzsche denounced the 'spell' of morality, the 'revenge' of the subaltern classes, or rather of the malformed, which worked to the detriment of the better, the elite (*supra*, 8 §6).

---

22   Kautsky 1908, 343–47 (cf. Lk 6, 20–21, 24–25 and Mt 5, 3–5).

But regardless of the immediate political objectives pursued by him, he had opened up a field of research that is extraordinarily fruitful: he drew attention to a hitherto largely unexplored front of the struggle among social classes, political parties and rival countries.

In a Berlin on which the Third Reich had already cast its shadow, Theodor Lessing analysed with explicit reference to Nietzsche the 'self-hatred [*Selbsthass*]' Jews had for centuries or millennia introjected as a consequence of defeat and the violence exercised, also psychologically, by the victors.[23] For all groups that for various reasons suffer discrimination and oppression, be it Jews, blacks, women or homosexuals, the rediscovery and reaffirmation of identity and difference constitute the salutary and joyful moment of the overcoming of the self-hatred imposed by the dominant group and internalised. It is the moment self-hatred turns into its opposite, and not just in the sense of a proud reaffirmation of one's own identity and difference but also in the sense of producing feelings of guilt in the dominant group, whose better or more sensitive members begin to experience the anxiety of bad conscience.

So, one can understand the efforts of this or that group to draw attention to the persecutions and tragedies they have suffered. There has been a remarkable diffusion in today's historiographical (and political) debate of the category of 'forgotten Holocaust', used to describe the Black Holocaust or the American Holocaust (suffered by Native Americans) or the massacres that decimated or wiped out the gypsies, the Armenians, the Australian Aborigines and so on.[24]

It is interesting to note that something similar occurs at the level of international relations. After Germany had already been unilaterally forced by the Treaty of Versailles to take the exclusive blame for starting the war and trampling on 'international morality', it was also prepared to acknowledge the horrors of the Third Reich. Countries like China, Korea, etc. wonder why Japan does not also freely admit to the terrible crimes of which it has been guilty in Asia. But why, objects Japan for its part, does the US stubbornly continue to view the nuclear annihilation of the civilian populations of Hiroshima and Nagasaki, perpetrated on the eve of the enemy's surrender, as legitimate? One could go on and on. The fact remains that none of these conflicts can be understood without taking into account the psychological dialectic analysed by Nietzsche. His greatness, once again, is that of an author who, far from being unpolitical, has smelled political and social conflict even in areas previously considered neutral.

---

23   Lessing 1984.
24   Cf. Losurdo 1996, 5, §13.

5 Women, Feelings and Subversion

But is it possible to emphasise the psychological dimension of the conflict without taking into account the role of women? When Nietzsche reconstructed the long history of subversion in the West, he was forced to ask himself another important question. In Taine he might have read the following analysis of an essential element of the crisis of the *ancien régime*:

> A formidable word, that of citizen, imported by Rousseau, has entered into common speech, and the matter is settled on the women adopting it as they would a cockade. [...] An inspiration of humanity animates these feminine breasts along with that of liberty. They interest themselves in the poor, in children, in the people.[25]

From this moment on, 'sensitive hearts' profoundly influenced public opinion; decisive battles were conducted and won 'owing to the women, to their sensibility and zeal, to a conspiracy of their sympathies'. Only thus could one understand the progressive weakening of the aristocracy and the *ancien régime*:

> It must be borne in mind that, in this century, the women were queens, setting the fashion, giving the tone, leading in conversation and naturally shaping ideas and opinions. When they take the lead on the political field we may be sure the men will follow them: each one carries her drawing room circle with her.[26]

Michelet reached similar conclusions, even though his political and ideological positions were quite different from those of Taine. The book he dedicated *To Women of the Revolution* emphasised from the very beginning the central role in the revolutionary upheavals of the 'new view' of 'motherhood' and 'compassion', whose carriers were women. This was because women were 'less spoiled than we by sophistic and scholastic habits'.[27] And, of the author particularly dear to the Jacobins: 'The true Rousseau is born of women.'[28]

Naturally, the analysis of the two French historians just quoted can be called into question, but there can be little doubt about the importance of women's

25 Taine 1899, Vol. 2, 146, 148.
26 Taine 1899, Vol. 2, 149.
27 Michelet 1980, 363, 367.
28 Histoire de France, 1867, XVII, 4, 44. Quoted in Barthes Barthes 1975, 149.

role in the abolitionist movement and, as regards the United States, in the ideological preparation of the abolitionist revolution, i.e., the Civil War. Between
the late eighteenth and the early nineteenth centuries, women for the first
time acquired a taste for political action and for expressing their personalities in the public arena, where they engaged in the agitation against slavery
and raised funds and signatures for petitions drawing attention to the tragedy
of the blacks.[29] A few decades later, the novel of a woman, Harriet Beecher-
Stowe, became an international bestseller: 'The heartbreak of families casually
separated by slave traders and owners under economic pressure inflamed the
universal audience for the book, especially among women whose prime belief
was the Christian sacredness of family.' The success of the novel was even
greater because it established a connection between slaves and the oppressed
of every race and condition: its full title was *Uncle Tom's Cabin Or, Life among
the Lowly*.[30]

Only in light of all that can we understand the balance-sheet drawn up by
Nietzsche:

> Continuation of Christianity by the French Revolution. Rousseau is the
> seducer: he again removes the chains of woman, who from then on is rep-
> resented in an ever more interesting way, as suffering. Then the slaves and
> Mistress Beecher-Stowe. Then the poor and the workers. Then the vicious
> and the sick – all that is brought to the fore.
>
> XI, 61

The 'aristocratic' seventeenth century was 'hard on the heart', 'aristocratism'
went hand in hand with the 'rule of reason'. The eighteenth century, on the
other hand, 'is rule by woman', by the 'heart' and all that follows: 'Feminism:
Rousseau, rule of feeling, witnessing the sovereignty of the senses (lying).' A
combination of feelings and ideas that 'subtly undermines all authorities'; the
pressure of the 'mob' was strongly felt (XII, 440–1). The intervention of women,
humanitarianism, the growing weight of feelings and compassion in shaping
public opinion – all that was for Nietzsche the same thing as the crisis of
the *ancien régime*. In this case too one should not lose sight of the specific
and penetrating historical analysis. We have seen how Tocqueville emphasised the role of 'general compassion' in undermining a society based on rigid
barriers of class and race. It is also significant that the American abolitionist

---

29   Bolt/Drescher 1980, 5 f.; Walwin 1982, 61 ff.; Kraditor 1989, 38–77; Ziegler 1992, 49.
30   Kazin 1994, 39.

movement, strongly marked by women's participation, felt the need to make a 'Declaration of Sentiments'.[31]

According to Nietzsche, the women most prone to moral indignation were 'the actresses' (FW, 361 [226]). Perhaps with the example of Michelet in mind, a fragment of the spring of 1888 notes: with her 'cult of piety, of compassion, love – the mother represents altruism convincingly' (XIII, 366). Since the morality of 'décadence' could not accept reality in all its harshness, it was 'visionary, sentimental, full of mysteries, it has women and "good feelings" for itself' (XIII, 422). With his sharp criticism of the role of women in the revolution, Nietzsche argued in a manner not unlike that of other more or less contemporary authors. After Le Bon had denounced the process of modern massification and maintained that 'the masses are [...] feminine', he defined their characteristics as follows: 'Impulsiveness, irritability, inability to reason, absence of judgement and critical spirit, exaggeration of feelings', love of 'moral virtues'.[32]

This again leads us back to Nietzsche. His originality lies in his effort to locate themes present in the culture of the time as part of his view of the *longue durée* of the cycle of subversion: long before 'the enthusiastic [*schwärmerisch*] spirit of the eighteenth century', women had been 'spoiled by Christianity' (FW, 362 [227]). Moreover, Christianity with its 'sentimentality' was 'a religion for women'; precisely because women were 'weak, typically sick', they needed 'a religion that exalts as divine being weak, loving, humble' (XIII, 364–6). Women were an integral part of the cycle of revolution, and were so from the very beginning: 'Woman has always conspired with the types of *décadence*, with the priests, against the "powerful", the "strong", the men' (XIII, 366). Throughout their 'whole history', women propagated the good moral sentiments that fed subversion (FW, 361 [226]). 'Femininities' and 'beautiful feelings' undermined 'rigorous self-discipline', the foundation of every aristocratic regime (EH, *Human, All Too Human*, 5 [119]).

We are familiar with the comparison of the condition of women and that of slaves, which Nietzsche had no intention whatsoever of criticising. Both groups tried to make up for their 'weakness' by cunning, deception and malice: women were 'incomparably more evil than man, cleverer too'; 'goodness in woman is a form of degeneration', of morbid detachment from one's own nature. Women's 'sensitivity to the needs of others' led them on the one hand to identify with subversion, but on the other it exposed them more easily to the moral indignation, the rancour, and thus to the blind violence inherent in subversion:

---

31   Kraditor 1989, 5.
32   Le Bon 1982, 22, 19, 37; Le Bon 1928, 26, 23, 43.

'Females are vengeful' (EH, Why I write such good books, 5 [105]; Why I am so clever, 7 [82]).

6   A Feminine Profile of the History of Subversion

Just as the figure of the slave and the woman resembled one another, so too the demands of both for emancipation had the same devastating effect and had therefore to be rejected with equal determination. And yet there is no lack of sympathetic explanations by certain feminists that seek from and find in Nietzsche the confirmation of their pathos of difference. Was it not Nietzsche that warned against assimilation under the sign of 'equal rights, equal education, equal entitlements and obligations' (JGB, 238 [127])? The emancipation of women led to 'weakening and softening of the most feminine instincts of all' and ended with 'defeminization' (JGB, 239 [128–9]). If women wanted to preserve their special nature, their true nature in its irreducible difference, they should above all beware of the movement that wanted to emancipate them:

> When, on principle, they start completely forgetting their discretion and their art – of grace, play, chasing-all-cares-away, of making things easier and taking them lightly, as well as their subtle skill at pleasant desires!
>
> JGB, 232 [124]

It was absurd and destructive to demand political rights for women, but for the rest they were 'something finer, more vulnerable, wilder, stranger, sweeter, more soulful' (JGB, 237 [127]).

The feminist interpretation of Nietzsche is very simple: for centuries, discrimination against women was based on their inability to argue in rigorously and abstractly logical terms and on their lack of courage and warrior spirit, their tendency to be guided by emotions and feelings, primarily compassion. It is enough to reverse the value judgement, and the innumerable theorists of female 'difference' (meant in a negative sense) turn if not into champions then into prophets of the cause of female 'difference' (meant this time in a positive sense). All this is quite simple, but for that very reason rather pointless.

Certainly, one can read with interest and enjoyment Nietzsche's mercilessly critical description of the condition of 'upper-class women' in the Victorian era: 'The whole world agrees that they should be brought up as ignorant as possible about matters erotic', and moreover to a sense of discomfort and guilt in respect of their sexuality (FW, 71 [74]). Compared to this 'soiling' of sexual intercourse and nature, the non-European and non-Christian religions were far superior: 'I do not know any book that says as many kind and delicate things to females as the law book of Manu', which could speak with naïveté and innocence of the 'mouth of a woman' or the 'breasts of a girl' (AC, 56 [57]). There was no room here for the view of women as a 'door of the devil [*diabolos ianua*]', to quote Tertullian,[33] an author Nietzsche knew and hated. When the philosopher praised the Manu Code as 'kind [...] to females' (AC, 56 [57]), he himself displayed a kindness, but a kindness that, far from attacking existing power relations, sought to confirm them.

On the other hand, we must not forget that the demand for a sex life for women not burdened by a sense of sin and oppressive social prohibitions was not a discourse universally applied: certainly not to those (men and women) doomed to be 'slaves of labour'. In this case, any seed of autonomous individuality could only be disruptive: the Manu Code had not only the merit of speaking tenderly and innocently about the 'mouth of a woman' or 'the breasts of a girl', but also that of not casting into crisis, with absurd egalitarian doctrines, the functioning of 'intelligent machines (men and women)', for which 'a mediocrity of ability and desire' was appropriate (AC, 57 [59]); its further merit was to provide for the 'removal of the labia for female children', and thus for the sexual mutilation of Chandala girls (GD, Improving humanity, 3 [185]).

We can understand what is new and important in Nietzsche from his political preoccupations. To emphasise the omnipresence of the will to power, he rejected the edifying vision of *eros* and love, and, with the usual psychological subtlety, albeit one-sidedly and emphatically, showed that *eros* also contained the element of *polemos*. In the attempt to draw a picture as complete as possible of the long cycle of upheavals devastating the West, and building on the lessons of a historian like Michelet, whose value judgement he reversed and radicalised, Nietzsche felt called upon to sketch a sort of female profile of the history of subversion. No few contemporary scholars deny Rousseau exercised a real influence on the ideological preparation of the French Revolution: after all, on the eve of it *Émile* and *The New Heloise* were his best-known books. Nietzsche had a far clearer vision when he stressed the role of 'beautiful feelings', certainly not lacking in Rousseau's novels, in undermining the rank-orderings and class barriers of the *ancien régime*.

---

33   Tertullian, De cultu feminarum 1, 1.

PART 7

Nietzsche and Us –
Radicality and Demystifying
Potential of the Reactionary Project

∴

Abolition of slavery – supposedly a tribute to 'human dignity', actually a destruction of a fundamentally different species (– undermining its values and happiness –)

XII, 437

• • •

Christianity, revolution, abolition of slavery, equal rights, philanthropy, love of peace, justice, truth – all these have value only in struggle, as standards: not as realities, but as flamboyant words for something completely different (even opposite!)

XIII, 62

• • •

No one lies as much the angry man.

JGB, 26 [28]

• • •

Schopenhauer, a thinker of integrity [...]; there are even moments when he sees with oriental eyes.

XI, 471

•
• •

CHAPTER 31

The Radical Aristocrat and the Great Moralist

1   Glorification of Slavery and Denunciation of the Fragmentation
     and Acrisia of Intellectual Labour

We know that, for Nietzsche, the work relationship is inevitably servile. However, the view of slavery (on the model of classical antiquity and in bitter
polemic with Christianity) as a condition for ensuring a small minority enjoys
the *otium* necessary for the development of culture makes it impossible for him
to identify with modern slavery. For both actual slavery, which had only just
been abolished in the United States and continued to exist in the colonies, and
the sort represented by factory workers were fully integrated into the capitalist
world, a world marked by the ideology of production and labour.

Illuminating in this regard is a fragment from the 1880s: '*Slavery in the
present*: a barbarity! *Where* are those *for whom* they work? – One must not
always expect a contemporaneity of the two mutually complementary castes.'
For what defined the modern world was the 'incapacity for *otium*' that had
infected the ruling classes, which in the meantime had tended to strike up a
chorus of the 'blessing of labour' (x, 296). This was apparent precisely in the
United States, where actual slavery had lasted longest in the West and where
the 'breathless haste in working' ruled supreme (FW, 329 [183]). In this respect,
the European country that could best be compared with the republic across the
Atlantic was Germany, because it belonged among the countries most terribly
ravaged by modernity.

Nietzsche's denunciation of the disappearance of *otium* was at the same
time an extraordinarily fruitful critical analysis of the division of labour in the
cultural sphere, with the consequent loss of perception of the whole as well
as of the need for it, and with the reduction of intellectual activity to mere
handicraft and fragmented production, conducted with a herd mentality and
incapable of a minimum of critical capacity.

From the very beginning, Nietzsche criticised a division of labour that had
lost its sense of the whole and the capacity for self-reflection led to acrisia and
the mutilation of the personality produced by it. We can already read in the
Basel lectures:

> Who still ventures to ask what may be the value of a science which con-
> sumes its minions in this vampire fashion? The division of labour in sci-

ence is practically struggling towards the same goal which religions in certain parts of the world are consciously striving after, – that is to say, towards the decrease and even the destruction of learning [*Bildung*].

BA, 1, I, 670 [40]

The intellectual could safely strike enlightened poses, but without the possibility of looking beyond the confined sector of specialisation he had carved out for himself, even the most open-minded intellectual was not so very different from the most obscurantist theologian. When Nietzsche denounced the narrowness and mediocrity of the 'mentality of specialists', this 'petty wisdom', derogatory metaphors hailed down: 'The tiny bit of brain open to knowledge of their world has nothing to do with the totality, it is a tiny limited talent'; we were dealing with 'camels of education on whose humps sit many good ideas and concepts, but the fact remains that the whole is, in fact, just a camel' (IX, 556). With 'his overestimation of the nook in which he sits and spins', the 'specialist' or 'scholar' was like the 'shop clerk of the spirit and the 'porter' of culture'; in his books, 'there is nearly always something oppressive, oppressed' (FW, 366 [230–1]). The 'modern cry of battle and sacrifice: "Division of labour! Line up!"' had had catastrophic results; intellectuals became 'slaves working' in the 'scientific factory', while knowledge as such was an integral part of a world dominated by 'the words "factory, labour market, supply, utilization"' (HL, 7, I, 300–1).

Together with the 'scientific factory', the *Stock Exchange Bulletin* marked the times and life styles of the intellectual; people were ashamed of rest, and 'long reflection almost gives [them] a bad conscience' (FW, 329 [183]). This analysis in many ways resembles that of Engels, who denounced the disappearance of the 'old reckless zeal for theory' and the bowing down of intellectuals before the 'temple' of the Stock Exchange.[1] Here, too, one senses a certain mourning of a time when great intellectuals 'were not yet in thrall to the division of labour' and did not suffer its 'restricting effects', including the 'production of one-sidedness, [that] we so often notice in their successors'.[2]

So, should we interpret Nietzsche as one of the great critics of the division of labour? It is hard to imagine a more arbitrarily selective view. In reality, we are dealing with a philosopher tirelessly committed to reiterating the inescapability of a drastic division of labour for the survival and development of culture. The model was the castes of the Aryan and Hindu world: 'the presupposition is here everywhere a true natural separation: the concept of caste sanctions only natural separation' (XIII, 395). So, it was a case not only of a division of labour

---

1 Marx and Engels 1975 ff., 26, 397.
2 Marx and Engels 1975 ff., 25, 319.

but of one rigidified to nature and that represented an insurmountable barrier. The catastrophe of the West went hand in hand with the decline of this world:

> There were times when men believed with unyielding confidence, even with piety, in their predestination for just this business, just this way of making a living, and utterly refused to acknowledge the element of accident, role, and caprice. With the help of this faith, estates, guilds, and inherited trade privileges were able to establish those monsters, the broad-based social pyramids that distinguished the middle ages and to which one can credit at least one thing: durability (and durability is a first-rank value on earth).
>
> FW, 356 [215]

The decline of this world had a long history, starting with Greece and ending with the 'Americans of today', who were unfortunately also developing a following in Europe (*supra*, 15, §5). In the course of his development, Nietzsche formulated an ever sharper rejection of a society based on social mobility, to the point of pressing a metaphysical seal onto this rejection in the shape of the doctrine of the eternal return of the same. The philosopher increasingly directed his attention and admiration to the caste model.

It would be just as one-sided to absolutise Nietzsche's theme of the critique of the ideology of labour and his glorification of *otium*. A fragment from the autumn of 1880 is unequivocally clear:

> The main achievement of labour is to prevent idleness [*Müssiggang*] in common [*gemein*] natures, also for example officials, merchants, soldiers, etc. The fundamental objection to socialism is that it wants to create idleness for common natures. The idle ordinary person is a burden to himself and to the world.
>
> IX, 221

Nothing could be further from Nietzsche than the idea of demanding *otium* or a minimum of *otium* for the slaves tied to the chariot of culture, i.e., for the vast majority of humanity. This theme must be sought in another, opposed cultural tradition. One might think of Lafargue, who theorised 'the right to idleness' and polemicised against the 'disastrous dogma' or 'mental folly' of 'love of labour'.[3] But, even before this, Marx identified as one of the central events of

---

3 Lafargue 1998, 20; Lafargue 1996, 43.

his time the campaign for the reduction of working hours and the rebellion of the white slaves or semi-slaves against social relations that forced them into 'working to death' and 'death from simple over-work'[4] (the other central event was the American Civil War, the struggle for the abolition of black slavery). One should go even further back, to Fichte, who was not stopped by his celebration of labour and of the social figure of the worker from demanding the right of all to 'rest and enjoyment, actually freedom and idleness'.[5] Rousseau too could be cited, for at least on one occasion (during his stay on the island of Saint-Pierre) he sang the praises of the 'blissful and necessary occupation of a man dedicated to idleness' and that could 'savour in all its sweetness' the 'delights of doing nothing'.[6]

In conclusion, we can reconstruct two opposing traditions of thought. The first, which began with Rousseau and led to Marx and Lafargue, although in frequently changing ways, presented the problem of labour and *otium* in universalistic terms. Nietzsche, on the other hand, radicalised a thread of thought already present in the liberal tradition and, in particular, in Constant: the *otium* of a small minority was based on semi-slave labour or the true slavery of the majority of people. Like Nietzsche, Lafargue, in his polemic against the ideology of labour, referred to ancient Greece, where 'contempt for labour' predominated and 'only slaves were allowed to work'.[7] Yet he recommended to the 'proletarians brutalized by the dogma of labour' reading Greek texts not affected by 'Christian hypocrisy' and 'capitalist utilitarianism', so they might find inspiration for the necessary struggle against 'the modern Minotaur, the capitalist factory'.[8] In Nietzsche's eyes, however, this minotaur was to be made more efficient and crueller, in order to ensure the exemption from labour and the full development of the personality of the privileged minority.

In this case, the celebration of *otium* was only one side of the coin: the other was the affirmation of the need for the hardest labour; similarly, the critique of the division of labour within the upper classes assumed an extremely rigid division of labour between the upper and the subaltern classes. To paraphrase Marx, one might say that in Nietzsche, as in the society he reflected, 'the surplus labour of the mass' or 'theft of others' labour time' were the condition of the 'non-labour of the few'. We are dealing here with a philosopher who was indeed the theorist of the 'non-labour of the few', but only because he was at

---

4 Marx and Engels 1975 ff., 35, 244, 261.
5 Fichte 1971, Vol. 4, 441; cf. Buhr 1991, 71 f.
6 Rousseau 1959 ff., Vol. 1, 223.
7 Lafargue 1998, 21; Lafargue 1996, 44.
8 Lafargue 1998, 57, 27; Lafargue 1996, 84 f., 51.

the same time the theorist of the 'surplus labour of the mass' and of the need, for the elite, to organise and develop 'the theft of others' labour time'. Nietzsche celebrated the Greeks as 'the people of *otium* [*Musse*]' (IX, 24), but also as the people that 'naïvely' and unproblematically accepted the inescapable reality of slavery and of the 'surplus labour' of the slave. And the talk of evoking a know-ledge capable of grasping the totality was certainly not directed at the slaves: to the contrary, in their case, the 'mastery of one thing, specialization as a natural instinct', was a destiny; this specialization was so pronounced it reduced the 'vast majority of people' to the significance of 'a wheel, a function' (AC, 57 [59]).

But the fact remains that the ideal figure of an intellectual or an individual freed from the constraints of work and the division of labour and therefore not mutilated by fragmentation, ready to question the meaning of his activity and capable of deploying all his critical potential, was analysed and celebrated by Nietzsche in a no less fascinating way than by Marx and Engels. And no one has been able to describe the dreadful consequences of the division of labour in such heartfelt terms as Zarathustra, echoing Hölderlin:[9] 'I walk among human beings as among the fragments and limbs of human beings! This is what is most frightening to my eyes, that I find mankind in ruins and scattered about as if on a battle field or a butcher field' (Za, II, On Redemption [110]).

The realisation that the capitalist bourgeoisie was incapable of *otium* be-came, in Nietzsche, the occasion to re-evoke in passionate tones the lost totality and to analyse in depth the process of the fragmentation of culture and its enslavement to the world of wealth and production. While nostalgia for *otium* led on the one hand to the demand for slavery, on the other it stimulated a mer-ciless critique of an essential aspect of capitalist society in which the division of labour penetrated more and more deeply into the ruling classes themselves and the intellectual layers.

2   Contempt for Democracy and Denunciation of the 'Nationalisation of the Masses'

The comprehensive critique of modernity, formulated from an observation post so elevated and so remote from the present in which Nietzsche lived, was not only an irrevocable liquidation of democracy but the anticipated denun-ciation of certain disquieting processes that would find their fullest and most tragic expression in the twentieth century. That which emerged from the furi-

---

9   Hölderlin 1978, Vol. 1, 739.

ous polemic against Wagner was that his music was not only mainly theatre, 'the art of the masses *par excellence*', but a theatre that required the presence of 'masses' and not of 'individuals'; the spectators were all transformed into 'people, public, herd, woman, pharisee, voting cattle, democrat, neighbour, fellow man, the idiots, the Wagnerians' (FW, 368, NW, Where I offer objections [266–70]).

Thus irrupted 'the theatrocracy [...], something secondary, cruder, bent into shape, lied into shape for the *masses*! [...] Theatre is a form of demonolatry in matters of taste, theatre is a rebellion of the masses, a *plebiscite* against good taste.' This is how Wagner 'won over the *crowds*' (WA, Postscript [256]), he 'had the *commanding* instinct of a great actor in absolutely everything' (FW, 368 [232]).

I have italicised the terms that point up the political nature of this analysis: it seems to condemn in advance the tableau that marks the process of the 'nationalization of the masses'.[10] And all this was supposed to stoke up their chauvinism and prepare them for the gigantic conflicts looming on the horizon:

> Wagner marches (amid the sound of drums and whistles) at the head of all performing artists, all presenters, all virtuosos. [...] The Wagnerian stage needs only one thing – Teutons! Definition of a Teuton: obedience and long legs. [...] There has never been more obedience – or better orders. Wagnerian music directors in particular are worthy of an age that posterity will one day refer to, with a sort of timid respect, as the classical age of war.
>
> WA, 11 [253–4]

It was a music that seemed particularly suited to the sacred rite or funeral rite of war: 'There was never a greater master in dull, hieratic fragrances' (WA, postscript [257]).

Together with what would later be called the 'nationalization of the masses', Nietzsche analysed and criticised crowd psychology, which developed and gained acceptance as a consequence of the process of democratisation. Things had changed decisively: 'It is not Corneille's public that Wagner needed to worry about: just the nineteenth century' (WA, 9 [249]). Now, everything was invented 'to persuade the masses' (WA, 7 [246]); Wagner 'wants effects, nothing but effects' (WA, 8 [248]). It was necessary to take note of a new and disturbing

---

10   Cf. Mosse 1974.

phenomenon: '[T]he great success, success with the masses, is not the prerogative of the genuine any more, – you have to be an actor to be successful! [...]
This ushers in the golden age for actors' (WA, 11 [253]). Wagner was precisely
'an excellent actor' (WA, 8 [247]). With his music, 'a theatrical rhetoric, a means
of expression, of intensifying gestures, of suggestion, of psychological pictur-
esque', gained acceptance (WA, 8 [247]).

The effect was deadly: there was no escape, 'even the most personal conscience is vanquished by the levelling magic of the "greatest number"' (FW, 368
[233], NW, Where I offer objections [266]). Wagner was a 'magnétiseur' or hyp-
notist, his only ambition as a musician was 'to persuade the nerves' (WA, 7), and
his music 'has the same effect as constant use of alcohol'; 'the corruption of the
nerves is the most uncanny thing of all'. All the conditions now existed for a
blind abandonment, especially as the 'belief in genius' spread. In this sense,
Wagner's music 'is the blackest obscurantism' shrouded 'inside the light of the
ideal' (WA, Postscript [256–7]).

There can be no doubt that, through this merciless critical analysis, Nietzsche was targeting democracy as such and, above all, the social protest movements in which, in one way or another, the concerns, the indignation, the hopes
of the subaltern classes and the masses, which for him were devoid of individuality, hopeless and intrinsically flawed, came to light: 'Savonarola, Luther,
Rousseau, Robespierre, Saint-Simon' were 'conceptual epileptics' but nevertheless 'can affect the great masses'. Unfortunately, 'the fanatics are pictur-
esque, humanity would rather see gestures than listen to reasons' (AC, 54 [54]).
Although this diagnosis is strongly compromised by Nietzsche's psychopathological reductionism, it ends by objectively drawing attention to the processes
of the nationalisation of the masses and the manipulation of crowd psychology that would unfold fully and completely in the course of the twentieth
century.

3   Elitism and Construction of Individual Personality

The relationship between the celebration of slavery and caste-order, as extreme
and naturalistically rigid expressions of the division of labour, and the condemnation of the division of labour within the caste of the free and idle can also
take other forms. We are dealing with a general problem. The radical aristocrat dramatically narrowed the circle of humanity, or of humanity equipped
with a sense of humanity and dignity. But, within this strictly limited circle, he
analysed with incomparable finesse the problems of individual life, of the free
and harmonious development of personality, of the meaning of life. In other

words, the aristocratic radical was also a great moralist. He was a figure that would seemingly like to incorporate the frenzy of the modern: 'Where has all that reflecting on moral issues ended up, which, after all, has at all times occupied every more nobly developed sociality?' (SE, 2; I, 344).

After Nietzsche had overcome the Germanomania of the years immediately following the triumphal ascent of the Second Reich, the great moralist was also revealed in the passion with which he condemned provincialism and ethnocentrism, and with which he called upon youth to liberate itself from these restrictions and chains in order to rediscover the taste of its own autonomy and freedom:

> We are accountable to ourselves for our own existence; consequently, we also want to be the real helmsmen of our existence and keep it from resembling a mindless coincidence. We have to approach existence with a certain boldness and willingness to take risks: especially since in both the worst and the best instances we are bound to lose it. Why cling to this clod of earth, to this trade; why heed what your neighbor says? It is so provincial to bind oneself to views that already a few hundred miles away are no longer binding. Orient and Occident are chalk lines drawn before our eyes in order to mock our timidity. 'I want to try to attain freedom', the young soul tells itself; and it is supposed to be hindered in this simply because by chance two nations hate and wage war on each other, or because two continents are separated by an ocean, or because a religion that did not even exist a few thousand years ago is now taught everywhere.
>
> SE, 1; I, 339 [173]

Perhaps no follower of the Enlightenment has so successfully exposed 'prejudice' and so seductively sung the praises of the freedom of spirit. One had to be able to resist not just chauvinistic intoxication but also the frenzy of labour and earning of the *Gründerjahre*:

> All of us know [...] how we hasten to sell our soul to the state, to money-making, to social life, or to scholarship just so that we will no longer possess it; how even in our daily work we slave away without reflection and more ardently than is necessary to make a living because it seems to us more necessary not to stop and reflect. [...] When we are quiet and alone we are afraid that something will be whispered into our ear, and hence we despise quiet and drug ourselves with sociability.
>
> SE, 5; I, 379 [210–11]

At times, it is as if one is reading Pascal, who, not by accident and in spite of his Christianity, is held up as a model: '[I]t might take somebody that is himself as deep, as wounded, and as monstrous as Pascal's intellectual conscience' (JGB, 45 [43]). Under the new conditions of modernity, the warning against *divertissement* was aimed primarily at intellectuals:

> Now, Pascal believes generally that human beings pursue their occupations and their scholarship and science so zealously only so as to flee from those all-important questions that every moment of solitude, every moment of true idleness would force upon them – from precisely those questions about why, whence and whither. The obvious question does not even occur to our scholars.

Such a 'fidgety scholarship that runs so frantically and breathlessly about' was shown to be 'poor and empty' (DS, 8, I, 203 [47]). Greatness was marked on the other hand by lack of haste, availability for long periods: 'For the thinker and for all inventive spirits, boredom is that disagreeable "lull" of the soul that precedes a happy voyage and cheerful winds; he has to endure it, must await its effect on him' (FW, 42 [57]).

To know how to say no to modern excitement was also the condition for the autonomous construction of one's own personality. He that 'does not want to be part of the masses' and did not want to be 'factory goods' was to pay great heed (SE, 1, I, 338). Certainly, to '"give style" to one's character [is] a great and rare art', which required an effort of self-discipline from which 'the weak characters with no power over themselves' flinched back (FW, 290 [163–4]). And here Nietzsche appealed to the youth: 'Always continue to become what you are – educator and moulder of yourself' (IX, 555).

To achieve this result, it was necessary never to lose sight of the 'true liberation of life', and to swim against the stream rather than chase blindly and recklessly after the ruling ideologies and myths of an age ruled not 'by living human beings, but instead by publicly opining pseudo-human beings' (SE, 1, I, 338 [172]). No doubt this appeal was part of a reactionary critique of modernity, but that in no way detracted from the charm of this lesson in living and this appeal for autonomy of judgement.

One's choice of profession and employment should aim primarily at spiritual satisfaction:

> Seeking work for the sake of wages – in this, nearly all people in civilized countries are alike; to all of them, work is just a means and not itself the end, which is why they are unrefined in their choice of work, provided it

yields an ample reward. Now there are rare individuals that would rather perish than work without taking pleasure in their work.

Here the teaching of the great moralist was not only linked to the gesture of distinction of the radical aristocrat but at times gave way to a disarming philistinism: 'this rare breed' ready to give up their lives rather than submit their spontaneity and creativity to the yoke of wage labour included not only 'artists and contemplative people of all kinds', but also 'men of leisure that spend their lives hunting, travelling, in love affairs, or on adventures'. The conclusion of the aphorism sounds decidedly false:

> All of them want work and misery as long as it is joined with pleasure, and the heaviest, hardest work, if need be. Otherwise they are resolutely idle, even if it spells impoverishment, dishonour, and danger to life and limb. They do not fear boredom as much as work without pleasure.
>
> FW, 42 [57]

Similar considerations could apply to the analysis of pain. Here too we were dealing with an important lesson, all the more persuasive since it proceeded from a direct and profound experience of life: 'Only great pain is the liberator of the spirit.' One emerged from it 'as a different person, with a few more question marks, above all with the will henceforth to question further, more deeply, severely, harshly, evilly, and quietly than one had previously questioned' (FW, Preface, 3 [6–7], NW, Epilogue, 1 [280]). Only now could the philosopher or individual really say with Augustine, *mihi quaestio factus sum*.

So, one can understand Nietzsche's disappointment with the fact that there was no longer any education in the ability to 'endure pain' (FW, 48 [61]). Thus, an essential condition of greatness was lost: the most severe school, misery, sickness were necessary, 'otherwise there would be no spirit on earth, and no ecstasy and exultation'. One was not to lose sight of a fundamental truth: 'Only those souls that pass through the tension of great trials [*grossgestimmte gespannte Seelen*] know what is art, what is serenity' (XI, 540).

But, once again, the great moralist gave way to the aristocratic radical. The argument continued by targeting those that would remedy actually existing pain by exaggerating and making an issue of it:

> The general inexperience with both sorts of pain and the relative rarity of the sight of suffering individuals have an important consequence: pain is hated much more now than formerly; one speaks much worse of it; indeed, one can hardly endure the presence of pain as a thought and

makes it a matter of conscience and a reproach against the whole of existence. The emergence of pessimistic philosophers is in no way the sign of
great, terrible states of distress [*Nothstände*]; rather, these question marks
about the value of all life are made in times when the refinement and ease
of existence make even the inevitable mosquito bites of the soul and the
body seem much too bloody and malicious.

> FW, 48 [61]

The quite particular suffering of the slaves chained to the chariot of culture
acknowledged or emphasised in other contexts was here denied or minimised.
Nietzsche could not do otherwise, for he believed there were no alternatives:

> There is a recipe against pessimistic philosophies and excessive sensit-
> ivity, things which seem to me to be the real 'distress of the present' –
> but this recipe may sound too cruel and would itself be counted among
> the signs that lead people to judge, 'existence is something evil.' Well, the
> recipe against this 'distress' is: distress.
>
> FW, 48 [61]

In this way, the theme of an education in the tolerance of pain, which Nietzsche had developed with the sensitivity and skill of a great moralist, became
an integral part of the political programme of aristocratic radicalism, which
vehemently rejected the suggestion that there could be a 'social question'. And
the criticism of a morality that made an education in the tolerance of pain
impossible, that had 'made all bodies and all souls weak and [...] shattered self-
reliant, independent, and unfettered individuals', also became an integral part
of this same political programme (M, 163 [120]). It was much more a question
of re-evaluating 'the affects of hatred, envy, greed, and power-lust, as the conditioning affects of life, as elements that fundamentally and essentially need
to be present in the total economy of life'. Again the great moralist revealed
himself, only to give way immediately and definitively to the radical aristocrat:

> [We are sailing straight over and away from morality; we are crushing and
> perhaps destroying the remnants of our own morality by daring to travel
> there – but what do we matter! Never before have intrepid voyagers and
> adventurers opened up a more profound world of insight.
>
> JGB, 23 [23–4]

The figures of the great moralists and the radical aristocrat were closely connected, since both catered to the same target group, a very limited circle, separated

by an insurmountable barrier from the mass of people, who served it as instruments of labour: 'Zarathustra can be happy only after the rank-ordering has been established.' Zarathustra himself explained: 'My gift can only be received when the recipient is there: for this purpose, rank-ordering' (XI, 541).

4   Zarathustra between Didactic Poem of the Free Spirit and Catechism of Aristocratic Radicalism

Rohde is right to define *Thus Spoke Zarathustra* as a sort of 'didactic poem' (B, III, 2, 412). It stands in the great German tradition of the *Bildungsroman*, the novel at whose centre is the process of formation and construction of the individual personality. In a fascinating way, the 'free spirit', or he that aspires to be one, is called upon to differentiate himself clearly from the 'last human being', which can only swim with the stream and lead a herd existence, whose subject is a completely impersonal 'one [*man*]':

> One [*man*] still loves one's neighbor and rubs up against him: for one [*man*] needs warmth. [...] One [*man*] still works, for work is a form of entertainment. But one sees to it that the entertainment is not a strain. [...] One [*Man*] has one's little pleasure for the day and one's little pleasure for the night: but one honors health.[11]
>
> Za, Zarathustra's Prologue, 5 [10]

The free spirit, who independently and consciously constructed his life and personality and was capable of swimming against the stream, was to adopt a very different way: 'The voice of the herd will still resonate in you too. And when you will say "I no longer am of one conscience with you", then it will be a lament and a pain' (Za, I, On the Way of the Creator [46]).

Together with form and style, content was also essential. The free spirit strove not only to rediscover the meaning of the earth and to rehabilitate the flesh but also to overcome provincialism and (intra-European) chauvinism; he wanted to be a wanderer in the best sense of the word: '[N]owhere did I find home; I am unsettled in every settlement, and a departure at every gate' (Za, II, On the Land of Education [95]); one had to be able to shift 'boundary stones' (Za, III, On the Spirit of Gravity, 2 [154]).

---

11   This is an analysis that must have deeply influenced the Heidegger of *Being and Time*, cf. Losurdo 1991, 2, §8.

The 'free spirit' was also called upon to turn his back on the fanatical taste of the absolute and unconditional: 'Must one curse right away where one does not love? That – seems to me in bad taste. [...] Get out of the way of all such unconditional ones! But that is how he acted, this unconditional one. He came from the rabble. That is a poor sick kind, a rabble kind. [...] Get out of the way of all such unconditional ones! They have heavy feet and sultry hearts – they do not know how to dance' (Za, IV, On the Higher Man, 16 [238]). A free spirit that had really assimilated the lesson of Zarathustra would set about independently constructing his own personality, and in so doing would free himself from every form of uncritical dependence on the master: 'You had not yet sought yourselves, then you found me. All believers do this; that's why all faith amounts to so little. Now I bid you lose me and find yourselves; and only when you have all denied me will I return to you' (Za, I, On the Bestowing Virtue, 3 [59]).

The free spirit was to aspire to a knowledge that had developed a sense of the whole, and thus did not allow itself to be reduced to 'one big eye, or one big maw or one big belly' or a 'big ear' (Za, II, On Redemption [109]); it could not be content with a pedantic knowledge that sought to avoid the big questions: the intellectual 'had not yet learned laughing and beauty' and was therefore 'gloomy' like Faust before his meeting with Mephistopheles (Za, II, On the Sublime Ones [91]). On the other hand, knowledge was not to be reduced to narcissistic enjoyment but was to be able to develop a passionate and fruitful relationship with life and reality. It was true that many intellectuals aspired to 'look upon life without desire' and with 'dead will'; they 'sit cool in their cool shade', they simply wanted to be 'spectators', so they 'take care not to sit where the sun burns on the steps' (Za, II, On Immaculate Perception [96] and On Scholars [98]). But, objected Zarathustra, 'I do not believe spirits that have cooled down' (Za, IV, On the Higher Man, 9 [235]). Ultimately, the true 'free spirit' or the 'overman' could identify with the world and enjoy it, without anxiously flinching in the face of the negative and the painful: '[O]nly where there are graves are there resurrections' (Za, II, The Grave Song [88]). The affirmation of life in its mixture of joy and pain meant affirming the theory of the eternal return: '"Was that – life?" I want to say to death. "Well then! One More Time!"' (Za, IV, The Sleepwalker Song, 1 [258]).

And yet, the great moralist represented only one side of the coin, the other being the radical aristocrat, seething with contempt and disgust for a world in which the common people 'have become ruler', and which was dominated by '[w]hat is effeminate, what comes from the servant's ilk' (Za, IV, On the Higher Man, 3 [233]). To deal with this catastrophe, a political struggle was necessary. Settling accounts with the socialist movement and its wretched ideals of justice was also settling accounts with the philistinism of the 'last human being': 'Break, break me the good and the just! – Oh my brothers, have you even understood these words?' Those against whom they were directed appeared to recoil in horror. Here, the moralist again intervened, but now he presented his disquieting face:

> You flee from me? You are frightened? You tremble before these words? My brothers, when I told you to break the good and the tablets of the good, then for the first time I launched mankind onto their high seas. [...]
> False coasts and false securities were taught you by the good; in the lies of the good you were born and bielded. Everything has been duplicitous and twisted from the ground up by the good.
>
> Za, III, On Old and New Tablets, 27–8 [171–2]

A change of course was absolutely necessary. One was not just to intervene in socio-political relations but also impose eugenic measures so radical that they did not even exclude the annihilation of the malformed. The latter, spreading their *ressentiment*, often also took the form of poisonous and voracious 'flies of the market place.' Even if the free spirit was aware of the danger, he did not seem to have acquired the determination the situation demanded. And again, the warning of the moralist and radical aristocrat can be heard: 'You are too proud to slay these sweet-toothed creatures. But beware, or it will become your doom to bear all their poisonous injustice!' (Za, I, On the Flies of the Market Place [38]). The still hesitant free spirit was urged not to allow himself to be hindered by unusable 'old tablets', which with the help of the biblical prohibition 'thou shalt not kill' ended up killing 'truth itself'; he was called upon to either drop or not to absolutise the biblical prohibition on killing, in order instead to affirm the 'supreme law of life' (*supra*, 19 §5).

In the meantime, it has become clear that in *Zarathustra* the levity of the novel or the didactic poem is inextricably linked with the harshness and brutality of the catechism of aristocratic radicalism. The picture Nietzsche sketched of Zarathustra (and of himself) is significant: '[T]his most yes-saying of all spirits' (EH, *Thus Spoke Zarathustra*, 6 [129]). The followers and '[c]ompanions' of Zarathustra 'shall be called' not just 'despisers of good and evil' but also 'annihilators [*Vernichter*]' (Za, I, Zarathustra's Prologue, 9 [14]). And no less significant is the picture Nietzsche drew of himself (and of Zarathustra): 'I am [...] the destroyer *par excellence*' (EH, Why I am a destiny, 2 [145]). This destroyer claimed for himself the 'right to annihilation' (*supra*, 19 §6). And yet he could add, with greater precision: 'I contradict and yet am the antithesis of a no-saying [*neinsagend*] spirit.' We are dealing with an objection that represents a powerful affirmation of life, liquidating 'many millennia' of the denial of life (the Jewish-Christian tradition as a whole) (B, III, 5, 503). The fact is that, in the case of the philosopher and the protagonist of his didactic poem, 'all oppositions are bound into a new unity'. So it is in reality too: 'The highest and the lowest forces of human nature, everything that is sweetest, most carefree, and most terrible, radiates from a single fountain with undying assurance' (EH, *Thus Spoke Zarathustra*, 6 [130]).

A few weeks after the appearance of *Beyond Good and Evil*, Nietzsche wrote to tell a 'dear friend' that his new work 'is a sort of commentary on my Zarathustra' (B, III, 3, 270). Meanwhile, Peter Gast had read the new book, and saw it as a 'campaign against the democratization, the debasement and lowering and diminishment of the modern human being'. The 'devoted disciple' or the 'grateful disciple', as he called himself in the letter, expressed his enthusiasm to his master:

> Magnificent are your political and moral theories, now clearly expressed. You will help out of their plight many of those that in our time did not know how to fight back against the rising tide of popular rule: I think there are still many human forces that are merely wrongly guided and feel themselves to be so, but who would find new life if someone were to clarify their role, something that only with great difficulty could occur to them in this morbid philanthropic air. Starting with you there will be a rising of the entire West.
>
> B, III, 4, 193–4 and 195–6

On the other hand, Peter Gast had already written in similar terms about *Zarathustra*: 'I hope this book is diffused as widely as the Bible, its canonical prestige, the series of commentaries on which in part its prestige rests.' The book was to be included among the 'sacred texts' and 'starting from it, time should be reckoned anew': sooner or later its author would be revered even more profoundly than the 'Asian founders of religions' (B, III, 2, 360–1 and 420). These were not just the gushings of an enthusiastic pupil. Basically, Nietzsche was of the same opinion. Now, in the vision of the world elaborated in the final phase of his development, he saw the turning point in world history, with the definitive conclusion of the two-thousand-year cycle of subversion and degeneration that began with the Jewish-Christian religion.

Both for teacher and pupil, *Zarathustra* and *Beyond Good and Evil* were one and the same. The first formulated in poetic language what the second expressed in a clearer prose. The attempts to immerse the figure of Zarathustra in an aura of innocence were pointless: here too we see at work the connection between the great moralist and the radical aristocrat, which marks Nietzsche as a whole.

The 'overman' announced by Zarathustra was on the one hand the 'free spirit', that had learned the best lessons of the didactic poem, and on the other hand the radical aristocrat, who did not hesitate to embrace a eugenics programme that pressed on to the frontier of the propagation of genocide. The free spirit, the overman, was called upon to free himself from any residue of 'anti-nature [*Widernatur*]' (XIII, 611), and to become fully aware that morality, the posture of the 'good', was nothing more than inner 'lies' and the inability to look reality in the face without hypocrisy; it was 'taking all measures to avoid seeing that reality is not constituted in a way that always invites benevolent instincts' (EH, Why I am a destiny, 4 [146]).

Like Rousseau, Nietzsche supported the 'return to nature' (WA, 3 [236]), but now the affirmation of nature was at the same time the affirmation of the terrible potential for negativity and violence inherent in it. Only the 'hypochondriac' flinched back, horrified and helpless. The denunciation of hypochondria played an important role in Hegel too, and his *Phenomenology of the Mind* was also in the tradition of the *Bildungsroman*. But here, and in Hegel's philosophy in general, hypochondria took the form not of the development of an ambitious project to transform the existing sociopolitical order starting from universal ideas and values but rather of the inability to understand that to build a new system, the universal was to be able to return to the particular and concrete, to relate to history and to take into account the resistances, difficulties, tortuosity, mediations, compromises, dilemmas and dramas that are part of the historical process and political action.[12] For Nietzsche, however, hypochondria was the inability to accept nature in its indissoluble intertwining of the beautiful and the terrible, it was the pretension to obstruct it by presumed moral rules that mortify the flesh, vitality, will to power. To the 'gloomy' one Zarathustra contrasted the human being 'eager for wars and festivals' (Za, IV, The Last Supper [231]). Rehabilitating the flesh meant restoring honour to war, as well as to '[h]atred, delight in the misfortunes of others, the lust to rob and rule, and whatever else is called evil' (FW, 1 [27]).

---

12   Losurdo 2001, III–XV and *passim*.

5   *Eros* and *Polemos*: Heine and Nietzsche

The denunciation of the 'austere morality' of Christianity was certainly not Nietzsche's newest and most important contribution. One can already read it in Heine, who celebrated the serene pagan acceptance of sensuality as against the 'Nazarene' worldview. One also finds it in Strauss, who, in reference to Buckle, commented: if the gospel damned wealth, which alone made *otium* possible, it also condemned 'science and art' and therefore turned out to be a 'principle hostile to culture'.[13] And yet the young Nietzsche polemicised strongly against Heine and his Jewish optimism, while the first *Unfashionable Observation* saw no problem in defending Christianity against Strauss's alleged philistine and Judaising optimism. Even beyond his early years, Nietzsche criticised both Buckle and the German author who quoted him. So, the red thread of Nietzsche's development is to be sought not in the critique of austere morality but in the struggle against the revolution he denounced from the very beginning but gradually researched in its various manifestations and remote origins.

Starting with his critique of austere morality, Heine also clearly identified the reactionary components of the Reformation:

> Leo x, the refined Florentine, the pupil of Politian, the friend of Raphael [...], Leo de' Medicis, how he must have smiled at the poor, chaste, simple monk, who fancied that the Gospel was the chart of Christendom and this chart must be true![14]

Luther appeared here as a sort of fundamentalist ayatollah, who would have liked to impose on a much more advanced and pluralistic culture the raw rigour he derived from the sacred text. In polemic not only against the papacy but also against luxury, lasciviousness and the paganism blamed on the Renaissance there arose the 'iconoclastically fanatical' attitude of the Reformation:[15] 'The enchanting images of the Madonna were destroyed.'[16] Opposite the fanatical monk stood a Pope who, in addition to expressing a more refined culture, was also decidedly 'more reasonable.'[17] Together with the needs of culture, Leo x also knew, wisely, how to lend an ear to the needs of the flesh:

---

13   Strauss 1872, 63 f. This observation by Strauss was also quoted by Lange, whom Nietzsche knew well, cf. Lange 1974, Vol. 2, 976.
14   Heine, 1982, 25.
15   Heine 1969–78, Vol. 6/1, 383 f.
16   Heine 1969–78, Vol. 3, 534.
17   Heine 1969–78, Vol. 3, 531.

For Luther did not comprehend the idea of Christianity, the utter destruction of Sensualism, was altogether too much in contradiction to human nature to be ever perfectly realised in life; he had not comprehended that Catholicism was a compromise between God and the devil, – that is, between spirit and matter, by which the autocracy of the spirit was theoretically declared, but the material element placed in such condition that it could practically exercise all its annulled rights. Hence the shrewd system of confession which the Church invented for the benefit of the senses, though always according to forms which discredit every act of sensuality, and secure to the spirit its arrogant usurpation.[18]

Except that Catholicism 'was a thing incomprehensible in the German North'. Here the 'Puritanism utterly hostile to all pleasures of the senses took possession of the land'; here '[o]ur climate facilitates the practice of Christian virtues', so that a Christianity took root 'that makes the fewest possible concessions to sensuality'.[19]

Clearly, this analysis reminds one in many ways of Nietzsche's. Heine contrasted the magnificence of Shakespeare with 'the levelling age of the Puritans, which, together with the monarchy, would put an end to every joy of life, all poetry and all serene art':[20] among the English Puritans, 'Republican fanaticism' was closely linked to the 'ascetic zeal of faith'.[21] Again, we are led back to Nietzsche and his denunciation of the potential for fanaticism, asceticism and the 'levelling' spirit in the Reformation and Puritanism, unable to understand the needs of art (and luxury) and the needs of the flesh. Yet Heine did not hesitate to praise Martin Luther and the Reformation as an essential chapter in the history of freedom.[22] Despite doubts and oscillations and not without inner torment, the great poet and disciple of Hegel did not take the regressive aspects of the great revolutions as a reason to dismiss them out of hand.

In this sense, Heine went deeper: he saw that this partly reactionary (or fundamentalist) movement that was the Reformation paved the way for the revolution not only with regard to freedom of thought but also at the level of sexuality:

18   Heine, 1982, 24.
19   Heine 1969–78, Vol. 3, 533 f.
20   Heine 1969–78, Vol. 4, 175 f.
21   Heine 1969–78, Vol. 4, 176.
22   Losurdo 1997a, 2, § 2–3.

I said earlier that at first it was spiritualism that in our country attacked Catholicism. But this applies only to the beginning of the Reformation; as soon as spiritualism had opened a breach in the old church building, sensualism sprang out in all its long restrained ardor, and Germany became the wildest playground of the intoxications of freedom and the joy of the senses. [...] Indeed, the external history of that period consisted almost exclusively of sensual émeutes.[23]

It was no accident that the Reformation demanded the abolition of clerical celibacy and thereby the full legitimation of conjugal sexuality. The peasants that rebelled against the landowners might also be motivated by ascetic enthusiasm, but what objective results did their uprising bring? 'In Münster sensualism ran naked through the streets in the figure of Jan van Leiden, and lay down with his twelve wives on that big bedstead that can still be seen in the town hall there.'[24] The same dialectic is developed in relation to art and culture in general: the original iconoclasm of the Reformation went in a completely opposite direction, with the unfolding of a magnificent period of art and culture.

The struggle initiated from anti-sensualist positions by the Reformation against the Catholic compromise with the flesh objectively favoured the subsequent struggle conducted against this same compromise, but from opposite positions, by the French Enlightenment. In the Catholic Church, spiritualism 'reigned nominally and *de jure*; whereas sensualism, through conventional subterfuges, exercised the real sovereignty and ruled *de facto*'. Luther's protest against the *de facto* suzerainty of sensuality ended up preparing the ground for the French philosophy of 'the seventeenth and eighteenth century', which in the course of its struggle against Catholicism protested against the *de jure* dominance of spiritualism.[25]

Heine proceeded in a similar way in his interpretation of Christianity. Once again, some aspects remind one of Nietzsche. It is a religion that establishes 'artificial discord' between the soul and the body and spreads 'with incredible rapidity, like a contagious disease, over the whole Roman empire.'[26] Thus Rome was defeated by Jerusalem, which it too had destroyed:

Did perhaps murdered Judea, by bequeathing its spiritualism to the Romans, seek to avenge itself on the victorious foe, as did the dying cen-

---

23   Heine 1969–78, Vol. 3, 335 f.
24   Heine 1969–78, Vol. 3, 536.
25   Heine, 1982, 157.
26   Heine, 1982, 148.

taur, who so cunningly wheedled the son of Jupiter into wearing the deadly vestment poisoned with his own blood? In truth, Rome, the Hercules among nations, was so effectually consumed by the Judaic poison that helm and armour fell from its decaying limbs, and its imperious battle tones degenerated into the prayers of snivelling priests and the trilling of eunuchs.[27]

On the other hand, 'the new, ruling, sad gods / gloating [*schadenfroh*] under the sheepskin of humility', were not nearly as innocent as they seemed.[28] The long period of Christianity still weighed on Europe with the 'general atmosphere of a lazaret'.[29] And yet, the advent of a new period of a general rehabilitation of the flesh was also realised through Christianity, with its affirmation of the unity of humankind and its positive effect on the 'over-robust races of the north, the ruddy barbarians'.[30]

> When once mankind shall have recovered its perfect life, when peace shall be again restored between body and soul, and they shall again interpenetrate each other with their original harmony, then it will be scarcely possible to comprehend the factitious feud which Christianity has instigated between them. Happier and more perfect generations, begot in free and voluntary embraces, blossoming forth in a religion of joy, will then smile sadly at their poor ancestors, who held themselves gloomily aloof from all the pleasures of this beautiful world, and through the deadening of all warm and cheerful sensuousness almost paled into cold spectres.[31]

One could say the 'overman' announced here was not very different from Nietzsche's. The philosopher constantly polemicised against those that 'have seduced us into the belief that man's natural inclinations are evil' (FW, 294 [167]). It was also from this point of view that Carmen was counterposed to Wagner's heroines: 'Finally, love, love that has been translated back into nature!' (WA, 2 [236]). And yet there remainrd deep-seated differences with Heine. And not just because the rehabilitation of the flesh of which Nietzsche spoke excluded the instruments of labour to which he continued to recommend a religion of renunciation and asceticism.

---

27   Heine, 1982, 72.
28   Heine 1969–78, Vol. 1, 207.
29   Heine 1969–78, Vol. 3, 518.
30   Heine, 1982, 73.
31   Heine, 1887, 148.

There is another reason. The love whose absence the philosopher regretted in the musician conditioned by the 'damp North' and still influenced by Christianity was 'love as fate, as fatality, cynical, innocent, cruel – and that is precisely what makes it nature!'; it was '[l]ove, whose method is war, whose basis is the deadly hatred between the sexes!' (WA, 2 [235–6]). We have seen already that the young Nietzsche distinguished between the imaginary good nature praised by Rousseau but also by Heine and nature captured in its real tragicness. This tragicness also manifests itself in *eros*.

We can now better understand the contrasting of Islam and Christianity, especially in the *Twilight of the Idols* and *The Antichrist*. Christianity was characterised by hostility to the body: 'The body is an object of hatred, hygiene is rejected as sensuousness; the church defends itself even against cleanliness (– the first Christian edict following the expulsion of the Moors was the closure of the public baths – there were some 270 in Cordoba alone)' (AC 21 [18]). Here Nietzsche reprised the attitude of the supporters of the Enlightenment, who set 'the greater sexual freedom of Islam [for males]' against Christian sexual phobia.[32] The wonderful world of Spain's Moorish culture, noted *The Antichrist*, demonstrated its superiority and spoke 'to our senses and tastes' (AC, 60 [63]). Lacking 'respectable, decent, cleanly instincts', the 'Church Fathers' were in truth 'not even men' (AC, 59 [63]). Yet unlike for supporters of the Enlightenment, for Nietzsche the rehabilitation of the body was not only the recognition of the value of sexuality, cleanliness, health: Islam said 'yes to life', both 'with the rare and refined preciousness of Moorish life' and with its 'noble, [...] masculine instincts' (AC, 60 [63]), because it knew how to acknowledge the values implicit in the figure of the male and the warrior. The same went for the Manu Code, similarly capable of feeling the attraction of the 'breasts of a girl' but also respectful of the figure of the warrior: 'noble values everywhere, a feeling of perfection, saying yes to life', a saying yes to the hierarchical, agonic, and virile worldview (AC, 56 [56]). On the opposite side, Christianity was dominated by a combination of sexual phobia and cowardice in the face of reality and its conflicts. Against 'bold realism', with its 'respect for everything objective', was set 'altruism', 'hyper-sentimentality', and 'feminism in taste' (GD, Skirmishes of an untimely man, 50 [223]). And then, '[n]ihilist and Christian: this rhymes, it does more than just rhyme' (AC, 58 [62]). This nihilism and this inability to recognise the values of *eros*, *polemos* and rank-ordering were characteristics of irredeemably rotten social strata, full of *ressentiment* towards the better and always ready to wave the banner of 'equality' and 'justice.'

---

32   Cf. Rodinson 1993, 72 ff.

Finally, Nietzsche's view of love as an event of nature must not be confused with Heine's 'embrace of free choice'. Carmen's story and the tragic end were the ultimate demonstration that there was no area of reality that eluded the *polemos*. The latter was so pervasive that it even shaped the deep structure of *eros*. And, once again, the figure of the great moralist, who warned against the edifying vision of *eros* and denounced the mutilation of personality implied in the mortification of the flesh, was inextricably tied to the figure of the radical and brutal aristocrat.

CHAPTER 32

Crisis of the Western Myth of Origin and of Imperial Universalism

1 The Glorification of Slavery and the Denunciation of the Idea of Mission

In confirmation of the fact that one can only can grasp Nietzsche's theoretical surplus by starting from a recognition of the *totus politicus* and consistently reactionary character of his thought, we return to the theme of slavery as the foundation of culture. In this case too, the metaphorical explanation casts a heavy shadow over the philosopher, despite its good intentions. It treats him as if he were completely naïve and unaware of the political debates and conflicts flaring up around him. But, as soon as one brings the historical context into play, even the glorification of slavery displays an unexpected critical effect. It fell at a time when European colonialism transfigured its expansion as a significant contribution to the struggle against the barbarism of slavery. The fact that it was first abolished in the British colonies and later in the United States lent impetus to the triumphant march of the West on a global scale; the most fervent abolitionist and evangelical circles saw in the 'Christianisation of Africa' the necessary reparation for the sin of the slave trade and the enslavement of blacks.[1] Thus a Crusade was summoned, sometimes understood in the literal and Christian sense of the word, except its progress went hand in hand with the subjection of the population to more or less forced labour, and even with an actual 'recrudescence of servile labour'[2] and the disintegration and destruction of indigenous culture.

So, Nietzsche's glorification of slavery was linked, paradoxically, with the demystification of the actual colonial practices of subjugation and ethnocide: 'Abolition of slavery – supposedly a tribute to "human dignity", actually a *destruction* of a fundamentally different *species* (– undermining its values and happiness –)' (XII, 437). It is a paradox that the theorist of the 'annihilation of decadent races' came, along with many of his contemporaries, to a conclusion similar to that of a great critic of colonialism and imperialism: according

---

1 Fogel 1991, 235 ff., 252.
2 Hobhouse 1904, 37.

to Hobson, the West had carried out a 'crowding out [of] the lower races [...]
by *forcing* upon *them* the *habits* of a *civilisation* equally *destructive* to *them*'.[3]
For Nietzsche, the theoretical rationale for slavery was at the same time praise
for the *otium* reserved for the elite and the consequent ridiculing of the alleged
'dignity of labour'; but precisely this was, in these years, the watchword with
whose help imperialism justified its expansionist march and the imposition of
forced labour on subjugated peoples.[4]

Nietzsche provided a pungent description of the modalities of the ethnocide
then being carried out: 'What do savage tribes today take over first of all from
the Europeans? Liquor and Christianity, the narcotics of Europe. And from
what do they perish most quickly? From European narcotics' (FW, 147 [129]).
This thesis was later reiterated: 'Christianity, alcohol – the two great means
of corruption' (AC, 60 [64]). The demystifying potential of Nietzsche's writings
is made clearer by a comparison. In 1790, Benjamin Franklin talked as follows
about the Indians:

> And, indeed, if it be the design of Providence to extirpate these savages in
> order to make room for cultivators of the earth, it seems not improbable
> that rum may be the appointed means. It has already annihilated all the
> tribes that formerly inhabited the sea-coast.[5]

This view was still very popular in the nineteenth century: the alleged providential design showed a very different face in Nietzsche. Here we can make a comparison with Marx. Let us pass over the well-known passages about the spreading of opium in China by Christian Britain; more important is the fact that he
too was of the opinion that Christianity, by virtue of its cult of the 'abstract
human being', destroyed communal and cultural ties and thus favoured capitalist and colonial penetration and disruption.[6]

But let us return to Nietzsche. In the last years of his conscious life, he
criticised Christianity with far greater severity than the religions (Hinduism,
Buddhism, Islam) in the countries consumed by European colonial expansion,
thus objectively undermining the ideology that underlay the abolitionist crusade and the practice of slavery. In Europe in these years, Islam was denounced
as synonymous with despotism and slavery. According to Nietzsche, however,
Christianity had made the serious mistake of depriving the West not only of

---

3   Hobson 1983, 253.
4   Hobson 1983, 157.
5   In Slotkin 1994, 79.
6   Marx and Engels 1975 ff., 26, 377 and 381 and 35, 90.

the 'fruits of ancient culture' but also of 'the fruits of Islamic culture'. A serious loss! 'Moorish Spain' in particular was 'a culture that makes even our nineteenth century seem very poor, very "late"'. So how was one to judge the Crusaders? 'Of course, they wanted loot: the Orient was rich ... Let us be fair! The crusades – a higher piracy, nothing else!' (AC, 60 [63]).

Here, too, it is worth venturing a comparison with Marx, who likened the Crusades to the discoveries and conquests made by Europe: both were driven by 'greed of gold' and the frantic search for the 'golden grail'.[7] Against the 'Crusades', of which it spoke with contempt, the *Communist Manifesto* set the far greater enterprises of the bourgeoisie, which has managed to realise a remarkable development of the productive forces also because it had drowned 'in the icy water of egotistical calculation' the 'most heavenly ecstasies of religious fervour, of chivalrous enthusiasm'.[8] We also come across this metaphor in Nietzsche: 'You refute a matter by putting it respectfully on ice – this is how you refute theologians too' (AC, 53 [53]).

2   A Critique *ante litteram* of 'Humanitarian War' and the 'Imperialism of Human Rights'

Along with *otium*, whose foundation was slavery and the surplus labour of the masses, Nietzsche also praised *bellum*. Except that, in this period, it was precisely in the name of the cause of peace that no few colonial wars were conducted. Even Cecil Rhodes had transfigured the wars of conquest promoted or desired by him as progressive steps towards the realisation of perpetual peace. Nietzsche denounced Christianity as an unwarlike and feminine religion; but his denunciation coincided precisely with the spread or the triumph of an 'imperial Christianity', in which the priest had the role of blessing the warrior's conquests and the merchant's penetration.[9] In similar terms, the immoralist philosopher indicted morality for hindering the full and free unfolding of the will to power; but this indictment came in the years when one of the eulogisers (Dilke) of British imperialism and the superiority of the Anglo-Saxon race claimed for it the right to exercise 'moral dictatorship over the globe'.[10]

---

7   Marx and Engels 1975 ff., 29, 389.
8   Marx and Engels 1975 ff., 6, 487.
9   Hobson 1983, 234.
10   Eldridge 1973, 48; Bodelsen 1968, 69.

Westerners, observes a fragment from the beginning of 1880, claimed dominion over the planet by virtue of their 'moral character'. For a while, during his
national-liberal and liberal phase, Nietzsche had shared this claim to moral
primacy (above, 9 §5). But, even then, doubts were beginning to emerge: 'It
is perhaps part of the essence of Jewish morality that it considers itself the first
and the highest; perhaps it is a conceit' (IX, 23). Subsequent developments radicalised the doubt to the point where the outcome of the comparison between
Europe and the non-European cultures was reversed. Westerners had taken
over from the Old Testament the proud self-consciousness that led them to
believe they were the chosen people, as the incarnation of absolute moral values. From this point of view, Kant's moral pathos, rather than pointing to a
single philosopher, was the ideology of the mission that underlay the West's
march of conquest:

> What? You admire the categorical imperative within you? This 'firmness'
> of your so-called moral judgement? This absoluteness of the feeling, 'here
> everyone must judge as I do'? Rather admire your selfishness here! And
> the blindness, pettiness, and simplicity of your selfishness [*Selbstsucht*]!
> For it is selfish to consider one's own judgement a universal law.
>
> FW, 335 [188–9]

It was Kant's mistake to 'scientify, under the concept of "practical reason"', 'this
form of corruption, this lack of intellectual rigour [*Gewissen*]', this claim to be
the immediate expression of universality:

> If you stop and think that among almost all peoples the philosopher is just
> a further development of the priestly type, then this legacy of the priests,
> the art of falling for your own forgeries, will not be particularly surprising.
> If you have a holy task like improving, saving, or redeeming mankind, if
> you carry God in your bosom and serve as the mouthpiece for imperat-
> ives issuing from the beyond, then this sort of a mission already puts you
> outside any merely rational assessment, – you are sanctified by a task like
> this, you are a type belonging to a higher order of things! ... Why should a
> priest care about science?
>
> AC 12 [11]

In this sense, Kantianism was shown to be a war machine: it was a constitutive element of the exalted self-consciousness of the West, of its inability
to view itself from the outside. The resistances of other peoples and cultures
were understandable: 'The Chinese are not at all disposed to admit that the

Europeans are distinguished from them by morality' (IX, 23). These objections were answered by referring to allegedly incontrovertible evidence not in need of any proof (JGB, 34 [34–5]). Thus, one sought refuge in dogmatism and ethnocentrism.

Of course, one must not forget that Nietzsche, in the conviction that slavery was insuperable and should be displaced, as far as possible, outside Europe, consistently unmasked the enslavement implicit in colonial expansionism but veiled by abolitionist slogans; similarly, he denounced Kantian 'egocentrism', as we have seen, only insofar as it was still 'petty and unambitious', self-mutilated by the search for universality. It is true we can read in Nietzsche that 'the character of Europeans, judging by their relationship with abroad, in colonization, is extremely cruel' (XI, 61). But, apart from some brilliant but only occasional impulses, the philosopher's merciless judgement was directed not at the brutality of colonial expansionism but at the philanthropic phrases that, despite everything, resonated in the metropolis. Once again, the flowers of the civilising and abolitionist ideology of colonialism were torn apart to affirm the inescapability of the chains; and the denunciation of the mystification of universalism was used to eliminate the very form of universality. Even so, the demystifying potential of Nietzsche's analysis remains undeniable.

In implacably deconstructing universality in all its forms, Nietzsche succeeded in denouncing imperial universalism in all its variants: 'Christianity, revolution, abolition of slavery, equal rights, philanthropy, love of peace, justice, truth – all these have value only in struggle, as standards: not as realities, but as flamboyant words for something completely different (even opposite!)' (XIII, 62). This fragment can be read as a critique ahead of its time of the ideologies of war that would collide in the twentieth century, including those that continue to reverberate to this day.

The fragment, which dates to the last months of the philosopher's conscious life, was contemporary with Bismarck's decision to launch a call for the abolition of slavery in the colonial world and for the expansion of culture and humanitarianism. He addressed his co-workers in these terms: 'Is it not possible to find details of gruesome cruelty against human beings?'[11] On the wave of moral indignation thus aroused it would be easier to call for a crusade against slave-owning Islam and consolidate Germany's international role. One could comment together with *Beyond Good and Evil*: 'No one lies as much as the angry man' (JGB, 26 [28]). There can be no doubt a critique of 'humanitarian war' and the 'imperialism of human rights' cannot skate over Nietzsche's lesson.

---

11   Morlang 2002.

3   The Crisis of the 'Jewish-Christian-Greek-Western' Myth of Origin

Along with the idea of the mission of the West, Nietzsche also deconstructed
the myth of origin upon which it rests. Starting out from the ambitious project to identify and uproot once and for all the modernity responsible for two
millennia of devastation in the West, Nietzsche contemptuously defined Christianity as a mere 'piece of oriental antiquity' (*supra*, 15 § 6), thus demonstrating
that he shared the exalted pathos of Europe and the West, a central element in
the dominant ideology in his (and not just his) time. But when he lamented
how much orientalising there was in the history of the West, and even in its
sacred history, he pointed up the porousness of the borders between West and
East or between culture and barbarism.

But why is Christianity or the entire Jewish-Christian tradition alien to the
true West? This god 'avid for honours in his heavenly seat', which sees a *crimen
laesae majestatis divinae* in sin and in the slightest offence against the norm sov-
ereignly emanating from him, is intrinsically and intolerably oriental. Despite
his immense power, he is also 'eager for revenge' and demands from everyone
equally a terrible humiliation as well as the complete renunciation of all sense
of dignity: to be 'spiritually crushed, degraded, wallowing in the dust – that
is the first and last condition of his grace' (FW, 135 [124]). In Nietzsche's eyes,
monotheism as such has something oriental about it, with its cult of one God,
omnipotent and perfect, whose infinite distance from human beings minim-
ises or cancels the differences between them: 'The one God as preparation for
herd-morality!' (XI, 542). There can be no aristocracy on earth if it is abolished
and negated in heaven: 'There must be many overmen. [...] One sole God would
always be a devil!' (XI, 541).

The idea of equality of which the West is so proud that it cites it as the reason
for its primacy and universal mission has its roots in an oriental religion at
whose centre lies the assertion of the universal subjugation of human beings
by one absolute Lord. The spread of Judaism and Christianity in the Hellenistic
and Roman world, the triumph of Christianity over polytheism and a world that
took the inequality of men and the slavery of the barbarians to be self-evident
and natural, all that meant for Nietzsche the triumph of the East over the West.
The oriental world is also the point of reference for the unilinear conception
of time and the more or less messianic awaiting of a *Novum*: in the ancient
world, it takes hold among slaves, servants and those of all kinds whose lives
have turned out badly, and later it has a devastating effect in the revolutionary
tradition.

Nietzsche set the Greek-Roman against the Hebrew-Christian origin of the
West. These two genealogies or myths of origin were implicitly joined and

remain so today. A long history lies behind this. The Europe of the seventeenth and eighteenth centuries interpreted and celebrated its struggle against the Ottoman Empire as a struggle against barbaric and oriental despotism. The clash between ancient Greece and Persia (and between Rome and the barbarians) was also re-interpreted in the same key. As soon as the slavery flourishing in Greece and Rome and the slave trade dominated principally by Britain and Spain was suppressed, Europe and the West could vaunt themselves as an exclusive island of freedom, which, by assuming the heritage of the Greco-Roman world as well as that of the *respublica christiana*, committed itself to the struggle against an incurably despotic Orient ranging from Persia at war with the Greeks to Islam at war with the Europeans and Christians.

Such an artificial construction could not fool a philologist and philosopher as attentive and uncompromising as Nietzsche, who from the very start drew up a quite different historical balance sheet:

> Hellenism weakened, Romanized, vulgarized, become decorative, then as decorative culture accepted as an ally by weakened Christianity, disseminated with violence among uncivilized peoples – this is the story of Western culture. The trick is achieved, and the Greek and the priestly are combined.
>
> VIII, 103

Together with the Christian-Germanic or the Christian-Aryan-Germanic myth of origin, Nietzsche had ended up also undermining the 'Jewish-Christian-Greco-Western' myth of origin, today cited to legitimise the West's global imperial mission. Both are equally ridiculous. If the first attempts to conceal the Jewish origins of Jesus, who against his will is turned into an Aryan and even a German, the second eliminates the oriental origins of Judaism and Christianity, which against their will become so Western they are made to justify the repeated crusades against the Orient. In polemic against the first myth, Nietzsche pointed out that the term 'German' originally meant 'pagan' (*supra*, 7 § 4): the two terms the Christian-Germanic myth of origin sought to unite in an inseparable binomial had been locked in bitter conflict. Nietzsche also highlighted the long-lasting opposition between classical antiquity and Judaism or Christianity, and took this opposition to the point where he interpreted the entire history of the West as a conflict between Rome and Judea. In this respect, one could summarise the philosopher's thinking in a famous aphorism: *Judaea capta Romam cepit*, the defeat suffered by Rome at the cultural level was the defeat of the pagan, polytheistic and aristocratic West.

On the other hand, Nietzsche also, though with oscillations and contradictions, drew attention to the conflicts between Judaism and Christianity, conflicts so acute that for a while the Jews were on friendlier terms with Islam than with Christianity. He found this confirmed, for example, by the beautiful Moorish culture, which he valued highly. On closer inspection, the 'Jewish-Christian-Greco-Western' myth of origin was a resumption, under new conditions, of the Christian-Aryan-Germanic myth: the 'Aryan' and 'Germanic' myth, long instrumental in the glorification of the West as a whole but then definitively compromised by the horrors of the Third Reich, has now given way to the 'Western' myth, but the mythological material and the ideological function remain fundamentally unchanged. Whatever the case, one must recognise that, whatever his own political opinion, Nietzsche has helped more than anyone to deconstruct and debunk the myth of origin and thus the war ideology of the West.

4   Denunciation of Revolution and Flight from the West

Together with the philological rigour with which the Western myth of origin was deconstructed as an expression of a mysterious Greco-Roman-Jewish-Christian soul, Nietzsche also undertook a spiritual flight from the West as the privileged site of the massification and devastation of modernity. The incessant upheavals in France, which seemed to sweep away any form of culture, placed counterrevolutionary thought before a dilemma. Should one view the West as a sacred place of culture, from which to exclude and excommunicate the protagonists of revolution, or should one challenge the West as such, seeking refuge from it in a faraway place not contaminated by revolution? The collapse of the *ancien régime* elicited both types of reaction. The Jacobins were likened successively to 'Turks', 'barbarians', 'savages', 'cannibals'. But there were also no few that denounced the corruption of the West. Such was the case, for example, with Maistre.[12]

This second sort of reaction spread particularly in a country like Germany, which formed the dividing-line between East and West. The upheavals in France and in Europe were sustained by the hope of realising, in a nearer or further future, spectacular improvements and fantastic ideal orders; from all that, Friedrich Schlegel took temporal and spatial distance, and pointed to the ancient 'wisdom of the Indians'. This wisdom showed how ridiculous was the

---

12   Losurdo 1996, 2, § 8 (on the first type of reaction); Berlin 1984, 64 f. (on Maistre).

'almost universally accepted opinion that the human being started from a state of animal stupidity' and thus refuted the idea of progress, which played such an essential role in the ideological preparation of revolution.[13]

Similarly, Schelling criticised the 'principle, considered to be sacred, of the permanent progress of humankind',[14] a view of history that 'lacks what is best, namely the beginning'.[15] To remedy this, one had to go in search of the 'original system of wisdom [*urweltlichen Weisheitssystems*]';[16] and again one was propelled far away from the West in the direction of the East and from the present to the past. According to Schelling, Egyptian, Hindu and Greek art demonstrated the absurdity of the idea of a start of the historical process from 'insignificant beginnings'.[17] So 'the dominant opinion' that humanity was 'left to fend for itself, that it blindly, *sine numine*, and at the mercy of mere chance, as if groping its way forward',[18] proceeded from an initial state of barbarism towards an objective at once both fantastic and tenuous, 'the realization of a perfect legal system, of the perfect development of the concept of freedom and the like', was to be rejected.[19]

But this road was taken with particular clarity by Schopenhauer. In his eyes, the West had the great disadvantage of being the place where the superstition of history and the 'philosophy of history' reigned, as witnessed especially by the great success of Hegel, who claimed to conceive 'universal history as a whole determined according to a plan', ultimately intended to lead to the creation of a wonderful worldly destiny for humanity.[20] Jointly responsible for the revolutionary catastrophe was not so much this or that philosopher but the religious tradition as a whole, which at a certain point, with its Jewish optimism and its Judaised and Pelagianised Christianity, imposed itself in the West: if the messianic tension foreshadowed the later progressive mythology, creationism prefigured, theologically, the revolution's ruinous experiments in social engineering. The flight from this West was at the same time the rediscovery of the authentic West, the place in which the extraordinary experience of the Aryans had its beginnings, a people unaffected by the sicknesses of the belief in progress and creationism that were part of the Jewish-Christian tradition. In conclusion, Europe was called upon to free itself of every Jewish mythology:

---

13   Schlegel 1975, 193.
14   Schelling 1856–61, Vol. 11, 239.
15   Schelling 1856–61, Vol. 11, 232.
16   Schelling 1856–61, Vol. 11, 236.
17   Schelling 1856–61, Vol. 11, 238.
18   Schelling 1856–61, Vol. 11, 239.
19   Schelling 1856–61, Vol. 11, 230.
20   Schopenhauer 1976–82b, 567 ff.; Schopenhauer 1976–82a, 523 f.

this was all the more necessary, and all the easier, because this mythology, despite its profound influence on German history, was the mythology of 'an alien, oriental people.'

As we have seen, the author of *The Birth of Tragedy* argued along the same lines. He too ejected from the authentic West, which he identified with the 'Aryan' version of original sin, not only the revolutionaries (this 'barbaric slave class') but also the followers of a superficial worldview of optimism and 'French-Jewish "elegance"'. The pathos of Europe and the West continued to be felt for a long time in Nietzsche's writings. Yet the progressive deepening of the critique of modernity led to an increasingly bitter indictment of Europe. Here 'a high, independent spiritedness', 'everything that raises the individual above the herd', would be perceived as dangerous (JGB, 201 [89]); 'for eighteen centuries, Europe was dominated by the single will to turn humanity into a sublime abortion'. 'European Christianity' in particular was the representative of this process of 'almost willful degeneration and atrophy of humanity' (JGB, 62 [57]); above all in Europe, in which Nietzsche also included the United States, the Jewish-Christian tradition had destroyed '*health* and racial strength'; the ascetic ideal can be defined as 'the *real catastrophe* in the history of the health of the European human being' (GM III, 21 [106–7]). So 'Christian-European morality' was particularly deserving of a place in the dock (JGB, 203 [92]).

There were further processes of degeneration that contributed to disfiguring the West and rendering it unrecognisable: 'To fend off boredom at any price is vulgar, just as work without pleasure is vulgar. Perhaps Asians are distinguished as above Europeans by their capacity for a longer, deeper calm' (FW, 42 [57–8]). In the West, on the other hand, the disastrous forward march of restlessness seemed unstoppable:

> The agitation of modern life becomes ever greater as we go westward, so that on the whole, the inhabitants of Europe present themselves to Americans as tranquil and pleasure-loving, even though they flit about like bees and wasps. This agitation has become so great that higher culture can no longer let its fruits ripen; it is as if the seasons followed on another too swiftly. Due to its lack of tranquillity, our civilisation is heading toward a new barbarism.
>
> MA, 285 [191–2]

So it was the West that exposed the entire world to the danger of barbarism. The only way of averting this threat was to mix 'Asian and Russian peasant blood with European and American blood' (XIV, 141). This was a decisive issue, and it could not be adequately tackled if one allowed oneself to be hampered by 'prejudices of hygiene and race' or prejudices of any other kind. The grafting of 'the contemplative element of the Russian peasant and of the Asian' onto 'European-American restlessness' would 'to a large extent correct the character of humanity' and even bring a 'solution to the riddle of the world' (VIII, 306). *Nulla salus nisi a Oriente!* Or at least: *nulla salus sine Oriente!*

For the ruling ideology this result is devastating. But this does not in any way justify interpreting Nietzsche in a 'progressive' sense. It is the flight from modernity and a Europe devastated by the ideology of progress and revolution that lead to a positive evaluation of an Orient so remote in space and time that it dissolves into a myth. A similar dialectic develops in Gobineau as well as in Schopenhauer. On the one hand the racial hierarchy constructed and used by him as a criterion for interpreting the whole of world history puts whites and Europeans at the top; on the other hand, he cannot but register that white Europeans' global expansion also contributed to the worldwide spread of an ideology that, at least in theory, pointed to the value of equality and was therefore antithetical to his *Essai sur l'inégalité des races humaines*. Similarly with Nietzsche. After calling on Europe to become master of the world, he was forced to draw a bitter conclusion: the 'herd morality' that had already triumphed in Europe took hold in 'the countries under Europe's influence', in the colonies (JGB, 202 [89]).

5   Denunciation of the Orientalising Christian Revolution and the Final Crisis of Eurocentrism

Christianity, which had grafted itself onto the trunk of post-exilic Judaism, came out worst in the comparison with other religions. Nietzsche's indictment concentrated above all on the social base to which Jesus and Paul turned. They encountered 'the life of the small people in the Roman province' and attributed 'the highest meaning and value' to its 'humble, virtuous, depressed life'; thus, they gave these wretches 'the courage to despise every other way of life' (FW, 353 [211]), to look with disdain on the upper classes. 'In Christianity, the instincts of the subjugated and oppressed come to the fore: the lowest classes are the ones that look to it for salvation' (AC 21 [18]). The self-consciousness thus achieved implied an irreducible hostility to the ruling elites. In the new religion 'the driving force remains: *ressentiment*, the popular uprising, the revolt of those whose lives have turned out badly' (XIII, 94); '[i]t is Christian to harbour a deadly hatred of the masters of the earth, the "nobles"' (AC, 21 [18]); 'the church waged moral combat on everything noble on earth' (AC, 60 [64]). This was the most democratic and subversive religion that had ever appeared in history: it erased the distinction between 'the exoteric and the esoteric' present in all higher cultures, 'among the Indians as well as among Greeks, Persians, and Muslims, [...] basically, everywhere that people believed in an order of rank and not in equality and equal rights' (JGB, 30 [31]).

From Nietzsche's point of view, the oriental religions were clearly preferable. Their social base was not plebeian. The Manu Code 'lets the noble classes, the philosophers and the warriors stand above the crowd', wherein lay 'the fundamental difference between it and every type of Bible' (AC, 56 [56]) and, in particular, the New Testament, this 'miserable' book, 'how bad it smells' (GD, 'Improving' humanity, 3 [184]).

Regarding Buddhism, it should be noted that the Buddha 'discovered [...] that type of person that is good and gracious (above all, inoffensive) out of laziness and who, also from laziness, lives abstinently and with nearly no needs at all' (FW, 353 [211]). To be more precise, it was the 'higher estates' (XIII, 163), the 'higher, even educated estates' that 'give a focus' to the Buddhist movement (AC 21 [17]). This was not the only difference from Christianity. Because of its different and better social base, Buddhism, far from articulating and stoking up *ressentiment*, denounced and combatted it in the interests of both society and the individual nurtured by it. While *ressentiment* 'stimulates to action' (XIII, 94), i.e., to subversion and the disastrous upheavals that characterised the history of the West, it was also fatal 'for the sick' affected by it:

> This was understood very well by that profound physiologist, the Buddha. His 'religion', which could be better described as a hygiene (so as not to confuse it with anything as pathetic as Christianity) – the effectiveness of this religion depends on conquering ressentiment: to free the soul of this – the first step to recovery. 'Enmity will not bring an end to enmity, friendship brings an end to enmity': this is how the Buddha's teaching begins – this is not the voice of morality, this is the voice of physiology.
>
> EH, Why I am so wise, 6 [81]

As 'hygiene' and therapy for the 'depression' that at a certain point arose, Buddhism 'has stopped saying "war against sin" and instead, giving reality its dues, says "war against suffering"'; instead of the senseless altruism of Christianity, 'egoism is a duty'. Because of its refusal to do violence to nature and its ability to 'give reality its dues', Buddhism 'is the only really positivistic religion in history'; it had left behind 'the self-deception of moral concepts'; in sharp contrast to the Jewish-Christian tradition, it was to a certain extent 'beyond good and evil' (AC, 20 [16–17]).

Clearly, the flight from Europe and the consequent crisis of Eurocentrism, driven by horror at modernity and democratisation, do not in themselves have a progressive meaning. It is dislike for *égalité* that lies at the bottom of the transfiguration of the Hindu world. The latter avoids any form of egalitarianism and affirms and consecrates the division of society into four castes or 'four races' (GD, 'Improving' humanity, 3 [184]).

Nietzsche's yearning for Asia was also driven by the emancipation of women, which in his view further devastated the West. A man worthy of the name

> will only ever be able to think about woman in an oriental manner. He needs to understand the woman as a possession, as property that can be locked up, as something predestined for servitude and fulfilled by it. In this he has to adopt the position of Asia's enormous rationality, Asia's superiority of instinct, just as the Greeks once did (being Asia's best heirs and students); we know that, from Homer up to the times of Pericles, while their culture was growing and their strength expanding, the Greeks were gradually becoming stricter with women too – in short, more oriental.
>
> JGB, 238 [127]

Paradoxically, this was an attitude previously represented by a personality hated with all his might by the mature Nietzsche, namely Luther. On the one hand, the protagonist of the Reformation glorified Christian Europe and denounced Islam and the Turks; on the other, horror at the growing arrogance and licentiousness that he notices in European women led him to look with favour on the Turkish-Islamic world, where a similar scandal was unthinkable.[21] Despite the enormous differences between the two authors here compared, their commonality consisted in the reaction to the crisis of Eurocentrism, which expressed itself in the condemnation of modernity, i.e., of the social processes and upheavals whose epicentre was precisely in Europe.

Finally, and in summary, in Nietzsche the flight from Europe took the form of distancing himself from a world of 'tame animals' that needed a moral disguise (FW, 352 [210]). Flight from this sick continent, ruled by 'the fear before death', this typical 'European sickness' (X, 662), went hand in hand with the quest for 'the tropical human being' or the 'human predator' not yet undermined by moral sickness. It was the search for a society and a culture where, to quote Kipling, 'there aren't no Ten Commandments' (*supra*, 14 § 3 and 23 § 3).

---

21   Luther 1883 ff., Vol. 30, 187 f., 190.

The protagonists and cantors of colonial expansion also perceived the charm of this other world, but only Nietzsche explicitly formulated the thesis that 'Asian human beings are a hundred times greater than the European' (XI, 573), than the 'most conscious Europeans' (FW, 354 [214]).

The motivations for this judgement are highly disturbing. The fact remains that the West's self-celebration as the seat of higher culture and, as Hegel would say, the 'absolute religion' enters into crisis. All the more so because Nietzsche criticised in Christianity and the Christian revolution, as well as in every other revolution, not just egalitarian subversion but also the regressive aspects. Beyond sexual phobia, a form of violence deflected inwardly and expressed as 'cruelty towards yourself' (AC, 21 [18]), this referred to the missionary, fanatical and violent potential of Christianity as such. The new religion, which had asserted itself on the ruins of the ancient world, awakened in the subaltern classes 'the clandestine subterranean self-confidence that grows and grows and is finally ready to "overcome the world [i.e. Rome and the upper classes throughout the empire]"' (FW, 353 [211]). Hence the 'hatred of heterodoxy; the will to persecute' (AC 21 [18]). Despite 'the call to love one's neighbour', 'the history of Christianity [...] is full of violence and drips with blood', in which sense it contrasted sharply with the 'Buddhist, rice-eating morality' (VIII, 460–1). In this context, a rice diet was no longer synonymous with 'weakening' and *décadence* (see above, 19, §1) but with a clear demarcation in respect of a history of senseless violence: the outcome of the comparison between Europe and Asia had been reversed in favour of the latter. Buddha 'does not try to root out heterodoxy; there is nothing his teachings resist more than feelings of revenge, aversion, *ressentiment* (– "enmity will not bring an end to enmity": the moving refrain of all Buddhism ...)' (AC 20 [17]). And further: Buddhism 'presupposes a very mild climate, extremely gentle and liberal customs, the complete absence of militarism' (AC 21 [17]). Again, what swings the comparison in Asia's favour is concern about the incessant slave revolt and the threat intra-European chauvinism poses for the master race as such.

However, two thousand years of Christianity and Jewish-Christian violence were nothing more than a 'piece of oriental antiquity'. On the one hand, Nietzsche confirmed by means of this attribution his pathos for the true West, on the other hand he ended up ridiculing any form of Eurocentrism by inserting such a 'piece' into a sequence of extremely long periods of time – in this way, past and present were radically shrunk to a brief moment of occurrence, which with its long and immeasurable periods of time clearly remained to be written. This is all the more so if one bears in mind that along with the expansion of historical time there is a corresponding and no less immeasurable expansion of the space in which the historical event is located. So-called 'world history' was merely the history of a 'clever animal' located 'in a remote corner of the universe glittering and poured out over countless solar systems'. True, this observation was part of the polemic against 'human rights' and the anthropocentrism that underlay them; just as the critique of the 'religion of historical power' was formulated on the basis of the need to call into question the results of the French Revolution and of modernity as such (*supra*, 2 § 4 and 6 § 3). But, here too, there was a theoretical surplus. It is evident in the fact that it is now possible to assert Nietzsche's methodology against his own political project and especially against today's dominant ideology. The latter transfigures the liberal West as a sort of *plenitudo temporum*, a fulfilment of the times, before which all must bow down, as the finally achieved goal of the human adventure, as the sole interpreter of culture, and as the exterminating angel called upon to eliminate by all means every real or perceived threat.

CHAPTER 33

Individualism and Holism, Inclusion and Exclusion: The Liberal Tradition, Nietzsche and the History of the West

1   Individualism and Anti-individualism from the Liberal Tradition to Nietzsche

According to today's dominant interpretation, Nietzsche marks the turning point to 'postmodern philosophy'.[1] But for the demystifying impulse of his philosophy, the end of the 'grand narratives [*grands récits*]' that defines the 'postmodern condition' would be unthinkable.[2] He would have been the first to launch a radical attack on the myths of Reason, History, Progress that characterised the development of modernity and shaped the theories of Hegel and Marx in their deep structure – even where the latter believed he was engaged in a radical critique of ideology. From this point of view, Nietzsche's destruction of these myths is a sort of metacritique of the Marxist critique of ideology, inspired by collective and meta-individual plans for liberation and emancipation and still wholly suffused by a 'modern' philosophy of history ready to sacrifice individuals on the altar of a theologising and holistic universal.

So, Nietzsche appears here as the great theorist of the individual, freed from the shackles of both premodern traditionalism and the modern 'Grand Narratives.' Many passages seem to support this interpretation. For example, *Human, All Too Human* speaks up for a 'morality of the mature individual':

> Admittedly, we all still suffer from having far too little consideration for what is personal in us; it has been badly developed – let's admit that to ourselves: we have instead forcibly diverted our attention from it and offered it up as a sacrifice to the state, to science, to the needy, as if it were something bad that had to be sacrificed.
>
> MA, 95 [72]

Primitive and savage peoples were 'determined most strongly by the law, by tradition: the individual is almost automatically bound to those things that move

---

1   Vattimo1985, 172.
2   Lyotard 1979, 65 (on Nietzsche) and *passim*.

with the uniformity of a pendulum' (MA, 111 [90]). The sense of individuality was a recent and precious acquisition: in the course of history, it had long been experienced as a curse and condemned. In the past, the sacrifice of the individual might also have had a real social function; a venerated tradition was created, 'above all for the purpose of preserving a community, a people' (MA, 96 [73]). But now the situation had changed: 'it is precisely the greatest regard for personal concerns that has the greatest general utility: so that strictly personal actions correspond exactly to the present conception of morality (as in general usefulness)' (MA, 95 [72]). So one had to do away with a morality that expressed the oppressive weight of tradition, custom, collectivity: 'With morality the individual is instructed to be a function of the herd and to ascribe value to himself only as a function' (FW, 116 [115]). And against the 'herd instincts' one could recommend 'selfishness', which in this case meant the defence of one's individuality (FW, 328 [183]).

But if Nietzsche on the one hand criticised socialism for being a moment of 'reaction to becoming individual', on the other he denounced it because it aimed, as 'a means of agitation of the individualist', to '*make possible many individuals*' (XII, 503). A similar ambivalence can be noted in the judgement concerning Christianity. On the one hand it was the religion of the herd as such; on the other, it could be blamed for having taught 'more fateful atomism' and individualism, conjugated in all its religious variations (*supra*, 21 § 7). The consequences for society and culture were catastrophic: following on the affirmation of the immortality of the individual and the equality of souls before God, 'the individual had become so important that one could no longer *sacrifice it*'; but 'that means to put the life of the species [*Gattung*] into question, in the most dangerous way'. Now the sides were reversed. Now Nietzsche defended the demands of society and the collectivity against the irresponsibility of socialism and the religion that stood behind it, both of which were focused on the individual: 'Although Christianity has brought to the fore the doctrine of disinterest and love, its actual historical effect remains the escalation of egoism, of individual-egoism, to the ultimate extreme.' One should not allow oneself to be distracted by appearances: 'the universal praise of "altruism"' was merely the ideological instrument employed by 'the egoism of the weak'; in this way, regardless of his value or disvalue, 'the individual is conserved in the best way'; the individual, any individual, had become more important than the need for the preservation and development of society (XIII, 218–19).

So, society and culture headed towards their ruin: 'The elements that have turned out badly (which everywhere preponderate) want to change the position of the species [*Art*], i.e., the quality of the species shall be diminished in favour of numbers' (XI, 513). The denunciation of 'degeneration [*Entartung*]', which deeply suffuses Nietzsche's philosophy, was directed against the monstrous egoism of the malformed and the insane complicity of the compassionate, who exposed the 'species' to mortal danger: the pathos of the 'species' was an essential element in the thinking of the presumed prophet of the postmodern. Far from being pronounced in the name of the individual, the condemnation of revolution indicted its ruinous individualistic effects: 'The revolution has destroyed the instinct for large organization, the possibility of a society' (XIII, 409). Finally, the charge of anti-individualism did not spare even the moralists: 'The stupid moralists [...] have thought about the individual and not about the perpetuation, through begetting, of what is noble'; but the main thing was precisely the creation and reproduction of a 'higher caste' or an 'elite humanity' (XI, 224).

So, should one attribute to Nietzsche a terrible incoherence? One must first of all note that he himself rejected the individualistic interpretation of his philosophy:

> My philosophy is aimed at rank-ordering [*Rangordnung*]: not at an individualistic morality. The sense of the herd must reign in the herd, but not extend beyond it: the leaders of the herd require a radically different assessment of their own actions.

Like 'collectivistic morality', 'individualistic morality' also had the drawback of asserting egalitarian parameters, insofar as it claimed 'the same freedom' and the same open-mindedness for all (XII, 280). Neither socialists nor Christians had a sense of reality. Not every human being as such qualified as an 'individual'. Culture and rule presupposed a 'need for slavery', and 'where there is slavery, there are few individuals' (FW, 149 [131]). This was a point Nietzsche never tired of making: 'One must in no way suppose that many human beings are "persons"' (XII, 491). 'Equality of the person' was the premise for 'socialism' (XIII, 70), an insane doctrine that dared not look reality in the eye:

> Most are *no* [persons]. Wherever the average characteristics predominate that determine whether a type survives, being a person would be a waste, a luxury; it would make no sense to wish for a 'person.' They are carriers, instruments of transmission.
>
> XII, 492

Like the Aristotelian slave, the 'instrument of transmission' could not be subsumed under the category of 'person' or individual, because in fact it did not fall under the category of human being. One can interpret Nietzsche as a theorist of individualism only if one half reads him. Let us consider a youthful text: 'The education of the masses cannot [...] be our aim; but rather the education of a few picked men [...]'. It is not difficult to interrupt the quotation arbitrarily, at this point. But perhaps it is better to continue reading: '[...] of a few picked men for great and lasting works'; or rather, 'great and lonely figures of the period', while most are born 'to serve and to obey', to serve as 'clay' (BA, 3; I, 698 [74–5]). The point of a culture and a social order worthy of respect was to make it 'possible for the few' (BA, 1, I, 665 [34]). Nietzsche stuck to this view throughout the course of his development.

And yet the problem we have set ourselves remains unresolved: was the philosopher individualistic or anti-individualistic? Before answering this question, it is worth posing another: was there any difference on this point between the philosopher of aristocratic radicalism and the representatives of proto-liberalism? Take Mandeville. Celebrated as the one for whom 'the arbitrary exercise of power by the government should be reduced to a minimum',[3] he is often seen as one of the first great theorists of 'individualism' and even of 'unbridled individualism'.[4] And it is true he was undoubtedly intolerant of the constraints of state power and traditional morality. However, even when professing an unprejudiced secular morality, Mandeville suggested making attendance at Sunday church services and religious instruction obligatory for the 'poor and illiterate', who on Sundays 'should be forbidden access to public entertainments that might seduce them away from the church'.[5] And all this, of course, so the poor, 'from childhood onwards', were inoculated with a sense of obedience to authority and respect for customs and traditions. Moreover, what was the condemnation of school teaching if not an attempt to prevent any manifestation of insubordination among the popular classes? What did the celebration of the 'poor, silly Country people' (who, admittedly, were distinguished by their 'innocence and honesty')[6] mean, if not the celebration of the herd mentality *par excellence*? As with Nietzsche so too with Mandeville, we encounter the problem of whether we are dealing with individualism or anti-individualism.

One encounters the same dilemma among many other representatives of proto-liberalism in particular: the defence of the inviolability of the individual sphere against monarchical absolutism could (as in the case of Locke) go hand in hand with a theoretical justification of slavery in the colonies or, more gen-

---

3 Hayek 1978, 259.
4 Colletti 1969, 287.
5 Mandeville 1924, 308.
6 Mandeville 1924, 269.

erally, with the reduction of the 'mass' to instruments of labour tools, devoid of personality and individuality, or, at best, eternal children, also unable to acquire a mature personality and individuality. In Sièyes we find the thesis that 'a small number, really small, of truly free and thinking heads' was inevitably set against the mass of 'bipedal tools' that had to passively accept their condition. We can easily find this thesis in Nietzsche, too (*supra*, 12 § 4). In both cases, a herd mentality of the many, which one may neither interfere with nor call into question, corresponds to the free development of individuality among the few.

2   The Individual as 'Collective Concept'

Aristocratic radicalism, which developed in the wake of the anti-democratic reaction of the second half of the nineteenth century, further narrowed the scope in which individuality was to develop and made the abyss that separated it from the mass of servants even more unbridgeable. Nietzsche spoke not only of 'tools of transmission' but also of 'dross and waste materials' (*supra*, 20 § 4), of this 'surplus of failures and degenerates, of the diseased and infirm', which existed 'with humans as with every other type of animal' (JGB, 62 [55]). We already know about the 'chasm' that exists 'between human being and human being, between estate and estate', and that there had to be a social apartheid (*supra*, 11 § 3). In fact, on closer inspection, even the language normally used to construct a rank-ordering was, despite its radical quality, affected by a residue of universalism; that is, it seemed, at the two ends of the scale, to presuppose a common nature that was entirely imaginary:

> For there is no health as such, and all attempts to define such a thing have failed miserably. [...] Thus there are innumerable healths of the body; and the more one allows the particular and incomparable to rear its head again, the more one unlearns the dogma of the 'equality of men', the more the concept of a normal health, along with those of a normal diet and normal course of an illness, must be abandoned by our medical men.
>
> FW, 120 [116–17]

Nietzsche criticised the categories that could bridge the gulf he had dug: 'The similar is not a degree of the like, but something completely different from the like' (IX, 505). Nominalism reached its extreme consequences. As for the 'neighbour', one was to bear in mind that 'the word is of Christian origin and does not correspond to the truth'. In any case, 'the conception of our neighbour [...] is very weak in us', for 'we feel ourselves nearly as free and irresponsible towards him as towards plants and stones' (MA, 101 [78]). One could say the intermediate categories between identity and radical otherness have disappeared, and this otherness, in its turn, has no difficulty in gearing itself up into an antithesis: 'All of us, in fact, when the difference between us and another being is quite large, no longer feel any sense of injustice, and so we kill a gnat, for instance without any remorse.' Xerxes had the son of a critic of his planned expedition torn apart: the victim 'ranks too low to be permitted to cause a world ruler any further annoying sensations' (MA, 81 [67]).

It made no sense to speak of a moral community that embraced everyone: 'Morality with universal prescriptions wrongs every individual' (IX, 465). Above all it had the disadvantage of confusing 'individuals, these true "in-and-for-themselves"', with 'their opposites, the herd people' (FW, 23 [48]). On the other hand, even the historical analysis reached a very significant conclusion: 'Justice (fairness) has its origin among people of approximately equal power. [...] Justice is therefore requital and exchange under the assumption of an approximately equal position of power' (MA 92 [70]). Hence it followed:

> As a good person, one belongs to the 'good', to the community that has a common feeling because all the individuals are entwined with one another by having a sense that requital is due. As a bad person, one belongs to the 'bad', to a mass of submissive, faint-hearted people that have no common feeling. The good are a caste, the bad a mass, like bits of dust. For a long time, good and bad man is the same as noble and base, master and slave. [...] In the community of the good, goodness is hereditary; it is impossible that a bad person could grow from such a good soil.
>
> MA, 45 [51]

In conclusion, 'All goodness develops only among like' (XI, 541). Let us see how 'proud natures' conduct themselves:

> [T]hey are often hard towards someone who is suffering, for he is not worthy of their contention and pride – but they are the more obliging toward their equals, against whom it would be honourable to fight and struggle if the occasion should arise. Spurred by the good feeling of this perspective, the members of the knightly caste became accustomed to treating each others with exquisite courtesy.
>
> FW, 13 [39]

And just as Nietzsche was brutal when digging and rendering unbridgeable the gulf between the 'higher caste' and the anonymous and impersonal mass of instruments of labour, he was seductive and 'courteous' when turning to members of a 'higher caste': 'I seek for myself and my like the sunny corner in the midst of the real world of now, those sunny notions that bring us well-being in excess. Let all do this for themselves, and leave aside general talking, for "society"' (IX, 455).

To understand the interweaving of individualism and anti-individualism in Nietzsche, let us once again analyse the tradition behind him. To justify his motion of 'reconciliation' with the American colonies rebelling in the name of freedom, Burke adduced a very important argument: one could not deny freedom to those that were part of 'a nation' in whose veins 'flows the blood of freedom', members of the 'chosen race of the sons of England', all worshippers of freedom; it was a matter of 'genealogy', against which 'human artifices' were useless.[7] An integral part of the chosen community of the free were the slave owners: in fact they particularly valued freedom and, unlike their slaves, saw it as something 'noble' and 'liberal'.[8] Far from contradicting the assertion or recognition of the institution of slavery, the value of freedom found its fullest incarnation precisely in the slave owners.

Heading further back into history in the reconstruction of this view, we encounter the classical antiquity whose return Nietzsche craved: when Aristotle set 'the race of the Hellenes' against the Asians, 'always in a state of subjection and slavery', he praised the former not only for their freedom but also for their ability to 'dominate everything'.[9] The glorification of freedom was linked to the glorification of mastery, which naturally entailed loss of freedom on the part of those forced to endure it. It was in this same sense that Cicero[10] celebrated the *liberi populi*, among whom Rome occupied a prominent place: but and at the same time Rome massively enslaved the defeated peoples, considered unworthy of freedom.

Let us now try to analyse the freedom/slavery dichotomy at the centre of both the liberal tradition and of Nietzsche's thinking, starting out from the etymological meaning of the two terms of the conceptual pair. *Doulos* and *servus* refer primarily to a condition of alienness, of exclusion. With regard to the Latin term *liber* (free), the original meaning is not, as one might be tempted to think, 'freed from something', but that of belonging to an ethnic group or race. This membership 'designated by means of a metaphor of plant growth' confers 'a

---

7   Burke 1826, Vol. 3, 66, 124.
8   Burke 1826, Vol. 3, 54.
9   Aristotle, Politics, 1327 b, 25–33.
10   Cicero, Republik, I, 48.

privilege the stranger or slave never knows'. 'Free' is a 'collective concept', a 'growth group', a 'lineage', 'the totality of those born and grown up together'. It is no accident that the etymon of *liber* is also that of *liberi*, children raised in the same family community. Freedom is a mark of distinction that applies to the 'well-born' and only to them.[11]

Paradoxical as it may seem at first sight, even the individual is a 'collective concept'. The celebration of the freedom of the individual can very well be linked, and is linked historically, to the formulation of rigid exclusion clauses. An ethnic or social group proclaims itself to be the privileged or exclusive interpreter of the value of freedom and individual autonomy. The pathos of the individual is not in contradiction with the pathos of the particular and privileged community to which its status as free human being and as individual in the strong sense of the term refers.

This dialectic is strongly represented in proto-liberalism. That Nietzsche took cognisance of it is again proof of his philosophical impartiality and acuity. But he took cognisance of this dialectic not to reject it but to reinforce and radicalise it, and this again proves the rigorously and consistently reactionary character of his thought. Now it is clear: to the individualism of a privileged minority, that lives freely and regardlessly in *otium*, corresponds functionally the herd mentality of the mass of slaves, destined to the toil and shame of labour and to discipline and subordination.

3   'Possessive Individualism', 'Aristocratic Individualism' and Anthropological Nominalism

To define this attitude, one sometimes speaks of the liberal or proto-liberal tradition and society of 'possessive individualism'.[12] This category is undoubtedly more compelling than that of individualism *tout court*, which fails to take into account the fact that entire social classes, the majority of the population, are collectively sacrificed on the altar of such a brilliant and ruthlessly 'individualistic' culture.

And yet, on closer analysis, even the category of 'possessive individualism' proves to be inadequate. Since it abstracts from the colonies, it focuses exclusively on the capitalist metropoles and the relationship or conflict between haves and have-nots. But how then should one explain the exclusion clauses

11   Benveniste 1969, 323 ff.
12   Macpherson 1962.

directed in their entirety and independent of the census at the 'races' John Stuart Mill had defined as in their 'nonage'? In this case, it is not social classes but whole peoples that are regarded as incapable of developing a mature individuality.

At first sight, the category of aristocratic individualism, which Rickert applied in relation to Nietzsche, seems more appropriate. It is wider and does not refer exclusively to property relations. Combining the two conceptual pairs (socialism/individualism and democracy/aristocracy), Rickert distinguished four possible 'tendencies': 'individualistic-democratic', i.e., 'liberalism', 'socialist-democratic', 'individualistic-aristocratic, whose best-known spokesperson is Friedrich Nietzsche', and, finally, the 'social aristocrats'. For the latter, Alexander Tille is named. We already know him: he was said to focus on the 'nation' and to elevate the Germans to the 'aristocratic people' *par excellence*. However, he was said thereby to combine aristocratism with socialism or collectivism, and, while declaring himself to be an admirer of Nietzsche, to fall back into the 'herd ideal' denounced by the latter.[13]

True, it is misleading and banally apologetic to equate liberalism and democratic individualism. Is the category of an aristocratic individualism set against social aristocratism more persuasive? In fact, as we have seen, Nietzsche condemned Christian and socialist 'individualism' or 'egoism', to which even some moralists are no strangers. Moreover, it is untrue that the 'tendency' favoured by the supposed theorist of aristocratic individualism recognised only individuals and never communities or collectives. For while Tille identified aristocracy primarily with the German people, Nietzsche identified it, as we know, with the 'upper caste' or 'elite humanity'. What primarily distinguished the two authors was not the presence or absence of a reference to a community, but the different demarcation of the community chosen.

It should be added that the community selected by the theorist of aristocratic radicalism was more sharply delineated than in all other cases. When underlining in the *Genealogy of Morals* the clear distance between 'higher' and 'lower' and celebrating 'the pathos of distance [that] ought to ensure that their tasks are kept separate for all eternity' (GM III, 14 [91]), Nietzsche perhaps had in mind the clinching argument with which Aristotle justified slavery: even within one single species beings were so 'removed [*diesteche*]' from one another that some are destined 'toward being ruled, others toward ruling'.[14] They were 'as different from other men as the soul from the body or man from

---

13   Rickert 1920, 81, 84f.
14   Aristotle, Politics, 1254a, 21–24.

beast'.[15] So the slave did not actually fall under the category of human being as such, a category that, on closer inspection, turned out to be empty and meaningless.

That is precisely what I have called 'anthropological nominalism'. Way beyond the demise of the ancient world, it continues to resonate in ever changing ways in modern thought and in the liberal tradition, as evidenced by the fact that efforts to define modern labour always revert to the categories classical antiquity has coined for slavery. Nietzsche's peculiarity is that in his case the reference to classical antiquity and the institution of slavery was consciously 'unfashionable' and in sharp opposition to the universal concept of human being, whose emergence represents, despite everything, a progressive achievement. Whereas, for Hegel, the fundamental limit of political thought in classical antiquity was its failure to construct a universal concept of the human being (it constructed only a limited one, under which the slave could not be subsumed[16]), Nietzsche saw the original sin of modern culture precisely in the fact that the nominalistic vision had been blurred or lost.

4   Anthropological Nominalism and Holism from the Liberal Tradition to Nietzsche

If by individualism one means the recognition of every individual, regardless of census, gender or race, as a subject that at the moral level has equal human dignity and possesses inalienable rights in the political field, there was no author more hostile to individualism than Nietzsche. The supposed prophet of postmodernism made his debut as a philosopher with a passionate call to return to classical antiquity and slavery, and by glorifying the caste society sanctified by the Manu Code. Regarding classical antiquity, Nietzsche's nostalgia was directed primarily towards pre-Socratic Greece, to a world in which, according to Hegel's analysis, 'the autonomous development of particularity' had not yet occurred, and where the rights of the 'self-sufficient and inherently infinite personality of the individual, the principle of subjective freedom', had not been recognised.[17] The reference to India came at roughly the same time as Marx warned against the tendency to idealise societies 'contaminated by distinctions of caste and slavery' – societies in which the individual was subjected to 'traditional rules' and enclosed within a narrow circle that appeared as 'a never

---

15   Aristotle, Politics, 1254b, 16–17; cf. Hildenbrand 1962, 405 f.
16   Cf. Losurdo 1992, 7, §5–6 and 10, §6.
17   Hegel 1969–79, Vol. 7, 342 (*Grundlagen der Philosophie des Rechts*, §185 A).

changing natural destiny', and in which the poor in particular were forced to lead an 'undignified, stagnatory, and vegetative life'.[18] As another contemporary of Nietzsche, a Protestant minister, confirmed, this was a society in which caste was a 'great social chain' that segregated the individual and prevented him from having any relationship outside the caste into which he was born and in which he was destined to die.[19]

It is interesting to see the passion with which Nietzsche, who longed for a return to a society in which the figure of the modern individual had not yet emerged, polemicised against Christians and socialists. Insofar as they gave expression to the 'egoism of the weak' and of the malformed, they lost sight of the 'general utility' (*supra*, 14 §5 and 33 §1), the need to ensure the 'life of the species [*Leben der Gattung*]', the 'preservation of the species [*Erhaltung der Gattung*]' (XIII, 218–19), the 'species interest [*Gattungs-Interest*]', the 'flourishing of the species [*Gedeihen der Gattung*]', the orderly 'overall breeding [*Gesammt-Züchtung*]', supposed to prevent the 'ruin of the species [*Ruin der Gattung*]'. Insofar as Christians and socialists were stubbornly attached to 'individual interest', they opposed the sacrifice of 'those whose lives have turned out badly, the weak, the degenerate' (XIII, 469–70).

Along with these perverse and destructive ideologies, it is also necessary to overcome any form of indulgence and weakness. The gravity of the situation calls for an unyielding severity:

> When the least organ inside an organism shows even the slightest neglect for its self-preservation, and rejuvenates its energies or asserts its 'egoism' with anything less than complete assurance, the whole organism will degenerate. The physiologist demands that the degenerate part be cut out, he refuses solidarity with anything degenerate, pity is the last thing on his mind.
>
> EH, *Daybreak*, 2 [122]

The organicistic metaphor was ubiquitous: 'Life itself recognizes no solidarity between the healthy and the degenerating parts of an organism: it must sever the latter, or all perish' (XIII, 612). The degenerating parts sometimes took on an even more repugnant form, that of the 'vomit' and 'excrement of society'. There was no sense in referring to classes or 'oppressed races' to explain the presence of 'anarchists' and socialists: 'society' had to regain the 'strength' to

---

18   Marx and Engels 1975 ff., 13, 132.
19   Warneck 1879, 150 and 198.

'excrete' them (XIII, 503–4). The organism, this totality that required the amputation of the affected parts or the defecation of its excrement, took a variety of names. We are already familiar with some: 'culture', 'species', 'life'. On other occasions, Nietzsche preferred to speak of 'society', called upon to exercise the most rigorous eugenic control over its members (XIII, 413 and 599), of the 'preservation of society' (AC, 57 [59]), to be ensured through the neutralisation of 'antisocial beings' (XIII, 430), of the 'general utility' (JGB, 61 [55]) or the 'public utility' (AC, 57 [59]). Are we witnessing a reversal of the previous positions regarding anthropological nominalism? No: precisely because servants, plebeians and, even more so, the malformed did not fall under the category of human being, they were expendable in the name of preserving a universality to which in reality they did not belong and from which they were excluded. An extreme anthropological nominalism and a voracious holism were merely two sides of the same coin.

The individualistic and postmodern interpretation of Nietzsche abstracted arbitrarily from the fate of those whose lives had turned out badly, the malformed, the defeated ones chained to the chariot of culture, i.e., from the fate of those that after all made up the great majority of humankind. On closer inspection, this interpretation bears many resemblances to the apologetics or self-apologetics that dominate today's liberal thinking. To clarify its misleading character, we quote Mandeville, who said: 'From what has been said, it is manifest, that, in a free nation, where slaves are not allowed of, the surest wealth consists in a multitude of laborious poor. [...] [I]t is requisite that great numbers of them should be ignorant as well as poor.' The same conclusion was reached in France by Destutt de Tracy: 'In poor nations the people are comfortable, in rich nations they are generally poor'.[20] Marx quoted these declarations in *Capital* to demonstrate the mystifying character of a universality that had the right to sacrifice the majority of its members, who in theory constituted it. One could add other passages to those Marx cited. In England in the eighteenth century, in the country that had emerged from the Glorious Revolution, Arthur Young said: 'Everyone but an idiot knows that the lower classes must be kept poor, or they will never be industrious'[21] and would not produce the 'wealth of nations' mentioned by Smith.

While Mandeville celebrated England's freedom, he had no difficulty in likening the condition of the slave to that of the nation's 'most wretched' (*supra*, 12 §4). Just as the 'wealth of nations' required the misery of the majority of

---

20   Marx and Engels 1975 ff., 35, 610 and 642.
21   In Tawney 1926, 270.

the population, so now what one might call the 'freedom of nations' required the substantial slavery of the same majority. The happiness, wealth and freedom of 'society' or the 'nation' were the unhappiness, poverty and slavery of the majority of its members. Why was this proposition not taken to be logically contradictory? The answer is obvious: because wage labourers were not really, i.e., fully, subsumed under the categories of 'society' and 'nation', under a universality that appealed to them only so they could serve as its sacrificial victims.

It is enough to replace the 'collective good', 'culture', 'life' or 'species' with 'society' or 'nation' to realise that the structure of the discourse is analogous in Nietzsche and proto-liberalism. This is the intertwining of radical anthropological nominalism and voracious holism with which we are already familiar. It is a discourse that falls short of the discourse of Marx (and, to a certain extent, even of Hegel). Despite its undeniable demystifying potential, Nietzsche's metacritique sought to restore the *status quo ante*, the uncontested domination of a monstrous universality that swallowed the vast majority of the population.

It was a universality that, on occasions, paradoxical as it may at first sight seem, assumed a moralising pose. We have already spoken of the charge of 'egoism' directed at Christians and socialists reluctant to amputate sick parts. They had lost sight of an essential point: 'True philanthropy demands sacrifice for the sake of the species', while rejection of such sacrifice was 'extreme immorality [*extreme Unmoralität*]' (XIII, 471–2). Egoism, immorality: these were the accusations traditionally levelled at the labour movement and socialism. Nietzsche's iconoclastic and immoral gestures now turned into their exact opposite, a sermon that did not shrink from demanding sexual abstinence from those whose lives had turned out badly. This reminds one of Malthus: the main difference from the Anglican clergyman was that Nietzsche would have preferred not to take risks and therefore called for 'castration' (*supra*, 19 §3).

Naturally, when it came to morality, one was to make the necessary distinctions: 'Virtue is our great misconception', and the misconception could only be cleared up by conceding a fundamental truth: 'Selection in the species, its purification of dross', was 'the virtue *par excellence*'; 'one must [*man soll*] amputate sick limbs: society's prime morality', 'society is a body of which no part may be sick [*an dem kein Glied krank sein darf*]' (XIII, 413). *Sollen, dürfen*: this is the language in which the ethical imperative is traditionally formulated, which in turn, also in accordance with tradition, requires the volition of universality. A universality, however, that, although from time to time otherwise configured, has the constant characteristic of not subsuming or not fully subsuming under itself the victims whose sacrifice it demands: the 'blind mole of culture' of which the early writings spoke, individuals degenerated from the *species*, the dross, the sick limbs of *society*, the excrement of the social organism. In conclusion, the liquidation of the idea of historical progress was pronounced in the name of a universality that stemmed essentially from modern thinking and that Marx had analysed as ideological and mystifying.

In Nietzsche, as in the proto-liberalism whose disappearance he lamented, lay a fundamental contradiction that was not, however, really logical in nature: it reflected two antithetical needs of bourgeois society of its time. When looking at the small elite of those 'that have turned out well', the aristocrats, the haves, the independent worth of the individual was forcefully underlined; but when it came to justifying the narrowness and exclusivity of the community of individuals, a holistic style of argumentation intervened. We have seen this in the case of Mandeville and Destutt de Tracy. But it also applied to Locke. For the 'preservation of the army, and in it of the whole common-wealth', the soldiers (from the people) had to show 'absolute obedience' to orders, 'even the most dangerous or unreasonable of them', of a 'superior officer' (from the aristocracy or the bourgeoisie), thus conferring on the latter the ultimate power of life and death. The defence of property coincided with the 'preservation of the whole', 'by cutting off those parts, and those only, which are so corrupt, that they threaten the sound and healthy'.[22] Here, too, we once again come up against the metaphor so cherished by Nietzsche.

5   Individualism as 'Grand Narrative' and Social Engineering

Does the advent of individualism or of its theoretical elaboration signify the end of 'grand narratives'? For Nietzsche, individualism, with its claim to construct the figure of the human being, the individual as such, and thereby to abstract from the extreme differences and inequalities that exist in nature, was precisely such a 'grand narrative'. To assume an equal dignity in individuals, or rather of natural beings that might be separated from one another by an abyss, was to affirm 'another world than that of life, nature, and history'. And just like the revolutionary political project, so too universalistic morality, which sought to construct the no less arbitrary figure of the moral subject as such, was a 'grand narrative', a disastrous act of social engineering that ignored and coerced nature: 'Why morality at all, if life, nature, and history are "immoral"?' (FW, 344 [201]).

The attempt to change and improve nature by eliminating or regulating the relations of rank ordering and violence that constituted it could lead only to

---

22   Locke 1970, 188f., 204f. (II, §139 and §171).

disaster: one was never to lose sight of the 'unusually uncanny historical consequences of optimism, that excrescence of the *homines optimi*'. If one wished
to rescue culture, one was not to put up with 'the interference of short-sighted,
good-natured hands'. The latter 'would mean robbing existence of its great
character, would mean castrating humanity and bringing it down to a miserable, Chinese level'. That is why 'Zarathustra sometimes calls the good men "the
last men"' (EH, Why I am a destiny, 4 [146]).

The subject that stood at the centre of revolutionary discourse and moral
discourse was the result of a dual procedure of social engineering: on the one
hand, a variety of vital processes were reduced to a unity, and on the other hand
this unity was detached from the natural world of which it was a constituent
part and merged with other similarly constructed unities. The critique of this
dual procedure of social engineering was on the one hand the destruction of
a purely 'imaginary' unity, and on the other the reconstruction of the actual
unity:

> We are buds on a single tree – what do we know of what can become of us
> in the interest of the tree! But in our consciousness we feel as if we wanted
> to and should be everything, a daydream of 'I' and 'not I.' Stop feeling like
> this fantastic ego! Learn step by step to rid yourself of this supposed indi-
> vidual! Discover the errors of the ego! Understand the ego as egoism! The
> opposite is in no sense to be understood as altruism! That would be love
> of other supposed individuals! No! Beyond 'me' and 'you'! feel cosmically!
>   IX, 443

As soon as the *Menschending*, the human-thing mentioned in the early writings
(*supra*, 2 §4), was re-immersed in nature, in the cosmic unity of which it was a
constituent part, it could claim no particular dignity, no inviolability, it was an
object alongside other objects and could be used like any other by that divine,
innocent child that was nature as a whole in its games of destruction and construction. The critique of plebeian and revolutionary social engineering paved
the way for the social engineering of 'aristocratic radicalism'. This emerges with
great clarity from Zarathustra's sermon:

> But my fervent will to create always drives me back to humanity; just as
> the hammer is driven to the stone. Oh, you humans, I see an image lying
> asleep in the stone, the image of images! [...] Now my hammer pounds on
> its prison with fury and cruelty. Pieces chip away from the stone: what do
> I care!
>   Za, II, On the Blessed Isles [67], EH, *Thus Spoke Zarathustra*, 8 [134]

Nietzsche-Zarathustra did not hide the potential for violence implicit in this enterprise, confirmed by the insistent return of the metaphor of hammer and stone. Thus a fragment from the spring of 1884 concerning *Zarathustra*:

> This is the hammer that vanquishes human beings
> Has the human being turned out badly? Well, let's see if can resist this hammer!
> This is the great noontide
> Those destined to decline bless themselves
> They predict the decline of countless individuals and races
> I am destiny
> I have vanquished compassion – the artist's exulting at the screaming of the marble.
>
> XI, 77

And again: 'I wander among people as among fragments of the future: the future that I see. This is my every writing and every wish, that I write and unite every riddle, everything that is fragmentary and at the terrible whims of chance' (Za, II, The Redemption; EH, *Thus Spoke Zarathustra*, 8 [133]). This was a project of social engineering that involved 'races' as well as 'individuals', and was certainly no less radical than that of which the revolutionaries were accused.

To read into Nietzsche an end to 'grand narratives' is colossally naïve. It is true he thought it made no sense to speak of historical progress: humankind had no common goals, it 'does not advance, it does not even exist' (XIII, 87 and 408). But the dissolution of the category of humankind (and of subject and individual), together with the emergence of the category of 'human-thing' and human-'stone', was precisely the precondition for Zarathustra's grand narrative and the aristocratic social engineering to which he strove. Against democratic social engineering, which undertook to 'transform humanity into One Organism', by subsuming into it all individuals and according each an equal value and equal dignity, human rights as such, Nietzsche set an opposite project: 'The greatest possible number of changing and diverse organisms that, having reached their maturity and putrefaction, drop their fruit: individuals of which certainly the greater part perishes, but the few count' (IX, 527). 'The last thing I would promise would be to "improve" humanity', said Nietzsche, but he went on to assert the need to transvalue all values, in order to 'to guarantee it prosperity, a future, a high right to a future' (EH, Prologue, 2 [71]). It is worth noting that this 'right to a future' did not pertain to the individual as such and not even to a humanity embracing all individuals. Because of their reluctance to sacrifice the malformed, 'the good [...] crucify those who write new values on new tablets, they sacrifice the future to themselves, they crucify all the futures of mankind!' (EH, Why I am a destiny, 4 [146]). It is hard to see why the reference to the 'great economy of the whole' or to 'life', to the 'supreme law of life', to the 'future' of the world as cosmic unity should be a less totalising explanation than that to the progress of humanity.

The postmodern interpretation of Nietzsche leads nowhere. One should seek, rather, to start out, according to the approach usually adopted, from his reactionary radicalism. Once again, it is worth bearing in mind the struggles after the French Revolution. We have seen how Maistre made fun of the figure of the human being as such and suggested that it was actually the result of an arbitrary construction, an artificial product of social engineering. Adopting a different and opposite value judgement, Hegel recognised that the human being in itself was in no way a natural and immediate given, but the result of almost two millennia of history. This did not mean, however, that slavery and serfdom were synonymous with nature: they too referred to history, or to a history called violently into question by the French Revolution.

A few decades later, these political and ideological struggles erupted with renewed intensity, particularly in the United States, during the Civil War and the subsequent Reconstruction, when an attempt was made, in vain, to secure blacks political and civil rights in the wake of the abolition of slavery. Which of the two warring parties now embodied the cause of spontaneous social development and which the cause of oppressive social engineering? For the theorists of slavery there could no doubt. It was enough to avoid abstract speculation and cast a glance at 'history': 'Slavery has been more universal than marriage and more permanent than liberty'; generalised freedom, on the other hand, was a 'limited and recent experiment'; but 'we do not we want a new world'.[23] After the Civil War, the theorists of white supremacy were in no doubt. In their eyes, the Union's attempt to impose equality and racial integration from above was foolish, for it annulled or drastically reduced the autonomy of the federal states, by recourse to a pedagogical dictatorship aimed at wiping out the racial 'prejudices' of the people of the South; all this was part of a mad experiment in social engineering designed to extinguish a centuries-old tradition and to trample underfoot the established values and customs of the vast majority of the (white) population, ultimately in violation of the natural order. It is not hard to imagine the objections levelled against this ideological campaign. Was the attempt to create a society based on equality and racial integration to be denounced as social engineering? Or was that not rather the case for slavery

---

23   Cobb 1858, xxxv.

and, later, apartheid and the legislation against miscegenation? Where was nature and where was artificial construct?[24] These questions acquired a new actuality with the colonial expansion of the West, which though often carried out in the name of the abolition of slavery led just as often to the imposition of forced labour on an even larger scale. Similar debates and struggles took place during the introduction of compulsory school attendance or social insurance, etc. Once again, where is nature and where artificial construct?

Because of his reactionary radicalism and his constant interest in history and politics, Nietzsche was in a position to problematise in advance the categories of 'grand narrative' and 'social engineering' that play such an important role in philosophical discourse and political ideology today. It is true that he betrays a residue of ideological distortion according to which the elimination of plebeian and revolutionary social engineering would be a sort of return to nature, to its authentically tragic and Dionysian dimension. The immoralist was the type of person that 'conceives of reality as it is: his type has the strength to do this –, it is not alienated, removed from reality, it is reality itself, it contains in itself everything terrible and questionable about reality'. The immoralist avoided flight and self-deception: '[T]he horrors of reality (in the affects, in the desires, in the will to power) are incalculably more necessary than that form of petty happiness called "goodness"'. He was able to recognise reality, and himself in it: 'Luckily the world is not built on instincts such that only good-natured herd animals can find their narrow bit of happiness in it'; he was well aware of the fact that 'negation and destruction are conditions of affirmation' (EH, Why I am a destiny, 4–5 [146–8]). Yes, '[b]ut in order for the creator to be, suffering is needed and much transformation' (Za, II, On the Blessed Isles [66]). And so: 'One of the preconditions of a Dionysian task is, most crucially, the hardness of a hammer, the joy even in destruction. The imperative "become hard!", the deepest certainty that all creators are hard is the true sign of a Dionysian nature' (EH, *Thus Spoke Zarathustra*, 8 [134]).

And yet, despite this remnant of self-deception, one would seek in vain in Nietzsche the naïveté of his postmodern interpreters, who believe they can celebrate with him the end of 'grand narratives'. Like other authors as different from him as Maistre and Hegel, Nietzsche was well aware that the category of human being or individual was the result of colossal revolutionary upheavals and a grand narrative that had unfolded across millennia.

---

24   Losurdo 1996, 2, §10.

6   Construction of General Concepts and Plebeian Social Engineering

Not only the concepts of an equal individual and equality as such violated nature, by denying or seeking to erase the inequalities, rank orderings, vitality and violence that constituted it. The very construction of general concepts was 'anthropomorphic through and through' (WL, 1, I, 883 [147]), i.e., functional to the dominion that the human being intended to exercise over nature. Here, 'shrewd and clever calculations and [...] overreachings of nature' were at work (BA, 4, I, 716 [96]). With its production of concepts, the intellect was only 'the means to preserve those weaker, less robust individuals who, by nature, are denied horns or the sharp fangs of a beast of prey with which to wage the struggle for existence' (WL, 1, I, 876 [142]). This was true of the relationship between the human world and the animal world but also of relationships within the human world as such. It was the servant and the plebeian that produced the 'conceptual hallucinations' regarding a presumed human being or individual as such; directly or indirectly, they stimulated science with its anti-aristocratic and anti-natural theory of concepts and laws equal for all.

So the transcendence that science attributed to itself of conflict and the struggle for power was illusory and mystifying:

> Logic and applied logic (like mathematics) [are part of] the artifices of the power that orders, subjects, simplifies and abbreviates, whose name is life, i.e., something practical and useful, that is to say, something life-sustaining, but precisely for this reason, not in the remotest sense something 'true'.
>
> XII, 238

The '[w]ill to truth' heralded by the 'wisest' was actually 'will to power': everything was to become 'smooth', so it could be mastered (Za, II, On Self-Overcoming [88]).

It is therefore understandable why, in the eyes of the postmodernists, Nietzsche has become the one that made the 'power relationship' the 'general focus' of 'philosophical discourse'. Starting from the thesis that '"truth" is linked in a circular relation with systems of power that produce and sustain it',[25] he was concerned more than any other to analyse 'what effects of power circulate among scientific statements'[26] – while, for Marx, relations of production were the focus, Nietzsche was the philosopher of power.

---

25   Foucault, 1977, 133.
26   Foucault, 1977, 113.

This is the conclusion Foucault reached. To start with, one should note the schematic character of the opposition thus established. For in fact, production relations were also, for Marx, power relations: the capitalist factory, where one can discover the secret of the creation of surplus value and capitalist accumulation, was also the place where the 'despotism' suffered by the workers was immediately palpable. The harshest criticism the *Communist Manifesto* levelled at the capitalist system was that it transformed the mass of workers into 'privates of the industrial army [...] placed under the command of a perfect hierarchy of officers and sergeants', with a minute control exercised by the 'overlooker' and especially by the individual bourgeois factory owner that happened 'daily and hourly'.[27]

But that is not the essential point. Far more serious is the shift that occurred in Foucault's analysis: Nietzsche was surreptitiously transformed from 'the philosopher of power' to a critic of power. The first definition is correct and ultimately confirms Nietzsche's character *totus politicus*. The second is deeply flawed. In fact, the factory relations Marx deprecated and abhorred would have been a model for the theorist of aristocratic radicalism, who would have loved to see the workers turned into real 'soldiers', Fundamentally, he not only propagated the ideal of *otium et bellum*, but repeatedly emphasised the educational value of military life (*supra*, 22 § 5).

Like slavery, the will to power was also something unavoidable. It was no less at work in the slave protesting in the name of 'reason' and 'justice' than in the master asserting his masterly right: 'Wherever I found the living, there I found the will to power; and even in the will of the serving I found the will to be master.' There was no point in appealing to justice as a higher resort: '[W]hat the people believe to be good and evil reveals to me an ancient will to power' (Za, II, On Self-Overcoming [88–9]). In the case of plebeians and servants, the will to power was manifested cunningly, by way of the construction of concepts at the moral, political and scientific level, with which they sought to stymie the greater vitality and strength of the better and of those that had turned out well. The presumed critic of power was strictly speaking the philosopher who demystified the servant's attempt to undermine or challenge the power of the master caste with the argument that this attempt was itself infused with the will to power and domination.

Behind Nietzsche, one senses the influence of Schopenhauer: for the latter, science, which served the practical purposes of the organisation of the phenomenal world or the 'preservation of the individual' and the 'propagation of

---

27   Marx and Engels 1975 ff., 6, 491.

the species', was a mere 'means', a *méchané* of the will to live, which constituted 'the first and original element'.[28] *The Gay Science* acknowledged the debt
owed by its author when it described the thesis of the 'instrumental nature
of the intellect' as Schopenhauer's 'immortal doctrine' (FW, 99 [95]). The two
philosophers had in common an emphasis on the dimension of power and
domination intrinsic to science, but, in the mature Nietzsche, power, domination and life were no longer to be denied and overcome in the *noluntas* but
unreservedly and joyfully accepted by the healthy. And yet, despite this reversal,
there remained an essential element of continuity connecting the two philosophers. When Schopenhauer emphasised the inherently instrumental character of reason and science, he saw this as demystification of social protest and
revolution, animated by the same desire for power they pilloried in the ruling
classes. For Nietzsche, not just reason and science but also morality was animated by the will to power and domination. This domination was transcendable
neither at the cognitive nor at the ethical level and was therefore protected
against any possible protest. Nietzsche's procedure was not a critique but a
metacritique, aimed at proving that any critique of the will to power and domination contradicted itself. The result was not a negation but an unconditional
affirmation without any form of hindrance: the 'lords of the earth must now
replace God and obtain the deep and absolute trust of the dominated' (XI, 620).

7   The Ambiguous History of the Critique of Calculating Thought

If Nietzsche reversed Schopenhauer regarding the analysis of science, Foucault
now performed a new reversal. But this reversal of the reversal or transvaluation of the transvaluation was not a return to the starting point. It is true that,
in the French author, power and will to power acquired an unambiguously negative meaning, but the target of the critique was quite different. In the case of
Schopenhauer and Nietzsche, it was a case of discovering the hidden and disguised presence of the will to power in science and reason and among followers
of the Enlightenment, to whom the revolution and social protest in the plebeian and subversive discourse appealed. Foucault's critique, however, referred
to the discourse, 'reason', 'truth' of power as such. The 'philosophy of power'
now paved the way for a sort of political-metaphysical anarchism.

Foucault proceeded similarly with regard to the dissolution of the subject.
As we have seen, in the second half of the nineteenth century this project

---

28   Schopenhauer 1976–82a, 403, 223.

stood on a line of continuity with the conservative and reactionary critique of the concept of the human being as such, among the human rights proclaimed by the French Revolution. Here too we encounter a game of reversals and transvaluations. The pathos of the subject or the human being had accompanied or supported the struggle against slavery and other sociopolitical relations accused of reifying the human being and disregarding his dignity. But the pathos of the subject was also the pathos of *homo faber*, who asserted a claim to master reality; it was the pathos of action that suffered no hindrances and resistances and tended to gear itself up to violence. So when, in this context, the theme of the dissolution of the subject or the critique of an emphatic idea of the human being was resumed, this happened with a value judgement the opposite of the original. Thus, Foucault and quite a few other postmodern authors believed 'one has to dispense with the constituent subject, and to get rid of the subject itself'.[29]

Through this reinterpretation of Nietzsche as critic of power and of the logic of power and domination implicit in scientific 'truth', Foucault and the postmodern interpreters in general believed they could set themselves clearly apart from the ideologies that had presided over the catastrophes of the twentieth century. However, Baeumler himself, who praised Nietzsche as 'the height of nominalism',[30] appreciated the rigour with which Nietzsche deconstructed the general concepts on which both the Enlightenment and the ideas of 1789 on the one hand and science on the other were founded. Whether one knelt down before 'the sacred' or before 'reason', commented Baeumler, the 'rational-Enlightenment' attitude was no less laden with force and violence than the 'priestly' one. In both cases, an 'absolute' demands its victims.[31]

This ideological theme was also clearly present in Böhm, a prominent ideologue of the Third Reich. In his eyes, a philosophy that sought to confer meaning and value only on the basis of a 'classifying consciousness' would lead to catastrophic results.[32] Starting out from the certainty of the *cogito*, Descartes had 'reduced concrete reality to *rationally controllable* reality, in fact has equated being controllable and being real'; and thus, 'through recourse to self-empowered reason [*selbstmächtige Vernunft*], the possibilities arise of mediated domination of the world'.[33] This had opened the way to a 'rational titanism' and to 'faith in infinite planning, which places the future unconditionally

---

29   Foucault 1977, 117.
30   Baeumler 1937a, 247.
31   Baeumler 1931a, 69 f.
32   Böhm 1938, 85 ff.
33   Böhm 1938, 106.

in human hands'.[34] Thus a continuous line led from Descartes to the positivism of Comte, who intended to transform human beings into 'masters and owners of nature [*maîtres et possesseurs de la nature*]' and to usher in that 'positive' age Nietzsche had exposed as the era of the 'last human'.[35] Böhm set 'disclosing thought [*erschliessendes Denken*], which opens up reality', a thought not permeated by the logic of domination but, on the contrary, 'revealing [*freilegend*]', against calculating thought, ultimately synonymous with 'nihilism',[36] and 'logical-systematic' thought: the thinking of the Germans, which appeared 'incomprehensible and mysterious to the West's rational sense for order'.[37]

The fact is that the critique of the 'constituent subject' (Foucault) or 'classifying consciousness' (Böhm) can be tied to a wide variety of contents. The categories of 'disclosing thought' and calculating thought are far from clear and extremely formal. The antidote to the latter is often identified by ideologues of Nazism in danger, sacrifice and war. This theme stems from Nietzsche, who believes calculating thought is embodied in the Jewish and English pacifistic and 'shopkeeper' spirit (*supra*, 18 §7 and 22 §3) and recommends living dangerously as a remedy for all that and for the hated 'civilization' (IX, 390).

Anyone who thinks it enough to bring the categories of 'calculating thought', 'constituent subject' and 'classifying consciousness' into the equation to explain the tragedies of the twentieth century (and today) or to appeal for the overcoming of these categories in order to leave these tragedies behind could perhaps be directed to a famous passage in the *German Ideology*:

> Once upon a time a valiant fellow had the idea that men were drowned in water only because they were possessed with the idea of gravity. If they were to get this notion out of their heads, say by avowing it to be a superstitious, a religious concept, they would be sublimely proof against any danger from water. His whole life long he fought against the illusion of gravity, of whose harmful consequences all statistics brought him new and manifold evidence. This valiant fellow was the type of the new revolutionary philosophers in Germany.[38]

---

34   Böhm 1938, 55 f.
35   Böhm 1938, 106 ff.
36   Böhm 1938, 80, 93.
37   Böhm 1938, 121, 126.
38   Marx and Engels 1975 ff., 5, 24.

8   Ancient, Modern and Postmodern

When Marx talked about the 'incessant human sacrifices from among the work-ing class'[39] or the 'mysterious rite of the religion of Moloch', which required 'child murder' and later, in modern times, developed an 'exclusive bias for the children of the poor', he had the 'political economy' of the liberal bourgeoisie in mind.[40] But he could just as easily have been talking of Nietzsche's 'great economy of the whole', which conferred an emphatically metaphysical formu-lation on that liberal political economy.

With their opposing views of the human being and of history, Marx and Nietzsche referred to the cultural and political struggles that have pervaded modernity, which is therefore far from being a homogeneous reality. From this point of view, the demarcation and contrasting of modernity and postmodern-ity is based upon a schema unsustainable in historiographical terms but that has a precise political and ideological significance. To grasp it, it might be use-ful to refer back to Constant's famous speech on the liberty of the ancients and the moderns, where he called for the Jacobin-Rousseauian tradition to be set aside once and for all, as irredeemably 'ancient'. Here, too, elements of instrumentalism can be found: when the liberal theorist sought to exclude from political rights the have-nots immersed in lowly labour, he demonstrated that he was much 'older' than the Jacobin-Rousseauian tradition. Robespierre, whom he accused of having forgotten, in his glorification of the *polis*, that the latter was based on slavery, not only abolished modern-day slavery in the colon-ies but accused the theorists of the property-owners' monopoly of political rights (thus Constant's predecessors) of wanting to revive the helotry of ancient Sparta. Although the liberal theorist's distortions are obvious, his speech was, politically, extraordinarily effective. The paradox is that Rousseauianism and Jacobinism, liquidated by Constant as 'ancient', are now ranged along a line of continuity with Hegel and Marx and in this way liquidated as 'modern'.

As we have seen, there is much one can and must learn from Nietzsche. But to do so, there is no need to suppress or palliate the radicalism of his reaction-ary project. Although the uncritical eulogists of the liberal tradition seem not to know it, slavery played an essential role even in Locke, who viewed it in the colonies as a self-evident and uncontroversial institution. But this does not pre-vent us from taking seriously his analyses about the need to limit government power within the sacred space of culture. Naturally, unlike the usual apologet-

39   Marx and Engels 1975 ff., 35, 490.
40   Marx and Engels 1975 ff., 21, 330.

ics, we must not lose sight of the fact that this sacred space, and the limitation
on power and the rule of law connected with it, excluded the great mass of
the profane or barbarians. Locke would have liked to see decreed in the constitution of an English colony in America the principle whereby 'every freeman
of Carolina shall have absolute power and authority over his negro slaves, of
what opinion or religion soever'.[41] He did not doubt that there were people 'by
the right of nature subjected to the absolute dominion and arbitrary power of
their masters'.[42] Locke displayed the same brutality in relation to wage labour
in the capitalist metropolis. Up until the middle of the nineteenth century,
the unemployed and the poor were locked up, often on a simple police order,
in 'workhouses' rightly described as 'concentration camps of the "enlightened
bourgeoisie"'.[43] At the end of the seventeenth century, in liberal England as it
emerged from the Glorious Revolution, Locke, in his capacity as a member of
the Commission on Trade, proposed a renewed crackdown: anyone forging a
pass was to have his ears cut off the first time and deported to the plantations
if it happened again, i.e., reduced in practice to the condition of a slave. But
there was an even easier solution, at least for those that had the misfortune
to be caught begging outside their parish and near a seaport: hand them over
to the Navy, and if they went ashore without permission or stayed longer than
allowed, punish them as deserters, with the death penalty.[44] All this is true. And
yet, the great theorist of the limitation of government power had left us with a
lesson it is impossible to ignore, even if the attempt to liberate it from its frightful exclusion clauses is by no means a straightforward and painless operation
at the level of concrete historical process and far from easy even at the purely
theoretical level: the exclusion clauses can appear in a variety of forms.

There is no reason to adopt a different attitude with respect to Nietzsche.
For him, in the wake of the aristocratic reaction of the late nineteenth century,
the sacred space of culture had become still narrower, while the great mass of
the profane or barbarians had grown immeasurably. The other side of the coin
is that the freedom of this space was conceived not only as freedom from an
oppressive power: it was also freedom from a narrow-minded herd morality as
well as from the intellectual mutilation implicit in the division of labour. In
this sense, Nietzsche had conceived of the freedom of the individual (i.e., of
the few, the very few, to whom he attributed this designation) in a more radical and fascinating way than Locke. But here it is more important than ever to

---

41   Locke 1963a, 196 (art. CX).
42   Locke 1970, 158 (II, § 85).
43   Colletti 1969, 280.
44   In Bourne 1969, Vol. 2, 377 ff.

bear in mind that if one lost sight of the whole, one also forfeited the chance to understand the separate parts. Is Nietzsche the theorist of the surmounting of the division of labour? Absolutely, providing one immediately adds that this surmounting, asserted in relation to a narrow sacred space, rests on a division of labour in its most extreme and brutal form, namely the caste system (the naturalisation of the division of labour) and slavery (a division of labour pushed to the point where the great mass of humankind is reduced to simple instruments of labour without individuality and dignity). Much the same can be said, for example, about the emancipation of the flesh and critical thinking: neither is theorised in general terms, the vast mass of the sacrificial victims of culture are irredeemably excluded from both. The freedom of the individual was conceived by Nietzsche in terms so radical they dissolved into the utopian; the reverse side of this fascinating utopia is of course a repugnant dystopia that not only degraded the vast majority of human beings to instruments of labour or, worse still, 'effluent and waste materials', but unhesitatingly contemplated their massive culling.

One can and must learn much from Locke and from Nietzsche, but precisely to that end, one must adopt a standpoint outside their political and theoretical world. Much can be learned from both authors about the development of a free individuality; but a prerequisite for this learning process is that we tear down the barrier that both erect between the sacred and the profane space, between culture and barbarism. Neither was in a position to universalise the category of the individual. But only Nietzsche realised that the freedom or fullness of the individual he celebrated presupposed slavery and the reduction to instruments of a mass of individuals or rather of *beings* by definition inherently incapable of individuality. While, at the political level, Nietzsche was much more 'reactionary' than the English liberal ('aristocratic radicalism' was the polemical response to the openness and concessions of the liberal world in the face of the offensive of the democratic popular movement), at the more strictly theoretical level he was clearly superior: he was well aware of how labour relations in capitalist society at the time and the relations between the Western metropolis and the colonies continued to be marked by servility and enslavement. He was fully aware of the terrible exclusion clauses that mark liberal thought and liberal society.

How One Constructs Nietzsche's Innocence: Publishers, Translators, Interpreters

The only valid tribute to thought such as Nietzsche's is precisely to use it, to deform it, to make it groan and protest. And if commentators then say that I am being faithful or unfaithful to Nietzsche, that is of absolutely no interest.[1]

• • •

His [Giorgio Colli's] thesis is moreover that one should listen to N[ietzsche] as one listens to music – well then, even in the case of music I am unable to tolerate an inexplicable and aesthetic way of hearing something. I am for the rational and explicable transposition or, better still, for the 'historical' (i.e., time-based) description of every fact: even if individualities like N[ietzsche] are evidently irreducible [*entelecheia*], and if I do not feel like negating the legitimacy of those who consider his forms of utterance to be timeless (this is for me an unresolved question). If Giorgio [Colli] speaks in this way, then it is because for him rationality has no significance and everything refers ultimately to the aesthetic unity of the individual.[2]

• • •

... the gravest misinterpretations and dangers of misunderstanding (and of self-misunderstanding) of Nietzsche's 'doctrine'.[3]

• •
•

These comments give us some idea of the spiritual climate in which today's dominant Nietzsche interpretation has arisen and become established. An extreme case is that of Giorgio Colli, who says we should read the philosopher while simply abandoning

---

1 Foucault 1977, 53–54.
2 From a note (3–5 October 1963) by Mazzino Montinari, in Campioni 1992, 82 f.
3 Vattimo 1983, 183.

ourselves to the musical charm of his magnificent prose. At the time, Montinari tries to resist. But we should not be deceived by the severe and mordant manner in which he expresses himself: we are on the eve of a capitulation. Colli's 'musical' interpretation, or a 'theoretical' interpretation that – as in Foucault's case – considers historical-philological reconstruction to be irrelevant or – as in Vattimo's case – seeks to correct Nietzsche's 'self-misunderstandings', has prevailed.

This spiritual climate has above all influenced the translations. But it is not the inaccuracies, oversights and errors that are the problem: no translation is flawless, and, of course, this also goes for the translations I have proposed in the Italian edition of my book. The problem is the 'method' that underlies the inaccuracies, oversights and errors in the Italian Colli-Montinari edition. This edition evinces a constant tendency to suppress the historical and political world as an alien and disruptive factor. This preoccupation is so pronounced that it has, at least in one instance, strongly influenced the editing.

1   The Young Nietzsche's Judeophobia

It is here we should start out, also because we have here a text that marks the beginning of Nietzsche's philosophical (and political) path. On 1 February 1870 he held a lecture in Basel titled 'Socrates and Tragedy' that concluded:

> *In conclusion, a single question. Is music drama really dead, dead for good? Should the German really not be allowed to put anything alongside that vanished work of art of the past other than 'great opera', much in the same way as the ape used to appear next to Hercules? This is the most serious question of our art, and who, as a German, does not understand the seriousness of this question* has fallen victim to the Socratism of our days, which undoubtedly cannot produce martyrs nor speak the language of the 'wisest among the Greeks' and which certainly blusters [like the historical Socrates] about not knowing anything, but really knows nothing. This Socratism is the Jewish press: I say nothing more.
>
> ST, I, 549 and XIV, 101

I have already dwelt at length on the reactions this text evoked in the Wagner household, as well as on Nietzsche's response (*supra*, 3 §1). It is worth quickly reviewing the incident, so the reader has to hand the elements essential for evaluating the editors' decisions. Invited by Cosima Wagner to avoid prematurely and recklessly provoking the Jewish community, Nietzsche replaced the term 'Jewish [*jüdische*]' with 'today's [*heutige*]' and, probably later, crossed out the first part of the paragraph (which I have italicised). The second part is on a page of the manuscript that has been torn out (by the philosopher or his sister Elisabeth, no one knows which). But so much is clear: the whole paragraph, as quoted here (with the explicit reference to the 'Jewish press') corresponds to the preparatory draft of the text, was delivered in the Basel lecture, was sent to Richard and Cosima Wagner and reflects without a doubt the original and young philosopher's true intention.

All this is clearly explained by Colli and Montinari (even though they have placed these clarificatory lines in such a way that they escape the reader's eyes). But let us see how they proceed in the edition prepared by them. The German edition gives only the first (italicised) part of the paragraph: to read the conclusion and the details of the matter, the reader must go to the trouble of checking in the volume devoted to variants and the critical apparatus. This procedure alone is highly questionable. Following Cosima's request, Nietzsche did not amend the written and spoken text because he had changed his mind but merely to carry out the temporary self-censorship urged on him by his correspondent. It is not clear why today's editors should follow Cosima's advice.

But things get even worse in the Italian version. Here the paragraph is quoted in full, save that the original 'Jewish press' has become 'today's press', while in the 'chronology' and 'notes' that accompany the text there is no reference to the original version. The 'chronology' (*Opere*, vol. III, II, 394–6) cites excerpts from Cosima's and Richard Wagner's letters in which they speak of the 'horror' and unease they had experienced on reading the text of the lecture; besides that, passages from Nietzsche's letter to Rohde are quoted, in which the philosopher explains that in future he wants to overcome the caution of the moment to express himself 'as seriously and frankly as possible'. But all this is made incomprehensible by the disappearance of the reference to the 'Jewish press' and Cosima's recommendations for caution on this point. The composer writes: 'You will receive absolution only if no one from *that side* understands anything. [...] I hope with all my heart you do not break your neck.' And Cosima: 'We were so upset that we no longer read anything that evening.' One can easily imagine the reader's questions. What 'side' is being referred to? And why should it be so threatening? Wagner continues: 'You could free me of a great part, even an entire half, of my mission.' Reader: what 'mission'? But the reader is left in the dark about the essential issue: the intellectual alliance the musician, after reading *Socrates and Tragedy*, offered the philologist in the common struggle against Judaism, a struggle to be conducted with the tactical skill the enemy's power and malice necessitated. In conclusion, the self-censorship recommended by Cosima and inexplicably included in the German version of the critical edition becomes real censorship in the Italian version (and in the widely available paperback edition published by the Piccola Biblioteca Adelphi).

But that is not the only example of censorship. The 'chronology' cites in relation to *The Birth of Tragedy* (*Opere*, vol. III, I, 468) passages from Nietzsche's letter to Wagner in which he attributes to him the merit of having, together with Schopenhauer, given voice to the 'Germanic seriousness of life', a 'more serious and soulful world-

view', threatened by 'clamant Judaism' (B, II, 1, 9). The quotation starts at an opportune moment: it reproduces the tribute paid to the 'Germanic seriousness of life', but
the reader once again learns nothing about the opposition of Judaism and Germanism that so profoundly characterised Nietzsche before the start of the 'Enlightenment'
phase, and nothing about the denunciation of Judaism that immediately preceded
it.

Now we come to the translation. I will confine myself to examples easy for non-
Italian readers to understand. *The Greek State* polemicised against 'a self-seeking, stateless money aristocracy' (CV, 3, I, 774 [171]). The allusion to Jewish finance, a constant
target of the anti-Jewish and anti-Semitic polemic, is transparent. But, in the Italian
version, the aristocracy changes from *apolide* [stateless] to *apolitika* [apolitical] (*Opere*,
vol. III, II, 234)! Taking up one of Wagner's favourite themes, the young Nietzsche
reproached Auerbach and authors of Jewish descent for using a form of German, 'due
to national reasons', characterised by 'natural foreignness' and therefore 'deplorable'
(VII, 598 [168]). In the Italian translation, *estraneità* [foreignness] becomes *inesperi-
enza* [inexperience] (*Opere*, III, III, II, 196), and so the young Nietzsche's Judeophobia
once again vanishes without trace.

2   The Suppression of Politics and History

The Germany celebrated by the Germanomaniacs, who would include the young Nietzsche, was synonymous with true 'culture', set against the banal 'civilization' of other
peoples, above all the Romans. The culture/civilisation dichotomy is wholly absent
from the Colli-Montinari Italian edition. Yet Nietzsche expressly emphasised the
'abysmal antagonism' between 'culture' and 'civilization' (*supra*, II §7).

Given the methodological assumptions represented especially by Giorgio Colli, little
attention is paid to history. Although the Puritan sect had sprung from an intrinsically plebeian Reformation, it succeeded in overcoming its origins and, thanks to the
inducements to self-overcoming contained within its religion, becoming a master-
race: 'Asceticism and Puritanism are almost indispensable means of educating and
ennobling a race that wants to gain control over its origins among the rabble' (JGB, 61
[55]), Nietzsche concluded. Not so, however, the Italian translation, which renders *Pur-
itanismus* as *castità* [chastity]! Even if one ignores the risk of transforming the immoralist philosopher into a eulogiser of purity and sexual abstinence, the fact remains that
the specific historical event to which he referred has vanished. Similarly, the 'visionary
[*schwärmerisch*]⁴ spirit of the eighteenth century' becomes in the Italian translation

---

4 *Schwärmerisch* is translated as 'enthusiastic' in the Cambridge translation.

a *spirito stravagante* [extravagant spirit] (FW, 362 [227]). Once again, the reference to the dreams of social regeneration that characterised the ideological preparation of the French Revolution tends to be obfuscated. The *Genealogy of Morals* (I, 5) criticised 'Europe's socialists' for their 'inclination towards the "Commune", the most primitive form of society': the Italian version has 'commune' in lowercase: will readers realise Nietzsche's target was the Paris Commune?

Luther, this plebeian, observed *The Gay Science*, 'lacked any inheritance from a ruling caste [*Kaste*] and instinct for power' (FW, 358 [222]). Caste becomes 'class' in the Italian translation (*Opere*, V, II, 272). The same happens in other even more significant contexts. It is 'is characteristic of every strong age', says *Twilight of the Idols*, to maintain 'the rift between people, between classes [*Stand*]' (GD, Skirmishes of an untimely man, 37 [212]). In the Italian translation too, 'class' again replaces *ceto* [caste] (*Opere*, VI, III, 136). As a result, we end up with the oxymoron of a chasm between class and class. One can speak of social class only when there is relative social mobility; but it is precisely this mobility Nietzsche aimed to eliminate. This is a trait that accompanied the philosopher in the entire course of his development, including the period of 'Enlightenment'.

3   Breeding, Physiology and Degeneration

A similar process occurs around the theme of 'breeding [*Züchtung*]'. As we know, Vattimo recommends its allegorical interpretation, with the help of an arbitrary abstraction from a historical context in which eugenic views were widespread, and an even more arbitrary abstraction from the interest, not to say enthusiasm, Nietzsche displayed for this new 'science'. It is interesting to observe how Vattimo immerses even the philosopher's most disquieting pages in a purifying bath. Zarathustra enounced the maxim 'Die at the right time' and then continued:

> To be sure, how could the person that never lives at the right time ever die at the right time? [Would that he were never born! – Thus I advise the superfluous. But even the superfluous boast about their dying [*thun noch wichtig mit ihrem Sterben*], and even the hollowest nut still wants to be cracked.] Everyone regards dying as important; but death is not yet a festival. As of yet people have not learned how to consecrate the most beautiful festivals.[5]
>
> Za, I, On Free Death [53]

---

5   Cf. Vattimo 1983, 244.

I have put square brackets around the passage Vattimo omits, indicated in his book in the traditional way, by means of an ellipsis in square brackets. In this way, it is not clear to the reader that, for Nietzsche, the importance of the death of the 'superfluous' was purely subjective and imaginary. They weighed unbearably on society and life; in one way or another, one was to urge them to end a worthless existence. Zarathustra insisted strongly on this in the excerpt, which – not for nothing – has been called the 'suicide chapter' (*supra*, 19 § 4). But there is no trace of this in Vattimo's commentary. Thus, he miraculously transforms a brutal eugenicist discourse that celebrates the suicide of the malformed as a festival of culture into purely moral reflection.

The process of volatilisation and sublimation concludes with the proposal to translate *Übermensch* as *oltreuomo* (*oltre*, 'above, beyond', *uomo*, 'man') rather than as *superuomo*, on the grounds that Nietzsche cared only about 'transcending the man of tradition'.[6] But when Zarathustra, in the speech that immediately follows, denounced 'the selfishness of the sick', who clung to a worthless life and thereby compound the 'degeneration [*Entartung*]', he continued: 'Upward goes our way, over from genus [*Art*] to super-genus [*Über-Art*]' (Za, I, On the Bestowing Virtue, 1 [56]). An essential aspect of Zarathustra's speech was his setting of the 'overman' and 'super-genus' against rampant 'degeneration'. Again, we find ourselves returning to a theme that, together and inextricably intertwined with the themes of the hereditary transmission of crime and eugenics, dominated European and Western culture in the second half of the nineteenth century and also played a central role in the circle of Nietzsche's treasured authors and friends. This is shown, for example, by the fact that the names of writers like Galton, Lombroso and Gobineau frequently cropped up in their correspondence (*supra*, 19 § 1). In Zarathustra to seek to separate the great fascinating moralist from the brutal theorist of aristocratic radicalism is an untenable enterprise.

The *oltreuomo* becomes the starting point for a dizzying process of transfiguration and sublimation. Vattimo refers to § 868 of the *Will to Power*, of which I here quote the central passage: 'A dominant race can grow only from terrible and violent beginnings. Problem: where are the barbarians of the twentieth century? Obviously, they will show and consolidate themselves only after enormous socialist crises.' This is one of Nietzsche's most brutally significant pages. Confronted with the challenge of what Nietzsche elsewhere called 'socialist wars' (*supra*, 11 § 7), with the 'choice' of 'either perish or win through', as he wrote in the last months of his conscious existence, a new caste or master race would form from those in a position, after putting aside democratic and humanitarian inhibitions, to apply barbaric means as the situation requires, and to demonstrate a 'will to terrible things' (this is also an allusion to the annihilation of the malformed, the basis of the slave revolt). Only then would the new 'dominant

---

6   Vattimo 1983, 183, fn. 11.

race' be able to dispose of the mass of human beings as the 'most intelligent slave animal'. '[T]errible and violent beginnings', the 'will to terrible things': these repeated expressions set the tone for this text (XIII, 17–18). But Vattimo refers to it only in order to read from it the evocation of 'a sort of 'new barbarians', whose barbarism consists essentially in the fact that they 'come from outside', they are abstracted from the logic of the system': this new species 'already anticipates the characteristics of the freedom achieved by the *oltreuomo*'.[7] As if by magic, the 'terrible and violent beginnings', the 'will to terrible things', the 'enormous socialist crises', and, of course, the reaffirmation of the necessity of slavery dissolve into thin air.

Sometimes the hermeneutics of innocence are so pronounced they end up provoking an actual reversal of meaning. *Ecce Homo* invites us to pay attention to 'all the things about life that deserve to be taken very seriously – questions of nutrition, residence, spiritual diet, treatment of the sick [*Krankenbehandlung*], cleanliness, weather!' Unfortunately, 'in the concept of the good person, [one has taken the side] of everything weak, sick, badly formed, suffering from itself, everything *that should be destroyed* [*zu Grunde gehen soll*], – defiance of the law of *selection*' (EH, Why I am a destiny, 8 [150–1]). In the Italian translation, *Krankenbehandlung*, which had a clearly eugenetic meaning, becomes '*cura dei malati* [healing of the sick]', despite Nietzsche's highlighting with italics the assertion that one was not artificially to keep alive in the world anything that ran counter to the 'law of *selection*' and that consequently 'should *perish*' (*Opere*, VI, III, 384–5).

4   Beyond the 'Nietzschean' Catechism

While some of the editorial choices are questionable and there are no few cases of political blocking in the translation, the 'chronology', and the 'notes' to the Italian version, the commentary in the *Opere* and the paperback editions published by Adelphi adopts an occasionally uplifting tone. Where *Twilight of the Idols* ('Improving' humanity, 4) points to the Manu Code and the Hindu world as an expression of an 'Aryan humanity', Colli and Montinari's commentary takes care to point out that the conceptual pair Aryan/anti-Aryan has an 'objective, descriptive character', void of 'value criteria.' While Nietzsche defines Christianity as 'the anti-Aryan religion *par excellence*', according to Colli and Montinari he had emphasised Jesus's Jewish origins merely in order to confront Christian anti-Semites trying to demonstrate that the founder of their religion was at least half-Roman and half-Aryan (*Opere*, VI, III, 502). In fact, in the text at issue it is crystal-clear that the opposition was between 'Chandala values'

---

7   Vattimo 1983, 374.

and 'Aryan values': while the former found their consecration in Christianity, the latter referred to an 'Aryan humanity, absolutely pure, absolutely original', which rejected
with horror 'the mishmash human beings', 'the fruit of adultery, incest, crime' (*supra*, 12
§ 8). According to Colli and Montinari, a master of prose used such emphatic language
to express an innocuously 'descriptive' concept! It is admittedly difficult to read in a
non-judgemental way a philosopher who, with his concept of perspectivism, tirelessly
emphasised that any theory involved the moment of decision, of choice, of the explicit
or implicit utterance of a value judgement. However, it is incomprehensible how one
can apply such an interpretation to a paragraph that even in the language it uses, in
every line and every word, exudes value judgements.

The hermeneutics of innocence treats history as an intruder that must immediately
be shown the door. At a time when the Aryan myth was running rampant, Nietzsche
was supposedly not only immune to it but did not even know about it. In the last phase
of his development, Nietzsche emphatically praised the Hindu world of castes, but was
supposedly unaware of the fact that the term *varna*, 'caste', also indicated colour, and
referred to the difference between the blond conquerors belonging to the higher races
and the subjugated coloured peoples of the lower castes. So a trained philologist and
passionate devotee of Hindu culture supposedly had no idea of what was perfectly clear
to both Treitschke and the circles of Christian missionaries Nietzsche hated and despised.[8] In fact, Aryan mythology, which had already made an appearance in *The Birth
of Tragedy*, played a growing role in Nietzsche's subsequent development.

As often happens in such cases, the outcome is a paradox. On the one hand, the apologetic zeal completely misses its target, for consistent anti-Semites have no problem in
acknowledging Jesus's Jewish descent, and at most take it as an occasion to denounce
Christianity along with Judaism, as, for example, Dühring did (*supra*, 18 § 6). On the
other hand, the apologetic zeal ends up achieving a result opposite to that pursued. In
their interpretation of the aphorism just quoted, Colli and Montinari seem to assume
that, for Nietzsche, 'Jewish' and 'Aryan' were opposites. In this case, the unavoidable
acknowledgement of a positive or negative value judgement of the two terms would
push in the direction of the most vehemently anti-Semitic circles the philosopher so
staunchly defended. And yet the antagonistic pole of the master-'race' was not the Jews
but the 'dark-haired native inhabitants' (GM, I, 5 [14]) who provided the mass of the servants or sudra.

The same apologetic zeal inspires the abandon with which the text *Socrates and
Tragedy* is presented and 'adjusted' and with which the traces of Judeophobia in the
young Nietzsche are erased. These are not the only cases of concealment and suppression with which the Piccola Biblioteca Adelphi can be reproached. One seeks in vain

---

8   Treitschke 1879, 468; Warneck 1879, 196.

in the more available volumes for the most disquieting or downright repulsive fragments, which provide a theoretical basis for annihilations on a massive scale. In this case, pedagogical and catechetical concern takes precedence over philological and historical rigour. That illustrious interpreters also resort to similar procedures is no reason for indulging in a method scientifically and ethically unacceptable.

As I have already explained several times, it is not at all a question of viewing Nietzsche as dated or uninteresting. On the contrary, his powerful demystifying potential can only be understood from the angle of the reactionary radicalism of his political programme. Moreover, his most repugnant sides refer to the most repugnant pages of the history the West wrote even before the start of the Third Reich. As in the history of the West as a whole, so too in the thought of this great philosopher, greatness and horror are two sides of the same coin: they point to the rigorous and unrelenting delimitation of the sacred space within which the right to the free unfolding of individuality is confined.

Nietzsche's Spectacles and Umbrella: An Answer to My Critics

So Nietzsche's philosophical significance is today manifoldly disputed. Perhaps some people want to believe that the new edition published by Colli and Montinari will be decisive here. It is true we are now for the first time acquainted with Nietzsche's notebooks in a reliable and chronological form, so we no longer depend on the editing and selection with which Nietzsche's sister and all later editors have edited Nietzsche's posthumous notes. However, *it is naïve to believe that now that we know the real Nietzsche, we are finally freed from the preoccupations of previous interpreters.* I illustrate my point with an example. A recent small book by Derrida, *Les éperons de Nietzsche*, devotes an entire chapter to a brief note by Nietzsche that goes: 'I have forgotten my umbrella.' Derrida writes an elegant essay about this line. Perhaps Nietzsche really did forget his umbrella. But who can know if anything important lies behind this fact? Whatever the case, *the example shows that such a comprehensive edition is at the same time an excellent way of hiding essential things behind inessential things.*[1]

∴

Colli and Montinari's editorial work is highly valuable, but it is not the hermeneutics of a fullness of time [*plenitudo temporum*] solemnly announced by the interpreters, eager to put an end to disquieting questions about reading Nietzsche. Gadamer's warning dates from 1986, and for a long time such questions were frowned upon in the name of political correctness and *bon ton*. And yet, even the Colli-Montinari edition confirms dimensions of the philosopher, however extraordinarily acute and stimulating he may have been, that today cannot but awaken the darkest memories: the glorification of eugenics and the 'super-species', the theorising on the one hand of slavery, on the other of the 'breeding' of the 'higher species of dominant Caesaric spirits', the demand for the 'annihilation of decadent races' and of 'millions of malformed', the assertion of the need for 'a hammer with which to smash degenerating and dying races, to remove them in order to make way for a new order of life'.

---

1   Gadamer 1986, 4; cf. Derrida 1978, 94–108.

1   Gadamer's Discomfiture

How to explain that Nietzsche's lost 'umbrella' arouses more attention than the themes just mentioned? Here the second part of Gadamer's warning, which I italicised, comes into play. So, should we view sceptically the fact that all the philosopher's notes are published in the same way and accorded the same weight, so that the most disquieting passages end up being overwhelmed by a mass of details regarding the most banal episodes in Nietzsche's life? Perhaps Gadamer goes too far here with his application of a hermeneutics of suspicion. Moreover, it is untrue that the Colli-Montinari edition publishes everything in the same way and without distinctions. In the third edition of Nietzsche's works, the so-called Grossoktav-Ausgabe (vol. XIII, 43), we can read this passage:

> He that as a knowing person has acknowledged that in us, alongside growth of all kinds, the law of perishing is at the same time in force, and that annihilation and decay inexorably impose themselves at the end of every creation and generation: he must learn to experience a kind of joy at such a sight, in order to *bear* it, or he is no longer good for knowing. That is, he must be capable of a refined cruelty and get used to it with a resolute heart. If his force is even higher in the rank-ordering of forces, he himself is one of the creators and not just a spectator: so it is not enough that he is capable of cruelty only in *seeing* so much suffering, so much extinction, so much destruction; such a human being must be able to create pain with pleasure, to be cruel with hand and deed (and not just with the eyes of the spirit).

This fragment, reproduced in a well-regarded edition, was included by Baeumler in his Nietzsche anthology, devoted to illustrating or celebrating the 'innocence of becoming'.[2] Later it was taken up again by Nolte, who used it to support his own interpretation: while Nietzsche reacted to Marx's demand for the 'destruction' of the bourgeoisie with a programme of 'counter-destruction', he 'provided the political radical anti-Marxism of fascism, [...] decades in advance, with the spiritual model even Hitler himself was never quite up to'.[3] This is a provocative thesis that would perhaps have deserved a wider discussion. But what happens with this fragment in the Colli-Montinari edition? As a preparatory draft of § 229 of *Beyond Good and Evil*, it is reproduced in the 'notices and notes' of the Adelphi edition of *Beyond Good and Evil* and in the volumes of the critical apparatus of the *Kritische Gesamtausgabe* and the *Kritische Studienausgabe*,

---

2   Baeumler 1931b, Vol. 1, 252.
3   Nolte 1963, 534 f.

while it disappears completely from the digital version of the *Kritische Studienausgabe*, because this has not, up to now (March 2009), reproduced the critical apparatus. For the same reason, it disappears from the digital version of the original conclusion of the lecture *Socrates and Tragedy*, with its polemic against the 'Jewish press'.

Thus, there emerges an even greater danger than that against which Gadamer warns. It is not the case that 'such a comprehensive edition' leads ultimately to 'hiding essential things behind inessential things'. What actually happens is rather that completely trivial notes (not just 'I have forgotten my umbrella' IX, 587] but also 'don't wear glasses in public!' [XIII, 579], 'warm clothes in the evening!' [XIII, 580], etc) tend to marginalise and even cause to disappear the hymn of the joy to destruction and to the unmasking of the Jewish press.[4]

2   'Persistence' and 'Improvement'

That these are serious problems is recognised by voices beyond suspicion. For example, Sossio Giametta, after a very critical reading of my Nietzsche study, notes:

> However, the book has one great merit: it puts an end, by applying the most historical, philological and critical tools, to the hermeneutics of innocence, which tear Nietzsche from his historical context and from his actual roots; this is a hermeneutic 'tendency' that 'has taken hold of even the best minds, including the two editors [Colli and Montinari]', and has led them to commit various errors that Losurdo persistently pursues.[5]

What should one say of this analysis? In the first place, one cannot but value the intellectual honesty of a researcher who, having made a first-rate contribution to the Italian version of the new critical edition, does not confine himself to recognising the (understandable and even inevitable) presence of errors of translation and other sorts. More important is the acknowledgement that these errors correspond to a certain extent to a logic, a precise interpretative 'tendency'. As for my supposed 'obstinacy', I would like to point out that, while I simply highlight the influence of the hermeneutics of innocence on the otherwise meritorious Colli-Montinari edition, Giametta is carried away to the point where he notes that this hermeneutics has 'taken hold' of the two editors.

On another occasion, Giametta formulates an even more drastic judgement on Montinari, in this case focusing more on his interpretation than on his editing:

4   Campioni 2002.
5   Giametta 2003.

In politics too he argues the need to take account of Nietzsche, his critique, his dimension. Not his blinding and lacerating truths. And not his errors and horrors, like the 'cannibal morality to be imposed dictatorially', as Rohde says, which bursts forth unmistakeably in *Beyond Good and Evil*. [...] All the things Montinari preaches about Nietzsche have the appearance of being important. But they are, sorry to say, insignificant if not false.[6]

I do not know if 'all' Montinari's observations are 'insignificant' or 'false', but it is certainly the case that his tendency to suppress 'errors and horrors' also shows up in his work as an editor, at least in the notes and commentary that accompany the Italian edition. My remarks are intended as a contribution to 'improving' the new critical edition. Here, I mention only the problems easiest to solve. Has the reader of the Italian edition the right to be informed of the fact that the lecture of 1 February 1870 ends with an indictment of the Jewish press? And is it acceptable that the reader is made aware of the agitation the lecture causes Cosima and Richard Wagner, but not of its cause (the public denunciation of Judaism as a synonym for Socratism)? Is it philologically accurate to quote only the glorification of the 'Germanic seriousness of life' from Nietzsche's letter to Wagner of 22 May 1869 but to remain silent about the contrasting of this worldview with 'clamant Judaism'? And, to return briefly to the problem of translation, would it not be right to put an end to the cheerful confusion of 'culture' and 'civilization', two terms to which Nietzsche ascribes quite different and even antithetical meanings? It is a good sign that some of my 'clarifications' regarding the translation 'can be accepted'.[7] It goes without saying I am not questioning Colli's and Montinari's 'good faith' and 'intellectual probity'.[8] But I fail to see why Lukács should be stripped of these characteristics, as the daily *La Repubblica* does in an anonymous article (a nice touch of elegance!) in which the adjective 'Lukácsian' is used practically synonymously with 'policing'.[9] To expose one's opponents to vile suspicion but to reject it with disdain for oneself or one's own side is the very nub of dogmatism!

3   Emerson and Nietzsche

Among those open to discussion that have reacted to the challenging of the hermeneutics of innocence is an interpreter whom I have criticised as a leading exponent of this hermeneutic. Gianni Vattimo recognises that, in spite of his admiration for

---

6   Giametta 1998, 260 f.
7   Campioni 2002.
8   Giametta 2002.
9   *La Repubblica* 2002.

Emerson, Nietzsche 'certainly did not share the latter's commitment to the abolition of slavery': so the celebration of slavery as an indispensable foundation of culture is not merely a metaphor! Moreover, Vattimo draws attention to 'certain contradictions of individualism with which we must still grapple even today'.[10] Can a worldview like that of Nietzsche and the liberal tradition behind him, which admittedly praised select individuals but labels the vast majority of humanity as instruments of labour and two-legged machines, truly be seen as individualistic? The emancipation of which the classical liberal tradition and – in a decidedly more radical and fascinating way – Nietzsche spoke never concerned the individual in his generality. That is precisely why the German philosopher, displaying a much greater critical awareness than his predecessor liberals, was careful not to profess individualism. On the contrary, he insisted that, just like 'collectivist morality', the 'individualistic' form had the disadvantage of asserting egalitarian measures, given that it demands the 'same freedom' and the same open-mindedness for all. The basic flaw of Christianity and socialism was, according to Nietzsche, to assume or invent souls and individuals where there were only instruments of labour. Vattimo is rightly concerned to valorise Nietzsche's 'less Nazistic traits of thought'. Yet the fact remains that we are not dealing with an unpolitical author; it is time to leave the hermeneutics of innocence behind us!

And yet there is no lack of shilly-shallying and vacillation. When Vattimo puts Nietzsche together with Emerson, he believes he can at least partially rescue the unpolitical interpretation: after all, who would want to assert against the American writer the suspicions and accusations levelled at the German philosopher? In reality, the hermeneutics of innocence prove unsustainable even with reference to Emerson. True, he had not experienced the trauma of the Paris Commune and an endlessly long revolutionary cycle that had devastated France in order to find its elective homeland in Germany in the late nineteenth century, where Social Democracy, a party celebrated or damned by the entire culture of the time as the spearhead of the revolution, was waxing menacingly. And yet disquieting themes are not absent from the American writer, above all when he praised great men (only they find sense in a world infested by 'pygmies' and therefore have the right to sacrifice 'millions of people' 'without sparing blood and without mercy'), insisted on the role of race ('we know what weight race has in history') and the fatal character of the expansion of the 'instinctive and heroic races', and praised the wars that 'rid the world of the corrupt races and the seats of disease'.[11]

Also significant is the history of Emerson's reception. Certain aspects of his thinking were recalled later by Chamberlain[12] and, with particular enthusiasm, by Henry Ford, the great scourge of the Jewish-Bolshevik conspiracy threatening the world, who

---

10   Vattimo 2003.
11   Emerson 1983a, 732–745, 950, 954, 1084.
12   Chamberlain 1937, 328.

for that very reason was highly successful in the Third Reich.[13] It is well known that Emerson had excellent relations with Carlyle, who along with Chamberlain was celebrated by the Nazi press in 1935 as the inspiration behind the new German regime: the two 'Britons' were jointly praised for having asserted the 'idea of the Führer and racial thought [*Führertum und Rassengedanke*]; thanks to this aristocratic worldview, they have tightened even further the links between the Germans and the English, the two peoples destined for leadership'.[14] This acknowledgement could also be extended to the American author, who for his part emphasised and celebrated the common racial origins and common imperial mission of Germans, English and Americans. So, the attempt to rescue at least Emerson on the grounds of pure culture hardly succeeds. The fact is that Vattimo, despite polemicising against Lukács, shares a basic premise with him: both argue as if the process of the formation of the most disquieting themes of the ideology of the late nineteenth century, later inherited, radicalised and transformed by the Nazis, were confined to Germany!

The history of Emerson's reception includes a chapter of surprising actuality. Immediately after the declaration of war on Spain, he was raised by excited chauvinists into the pantheon of 'imperial intellects of his race', that superb 'conquering race', champion of the unstoppable expansion of the United States.[15] Against that, he was later mercilessly reinterpreted by critics of the Vietnam War: it was Emerson who removed from our politics and our politicians 'any sense of restriction'.[16]

4   The Public Prosecutor and the Defendant: A Strange Convergence

And yet, despite my persisting differences with Vattimo, the fact remains that his contribution is symptomatic: the hermeneutics of innocence regarding Nietzsche is no longer taboo. Perhaps the tendency to get rid of the 'preoccupations' Gadamer mentions by finding two scapegoats for them has begun to falter. The first is, of course, Elisabeth, accused of having adapted Nietzsche's philosophy to the needs of Nazism. Even today, few dare question this thesis. What does it matter if her biography of the philosopher appeared at the turn of the century, and if *The Will to Power* was published in 1901 or, in its second edition, in 1906, in the Europe of the *belle époque*, when no one was yet able to predict the outbreak of the First World War, let alone the rise of Hitler? To avoid troubling their conscience, the hermeneuts of innocence readily attribute extraordinary powers of divination to the despised Elisabeth. The result is to expose

---

13   Baldwin 2001, 45 ff.
14   Vollrath 1935, Foreword.
15   Thus, for example, Albert J. Beveridge, in Bairati 1975, 242.
16   Cf. Lopez 1999, 198.

her as a sort of female Nostradamus, who, far from merely predicting a distant future, worked actively and successfully for its fateful realisation.

The interesting thing is that, despite the harshness of the indictment, the prosecutor ends up displaying some unexpected resemblances to the unfortunate accused. Vattimo, in his attempt to rescue the hermeneutics of innocence though in a weaker version, links Nietzsche to Emerson, but Elisabeth, in her biography, had already said the philosopher 'particularly loved' the American writer.[17] Do not Colli and Montinari insist that Nietzsche had nothing to do with anti-Semitism and Judeophobia? This was exactly Elisabeth's standpoint. If the two editors, in their rendition of *Socrates and Tragedy*, confine the conclusion ('this Socratism is the Jewish press') to the critical apparatus or delete it altogether, the philosopher's scorned sister proceeded similarly. In her biography, she reported in detail on the lecture, but said nothing about its conclusion; she said Cosima and Richard Wagner reacted with both admiration and concern, but without specifying that this reaction was brought about by the explicit identification of Socratism and Judaism. Moreover, it is precisely Colli and Montinari that suggest, in the critical apparatus to the German edition, that it might not have been the author who tore out the final page, with its already familiar conclusion, from *Socrates and Tragedy*. And how could one explain by Elisabeth's intervention, if not by a desire to shield the philosopher from the accusation of anti-Semitism?

Elisabeth was the recipient of the letters in which the young Nietzsche gave free rein to his Judeophobia: he was glad 'finally' to have found an inn where one could enjoy a meal without having to endure the sight of 'Jewish ugly mugs', or, again with reference to the Jews, of 'disgusting soulless apes and other merchants'; he expressed his disgust at seeing 'Jews and cronies of Jews wherever one looks' at a performance of the *Afrikanerin* by Meyerbeer (the musician of Jewish origin mocked by Wagner). He even wrote to ask his sister: 'How can you expect from me that I order a book from a scandalous Jewish antiquarian?' Elisabeth took care not to trumpet these letters abroad, but rather extended a veil of silence over them: but does not the Colli-Montinari edition do the same? There is another interesting detail. After Wilamowitz had torn into the *Birth of Tragedy* in a review, Nietzsche denounced him as a 'youngster suffering from Jewish arrogance', while he mocked the coldness of his teacher or ex-teacher Ritschl, blaming it on his Alexandrian or 'Jewish-Roman' culture. The philologist-philosopher's circle of friends reacted similarly. Elisabeth responded more coolly in her biography, where she merely criticised the philologist's limited horizons. That the young Nietzsche's violent Judeophobia has remained so long in shadow is, ultimately, thanks to the curtain his loving sister drew over it.

---

17   Förster-Nietzsche 1885–1904, Vol. 2, 176.

Far from adapting her brothers thinking to the ideological demands of Nazism (and moreover decades in advance of it!), Elisabeth tended rather to soften or remove the most repugnant declarations. On the other hand, Nietzsche's esteemed disciple Brandes provided an interpretation that made Nietzsche a champion of the most radical and repugnant forms of eugenics (later adopted by the Nazis): 'The hygiene that keeps alive millions of weak and useless beings that should rather die is, for him, not true progress.' In reality, 'one must measure the greatness of a movement by the sacrifices it requires'. In the end, the same preoccupation inspires today's apologists as inspired Nietzsche's sister: one should erect a monument to him, although it goes without saying that a postmodern monument would have to look very different from one designed to suit the Wilhelmine age.

The sole toehold for the idea of a plot by Elisabeth is the homage paid her by Hitler 1934, while she was still alive, and a year later, after her death. But this evidence carries little weight. Clearly, Hitler's tribute was meant not for the widow of Bernhard Förster but for Nietzsche's sister. And not entirely without reason, at least according to Heidegger, who in 1936 observed: 'Mussolini and Hitler, the two men that brought in a counter-movement against nihilism, both learned from Nietzsche, though in essentially different ways.' It is true Elisabeth seems to like the obeisances: at last her brother had become a national monument! And yet there was no lack of reservations and even of a certain irony: after Hitler's visit to Weimar, Elisabeth noted he had given 'the impression of a person more significant religiously than politically'.[18] Heidegger was far less reserved in his enthusiasm: he was so fascinated by the Führer that he silenced Jaspers's doubts and timid objections by exclaiming: 'But look at his wonderful hands.'[19] So why blame a poor woman rather than one of the great interpreters for shattering the magic of the unpolitical interpretation of Nietzsche? The hermeneuts of innocence do not allow themselves to be impressed by such an objection and withdraw from the affair, while effortlessly dipping Heidegger too into a purifying bath that washes away all political debris.

5   The Conflict of the Faculties: Philosophers and Historians

To realise how unsustainable is the second myth (the one that makes not Elisabeth but Lukács the scapegoat), it is enough to carry out a simple intellectual experiment. Let us imagine a student who wants to study Nietzsche, and starts by visiting a department of philosophy. There, Kaufmann, Deleuze, Foucault, Bataille, Vattimo and Cacciari prac-

---

18   In Fest 1973, 458 f.
19   Jaspers 1984, 101.

tically rule the roost, all working in different ways to unmask Elisabeth's conspiracy and Lukács's ideological delirium. But should the student happen to cross over into a history classroom, he would encounter a completely different line of interpretation: eminent historians like Ritter, Hobsbawm, Elias, Mayer and Nolte all agree, though from quite different positions, on placing Nietzsche in the ranks of the anti-democratic reaction of the late nineteenth century, from which stems the movement that later led to fascism. In the philosophy classrooms, the hermeneutics of innocence are obligatory. On the other hand, Mayer says the following about Nietzsche's philosophy: 'In this sense the new *Weltanschauung* was anything but innocent.' And if you think the historian quoted here is too leftwing (his book is dedicated to Marcuse), you can turn to Nolte: as we have seen, for the representative of historical revisionism, Hitler was a sort of shy and awkward follower of Nietzsche!

Instead of getting exercised about Lukács, the hermeneuts of innocence would do better to choose the targets of their criticism with greater care. George Lichtheim also displayed the highest contempt for the Hungarian Marxist philosopher, but then declared that '[i]t is not too much to say that but for Nietzsche the SS – Hitler's shock troops and the core of the whole movement – would have lacked the inspiration to carry out their programmes of mass murder in Eastern Europe'. The thesis is mistaken. Nietzsche was certainly not thinking of the Slavs when he elaborated his theory of the 'annihilation of the decadent races', for at the end of the nineteenth century the Slavs were still considered an integral part of the 'civilised' world (this view was also Chamberlain's). On the other hand, establishing an immediate and exclusive relationship between this 'annihilation' and the Third Reich helps to embellish the colonial tradition and the liberal West, as if the extermination of the Native Americans or the aborigines of Australia and South Africa had not already taken place by the end of the nineteenth century!

Even so, a problem arises: why do the hermeneuts of innocence attack only Lukács and not the historians mentioned above or more recent and authoritative scholars of the Third Reich (e.g., Kershaw), who stress Nietzsche's strong influence on Hitler's ideological formation? Earlier, there was much debate and widespread unease about the big gap between the natural sciences and the humanities, and people criticised the lack of communication between them. Now, however, there seems to be a lack of communication even within the humanities, between philosophical and historical research, whereby the latter signifies in the eyes of the philosopher-priests of the Nietzsche cult the desecration of a sacred ritual.

6   The Suppressions of the 'New Right' and of the Postmodern Left

Thus, the traditional criticism of Lukács, that he repeated, albeit with a reversed value judgement, Baeumler's[20] picture of Nietzsche, turns out to be completely unsustainable. The charge ignores Heidegger of the 1930s on the one hand, and a whole range of contemporary historians on the other.

Nowadays, not only the postmodern left tends to suppress Nietzsche's most repugnant statements. So do the new rightists, whose efforts to gain a new respectability are seriously hampered by the demand for the 'annihilation of decadent races' and of 'millions of deformed'. This emerges with particular clarity from the recently published Italian translation of the book Alfred Baeumler, who two years later joined the Nazi party, dedicated to the philosopher in 1931. Here Nietzsche's *Zucht* and *Züchtung* are rendered as *addestramento*, '[military] training'. The term has military and warlike connotations and is thereby distinguished from the banal and philistine *educazione* ('education'), which the postmodern translators and interpreters like to use. However, neither *addestramento* nor *educazione* convey the eugenics programme of Nietzsche's 'new party of life', which aimed at encouraging the fertility of healthy couples while seeking to stop the malformed from getting married and even to 'castrate' or 'annihilate' them. This is why the 'new party of life', with an explicit reference to Galton, did not stop at recommending the 'education' or 'training' of the master race and the race of servants, but called for their 'breeding'. But Nietzsche's eugenicist ideas are a burden not only for the postmodern left, which would dearly love to see the back of them, but also for the new right, which seeks to define its anti-egalitarian programme in cultural rather than in naturalistic and biological terms, as in the past.

Similarly, *Übermensch* is no longer rendered in the recent Italian translation of Baeumler by the traditional *superuomo* but by *sovrauomo*.[21] In this case too, the similarity with Vattimo's *oltreuomo*, meant to convey the transcendence of the human being of tradition, is striking. In Zarathustra's speech, 'overman' refers to the 'super-species': and again, the shadow of eugenics looms into view. But in the background lurks an even more disturbing shadow, that projected by a central and particularly sinister category of Nazi ideological discourse, namely, the category of *Untermensch*, which can be separated from *Übermensch* only with great difficulty: the two terms constitute a single conceptual dichotomy. A journalist who had read Nietzsche or was at least superficially acquainted with his writings pointed to the great danger posed to culture by such an *Untermensch* (the mass of 'savages and barbarians', 'essentially incapable of culture and obstinately hostile to culture'). Referring to Nietzsche (also in terms of his language

---

20   Baeumler 1931a.
21   Baeumler 2003.

and sources), he polemicised against the 'fetish' or 'idol' of 'democracy', evoked a 'new aristocracy' or 'new nobility', and expressed his admiration for Theognis and his battle against mixed marriages between the nobility and the common people. Here not just eugenics but the *oltreuomo* of the postmodern left or the *sovrauomo* of the new right was invoked to perform a miracle and above all eliminate the *Untermensch*!

Surprising in this linguistic-ideological story is the fact that the author in question was not a German but a North American who had studied in Germany: Lothrop Stoddard was the first to coin the term 'Under Man' in 1922, in a book subtitled *The Menace of the Under-Man*. The book was immediately translated into German, and Under Man became *Untermensch*. Rosenberg passionately embraced the category and admitted taking it over from Stoddard, upon whom two American presidents, Harding and Hoover, also lavished praise. Evidently, the alternative to the hermeneutics of innocence does not take the form of drawing a straight line of continuity from Nietzsche to Hitler. The *Untermensch* of the North American ideologue referred, well before its application to the oriental and Asiatic Bolsheviks, to blacks and Native Americans, who in the years following the Civil War were the object of terrorist violence and genocide. Similar considerations apply to the other term in the conceptual dichotomy. At the beginning of the twentieth century an English poet, John Davidson, referred positively to the theory of the overman, but criticised it on account of its cosmopolitan character. According to Davidson, Nietzsche missed a fundamental truth: 'The Englishman is the overman and the history of England is the history of his development.' A different opinion was represented by the Italian writer Angelo Mosso, another eulogiser of imperialism, who was fascinated above all by the epic of the Far West: 'The Yankee is the *superuomo*.'[22]

So, to understand the repugnant aspects of Nietzsche's philosophy (the reverse side of his radical and fascinating project of emancipation, designated for a very small elite of the aristocratic caste and overmen), one must not only start from the end of the nineteenth century (rather than 1933), but one must also take into account the fact that this grim ideology of the turn of the century had spread not only across Germany but across the West as a whole, before being inherited and radicalided by the Nazis.

We thus return to the 'preoccupations' and the disquieting questions to which Gadamer had pointed: would it not make sense to take them up once again and discuss them from a new perspective, rather than give in to the compulsion to suppress them? Or will Nietzsche's spectacles and umbrella continue to make the running?

---

22   In Losurdo 1997c, 82.

Abbreviations Used in Citing Nietzsche's writings

In quotations from Nietzsche and other authors, italics are retained, removed or modified depending on the needs of the text. Nietzsche's works and correspondence are referred to directly in the text. Unless otherwise stated, the most widely used edition (including digital editions) is cited: *Sämtliche Werke* (Complete works), *Kritische Studienausgabe* (KSA) (Critical Studies Edition), edited by Giorgio Colli and Mazzino Montinari, 15 vols, Munich-Berlin 1980. The 15 vols are referenced with simple Roman numerals (I–XV). This abbreviation is followed where appropriate by a reference to the internal division of the text and, if necessary, the volume number and page of the cited edition. If further details are not given, the vol. and page number refer to the *Nachgelassene Fragmente* (Posthumous Fragments) or to variants subsequently dropped (KSA 14). The correspondence is based on *Briefwechsel. Kritische Gesamtausgabe* (Correspondence. Critical Complete Edition), edited by Giorgio Colli and Mazzino Montinari, Berlin-New York, 1975 ff. In the case of the correspondence, the letter B is followed by an indication of the volume, the semi-volume and the page reference.

Nietzsche quotations are either translated into English directly from the German, sometimes guided by Losurdo's Italian rendering, or follow existing published translations, sometimes slightly modified in the interests of consistency. In the case of borrowed translations, the translations used are indicated in the list immediately below. In the subsequent list of the original German sources, the translation used is indicated in abbreviated form. The number of the page from which the translation comes is indicated in square brackets in the citation in the text, following the reference to the original German work. In the case of the *Nachgelassene Fragmente*, quotations follow the translation in *Unpublished Writings from the Period of Unfashionable Observations*, Stanford 1999 (see list, below), where available: otherwise, they are translated directly from the German.

Nietzsche, *Beyond Good and Evil* (edited by Rolf-Peter Horstmann and Judith Norman), Cambridge: Cambridge University Press, 2002

Nietzsche, *Dawn, Thoughts on the Presumptions of Morality* (translated by Brittain Smith, Afterword by Keith Ansell-Pearson), Stanford: Stanford University Press, 2011

Nietzsche, *Human, All Too Human I / A Book For Free Spirits* (translated, with an Afterword, by Gary Handwerk), Stanford: Stanford University Press, 1997

Nietzsche, *Human, All Too Human II and Unpublished Fragments from the Period of Human, All Too Human II* (*Spring 1878–Fall 1879*) (translated, with an Afterword, by Gary Handwerk), Stanford: Stanford University Press, 2012

Nietzsche, *On the Genealogy of Morality* (edited by Keith Ansell-Pearson, translated by Carol Diethe), Cambridge: Cambridge University Press, 1997

Nietzsche, *The Antichrist, Ecce Homo, Twilight of the Idols and Other Writings* (edited by Aaron Ridley and Judith Norman), Cambridge: Cambridge University Press, 2005

Nietzsche, *The Birth of Tragedy and Other Writings* (edited by Raymond Geuss and Ronald Speirs), Cambridge: Cambridge University Press, 1999

Nietzsche, *The Dionysian World View*, https://archive.org/stream/Nietzsche-TheDionysianWorldView#page/no/mode/2up

Nietzsche, *The Gay Science* (edited by Bernard Williams, translated by Josefine Nauckhoff), Cambridge: Cambridge University Press, 2001

Nietzsche, *Thus Spoke Zarathustra* (edited by Adrian Del Caro and Robert B. Pippin), Cambridge: Cambridge University Press, 2006

Nietzsche, *Unfashionable Observations* (translated, with an Afterword, by Richard T. Gray), Stanford: Stanford University Press, 1995

Nietzsche, *Unpublished Writings from the Period of Unfashionable Observations* (translated, with an Afterword, by Richard T. Gray), Stanford: Stanford University Press, 1999

Nietzsche, *Writings from the Late Notebooks* (edited by Rudiger Bittner, translated by Kate Sturge), Cambridge: Cambridge University Press, 2003

I–XV	Samtliche Werke. *Kritische Studienausgabe* (KSA) (Critical Studies Edition), ed. by Giorgio Colli and Mazzino Montinari, Munich-Berlin: De Gruyter, 1980
A	*Autobiographisches aus den Jahren 1856 bis 1869* (Autobiographical from the years 1856 to 1869), in *Werke in drei Bänden*, edited by Karl Schlechta, Munich: Hanser, 1976, vol. 3
AC	*Der Antichrist*, finished end of 1888 (KSA 6). *The Antichrist, Ecce Homo, Twilight of the Idols and Other Writings*, Cambridge 2005.
B	*Briefwechsel. Kritische Gesamtausgabe* (Correspondence. Critical Complete Edition) edited by Giorgio Colli and Mazzino Montinari, Berlin-New York: De Gruyter, 1975 ff.
BA	*Ueber die Zukunft unserer Bildungsanstalten* (On the future of our educational institutions) 1872 (KSA 1)
CV	*Fünf Vorreden zu fünf ungeschriebenen Büchern* (Five prefaces for five unwritten books) Christmas 1872 (KSA 1)
CV 1	*Über das Pathos der Wahrheit* (On the pathos of truth)
CV 2	*Gedanken über die Zukunft unserer Bildungsanstalten* (Thoughts on the future of our educational institutions)
CV 3	*Der griechische Staat. The Greek State*, https://archive.org/details/NietzscheHomersContestTheGreekState
CV 4	*Das Verhältniss der Schopenhauerschen Philosophie zu einer deutschen Cultur* (The relationship of Schopenhaurian philosophy to a German culture)
CV 5	*Homer's Wettkampf* (Homer's contest)

DS   *David Strauss der Bekenner und der Schriftsteller* (David Strauss the confessor and the writer), *Unzeitgemässe Betrachtungen* I, 1873 (KSA 1). *Unfashionable Observations*, Stanford 1995

DTM   *Dissertatio de Theognide Megarensi*, 1864, in FS 3 *Schriften der Studenten- und Militärzeit*, 1935

DW   *Die dionysische Weltanschauung* (The Dionysian worldview) June–July 1870 (KSA 1). *The Dionysian World View.*

EH   *Ecce homo. Wie man wird, was man ist*, finished end of 1888 (KSA 6). *The Antichrist, Ecce Homo, Twilight of the Idols and Other Writings*, Cambridge 2005

FG   *Fatum und Geschichte. Gedanken* (Fate and history. Thoughts) 1862 (KGA 1/2)

FS   *Frühe Schriften* (Five writings) C.H. Beck, Munich, 1994 (photographic impression of *Werke und Briefe, Historisch-kritische Gesamtausgabe*, edited by Hans Joachim Mette and Karl Schlechta, Munich: Beck, 1933–40, interrupted after the first five vols)

FW   *Die fröhliche Wissenschaft*, 1882; Preface of 1887 (KSA 3). *The Gay Science*, Cambridge 2001

GD   *Götzendämmerung*, 1888 (KSA 6). *The Antichrist, Ecce Homo, Twilight of the Idols and Other Writings*, Cambridge 2005

GM   *Zur Genealogie der Moral*, 1887 (KSA 5). *On the Genealogy of Morality*, Cambridge 1997

GMD   *Das griechische Musikdrama* (Greek musical drama), lecture in Basel, 18 January 1870 (KSA 1)

GT   *Die Geburt der Tragödie*, 1872; the new edition of 1886 is prefaced by the *Versuch einer Selbstkritik* (KSA 1). *The Birth of Tragedy and Other Writings*, Cambridge 1999

HKP   *Homer und die klassische Philologie* (Homer and classical philology), Christmas 1869 (KGA 2/1)

HL   *Vom Nutzen und Nachtheil der Historie für das Leben* (On the utility and liability of history for life), *Unzeitgemässe Betrachtungen* II, 1874 (KSA 1). *Unfashionable Observations*, Stanford 1995

JGB   *Jenseits von Gut und Böse. Vorspiel einer Philosophie der Zukunft*, 1886 (KSA 5). *Beyond Good and Evil*, Cambridge 2002

KGA   *Kritische Gesamtausgabe* (Critical Complete Edition) edited by Giorgio Colli and Mazzino Montinari, Berlin-New York: De Gruyter, 1964 ff.

KZD   *Die kirchlichen Zustände der Deutschen in Nordamerika* (Religious conditions of the Germans in North America), 1865 (KGA 1/4)

M   *Morgenröthe. Gedanken über die moralischen Vorurtheile*, 1881; Preface of 1887 (KSA 3). *Dawn, Thoughts on the Presumptions of Morality*, Stanford 2011

MA   *Menschliches, Allzumenschliches. Ein Buch für freie Geister*, 1878; Preface of 1886 (KSA 2). *Human, All Too Human I*, Stanford 1997

MD   *Mahnruf an die Deutschen* (Appeal to the Germans), 1873 (KSA 1)

NW   *Nietzsche contra Wagner. Aktenstücke eines Psychologen* (Nietzsche against Wagner. Processual documents of a psychologist), finished end of 1888 (KSA 6)

Opere *Opere di Friedrich Nietzsche,* edited by Giorgio Colli and Mazzino Montinari, Milano: Adelphi, 1964 ff. (Italian edition of KGA)

PHG   *Die Philosophie im tragischen Zeitalter der Griechen* (Philosophy in the tragic age of the Greeks) 1873 (KSA 1)

SE   *Schopenhauer als Erzieher* (Schopenhauer as educator), *Unzeitgemässe Betrachtungen* III, 1874 (KSA 1). *Unfashionable Observations,* Stanford 1995

SGT   *Sokrates und die griechische Tragödie* (Socrates and Greek tragedy), 1871 (KSA 1)

ST   *Sokrates und die Tragödie* (Socrates and tragedy), lecture in Basel, 1 February 1870 (KSA 1)

VM   *Vermischte Meinungen und Sprüche,* (Mixed opinions and maxims), 1879 (KSA 2). *Human, All Too Human II,* Stanford 2012

WB   *Richard Wagner in Bayreuth* (Richard Wagner in Bayreuth), *Unzeitgemässe Betrachtungen* IV, 1876 (KSA 1). *Unfashionable Observations,* Stanford 1995

WL   *Über Wahrheit und Lüge im aussermoralischen Sinne* (On truth and lie in the extra-moral sense), 1873 (KSA 1)

WS   *Der Wanderer und sein Schatten* (The wanderer and his shadow), 1880; in the edition of 1886, *Menschliches, Allzumenschliches,* VM and WS form the second part, which also has a Preface (KSA 2). *Human, All Too Human II,* Stanford 2012

WA   *Der Fall Wagner* (The case of Wagner), 1888 (KSA 6)

WzM   *Der Wille zur Macht* (The will to power), 1901; second extended edition 1906

Za   *Also sprach Zarathustra,* 1883–1885 (KSA 4). *Thus Spoke Zarathustra,* Cambridge 2006

Bibliography

Allard, Paul 1974, *Les esclaves chrétiens depuis les premiers temps de l'Église jusqu'à la fin de la domination romaine en Occident* (1876), photocopy of the fifth completely revised edition, 1914, Hildesheim-New York: Olms

Altman, William 2014, *Friedrich Wilhelm Nietzsche: The Philosopher of the Second Reich*, Maryland: Lexington Books

Appel, Fredrick 1999, *Nietzsche Contra Democracy*, Cornell: Cornell University Press

Andler, Charles 1958, *Nietzsche. Sa vie et sa pensée* (1920–31), Paris: Gallimard

Andreas-Salomé, Lou 1970, 'Tagebuch für Paul Rée', in *Friedrich Nietzsche, Paul Rée, Lou von Salomé. Die Dokumente ihrer Begegnung*, ed. Ernst Pfeiffer, Frankfurt/M.: Insel

Andreas-Salomé, Lou 1983, *Friedrich Nietzsche in seinen Werken*, ed. Ernst Pfeiffer, Frankfurt/M.: Insel

Appiah, Kwame Anthony 1992, *In My Father's House. Africa in the Philosophy of Culture*, New York-Oxford: Oxford University Press

Arendt, Hannah 1945, 'Organized Guilt and Universal Responsibility', *Jewish Frontier*, January 1945: 19–23

Arendt, Hannah 1959, *Rahel Varnhagen. Lebensgeschichte einer deutschen Jüdin aus der Romantik*, Munich: Piper

Arendt, Hannah 1966, *The Origins of Totalitarianism* (first edn 1951), New York: Harcourt, Brace and World

Arendt, Hannah 1981, *On Revolution* (1963), New York: Viking Press

Aristotle 2002, *Nicomachean Ethics*, translated by Joe Sachs, Focus Philosophical Library, Pullins Press

Aristotle (English) 2013, *Aristotles's Politics*, translated by Carnes Lord, Chicago: University of Chicago Press.

Arndt, Ernst Moritz 1963, 'Der Rhein. Deutschlands Strom, aber nicht Deutschlands Grenze' (1813), in *Dokumente zur deutschen Politik 1808–1870*, ed. Harry Pross, Frankfurt/M.: Fischer

Arnim, Ludwig Achim von 1978, 'Von Volksliedern' (1805), in *Deutsche Literaturkritik*, ed. Hans Mayer, Frankfurt/M.: Fischer

ASC = *Antisemitische Correspondenz und Sprechsaal für innere Partei-Angelegenheiten*, Leipzig, 1885 ff. (cited as ASC, followed by number and page)

Aschheim, Steven E. 1997, 'Nietzsche, Anti-Semitism and the Holocaust', in Jacob Golomb (ed.), *Nietzsche and Jewish Culture*, London-New York: Routledge

Aulard, Alphonse 1977, *Histoire politique de la Révolution française* (1926), photocopy, Aalen: Scientia

Baader, Benedikt Franz Xavier von 1963, 'Über Katholicismus und Protestantismus'

(1824), in *Sämtliche Werke*, ed. Franz Hoffmann, Julius Hamberger et al. (Leipzig 1851–60), vol. I, photocopy, Aalen: Scientia

Babeuf, Francois Noel 1988, *Écrits*, ed. Claude Mazauric, Paris: Messidor/Éditions sociales

Baczko, Bronislaw 1989, *Comment sortir de la Terreur. Thérmidor et la Révolution*, Paris: Gallimard

Baeumler, Alfred 1931a, *Nietzsche, der Philosoph und Politiker*, Leipzig: Reclam

Baeumler, Alfred 1931b (ed.), *Friedrich Nietzsche. Die Unschuld des Werdens*, Leipzig: Kröner

Baeumler, Alfred 1937a, 'Nietzsche' (1930), in Baeumler, *Studien zur deutschen Geistesgeschichte*, Berlin: Junker and Dünnhaupt

Baeumler, Alfred 1937b, 'Nietzsche und der Nationalsozialismus' (1934), in Baeumler, *Studien zur deutschen Geistesgeschichte* [cf. Baeumler 1937a]

Baeumler, Alfred 1937c, 'Hellas und Germanien' (1937), in Baeumler, *Studien zur deutschen Geistesgeschichte* [cf. Baeumler 1937a]

Bagehot, Walter 1974a, 'The English Constitution. Introduction to Second Edition' (1872), in *Collected Works*, vol. 5, ed. Norman St John-Stevas, London: The Economist

Bagehot, Walter 1974b, 'The English Constitution' (1867; second edn 1872), in *Collected Works* [cf. Bagehot 1974a], vol. 5

Bagehot, Walter 1974c, 'The Destruction in Paris of What the World Goes to See at Paris' (1871), in *Collected Works* [cf. Bagehot 1974a], vol. 8

Bairati, Piero 1975 (ed.), *I profeti dell'impero americano. Dal periodo coloniale ai nostri giorni*, Turin: Einaudi

Baldensperger, Fernand 1968, *Le mouvement des idées dans l'émigration française* (1924), New York: Burt Franklin

Baldwin, Neil 2001, *Henry Ford and the Jews. The Mass Production of Hate*, New York: Public Affairs

Balfour, Michael 1964, *The Kaiser and His Times*, London: The Cresset Press

Bamberger, Ludwig 1965, 'Deutschthum und Judenthum' (1880), in Boehlich 1965

Barie, Ottavio 1953, *Idee e dottrine imperialistiche nell'Inghilterra vittoriana*, Bari: Laterza

Barthes, Roland 1975, *Michelet*, Paris: Seuil

Bastid, Paul 1939 (ed.), *Les discours de Sieyès dans les débats constitutionnels de l'an III*, Paris: Hachette

Bataille, Georges 1973, 'Nietzsche et le national-socialisme' (1944), in *Oeuvres complètes*, vol. 6, second half-vol., Paris: Gallimard

Baumgarten, Hermann 1974, *Der deutsche Liberalismus. Eine Selbstkritik* (1866), ed. Adolf M. Birke, Frankfurt/M.-Berlin-Vienna: Ullstein

Baxa, Jakob 1966 (ed.), *Adam Müllers Lebenszeugnisse*, Munich-Paderborn-Vienna: Schöningh

Bebel, August 1964, *Die Frau und der Sozialismus* (1883), 60th edn, Berlin: Dietz

Bebel, August 1995, 'Sozialdemokratie und Antisemitismus' (1893), in *Ausgewählte Reden und Schriften*, vol. 3, ed. Gustav Seeber, Munich-New Providence-London-Paris: K.G. Saur

Becker, August 1844, *Was wollen die Kommunisten? Eine Rede*, Lausanne: Kommunisten Verein

Beiner, Ronald 2018, *Dangerous Minds: Nietzsche, Heidegger, and the Return of the Far Right*, Philadelphia: University of Pennsylvania Press.

Bensen, Heinrich Wilhelm 1965, 'Die Proletarier. Eine historische Denkschrift', Stuttgart 1847, reprinted in Carl Jantke and Dietrich Hilger (eds.), *Die Eigentumslosen. Der deutsche Pauperismus und die Emanzipationskrise in Darstellungen und Deutungen der zeitgenössischen Literatur*, Freiburg-Munich: Alber

Bentham, Jeremy 1838–43, *The Works*, ed. John Bowring, Edinburgh: Tait

Benveniste, Émile 1969, *Le vocabulaire des institutions indo-européennes*, Paris: Éditions de Minuit

Berlin, Isaiah 1984, *Russian Thinkers* (1948 ff.), London: Penguin Books

Bernoulli, Carl Albrecht 1908, *Franz Overbeck und Friedrich Nietzsche. Eine Freundschaft*, Jena: Diederichs

Bertram, Ernst 1919, *Nietzsche. Versuch einer Mythologie*, Berlin Georg Bondi

Bismarck, Otto von 1919, *Gedanken und Erinnerungen* (1898), Stuttgart-Berlin: Cotta

Bismarck, Otto von (n. d).: *Gespräche* (1924–26), ed. Willy Andreas, with K.F. Reinking, Birsfelden-Basel: Schibli–Doppler

Blackburn, Robin 1990, *The Overthrow of Colonial Slavery 1776–1848* (1988), London-New York: Verso

Blanqui, Auguste 1973, L'éternité par les astres. Hypothèse astronomique (1872), in *Instructions pour une prise d'armes, L'éternité par les astres. Hypothèse astronomique et autres textes*, ed. Miguel Abensour and Valentin Pelosse, Paris: Éditions de la Tête de Feuilles

Bloch, Ernst 1962, *Erbschaft dieser Zeit*, Frankfurt/M.: Suhrkamp

Bloch, Ernst 1973, *Das Prinzip Hoffnung* (1938–1947), Frankfurt/M.: Suhrkamp

Bodelsen, Carl A. 1968, *Studies in Mid-Victorian Imperialism* (1924), New York: Howard Fertig

Boehlich, Walter 1965 (ed.), *Der Berliner Antisemitismusstreit*, Frankfurt/M.: Insel

Bohm, Franz 1938, *Anti-Cartesianismus. Deutsche Philosophie im Widerstand*, Leipzig: Meiner

Bolt, Christine, and Seymour Drescher 1980, 'Introduction', in Christine Bolt and Seymour Drescher (eds.), *Anti-Slavery, Religion and Reform*, Kent, Connecticut (USA): Dawson-Archon

Bosc, Yannick 2000, *Le conflit des libertés. Thomas Paine et le débat sur la Déclaration et la Constitution de l'an III*, Dissertation, Université Aix–Marseille I

Boulainvilliers, Comte de 1727, *Histoire de l'ancien gouvernement de la France*, The Hague-Amsterdam: Aux dépends de la Compagnie

Bourne, Henry Richard Fox 1969, *The Life of John Locke* (1876), photocopy, Aalen: Scientia

Bowen, David Warren 1990, *Andrew Johnson and the Negro*, Knoxville: The University of Tennessee Press

Bowman, Shearer Davis 1993, *Masters and Lords. Mid-19th Century US Planters and Prussian Junkers*, New York-Oxford: Oxford University Press

Bracher, Karl Dietrich 1982, *Zeit der Ideologien. Eine Geschichte politischen Denkens im 20. Jahrhundert*, Berlin: Deutsche Verlags-Anstalt

Bracher, Karl Dietrich 1999, 'Zeit der Ideologien. Ende oder Dauer? Erfahrungen aus dem Jahrhundert der Totalitarismen', in *Macht und Zeitkritik: Festschrift für Hans-Peter Schwarz zum 65. Geburtstag*, ed. Peter R. Weilemann, Hanns Jürgen Kusters, Günter Buchstab, Paderborn-Munich-Vienna-Zurich: Schöningh

Brandes, George 2004, *Nietzsche. Eine Abhandlung über aristokratischen Radikalismus* [Danish 1899], Berlin: Berenberg

Bravo, Gian Mario 1973 (ed.), *Il socialismo prima di Marx. Antologia di scritti di riformatori, socialisti, utopisti, comunisti e rivoluzionari premarxisti*, Rome: Editori Riuniti

Bravo, Gian Mario 1976, *Storia del socialismo 1789–1848. Il pensiero socialista prima di Marx* (1971), Rome: Editori Riuniti

Brennan, Timothy 2004, *Borrowed Light: Vico, Hegel, and the Colonies*, Stanford: Stanford University Press.

Brie, Friedrich 1928, *Imperialistische Strömungen in der englischen Literatur* (1916), second revised edn, Halle/Saale: Niemeyer

Brinton, Crane 1953, *The Anatomy of Revolution*, London: Jonathan Cape

Brobjer, Thomas J. 2008, *Nietzsche's Philosophical Context: An Intellectual Biography*, Illinois: University of Illinois

Broszat, Martin 1952, *Die antisemitische Bewegung im Wilhelminischen Deutschland*, Dissertation, University of Cologne

Bucholtz, Franz Ritter von 1967, 'Über Stolbergs letzte Schriften', in *Concordia* (1823), ed. Ernst Behler, photocopy, Darmstadt: Wissenschaftliche Buchgesellschaft

Buhr, Manfred 1991, 'Die Philosophie Johann Gottlieb Fichtes und die Französiche Revolution', in Manfred Buhr and Domenico Losurdo, *Fichte, die Französische Revolution und das Ideal vom ewigen Frieden*, Berlin: Akademie Verlag

Bull, Malcolm 2014, *Anti-Nietzsche*, London: Verso

Burckhardt, Jacob 1978a, 'Weltgeschichtliche Betrachtungen', ed. Jacob Oeri, in *Gesammelte Werke*, vol. 4, Basel-Stuttgart: Schwabe

Burckhardt, Jacob 1978b, 'Historische Fragmente aus dem Nachlass', in *Gesammelte Werke* [cf. Burckhardt 1978a]

Burke, Edmund 1826, *The Works. A New Edition*, London: Rivington

Burleigh, Michael, and Wolfgang Wippermann 1991, *The Racial State. Germany 1933–1945*, Cambridge: Cambridge University Press

Calhoun, John C. 1992, *Union and Liberty: The Political Philosophy of John C. Calhoun*, ed. Ross M. Lence, Indianapolis: Liberty Classics

Campioni, Giuliano 1992, *Leggere Nietzsche. Alle origini dell'edizione critica Colli-Montinari*, Pisa: ETS

Campioni, Giuliano 2002, 'Il frammento scomparso', *La* Repubblica, 1 October: 43

Cancik, Hubert 1997, '"Mongols, Semites, and the Pure-Bred Greeks". Nietzsche's Handling of the Racial Doctrines of His Time', in Jacob Golomb [cf. Aschheim 1997]

Canfora, Luciano 1980, *Ideologie del classicismo*, Turin: Einaudi

Canfora, Luciano 1986, *Storia della letteratura greca*, Rome-Bari: Laterza

Cannadine, David 1990, *The Decline and Fall of the British Aristocracy*, New Haven: Yale University Press

Caprivi, Graf Georg Leo 1894, 'Rede in der Reichstagssitzung vom 30. November 1893', in *Stenographische Berichte über die Verhandlungen des Reichstags*, vol. 153, IXth Legislative period, IInd Session 1893/94, Berlin

Carducci, Giosue 1964, 'Giambi ed epodi' (1867–79), in *Tutte le poesie*, ed. Luigi Banfi, vol. 2, Milan: BUR

Carlyle, Thomas 1983, *Latter-Day Pamphlets* (1850), ed. Michael K. Goldberg and Jules Seigel, Ottawa: Canadian Federation for the Humanities

Carlyle, Thomas 1934, 'On Heroes, Hero-Worship, and the Heroic in History' (1841), in Seigel, *Sartor Resartus, On Heroes, Hero Worship*, London: Dent and Sons

Carus, Carl Gustav 1849, *Über ungleiche Befähigung der verschiedenen Menschheitsstämme für höhere geistige Entwicklung*, Leipzig: Brockhaus

Cassagnac, Adolphe Granier de 1977, *Histoire des classes ouvrières et des classes bourgeoisies* (1838), German translation: *Geschichte der arbeitenden und der bürgerlichen Classen* (1839), photocopy, Hildesheim-New York: Olms

Cassirer, Ernst 1946, *The Myth of the State*, New Haven: Yale University Press

Cavour, Camillo Benso conte di 1970, 'Des idées communistes et des moyens d'en combattre le développement' (1845), in Gastone Manacorda (ed.), *Il socialismo nella storia d'Italia*, Bari: Laterza

Cecil, Lamar 1989, *Wilhelm II*, Chapel Hill: University of North Carolina Press

Celsus, in Origen 1953, *Contra Celsum*, translated by Henry Chadwick, Cambridge: Cambridge University Press

Césaire, Aimé 1961, *Toussaint Louverture. La révolution française et le problème colonial*, Paris: Présence Africaine

Chabod, Federico 1989, *Storia dell'idea d'Europa*, ed. Ernesto Sestan and Armando Saitta, Rome-Bari: Laterza

Chamberlain, Houston S. 1914, *Kriegsaufsätze*, Munich: Bruckmann

Chamberlain, Houston S. 1937, *Die Grundlagen des neunzehnten Jahrhunderts. Ungekürzte Volksausgabe* (1898), Munich: Bruckmann

Chateaubriand, Francois-Réneé 1973, *Mémoires d'outre-tombe* (1849), ed. Pierre Clarac, Paris: Le Livre de Poche

Chateaubriand, Francois-Réneé 1978, *Essai historique sur les révolutions anciennes et modernes, considérées dans leurs rapports avec la Révolution Française* (1797), ed. Maurice Regard, Paris: Gallimard

Chesneaux, Jean, and Marianne Bastid 1969 (ed.), *Histoire de la Chine*, vol. 1: *Des guerres de l'opium à la guerre franco-chinoise 1840–1885*, Paris: Hatier Université

Claussen, Detlev 1987, *Vom Judenhass zum Antisemitismus, Materialien einer verleugneten Geschichte*, Darmstadt-Neuwied: Luchterhand

Cloots, Anacharsis 1980, *Oeuvres*, ed. Albert Soboul, Munich: Kraus Reprint

Cobb, Thomas R.R. 1858, *An Inquiry into the Law of Negro Slavery*, Philadelphia: T. & J.W. Johnson & Co.

Cobet, Christoph 1973, *Der Wortschatz des Antisemitismus in der Bismarckzeit*, Munich: Fink

Cochin, Augustin 1978, *Les sociétés de pensée et la démocratie moderne. Études d'histoire révolutionnaire* (1921), Paris: Copernic

Cochin, Augustin 1979, *La révolution et la libre pensée* (1924), Paris: Copernic

Colajanni, Napoleone 1906, *Latini e Anglo-Sassoni (Razze inferiori e razze superiori)*, second edn, Rome-Naples: Rivista Popolare

Colletti, Lucio 1969, *Ideologia e società*, Bari: Laterza

Comte, Auguste 1969, *Cours de philosophie positive* (1839), vol. 4, photocopy, Brussels: Culture et Civilisation

Comte, Auguste 1985, 'Discours préliminaire sur l'esprit positif' (1844) in Comte, *Traité philosophique d'astronomie populaire*, Paris: Fayard

Conrad, Joseph 1989, *Heart of Darkness* (1899), London: Penguin Books

Conrad-Martius, Hedwig 1955, *Utopien der Menschenzüchtung. Der Sozialdarwinismus und seine Folgen*, Munich: Kösel

Constant, Benjamin 1957, *Oeuvres*, ed. Alfred Roulin, Paris: Gallimard

Constant, Benjamin 1988, *De la force du gouvernement actuel de la France et de la nécessité de s'y rallier* (1796), Paris: Flammarion

Croce, Benedetto 1959, 'Lo Hölderlin e i suoi critici' (1943), in Croce, *Discorsi di varia filosofia*, vol. 1, Bari: Laterza

Croce, Benedetto 1965, *Storia d'Europa nel secolo decimonono* (1932), Bari: Laterza

Cronholm, Anna Christie 1958, *Die nordamerikanische Sklavenfrage im deutschen Schrifttum des 19. Jahrhunderts*, Berlin: Freie Universität

Crummel, Alexander 1897, 'The Attitude of the American Mind toward the Negro Intellect', address as president of the American Negro Academy, 1897, quoted in Henry Louis Gates Jr., *Loose Canons: Notes in the Culture Wars* (New York: Oxford University Press, 1992), 72–73 in Nussbaum, Martha C. (1997), *Cultivating Humanity. A Classical Defense of Reform in Liberal Education*, Cambridge, MA, Harvard University Press, p. 155

Daniels, Roger 1997, *Not Like Us. Immigrants and Minorities in America, 1890–1924*, Chicago: Dee

Darwin, Charles 1984, 'The Descent of Man' (1871), in Robert Maynard Hutchins (ed).,
  Great Books of the Western World, vol. 49: *Darwin* (1952), Chicago-London: Encyclopaedia Britannica

Davis, David Brion 1966, *The Problem of Slavery in Western Culture*, Ithaca: Cornell University Press

De Felice, Renzo 1981, *Mussolini il duce. II. Lo Stato totalitario 1936–1940*, Turin: Einaudi

Deleuze, Gilles 1962, *Nietzsche et la philosophie*, Paris: PUF

Derrida, Jacques 1978, *Éperons. Les styles de Nietzsche* (quadrilingual edn), Venice:
  Corbo e Fiore

Derrida, Jacques 1986, 'Interpreting Signatures (Nietzsche/Heidegger): Two Questions',
  Philosophy and Literature, 10, 2: October

Detwiler, Bruce 1990, *Nietzsche and the Politics of Aristocratic Radicalism*, Chicago: University of Chicago Press

Deussen, Paul 1901, *Erinnerungen an Friedrich Nietzsche*, Leipzig: Brockhaus

Diderot, Denis 1994, 'Réfutation suivie de l' ouvrage d' Helvétius intitulé "L' homme"', in
  Oeuvres, ed. Laurent Versini, vol. 1, Paris: Laffont

Digeon, Claude 1959, *La crise allemande de la pensée française (1870–1914)*, Paris: PUF

Dilthey, Wilhelm 1914–36, 'Die Reorganisation des preussischen Staats. III. Wilhelm von
  Humboldt' (1872), in *Gesammelte Schriften*, vol. 12, Leipzig-Berlin: Teubner

Disraeli, Benjamin 1982, *Coningsby or the New Generation* (1844), ed. Sheila M. Smith,
  Oxford: Oxford University Press

Dombowsky, Don 2004, *Nietzsche's Machiavellian Politics*, London: Palgrave

Donoso Cortés, Juan 1946a, 'Los sucesos de Roma' (30 November 1848), in *Obras Completas*, ed. Don Juan Juretschke, vol. 2, Madrid: La Editorial Católica

Donoso Cortés, Juan 1946b, 'Discurso sobre la dictadura' (4 January 1849), in *Obras Completas* [cf. Donoso Cortés 1946a], vol. 2

Donoso Cortés, Juan 1946c, 'Letter to Montalembert of 4 June 1849', in *Obras Completas*
  [cf. Donoso Cortés 1946a], vol. 2

Donoso Cortés, Juan 1946d, 'Letter to Director of "Heraldo" of 15 April 1852', in *Obras
  Completas* [cf. Donoso Cortés 1946a], vol. 2

Donoso Cortés, Juan 1946e, 'Ensayo sobre el catolicismo, el liberalismo y el socialismo'
  (1851), in *Obras Completas*, [cf. Donoso Cortés 1946a], vol. 2

Donoso Cortés, Juan 1874, *Essays on Catholicism, Liberalism and Socialism*, translated
  by W. McDonald, Dublin: William B. Kelly

Dostoyevsky, Fyodor 1994, *Demons*, translated by Pevear and Volokhonsky, London:
  Everyman

Drochon, Hugo 2018, *Nietzsche's Great Politics*, Princeton: Princeton University Press

Duboc, Julius 1896, *Jenseits vom Wirklichen. Eine Studie aus der Gegenwart*, Dresden:
  Henkler

Dühring, Eugen 1871, *Kritische Geschichte der Nationalökonomie und des Sozialismus*, Berlin: Grieben

Dühring, Eugen 1873, *Cursus der National- und Socialökonomie einschliesslich der Hauptpunkte der Finanzpolitik*, Berlin: Grieben

Dühring, Eugen 1875, *Cursus der Philosophie als streng wissenschaftlicher Weltanschauung und Lebensgestaltung*, Leipzig: Koschny (Heimann's Verlag)

Dühring, Eugen 1881a, *Der Werth des Lebens populär dargestellt* (1865), third edn, Leipzig: Fue's Verlag (Reisland)

Dühring, Eugen 1881b, *Die Judenfrage als Racen-, Sitten- und Culturfrage*, Leipzig: Reuther

Dühring, Eugen 1897, *Der Ersatz der Religion durch Vollkommneres und die Ausscheidung alles Judäerthums durch den modernen Völkergeist* (1882), second revised edn, Berlin: Kufahl

Duncan, David 1996 (ed.), *The Life and Letters of Herbert Spencer* (1908), London: Routledge/Thoemmes Press

Duttenhofer, A. 1855, *Über die Emanzipation der Neger. Ein Versuch zur Aufstellung humaner Principien in dieser Frage*, Nördlingen: Beck'sche Buchhandlung

Eckermann, Johann Peter 1981, *Gespräche mit Goethe in den letzten Jahren seines Lebens* (1835), ed. Fritz Bergemann, Frankfurt/M.: Insel

Eldridge, Colin C. 1973, *England's Mission. The Imperial Idea in the Age of Gladstone and Disraeli 1868–1880*, Chapel Hill: University of North Carolina Press

Elias, Norbert 1989, *Studien über die Deutschen. Machtkämpfe und Habitusentwicklung im 19. und 20. Jahrhundert*, ed. Michael Schroter, Frankfurt/M.: Suhrkamp

Emerson, Ralph Waldo 1983a, 'Representative Men' (1850), in *Essays and Lectures*, ed. Joel Porte, New York: The Library of America

Emerson, Ralph Waldo 1983b, 'The Conduct of Life' (1860), in *Essays and Lectures* [cf. Emerson 1983a]

Epstein, Klaus 1966, *The Genesis of German Conservatism*, Princeton: Princeton University Press

Evola, Julius 1964, *Il fascismo. Saggio di una analisi critica dal punto di vista della Destra*, Rome: Volpe

Evola, Julius 1978, *Imperialismo pagano* (1928), Padua: Edizioni di Ar

Evola, Julius 1984, *Rivolta contro il mondo moderno* (1934), Rome: Edizioni Mediterranee

Evola, Julius 1995a, *Il mito del sangue* (1937; 1942, second revised edn), Borzano: SeaR

Evola, Julius 1995b, *Lo Stato* (1934–43), ed. Gian Franco Lami, Rome: Fondazione Julius Evola

Eyck, Erich 1976, *Bismarck und das Deutsche Reich*, third edn, Munich: Heyne

Faulhaber, Michael (Kardinal) 1934, *Judentum, Christentum, Germanentum*, Munich: Huber

Fenske, Hans 1977 (ed.), *Der Weg zur Reichsgründung 1850–1870*, Darmstadt: Wissenschaftliche Buchgesellschaft

Fenske, Hans 1978 (ed.), *Im Bismarckschen Reich*, Darmstadt: Wissenschaftliche Buchgesellschaft

Ferguson, Adam 1966, *An Essay on the History of Civil Society* (1767), Edinburgh: Edinburgh University Press

Ferrari Zumbini, Massimo 2001, *Le radici del male. L'antisemitismo in Germania: Da Bismarck a Hitler*, Bologna: Il Mulino

Ferraris, Maurizio 1995, 'Storia della "Volontà di Potenza"', in Friedrich Nietzsche, *La volontà di potenza*, new Italian edn, ed. Maurizio Ferraris and Pietro Kobau (1992), Milan: Bompiani

Ferry, Luc, and Alain Renaut 1985, *La pensée 68. Essai sur l'anti-humanisme contemporain*, Paris: Gallimard

Fest, Joachim C. 1973, *Hitler. Eine Biographie*, Frankfurt/M.-Berlin-Vienna: Ullstein

Feuerbach, Ludwig 1966, 'Grundsätze der Philosophie der Zukunft' (1843), in *Kleine Schriften*, ed. Karl Lowith, Frankfurt/M.: Suhrkamp

Feuerbach, Ludwig 1967, 'Die Naturwissenschaft und die Revolution' (1850), in *Anthropologischer Materialismus. Ausgewählte Schriften*, ed. Alfred Schmidt, vol. 2, Frankfurt/M.-Vienna: Europäische Verlagsanstalt

Fichte, Johann G. 1967, *Briefwechsel*, ed. Hans Schulz (Leipzig 1930), photocopy, Hildesheim: Olms

Fichte, Johann G. 1971, *Werke* (1845), ed. Immanuel Hermann Fichte, Berlin: De Gruyter

Figes, Orlando 1996, *A People's Tragedy. The Russian Revolution 1891–1924*, London: Jonathan Cape

Fink, Arthur E. 1962, *Causes of Crime. Biological Theories in the United States 1800–1915* (1938), New York: Perpetua

Fink, Eugen 1993, *Nietzsches Philosophie* (1960), third revised edn, Stuttgart-Berlin-Cologne-Mainz: Kohlhammer

Fischer, Kuno 1911, *Geschichte der neueren Philosophie*, vol. 8/1: *Hegel's Leben, Werke und Lehre*, second edn, Heidelberg: Carl Winter's Universitätsbuchhandlung

Fitzhugh, George 1854, *Sociology for the South or The Failure of Free Society*, Richmond: Morris

Fitzhugh, George 1960, *Cannibals All! or Slaves Without Masters* (1856), ed. and with an introduction by C. Wann Woodward, Cambridge, MA: The Belknap Press of Harvard University Press

Flaubert, Gustave 1912, *Correspondence*, vol. 3, Paris: Fasquelle

Fleischmann, Eugene 1970, *Le Christianisme 'mis à nu'*, Paris: Plon

Fogel, Robert William 1991, *Without Consent or Contract. The Rise and Fall of American Slavery* (1989), New York: Norton

Forster-Nietzsche, Elisabeth 1895–1904, *Das Leben Friedrich Nietzsche's*, Leipzig: Naumann

Foucault, Michel 1967, 'Nietzsche, Freud, Marx', in *Nietzsche, Cahiers de Royaumont, Philosophie*, Nr. 6, Paris: Éditions de Minuit

Foucault, Michel 1977, *Power/Knowledge: Selected Interviews and Other Writings, 1972–1977*, Sussex: Harvester Press

Frankel, Jonathan 1981, *Prophecy and Politics. Socialism, Nationalism and the Russian Jews, 1862–1917*, Cambridge: Cambridge University Press

Frantz, Konstantin 1881, 'Zur Philosophie des Militarismus', *Bayreuther Blätter*, March: 66–70

Frantz, Konstantin 1970, *Die Religion des Nationalliberalismus* (1872), photocopy, Aalen: Scientia

Fréderic II Roi de Prusse 1791, *Oeuvres posthumes*, vol. xx: *Correspondance de Monsieur D'Alembert avec Fréderic II Roi de Prusse*, Berlin: Chez Voss et fils

Fredrickson, George M. 1995, *Black Liberation. A Comparative History of Black Ideologies in the United States and South Africa*, Oxford: Oxford University Press

Freud, Sigmund 1964, *Moses and Monotheism* (1939), translated by James Strachey, London: Hogarth Press

Frigessi, Delia 1995, 'La scienza della devianza', in Lombroso 1995

Fritsch, Theodor 1893, *Antisemiten-Katechismus. Eine Zusammenstellung des wichtigsten Materials zum Verständniss der Judenfrage*, 25th extended edn (first edn 1887, under pseudonym Thomas Frey), Leipzig: Beyer

Fritsch, Theodor 1911, *Mein Beweis-Material gegen Jahvé*, second edn, Leipzig: Hammer

Fritsch, Theodor 1943, *Handbuch der Judenfrage. Die wichtigsten Tatsachen zur Beurteilung des jüdischen Volkes* (revised edn by Fritsch 1893, practically a new book), 48th edn, Leipzig: Hammer

Fuchs, Dieter 1998, '*Der Wille zur Macht*: Die Geburt des "Hauptwerkes" aus dem Geiste des Nietzsche-Archivs', *Nietzsche-Studien*, 26: 384–401

Gadamer, Hans-Georg 1986, 'Das Drama Zarathustras', *Nietzsche-Studien*, 15: 1–15

Gager, John G. 1985, *The Origins of Anti-Semitism. Attitudes Toward Judaism in Pagan and Christian Antiquity*, Oxford: Oxford University Press

Gall, Lothar 1980, *Bismarck. Der weisse Revolutionär*, Frankfurt/M.-Berlin-Vienna: Propyläen

Galton, Francis 1869, *Hereditary Genius. An Inquiry into its Laws and Consequences*, London: Macmillan

Galton, Francis 1874, *English Men of Science: Their Nature and Nurture*, London: Macmillan

Galton, Francis 1907, *Probability, the Foundation of Eugenics*, Oxford: Frowde

Gandhi, Mohandas K. 1969–2001, 'An Autobiography or The Story of My Experiments with Truth' (1925), in *The Collected Works of Mahatma Gandhi* (new edn in 100 vols), vol. 44, New Delhi: Government of India, Ministry of Information and Broadcasting, Publications Division

Gay, Peter 1965, *Voltaire's Politics. The Poet as Realist*, New York: Vintage Books

Genovese, Eugene D. 1978, 'L'economia schiavista americana in una prospettiva mondiale', in Raimondo Luraghi (ed)., *La guerra civile americana*, Bologna: Il Mulino

Genovese, Eugene D. 1995a, *The Southern Front. History and Politics in the Cultural War*, Columbia: University of Missouri Press

Genovese, Eugene D. 1995b, *The Slaveholders' Dilemma. Freedom and Progress in Southern Conservative Thought, 1820–1860* (1992), Columbia: University of South Carolina Press

Genovese, Eugene D. 1998, *A Consuming Fire. The Fall of the Confederacy in the Mind of the White Christian South*, Athens, GA: University of Georgia Press

Gentz, Friedrich von 1800, 'Der Ursprung und die Grundsätze der Amerikanischen Revolution, verglichen mit dem Ursprunge und den Grundsätzen der Französischen', *Historisches Journal*, 2

Gentz, Friedrich von 1836–8, *Ausgewählte Schriften*, ed. Wilderich Weick, Stuttgart-Leipzig: Rieger and Comp.

Gentz, Friedrich von 1967, *Betrachtungen über die französische Revolution* (1793) [this is the often free German translation of *Reflections on the Revolution in France*, in Burke 1826; we use the reprint of the second edn (1794)], ed. Lore Iser, with an introduction by Dieter Henrich, Frankfurt/M.: Suhrkamp

Gernet, Jacques 1972, *Le monde chinois*, Paris: Colin

Giametta, Sossio 1998, *Saggi nietzscheani*, Naples: La Città del Sole

Giametta, Sossio 2002, 'L'antisemitismo nostalgico di Nietzsche', *Il Giornale*, 31 January

Giametta, Sossio 2003, 'L'individuo scatenato', *Il domenicale*, 12 April: 7

Gioberti, Vincenzo 1938–42a, 'Del primato morale e civile degli italiani' (1846), in *Opere edite e inedite*, ed. Enrico Castelli et al., vol. 3, Milan: Bocca

Gioberti, Vincenzo 1938–42b, 'Il gesuita moderno' (1846–7), in *Opere edite e inedite* [cf. Gioberti 1938–1942 a], vol. 17 and 18

Gioberti, Vincenzo 1969, *Del rinnovamento civile degli italiani* (1851), ed. Luigi Quattrocchi, Rome: Abete

Giordani, Igino 1956 (ed.), *Le encicliche sociali dei Papi. Da Pio IX a Pio XII (1864–1956)*, fourth revised edn, Rome: Studium

Girardet, Raoul 1983, *Le nationalisme français. Anthologie 1871–1914*, Paris: Seuil

Glanz, James 1999, 'In Science vs. Bible Wrangle, Debate Moves to the Cosmos', *International Herald* Tribune, 11 October: 2

Gobineau, Arthur de 1917, *Ce qui est arrivé à la France en 1870* (1907, postum), German translation by Rudolf Schlosser, *Frankreichs Schicksale im Jahre 1870*, Leipzig: Reclam

Gobineau, Arthur de 1983, 'Essai sur l'inégalité des races humaines' (1853–5), in *Oeuvres*, ed. Jean Gaulmier, vol. 1 (with Jean Boissel), Paris: Gallimard

Godechot, Jacques 1956, *La Grande Nation. L'expansion de la France révolutionnaire dans le monde 1788–1799*, vol. 1, Paris: Aubier

Godechot, Jacques 1984, *La contre-révolution 1789–1804*, second edn, Paris: PUF

Goebbels, Joseph 1991a, *Tagebücher*, ed. Ralf Georg Reuth, Munich-Zurich: Piper

Goebbels, Joseph 1991b, *Reden 1932–1945*, ed. Helmut Heiber (1971–2), Bindlach: Gondrom

Goudsblom, Johan 1960, *Nihilisme en Culture*, Amsterdam: N.V. De Arbeiderspers

Graetz, Heinrich 1965a, 'Erwiderung an Herrn von Treitschke' (7 December 1879), in Boehlich 1965

Graetz, Heinrich 1965b, 'Mein letztes Wort an Professor von Treitschke' (28 December 1879), in Boehlich 1965

Gramsci, Antonio 1975, *Quaderni del carcere*, 4 vols, ed. Valentino Gerratana, Turin: Einaudi

Griesinger, Theodor 1863, *Land und Leute in Amerika. Skizzen aus dem amerikanischen Leben*, second edn, Stuttgart: Kröner

Grimm, Herman 1871, 'Voltaire und Frankreich. Ein Versuch', *Preussische Jahrbücher*, 27, parts 1 and 5: 1–25, 566–613

Groethuysen, Bernard 1956, *Origines de l'esprit bourgeois en France*, vol. 1: *L'Église et la bourgeoisie* (1927), fifth edn, Paris: Gallimard

Grotius, Hugo 1913, *De jure belli ac pacis libri tres* (reproduction of edn of 1646), ed. James Brown Scott, Washington: Carnegie Institution

Guillemin, Henri 1958, *Benjamin Constant muscadin 1795–1799*, 6. edn, Paris: Gallimard

Guizot, Francois 1849, *De la démocratie en France* (January 1849), second edn, Naples: Nobile

Gumplowicz, Ludwig 1883, *Der Rassenkampf. Soziologische Untersuchungen*, Innsbruck: Wagner'sche Universitätsbuchhandlung

Gumplowicz, Ludwig 1885, *Grundriss der Soziologie*, Vienna: Manz'sche K.K. Hof-Verlags- und Universitäts-Buchhandlung

Gutman, Robert W. 1971, *Richard Wagner. The Man, His Mind and His Music* (1968), London: Penguin Books

Gutzkow, Karl 1974, 'Onkel Toms Hütte' (1852–3), in Demetz, Peter (ed)., *Liberale Energie. Eine Sammlung seiner kritischen Schriften*, Frankfurt/M.-Berlin-Vienna: Ullstein

Haase, Marie-Luise 1989, 'Friedrich Nietzsche liest Francis Galton', *Nietzsche-Studien*, 18: 633–58

Habermas, Jurgen 1968a, *Erkenntnis und Interesse*, Frankfurt/M.: Suhrkamp

Habermas, Jurgen 1968b, 'Afterword to Friedrich Nietzsche, *Erkenntnistheoretische Schriften*', Frankfurt/M.: Suhrkamp

Hammer, Karl 1971, *Deutsche Kriegstheologie (1870–1918)*, Munich: Kösel

Hammer, Karl 1978, *Weltmission und Kolonialismus. Sendungsideen des 19. Jahrhunderts im Konflikt*, Munich: Kösel

Harrington, J. Drew 1989, 'Classical Antiquity and the Proslavery Argument', *Slavery and Abolition*, 10, 1: 60–72

Hartmann, Eduard von 1989, *Philosophie des Unbewussten. Versuch einer Weltanschauung* (1869), photocopy, Hildesheim-Zurich-New York: Olms

Hartz, Louis 1955, *The Liberal Tradition in America. An Interpretation of American Political Thought Since the Revolution*, New York: Harcourt, Brace and World

Havens, George Remington 1933, 'Voltaire's Marginalia on the Pages of Rousseau', *Ohio State University Studies*, VI

Hayek, Friedrich A. von 1978, *New Studies in Philosophy, Politics, Economics and the History of Ideas*, London: Routledge and Kegan Paul

Hayek, Friedrich A. von 1982, *Law, Legislation and Liberty* (1973/1976/1979), London: Routledge and Kegan Paul

Haym, Rudolf 1854, 'Friedrich von Gentz', in *Allgemeine Encyclopädie der Wissenschaften und Künste*, ed. J.S. Ersch and J.G. Gruber, first Sektion, vol. 5, Leipzig: Gleditsch

Haym, Rudolf 1861, 'Gespräche Huttens (Rezension von D.F. Strauss)', *Preussische Jahrbücher*, 6: 307 ff.

Haym, Rudolf 1902, *Aus meinem Leben. Erinnerungen*, Berlin: Gaertner

Haym, Rudolf 1903a, 'Arthur Schopenhauer' (1864), in *Gesammelte Aufsätze*, ed. Wilhelm Schrader, Berlin: Weidmannsche Buchhandlung

Haym, Rudolf 1903b, Hermann Baumgarten (1894), in *Gesammelte Aufsätze* [cf. Haym 1903a]

Haym, Rudolf 1906, *Die romantische Schule* (1870), second edn, Berlin: Weidmannsche Buchhandlung

Haym, Rudolf 1927, 'An Hegels hundertstem Geburtstag' (in *Grenzboten* 1870, second semester, vol. 1), newly published in the appendix to the second edn of *Hegel und seine Zeit*, ed. Hans Rosenberg, Leipzig: Heims

Haym, Rudolf 1930, *Ausgewählter Briefwechsel*, ed. Hans Rosenberg, Berlin-Leipzig: Deutsche Verlags-Anstalt

Haym, Rudolf 1974, *Hegel und seine Zeit* (1857), photocopy of first edn, Darmstadt: Wissenschaftliche Buchgesellschaft

Hayman, Ronald 1980, *Nietzsche. A Critical Life*, New York: Penguin

Hegel, Georg W.F. 1919–20, *Vorlesungen über die Philosophie der Weltgeschichte*, ed. Georg Lasson, Leipzig: Meiner

Hegel, Georg W.F. 1956a, *Sämtliche Werke*, ed. Hermann Glockner, vol. 6, third edn, Stuttgart: Frommann

Hegel, Georg W.F. 1956b, *Berliner Schriften*, ed. Johannes Hoffmeister, Hamburg: Meiner

Hegel, Georg W.F. 1966, *Vorlesungen über die Philosophie der Religion* (1925), ed. Georg Lasson, second edn, Hamburg: Meiner

Hegel, Georg W.F. 1969–79, *Werke in zwanzig Bänden*, ed. Eva Moldenhauer and Karl Markus Michel, Frankfurt/M.: Suhrkamp

Hegel, Georg W.F. 1973f., *Vorlesungen über Rechtsphilosophie*, ed. Karl Heinz Ilting, Stuttgart-Bad Cannstatt: Frommann-Holzboog

Hegel, G.W.F. 1975, *Natural Law, The Scientific Ways of Treating Natural Law, Its Place in Moral Philosophy, and Its Relation to the Positive Sciences of Law*, translated by T.M. Knox, Philadelphia: University of Pennsylvania Press

Hegel, G.W.F. 1978, *Religionsphilosophie: Die Vorlesung von 1821*, ed. Karl Heinz Ilting, Naples: Bibliopolis

Heidegger, Martin 1961, *Nietzsche*, vol. 1, Pfullingen: Günther Neske

Heidegger, Martin 1981, 'Aristoteles, Metaphysik IX, 1–3. Von Wesen und Wirklichkeit der Kraft' (1931), in *Gesamtausgabe*, vol. 33, Frankfurt/M.: Klostermann

Heine, Heinrich 1887, *Prose Writings*, London: Camelot Series

Heine, Heinrich 1969–78, *Sämtliche Schriften*, ed. Klaus Briegleb, Munich: Hanser

Heine, Heinrich 1982, *History of Religion and Philosophy in Germany*, North Queensland: James Cook University

Herder, Johann G. 1978, 'Briefe zur Beförderung der Humanität. Siebente Sammlung' (1796), in *Sämtliche Werke*, ed. Bernhard Suphan, Berlin 1881, vol. 18, photocopy, Hildesheim-New York: Olms

Herf, Jeffrey 1984, *Reactionary Modernism. Technology, Culture and Politics in Weimar and the Third Reich*, Cambridge: Cambridge University Press

Herre, Franz 1983, *Deutsche und Franzosen*, Bergisch Gladbach: Lübbe

Herzen, Alexander (Gercen, Aleksandr Ivanovič) 1851, *Du développement des idées révolutionnaires en Russie*, Nice: Canis Frères

Herzen, Alexander (Gercen, Aleksandr Ivanovič) 1852, *Le peuple russe et le socialisme. Lettre à Monsieur J. Michelet*, Paris: A. Franck

Herzen, Alexander (Gercen, Aleksandr Ivanovič) 1871, De *l'autre rive*, tr. by Alexandre Herzen junior, third edn, first French edn, Geneva: Impr. de Czerniecki

Herzen, Alexander (Gercen, Aleksandr Ivanovič) 1950, 'Mémoires et Pensées' (1855–62), in *Textes philosophiques choisis*. Moscow: Éditions en langues etrangeres

Hildenbrand, Karl 1962, *Geschichte und System der Rechts- und Staatsphilosophie* (1860), Aalen: Scientia

Hillebrand, Karl 1892, *Zeiten, Völker und Menschen*, vol. 2: *Wälsches und Deutsches* (1875), second revised edn, Strasbourg: Trübner

Hillgruber, Andreas 1994, *Der Zweite Weltkrieg 1939–1945. Kriegsziele und Strategie der grossen Mächte*, Stuttgart-Berlin-Cologne-Mainz: Kohlhammer

Himmelfarb, Gertrude 1985, *The Idea of Poverty. England in the Early Industrial Age* (1983), New York: Vintage Books

Hirschman, Albert O. 1982, *Shifting Involvements. Private Interest and Public Action*, Princeton: Princeton University Press

Hitler, Adolf 1935, 'Kein Volk lebt länger als die Dokumente seiner Kultur' (Nurnberg, 12 September), *Völkischer Beobachter*, 13 September: 3–5

Hitler, Adolf 1939a, 'Rede zur Eröffnung der Grossen Deutschen Kunstausstellung' (Munich, 16 July), *Völkischer Beobachter*, 17 July: 1–2

Hitler, Adolf 1939b, *Mein Kampf* (1925–7), Munich: Zentralverlag der NSDAP

Hitler, Adolf 1980, *Monologe im Führerhauptquartier 1941–1944. Die Aufzeichnungen Heinrich Heims*, ed. Werner Jochmann, Hamburg: Albrecht Knaus

Hitler, Adolf 1989, *Tischgespräche*, ed. Henry Picker (1951), Frankfurt/M.-Berlin: Ullstein

Hobhouse, Leonard Trelawney 1904, *Democracy and Reaction*, London: Fisher Unwin

Hobsbawm, Eric J. 1959, *Primitive Rebels. Studies in Archaic Forms of Social Movement in the 19th and 20th Centuries*, Manchester: Manchester University Press

Hobsbawm, Eric J. 1987, *The Age of Empire. 1875–1914*, London: Abacus

Hobson, John A. 1983, *Imperialism. A Study* (1902), Ann Arbor: University of Michigan Press

Hoffmann, Geza von 1913, *Die Rassenhygiene in den Vereinigten Staaten von Nordamerika*, Munich: Lehmanns

Hofstadter, Richard 1944–5, *Social Darwinism in American Thought*, Philadelphia: University of Pennsylvania Press

Hölderlin, Friedrich 1978, *Sämtliche Werke und Briefe* (1970), ed. Günther Mieth, Munich: Hanser

Holub, Robert 2015, *Nietzsche's Jewish Problem: Between Anti-Semitism and Anti-Judaism*, Princeton: Princeton University Press

Horkheimer, Max, and Theodor W. Adorno 1947, *Dialektik der Aufklärung*, Amsterdam: Querido

Huard, Raymond 1991, *Le suffrage universel en France 1848–1946*, Paris: Aubier

Hugo, Gustav 1819, *Lehrbuch eines civilistischen Cursus*, vol. 2, *Lehrbuch des Naturrechts als einer Philosophie des positiven Rechts, besonders des Privatrechts*, fourth edn, Berlin: Mylius

Humboldt, Wilhelm von 1903–36a, 'Ideen zu einem Versuch, die Gränzen der Wirksamkeit des Staates zu bestimmen' (1792), in *Gesammelte Schriften*, vol. 1, Berlin: Akademieausgabe

Humboldt, Wilhelm von 1903–36b, 'Über das Studium des Altertums und des griechischen insbesondere' (1793), in *Gesammelte Schriften* [cf. Humboldt 1903–36a]

Hume, David 1971, 'Of the Populousness of Ancient Nations' (1752), in *Opere*, ed. Eugenio Lecaldano and Enrico Mistretta, vol. 2, Bari: Laterza

Hume, David 1983, *The History of England* (on the basis of the edn of 1778), Indianapolis: Liberty Classics

Iggers, Georg 1973, 'Heinrich von Treitschke', in Hans-Ulrich Wehler (ed.), *Deutsche Historiker*, Göttingen: Vandenhoeck and Ruprecht

Jacobi, Friedrich Heinrich 1980, 'David Hume über den Glauben, oder Idealismus und Realismus. Ein Gespräch' (1787; 1815), in *Werke*, ed. Friedrich Roth and Friedrich Köp-

pen (Leipzig 1812–25), vol. 2, photocopy, Darmstadt: Wissenschaftliche Buchgesellschaft

Jacobsen, Hans-Adolf 1989, 'Kommissarbefehl und Massenexekutionen sowjetischer
Kriegsgefangener', in Hans Buchheim et al. (ed)., *Anatomie des ss-Staates* (1967),
fifth edn, vol. 2, Munich: dtv

Jacoby, Johann 1978, *Briefwechsel 1850–1877*, ed. Edmund Silberner, Bonn: Neue Gesellschaft

Jaeger, Werner 1934, *Paideia. Die Formung des griechischen Menschen*, Berlin-Leipzig:
De Gruyter

Janz, Curt Paul 1981, *Friedrich Nietzsche Biographie* (1978), Munich: dtv

Jardin, Andre 1984, *Alexis de Tocqueville 1805–1859*, Paris: Hachette

Jaspers, Karl 1936, *Nietzsche. Einführung in das Verständnis seines Philosophierens*, Berlin-Leipzig: De Gruyter

Jaspers, Karl 1984, *Philosophische Autobiographie* (1977), revised edn, Munich-Zurich:
Piper

Jaspers, Karl 1985, *Psychologie der Weltanschauungen* (1919), Munich-Zurich: Piper

Jean Paul 1879, 'Vorschule der Aesthetik' (1804), in *Jean Pauls Werke*, 49–53 part, Berlin:
Hempel

Jefferson, Thomas 1955, *Notes on the State of Virginia* (1787), ed. William Peden, Chapel
Hill: University of North Carolina Press

Joho, Wolfgang 1958, *Traum von der Gerechtigkeit. Die Leidensgeschichte des Handwerks-
gesellen, Rebellen und Propheten Wilhelm Weitling*, Berlin: Neues Leben

Jordan, Winthrop D. 1968, *White Over Black. American Attitudes Toward the Negro 1550–
1812*, New York: Norton and Company

Kant, Immanuel 1900 ff., *Gesammelte Schriften*, Berlin: Akademieausgabe

Kant, Immanuel 1970, *Political Writings*, translated by H.B. Nisbet, Cambridge: Cambridge University Press

Kant, Immanuel 2009, *Kant's Idea for a Universal History with Cosmopolitan Aim: A
Critical Guide*, translated by Allen Wood, edited by Rorty and Schmidt, Cambridge:
Cambridge University Press

Karnow, Stanley 1989, *In Our Image*, New York: Random House

Kaufmann, Walter A. 1950, *Nietzsche: Philosopher, Psychologist, Antichrist*, Princeton:
Princeton University Press

Kautsky, Karl 1888, 'Arthur Schopenhauer', *Die Neue Zeit*, VI: 66–78, 97–109

Kautsky, Karl 1908, *Der Ursprung des Christentums. Eine historische Untersuchung*, Stuttgart: Dietz

Kazin, Alfred 1994, 'Her Holiness', *The New York Review of Books*, 1 December: 39–40

Kershaw, Ian 1998, *Hitler 1889–1936: Hubris*, London: Penguin

Ketteler, Wilhelm Emmanuel Freiherr von 1864, *Die Arbeiterfrage und das Christen-
thum*, Mainz: Franz Kirchheim

Ketteler, Wilhelm Emmanuel Freiherr von 1967, 'Die Katholiken im Deutschen Reiche. Entwurf zu einem politischen Programm' (1873), in Karl H. Hoefele (ed.), *Geist und Gesellschaft der Bismarckzeit*, Göttingen-Berlin-Frankfurt/M.: Musterschmidt

Kidd, Benjamin 1902, *Principles of Western Civilisation*, London: Macmillan

Kierkegaard, Soren 1962 ff., *Die Tagebücher*, Düsseldorf-Cologne: Eugen Diederichs

Kiernan, Victor G. 1988, *The Duel in European History. Honour and the Reign of Aristocracy*, Oxford: Oxford University Press

Kleist, Heinrich von 1961, *Sämtliche Werke und Briefe*, ed. Helmut Sembdner, Munich: dtv

Kleist, Heinrich von 1973, 'Über den Zustand der Schwarzen in Amerika', in *Berliner Abendblätter*, ed. Heinrich von Kleist, 1810–11, photocopy, ed. Helmut Sembdner, vol. 2, 38–39 (Nr. 10; 12. January 1811) and 47–48 (Nr. 12; 15. January 1811), Darmstadt: Wissenschaftliche Buchgesellschaft

Knapp, Georg Friedrich 1891, *Die Landarbeiter in Knechtschaft und Freiheit. Vier Vorträge*, Leipzig: Duncker and Humblot

Kolchin, Peter 1987, *Unfree Labor. American Slavery and Russian Serfdom*, Cambridge, MA.: The Belknap Press of Harvard University Press

Köselleck, Reinhart 1975, *Preussen zwischen Reform und Revolution* (1967), second revised edn, Stuttgart: Klett

Kraditor, Aileen S. 1989, *Means and Ends in American Abolitionism. Garrison and His Critics on Strategy and Tactics, 1834–1850* (1967), Chicago: Dee

Kraus, Otto 1894, 'Aus Heinrich Leos geschichtlichen Monatsberichten und Briefen', *Allgemeine Konservative Monatsschrift für das christliche Deutschland*, Leipzig, July–December

Krug, Wilhelm Traugott 1969, *Allgemeines Handwörterbuch der philosophischen Wissenschaften nebst ihrer Literatur und Geschichte* (1828), vol. 5/2, photocopy, Stuttgart-Bad Cannstatt: Frommann-Holzboog

Kuhl, Stefan 1994, *The Nazi Connection. Eugenics, American Racism and German National Socialism*, Oxford: Oxford University Press

Kunnas, Tarmo 1972, *Drieu, Céline, Brasillach et la tentation fasciste*, Paris: Les Sept couleurs

Kupisch, Karl 1965 (ed.), *Quellen zur Geschichte des deutschen Protestantismus 1871 bis 1945* (1960), Munich-Hamburg: Siebenstern

Lafargue, Paul 1996, *Le droit à la paresse* (1883), Paris: Le Temps des Cerises

Lafargue, Paul 1998, *Das Recht auf Faulheit* [French 1996/1883], Grafenau: Trotzdem-Verlag

Lagarde, Paul de 1937, *Schriften für das deutsche Volk*, ed. Karl August Fischer, Munich: Lehmanns

Lamennais, Félicité R. de 1978, 'De l'esclavage moderne' (1840), in *De l'absolutisme et de la liberté et autres essais*, ed. Henri Guillemin, Paris: Ramsay

Lampl, Hans Erich 1986, 'Ex oblivione: Das Fere-Palimpsest', *Nietzsche-Studien*, 15: 225–64

Landa, Ishay 2009, *The Overman in the Marketplace: Nietzschean Heroism in Popular Culture*, Maryland: Lexington Books

Langbehn, Julius 1922, *Rembrandt als Erzieher. Von einem Deutschen* (1890), Illustrierte Volksausgabe, Weimar: Duncker

Lange, Friedrich Albert 1974, *Geschichte des Materialismus* (1873; second edn), Frankfurt/M.: Suhrkamp

Lange, Friedrich Albert 1975, *Die Arbeiterfrage* (1865), ed. Julius H. Schoeps, Duisburg: Braun

Lanternari, Vittorio 1960, *Movimenti religiosi di libertà e di salvezza dei popoli oppressi*, Milan: Feltrinelli

Lapouge, Georges Vacher de 1896, *Les sélections sociales*, Paris: Thorin and Fils

Lapouge, Georges Vacher de 1977, *L'Aryen. Son rôle social* (1899), Bologna: Forni

La Repubblica 2002, 'Quale Nietzsche e stato censurato?', 27 December: 39

Larizza, Mirella 1999, *Bandiera verde contro bandiera rossa. Auguste Comte e gli inizi della Société positiviste (1848–1852)*, Bologna: Il Mulino

Lassalle, Ferdinand 1919, 'Das Arbeiterprogramm' (1862–3), in *Gesammelte Reden und Schriften*, ed. Eduard Bernstein, vol. 2, Berlin: Cassirer

Lassalle, Ferdinand 1864, *Herr Bastiat-Schulze von Delitzsch, der ökonomische Julian, oder Kapital und Arbeit*, Berlin: Reinhold Schlingmann

Laube, Heinrich 1845–7, *Ausgewählte Werke in zehn Bänden*, ed. Hubert Houben, vol. 9, Leipzig: Max Hesse Verlag

Lazare, Bernard 1969, *L'antisémitisme. Son histoire et ses causes* (1894), Paris: Documents et Témoignages

Le Bon, Gustave 1894, *Les lois psychologiques de l'évolution des peuples*, Paris: Félix Alcan

Le Bon, Gustave 1920, *Psychologie du socialisme* (1896), third edn, Paris: Félix Alcan

Le Bon, Gustave 1925, *La Révolution française et la psychologie des Révolutions* (1912), Paris: Flammarion

Le Bon, Gustave 1928, *Psychologie des foules* (1895), Paris: Félix Alcan

Lecky, William E.H. 1883–8, *A History of England in the Eighteenth Century*, third edn, London: Longmans-Green

Lémonon, Michel 1971, *Le rayonnement du gobinisme en Allemagne* (PhD, Strasbourg II)

Lenin, Vladimir Ilich 1953–, *Collected Works*, Moscow: Progress

Lerda, Gennaro V. 1976, 'La schiavitù e la guerra civile nelle pagine della "Civiltà Cattolica" (1850–1865)', in Giorgio Spini et al., *Italia e America dal Settecento all'età dell'imperialismo*, Venice: Marsilio

Lessing, Theodor 1984, *Der jüdische Selbsthass* (1930), new edn, with introduction by Boris Groys, Munich: Matthes and Seitz

Lichtenberg, Georg Christoph 1949, *Gesammelte Werke*, ed. Wilhelm Grenzmann, Frankfurt/M.: Holle

Lichtheim, George 1974, *Europe in the Twentieth Century*, London: Cardinal

Lifton, Robert Jay 1988, *Ärzte im Dritten Reich* [English 1986], tr. by Annegrete Lösch, Stuttgart: Klett-Cotta

Linguet, Simon Nicolas Henri 1984, *Théorie des lois civiles ou principes fondamentaux de la société* (1767), Paris: Fayard

Livingstone, David 1858, *Missionsreisen und Forschungen in Süd-Afrika während eines sechzehnjährigen Aufenthalts im Innern des Continents*, from the English by Hermann Lotze, Leipzig: Hermann Costenoble

Locke, John 1963a, 'The Fundamental Constitutions of Carolina' (1669), in *The Works* (London 1823), vol. 10, photocopy, Aalen: Scientia

Locke, John 1963b, 'An Essay Concerning Human Understanding' (1689), in *The Works* [cf. Locke 1963a], vol. 3

Locke, John 1970, *Two Treatises of Civil Government* (1690), ed. W.S. Carpenter, New York: Everyman's Library

Lombroso, Cesare 1995, *Delitto, genio, follia. Scritti scelti*, ed. Delia Frigessi, Ferruccio Giacanelli, Luisa Mangoni, Turin: Bollati Boringhieri

Lopez, Michael 1999, 'La retorica della guerra in Emerson', in Giorgio Mariani (ed)., *Le parole e le armi. Saggi su guerra e violenza nella cultura e letteratura degli Stati Uniti d'America*, Milan: Marcos y Marcos

Losurdo, Domenico 1983b *Autocensura e compromesso nel pensiero politico di Kant*, Naples: Istituto Italiano per gli Studi Filosofici-Bibliopolis

Losurdo, Domenico 1983a, *Tra Hegel e Bismarck. La rivoluzione del 1848 e la crisi della cultura tedesca*, Rome: Editori Riuniti

Losurdo, Domenico 1992, *Hegel e la libertà dei moderni*, Rome: Editori Riuniti

Losurdo, Domenico 1993b *Democrazia o bonapartismo. Trionfo e decadenza del suffragio universale*, Turin: Bollati Boringhieri

Losurdo, Domenico 1995, *La comunità, la morte, l'Occidente. Heidegger e l'"ideologia della Guerra"*, Turin: Bollati Boringhieri

Losurdo, Domenico 1996, *Il revisionismo storico. Problemi e miti*, Rome-Bari: Laterza

Losurdo, Domenico 1997a, *Hegel e la Germania. Filosofia e questione nazionale tra rivoluzione e reazione*, Milan: Guerini-Istituto Italiano per gli Studi Filosofici

Losurdo, Domenico 1997b, *Dai fratelli Spaventa a Gramsci. Per una storia politico-sociale della fortuna di Hegel in Italia*, Naples: La Città del Sole

Losurdo, Domenico 1997c, *Antonio Gramsci dal liberalismo al 'comunismo critico'*, Rome: Gamberetti

Losurdo, Domenico 1998, *Il peccato originale del Novecento*, Rome-Bari: Laterza

Losurdo, Domenico 1999a, 'Antigiudaismo, giudeofobia, antisemitismo', *I viaggi di Erodoto*, XIII, 38/39: 139–160

Losurdo, Domenico 1999b, 'La crisi del processo di emancipazione degli ebrei: per un'analisi comparata', in Alberto Burgio (ed)., *Nel nome della razza. Il razzismo nella storia d'Italia 1870–1945*, Bologna: Il Mulino

Losurdo, Domenico 2001, *L'ipocondria dell'impolitico. La critica di Hegel ieri e oggi*, Lecce: Milella

Losurdo, Domenico 2014, *Liberalism: A Counter-History*, translated by Gregory Elliott, London: Verso

Lovejoy, Arthur O. 1961, *The Great Chain of Being. A Study of the History of an Idea*, Cambridge, M.A.: Harvard University Press

Löwith, Karl 1961, *Weltgeschichte und Heilsgeschehen. Die theologischen Voraussetzungen der Geschichtsphilosophie* (1953), fourth edn, Stuttgart: Kohlhammer

Lukács, Georg 1980, *The Destruction of Reason*, translated by Peter Palmer, London: Merlin Press

Ludendorff, Erich 1928, *Kriegshetze und Völkermorden in den letzten 150 Jahren im Dienste des 'allmächtigen Baumeisters aller Welten'*, Munich: Self-published

Ludendorff, Erich 1934, *Deutsche Abwehr. Antisemitismus gegen Antigojismus*, Munich: Self-published

Ludendorff, Erich 1935, *Der totale Krieg*, Munich: Ludendorffs Verlag

Ludendorff, Mathilde 1931, *Erlösung von Jesu Christo*, Munich: Ludendorffs Volkswarte-Verlag

Ludwig, Emil 2000, *Colloqui con Mussolini* (1932), Milan: Mondadori

Lukács, György 1954, *Die Zerstörung der Vernunft*, Berlin: Aufbau

Lukács, György 1948, *Der junge Hegel und die Probleme der kapitalistischen Gesellschaft*, Berlin: Aufbau

Luthardt, Christoph E. 1967, 'Die modernen Weltanschauungen und ihre praktischen Konsequenzen. Vorträge' (1880), in Karl H. Hoefele [cf. Ketteler 1967]

Luther, Martin 1883 ff., *Werke. Kritische Gesamtausgabe*, Weimar: Bohlau

Lutz, Ralph 1911, *Die Beziehungen zwischen Deutschland und den Vereinigten Staaten während des Sezessionskriegs*, Heidelberg: Winter's Universitätsbuchhandlung

Lyotard, Jean-Francois 1979, *La condition postmoderne*, Paris: Éditions de Minuit

Macpherson, Crawford B. 1962, *The Political Theory of Possessive Individualism: Hobbes to Locke*, Oxford: Oxford University Press

Maistre, Joseph de 1984, *Oeuvres complètes* (Lyons 1884), photocopy, Hildesheim-Zurich-New York: Olms

Malthus, Thomas Robert 1826, *An Essay on the Principle of Population*, vol. 2, sixth edn, London: John Murray

Malthus, Thomas Robert 1986, *An Essay on the Principle of Population. The first edition* (*1798*), London: Pickering and Chatto

Mandeville, Bernard 1924, 'An Essay on Charity and Charity Schools', in *The Fable of the Bees*, Oxford: Clarendon Press.

Mann, Thomas 1986, 'Nietzsche's Philosophie im Lichte unserer Erfahrung' (1947), in *Essays*, ed. Hermann Kurzke, vol. 3, Frankfurt/M.: Fischer

Manzoni, Alessandro 1963, 'Dell'invenzione' (1850), in *Tutte le opere*, ed. Alberto Chiari and Fausto Ghisalberti, vol. 3, Milan: Mondadori

Mao Tsetung 1967, 'On Correcting Mistaken Ideas in the Party' [Chinese 1929], in *Selected Writings*, volume I, Peking: Foreign Language Press

Marr, Wilhelm 1862, *Der Judenspiegel*, Hamburg: Self-published

Martini, Fritz 1963, *Deutsche Literaturgeschichte*, Stuttgart: Kröner

Marwitz, Friedrich August Ludwig von der 1965, 'Von der Schrankenlosigkeit' (1836), in Carl Jantke and Dietrich Hilger [cf. Bensen 1965]

Marx, Karl, and Friedrich Engels 1955 ff., *Werke*, Berlin: Dietz

Marx, Karl, and Friedrich Engels 1975 ff., *Collected Works*, New York: International Publishers

Mason, Haydn 1981, *Voltaire. A Biography*, London: Paul Elek Granada Publishing

Massara, Massimo 1972 (ed.), *Il marxismo e la questione ebraica*, Milan: Edizioni del Calendario

Matteucci, Nicola 1957, *Jacques Mallet-Du Pan*, Naples: Istituto Italiano per gli Studi Storici

Mauzi, Robert 1960, *L'idée du bonheur dans la littérature et la pensée françaises au XVIII siècle*, Paris: Colin

Maximilian II König von Bayern und Schelling 1890, *Briefwechsel*, ed. Ludwig Trost and Friedrich Leist, Stuttgart: Cotta

Mayer, Arno J. 1981, *The Persistence of the Old Regime. Europe to the Great War*, New York: Pantheon Books

Mayer, Arno J. 1988, *Why Did the Heavens not Darken? The Final Solution in History*, New York: Pantheon Books

Mayeur, Jean-Marie 1973, *Les débuts de la IIIe République 1871–1898*, Paris: Seuil

Mehring, Franz 1898, *Geschichte der deutschen Sozialdemokratie* (1897–98), vol. 3, second part, Stuttgart: Dietz

Mehring, Franz 1961 ff., *Gesammelte Schriften*, ed. Thomas Höhle, Hans Koch and Josef Schleifstein, Berlin: Dietz

Menzel, Wolfgang 1869, *Kritik des modernen Zeitbewusstseins*, Frankfurt/M.: Heyder and Zimmer

Merriam, Charles E. 1969, *A History of American Political Theories* (1903), New York: Kelley

Meyer, Eduard 1895, 'Untersuchung zum Ursprung des Odysseus-Mythus', *Hermes*, 30

Meysenbug, Malwida von 1901, *Individualitäten*, Berlin-Leipzig: Schuster und Loeffler

Michelet, Jules 1980, 'Les Femmes de la Révolution' (1854), in *Oeuvres complètes*, ed. Paul Viallaneix, vol. 16, Paris: Flammarion

Mill, John Stuart 1965a, 'Carlyle's French Revolution' (1837), in *Collected Works*, ed.

John M. Robson, vol. 20, London: University of Toronto Press, Routledge and Kegan Paul

Mill, John Stuart 1965b, 'Autobiography' (1853–70; first edn 1873), in *Collected Works* [cf. Mill 1965a], vol. 1

Mill, John Stuart 1965c, 'A System of Logic Ratiocinative and Inductive' (1843, eighth edn), in *Collected Works* [cf. Mill 1965a], vol. 7–8

Mill, John Stuart 1972a, 'On Liberty' (1858), in *Utilitarianism, Liberty, Representative Government*, ed. H.B. Acton, London: Dent

Mill, John Stuart 1972b, 'Representative Government' (1861), in *Utilitarianism, Liberty, Representative Government* [cf. Mill 1972a]

Miller, Randall M., Harry S. Stout and Charles Reagan Wilson 1998, *Religion and the American Civil War*, Oxford: Oxford University Press

Mises, Ludwig von 1956, *The Anticapitalistic Mentality*, Princeton: D. von Nostrand Co.

Mohl, Robert von 1981, 'Gewerbe- und Fabrikwesen', in *Staatslexikon oder Encyclopädie der Staatswissenschaften*, ed. Carl von Rotteck and Carl Theodor Welcker, now in *Der europäische Liberalismus im 19. Jahrhundert*, ed. Lothar Gall and Rainer Koch, vol. 4, Frankfurt/M.-Berlin-Vienna: Ullstein

Mohler, Armin 1989, *Die konservative Revolution in Deutschland 1918–1932. Ein Handbuch* (1949; 1972), third extended edn, Darmstadt: Wissenschaftliche Buchgesellschaft

Moissonnier, Maurice 2001, '1774–1849. Un siècle lyonnais: les canuts face aux cannibales du profit', in Gilles Perrault et al., *Le livre noir du capitalisme* (1999), Paris: Le Temps des cerises

Mommsen, Theodor 1965, *Auch ein Wort über unser Judenthum*, in Boehlich 1965

Montaigne, Michel de 1965, *Essais* (1580–1588), ed. Pierre Michel, with a foreword by Maurice Merleau-Ponty, Paris: Gallimard

Montaigne, Michel de 2002, *Essais* [French 1965], tr. by H. Stilett, Munich: Goldmann

Montesquieu, Charles-Louis de Secondat de 1949–51, 'De l'esprit des lois' (1748), in *Oeuvres complètes*, vol. 2, ed. Roger Caillois, Paris: Gallimard

Montinari, Mazzino 1999, *Che cosa ha detto Nietzsche* (1975), Milan: Adelphi

Moravia, Sergio 1986, *Il tramonto dell'illuminismo*, second edn, Rome-Bari: Laterza

Morgan, Edmund S. 1975, *American Slavery American Freedom. The Ordeal of Colonial Virginia*, New York: Norton

Morison, Samuel E. 1953 (ed.), *Sources and Documents Illustrating the American Revolution and the Formation of the Federal Constitution 1764–1788* (1923), second edn, Oxford: Clarendon Press

Morlang, Thomas 2002, 'Ein Schlag ins Wasser. Schon einmal, 1888/89, überwachte Deutschlands Marine im Namen der Freiheit die ostafrikanische Küste', *Die Zeit*, 17 January: 86

Möser, Justus 1842, 'Patriotische Phantasien: Der jetzige Hang zu allgemeinen Gesetzen und Verordnungen ist der gemeinen Freiheit gefährlich' (1772), in *Sämtliche Werke*, ed. B.R. Abeken and J.W.J. von Voigts, vol. 2, Berlin: Nicolaische Buchhandlung

Mosse, George L. 1966, *The Crisis of German Ideology* (1964), London: Weidenfeld and Nicholson

Mosse, George L. 1974, *The Nationalization of the Masses. Political Symbolism and Mass Movements in Germany from the Napoleonic Wars through the Third Reich*, New York: Howard Fertig

Mosse, George L. 1990, *Fallen Soldiers. Reshaping the Memory of the World Wars*, Oxford: Oxford University Press

Mounier, Jean Joseph 1801, *De l'influence attribuée aux philosophes, aux francs-maçons et aux illuminés, sur la Révolution de France*, Tübingen: Cotta

Müller, Adam 1935, 'Elemente der Staatskunst' (1808–9) in Paul Kluckhohn (ed.), *Deutsche Vergangenheit und deutscher Staat* (Deutsche Literatur, Reihe Romantik, vol. 10), Leipzig: Reclam

Musil, Robert 1952, *Der Mann ohne Eigenschaften*, Reinbek bei Hamburg: Rowohlt

Necker, Jacques 1970, 'Sur la législation et le commerce des grains' (1775), in *Oeuvres complètes*, ed. Auguste Louis de Stael-Holstein (Paris 1820), vol. 1, photocopy, Aalen: Scientia

Negri, Antimo 1978, *Nietzsche. Storia e cultura*, Rome: Armando

Nevins, Allan, and Henry S. Commager 1943, *America. The Story of a Free People*, Boston: Little, Brown and Company

Newfield, Christopher 2012, *The Emerson Effect: Individualism and Submission in America*, Chicago: University of Chicago Press

Nietzsche, Friedrich 2003, *Writings from the Late Notebooks*, Cambridge: Cambridge University Press

Nissen, Benedikt Momme 1926, *Der Rembrandtdeutsche Julius Langbehn*, Freiburg: Herder

Nolte, Ernst 1960, 'Marx und Nietzsche im Sozialismus des jungen Mussolini', *Historische Zeitschrift*, 191, 2, October: 249–335

Nolte, Ernst 1963, *Der Faschismus in seiner Epoche*, Munich: Piper

Nolte, Ernst 1990, *Nietzsche und der Nietzscheanismus*, Frankfurt/M.-Berlin: Propyläen

Nolte, Ernst 1991, *Lehrstück oder Tragödie? Beiträge zur Interpretation der Geschichte des 20. Jahrhunderts*, Cologne-Weimar-Vienna: Bohlau

Nordau, Max (n.d.): *Entartung* (1892), Berlin: Duncker

Norddeutsche Allgemeine Zeitung of 26 October 1888, evening edn: 1

Novalis 1978, 'Die Christenheit oder Europa' (1799), in *Werke, Tagebücher und Briefe*, ed. Hans-Joachim Mahl and Richard Samuel, vol. 2, Munich: Hanser

Nussbaum, Martha C. 1997, *Cultivating Humanity. A Classical Defense of Reform in Liberal Education*, Cambridge, MA: Harvard University Press

Olender, Maurice 1989, *Les langues du Paradis. Aryens et Sémites: un couple providentiel*, Paris: Seuil

Omodeo, Adolfo 1974, *Studi sull'età della Restaurazione*, second edn, Turin: Einaudi

Opitz, Reinhard 1977 (ed.), *Europastrategien des deutschen Kapitals 1900–1945*, Cologne: Pahl-Rugenstein

Orsucci, Andrea 1996, *Orient – Okzident. Nietzsches Versuch einer Loslösung vom europäischen Weltbild*, Berlin: De Gruyter

Ottmann, Henning 1999, *Philosophie und Politik bei Nietzsche* (1987), second edn, Berlin: De Gruyter

Overbeck, Franz 1906, 'Erinnerungen an Friedrich Nietzsche', *Die neue Rundschau*, vol. 1: 209–31, 320–30

Overbeck, Franz and Erwin Rohde 1990, 'Briefwechsel', in *Supplementa Nietzscheana*, vol. 1, Berlin: De Gruyter

Overbeck, Franz 1994–95a, 'Über das Verhältnis der alten Kirche zur Sclaverei im römischen Reiche' (1875), in *Werke und Nachlass*, ed. Ekkehard W. Stegemann et al., vol. 2, Stuttgart-Weimar: Metzler

Overbeck, Franz 1994–95b, 'Einleitung' (1903) to *Über die Christenheit unserer heutigen Theologie* (1873), in *Werke und Nachlass* [cf. Overbeck 1994–95a], vol. 1

Overbeck, Franz 1994–95c, 'H. St. Chamberlain', in *Werke und Nachlass* [cf. Overbeck 1994–95a], vol. 6/1

Pareto, Vilfredo 1974, *I sistemi socialisti* (1901), ed. Giovanni Busino, Turin: UTET

Pareto, Vilfredo 1988, *Trattato di sociologia generale* (1916), ed. Giovanni Busino, Turin: UTET

Pareyson, Luigi 1977 (ed.), *Schellingiana rariora*, Turin: Bottega d'Erasmo

Parrington, Vernon L. 1954, *Main Currents in American Thought. An Interpretation of American Literature from the Beginnings to 1920*, vol. 2: *1800–1860: The Romantic Revolution in America*, New York: Harcourt, Brace and World

Pascal, Blaise 1954, 'Pensées' (1670), in *Oeuvres complètes*, ed. Jacques Chevalier, Paris: Gallimard

Pascoli, Giovanni 1994, 'L'avvento' (1901), in *L'Era Nuova. Pensieri e discorsi*, ed. Rocco Ronchi, Milan: EGEA

Perrot, Michelle 1984, 'Introduction to Alexis de Tocqueville, *Le système pénitentiaire aux Étas-Unis et son application en France* (1833)', in *Oeuvres complètes*, ed. Jacob Peter Mayer, 1951 ff., vol. 4/1, Paris: Gallimard

Pick, Daniel 1989, *Faces of Degeneration: A European Disorder, c. 1848–c. 1918*, Cambridge: Cambridge University Press

Pick, Daniel 1993, *War Machine. The Rationalization of Slaughter in the Modern Age*, New Haven: Yale University Press

Plato 1955, *The Republic*, translated by Desmond Lee, London: Penguin

Plato 2010, *Gorgias, Menexenus, Protagoras*, edited by Malcolm Schofield, translated by Tom Griffith, Cambridge: Cambridge University Press

Plitt, Gustav L. 1869–70 (ed.), *Aus Schellings Leben in Briefen*, Leipzig: Hirzel

Ploetz, Alfred 1895, *Grundlinien einer Rassenhygiene*, Berlin: Fischer

Podach, Erich F. 1932, *Gestalten um Nietzsche*, Weimar: Lichtenstein

Pöggeler, Otto 1974, 'Hegel und die Anfänge der Nihilismus-Diskussion', in Dieter Arendt (ed.), *Der Nihilismus als Phänomen der Geistesgeschichte in der wissenschaftlichen Diskussion unseres Jahrhunderts*, Darmstadt: Wissenschaftliche Buchgesellschaft

Polanyi, Karl 1957, *The Great Transformation* (1944), Boston: Beacon Press

Poliakov, Léon 1968, *Histoire de l'antisémitisme*, vol. 3, Paris: Calmann-Lévy

Poliakov, Léon 1987, *Le mythe aryen. Essai sur les sources du racisme et des nationalismes* (1971), revised edn, Brussels: Complexe

Poliakov, Léon and Josef Wulf 1978, *Das dritte Reich und seine Denker* (1959), Munich: Saur

Proudhon, Pierre-Joseph 1858, *De la justice dans la révolution et dans l'église*, vol. 2, Paris: Librairie de Garnier Frères

Proudhon, Pierre-Joseph 1926, 'Qu'est-ce que la propriété?' (1840), in *Oeuvres complètes*, vol. 4, Paris: Rivières

Radowitz, Joseph Maria von 1851, *Gespräche aus der Gegenwart über Staat und Kirche*, fourth edn, Stuttgart: Becher

Ranke, Leopold von 1975, Vorlesungseinleitung (winter semester 1855–56), in *Aus Werk und Nachlass*, vol. 4, Munich-Vienna: Oldenbourg

Ranke, Leopold von 1980, *Über die Epochen der neueren Geschichte* (1854), Darmstadt: Wissenschaftliche Buchgesellschaft

Ratner-Rosenhagen, Jennifer 2012, *American Nietzsche: A History of an Icon and His Ideas*, Chicago: University of Chicago Press

Rauschning, Hermann 1938, *Die Revolution des Nihilismus*, fifth edn, Zurich-New York: Europa

Raynal, Guillaume Th. 1981, *Histoire philosophique et politique des Deux Indes*, ed. Yves Benot, Paris: Maspero

Rée, Paul 1877, *Der Ursprung der moralischen Empfindungen*, Chemnitz: Schmeitzner

Rée, Paul 2004, 'Psychologische Beobachtungen' (1875), in Rée, *Gesammelte Werke 1875–1885*, Supplementa Nietzscheana, vol. 7, Berlin: De Gruyter

Rehmann, Jan 2004, *Postmoderner Links-Nietzscheanismus: Deleuze & Foucault. Eine Dekonstruktion*, Hamburg: Argument

Renan, Ernest 1947 ff., *Oeuvres complètes*, ed. Henriette Psichari, Paris: Calmann–Lévy

Renault, François 1971, *Lavigerie, l'esclavage africain et l'Europe*, Paris: Boccard

Reuth, Ralf G. 1991, *Goebbels*, second edn, Munich: Piper

Rickert, Heinrich 1920, *Die Philosophie des Lebens. Darstellung und Kritik der philosophischen Modeströmungen unserer Zeit*, Tübingen: Mohr Siebeck

Ricoeur, Paul 1965, *De l'interprétation. Essai sur Freud*, Paris: Seuil

Riedel, Manfred 1978, 'Nihilismus', in Otto Brunner, Werner Conze and Reinhart

Köselleck, *Geschichtliche Grundbegriffe. Historisches Lexikon zur politisch-sozialen Sprache in Deutschland*, vol. 4, Stuttgart: Klett-Cotta

Rieffer, G. 1858, 'Amerikanische Anschauungen und Studien I', *Preussische Jahrbücher*, vol. 1: 300–1

Riehl, Alois 1920, *Friedrich Nietzsche. Der Künstler und der Denker* (1897), sixth edn, Stuttgart: Frommans (Kurtz)

Ritter, Gerhard 1960, *Staatskunst und Kriegshandwerk. Das Problem des 'Militarismus' in Deutschland*, second vol.: *Die Hauptmächte Europas und das wilhelminische Reich (1890–1914)*, Munich: R. Oldenbourg

Robin, Corey 2013, 'Nietzsche's Marginal Children: On Friedrich Hayek', *The Nation*, May Issue

Rodinson, Maxime 1993, *La fascination de l'Islam* (1980; 1989), Paris: La Découverte

Rohde, Erwin 1989a, 'Anzeige für "Das Litterarische Centralblatt" [1872]', in *Der Streit um Nietzsches 'Geburt der Tragödie': die Schriften von E. Rohde, R. Wagner, and v. Wilamowitz-Möllendorff*, ed. Karlfried Gründer (1969), reprint of first edn, Hildesheim: Olms

Rohde, Erwin 1989b, 'Anzeige für die "Norddeutsche Allgemeine Zeitung"' (1872), in *Der Streit um Nietzsches 'Geburt der Tragödie'* [cf. Rohde 1989a]

Rohde, Erwin 1989c, 'Afterphilologie', in *Der Streit um Nietzsches 'Geburt der Tragödie'* [cf. Rohde 1989a]

Röhl, John C.G. 1993, *Wilhelm II. Die Jugend des Kaisers, 1859–1888*, Munich: Beck

Röhl, John C.G. 2001, *Wilhelm II. Der Aufbau der Persönlichen Monarchie, 1888–1900*, Munich: Beck

Rose, Paul Lawrence 1992, *Wagner: Race and Revolution*, London: Faber and Faber

Rosenberg, Alfred 1935, *An die Dunkelmänner unserer Zeit. Eine Antwort auf die Angriffe gegen den 'Mythus des 20. Jahrhunderts'*, Munich: Hoheneichen

Rosenberg, Alfred 1937a, *Der Mythus des 20. Jahrhunderts* (1930), Munich: Hoheneichen

Rosenberg, Alfred 1937b, *Protestantische Rompilger. Der Verrat an Luther und der 'Mythus des 20. Jahrhunderts'*, Munich: Hoheneichen

Rosenkranz, Karl 1854, *Aus einem Tagebuch. Königsberg Herbst 1833 bis Frühjahr 1846*, Leipzig: Brockhaus

Rosenkranz, Karl 1862, *Wissenschaft der logischen Idee*, Königsberg: Bornträger

Rosenkranz, Karl 1963, *Hegels Leben* (1844), photocopy, Darmstadt: Wissenschaftliche Buchgesellschaft

Rosenkranz, Karl 1969, *Schelling. Vorlesungen gehalten im Sommer 1842 an der Universität zu Königsberg* (Danzig 1843); photocopy, Aalen: Scientia

Rosmini, Antonio 1840–57a, 'Introduzione alla filosofia' (1850), in *Opere edite e inediti*, vol. 1, Milan (et al).: Poliani, Casuccio et al.

Rosmini, Antonio 1840–57b, 'Logica' (1854), in *Opere edite e inedite* [cf. Rosmini 1840–57a]

Rosmini, Antonio 1840–57c, 'Il Comunismo e il Socialismo' (1849), in *Opere edite ed ined-ite* [cf. Rosmini 1840–57a], vol. 37 (*Filosofi a della politica*: vol. 4)

Ross, Werner 1984, *Der ängstliche Adler. Friedrich Nietzsches Leben* (1980), Munich: dtv

Rousseau, Jean-Jacques 1959 ff., *Oeuvres complètes*, ed. Bernard Gagnebin and Marcel Raymond, Paris: Gallimard

Rousseau, Jean-Jacques 1971, *Discours sur les richesses ou Lettre à Crysophile*, in *Oeuvres complètes*, ed. Michel Launay, vol. 2, Paris: Seuil

Ruge, Arnold 1847–8, 'Was wird aus der Religion?' (1841), in *Sämmtliche Werke*, Man-nheim: Grohe

Ruge, Arnold 1886, *Briefwechsel und Tagebuchblätter aus den Jahren 1825–1880*, ed. Paul Nerrlich, Berlin: Weidmannsche Buchhandlung

Ruge, Wolfgang, and Wolfgang Schumann 1977 (ed.), *Dokumente zur deutschen Ge-schichte. 1939–1942*, Frankfurt/M.: Roderberg

Sade, Donatien A. François Marquis de 1998, *'Que suis-je à présent? ...'*, ed. Maurice Lever, Paris: Bartillat

Saint-Just, Louis Antoine Léon de 1984, *Oeuvres complètes*, ed. Michèle Duval, Paris: Lebovici

Saint-Simon, Claude-Henri de 2003, *Nouveau Christianisme* (1825), photocopy, Milan: Fondazione Giangiacomo Feltrinelli

Santaniello, Weaver 1994, *Nietzsche, God and the Jews. His Critique of Judeo-Christianity in Relation to the Nazi Myth*, New York: State University of New York Press

Santaniello, Weaver 1997, 'A Post-Holocaust Re-Examination of Nietzsche and the Jews. Vis-à-vis Christendom and Nazism', in Jacob Golomb [cf. Aschheim 1997]

Sautet, Marc 1981, *Nietzsche et la Commune*, Paris: La Sycomore

Savigny, Friedrich Karl von 1967, *Vom Beruf unserer Zeit für Gesetzgebung und Recht-swissenschaft* (1840), photocopy, Hildesheim: Olms

Schelling, Friedrich Wilhelm Joseph 1856–61, *Sämtliche Werke*, Stuttgart-Augsburg: Cotta

Schelling, Friedrich Wilhelm Joseph 1972, *Grundlegung der positiven Philosophie. Münchner Vorlesung WS 1832/33 und SS 1833*, ed. Horst Fuhrmans, Turin: Bottega D'Erasmo

Schieder, Theodor 1979, *Vom Deutschen Bund zum Deutschen Reich* (1970), fourth edn, Munich: dtv

Schlegel, Friedrich 1963, 'Philosophische Lehrjahre 1796–1806', part one, in *Kritische Ausgabe seiner Werke*, ed. Ernst Behler, vol. 18, Munich-Paderborn-Vienna: Schön-ingh

Schlegel, Friedrich 1975, 'Über die Sprache und Weisheit der Indier' (1808), in *Kritische Ausgabe seiner Werke*, ed. Ernst Behler and Ursula Struc-Oppenberg, vol. 8, Munich-Paderborn-Vienna: Schöningh

Schmuhl, Hans-Walter 1992, *Rassenhygiene, Nationalsozialismus, Euthanasie* (1987), second edn, Göttingen: Vandenhoeck and Ruprecht

Schnabel, Franz 1954, *Deutsche Geschichte im neunzehnten Jahrhundert*, vol. 3: *Erfahrungswissenschaften und Technik*, third edn, Freiburg: Herder

Schoeck, Helmut 1980, *Der Neid. Die Urgeschichte des Bösen* (1969), Munich-Vienna: Herbig

Schopenhauer, Arthur 1929–33, *Briefwechsel*, ed. Carl Gebhardt and Arthur Hübscher, Munich: Piper

Schopenhauer, Arthur 1971, *Gespräche*, ed. Arthur Hubscher, Stuttgart-Bad Cannstatt: Frommann-Holzboog

Schopenhauer, Arthur 1976–82a, 'Die Welt als Wille und Vorstellung' (1818), in *Sämtliche Werke*, ed. Wolfgang Frhr. von Lohneysen, vol. 1, Darmstadt: Wissenschaftliche Buchgesellschaft

Schopenhauer, Arthur 1976–82b, 'Die Welt als Wille und Vorstellung. Ergänzungen' (1844 and 1858), in *Sämtliche Werke* [cf. Schopenhauer 1976–82a], vol. 2

Schopenhauer, Arthur 1976–82c, 'Parerga und Paralipomena' (1851), in *Sämtliche Werke* [cf. Schopenhauer 1976–82a], vols 4 and 5

Schopenhauer, Arthur 1976–82d, 'Über die Grundlage der Moral' (1840), in *Sämtliche Werke* [cf. Schopenhauer 1976–82a], vol. 3

Schopenhauer, Arthur 1976–82e, 'Über den Willen in der Natur' (1854), in *Sämtliche Werke* [cf. Schopenhauer 1976–82a], vol. 3

Seccombe, Wally 1992, *Millennium of Family Change: Feudalism to Capitalism in Northwestern Europe*, London: Verso

See, Klaus von 1994, *Barbar, Germane, Arier. Die Suche nach der Identität der Deutschen*, Heidelberg: Universitätsverlag C. Winter

Seier, Hellmut 1973, 'Heinrich von Sybel', in *Deutsche Historiker*, ed. Hans-Ulrich Wehler, Göttingen: Vandenhoeck and Ruprecht

Sengupta, Somini 2002, 'Hindu Right Reaches for Young Minds', *International Herald Tribune*, 15 May: 2

Sieyès, Emmanuel-Joseph 1985a, 'Essai sur les privilèges' (November 1788), in *Écrits politiques*, ed. Roberto Zapperi, Paris: Éditions des archives contemporaines

Sieyès, Emmanuel-Joseph 1985b, 'Qu'est-ce que le Tiers État?' (January 1789), in *Écrits politiques* [cf. Sieyès 1985a]

Sieyès, Emmanuel-Joseph 1985c, 'Notes et fragments inédits', in *Écrits politiques* [cf. Sieyes 1985a]

Sieyès, Emmanuel-Joseph 1985d, 'Dire sur la question du veto royal' (September 1789), in *Écrits politiques* [cf. Sieyes 1985a]

Silberner, Edmund 1976, *Johann Jacoby. Politiker und Mensch*, Bonn: Neue Gesellschaft

Simon, Walter M. 1963, *European Positivism in the Nineteenth Century. An Essay in Intellectual History*, Ithaca: Cornell University Press

Slotkin, Richard 1994, *The Fatal Environment. The Myth of the Frontier in the Age of Industrialization 1800–1890* (1985), New York: Harper Perennial

Smith, Adam 1981, *An Inquiry into the Nature and the Causes of the Wealth of Nations* (1775–7), Indianapolis: Liberty Classics

Sombart, Werner 1915, *Händler und Helden. Patriotische Besinnungen*, Munich-Leipzig: Duncker and Humblot

Sombart, Werner 1987, *Der moderne Kapitalismus* (1927), Munich: dtv

Sorel, Georges 1973, 'Da Proudhon a Lenin' and 'L'Europa sotto la tormenta', in appendix to *Lettres à Mario Missiroli*, foreword by Gabriele De Rosa, Rome: Edizioni di Storia e Letteratura

Spaventa, Bertrando 1972a, 'False accuse contro l'hegelismo' (1851), in *Opere*, ed. Giovanni Gentile, vol. 3, Florence: Sansoni

Spaventa, Bertrando 1972b, 'La politica dei gesuiti nel secolo XVI e nel XIX' (1854–5), in *Opere* [cf. Spaventa 1972a], vol. 2

Spence, Jonathan 1998, *God's Chinese Son. The Taiping Heavenly Kingdom of Hong Xiuquan*, London: Harper Collins

Spencer, Herbert 1865, *Social Statics* (1850), New York: Appleton

Spencer, Herbert 1981, *The Man versus the State with Six Essays on Government, Society and Freedom* (1843–84), Indianapolis: Liberty Classics

Spengler, Oswald 1937, 'Frankreich und Europa' (1924), in *Red und Aufsätze*, ed. Hildegard Kornhardt, Munich: Beck

Stahl, Friedrich J. 1963, 'Preface (1829) to *Die Philosophie des Rechts*', photocopy of the fifth edn (1878), vol. 1, Hildesheim: Olms

Steding, Christoph 1938, *Das Reich und die Krankheit der europäischen Kultur*, Hamburg: Hanseatische Verlagsanstalt

Stegmaier, Werner, and Daniel Krochmalnik 1997 (ed.), *Jüdischer Nietzscheanismus*, Berlin: De Gruyter

Stein, Lorenz von 1959, *Geschichte der sozialen Bewegung in Frankreich von 1789 bis auf unsere Tage* (1849), photocopy of the edn published by Gottfried Salomon in 3 vols (Munich 1921), Hildesheim: Olms

Stein, Ludwig 1893, *Nietzsche's Weltanschauung und ihre Gefahren*, Berlin: Reimer

Stendhal (Henry Beyle) 1973, *Le rouge et le noir* (1830), Paris: Éditions Garnier Frères

Sternhell, Zeev 1978, *La droite révolutionnaire. Les origines françaises du fascism 1885–1914*, Paris: Seuil

Stirner, Max 1967, *Geschichte der Reaktion* (1852), photocopy, Aalen: Scientia

Stirner, Max 1981, *Der Einzige und sein Eigentum* (1844), Stuttgart: Reclam

Stöcker, Adolf 1890, *Christlich-Sozial. Reden und Aufsätze* (1884), second edn, Berlin: Verlag der Buchhandlung der Berliner Stadtmission

Stöcker, Adolf 1891a, *Sozialdemokratie und Sozialmonarchie*, Leipzig: Grunow

Stöcker, Adolf 1891b, *Arm und Reich*, Basel: Geering

Stöcker, Adolf 1899, *Über Frauenarbeit*, Berlin: Verlag der Buchhandlung der Berliner Stadtmission

Stoddard, Lothrop 1925, *Der Kulturumsturz. Die Drohung des Untermenschen* [English 1922], tr. by Wilhelm Heise, Munich: Lehmanns

Stoddard, Lothrop 1984, *The Revolt against Civilization. The Menace of the Under Man* (1922), reprint, New York: Scribner

Stolberg-Wernigerode, Otto Graf zu 1933, *Deutschland und die Vereinigten Staaten von Amerika im Zeitalter Bismarcks*, Berlin-Leipzig: De Gruyter

Stoll, Adolf 1929 (ed.), *F.C. v. Savigny. Ein Bild seines Lebens mit einer Sammlung seiner Briefe*, vol. 2, Berlin: Heymanns

Strauss, David Friedrich 1835–6, *Das Leben Jesu, kritisch bearbeitet*, Tübingen: Osiander

Strauss, David Friedrich 1872, *Der alte und der neue Glaube. Ein Bekenntniss*, second reprint, Leipzig: Hirzel

Struve, Walter 1973, *Élites against Democracy. Leadership Ideals in Bourgeois Political Thought in Germany, 1890–1933*, Princeton: Princeton University Press

Sumner, William Graham 1992, 'Democracy and Plutocracy', in *On Liberty, Society and Politics*, ed. Robert C. Bannister, Indianapolis: Liberty Classics

Taine, Hippolyte 1899, *Les origines de la France contemporaine* (1876–94), Paris: Hachette

Tal, Uriel 1975, *Christians and Jews in Germany. Religion, Politics and Ideology in the Second Reich, 1870–1914* [Hebrew 1969], tr. by Noah Jonathan Jacobs, Ithaca: Cornell University Press

Taureck, Bernhard H.F. 1989, *Nietzsche und der Faschismus*, Hamburg: Junius

Taureck, Bernhard H.F. 2000, *Nietzsche und der Faschismus: Ein Politikum*, Leipzig: Reclam

Tawney, Richard H. 1926, *Religion and the Rise of Capitalism: A Historical Study*, London: Murray

Teti, Vito 1993, *La razza maledetta. Origini del pregiudizio antimeridionale*, Rome: Manifesto Libri

Thucydides 1998, *The Peloponnesian War*, translated by Steven Lattimore, Indianapolis/Cambridge: Hackett Press

Tille, Alexander 1893, *Volksdienst. Von einem Sozialaristokraten*, Berlin-Leipzig: Viennaer'sche Verlagsbuchhandlung

Tille, Alexander 1895, *Von Darwin bis Nietzsche. Ein Buch Entwicklungsethik*, Leipzig: Naumann

Tocqueville, Alexis de 1864–7, *Oeuvres complètes*, ed. by Tocqueville's widow and Gustave de Beaumont, Paris: Michel Levy Frères

Tocqueville, Alexis de 1951 ff., *Oeuvres complètes*, ed. Jacob Peter Mayer, Paris: Gallimard

Todorov, Tzvetan 1989, *Nous et les autres. La réflexion française sur la diversité humaine*, Paris: Seuil

Tonnies, Ferdinand 1897, *Der Nietzsche-Kultus. Eine Kritik*, Leipzig: O.R. Reisland

Townsend, Joseph 1971, *A Dissertation on the Poor Laws by a Well-Wisher to Mankind* (1786), Oakland: University of California Press

Toynbee, Arnold 1951–4, *A Study of History* (1934–54), vol. 1, London: Oxford University Press

Toynbee, Arnold 1952, *The World and the West*, Oxford: Oxford University Press

Toynbee, Arnold 1959, *Hellenism. The History of a Civilisation*, Oxford: Oxford University Press

Treitschke, Heinrich von 1865, 'Der Bonapartismus', *Preussische Jahrbücher*, 16

Treitschke, Heinrich von 1878, 'Der Socialismus und der Meuchelmord', *Preussische Jahrbücher*, 41, reprint in *Zehn Jahre deutscher Kämpfe. Schriften zur Tagespolitik*, second edn, Berlin: Reimer

Treitschke, Heinrich von 1879, 'Der Socialismus und seine Gönner' (1874), in *Zehn Jahre deutscher Kämpfe. Schriften zur Tagespolitik*, second edn, Berlin: Reimer

Treitschke, Heinrich von 1886, 'Die Freiheit' (1861), in *Historische und politische Aufsätze*, vol. 3, Leipzig: Hirzel

Treitschke, Heinrich von 1897–8, *Politik. Vorlesungen gehalten an der Universität zu Berlin*, ed. Max Cornicelius, Leipzig: Hirzel

Treitschke, Heinrich von 1965a, 'Unsere Aussichten' (7 December 1879), in Boehlich 1965

Treitschke, Heinrich von 1965b, 'Herr Graetz und sein Judenthum' (15 December 1879), in Boehlich 1965

Treitschke, Heinrich von 1965c, 'Noch einige Bemerkungen zur Judenfrage' (10 January 1880), in Boehlich 1965

Treitschke, Heinrich von 1978, 'Zwei Kaiser' (*Preussische Jahrbücher*, July 1888), in Fenske 1978

Treitschke, Heinrich von 1981, *Deutsche Geschichte im neunzehnten Jahrhundert* (1879–94), Königstein/Ts.: Athenäum/Droste

Trendelenburg, Friedrich Adolf 1964, *Logische Untersuchungen*, photocopy of third edn 1870, Hildesheim: Olms

Treue, Wilhelm 1958, *Deutsche Geschichte. Von den Anfängen bis zum Ende des Zweiten Weltkrieges*, second edn, Stuttgart: Kröner

Trotsky, Leon 1971, *Nineteen Hundred and Five*, translated by Anya Bostock, London: Allen Lane

Trotsky, Leon 1979, 'A propos de la philosophie du surhomme', *Cahiers Léon Trotsky*, 1: 105–20

Tucholsky, Kurt 1932, 'Fräulein Nietzsche. Vom Wesen des Tragischen', in *Gesammelte Werke in 10 Bänden*, ed. Mary Gerold-Tucholsky and Fritz J. Raddatz, vol. 10 (1985), Reinbek bei Hamburg: Rowohlt

Turgenev, Ivan 1999, *Fathers and Sons*, translated by Richard Freeborn, Oxford: Oxford University Press

Untersteiner, Mario 1954, *Sofisti. Testimonianze e frammenti*, vol. 3, Florence: La Nuova Italia

Varela, Nicolas Gonzalez 2010, *Nietzsche Contra La Democracia: El Pensamiento Politico de Friedrich Nietzsche 1862–1872*, Barcelona: Montesinos

Vattel, Emer de 1916, *Le droit des gens ou principes de la loi naturelle* (1758), 'The Classics of International Law', ed. James Brown Scott, Washington: Carnegie Institution

Vattimo, Gianni 1983, *Il soggetto e la maschera. Nietzsche e il problema della liberazione* (1974), Milan: Bompiani

Vattimo, Gianni 1985, *La fine della modernità*, Milan: Garzanti

Vattimo, Gianni 2000, *Introduzione a Nietzsche* (1985), Rome-Bari: Laterza

Vattimo, Gianni 2003, 'Anticipatore di Nietzsche ci aiuta a capirlo meglio', *La Stampa*, 25 May: 19

Veblen, Thorstein 1904, *The Theory of Business Enterprise*, New York: Scribner's

Venturi, Franco 1972, *Il populismo russo* (1952), Turin: Einaudi

Venturi, Franco 1969–87, *Settecento riformatore*, Turin: Einaudi

Venturi, Franco 1978, *La catastrofe di Nietzsche a Turin*, Turin: Einaudi

Venturi, Franco 1986, *Zarathustras Ende. Die Katastrophe Nietzsches in Turin* [Italian 1978], Vienna-Cologne-Graz: Bohlau

Vincent, John 1990, *Disraeli*, Oxford: Oxford University Press

Vivarelli, Vivetta 1984, 'Das Nietzsche-Bild in der Presse der deutschen Sozialdemokratie', *Nietzsche-Studien*, 13: 521–69

Vollrath, Wilhelm 1935, *Th. Carlyle und H. St. Chamberlain, zwei Freunde Deutschlands*, Munich: Lehmanns

Volpi, Franco 1996, *Il nichilismo*, Rome-Bari: Laterza

Voltaire 1834, 'Dictionnaire philosophique' (1764 ff.)., in *Oeuvres complètes de Voltaire*, ed. M.F. Tissot, vol. 56, Paris: Pourrat Frères Éditions

Voltaire 1906, *Siècle de Louis XIV* (1751), ed. Émile Bourgeois, Paris: Hachette

Voltaire 1989, *Traité sur la tolérance* (1762–5), Paris: Flammarion

Voltaire 1991, 'Premier discours sur l'homme' (1775, final version), in *The Complete Works of Voltaire*, vol. 17, Oxford: The Voltaire Foundation/Taylor Institution

Wagner, Cosima 1882, 'Ein Erinnerungsbild aus Wahnfried', *Bayreuther Blätter*, December

Wagner, Cosima 1977, *Die Tagebücher, 1878–1883*, edited and with a commentary by Martin Gregor-Dellin and Dietrich Mack, vol. 2, Munich-Zurich: Piper

Wagner, Cosima 1976–82, *Die Tagebücher*, edited and with a commentary by Martin Gregor-Dellin and Dietrich Mack, Munich-Zurich: Piper

Wagner, Richard 1910a, 'Die Kunst und die Revolution' (1849), in *Sämtliche Schriften und Dichtungen. Volks-Ausgabe*, sixth edn, vol. 3, Leipzig: Breitkopf und Hartel

Wagner, Richard 1910b, 'Das Judentum in der Musik' (1850), in *Sämtliche Schriften und Dichtungen* [cf. Wagner 1910a], vol. 5

Wagner, Richard 1910c, 'Oper und Drama' (1851), in *Sämtliche Schriften und Dichtungen* [cf. Wagner 1910a], vol. 3

Wagner, Richard 1910d, 'Zensuren (Zensur von Eduard Devrient, 1869)', in *Sämtliche Schriften und Dichtungen* [cf. Wagner 1910a], vol. 8

Wagner, Richard 1910e, 'Zensuren (Aufklärungen über das Judentum in der Musik, 1869)', in *Sämtliche Schriften und Dichtungen* [cf. Wagner 1910a], vol. 8

Wagner, Richard 1910f, 'Beethoven' (1870), in *Sämtliche Schriften und Dichtungen* [cf. Wagner 1910a], vol. 9

Wagner, Richard 1910g, 'Über das Dirigieren' (1870), in *Sämtliche Schriften und Dichtungen* [cf. Wagner 1910a], vol. 8

Wagner, Richard 1910h, 'An das deutsche Heer von Paris' (January 1871), in *Sämtliche Schriften und Dichtungen* [cf. Wagner 1910a], vol. 9

Wagner, Richard 1910i, 'Deutsche Kunst und deutsche Politik' (1867–8), in *Sämtliche Schriften und Dichtungen* [cf. Wagner 1910a], vol. 8

Wagner, Richard 1910l, 'Was ist deutsch?' (1865–78), in *Sämtliche Schriften und Dichtungen* [cf. Wagner 1910a], vol. 10

Wagner, Richard 1910m, 'Modern' (1878), in *Sämtliche Schriften und Dichtungen* [cf. Wagner 1910a], vol. 10

Wagner, Richard 1910n, 'Religion und Kunst' (1880), in *Sämtliche Schriften und Dichtungen* [cf. Wagner 1910a], vol. 10

Wagner, Richard 1910o, 'Was nutzt diese Erkenntnis? Ein Nachtrag zu "Religion und Kunst"' (1800), in *Sämtliche Schriften und Dichtungen* [cf. Wagner 1910a], vol. 10

Wagner, Richard 1910p, Erkenne dich selbst (1881), in *Sämtliche Schriften und Dichtungen* [cf. Wagner 1910a], vol. 10

Wagner, Richard 1910r, 'Heldentum und Christentum' (1881), in *Sämtliche Schriften und Dichtungen* [cf. Wagner 1910a], vol. 10

Wagner, Richard 1911, *Mein Leben* (1870), Munich: Bruckmann

Waite, Geoffrey 1996, *Nietzsche's Corps/e: Aesthetics, Politics, Prophecy, or, the Spectacular Technoculture of Everyday Life*, Duke: Duke University Press

Walicki, Andrzej 1996, 'I due volti di Alexandr Herzen', Introduction to Alexandr Herzen, *Il passato e i pensieri*, ed. Lia Wainstein, Turin: Einaudi

Wallon, Henri Alexandre 1974a, 'Introduction to *Histoire de l'esclavage dans l'antiquité*' (Paris 1879, second edn), vol. 1, photocopy, Aalen: Scientia

Wallon, Henri Alexandre 1974b, 'Avertissement de la prèmière édition (1847)', in *Histoire de l'esclavage dans l'antiquité* [cf. Wallon 1974a]

Walwin, James 1982, 'The Propaganda of Anti-Slavery', in James Walvin (ed).: *Slavery and British Society 1776–1846*, London: Macmillan

Warneck, Gustav 1879, *Die gegenseitigen Beziehungen zwischen der modernen Mission und Cultur. Auch eine Culturkampfstudie*, Gütersloh: Bertelsmann

Warneck, Gustav 1889, *Die Stellung der evangelischen Mission zur Sklavenfrage*, Gütersloh: Bertelsmann

Weaver, Richard M. 1987, *The Southern Essays*, ed. G.M. Curtis III and J.J. Thompson Jr., Indianapolis: Liberty Press

Weber, Max 1971, *Gesammelte politische Schriften* (1958), ed. Johannes Winckelmann, third edn, Tübingen: Mohr (Siebeck)

Weber, Max 1972, Die Wirtschaftsethik der Weltreligionen (1915–19), in *Gesammelte Aufsätze zur Religionssoziologie*, vol. 1, Tübingen: Mohr (Siebeck)

Weber, Max 1985, *Wirtschaft und Gesellschaft* (1921), ed. Johannes Winckelmann, fifth revised edn, Tübingen: Mohr (Siebeck)

Wehler, Hans-Ulrich 1969 (ed.), *Friedrich Kapp. Vom radikalen Frühsozialisten des Vormärz zum liberalen Parteipolitiker des Bismarckreichs. Briefe. 1843–1884*, Frankfurt/M.: Insel

Wehler, Hans-Ulrich 1985, *Bismarck und der Imperialismus* (1969), Frankfurt/M.: Suhrkamp

Weichelt, Hans 1922, *Zarathustra-Kommentar* (1910), second extended edn, Leipzig: Meiner

Weil, Simone 1962, *Selected Essays 1934–43*, translated by Richard Rees, London: Oxford University Press

Weingart, Peter, Jurgen Kroll and Kurt Bayertz 1992, *Rasse, Blut und Gene. Geschichte der Eugenik und Rassenhygiene in Deutschland* (1988), Frankfurt/M.: Suhrkamp

Weisse, Christian Hermann 1832, *Über das Verhältnis des Publikums zur Philosophie in dem Zeitpunkt von Hegels Abscheiden*, Leipzig: Schaarschmidt und Volkmar

Weismann, Karlheinz 1995, *Der Weg in den Abgrund. Deutschland unter Hitler 1933 bis 1945*, Berlin: Propyläen

Weitling, Wilhelm 1845, *Die Menschheit wie sie ist und wie sie sein soll*, second edn, Berne: Jenni

Weitling, Wilhelm 1849, *Das Evangelium eines armen Sünders* (1843), Munich: Ernst

Westernhagen, Curt von 1936, *Nietzsche, Juden, Antijuden*, Weimar: Duncker

Westphal, Otto 1964, *Welt- und Staatsauffassung des deutschen Liberalismus* (1919), photocopy, Aalen: Scientia

Widemann, Paul Heinrich 1885, *Erkennen und Sein*, Karlsruhe-Leipzig: Reuther

Widmaier, Rita 1990 (ed.), *Leibniz korrespondiert mit China. Der Briefwechsel mit Jesuitenmissionaren (1689–1714)*, Frankfurt/M.: Klostermann

Wilamowitz-Mollendorff, Ulrich von 1989a, 'Zukunftsphilologie!' (1872), in *Streit um Nietzsches 'Geburt der Tragödie'* [cf. Rohde 1989a]

Wilamowitz-Mollendorff, Ulrich von 1989b, 'Zukunftsphilologie! Zweites Stück' (1873), in *Streit um Nietzsches 'Geburt der Tragödie'* [cf. Rohde 1989a]

Willard, Claude 2001, '1871: Trahison de classe et semaine sanglante', in Gilles Perrault et al. [cf. Moissonnier 2001]

Williams, Basil 1921, *Cecil Rhodes*, London: Constable and Co Ltd

Williams, Eric 1990, *Capitalism and Slavery* (1944), London: Deutsch

Wood, Forrest G. 1968, *Black Scare. The Racist Response to Emancipation and Reconstruction*, Oakland: University of California Press

Woodward, C. Vann 1960, 'George Fitzhugh, Sui Generis' [cf. Fitzhugh 1960]

Zelinsky, Hartmut 1983, *Richard Wagner – ein deutsches Thema. Eine Dokumentation zur Wirkungsgeschichte Richard Wagners 1876–1976*, Berlin–Vienna: Medusa

Ziegler, Valerie H. 1992, *The Advocates of Peace in Antebellum America*, Bloomington: Indiana University Press

Index

CPSIA information can be obtained
at www.ICGtesting.com
Printed in the USA
JSHW031156280621
16185JS00003B/6

9 781642 593402